UNIVERSITY CASEBOOK SERIES

EDITORIAL BOARD

ROBERT C. CLARK
DIRECTING EDITOR
Dean & Royall Professor of Law
Harvard University

DANIEL A. FARBER
Sho Sato Professor of Law
University of California at Berkeley

OWEN M. FISS
Sterling Professor of Law
Yale University

THOMAS H. JACKSON
President
University of Rochester

HERMA HILL KAY
Dean & Barbara Nachtrieb Armstrong Professor of Law
University of California, Berkeley

HAROLD HONGJU KOH
Gerard C. & Bernice Latrobe Smith Professor of International Law
Yale Law School

DAVID W. LEEBRON
Dean & Lucy G. Moses Professor of Law
Columbia University

SAUL LEVMORE
Dean & William B. Graham Professor of Law
University of Chicago

ROBERT L. RABIN
A. Calder Mackay Professor of Law
Stanford University

CAROL M. ROSE
Gordon Bradford Tweedy Professor of Law & Organization
Yale University

DAVID L. SHAPIRO
William Nelson Cromwell Professor of Law
Harvard University

KATHLEEN M. SULLIVAN
Dean and Richard E. Lang Professor and
Stanley Morrison Professor of Law
Stanford University

CASES AND MATERIALS

TAXATION OF NONPROFIT ORGANIZATIONS

by

JAMES J. FISHMAN
Professor of Law,
Pace University School of Law

STEPHEN SCHWARZ
Professor of Law,
Hastings College of the Law

FOUNDATION PRESS

NEW YORK, NEW YORK

2003

Foundation Press, a Thomson business, has created this publication to provide you with accurate and authoritative information concerning the subject matter covered. However, this publication was not necessarily prepared by persons licensed to practice law in a particular jurisdiction. Foundation Press is not engaged in rendering legal or other professional advice, and this publication is not a substitute for the advice of an attorney. If you require legal or other expert advice, you should seek the services of a competent attorney or other professional.

COPYRIGHT © 2003 By FOUNDATION PRESS

        395 Hudson Street
        New York, NY 10014
        Phone Toll Free 1–877–888–1330
        Fax (212) 367–6799
        fdpress.com

Printed in the United States of America

ISBN 1–58778–595–1

TEXT IS PRINTED ON 10% POST CONSUMER RECYCLED PAPER

To Liz, Lisi, and Diana

           JJF

To F.K.G.

           SS

*

PREFACE

This text has been adapted from the Second Edition of our casebook, Nonprofit Organizations: Cases and Materials. It is offered as an alternative for specialized J.D. and LL.M courses and seminars on the taxation of charitable and other nonprofit organizations. Coverage is up to date through April, 2003.

Before our first edition was published in 1995, a handful of law schools offered courses in nonprofit organizations, ranging from global surveys to more specialized tax offerings, but instructors (and curricular growth) were hindered by a dearth of published teaching materials. Our goal was to help fill this void by crafting a book that eased the burden on experienced teachers and enticed newcomers to teach, study and practice in this fascinating and topical area.

Over the past decade, the law of the nonprofit sector has emerged from the shadows and become recognized as a distinct and dynamic legal discipline. Our publication of the first comprehensive law school text in the field was an important step in this evolution. And the response—adoption at over 70 law schools—has been gratifying.

The field of nonprofit organizations has appeal to students and professors with interests in wide-ranging areas such as corporations, taxation, estate planning, constitutional law, antitrust, law and economics, environmental law, health law, and public interest law. The law of nonprofits also is increasingly of interest, we think, because so many lawyers and law students become involved with nonprofit organizations as directors, trustees, members, and volunteers, and in those capacities they are frequently called upon for legal advice.

With such a potentially broad constituency, we were faced with the challenge of covering those topics of greatest importance and yet preserving flexibility for instructors with different emphasis and expertise, all while keeping the book to a manageable length. To that end, we provided a teaching tool that is readily adaptable to a two or three-unit survey course, a policy-oriented seminar, or a more specialized J.D. or LL.M tax-exempt organizations class. Based on our collective experience, we continue to think that the best J.D. level nonprofits courses are "interdisciplinary," covering both the state law perspective (formation, dissolution, operation and governance, with an emphasis on the fiduciary obligations of officers and directors) and federal tax issues. Even in tax-focused courses, students will benefit greatly from exposure to full range of legal issues.

But as the field has grown, so has the range of more specialized law school courses (and even some new competing casebooks). This spin-off edition accommodates the needs of instructors who are seeking efficient tax-focused coverage and who teach by the problem method. As with the mother text, it includes a variety of materials, including carefully edited cases, excerpts from leading scholarly articles and books, some writings from other disciplines, and authoritative IRS administrative materials. Most topics include extensive authors' text, notes, questions, bibliographic references for further reading, and problems for class discussion. To enliven the coverage, the notes and questions include frequent references to the rich array of real world controversies involving nonprofits, thus offering an opportunity for students to evaluate critically the increasingly publicized "darker side" of the sector.

Turning to the specifics of organization and coverage, the book consists of four parts. Part One (Chapter 1), an introduction, bridges theory and practice. It begins by describing the universe of nonprofits and addressing the principal theoretical rationales for the nonprofit sector. If the study of the nonprofit sector has serious academic merit, as we believe it does, theoretical questions such as why the nonprofit sector exists should be addressed at an early point and revisited frequently. This approach is as valid in a specialized tax offering as in a more global survey course. Chapter 1 concludes on a practical note, providing a concise overview of the nontax considerations affecting choice of legal form for a nonprofit organization and an introductory problem.

Part Two (Chapters 2-4) is devoted to the rules for obtaining and maintaining federal tax exemption. In organizing the coverage of qualification for exempt status, we employ the familiar (and we think, useful) distinction between public benefit and mutual benefit organizations. Chapter 2 addresses the affirmative requirements and operational limitations faced by organizations seeking tax-exempt status under § 501(c)(3), with more abbreviated coverage of § 501(c)(4) social welfare organizations and state and local tax exemption issues. It includes updated coverage of the § 4958 intermediate sanctions regime and expanded discussion of joint ventures and the impact of commercial activities on exempt status. Chapter 3 provides more focused consideration of private foundations, a sub-species within § 501(c)(3). A major goal of this chapter is to demonstrate the distinction between private foundations and public charities, the various routes to avoiding private foundation status, and how to navigate the regulatory regime if an organization is unable to do so. This chapter employs a two-track approach to make this challenging material accessible both to those who desire a more policy-oriented overview while offering the additional detailed coverage that is essential in a more advanced or graduate-level class. Chapter 4 offers an overview of the exemption requirements for the most familiar types of mutual benefit organizations, such as labor unions, trade associations, social clubs, and fraternal lodges.

Part Three (Chapter 5) is devoted to the taxation of business and investment income of nonprofits—specifically, the unrelated business income tax. Part Four (Chapter 6) covers the charitable contributions deduction. Each of these chapters, more or less, also employ a "two track" approach, beginning with a policy-oriented nontechnical overview, then turning to basic tax principles, and concluding with the most technical material. Instructors can easily pick and choose the depth of their coverage.

To complement the main casebook and this spin-off version, we have prepared a separate softbound supplement (Nonprofit Organizations: Selected Statutes, Regulations and Forms), now in its Second Edition, which contains excerpts from the Revised Model Nonprofit Corporation Act, the nonprofit corporation laws of several leading jurisdictions, the Uniform Prudent Investor Act, selected sections of the Restatements of Trusts and other statutes; relevant sections of the Internal Revenue Code and Treasury Regulations; important IRS forms, including the application for exemption under § 501(c)(3); sample articles and bylaws for a nonprofit corporation; and a simple charitable trust instrument. Suggested assignments to the statutory supplement are provided in bold type at the beginning of most sections of the casebook.

As for other matters of style and format, we have edited cases and other original sources freely to make them more accessible to students. Citations and internal cross references in excerpted materials have been deleted without so indicating. Textual omissions are indicated by asterisks, and editorial additions are in brackets. Many footnotes from original sources have been omitted without renumbering those that remain. Our goal was to make the text gender neutral, and we have tried to alternate between masculine and feminine pronouns to represent both sexes.

This has been a collaborative effort in the best sense, and many people who teach, write and practice in the field have graciously offered their advice and encouragement during the gestation period of this project and beyond. We owe special thanks to John Simon, who has done so much to nurture the field, for his many helpful insights; to Harvey Dale, the director of the National Center on Philanthropy and the Law at New York University School of Law, who has encouraged this project at every stage and offered us the unique opportunity to present our work-in-progress to leading scholars and practitioners at an invitational conference at NYU; and to Bill Hutton, who generously allowed us to adapt problems and colorful characters that he has developed and refined over the years. We also are grateful to the other participants in the NYU conference: Bob Boisture, Laura Brown Chisolm, Marion Fremont-Smith, Harvey Goldschmid, Carlyn McCaffrey, Jill Manny, and Peter Swords. And thanks too to Rob Atkinson, whose views on the appropriate model for a law school nonprofits course greatly stimulated our thinking, and to John Colombo and Mike Klausner, whose insights and questions helped us to improve our analysis of several topics. Any errors or other transgressions, of course, remain those of the authors— and for this edition, that means Professor Schwarz, who bears primary responsibility for the tax chapters.

Professor Fishman also wishes to thank Pace University and the Charles A. Frueauff Foundation for their research support; the National

Center on Philanthropy and the Law, which provided access to its philanthropy library at NYU School of Law; Judith Jaeger, who has typed much of his portions of the manuscript; and his students, whose bracing critiques and untoward enthusiasm in finding typos were of invaluable assistance. Professor Schwarz wishes to thank Hastings College of the Law for its research support. He also is indebted to his former students, Adele Dorison and Barbara Rosen, for their invaluable work as editors and research assistants.

And last but hardly least, we are grateful for the support of our families, friends, colleagues, and students.

JAMES J. FISHMAN
STEPHEN SCHWARZ

May 2003

ACKNOWLEDGEMENTS

With appreciation, the authors acknowledge the following authors, publishers, and other copyright holders who gave permission to reprint excerpts from their works:

American Bar Association, Introduction to Revised Model Nonprofit Corporation Act xxiv-xxix (1988). Reprinted with permission of Panel Publishers, a division of Aspen Publishers, Inc., 36 W. 44th St., Suite 1316, New York, N.Y. 10036. All rights reserved.

William D. Andrews, Personal Deductions in an Ideal Income Tax, 86 Harvard Law Review 309, 344-348, 356-358, 371-372, 374-375 (1972). Copyright © 1972 by the Harvard Law Review Association.

Boris I. Bittker and George K. Rahdert, The Exemption of Nonprofit Organizations from Federal Income Taxation, 85 Yale Law Journal 299, 307-316, 348-357 (1976), reprinted with permission of the Yale Law Journal Company and Fred B. Rothman & Co.

Developments in the Law—Nonprofit Corporations, 105 Harvard Law Review 1578, 1649-51 (1992). Copyright © 1992 by the Harvard Law Review Association.

John A. Edie, First Steps in Starting a Foundation 6-10, 25-27 (3d ed.). Copyright © 1993 by The Council on Foundations, Inc.

David F. Freeman and The Council on Foundations, The Handbook on Private Foundations 1-9, 248-253 (rev. ed. 1991). Copyright © 1991 by The Council on Foundations, Inc.

John W. Gardner, The Independent Sector, in America's Voluntary Spirit xiii-xv (Brian O'Connell ed., The Foundation Center, 1983). Copyright © 1983 by Brian O'Connell.

Gilbert M. Gaul & Neill A. Borowski, Free Ride: The Tax-Exempt Economy (Andrews & McMeel, 1993).

Mark A. Hall & John D. Colombo, The Donative Theory of the Charitable Tax Exemption, 52 Ohio State Law Journal 1379, 1381-1389 (1991).

Henry Hansmann, The Role of Nonprofit Enterprise, 89 Yale Law Journal 835, 835-845 (1980), reprinted by permission of the Yale Law Journal Company and Fred B. Rothman & Co.

Henry Hansmann, The Rationale for Exempting Nonprofit Organizations from Corporate Income Taxation, 91 Yale Law Journal 54, 72-75 (1981), reprinted by permission of the Yale Law Journal Company and Fred B. Rothman & Co.

Henry Hansmann, Reforming Nonprofit Corporation Law, 129 University of Pennsylvania Law Review 497, 504-509 (1981), with permission of Fred B. Rothman & Co. Copyright © 1981 by Henry B. Hansmann.

Monica Langley, The SO Trend: How to Succeed in Charity Without Really Giving: A "Supporting Organization" Lets Wealthy Donate Assets, Still Keep Control, Wall St. Journal, May 29, 1998, p. A1. Republished by permission of Dow Jones, Inc. via Copyright Clearance Center, Inc. © 1998 Dow Jones and Company, Inc. All Rights Reserved Worldwide.

Waldemar A. Nielsen, The Big Foundations 7-17 (1972), reprinted with permission of The Twentieth Century Fund, New York.

Teresa Odendahl, Charity Begins at Home: Generosity and Self-Interest Among the Philanthropic Elite 3-5, 232-240 (1990). Copyright © 1990 by Basic Books, Inc. Reprinted by permission of Basic Books, a division of HarperCollins Publishers, Inc.

Marilyn E. Phelan, Nonprofit Enterprise: Law and Taxation § 1.11 at 32 (1993). Published by Clark Boardman Callaghan, 155 Pfingsten Road, Deerfield, Ill. 60015.

Lester M. Salamon, The Nonprofit Sector: A Primer 11-13, 31-35, 77-81, 84-85, 87, 95-99, 110-112 (2d ed. 1999). Copyright © 1999 by Lester M. Salamon. Published by The Foundation Center, 79 Fifth Avenue, New York, N.Y. 10003.

Lester A. Salamon, The Rise of the Nonprofit Sector, Foreign Affairs, July/August 1994. Reprinted by permission of Foreign Affairs. Copyright © 1994 by the Council on Foreign Relations, Inc.

John G. Simon, The Tax Treatment of Nonprofit Organizations: A Review of Federal and State Policies, in Walter W. Powell (ed.), The Nonprofit Sector: A Research Handbook 68-73 (1987), Yale University Press. Copyright © 1987 by Yale University.

Burton A. Weisbrod, To Profit or Not to Profit: The Commercial Transformation of the Nonprofit Sector 1-4 (1999). Reprinted with the permission of Cambridge University Press and Burton A. Weisbrod.

SUMMARY OF CONTENTS

TABLE OF CONTENTS

CHAPTER 4   Tax Exemption: Mutual Benefit Organizations   508

*

TABLE OF CASES

Principal cases are in bold type. Non-principal cases are in roman type. References are to Pages.

TABLE OF STATUTES

TABLE OF TREASURY REGULATIONS

TABLE OF REVENUE RULINGS

*

TABLE OF MISCELLANEOUS RULINGS

*

TABLE OF AUTHORITIES

profit Organizations with Small Business: An Issue for the 1980s (1984), 575.

Vise, David A., District to Go After Tax-Exempt Groups, Wash. Post, Jan. 25, 1995, p. 213.

Wallace, John A. & Robert W. Fisher, The Charitable Deduction Under Section 170 of the Internal Revenue Code, in IV Research Papers Sponsored by the [Filer] Commission on Private Philanthropy and Public Needs 2131 (1977), 672.

Weisbrod, Burton A., The Nonprofit Economy (1988), 48.

Weisbrod, Burton A., The Voluntary Nonprofit Sector: An Economic Analysis (1977), 45.

Weisbrod, Burton A. (ed.), To Profit or Not to Profit: The Commercial Transformation of the Nonprofit Sector (1998), 44, 563.

Weitzman, Murray S. & Nadine T. Jaladoni, Linda M. Lampkin & Thomas H. Pollak, The New Nonprofit Almanac and Desk Reference (2002), 11.

Wellford, W. Harrison & Janne G. Gallagher, Unfair Competition? The Challenge to Tax Exemption (1988), 211, 575.

Wermeil, U.S. Can't Grant Biased Schools Tax Exemptions, Wall St. J., May 25, 1983, p. 115.

Whelan, Charles M., "Church" in the Internal Revenue Code: The Definitional Problem, 45 Ford. L.Rev. 885 (1977), 201.

Wiggins, A.M., Jr. & Bert W. Hunt, Tax Policy Relating to Environmental Activities and Public Interest Litigation, in IV Research Papers Sponsored by the [Filer] Commission on Private Philanthropy and Public Needs 2045 (1977), 145.

Williams, Grant, New Pa. Law and Court Ruling Specify Standards for Tax Exemption, Chron. Philanthropy, Dec. 11, 1997, p. 215.

Williams, Laurens & Donald V. Moorehead, An Analysis of the Federal Tax Distinctions Between Public and Private Charitable Organizations, in IV Research Papers Sponsored by the [Filer] Commission on Private Philanthropy and Public Needs 2099 (1977), 382.

Wirtschafter, Nathan, Note, Fourth Quarter Choke: How the IRS Blew the Corporate Sponsorship Game, 27 Loy. L.A. L. Rev. 1465 (1994), 610.

Wright, Carolyn D., Christian Coalition Fails to Obtain Tax-Exempt Status, 25 Exempt Org. Tax Rev. 9 (1999), 344.

Wright, Carolyn D., IRS Looking to Pursue Sierra Club Issues in Another Case, Owens Says, 16 Exempt Org. Tax Rev. 564 (1997), 627.

Wright, Carolyn D., UCC, IRS Settle Decade-Long Exemption Dispute: 501(c)(3) Status Revoked for Three Years, 28 Exempt Org. Tax Rev. 189 (2000), 234.

*

CASES AND MATERIALS

TAXATION OF NONPROFIT ORGANIZATIONS

*

INTRODUCTION

CHAPTER 1

An Overview of the Nonprofit Sector

A. Introduction

Revised Model Nonprofit Corporation Act § 13.01.

Cal. Corp. Code § 5410.

The vast array of organizations in the United States that share the designation "nonprofit" are said to inhabit a "sector" of American society—commonly referred to as "the nonprofit sector" and also variously labeled as the "third," "independent," "charitable," "voluntary," "philanthropic," "civil society," and "tax-exempt" sector. The operative assumption is that nonprofits play a societal role that is distinct from that of government and the private, for-profit sector, but much of this terminology is misleading or incomplete. Far from being independent, many nonprofit organizations have a close programmatic and financial relationship with government or private business. Not all nonprofits are charitable or rely on volunteers, nor do all charities derive the bulk of their support from private philanthropy. And nonprofits may and often do earn a profit.

The diversity of the nonprofit sector is evident from this list of familiar and obscure organizations culled from the Internal Revenue Service's list of nonprofits eligible to receive tax-deductible charitable contributions: American Acupuncture and Herbs Research Institute, Phillips Exeter Academy, Girl Scouts of America, Talmudic Research Institute, Museum of Neon Art (Los Angeles), Meditation Center of Michigan, Polynesian Cultural Center, Mothers Club of Grosse Point South High School, The Eucalyptus Foundation, Lincoln Center for the Performing Arts, Planned Parenthood, Church of Scientology International, and the Summit (N.J.) Association for Gerontological Endeavor.

The nonprofit form of organization extends well beyond the charitable, religious, and educational organizations in the above list. Nonprofits include labor unions, fraternal lodges, social clubs, college fraternities, trade associations, and even professional sports leagues. They range from modest entities such as a three-person dance company or a neighborhood free medical clinic, to substantial institutions such as Harvard University, the Ford Foundation or the Mayo Clinic, with revenues and assets in the billions.

Uniting this diverse population and distinguishing nonprofits from for-profit entities is one defining characteristic: the "nondistribution constraint." As explained by Professor Henry Hansmann:

> A nonprofit organization is, in essence, an organization that is barred from distributing its net earnings, if any, to individuals who exercise control over it, such as members, officers, directors, or trustees. By "net earnings" I mean here pure profits—that is, earnings in excess of the amount needed to pay for services rendered to the organization; in general, a nonprofit is free to pay reasonable compensation to any person for labor or capital that he provides, whether or not that person exercises some control over the organization. It should be noted that a nonprofit organization is not barred from earning a profit. Many nonprofits in fact consistently show an annual accounting surplus. It is only the distribution of the profits that is prohibited. Net earnings, if any, must be retained and devoted in their entirety to financing further production of the services that the organization was formed to provide. Since a good deal of the discussion that follows will focus upon this prohibition on the distribution of profits, it will be helpful to have a term for it; I shall call it the "nondistributional constraint."

> Most nonprofits of any significance are incorporated. For these organizations, the nondistribution constraint is imposed, either explicitly or implicitly, as a condition under which the organization receives its corporate charter. Thus a nonprofit corporation is distinguished from a for-profit (or "business") corporation primarily by the absence of stock or other indicia of ownership that give their owner a simultaneous share in both profits and control.

> In the corporation law of some states, the nondistribution constraint is accompanied or replaced by a simple statement to the effect that the organization must not be formed or operated for the purpose of pecuniary gain. Often such a condition as applied is equivalent to the nondistribution constraint. Occasionally, however, it is interpreted more restrictively to mean that an organization may not be incorporated as a nonprofit even if it is intended to assist in the pursuit of pecuniary gain in a more indirect manner.

* * *

> Sometimes nonprofit organizations are formed as charitable trusts without being incorporated, although for operating nonprofits this approach is uncommon in the United States. In such cases, control over the organization lies with the trustees, and the nondistribution constraint is imposed by the law of trusts, which prohibits trustees from taking from the trust anything beyond reasonable compensation for services rendered.

Henry Hansmann, The Role of Nonprofit Enterprise, 89 Yale L.J. 837, 840 (1980).

A study of the taxation of nonprofit organizations is enhanced by having a broader perspective at the outset. To that end, this introductory chapter marks the boundaries of the nonprofit sector, describes its inhabitants, explains its widespread presence in our society, and previews the distinctive state and federal legal regimes that govern and regulate nonprofit organizations in the United States.

John W. Gardner, The Independent Sector

in America's Voluntary Spirit ix, xiii–xv (Brian O'Connell ed., 1983).

In a totalitarian state, most organized activity is governmental—and the little that is not is heavily controlled or influenced by government. Almost everything is bureaucratized and subject to central goal-setting and rule-making.

In the nations that the world thinks of as democracies, there is, in contrast, a large area of activity outside of government. The United States probably outstrips all others in the size and autonomy of its nongovernmental sector. The major portion of our private sector consists of activities designed for profit; a smaller portion consists of nonprofit activities. Both profit and nonprofit segments have many dealings with government, but both recognize that their vitality depends in part on their success in holding themselves free of central bureaucratic definition of goals.

Our subject here is the nonprofit segment. It has been variously labelled the voluntary sector, the third sector or—more recently—the independent sector.

In its diversity and strength the voluntary sector is uniquely American—not in the fact of its existence, because it exists elsewhere, but in its extraordinary richness and variety. It encompasses a remarkable array of American institutions—libraries, museums, religious organizations, schools and colleges, organizations concerned with health and welfare, citizen action groups, neighborhood organizations and countless other groups such as Alcoholics Anonymous, the Urban League, the 4H Clubs, the Women's Political Caucus, the Salvation Army, and the United Way. * * *

Attributes of the Sector

It is worth reviewing some of the characteristics of the independent sector that make it a powerfully positive force in American life. There is no point in comparing it favorably or unfavorably with other sectors of the society. Each has its function.

Perhaps the most striking feature of the sector is its relative freedom from constraints and its resulting pluralism. Within the bounds of the law, all kinds of people can pursue any idea or program they wish. Unlike government, an independent sector group need not ascertain that its idea or philosophy is supported by some large constituency, and unlike the business sector, they do not need to pursue only those ideas which will be profitable. If a handful of people want to back a new idea, they need seek no larger consensus.

Americans have always believed in pluralism—the idea that a free nation should be hospitable to many sources of initiative, many kinds of institutions, many conflicting beliefs, and many competing economic units. Our pluralism allows individuals and groups to pursue goals that they themselves formulate, and out of that pluralism has come virtually all of our creativity.

Every institution in the independent sector is not innovative, but the sector provides a hospitable environment for innovation. Ideas for doing things in a different, and possibly better, way spring up constantly. If they do not fill a need, they quickly fall by the wayside. What remains are the few ideas and innovations that have long-term value. New ideas and new ways of doing things test the validity of accepted practice and build an inventory of possible alternative solutions which can be used if circumstances change.

Government bureaucracies are simply not constructed to permit the emergence of countless new ideas, and even less suited to the winnowing out of bad ideas. An idea that is controversial, unpopular, or "strange" has little chance in either the commercial or the political marketplace. In the nonprofit sector, someone with a new idea or program may very well find the few followers necessary to help nurse it to maturity. Virtually every significant social idea of the past century in this country has been nurtured in the nonprofit sector.

The sector is the natural home of nonmajoritarian impulses, movements, and values. It comfortably harbors innovators, maverick movements, groups which feel that they must fight for their place in the sun, and critics of both liberal and conservative persuasion.

Institutions of the nonprofit sector are in a position to serve as the guardians of intellectual and artistic freedom. Both the commercial and political marketplaces are subject to leveling forces that may threaten standards of excellence. In the nonprofit sector, the fiercest champions of excellence may have their say. So may the champions of liberty and justice.

The sector preserves individual initiative and responsibility. As in the for-profit sector, there are innumerable opportunities for the resourceful— to initiate, explore, grow, cooperate, lead, make a difference. At a time in history when individuality is threatened by the impersonality of large-scale social organization, the sector's emphasis on individual initiative is a priceless counterweight.

To deal effectively with the ailments of our society today, individual initiative isn't enough, there has to be some way of linking the individual with the community. In the independent sector, such linkages are easily forged. Citizens banding together can tackle a small neighborhood problem or a great national issue.

The past century has seen a more or less steady deterioration of American communities as coherent entities with the morale and binding values that hold people together. Our sense of community has been badly battered, and every social philosopher emphasizes the need to restore it. What is at stake is the individual's sense of responsibility for something beyond the self. A spirit of concern for one's fellows is virtually impossible to sustain in a vast, impersonal, featureless society. Only in coherent human groupings (the neighborhood, the family, the community) can we keep alive our shared values and preserve the simple human awareness that we need one another. We must recreate a society that has its social and spiritual roots firmly planted in such groupings—so firmly planted that those roots cannot be ripped out by the winds of change, nor by the dehumanizing, automatizing forces of the contemporary world.

This is not to express a sentimental aversion to large-scale organization or national action. Many of the forces acting upon us can only be dealt with by large-scale organizations, national in scope, including a vigorous government. But if we intend that the overarching governmental organizations we create be our servants and not our masters, we must have vital communities.

The Great Shared Task

My observations about the positive aspects of the sector are not intended to gloss over the flaws that are evident in its institutions and organizations. Some nonprofit institutions are far gone in decay. Some are so badly managed as to make a mockery of every good intention they might have had. There is fraud, mediocrity, and silliness. In short, the human and institutional failures that afflict government and business are also present in the voluntary sector. Beyond that, it is the essence of pluralism (in the society as a whole as well as in this sector) that no particular observer will approve of everything that goes on. If you can't find a nonprofit institution that you can honestly disrespect, then something has gone wrong with our pluralism.

But these considerations are trivial compared to the attributes that make the independent sector a source of deep and positive meaning in our national life. If it were to disappear from our national life, we would be less distinctly American. The sector enhances our creativity, enlivens our communities, nurtures individual responsibility, stirs life at the grassroots, and reminds us that we were born free. Its vitality is rooted in good soil—civic pride, compassion, a philanthropic tradition, a strong problem-solving impulse, a sense of individual responsibility and, despite what cynics may say, an irrepressible commitment to the great shared task of improving our life together.

Gilbert M. Gaul & Neill A. Borowski, Free Ride: The Tax–Exempt Economy

1–13 (1993).

The National Football League, that bastion of free enterprise and million-dollar quarterbacks, doesn't look like a nonprofit organization.

Then again, it doesn't act like one, either. The NFL spends less than 1 percent of its $35 million budget on charitable activities, pays its commissioner $1.5 million a year, and spends another $1.5 million to lease seven floors of a Park Avenue office tower. Or take the Motion Picture Academy of Arts and Sciences, which spent $6 million to put on the dazzling Oscars show. You thought nonprofit organizations had to be charities, run by meagerly paid managers and volunteers? Not anymore..

Thanks to the remarkable largess of Washington lawmakers, an ever-expanding definition of charity and a near-total collapse of government supervision, America's nonprofit economy has become a huge, virtually unregulated industry. Within it, almost anything and anybody qualifies for tax-exempt status. Auto racing promoters. Collection agencies. Country clubs. Criminals. A half-billion-dollar defense research corporation. Investment houses. Mail-order colleges. A polo museum. Retail stores. Professional surfers. An association of Druids. Foreign real estate investors. Space explorers. Even a chili appreciation society.

Each year for the last dozen years, an average of 29,000 new groups have been declared nonprofit and gone off the tax rolls. Today, an estimated 1.2 million organizations are exempt from taxes—not counting churches, which don't even have to apply.

Think of it as Congress' contribution to charity. And you make up for the taxes they don't pay. A major but little-noticed change has taken place in the American economy in the last 20 years: the dramatic growth of nonprofit businesses. These businesses had an estimated $500 billion in revenues in 1990—nearly six times the income of farms, five times that of utilities and twice as much as the construction industry. They represented roughly 6 percent of the nation's total economic output and employed about 7 million people. Since 1970, this tax-exempt sector has grown four times as fast as the rest of the economy.

Nonprofit hospitals, universities, museums and churches own large parcels of real estate, on which they pay no property or income taxes. Even the most dramatic building on the Philadelphia skyline, One Liberty Place, was built with financing help from a nonprofit pension fund. Nationally, nonprofits control property, cash and investments worth more than $850 billion—and that is a conservative estimate. Because neither churches nor smaller nonprofit groups have to report income or assets, the true figure probably exceeds $1 trillion. Government economists acknowledge that they don't track the tax-free economy or its impact. To put $850 billion in perspective, if the holdings of nonprofit groups and foundations were liquidated tomorrow, there would be enough to write a $3,401 check for each man, woman and child in America. Or enough to pay off last year's federal deficit and have more than $500 billion left over for Bill Clinton to spend.

These exemptions are costing more than $36.5 billion a year in lost tax revenue * * *. That is the equivalent of the income taxes paid by 25 million taxpayers. At the local level, the exclusion of billions of dollars worth of property from the tax rolls of cash-starved school districts and municipalities is increasing budget woes and straining social services.

The transformation of this nonprofit economy has happened largely without notice, forethought or national debate about the consequences and public policy implications for the country. Nonprofit groups do a lot of good in a lot of areas for a lot of people. That's why they were granted exemption from taxation. But as Congress has become more and more liberal with the nonprofit designation, and as the Internal Revenue Service has become swamped, abuses have grown.

An 18–month study by The [Philadelphia] Inquirer, which included examination of tax returns of 6,000 exempt organizations, found that:

• Many nonprofits operate just like for-profit businesses. They make huge profits, pay handsome salaries, build office towers, invest billions of dollars in stocks and bonds, employ lobbyists and use political action committees to influence legislation. And increasingly they compete with taxpaying businesses.

• Executives at some large nonprofit businesses make more than $1 million a year. Of 25,000 salaries examined of executives of big nonprofit organizations, nearly half were at least $100,000 a year. The top compensation in 1991 was NFL commissioner Paul Tagliabue, who was paid $1,511,731 in salary and benefits. Many also received such perks as free housing, maid services, luxury cars and chauffeurs, and no-interest loans.

• Nonprofit hospitals, which originally were exempted from taxes because of their charity care, now devote an average of 6 percent of expenditures to caring for the poor. In the Philadelphia area, the figure is even less. Meanwhile, more than $1 billion in hospital profits have been shifted to commercial spinoffs—hotels, restaurants, health spas, laundries, marinas, parking garages.

• Private, nonprofit colleges and universities have more than doubled their tuition in the last decade, even though their income from investments was doubling and tripling in the 1980s. Some schools—including MIT, CalTech and Penn State's main campus—now spend more on research than on teaching; these schools collect millions of dollars for work done under contract to commercial companies. This income is shielded from taxes, and the companies get a tax write-off.

• Private foundations have become great warehouses of untaxed wealth. Most foundations give away only the minimum required by law, 5 percent of their [net] assets each year, while earning much more on investments. With $163 billion in assets, they are operated like private banks, with elite, self-perpetuating boards of directors. Where they invest their money and how they vote their stock give these boards great economic power.

• A multibillion-dollar pool of cheap money, available through low-interest loans to tax-exempt organizations and subsidized by taxpayers, has financed a massive expansion of hospitals and universities. Some have overbuilt: On any given night, one third of the hospital beds in America are empty. In Pennsylvania, more than 100 government authorities issue low-interest tax-exempt bonds, with few questions about whether the projects are needed.

• Dozens of directors and executives of nonprofit institutions own or are officers of outside companies that do business with the nonprofit. The services they provide range from legal and financial advice to selling the nonprofit food or other goods. The IRS requires disclosure of such relationships, but only minimal details about finances.

• The Internal Revenue Service, which is charged with policing nonprofits, is so understaffed—and the number of exempt organizations so large—that it would take 79 years to audit them all at the present rate. Most applications for nonprofit status are rubber-stamped by IRS; even convicted felons have been approved.

"Until I looked, I thought being declared a nonprofit was pretty hard. Then I found something like 95 or 99 percent who apply get approved. It's like getting your driver's license," said Ted Chapler, executive director of the Iowa Finance Authority, which arranges tax-exempt financing for nonprofit organizations.

* * *

[O]ver the years, three basic changes have occurred with large nonprofits. Instead of depending on charitable contributions, many tax-exempt businesses began charging fees for services. And the fees kept rising. Also, federal programs—Medicaid, Medicare, Social Security disability—began paying for many of the services once provided by charities. And Congress, responding to special interests, expanded its definition of nonprofit to include many new categories, such as fraternal groups, trade associations, mutual life insurance companies, health insurance firms, labor unions, retirement funds, cemeteries and credit unions.

Today there are 25 categories of nonprofits—including the one that covers the NFL. Congress rewrote the tax laws in 1966 to declare the professional football league a not-for-profit enterprise, inserting the NFL in the same section of the tax code that exempts boards of trade and local chambers of commerce from federal taxes. The exemption covers only the league organization, not the teams and players within it. Nor is the NFL the only professional sports organization to benefit. The National Hockey League, Professional Bowling Association, Professional Golf Association, U.S. Tennis Association and the players' associations of football and major league baseball are among the many tax-exempt sports groups. Then there's the National Museum of Polo & Hall of Fame. Its exempt purpose "relates to the operation of the Polo Museum and Hall of Fame at the Kentucky Horse Park in Lexington, Ky." Among its major 1990 expenses: tent rental, catering and dinner at the Club Collette in Palm Beach, Fla.

* * *

For most companies, earning 10 cents in profit on every dollar in revenue would be considered a very good year. Many large nonprofits make that much and more. In 1991, the University of Pennsylvania made 11 cents in profit for each dollar it took in—$153 million profit on revenues of $1.3 billion. A year before, it made 13 cents on the dollar. During most of the 1980s, Penn enjoyed double-digit profit margins.

Princeton University has done even better. In 1990, it made 32 cents profit on every dollar of revenue—$197 million on revenues of about $613 million. Only one public company, Newmont Mining Inc., had a higher profit margin in the Fortune 500 rankings that year. Then there's the Bible business. In 1991 the nonprofit American Bible Society made 55 cents on each dollar of revenue—$52 million on revenues of $95 million. The Society's $350 million in investments was enough to run the business for eight years. As these examples show, many nonprofit businesses are highly profitable. An Inquirer computer analysis of 630 large nonprofits found that they had an average profit margin of 9 percent in 1990—more than double the average of Fortune 500 companies.

* * *

Harvard University, which has an investment portfolio worth [$17.5 billion as of June 30, 2002, had a 15.2 percent average annual total return for the ten years ending June 30, 2002, Eds.]. Not every nonprofit made money. Mt. Sinai Hospital in Philadelphia, a division of the Graduate Health System, recorded a loss of $16.8 million. As a group, however, hospitals and health-care organizations were among the most profitable. The Mayo Clinic Foundation in Rochester, Minn., had a profit of nearly $90 million on revenues of $642 million. Mayo's 14 percent profit margin would have ranked it ahead of such pharmaceutical companies as Johnson & Johnson Inc., Pfizer Inc. and Warner Lambert Inc. And the drug industry is considered the most profitable business in America. Mayo was so wealthy, it ended 1991 with $979 million in unrestricted funds, money it could use for whatever it chose. It operated 11 taxable subsidiaries, including an airport management company, and had 28 companies in all. Mayo owned buildings, property and equipment valued at $773 million, including spinoff clinics in Jacksonville, Fla., and Scottsdale, Ariz.

Another charity that fared well was Father Flanagan's Boys Home, better known as Boys Town, near Omaha, Neb. In fiscal 1989, it had a profit of $29 million on income of $93 million—a 32 percent margin. That would have dwarfed margins of IBM, General Motors, Reebok or Time–Warner. Boys Town, popularized in a 1938 film featuring Spencer Tracy and Mickey Rooney, owned stocks, bonds, property and Treasury bills worth nearly $423 million. It had four outside advisers to manage its investment portfolio. In 1990, Boys Town officials set up a separate tax-exempt foundation, Father Flanagan's Foundation Fund, Inc., and transferred $371 million in investment holdings. Since then, the value of the foundation's holdings has increased to $478 million. Boys Town's treasurer, Jim Schmidt, said the goal was to build up the foundation's wealth and use a portion of the interest income to help support Boys Town's expanding services to troubled children.

B.   Dimensions of the Nonprofit Sector

The dimensions of the nonprofit sector are constantly being measured. Bean counting abounds on the number and categories of nonprofits, their sources of support, income, expenses, employees, and share of the gross national product. The Independent Sector, an organization formed to conduct research on nonprofits, estimates that there are approximately 1.6 million nonprofit organizations in the United States. If one counts local chapters of regional or national groups, the number grows to over 6 million. In 1998, nonprofits had 10.9 million paid employees and 5.8 million volunteers, representing 7.1 percent of the total employment in the United States. The nonprofit sector's share of national income in 1998 was 6.7 percent or $443.6 billion compared to the for-profit sector's 80 percent and government's 13.3 percent. According to the latest survey by the Chronicle of Philanthropy, the largest charitable nonprofit (based on private donations) was The Salvation Army, which received $1.391 billion in donations and had a total income of $1.9 billion in its 2001 fiscal year. The second ranked charity measured by private support was the Fidelity Investments Charitable Gift Fund at $1.055 billion. Rounding out the "top five" were the Stowers Institute for Medical Research ($950 million), Lutheran Services in America ($848 million), and YMCA of the USA ($791 million). See The Tide Turns, Chron. of Philanthropy, Oct. 31, 2002, at 28.

NOTE: WHERE THE MONEY COMES FROM—SOURCES OF FUNDING OF THE CHARITABLE SECTOR

It may come as a surprise, but the major sources of funds derived by what we will come to know as public benefit organizations are fees, dues, and charges for services provided. As reflected in Table 1.1, below, in 1997 private contributions accounted for only 20 percent of revenue compared to 38 percent from fees for services and 31 percent from government.

Table 1.1

Sources of Nonprofit Sector's Funds 1997

Source	Amount (in Billions) of Dollars	Percentage of Total
Dues Fees & Charges	249.0	37.5
Contributions	132.1	19.9
Government	207.8	31.3
Other (net profit from sales and investment income)	75.9	11.4
TOTAL	$664.8	100%

Source: Murray S. Weitzman, Nadine T. Jalandoni, Linda M. Lampkin & Thomas H. Pollak, The New Nonprofit Almanac and Desk Reference (2002). Dollar figures are rounded off.

• *Fees, service charges, and other commercial income.* The major source of support of America's nonprofit, public-benefit, service organizations are fees, service charges, and other commercial income. Included here are college tuition payments, charges for hospital care not covered by government health insurance, other direct payments for services, and income from investments and sales of products. This source alone accounts for over half of all nonprofit service-organization revenues.

• *Government.* The second most important source of income of nonprofit, public-benefit, service organizations is government. Government grants, contracts, and reimbursements account for 31.3 percent of nonprofit service-organization income. This reflects a widespread pattern of partnership between government and the nonprofit sector in carrying out public purposes, from the delivery of health care to the provision of education.

• *Private Giving.* The 19.9 percent of total income that nonprofits receive from private giving makes this the third largest source of nonprofit service-organization income.

As summarized in Tables 1.2 and 1.3, which reflect the most recent available data, individuals were the major source of charitable giving, and most of those gifts were made to churches. Total charitable giving in 2001 was $212 billion, a modest 0.5 percent increase over the previous year. Table 1.3 ranks the recipients of charitable gifts, with religious organizations at the top with 38.2 percent of total gifts in 2001.

Table 1.2

Sources of Charitable Giving, 2001

Source	Amount (in Billions) of Dollars	Percentage of Total
Individuals	$160.72	75.8
Foundations	25.90	12.2
Bequests	16.33	7.7
Corporations	9.05	4.3
TOTAL	$212.00	100%

Source: American Association of Fund–Raising Counsel, Giving USA 2002 (2002). Data available at http://www.aafrc.org/images/graphics/chart1.gif

Table 1.3

Recipients of Charitable Giving, 2002

Recipient	Amount (in Billions) of Dollars	Percentage of Total
Religion	$ 80.96	38.2
Education	31.84	15.0
Foundations	25.55	12.1
Health	18.43	8.7

Human services	20.71	9.3
Public/society benefit	11.82	5.6
Arts, culture, humanities	12.14	5.7
Environment, wildlife	6.41	3.0
International affairs	4.14	2.0
TOTAL	$212.00 *	

Source: American Association of Fund–Raising Counsel, Giving USA 2002 (2002). Data available at http://www.aafrc.org/images/graphics/chart2.gif 2002 (2002)

* The total and percentages exceed the sources of charitable giving because some nonprofits, the United Way is an example, support other nonprofits.

The largest subsectors of the charitable branch of the nonprofit sector are religious congregations and service-providing organizations in fields such as health care, education, and other social services. The excerpts that follow offer an overview of these areas in both the domestic and international settings.

Lester M. Salamon, America's Nonprofit Sector: A Primer

31–35, 77–81, 84–85, 87, 95–99, 110–112 (2d ed. 1999).

SCOPE AND STRUCTURE: THE ANATOMY OF AMERICA'S NON-PROFIT SECTOR

Religious Congregations

In addition to the funding intermediaries [foundations, united ways], a second broad class of public-serving nonprofit organizations are the numerous sacramental religious organizations. Included here are the close to 350,000 religious congregations—churches, mosques, synagogues, and other places of worship—as well as an assortment of conventions of churches, religious orders, apostolic groups, and religious auxiliaries. * * *

Although they often engage in a variety of service functions, religious congregations really exist primarily to serve the needs of their members rather than the public more generally. * * * They are the only organizations that are automatically entitled to tax exemption under Section 501(c)(3) of the tax code, and thus to the receipt of tax deductible donations, without even having to file an application for formal recognition from the Internal Revenue Service. They are also exempt from the reporting requirements that the law places on other types of 501(c)(3) organizations.

This favored position reflects the strong separation of church and state built into the American constitution. Because the power to tax is the power to destroy, it is felt that to require religious congregations to secure approval from government to be incorporated or exempted from taxation would be to give government too much potential control over them. A self-declared religious congregation is therefore automatically treated as a 501(c)(3) organization exempt from taxes and eligible to receive tax-deductible gifts.

What constitutes a religious congregation or church for this purpose is open to dispute, however. Federal authorities have historically been loath to define the term very precisely in view of the First Amendment's prohibition on any laws regarding the establishment of religion or the free exercise thereof. But the appearance of various self-styled religious organizations that turn out to be fronts for nonexempt activities has led the courts and the Internal Revenue Service to be somewhat more precise. Thus, churches and religious organizations are expected, among other things, to have some recognized creed or form of worship, to be sacerdotal in character, to have regular religious services, and to operate, like other 501(c)(3) organizations, for other than private gain.

Service Providers

We come now to what in many respects is the heart of the public-serving nonprofit sector: the broad assortment of organizations that are neither funding intermediaries nor sacramental religious congregations but rather service-providing organizations. Included are providers of health services, education, day care, adoption services, counseling, community organization, employment and training, arts, culture, music, theater, and hundreds of others. Also included, however, are research institutes, advocacy organizations seeking to promote particular causes or call attention to social and economic ills, community-based organizations, and organizations involved in overseas relief and development.

To make sense of this welter of organizations, it is useful to group them into five basic categories:

- health care, including hospitals, clinics, nursing and personal care facilities, home health care centers, and specialty facilities (e.g., kidney dialysis units);
- education, including elementary and secondary education, higher education, libraries, vocational schools, noncommercial research institutes, and related educational services;
- social and legal services, including individual and family social services, job training and vocational rehabilitation services, residential care, day care, and legal aid services;
- civic and social, including advocacy organizations, civil rights organizations, neighborhood based organizations; and
- arts and culture, including bands, orchestras, theater groups, museums, art galleries, and botanical and zoological gardens.

* * *

Numbers of Organizations

Solid data on the scope of this nonprofit service sector, or of its constituent parts, are difficult to piece together and sensitive to differences in record-keeping (e.g., some organizations treat their branches as separate organizations and others as integral parts of a single parent organization;

many organizations carry out a multitude of activities and cannot easily be classified in one category). [As of the end of 2001, 1,567,580 organizations were registered with the IRS as tax-exempt under § 501(c) of the Internal Revenue Code.₁ Many of the organizations on the IRS master list are small or inactive; many other organizations, such as churches or local chapters, are not required to register with the IRS and are not included in these totals. At the end of 2002, approximately 55 percent of all IRS-recognized organizations were exempt from taxation under § 501(c)(3) of the Internal Revenue Code. These organizations are organized and operated exclusively for religious, charitable, scientific, literary or educational purposes. See Table 1.4, infra, p. 57. Eds.] [T]hese organizations are not distributed evenly among the various service fields. Rather:

- The *social service agencies* are the most numerous. Close to 40 percent of nonprofit service organizations fall into this category. Included here are child day care centers, individual or family counseling agencies, job training and vocational rehabilitation facilities, residential care institutions, and the like.

- The next largest group of nonprofit service agencies are *educational and research institutions*, including private elementary and secondary schools as well as private universities and colleges, libraries, and research institutes. Close to 38,000 such nonprofit educational institutions exist and they comprise 22 percent of the sector's institutions.

- The third most numerous type of nonprofit agencies are the *civic organizations*, which includes neighborhood associations, advocacy organizations, community improvement agencies, civil rights organizations and the like. Seventeen percent of nonprofit service organizations take this form.

- *Health organizations*, including hospitals, nursing homes, and clinics, comprise 14 percent of the organizations.

- The smallest component of the nonprofit service sector is the arts and recreation component, which includes symphonies, art galleries, theaters, zoos, botanical gardens, and other cultural and recreational institutions. Together, these cultural and recreational organizations represent 8 percent of the known nonprofit organizations.

Expenditures: A Major Economic Force

Because of the growth of government spending in recent decades and the prominence given to government policies, it is widely believed that this nonprofit service sector has shrunk into insignificance. Yet nothing could be further from the truth. To the contrary, in addition to their social value, nonprofit organizations are also a major economic force. In particular, these nonprofit public-benefit service organizations had expenditures in

---

1. This information is derived primarily from the most recently available IRS data, and research by Professor Lester Salamon and others. See 2002 Internal Revenue Service Data Book, Publication 55B.

1996 of approximately $460 billion, or almost 6 percent of the country's gross national product and more than 30 percent of total expenditures on services. * * *

The distribution of expenditures differs widely, however, from the distribution of organizations * * *:

- *Health dominance.* The health subsector, composed in part of huge hospital complexes, accounts for the lion's share of the sector's total resources even though it comprises a relatively small proportion of the organizations. In particular, with 14 percent of the organizations the health subsector accounts for 62 percent of all nonprofit service-organization expenditures.

- *Significant education presence.* The education subsector accounted for another 21 percent of the expenditures. Health and education organizations alone thus control over 80 percent of the sector's expenditures.

- *Balance of the sector.* By contrast, the social service, civic and social, and arts organizations, which represent altogether two out of every three (65 percent) of the organizations, accounted for only 17 percent of the expenditures.

Quite clearly, this is a sector with a great deal of diversity in the size of its component organizations.

* * *

HEALTH CARE

Of all the components of the nonprofit service sector, the largest by far is health care. * * * [N]onprofit health providers absorbed close to 60 percent of all nonprofit revenues in 1996 and over 25 percent of all private charitable contributions. This reflects the tremendous scale of the health care field. But it also reflects the substantial role that nonprofit organizations play in this field.

* * *

Overview: National Health Spending

Basic Contours

Health has emerged in recent years as one of the largest and fastest growing components of national spending. * * * [C]lose to 30 percent of government social welfare spending goes for health care, and an even larger amount of private spending goes into this field as well. As of 1996, in fact, health care accounted for 13.6 percent of the U.S. gross national product—a total of $1.035 trillion in spending.

Recent Growth

Health expenditures are not only large, but they have also been growing rapidly. [T]otal health spending grew nearly fivefold between 1965 and 1996, after adjusting for inflation, roughly twice as fast as the nation's overall gross national product. As a result, health expenditures went from about 6 percent of gross national product in 1965 to nearly 14 percent by 1996.

Although health expenditures have grown rapidly over this 30–year period, the pace of growth seems to have slowed somewhat in the 1990s, largely as a result of the so-called "managed care revolution," the widespread replacement of fee-for-service insurance by managed care insurance plans that impose more severe limits on the amounts that health care providers can charge for various services. After expanding at an average rate of 10–13 percent (before adjusting for inflation) during the 1970s and 1980s, therefore, health spending growth dropped to 4–5 percent per year in the mid–1990s.

Sources of Growth

A principal source of the growth in health spending between 1965 and 1996 * * * was the increase that occurred in *government* health spending. Such spending grew eightfold between 1965 and 1996, after adjusting for inflation, compared to a threefold increase in private health spending. This reflects primarily the creation of the federal Medicare and Medicaid programs in 1965. As a result, government spending on health increased from 26 percent of the total in 1965 to 47 percent of a much larger total in 1996.

Even so, the private-sector contribution to the growth was larger in absolute terms, so that private sources remained dominant by the end of the period. At the same time the growth rate of non-private health spending dropped especially extensively in the 1990s, from more than 10 percent a year in the 1970s and 1980s to under 3 percent in the mid–1990s.

The Role of Philanthropy

Although the nonprofit sector plays a major role in the health field, as will be documented more fully below, very little of the revenue in this field comes from private philanthropy. In particular, of the $1.035 trillion in health care spending in 1996, only $16.3 billion, or less than 2 percent, came from private philanthropic giving. Such giving is somewhat more important in financing certain subfields, such as medical research and construction, but even here it is far from the dominant source.

The Role of Nonprofit Providers

While private philanthropy may constitute a relatively limited part of overall health finance, however, the private, nonprofit sector nevertheless plays a very significant role in health care delivery. To understand this role, however, it is necessary to divide the health sector into its component parts and look more closely at the four components where nonprofit organizations are most important: hospital care, clinic care, nursing home care, and insurance.

Hospital Care

Overview

Scale. Hospital care represents the largest single component of health care in the United States, and also the one where nonprofit organizations are most prominent. [J]ust over one-third of all health spending goes for hospital care—a total of $358.5 billion in 1996. By comparison, private practitioners (dentists and physicians) received 24 percent of total health expenditures, while nursing homes received 8 percent.

Sources of funding. Unlike health care as a whole, government is the dominant source of funding for hospitals. * * * More than 60 percent of all hospital revenue comes from government, up from 55 percent just a decade before. Of this total, the federal government contributes by far the lion's share—51 percent of total hospital income—with state and local governments providing 11 percent. The remaining funding, about 38 percent in 1996, comes from private sources, including 34 percent from private fees and insurance payments and 4 percent from private philanthropy and miscellaneous sales.

Number and types of hospitals. * * * As of 1996, there were about 6,363 hospitals in the United States registered with the American Hospital Association. Of these, the overwhelming majority (83 percent) are general hospitals, the type with which most people are familiar. The remainder include some 710 psychiatric hospitals and another 385 other specialized hospitals.

Nonprofit vs. Government, and For–Profit Roles in the Hospital Industry

Nonprofit hospitals. While government provides most of the hospital spending, nonprofit institutions deliver most of the hospital services. Just about half (50 percent) of all hospitals in the country are organized as nonprofits. These nonprofit hospitals account for 56 percent of the country's hospital beds, and 70 percent of all hospital expenditures.

Nonprofits are especially prominent among the country's general hospitals, which form the heart of the nation's hospital industry. Despite a flurry of for-profit hospital formations in the 1980s, 55 percent of these institutions remain private, nonprofit organizations and they account for 64 percent of the general hospital beds and 72 percent of the general hospital expenditures. By contrast, only 25 percent of the specialty hospitals are nonprofit organizations and they account for only 15 percent of the specialty hospital beds.

Government hospitals. About a third (31 percent) of all hospitals are operated by governmental authorities, chiefly at the state and local levels. * * * Most of these are general hospitals, many of them in central city areas. However, government is also quite prominent in the specialty hospital field. Thus, 31 percent of the specialty hospitals are operated by governmental authorities, and these government institutions account for 53 percent of all specialty hospital expenditures and 62 percent of specialty hospital beds.

For-profit hospitals. For-profit corporations play a considerably smaller role in the hospital field, with 19 percent of all hospitals and 14 percent of all hospital beds. However, for-profit corporations have carved out a particular niche for themselves in the specialty hospital field. Forty-four percent of all specialty hospitals are for-profit institutions. Although these institutions tend to be smaller than the typical public hospital, they are nevertheless a significant component of the industry.

* * *

Clinics and Home Health Care

Overview

The second largest component of the health field in which nonprofit organizations have a substantial role is outpatient care other than in doctors' offices. Included here is a wide assortment of activities including clinic care, home health care, kidney dialysis centers, drug and alcohol treatment centers, public health services, school health, and a variety of miscellaneous health services. * * * [T]his component of the health care field accounted for 15 percent of all health expenditures in 1996, or about $150 billion.

Of this total, nearly one-fourth goes for *government public health activities*, which include local public health screening and the federal government's Public Health Service and Center for Disease Control. An even larger share (nearly 40 percent) goes for a variety of *outpatient clinics* (e.g., kidney dialysis centers, drug treatment centers, rehabilitation centers). These institutions bear a strong resemblance to the short-term specialty facilities that are gaining ground within the hospital industry, except that these facilities are tailored to "outpatient" care. Another 20 percent of this portion of health care spending goes for the relatively new field of *home health care* (i.e., skilled nursing or medical care provided in the home). Finally, the remaining 18 percent went for *other personal health services*, such as drug abuse treatment and school health.

Like hospital care, clinic and home health care spending is mostly financed by government. [G]overnment provides 60 percent of all the spending in this field. This is partly due to the fact that this field includes the direct public health activities and school health services. But it also reflects the broadening of Medicare coverage, beginning in the late 1980s, to include home health services. This triggered a considerable surge in the home health care industry.

Nonprofit Role

Nonprofit organizations play a major role in the provision of outpatient and home health care, although they have recently faced considerable competition from for-profit providers * * * . [N]onprofit organizations represent a third of the roughly 37,000 private health clinics identified by the U.S. Census Bureau in its latest *Census of Service Industries*. What is more, the nonprofit facilities seem to be larger on average than the for-profit ones, so that they account for 45 percent of the employees and, as of 1996, 44 percent of the revenues.

* * *

Nursing Home Care

Overview

Nursing home care is the third major component of the health field where nonprofit organizations are active. * * * [N]ursing homes absorbed about 8 percent of all health spending in 1996, a total of some $80 billion. Of this, over 60 percent now comes from government and about 40 percent from private sources, all but 2 percent of this in the form of fees. Most of the government revenue comes from the Medicaid program, but Medicare has recently increased its funding of nursing home care as well.

* * *

EDUCATION

If health is the largest component of the American nonprofit sector, education is the second largest. One out of every five dollars of nonprofit expenditures are made by nonprofit education institutions. * * * What is more, nonprofit institutions play important roles in all four major segments of the educational system: (1) higher education, (2) elementary and secondary education, (3) vocational education, and (4) library services.

* * *

Education Spending

Overview

Scale and Uses. Americans spent $518 billion on education in the 1995–96 academic year, about half as much as on health, but still a significant 7 percent of the gross national product. [T]he bulk of this spending (58 percent) went for elementary and secondary education. Higher education absorbed another 39 percent. The balance (about 3 percent) went for vocational education and library services.

Sources of spending. Unlike the situation in the health sphere, where private spending is the dominant source of revenue, in the education sphere most of the spending originates with government. As of 1995, close to 70 percent of total education spending in the United States came from government, almost 90 percent of it from the state and local level. By comparison, private fees and payments accounted for 28 percent of the total and private philanthropy for about 3 percent.

[T]his situation is largely a reflection of the major role that government plays in the financing of elementary and secondary education in the United States. Thus, 90 percent of all elementary and secondary education funds come from government. By contrast, government provides only 39 percent of the funding for higher education, while 55 percent comes from tuition and fees.

* * *

The Role of Philanthropy and the Nonprofit Sector

Although philanthropy plays a relatively minor role in the *financing* of education, as in the case of health the nonprofit sector nevertheless plays a significant role in the *delivery* of education. Overall, nonprofit organizations absorb close to one in every five dollars of education spending. In some fields, such as higher education, moreover, the nonprofit share is considerably larger than this.

* * *

Sources of Funds

[T]he pattern of funding of higher education in the United States differs considerably from that for other levels of education. In particular, fees and charges play a significantly more important role in the funding of higher education than they do for elementary and secondary education, where government is the dominant source of support.

[T]his distinctive higher education funding pattern is largely a product of the nonprofit institutions. Fully 70 percent of the income of these institutions comes from fees and other sales. Government is a distant second as a source of support, with 17 percent of the revenue. Private gifts, grants, contracts, and endowment earnings together account for the remaining 13 percent of support. Even for the private institutions, therefore, private philanthropy is only the third most important source of support.

The public institutions of higher education, by contrast, rely more heavily on government support, though even here government's contribution is somewhat smaller than might be assumed. Half of the revenue of the public institutions comes from government. But fee and sale income is also significant, accounting for about 44 percent of the total. Finally, private gifts, grants, contracts, and endowment income provide the remaining 5 percent.

* * *

SOCIAL SERVICES

Definition

Although the term "social services" is somewhat amorphous, the basic concept behind it is fairly straightforward. Social services are essentially forms of assistance, other than outright cash aid, that help individuals and families to function in the face of social, economic, or physical problems or needs. Included are day-care services, adoption assistance, family counseling, residential care for the elderly or the physically or mentally handicapped, vocational rehabilitation, disaster assistance, refugee assistance, emergency food assistance, substance abuse treatment, and many more.

Overall Scale

Although the social services field has expanded considerably since the 1960s—the product of some major economic and demographic changes as well as the launching of a number of new government programs—the scale of this field still lags far behind that of either health or education. Thus, of the $1.434 trillion in government social welfare spending as of 1994, only $28.2 billion, or about 2 percent, went for social services. By comparison, education absorbed $345.3 billion in government funding and health $391.1 billion—both well over ten times as much.

Government is only one source of social service spending, of course, but even with nongovernmental funds included, social service spending is a pale reflection of the spending on either health or education. Thus, as of 1994, social services absorbed approximately $73.6 billion in total spending, or a mere 1 percent of gross domestic product. By comparison, as previous chapters have shown, health spending totaled $1.035 billion, or almost 14 percent of the gross domestic product; and education spending totaled $518 billion, or 7 percent of gross domestic product.

Sources of Social Service Spending

[T]he largest single source of social service spending is fees and charges. As of the mid–1990s, this source accounted for 49 percent of total social service spending in the United States. The second largest source of such spending is government which accounted for 38 percent of the total as of 1994. By contrast, private giving from all sources—individuals, foundations, and corporations—accounted for a considerably smaller 13 percent of social service spending.

The substantial role that fees and service charges play in the financing of social services at the present time reflects the changing character of the social services market in recent years. The aging of the population, the increased labor force participation of women, and the proliferation of drug abuse and related forms of addiction have increased the demand for residential care, counseling, day-care, and related social services on the part of populations that can pay for such services, either directly or through expanded health insurance programs. Also at work have been the general retrenchment in government social welfare expenditures, which put a lid on the expansion on government support, at least in the social services field; and the relatively limited ability of private charity to fill the resulting gap.

Nonprofit, Government, and For–Profit Roles

Despite the dominant role of fees and government support in the *funding* of social services, private, nonprofit organizations still play the dominant role in the actual *delivery* of such services. At the same time, government agencies and for-profit providers also play important roles.

The Nonprofit Role

Overall role. As noted earlier, there were approximately 66,000 nonprofit organizations providing social services in the United States as of the early 1990s. Of these, the most numerous were providers of individual and family services (44 percent) and child day-care (24 percent). The rest provided residential care (23 percent), and job training (9 percent). Individual and family service agencies also rank highest in financial terms, with 45 percent of the total revenues; but day-care, with 24 percent of the agencies, accounts for only 10 percent of the revenues. Of the balance, residential care accounts for 29 percent and job training 16 percent.

[T]hese nonprofit agencies play a very significant role in the provision of social services in the United States. In particular, they account for:

- 53 percent of the private social service agencies.
- 61 percent of all social service revenues.
- 55 percent of all social service agency employment—an estimated 1.2 million employees in all.

In addition, nonprofit social service organizations also engage the energies of a sizable army of volunteers. According to recent estimates, these volunteers contribute time that is equivalent to another 840,000 full-time employees in addition to the estimated 1.2 million paid employees of these agencies.

Lester M. Salamon, The Rise of the Nonprofit Sector

For. Aff. 109 (July/Aug. 1994).

A striking upsurge is under way around the globe in organized voluntary activity and the creation of private, nonprofit or nongovernmental organizations. From the developed countries of North America, Europe and Asia to the developing societies of Africa, Latin America and the former Soviet bloc, people are forming associations, foundations and similar institutions to deliver human services, promote grass-roots economic development, prevent environmental degradation, protect civil rights and pursue a thousand other objectives formerly unattended or left to the state. * * *

In the developed countries, for example, a significant expansion of citizen activism has been evident for several decades. A 1982 survey of nonprofit human service organizations in 16 American communities showed that 65 percent had been created since 1960. The number of private associations has similarly skyrocketed in France, with more than 54,000 formed in 1987 alone, compared to about 11,000 per year in the 1960s. Recent estimates record some 275,000 charities in the United Kingdom, with income approaching five percent of gross national product. In Italy, research conducted in 1985 showed that 40 percent of the organizations had been formed since 1977.

This phenomenon is even more dramatic in the developing world, where some 4,600 Western voluntary organizations are now active, providing support to approximately 20,000 indigenous nongovernmental organizations. In India, the Village Awakening Movement, which grew out of the Gandhian tradition, is active in thousands of villages. Bangladesh boasts approximately 10,000 registered nongovernmental organizations. In Sri Lanka, the Sarvodala Shramadana movement has organized more than 8,000 villages to produce small-scale improvement projects. Elsewhere, some 21,000 nonprofit organizations have formed in the Philippines; nearly 100,000 Christian Base Communities built on local action groups now dot the Brazilian countryside; some 27,000 nonprofit organizations are now reported in Chile and 2,000 in Argentina; and recent estimates indicate that 30 percent of Kenya's capital development since the 1970s has come from the Harambee movement, which has led local communities to initiate a wide variety of development projects.

Similar developments have also been evident in Eastern Europe and the former Soviet Union. Well before the dramatic political events that captured world attention in 1989, important changes were taking place beneath the surface of East European society, and voluntary organizations were very much at the center of them. Indeed, a veritable "second society" had come into existence, consisting of thousands, perhaps millions, of networks of people who provided each other mutual aid to cope with the economy of scarcity in which they lived. By the late 1970s, these networks were already acquiring political significance.

This process has only accelerated since the overthrow of the communist governments. As of 1992, several thousand foundations were registered with governmental authorities in Poland. In Hungary, 6,000 foundations and 11,000 associations had been registered by mid–1992. A Foundation Forum was established in Bulgaria in 1991, linking close to 30 newly created private groups. Although slower in the former Soviet Union, this process has recently accelerated there as well. A Foundation for Social Innovations was formed in 1986, in the second year of perestroika, as a way to translate citizen initiatives into effective social action. Since then dozens of other foundations and nonprofit organizations have been created into assist gifted and talented children, to protest the Chernobyl nuclear disaster, to call attention to the disappearance of the Aral Sea, to encourage cultural heterogeneity, and for dozens of other purposes.

How can we explain the extraordinary growth and pervasiveness of this phenomenon? Pressures to expand the voluntary sector seem to be coming from at least three different sources: from "below" in the form of spontaneous grass-roots energies, from the "outside" through the actions of various public and private institutions, and from "above" in the form of government policies. * * *

Why has this flourishing of third-sector activity occurred now? Four crises and two revolutionary changes have converged both to diminish the hold of the state and to open the way for this increase in organized voluntary action.

The first of these impulses is the perceived crisis of the modern welfare state. Over the past decade or so the system of governmental protection against old age and economic misfortune that had taken shape by the 1950s in the developed West no longer appeared to be working. * * *

Accompanying the crisis of the welfare state has been a crisis of development. The oil shocks of the 1970s and the recession of the early 1980s dramatically changed the outlook for developing countries. In sub-Saharan Africa, Western Asia and parts of Latin America average per capita incomes began to fall. * * *

A global environmental crisis has also stimulated greater private initiative. The continuing poverty of developing countries has led the poor to degrade their immediate surroundings in order to survive. * * *

Finally, a fourth crisis—that of socialism—has also contributed to the rise of the third sector. * * *

Beyond these four crises, two further developments also explain the recent surge of third-sector organizing. The first is the dramatic revolution in communications that took place during the 1970s and 1980s. * * *

The combined expansion of literacy and communications has made it far easier for people to organize and mobilize.

The final factor critical to the growth of the third sector was the considerable global economic growth that occurred during the 1960s and early 1970s, and the bourgeois revolution that it brought with it. * * *

NOTE: INTERNATIONAL CHARITIES AND TERRORIST ACTIVITY

We normally think of charities as reflecting the highest motives of human impulse and generosity. But nonprofits have also been used as covers for illicit activities. Investigations in the aftermath of September 11th have revealed the frequent use of Muslim charitable organizations to funnel money, aid, and material for terrorist uses. The Benevolence International Foundation of Illinois, which operated in Bosnia, has been accused of financing Osama Bin Laden and the Al Qaeda terrorist network. Several Saudi Arabian charities are alleged to have supported terrorist activities. This is a nondenominational problem. For instance, when the gang of organized crime boss John Gotti moved from Brooklyn to Queens, N.Y., it incorporated itself as a mutual benefit organization, the Bergin Hunting and Fishing Association.[1] As early as 1996, groups such as Hamas, a radical Islamic organization; Kahane Chai (right wing Jewish group); the Liberation Tigers of Tamil Eelam (Sri Lankan terrorist organization); and the Provisional Irish Republican Army were known to have engaged in fundraising in the United States through purported charitable organizations. William Patton, Preventing Terrorist Fundraising in the United States, 30 Geo. Wash. J.Int'l L & Econ. 127,129 (1996). Charitable organizations have been used to launder drug money and as a front for arms purchases. In response to these problems, the United States and other governments have attempted to freeze the assets of such groups. Separating ''bad dollars''

---

1. The gang could shoot but not spell straight. It was named for the street of its former venue, Bergan Avenue. Selwyn Raab, ''John Gotti Dies in Prison at 61,'' N.Y. Times, June 11, 2002, at A1.

from "good dollars" can be difficult. Some charities, not engaged in funding terrorist activities, have claimed they have been victims of ethnic profiling or guilt by a similar-sounding name. See Glenn R. Simpson & Robert Block, Politics & Policy: U.S. Moves to Stop Terror Funding Pose Risks With Allies, Wall St.J., Oct. 9, 2001, at A24; Glenn R. Simpson, Hesitant Agents: Why the FBI Took Nine Years to Shut Group It Tied to Terror, Wall St. J. Feb. 27, 2002, at A1.

NOTES

1. *The National Taxonomy of Exempt Entities.* Given the diversity of the nonprofit sector in the United States, it should surprise that until recently there has been no generally accepted classification or taxonomy of its members or even an agreed upon definition of nonprofit. The most complete statistical profile can be found in the publication, Nonprofit Almanac, which is published periodically by the Independent Sector in partnership with the Urban Institute. The Nonprofit Almanac examines the nonprofit sector in relation to other sectors of the economy from a variety of perspectives.

The National Center for Charitable Statistics (NCCS) at Independent Sector has developed a classification system for tax-exempt organizations known as the National Taxonomy of Exempt Entities. Since 1987, the NCCS in cooperation with the Statistics of Income Division of the Internal Revenue Service has completed the initial classification of over 1.1 million tax-exempt organizations. The NTEE System identifies organizations by primary purpose, major program, type of governance, area of service, and clientele, beneficiaries or members served. There are 26 major groups in the NTEE system, ranging from arts, culture, and humanities to mutual/membership benefit organizations. A second level of analysis focuses on the major mission or the major areas in which the organization operates. A third level of the taxonomy identifies the governance of the organization, whether the ownership or affiliation is private nonsectarian, religious, or governmental. The fourth level of the taxonomy identifies specific characteristics of the organization's target population-gender, age, racial or ethnic characteristics, defined groups—and geographical area of service or impact. See Virginia Ann Hodgkinson, Murray S. Weitzman, John A. Abrahams, Eric A. Crutchfield and David R. Stevenson, Nonprofit Almanac 1996–1997, ch. 5; App. A (1996); Virginia A. Hodgkinson, Mapping the Nonprofit Sector in the United States: Implications for Research, 1 Voluntas 6 (1990).

For a criticism of the NTEE see Sarah E. Turner, Thomas I. Nygren & William G. Bowen, The NTEE Classification System: Tests of Reliability/Validity in the Field of Higher Education, 4 Voluntas 73–94 (1993) (the New York Shakespeare *Festival* is classified as a "fair, county, other"; the "Southern California–Southern Nevada End *Stage* Renal Disease Network" and the Association of Professional Ball *Players* of America are classified as "theatres." Id. at 86).

2. *An International Taxonomy*. Problems of definition are even greater from a global perspective because of the patterns of differentiation of societies, levels of developments, differing legal systems, historical factors and other traditions. Lester M. Salamon & Helmut K. Anheier, In Search of the Nonprofit Sector I: The Question of Definitions (Johns Hopkins Comparative Nonprofit Sector Project, Working Paper No. 1, 1992). On the international level, the Johns Hopkins Comparative Nonprofit Sector Project is attempting to understand the scope, structure, and role of the nonprofit sector by developing a common framework and approach. This project adopts a structural/operational definition which identifies a broad range of organizations by five characteristics: formally constituted; nongovernmental in basic nature; self-governing; non-profit distributing; and voluntary to some meaningful extent. Salamon and Anheier developed an International Classification of Nonprofit Organizations (ICNPO) drawing on Standard Industrial Classification (SIC) systems embodied in national income accounting around the world, but modified to accommodate key components of the nonprofit sector overlooked in SIC. This classification scheme identifies twelve broad groups of organizations: culture and recreation; education and research; health; social services; environment; development and housing; law, advocacy, and politics; philanthropic intermediaries and volunteerism promotion; international; religion; business, professional associations, unions; and not elsewhere classified. Lester M. Salamon & Helmut K. Anheier, In Search of the Nonprofit Sector II: The Problem of Classification (Johns Hopkins Comparative Nonprofit Sector Project, Working Paper No. 3, 1992).

3. *The Nonprofit Sector in New York City*. The most complete survey of the impact of the nonprofit sector in a community is The Nonprofit Sector in New York City, a study published in 1992 by the Nonprofit Coordinating Committee, which counted a total of 19,500 organizations employing 450,000 in New York City. The total included 2,500 arts and cultural groups, and 7,600 social services and educational services organizations. Nonprofits employed 12.5 percent of the city's labor force and total operating expenditures in fiscal 1989 were more than $31 billion. Forty percent of the nonprofits had annual budgets under $125,000 while 21 percent had budgets of more than $1 million.

4. *For Further Reading*. Michael O'Neill, Non Profit Nation (2002); Helmut K. Anheier & Kusuma Cunningham, Internationalization of the Nonprofit Sector, in The Jossey–Bass Handbook of Nonprofit Leadership and Management (Robert D. Herman ed., 1994); William G. Bowen, Thomas I. Nygren, Sarah E. Turner, & Elizabeth A. Duffy, The Charitable Nonprofits (1994); The Nonprofit Sector in the Mixed Economy (Avner Ben–Ner & Benedetto Gui eds., 1993); America's Voluntary Spirit: A Book of Readings (Brian O'Connell ed., 1983); Virginia A. Hodgkinson & Richard W. Lyman, The Future of the Nonprofit Sector: Challenges, Changes and Policy Considerations (1989); The Nonprofit Sector in International Perspective: Studies in Comparative Culture and Policy (Estelle James ed., 1989); Kathleen D. McCarthy, Virginia A. Hodgkinson, Russy D. Sumariwalla et al., The Nonprofit Sector in the Global Community (1992); Michael

O'Neill, The Third America: The Emergence of the Nonprofit Sector in the United States (1989); The Nonprofit Sector: A Research Handbook (Walter W. Powell ed., 1987); Research Papers Sponsored by the [Filer] Commission on Private Philanthropy and Public Needs (1977).

C.   Charity, Philanthropy and Nonprofit Organizations: An Historical Introduction

Preamble to the Statute of Charitable Uses

43 Eliz., ch. 4 (1601).

> Whereas lands, tenements, rents, annuities, profits, hereditaments, goods, chattels, money and stocks of money have been heretofore given, limited, appointed, and assigned as well by the Queen's most excellent Majesty, and her most noble progenitors, as by sundry other well-disposed persons; some for relief of aged, impotent and poor people, some for maintenance of sick and maimed soldiers and mariners, schools of learning, free schools and scholars in universities, some for repair of bridges, ports, havens, causeways, churches, sea-banks, and highways, some for education and preferment of orphans, some for or towards relief, stock or maintenance for houses of correction, some for marriages of poor maids, some for supportation, aid and help of young tradesmen, handicraftsmen, and persons decayed; and others for relief or redemption of prisoners or captives, and for aid or ease of any poor inhabitants concerning payments of fifteens, setting out of soldiers and other taxes; * * *

NOTE: THE STATUTE OF CHARITABLE USES AND THE MEANING OF CHARITY

Although gifts had been made for so called "pious causes" for centuries before, the modern law of charity commenced in 1601 when Parliament enacted the Statute of Charitable Uses, 43 Eliz. ch. 4, officially titled "An Act to Redress Misemployment of Lands, Goods and Stocks of Money Heretofore Given to Charitable Uses." The Statute had two main objectives: the first was to reform the administration of charity by establishing commissions in each English county to inquire into the misapplication of trusts established for charitable purposes. The second, and historically most important, was fulfilled in the statute's preamble: the specification of those purposes which were considered charitable and therefore within the jurisdiction of the commissions. The categories of charitable uses were never regarded as exclusive but as typical of the kinds of philanthropic activities which the state wished to encourage. Public benefit was the key to the statute, and the relief of poverty its principal manifestation. Gareth Jones, History of the Law of Charity 1532–1827 26–27 (1969). Other uses, principally religious, fell outside the preamble but also were considered charitable. Id. at 56–57.

Over the intervening centuries a number of broad categories of activities have been recognized as charitable, including the relief of poverty, the advancement of education, religion and science, the promotion of health, and lessening the burdens of government. The common law origins of charity have had a lasting influence on the evolution of "charitable" activities under corporate and tax codes. As these materials will demonstrate, charity is an evolving concept constantly changing to meet the needs of society. This flexibility has been recognized by the courts and the Internal Revenue Service. See John P. Persons, John J. Osborn, Jr. & Charles F. Feldman, Criteria for Exemption Under Section 501(c)(3), IV Research Papers Sponsored by the [Filer] Commission on Private Philanthropy and Public Needs 1909 (1977), and Chapter 2C4, infra, at pp. 121–167.

NOTE: THE DEVELOPMENT OF NONPROFIT LAW IN THE UNITED STATES

The immediate stimulus for the benevolent atmosphere to charity in the new world was the pressing need for the establishment of public facilities such as hospitals, churches, and schools: "[The colonists] did not debate the question of public versus private responsibility * * * public and private philanthropy were so completely intertwined as to become almost indistinguishable. The law itself reflected a pragmatic approach to the solving of social problems through philanthropy. Colonial assemblies went out of their way to remove obstacles in the way of charities. The courts valuing social betterment above legal technicalities, asserted a permissive charity doctrine that supported donors' benevolent intentions, even when the formulation of their plans was clearly imperfect." Howard S. Miller, The Legal Foundations of American Philanthropy 1776–1844, at xi (1961).

Philanthropic approaches in Colonial America were not uniform. From the beginning, public and private philanthropy coexisted. In Boston and other Massachusetts towns, public spending for poverty relief combined with private contributions and legacies. The typical vehicle for private philanthropic efforts was the English charitable use, which enjoyed universal approval.

In the immediate post-Revolutionary period, the favorable attitude toward charity continued. The law relating to charities reflected the general uncertainty and transition that characterized all American law in the post-Revolutionary period. Miller, supra, at 15. Cf. William Nelson, Americanization of the Common Law: The Impact of Legal Change on Massachusetts Society 1760–1830, at 68 (1975). Each state utilized an approach reflective of its local needs and customs. Most state constitutions were silent about philanthropy. The Massachusetts constitution of 1780, however, provided: "It shall be the duty of legislatures and magistrates, in all future periods of this Commonwealth * * * to countenance and inculcate the principles of humanity and general benevolence, public and private charity * * * and all social affections, and generous sentiments among the people.''

Pennsylvania, Vermont, and New Hampshire also gave constitutional protection to charities. Other states passed statutes facilitating and reaffirming the benefits of charities to the community. In part, the retention of prior statutes and practices resulted from the general continuation of English law and precedent in the first years following Independence.

In England the charitable trust rather than the corporation has been the predominant form of organization for charitable activities. The reason was that the state historically was the source of power to create corporations whereas the creator of the charitable trust was afforded greater freedom. Marion Fremont–Smith, Foundations and Government 34–35 (1965). The charitable trust has had a more uncertain use in the United States because of quirks of our history and early ignorance as to its origins. In the aftermath of the Revolution, many states repealed all British statutes. Several states refused to uphold the validity of charitable trusts. Courts in those jurisdictions mistakenly concluded that since the Statute of Charitable Uses was no longer in effect, trusts could not be upheld because equitable powers for their enforcement did not exist at common law and were not exercised by Chancellors prior to 1601. Though this historical error was corrected in Vidal v. Girard's Executors, 43 U.S. (2 How.) 127, 11 L.Ed. 205 (1844), throughout the nineteenth century charitable trusts remained under a cloud and were construed strictly in several jurisdictions. In their place the charitable corporation was used for eleemosynary organizations.

Another reason the charitable corporation was favored over the charitable trust was the power of the legislature or executive of a state to dictate the terms of corporate privilege. Regulation of that privilege was thought to provide the state with greater control over charitable activities than the charitable trust, control of which would be exercised by an equity court. Cf. Levy v. Levy, 33 N.Y. 97, 112 (1865); Dallin Oaks, Trust Doctrines in Church Controversies, 1981 B.Y.U.L. Rev. 805, 858–60.

As early as the 17th century, the corporation was used in the New World as an organizational form for charitable activities. Almost all colonial corporations had charitable purposes. They were churches, charities, educational institutions, or municipal corporations. Lawrence M. Friedman, A History of American Law at 188 (2d ed. 1985). The practice of executive or legislative branches in the colonies from the beginning of the eighteenth century was to confer upon owners or inhabitants of political divisions or organizations with political or governmental functions the attribute of legal personality, the essence of corporateness. This line of reasoning led to the incorporation of religious societies. At the beginning of the eighteenth century several colonies, borrowing from an English 1597 statute, 39 Eliz., ch. 5 (1597), which allowed for the automatic incorporation of hospitals and houses of correction, provided for self-incorporation of some religious, charitable or municipal institutions.

The early colonial corporations were of two kinds. The first was the public corporation-municipal corporations chartered by the towns or a few administrative boards charged with the oversight of public education, charity, and the like on behalf of local units of government. The second kind, private corporations, included ecclesiastical, educational, charitable, and business corporations. The most numerous in this second category were corporations concerned with religious worship. Next in numerical size were those formed for charitable or educational purposes, although they still might have a religious nature. Business corporations were few and of little importance. Many of the colonial business corporations would be considered cooperatives or quasi-philanthropic today. They were incorporated for the purpose of erecting bridges, building or repairing roads, or promoting ends of general public utility.

From the first years of the Republic, most states actively encouraged the incorporation of private associations that performed vital public services. Robert Seavoy, The Origins of the American Business Corporation 1784–1855, 255 (1982). Upon Independence, several state legislatures passed statutes permitting general incorporation of charitable organizations such as churches, schools, and literary societies.

The rationale motivating the passage of early general incorporation acts included advantage to the public if such incorporations were increased; convenience to individuals desiring to incorporate; relief of legislative workload; and promotion of freedom of religion. Incorporation also enabled the trustees of a charitable organization to receive legacies and bequests, and it provided cheap legal process at the local level to ensure property was held in the corporate name, thus enabling title in such property to be defended at law in the name of the corporation. The local public service function of early American corporations distinguished them from their English counterparts and led to their legislative encouragement. By the second decade of the nineteenth century, general incorporation statutes existed in New York for educational institutions, libraries, agricultural societies, medical societies, and Bible and common prayer organizations. Other charitable and benevolent organizations were readily granted incorporation by special legislative charter. Whenever a class of benevolent organizations was recognized as being essentially nonpolitical and noncontroversial, a general incorporation law for that activity was readily passed.

Despite the encouragement of corporateness, legislatures retained a tight control over corporate purposes and activities. The New York general incorporation statute of 1784 for the incorporation of religious societies had limitations upon the amount of an estate these bodies could accumulate and required trustees to render stated accounts to the Chancellor. All of the early general incorporation statutes contained limitations upon the amounts of revenue to be held by such organizations and the purposes for which such revenue was to be applied and requirements for furnishing inventories and reporting any excess property to the legislature. The legislative policy was to enforce within certain limits the accumulation of property.

New York, which interpreted charitable trusts strictly, developed a broad legislative scheme for public charities through the medium of corporate bodies. Beginning in 1790 the New York legislature, concurrently with the general incorporation statutes, incorporated by special charters societies for a variety of religious, literary, scientific, benevolent, and charitable purposes. The corporate body thus was kept under tight legislative control and supervision.

In 1840 the New York legislature passed an act authorizing gifts of real and personal property to any incorporated college or other charitable institution. In 1848 the legislature passed a general incorporation statute for all classes of charitable organizations. 1848 N.Y. Laws 319. A similar movement toward the consolidation of charitable corporations into one general incorporation statute occurred in other states in the middle of the nineteenth century.

Other states' charitable corporation statutes evolved similarly. In California in 1850, the first legislature enacted an "Act Concerning Corporations" which specifically allowed charitable organizations to incorporate. 1850 Cal. Stat. §§ 175–84. Thereafter, a variety of piecemeal legislation was passed expanding the types of organizations that could incorporate. California nonprofit legislation was generally skeletal, outlining purposes specifically permitted, elections of directors, bylaw provisions, and the requirements for the holding and mortgaging of property. In 1931, California enacted a General Nonprofit Corporation Law, Cal. Civ. Code, Title 12, Art. I (1931), based largely upon an Ohio act, which in turn had been drafted on the basis of the nonprofit statutes of New York, Maryland, Illinois and Michigan. 1 H.W. Ballantine & R. Sterling, California Corporation Laws 529 (1949). The General Nonprofit Corporation Law abandoned many of the restrictions on charitable corporations, and gave nonprofit corporations greater flexibility in internal affairs. Nonprofit corporations were, however, also bound by the General Corporation Law, thereby carrying into nonprofit corporation law an undefined body of business corporate law. In other areas, such as the law relating to standards of conduct of directors, trust principles governed. The General Nonprofit Corporation Law was largely incorporated into the Corporation Code of 1947. In 1980, the current Nonprofit Corporation Law became effective and for the first time treated California nonprofit corporation law as a coherent whole. The American Bar Association's Revised Model Nonprofit Act, completed in 1987, largely is based on the California statute.

For Further Reading. Henry Hansmann, The Evolving Law of Nonprofit Organizations: Do Current Trends Make Good Policy?, 39 Case W.Res.L.Rev. 807 (1988); F. Emerson Andrews, Philanthropy in the United States (1974); Robert H. Bremner, American Philanthropy (2d ed. 1988); Merle Curti, American Philanthropy and the National Character, 10 American Quarterly 420–437 (Winter, 1958) reprinted in America's Voluntary Spirit (Brian O'Connell ed., 1983); James J. Fishman, The Development of Nonprofit Corporation Law and an Agenda for Reform, 34 Emory L.J. 619 (1985); Peter Dobkin Hall, Historical Perspectives on Nonprofit Organizations, in The Jossey–Bass Handbook of Nonprofit Leadership and Management (Robert D. Herman ed., 1994); Peter Dobkin Hall, A Historical Overview of the Private Nonprofit Sector, in The Nonprofit Sector: A Research Handbook (Walter W. Powell ed., 1987); Howard S. Miller, The Legal Foundations of American Philanthropy 1776–1844 (1961).

D. RATIONALES FOR THE NONPROFIT SECTOR

What explains the existence of the nonprofit sector? Why does the legal system confer special treatment, such as tax exemptions and other benefits, on nonprofit organizations? In addressing these threshold questions, Lester Salamon has suggested that at least five major considerations are involved:

1. *Historical.* The nonprofit sector's existence can be explained by historical factors, such as the growth of voluntary organizations in the American colonies that predated government.

2. *Market Failure.* As elaborated in the excerpts below, nonprofit organizations exist in response to certain inherent limitations of the American market economy.

3. *Government Failure.* A vibrant nonprofit sector springs from the failure of government to provide collective goods because much government action requires majority support. Nonprofit organizations are formed by smaller groups of people to address needs that government is unwilling or unable to support.

4. *Pluralism/Freedom.* As demonstrated by the many reforms in American society that originated in the nonprofit sector, nonprofit organizations play a valuable role in promoting the values of pluralism and freedom.

5. *Solidarity.* The nonprofit sector is a mechanism through which an individualistic democratic society can express solidarity through joint action.

The excerpts below elaborate on the questions—what is the nonprofit sector and why do we have it?

Lester M. Salamon, America's Nonprofit Sector: A Primer
11–13 (2d ed. 1999).

The Rationale: Why Do We Have a Nonprofit Sector?

Why does the nonprofit sector exist in the United States, or any other country? Why did such organizations come into existence, and why do we give these organizations special tax and other advantages? * * *

Market Failure

[T]he creation of nonprofit organizations has been motivated by certain inherent limitations of the market system that dominates the American economy. Economists refer to these as *market failures*. Essentially, the problem is this: The market is excellent for handling those things we consume individually, such as shoes, cars, clothing, food. For such items, consumer choices in the marketplace send signals to producers about the prices that consumers are willing to pay and the quantities that can be sold at those prices. By contrast, the market does not handle very well those things that can only be consumed collectively, such as clean air, national defense, or safe neighborhoods. These so-called public goods involve a serious "free-rider" problem because, once they are produced, everyone can benefit from them even if they have not shared in the cost. Therefore, it is to each individual's advantage to let his or her neighbor bear the cost of these public goods because each individual will be able to enjoy them whether he or she pays for them or not. The inevitable result, however, will be to produce far less of these collective goods than people really want and thus to leave everyone worse off.

To correct for this, some form of nonmarket mechanism is needed. One such mechanism is government. By imposing taxes on individuals, government can compel everyone to share in the cost of collective goods. Indeed, in classical economic theory the problem of providing collective goods is the major rationale for the existence of government.

But in a democracy government will only supply those collective goods desired by a majority. Where such support is lacking, another mechanism is needed, and one such mechanism is the nonprofit sector. Nonprofit organizations allow groups of individuals to pool their resources to produce collective goods they mutually desire but cannot convince a majority of their countrymen to support. This can happen, for example, when particular subgroups share certain cultural, social, or economic characteristics or interests not shared by all or most citizens of a country. Through nonprofit organizations such subgroups can provide the kinds and levels of collective goods they desire. The greater the heterogeneity of the population, therefore, the larger the nonprofit sector is likely to be.

A slightly different kind of market failure occurs where information asymmetries exist, e.g., where the purchasers of services are not the same as the consumers, a situation economists refer to as *contract failure*. This is the case, for example, with nursing homes, where the consumers are often elderly people with limited consumer choice or ability to discriminate among products and the purchasers are their children. In such situations, the purchasers, unable to assess the adequacy of services themselves, seek some substitute for the market mechanism, some provider they can trust. Because nonprofits do not exist principally to earn profits, they often are preferred providers in such situations.

Government Failure

Since the existence of "market failures"—of inherent limitations of the market system—serves, in classical economic theory, as the justification for reliance on government, it is clear that market failures alone cannot explain the existence of a nonprofit sector. Also important are "government failures," inherent limitations of government that help to explain why nonprofit organizations are needed. In the first place, even in a democracy it is often difficult to get government to act to correct "market failures" because government action requires majority support. By forming nonprofit organizations, smaller groupings of people can begin addressing needs that they have not yet convinced others to support. In short, it is not market failure alone that leads to a demand for nonprofit organizations. Rather, it is the failure of *both* the market and the state to supply collective goods desired by a segment of the population, but not by enough to trigger a governmental response.

Even when majority support exists, however, there is still often a preference for some nongovernmental mechanism to deliver services and respond to public needs because of the cumbersomeness, unresponsiveness, and bureaucratization that often accompanies government action. This is particularly true in the United States because of a strong cultural resistance to the expansion of government. Even when government financing is viewed as essential, therefore, it is often the case that private, nonprofit organizations are utilized to deliver the services that government finances. The result * * * is a complex pattern of cooperation between government and the nonprofit sector.

Henry Hansmann, The Role of Nonprofit Enterprise

89 Yale L.J. 835, 840–845 (1980).

B.   *A Categorization of Nonprofit Organizations*

The flexibility of the corporation statutes permits nonprofit organizations to assume a wide variety of forms. Consequently, for the sake of simplifying exposition and analysis, it will help us to develop a basic subcategorization of nonprofits according to the manner in which they are financed and controlled.

1.   Financing: Donative Versus Commercial Nonprofits

Nonprofits that receive most or all of their income in the form of grants or donations I shall call "donative" nonprofits. Organizations for the relief of the needy, such as the Salvation Army, the American Red Cross, and CARE, are perhaps the most obvious examples. Those nonprofits that, on the other hand, receive the bulk of their income from prices charged for their services I shall call "commercial" nonprofits. Many nursing homes, most hospitals, and the American Automobile Association would clearly fall within this latter category.

Of course, not all nonprofits fit neatly into one or the other of these two categories. For example, most universities rely heavily upon donations as well as upon income from the sale of services—*i.e.,* tuition—and thus lie somewhere between the two. Consequently, donative and commercial nonprofits should be considered polar or ideal types rather than mutually exclusive and exhaustive categories.

In this Article I shall use the word "patrons" to refer to those persons who constitute the ultimate source of a nonprofit's income. Thus, in the case of a donative nonprofit, by "patrons" I mean the organization's donors, while in the case of commercial nonprofits I use the term to refer to the organization's customers; when the organization receives income from both customers and donors, the term comprises both.

2.   *Control: Mutual Versus Entrepreneurial Nonprofits*

Nonprofits that are controlled by their patrons I shall call "mutual" nonprofits. Country clubs provide an example: generally their directors are elected by the membership, which comprises the organization's customers. Common Cause, the citizens' lobby, presents another example: the board of directors of that organization ultimately is selected by the membership, which consists of all individuals who donate at least fifteen dollars annually to the organization.[30] On the other hand, nonprofits that are largely free from the exercise of formal control by their patrons I shall term "entrepreneurial" nonprofits. Such organizations are usually controlled by a self-perpetuating board of directors. Most hospitals and nursing homes, for example, belong within this latter category. Again, the two categories are really the ends of a continuum. For example, the board of trustees of some universities is structured so that roughly half is elected by the alumni—which constitutes the bulk of past customers and present donors—while the other half is self-perpetuating.

It is important to recognize that, while the organizations that I have termed "mutual" nonprofits may bear some resemblance to cooperatives, they are by no means the same thing. Cooperatives are generally formed under state cooperative corporation statutes that are quite distinct from both the nonprofit corporation statutes and the business corporation statutes. Cooperative corporation statutes typically permit a cooperative's net earnings to be distributed to its patrons or investors, who may in turn exercise control over the organization. Thus, cooperatives are not subject to the non distribution constraint that is the defining characteristic of nonprofit organizations.

30. It should be recognized that there are many nonprofits that have "members" but that are most appropriately characterized as entrepreneurial rather than mutual nonprofits. For example, many nonprofits designate their patrons as members but offer them no control over the organization. In such organizations one is a member in precisely the same sense that one becomes a member of the distinctly proprietary Book-of-the-Month Club. Other nonprofits, in turn, are controlled by a group of persons who are designated members, but who are not the organization's patrons. For example, control over local United Way organizations resides in its member agencies, which are the service organizations that receive the funds that United Way collects from individual patrons; the patrons themselves have no direct voice in United Way's affairs. In fact, the term "member," as it is used in the nonprofit corporation statutes and by nonprofit organizations themselves, often is applied so broadly as to have little definite meaning. For example: the Model Act gives the incorporators of a nonprofit complete freedom in establishing criteria for membership and in determining what rights (including voting rights), if any, the members are to have. See ALI–ABA Model Nonprofit Corporation Act §§ 8, 15, 34, 40, 45 (1964).

3. *The Four Resulting Categories*

The intersection of the preceding divisions in terms of finance and control produces four categories of nonprofits: (1) donative mutual; (2) donative entrepreneurial; (3) commercial mutual; and (4) commercial entrepreneurial. The following diagram displays some typical examples of these four types of organization.

	Mutual	Entrepreneurial
donative	Common Cause National Audubon Society political clubs	CARE March of Dimes art museums
commercial	American Automobile Association Consumers Union * country clubs	National Geographic Society ** Educational Testing Service community hospitals nursing homes

* Publisher of *Consumer Reports*
** Publisher of *National Geographic*

With these bits of nomenclature at our service, we can now turn to more substantive matters.

II.   Toward a General Theory of the Role of Nonprofit Enterprise

Undoubtedly many factors help explain why nonprofit institutions have proliferated in some areas of activity and not in others. Some of these factors are peculiar to particular types of nonprofits and will be considered below when we focus on individual sectors. There is, however, a rather general answer to the questions, what makes a given activity more suitable to nonprofit than to for-profit organizations?[32]

Economic theory tells us that, when certain conditions are satisfied, profit-seeking firms will supply goods and services at the quantity and price

32. The way I am approaching this question may appear a bit backward from a historical perspective. At least where corporations are concerned, nonprofits long antedate their for-profit counterparts, which are in fact relative latecomers on the organizational scene. Thus, while the modern American university can trace its ancestry directly to the chartering of the university of Oxford in the twelfth century, and ecclesiastical corporations such as monasteries go back even further, the first charters for profit-seeking corporations were not issued until nearly half a millennium later. See J. Davis, Corporations (1961) (surveying early development of corporate form in Anglo–American law). Viewed historically, then, we might well be tempted to ask why it was that large profit-seeking organizations arose. Yet today we are confronted with a well-articulated rationale for organizing economic activity along profit-seeking lines, and it is the nonprofits that seem to call for explanation. That explanation, I believe, can in large part be discovered by considering some of the limitations of the for-profit form.

that represent maximum social efficiency. Among the most important of these conditions is that consumers can, without undue cost or effort, (a) make a reasonably accurate comparison of the products and prices of different firms before any purchase is made, (b) reach a clear agreement with the chosen firm concerning the goods or services that the firm is to provide and the price to be paid, and (c) determine subsequently whether the firm complied with the resulting agreement and obtain redress if it did not.

In many cases—most notably with standardized industrial goods and farm produce—these requirements are reasonably well satisfied. Yet occasionally, due either to the circumstances under which the product is purchased and consumed or to the nature of the product itself, consumers may be incapable of accurately evaluating the goods promised or delivered. As a consequence, they will find it difficult to locate the best bargain in the first place or to enforce their bargain once made. In such circumstances, market competition may well provide insufficient discipline for a profit-seeking producer; the producer will have the capacity to charge excessive prices for inferior goods. As a consequence, consumer welfare may suffer considerably.

In situations of this type, consumers might be considerably better off if they deal with nonprofit producers rather than with for-profit producers. The nonprofit producer, like its for-profit counterpart, has the capacity to raise prices and cut quality in such cases without much fear of customer reprisal; however, it lacks the incentive to do so because those in charge are barred from taking home any resulting profits. In other words, the advantage of a nonprofit producer is that the discipline of the market is supplemented by the additional protection given the consumer by another, broader "contract," the organization's legal commitment to devote its entire earnings to the production of services. As a result of this institutional constraint, it is less imperative for the consumer either to shop around first or to enforce rigorously the contract he makes.

Of course, one would expect that when the profit motive is eliminated a price is paid in terms of incentives. For example, nonprofit firms might be expected to be slower in meeting increased demand and to be less efficient in their use of inputs than for-profit firms. In addition, in spite of the limitations imposed upon them, nonprofits may succeed in distributing some of their net earnings through inflated salaries, various perquisites granted to employees, and other forms of excess payments. However, in situations in which the consumer is in a poor position to judge the services he is receiving, any approach to organizing production is likely to be a question of "second best." Moreover, it is plausible that the discipline of the market is in many cases sufficiently weak so that the efficiency losses to be expected from any industry of for-profit producers are considerably greater than those to be expected from nonprofit producers. In sum, I am suggesting that nonprofit enterprise is a reasonable response to a particular kind of "market failure," specifically the inability to police producers by ordinary contractual devices, which I shall call "contract failure."

If this line of reasoning at first seems a bit foreign, it is probably due in large part to the economic terminology in which it has been couched. In essence, it is saying nothing more than that we can view all nonprofits in much the same way that we have always viewed charitable trusts—that is, as fiduciaries. The only novel element is that in the case of many nonprofits—notably the ones that I have labeled "commercial"—the donors and the beneficiaries are one and the same group.

There are, to be sure, some isolated cases in which the nonprofit form has been adopted for reasons other than contract failure; social clubs, as I shall discuss later, provide the most important example. In general, however, contract failure is the essential factor in the role of nonprofit enterprise.

It follows from these basic notions that the corporate charter serves a rather different function in nonprofit organizations than it does in for-profit organizations. In the case of the business corporation, the charter, and the case law that has grown up around it, protect the interests of the corporation's shareholders from interference by those parties—generally corporate management and other shareholders—who exercise direct control over the organization. In the case of the nonprofit corporation, on the other hand, the purpose of the charter is primarily to protect the interests of the organization's *patrons* from those who control the corporation. For this fundamental reason, the corporate law that has been developed for business corporations, and particularly that which concerns the fiduciary obligations of corporate management, often provides a poor model for nonprofit corporation law. This fact has not always been appreciated.

Henry Hansmann, Reforming Nonprofit Corporation Law

129 U.Pa.L.Rev. 497, 504–509 (1981).

B.   The Role of Nonprofit Organizations

To understand the unique functions served by the nonprofit form of organization, it is helpful to compare the role of nonprofits with that of profit-seeking (or "for-profit" or "business") organizations.

Like for-profit organizations, virtually all nonprofit organizations are, in a sense, engaged in the sale of services. This is, of course, true by definition for commercial nonprofits. Yet donative nonprofits, too, "sell" their services—and it is the donors who are the purchasers. For example, when an individual makes a contribution to the American Red Cross, or to the Metropolitan Opera, it is not quite a pure gift in the sense that the directors of the organization are free to do anything that they wish with the money. Rather, the contribution is a payment made with the understanding that it is to be devoted entirely to assisting disaster victims, or to presenting more and better opera productions. That is, such contributions are essentially efforts to "buy" disaster relief, or opera, and this is what the organizations in question exist to provide and "sell."

Why is it necessary that organizations such as these be nonprofit? In particular, why could not a for-profit firm provide the same services? The reason, in most cases, appears to be that either the nature of the service in question, or the circumstances under which it is provided, render ordinary contractual devices inadequate to provide the purchaser of the service with sufficient assurance that the service was in fact performed as desired. The advantage of the nonprofit form in such circumstances is that it makes the producer a fiduciary for its purchasers, and thus gives them greater assurance that the services they desire will in fact be performed as they wish.

1. Clarifying Examples

Some examples may help to make this clear.

a. Third Party Payment

Consider, initially, those donative nonprofits, such as CARE, the Salvation Army, and the American Red Cross, that collect contributions with which to provide relief to the poor and distressed. Why is it necessary that these organizations be nonprofit? Could not profit-seeking firms instead provide the same service—whether dried milk for hungry children in Africa, or bandages for disaster victims, or food for derelicts—in return for payments from philanthropically included individuals?

The answer, in considerable part, apparently lies in the fact that the individuals who receive the services in question have no connection with the individuals who pay for them. Thus, for example, suppose that a profit-seeking counterpart to CARE were to promise to provide one hundred pounds of dried milk to hungry children in Africa in return for a payment of ten dollars. Because the patron has no contact with the intended recipients, he or she would have no simple way of knowing whether the promised service was ever performed, much less performed well. Consequently, the owners of the firm would have both the incentive and the opportunity to provide inadequate service and to divert the money thus saved to themselves.

The advantage of the nonprofit form in such circumstances is that, because the nondistribution constraint prohibits those who control the organization from distributing to themselves out of the organization's income anything beyond reasonable compensation for services they render to the organization, they have less opportunity and incentive than would the managers of a for-profit firm to use the organization's patrons intend it to be used for. In these circumstances, therefore, an individual would presumably much prefer to patronize a nonprofit organization than a for-profit organization. Consequently, it is not surprising that such redistributive services are provided almost exclusively by nonprofit firms.

b. Public Goods

Similar reasoning applies to the provision of what economists term a "public good"—that is, a good or service such that (1) the cost of providing the good to many persons is not appreciably more than the cost of providing it to one; and (2) once the good has been provided to one person, it is difficult to prevent others by enjoying it as well.[7] Typical examples are noncommercial broadcasting, public monuments, and scientific research.

Even if individual consumers are willing to contribute to the cost of such services, rather than yielding to the incentive to be "free-riders" on the contributions of others, it is likely that they will do so only if the services are provided by a nonprofit. The reason for this is simply that, owing to the indivisible nature of the service involved, the consumer generally has no simple means of observing whether his or her contribution has increased the level of the service provided. Rather, the consumer must take the producer's word that the contribution will be used to purchase more of the good, rather than simply going into someone's pocket. Such a promise will be easier to believe if the producing firm is subject to the nondistribution constraint. Thus, listener-supported radio, tax reform lobbying, and heart research are all typically financed through nonprofit organizations.

c.   Complex Personal Services

Those organizations—most of which we would classify as commercial nonprofits—that provide complex and vital personal services, such as nursing care, day care, education, and hospital care, offer yet another example. The patients at a nursing home, for example, are often too feeble or ill to be competent judges of the care they receive. Likewise, hospital patients and consumers of day care, owing to the difficulty of making an accurate personal appraisal of the kind and quality of services they need and receive, must necessarily entrust a great deal of discretion to the suppliers of those services. The nondistribution constraint reduces a nonprofit supplier's incentive to abuse that discretion, and, consequently, consumers might reasonably prefer to obtain these services from a nonprofit firm.

2.   "Contract Failure"

In short, nonprofit firms serve particularly well in situations characterized by what I shall refer to, for simplicity, as "contract failure"—that is, situations in which, owing either to the nature of the service in question or to the circumstances under which it is produced and consumed, ordinary contractual devices in themselves do not provide consumers with adequate means for policing the performance of producers. In such situations, the nonprofit form offers consumers the protection of another, broader "contract"—namely, the organization's commitment, through its nonprofit charter, to devote all of its income to the services it was formed to provide.

It follows that the charter of a nonprofit corporation serves a rather different purpose than does the charter of a business corporation. In a

---

7. Public goods, because of these characteristics, are often, but need not be, provided by the government. See generally E. Mansfield, Microeconomics 470–94 (3d ed. 1979).

business corporation, the charter, and the statutory and decisional law in which it is embedded, serves primarily to protect the interests of the corporation's shareholders from invasion by those immediately in control of the corporation, including management and other shareholders. In a nonprofit corporation, on the other hand, the restrictions imposed on controlling individuals by the charter and the law are primarily for the benefit of the organization's patrons. As a consequence, business corporation law is often a poor model for nonprofit corporation law. * * *

3. Countervailing Considerations

The nonprofit form brings with it costs as well as benefits. The curtailment of the profit motive that results from the nondistribution constraint can reduce incentives for cost efficiency, for responsiveness to consumers, and for expansion or creation of new firms in the presence of increasing demand. Moreover, the inability of nonprofits to raise equity capital through the issuance of stock can severely hamper their ability to meet needs for new capital. Only when contract failure is relatively severe is it likely that the advantages of nonprofits as fiduciaries will clearly outweigh these corresponding disadvantages, and thus give the nonprofit firm a net advantage over its for-profit counterpart.

Further, the nondistribution constraint is obviously not airtight. Indeed, as will be emphasized below, the constraint is often poorly policed and even, in many cases, poorly defined. As a consequence, the managers of nonprofits often find, and take advantage of, the opportunity to profit at the expense of the organization. Such behavior, of course, further reduces the advantages offered to patrons by nonprofit as opposed to for-profit firms in situations of contract failure.

In the case of services for the needy, public goods, and other services commonly provided by donative nonprofits, the need for a fiduciary organization is so obvious that for-profit firms are virtually unheard of. On the other hand, contract failure is not so obviously a critical problem for many consumers of the services that are often provided by commercial nonprofits, such as day care, nursing care, hospital care, and education. As a consequence, these services are commonly provided by for-profit as well as nonprofit firms.

D. Summary

In sum, I am suggesting that the essential role of the nonprofit organization is to serve as a fiduciary for its patrons in situations of contract failure. This statement, it should be emphasized, has both a positive (descriptive) and a normative aspect. Taken descriptively, it is an assertion that nonprofit organizations tend to arise in situations in which there is evidence of contract failure and not in cases in which contract failure is absent. Casual empiricism appears to support this conclusion, at least in its broad contours. More important for the purposes at hand, however, is the normative aspect of this analysis—namely, the assertion that the fiduciary role described here is the *appropriate* role for nonprofit organizations.

NOTES AND QUESTIONS

1. *Contract Failure*. Does contract failure fully explain the origins and development of the nonprofit sector? How do we explain that some nonprofits, such as hospitals, nursing homes and some educational institutions, coexist as for-profit, nonprofit, and government entities? What is the relationship of government to the nonprofit sector? Doesn't the government often serve the role of intervening when there is contract failure? Are there incentives for managers of nonprofits to cheat by avoiding the nondistribution constraint?

2. *Another View of the Governmental Role*. Economic theories of market and contract failure assume that nonprofit organizations fill a gap between the business and government sectors. However, government has turned more of the responsibilities for delivery of publicly financed services over to nonprofit organizations than it has retained for itself. In the process government is the most important source of income for most social service agencies. Lester M. Salamon, Partners in Public Service: The Scope and Theory of Government–Nonprofit Relations, in The Nonprofit Sector: A Research Handbook 99, 100 (Walter W. Powell, ed. 1987). Thus, one may view government and the nonprofit sector as a partnership or independent contractor relationship. Professor Salamon has suggested that rather than view the voluntary sector as a residual response to the failures of the market and government, it is the preferred mechanism for providing collective goods. Id. at 111. From this perspective the government is the residual provider when the voluntary sector is unable or unwilling to carry the burden. In theory the government provides a steady stream of financial support, sets priorities based on political consensus, and distributes benefits more equitably than the private sector. Voluntary organizations, however, can operate more efficiently and personally on a smaller scale than government. Salamon notes that the partnership may not work so well in practice as voluntary agencies may lose their independence, or could distort their missions by going where the money is, or become bureaucratized. Id. at 114–116.

3. *Responses to Hansmann*. Hansmann's work has been enormously influential. For critiques see Rob Atkinson, Altruism in Nonprofit Organizations, 31 B.C.L. Rev. 501 (1990); Ira Mark Ellman, Another Theory of Nonprofit Corporations, 80 Mich. L. Rev. 999 (1982); Richard Steinberg & Bradford Gray, The Role of Nonprofit Enterprise in 1993: Hansmann Revisited, 22 Nonprofit & Voluntary Sector Q. 297–317 (1993).

4. *Political and Social Theories*. Economists have more easily generated theories that attempt to account for the development of nonprofits than have political and social theorists. James Douglas has written: "The task of devising a political analogue to market failure bristles with difficulties. At a fundamental level economists have a common criterion or

measuring rod—that of 'utility' for judging the desirability of a form of organization." Economists can claim that market failure occurs when pursuit by individuals of their own utility is calculated not to result in maximum utility for society. No similar unifying measure can be applied to political institutions. Political Theories of Nonprofit Organization, in The Nonprofit Sector: A Research Handbook 43 (Walter W. Powell ed., 1987).

Yet economic theories are not free of criticism. They neglect the role of government and government policy by assuming that government policy-makers merely implement the demand of the people for collective goods and have no independent role to play in shaping the nonprofit sector. Steven Rathgeb Smith & Michael Lipsky, Nonprofits for Hire 31–32 (1993). Economic theories underestimate the fact that our voluntary sector has emerged because of historical and political factors as well as economic needs.

Political and social theorists attempt to answer such questions as: given the wealth of services provided by government at all levels why do we need nonprofits at all, particularly those that carry out a public function or coexist with governmental organizations that provide the same services? Why does government provide direct subsidies to many nonprofit organizations in the form of grants plus indirect assistance through tax exemption? Do nonprofits play a particular role in our democratic system?

Political theory offers several justifications for the emergence and roles of nonprofits in democratic societies. Government action is bounded by political feasibility whereas private organizations need not heed the majority's will. Nonprofits can engage in experimentation and innovative projects for which government would need to build a certain level of support among the electorate. Additionally, governmental benefits must be distributed equitably which can have a confining effect on their supply. For instance, if the public voted regularly to provide funds for AIDS research, would the same level of assistance be provided? Thus, governments tend to be more constrained, bureaucratic, and less innovative than nonprofits. As John Stuart Mill noted: "Government operations tend to be everywhere alike. With individuals and voluntary associations, on the contrary, there are varied experiments, and endless diversity of experience." On Liberty 135 (Oxford: World Classics ed. 1912) (1859).

The nonprofit sector is also a force for democracy. It promotes a diversity of views and support, complementing government efforts in some areas and filling gaps in others. Nonprofits play a crucial role in promoting the values of freedom and pluralism, by encouraging individual initiatives for the public good. Lester Salamon, America's Nonprofit Sector: A Primer 14 (2d ed. 1999). Nonprofits are also manifestations of community. As Alexis DeTocqueville and others have noted, voluntary associations mediate between the bureaucratic institutions of government and the individual. See Peter L. Berger & Richard J. Neuhaus, To Empower People: The Role of Mediating Structures in Public Policy (1977).

5. *For Further Reading.* To Profit or Not to Profit: The Commercial Transformation of the Nonprofit Sector (Burton A. Weisbrod ed., 1998);

Avner Ben–Ner, Nonprofit Organizations: Why Do They Exist in Market Economies?, in The Economics of Nonprofit Institutions: Studies in Structure and Policy (Susan Rose–Ackerman, ed. 1986); William J. Baumol & William G. Bowen, Performing Arts—The Economic Dilemma 378–386 (1966); Henry Hansmann, Economic Theories of Nonprofit Organization, in The Nonprofit Sector: A Research Handbook 27–42 (Walter W. Powell ed., 1987); Estelle James & Susan Rose–Ackerman, The Nonprofit Enterprise in Market Economics (1986); The Economics of Nonprofit Institutions: Studies in Structure and Policy (Susan Rose–Ackerman ed., 1986); Burton A. Weisbrod, The Voluntary Nonprofit Sector: An Economic Analysis (1977); and Burton A. Weisbrod, The Nonprofit Economy (1988); Barbara K. Bucholtz, Reflections on the Role of Nonprofit Associations in a Representative Democracy, 7 Cornell J. Law & Pub. Policy 555, 571–583 (1998); James Douglas, Why Charity?: The Case for a Third Sector (1983); Waldemar A. Nielsen, The Endangered Sector (1979); Alan Pifer, Philanthropy in an Age of Transition: The Essays of Alan Pifer (1984); Lester M. Salamon, Partners in Public Service, in The Nonprofit Sector: A Research Handbook 99 (Walter W. Powell ed., 1987).

E.   THE LEGAL FRAMEWORK: ORGANIZATION AND GOVERNANCE

1.   INTRODUCTION

Like their for-profit counterparts, nonprofit organizations are governed by a variety of legal regimes. These evolving bodies of law can be broadly (and rather arbitrarily) divided into three categories: organization and governance, other regulatory law, and the subject of this text—taxation.

Organization and governance are primarily matters of state law. Many states have enacted distinct nonprofit corporation statutes that address the mechanics of forming a nonprofit corporation, operational issues, fiduciary obligations and liabilities of officers and directors, structural changes such as mergers and conversions to for-profit status, dissolution, and the oversight role of the state Attorney General. Among the goals of modern nonprofit corporation statutes is to recognize the unique and diverse nature of nonprofits, to promote ease of formation and operation, to provide practical answers to everyday problems faced by nonprofit organizations and their managers, and to recognize the different roles played by nonprofit corporations.

2.   CHOICE OF THE LEGAL FORM OF A NONPROFIT ORGANIZATION

a.   IN GENERAL

A threshold decision for the founders of a nonprofit entity is the legal structure the organization will adopt. Both tax and non-tax considerations must be evaluated. Tax considerations include: the appropriate type of federal tax exemption, the organization's classification as a public charity or private foundation, the forms of organization permitted under the Internal Revenue Code, and the consequences of each type.[1] Non-tax factors include the speed with which one needs to establish the organization, concerns with limited liability, the sophistication and goals of the organizers, financial resources, and the type and scale of activities to be conducted. Among other considerations are the capacity to own property and contract, the capacity to sue and be sued, liabilities to third parties, the permanence of the organization and ease of dissolution, and governance requirements. See generally Harry G. Henn & Michael George Pfeiffer, Nonprofit Groups: Factors Influencing Choice of Form, 11 Wake Forest L. Rev. 181 (1975); Kenneth L. Guernsey & Michael Traynor, Nontax Considerations Before Incorporation, in Advising California Nonprofit Corporations, ch. 2 (California Continuing Education of the Bar, 1998).

Assuming that the entity will apply for some type of federal income tax exemption, it must choose from the organizational forms recognized by the Internal Revenue Code. To obtain exempt status under § 501(c)(3), the most desirable exempt status because the organization is eligible to receive tax-deductible contributions, a nonprofit entity must be a corporation, trust, or unincorporated association. Section 501(c)(3) refers to a "corporation, community chest, fund or foundation," but does not specify how any of those organizations must be formed. It has long been established that trusts, though not mentioned in the statute, are included in the terms "fund" or "foundation".[2] Most exempt organizations are corporations and a few are unincorporated associations.[3] It is not possible to operate an exempt organization as an individual[4] or as a partnership,[5] but limited liability companies are becoming more accepted as an organizational form.

b. UNINCORPORATED ASSOCIATIONS

Uniform Unincorporated Association Act.

Many smaller nonprofits are unincorporated associations, a form that involves nothing more than two or more persons organized for a common purpose. The most prominent and substantial unincorporated associations are labor unions and political organizations. The American Bar Association once was an unincorporated association. More typically, the unincorporated association form is used by newly formed entities or those commencing the incorporation process. This form may be suitable for fledgling organizations with uncertain prospects, a limited expected duration, or founders who are unlikely to bring the activity or project to fruition.

The advantages of unincorporated associations are their informality and flexibility. Unlike a nonprofit corporation, no governmental approvals

---

1. These issues are considered in Chapter 2, infra.

2. Fifth–Third Union Trust Co. v. Commissioner, 56 F.2d 767 (6th Cir.1932); G.C.M. 15778, XIV–2 C.B. 118 (1935).

3. For federal tax purposes, the corporate form includes unincorporated associations which are taxed as corporations under I.R.C. § 7701(a)(3).

4. I.R.S. Exempt Orgs. Handbook, § 321.1 (1977).

5. Emerson Inst. v. U.S., 356 F.2d 824 (D.C.Cir.1966).

must be obtained in order to form or dissolve unincorporated associations. They can obtain recognition of federal tax exemption under § 501(c)(3) and are required to follow the filing requirements binding exempt entities.[6] An unincorporated association needs neither a constitution nor bylaws except if it seeks recognition of exempt status under § 501(c)(3).[7]

The disadvantages of unincorporated association status outweigh the benefits. Although an Unincorporated Nonprofit Association Act was approved by the Commissioners on Uniform State Laws in 1992, it has not been widely adopted. Few statutory rules govern or guide unincorporated associations, and there is little case law. Section 6 of the Uniform Unincorporated Association Act grants members limited liability, but it has not been widely followed. The law of agency governs most legal relationships. Unincorporated associations have no separate legal existence apart from their members, and individual members may be found personally liable. Absent an enabling statute, an unincorporated association cannot receive or hold property in the association's name. The organization has no perpetual duration, nor can it contract in its own name or hold title to property. Upon dissolution, members are entitled to their pro rata share of assets unless the articles of association provide otherwise. Since an unincorporated association is not a separate legal entity, all members are parties defendant of an alleged liability of the association. A majority of jurisdictions have passed legislation treating the unincorporated association as an entity for legal purposes such as capacity to sue or be sued. A final disadvantage is that banks, creditors, and other vendors, which all are more accustomed to dealing with corporations, may be reluctant to conduct business with an unincorporated association.

c.   CHARITABLE TRUSTS

Sample Form of Charitable Trust.

The oldest type of nonprofit entity is the charitable trust whose existence has been traced back prior to the Statute of Uses of 1601.[8] A charitable trust is a fiduciary relationship with respect to property arising as a result of the manifestation of an intention to create it. The person

---

6. Under I.R.C. § 7701, associations generally are treated as corporations for purposes of § 501(c)(3). The Internal Revenue Service tends to look more closely at applications from unincorporated associations. The organizing documents must be signed by a minimum of two people associated under its terms. I.R.S. Exempt Orgs. Handbook § 321.5 (1985). If the unincorporated association has received recognition of exemption and later incorporates, it must file a new application for recognition of exemption. Bruce R. Hopkins, The Law of Tax Exempt Organizations § 24.1(b) (7th ed. 1998).

7. "A formless aggregation of individuals without some organizing instrument, governing rules, and regularly chosen officers would not be a tax exempt charitable entity for purposes of § 501(c)(3)." IRS Exempt Organizations Handbook § 321.4. The written articles of association must include a clause that provides that upon dissolution, the organization's assets will be transferred to another exempt organization. Treas. Reg. § 1.501(c)(3)–1(b)(4).

8. 43 Eliz. ch. 4. George G. Bogert & George T. Bogert (Rev. 2d ed. 1988) § 321. Exempt organizations such as churches existed far back into antiquity.

holding the trust property (the trustee) is subjected to equitable duties to deal with the property for a charitable purpose. Restatement Second of Trusts § 348. Charitable trusts differ from private trusts in several ways. Their object is to benefit the community rather than private individuals. Assets of a charitable trust must be irrevocably dedicated to the purposes of that trust. Therefore, no disposition of property for an otherwise valid purpose will be invalid because of the indefiniteness, lack of existence or capacity, or uncertainty of the beneficiaries. Charitable trusts are enforced by the attorney general rather than by the trust's beneficiaries, and they can be of unlimited duration unhindered by the rule against perpetuities.

Charitable trusts are suitable for holding property for charitable purposes and often are used for private foundations that are engaged solely in making grants. The charitable trust form offers: ease and swiftness of formation, administration with fewer formalities than the corporate form, fewer housekeeping requirements, perpetual or indefinite period of existence, and the possibility of continuing control by the grantor. Charitable trusts may be less expensive to maintain than a nonprofit corporation.

A charitable trust instrument names the trustees, states the charitable purpose, establishes policies for administration, distribution of assets and dissolution, names successor trustees or method of selection, and states the duration of the trust.[9] Management of the charitable trust rests in the trustees. They may be selected by the settlor, by a court in certain circumstances, and may be self-perpetuating if the trust instrument so provides. Henn & Pfeiffer, supra, at 202–203.

Where time is of the essence for the receipt of assets, a trust is easily and quickly formed. Unlike the corporation there is no need for prior governmental approval to create a trust. The requisites for effective formation of a charitable trust are essentially the same as those applicable to private trusts except there is no requirement of identifiable beneficiaries. The settlor must only describe with definiteness a purpose which is legally charitable. The naming or describing of individuals or classes of persons is merely to show the conduit through which the benefit is to flow.[10] A trust may be created by the declaration of the settlor, by conveyance, by deed or will to a trustee, or by making a contract by the settlor in favor of a trustee.

d. NONPROFIT CORPORATIONS

Rev. Model Nonprofit Corp. Act §§ 1.40(6), (10), (21), (23), (28), (30), 2.02.

N.Y. Not-for-Profit Corp. L. § 201.

The predominant nonprofit organizational form used in the United States is the nonprofit corporation. Its primary distinction from the busi-

---

9. Charitable trusts can be indefinite in duration unless the grantor has reserved a right of revocation or power to modify. Austin W. Scott & William F. Fratcher, Scott on Trusts, § 367, at 113–115 (4th ed. 1989 & Supp. 1998).

10. The theory is that in the case of the charitable trust, the beneficial property interest is devoted to the accomplishment of purposes that are beneficial or supposed to be beneficial to the community. Therefore the persons receiving such benefits need not be designated. Scott on Trusts, supra § 364.

ness corporation is the nondistribution constraint.[11] This does not preclude nonprofit corporations from earning a profit; it only prevents them from distributing any net profit to their members, who are the nonprofit equivalent of corporate shareholders. A particular advantage of the nonprofit corporate form is that the governing statutes are comparable to state corporate law. This similarity offers a familiar model to a nonprofit corporation's legal counsel as well as a body of analogous case law that often can be transported to the nonprofit context.

Compared to the unincorporated association or charitable trust, the charitable corporation must conform to more formalities in its creation and dissolution, but internal governance normally is more flexible, making it easier to react to changed circumstances such as the resignation or death of a director. A corporation can hold new elections while a change in trustee may require application to a court. It can easily amend corporate governing instruments.[12] The corporation is an artificial entity that can sue and be sued, contract, and hold property in its own name. It has an indefinite existence, and a centralized management known as the board of directors. Directors of a nonprofit corporation are held to a lower standard of care than charitable trustees. Directors also enjoy the advantage of limited liability. The corporation offers more established patterns than the trust for determining the legal consequences of engaging in multiple operations (consolidations and mergers, reorganizations).

The circumstances under which proceedings by which creditors can reach property differ. If a charitable corporation incurs a liability in contract or tort, an action at law lies against the corporation, while it is in equity, if at all, that a creditor can reach trust property.[13]

When property is conveyed to a charitable corporation, the organization usually has full ownership rights in the property. However, a charitable corporation does not hold property beneficially in the same sense as a business corporation, because the Attorney General can sue to prevent a

11. Consumer cooperatives, a specialized breed of nonprofit, do permit dividend distributions to their members. Cooperative corporation statutes typically limit the purposes for which such corporations can be formed to agricultural, housing, or medical activities. See N.Y. Coop. Corp. Law § 13; Mo. Ann. Stat. § 357.010; Henry B. Hansmann, Reforming Nonprofit Corporation Law, 129 U.Pa. L.Rev. 497, 595–596 (1981).

12. However, corporate flexibility is not unlimited. In Alco Gravure, Inc. v. Knapp Foundation, 64 N.Y.2d 458, 490 N.Y.S.2d 116, 479 N.E.2d 752 (1985), the court held that directors of a not-for-profit corporation did not have unlimited power of amendment as to how assets were to be administered or to effectuate a transfer of assets on dissolution of a nonprofit corporation where amendment would have changed the purpose for which funds were given to the corporation. Many features of corporate flexibility such as the ability to delegate to officers and agents and amending rules of procedure can be incorporated in a trust by carefully drafted powers in the governing trust instrument. Carolyn C. Clark & Glenn M. Trost, Forming a Foundation: Trust vs. Corporation, 3 Prob. & Prop. Rev. 32 (May/June 1989).

13. Scott on Trusts, supra note 9, at § 348.1.

diversion of property from the purposes for which it was given.[14] When property is left by will to a charitable corporation or property is conveyed to a corporation by an executor, the corporation is not thereafter bound to account as if it were a testamentary trustee.

3.   NONPROFIT CORPORATIONS: A CLOSER LOOK

Model Nonprofit Corporation Act § 4.

Cal. Corp. Code §§ 5111, 5130, 5410.

Ill. Comp. Stat. ch. 805, § 105/103.05.

N.Y. Not-for-Profit Corp. L. §§ 201–02, 204–05, 404–06, 508, 515.

Rev. Model Nonprofit Corp. Act §§ 3.01–02.

a.   IN GENERAL

States have adopted widely differing approaches in their statutory treatment of nonprofit corporations. A decreasing majority still follow in whole or in part the original Model Nonprofit Corporation Act, which was adopted in 1952 and revised in 1957 and 1964.[1] Those states having no separate statute for nonprofits often subsume them under the general corporate law, in a section for nonstock corporations.[2] New York and California have their own very different statutes particularly as to how nonprofits should be classified. An increasing number of jurisdictions are adopting the Revised Model Nonprofit Corporation Act (RMNCA), which was approved by the American Bar Association in 1987. The Revised Model Act's classification of nonprofits, based upon the California approach,[3] has attracted less favor than has the remainder of the statute, which follows the ABA's Revised Model Business Corporation Act.[4]

---

14. Id. But see Lefkowitz v. Lebensfeld, 68 A.D.2d 488, 417 N.Y.S.2d 715 (1979), aff'd 51 N.Y.2d 442, 415 N.E.2d 919, 434 N.Y.S.2d 929 (1980), where the attorney general, purporting to represent the ultimate beneficiaries of charities which had received an unrestricted gift of corporate stock, sued the corporation that issued the stock to compel the declaration and payment of dividends and payment of the market value of the shares which had been purchased from the charities at a price below market value. The court dismissed the action, because the attorney general did not have standing to sue third parties who allegedly were liable to the charitable organizations.

1. See 1 Marilyn E. Phelan, Nonprofit Enterprises §§ 1:11–1:62 for a description of state nonprofit statutes (1995 & Supp. 1997).

2. Del. Code Ann. tit. 8, § 102(a)(4); Kansas Stat. Ann. § 17–6002(a)(4); Md. Code

Ann. Corps. & Ass'ns §§ 5–201 to 5–208, Okla. Gen. Corp. Act. § 1002.

3. Compare RMNCA § 2.02 with Cal. Corp. Code §§ 5111, 7111, 9111.

4. See introduction to RMNCA at xx; Texas has adopted the Revised Model Act's standards for directors Tex. Rev. Civ. Stat. Ann. Art 1396–3.02; Idaho and Mississippi have adopted the Revised Model Act but did not incorporate the provisions that differentiated between mutual and public benefit corporations. Jurisdictions adopting the Revised Model Act include: Idaho (Idaho Code §§ 30–3–1 to 30–3–145); Mississippi (Miss. Code Ann. §§ 79–11–101 to 79–11–399); Montana (Mont. Code Ann. §§ 35–2–113 to 35–2–1402); Oregon (Or. Rev. Stat. §§ 65.001 to 65.990); Tennessee (Tenn. Code Ann. §§ 48–51–101 to 48–68–105); and Wyoming (Wyo. Stat. §§ 17–19–101 to 17–19–1807).

Some jurisdictions have separate provisions for specific types of non-profits. For example, religious corporations or hospital service institutions utilize the general nonprofit statute only for matters dealing with internal governance or corporate housekeeping.[5] Several states limit the purposes for which nonprofit corporations may be formed.[6] Others allow incorporation for any lawful purpose, limited only by the nondistribution constraint.[7] The trend is in favor of liberalization of purposes.[8]

A leading treatise summarizes some of the other differences in approach:

> While the states have some common themes in their nonprofit corporate statutes, there are many differences. All the state statutes prohibit the payment of dividends. Most prohibit the issuance of stock; however, some do permit it.[9] State statutes do not prohibit the making of a profit by a nonprofit corporation. Most provide for the payment of a reasonable compensation to officers and directors, and for the payment of other non cash benefits to their members.[10] In addition most states provide for the distribution of the assets to the members upon liquidation or upon final dissolution, except for those charitable organizations for which a charitable trust is placed upon the assets.[11] Some states classify nonprofit corporations into categories, whereas most do not. Some states provide standards of conduct for the officers and directors; others do not. The newer state statutes provide for member derivative actions,[12] whereas many of the states do not have such a provision.

Marilyn Phelan, 1 Nonprofit Enterprises § 1:11 at 34 (1995 & Supp. 1997) (footnotes renumbered).

b.   PUBLIC BENEFIT v. MUTUAL BENEFIT

In studying the law of nonprofit organizations, a useful distinction can be made between "public benefit" and "mutual benefit" organizations. These categories, though not universally accepted, have been adopted by the California Nonprofit Corporations Code and the American Bar Association's Revised Model Nonprofit Corporation Act.[13]

5. See N.Y. Not-for-Profit Corp. L. § 201(b); N.Y. Relig. Corp. L. § 2(b).

6. See Alaska Stat. § 10.20.005; Fla. Stat. Ann. § 617.0301; 805 Ill. Comp. Stat. Ann. § 105/103.05.

7. Thus, Indiana provides: "A corporation incorporated under this article [Nonprofit Corporations] has the purpose of engaging in any lawful activity unless a more limited purpose is set forth in the articles of incorporation." Ind. Code Ann. § 23–17–4–1–(a) (West 1998); see also Ohio Rev. Code Ann. § 1702.03 (West 1998); Wis. Stat. Ann. § 181.03 (West 1998).

8. Henry Hansmann, Reforming Nonprofit Corporation Law, 129 U.Pa.L. Rev. 497, 510 (1981). The RMNCA (§ 3.01(a)) also adopts the permissive approach.

9. See, e.g., Ala. Code § 10–3A–44; Pa. Stat. Ann. tit. 15, § 5752.

10. See D.C. Code Ann. § 29–5279.

11. See, e.g., Ariz. Rev. Stat. Ann. §§ 10–2326, 10–2422.

12. Calif. Corp. Code § 5710; Nebraska Nonprofit Corp. Act § 21–1949 (1997).

13. Each of these Codes also includes "religious corporations" as a separate category. In general, rules applicable to public

A public benefit organization can be defined as a group serving what may loosely be called a public or charitable purpose—to do good works, benefit society or improve the human condition. This category embraces what are known for tax purposes as § 501(c)(3) public charities (including charitable, religious, educational and other organizations that derive their support from the general public) and private foundations, which also derive their exempt status from § 501(c)(3) of the Internal Revenue Code but are subject to special regulatory controls and sanctions. Also included are § 501(c)(4) social welfare organizations which are tax-exempt but, unlike § 501(c)(3) charities, are not eligible to receive tax-deductible charitable contributions or bequests.

A distinctive characteristic of mutual benefit organizations is that they are formed primarily to further the common goals of their members rather than for profit or a public or religious purpose. Many of these groups exist to serve rather narrow interests. The bond may be economic, as with chambers of commerce and labor unions, or social, as with country clubs and fraternal lodges. In theory, the members of these organizations have pooled their resources to do what they might have chosen to do separately without additional tax consequences. As such, they are not appropriate objects of taxation. In practice, of course, mutual benefit organizations may do much more. The conduct of a business with non-members and investment in securities or real estate are familiar examples of extracurricular behavior.

The public v. mutual benefit dichotomy will be used frequently in this text to distinguish between these two broad categories of nonprofits. The excerpt below provides a more detailed summary of the distinctive aspects of public and mutual benefit corporations for state corporate law purposes.

Introduction to Revised Model Nonprofit Corporation Act

American Bar Association, pp. xxiv–xxix (1988).

Public Benefit Corporations

Corporations which have 501(c)(3) status must be public benefit or religious corporations. Other corporations may be public benefit corporations if they elect to be governed by rules appropriate to organizations holding themselves out as promoting the public good. For example, an environmental organization ineligible for tax exempt status because it intends to engage in extensive lobbying or endorse candidates could be formed as a public benefit corporation. Even if a corporation engages in controversial activities, it may be a public benefit corporation if its activities are lawful and it complies with the rules applicable to public benefit corporations.

benefit corporations also apply to religious corporations, but religious corporations, in recognition of their special constitutional status, are afforded more flexibility and are subject to less governmental oversight. As of this writing, relatively few jurisdictions have adopted the Revised Model Act's approach.

One general rule is that members, unlike shareholders in business corporations, can have no ownership interest in their corporation. The assets of a public benefit corporation are held for public or charitable purposes and not to benefit members, directors, officers or controlling persons. The assets cannot be distributed to members, directors or officers either while the public benefit corporation is operating or upon its dissolution. A membership, unlike a security, cannot be sold or otherwise transferred by a member. A public benefit corporation may not purchase any of its memberships or rights arising from its memberships. Even if a member resigns or his or her membership is terminated, a public benefit corporation cannot make a payment to the member for such membership.

Because members cannot have an economic interest in public benefit corporations, their right to vote on amendments to bylaws is not as broad as the right of members of mutual benefit corporations who can have a certain economic interest in mutual benefit corporations.

To protect the assets held by public benefit corporations, the Revised Act places restrictions on the type of corporations with which they can merge and the conditions of the merger. The clearest sort of abuse would result if a public benefit corporation merged with a business corporation and the members of the public benefit corporation received stock or something else in exchange for their membership. The Revised Act prohibits this from happening.

Public benefit corporations hold themselves out as benefiting society. Donations to public benefit corporations are made with the expectation that the money will be used for the public good and not to benefit individual directors. Consequently, the Revised Act holds directors of public benefit corporations to a high standard when they engage in economic transactions with their corporations. This will help ensure potential donors that their contributions will be dedicated to the corporation's public purposes and will not be used for private gain of the corporation's members or managers. The Revised Act distinguishes between public benefit corporations and mutual benefit corporations. It applies the business standard to economic transactions between directors of mutual benefit corporations and their corporations, but applies a more rigorous standard to the directors of public benefit corporations.

Since members of public benefit corporations have no economic interest in their corporations, they have no personal economic incentive to monitor corporate activities and prevent abuses. Many public benefit corporations do not even have members. While contributors have an incentive to monitor corporate activities, they may have no practical means of doing so. Consequently there may be no private individual with an economic incentive to review decisions made by a public benefit corporation's directors.

The Revised Act seeks to fill this void by statutorily clarifying existing common law and statutory authority of the attorney general. It does this by authorizing the attorney general to monitor and exercise oversight powers over public benefit corporations. The attorney general has authority to bring, must receive notice of, and may join in, derivative actions on behalf of public benefit corporations. The attorney general may approve conflict of interest transactions. The attorney general may sue former or incumbent directors and officers for ultra vires acts, and may bring an action for breach of their duty of care or loyalty. The attorney general may commence proceedings to hold an annual, regular or special meeting of members.

The standards, rules and procedures applicable to public benefit corporations are appropriate in light of the role they play in society and the representations they make to the public. Moreover, the rules prohibiting members from having an economic interest in public benefit corporations, providing scrutiny for director conflict of interest transactions and authorizing attorney general oversight mitigate against potential abuses by those operating public benefit corporations.

Mutual Benefit Corporations

Trade associations, social clubs and fraternal organizations are typical examples of mutual benefit corporations. Mutual benefit corporations hold themselves out as benefitting, representing and serving a group of individuals or entities. These individuals or entities are usually referred to as "members."

Members may have an economic interest in mutual benefit corporations. Members may not receive distributions while a mutual benefit corporation is operating, but their membership interests may be sold or transferred to the corporation or third parties, and they may receive distributions when the corporation dissolves.

Members have broad rights to vote on bylaw amendments to protect their economic and other interests. If members do not approve of the manner in which their corporation is operating, they may elect new directors or take other action to protect their position as members. As the members form a countervailing force roughly equivalent to shareholders, there is little need to give the attorney general broad jurisdiction over the activities of mutual benefit corporations.

Mutual benefit corporations may operate with a self-perpetuating board of directors. Individuals may be called "members" even if they do not have the right to vote for directors. As these "members" do not have the right to elect directors, the Revised Act does not treat them as "members" and does not give them statutory rights.

The Subcommittee [on the Model Nonprofit Corporation Law] rejected the idea of requiring all mutual benefit corporations to have members who could elect directors and therefore have statutory rights. Consequently some mutual benefit corporations may have individuals who are called members, but who do not have statutory membership rights under the Revised Act. The rights of these individuals are left to development on a state by state basis.

c.   FORMING A NONPROFIT CORPORATION

Rev. Model Nonprofit Corporation Act §§ 2.01–2.06.
Sample Certificate of Incorporation and Bylaws.

Once a decision has been made to form a nonprofit corporation, the next step is to select the state of incorporation. That typically will be the jurisdiction in which the organization intends to conduct its activities.[1] The law of the state of incorporation normally governs internal organizational affairs. After the state of incorporation has been selected, the corporation then must be formally organized. The first stage of the organization process is to prepare a "certificate of incorporation" or "articles of incorporation" or "charter" (the statutory language differs from state to state but the phrase means the same thing). The certificate of incorporation is eventually filed with the appropriate state official, usually the secretary of state. Though the requirements differ somewhat by jurisdiction, the nonprofit statutes generally require the certificate to contain the name of the organization,[2] a statement and description of the purposes of the organization, the name of an agent for service of process, and the names and addresses of the original incorporators or directors. If the organization will be a public benefit corporation there will be a provision stating that upon dissolution the organization will distribute its assets to other public benefit organizations to meet the requirements of § 501(c)(3) of the Internal Revenue Code, and if the nonprofit is a private foundation it will act or refrain from acting so as not to subject itself to various excise taxes. If the corporation has members, a provision relating thereto may be in the certificate. Several jurisdictions permit limitation of the liability of unpaid directors of the organization if the corporation places this limitation in the certificate.[3] Additionally, there are any number of optional provisions that may be included.

After the articles of incorporation have been drafted, the nonprofit corporation may be required to obtain certain consents for particular types of organizations such as hospitals, educational organizations, or a particular type of nonprofit. After the consents are obtained, and in certain jurisdictions after the attorney general is notified, the certificate is filed with the secretary of state and the organization's corporate existence commences.

A nonprofit corporation also requires a set of bylaws, which are the procedures or internal rules governing the entity. The bylaws generally are a more detailed and flexible document than the articles of incorporation, and they may contain any provision not inconsistent with the corporate law of the jurisdiction. Typically, bylaws contain notice requirements for special

---

1. There may be occasions where speed of incorporation is critical. In some states, such as New York, the incorporators must obtain a consent or waiver of consent by specified authority that the proposed organization is or is not a particular activity such as a school or hospital. N.Y. Not-for-Profit Corp. L. § 404. In that situation the incorporation takes some time. Delaware, which has no separate nonprofit corporate statute, may be a viable alternative. Incorporation in Delaware can be accomplished virtually overnight, and the organization then may apply for authority to do business in the home jurisdiction as a registered foreign corporation.

2. Statutes often require specific language, such as "association," "club," "foundation," or words that cannot be used absent approvals from the appropriate bodies. See Cal. Corp. Code § 5122; N.Y. Not-for-Profit Corp. L. § 301.

3. See Va. Code Ann. § 13.1–870.1.

and annual meetings, definitions of members if a membership corporation, the date of the annual meeting, quorum requirements for conducting business, member tenure, election procedures, removal and filling vacancies of directors. The bylaws will also specify the number and responsibilities of officers, the fiscal year, committees of the board, indemnification provisions, whether informal actions by the board or members are permitted, and procedures for amendment. See Barbara L. Kirschten, Nonprofit Corporation Forms Handbook (1993). Though most of the clauses in the articles of association and bylaws are standardized "boilerplate" provisions, careful drafting is important, particularly if the organization's charitable purposes come under challenge. See Matter of Troy, 364 Mass. 15, 57, 306 N.E.2d 203, 227 (1973), where the mere fact that a corporation was formed under a nonprofit statute did not by itself establish it was a charitable corporation. A court must consider language of constitution, articles of organization, bylaws, purposes and actual work performed.

After the articles of association have been accepted by the appropriate state official, an organizational meeting is held. The initial board of directors are elected, officers are appointed, the bylaws are approved, and authorization to open a bank account is granted. The corporation then should apply for recognition of exemption from federal income taxation by the Internal Revenue Service. When recognition of exemption and the category of exemption is received by the organization, the exemption letter relates back to the founding date of the organization if the application was filed within 15 months (or, in some cases, 27 months) after the end of the month in which it was formed. See Chapter 2C2, infra, at pp. 91–93. Some jurisdictions also require a separate application in order to obtain state income and property tax exemptions.

4. Taxation

Nonprofit corporations and charitable trusts have long enjoyed exemptions from income, real property, sales, and other more specialized taxes. Nonprofits qualifying as "charitable" are eligible to receive tax-deductible contributions. The influence of this large and complex body of "fiscal law" is considerable, often shaping a nonprofit's organizational structure, the compensation paid to its officers and employees, its ability to engage in commercial or political advocacy activities, and its fundraising practices. Table 1.4, below, is a list of the categories of nonprofit organizations eligible for exemption from federal income tax and the number of organizations registered with the Internal Revenue Service in each category.

Table 1.4

Tax–Exempt Organizations Registered with the IRS—2001

	Applications				Organizations Registered	
	Approved	Denied	Other[1]	Total	2000	2001
Section 501(c) by subsection:						
(1) Corporations organized under act of Congress	58	0	5	63	20	48
(2) Titleholding corporations	171	0	41	212	7,009	6,984
(3) Religious, charitable, etc.	59,909	629	13,823	74,361	819,008	865,096
(4) Social welfare	1,471	2	566	2,039	137,037	136,882
(5) Labor, agriculture organizations	295	2	64	361	63,456	62,944
(6) Business leagues	1,473	8	314	1,795	82,246	82,706
(7) Social and recreation clubs	767	4	475	1,246	67,246	67,289
(8) Fraternal beneficiary societies	19	0	18	37	81,980	81,112
(9) Voluntary employees' beneficiary associations	272	0	86	358	13,595	13,292
(10) Domestic fraternal beneficiary societies	18	0	30	48	23,487	23,531
(11) Teachers' retirement funds	0	0	1	1	15	15
(12) Benevolent life-insurance associations	98	1	48	147	6,489	6,500
(13) Cemetery companies	191	0	23	214	10,132	10,269
(14) State-chartered credit unions	32	0	4	36	4,320	4,409
(15) Mutual-insurance companies	209	0	10	219	1,342	1,423
(16) Corporations to finance crop operations	1	0	0	1	22	23
(17) Supplemental unemployment benefit trusts	5	0	0	5	501	490
(18) Employee-funded pension trusts	0	0	0	0	2	1
(19) War-veterans' organizations	117	0	47	164	35,249	35,263
(20) Legal-service organizations	0	0	0	0	N/A	N/A
(21) Black-lung trusts	0	0	0	0	28	28
(22) Multi-employer pension plans	0	0	0	0	0	0
(23) Veterans' associations founded prior to 1880	0	0	0	0	2	2
(24) Trusts described in section 4049 of ERISA	0	0	0	0	1	1
(25) Holding companies for pensions, etc.	265	0	8	273	1,192	1,236
(26) State-sponsored high-risk health insurance orgs.	0	0	0	0	9	9
(27) State-sponsored workers' comp. reinsur. orgs.	2	0	0	2	7	5
Total	**65,371**	**646**	**15,568**	**81,585**	**1,354,395**	**1,567,580**

SOURCE: IRS Data Book, FY 2001. All § 501(c)(3) organizations are not included because certain organizations (e.g., churches) need not apply for recognition of exemption unless they desire a ruling; § 501(c)(3) totals include private foundations.

[1]"Other" includes applications withdrawn, incomplete, or which failed to provide required information to IRS; and other.

For Further Reading. Bazil Facchina, Evan Showell & Jan E. Stone, Privileges and Exemptions Enjoyed by Nonprofit Organizations: A Catalog and Some Thoughts on Nonprofit Policymaking (N.Y.U. School of Law Program on Philanthropy and the Law, 1993); Thomas Silk, The Legal Framework of the Nonprofit Sector in the United States, in The Jossey–Bass Handbook of Nonprofit Leadership and Management (Robert D. Herman ed. 1994); Developments in the Law–Nonprofit Corporations, 105 Harv.L.Rev. 1578 (1992).

5. AN INTRODUCTORY PROBLEM

The legal framework governing nonprofits brings with it benefits, such as tax exemptions, and burdens, such as the nondistribution constraint. In meeting with the founders of a new enterprise that might qualify for nonprofit status, a lawyer must inquire about their purposes and goals, proposed activities, the sources of funding, and the desired relationship of the founders and others to the organization. The problem below offers an opportunity to address some of these pre-formation issues.

Specifically, the problem is intended to launch a general discussion of some preliminary considerations relating to the decision whether to form an organization as a for-profit business or a nonprofit entity and, if nonprofit, to consider options on choice of organizational form (corporation, trust, unincorporated association) and, if a nonprofit corporation, choice of category under state law (e.g., public or mutual benefit) and, finally, type of tax-exempt status—e.g. § 501(c)(3) or some other section of the Code.

PROBLEM

Leona Read and Tom O'Brien, both full-time law professors with considerable practical experience, are interested in forming and operating an entity that will conduct continuing legal education programs to attorneys in your state. They plan to call their entity "Lear's Council." The impetus is the continuing education that has been mandated by your state's bar for all lawyers. For now, Leona and Tom intend to remain as full-time faculty members, but ultimately they may devote more time to continuing education if it proves to be successful.

Leona and Tom are seeking some general advice as to what factors should be considered in deciding whether to conduct their continuing education activity as a for-profit business or a nonprofit educational organization. If nonprofit, they would like some advice as to the appropriate form for their entity and the formal organizational steps required under your jurisdiction's law.

PART TWO

TAX EXEMPTION

CHAPTER 2

Tax Exemption: Public Benefit Organizations

A. Introduction

The Internal Revenue Code long ago emerged as a significant regulator of nonprofit activity. The requirements for obtaining federal tax exempt status, the Code's elaborate system of classifying nonprofits, and the accompanying maze of charitable deduction rules are a constant presence for nonprofit directors, managers, fundraisers, philanthropists—and scholars. As Professor John Simon has so aptly put it, "[c]harity seems destined to be enmeshed in tax policy debate not only because so is everything in our society but also because, over the years, we have come to entrust to the tax system a central role in the nourishment and regulation of the nonprofit sector." John G. Simon, The Tax Treatment of Nonprofit Organizations: A Review of Federal and State Policies, in The Nonprofit Sector: A Research Handbook 68 (Walter W. Powell ed., 1987).

Tax benefits for nonprofit organizations have a venerable history, perhaps as old as civilization itself.[1] As chronicled in the Bible, "Joseph made it a law over the land of Egypt unto this day, that Pharaoh should have the fifth part; except the land of the priests only, which became not Pharaohs * * *." Genesis 47:24. Historical studies have reported that religious institutions were not taxed in ancient civilizations because they were thought to be owned by the gods themselves and thus beyond the reach of mortal taxing authorities. Although for a time churches were subject to taxation in England and church property was confiscated during the Reformation, the practice of granting tax exemptions ultimately spread to secular charities, culminating with the British Statute of Charitable Uses of 1601. Long regarded as the model for what was to come in America, the 1601 Statute was the first codification of charitable trust law, offering in its preamble one of the earliest lists of charitable purposes and relaxing the technical conveyancing rules of the common law to facilitate charitable transfers.[2]

---

1. Much of this discussion of the history of tax exemptions is derived from Chauncey Belknap, The Federal Income Tax Exemption of Charitable Organizations: Its History and Underlying Policy, in IV Research Papers Sponsored by the [Filer] Commission on Private Philanthropy and Public Needs 2025 (1977). See also John D. Colombo & Mark A. Hall, The Charitable Tax Exemption (1995).

2. See Chapter 1C, supra, at pp. 28–29.

The American colonists adopted the European tradition of providing tax exemptions for church property. Most of the colonies extended these benefits to higher education, with Rhode Island going so far as to exempt all the properties of the professors of Brown University from taxation. Federal income tax exemptions made their debut in 1894 with the enactment of the first corporate income tax, which included an explicit exemption for " * * * corporations, companies, or associations organized and conducted solely for charitable, religious or educational purposes * * * [and] stocks, shares, funds or securities held by any fiduciary or trustee for charitable, religious, or educational purposes * * *." Revenue Act of 1894, ch. 349, 32, 28 Stat. 556. A comparable provision has been included in every subsequent federal income tax act. The deduction for charitable contributions, proposed but rejected in 1913, was adopted in 1917 (with a limit of 15 percent of income) in response to the fear that higher tax rates would cause philanthropy to decline. It since has become one of the most entrenched features of our federal tax system.[3]

The early history of the law of tax–exempt organizations is relatively uninformative. Congress, courts, and the tax collectors paid scant attention to the nonprofit sector, preferring to concentrate on profit–seeking individuals and entities whose activities offered a more promising source of revenue. As Professor Boris Bittker has observed, in the early days of the income tax law "all nonprofit organizations were lumped together and exempted from tax as though fungible members of an undifferentiated mass." Boris I. Bittker & Lawrence Lokken, 4 Federal Taxation of Income, Estates and Gifts ¶ 100.1.1 (2d ed. 1992). Beginning after World War II and continuing to the end of the 20th century and beyond, however, nonprofit organizations have come under increasing scrutiny. As nonprofits gained wealth and influence, the wisdom of unbridled tax exemption and the accountability of the nonprofit sector have become recurring subjects of controversy. The excerpt below offers an introductory perspective on these developments and previews the Internal Revenue Code's intricate scheme for classifying nonprofit organizations.

John G. Simon, The Tax Treatment of Nonprofit Organizations: A Review of Federal and State Policies

in The Nonprofit Sector: A Research Handbook 68–73 (Walter W. Powell ed., 1987).

AN OUTLINE OF THE TAX TREATMENT OF THE NONPROFIT SECTOR

A Federal Tax Taxonomy

The nonprofit sector is subject to special treatment under federal individual and corporate income taxes, estate and gift taxes, and certain

---

3. The background and policy aspects of the charitable deduction are discussed in Chapter 6A, infra, at pp. 673–691.

excise taxes. There are, in fact, four separate treatments, one for each of four principal categories into which the federal tax laws divide the nonprofit sector. In Figure 5.1 [below] each category is represented by a ring embracing a set of organizations that are subject to a substantially similar tax regime, distinct from the regimes applicable to the adjoining rings. The rings are so arranged that together they make up a group of concentric circles, which, as one moves outward from Ring IV, contain increasingly larger portions of the nonprofit world.

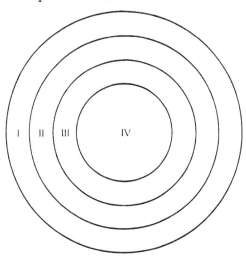

FIGURE 5.1   A SCHEMATIC SKETCH OF NONPROFIT TAX CATEGORIES

Thus, the full circle, encompassing Rings I through IV, includes all entities that are exempt from federal income tax (the tax otherwise imposed on corporations, unincorporated associations, or trusts) under the principal exemption statute, § 501 of the Internal Revenue Code. Almost all these groups share the condition of being organized on a not–for–profit basis, which means not that the entity is forbidden to generate a profit but that any such profits may not be distributed to owners or other private persons; Hansmann refers to this rule as the "nondistribution constraint." This constraint is imposed on these institutions by the legal instrument under which they are organized under state law—the "charter" or "articles" in the case of a nonprofit corporation or an unincorporated association, or the "deed of trust" or other trust instrument in the case of a charitable trust (Fremont–Smith 1965). (Which of these legal forms of organization a nonprofit group adopts is almost wholly irrelevant for determining that group's federal tax treatment.)

The Charitable–Noncharitable Distinction

There is a basic distinction between Ring I and the Rings II–IV circle, however. Groups in Rings II–IV are not only nonprofit but also what are loosely referred to by tax lawyers as the "charitables"—organizations described in § 501(c)(3) of the code as serving "religious, charitable, scientific, testing for public safety, literary or educational purposes." The shorthand "charitable" is used for these Rings II–IV groups, even though it is only one of several adjectives used in § 501(c)(3), because "charitable" is the residual category used to classify these groups when they do not fit under any of the other adjectives and also because the Supreme Court has held that all § 501(c)(3) groups must conform to common–law charitable criteria.

In Ring I are the *non*charitable nonprofits that are listed throughout the succeeding subsections of the exemption statute, in §§ 501(c)(4)–(21); here we have social clubs, veterans' organizations, labor unions, burial societies, chambers of commerce, marketing cooperatives, and other associations that may roughly be described as carrying forward the private interests of the members but subject to the nondistribution constraint. Bittker and Rahdert describe these as "mutual benefit" organizations, as distinct from the § 501(c)(3) charitable groups, which they characterize as "public service" organizations. Weisbrod distinguishes the Ring I from the Rings II–IV groups (to use our labels) on the basis of the greater tendency of the latter groups to provide "collective goods," often referred to as "public goods"—benefits that are not captured only by the persons or institutions generating the benefits. The tax system criteria for § 501(c)(3)—Rings II–IV—treatment will be further described later in this chapter. Apart from criteria, what are the *results* of landing in the Rings II–IV circle—within the charitable § 501(c)(3) set? Several consequences will be described below, but the most celebrated one is that contributions of cash or property (but not services) to these charitable groups are deductible by individuals and corporations for income tax purposes (under § 170 of the Code) and also deductible for estate and gift tax purposes (under §§ 2055, 2522). Gifts to Ring I organizations are not deductible, except for veterans' groups, nonprofit cemetery companies, and fraternal beneficiary organizations that use the gift for charitable purposes. * * *

Distinctions Within the Charitable World

Starting in 1954, and more ambitiously in 1969, Congress made distinctions—created a class system, some would say—*within* the § 501(c)(3) charitable world, which is why it is shown as a three–ring circle (II–IV) in our diagram. The charity world was first divided into two parts: the "private foundations" (Rings III and IV) and the groups that were *not* private foundations (Ring II). The private foundations were defined as constituting all groups that flunked certain tests set up by § 509 of the code. To pass these tests, a group must be a school, a church, a hospital (or hospital–related research entity), or a group that meets one of several alternative (and fairly complicated) definitions of a "publicly supported" organization. Organizations meeting these tests (and certain variations upon them) are, in the language of the tax bar, "public charities" (not to be confused with the broader set of § 501(c)(3) charities), and they escape private foundation classification, with all the disabilities that attach to that status. This subdivision was meant to separate grant–making organizations (embracing the Ford Foundation and lesser dispensers) from the operating charities. It was in the former camp that more fiscal abuses were thought to lie, more political activism, more "unaccountable" wealth, more of all kinds of other problems, and, in any event, it was thought that dollars given to grant–making foundations entered the stream of active charitable use more slowly than gifts to operating nonprofits (a proposition discussed below).

Distinctions Within the Foundation Category

In the midst of the 1969 congressional deliberations, however, it was discovered that the private foundation category, as pending legislation defined it, included all kinds of non–grant–making bodies that did not happen to be schools, churches, hospitals, or publicly supported. Many research institutions, social action groups, museums, and other nonprofits would fall afoul of the private foundation strictures. Congress could have moved them into public charity (Ring II) status, but, instead, it subdivided the foundation world (the Rings III–IV circle) into the "operating founda- tions"—Ring III—and the "nonoperating foundations" (the grant–making ones)—Ring IV. Probably the most important legal feature of the operating foundation is that it spends 85 percent of its income on the active conduct of its charitable program (as compared to grant making). Operating founda- tions receive more favorable treatment in several respects than do their nonoperating counterparts, as we shall see when we summarize the ring– to–ring progression in terms of tax benefit and regulatory burden.

This somewhat amoebic subdivision repeated itself in August 1984. For the purpose of giving certain operating foundations the benefit of public charity treatment in two respects (cited below), Congress carved out a subset of the Ring III world and called it the "exempt operating founda- tion"—an operating foundation that (1) had that status at the start of 1983 or, if not, had a past history of being publicly supported, and (2) had a board that was "broadly representative of the general public" and was not donor controlled—no officers and not more than a quarter of the board were persons related to major donors. Because of the limited (though not trivial) legal consequences of exempt operating foundation status, we have not created a separate ring (perhaps Ring II.5) for this subspecies.

Other Nonprofit Species

The reader may wonder where among these rings certain nonprofits reside. Take community foundations, for example. These grant–making pools of many endowed funds dedicated to local or statewide purposes and administered by a broadly representative distribution committee (for phi- lanthropic decisions) and by trustee banks (for investment decisions) quali- fy, for the most part, as public charities (Ring II) because of the multiplicity of their funders. They are not to be confused with community chests (typically part of the United Way system), another form of Ring II organi- zation that solicits mainly nonendowment contributions from the public and channels them largely to member agency public charities. Corporate foundations are treated like any other grantmaking Ring IV foundation, except that their resources come from a corporate donor (which often provides trustees and staff to the foundation from among company personnel). Lying outside these rings are still other nonprofits. Political parties are treated by a separate part of the code that both exempts part of their income and taxes part of it (for example, investment income). The funds that finance pension plans are covered by yet other code sections that exempt their investment income if they meet various qualifying criteria. Although some cooperatives are found within Ring I, consumer and farmer cooperatives are covered by special sections that, directly or indirectly, permit cooperative income to go untaxed.

Consequences of the Categories

What consequences attach to landing in one or another of the four rings? Table 5.1 [the Table is omitted, but the information it contains will be revealed gradually in this and subsequent chapters, Eds.] answers this question in summary fashion * * *. With respect to the *degree of regulation*, the reader will notice that here, as in Dante's circles of hell, the situation worsens (from the perspective of the nonprofit organization) as we move from outer to inner circles: the scope of the regulation, the strictness of standards, the strength of sanctions, and the obligations of disclosure all increase. When we look at the *degree of tax benefit*, however, the progression across the rings is rather different. We travel from the least–favored–nation status of Ring I to the most–favored position of Ring II and then part (but not all) of the way back down the benefit scale as we cross Rings III and IV. Combining these patterns, we see that, as we go from mutual benefit groups (Ring I) to the public interest organizations (Rings II–IV), Congress increases the level of benefit and, in rough exchange, imposes a higher behavioral standard. However, *within* the public interest or § 501(c)(3) realm (the Rings II–IV circle), the benefit–regulation trade–off ends, resulting in decreasing benefits *and* increasing regulation as we move from the most—to the least–favored charitable classes—from the public charities of Ring II to the grant–making foundations of Ring IV. * * *

NOTES

1. *The Role of the Tax System.* In surveying the federal and state policies that shape the tax treatment of nonprofits, Professor Simon has identified four essential functions that are useful reference points for the material to come. Those functions are: support, equity, police, and border patrol.

The support function encourages the continuation and expansion of the nonprofit sector through relief from tax. As discussed in the next section of this chapter and again in Chapter 6 (Charitable Contributions), a central policy issue is whether tax exemptions and charitable deductions are subsidies and, if so, whether this type of support is justified and appropriately provided by the tax system.

The equity function, with its goal of redistributing resources and opportunities, has its roots in the history of charity. The debate here is over the extent to which tax benefits should depend upon an organization's redistributional mission. For example, should exempt status be conditioned on service to the poor and disadvantaged? What is the appropriate degree of private benefit that may be derived by donors, and how much influence may donors wield?

The tax system exercises its police function by regulating the fiduciary behavior of a nonprofit's trustees, managers and donors. At the outset, this raises a recurring jurisdictional question: is the federal tax system, which is intended primarily to collect revenue, the most appropriate police officer? Why shouldn't the states play a more active role? The Internal Revenue Service's dominant regulatory role pervades the law of exempt organizations, most prominently in the special regime governing private foundations.

Finally, the border patrol function shapes what nonprofits may and may not do if they wish to secure and maintain their exempt status. The constraints on lobbying and political campaign activity, for example, limit the involvement of § 501(c)(3) charities in various aspects of the political process, while the restrictions on commercial activity and the unrelated business income tax patrol the nonprofit–business border.

The functions identified by Professor Simon undoubtedly influence the behavior of the nonprofit sector. The challenge for nonprofit students and scholars is to discern a coherent rationale for these policies. See John G. Simon, The Tax Treatment of Nonprofit Organizations: A Review of Federal and State Policies, in The Nonprofit Sector: A Research Handbook 73–95 (Walter W. Powell ed., 1987).

2. *For Further Reading.* The leading treatises on taxation of exempt organizations are Frances R. Hill & Douglas M. Mancino, Taxation of Exempt Organizations (2002 & current Supp.) and Bruce R. Hopkins, The Law of Tax–Exempt Organizations (7th ed. 1998). An excellent survey of the area also can be found in Boris I. Bittker & Lawrence Lokken, 4 Federal Taxation of Income, Estates and Gifts, chs. 100–104 (3d ed. 1999 with current Supp.). The Internal Revenue Service's perspective on substantive and procedural issues affecting exempt organizations is revealed periodically in the Service's Exempt Organizations Continuing Professional Education Technical Instruction Program Textbook. The textbook is available on line at <www.irs.ustreas.gov/charities/index.html> and is reprinted and sold by Commerce Clearing House and Tax Analysts. Encyclopedic coverage of current developments is provided by The Exempt Organizations Tax Review, published monthly by Tax Analysts. A good practice–oriented periodical is the Journal of Exempt Organizations, published by Warren, Gorham & Lamont.

THE ROAD AHEAD

Professor Simon's aerial view of the tax treatment of nonprofits has prepared us for the landing that is about to occur. The remainder of this chapter considers in detail the federal tax exemption standards for "public benefit organizations"—the "§ 501(c)(3) charities" described in Rings II–IV of Simon's schematic sketch and § 501(c)(4) social welfare organizations, which are exempt from federal income tax but not eligible to receive tax–deductible contributions. Chapters 3 and 4 consider the special problems of private foundations (Rings III and IV) and the exemption requirements for "mutual benefit organizations" (Ring I). Chapter 5 turns to the unrelated business income tax, the principal statutory watchdog patrolling the nonprofit–business border. Chapter 6 concludes the text with a survey of the charitable contributions deduction. Issues of state and local taxation are discussed selectively, with greatest emphasis placed on the real property tax exemption.

B. THE RATIONALE FOR CHARITABLE TAX EXEMPTIONS

Virtually all public benefit organizations derive their tax–exempt status under § 501(c)(3) of the Internal Revenue Code, which encompasses organizations "organized and operated exclusively for religious, charitable, scientific, testing for public safety, literary, or educational purposes, or to foster national or international amateur sports competition * * * or for the prevention of cruelty to children or animals * * * "provided that: (1) no part of the net earnings of the organization inures to the benefit of any private shareholder or individual, (2) no substantial part of its activities may consist of certain activities aimed at influencing legislation, and (3) the organization does not participate or intervene in any political campaign on behalf of any candidate for public office.

Exemption under § 501(c)(3) brings with it a wide range of additional tax benefits and exemptions from other forms of government regulation. Most importantly, virtually all § 501(c)(3) organizations qualify to receive tax–deductible contributions for income, estate and gift tax purposes. I.R.C. §§ 170; 2055; 2522. With very few exceptions, other exempt organizations are not eligible to receive tax–deductible gifts. Section 501(c)(3) organizations also are allowed to issue tax–exempt bonds to finance some of their activities (I.R.C. § 145), are exempt from federal unemployment taxes (I.R.C. § 3306(c)(8)), enjoy preferred postal rates (39 C.F.R. § 111.1 (1990)), qualify to provide tax–deferred retirement plans for their employees (I.R.C. § 403(b)), are likely to qualify for exemption from various state and local taxes, and may be entitled to exemption under antitrust, securities, labor, bankruptcy, and other regulatory regimes.[1]

---

1. For a comprehensive catalog of the privileges and benefits accorded nonprofit organizations by federal, state, and local governments, see Bazil Facchina, Evan Showell & Jan E. Stone, Privileges and Exemptions Enjoyed by Nonprofit Organizations: A Catalog and Some Thoughts on Nonprofit Policymaking (N.Y.U. School of Law, Prog. on Philanthropy and the Law, 1993).

What is the rationale for all this largesse? Are tax exemptions equivalent to a government "subsidy" to the benefited groups and, if so, what makes nonprofits worthy of this government support? If it is appropriate to subsidize nonprofits, why should the support come from the tax system? What are the implications of accepting or rejecting a particular rationale for exemption? These questions are not wholly theoretical. Advisors to exempt organizations and their donors often must defend the tax benefits enjoyed by their clients. And as we shall discover shortly, the resolution of exemption qualification controversies often turns on the perceived rationale for exempt status. It is thus appropriate to introduce the policy dimension at the outset and revisit these normative questions frequently in studying the taxation of exempt organizations.

1.   Traditional Public Benefit Subsidy Theory

The early history of the charitable tax exemption in the United States is surprisingly uninformative. Congress, preoccupied with the wisdom and constitutionality of an income tax, appears to have been acting based on some intuitive sense that it was simply not appropriate as a matter of history or tax policy to tax charitable organizations. Courts and commentators, when called upon to explain tax exemptions, developed what is variously referred to as the "public benefit" or "traditional subsidy" theory, justifying charitable tax exemptions on the basis of the public benefits conferred by the organizations–benefits which relieve the burdens of government by providing goods or services that society or government is unable or unwilling to provide. A variation of this traditional "quid pro quo" theory emphasizes the secondary community benefits offered by nonprofit organizations by their contributions to a robust and pluralistic American society and their role as innovators and efficient providers of public benefits.

The brief excerpt that follows summarizes the conventional wisdom. It was prepared in 1954 for the Rockefeller Foundation by its legal counsel and later published by The Commission on Private Philanthropy and Public Needs (the Filer Commission), a panel of prominent citizens formed in 1973 to study private philanthropy.

Chauncey Belknap, The Federal Income Tax Exemption of Charitable Organizations: Its History and Underlying Policy

IV Research Papers Sponsored by the [Filer] Commission on Private Philanthropy and Public Needs 2025, 2039 (1977).

Since medieval times, certain activities rating high in the scale of contemporary values have been accorded tax exemption. From the time when old world culture was first transplanted to America, charitable activities have been granted various forms of tax favors. The basic motive for these tax favors has been a wish to encourage activities that were recognized as inherently meritorious and conducive to the general welfare. In some cases it was also true that the exempted organizations performed activities that government would otherwise be forced to undertake, but it is believed that governmental saving has not been the decisive factor influencing the exemption of charitable activities from tax.

Some of these activities, as a matter of law and tradition, fall outside the scope of government action. Others, although within the area where government action would be permissible, are regarded as better left in private hands, for two reasons. The first reason is that private enterprise and diversity of action are believed to do the specific job better. The second reason is that the preservation of the American policies of individual initiative and of decentralization is deemed vital in itself.

The co–ordinate privileges of tax exemption and deductibility for tax purposes of gifts to tax–exempt organizations are remarkably well–conceived devices by which government can aid and stimulate private charitable enterprise, without subjecting it to control.

The essence of the advantage of this system is that it is automatic. The government does not control the flow of funds to the various organizations; the receipts of each organization are determined by the values and the choices of private givers. The donors determine the direction of their own funds, and the distribution of "tax savings" as well. The income of each individual organization is a product of donations it receives and the investment wisdom of its managers. Since all of these operations are out of the hands of government under the exemption and deduction statutes, the beneficiary organizations receive their governmental aid without having to petition for it. They are, therefore, in [Harvard] President Eliot's words " * * * untrammelled in their action, and untempted to unworthy acts or mean compliances."

Similarly, under the automatic system of tax exemptions and deductions, private bodies, and not government, determine the application of the funds. Private conviction and inspiration, in all of their diversity, are free to inquire, to experiment, and to take action. Effort may be wasted, mistakes may be made, agencies may even work at cross–purposes; but in the long run the well–being of mankind is thus fostered. The basic premise of the system is that progress comes through freedom.

NOTES AND QUESTIONS

1. *Tax Expenditures*. Under traditional theory, tax exemptions and charitable deductions are viewed as government subsidies to the organizations and their donors. This form of financial support is known as a "tax expenditure" in modern tax policy parlance. As first defined by the Congressional Budget and Impoundment Control Act of 1974, P.L. 93–344, "tax expenditures" are "revenue losses attributable to exclusion, exemption, or deduction from gross income or which provide a special credit, a preferential rate of tax, or a deferral of tax liability." Id. at § 3.3. Proponents of this

mode of analysis contend that tax expenditures are analogous to direct outlay programs and thus are an alternative means by which the government spends its money.

Tax expenditures are distinguished from "structural" provisions of an income tax system. Implicit in our normative structure, for example, is that a tax will be imposed on a proper yet practical concept of net income. The Internal Revenue Code thus permits taxpayers to deduct ordinary and necessary business expenses and excludes from the tax base a variety of economic benefits (e.g., certain fringe benefits) that would be impractical to include in the tax base. But many deductions, exclusions and other preferences are not compelled by structural or practical considerations. Rather, they are designed to encourage certain economic behavior or to reduce the tax liabilities of taxpayers in special circumstances. These are "tax expenditures." Familiar examples include the deductions for home mortgage interest, state and local income and property taxes, accelerated depreciation, and the exclusion from gross income for interest on state and local municipal bonds.

Harvard President Charles William Eliot, who is quoted in Belknap's excerpt above, questioned the notion of tax expenditures as far back as 1874. "It has been often asserted," Eliot said, "that to exempt an institution from taxation is the same thing as to grant it money directly from the public treasury. This statement is sophistical and fallacious." Contrasting tax exemptions with direct government grants, Eliot added:

> The exemption method is comprehensive, simple and automatic; the grant method, as it has been exhibited in this country, requires special legislation of a peculiarly dangerous sort, a legislation which inflames religious quarrels, gives occasion for acrimonious debates, and tempts to jobbery. The exemption method leaves the trustees of the institutions fostered untrammelled in their action, and untempted to unworthy arts or mean compliances.
>
> The exemption method is emphatically an encouragement to public benefactions. On the contrary, the grant method extinguishes public spirit. No private person thinks of contributing to the support of an institution which has once got firmly saddled on the public treasury. The exemption method fosters the public virtues of self–respect and reliance; the grant method leads straight to an abject dependence upon that superior power–Government. The proximate effects of the two methods of state action are as different as well–being from pauperism, as republicanism from communism. It depends upon the form which the action of the State takes, and upon the means which must be used to secure its favor, whether the action of the State be on the whole wholesome or pernicious. The exemption is wholesome while the direct grant is, in the long run, pernicious.

Charles William Eliot, Views Respecting Present Exemption from Taxation of Property Used for Religious, Educational and Charitable Purposes 392 (1874), quoted in Chauncey Belknap, The Federal Income Tax Exemption of Charitable Organizations: Its History and Underlying Policy, in IV Research Papers Sponsored by the [Filer] Commission on Private Philanthropy and Public Needs 2025, 2038–2039 (1977).

The staff of the Joint Committee on Taxation annually prepares a report as part of the federal budget process estimating tax expenditures. It is notable that under the Joint Committee's methodology, tax exemption under § 501(c)(3) is not classified as a tax expenditure because "the nonbusiness activities of [tax-exempt] organizations generally must predominate and * * * [i]n general, the imputed income derived from nonbusiness activities conducted by individuals or collectively by certain nonprofit organizations is outside the normal income tax base." Joint Committee on Taxation, Estimates of Federal Tax Expenditures for Fiscal Years 2003–2007 (JCS–5–02) 11, Dec. 19, 2002. This significant concession is not universally shared by tax expenditure purists. The charitable deduction, however, is classified as a tax expenditure, as is the exclusion from income available to holders of tax-exempt bonds issued by § 501(c)(3) organizations. See id. at 11–12.

2. *Why a Subsidy?* If tax exemptions are subsidies, what justifies the support? Would a system of direct grants be preferable? One frequently articulated justification for tax exemptions is that the benefited organizations relieve government from burdens that it otherwise would have to bear. Is that explanation underinclusive? Does § 501(c)(3) confer exempt status on organizations conducting activities that government is not obligated to undertake? Another justification is that tax exemptions support activities that provide a community benefit. Is this overinclusive? What is a "community benefit" and what agency of government is best equipped to make that determination? Do nonprofits that charge for their services, such as hospitals, theaters, and many private schools, provide a community benefit?

3. *Equitable Considerations.* When viewed as a subsidy, tax benefits for charities are challenged on equitable grounds because the economic benefit derived by donors increases proportionally to their marginal tax bracket. Under classical tax expenditure theory, the government "spends" more for charitable gifts by high–bracket taxpayers and provides little or no subsidy for gifts by low–income taxpayers, many of whom do not even itemize deductions. Put differently, the government adds proportionately more of the subsidy to a high–income taxpayer's giving and proportionately less to the low–income taxpayer's contribution. So viewed, the charitable deduction is said to have an "upside-down" effect. See, e.g., Giving in America: Toward a Stronger Voluntary Sector, Report of the [Filer] Commission on Private Philanthropy and Public Needs 109 (1975). Do these equitable concerns apply with equal force to the § 501(c)(3) income tax exemption and the charitable deduction? For additional discussion of the rationale for the charitable deduction, see Chapter 6A2, infra, at pp. 673–691.

2.   INCOME MEASUREMENT THEORY

Beginning in the 1970's, legal scholars began rethinking the rationale for charitable tax exemptions. In a seminal article, Boris Bittker and

George Rahdert took issue with the mainstream subsidy theory, arguing that the exemption for public benefit nonprofits is simply a natural outgrowth of a taxing system aimed at measuring income. Under this income measurement or tax base theory, public benefit organizations are exempt because they are inappropriate objects of income taxation. If public benefit organizations were not exempt, the authors asked, how would they be taxed? Would contributions to a church or school be income? Would church property be eligible for the depreciation allowance? Would expenditures for social services be deductible as ordinary and necessary business expenses? And would it be possible to devise an appropriate tax rate? Historically, charitable tax exemptions often were justified by tax base theories—e.g., an early rationale for federal tax exemption appears to be that charities had no income. Is this historical justification still valid? The excerpt below summarizes Bittker and Rahdert's modern income measurement theory.

Boris I. Bittker and George K. Rahdert, The Exemption of Nonprofit Organizations from Federal Income Taxation

85 Yale L.J. 299, 307–316 (1976).

A.   Measuring the "Income" of Public Service Organizations

Though differing in form and in the boundaries of their permissible activity, all exempt organizations engaged in public service activities share one common feature: if they were deprived of their exempt status and treated as taxable entities, computing their "net income" would be a conceptually difficult, if not self–contradictory task. From its inception, the federal income tax has been imposed not on gross receipts or gross income, but on an adjusted net amount—roughly speaking, gross income less business expenses. As a guide in computing "net" or "taxable" income, an extensive body of legal and accounting principles derived from business and financial practice has been developed. But these principles rest on the premise that the organization seeks to maximize its profit, and hence are not a satisfactory way of measuring the success of organizations that reject this basic premise. When the familiar methods of income measurement prescribed by the Internal Revenue Code, the accounting profession, or administrative practice are applied to nonprofit organizations, these methods must be stretched to, or beyond, the breaking point.

This result can be readily illustrated by a simple example. Assume that a charitable organization's receipts and disbursements for the year are as follows:

Receipts:	*(thousands)*
1. Interest from endowment	$100
2. Membership dues	25
3. Gifts and bequests	75
4. Total receipts	200

Disbursements:

5.	Salaries of staff	$ 25
6.	Medical welfare programs for indigent persons	125
7.	Total disbursements	$150

Net:

8.	Receipts less disbursements (line 4 minus line 7)	$ 50

The first step in computing the organization's hypothetical taxable income is to take account of its endowment income (line 1), but nothing else is this simple. Should the dues paid by its members (line 2) be treated as gifts to the organization and excluded from gross income under § 102, which provides that gifts and bequests are not taxable? Or are dues the functional equivalent of business income because the organization has obtained them by advertising its activities, promising to apply the funds to its announced charitable purposes, and allowing the members to participate in its affairs in the manner specified by its charter and by–laws? Similarly, do the gifts and bequests (line 5) qualify for exclusion from the organization's gross income under § 102, or should that provision be restricted to gifts and bequests received by individuals in a personal context, and not applied to amounts received by an organization as a result of its systematic solicitation of contributions? To the extent that dues, gifts, and bequests are used to increase the organization's endowment, should they be treated as contributions to capital, excluded from gross income under § 118?

At a more fundamental level, in view of the organization's duty to use contributions for its charitable purposes, should it be regarded as a mere conduit through which the funds move from the donor to the ultimate recipients, without creating any tax consequences for the intermediary? If an individual puts funds into a separate bank account to be used by him for charitable purposes, the deposit itself (as distinguished from interest thereon) could hardly be regarded as creating income. Should the dues and contributions received by a charitable organization be seen as a series of such individual deposits, which do not become taxable income simply because they are jointly administered by, or for, the benefactors? Or should the organization be treated as having a life of its own, separate from its contributors, and thus as having "income" when it collects funds that will be disbursed in a significantly different manner, given the natural evolution of bureaucracies, from the way the individuals would have spent their own funds if acting independently.

Once these puzzles in the definition of the organization's gross income have been solved, we must then decide which expenses may be deducted to arrive at net income. Do staff salaries (line 5) constitute "ordinary and necessary business expenses" under § 162, when paid by an organization that does not seek profits? Individuals who engage in such benevolent activities as giving money to needy relatives, acquaintances, or beggars cannot deduct their contributions, let alone any expenses for travel, advice, or bookkeeping incurred in distributing their largesse, no matter how extensive and systematic their generosity may be. Is this the proper analogy in deciding whether a charity can deduct its expenses, or should it instead be treated as an enterprise whose "business" is benevolence? The answer to these questions will bear on the proper classification of the medical and welfare program (line 6). If the salaries paid to the organization's staff are deductible business expenses because the charity's "business" is charity, then the funds given by it to the indigent should also be treated as business expenses.

The Internal Revenue Service has persistently asserted, with substantial success in the litigated cases, that expenditures not motivated by the desire for profit cannot be deducted as business expenses under § 162. For example, the taxpayer is allowed to offset any receipts generated by his "hobbies" against his related expenditures, but cannot deduct the loss if expenditures exceed receipts. If applied to non–profit organizations, this interpretation of § 162 would lead to a bizarre result, which can be illustrated by a simple example. Assume two retirement homes for the poor, each of which is operated by a nonprofit (but nonexempt) corporation and has 100 guests whose maintenance costs $3,000 per year each. If the first home operates at the breakeven point because it charges each guest $3,000 annually, it will, like the hobby farmer operating a breakeven farm, have neither income nor loss. If the second home has an endowment of $3 million, producing $300,000 interest per year, and is hence able to open its doors to guests who cannot afford to pay at all, it will have $300,000 of gross income but no deductible expenditures, because its maintenance charges do not arise in a profit–seeking venture. It will, therefore, be subject to a corporate tax of $138,500 (at current rates), or more than 45 percent of gross income, even though its guests are wholly indigent, while the other institution, whose guests may have been better off to begin with, will have no taxes to pay.

At first blush, the comparison may seem incomplete, since the personal tax status of the paying guests of the first institution has not been taken into account. Is the tax on the free institution simply a substitute for the income taxes paid by the paying guests of the first institution on their personal income, so that their $3,000 annual fees are after–tax amounts, while the expenditures of the free institution are also after–tax amounts? The trouble with this effort to reconcile the two cases is that the paying guests may be below the taxable income level, or derive their $3,000 fees from exempt social security benefits, gifts from members of their families, or other exempt sources. And even if their income had been fully taxed, their effective rate would not have been comparable to the 45 percent tax imposed on the free institution (and hence indirectly on its guests) unless they came from the upper reaches of the income ladder—$75,000 or above. Moreover, this way of analyzing the two cases suggests that the endowment income of the free institution should be imputed to the guests it supports, and this in turn implies that if they are below, or even substantially above, the poverty level, they are being grossly overtaxed.

In an effort to avoid this unpalatable dilemma, it might be argued that the concept of "business expenses" should be enlarged, by statutory amendment if necessary, to permit nonprofit institutions to deduct all amounts expended to advance their charitable or other nonprofit objectives. This would achieve substantially the same result as tax exemption, save for amounts earned in one year and either accumulated for future expenditure or spent on buildings and equipment. Since these accumulations and capital outlays are irrevocably dedicated to the institution's nonprofit objectives, however, we do not regard this alternative mode of computing a nonprofit organization's income as very appealing; nor can we see that it has any economic or social advantages over a regime of complete exemption.

If, as we believe, any attempt to treat charitable activity as a "business" is self–contradictory, can the income of a charitable organization be computed by treating its disbursements as charitable contributions, to be deducted under the rules applicable to other philanthropically inclined taxpayers? Although this approach seems more promising at the outset as a method of computing income than the § 162 route just examined, it proves on further analysis hardly more satisfactory.

To begin with, if the charity must rely on the current statutory provision (§ 170) for its right to deduct charitable contributions, it would encounter the obstacle that § 170 permits contributions to be deducted only if they are channeled by the taxpayer claiming the deduction through a nonprofit organization. Natural persons and business organizations cannot deduct charitable contributions made directly to needy individuals; and since philanthropic organizations are themselves tax–exempt, there has heretofore been no need to allow them to deduct such benefactions. If they had to rely on § 170, and it could be twisted to allow a deduction for direct grants to needy persons when paid by a charitable organization, another obstacle is encountered: taxpayers are allowed to deduct charitable contributions only up to specified percentages of their adjusted gross or taxable income—five percent [now ten percent, Ed.], in the case of corporations. If charitable organizations were subject to these percentage restrictions, they would no doubt consistently report higher profit margins on their gross receipts than the nation's most successful business corporations. A charity with $100,000 of income, for example, could deduct only $5,000 of charitable contributions if the five percent limit of § 170(c) applied, leaving 95 percent of its income as taxable "profit" even if the entire amount was spent to advance its eleemosynary objectives. Yet removal of the percentage limit for charities would mean that charities using all of their receipts for charitable purposes would be "unprofitable" as judged by Internal Revenue Code standards, while, conversely, those making the smallest current contributions would be the most "profitable," even though the retained funds were allocated for charitable expenditures in the immediate future.

* * *

So far, we have not complicated the problem of measuring a nonprofit organization's income by assuming any expenditures for nondeductible capital outlays, but the effect of such investments must be examined. If the

Church of the Gospel spends all of its receipts to support missionaries who live in tents, does it have less "net income" than the Church of the Adoration, which uses some of its receipts to construct a basilica (with an estimated useful life of 50 years) and to purchase a reliquary whose useful life cannot be predicted, at least not by the secular engineering methods with which the Internal Revenue Service is conversant? If both churches were ordinary business enterprises, the former could deduct all of its expenses currently, and hence would have no net income, while the latter would have to report income currently, because it could neither deduct nor depreciate the cost of the reliquary and could depreciate only a small fraction of the cost of the basilica. No doubt a church with reliquaries and buildings is "rich" in certain senses; Savanarola might denounce its possessions as an affront to the Almighty and Sotheby's could sell them on the auction block. But in the more modest framework of an income tax system, much can be said for treating both churches alike, even if equality is not compelled by the establishment clause of the First Amendment.

Depending, then, on the answers to these riddles, and depending also on such statutory clarification as might be forthcoming, the "net income" or "loss" of our hypothetical charity is one of a dozen different amounts. By itself, this possibility, though exasperating, is not unprecedented; "income" is a vaguer concept than the layman imagines. But our excursion has taken us through several unusually murky caverns, leaving—in our view—no escape from the conclusion that the very concept of "taxable income" for charitable or other public service organizations is an exotic subject more suited to academic speculation than to practical administration.

B. The Appropriate Tax Rate for Public Service Organizations

If despite these conceptual difficulties a satisfactory measure of the income of a charitable organization can be found, or if the difficulties are simply overridden by legislative fiat in favor of an arbitrary formula, we then face the problem of prescribing a suitable tax rate. This should not be plucked from the sky, nor should the rates prescribed for other taxpayers be applied to public service organizations unless their circumstances are comparable. Contemporary tax theorists would want a rate schedule that was consonant with either the "benefit" or the "ability to pay" theories of taxation. Though vague and malleable, these efforts to match the burden with the taxpayer's circumstances are less arbitrary than any alternative standard.

Ideally, since the economic burden of the tax will fall on the organization's ultimate beneficiaries (unless the tax prompts the benefactors to increase their gifts), the organization's income should be imputed to these recipients so it can be taxed at each one's personal tax rate. The difficulty with this approach, of course, is that the identity of the beneficiaries will rarely be known when the income is received by the organization; in this respect, they resemble the beneficiaries of a "sprinkling" trust. Recognizing that the beneficiaries of a charitable organization are usually too widely dispersed to allow an accurate imputation of the association's income, Congress might tax the entity itself, as a surrogate for its beneficiaries, at the estimated average rate at which the income would be taxed to the individuals if an imputation were feasible. As an alternative, Congress might conclude that justice would be better served by foregoing any tax on the entity's income, lest the estimated rate be higher than an accurate imputation would have produced. This decision would draw strength from the fact than an average rate, even if low, is bound to overtax the most needy beneficiaries of most philanthropic organizations.

The fact that recipients of gifts, whether they benefit from personal generosity or institutional philanthropy, are allowed by § 102 of the Internal Revenue Code to exclude these receipts from their gross income provides independent support for a decision to exempt charitable organizations. Since direct gifts from the original donor to the ultimate recipients would be excluded from their gross income, it would not be inappropriate to allow the same amount to pass untaxed through the organization, viewing it as a conduit to convey gifts from donors to their beneficiaries, rather than as an entity with independent taxpaying ability. Moreover, the benefits of a vast range of government services are received tax–free by citizens; this state of affairs has long been accepted as unavoidable, because it is simply not feasible to measure and impute the value of these benefits to the recipients in order to tax each person at an appropriate marginal rate. The largesse of public service organizations is not much different, and this analogy argues for exempting their income from taxation, thus allowing their resources to pass intact to the beneficiaries.

QUESTIONS

1. Does the income measurement theory provide an acceptable normative standard for charitable tax exemptions? Does it tell us anything about what makes public benefit organizations worthy of preferred treatment or why tax exemptions are an appropriate reward? Or would Bittker and Rahdert say that these questions are irrelevant?

2. Is it accurate to say that all charitable organizations have no measurable income? What about a hospital that derives most of its revenue from fees, or a school that relies primarily on tuition?

3. Is the income measurement theory limited to the income tax exemption for nonprofits? Does it also justify other tax benefits, such as eligibility to receive deductible contributions and real property tax exemptions? To be acceptable, should a rationale explain all the privileges and exemptions enjoyed by nonprofits?

4. As a technical and practical matter, would it be such an insurmountable task to tax nonprofit organizations?

3.   CAPITAL SUBSIDY THEORY

Bittker and Rahdert's attempt to articulate a more rigorous theory to justify charitable income tax exemptions went largely unnoticed beyond a small segment of the academic community. Those who absorbed it were stimulated but left dissatisfied. Professor Bittker's Yale Law School colleague, Henry Hansmann, was one of the first scholars to argue that Bittker and Rahdert had overstated the difficulties of determining the appropriate tax base for a nonprofit. For those organizations deriving all or nearly all of their revenue from the sale of goods or services, Hansmann argued, it would be no great task to import conventional tax concepts and come up with a meaningful net earnings figure. Even for nonprofits that relied on donations for their support, traditional tax concepts might be adapted by treating donations as includable in gross income and allowing deductions for the expenses of providing services related to the organization's exempt purposes. To be sure, there would be unique issues and some difficulties, but Hansmann argued persuasively that it would be possible to construct a definition of taxable income for all types of nonprofits that was consistent with the concepts employed in defining taxable income for business entities.

In a pioneering series of articles, Professor Hansmann employed law and economics methodology, first to explain the existence of nonprofit enterprises and then to examine the rationale for exemption. As previewed in Chapter 1, Hansmann concluded that nonprofit firms typically arise as the most efficient providers of goods and services in situations where, because of the circumstances under which goods or services are purchased or consumed or the nature of the service itself, consumers have difficulty evaluating the quantity or quality of the product or service. In these "contract failure" situations, for–profit firms may have an incentive and opportunity to exploit consumers, while nonprofits are viewed as more trustworthy because the nondistribution constraint prevents their founders, managers or members from diverting profits for personal use. See Chapter 1D1, supra, at pp. 35–43. Hansmann links the contract failure theory to the rationale for tax exemptions by arguing that income tax exemptions are a necessary tool to compensate nonprofits for the constraints they face in gaining access to capital markets by virtue of their inability to offer profit shares to private investors ("the nondistribution constraint") and their inadequate access to debt financing. Tax exemptions thus act as a capital formation subsidy, enabling nonprofits to finance growth through retained earnings, and they enhance the ability of nonprofits to borrow. Hansmann's theory is summarized in the following excerpt.

Henry Hansmann, The Rationale for Exempting Nonprofit Organizations from Corporate Income Taxation

91 Yale L.J. 54, 72–75 (1981).

There is an efficiency rationale for the exemption that is more appealing than [the public benefit and income measurement rationales], although it seems never to have been expressly offered before. That rationale is that the exemption serves to compensate for difficulties that nonprofits have in raising capital, and that such a capital subsidy can promote efficiency when employed in those industries in which nonprofit firms serve consumers better than their for–profit counterparts.

Nonprofit organizations lack access to equity capital since, by virtue of the nondistribution constraint [the rule that prohibits nonprofits from distributing their earnings to shareholders, Eds.], they cannot issue owner-ship shares that give their holders a simultaneous right to participate in both net earnings and control. Consequently, in raising capital, nonprofits are limited to three sources: debt, donations, and retained earnings. These three sources may, in many cases, prove inadequate to provide a nonprofit with all of the capital that it needs.

Donations are commonly an uncertain source of capital for nonprofits, and an inadequate one as well. Free–rider incentives presumably keep the flow of contributions to donative nonprofits—many of which provide public goods—well below the socially optimal level, and commercial nonprofits, by definition, receive few gifts of any sort. Debt, too, has distinct limits as a source of capital for most nonprofits. Lenders are commonly unwilling to provide anything near 100% of the capital needs even of proprietary firms, and are evidently even more conservative in lending to nonprofit firms. One reason for this is that, as debt comes to account for something close to 100% of a nonprofit's capital, it becomes increasingly unlikely that the organization's assets will provide adequate security for the debt. Of course, such a lack of security need not rule out debt financing. Debt, like equity, can be used as an instrument for risky investments; one need simply run up the interest rate on loans and bonds as they come to account for a larger fraction of the organization's capital. However, the transaction costs of using debt instruments for capital financing under conditions of substantial risk are high, and presumably prohibitive beyond some point well short of 100% debt financing.

As a consequence of these restrictions on external financing, a nonprof-it organization's ability to accumulate retained earnings is of substantial importance as a means of capital expansion. The reason for this is twofold. First, accumulated earnings can be used directly to finance capital improve-ments. Second, the amount of debt financing that a nonprofit can obtain is proportional to some extent on the amount of revenue it can derive from retained earnings, since capital purchased with such earnings provides an extra margin of security for the debt, and since the cash flow from such earnings is evidence to lenders that interest payments on the debt can be covered. To be sure, retained earnings, even when added to the sources of external financing available to nonprofits, are likely to prove an inadequate source of capital where the need for expansion is strong. But at least such earnings have the advantage that they are likely to be proportional to the degree to which demand for the organization's services exceed its ability to supply them, since excess demand will generally permit the organization to raise its prices (or attract larger donations).

A case therefore can be made against an income tax on nonprofits on the ground that such a tax would (at current corporate rates) cut retained earnings roughly in half, and hence would further cripple a group of organizations that is already capital–constrained. Or, put differently, the exemption can be understood as a subsidy to capital formation.

Of course, the mere fact that nonprofits as a class have difficulty raising adequate amounts of capital does not in itself constitute a justification for providing them with a capital subsidy. Quite the contrary: if the only thing distinguishing nonprofit from for–profit providers of a given service is that the nonprofits have difficulty raising adequate amounts of capital, then a capital subsidy to the nonprofits would simply be wasteful; the industry should be left to the for–profit firms. Indeed, presumably the reason why most sectors of our economy are dominated by for–profit firms is that they constitute, overall, the most efficient means of mobilizing productive resources—including, in particular, capital.

The problem, however, is that often nonprofits are, aside from problems of capital formation, more efficient than their for–profit counterparts in providing those services characterized by contract failure. For such services, the cost of capital subsidy provided by corporate tax exemption may be more than compensated for by the efficiency gains deriving from the expansion of nonprofit producers that the subsidy encourages.

Thus, the need for capital subsidies provides some justification for exempting nonprofits from corporate income taxation in those industries in which, owing to contract failure, nonprofits have important efficiency advantages over for–profits. And this, it appears, is the strongest argument that can be offered for the current policy of exempting many, but not all, nonprofits from taxation.

This argument is not without difficulties. For one thing, as already noted, it is not obvious that the exemption as currently administered is confined to those industries characterized by contract failure. This objection could be met, however, by redefining the contours of the exemption as suggested below.

More importantly, an exemption from income taxation is a crude mechanism for subsidizing capital formation in the nonprofit sector. The extent to which nonprofit firms are capital constrained evidently varies considerably from one industry to another, and, even within industries, from one firm to another. Although direct evidence of the degree of under- or over-investment among nonprofit firms is largely lacking, there is strong indirect evidence suggesting that nonprofit firms in rapidly growing service industries, such as nursing care, have had their growth noticeably hampered by an inadequate supply of capital. At the same time, there is good reason to believe that in many cases nonprofit firms are substantially overcapitalized; this often seems to be the case today, for example, with nonprofit hospitals. Simply granting or denying income tax exemption will obviously fail to eliminate all such disparity in access to capital among nonprofit firms. The exemption alone can only ameliorate, not eliminate, severe cases of capital constraint, while, in turn, denial of the exemption will in itself be inadequate to insure that a nonprofit does not accumulate capital far in excess of the efficient level of investment.

NOTES AND QUESTIONS

1. *A Crude Subsidy?* Some critics contend that Hansmann's capital subsidy theory is flawed because it is not sensitive to differences in capital needs among different deserving nonprofits. A more direct and efficient method for subsidizing capital formation, so the argument goes, exists through direct grants or the issuance of tax–exempt bonds. See, e.g., Mark A. Hall & John D. Colombo, The Charitable Status of Nonprofit Hospitals: Toward a Donative Theory of Tax Exemption, 66 Wash.L.Rev. 307, 388 (1991). Why aren't consumers naturally drawn to nonprofits in contract failure situations even without a tax subsidy?

2. *And What About Altruism?* Professor Hansmann's rationale for tax exemptions is grounded in notions of economic efficiency. Is this perspective too narrow? Professor Rob Atkinson challenged Hansmann's "emerging orthodoxy" by arguing that tax exemptions are justified as an appropriate subsidy rewarding the altruistic decision by a nonprofit's founders to forego profits. Rob Atkinson, Altruism in Nonprofit Organizations, 31 B.C.L.Rev. 501 (1990). Atkinson defines altruistic organizations as all nonprofits other than "mutual commercial" nonprofits (such as parent-controlled day care centers where the founders directly benefit from the organization's production). Under his altruism theory, any nonprofit organization whose income is being used to subsidize consumption by someone other than those who control the organization would be entitled to a tax exemption without any inquiry into the merits of the consumption or the public benefits flowing from it. "The metabenefit of altruistic production would suffice." Id. at 619. As long as the organization remains nonprofit, Atkinson argues, this element of altruism remains, even if all other factors of production must be purchased at market prices. Atkinson's theory has the virtue of certainty and it would be relatively easy to administer, but it is far more expansive than the other theories.

Does altruism adequately explain why the founders of an organization choose to adopt the nonprofit form? Should any nonprofit organization be entitled to tax–exempt status simply because it agrees, by adopting the nonprofit form, to refrain from distributing any profits to private individuals? Or should there be some more limiting principle? If so, is the appropriate criterion related to the nature of the organization's activities, the sources of its financial support, or other factors?

4. DONATIVE THEORY

Another attempt to articulate a rationale comes from Professors Mark Hall and John Colombo. Their first article addressed the question in the context of the exempt status of nonprofit hospitals. Professors Hall and Colombo argued that "the primary rationale for the charitable exemption is to subsidize those organizations capable of attracting a substantial level of donative support from the public." Mark A. Hall & John D. Colombo, The Charitable Status of Nonprofit Hospitals: Toward a Donative Theory of Tax Exemption, 66 Wash. L. Rev. 307, 390 (1991). In a second article, from which the excerpt below is taken, Hall and Colombo elaborate on the donative theory and describe how it should be implemented.

Mark A. Hall and John D. Colombo, The Donative Theory of the Charitable Tax Exemption

52 Ohio St.L.J. 1379, 1381–1389 (1991).

It is extraordinary that no generally accepted rationale exists for the multibillion dollar exemption from income and property taxes that is universally conferred on "charitable" institutions. Due primarily to the vast array of activities to which the exemption has been applied, it has defied all past attempts to formulate a synthesizing concept of charitable. Most commentators therefore have resorted to a theoretic pluralism, or agnosticism, maintaining that no single theory is capable of capturing the nuanced contours that historically have shaped the charitable exemption. This is an unsatisfactory explanation, however, for it ignores the unitary structure of the charitable exemption, which uses the single concept of charity to define its scope. Denying that this concept has any definitional content means that "charitable" is applied as a completely open–textured term to activities that are considered deserving of an exemption for a multitude of undisclosed policy reasons. Because we lack a coherent descriptive concept of what charities are, no normative explanation for why they should be exempt from taxes emerges for critical examination.

This unprincipled state of affairs is so taken for granted that the fundamental basis for the exemption is hardly discussed. In a previous article, we helped fill this void by critiquing the conventional and academic theories of the exemption. We applied four evaluative criteria to demonstrate that each of the previously expounded theories fails to explain why the activities the exemption encompasses should receive an implicit subsidy through the tax system. In order to place the exemption on firmer theoretical footing, we then proposed a donative theory of the charitable exemption—one that considers as charities only those institutions that are capable of attracting a substantial level of donative support from the public. We then demonstrated that this theory convincingly meets each of the four criteria that other exemptions fail. This Article expands on the donative theory of the charitable exemption, first by summarizing the basic theory as it contrasts with conventional alternatives, then testing this theory against a number of possible objections, and finally describing how the exemption should be administered under this theory.

I.   The Donative Theory in Broad Outline

A.   Deservedness

The most important criterion for evaluating a theory of the charitable tax exemption is deservedness, which has two distinct components: whether the theory identifies activities that are both worthy of, and in need of, a social subsidy. The chief example of a conventional theory that fails the first component of deservedness–worthiness—is the theory that uses charitable trust law to define the scope of the tax exemption. This body of law, which has evolved since before the enactment of the 1601 Statute of Charitable Uses, contains essentially no subject matter limits to its coverage. It indiscriminately enforces trusts that pursue any public purpose that a founder might choose. As one court has declared, charity, so conceived, is "broad enough to include whatever will promote, in a legitimate way, the comfort, happiness, and improvement of an indefinite number of persons." It is manifestly absurd to confer billions of dollars of public subsidy on activities for no other reason than that, if they were organized as trusts, the law would not refuse to enforce the trust terms.

Other theories more discriminating in their determination of worthiness are nevertheless flawed under the deservedness criterion because they do not explain why valued activities need support to exist at a socially optimal level. A prime example is the community benefit theory, which seeks to ascertain which activities are more desirably offered on a nonprofit than a for–profit basis. This theory is flawed because, even assuming society has a preference for nonprofit enterprise, it fails to explain why a subsidy is needed to effectuate this preference. For instance, even if we accept the (unproven) argument that nonprofit hospitals are superior to for–profits, doctors and patients are free to patronize nonprofits to the full extent they desire. Therefore, there is no basis for providing a social subsidy to assist in realizing this choice. The exemption is either a waste or a windfall.

The donative theory avoids these twin pitfalls in the deservedness criterion by deriving its concept of charity from the failure of the private sector to supply goods and services that are not sold efficiently through individual transactions. It reasons that donative institutions deserve a tax subsidy because the willingness of the public to contribute demonstrates both worthiness and neediness. Donors' selections of particular objects of philanthropy from the many available alternatives reveal those that are of special worth in the public's estimation. The institution's resort to solicitations evidences that its needs are not being met elsewhere. We can be assured that donations themselves will not fully satisfy this need since donors do not lightly relinquish their assets; in the absence of a quid pro quo return, the free rider incentive that affects the motivation to give tells us that donors systematically will give less than the deservedness that they perceive (as measured hypothetically by their willingness to purchase the good if it were capable of being delivered in ordinary market transactions). Hence, the existence of substantial donative support from the public at large signals the need for an additional, shadow subsidy to take up the donative slack.

B. Proportionality

After determining what activities deserve a social subsidy, the next difficulty in understanding the charitable exemption is formulating a theory that reasonably tailors the level of subsidy to the level of deservedness so as not to grossly over– or under–subsidize the activity. The primary hurdle this second inquiry presents is why should deserving activities be subsidized through the tax system rather than by a more targeted form of direct subsidy that would almost surely be more accurate? A leading example of a theory that fails this proportionality criterion is one that limits the exemption to organizations that provide some measure of free services to the poor. Under this theory of the exemption, a tax subsidy produces an upside down effect as between qualifying entities that provide a small percentage of free services and those that provide a large percentage: those charities that provide the least free services will have the most exempt property and income, all else being equal. Therefore, the charity–care theory perversely provides the most aid to those activities that least deserve support, among the entities that qualify.

The donative theory on first inspection also appears to suffer somewhat under the proportionality criterion. While a donative subsidy is not perverse in its effect, at best there is only a rough relationship between an institution's donative support and the amount of its exempt property or income. There is an approximate relationship with respect to exempt property, but there is some question whether the income tax exemption provides a subsidy at all, given that gifts would not count as income even absent the exemption. However, a second aspect of the donative theory— government failure—explains that, by definition, no superior subsidy alternative exists. The donative theory operates at the intersection of the failure of both private markets and the government. Only when neither sector is capable of providing a shared social benefit at the desired level will a substantial number of people resort to philanthropy. This observation establishes why the donative theory elegantly satisfies the proportionality criterion: The political stalemate that prevents a direct government subsidy means that, however flawed, an implicit subsidy through the tax system is the only available mechanism for subsidy.

C.   Universality and Historical Consistency

A fully successful theory of the exemption must also satisfy two criteria of secondary, but still considerable, importance. The first, a criterion of universality, derives from the fact that the charitable exemption is structured as a unitary, coordinated system composed of a host of benefits and burdens that flow automatically from the determination of charitable status. Charitable organizations at once qualify for exemptions from both local property taxes and federal corporate income tax; these "501(c)(3) organizations" are also eligible under Code section 170 to receive contributions that are deductible in computing the donor's personal income tax. Tax–exempt status carries with it the requirements that the organization be truly nonprofit, that it limit its political lobbying and campaigning activities, and that it pay taxes on earnings unrelated to its exempt purpose. A successful theory of the exemption should explain most or all of these tax benefits and burdens.

A satisfactory theory of the charitable exemption should also be historically consistent with the major categories of exempt activities. Because the concept of charity explicitly refers to over 400 years of legal precedent, it would constitute an abandonment, not an explanation, of the charitable exemption to construct a theory that is oblivious to this history.

Some existing theories of the exemption fail to account for either of these considerations. For instance, Professors Bittker and Hansmann have proposed competing theories that would explain the federal income tax exemption but that have no relationship to the state property tax exemption. Moreover, their theories fail to explain major restrictions on the exemption and give no coherent meaning to the term "charitable" that accords with established history and common sense understandings.

In contrast, the outline form of the donative theory nicely satisfies the universality criterion. Those institutions that receive donative support deserve subsidy through all available tax mechanisms: income, property, and sales tax exemptions as well as the charitable deduction. The theory therefore avoids treating each of these as a separate problem. Moreover, defining charities as those activities that receive substantial donative support is consistent with our intuitive and historical concepts of this term.

In particular, only the donative theory is capable of reconciling the charitable exemption's historical connection with the law of charitable trusts. On first inspection, it makes no sense for tax law to borrow its concept of charity from trust law, as it purports to do, since the functions of these two bodies of law, and the social costs of charitable characterization, are entirely different. Focus on the donative element, however, explains this historical connection. Charitable trusts receive legal protection because of their donative status: the self–sacrifice entailed in the founder's formation of the trust ensures that the object of the trust deserves at least the limited social support of legal enforcement. We argue that a donative act also deserves the additional social support entailed in the tax exemption. Only when we lose sight of this donative aspect of charitable trust law and blindly transplant its subject matter to tax law do we lose any rational subject matter limits. Therefore, retaining the crucial donative element maintains contact between modern tax law and the centuries of trust law precedent.

D. The Challenge That Lies Ahead

In broad perspective, the donative theory stands in fundamental contrast to other theories of the charitable exemption in the social engine that it uses to establish the exemption's proper scope. The theory that refers to the law of charitable trusts unsuccessfully employs a common law judicial process to define the subject matter limits of the exemption. Other approaches employ a political process to make ad hoc, normative judgments of which activities deserve the exemption based on intensely empirical inquiries, despite the absence of any political structure other than taxing agencies to make these judgments. Only the donative theory employs a market–like process that relies on the self–interest of donors to choose for themselves the objects of charity that deserve public support. Donors "vote" for an indirect subsidy by participating in a "market in altruism" when they have been unsuccessful in obtaining direct provision through actual political or market mechanisms.

However attractive the donative theory is in broad outline, its acceptability turns on a host of minute inquiries such as precisely what acts constitute a donation, and exactly how the exemption should be administered. The donative theory still has not been subjected to the same detailed scrutiny that we have given the more conventional theories of the exemption. This unfinished task leaves a number of objections and imperfections to be addressed in the specific application and implementation of the donative theory. This Article undertakes this task by expanding on the donative theory in two dimensions: the theoretical and the practical. We develop more rigorously the theory for subsidizing donative institutions in order to repel attacks that it either goes too far or does not go far enough, and we define more carefully how donative institutions should be identified and subsidized in order to understand how the exemption should be administered. Our aim here is to present a fully–articulated conception of the charitable exemption that is capable of immediate implementation.

NOTES AND QUESTIONS

1. *How Much Donative Support?* Under the donative theory, only institutions capable of attracting a "substantial level" of donative support from the public qualify for tax-exempt status. Setting this donative threshold raises a host of practical questions. For example, against what base is donative support measured? What percentage of that base must come from donations for an organization to qualify as charitable? What donations count? Is it sufficient if they all come from one person or family, or must donative support be from the general public? Who is the public? Acknowledging that the appropriate threshold is a value judgment that ultimately must be resolved in the political arena, Hall and Colombo generally conclude that one–third of an organization's gross revenues should come from public donations over a four–year measuring period. Mark A. Hall & John D. Colombo, The Donative Theory of the Charitable Tax Exemption, 52 Ohio St.L.J. 1379, 1450–1452 (1991). They would be willing to relax the one–third threshold to 10 or 20 percent for certain categories of historically exempt organizations, such as schools or hospitals. See John D. Colombo & Mark A. Hall, The Charitable Tax Exemption 200 (1995), which includes numerous other refinements and implementation details. Why is one–third the magic number? Would it be more appropriate to condition exempt status on the number of donors? In the last analysis, is the donative theory inherently arbitrary or imprecise? Hall and Colombo defend the one–third test as consistent with historical experience. For example, in Chapter 3 we will see that a one–third threshold is consistent with several tests used to determine whether a § 501(c)(3) organization qualifies as a "public charity," thus avoiding private foundation status. See I.R.C. §§ 509(a)(1), (2); 170(b)(1)(A)(vi); Treas. Reg. § 1.170A–9(e)(2). But the private foundation regulations also permit an organization to qualify as a public charity with only 10 percent public support if it engages in active fundraising and has

other attributes that ensure accountability to the public. Treas. Reg. § 1.170A–9(e)(3).

2. *Practical Implementation.* The donative theory presents a host of other practical implementation issues, most of which are considered by Hall and Colombo. The base (denominator) for their one–third support test is an organization's gross revenues, including gifts, investment income, receipts for goods and services, gains from the sale or exchange of capital assets, and net income from unrelated business income. As for the numerator of the support fraction, Hall and Colombo would import the well–developed body of law that determines what constitutes a gift for charitable deduction purposes. Any payments received by the organization for goods and services (e.g., tuition, fees paid to a hospital) would not qualify as donative support, but Hall and Colombo would include the fair market value of donated labor, using a crude but practical standard measure. Government grants would not count but grants from other private entities (e.g., private foundations) would qualify as donations. To ensure a sufficiently broad base of donative support, Hall and Colombo—again borrowing from the private foundation rules (see Treas. Reg. § 1.170A–9(e)(6))—would include donations from any one source in the "good support" numerator only to the extent they did not exceed two percent of the organization's annual gross revenue. But what of the punitive effect of this two percent rule if an organization receives a particularly large single donation? Professors Hall and Colombo propose to exclude these disproportionate gifts from both the top and bottom of the support fraction, at least if the gift is "innocent" (e.g., from a source unrelated to the organization's management or founder) but not if it is "suspicious." Nothing is easy! To their credit, Hall and Colombo tackle these and other problems of practical implementation. See John D. Colombo & Mark A. Hall, The Charitable Tax Exemption 193–224 (1995). How would traditional charities, such as churches, private schools, health care organizations, and cultural organizations fare under the donative theory?

3. *For Further Reading.* Rob Atkinson, Theories of the Special Tax Treatment of Nonprofit Organizations, ch. 15 in Frances R. Hill & Barbara L. Kirschten, Federal and State Taxation of Exempt Organizations (1994); Evelyn Brody, Of Sovereignty and Subsidy: Conceptualizing the Charity Tax Exemption, 23 J. Corp. L. 585 (1998); Nina J. Crimm, An Explanation of the Federal Income Tax Exemption for Charitable Organizations: A Theory of Risk Compensation, 50 Fla.L.Rev. 419 (1998).

5.   PROPERTY TAX EXEMPTIONS

Many nonprofits do not earn a significant net profit or rely on charitable contributions as a major source of their support. State and local tax exemptions may be the most significant governmental benefit for these organizations, especially if they own real property. Property tax exemptions have received less scrutiny than federal income tax exemptions, but they are assuming greater importance as state and local governments seek new sources of revenue. Like income tax exemptions, property tax exemptions are justified as appropriate government subsidies to support and encourage the public benefits and service provided by the nonprofit sector. Critics emphasize the inroads from tax–exempt property into the tax base of a local municipality and the lack of any corresponding return benefits from many nonprofits to the community bearing the exempt burden. Others stress the need for all nonprofits to pay their "fair share" for essential state and local government services.

Defenders of property tax exemptions have challenged the notion of a subsidy and attempted to explain the exemption based on a "tax base defining" rationale. In a leading study, Professor Thomas Heller proposed five alternatives to the conventional wisdom: (1) if property taxes are an indirect charge for government benefits, nonprofits are exempt because it is not clear that they are substantial consumers of those benefits; (2) property taxes serve to correct deficiencies in the federal income tax, such as the failure to tax imputed income from owner–occupied housing, and no such correction is needed for nonprofit organizations; (3) property taxes are a tool of land use planning, forcing owners to convert their property toward market preferred uses—a regulatory policy that is inappropriate when applied to nonprofit landowners; (4) the property tax is a wealth tax based on redistributional principles that do not apply to nonprofit organizations; and (5) the property tax, as customarily defined, is a vestige of history without any normative principles and, under this "customary definition," nonprofits do not belong in the tax base. See, e.g., Thomas C. Heller, Is the Charitable Exemption from Property Taxation an Easy Case? General Concerns About Legal Economics and Jurisprudence, in Essays on the Law and Economics of Local Government 183 (D. Rubinfeld ed., 1979).

In a landmark study of property tax exemptions in New York, Peter Swords has argued that the incidence of property tax must fall either on an exempt organization's beneficiaries or its donors. Since beneficiaries tend to be poor, imposing taxes on nonprofit property would not pass muster under an "ability to pay" criterion. Swords also points to various secondary benefits, such as the economic efficiency that flows from the ability of nonprofits to supply public goods that otherwise would not be produced in sufficient quantities. See Peter L. Swords, Charitable Property Tax Exemptions in New York State 191–209 (1981).

For further discussion of state tax issues, see Section C8 of this chapter, infra, at pp. 211–216.

For Further Reading: Property Tax Exemption for Charities: Mapping the Battlefield (Evelyn Brody ed. 2002); L. Richard Gabler & John F. Shannon, The Exemption of Religious, Educational, and Charitable Institutions from Property Taxation, in IV Research Papers Sponsored by the [Filer] Commission on Private Philanthropy and Public Needs 2535 (1977); Rebecca S. Rudnick, State and Local Taxes on Nonprofit Organizations, 22 Cap.U.L.Rev. 321 (1993); William R. Ginsberg, The Real Property Tax Exemption of Nonprofit Organizations: A Perspective, 53 Temple L.Q. 291 (1980); Robert T. Bennett, Real Property Tax Exemptions of Non–Profit Organizations, 16 Clev.–Mar.L.Rev. 150 (1967).

C. BASIC REQUIREMENTS FOR CHARITABLE TAX EXEMPTION

1. ORGANIZATIONAL AND OPERATIONAL TESTS

Internal Revenue Code: § 501(c)(3).

Treasury Regulations: § 1.501(c)(3)–1(a), (b), (c).

As previewed earlier, the "charitable nonprofits"—those that derive their exemption from § 501(c)(3)—are by far the most important category within the nonprofit sector. They include churches, schools, hospitals, arts and environmental groups, and the broad array of other organizations that fall under the rubric of "charity." To qualify for exempt status under § 501(c)(3), an organization must meet the following requirements:

1. It must be organized as a nonprofit corporation, or as a "community chest, fund, or foundation." "Corporation," for this purpose, is construed to include unincorporated associations, and "fund or foundation" includes wholly charitable trusts.

2. It must be organized and operated exclusively for religious, charitable, scientific, testing for public safety, literary, or educational purposes, to foster national or international amateur sports competition (as long as the activity does not involve the furnishing of athletic facilities or equipment), or to prevent cruelty to children or animals.

3. No part of its "net earnings" may inure to the benefit of any private shareholder or individual.

4. No "substantial part" of the organization's activities may consist of certain lobbying activities, with substantiality being measured either by a vague balancing standard or, for eligible electing charities, by more objective expenditure tests.

5. The organization may not participate or intervene in any political campaign on behalf of or in opposition to any candidate for public office.

The Treasury Regulations expand upon these requirements, providing that an organization must satisfy a formalistic "organizational test" and an objective "operational test." Treas. Reg. § 1.501(c)(3)–1. Although these regulations have largely been overshadowed by an increasingly developed body of case law, they are the obligatory starting point for a study of the requirements for exemption under § 501(c)(3).

The Organizational Test. The organizational test relates solely to the language used in the organization's governing (e.g., trust instrument, articles of incorporation or association, charter, etc.), which must (1) limit the purposes of the organization to one or more exempt purposes described in § 501(c)(3), and (2) not expressly empower the organization to engage (except to an insubstantial degree) in any activities which do not further one or more exempt purposes. Treas. Reg. § 1.501(c)(3)–1(b)(1)(i).

The organization's purposes as stated in its governing document may be as broad as the statute itself ("formed for charitable and educational purposes within the meaning of § 501(c)(3) of the Code"), or more limiting ("formed to operate a school for adult education"), but may not be overly broad ("to promote the health and welfare of the human race") or authorize non–exempt activities ("to engage in the operation of a social club"). Treas. Reg. § 1.501(c)(3)–1(b)(1)(ii) & (iii). Nor may the articles empower the organization to engage in any impermissible activities, such as more than an insubstantial amount of lobbying or any participation in political campaigns. Treas. Reg. § 1.501(c)(3)–1(b)(3). Indeed, a properly drafted governing document should expressly prohibit the organization from engaging in impermissible political activities.

The regulations are principally concerned with the magic language in the organizational documents. Under the organizational test, it is not enough to show that an organization is actually operated for exempt purposes (Treas. Reg. § 1.501(c)(3)–1(b)(1)(iv)), although a few cases have permitted extrinsic evidence to help an organization cure a technical foot fault and preserve its exempt status (see, e.g., Blake v. Commissioner, 30 T.C.M. 781 (1971)).

Another critical element of the organizational test looks to the distribution of assets on dissolution. Either in its charter or under applicable state law, the organization must expressly dedicate its assets to one or more exempt purposes in the event of dissolution. The required dedication does not exist if assets may be distributed to the organization's members. This requirement is easily met by providing that upon dissolution the assets will be distributed to another § 501(c)(3) organization in furtherance of an exempt purpose. Treas. Reg. § 1.501(c)(3)–1(b)(4). Even if the charter is not explicit on this point, the test is met if state law requires that the organization's assets must be dedicated to a charitable purpose on dissolution. The Service has published a list of states that provide for the distribution of a nonprofit's assets by operation of law in a manner that satisfies the organizational test. See Rev. Proc. 82–2, 1982–1 C.B. 367. It also has stated that the following language will satisfy the dissolution requirement of the organizational test:

> Upon dissolution of [this organization], assets shall be distributed for one or more exempt purposes within the meaning of Section 501(c)(3) of the Internal Revenue Code, or corresponding section of any future Federal tax code, or shall be distributed to the Federal government or to a state or local government, for a public purpose.

Rev. Proc. 82–2, supra, § 2.05. See also I.R.S. Publication 557 at 18–20 for sample organizational documents for nonprofit corporations and charitable trusts.

The Operational Test. The operational test requires the organization to engage "primarily in activities that accomplish one or more of [the] exempt purposes specified in section 501(c)(3)." Treas. Reg. § 1.501(c)(3)–1(c)(1). This test is not met if "more than an insubstantial part of [the organization's] activities is not in furtherance of an exempt purpose." Id. Examples of impermissible conduct include inurement of net earnings to private individuals and operating as an "action organization"—i.e., engaging in the substantial lobbying or political campaign activities proscribed by the Code. Treas. Reg. § 1.501(c)(3)–1(c)(2) & (3).

The operational test does little more than paraphrase the statute. Far more instructive are the evolving definitions of the "exempt" purposes specified in § 501(c)(3), as applied to fact patterns illustrated in the materials that follow, and the interpretations of the inurement and political activity prohibitions also covered later in this chapter. The "operational test" regulations, however, make one notable concession. In focusing on an organization's "primary" activities and suggesting that an "insubstantial" part of those activities may further a non–exempt purpose, they confirm that operated "exclusively" means operated "primarily" for exempt purposes. Treas. Reg. § 1.501(c)(3)–1(c)(1). Insubstantial non–exempt operations have long been tolerated by the Service, despite the seeming inflexibility of the term "exclusively." See Better Business Bureau v. United States, 326 U.S. 279, 66 S.Ct. 112, 90 L.Ed. 67 (1945). For example, a § 501(c)(3) organization may engage in insubstantial business activities unrelated to its exempt purposes without risking loss of exemption, but the net income from any such business is potentially subject to the unrelated business income tax. See I.R.C. § 511 et seq. and Chapter 5, infra.

2.   APPLICATION FOR § 501(c)(3) EXEMPTION

Internal Revenue Code: § 508(a)–(c).

Treasury Regulations: § 1.508–1(a)(1), (2)(i), (3)(i).

The Notice Requirement. Most nonprofit organizations seeking recognition as tax–exempt under § 501(c)(3) and as eligible to receive tax–deductible contributions under § 170 must "notify" the Internal Revenue Service that they are applying for exemption and obtain a favorable determination of their exempt status. These requirements apply to all aspiring § 501(c)(3) organizations formed after October 9, 1969, except for churches, their integrated auxiliaries, conventions and associations of churches, and organizations other than private foundations that normally have gross receipts of $5,000 or less. I.R.C. § 508(a), (c)(1); Treas. Reg. 1.508–1(a)(3).[1] Organizations covered by a group exemption letter also are exempt from filing. A group exemption letter is a ruling issued to a central organization recognizing the exemption of a group of "subordinate" organizations—for example, Boy or Girl Scout chapters, local church parishes, and the like. Treas. Reg. 1.508–1(a)(3)(i)(C).

The notice requirement also applies to § 501(c)(3) organizations that seek to avoid private foundation status. See I.R.C. § 509(a). In general, any § 501(c)(3) organization formed after October 9, 1969 is presumed to be a

---

1. An organization's annual gross receipts are "normally" less than $5,000 if they do not exceed $7,500 for its first taxable year, an aggregate of $12,000 for its first two taxable years, and $15,000 for its first three years. Treas. Reg. § 1.508–1(a)(3)(ii).

private foundation unless it notifies the IRS that it is not a private foundation. I.R.C. § 508(b); Treas. Reg. § 1.508–1(b). The substantive rules and procedures for avoiding private foundation status are discussed in Chapter 3, infra.

Form 1023. A § 501(c)(3) organization meets the notice requirement by filing an Application for Recognition of Exemption on IRS Form 1023 within 15 months from the end of the month in which it was organized. Treas. Reg. § 1.508–1(a)(2)(i).[2] Preparing Form 1023 can be a daunting experience. The IRS requires the organization to provide a narrative description of its past, present and future activities; detailed financial data, including a proposed 2–year budget for new organizations; and answers to a long list of questions relating to the organization's governing body, its relationship to other organizations, and its actual and proposed fund raising activities. Certain organizations, such as churches, schools, hospitals, homes for the aged, child care providers, and successors to for–profit organizations, must provide additional information on special schedules. Even more detailed information is requested from organizations seeking to avoid private foundation status. Form 1023 also requires the organization to submit numerous attachments, including a conformed copy of its articles of organization or other enabling documents and its by–laws. Complete copies of Form 1023 and its instructions are included in the Statutes, Regulations and Forms Supplement.

Completed exemption applications formerly were filed with the IRS key district office where the organization's principal place of business was located, but they now are all routed to a central location in Cincinnati, Ohio. If the application raises unique or unsettled issues, the case may be referred to the IRS National Office in Washington, D.C. The application must be accompanied by a "user fee," which is $150 both for organizations with annual gross receipts averaging not more than $10,000 during the preceding four years and for new organizations that anticipate not more than $10,000 gross receipts over their first four years. The fee for all other applicants is $500.

An organization that files its application for exemption within the required notice period (including extensions) and receives a favorable determination letter from the IRS will be recognized as exempt from the date of its creation. The organization's donors then will be assured that gifts made from the date of creation are tax–deductible, and the organization's name will be added to IRS Publication 78, a bulky two–volume "cumulative list" of all organizations recognized as eligible to receive charitable contributions under § 170. Publication 78's list of eligible organizations also is included on the IRS's web site at <www.irs.ustreas.gov> and is available through several on-line services. If the organization was required to alter its activities or organizational documents during the

2. Organizations automatically may extend the filing period to 27 months if they file a completed application within the extended period and indicate that the form is being filed pursuant to Rev. Proc. 92–85, 1992–2 C.B. 490. An additional extension may be granted for good cause. Id.

application process, its exemption will be effective as of the date specified in the favorable determination letter. If the application was untimely but the organization qualifies for exemption, the IRS's normal practice is to grant § 501(c)(4) exempt status up to the date when the application was filed and § 501(c)(3) status thereafter. See Rev. Rul. 80–108, 1980–1 C.B. 119. In that event contributions made before the application was filed are not tax–deductible. I.R.C. § 508(d)(2)(B).

An organization that receives an adverse determination letter will be advised of its right to file a protest with the IRS Appeals Office. Filing the protest invokes the usual IRS appeals procedures, including the right to a conference and the ability to request "technical advice" from the National Office. An organization that anticipates difficulties in obtaining a favorable determination should make its best and most complete case during this administrative process. As discussed below, exhaustion of all administrative remedies is essential to set the stage for a judicial determination through the declaratory judgment procedure authorized by § 7428 of the Code.

For other procedural issues, see Section H of this chapter, infra, at pp. 351–372.

3.   THE PUBLIC POLICY LIMITATION

Treasury Regulations: § 1.501(c)(3)–1(d)(1) & (2).

To qualify for exemption under § 501(c)(3), an organization must be organized and operated exclusively for one or more of the specified exempt purposes. Treas. Reg. § 1.501(c)(3)–1(d)(1). The term "charitable" is the broadest of those purposes. Although Congress has never specifically defined "charitable," the regulations—borrowing principles from charitable trust law—expansively construe it in its "generally accepted legal sense" by providing that charity includes such divergent activities as: relief of the poor and distressed; promotion of social welfare; advancement of religion, education and science; promotion of health; erection of public buildings; and lessening of burdens of government. Included within the ambit of "social welfare" are activities designed to lessen neighborhood tensions, eliminate prejudice or discrimination, defend human and civil rights, and combat community deterioration and juvenile delinquency. Treas. Reg. § 1.501(c)(3)–1(d)(2). In short, "charitable" has been construed to mean far more than benevolence or philanthropy, and it is an evolving concept that expands to meet changing societal needs.

A distinct aspect of the "charitable" requirement is a loosely defined public policy limitation that is superimposed over the list of exempt purposes in 501(c)(3). An outgrowth of the common law of charitable trusts, this broader concept of "charitable" requires a 501(c)(3) organization to serve a public purpose and disqualifies any organization that is operated for illegal purposes or engages in activities contrary to a clearly established public policy. The Supreme Court first applied the public policy standard to deny exemption to a racially discriminatory religious school in the celebrated *Bob Jones University* case. As illustrated by the case and the materials following it, it remains uncertain to what extent this limitation extends beyond racial discrimination in education.

Bob Jones University v. United States

Supreme Court of the United States, 1983.
461 U.S. 574, 103 S.Ct. 2017, 76 L.Ed.2d 157.

■ CHIEF JUSTICE BURGER delivered the opinion of the Court.

We granted certiorari to decide whether petitioners, nonprofit private schools that prescribe and enforce racially discriminatory admissions standards on the basis of religious doctrine, qualify as tax–exempt organizations under § 501(c)(3) of the Internal Revenue Code of 1954.

I

A

* * *

[Even after the Supreme Court's landmark decision in Brown v. Board of Education, the Internal Revenue Service routinely granted exempt status under § 501(c)(3) to private schools, without regard to their racial admissions policies. That policy began to shift in 1967, when the Service announced that it would deny tax exemptions to racially discriminatory private schools that received state aid. Two years later, parents of black public school children in Mississippi sued to enjoin the Service from granting exemptions or allowing charitable contributions to any discriminatory school within that state. In the midst of the litigation, the Service announced that it could no longer justify granting tax–exempt status to discriminatory schools, whether or not they received state aid or were church–related. But the case had become complicated by the intervention of parents and children who supported or attended private segregated Mississippi schools. It proceeded to a three–judge district court, which held in Green v. Connally, 330 F.Supp. 1150 (D.D.C.1971), aff'd mem. sub nom. Coit v. Green, 404 U.S. 997, 92 S.Ct. 564, 30 L.Ed.2d 550 (1971) that racially discriminatory schools in Mississippi did not qualify for exempt status because they violated a sharply defined federal policy against discrimination in education. In Rev. Rul. 71–447, 1971–2 C.B. 230, the Service extended the policy nationwide, basing its position on the common law requirement that the purpose of a charitable trust may not be illegal or contrary to public policy.

Following the mandate in Green, the Service issued guidelines aimed at enforcing the nondiscriminatory policy and extending it even to church–related schools that claimed their discriminatory policies were motivated by sincere religious beliefs. See Rev. Rul. 75–231, 1975–1 C.B. 159. In the early 1970's, the Service revoked the exemption of Bob Jones University, a fundamentalist Christian institution that had admitted a few black students but prohibited interracial dating and marriage, and denied exempt status to Goldsboro Christian Schools, which refused to admit blacks on religious grounds. Bob Jones filed suit seeking to enjoin the Service's revocation. The case wended its way up to the Supreme Court, which held in Bob Jones University v. Simon, 416 U.S. 725, 94 S.Ct. 2038, 40 L.Ed.2d 496 (1974) that the Anti–Injunction Act (§ 7421(a) of the Internal Revenue Code) prohibited the University from obtaining judicial review of the Service's action before the assessment or collection of any tax. As a result, Bob Jones regrouped, challenging the revocation in a suit for refund of federal unemployment taxes paid with respect to its employees. Goldsboro Christian Schools initiated its action with a similar refund suit. At the time these cases were commenced, exempt organizations generally were unable to obtain a declaratory judgment with respect to adverse IRS determinations and were forced to await a specific tax deficiency and then sue for a refund. As discussed in Section H1 of this chapter, infra, at pp. 351–353, § 7428 now eases the path to judicial review of adverse IRS exemption rulings. Eds.]

B

No. 81–3, Bob Jones University v. United States

Bob Jones University is a nonprofit corporation located in Greenville, South Carolina. Its purpose is "to conduct an institution of learning * * * giving special emphasis to the Christian religion and the ethics revealed in the Holy Scriptures." The corporation operates a school with an enrollment of approximately 5,000 students, from kindergarten through college and graduate school. Bob Jones University is not affiliated with any religious denomination, but is dedicated to the teaching and propagation of its fundamentalist Christian religious beliefs. It is both a religious and educational institution. Its teachers are required to be devout Christians, and all courses at the University are taught according to the Bible. Entering students are screened as to their religious beliefs, and their public and private conduct is strictly regulated by standards promulgated by University authorities.

The sponsors of the University genuinely believe that the Bible forbids interracial dating and marriage. To effectuate these views, Negroes were completely excluded until 1971. From 1971 to May 1975, the University accepted no applications from unmarried Negroes,[5] but did accept applications from Negroes married within their race.

Following the decision of the United States Court of Appeals for the Fourth Circuit in McCrary v. Runyon, prohibiting racial exclusion from private schools, the University revised its policy. Since May 29, 1975, the University has permitted unmarried Negroes to enroll; but a disciplinary rule prohibits interracial dating and marriage. That rule reads:

"There is to be no interracial dating.

5. Beginning in 1973, Bob Jones University instituted an exception to this rule, allowing applications from unmarried Ne- groes who had been members of the University staff for four years or more.

"1. Students who are partners in an interracial marriage will be expelled.

"2. Students who are members of or affiliated with any group or organization which holds as one of its goals or advocates interracial marriage will be expelled.

"3. Students who date outside their own race will be expelled.

"4. Students who espouse, promote, or encourage others to violate the University's dating rules and regulations will be expelled."

The University continues to deny admission to applicants engaged in an interracial marriage or known to advocate interracial marriage or dating.

Until 1970, the IRS extended tax–exempt status to Bob Jones University under § 501(c)(3). By the letter of November 30, 1970, that followed the injunction issued in Green v. Kennedy, the IRS formally notified the University of the change in IRS policy, and announced its intention to challenge the tax–exempt status of private schools practicing racial discrimination in their admissions policies.

* * *

Thereafter, on April 16, 1975, the IRS notified the University of the proposed revocation of its tax–exempt status. On January 19, 1976, the IRS officially revoked the University's tax–exempt status, effective as of December 1, 1970, the day after the University was formally notified of the change in IRS policy. * * *

The United States District Court for the District of South Carolina held that revocation of the University's tax–exempt status exceeded the delegated powers of the IRS, was improper under the IRS rulings and procedures, and violated the University's rights under the Religion Clauses of the First Amendment. 468 F.Supp. 890, 907 (D.S.C.1978). * * *

The Court of Appeals for the Fourth Circuit, in a divided opinion, reversed. * * *

C

No. 81–1, Goldsboro Christian Schools, Inc. v. United States

Goldsboro Christian Schools is a nonprofit corporation located in Goldsboro, North Carolina. Like Bob Jones University, it was established "to conduct an institution or institutions of learning * * *, giving special emphasis to the Christian religion and the ethics revealed in the Holy scriptures." * * * The school offers classes from kindergarten through high school, and since at least 1969 has satisfied the State of North Carolina's requirements for secular education in private schools. The school requires its high school students to take Bible–related courses, and begins each class with prayer.

Since its incorporation in 1963, Goldsboro Christian Schools has maintained a racially discriminatory admissions policy based upon its interpretation of the Bible.[6] Goldsboro has for the most part accepted only Caucasians. On occasion, however, the school has accepted children from racially mixed marriages in which one of the parents is Caucasian.

Goldsboro never received a determination by the IRS that it was an organization entitled to tax exemption under § 501(c)(3). Upon audit of Goldsboro's records for the years 1969 through 1972, the IRS determined that Goldsboro was not an organization described in § 501(c)(3), and therefore was required to pay taxes under the Federal Insurance Contribution Act and the Federal Unemployment Tax Act.

* * *

The District Court for the Eastern District of North Carolina * * * assumed that Goldsboro's racially discriminatory admissions policy was based upon a sincerely held religious belief. The court nevertheless rejected Goldsboro's claim to tax–exempt status under § 501(c)(3), finding that "private schools maintaining racially discriminatory admissions policies violate clearly declared federal policy and, therefore, must be denied the federal tax benefits flowing from qualification under Section 501(c)(3)." The court also rejected Goldsboro's arguments that denial of tax–exempt status violated the Free Exercise and Establishment Clauses of the First Amendment. Accordingly, the court entered summary judgment for the Government on its counterclaim. The Court of Appeals for the Fourth Circuit affirmed, 644 F.2d 879 (CA4 1981)(per curiam). That court found an "identity for present purposes" between the Goldsboro case and the Bob Jones University case, which had been decided shortly before by another panel of that court, and affirmed for the reasons set forth in Bob Jones University. We granted certiorari in both cases,[9] and we affirm in each.

II

A

In Revenue Ruling 71–447, the IRS formalized the policy first announced in 1970, that § 170 and § 501(c)(3) embrace the common law

6. According to the interpretation espoused by Goldsboro, race is determined by descendance from one of Noah's three sons— Ham, Shem and Japheth. Based on this interpretation, Orientals and Negroes are Hamitic, Hebrews are Shemitic, and Caucasians are Japhethitic. Cultural or biological mixing of the races is regarded as a violation of God's command. * * *

9. After the Court granted certiorari, the Government filed a motion to dismiss, informing the Court that the Department of Treasury intended to revoke Revenue Ruling 71–447 and other pertinent rulings and to recognize § 501(c)(3) exemptions for petitioners. The Government suggested that these actions were therefore moot. Before this Court ruled on that motion, however, the

United States Court of Appeals for the District of Columbia Circuit enjoined the Government from granting § 501(c)(3) tax–exempt status to any school that discriminates on the basis of race. Wright v. Regan, No. 80–1124 (CADC Feb. 18, 1982)(per curiam order). Thereafter, the Government informed the Court that it would not revoke the revenue rulings and withdrew its request that the actions be dismissed as moot. The Government continues to assert that the IRS lacked authority to promulgate Revenue Ruling 71–447, and does not defend that aspect of the rulings below. [The background and import of this rather understated version of the Government's change of position are discussed in the Notes following the case. Eds.]

"charity" concept. Under that view, to qualify for a tax exemption pursuant to § 501(c)(3), an institution must show, first, that it falls within one of the eight categories expressly set forth in that section, and second, that its activity is not contrary to settled public policy.

Section 501(c)(3) provides that "[c]orporations * * * organized and operated exclusively for religious, charitable * * * or educational purposes" are entitled to tax exemption. Petitioners argue that the plain language of the statute guarantees them tax–exempt status. They emphasize the absence of any language in the statute expressly requiring all exempt organizations to be "charitable" in the common law sense, and they contend that the disjunctive "or" separating the categories in § 501(c)(3) precludes such a reading. Instead, they argue that if an institution falls within one or more of the specified categories it is automatically entitled to exemption, without regard to whether it also qualifies as "charitable." The Court of Appeals rejected that contention and concluded that petitioners' interpretation of the statute "tears section 501(c)(3) from its roots." 639 F.2d, at 151.

It is a well–established canon of statutory construction that a court should go beyond the literal language of a statute if reliance on that language would defeat the plain purpose of the statute:

> "The general words used in the clause * * *, taken by themselves, and literally construed, without regard to the object in view, would seem to sanction the claim of the plaintiff. But this mode of expounding a statute has never been adopted by any enlightened tribunal—because it is evident that in many cases it would defeat the object which the legislature intended to accomplish. And it is well settled that, in interpreting a statute, the court will not look merely to a particular clause in which general words may be used, but will take in connection with it the whole statute * * * and the objects and policy of the law * * *." Brown v. Duchesne, 19 how. 183, 194 (1857)(emphasis added).

Section 501(c)(3) therefore must be analyzed and construed within the framework of the Internal Revenue Code and against the background of the Congressional purposes. Such an examination reveals unmistakable evidence that, underlying all relevant parts of the Code, is the intent that entitlement to tax exemption depends on meeting certain common law standards of charity—namely, that an institution seeking tax–exempt status must serve a public purpose and not be contrary to established public policy.

This "charitable" concept appears explicitly in § 170 of the Code. That section contains a list of organizations virtually identical to that contained in § 501(c)(3). It is apparent that Congress intended that list to have the same meaning in both sections.[10] In § 170, Congress used the list of

---

10. The predecessor of § 170 originally was enacted in 1917, as part of the War Revenue Act of 1917, ch. 63, 1201(2), 40 Stat. 300, 330 (1917), whereas the predecessor of § 501(c)(3) dates back to the income tax law of 1894, Act of August 27, 1894, ch. 349, 28 Stat. 509, see n. 14, infra. There are minor differences between the lists of organizations in the two sections, see generally Liles & Blum, Development of the Federal Tax Treat-

organizations in defining the term "charitable contributions." On its face, therefore, § 170 reveals that Congress' intention was to provide tax benefits to organizations serving charitable purposes. The form of § 170 simply makes plain what common sense and history tell us: in enacting both § 170 and § 501(c)(3), Congress sought to provide tax benefits to charitable organizations, to encourage the development of private institutions that serve a useful public purpose or supplement or take the place of public institutions of the same kind.

Tax exemptions for certain institutions thought beneficial to the social order of the country as a whole, or to a particular community, are deeply rooted in our history, as in that of England. The origins of such exemptions lie in the special privileges that have long been extended to charitable trusts.[12]

More than a century ago, this Court announced the caveat that is critical in this case:

> [I]t has now become an established principle of American law, that courts of chancery will sustain and protect * * * a gift * * * to public charitable uses, provided the same is consistent with local laws and public policy * * *.

Soon after that, in 1878, the Court commented:

> A charitable use, where neither law nor public policy forbids, may be applied to almost any thing that tends to promote the well–doing and well–being of social man.

In 1891, in a restatement of the English law of charity[13] which has long been recognized as a leading authority in this country, Lord MacNaghten stated:

---

ment of Charities, 39 L. & Contemp. Prob. 6, 24–25 (No. 4, 1975) (hereinafter Liles & Blum). Nevertheless, the two sections are closely related; both seek to achieve the same basic goal of encouraging the development of certain organizations through the grant of tax benefits. The language of the two sections is in most respects identical, and the Commissioner and the courts consistently have applied many of the same standards in interpreting those sections. * * * To the extent that § 170 "aids in ascertaining the meaning" of § 501(c)(3), therefore, it is "entitled to great weight," * * *.

12. The form and history of the charitable exemption and deduction sections of the various income tax acts reveal that Congress was guided by the common law of charitable trusts. See Simon, The Tax–Exempt Status of Racially Discriminatory Religious Schools, 36 Tax L.Rev. 477, 485–489 (1981)(hereinafter Simon). Congress acknowledged as much in

1969. The House Report on the Tax Reform Act of 1969, Pub.L. 91–172, 83 Stat. 487, stated that the § 501(c)(3) exemption was available only to institutions that served "the specified charitable purposes," H.R.Rep. No. 413 (Part 1), 91st Cong., 1st Sess. 35 (1969), U.S.Code Cong. & Admin.News 1969, p. 1645, and described "charitable" as "a term that has been used in the law of trusts for hundreds of years." * * * We need not consider whether Congress intended to incorporate into the Internal Revenue Code any aspects of charitable trust law other than the requirements of public benefit and a valid public purpose.

13. The draftsmen of the 1894 income tax law, which included the first charitable exemption provision, relied heavily on English concepts of taxation; and the list of exempt organizations appears to have been patterned upon English income tax statutes. See 26 Cong.Rec. 584–588, 6612–6615 (1894).

"Charity" in its legal sense comprises four principal divisions: trusts for the relief of poverty; trusts for the advancement of education; trusts for the advancement of religion; and trusts for other purposes beneficial to the community, not falling under any of the preceding heads.

These statements clearly reveal the legal background against which Congress enacted the first charitable exemption statute in 1894: charities were to be given preferential treatment because they provide a benefit to society.

What little floor debate occurred on the charitable exemption provision of the 1894 Act and similar sections of later statutes leaves no doubt that Congress deemed the specified organizations entitled to tax benefits because they served desirable public purposes. In floor debate on a similar provision in 1917, for example, Senator Hollis articulated the rationale:

For every dollar that a man contributes to these public charities, educational, scientific, or otherwise, the public gets 100 percent.

In 1924, this Court restated the common understanding of the charitable exemption provision:

Evidently the exemption is made in recognition of the benefit which the public derives from corporate activities of the class named, and is intended to aid them when not conducted for private gain. Trinidad v. Sagrada Orden, 263 U.S. 578, 581, 44 S.Ct. 204, 205, 68 L.Ed. 458 (1924).

In enacting the Revenue Act of 1938, ch. 289, 52 Stat. 447 (1938), Congress expressly reconfirmed this view with respect to the charitable deduction provision:

The exemption from taxation of money and property devoted to charitable and other purposes is based on the theory that the Government is compensated for the loss of revenue by its relief from financial burdens which would otherwise have to be met by appropriations from other public funds, and by the benefits resulting from the promotion of the general welfare.

A corollary to the public benefit principle is the requirement, long recognized in the law of trusts, that the purpose of a charitable trust may not be illegal or violate established public policy. In 1861, this Court stated that a public charitable use must be "consistent with local laws and public policy," * * *. Modern commentators and courts have echoed that view.

When the Government grants exemptions or allows deductions all taxpayers are affected; the very fact of the exemption or deduction for the donor means that other taxpayers can be said to be indirect and vicarious "donors." Charitable exemptions are justified on the basis that the exempt entity confers a public benefit—a benefit which the society or the community may not itself choose or be able to provide, or which supplements and advances the work of public institutions already supported by tax revenues.[18] History buttresses logic to make clear that, to warrant exemption under § 501(c)(3), an institution must fall within a category specified in that section and must demonstrably serve and be in harmony with the public interest.[19] The institution's purpose must not be so at odds with the common community conscience as to undermine any public benefit that might otherwise be conferred.

B

We are bound to approach these questions with full awareness that determinations of public benefit and public policy are sensitive matters with serious implications for the institutions affected; a declaration that a given institution is not "charitable" should be made only where there can be no doubt that the activity involved is contrary to a fundamental public policy. But there can no longer be any doubt that racial discrimination in education violates deeply and widely accepted views of elementary justice. Prior to 1954, public education in many places still was conducted under the pall of Plessy v. Ferguson, 163 U.S. 537, 16 S.Ct. 1138, 41 L.Ed. 256 (1896); racial segregation in primary and secondary education prevailed in many parts of the country. See, e.g., Segregation and the Fourteenth Amendment in the States (B. Reams & P. Wilson, eds. 1975).[20] This Court's

18. The dissent acknowledges that "Congress intended * * * to offer a tax benefit to organizations * * * providing a public benefit," * * * but suggests that Congress itself fully defined what organizations provide a public benefit, through the list of eight categories of exempt organizations contained in § 170 and § 501(c)(3). Under that view, any nonprofit organization that falls within one of the specified categories is automatically entitled to the tax benefits, provided it does not engage in expressly prohibited lobbying or political activities. The dissent thus would have us conclude, for example, that any nonprofit organization that does not engage in prohibited lobbying activities is entitled to tax exemption as an "educational" institution if it is organized for the "instruction or training of the individual for the purpose of improving or developing his capabilities," 26 CFR § 1.501(c)(3)–1(d)(3). As Judge Leventhal noted in Green v. Connally, Fagin's school for educating English boys in the art of picking pockets would be an "educational" institution under that definition. Similarly, a band of former military personnel might well set up a school for intensive training of subversives for guerrilla warfare and terrorism in other countries; in the abstract, that "school" would qualify as an "educational" institution. Surely Congress had no thought of affording such an unthinking, wooden meaning to § 170 and § 501(c)(3) as

to provide tax benefits to "educational" organizations that do not serve a public, charitable purpose.

19. The Court's reading of § 501(c)(3) does not render meaningless Congress' action in specifying the eight categories of presumptively exempt organizations, as petitioners suggest. * * * To be entitled to tax–exempt status under § 501(c)(3), an organization must first fall within one of the categories specified by Congress, and in addition must serve a valid charitable purpose.

20. In 1894, when the first charitable exemption provision was enacted, racially segregated educational institutions would not have been regarded as against public policy. Yet contemporary standards must be considered in determining whether given activities provide a public benefit and are entitled to the charitable tax exemption. In Walz v. Tax Comm'n, 397 U.S. 664, 672–673, 90 S.Ct. 1409, 1413, 25 L.Ed.2d 697 (1970), we observed: "Qualification for tax exemption is not perpetual or immutable; some tax–exempt groups lose that status when their activities take them outside the classification and new entities can come into being and qualify for the exemption." Charitable trust law also makes clear that the definition of "charity" depends upon contemporary standards. See, e.g., Restatement (Second) of

decision in Brown v. Board of Education, 347 U.S. 483, 74 S.Ct. 686, 98 L.Ed. 873 (1954), signalled an end to that era. Over the past quarter of a century, every pronouncement of this Court and myriad Acts of Congress and Executive Orders attest a firm national policy to prohibit racial segregation and discrimination in public education.

An unbroken line of cases following Brown v. Board of Education establishes beyond doubt this Court's view that racial discrimination in education violates a most fundamental national public policy, as well as rights of individuals.

* * *

Congress, in Titles IV and VI of the Civil Rights Act of 1964, clearly expressed its agreement that racial discrimination in education violates a fundamental public policy. Other sections of that Act, and numerous enactments since then, testify to the public policy against racial discrimination.

The Executive Branch has consistently placed its support behind eradication of racial discrimination. * * *

Few social or political issues in our history have been more vigorously debated and more extensively ventilated than the issue of racial discrimination, particularly in education. Given the stress and anguish of the history of efforts to escape from the shackles of the "separate but equal" doctrine of Plessy v. Ferguson, supra, it cannot be said that educational institutions that, for whatever reasons, practice racial discrimination, are institutions exercising "beneficial and stabilizing influences in community life," Walz v. Tax Comm'n, 397 U.S. 664, 673, 90 S.Ct. 1409, 1413, 25 L.Ed.2d 697 (1970), or should be encouraged by having all taxpayers share in their support by way of special tax status.

There can thus be no question that the interpretation of § 170 and § 501(c)(3) announced by the IRS in 1970 was correct. That it may be seen as belated does not undermine its soundness. It would be wholly incompatible with the concepts underlying tax exemption to grant the benefit of tax-exempt status to racially discriminatory educational entities, which "exer[t] a pervasive influence on the entire educational process." Norwood v. Harrison, supra, 413 U.S., at 469, 93 S.Ct., at 2812. Whatever may be the rationale for such private schools' policies, and however sincere the rationale may be, racial discrimination in education is contrary to public policy. Racially discriminatory educational institutions cannot be viewed as conferring a public benefit within the "charitable" concept discussed earlier, or within the Congressional intent underlying § 170 and § 501(c)(3).[21]

Trusts, § 374, comment a (1959); Bogert § 369, at 65–67; 4 Scott § 368, at 2855–2856.

21. In view of our conclusion that racially discriminatory private schools violate fundamental public policy and cannot be deemed to confer a benefit on the public, we need not decide whether an organization providing a public benefit and otherwise meeting the requirements of § 501(c)(3) could nevertheless be denied tax–exempt status if certain of its activities violated a law or public policy.

C

Petitioners contend that, regardless of whether the IRS properly concluded that racially discriminatory private schools violate public policy, only Congress can alter the scope of § 170 and § 501(c)(3). Petitioners accordingly argue that the IRS overstepped its lawful bounds in issuing its 1970 and 1971 rulings.

Yet ever since the inception of the tax code, Congress has seen fit to vest in those administering the tax laws very broad authority to interpret those laws. In an area as complex as the tax system, the agency Congress vests with administrative responsibility must be able to exercise its authority to meet changing conditions and new problems. Indeed as early as 1918, Congress expressly authorized the Commissioner "to make all needful rules and regulations for the enforcement" of the tax laws. Revenue Act of 1918, ch. 18, § 1309, 40 Stat. 1057, 1143 (1919). The same provision, so essential to efficient and fair administration of the tax laws, has appeared in tax codes ever since, see 26 U.S.C.A. § 7805(a) (1976); and this Court has long recognized the primary authority of the IRS and its predecessors in construing the Internal Revenue Code, * * *.

Congress, the source of IRS authority, can modify IRS rulings it considers improper; and courts exercise review over IRS actions. In the first instance, however, the responsibility for construing the Code falls to the IRS. Since Congress cannot be expected to anticipate every conceivable problem that can arise or to carry out day–to–day oversight, it relies on the administrators and on the courts to implement the legislative will. Administrators, like judges, are under oath to do so.

In § 170 and § 501(c)(3), Congress has identified categories of traditionally exempt institutions and has specified certain additional requirements for tax exemption. Yet the need for continuing interpretation of those statutes is unavoidable. For more than 60 years, the IRS and its predecessors have constantly been called upon to interpret these and comparable provisions, and in doing so have referred consistently to principles of charitable trust law. In Treas.Reg. 45, art. 517(1)(1921), for example, the IRS denied charitable exemptions on the basis of proscribed political activity before the Congress itself added such conduct as a disqualifying element. In other instances, the IRS has denied charitable exemptions to otherwise qualified entities because they served too limited a class of people and thus did not provide a truly "public" benefit under the common law test. Some years before the issuance of the rulings challenged in these cases, the IRS also ruled that contributions to community recreational facilities would not be deductible and that the facilities themselves would not be entitled to tax–exempt status, unless those facilities were open to all on a racially nondiscriminatory basis. These rulings reflect the Commissioner's continuing duty to interpret and apply the Internal Revenue Code.

Guided, of course, by the Code, the IRS has the responsibility, in the first instance, to determine whether a particular entity is "charitable" for purposes of § 170 and § 501(c)(3).[22] This in turn may necessitate later determinations of whether given activities so violate public policy that the entities involved cannot be deemed to provide a public benefit worthy of "charitable" status. We emphasize, however, that these sensitive determinations should be made only where there is no doubt that the organization's activities violate fundamental public policy.

On the record before us, there can be no doubt as to the national policy. In 1970, when the IRS first issued the ruling challenged here, the position of all three branches of the Federal Government was unmistakably clear. The correctness of the Commissioner's conclusion that a racially discriminatory private school "is not 'charitable' within the common law concepts reflected in * * * the Code," Rev.Rul. 71–447, 1972–2 Cum.Bull., at 231, is wholly consistent with what Congress, the Executive and the courts had repeatedly declared before 1970. Indeed, it would be anomalous for the Executive, Legislative and Judicial Branches to reach conclusions that add up to a firm public policy on racial discrimination, and at the same time have the IRS blissfully ignore what all three branches of the Federal Government had declared.[23] Clearly an educational institution engaging in practices affirmatively at odds with this declared position of the whole government cannot be seen as exercising a "beneficial and stabilizing influenc[e] in community life," and is not "charitable," within the meaning of § 170 and § 501(c)(3). We therefore hold that the IRS did not exceed its authority when it announced its interpretation of § 170 and § 501(c)(3) in 1970 and 1971.[24]

D

The actions of Congress since 1970 leave no doubt that the IRS reached the correct conclusion in exercising its authority. It is, of course, not unknown for independent agencies or the Executive Branch to misconstrue the intent of a statute; Congress can and often does correct such misconceptions, if the courts have not done so. Yet for a dozen years Congress has been made aware—acutely aware—of the IRS rulings of 1970 and 1971. As we noted earlier, few issues have been the subject of more

22. In the present case, the IRS issued its rulings denying exemptions to racially discriminatory schools only after a three–judge District Court had issued a preliminary injunction. * * *

23. Justice Powell misreads the Court's opinion when he suggests that the Court implies that "the Internal Revenue Service is invested with authority to decide which public policies are sufficiently 'fundamental' to require denial of tax exemptions." The Court's opinion does not warrant that interpretation. Justice POWELL concedes that "if any national policy is sufficiently fundamental to constitute such an overriding limitation on the availability of tax–exempt status under § 501(c)(3), it is the policy against racial discrimination in education." Since that policy is sufficiently clear to warrant Justice POWELL's concession and for him to support our finding of longstanding Congressional acquiescence, it should be apparent that his concerns about the Court's opinion are unfounded.

24. Many of the amici curiae, including Amicus William T. Coleman, Jr. (appointed by the Court), argue that denial of tax–exempt status to racially discriminatory schools is independently required by the equal protection component of the Fifth Amendment. In light of our resolution of this case, we do not reach that issue. * * *

vigorous and widespread debate and discussion in and out of Congress than those related to racial segregation in education. Sincere adherents advocating contrary views have ventilated the subject for well over three decades. Failure of Congress to modify the IRS rulings of 1970 and 1971, of which Congress was, by its own studies and by public discourse, constantly reminded; and Congress' awareness of the denial of tax–exempt status for racially discriminatory schools when enacting other and related legislation make out an unusually strong case of legislative acquiescence in and ratification by implication of the 1970 and 1971 rulings.

* * *

Non–action by Congress is not often a useful guide, but the non–action here is significant. During the past 12 years there have been no fewer than 13 bills introduced to overturn the IRS interpretation of § 501(c)(3). Not one of these bills has emerged from any committee, although Congress has enacted numerous other amendments to § 501 during this same period, including an amendment to § 501(c)(3) itself. It is hardly conceivable that Congress—and in this setting, any Member of Congress—was not abundantly aware of what was going on. In view of its prolonged and acute awareness of so important an issue, Congress' failure to act on the bills proposed on this subject provides added support for concluding that Congress acquiesced in the IRS rulings of 1970 and 1971. * * *.

The evidence of Congressional approval of the policy embodied in Revenue Ruling 71–447 goes well beyond the failure of Congress to act on legislative proposals. Congress affirmatively manifested its acquiescence in the IRS policy when it enacted the present 501(i) of the Code * * *. That provision denies tax–exempt status to social clubs whose charters or policy statements provide for "discrimination against any person on the basis of race, color, or religion."[25] Both the House and Senate committee reports on that bill articulated the national policy against granting tax exemptions to racially discriminatory private clubs.

Even more significant is the fact that both reports focus on this Court's affirmance of Green v. Connally, supra, as having established that "discrimination on account of race is inconsistent with an educational institution's tax exempt status." * * * These references in Congressional committee reports on an enactment denying tax exemptions to racially discriminatory private social clubs cannot be read other than as indicating approval of the standards applied to racially discriminatory private schools by the IRS subsequent to 1970, and specifically of Revenue Ruling 71–447.

III

Petitioners contend that, even if the Commissioner's policy is valid as to nonreligious private schools, that policy cannot constitutionally be ap-

---

25. Prior to the introduction of this legislation, a three–judge district court had held that segregated social clubs were entitled to tax exemptions. McGlotten v. Connally, 338 F.Supp. 448 (D.D.C.1972). Section 501(i) was enacted primarily in response to that decision. * * *

plied to schools that engage in racial discrimination on the basis of sincerely held religious beliefs. As to such schools, it is argued that the IRS construction of § 170 and § 501(c)(3) violates their free exercise rights under the Religion Clauses of the First Amendment. This contention presents claims not heretofore considered by this Court in precisely this context.

* * *

[Noting that not all burdens on religion are unconstitutional if justified by an overriding governmental interest, the Court held that the interest of eradicating racial discrimination in education substantially outweighs whatever burden denial of tax benefits may place on the exercise of their religious beliefs. The Court summarily rejected the University's Establishment Clause challenge, observing that the Service's policy was founded on a neutral, secular basis. Eds.]

IV

The remaining issue is whether the IRS properly applied its policy to these petitioners. Petitioner Goldsboro Christian Schools admits that it "maintain[s] racially discriminatory policies," but seeks to justify those policies on grounds we have fully discussed. The IRS properly denied tax–exempt status to Goldsboro Christian Schools. Petitioner Bob Jones University, however, contends that it is not racially discriminatory. It emphasizes that it now allows all races to enroll, subject only to its restrictions on the conduct of all students, including its prohibitions of association between men and women of different races, and of interracial marriage.[31] Although a ban on intermarriage or interracial dating applies to all races, decisions of this Court firmly establish that discrimination on the basis of racial affiliation and association is a form of racial discrimination, * * *. We therefore find that the IRS properly applied Revenue Ruling 71–447 to Bob Jones University.[32]

The judgments of the Court of Appeals are, accordingly,

Affirmed.

■ Justice Powell, concurring in part and concurring in the judgment.

I join the Court's judgment, along with part III of its opinion holding that the denial of tax exemptions to petitioners does not violate the First

---

31. This argument would in any event apply only to the final eight months of the five tax years at issue in this case. Prior to May 1975, Bob Jones University's admissions policy was racially discriminatory on its face, since the University excluded unmarried Negro students while admitting unmarried Caucasians.

32. Bob Jones University also argues that the IRS policy should not apply to it because it is entitled to exemption under § 501(c)(3) as a "religious" organization, rather than as an "educational" institution. The record in this case leaves no doubt, however, that Bob Jones University is both an educational institution and a religious institution. As discussed previously, the IRS policy properly extends to all private schools, including religious schools. The IRS policy thus was properly applied to Bob Jones University.

Amendment. I write separately because I am troubled by the broader implications of the Court's opinion with respect to the authority of the Internal Revenue Service (IRS) and its construction of §§ 170(c) and 501(c)(3) of the Internal Revenue Code.

I

Federal taxes are not imposed on organizations "operated exclusively for religious, charitable, scientific, testing for public safety, literary, or educational purposes * * *." 26 U.S.C.A. § 501(c)(3). The Code also permits a tax deduction for contributions made to these organizations. § 170(c). It is clear that petitioners, organizations incorporated for educational purposes, fall within the language of the statute. It also is clear that the language itself does not mandate refusal of tax–exempt status to any private school that maintains a racially discriminatory admissions policy. Accordingly, there is force in Justice Rehnquist's argument that §§ 170(c) and 501(c)(3) should be construed as setting forth the only criteria Congress has established for qualification as a tax–exempt organization. * * * Indeed, were we writing prior to the history detailed in the Court's opinion, this could well be the construction I would adopt. But there has been a decade of acceptance that is persuasive in the circumstances of this case, and I conclude that there are now sufficient reasons for accepting the IRS's construction of the Code as proscribing tax exemptions for schools that discriminate on the basis of race as a matter of policy.

I cannot say that this construction of the Code, adopted by the IRS in 1970 and upheld by the Court of Appeals below, is without logical support. The statutory terms are not self–defining, and it is plausible that in some instances an organization seeking a tax exemption might act in a manner so clearly contrary to the purposes of our laws that it could not be deemed to serve the enumerated statutory purposes. And, as the Court notes, if any national policy is sufficiently fundamental to constitute such an overriding limitation on the availability of tax–exempt status under § 501(c)(3), it is the policy against racial discrimination in education. Finally, and of critical importance for me, the subsequent actions of Congress present "an unusually strong case of legislative acquiescence in and ratification by implication of the [IRS'] 1970 and 1971 rulings" with respect to racially discriminatory schools. In particular, Congress' enactment of § 501(i) in 1976 is strong evidence of agreement with these particular IRS rulings.

II

I therefore concur in the Court's judgment that tax–exempt status under § 170(c) and § 501(c)(3) is not available to private schools that concededly are racially discriminatory. I do not agree, however, with the Court's more general explanation of the justifications for the tax exemptions provided to charitable organizations. The Court states:

> Charitable exemptions are justified on the basis that the exempt entity confers a public benefit—a benefit which the society or the community may not itself choose or be able to provide, or which supplements and

advances the work of public institutions already supported by tax revenues. History buttresses logic to make clear that, to warrant exemption under 501(c)(3), an institution must fall within a category specified in that section and must demonstrably serve and be in harmony with the public interest. The institution's purpose must not be so at odds with the common community conscience as to undermine any public benefit that might otherwise be conferred.

Applying this test to petitioners, the court concludes that "[c]learly an educational institution engaging in practices affirmatively at odds with [the] declared position of the whole government cannot be seen as exercising a 'beneficial and stabilizing influenc[e] in community life,' * * * and is not 'charitable,' within the meaning of § 170 and § 501(c)(3)," Quoting Walz v. Tax Comm'n, 397 U.S. 664, 673, 90 S.Ct. 1409, 1413, 25 L.Ed.2d 697 (1970).

With all respect, I am unconvinced that the critical question in determining tax–exempt status is whether an individual organization provides a clear "public benefit" as defined by the Court. Over 106,000 organizations filed § 501(c)(3) returns in 1981. Internal Revenue Service, 1982 Exempt Organization/Business Master File. I find it impossible to believe that all or even most of those organizations could prove that they "demonstrably serve and [are] in harmony with the public interest" or that they are "beneficial and stabilizing influences in community life." Nor I am prepared to say that petitioners, because of their racially discriminatory policies, necessarily contribute nothing of benefit to the community. It is clear from the substantially secular character of the curricula and degrees offered that petitioners provide educational benefits.

Even more troubling to me is the element of conformity that appears to inform the Court's analysis. The Court asserts that an exempt organization must "demonstrably serve and be in harmony with the public interest," must have a purpose that comports with "the common community conscience," and must not act in a manner "affirmatively at odds with [the] declared position of the whole government." Taken together, these passages suggest that the primary function of a tax–exempt organization is to act on behalf of the Government in carrying out governmentally approved policies. In my opinion, such a view of § 501(c)(3) ignores the important role played by tax exemptions in encouraging diverse, indeed often sharply conflicting, activities and viewpoints. As Justice Brennan has observed, private, nonprofit groups receive tax exemptions because "each group contributes to the diversity of association, viewpoint, and enterprise essential to a vigorous, pluralistic society." Far from representing an effort to reinforce any perceived "common community conscience," the provision of tax exemptions to nonprofit groups is one indispensable means of limiting the influence of governmental orthodoxy on important areas of community life.[3] Given the importance of our tradition of pluralism, "[t]he interest in preserving an area of untrammeled choice for private philan-

---

3. Certainly § 501(c)(3) has not been applied in the manner suggested by the Court's analysis. The 1,100-page list of exempt organizations includes—among count-

thropy is very great." Jackson v. Statler Foundation, 496 F.2d 623, 639 (C.A.2 1973)(Friendly, J., dissenting from denial of reconsideration en banc).

I do not suggest that these considerations always are or should be dispositive. Congress, of course, may find that some organizations do not warrant tax–exempt status. In this case I agree with the Court that Congress has determined that the policy against racial discrimination in education should override the countervailing interest in permitting unorthodox private behavior.

I would emphasize, however, that the balancing of these substantial interests is for Congress to perform. I am unwilling to join any suggestion that the Internal Revenue Service is invested with authority to decide which public policies are sufficiently "fundamental" to require denial of tax exemptions. Its business is to administer laws designed to produce revenue for the Government, not to promote "public policy." As former IRS Commissioner Kurtz has noted, questions concerning religion and civil rights "are far afield from the more typical tasks of tax administrators—determining taxable income." Kurtz, Difficult Definitional Problems in Tax Administration: Religion and Race, 23 Catholic Lawyer 301, 301 (1978). This Court often has expressed concern that the scope of an agency's authorization be limited to those areas in which the agency fairly may be said to have expertise, and this concern applies with special force when the asserted administrative power is one to determine the scope of public policy. As Justice Blackmun has noted,

> where the philanthropic organization is concerned, there appears to be little to circumscribe the almost unfettered power of the Commissioner. This may be very well so long as one subscribes to the particular brand of social policy the Commissioner happens to be advocating at the time * * *, but application of our tax laws should not operate in so fickle a fashion. Surely, social policy in the first instance is a matter for legislative concern.

* * *

less examples—such organizations as American Friends Service Committee, Inc., Committee on the Present Danger, Jehovah's Witnesses in the United States, Moral Majority Foundation, Inc., Friends of the Earth Foundation, Inc., Mountain States Legal Foundation, National Right to Life Educational Foundation, Planned Parenthood Federation of America, Scientists and Engineers for Secure Energy, Inc., and Union of Concerned Scientists Fund, Inc. See Internal Revenue Service, Cumulative List of Organizations Described in Section 170(c) of the Internal Revenue Code of 1954, at 31, 221, 376, 518, 670, 677, 694, 795, 880, 1001, 1073 (Rev'd Oct. 1981). It would be difficult indeed to argue that each of these organizations reflects the views of the "common community conscience" or "demonstrably * * * [is] in harmony with the public interest." In identifying these organizations, largely taken at random from the tens of thousands on the list, I of course do not imply disapproval of their being exempt from taxation. Rather, they illustrate the commendable tolerance by our Government of even the most strongly held divergent views, including views that at least from time to time are "at odds" with the position of our Government. We have consistently recognized that such disparate groups are entitled to share the privilege of tax exemption.

■ Justice Rehnquist, dissenting.

The Court points out that there is a strong national policy in this country against racial discrimination. To the extent that the Court states that Congress in furtherance of this policy could deny tax–exempt status to educational institutions that promote racial discrimination, I readily agree. But, unlike the Court, I am convinced that Congress simply has failed to take this action and, as this Court has said over and over again, regardless of our view on the propriety of Congress' failure to legislate we are not constitutionally empowered to act for them.

In approaching this statutory construction question the Court quite adeptly avoids the statute it is construing. This I am sure is no accident, for there is nothing in the language of § 501(c)(3) that supports the result obtained by the Court. * * * With undeniable clarity, Congress has explicitly defined the requirements for § 501(c)(3) status. An entity must be (1) a corporation, or community chest, fund, or foundation, (2) organized for one of the eight enumerated purposes, (3) operated on a nonprofit basis, and (4) free from involvement in lobbying activities and political campaigns. Nowhere is there to be found some additional, undefined public policy requirement.

The Court first seeks refuge from the obvious reading of § 501(c)(3) by turning to § 170 of the Internal Revenue Code which provides a tax deduction for contributions made to § 501(c)(3) organizations. * * * The Court seizes the words "charitable contribution" and with little discussion concludes that "[o]n its face, therefore, § 170 reveals that Congress' intention was to provide tax benefits to organizations serving charitable purposes," intimating that this implies some unspecified common law charitable trust requirement. * * *

The Court would have been well advised to look to subsection (c) where, as § 170(a)(1) indicates, Congress has defined a "charitable contribution":

> For purposes of this section, the term "charitable contribution" means a contribution or gift to or for the use of * * * [a] corporation, trust, or community chest, fund, or foundation * * * organized and operated exclusively for religious, charitable, scientific, literary, or educational purposes, or to foster national or international amateur sports competition (but only if no part of its activities involve the provision of athletic facilities or equipment), or for the prevention of cruelty to children or animals; * * * no part of the net earnings of which inures to the benefit of any private shareholder or individual; and * * * which is not disqualified for tax exemption under section 501(c)(3) by reason of attempting to influence legislation, and which does not participate in, or intervene in (including the publishing or distributing of statements), any political campaign on behalf of any candidate for public office. 26 U.S.C.A. § 170(c).

Plainly, § 170(c) simply tracks the requirements set forth in § 501(c)(3). Since § 170 is no more than a mirror of § 501(c)(3) and, as the Court points out, § 170 followed § 501(c)(3) by more than two decades, it is at best of little usefulness in finding the meaning of § 501(c)(3).

Making a more fruitful inquiry, the Court next turns to the legislative history of § 501(c)(3) and finds that Congress intended in that statute to offer a tax benefit to organizations that Congress believed were providing a public benefit. I certainly agree. But then the Court leaps to the conclusion that this history is proof Congress intended that an organization seeking § 501(c)(3) status "must fall within a category specified in that section and must demonstrably serve and be in harmony with the public interest." * * * To the contrary, I think that the legislative history of § 501(c)(3) unmistakably makes clear that Congress has decided what organizations are serving a public purpose and providing a public benefit within the meaning of § 501(c)(3) and has clearly set forth in § 501(c)(3) the characteristics of such organizations. In fact, there are few examples which better illustrate Congress' effort to define and redefine the requirements of a legislative act.

* * *

The Court suggests that unless its new requirement be added to § 501(c)(3), nonprofit organizations formed to teach pickpockets and terrorists would necessarily acquire tax exempt status. * * * Since the Court does not challenge the characterization of petitioners as "educational" institutions within the meaning of § 501(c)(3), and in fact states several times in the course of its opinion that petitioners are educational institutions, * * * it is difficult to see how this argument advances the Court's reasoning for disposing of petitioners' cases.

But simply because I reject the Court's heavy–handed creation of the requirement that an organization seeking § 501(c)(3) status must "serve and be in harmony with the public interest," does not mean that I would deny to the IRS the usual authority to adopt regulations further explaining what Congress meant by the term "educational." The IRS has fully exercised that authority in 26 CFR § 1.501(c)(3)–1(d)(3), which provides:

> "(3) Educational defined—(i) In general. The term 'educational,' as used in section 501(c)(3), relates to—

>> "(a) The instruction or training of the individual for the purpose of improving or developing his capabilities; or

>> "(b) The instruction of the public on subjects useful to the individual and beneficial to the community.

> "An organization may be educational even though it advocates a particular position or viewpoint so long as it presents a sufficiently full and fair exposition of the pertinent facts as to permit an individual or the public to form an independent opinion or conclusion. On the other hand, an organization is not educational if its principal function is the mere presentation of unsupported opinion.

"(ii) Examples of educational organizations. The following are examples of organizations which, if they otherwise meet the requirements of this section, are educational:

"*Example (1).* An organization, such as a primary or secondary school, a college, or a professional or trade school, which has a regularly scheduled curriculum, a regular faculty, and a regularly enrolled body of students in attendance at a place where the educational activities are regularly carried on.

"*Example (2).* An organization whose activities consist of presenting public discussion groups, forums, panels, lectures, or other similar programs. Such programs may be on radio or television.

"*Example (3).* An organization which presents a course of instruction by means of correspondence or through the utilization of television or radio.

"*Example (4).* Museums, zoos, planetariums, symphony orchestras, and other similar organizations."

I have little doubt that neither the "Fagin School for Pickpockets" nor a school training students for guerrilla warfare and terrorism in other countries would meet the definitions contained in the regulations.

Prior to 1970, when the charted course was abruptly changed, the IRS had continuously interpreted § 501(c)(3) and its predecessors in accordance with the view I have expressed above. This, of course, is of considerable significance in determining the intended meaning of the statute. [Justice Rehnquist proceeded to conclude that the position adopted by the IRS in 1970 was not entitled to any deference and that there was little or no evidence that Congress acquiesced by its failure to enact legislation to reverse the policy. Eds.]

* * *

I have no disagreement with the Court's finding that there is a strong national policy in this country opposed to racial discrimination. I agree with the Court that Congress has the power to further this policy by denying § 501(c)(3) status to organizations that practice racial discrimination. But as of yet Congress has failed to do so. Whatever the reasons for the failure, this Court should not legislate for Congress.[1]

Petitioners are each organized for the "instruction or training of the individual for the purpose of improving or developing his capabilities," 26 CFR § 1.501(c)(3)–1(d)(3), and thus are organized for "educational purposes" within the meaning of § 501(c)(3). Petitioners' nonprofit status is uncontested. There is no indication that either petitioner has been involved in lobbying activities or political campaigns. Therefore, it is my view that

---

1. Because of its holding, the Court does not have to decide whether it would violate the equal protection component of the Fifth Amendment for Congress to grant § 501(c)(3) status to organizations that practice racial discrimination. I would decide that it does not. The statute is facially neutral; absent a showing of a discriminatory purpose, no equal protection violation is established.

unless and until Congress affirmatively amends § 501(c)(3) to require more, the IRS is without authority to deny petitioners § 501(c)(3) status. For this reason, I would reverse the Court of Appeals.

NOTES AND QUESTIONS

1. *A Legislative Solution?* The opinion in *Bob Jones* does not adequately capture the political firestorm that followed the Reagan Administration's decision, on the eve of filing its brief in the Supreme Court, to abandon the Service's position denying exemptions to discriminatory schools. While insisting that it was against race discrimination in any form, the Justice Department concluded that the Service could not deny tax exemptions to discriminatory schools without specific statutory authority. Conceding defeat, it requested the Supreme Court to dismiss the cases as moot. Several days later, in the face of a wave of protest, President Reagan proposed legislation that would have given the Service express authority to deny tax–exempt status to schools with racially discriminatory policies. A statement by a Treasury Department official at hearings to consider this proposal sheds some light on the Reagan Administration's thinking:

> The Justice Department has prepared and delivered to the Treasury Department a memorandum of law which describes the legal deficiencies in the Service's position. As the Justice Department memorandum concludes, there is no adequate basis in law for the Service's position that it has the authority to select certain Federal public policies and impose these policies on tax exempt organizations * * *.

> The implications of continuing the policy of allowing the IRS to determine on its own those public policies denying tax exemptions was well stated by the district court in the Bob Jones case. There, the judge pointed out that Section 501(c)(3) does not endow the IRS with authority to discipline wrongdoers or to promote social change by denying exemptions to organizations that offend federal public policy. Voicing apprehension over such broad power, the district court observed:

>> Federal public policy is constantly changing. When can something be said to become federal public policy? Who decides? With a change of federal public policy, the law would change without congressional action—a dilemma of constitutional proportions. Citizens could no longer rely on the law of Section 501(c)(3) as it is written, but would then rely on the IRS to tell them what it had decided the law to be for that particular day. Our laws would change at the whim of some nonelected IRS personnel, producing bureaucratic tyranny.

For example, if we were to endorse the theory on which the Service was proceeding before the Supreme Court, what would prevent the Service from revoking the tax exempt status of Smith College, a school open only to women? Does sex discrimination violate a clearly enunciated public policy? Apparently someone in the state of Massachusetts thinks so, because litigation on this issue is currently going forward in the state courts of Massachusetts.

What about religious organizations that refuse to ordain priests of both sexes? And could the Commissioner decide that if Black Muslim organizations refuse to admit whites they should be denied a tax exempt status because they discriminate?

Further, should the IRS Commissioner be permitted—in the absence of legislation—to determine what is national policy on abortion? Should hospitals that refuse to perform abortions be denied their tax exempt status? Or, reading Federal policy another way, should hospitals that do perform abortions be denied their tax exempt status?

Finally, I turn to a description of the Administration's bill, which is before the committee this morning. Section one of that bill directly addresses the issue before us. Specifically, a new Section 501(j) would be added to the Internal Revenue Code to deny 501(c)(3) treatment and 501(a) treatment if the school practices racial discrimination.

New Code Section 501(j)(2) defines "racially discriminatory policy." Generally, under the bill, a school has such a policy if it refuses to admit students of all races (defined to include also color and national origin) to the rights, privileges, programs, and activities usually accorded or made available to students by that organization, or if the organization refuses to administer its educational policies, admission policies, scholarship and loan programs, or other programs in a manner that does not discriminate on the basis of race. This definition generally conforms to that first established by the court in the Green litigation and carried forward by the IRS in Rev. Rul. 71–447 and subsequent pronouncements.

Additionally, Section 501(j)(2) contains an explicit provision in recognition of the legitimate interests of religious–based schools. Thus, under the bill, an admission policy or a program of religious training or worship that is limited to, or grants preference or priority to, members of a particular religious organization or belief would not be considered a racially discriminatory policy. Thus, schools may confine admission and training to persons of a particular religion. The protection, however, will not apply if the policy, program, preference or priority is based upon race or upon a belief that requires discrimination on the basis of race. Pursuant to this rule, we expect that Bob Jones and Goldsboro would be denied their tax exempt status if they continue their past racial practices.

Statement of R.T. McNamar, Deputy Secretary of the Treasury, Hearings on Legislation to Deny Tax Exemption to Racially Discriminatory Private Schools, 97th Cong., 2d Sess. 225, 229–232 (1982).

After the Justice Department's concession, the Court of Appeals for the District of Columbia Circuit, in related litigation, enjoined the Service from restoring exempt status to any racially discriminatory school. Wright v. Regan, Nos. 80–1124 & 82–1134 (D.C. Cir. Feb. 18, 1982)(per curiam). The

Government then withdrew its request to dismiss the pending cases as moot and suggested that the court appoint counsel to support the judgments of the Fourth Circuit. The Supreme Court agreed, appointing William T. Coleman, a distinguished civil rights attorney and former Secretary of Transportation, to defend what had become the Service's former position.

Suppose you had been the Justice Department attorney who had successfully argued for denial of exempt status in the court of appeals. You are told by your superiors that you now must draft and sign a brief taking the opposite position. You like your job. What do you do?

2.   *Post-Decision Press Conference.* After the Supreme Court handed down its 8–1 decision in *Bob Jones University*, the Justice Department conceded that additional legislation was unnecessary to give the IRS authority to deny tax exemptions to discriminatory schools, and President Reagan told reporters, "We will obey the law." See Stephen Wermiel, U.S. Can't Grant Biased Schools Tax Exemptions, Wall St. J., May 25, 1983, at 2. The Reverend Bob Jones, Jr., whose father founded the university in 1927, was less respectful. After hearing of the decision, Rev. Jones reportedly preached a sermon in the college chapel, declaring: "We're in a bad fix when eight evil old men and one vain and foolish woman can speak a verdict on American liberties. Our nation from this day forward is no better than Russia insofar as expecting the blessings of God is concerned." See William H. Honan, Obituary of Bob Jones, Jr., N.Y. Times, Nov. 13, 1998, at C24 (national edition).

3.   *IRS Enforcement Policy.* It is one thing for a court to rule that racially discriminatory schools do not qualify for tax exemption but quite another matter to implement the court's mandate. The Service's early enforcement efforts proved to be controversial. After the three–judge court's 1971 decision in Green v. Connally, the Service released guidelines for determining whether private schools had adequately publicized their racially nondiscriminatory policy. Rev. Proc. 72–54, 1972–2 C.B. 834. As amplified in Rev. Proc. 75–50, 1975–2 C.B. 578, these guidelines required schools to demonstrate their racially nondiscriminatory policy in governing documents and catalogues; to make their policy known to all segments of the community through newspapers and the broadcast media; and to keep detailed records evidencing compliance with the guidelines. No actual minority quotas were imposed, however, and a school practicing de facto discrimination could qualify for exemption as long as it met the publicity and recordkeeping requirements.

These guidelines did not always identify schools that in actual operation discriminated against minority students, even though the schools may have professed to have an open enrollment policy and complied with the publication and recordkeeping requirements of Rev. Proc. 75–50. Against that background, the *Green* plaintiffs reopened that case in 1976, asserting that the Service was not complying with the court's continuing injunction against granting exemptions to discriminatory private schools in Mississippi. A companion suit was filed asserting that the Service's enforcement of the nondiscrimination requirements on a nationwide basis was ineffective.

In August, 1978, the Carter Administration proposed a set of stricter standards, including numerical quotas, to be applied primarily to private elementary and secondary schools that had been adjudicated by a court or agency to be racially discriminatory or that were created or substantially expanded at or about the time of public school desegregation in the community and had little or no minority enrollment. The reaction to this proposal was hostile. The Service was bombarded with more than 115,000 letters of protest—"the biggest reaction anyone here can remember," according to an I.R.S. spokesman at the time. See Sanford L. Jacobs, Private Schools Pounce on IRS Proposal, Wall St.J., Nov. 6, 1978, at 13. Religious groups were particularly upset, believing the percentage test to be a quota system that was a threat to religious freedom. Jewish groups claimed that the procedure would deny an exemption to a Hebrew school because it did not have black or Spanish–speaking students.

Responding to this public outcry, the Service regrouped and issued more flexible guidelines under which a school satisfied a "safe harbor" if minority enrollment was 20 percent of the percentage of minority age school population in the "community." Otherwise, schools were required to show steps taken to attract minority students. But these policies never became effective because Congress passed successive measures providing that no government funds could be used "to formulate or carry out any rule, policy, procedure, guideline, regulation, standard, or measure which would cause the loss of tax–exempt status to private, religious, or church–operated schools under section 501(c)(3) of the Internal Revenue Code of 1954 unless in effect prior to August 22, 1978," and, specifically, that no funds could be used to implement the 1979 revenue procedure. See, e.g., P.L. 96–74, § 103, 615–616, 93 Stat. 559, 577 (1979). The Supreme Court considered the significance of these appropriations freezes in *Bob Jones University*. The majority concluded that Congress only intended to limit the Service's more aggressive enforcement procedures without altering the substantive standards, while Justice Rehnquist saw the freezes as inconclusive and surely not evidence of Congressional acquiescence to the Service's substantive policy.

4. *Meanwhile, Back in the Courts.* After the decision in *Bob Jones*, the Service faced inconsistent directives from Congress and the courts. Parents of black children attending public schools in several Southern states sued to compel the Service to strengthen its enforcement efforts and to deny exempt status to racially discriminatory schools throughout the United States. Reversing the D.C.Circuit, the Supreme Court held that the parents lacked standing to sue. Allen v. Wright, 468 U.S. 737, 104 S.Ct. 3315 (1984). The Court stated that the Article III doctrine of standing requires a plaintiff to allege personal injury fairly traceable to the defendant's allegedly unlawful conduct and likely to be redressed by the requested relief. It concluded that the injuries alleged by the plaintiffs were neither "judicially cognizable" nor fairly traceable to any unlawful conduct of the IRS. Id. at

753. For additional discussion of the obstacles facing third parties who seek to challenge an organization's exempt status, see Section H3 of this chapter, infra, at pp. 586–601.

Did Congressional hostility to the Carter Administration's 1978 enforcement guidelines and the Supreme Court's decision in *Wright* mean that *Bob Jones* was a hollow victory? Probably not. Revenue Procedure 75–50 (see Note 3, above) is still on the books, and subsequent developments discussed below indicate that the Service has enforced and cautiously extended the public policy limitation.

5. *Subsequent Judicial Developments*. In Calhoun Academy v. Commissioner, 94 T.C. 284 (1990), the Tax Court upheld the Service's denial of exempt status to a private school in South Carolina because the school failed to show that it operated in good faith in accordance with a nondiscriminatory policy toward black students. Despite a sizable local black population, Calhoun Academy never had an enrolled black student or a black applicant; it never had any employment applications from black teachers; and it did not actively recruit teachers. It did have several Asian–American students, however, and published a statement of nondiscriminatory policy in local newspapers and its own publications. In discussing the appropriate burden of proof, the court stated (94 T.C. at 297):

> Concerning what petitioner must prove, its burden in this proceeding, in broad terms, is to establish that it has a racially nondiscriminatory policy as to students. * * * More precisely, petitioner must show that it has adopted a racially nondiscriminatory policy as to students and operates in good faith in accordance with that policy. * * * If adoption of the policy is defined to mean adoption in substance rather than merely in form, then the adoption and operation elements are largely redundant. Adoption in form also does not reasonably stand as a separate element, instead serving most appropriately as a fact that contributes to an inference of good faith operation in a racially nondiscriminatory manner. Therefore, to have a separate and meaningful existence, the adoption element must be something more than adoption in form, yet something less than adoption in substance. Specifically, we define the adoption element to require more than mere adoption in form on the books of the organization, coupled with appropriate publicity and notification to the various relevant groups in the community so that adoption of the policy is known publicly.

The court went on to state that a private school may meet its burden of proof under § 501(c)(3) without establishing that it took affirmative steps on its own initiative to attract students and teachers of underrepresented races, but that "[a] conclusion that a private school generally is not required to take the specific affirmative acts suggested by [the Service] * * * does not equate with a conclusion that petitioner on the record in the instant case has satisfied its burden of proving that its operations qualify for tax–exempt status." 94 T.C. at 304. The smoking pistol, it appears, was the absence of any black students and the inability to attract them, which created an unfavorable "inference of discrimination" in view of the school's all–white history.

6. *Discriminatory Trusts*. In Private Letter Ruling 8910001 (Nov. 30, 1988), the Service ruled that a privately administered trust that otherwise qualifies for exemption under § 501(c)(3) will not be recognized as exempt if its governing instrument restricts beneficiaries to "worthy and deserving white persons." The trust had been established under a will which provided for a charitable trust " * * * for the benefit and relief of worthy and deserving white persons over the age of sixty years who were residents of a certain city and did not have sufficient income from other sources for their comfort and support." Noting that the Supreme Court's opinion in *Bob Jones* required the Service to ask whether, first, there is a public policy against a particular activity and, second, whether that public policy is so fundamental as to require the denial or revocation of exempt status for organizations participating in that activity, the ruling concluded:

> The Court's opinion in *Bob Jones* leaves little doubt that discrimination on the basis of race, whether in an educational context or otherwise, violates a public policy so fundamental as to justify denial of charitable status to any organization otherwise described in section 501(c)(3). However, this does not mean that every racially restrictive provision justifies denial of exemption. The racial restriction must be of the type against which Federal policy is directed. It is of a type that excludes from participation in or denies the benefits of a program or activity to individuals solely on the basis of race so that it can reasonably be expected to aggravate the disparity in the educational, economic, or social levels of that group when compared with society as a whole.

> In this case, the trust's charitable program consists of making available a variety of goods and services to a charitable class consisting of needy persons over the age of sixty who are residents of the city of S. Potential beneficiaries, however, are restricted to white persons. The trust denies eligibility for benefits to members of the charitable class solely because of the race of the individual. This denial aggravates the burdens placed on those who have traditionally been the subject of discrimination and thereby fosters racial discrimination. This situation is not unlike that presented in Rev. Rul. 67–325, 1967–2 C.B. 113, wherein a racially restricted community facility was not deemed to be charitable unless all members of the community were eligible for the benefits provided. Based on the facts and circumstances of this case, the trust's activities are contrary to the clearly defined Federal public policy against racial discrimination. Therefore, the trust is [not] described in * * * section 501(c)(3) * * *.

The ruling went on to state the Service's view that *Bob Jones* "was not limited to racial discrimination in education but encompassed the eradication of racial discrimination in general." Id.

7. *Lingering Questions*. The reach of the public policy limitation articulated in *Bob Jones University* remains uncertain. As Justice Powell

put it in his concurring opinion, "[m]any questions remain." 461 U.S. 574, 612, 103 S.Ct. 2017 (1983). For example, would a church that discriminated on the basis of race fail to qualify for § 501(c)(3) exemption? What about a single-sex school, a private university that excluded gays and lesbians, or scholarship programs targeted for racial minorities, immigrants, or white males from the suburbs? Do recent successful challenges to state-supported affirmative action programs affect the tax-exempt status of private nonprofit organizations with a significant affirmative action mission? Many of these questions are raised in the problems following this Note. The Service has remained silent on most of them, preferring to avoid any formal pronouncements on issues that remain unsettled in the larger world beyond the tax code.

As for the sources of public policy that should inform these tax exemption questions, presumably they include the Constitution, federal and state statutes, administrative regulations and executive orders, and definitive court opinions. For some recent judicial developments that may be among these sources, see U.S. v. Virginia, 518 U.S. 515, 116 S.Ct. 2264 (1996) (categorical exclusion of women from educational opportunities provided by state-supported military school was denial of equal protection; proposed remedy of separate program for women did not cure constitutional violation); Faulkner v. Jones, 51 F.3d 440 (4th Cir.1995), cert. denied, 516 U.S. 910, 116 S.Ct. 331 (1995) (state's support of the Citadel, a male-only military college, violated equal protection rights of women); Podberesky v. Kirwan, 38 F.3d 147 (4th Cir.1994), cert. denied, 514 U.S. 1128, 115 S.Ct. 2001 (1995) (merit-based scholarship program limited to African–Americans at University of Maryland was unconstitutional; court rejected university's claim that program was justified by sufficient evidence of past discrimination); Hopwood v. State of Texas, 78 F.3d 932 (5th Cir.1996), reh. denied, 84 F.3d 720 (1996), cert. denied, 518 U.S. 1033, 116 S.Ct. 2580, 135 L.Ed.2d 1094 (1996) (state law school may not consider applicant's minority status or otherwise use race-based preference in admissions policies).

Additional guidance may (or may not) be forthcoming when the Supreme Court decides two major affirmative action cases involving constitutional challenges to the undergraduate and law school admissions policies at the University of Michigan. See Gratz v. Bollinger, 122 F.Supp.2d 811 (E.D.Mich.2000), cert. granted, 123 S.Ct. 617 (2002); Grutter v. Bollinger, 288 F.3d 732 (6th Cir.2002), cert. granted, 123 S.Ct. 617 (2002). Decisions are expected in July 2003.

8. *Bob Jones Museum.* Despite losing its tax exemption, Bob Jones University lives on, with 5,000 students. The university has admitted a handful of African–American and Asian–American students, but it continues to enforce its interracial dating ban. Through the efforts of Rev. Bob Jones, Jr., the university assembled a prominent collection of religious art that was housed in a museum and gallery. In 1992, the university "spun off" the museum, which was located on campus and attracted 20,000 visitors annually. The museum paid below market rent for its use of school

property and displayed the art collection, which was "on loan" from the university. In Bob Jones University Museum and Gallery, Inc., 71 T.C.M. 3120 (1996), the Tax Court held that the museum qualified for exemption under § 501(c)(3) despite its close affiliation with Bob Jones University. The museum's five-person board included Bob Jones, Jr.; the chancellor's son, Bob Jones III; an attorney; an accountant; and a local businessman.

Finding that the museum was a bona fide educational organization, the Tax Court rejected the Service's argument that the museum furthered a substantial non-exempt purpose by providing a "reputational benefit" and funneling tax-deductible contributions to the university. The court concluded that neither the rent payments nor the payment of salaries to former university employees provided an impermissible financial benefit to the nonexempt university and that any other benefits were incidental. Without much explanation of its reasoning, the court stated that a museum was not an "essential part" of a university, suggesting that the result might have been different if the spin-off had involved a library, cafeteria, or bookstore.

9. *Constitutional Aspects*. Apart from the Court's brief dismissal of the First Amendment religion clause issues, *Bob Jones* was a statutory interpretation case, not a constitutional law decision. Would any constitutional problem be presented if federal tax exemptions were granted to racially discriminatory schools? Does the answer depend on your view of the rationale for tax exemptions? Consider, for example, the conventional view that tax exemptions are government subsidies to the benefited organizations.

10. *For Further Reading*. David A. Brennen, The Power of the Treasury: Racial Discrimination, Public Policy, and "Charity" in Contemporary Society, 33 U.C. Davis L. Rev. 389 (2000); Donald C. Alexander, Validity of Tax Exemptions & Deductible Contributions for Private Single–Sex Schools, 70 Tax Notes 225 (1996); Miriam Galston, Public Policy Constraints on Charitable Organizations, 3 Va. Tax Rev. 291 (1984); Douglas Laycock, Observation: Tax Exemptions for Racially Discriminatory Religious Schools, 60 Tex. L. Rev. 249 (1982); Karla W. Simon, The Tax–Exempt Status of Racially Discriminatory Religious Schools, 36 Tax L. Rev. 477 (1981).

PROBLEMS

Consider whether the following organizations qualify for exemption under § 501(c)(3):

(a) The Fields Aryan Church, which has never permitted African–Americans to become members or attend Sunday worship services in its 75 years as a congregation.

(b) The Role Model School, a private secondary school that restricts its faculty and student body to African–American males. A central purpose of the School is to provide a distinctive educational environment and positive role models for its students.

(c) Clara Foltz College, a private liberal arts college that only admits women as students.

(d) Blue Prep, a private high school in the New York suburbs, which has publicized its open–door policy, but only has one non–white student (the son of a United Nations delegate). Tuition is $15,000 per year, and financial aid is limited.

(e) Yeshiva Brooklyn, a high school for Orthodox Jews. No person of color has ever attended the school.

(f) The Welk Scholarship Trust, which awards college scholarships to academically distinguished male graduates of high schools in Southern California who are of Scandinavian descent.

(g) The Johnson Scholarship Trust, which awards scholarships to deserving African–American graduates of colleges and universities in California who plan to continue their education at the graduate school level.

4.   THE SCOPE OF CHARITY: THE COMMUNITY BENEFIT STANDARD

a.   NONPROFIT HOSPITALS AND OTHER HEALTH CARE PROVIDERS

The public policy standard articulated by the Supreme Court in *Bob Jones University* is only one aspect of the concept of "charitable" and applies to all organizations seeking exemption under § 501(c)(3). The focus shifts here to the very different question of whether an organization is organized and operated for "charitable" purposes. The tax definition of "charitable" has evolved considerably from its earliest English origins. Proposed Treasury regulations issued in 1956, following the Service's historically restrictive interpretation, employed a "relief of the poor" concept, providing that "[o]rganizations formed and operated exclusively for charitable purposes include generally organizations for the relief of poverty, distress, or other conditions of similar public concern." Prop. Treas. Reg. § 1.501(c)(3)–1(b), 21 Fed. Reg. 460, 463 (1956). When final regulations were issued in 1969, however, the Service adopted the more expansive "community benefit" standard that owes its origins to Lord MacNaghten's venerable articulation in the 1891 case of Commissioners of Income Tax v. Pemsel, 22 Q.B.D. 296, A.C. 532. See Treas. Reg. § 1.501(c)(3)–1(d)(2).

The evolution of the concept of charity from "relief of the poor" to "community benefit" is best illustrated by the history of tax exemption standards for nonprofit hospitals and other health care providers. When § 501(c)(3) was first enacted, most nonprofit hospitals operated like traditional charities by treating indigent patients and relying on volunteer labor. The Service's first articulation of a standard for hospital tax exemptions was consistent with this traditional concept of charitable. In a 1956 ruling, the Service relied on "relief of poverty" as the underlying rationale for exemption and required a tax-exempt hospital to treat indigent patients without regard to their ability to pay. Rev. Rul. 56–185, 1956–1 C.B. 202. The ruling also required tax-exempt hospitals to adopt an "open staff" policy.

The growth of private and employer-provided health insurance and the introduction in 1965 of government programs such as Medicare and Medicaid altered the economics of the health care sector and transformed the American hospital. In response to these changes and over the objections of poverty rights advocates, the Service discarded the charity care requirement, replacing it with a community benefit standard that mirrored the "charitable" concept articulated in the 1969 Treasury Regulations. These and later developments are surveyed in the materials below.

Revenue Ruling 69–545

1969–2 Cum.Bull. 117.

Advice has been requested whether the two nonprofit hospitals described below qualify for exemption from Federal income tax under section 501(c)(3) of the Internal Revenue Code of 1954. * * *

Situation 1. Hospital A is a 250–bed community hospital. Its board of trustees is composed of prominent citizens in the community. Medical staff privileges in the hospital are available to all qualified physicians in the area, consistent with the size and nature of its facilities. The hospital has 150 doctors on its active staff and 200 doctors on its courtesy staff. It also owns a medical office building on its premises with space for 60 doctors. Any member of its active medical staff has the privilege of leasing available office space. Rents are set at rates comparable to those of other commercial buildings in the area.

The hospital operates a full time emergency room and no one requiring emergency care is denied treatment. The hospital otherwise ordinarily limits admissions to those who can pay the cost of their hospitalization, either themselves, or through private health insurance, or with the aid of public programs such as Medicare. Patients who cannot meet the financial requirements for admission are ordinarily referred to another hospital in the community that does serve indigent patients.

The hospital usually ends each year with an excess of operating receipts over operating disbursements from its hospital operations. Excess funds are generally applied to expansion and replacement of existing facilities and equipment, amortization of indebtedness, improvement in patient care, and medical training, education, and research.

Situation 2. Hospital B is a 60–bed general hospital which was originally owned by five doctors. The owners formed a nonprofit organization and sold their interests in the hospital to the organization at fair market value. The board of trustees of the organization consists of the five doctors, their accountant, and their lawyer. The five doctors also comprise the hospital's medical committee and thereby control the selection and the admission of other doctors to the medical staff. During its first five years of operations, only four other doctors have been granted staff privileges at the hospital. The applications of a number of qualified doctors in the community have been rejected.

Hospital admission is restricted to patients of doctors holding staff privileges. Patients of the five original physicians have accounted for a large majority of all hospital admissions over the years. The hospital maintains an emergency room, but on a relatively inactive basis, and primarily for the convenience of the patients of the staff doctors. The local ambulance services have been instructed by the hospital to take emergency cases to other hospitals in the area. The hospital follows the policy of ordinarily limiting admissions to those who can pay the cost of the services rendered. The five doctors comprising the original medical staff have continued to maintain their offices in the hospital since its sale to the nonprofit organization. The rental paid is less than that of comparable office space in the vicinity. No office space is available for any of the other staff members.

Section 501(c)(3) of the Code provides for exemption from Federal income tax or organizations organized and operated exclusively for charitable, scientific, or educational purposes, no part of the net earnings of which inures to the benefit of any private shareholder or individual.

Section 1.501(c)(3)–1(d)(1)(ii) of the regulations provides that an organization is not organized or operated exclusively for any purpose set forth in section 501(c)(3) of the Code unless it serves a public rather than a private interest.

Section 1.501(c)(3)–1(d)(2) of the regulations states that the term "charitable" is used in section 501(c)(3) of the Code in its generally accepted legal sense.

To qualify for exemption from Federal income tax under section 501(c)(3) of the Code, a nonprofit hospital must be organized and operated exclusively in furtherance of some purpose considered "charitable" in the generally accepted legal sense of that term, and the hospital may not be operated, directly or indirectly, for the benefit of private interests.

In the general law of charity, the promotion of health is considered to be a charitable purpose. Restatement (Second), Trusts, sec. 368 and sec. 372; IV Scott on Trusts (3rd ed. 1967), sec. 368 and sec. 372. A nonprofit organization whose purpose and activity are providing hospital care is promoting health and may, therefore, qualify as organized and operated in furtherance of a charitable purpose. If it meets the other requirements of section 501(c)(3) of the Code, it will qualify for exemption from Federal income tax under section 501(a).

Since the purpose and activity of Hospital A, apart from its related educational and research activities and purposes, are providing hospital care on a nonprofit basis for members of its community, it is organized and operated in furtherance of a purpose considered "charitable" in the generally accepted legal sense of that term. The promotion of health, like the relief of poverty and the advancement of education and religion, is one of the purposes in the general law of charity that is deemed beneficial to the community as a whole even though the class of beneficiaries eligible to receive a direct benefit from its activities does not include all members of the community, such as indigent members of the community, provided that the class is not so small that its relief is not of benefit to the community. Restatement (Second), Trusts, sec. 368, comment (b) and sec. 372, comments (b) and (c); IV Scott on Trusts (3rd ed. 1967), sec. 368 and sec. 372.2. By operating an emergency room open to all persons and by providing hospital care for all those persons in the community able to pay the cost thereof either directly or through third party reimbursement, Hospital A is promoting the health of a class of persons that is broad enough to benefit the community.

The fact that Hospital A operates at an annual surplus of receipts over disbursements does not preclude its exemption. By using its surplus funds to improve the quality of patient care, expand its facilities, and advance its medical training, education, and research programs, the hospital is operating in furtherance of its exempt purposes.

Furthermore, Hospital A is operated to serve a public rather than a private interest. Control of the hospital rests with its board of trustees, which is composed of independent civic leaders. The hospital maintains an open medical staff, with privileges available to all qualified physicians. Members of its active medical staff have the privilege of leasing available space in its medical building. It operates an active and generally accessible emergency room. These factors indicate that the use and control of Hospital A are for the benefit of the public and that no part of the income of the organization is inuring to the benefit of any private individual nor is any private interest being served.

Accordingly, it is held that Hospital A is exempt from Federal income tax under section 501(c)(3) of the Code.

Hospital B is also providing hospital care. However, in order to qualify under section 501(c)(3) of the Code, an organization must be organized and operated exclusively for one or more of the purposes set forth in that section. Hospital B was initially established as a proprietary institution operated for the benefit of its owners. Although its ownership has been transferred to a nonprofit organization, the hospital has continued to operate for the private benefit of its original owners who exercise control over the hospital through the board of trustees and the medical committee. They have used their control to restrict the number of doctors admitted to the medical staff, to enter into favorable rental agreements with the hospital, and to limit emergency room care and hospital admission substantially to their own patients. These facts indicate that the hospital is operated for the private benefit of its original owners, rather than for the exclusive benefit of the public. See Sonora Community Hospital v. Commissioner, 46 T.C. 519 (1966), aff'd. 397 F.2d 814 (1968).

Accordingly, it is held that Hospital B does not qualify for exemption from Federal income tax under section 501(c)(3) of the Code. In considering whether a nonprofit hospital claiming such exemption is operated to serve a private benefit, the Service will weigh all of the relevant facts and circumstances in each case. The absence of particular factors set forth above or the presence of other factors will not necessary be determinative.

* * *

Eastern Kentucky Welfare Rights Organization v. Simon

United States Court of Appeals, District of Columbia Circuit, 1974.
506 F.2d 1278.

■ JAMESON, SENIOR DISTRICT JUDGE:

[This case, a challenge to the validity of Revenue Ruling 69–545, was brought by a group of health and welfare organizations and indigent individuals. The coalition found a sympathetic audience in the district court but ultimately lost on procedural grounds in the Supreme Court, which held that the plaintiffs lacked standing. Simon v. Eastern Kentucky Welfare Rights Organization, 426 U.S. 26, 96 S.Ct. 1917 (1976). The Supreme Court never reached the merits, but the D.C. Circuit upheld the Service's ruling policy. Its opinion remains as an influential (and controversial) affirmation of the Service's community benefit standard for nonprofit hospitals. Eds.]

* * *

III.   VALIDITY OF REVENUE RULING 69–545

In holding that "Revenue Ruling 69–545 was improperly promulgated and is without effect", the district court concluded that "based on relevant judicial, legislative, and administrative decisions" the new Ruling constituted an unauthorized reversal of a long-established policy of requiring exempt hospitals "to offer special financial consideration to persons unable to pay." The court recognized that "as a matter of jurisdiction and efficient tax administration * * * courts have regularly paid deference to the expertise attributed to the I.R.S. in tax related matters and therefore judicial interference has been reluctantly employed." The court continued: "However, this exhibition of restraint is predicated upon the assumption that administrative rulings will do no more than effectuate, implement and clarify the provisions of the Code which have been Congressionally enacted * * * . When this assumption is proven wrong, the courts must act to rectify any administrative determination which is not in accord with the Code."

We do not disagree with these principles of judicial interpretation of administrative rulings, but our own analysis of the judicial, legislative, and administrative decisions leads to a contrary result. We conclude that Revenue Ruling 69–545 is not inconsistent with 26 U.S.C. § 501(c)(3) and that the modification of the prior ruling was authorized.

The definition of the term "charitable" has never been static and has been broadened in recent years. Prior to 1959, Treasury Regulations generally defined charitable organizations as those operated for the relief of the poor. In 1959, however, a comprehensive set of regulations interpreting § 501(c) (3) was issued. These regulations adopted a broad concept of "charitable." * * *

This Treasury Regulation was cited in Green v. Connally, supra, wherein the three-judge district court stated with respect to § 501(c)(3):

> * * * clearly, the term "charitable" is used "in its generally accepted legal sense," Treas.Reg. § 1.501(c)(3)–1(d)(2), and not in a street or popular sense (such as, e.g., benevolence to the poor and suffering). Thus "strong analogy" can be derived from the general common law of charitable trusts, at least for close interpretative questions.

330 F.Supp. at 1157.

In promulgating Revenue Ruling 69–545, the Commissioner did rely on an analogy to the law of charitable trusts. As indicated earlier, the Commissioner cited both the Restatement (Second) of Trusts, sec. 368 and sec. 372, and IV Scott on Trusts (3rd ed. 1967) sec. 368 and sec. 372 in holding that the promotion of health is a charitable purpose within the meaning of § 501(c)(3).

The term "charitable" is thus capable of a definition far broader than merely the relief of the poor. The law of charitable trusts supports the broader concept. The question involved here then is whether the term "charitable" as used in § 501(c)(3) may be broadly interpreted as was done in Revenue Ruling 69–545 or is to be restricted to its narrow sense of relief of the poor.

We cannot conclude, as did the district court, that Congress intended the latter construction. While it is true that in the past Congress and the federal courts have conditioned a hospital's charitable status on the level of free or below cost care that it provided for indigents, there is no authority for the conclusion that the determination of "charitable" status was always to be so limited. Such an inflexible construction fails to recognize the changing economic, social and technological precepts and values of contemporary society.

In the field of health care, the changes have been dramatic. Hospitals in the early part of this nation's history were almshouses supported by philanthropy and serving almost exclusively the sick poor. Today, hospitals are the primary community health facility for both rich and poor. Philanthropy accounts for only a minute percentage of the hospital's total operating costs. Those costs have soared in recent years as constant modernization of equipment and facilities is necessitated by the advances in medical science and technology. The institution of Medicare and Medicaid in the last decade combined with the rapid growth of medical and hospital insurance has greatly reduced the number of poor people requiring free or below cost hospital services. Much of that decrease has been realized since the promulgation of Revenue Ruling 56–185. Moreover, increasingly counties and other political subdivisions are providing nonemergency hospitalization and medical care for those unable to pay. Thus, it appears that the rationale upon which the limited definition of "charitable" was predicated has largely disappeared. To continue to base the "charitable" status of a hospital strictly on the relief it provides for the poor fails to account for these major changes in the area of health care.

In holding Revenue Ruling 69–545 void, the district court placed undue emphasis on the fact that Congress in 1969 failed to amend the Internal Revenue Code by including language which would have conformed the Code to the new ruling. The Senate Finance Committee in deleting a House provision which would have allowed exempt status to institutions "organized and operated exclusively for the providing of hospital care" stated:

> The committee deleted from the bill those provisions which would have conformed the code to the result reached by the 1969 ruling. The committee decided to reexamine this matter in connection with pending legislation on Medicare and Medicaid.

This action or inaction by Congress cannot be interpreted as disapproving the new ruling. Congress could have rejected the ruling had it determined that it was not in conformity with the Code. Instead, it committed the matter for further study in the light of Medicare and Medicaid. No further action has been taken by Congress since the ruling became effective in 1969.

It is important to note also that Revenue Ruling 69–545 rather than overruling Revenue Ruling 56–185 simply provides an alternative method whereby a nonprofit hospital can qualify as a tax exempt charitable organization. That method entails the operation of an emergency room open to all regardless of their ability to pay and providing hospital services to those able to pay the cost either directly or through third party reimbursement. Thus, to qualify as a tax exempt charitable organization, a hospital must still provide services to indigents.

The required provision of emergency room services is of great import to the indigent. Emergency room service is often the only means of access that the poor have to medical care. Furthermore, the fact that hospitals seeking to qualify as charities pursuant to Revenue Ruling 69–545 must accept Medicare and Medicaid patients is also significant. A large percentage of the indigent populace of the nation is now covered by either Medicare or Medicaid. In the final analysis, Revenue Ruling 69–545 may be of greater benefit to the poor than its predecessor Ruling 56–185. Certainly Ruling 69–545 is more in conformity with the concept of "charitable" as defined in the Treasury Regulation adopted, after extensive study, in 1959 and interpreting § 501(c)(3).

In summary, we conclude that Revenue Ruling 69–545 is founded on a permissible definition of the term "charitable" and is not contrary to any express Congressional intent.

* * *

[The opinion denying rehearing en banc, and the accompanying statements by the judges, are omitted.]

IHC Health Plans, Inc. v. Commissioner

United States Court of Appeals, Tenth Circuit, 2003.
325 F.3d 1188.

■ Tacha, Chief Circuit Judge.

I. Background

IHC Health Plans, Inc. ("Health Plans"), on its own behalf and as successor in interest to IHC Care, Inc. ("Care") and IHC Group, Inc. ("Group") (collectively "petitioners"), appeals the Tax Court's decision denying petitioners' request for tax exemption under 26 U.S.C. § 501(c)(3). We have jurisdiction to review the Tax Court's decision under 26 U.S.C. § 7482(a)(1). The sole issue presented in this appeal is whether petitioners qualify for tax-exempt status under 26 U.S.C. § 501(c)(3) as organizations operated exclusively for charitable purposes.

A. The IHC Integrated Delivery System

1. The formation of IHC

In 1970, the Church of Jesus Christ of Latter Day Saints ("LDS Church") formed Health Services Corporation, later renamed Intermountain Health Care, Inc. ("IHC"), as a Utah nonprofit corporation. IHC assumed ownership and control of fifteen hospitals previously owned by the LDS Church. In 1975, the LDS Church transferred control of IHC to an independent board of trustees, comprised of persons representative of the community. The Internal Revenue Service ("IRS") has consistently recognized IHC as a charitable, tax-exempt organization.

2. The formation of Health Services

As part of its plan to streamline and integrate its provision of health-care services, IHC formed IHC Health Services, Inc. ("Health Services") in 1982 as a Utah nonprofit corporation. In 1983, IHC transferred its hospitals and substantially all the assets necessary to its operation to Health Services. IHC then ceased operating hospitals directly and assumed the role of a parent company, with Health Services as IHC's principal health-care services organization. IHC is Health Services' sole corporate member and the board of trustees of IHC and Health Services are comprised of the same individuals.

At the end of 1999, Health Services operated twenty-two hospitals located in Utah and Idaho, employing approximately 300 primary care physicians and 100 specialist physicians in its Physician Division; it separately employed approximately 120 physicians in its Hospital Division. All Health Services hospitals participated in the Medicare and Medicaid programs for inpatient and outpatient hospital services. Between 1997 and 1999, Health Services provided nearly $1.2 billion in health-care services, without reimbursement, to patients covered by Medicare, Medicaid, and other governmental programs. During that same period, Health Services furnished more than $91 million in free health-care services to indigent patients.

The Commissioner has recognized Health Services as a tax-exempt organization under section 501(c)(3).

3. Health Plans, Care, and Group

In order to further integrate its provision of health-care services, IHC formed Health Plans, Care, and Group to operate as health maintenance organizations ("HMOs") within the IHC Integrated Delivery System. A detailed description of each organization is set forth in Sections I(B)–(D), infra.

4. IHC's role as parent company

IHC's board of trustees maintained governance power and control over Health Plans, Care, and Group. In particular, IHC had the authority, directly and indirectly, to elect petitioners' boards of trustees. IHC, Health Services, and petitioners shared many of the same corporate officers. IHC conducted petitioners' strategic planning, established their priorities, and attempted to implement their business plans on an enterprise basis. Also, Health Services provided petitioners with centralized management services, including human resources, legal services, public relations, and treasury functions.[4]

B. Health Plans

In 1983, IHC created Health Plans to operate as a state-licensed HMO and preferred provider organization ("PPO"). IHC was the sole corporate member of Health Plans and possessed the power to remove members from Health Plans' board of trustees. Health Plans offered health plans to small-employer groups, large-employer groups, and individuals, including Medicaid recipients.

In 1999, the population of Utah was approximately 2,130,000. Health Plans enrolled 416,370 Utahans in its various plans, or approximately twenty percent of Utah's total population. In 1999, approximately 73,503 Utahans were enrolled in a Medicaid managed-care program. Health Plans enrolled 35,902 of these individuals, or approximately fifty percent of Utah's total Medicaid population.

In determining premiums, Health Plans applied an "adjusted community rating" for individuals and small-employer groups, adjusting its rates for risk factors such as age and gender. For large-employer groups, Health Plans used a "past claims experience" method in determining premiums.

---

4. Health Plans provided specialized management and administrative services to Care and Group. Neither Care nor Group had any employees, facilities, or equipment, and both relied on Health Services and Health Plans for their operational requirements.

In June 1985, the IRS recognized Health Plans as tax exempt under section 501(c)(3). The Commissioner subsequently revoked Health Plans' tax exemption in 1999.

C.   Care

In 1985, IHC formed Care to operate as a "direct contract" HMO, offering federally-qualified health plans in conjunction with Health Plans.[6] Health Plans incorporated Care as a subsidiary because the HMO Act of 1973, 42 U.S.C. § 300e–9, precluded Health Plans from operating a federally-qualified HMO within the same corporate entity in which it operated a state-licensed HMO. Health Plans was Care's sole corporate member, and Care used the same network of health-care providers as Health Plans.

Care only offered its IHC Care health plan to employers with more than 100 employees. Care used an adjusted community rating methodology to determine IHC Care premiums, as required for all federally-qualified HMOs. See 42 C.F.R. § 417.104(a)(3), (b). Between 1996 and 1998, Care also offered IHC Senior Care, a Medicare "risk" health plan it has since discontinued.

On April 28, 1986, Care applied for tax exemption under section 501(c)(3). The Commissioner denied Care's request in a final adverse determination letter on June 16, 1999.

D.   Group

In 1991, IHC formed Group to operate as a federally-qualified "group" model HMO. IHC separately incorporated Group because, at the time of Group's formation, the Health Care Financing Administration prohibited a single corporation from operating two different types of federally-qualified HMOs. Health Plans was Group's sole corporate member.

Group offered its SelectMed health plan exclusively to employers with 100 or more employees. To determine the amount of the premium under the SelectMed plan, Group relied upon an adjusted community rating methodology. Enrollees in the SelectMed plan received a variety of health-care services at no additional charge through Group's "Core Wellness Program." Between 1993 and 1998, Group also offered a Medicare "cost" health plan, IHC Senior Care, which it has since discontinued.

In 1991, Group filed an application for tax exemption under section 501(c)(3). The Commissioner denied Group's request in a final adverse determination letter on June 16, 1999.

E.   The Commissioner's Decision

In 1999, the Commissioner concluded that neither Health Plans, Care, nor Group operated exclusively for exempt purposes under section 501(c)(3). The Commissioner alternatively concluded that Health Plans and

---

6. The HMO Act of 1973 provided certain marketing advantages to "qualified" HMOs. In particular, under 42 U.S.C. § 300e–9, certain employers were required to offer their employees the option of enrolling in a federally-qualified HMO.

Care were not entitled to tax-exempt status under section 501(m)(1), which precludes tax-exempt status where a "substantial part of [an organization's] activities consists of providing commercial-type insurance." 26 U.S.C. § 501(m)(1). Accordingly, the Commissioner revoked Health Plans' tax-exempt status, retroactive to January 1, 1987, and denied exemptions to Care and Group.

Health Plans, Care, and Group brought suit in the United States Tax Court, seeking a declaratory judgment reversing the Commissioner's adverse determinations. On September 25, 2001, the Tax Court affirmed the Commissioner's conclusions in three separate opinions. * * * This appeal followed.

II. Discussion

* * *

B. Overview of Applicable Law

"Our analysis must start from the proposition that exemptions from income tax are a matter of legislative grace." Mutual Aid Ass'n of Church of the Brethren v. United States, 759 F.2d 792, 794 (10th Cir.1985) (citation omitted). Thus, we must narrowly construe exemptions from taxation. * * * In this case, petitioners seek exemption under 26 U.S.C. § 501(c)(3).

Under section 501(c)(3), an organization must meet three requirements in order to qualify for tax exemption: "(1) the corporation must be organized and operated exclusively for exempt purposes; (2) no part of the corporation's net earnings may inure to the benefit of any shareholder or individual; and (3) the corporation must not engage in political campaigns or, to a substantial extent, in lobbying activities." Hutchinson Baseball Enters., Inc. v. C.I.R., 696 F.2d 757, 760 (10th Cir.1982). In this case, the sole question we must consider is whether Health Plans, Care, and Group operated exclusively for exempt purposes within the meaning of section 501(c)(3).

C. Whether Health Plans, Care, and Group Operated for a Charitable Purpose.

This inquiry requires us to address two basic questions. First, we must consider whether the purpose proffered by petitioners qualifies as a "charitable" purpose under section 501(c)(3). "The term 'charitable' is used in section 501(c)(3) in its generally accepted legal sense and is ... not to be construed as limited by the separate enumeration in section 501(c)(3)." 26 C.F.R. § 1.501(c)(3)–1(d)(2). An organization will not be considered charitable, however, "unless it serves a *public rather than a private interest*." 26 C.F.R. § 1.501(c)(3)–1(d)(1)(ii) (emphasis added).

Second, we must determine whether petitioners in fact operated *primarily* for this purpose. Geisinger Health Plan v. C.I.R., 985 F.2d 1210, 1219 (3d Cir.1993) (Geisinger I). Under the "operational test" set forth in the IRS regulations, "[a]n organization will be regarded as 'operated exclusively' for one or more exempt purposes only if it engages primarily in activities which accomplish one or more of such exempt purposes specified in section 501(c)(3). An organization will not be so regarded if more than an insubstantial part of its activities is not in furtherance of an exempt purpose." 26 C.F.R. § 1.501(c)(3)–1(c)(1).

In this case, the Tax Court concluded that "the promotion of health for the benefit of the community is a charitable purpose," but found that neither Health Plans, Care, nor Group operated primarily to benefit the community. For the reasons set forth below, we agree.

1. The promotion of health as a charitable purpose

In defining "charitable," our analysis must focus on whether petitioners' activities conferred a *public* benefit. 26 C.F.R. § 1.501(c)(3)-1(d)(1)(ii) ("An organization is not organized or operated exclusively for [an exempt purpose] ... unless it serves a public rather than a private interest."). The public-benefit requirement highlights the *quid pro quo* nature of tax exemptions: the public is willing to relieve an organization from the burden of taxation in exchange for the public benefit it provides. Geisinger I, 985 F.2d at 1215; cf. Flat Top Lake Ass'n v. United States, 868 F.2d 108, 112 (4th Cir.1989) ("In many ways, exemption from taxation may be seen as a democratic commonwealth's method of acknowledging the conferral of a universal benefit."). As the Supreme Court has recognized, "[c]haritable exemptions are justified on the basis that the exempt entity confers a public benefit—a benefit which the society or the community may not itself choose or be able to provide, or which supplements and advances the work of public institutions already supported by tax revenues." Bob Jones Univ. v. United States, 461 U.S. 574, 591 (1983) (emphasis added).

a. Evolution of the "community benefit" standard

The IRS has long recognized that nonprofit hospitals may be exempt as "charitable" entities under section 501(c)(3). See generally John D. Colombo, Health Care Reform and Federal Tax Exemption: Rethinking the Issues, 29 Wake Forest L. Rev. 215, 218 (1994). "Exemption for hospitals, in fact, is so ingrained in the lore of taxation that today about half the states specifically enumerate hospitals as exempt entities, alongside such traditional exemption bulwarks as churches and educational institutions." Id. at 215. Early on, the touchstone for exemption was the provision of free or below-cost care. Id. at 217. In 1956, the IRS published Rev. Rul. 56–185, which provided that a hospital "must be operated to the extent of its financial ability for those not able to pay for the services rendered and not exclusively for those who are able and expected to pay."

By the last part of the twentieth century, however, with the advent of Medicare and Medicaid and the increased prevalence of private insurance, nonprofit hospitals moved away from this "relief of poverty" function. Colombo, supra, at 218. "The financing of their services evolved in parallel, from primary dependence on the generosity of religious orders and charitable donors, to almost exclusive reliance on payments for services rendered."

M. Gregg Bloche, Health Policy Below the Waterline: Medical Care and the Charitable Exemption, 80 Minn. L. Rev. 299, 300 (1995).

In 1969, in response to the nonprofit hospital's changing function, the IRS modified its position regarding charity care. In Rev. Rul. 69–545, which modified 56–185, the IRS removed "the requirement[ ] relating to caring for patients without charge or at rates below cost." In its discussion, the IRS stated:

> The promotion of health, like the relief of poverty and the advancement of education and religion, is one of the purposes in the general law of charity that is deemed beneficial to the community as a whole even though the class of beneficiaries eligible to receive a direct benefit from its activities does not include all members of the community, such as indigent members of the community, provided that the class is not so small that its relief is not of benefit to the community.

Rev. Rul. 69–545. The hospital in question provided hospital care for all persons in the community able to pay either directly or through third-party insurers. The IRS also noted, however, that the hospital operated an emergency room open to all persons *regardless of ability to pay*.[13] In addition, the hospital used surplus funds to improve patient care and finance medical training, education, and research. Based on these factors, the IRS concluded that the hospital was "promoting the health of a class of persons . . . broad enough to benefit the community." Id.

Finally, in Revenue Ruling 83–157, the IRS amplified its prior ruling in 69–545. The hospital in 83–157 was identical to the hospital in 69–545, except that it did not operate an emergency room open to all regardless of ability to pay. In eschewing any rigid test under section 501(c)(3), the IRS made clear that although "[g]enerally, operation of a full time emergency room providing emergency medical services to all members of the public regardless of their ability to pay for such services is strong evidence that a hospital is operating to benefit the community . . . other significant factors . . . may be considered." Rev. Rul. 83–157. The IRS went on to conclude that the hospital did in fact operate for the benefit of the community, noting that the hospital treated patients participating in Medicare and Medicaid and applied any surplus funds to improve facilities, equipment, and patient care, and advance its medical training, education, and research.

Thus, under the IRS's interpretation of section 501(c)(3), in the context of health-care providers, we must determine whether the taxpayer operates *primarily for the benefit of the community*.[16] And while the concept

---

13. In a subsequent ruling, the IRS characterized the hospital's open emergency room as a "major factor" in its determination. Rev. Rul. 83–157.

16. In interpreting these three rulings, court decisions have highlighted several factors relevant under the "community benefit" analysis. These factors include:

(1) size of the class eligible to benefit;

(2) free or below-cost products or services; (3) treatment of persons participating in governmental programs such as Medicare or Medicaid;

(4) use of surplus funds for research or educational programs; and

(5) composition of the board of trustees.

of "community benefit" is somewhat amorphous, we agree with the IRS, the Tax Court, and the Third Circuit that it provides a workable standard for determining tax exemption under section 501(c)(3).

b.   Defining "community benefit"

In giving form to the community-benefit standard, we stress that "not every activity that promotes health supports tax exemption under § 501(c)(3). For example, selling prescription pharmaceuticals certainly promotes health, but pharmacies cannot qualify for . . . exemption under § 501(c)(3) on that basis alone." Rev. Rul. 98–15. In other words, engaging in an activity that promotes health, *standing alone,* offers an insufficient indicium of an organization's purpose. Numerous for-profit enterprises offer products or services that promote health.

Similarly, the IRS rulings in 69–545 and 83–157 demonstrate that an organization cannot satisfy the community-benefit requirement based solely on the fact that it offers health-care services to all in the community[17] in exchange for a fee.[18] Although providing health-care products or services to all in the community is necessary under those rulings, it is insufficient, standing alone, to qualify for tax exemption under section 501(c)(3). Rather, the organization must provide some additional "plus."

This plus is perhaps best characterized as "a benefit which the society or the community may not itself choose or be able to provide, or which supplements and advances the work of public institutions already supported by tax revenues." Bob Jones Univ., 461 U.S. at 591. Concerning the former, the IRS rulings provide a number of examples: providing free or below-cost services, see Rev. Rul. 56–185; maintaining an emergency room open to all, regardless of ability to pay, see Rev. Rul. 69–545; and devoting surpluses to research, education, and medical training, see Rev. Rul. 83–157. These services fall under the general umbrella of "positive externalities" or "public goods." Bloche, supra, at 312.[19] Concerning the latter, the

See, e.g., Geisinger I, 985 F.2d at 1218; see generally Sound Health Ass'n v. C.I.R., 71 T.C. 158 (1978); Douglas M. Mancino, Income Tax Exemption of the Contemporary Nonprofit Hospital, 32 St. Louis U. L. J. 1015, 1037–70 (1988).

17. We recognize that certain health-care entities provide specialized services, which are not required by "all" in the community, and we do not mean to foreclose the possibility that such entities may qualify as "charitable" under section 501(c)(3). As the IRS recognized in Rev. Rul. 83–157:

> Certain specialized hospitals, such as eye hospitals and cancer hospitals, offer medical care limited to special conditions unlikely to necessitate emergency care and do not, as a practical matter, maintain emergency rooms. These organizations

may also qualify under section 501(c)(3) if there are present similar, significant factors that demonstrate that the hospitals operate exclusively to benefit the community.

18. At least where the fee is above cost. We express no opinion on whether an enterprise that sold health-promoting products or services entirely at or below cost would qualify for tax exemption under 501(c)(3).

19. Under the Treasury Department's view, for-profit enterprises are unlikely to provide such services since " 'market prices . . . do not reflect the benefit [these services] confer on the community as a whole.' " Bloche, supra, at 312 (quoting Tax-Exempt Status of Hospitals, and Establishment of Charity Care Standards: Hearing before the House Comm. on Ways and Means, 102d

primary way in which health-care providers advance government-funded endeavors is the servicing of the Medicaid and Medicare populations.

c. Quantifying "community benefit"

Difficulties will inevitably arise in quantifying the required community benefit. The governing statutory language, however, provides some guidance. Under section 501(c)(3), an organization is not entitled to tax exemption unless it operates for a charitable purpose. Thus, the existence of some incidental community benefit is insufficient. Rather, the magnitude of the community benefit conferred must be sufficient to give rise to a strong inference that the organization operates *primarily for the purpose of benefitting the community*. Geisinger I, 985 F.2d at 1219.

Thus, our inquiry turns "not [on] the nature of the activity, but [on] the *purpose* accomplished thereby." Bethel Conservative Mennonite Church v. C.I.R., 746 F.2d 388, 391 (7th Cir.1984) (emphasis added). Of course, because of the inherent difficulty in determining a corporate entity's subjective purpose, we necessarily rely on objective indicia in conducting our analysis. In determining an organization's purpose, we primarily consider the manner in which the entity carries on its activities.

d. The resulting test

In summary, under section 501(c)(3), a health-care provider must make its services available to all in the community *plus* provide additional community or public benefits. The benefit must either further the function of government-funded institutions or provide a service that would not likely be provided within the community but for the subsidy. Further, the additional public benefit conferred must be sufficient to give rise to a strong inference that the public benefit is the *primary purpose* for which the organization operates. In conducting this inquiry, we consider the totality of the circumstances. With these principles in mind, we proceed to review the Tax Court's decision in the present case.

2. The Tax Court correctly defined "charitable" and applied the appropriate legal test under 501(c)(3).

Petitioners first contend that the Tax Court erred in its conclusion regarding the applicable law. Based upon our discussion supra, we disagree. The Tax Court correctly recognized the "promotion of health for the benefit of the community" as a charitable purpose. Health Plans, 82 T.C.M. at 602 ("[I]t is now well settled that the promotion of health for the benefit of the community is a charitable purpose."). Further, the Tax Court considered the community-benefit requirement based on the totality of the

Cong., 1st Sess. 34–37 (1991) (statement of Michael J. Graetz, Deputy Assistant Secretary for Tax Policy, U.S. Dep't of the Treasury)). Thus, the provision of such "public goods"—at least when conducted on a suffi- ciently large scale—arguably supports an inference that the enterprise is responding to some inducement that is not market-based. Cf. id.

circumstances.[21] Id. at 604 ("The community benefit test requires consideration of a variety of factors that indicate whether an organization is involved in the charitable activity of promoting health on a communitywide basis.... Considering all the facts and circumstances ... we conclude that petitioner did not provide a meaningful community benefit."). Thus, the Tax Court did not err in determining the applicable law.

3.   The Tax Court correctly concluded that petitioners do not operate primarily to promote health for the benefit of the community .

Petitioners next argue that the Tax Court erred in concluding that petitioners did not operate primarily for the benefit of the community. We disagree.

a.   Nature of the product or service and the character of the transaction

In this case, we deal with organizations that do not provide health-care services directly. Rather, petitioners furnish group insurance entitling enrollees to services of participating hospitals and physicians. [The court then discussed how the IHC group determined premiums based on the risk assumed and cited cases where the commercial nature of an activity cast doubt as to an entity's charitable purpose. Eds.]

b.   Free or below-cost products or services

The fact that an activity is normally undertaken by commercial for-profit entities does not necessarily preclude tax exemption, particularly where the entity offers its services at or below-cost. Cf. Bloche, supra, at 311 n. 31. But petitioners provide virtually no free or below-cost health-care services. All enrollees must pay a premium in order to receive benefits. As the Eighth Circuit has recognized, "[a]n organization which does not extend some of its benefits to individuals financially unable to make the required payments [generally] reflects a commercial activity rather than a charitable one." Federation Pharmacy Servs., Inc. v. C.I.R., 625 F.2d 804, 807 (8th Cir.1980). Further, the fact that petitioners in no way subsidize dues for those who cannot afford subscribership distinguishes this case from the HMOs in Sound Health Ass'n v. C.I.R., 71 T.C. 158 (1979), and Geisinger I, 985 F.2d at 1219.

We acknowledge, as did the Tax Court, that petitioners' "adjusted community rating system likely allowed its enrollees to obtain medical care at a lower cost than might otherwise have been available." Care, 82 T.C.M. at 625; Group, 82 T.C.M. at 615. Again, however, selling services at a discount tells us little about the petitioners' *purpose*. "Many profitmaking organizations sell at a discount." Federation Pharmacy, 72 T.C. at 692, *aff'd* 625 F.2d 804 (8th Cir.1980). In considering price as it relates to an organization's purpose, there is a qualitative difference between selling at a discount and selling below cost.

21. Because the community-benefit requirement is considered under a totality-of-the-circumstances test, we reject petitioners' challenge to the Tax Court's reliance on any one of the numerous factors cited in support of its conclusion.

In sum, petitioners sole activity is arranging for health-care services in exchange for a fee. To elevate the attendant health benefit over the character of the transaction would pervert Congress' intent in providing for charitable tax exemptions under section 501(c)(3). Contrary to petitioners' insinuation, the Tax Court did not accord dispositive weight to the absence of free care. Neither do we. Rather, it is yet another factor that belies petitioners' professions of a charitable purpose.[27]

c.   Research and educational programs

Nothing in the record indicates that petitioners conducted research or offered free educational programs to the public. This bolsters our conclusion that petitioners did not operate for the purpose of promoting health for the benefit of the community.

d.   The class eligible to benefit

(1)   Health Plans

As the Tax Court noted, "[Health Plans] offered its [coverage] to a broad cross-section of the community including individuals, the employees of both large and small employers, and individuals eligible for Medicaid benefits." Health Plans, 82 T.C.M. at 604. In fact, in 1999, Health Plans' enrollees represented twenty percent of Utah's total population and fifty percent of Utah residents eligible for Medicaid benefits.[29]

Nevertheless, even though almost all Utahans were potentially eligible to enroll for Health Plans coverage, the self-imposed requirement of membership tells us something about Health Plans' operation. As the Third Circuit noted in Geisinger I:

> The community benefitted is, in fact, limited to those who belong to [the HMO] since the requirement of subscribership remains a condition precedent to any service. Absent any additional indicia of a charitable purpose, this self-imposed precondition suggests that [the HMO] is primarily benefitting itself (and, perhaps, secondarily benefitting the community) by promoting subscribership throughout the areas it serves.

985 F.2d at 1219. Further, while the absence of a large class of potential beneficiaries may preclude tax-exempt status, its presence standing alone provides little insight into the organization's purpose. Offering products

---

27. As the Eighth Circuit has noted, "a 'charitable' hospital may impose charges or fees for services rendered, and indeed its charity record may be comparatively low depending upon all the facts ... but a serious question is raised where its charitable operation is virtually inconsequential." Federation Pharmacy, 625 F.2d at 807 (8th Cir.1980) (quoting Sonora Cmty. Hosp. v. C.I.R., 46 T.C. 519, 526 (1966)) (internal quotation marks omitted).

29. We acknowledge that Health Plans' service to Utah's Medicaid community provides some community benefit. The relevant inquiry, however, is not "whether [petitioner] benefitted the community at all ... [but] whether it primarily benefitted the community, as an entity must in order to qualify for tax-exempt status." Geisinger I, 985 F.2d at 1219.

and services to a broad segment of the population is as consistent with self promotion and profit maximization as it is with any "charitable" purpose.

(2) Care and Group

Neither Care nor Group offered their health plans to the general public. Rather, both Care and Group limited their enrollment to employees of large employers (employers with 100 or more employees). Thus, as the Tax Court found, "[Care and Group] operate[d] in a manner that substantially limit[ed] [the] universe of potential enrollees." Care, 82 T.C.M. at 625; Group, 82 T.C.M. at 615. Based on this finding, the Tax Court correctly concluded that neither Care nor Group promoted health for the benefit of the community.

e.   Community board of trustees

Finally, we consider petitioners' board composition. Prior to 1996, Health Plans' bylaws provided that "[a] plurality of Board members shall represent the buyer-employer community and an approximately equal number of physicians and hospitals representatives shall be appointed." As the IRS noted, Health Plans' pre–1996 bylaws skewed control towards subscribers, rather than the community at large. In 1996, however, Health Plans amended its bylaws to require that a majority of board members be disinterested and broadly representative of the community.

It makes little difference whether we consider petitioners' board prior to 1996 or following the amendments. Even if we were to conclude petitioners' board broadly represents the community, the dearth of any actual community benefit in this case rebuts any inference we might otherwise draw.

4.   Conclusion

For the above reasons, we agree with the Tax Court's conclusion that petitioners, standing alone, do not qualify for tax exemption under section 501(c)(3).

[The court then considered the taxpayers' alternative argument that they qualified for exemption based on the fact that their activities were an "integral part" of Health Services and essential to Health Services in accomplishing its tax-exempt purpose. Under the "integral part doctrine," if an organization's sole activity is an "integral part" of an exempt affiliate's activities, the organization may derive its exemption vicariously from the affiliate. The court rejected any application of this doctrine insofar as it rested on a derivative theory of exemption. But it accepted an interpretation of the doctrine that, based on the totality of facts and circumstances, recognized that the performance of a particular activity that is not inherently charitable may nonetheless further a charitable purpose. See Reg. § 1.502–1(b), in which a subsidiary operated for the sole purpose of providing electric power to its clearly tax-exempt parent was itself recognized as exempt. The court concluded that the requisite nexus between the taxpayers and their affiliate, Health Services, was lacking here because they contracted approximately 80 percent of physician services from independent physicians with no direct link to Health Services. As a result, it held that the taxpayers did not function solely to further Health Services' performance of its exempt activities. Eds.]

III. Conclusion

Based on the foregoing, we AFFIRM the Tax Court's decision denying petitioners tax-exempt status under 26 U.S.C. § 501(c)(3).

NOTES

1. *Other Qualification Issues.* The health care sector raises a wide variety of tax issues, beginning with the basic exemption standards considered here. Health care providers do not qualify for exempt status under § 501(c)(3) if any part of their net earnings inures to the benefit of "insiders" such as officers, trustees, and influential physicians, or if they provide a more than incidental private benefit to noninsiders. Insiders and organization managers also may be subject to intermediate sanctions in the form of an excise tax under § 4958 if they receive or authorize excess economic benefits as a result of their position with the organization. Revenue from activities that are not substantially related to a health care provider's charitable or other exempt purposes may be subject to the unrelated business income tax. Inurement and private benefit issues, including hospital joint ventures with for-profit organizations, are discussed in Sections D and E of this chapter, infra, at pp. 216–285. The unrelated business income tax is covered in Chapter 5, infra, at p. 562 et seq.

2. *Emergency Rooms.* In Revenue Ruling 69–545, the Service ruled that a tax–exempt hospital must maintain an emergency room that is open to all persons regardless of ability to pay. What if a hospital does not operate an emergency room because state health officials have determined that such facilities would duplicate emergency services and facilities that are adequately provided by another medical institution in the community? Certain specialized hospitals, such as eye and cancer facilities, offer medical care limited to special conditions that are unlikely to necessitate emergency care and thus do not, as a practical matter, operate emergency rooms. In Revenue Ruling 83–157, 1983–2 C.B. 94, the Service ruled that these specialized hospitals qualify for § 501(c)(3) exemption despite their lack of emergency facilities. The ruling requires other "significant factors," however, that evidence the hospital's commitment to community health care. These may include a broad–based board of directors, an open medical staff policy, treatment of medicare and medicaid patients, and the application of any operating surplus to improving facilities, equipment, patient care and medical research.

3. *State Property Tax Exemptions.* The abandonment of charity care as the proper standard for hospital tax exemptions has been questioned in a handful of states. In a leading case, the Utah Supreme Court upheld the denial of a state property tax exemption to two nonprofit hospitals that

failed to provide any significant care to indigent patients. Utah County ex rel. County Board of Equalization v. Intermountain Health Care, Inc., 709 P.2d 265 (Utah 1985). The case caused a stir and prompted a few other state tax collectors to reconsider their tax exemption standards for nonprofit hospitals. Other state courts or legislatures have not followed Utah's lead in resurrecting the charity care standard. See, e.g., Medical Center Hosp. of Vt., Inc. v. City of Burlington, 152 Vt. 611, 566 A.2d 1352 (1989). For additional discussion of state property tax exemptions, see Section C8 of this chapter, infra, at pp. 211–216.

4. *IRS Examination Guidelines.* The Service has issued instructive guidelines for use by revenue agents in determining whether a hospital qualifies for tax–exempt status. Ann. 92–83, 1992–22 I.R.B. 59. The following factors are to be considered in determining whether a hospital meets the community benefit standard articulated in Rev. Rul. 69–545:

(a) Does the hospital have a governing board composed of prominent civic leaders rather than hospital administrators, physicians, etc.?

(b) If the hospital is part of a multi–entity system, do the minutes reflect corporate separateness? Do they show that the board members understand the purposes and activities of the various entities?

(c) Is admission to the medical staff open to all qualified physicians in the area?

(d) Does the hospital operate a full–time emergency room open to everyone, regardless of ability to pay?

(e) Does the hospital provide non–emergency care to everyone in the community who is able to pay either privately or through third parties including Medicare and Medicaid?

The guidelines encourage agents to ascertain whether the hospital has an open staff policy for physicians by identifying staff admission qualification requirements and by reviewing application procedures and minutes of medical staff meetings. Emergency room procedures are to be scrutinized by reviewing operations manuals and interviewing ambulance drivers to determine whether they have been instructed to take indigent patients to another hospital. Agents also are told to investigate whether hospitals that participate in Medicare programs have violated regulations that prohibit "dumping" of indigent emergency patients on other hospitals. The audit guidelines are extremely influential and make it clear that nondiscriminatory treatment of Medicare and Medicaid patients has become a condition for obtaining § 501(c)(3) exemption.

These guidelines also address issues discussed later in this text, such as private inurement and private benefit, unreasonable compensation, joint ventures between taxable and tax–exempt parties, and unrelated business tax questions.

5. *Health Maintenance Organizations.* Does Revenue Ruling 69–545 provide that promotion of health is per se a charitable purpose? How broad must be the benefited community be for a health care provider to qualify as

"charitable?" Does the community benefit standard require more than providing health care services to paying patients and maintaining an open emergency rooms? As new forms of health care providers emerge, the Service has been forced to confront these issues. In doing so, it has refined and retreated from the permissive standard suggested by Revenue Ruling 69–545.

As evidenced by the *IHC* case, the Service's attitude toward health maintenance organizations illustrates its more cautious approach. HMOs come in many forms, but two common characteristics have troubled the Service: a membership structure (excessive private benefit?), and the resemblance of HMOS to insurance programs (substantial nonexempt purpose?). The early HMOs were group practice plans providing comprehensive health care services to members for a prepaid fee using salaried in-house staff. The Service ruled that this type of HMO was relegated to less favored tax-exempt status as a § 501(c)(4) social welfare organization. The principal rationale for denying exemption under § 501(c)(3) was that HMOs, as membership organizations, did not serve a sufficiently broad community.

In Sound Health Ass'n v. Commissioner, 71 T.C. 158 (1978), the Tax Court rejected the Service's position, but the HMO in *Sound Health* was somewhat unique and presented a poor test case for denial of exemption. Sound Health provided health services at a clinic facility using primarily a salaried staff. It was open both to its subscribers, who paid a fixed premium, and also to nonmembers on a fee-for-service basis. Emergency cases were handled without regard to a patient's membership status, and free or reduced rate care was provided to a limited number of indigent patients. All members of the community who could pay the premiums were eligible for membership, and a subsidized dues program accommodated some low-income patients. Sound Health also had an educational and research program. The Tax Court concluded that Sound Health made at least as strong a case of community benefit as the IRS-blessed "Hospital A" in Revenue Ruling 69–545. It also held that the prepayment feature was a valid risk-spreading device that was similar to insurance but did not result in any impermissible private benefit.

The Service ultimately acquiesced to the result in *Sound Health* (1981–1 C.B. 2), but remained hostile to any HMO that failed to meet a 14–factor test including criteria such as actual delivery of health care services, free care and reduced rates for indigent patients, a meaningful subsidized dues program, a broad community board, and health education programs open to the entire community. G.C.M. 39828 (Sept. 30, 1987). Particularly targeted were HMOs that arranged for the delivery of health care through agreements with physicians or other entities but did not actually provide medical services. The Service's position has been accepted by the Tenth Circuit in *IHC* and also by the Third Circuit, which held that a Pennsylvania nonprofit HMO serving a predominantly rural population of paying subscribers did not qualify for exemption under § 501(c)(3). Geisinger Health Plan v. Commissioner, 985 F.2d 1210 (3d Cir.1993). The court found that the Geisinger Health Plan (GHP), which contracted with a network of § 501(c)(3) affiliates (a clinic and two hospitals) to provide physician and hospital services to its subscribers, did no more than arrange for its paying subscribers to receive health care services. A small subsidized dues program for low-income members was not enough to establish the requisite community benefit. Despite the fact that GHP enhanced health care in an underserved rural area, the court concluded that it primarily benefited itself rather than the community.

The Third Circuit remanded *Geisinger Health Plan* to the Tax Court for a determination of whether GHP nonetheless vicariously qualified under § 501(c)(3) because it was an integral part of a larger system of qualified organizations. Under the integral part doctrine, an organization that provides services to an affiliated exempt organization is itself exempt if the services would not constitute an unrelated trade or business if performed by the affiliate. See Treas. Reg. § 1.502–1(b). Therefore, a subsidiary formed to provide electric power to its tax-exempt parent also would qualify for exemption as long as it did not provide substantial services to third parties. Id. On remand, the Tax Court held that GHP did not meet the integral part test. The court was unable to determine whether GHP had performed substantial services for individuals who were not patients of its tax-exempt affiliates. It thus found that GHP failed to prove that its activities would not have been considered an unrelated trade or business if they had been carried on by the related entities. Geisinger Health Plan v. Commissioner, 100 T.C. 394 (1993). The Third Circuit affirmed on a different theory, finding that GHP's relationship to its affiliates did not enhance its own charitable character, as required by the regulations, because the affiliation did nothing to increase the portion of the community for which the GHP system promoted health. Geisinger Health Plan v. Commissioner, 30 F.3d 494 (3d Cir.1994).

The result in *Geisinger Health Plan* is strange because the organizational structure of the Geisinger system appears to have been mandated by state licensing requirements. As an integrated unit, GHP and its affiliates satisfied most of the Service's criteria for community benefit, but the Third Circuit was unwilling to grant exempt status to a stand-alone entity that performed no health services itself. The best that can be gleaned from this muddled controversy is that the Service's current concept of community benefit requires more than simply providing health care services to paying customers, and that the tax law is having difficulty keeping up with the transformation of the health care sector.

6. *Integrated Delivery Systems.* With the rapid changes in the American health care industry, the self–standing community hospital has become an anachronism. In many parts of the country, "integrated delivery system" ("IDS") models offer full–service health care, including physician office visits, diagnostic tests, acute hospital care, long–term nursing care, and pharmaceutical sales. A typical IDS might own one or more hospitals and the assets necessary to operate clinics and private physician practices. An IDS normally enters into contracts with third–party payors (e.g.,

insurance companies) to provide all essential health care services, and employs private physicians and other health care professionals.

A common structure for an IDS is the "foundation model" (the term "foundation" is used generically and is not to be confused with "private foundation"), where a parent foundation controls and manages a variety of medical facilities in the network. The tax-exempt foundation often acquires its facilities from a for-profit taxpayer in a debt-financed transaction that relies heavily on the foundation's ability, as a § 501(c)(3) organization, to issue tax–exempt bonds. These transactions raise a number of legal questions, including the fairness of the original purchase price, the composition of the network parent's governing board, compensation levels of physicians, the relationship between the tax–exempt health providers and their for-profit subsidiaries, and the breadth of the community served by the network. Notable aspects of these rulings are the requirement of no more than 20 percent physician participation on the parent "foundation's" governing board, and the implication that each component in the system must independently demonstrate the requisite "community benefit" in order to obtain exempt status. Thus, an organization that simply aligns itself with an affiliated charitable entity is not enough, in itself, to qualify under § 501(c)(3). Favorable factors include an open emergency room, acceptance of Medicare and Medicaid patients, a commitment to some charity care, and meaningful research and education programs.

In several rulings in the mid–1990's, the Service signaled a more flexible policy regarding physician representation on governing boards. A board still must have a majority of "disinterested" directors but could satisfy a facts and circumstances test by adopting a conflict of interest policy and periodically monitoring its compliance with a "charitable" mission. See, e.g., Marlis L. Carson, Fred Stokeld & Carolyn D. Wright, IRS Takes More Flexible Approach to Physician Board Representation, 71 Tax Notes 733 (1996).

7. *Health Insurance Providers*. At one time, nonprofit health insurance providers qualified for tax exemption as § 501(c)(4) social welfare organizations. The Service's longstanding policy gave shelter to organizations such as Blue Cross and Blue Shield and their affiliates. In 1986, Congress intervened by enacting § 501(m), which disqualifies an organization from exemption under either § 501(c)(3) or § 501(c)(4) if a "substantial part of its activities consists of providing commercial-type insurance." I.R.C. § 501(m)(1). An "insubstantial" commercial insurance activity will not cause a loss of exemption, but any net revenue will be subject to the unrelated business income tax.

8. *Congressional Scrutiny*. The tax–exempt status of nonprofit hospitals came under increasing scrutiny in the early 1990's. Bills (H.R. 1374 and H.R. 790) were introduced in the House by Representatives Donnelly and Roybal that would have denied 501(c)(3) status and certain other tax benefits for hospitals not meeting a "community benefit" or "charity care" standard. The Donnelly proposal would have required hospitals to provide adequate emergency medical services (e.g., a full–time emergency room

open to all members of the public regardless of ability to pay), service to
Medicaid patients, and charity care or other community benefits. Sanctions
would include loss of exempt status, ineligibility to receive tax–deductible
contributions but, in some situations, an interim monetary penalty would
be imposed before exemption was stripped. Hearings on these proposals
were held in July, 1991, before the House Ways and Means Committee, but
Congress did not take action, and Representatives Roybal and Donnelly
have both retired from the House. An effort in 1994 to enact a charity care
standard for nonprofit health care providers as part of comprehensive
health care reform legislation also was unsuccessful.

9. *For Further Reading.* Douglas Mancino, Income Tax Exemption of
the Contemporary Nonprofit Hospital, 32 St. Louis U.L.J. 1015 (1988);
Robert C. Clark, Does the Nonprofit Form Fit the Hospital Industry, 93
Harv. L. Rev. 1417 (1980); Daniel M. Fox & Daniel C. Schaffer, Tax
Administration as Health Policy: Hospitals, the Internal Revenue Service,
and the Courts, 16 Duke Journal of Health Politics, Policy and Law 251
(1991); John D. Colombo, Health Care Reform and Federal Tax Exemption:
Rethinking the Issues, 29 Wake F. Law Rev. 215 (1994); John D. Colombo
& Mark A. Hall, The Future of Tax–Exemption for Nonprofit Hospitals and
Other Health Care Providers, 7 Exempt Org. Tax Rev. 395 (1993); Nina J.
Crimm, Evolutionary Forces: Changes to For–Profit and Non-for-Profit
Health Care Delivery Structures: A Regeneration of Tax Exemption Stan-
dards, 37 Bos. C. L. Rev. 1 (1995); John D. Colombo, The IHC Cases: A
Catch–22 for Integral Part Doctrine, A Requiem for Rev. Rul. 69–545, 34
Exempt Org. Tax Rev. 401 (2001).

PROBLEMS

Keeping in mind the competing views on the rationale for tax exemption discussed earlier in the text, consider, from a policy standpoint and
under the standards of current law, whether the following organizations
qualify for federal tax exemption under § 501(c)(3):

(a) Suburban General Hospital ("Hospital") is a 500–bed nonprofit
regional facility, with a broad community–based board of directors
and medical staff privileges open to all qualified physicians. Hospital only accepts patients who can pay for their health care, either
directly or through private insurance or Medicare. Except in the
most extreme emergencies, Hospital routinely refers emergency
room patients who are unable to pay for their care to a nearby
county hospital.

(b) Same as (a), above, except that Hospital has an open emergency
room, but it routinely diverts non-emergency patients to a nearby
county hospital.

(c) Same as (b), above, except Hospital acquired its assets at fair
market value from a for–profit partnership operated by a group of
physicians. Physician services at Hospital are provided by an exclusive contract with a for–profit group practice consisting primarily of

the doctors who owned the facility before it was acquired by Hospital. These doctors represent 40 percent of the Hospital's board of trustees.

(d) Community Drug Store, a nonprofit pharmacy not affiliated with a hospital or clinic, sells prescription drugs, orthopedic shoes, walkers and other medical products at cost to elderly and handicapped persons near a large urban low–income housing development.

b.   PUBLIC INTEREST LAW FIRMS AND OTHER LEGAL SERVICES

Traditional legal aid organizations qualify as charitable because they provide free services to low–income individuals or charge modest fees based on a client's ability to pay. See Rev. Rul. 69–161, 1969–1 C.B. 149, amplified by Rev. Rul. 78–428, 1978–2 C.B. 177. The more controversial question considered in this section is whether organizations that engage in "public interest" litigation are charitable and, if so, what constitutes the "public interest." In the early 1970's, the Service announced that it was "studying" whether public interest law firms would continue to qualify for exempt status under § 501(c)(3). The public interest bar viewed the announcement as a veiled threat and, after a firestorm of protest, the Service gradually retreated.[1] The rulings that follow articulate the current policy.

Revenue Ruling 75–74
1975–1 Cum. Bull. 152.

Advice has been requested whether the nonprofit organization described below, which otherwise qualifies for exemption from Federal income tax under section 501(c)(3) of the Internal Revenue Code of 1954, is operated exclusively for charitable purposes.

The organization is organized and operated as a public interest law firm in accordance with the guidelines set forth in Rev. Proc. 71–39, 1971–2 C.B. 575 and Rev. Proc. 75–13. The organization represents clients in court and in proceedings before administrative agencies. The organization has engaged in "public interest" litigation in areas such as environmental protection, urban renewal, prison reform, freedom of information, injunction suits challenging governmental and private action or inaction, and "test" cases of significance to the public.

Under its articles of incorporation and by–laws, the overall management of the organization is vested in a board of governors, the majority of whom are attorneys. The members of the board are prominent attorneys, law professors, and leaders of public interest organizations.

Several members of the board of governors comprise a litigation committee, whose function is to determine, for each proposed case, whether

---

1. For a comprehensive survey of these developments, see A.M. Wiggins, Jr. & Bert W. Hunt, Tax Policy Relating to Environmental Activities and Public Interest Litigation, in IV Research Papers Sponsored by the [Filer] Commission on Private Philanthropy and Public Needs 2045 (1977).

the case meets certain criteria for selection. The criteria of the Committee include: whether the case involves a matter of important public interest; whether the individuals or groups involved cannot afford competent private legal counsel; whether the case affords opportunities for participation by law students; and whether the organization's resources are adequate in view of the complexity of the case.

The organization does not accept cases in which private persons have a sufficient economic interest in the outcome of the litigation to justify the retention of private counsel. The organization's financial support is derived from grants and contributions. Section 501(c)(3) of the Code provides for the exemption from Federal income tax of organizations organized and operated exclusively for charitable purposes.

Section 1.501(c)(3)–1(d)(2) of the Income Tax Regulations provides that the term 'charitable' is used in section 501(c)(3) of the Code in its generally accepted legal sense.

In Rev. Proc. 71–39, 1971–2 C.B. 575, the Internal Revenue Service announced guidelines pursuant to which it would recognize public interest law firms as exempt from the Federal income tax as organizations described in section 501(c)(3) of the Code.

Organizations meeting the guidelines of Rev. Proc. 71–39 are recognized as charities because they provide a service which is of benefit to the community as a whole. They provide legal representation on issues of significant public interest where such representation is not ordinarily provided by traditional private law firms. In this way, the courts and administrative agencies are afforded the opportunity to review issues of significant public interest and to identify and adjudicate that interest.

Charitability rests not upon the particular positions advocated by the firm, but upon the provision of a facility for the resolution of issues of broad public importance. For this reason, section 3.05 of Rev. Proc. 71–39 recognizes that it is for the public interest law firm itself, through a board or committee representative of the public interest, to select the cases in which representation is warranted.

Charitability is also dependent upon the fact that the service provided by public interest law firms is distinguishable from that which is commercially available. It is a general rule of charity law that the providing of an ordinary commercial service to the members of a community, even if done on a not–for–profit basis, is not regarded as charitable.

It is generally recognized that public interest representation is not ordinarily provided on a continuing basis by private law firms. Although a number of reasons have been given for the inability of private firms to provide sufficient representation of this type, it is primarily due to the fact that this type of representation is not economically feasible for private firms. In the typical public interest case, no individual plaintiff has a sufficient economic interest to warrant his bearing the cost of retaining private counsel. Even if the community as a whole has a significant cumulative economic interest, individual interests are generally so varied and diffused that it is not practical to rely upon collective financing of such cases.

This lack of economic feasibility in public interest cases is an essential characteristic distinguishing the work of public interest law firms from that of private firms and is a prerequisite of charitable recognition. For this reason section 3.01 of Rev. Proc. 71–39 provides that the activity of public interest law firms would not normally extend to direct representation of litigants in actions between private persons where their financial interests at stake would warrant representation from private legal sources.

The above described organization, which otherwise qualifies for exemption and which is operated in conformity with the guidelines of Rev. Proc. 71–39, provides representation in cases of important public interest that are not economically feasible for private firms. Accordingly, it is operated exclusively for charitable purposes and qualifies for exemption under section 501(c)(3) of the Code. * * *

Revenue Procedure 92–59

1992–2 Cum. Bull. 411.

SEC. 1. PURPOSE

The purpose of this revenue procedure is to supersede Rev. Proc. 71–39, 1971–2 C.B. 575, to modify and supersede Rev. Proc. 75–13, 1975–1 C.B. 662, to revoke Rev. Rul. 75–75, 1975–1 C.B. 154, and to amplify Rev. Rul. 75–76, 1975–1 C.B. 154, by setting forth guidelines for public interest law firms, including procedures under which a public interest law firm may accept fees for its services. The Internal Revenue Service will issue rulings and determinations regarding exemption to new public interest law firms and test the charitable character of such organizations already holding such rulings based on the guidelines set forth in this revenue procedure. These guidelines are not inflexible and an organization will be given the opportunity to demonstrate that under the facts and circumstances of its particular program, adherence to the guidelines is not required in certain respects in order to ensure that the operations are totally charitable.

SEC. 2. BACKGROUND

.01 In Rev. Proc. 71–39, the Service announced guidelines pursuant to which it would recognize public interest law firms as exempt from federal income tax under section 501(c)(3) of the Internal Revenue Code. Section 3.02 of Rev. Proc. 71–39 provides that the public interest law firm does not accept fees for its services except in accordance with procedures approved by the Service.

.02 Rev. Rul. 75–74, 1975–1 C.B. 152, provides that the recognition of public interest law firms as charitable is based on their provision of legal representation for the resolution of issues of broad public importance where such representation is not ordinarily provided by private law firms because the cases are not economically feasible.

.03   Rev. Rul. 75–75 holds that charging or accepting fees from clients makes the organization indistinguishable from a private law firm. The revenue ruling indicates that the expectation of fees for services might influence which cases are accepted.

.04   Rev. Rul. 75–76 holds that the acceptance of fees awarded by a court or an administrative agency and paid by opposing parties does not preclude a public interest law firm that derives most of its support from grants and contributions from exemption under section 501(c)(3) of the Code. However, exemption would only be justified if it is clear that neither the expectation nor the possibility, however remote, of an award of fees is a substantial motivating factor in the selection of cases. In addition, the firm must cease to handle issues with a strong possibility of a fee award if these become economically feasible for private litigants.

.05   Rev. Proc. 75–13 sets forth procedures under which a public interest law firm may accept fees for its services. Under these procedures, the organization may not receive or request fees from its clients for the provision of legal services. Attorney fees paid by opposing parties, however, are permissible if awarded by a court or administrative agency in a case or settlement agreement.

.06   The procedures of Rev. Proc. 75–13 were published to eliminate the possibility that a decision to litigate might rest on the payment the firm receives instead of the economic feasibility or the litigants and thus render a public interest law firm's practice indistinguishable from a private firm's. The Service has reconsidered these procedures and concluded that safeguards sufficient to distinguish a public interest law firm's practice from the private practice of law can be implemented without absolutely prohibiting public interest law firms from receiving client–paid fees.

.07   Section 3 below sets forth general guidelines under which the Service will determine whether a public interest law firm meets the test of being exclusively charitable and thus is entitled to recognition of exemption as an organization described in section 501(c)(3) of the Code. Section 4 below sets forth approved procedures for the acceptance of court awarded attorneys' fees. Section 5 below sets forth additional procedures to apply in the case of client–paid fees to assure that the public interest law firm that accepts client–paid fees remains distinguishable from a private law firm. The procedures in Section 5 are not applicable to out–of–pocket costs incurred in litigation.

SEC. 3. GENERAL GUIDELINES

.01   The engagement of the organization in litigation can reasonably be said to be in representation of a broad public interest rather than a private interest. Litigation will be considered to be in representation of a broad public interest if it is designed to present a position on behalf of the public at large on matters of public interest. Typical of such litigation may be class actions in which the resolution of the dispute is in the public interest; suits for injunction against action by government or private interests broadly affecting the public; similar representation before administrative boards and agencies; test suits where the private interest is small; and the like.

.02   The litigation activity does not normally extend to direct representation of litigants in actions between private persons where the financial interests at stake would warrant representation from private legal sources. In such cases, however, where the issue in litigation affects a broad public interest or will have an impact on the broad public interest, the organization may serve as a friend of the court.

.03   The organization does not attempt to achieve its objectives through a program of disruption of the judicial system, illegal activity, or violation of applicable canons of ethics.

.04   The organization files with its annual information return a description of cases litigated and the rationale for the determination that they would benefit the public generally.

.05   The policies and programs of the organization (including compensation arrangements) are the responsibility of a board or committee representative of the public interest, which is not controlled by employees or persons who litigate on behalf of the organization nor by any organization that is not itself an organization described in section 501(c)(3) of the Code.

.06   The organization is not operated, through sharing of office space or otherwise, in a manner so as to create identification or confusion with a particular private law firm.

.07   There is no arrangement to provide, directly or indirectly, a deduction for the cost of litigation that is for the private benefit of the donor.

.08   The organization does not accept fees for its service except in accordance with the procedures set forth in Sections 4 and 5 below.

.09   The organization must otherwise comply with the provisions of section 501(c)(3) of the Code, that is, it may not participate in, or intervene in, any political campaign on behalf of (or in opposition to) any candidate for public office, no part of its net earnings may inure to the benefit of any private shareholder or individual, and no substantial part of its activities may consist of carrying on propaganda or otherwise attempting to influence legislation, (except as otherwise provided in section 501(h)).

.10   A public interest law firm may accept reimbursement from clients or from opposing parties for direct out–of–pocket expenses incurred in the litigation. Courts have traditionally distinguished out–of–pocket costs such as filing fees, travel expenses, and expert witness fees from attorneys' fees. These expenses are usually nominal in comparison to the amount of attorneys' fees.

SEC. 4. ACCEPTANCE OF ATTORNEYS' FEES

.01   The organization may accept attorneys' fees in public interest cases if such fees are paid by opposing parties and are awarded by a court or administrative agency or approved by such a body in a settlement agreement.

.02   The organization may accept attorneys' fees in public interest cases if such fees are paid directly by its clients provided it adopts additional procedures as set forth in Section 5 of this revenue procedure.

.03   The likelihood or probability of a fee, whether court awarded or client–paid, may not be a consideration in the organization's selection of cases. The selection of cases should be made in accordance with the procedures set forth in Section 3 of this revenue procedure.

.04   Cases in which a court awarded or client–paid fee is possible may not be accepted if the organization believes the litigants have a sufficient commercial or financial interest in the outcome of the litigation to justify retention of a private law firm. The organization may, in cases of sufficient broad public interest, represent the public interest as amicus curiae or intervenor in such cases.

.05   The total amount of all attorneys' fees (court awarded and received from clients) must not exceed 50 percent of the total cost of operation of the organization's legal functions. This percentage will be calculated over a five–year period, including the taxable year in which any fees are received and the four preceding taxable years (or any lesser period of existence). Costs of legal functions include: attorneys' salaries, nonprofessional salaries, overhead, and other costs directly attributable to the performance of the organization's legal functions. An organization may submit a ruling request where an exception to the above 50 percent limitation appears warranted.

.06   The organization will not seek or accept attorneys' fees in any circumstances that would result in a conflict with state statutes or professional canons of ethics.

.07   All attorneys' fees will be paid to the organization, rather than to individual staff attorneys. All staff attorneys and other employees will be compensated on a straight salary basis, not exceeding reasonable salary levels and not established by reference to any fees received in connection with the cases they have handled.

.08   In addition to the information required by Section 3.04 of this revenue procedure, the organization will file with its annual information return a report of all attorneys' fees sought and recovered in each case.

SEC. 5. ADDITIONAL RULES APPLICABLE TO CLIENT–PAID FEES

.01   Client–paid fees may not exceed the actual cost incurred in each case, viz., the salaries, overhead, and other costs fairly allocable to the litigation in question. Costs may be charged against a retainer, with any balance remaining after the conclusion of the litigation refunded to the litigant.

.02   Once having undertaken a representation, a public interest law firm may not withdraw from the case because the litigant is unable to pay the contemplated fee.

* * *

PROBLEMS

Consider whether the following organizations qualify for exemption under § 501(c)(3):

(a) The Free Market Legal Foundation, a nonprofit organization established by wealthy individuals and private foundations to counter the impact of "liberal" public interest law firms. Its programs include litigation of precedent-setting cases, research, and public education. The organization's recent litigation has included: a suit to challenge several Environmental Protection Agency regulations regarding strip mining in the West; a suit to challenge on constitutional grounds a minority scholarship program at a state university; an action on behalf of a Georgia factory owner who refused to allow an OSHA inspector into his plant without a search warrant; defense of a state initiative ending bilingual education; representation of students at various major universities who have been charged with violation of "hate speech" codes; and handling an appeal in a sexual harassment suit brought by a woman against a high governmental official. The Foundation is dedicated to the principles of free enterprise, private property rights, limited government, free speech, and reform of the civil and criminal justice systems.

(b) The Litigious Naturalists, an organization that institutes and maintains environmental litigation as a party plaintiff under state and federal environmental laws. It does not have its own staff or attorneys but employs private counsel to represent its interests.

(c) Middle Class Legal Services ("MCLS"), a nonprofit organization formed by five recent law school graduates to provide routine legal services in areas such as family law, bankruptcy, landlord–tenant, probate and simple tax controversies, to individuals and small businesses who are able to pay below–market fees ranging from $65 to $150 per hour. The stated purpose of MCLS is to provide services to those who are not poor enough to qualify for traditional legal services organizations and yet are unable to pay the prevailing rates charged by law firms and sole practitioners in the community.

(d) The Local Bar Association ("LBA"), a voluntary membership organization formed to promote the interests of the legal profession in a major American city. LBA's primary activity is the operation of a lawyer referral service that provides low and middle income persons with an opportunity to obtain representation from a panel of participating attorneys on matters such as divorce, probate, bankruptcy, landlord–tenant, and employment law matters. Other activities include the maintenance of a public law library, continuing legal education seminars and a tribunal to inquire into complaints of ethical and unauthorized practices and to report violations to the state bar association.

c.   COMMUNITY DEVELOPMENT AND LOW–INCOME HOUSING

The charitable sector includes many organizations seeking to ameliorate the problems of urban poverty through community economic development and affordable housing projects. Organizations operated for "[r]elief of the poor and distressed or of the underprivileged" have long qualified as "charitable" under § 501(c)(3). The more difficult questions are whether charitable status extends to nonprofit organizations that form effective economic partnerships with government and the private sector. Beginning in the early 1970's, the Service recognized that arresting urban problems through philanthropic venture capital could be a charitable purpose even if it might involve some incidental private benefit extending beyond the charitable class. The rulings below illustrate the Service's general approach in these areas, and the subsequent problems provide an opportunity to apply these broad guidelines to some typical fact patterns.

Revenue Ruling 74–587

1974–2 Cum. Bull. 162.

Advice has been requested whether a nonprofit organization formed and operated in the manner described below is exempt from Federal income tax under section 501(c)(3) of the Internal Revenue Code of 1954.

The organization's charter provides that it is organized exclusively for charitable purposes and restricts its activities to those not proscribed by section 501(c)(3) or other related provisions of the Code. The declared objectives of the organization are the relief of poverty, the elimination of prejudice, the lessening of neighborhood tensions, and the combating of community deterioration in certain economically depressed areas through a program of financial assistance and other aid designed to improve economic conditions and economic opportunities in these areas.

In furtherance of such objectives the organization devotes its resources to programs designed to stimulate economic development in high density urban areas inhabited mainly by low–income minority or other disadvantaged groups. Because of the lack of capital for development, the limited entrepreneurial skills of the owners, the social unrest and instability of the area, and the depressed market within which they operate, many of the businesses located in these high density urban areas have declined or fallen into disrepair, and others have ceased to operate.

The organization undertakes to combat such conditions by providing funds and working capital to corporations or individual proprietors who are not able to obtain funds from conventional commercial sources because of the poor financial risks involved in establishing and operating enterprises in these communities or because of their membership in minority or other disadvantaged groups. The program is designed to enable the recipient of funds or capital to start a new business or to acquire or improve an existing business. Depending upon the circumstances, the financial assistance may be in the form of low–cost or long–term loans or the purchase of equity interests in the various enterprises. The terms of any loan will be reasonably related to the needs of the particular business. Where the financial assistance takes the form of acquiring an equity interest, the organization disposes of such interest as soon as the success of the business is reasonably assured.

In selecting recipients for aid, the organization consults with other nonprofit and governmental organizations operating anti–poverty and anti–discrimination programs to identify particular undertakings that will fill a community need and offer the greatest potential community benefit. Preference is given to businesses that will provide training and employment opportunities for the unemployed or under–employed residents of the area. In selecting a recipient for financial assistance, the organization considers the applicant's motivation, education, experience, and prior participation in management and job training programs. It also considers recommendations from other organizations conducting rehabilitation and training programs.

The organization does not actively participate in the day–to–day operation of the businesses to which it provides financial assistance; however, it does review their progress periodically to assure that the funds are used for the organization's purposes. In addition, when appropriate, the organization provides technical assistance and counseling.

The facts relating to the financial activities undertaken by the organization in carrying out this program established that these loans and purchases of equity interest are not undertaken for purpose of profit or gain but for the purpose of advancing the charitable goals of the organization and are not investments for profit in any conventional business sense.

The organization is financed by grants from foundations and by public contributions.

Section 501(c)(3) of the Code provides for the exemption from Federal income tax of organizations organized and operated exclusively for charitable purposes.

Section 1.501(c)(3)–1(a) of the Income Tax Regulations provides that in order to be exempt as an organization described in section 501(c)(3) of the Code, the organization must be one that is both organized and operated exclusively for one or more of the purposes specified in that section. An organization that fails to meet either the organizational or the operational test is not exempt.

Section 1.501(c)(3)–1(d)(2) of the regulations defines the term "charitable" as including the promotion of social welfare by organizations designed to relieve the poor and distressed or the underprivileged, to lessen neighborhood tensions, to eliminate prejudice and discrimination, or to combat community deterioration.

The corporate charter declares the purposes of the organization to be exclusively charitable and contains appropriate restrictions against engaging in any activities proscribed under section 501(c)(3) or related provisions of the Code. To that extent, therefore, the organization meets the organizational requirements of the applicable regulations provisions.

To satisfy the "operational test" the organization's resources must be devoted to programs that qualify as exclusively charitable within the meaning of section 501(c)(3) of the Code and applicable regulations.

Through its program of financial assistance, the organization is devoting its resources to uses that benefit the community in a way that the law regards as charitable. Such conclusion follows from the fact that the organization's described program of aiding minority–owned businesses promotes the social welfare of the community, since it helps to lessen prejudice and discrimination against minority groups by demonstrating that the disadvantaged residents of an impoverished area can operate businesses successfully if given the opportunity and proper guidance. It also helps to relieve poverty, while at the same time lessening neighborhood tensions and dissatisfaction arising from the lack of employment opportunities by assisting local businesses that will provide a means of livelihood and expanded job opportunities for unemployed or underemployed area residents. Finally, it combats community deterioration by helping to establish businesses in the area and by rehabilitating existing businesses that have deteriorated.

Although some of the individuals receiving financial assistance in their business endeavors under the organization's program may not themselves qualify for charitable assistance as such, that fact does not detract from the charitable character of the organization's program. The recipients of loans and working capital in such cases are merely the instruments by which the charitable purposes are sought to be accomplished.

Accordingly, the organization is exempt from Federal income tax under section 501(c)(3) of the Code.

Revenue Ruling 70–585

1970–2 Cum.Bull. 115.

Advice has been requested whether nonprofit organizations created to provide housing for low or moderate income families under Federal and State programs qualify for exemption from Federal income tax as charitable organizations described in section 501(c)(3) of the Internal Revenue Code of 1954.

Section 501(c)(3) of the Code provides for the exemption from Federal income tax of organizations organized and operated exclusively for charitable purposes.

Section 1.501(c)(3)–1(d)(2) of the Income Tax Regulations defines the term "charitable" as including the relief of the poor and distressed or of the underprivileged, and the promotion of social welfare by organizations designed to lessen neighborhood tensions, to eliminate prejudice and discrimination, or to combat community deterioration.

It is held generally that where an organization is formed for charitable purposes and accomplishes its charitable purposes through a program of providing housing for low and, in certain circumstances, moderate income families, it is entitled to exemption under section 501(c)(3) of the Code. The fact that an organization receives public funds under State or Federal programs for housing is not determinative; qualification is based on whether or not the organization is charitable within the meaning of section 501(c)(3).

The following situations are illustrative of the foregoing principle.

Situation 1. An Organization Formed to Aid Low Income Families

An organization was formed to develop a program for new home construction and the renovation of existing homes for sale to low income families on long–term, low–payment plans. It purchases homes for renovation and lots for building new homes throughout the city in which it is located. It builds new homes for sale to low income families who qualify for loans under a Federal housing program and who cannot obtain financing through conventional channels. It also aids financially those families eligible for the loans who do not have the necessary down payment. Rehabilitated homes are made available to families who cannot qualify for any type of mortgage loan. The cost of these homes is recovered, if possible, through very small periodic payments. The organization derives its operating funds through Federal loans and contributions from the general public. Where possible, renovations are made with volunteer help.

By providing homes for low income families who otherwise could not afford them, the organization is relieving the poor and distressed. Thus, it is held that this organization is organized and operated exclusively for charitable purposes, and it is exempt from Federal income tax under section 501(c)(3) of the Code. The determination of what constitutes low income is a factual question based on all of the surrounding circumstances.

Situation 2. An Organization Formed to Eliminate Prejudice and Discrimination

An organization was formed to ameliorate the housing needs of minority groups by building housing units for sale to persons of low and moderate income on an open occupancy basis. It constructs new housing that is available to members of minority groups with low and moderate income who are unable to obtain adequate housing because of local discrimination. These housing units are so located as to help reduce racial and ethnic imbalances in the community. They are sold at or below cost to low or moderate income families or rented, with options to purchase, to families who cannot presently afford to purchase. Preference is to be given to families previously located in ghetto areas. The organization also informs the public regarding integrated housing as a means of minimizing potential misunderstanding and stabilizing integrated neighborhoods. It is financed by contributions from the general public and by funds obtained under Federal and State housing programs.

As the organization's activities are designed to eliminate prejudice and discrimination and to lessen neighborhood tensions, it is engaged in charitable activities within the meaning of section 501(c)(3) of the Code. See Rev. Rul. 68–655, C.B. 1968–2, 213. Accordingly, it is held that this organization is exempt from Federal income tax under section 501(c)(3) of the Code.

Situation 3. An Organization Formed to Combat Community Deterioration

An organization was formed to formulate plans for the renewal and rehabilitation of a particular area in a city as a residential community. Studies of the area showed that the median income level in the area is lower than in other sections of the city and the housing located in the area is generally old and badly deteriorated.

The organization's membership is composed of the residents, businesses, and community organizations in the area. The organization cooperates with the local redevelopment authority in providing residents of the area with decent, safe, and sanitary housing without relocating them outside the area. The organization has developed an overall plan for the rehabilitation of the area; it sponsors a renewal project in which the residents themselves take the initiative; and it arranges monthly meetings to involve residents in the planning for the renewal of the area. As part of the renewal project, it purchased an apartment house that it plans to rehabilitate and rent at cost to low and moderate income families with preference given to residents of the area. The organization is supported by Federal funds, membership fees, and contributions.

Since the organization's purposes and activities combat community deterioration by assisting in the rehabilitation of an old and run–down residential area, they are charitable within the meaning of section 501(c)(3) of the Code. Thus, it is held that the organization is exempt from Federal income tax under section 501(c)(3) of the Code.

Situation 4. An Organization Formed to Provide Moderate Income Families With Housing in a Particular Community

An organization was formed to build new housing facilities for the purpose of helping families to secure decent, safe, and sanitary housing at prices they can afford. Its membership is composed of community organizations that are concerned with the growing housing shortage in the community. A study of the area shows that because of the high cost of land, increased interest rates, and the growing population, there is a shortage of housing for moderate income families in the community. The organization plans to erect housing that it to be rented at cost to moderate income families. The organization is financed by mortgage money obtained under Federal and State programs and by contributions from the general public.

Since the organization's program is not designed to provide relief to the poor or to carry out any other charitable purpose within the meaning of the regulations applicable to section 501(c)(3) of the Code, it is held that it is not entitled to exemption from Federal income tax under section 501(c)(3) of the Code.

* * *

NOTES

1. *The Age of Specialization*. Community development and low–income housing have become highly technical sub–specialties, requiring expertise in sources of government funding, debt financing techniques, partnership tax, and the real estate development process—all areas going well beyond the scope of this text. Particularly important is the low–income housing tax credit, which helps for–profit and nonprofit developers raise equity to purchase, rehabilitate, and construct affordable housing. See I.R.C. 42. In introducing this topic, a leading treatise has warned:

> Nonprofit developers should be aware that this [low–income housing tax credit] program is extremely complicated and rife with land mines for those uninitiated in this type of financing. Early in the development process, sponsors who are seriously considering a tax credit project should retain tax counsel experienced in the low–income housing tax credit. Bennett L. Hecht, Developing Affordable Housing: A Practical Guide for Nonprofit Organizations 148 (1994).

2. *Low-Income Housing Safe Harbor*. In Rev. Proc. 96–32, 1996–1 C.B. 717, the Service clarified the standards for low-income housing organizations seeking to qualify for exemption under § 501(c)(3). The procedure includes a bright line test providing that an organization will qualify for exemption if at least 75 percent of its units are occupied by families who are low-income (80 percent of the areas's median income) under federal housing guidelines. At least 20 percent of those units must be occupied by residents who are "very-low income" (50 percent of the areas's median), or 40 percent of those units must be occupied by residents whose incomes do not exceed 120 percent of the areas's very low-income limit. The safe harbor requires that the housing must be "affordable" to its charitable beneficiaries but permits an organization to evict tenants for failure to pay rent or misconduct. Any organization unable to meet the safe harbor may rely on a facts and circumstances test that looks to other factors demonstrating the organization's charitable purposes. Finally, the revenue procedure warns that the Service will carefully scrutinize situations where arrangements involving private developers or management companies may result in impermissible inurement or private benefit.

3. *For Further Reading*. Herbert Stevens and Thomas Tracy, A Developer's Guide to the Low Income Housing Tax Credit (1992).

PROBLEMS

Consider whether each of following nonprofit organizations qualify for exemption under § 501(c)(3) and, if not, what structural and operational changes would improve its chances:

(a) Urban Renewal, Inc. ("URI") was formed to increase business patronage in a ten square mile section of South Central Gotham City, an inner–city neighborhood that is primarily inhabited by African–Americans and Korean–Americans. URI accomplishes its purposes by: presenting television and radio advertisements describing the advantages of shopping in the area, informing news media on the area's problems and potentials, operating a telephone service to provide information to prospective shoppers on transportation in the area, and providing financial assistance through low–interest loans and the purchase of equity interests in business enterprises in the area. The organization is run by a board of directors consisting of five members of the Gotham City business community (three are white, one is Korean–American and one is Latino). Two members of the board own businesses in South Central Gotham City.

(b) Affordable Housing, Inc., which was formed to develop a program for new home construction and the renovation of existing homes for sale to low–income families. The organization purchases and renovates existing homes and builds new homes for sale to low–income families who qualify for loans under various federal housing assistance programs.

(c) Same as (b), above, except that the organization was formed to assist moderate–income families to secure decent, safe and sanitary housing at an affordable price. The organization will construct housing and rent it at cost to qualifying families.

d. PROTECTION OF THE ENVIRONMENT

Revenue Ruling 76–204

1976–1 Cum. Bull. 152.

Advice has been requested whether the nonprofit organization described below, which otherwise qualifies for exemption from Federal income tax under section 501(c)(3) of the Internal Revenue Code of 1954, is operated exclusively for charitable purposes.

The organization was formed by scientists, educators, conservationists, and representatives of the community–at–large for the purpose of preserving the natural environment. It accomplishes this purpose by acquiring and maintaining ecologically significant undeveloped land such as swamps, marshes, forests, wilderness tracts, and other natural areas. The organization acquires the land either as a recipient of a charitable gift or bequest, or as a purchaser. In order to be constantly aware of the availability of significant undeveloped areas, the organization works closely with Federal, state, and local government agencies, and private organizations concerned with environmental conservation.

Some of the land is maintained by the organization itself for the purpose of preserving it in its natural state. Generally, public access to such land is limited so that the delicate balance of the ecosystem remains undisturbed. In these situations the organization will allow educational and scientific research or study as long as such use will not disrupt the particular ecosystem.

Other tracts of land are merely held and preserved by the organization until arrangements can be made to transfer title to the land to a government conservation agency. This usually occurs when the agency is presently unable to acquire the land itself, but where the parcel is particularly suited for inclusion into a new or existing park, wilderness area, or wildlife preserve. Depending upon the circumstances surrounding the organization's initial acquisition of the land, and the restrictions on the particular government agency involved, the organization either makes an outright gift of the land to the agency, or is reimbursed by the agency for the cost of the land. Aside from this occasional reimbursement, the organization does not regularly receive any support from the government, but receives most of its funding from the general public.

Section 501(c)(3) of the Code provides for the exemption from Federal income tax of organizations organized and operated exclusively for charitable purposes.

Section 1.501(c)(3)–1(d)(2) of the Income Tax Regulations states that the term 'charitable' is used in section 501(c)(3) of the Code in its generally accepted legal sense and includes the advancement of education and science.

It is generally recognized that efforts to preserve and protect the natural environment for the benefit of the public serve a charitable purpose. Restatement (Second) of Trusts § 375 (1959). In Noice v. Schnell, 101 N.J. Eq. 252, 137 A. 582 (E. & A. 1927), the court held that a bequest, in trust, to preserve and protect from commercial development the Palisades along the Hudson River was a valid charitable trust. In addition, in President and Fellows of Middlebury College v. Central Power Corporation of Vermont, 101 Vt. 325, 143 A. 384 (1928), the court found that a devise of land to preserve a specimen of original Vermont forest was a charitable bequest. Similar charitable bequests have been upheld in other cases dealing with environmental preservation. See, e.g., Richardson v. Essex Institute, 208 Mass. 311, 94 N.E. 262 (1911); Cresson's Appeal, 30 Pa. 437 (1858); and Staines v. Burton, 17 Utah 331, 53 P. 1015 (1898).

Several published Revenue Rulings have also recognized the charitable and educational nature of organizations designed to preserve and promote the natural environment. For example, Rev. Rul. 70–186, 1970–1 C.B. 128, holds that an organization formed to preserve a lake as a public recreational facility and to improve the condition of the water in the lake to enhance its recreational features qualifies for exemption under section 501(c)(3) of the Code. In addition, Rev. Rul. 67–292, 1967–2 C.B. 184, holds that an organization formed for the purpose of purchasing and maintaining a sanctuary for wild birds and animals for the benefit of the public may qualify as exempt from Federal income tax under section 501(c)(3).

Furthermore, the promotion of conservation and protection of natural resources has been recognized by Congress as serving a broad public benefit. For example, Congress declared in the National Environmental Policy Act of 1969, 42 U.S.C.A. 4321 (1969), that the prevention and elimination of damage to the environment stimulates the health and welfare of man and enriches the understanding of ecological systems and natural resources important to the nation.

The benefit to the public from environmental conservation derives not merely from the current educational, scientific, and recreational uses that are made of our natural resources, but from their preservation as well. Only through preservation will future generations be guaranteed the ability to enjoy the natural environment. A national policy of preserving unique aspects of the natural environment for future generations is clearly mandated in the Congressional declarations of purpose and policy in numerous Federal conservation laws. See, e.g., Wilderness Act, 16 U.S.C.A. § 1131 (1964)(wilderness areas); Estuarine Areas Act, 16 U.S.C.A. § 1221 (1968)(estuaries); Wild and Scenic Rivers Act, 16 U.S.C.A. § 1271 (1968)(rivers); Water Bank Act, 16 U.S.C.A. § 1301 (1970)(wetlands). While the public benefits from environmental conservation are clearly recognized and measurable, an equally important public purpose is served by preserving natural resources for future generations.

In this case, by acquiring and preserving (whether by self–maintenance or through transfer to a governmental agency) ecologically significant undeveloped land, the organization is enhancing the accomplishment of the express national policy of conserving the nation's unique natural resources. In this sense, the organization is advancing education and science and is benefiting the public in a manner that the law regards as charitable. The restrictions on current access to the lands maintained by the organization are essential to the preservation of their natural state, and are therefore essential to the fulfillment of the organization's charitable purpose. A similar principle is set forth in Rev. Rul. 75–207, 1975–1 C.B. 361, which holds that the value of an island, owned by a private foundation dedicated to preserve the natural ecosystems on the island to which access is limited to invited public and private researchers, may be excluded from the foundation's minimum investment return under section 4942(e) of the Code.

Accordingly, the organization is operated exclusively for charitable purposes and qualifies for exemption from Federal income tax under section 501(c)(3) of the Code.

* * *

Revenue Ruling 78–384

1978–2 Cum.Bull. 174.

Advice has been requested whether the nonprofit organization described below is operated exclusively for charitable purposes, and thus qualifies for exemption from federal income tax under section 501(c)(3) of the Internal Revenue Code of 1954.

The organization is a nonprofit corporation that owns farm land. It restricts the use of its farm land to farming or such other uses as the organization deems ecologically suitable for the land. The organization states that it benefits the public by restricting its land to uses compatible with the ecology of the area.

Section 501(c)(3) of the Code provides for the exemption from federal income tax of organizations organized and operated exclusively for charitable purposes.

Section 1.501(c)(3)–1(d)(2) of the Income Tax Regulations states that the term "charitable" is used in section 501(c)(3) of the Code in its generally accepted legal sense.

Rev. Rul. 76–204, 1976–1 C.B. 152, holds that an organization preserving ecologically significant land for the benefit of the public is operated exclusively for charitable purposes under section 501(c)(3) of the Code.

Although the organization described above restricts its land to uses that do not change the environment, it is not preserving land that has any distinctive ecological significance within the meaning of Rev. Rul. 76–204. In addition, any benefit to the public from this organization's self–imposed restriction on its own land is too indirect and insignificant to establish that the organization serves a charitable purpose within the meaning of section 1.501(c)(3)–1(d)(2) of the regulations.

Accordingly, because the organization does not preserve ecologically significant land and has not otherwise established that it serves a charitable purpose, it is not operated exclusively for charitable purposes, and thus does not qualify for exemption from federal income tax under section 501(c)(3) of the Code.

Rev. Rul. 76–204 is distinguished.

NOTES

1. *Land Trusts*. The nonprofit land trust has emerged as a popular land conservation vehicle. Proponents of land trusts point to their flexibility, and their ability to act more quickly than government agencies and negotiate more discretely with landowners. Donations to land trusts often entitle donors to substantial tax savings. Local property tax benefits also may be available. A leading guidebook in the field describes a land trust as follows:

> Land trusts are local, state, or regional nonprofit organizations directly involved in protecting land for its natural, recreational, scenic, histori-

cal, or productive value. Most land trusts are private, nonprofit corporations. There are also a few governmental or quasi–governmental bodies called land trusts that operate with the freedom and flexibility of a private trust, some of which have a private board or the ability to use private funds. Land trusts are not "trusts" in the legal sense, and may also be called "conservancies," "foundations," or any number of other names descriptive of their purposes.

Land trusts are distinguished by their first–hand involvement in land transactions or management. This involvement can take many forms. Some land trusts purchase or accept donations of land or of conservation easements (permanent, binding agreements that restrict the uses of a piece of land to protect its conservation resources). Some manage land owned by others or advise landowners on how to preserve their land. Some land trusts help negotiate conservation transactions in which they play no other role. Land trusts often work cooperatively with government agencies by acquiring or managing land, researching open space needs and priorities, and assisting in the development of open space plans. They also may work with other non–profit organizations and sometimes with developers. A land trust may do one, several, or all of these things.

Some land trusts are organized to protect a single piece of property, but the more active trusts have a larger land protection agenda. They may focus their efforts in a community, in a region, on a particular type of resource, or on a protection project. Some operate statewide and work cooperatively with local land trusts in addition to conducting their own land conservation projects. Resources protected by land trusts include forests, prairie grasslands, islands, urban gardens, river corridors, farmland, watersheds, parklands, marshes, ranchland, scenic vistas, cultural landscapes, Civil War battlefields, and hiking trails.

Land Trust Alliance, Starting a Land Trust: A Guide to Forming a Land Conservation Organization (1990).

2. *For Further Reading.* Janet Diehl, Thomas S. Barrett, et al., The Conservation Easement Handbook (1988); Stephen J. Small, Federal Tax Law of Conservation Easements (1996 & current Supp.). A leading periodical on current developments in land conservation law and related topics is The Back Forty, a publication of The Hyperion Society, a land conservation law center operated in connection with the University of California, Hastings College of the Law.

PROBLEMS

Consider whether the following organizations qualify for tax exemption under § 501(c)(3):

(a) The Mt. Sutro Preservation League, an organization formed by property owners in a residential area to acquire and hold about 100 acres of undeveloped woods adjoining their homes. The League seeks to prevent further commercial development of the area and to support a lawsuit enjoining the construction of a hospital building by a nearby medical center.

(b) The Martinez Agricultural Trust, an organization that owns and operates 500 acres of Kansas farmland as a demonstration conservation project. The Trust tests experimental farming methods and soil restoration techniques, and develops new strains of crops. Results of its research are made available to area farmers. The land has no significant environmental attributes and is adjacent to a larger property owned by the Martinez family, who donated the farmland to the Trust and control its board of directors.

(c) The Hardscrabble County Land Conservancy, an organization empowered to acquire, hold, manage, and dispose of land in a manner designed to preserve and enhance farms and ranches and protect them against conversion to nonagricultural uses. The Conservancy's programs are designed to advance clearly delineated federal and state land conservation policies. The Conservancy intends to acquire, through charitable donations and purchases from farmers and other landowners, easements that restrict the use of the affected property to exclusively agricultural land.

e.   DISASTER RELIEF

The enormous outpouring of philanthropy following the September 11, 2001 terrorist attacks raised a number of questions about the legal requirements for a disaster-relief organization to qualify as "charitable" under § 501(c)(3) and the tax consequences for individuals and businesses receiving financial assistance.

Some of these issues had been addressed by the IRS in response to earlier disasters,[1] and the Treasury regulations have long provided that the concept of "charitable" includes "relief of the poor and distressed or of the under privileged . . ." Treas. Reg. § 1.501(c)(3)–1(d)(2). Within a week after the attacks, the IRS elaborated by releasing the advance text of a publication, "Disaster Relief: Providing Assistance Through Charitable Organizations" (hereinafter "Disaster Relief"), clarifying its view of the rules for existing organizations and new charities formed specifically in the wake of September 11th.[2] Legislation enacted by Congress in early 2002 further clarified and liberalized the rules. This Note highlights some of the major tax issues, beginning with general tax principles and then turning to the specific September 11th relief legislation.

---

1. In 1999, for example, the Service published an article in its annual training manual on the subject. See Ruth Rivera Huetter & Marvin Friedlander, Disaster Relief and Emergency Hardship Programs, Exempt Organizations Continuing Professional Education Technical Instruction Program for FY 1999, at 219.

2. The publication (Pub. 3833) was updated in March 2002. It is available on the IRS web site <www.irs.gov> and has been reprinted in 36 Exempt Org. Tax Rev. 60 (2002).

Disaster Relief as a Charitable Purpose. The IRS disaster relief publication begins by stating the obvious: providing aid to relieve distress caused by a natural or civil disaster (e.g., fire, flood, hurricane, earthquake, riot and the like) or emergency hardship "is charity in its most basic form." Disaster Relief, at 1. Disaster relief can include loans, grants of money, or providing basic necessities such as food, clothing, housing, medical assistance and psychological counseling. Immediately following a disaster, providing these types of essential aid is considered charitable regardless of a recipient's financial resources, but long-term assistance only can be provided to persons who are "appropriate recipients of charity." Disaster Relief, at 4–5.

In determining those who may properly receive assistance from a charitable organization, the critical question narrows to—what constitutes a "charitable class" of beneficiaries. A charitable class must be large or indefinite enough that providing aid to its members benefits the community as a whole. For that reason, a disaster-relief organization never can qualify as charitable if its benefits are limited to a few specified individuals or families, and in theory donors may not earmark contributions for a particular victim.[3] The following examples from the IRS publication are instructive:

Example 1: Linda's baby, Todd, suffers a severe burn from a fire requiring costly treatment that Linda cannot afford. Linda's friends and co-workers form the Todd Foundation to raise funds from fellow workers, family members, and the general public to meet Todd's expenses. Since the organization is formed to assist a particular individual, it would not qualify as a charitable organization.

Consider this alternative case: Linda's friends and co-workers form an organization to raise funds to meet the expenses of an open-ended group consisting of all children in the community injured by disasters where financial help is needed. Neither Linda nor members of Linda's family control the charitable organization. The organization controls the selection of aid recipients and determines whether any assistance for Todd is appropriate. Potential donors are advised that, while funds may be used to assist Todd, their contributions might well be used for other children who have similar needs. The organization does not accept contributions specifically earmarked for Todd or any other individual. The organization, formed and operated to assist an indefinite number of persons, qualifies as a charitable organization.

* * *

Example 2: A hurricane causes widespread damage to property and loss of life in several counties of a coastal state. Over 100,000 homes

---

3. We say "in theory" because, in practice, earmarking is not uncommon—e.g., "send your donation to the Jane Doe Trust Fund at XYZ Bank (clearly not tax-deductible), or to the Jane Doe Relief Fund at Community Foundation (technically, the wrong way to solicit, but donors often get a receipt telling them their gift is tax-deductible)."

are damaged or destroyed by high winds and floods. The group of people affected by the disaster is large enough so that providing aid to this group benefits the public as a whole. Therefore, a charitable organization can be formed to assist persons in this group since the eligible recipients comprise a charitable class.

Example 3: A hurricane causes widespread damage to property and loss of life in several counties of a coastal state. In one of the affected counties, an existing charitable organization has an ongoing program that provides emergency assistance to residents of the county. A small number of residents of this county suffered significant injury or property damage as a result of the storm. The organization provided assistance to some of these individuals. The organization's assistance was provided to a charitable class because the group of potential recipients is indefinite in that it is open-ended to include other victims of future disasters in the county.

Disaster Relief 6–7.

Needy or Distressed Test. One of the more sensitive questions to arise out of the September 11th attacks was the extent to which a victim or victim's family must demonstrate financial need to become part of an appropriate charitable class. Some victims of the World Trade Center disaster were quite affluent, and others had ample life insurance or were covered by generous employee benefit programs. While awaiting legislation,[4] the Service initially expressed serious concern that organizations disbursing funds to victims of the attacks would risk their charitable status if distributions were made without regard to the victims' financial need. See Diana B. Henriques & David Barstow, Victims' Funds May Violate U.S. Tax Law, N.Y. Times, Nov. 12, 2001, at B1. The Service's traditional view was that disaster victims need not be totally destitute to be needy and they can qualify as "distressed" even if they are not poor. But an outright transfer of funds based solely on an individual's involvement in a disaster without regard to the individual's particular needs or distress was viewed by the Service as impermissible private benefit. After a disaster, need or distress often depends on timing and context—e.g., a charity distributing short-term assistance in the few days or weeks following a disaster, such as housing, food, or crisis counseling, would require far less documentation of financial need than an organization distributing longer-term aid. See Disaster Relief 7–10.

In response to concerns raised by New York City's Twin Towers Fund and other large charities, the IRS reconsidered and shifted to a more permissive stance, announcing that it would treat relief payments from charities as related to the organization's exempt purposes if "made in good faith using objective standards." I.R.S. Notice 2001–78, 2001–50 I.R.B. 1. See also David Barstow & Diana B. Henriques, I.R.S. Makes An Exception

---

4. For the special statutory rules for September 11 disaster relief, see infra pp. 167–168.

on Terror Aid, N.Y. Times, Nov. 17, 2001, at B1. Was the Service's change of its long-held position a compassionate response to the September 11th tragedy, or a capitulation to public pressure that distorts the concept of charity and creates serious inequities? Should the change of position apply to all future disasters or be limited to the September 11 funds?

See also the discussion below of the Victims of Terrorism Tax Relief Act of 2001, which codifies the Service's liberalized stance in some circumstances.

Employer-Related Assistance. Special problems are raised by organizations formed by a particular employer to provide relief for employees and their families. Consider, for example, a financial services firm at the World Trade Center with 1,000 employees many of whom died in the attack. May the company establish a charitable organization (or use an existing corporate foundation) to provide financial assistance to families of employees, or would this result in impermissible private benefit? Does it matter if the organization is a public charity or a private foundation? And do the benefits provided constitute taxable compensation? The first draft of the IRS disaster relief publication listed criteria to be weighed in determining whether employer-related assistance programs were charitable. The key seemed to be that employment must be merely a "qualifying factor" for relief (it gets you in the door) and that a sufficiently large or "indefinite" charitable class must exist (e.g., small companies with only a few employees couldn't qualify). In the case of employer-sponsored public charities, the current IRS position is that payments made to employees for employer-sponsored disaster relief will be considered consistent with charitable purposes if: (1) the class of beneficiaries is larger or indefinite (i.e., an appropriate "charitable class"), and (2) the recipients are selected based on an objective determination of need by an independent committee controlled by individuals who are not in a position to exercise substantial influence over the employee's affairs. If these requirements are met, any financial assistance received by employees or their families are excluded from gross income as gifts. Disaster Relief, at 18–19.

Private Foundations: Special Problems. As discussed in Chapter 6, private foundations are subject to a stricter regulatory regime than public charities. For a brief discussion of the special problems faced by private foundations providing disaster relief, see Chapter 3C2a, infra, pp. 458–459.

Assistance to Businesses. Many businesses near the World Trade Center, large and small, suffered severe economic dislocation as a result of the terrorist attacks. Are grants or loans (e.g., to meet payroll or relocate) to those businesses consistent with the concept of charity, or do they result in impermissible private benefit? Put more succinctly, can a business be an appropriate object of charity? Prior to September 11, 2001, the Service's view was that, apart from helping a business owner meet the most basic needs, any more general financial assistance was inconsistent with the concept of charity. After receiving submissions from the American Bar Association Tax Section and others, however, the Service moderated this restrictive view and announced that affected businesses could treat grants from charitable organizations as tax-free gifts if the charity had donative intent and was not expecting anything of value in return. See Letter from Lewis J. Fernandez, Deputy Associate Chief Counsel, Internal Revenue Service to Richard M. Lipton, Chair, ABA Section of Taxation, April 15, 2002, reprinted in 36 Exempt Org. Tax Rev. 522 (2002).

Legislation. Some of the issues with which the IRS was grappling were specifically resolved by the Victims of Terrorism Tax Relief Act, P.L. 107–134 ("the Act"), which became law in January 2002. The Act includes tax relief for those who died or were injured in the September 11th terrorist attacks and the anthrax bioterrorism in late 2001. Provisions of particular interest to the nonprofit sector include:

(1) Section 104 of the Act clarifies that payments made by § 501(c)(3) charities, including private foundations, as a result of the September 11th terrorist attacks or the anthrax bioterrorism (no other disasters qualify) are considered to be made for an exempt purpose even without a specific assessment of financial need if the payments are made in good faith under an objective formula consistently applied. For example, a charitable organization that assists families of firefighters killed in the line of duty could make a pro-rata distribution to the families of firefighters killed in the attacks, even though the specific financial needs of each family are not directly considered. This important provision is only part of the Act and was not codified in the Internal Revenue Code.

(2) If the rules and criteria in (1), above, are met, the Act describes the circumstances under which employers may create and control private foundations for the purpose of making payments to families of deceased employees.

(3) The Act adds to the Internal Revenue Code new § 139, which provides that "qualified disaster relief payments" received from any payor (a charity, an employer or a third party) by individuals for personal, family, living or funeral expenses, and for repair or replacement of items lost in a disaster, are excluded from gross income. Thus, for example, payments made by commercial airlines to families of passengers killed as a result of a qualified disaster would be excluded from gross income. The legislative history elaborates considerably on the scope of this new exclusion, which is not limited to victims of the September 11th attacks or the subsequent anthrax episode. See Joint Committee on Taxation, Technical Explanation of the Victims of Terrorism Tax Relief Act of 1001 (JCX–93–01), 107th Cong., 2d Sess. (2002).

For Further Reading. Catherine E. Livingston, Disaster Relief Activities of Charitable Organizations, presentation to New York State Bar Association Section of Taxation, reprinted in 35 Exempt Org. Tax Rev. 153 (2002); Betsy Buchalter Adler & Barbara A. Rosen, Disaster! Practices and Procedures for Charities Providing Relief After 9/11: A Case Study, 96 J. Tax'n 297 (May 2002).

5.   EDUCATIONAL ORGANIZATIONS

Treasury Regulations: § 1.501(c)(3)–1(d)(3).

The promotion of education has long been regarded as a charitable purpose, and tax exemptions have been granted to nonprofit private schools, with little or no controversy, ever since colonial times. Although educational organizations are a sub–set of the broader "charitable" category, they raise distinct issues of interpretation under § 501(c)(3). The central question is what activities are "educational."

The regulations define "educational" purposes as (1) the instruction or training of individuals for the purpose of improving or developing their capabilities, or (2) the instruction of the public on subjects useful to individuals and beneficial to the community. Treas. Reg. § 1.501(c)(3)–1(d)(3). Examples include traditional schools and colleges; public discussion groups; and cultural institutions such as museums, zoos, planetariums, and symphony orchestras. Treas. Reg. § 1.501(c)(3)–1(d)(3)(ii). The Service has adopted a broad view of education, granting exemption to day care centers for infant children, trade schools, college bookstores, alumni associations, a jazz festival, organizations providing continuing education to doctors or lawyers, and marriage counseling services. See, e.g., San Francisco Infant School, Inc. v. Commissioner, 69 T.C. 957 (1978) (child care center); Rev. Rul. 69–538, 1969–2 C.B. 116 (bookstore); Rev. Rul. 60–143, 1960–1 C.B. 192 (alumni organization); Rev. Rul. 65–271, 1965–2 C.B. 161 (jazz festival); Rev. Rul. 65–298, 1965–2 C.B. 163 (updates for physicians). A dog obedience school was denied exemption, however, apparently on the theory that educating animals is not a valid exempt purpose. Ann Arbor Dog Training Club, Inc. v. Commissioner, 74 T.C. 207 (1980).

Organizations advocating particular viewpoints raise special problems. The regulations recognize advocacy groups as "educational" as long as they present a "sufficiently full and fair exposition of the pertinent facts" to permit a listener to form an independent opinion but not if their principal function is the mere presentation of unsupported opinion. Reg. § 1.501(c)(3)–1(d)(3). As illustrated by the materials that follow, these hazy distinctions are problematic in application and have raised constitutional questions.

Revenue Ruling 75–384

1975–2 Cum. Bull. 204.

Advice has been requested whether a nonprofit organization formed to promote world peace and disarmament by nonviolent direct action including acts of civil disobedience qualifies for exemption from Federal income tax under section 501(c)(3) or 501(c)(4) of the Internal Revenue Code of 1954.

The purposes of the organization are to educate and inform the public on the principles of pacifism and nonviolent action including civil disobedience. Its primary activity is the sponsoring of protest demonstrations and nonviolent action projects in opposition to war and preparations for war.

Protest demonstrations are conducted at military establishments, Federal agencies, and industrial companies involved with military and defense operations. Other activities consist of peace marches and protests against the use of tax monies for war purposes. The protest demonstrations constitute the primary activity of the organization. They are designed to draw public attention to the views of the organization and to exert pressure on governmental authorities. To derive the maximum publicity of an event, demonstrators are urged to commit acts of civil disobedience. Participants deliberately block vehicular or pedestrian traffic, disrupt the work of government, and prevent the movement of supplies. These activities are violations of local ordinances and breaches of public order. Incidental to demonstrations, leaflets are dispersed presenting the views of the organization.

Section 501(c)(3) of the Code provides for the exemption from Federal income tax of organizations organized and operated exclusively for charitable purposes.

Section 1.501(c)(3)–1(d)(2) of the Income Tax Regulations provides that the term "charitable" is used in section 501(c)(3) of the Code in its generally accepted legal sense. The regulation further states that the term "charity" includes lessening the burdens of government and the promotion of social welfare by organizations designed (i) to lessen neighborhood tensions; (ii) to eliminate prejudice and discrimination; (iii) to defend human and civil rights secured by law; or (iv) to combat community deterioration and juvenile delinquency.

As a matter of trust law, one of the main sources of the general law of charity, no trust can be created for a purpose which is illegal. The purpose is illegal if the trust property is to be used for an object which is in violation of the criminal law, or if the trust tends to induce the commission of crime, or if the accomplishment of the purpose is otherwise against public policy. IV Scott on Trusts Sec. 377 (3d. ed. 1967). Thus, all charitable trusts (and by implication all charitable organizations, regardless of their form) are subject to the requirement that their purposes may not be illegal or contrary to public policy. See Rev. Rul. 71–447, 1971–2 C.B. 230; Restatement (Second), Trusts (1959) Sec. 377, Comment (c).

In this case the organization induces or encourages the commission of criminal acts by planning and sponsoring such events. The intentional nature of this encouragement precludes the possibility that the organization might unfairly fail to qualify for exemption due to an isolated or inadvertent violation of a regulatory statute. Its activities demonstrate an illegal purpose which is inconsistent with charitable ends. Moreover, the generation of criminal acts increases the burdens of government, thus frustrating a well recognized charitable goal, i.e., relief of the burdens of government. Accordingly, the organization is not operated exclusively for charitable purposes and does not qualify for exemption from Federal income tax under section 501(c)(3) of the Code.

Section 501(c)(4) of the Code describes civic leagues or organizations not organized for profit but operated exclusively for the promotion of social welfare.

Section 1.501(c)(4)–1(a)(2)(i) of the regulations provides that an organization is operated exclusively for the promotion of social welfare if it is primarily engaged in promoting in some way the common good and general welfare of the people of the community. An organization embraced within this section is one which is operated primarily for the purpose of bringing about civic betterments and social improvements.

Illegal activities, which violate the minimum standards of acceptable conduct necessary to the preservation of an orderly society, are contrary to the common good and the general welfare of the people in a community and thus are not permissible means of promoting the social welfare for purposes of section 501(c)(4) of the Code. Accordingly, the organization in this case is not operated exclusively for the promotion of social welfare and does not qualify for exemption from Federal income tax under section 501(c)(4).

Revenue Ruling 78–305

1978–2 Cum.Bull. 172.

Advice has been requested whether the nonprofit organization described below, which otherwise qualifies for exemption from Federal income tax under section 501(c)(3) of the Internal Revenue Code of 1954, is operated exclusively for charitable and educational purposes.

The organization was formed to educate the public about homosexuality in order to foster an understanding and tolerance of homosexuals and their problems. The organization collects factual information relating to the role of homosexual men and women in society and disseminates this information to the public.

The organization presents seminars, forums, and discussion groups, all of which are open to the public. Materials distributed to the public include copies of surveys, summaries of opinion polls, scholarly statements, publications of government agencies, and policy resolutions adopted by educational, medical, scientific, and religious organizations. The organization accumulates factual information through the use of opinion polls and independently compiled statistical data from research groups and clinical organizations. All materials disseminated by the organization contain a full documentation of the facts relied upon to support conclusions contained therein.

The organization does not participate in any political campaign, nor does it attempt to influence legislation. The organization does not advocate or seek to convince individuals that they should or should not be homosexuals.

Section 501(c)(3) of the Code provides for the exemption from federal income tax of organizations organized and operated exclusively for charitable and educational purposes.

Section 1.501(c)(3)–1(d)(3) of the Income Tax Regulations provides in relevant part that the term 'educational' as used in section 501(c)(3) of the Code relates to the instruction of the public on subjects useful to the individual and beneficial to the community. The regulations further provide that an organization may be educational even though it advocates a particular position or viewpoint, so long as it presents a sufficiently full and fair exposition of pertinent facts to permit the public to form an independent opinion or conclusion.

The presentation of seminars, forums, and discussion groups is a recognized method of educating the public. See section 1.501(c)(3)–1(d)(3)(ii) of the regulations. By disseminating information relating to the role of homosexuals in society, the organization is furthering educational purposes by instructing the public on subjects useful to the individual and beneficial to the community. The method used by the organization in disseminating materials is designed to present a full and fair exposition of the facts to enable the public to form an independent opinion or conclusion. The fact that the organization's materials concern possibly controversial topics relating to homosexuality does not bar exemption under section 501(c)(3) of the Code, so long as the organization adheres to the educational methodology guidelines of section 1.501(c)(3)–(1)(d)(3).

Accordingly, the organization is operated exclusively for charitable and educational purposes and thus qualifies for exemption from federal income tax under section 501(c)(3) of the Code.

Big Mama Rag v. United States

United States Court of Appeals, District of Columbia Circuit, 1980.
631 F.2d 1030.

■ MIKVA, CIRCUIT JUDGE:

Plaintiff, Big Mama Rag, Inc. (BMR, Inc.), appeals from the order of the court below granting summary judgment to defendants and upholding the IRS's rejection of plaintiff's application for tax-exempt status. Specifically, BMR, Inc. questions the finding that it is not entitled to tax exemption as an educational or charitable organization under section 501(c)(3) of the Internal Revenue Code, 26 U.S.C. § 501(c)(3) (1976), and Treas. Reg. § 1.501(c)(3)–1(d)(2) & (3) (1959). Appellant also challenges the constitutionality of the regulatory scheme, arguing that it violates the First Amendment and the equal protection component of the Fifth Amendment and that it unconstitutionally conditions tax-exempt status on the waiver of constitutional rights.

Because we find that the definition of "educational" contained in Treas. Reg. § 1.501(c)(3)–1(d)(3) is unconstitutionally vague in violation of the First Amendment, we reverse the order of the court below.

I.   Background

BMR, Inc. is a nonprofit organization with a feminist orientation. Its purpose is "to create a channel of communication for women that would educate and inform them on general issues of concern to them." To this end, it publishes a monthly newspaper, Big Mama Rag (BMR), which prints articles, editorials, calendars of events, and other information of interest to women. BMR, Inc.'s primary activity is the production of that newspaper, but it also devotes a considerable minority of its time to promoting women's rights through workshops, seminars, lectures, a weekly radio program, and a free library.

BMR, Inc. has a predominantly volunteer staff and distributes free approximately 2100 of 2700 copies of Big Mama Rag's monthly issues. Moreover, the organization has severely limited the quantity and type of paid advertising. As the district court found, BMR, Inc. neither makes nor intends to make a profit and is dependent on contributions, grants, and funds raised by benefits for over fifty percent of its income.

Because of its heavy reliance on charitable contributions, BMR, Inc. applied in 1974 for tax-exempt status as a charitable and educational institution. That request was first denied by the IRS District Director in Austin, Texas, on the ground that the organization's newspaper was indistinguishable from an "ordinary commercial publishing practice." After BMR, Inc. filed a protest and a hearing was held in the IRS National Office, the denial of tax-exempt status was affirmed on three separate grounds:

1. the commercial nature of the newspaper; 2. the political and legislative commentary found throughout; and 3. the articles, lectures, editorials, etc., promoting lesbianism.

To enable BMR, Inc. to obtain judicial review of the IRS decision, the IRS District Director issued a final determination letter, which denied tax-exempt status on the grounds that, inter alia, the content of BMR was not educational and the manner of distribution was that of ordinary commercial publishing organizations.[4]

Appellant then brought a declaratory judgment action in the District Court for the District of Columbia. On cross-motions for summary judgment, the judge granted appellees' motion. Although the court rejected appellees' argument that BMR, Inc. was not entitled to tax-exempt status because it was a commercial organization, it agreed that appellant did not satisfy the definitions of "educational" and "charitable" in Treas. Reg. § 1.501(c)(3)–1(d)(2) & (3). The court found no constitutional basis for disturbing the IRS's decision.

II. THE REGULATORY SCHEME

Tax exemptions are granted under section 501(c) of the Internal Revenue Code to a variety of socially useful organizations, including the

---

4. The District Director's reasoning stated in full: The organization in publishing the newspaper is not operated exclusively for educational purposes as required by Code section 501(c)(3) as the content of the publication is not educational, the preparation of the material does not follow methods educational in nature, the distribution of the material is not valuable in achieving an educational purpose and/or the manner in which the distribution is accomplished is not distinguishable from ordinary commercial publishing practices.

charitable and the educational. The Code forbids exemption of an organization if any part of its net earnings inures to the benefit of private persons or if it is an "action organization"—one that attempts to influence legislation or participates in any political campaign. Treasury regulations impose additional requirements: exempt status is accorded only to applicants whose articles of organization limit their activities to furtherance of exempt purposes (the "organizational test") or whose activities are in fact aimed at accomplishment of exempt purposes (the "operational test"). Treas.Reg. § 1.501(c)(3)–1(b) & (c) (1959).

The Treasury regulations also define some of the exempt purposes listed in section 501(c)(3) of the Code, including "charitable" and "educational." The definition of "educational" is the one at issue here: The term "educational," as used in section 501(c)(3), relates to-(a) The instruction or training of the individual for the purpose of improving or developing his capabilities; or (b) The instruction of the public on subjects useful to the individual and beneficial to the community. An organization may be educational even though it advocates a particular position or viewpoint so long as it presents a sufficiently full and fair exposition of the pertinent facts as to permit an individual or the public to form an independent opinion or conclusion. On the other hand, an organization is not educational if its principal function is the mere presentation of unsupported opinion. Treas. Reg. § 1.501(c)(3)–1(d)(3)(i) (1959).

The district court found that BMR, Inc. was not entitled to tax-exempt status because it had "adopted a stance so doctrinaire" that it could not meet the "full and fair exposition" standard articulated in the definition quoted above. Appellant's response is threefold. First, it argues, the "full and fair exposition" hurdle is not applicable at all here because BMR, Inc. is not an organization whose primary activity or principal function is advocacy of change. Second, BMR, Inc. contends that its publication does satisfy the requirements of the "full and fair exposition" standard. Finally, appellant maintains that denial of its application for tax-exempt status on the basis of the "full and fair exposition" standard is unconstitutional for a number of reasons.

Even though tax exemptions are a matter of legislative grace, the denial of which is not usually considered to implicate constitutional values, tax law and constitutional law are not completely distinct entities. In fact, the First Amendment was partly aimed at the so-called "taxes on knowledge," which were intended to limit the circulation of newspapers and therefore the public's opportunity to acquire information about governmental affairs. In light of their experience with such taxes, the framers realized, in the words of Mr. Justice Douglas, that "(t)he power to tax the exercise of a privilege is the power to control or suppress its enjoyment." Murdock v. Pennsylvania, 319 U.S. 105, 112, 63 S.Ct. 870, 874, 87 L.Ed. 1292 (1943). Thus, although First Amendment activities need not be subsidized by the state, the discriminatory denial of tax exemptions can impermissibly infringe free speech. Similarly, regulations authorizing tax exemptions may not be so unclear as to afford latitude for subjective application by IRS officials. We find that the definition of "educational," and in particular its "full and fair exposition" requirement, is so vague as to violate the First Amendment and to defy our attempts to review its application in this case.

III. VAGUENESS ANALYSIS

Vague laws are not tolerated for a number of reasons, and the Supreme Court has fashioned the constitutional standards of specificity with these policies in mind. First, the vagueness doctrine incorporates the idea of notice-informing those subject to the law of its meaning. A law must therefore be struck down if "men of common intelligence must necessarily guess at its meaning."

Second, the doctrine is concerned with providing officials with explicit guidelines in order to avoid arbitrary and discriminatory enforcement. To that end, laws are invalidated if they are "wholly lacking in 'terms susceptible of objective measurement.'"

These standards are especially stringent, and an even greater degree of specificity is required, where, as here, the exercise of First Amendment rights may be chilled by a law of uncertain meaning. Vague laws touching on First Amendment rights, noted the Supreme Court in Baggett, require (those subject to them) to "steer far wider of the unlawful zone," than if the boundaries of the forbidden areas were clearly marked, * * * by restricting their conduct to that which is unquestionably safe. Free speech may not be so inhibited. Measured by any standard, and especially by the strict standard that must be applied when First Amendment rights are involved, the definition of "educational" contained in Treas.Reg. § 1.501(c)(3)–1(d)(3) must fall because of its excessive vagueness.

We do not minimize the difficulty and delicacy of the task delegated to the Treasury by Congress under section 501(c)(3) of the Code. Words such as "religious," "charitable," "literary," and "educational" easily lend themselves to subjective definitions at odds with the constitutional limitations we describe above. Treasury bravely made a pass at defining "educational," but the more parameters it tried to set, the more problems it encountered.

The first portion of the regulation relied upon to deny BMR, Inc.'s request for tax-exempt status measures an applicant organization by whether it provides "instruction of the public on subjects useful to the individual and beneficial to the community." Treas.Reg. § 1.501(c)(3)–1(d)(3)(i)(b) (1959). The district court rejected that test with barely a murmur of disagreement from appellees. That standard, held the court below, "would be far too subjective in its application to pass constitutional muster."

We find similar problems inherent in the "full and fair exposition" test, on which the district court based affirmance of the IRS's denial of tax-exempt status to BMR, Inc. That test lacks the requisite clarity, both in explaining which applicant organizations are subject to the standard and in articulating its substantive requirements.

A.   Who Is Covered by the "Full and Fair Exposition" Test?

According to the terms of the Treasury regulation, only an organization that "advocates a particular position or viewpoint" must clear the "full and fair exposition" hurdle. Appellant maintains that the definition of an advocacy organization is to be found in the preceding subsection of the regulation, which defines the term "charitable": The fact that an organization, in carrying out its primary purpose, advocates social or civic changes or presents opinion on controversial issues with the intention of molding public opinion or creating public sentiment to an acceptance of its views does not preclude such organization from qualifying under section 501(c)(3) so long as it is not an "action" organization of any one of the types described in paragraph (c)(3) of this section. Treas.Reg. § 1.501(c)(3)–1(d)(2) (1959). The district court held that this part of the regulation was designed to cover charitable institutions and that BMR, Inc., an educational rather than a charitable organization, must meet the "full and fair exposition" standard rather than the more lenient "action organization" standard of section 1.501(c)(3)–1(d)(2). Obviously, if BMR, Inc. is an advocacy group and is not a charitable organization, it may not take cover under the "action organization" standard but must instead meet the "full and fair exposition" test.

The initial question, however, is whether or not BMR, Inc. is an advocacy group at all. What appellant turns to Treas. Reg. § 1.501(c)(3)–1(d)(2) for is the definition of "advocacy," not for the appropriate standard to be applied to advocacy organizations seeking tax-exempt status. The district court did not deal with that question, and, indeed, it is difficult to ascertain from the language of the regulation defining "educational" exactly what organizations are intended to be covered by the "full and fair exposition" standard and whether or not the definitions of advocacy groups are the same for both educational and charitable organizations.

The uncertainty of the coverage of the "full and fair exposition" standard is evidenced by its application over the years by the IRS. The Treasury Department's Exempt Organizations Handbook has defined "advocates a particular position" as synonymous with "controversial." Such a gloss clearly cannot withstand First Amendment scrutiny. It gives IRS officials no objective standard by which to judge which applicant organizations are advocacy groups-the evaluation is made solely on the basis of one's subjective notion of what is "controversial." And, in fact, only a very few organizations, whose views are not in the mainstream of political thought, have been deemed advocates and held to the "full and fair exposition" standard. The one tax-exempt homosexual organization cited by the Government as evidence that the IRS does not discriminate on the basis of sexual preference was required to meet the "full and fair exposition" standard even though it admittedly did not "advocate or seek to convince individuals that they should or should not be homosexuals." Rev.Rul. 78–305, 1978–2 C.B. 172, 173.

The Treasury regulation defining "educational" is, therefore, unconstitutionally vague in that it does not clearly indicate which organizations are advocacy groups and thereby subject to the "full and fair exposition" standard. And the latitude for subjectivity afforded by the regulation has seemingly resulted in selective application of the "full and fair exposition" standard-one of the very evils that the vagueness doctrine is designed to prevent.

B.   What Does the "Full and Fair Exposition" Test Require?

The Treasury definition of "educational" may also be challenged on the ground that it fails to articulate with sufficient specificity the requirements of the "full and fair exposition" standard. The language of the regulation gives no aid in interpreting the meaning of the test: An organization may be educational even though it advocates a particular position or viewpoint so long as it presents a sufficiently full and fair exposition of the pertinent facts as to permit an individual or the public to form an independent opinion or conclusion. On the other hand, an organization is not educational if its principal function is the mere presentation of unsupported opinion. Treas.Reg. § 1.501(c)(3)–1(d)(3) (1959). What makes an exposition "full and fair"? Can it be "fair" without being "full"? Which facts are "pertinent"? How does one tell whether an exposition of the pertinent facts is "sufficient * * * to permit an individual or the public to form an independent opinion or conclusion"? And who is to make all of these determinations?

The regulation's vagueness is especially apparent in the last clause quoted above. That portion of the test is expressly based on an individualistic-and therefore necessarily varying and unascertainable-standard: the reactions of members of the public. The Supreme Court has recognized that statutes phrased in terms of individual sensitivities are suspect and susceptible to attack on vagueness grounds. * * *

An additional source of unclarity lies in the relationship between the two sentences comprising the "full and fair exposition" test. Appellant argues that the two should be read as counter–examples—an organization fails to satisfy the test only if "its principal function is the mere presentation of unsupported opinion." The Government, on the other hand, contends that tax-exempt status must be denied BMR, Inc. if a substantial portion of its newspaper consists of unsupported opinion. Again, the language of the regulation does not resolve this issue.[13]

The district court's interpretation of the "full and fair exposition" test, and the one advocated by the Government, is no more precise. The district court found the Treasury regulation "capable of objective application"

---

13. The IRS has adopted a list of specific guidelines to implement the Treasury definition of "educational." But those guidelines use the same conclusory terms as the regulation and are not helpful in clarifying its meaning: An organization * * * may qualify * * * if (1) the content of the publication is educational, (2) the preparation of material follows methods generally accepted as "educational" in character, (3) the distribution of the materials is necessary or valuable in achieving the organization's educational and scientific purposes, and (4) the manner in which the distribution is accomplished is distinguishable from ordinary commercial publishing practices. Rev.Rul. 67–4, 1967–1 C.B. 121, 122; see Rev.Rul. 77–4, 1977–1 C.B. 141.

because "it asks only whether the facts underlying the conclusions are stated." But distinguishing facts, on the one hand, and opinion or conclusion, on the other, does not provide an objective yardstick by which to define "educational." The distinction is not so clear-cut that an organization seeking tax–exempt status—or an IRS official reviewing an application for exemption—will be able to judge when any given statement must be bolstered by another supporting statement.

One of the five examples cited by the Government as evidence of BMR's failure to meet the "full and fair exposition" test may be used to illustrate our point. Most of the article, discussing Susan Saxe's 1975 plea of guilty to charges stemming from a bank robbery in Philadelphia, is simple journalistic reporting. It discusses the terms of the plea bargain, the reaction of local feminists, the differential treatment accorded Saxe supporters and white men who went to observe the pretrial hearing, and police questioning of women in Philadelphia. In return for Saxe's plea, the Government apparently agreed, among other things, to "call off its investigation of the women's and lesbian communities" in the area and not to ask Saxe to testify against "anyone she has known or know (sic) about in the last five years." By forcing Saxe to choose between her own interests and those of other women, the article continues, "the Government has clarified for us, once again, that we, as women, are inextricably bound up with each other in the struggle."

Certainly, the author's viewpoint is not disguised in the last sentence. But is the statement one of fact or opinion? If the latter, is the author's description of the terms of the guilty plea sufficient to inform readers of the basis underlying her opinion? Or is further proof of the existence of "the struggle" necessary? If so, would the article satisfy the "full and fair exposition" test without that final statement? Neither the Treasury regulation nor the proposed fact/opinion distinction is responsive to these questions. And one's answers will likely be colored by one's attitude towards the author's point of view.

The futility of attempting to draw lines between fact and unsupported opinion is further illustrated by the district court's application of that test. The court did not analyze the contents of BMR under its proposed test but merely stated, without further explication, that the publication was not entitled to tax-exempt status because it had "adopted a stance so doctrinaire that it cannot satisfy this standard." Instead of applying the purportedly objective test the court had formulated, it was forced to resolve the case by resorting to the subjective notion of whether the publication was "doctrinaire." We can conceive of no value-free measurement of the extent to which material is doctrinaire, and the district court's reliance on that evaluative concept corroborates for us the impossibility of principled and objective application of the fact/opinion distinction.

Appellees suggest that the Treasury regulation at issue here embodies a related distinction—between appeals to the emotions and appeals to the mind.[16] Material is educational, they argue, if it appeals to the mind, that is, if it reasons to a conclusion from stated facts. Again, the required linedrawing is difficult, a problem which is compounded if the difference between the two relies on the aforementioned fact/opinion distinction.

Moreover, the Treasury regulation does not support such a narrow concept of "educational" and we cannot approve it. Nowhere does the regulation hint that the definition of "educational" is to turn on the fervor of the organization or the strength of its language. As the Supreme Court has recognized in another context, the emotional content of a word is an important component of its message.

An example raised by appellees in their brief and discussed at oral argument is illustrative. The American Cancer Society's cause may be better served by a bumper sticker picturing a skull and crossbones and saying "Smoking rots your lungs" than by one that merely states "Smoking is hazardous to your health." Both are intended to impart the same message, and they are identical in degree of specificity of the underlying facts. Although the first may be said to appeal more to the emotions, and the second to the mind, that distinction should not obscure the similarities between the two. They should be considered equal in educational content.

Even if one could in fact differentiate fact from unsupported opinion, or emotional appeals from appeals to the mind, these proposed distinctions would be inadequate definitions of "educational" because material often combines elements of each. In such cases, appellees suggested at oral argument, a quantitative test would be appropriate. But the Treasury regulation makes no mention of such a test. Even if a quantitative approach were authorized, it is unclear how much of a publication's content would have to be factual, or appeal to the mind, in order to satisfy the "full and fair exposition" standard. Also unanswered is who would apply the test and determine the requisite amount of factual material. Certainly, the Treasury regulation itself gives no clue.[18]

Thus, neither of the distinctions proposed here remedies the imprecise language of the "full and fair exposition" standard or clarifies the requirements imposed by that test.

IV. CONCLUSION

The definition of "educational" contained in Treas.Reg. § 1.501(c)(3)–1(d)(3) lacks sufficient specificity to pass constitutional muster. Its "full

16. The court below also seemed to endorse this distinction: it read the Treasury regulation as requiring that a publication be "sufficiently dispassionate as to provide its readers with the factual basis from which they may draw independent conclusions." One can only speculate how a poetry publication would be classified under such a dichotomy.

18. In addition to advancing the two distinctions discussed above to elucidate the Treasury's definition of "educational," appellees also rely on the notion of onesidedness. They point to BMR's editorial policy of "not print(ing) any material which, by our judgment, does not affirm our struggle." We agree with the court below that the Treasury regulation may not be read to compel an educational organization to "present views inimical to its philosophy."

and fair exposition" standard, on the basis of which the denial of BMR, Inc.'s application for tax exemption was upheld by the court below, is vague both in describing who is subject to that test and in articulating its substantive requirements.

The history of appellant's application for tax-exempt status attests to the vagueness of the "full and fair exposition" test and evidences the evils that the vagueness doctrine is designed to avoid. The district court's decision was based on the value-laden conclusion that BMR was too doctrinaire. Similarly, IRS officials earlier advised appellant's counsel that an exemption could be approved only if the organization "agree(d) to abstain from advocating that homosexuality is a mere preference, orientation, or propensity on par with heterosexuality and which should otherwise be regarded as normal." Whether or not this view represented official IRS policy is irrelevant. It simply highlights the inherent susceptibility to discriminatory enforcement of vague statutory language.

We are sympathetic with the IRS's attempt to safeguard the public fisc by closing revenue loopholes. And we by no means intend to suggest that tax-exempt status must be accorded to every organization claiming an educational mantle. Applications for tax exemption must be evaluated, however, on the basis of criteria capable of neutral application. The standards may not be so imprecise that they afford latitude to individual IRS officials to pass judgment on the content and quality of an applicant's views and goals and therefore to discriminate against those engaged in protected First Amendment activities.

We are not unmindful of the burden involved in reformulating the definition of "educational" to conform to First Amendment requirements. But the difficulty of the task neither lessens its importance nor warrants its avoidance. Objective standards are especially essential in cases such as this involving those espousing nonmajoritarian philosophies. In this area the First Amendment cannot countenance a subjective "I know it when I see it" standard. And neither can we.

This case is accordingly reversed and remanded for further proceedings consistent with this opinion.

Revenue Procedure 86–43

1986–2 Cum.Bull. 729.

SECTION 1. PURPOSE

The purpose of this revenue procedure is to publish the criteria used by the Internal Revenue Service to determine the circumstances under which advocacy of a particular viewpoint or position by an organization is considered educational within the meaning of section 501(c)(3) of the Internal Revenue Code, and within the meaning of section 1.501(c)(3)–1(d)(3) of the Income Tax Regulations.

SECTION 2. BACKGROUND

.01 Section 501(c)(3) of the Code provides for exemption from federal income tax for organizations that are organized and operated exclusively for purposes specified in that section, including educational purposes. Section 1.501(c)(3)–1(d)(3) of the regulations provides that the term "educational" relates to a) the instruction or training of the individual for the purpose of improving or developing his capabilities; or b) the instruction of the public on subjects useful to the individual and beneficial to the community. Under this regulation, an organization may be educational even though it advocates a particular position or viewpoint, so long as it presents a sufficiently full and fair exposition of the pertinent facts as to permit an individual or the public to form an independent opinion or conclusion. On the other hand, an organization is not educational if its principal function is the mere presentation of unsupported opinion.

.02 In applying section 1.501(c)(3)–1(d)(3) of the regulations, the Service has attempted to eliminate or minimize the potential for any public official to impose his or her preconceptions or beliefs in determining whether the particular viewpoint or position is educational. It has been, and it remains, the policy of the Service to maintain a position of disinterested neutrality with respect to the beliefs advocated by an organization. The focus of section 1.501(c)(3)–1(d)(3), and of the Service's application of this regulation, is not upon the viewpoint or position, but instead upon the method used by the organization to communicate its viewpoint or positions to others.

.03 Two recent court decisions have considered challenges to the constitutionality of section 1.501(c)(3)–1(d)(3) of the regulations. One decision held that the regulation was unconstitutionally vague. Big Mama Rag, Inc. v. United States, 631 F. 2d. 1030 (D.C.Cir.1980). However, in National Alliance v. United States, 710 F. 2d 868 (D.C.Cir.1983), the court upheld the Service's position that the organization in question was not educational. Although the latter decision did not reach the question of the constitutionality of section 1.501(c)(3)–1(d)(3), it did note that the methodology test used by the Service when applying the regulation "tend[s] toward ensuring that the educational exemption be restricted to material which substantially helps a reader or listener in a learning process." The court also noted that the application of this test reduced the vagueness found in the earlier Big Mama Rag decision.

.04 The methodology test cited by the court in National Alliance reflects the long-standing Service position that the method used by an organization in advocating its position, rather than the position itself, is the standard for determining whether an organization has educational purposes. This methodology test is set forth in Section 3 of this revenue procedure, and is used in all situations where the educational purposes of an organization that advocates a particular viewpoint or position are in question. Publication of this test represents no change either to existing procedures or to the substantive position of the Service.

SECTION 3. CRITERIA USED TO DETERMINE WHETHER ADVOCACY BY AN ORGANIZATION IS EDUCATIONAL

.01 The Service recognizes that the advocacy of particular viewpoints or positions may serve an educational purpose even if the viewpoints or positions being advocated are unpopular or are not generally accepted.

.02 Although the Service renders no judgment as to the viewpoint or position of the organization, the Service will look to the method used by the organization to develop and present its views. The method used by the organization will not be considered educational if it fails to provide a factual foundation for the viewpoint or position being advocated, or if it fails to provide a development from the relevant facts that would materially aid a listener or reader in a learning process.

.03 The presence of any of the following factors in the presentations made by an organization is indicative that the method used by the organization to advocate its viewpoints or positions is not educational.

1. The presentation of viewpoints or positions unsupported by facts is a significant portion of the organization's communications.

2. The facts that purport to support the viewpoints or positions are distorted.

3. The organization's presentations make substantial use of inflammatory and disparaging terms and express conclusions more on the basis of strong emotional feelings than of objective evaluations.

4. The approach used in the organization's presentations is not aimed at developing an understanding on the part of the intended audience or readership because it does not consider their background or training in the subject matter.

.04 There may be exceptional circumstances, however, where an organization's advocacy may be educational even if one of more of the factors listed in section 3.03 are present. The Service will look to all the facts and circumstances to determine whether an organization may be considered educational despite the presence of one or more of such factors.

SECTION 4. OTHER REQUIREMENTS

Even if the advocacy undertaken by an organization is determined to be educational under the above criteria, the organization must still meet all other requirements for exemption under section 501(c)(3), including the restrictions on influencing legislation and political campaigning contained therein.

NOTES

1. *Hate Groups.* Shortly after deciding *Big Mama Rag*, the D.C. Circuit considered the tax-exempt status of National Alliance, a neo-Nazi organization that sought to arouse in white Americans of European ancestry an understanding of and pride in their racial and cultural heritage.

National Alliance v. United States, 710 F.2d 868 (D.C.Cir.1983). Central themes of National Alliance's principal publication (Attack!) were: non-whites are inferior to white Americans of European ancestry; blacks are aggressively brutal and dangerous; Jews, through their control of the media, cause U.S. policies to be harmful to the interests of whites; and communists are at fault for persuading neo-liberals that integration and equality are desirable. National Alliance called for armed confrontations between the races. Id. at 869–872.

Despite its *Big Mama Rag* precedent, the court upheld the Service's denial of exemption to National Alliance on the ground that it was not "educational." The court found that National Alliance did not rationally develop a point of view and failed to engage in "intellectual exposition." Applying what is best described as "I know it when I see it" jurisprudence, the court concluded that "the National Alliance material is far outside the range Congress could have intended to subsidize in the public interest by granting tax exemption." Id. at 873.

To help cure the constitutional infirmities of the regulations, the Service unveiled the Methodology Test, which later was promulgated as Rev. Proc. 86–43, in the *National Alliance* litigation. While noting that the Methodology Test reduced the vagueness found in *Big Mama Rag*, the court declined to rule whether the constitutional malady had been cured. It need not reach the vagueness issue, the court said, because National Alliance did not qualify as "educational" under any reasonable interpretation of the term. Id.

In The Nationalist Movement v. Commissioner, 102 T.C. 558, aff'd per curiam, 37 F.3d 216 (5th Cir.1994), the Tax Court upheld the constitutionality of the Methodology Test. The Nationalist Movement espoused a pro-majority philosophy. It favored white Americans and skinheads, and opposed foreigners, domestic minorities, Jews, homosexuals, immigrants, the Martin Luther King Day holiday, and Black History Month. The Tax Court found that the Methodology Test was neither aimed at the suppression of ideas nor vague or overbroad on its face, and concluded:

> Its provisions are sufficiently understandable, specific, and objective both to preclude chilling of expression protected under the First Amendment and to minimize arbitrary or discriminatory application by the IRS. The revenue procedure focuses on the method rather than the content of the presentation. In contrast, it was the potential for discriminatory denials of tax exemption based on speech content that caused the Court of Appeals for the District of Columbia Circuit to hold that the vagueness of the "full and fair exposition" standard violates the First Amendment. Petitioner has not persuaded us that either the purpose or the effect of the revenue procedure is to suppress disfavored ideas.

Id. at 588–589.

The Tax Court went on to find that The Nationalist Movement's methodology had failed all four factors because the organization failed to support its viewpoints with facts, distorted the facts, used inflammatory and disparaging terms, and failed to educate its young followers by developing an understanding based on their background and training. Id. at 589–594.

2. *Commerciality, Inurement and Private Benefit.* Many educational organizations, such as museums, theaters and publishers, derive the bulk of their support from admission fees, subscriptions and other revenue–generating activities. Under current exemption standards, it is not inconsistent with "educational" status to raise revenue in this manner, provided that the organization's primary purpose remains educational and its net earnings neither inure to the benefit of insiders nor provide some other form of private benefit. The "commerciality," inurement and private benefit limitations, which are not unique to educational organizations, are considered in Sections D and E of this chapter, infra, at pp. 216–285.

3. *College and University Audit Guidelines.* The IRS has made colleges and universities its second most important audit priority (behind health care organizations). The Service's attitude is reflected in a detailed set of audit guidelines first published in 1992 and finalized in 1994. Revenue agents are instructed to examine a wide range of activities, including financial statements, fringe benefit and retirement plans, scholarships, fundraising solicitations, investments, government–funded research contracts, political activities, college bookstore product lines, and transactions with related entities. See Internal Revenue Service, College and University Examination Guidelines, reprinted in 10 Exempt Org. Tax Rev. 618 (1994). The guidelines suggest that agents should review student newspapers and alumni publications because they may "offer a different perspective" on the operations of the institution. Id. at 343.32 (4) & (5).

4. *Child Care Organizations.* Section 501(k), which was added in 1984, makes it clear that the term "educational" purposes includes providing care for children away from their homes if: (1) substantially all of the care is to enable individuals, such as the child's parents or guardian, to be gainfully employed, and (2) the services provided are available to the general public. Prior to this amendment, the Service sometimes took the position that a child care organization did not qualify for exemption if provided only custodial care without a formal educational program.

5. *For Further Reading.* John D. Colombo, Why is Harvard Tax–Exempt? (And Other Mysteries of Tax Exemption for Private Educational Institutions), 35 Ariz.L.Rev. 841 (1993); Daniel Shaviro, From Big Mama Rag to National Geographic: The Controversy Regarding Exemptions for Educational Publications, 41 Tax L. Rev. 693 (1986); Tommy F. Thompson, The Availability of the Federal Educational Tax Exemption for Propaganda Organizations, 18 U.Cal.Davis L. Rev. 487 (1985).

PROBLEMS

Consider whether the following organizations qualify for exemption under § 501(c)(3):

(a) Students Together for Individual Rights ("STIR"), an organization of law students formed to educate the public about homosexuality in order to promote understanding and tolerance of the gay and lesbian community. STIR presents seminars, forums and discussion groups, and publishes a magazine.

(b) Same as (a), above, except that a principal activity of STIR is to organize demonstrations to protest actions of businesses and government agencies that it considers to be discriminatory against gays and lesbians. Leaders of STIR often urge followers to block traffic, disrupt the activities of targeted businesses, and engage in other acts of civil disobedience.

(c) The Heredity Research Fund, an educational organization founded by a group of prominent scientists to conduct research in the area of "racial betterment" and to award grants to universities and other foundations for heredity research. The Fund specializes in research on "eugenics," a movement devoted to improving the human species through control of heredity factors in mating. Several major recipients of Heredity Research Fund grants have espoused the theory that whites are inherently more intelligent than blacks and have used their funds to conduct seminars on the subject.

(d) Right to Life, Inc., a nonprofit educational organization that sponsors forums, lectures and other programs dealing with abortions and pro–life alternatives. Its goals are to educate the public on the rights of the unborn. Assume that the organization does not violate the limitations on lobbying or political campaigning in § 501(c)(3) but does engage in frequent picketing and demonstrations near clinics that perform abortions.

(e) Family Planning Alternatives, an organization that provides free counseling to women on methods of avoiding unwanted pregnancies and operates an abortion clinic.

6.   RELIGIOUS ORGANIZATIONS

Since colonial times in America, and long before then in other cultures, churches and other religious organizations have enjoyed exemption from income and property taxes. Section 501(c)(3) is faithful to that tradition by granting exempt status to organizations organized and operated for "religious purposes," a category that is not limited to traditional houses of worship. Religious exemptions extend to book publishers, broadcasters, organizations conducting genealogical research, and burial societies. The exempt purposes listed in § 501(c)(3) also are not mutually exclusive. A separately incorporated parochial school may be both "religious" and "educational," and many typical "charitable" activities may be under the control or sponsorship of a particular religion or church.

Although religious tax exemptions are firmly rooted in American law and tradition, they have engendered an ongoing controversy. For a time, the debate centered on whether religious tax exemptions were constitutional. The Supreme Court settled that issue in Walz v. Tax Commission, 397 U.S. 664, 90 S.Ct. 1409 (1970), when it held that the Establishment Clause of the First Amendment was not violated by an exemption from property taxation for land and buildings owned by churches and used solely for religious worship. In upholding a New York statute that also exempted property owned by charitable, educational and other nonprofit organizations, the Court declined to justify religious tax exemptions on the social welfare services or "good works" performed by many churches. It reasoned that to emphasize so variable an aspect of the work of religious bodies would introduce an intrusive element of governmental evaluation that would undermine the constitutional policy of neutrality. The Court characterized property tax exemptions as the product of a "benevolent neutrality" that neither advanced nor inhibited religion and created only a minimal and remote "entanglement" between church and state. Although *Walz* involved a state property tax exemption, the Court suggested that the tax benefits provided by the Internal Revenue Code similarly were immune from a First Amendment challenge, but it declined to rule that religious tax exemptions were constitutionally required.

Highly sensitive questions arise when a governmental taxing authority attempts to deny exempt status to an organization that claims to be "religious" or a "church." The vast panoply of beliefs in the United States makes this definitional task inordinately delicate, which may explain why definitions of "religious purpose" or "church" are conspicuously absent from the regulations. Recognizing the constitutional difficulties that would be presented by a narrow definition, the Internal Revenue Service has advised its revenue agents to interpret "religion" broadly, encompassing even those sects that do not believe in a Supreme Being. This reluctance to define religion is necessitated by constitutional constraints. In United States v. Ballard, which involved the mail fraud prosecution of the leader of a sect who claimed to be a divine messenger with supernatural powers, the Supreme Court admonished fact finders to avoid entering the definitional quagmire:

> Man's relation to his God was made no concern of the state. He was granted the right to worship as he pleased and to answer to no man for the verity of his religious views. The religious views espoused by respondents might seem incredible, if not preposterous, to most people. But if those doctrines are subject to trial before a jury charged with finding their truth or falsity, then the same can be done with the religious beliefs of any sect. When the triers of fact undertake that task, they enter a forbidden domain.

322 U.S. 78, 87, 64 S.Ct. 882, 886 (1944).

As demonstrated by the following materials, the courts generally have avoided making value judgments on the bona fides of a religious organization except in the most egregious cases.

Holy Spirit Association v. Tax Commission

New York Court of Appeals, 1982.
55 N.Y.2d 512, 450 N.Y.S.2d 292, 435 N.E.2d 662.

■ Jones, Judge:

[This case, which involved a real property tax exemption, illustrates the difficulty of denying a governmental benefit to a "controversial" religious group. The Internal Revenue Service never litigated the question of the Unification Church's federal tax–exempt status, but it did succeed in convicting the church's leader, Reverend Sun Myung Moon, of criminal tax fraud. See United States v. Sun Myung Moon, 718 F.2d 1210 (2d Cir.1983), cert. denied, 466 U.S. 971, 104 S.Ct. 2344 (1984). Eds.]

OPINION OF THE COURT

In determining whether a particular ecclesiastical body has been organized and is conducted exclusively for religious purposes, the courts may not inquire into or classify the content of the doctrine, dogmas, and teachings held by that body to be integral to its religion but must accept that body's characterization of its own beliefs and activities and those of its adherents, so long as that characterization is made in good faith and is not sham. On this principle it must be concluded that the Unification Church has religion as its "primary" purpose inasmuch as much of its doctrine, dogmas, and teachings and a significant part of its activities are recognized as religious, and in good faith it classifies as religious the beliefs and activities which the Tax Commission (Commission) and the court below have described as political and economic.

The Holy Spirit Association for the Unification of World Christianity (the Church) is one of more than 120 national Unification Churches throughout the world propagating a common religious message under the spiritual guidance of the Reverend Sun Myung Moon, the Unification movement's founder and prophet. The Church was organized as a California nonprofit corporation in 1961, and since 1975 has maintained its headquarters in New York City.

In March, 1976 the Church applied to the Tax Commission of the City of New York under section 421 (subd. 1, par. [a])of the New York Real Property Tax Law[1] for exemption from real property taxes for the tax year beginning July 1, 1976 of three properties title to which it had acquired in 1975. The three properties are: the Church headquarters, located at 4 West 43rd Street in the Borough of Manhattan; the missionary residence, located at 305 West 107th Street in Manhattan; and the maintenance and storage facility, located at 38–38 Ninth Street in the Borough of Queens. Following

---

1. New York Real Property Tax Law (§ 421): "1. (a) Real property owned by a corporation or association organized or conducted exclusively for religious, charitable, hospital, educational, moral or mental improvement of men, women or children or cemetery purposes, or for two or more such purposes, and used exclusively for carrying out thereupon one or more of such purposes either by the owning corporation or association or by another such corporation or association as hereinafter provided shall be exempt from taxation as provided in this section."

hearings, the Tax Commission on September 21, 1977, by a vote of 4 to 3 denied the application. The majority concluded that, "although the applicant association does in certain respects bespeak of a religious association, it is in our opinion so threaded with political motives that it requires us to deny its application." Having concluded that the Church was not organized or conducted exclusively for religious purposes, the majority of the Commission had no occasion to consider whether the three properties were used exclusively for religious purposes. The dissenting members of the Tax Commission, explicitly declining to judge the validity or content of the religious beliefs of the Church or its adherents or to submit the Church's theology to analysis, concluded that the Church was organized exclusively for religious purposes and that the three properties in question were used exclusively for statutory purposes. The dissenters would therefore have granted the application.

[After reviewing a report of a Special Referee, the Appellate Division of the New York Supreme Court upheld the denial of the exemption because the Church was "inextricably interwoven with political motives and activities as to warrant denial of tax exemption." Eds.]

It is appropriate at the threshold to delineate our holding in this case—to make explicit what we are not as well as what we are called on to decide. We are not called on to determine whether the Church has any real religious purpose or whether any of its doctrine, dogmas, and teachings constitute a religion. In this case it is recognized that at least many of the beliefs and a significant part of the activities of the Church are religious and that the Unification movement at least in part is a religion. The determination of the Tax Commission, the report of the Special Referee, the opinion at the Appellate Division and now the arguments of the Tax Commission in our court all, at least implicitly, accept this proposition.

The issue that we confront is a narrower one—is the Church, many of whose beliefs and activities are religious, organized and conducted primarily[2] for religious purposes within the contemplation of section 421 (subd. 1, par. [a])? This, as understood by the Tax Commission and the Appellate Division, turns on whether the Church is engaged in so many or such significant nonreligious activities as to warrant the conclusion that its purpose is not primarily religious. More specifically the issue is whether the activities which have been found to be "political" and "economic" are for the purposes of that statute to be classified as secular rather than religious.

When, as here, particular purposes and activities of a religious organization are claimed to be other than religious, the civil authorities may engage in but two inquiries: Does the religious organization assert that the challenged purposes and activities are religious, and is that assertion bona fide? Neither the courts nor the administrative agencies of the State or its subdivisions may go behind the declared content of religious beliefs any

---

2. The statute uses the adverb "exclusively", but we have held that it connotes "principally" or "primarily" (Matter of Association of Bar of City of N.Y. v. Lewisohn, 34 N.Y.2d 143, 153, 356 N.Y.S.2d 555, 313 N.E.2d 30).

more than they may examine into their validity. This principle was firmly established in Watson v. Jones, 13 Wall. [80 U.S.] 679, 728, 20 L.Ed. 666, when the Supreme Court declared that "[t]he law knows no heresy, and is committed to the support of no dogma, the establishment of no sect." That court again condemned the judicial pursuit of any such investigation in Board of Educ. v. Barnette, 319 U.S. 624, 640–642, 63 S.Ct. 1178, 1186–1187, 87 L.Ed. 1628, n. omitted:

> Struggles to coerce uniformity of sentiment in support of some end thought essential to their time and country have been waged by many good as well as by evil men * * * As first and moderate methods to attain unity have failed, those bent on its accomplishment must resort to an ever–increasing severity. As governmental pressure toward unity becomes greater, so strife becomes more bitter as to whose unity it shall be * * * Ultimate futility of such attempts to compel coherence is the lesson of every such effort from the Roman drive to stamp out Christianity as a disturber of its pagan unity [to] the Inquisition, as a means to religious and dynastic unity * * *. Compulsory unification of opinion achieves only the unanimity of the graveyard.

> It seems trite but necessary to say that the First Amendment to our Constitution was designed to avoid these ends by avoiding these beginnings * * *.

> If there is any fixed star in our constitutional constellation, it is that no official, high or petty, can prescribe what shall be orthodox in politics, nationalism, religion, or other matters of opinion * * * If there are any circumstances which permit an exception, they do not now occur to us. The articulation of the Supreme Court in foreclosing judicial inquiry into the truth or falsity of religious beliefs is equally applicable to judicial inquiry as to the content of religious beliefs.

> Freedom of thought, which includes freedom of religious belief, is basic in a society of free men. * * * It embraces the right to maintain theories of life and of death and of the hereafter which are rank heresy to the followers of the orthodox faiths. Heresy trials are foreign to our Constitution. Men may believe what they cannot prove. They may not be put to the proof of their religious doctrines or beliefs * * * Many take their gospel from the New Testament. But it would hardly be supposed that they could be tried before a jury charged with the duty of determining whether those teachings contained false representations * * * The religious views espoused by respondents might seem incredible, if not preposterous, to most people. But if these doctrines are subject to trial before a jury charged with finding their truth or falsity, then the same can be done with the religious beliefs of any sect. When the triers of fact undertake that task, they enter a forbidden domain. * * *

The reliance by the Tax Commission and by the Appellate Division on Christian Echoes Nat. Ministry v. United States, 10th Cir., 470 F.2d 849 as authority for their examination and consequent characterization of the activities of the Church is misplaced (aside from whether the holding in that case has been subsequently eroded). The issue in that case was the entitlement of a religious organization to tax exemption under the Internal Revenue Code. The statute there involved [§ 501(c)(3)] in effect deprived a religious organization which would otherwise be tax exempt of that exemption if a substantial part of its activities was carrying on propaganda or otherwise attempting to influence legislation or if it participated in political campaigns on behalf of candidates for public office. We are not here concerned with whether the Legislature has authority, should it choose to do so, to deny exemption to an organization whose purpose is primarily religious but which as part of its religious program devotes a substantial portion of its activities to political objectives. It suffices for our present purposes to note that section 421 (subd. 1, par. [a])includes no such provision.[3]

We turn then to the first avenue of inquiry allowed us, namely, whether the Church asserts that its religious doctrine and teachings embrace the challenged activities. We quote the statement with respect to the history and doctrine, dogmas and teachings of the Church from the brief of the Church in our court (without its footnote references to sources in the record).

> The Unification movement has its origins in Korea as one of the host of revivalist Christian religions that flourished there in the aftermath of the forty–year Japanese occupation (1905–1945), during which Korean religions were suppressed. Common to many of these new, patriotic religions was the theme of Korea as the modern Holy Land, birthplace of the new Messiah. This theme likewise animates the religion founded by the Reverend Moon.

> Unification theology is based on the teachings of the Old and New Testaments as clarified by revelations held to have been received by the Reverend Moon directly from Jesus Christ beginning in 1936, and subsequently recorded by his followers in the book Divine Principle. Central to Divine Principle is the millenialist conviction that the time has come for the forces of God to reclaim the earth from the forces of Satan, and to restore "the Kingdom of God on earth."

> According to Unification theology, the "great promise of Christianity" is "the return of Christ"—"not as a visiting God but as a sinless man"—to complete the work Jesus began 2,000 years ago. Unification faith holds that "when Jesus came he was the Messiah," the perfect image of God. Through the Resurrection, the Church believes, Jesus

---

3. Nor are we here concerned with cases (quotations from which are relied on by the Tax Commission), relating to the authority of the State in the employment of its police power to regulate or restrict the exercise of what are concededly religious principles, in which the courts deny the right of the religious group to be final arbiter of the issue (e.g., Wisconsin v. Yoder, 406 U.S. 205, 92 S.Ct. 1526, 32 L.Ed.2d 15 [holding Wisconsin's compulsory school–attendance law unconstitutional as applied to members of the Amish religion because contrary to their religious beliefs]; United States v. Seeger, 380 U.S. 163, 85 S.Ct. 850, 13 L.Ed.2d 733 [upholding claims by conscientious objectors to exemption from universal military service]).

brought "spiritual salvation," but the physical institutions of this world—beginning with the family—remained unredeemed; in the Church's view, it is for the new Messiah to restore a Bride and establish the True Family serving as the foundation for ending "the existence of evil in the world," and to accomplish "not only spiritual but also physical" salvation for mankind. Adherents of the Unification faith look to the Reverend Moon to accomplish this task.

In Unification doctrine, every temporal sphere—political, cultural, and economic—is a battleground for the forces of God and the forces of Satan. God–denying Communism is deemed a singularly potent evil, threatening to overwhelm the forces of God just as Cain overwhelmed Abel; the division between North and South Korea is seen as a central providential instance of the struggle between the sons of Adam. Other temporal controversies also assume crucial spiritual significance in Unification theology.

Committed to the view that men and women need no "mediator between themselves and God," Unification faith makes no provision for a "priestly class." All members of the Church, for example, are qualified to conduct prayer services and other religious activities. Church members fall into two categories—some 7,000 members, serving the Church full–time, are engaged in some combination of evangelical, educational, pastoral, and fund–raising activities, and rely upon the Church or local Church units to meet their material needs; the remaining 30,000 members accept the tenets of the Church as their faith but devote less than full–time efforts to the Church. Representing a movement that proclaims an urgent millenialist gospel, the Church appeals primarily, but not exclusively, to the young.

There can be no doubt on the record before us that the Church has amply demonstrated that it does indeed assert that those beliefs and activities which the Tax Commission and the Appellate Division have found to be political and economic are of the essence of its religious doctrine and program. This has been the finding at every stage of this matter. The Special Referee reported that "the petitioner's theological doctrines bind petitioner to a course of political activism," that "petitioner believes that the physical world consisting of science and economics as well as the spiritual world consisting of religion have developed in accordance with 'God's providence' and that 'religion and economy relate to social life through politics'," that "it is petitioner's religious tenet that the republican form of government with separate or coequal powers held by the legislative, judicial and executive branches of government is a Satanic principle and that these three governmental branches under the present political system must be brought under a single controlling force as a condition for the second coming of the Messiah;" that "according to the Divine Principle, the forces of Satan must be subdued and Korea unified under the type of political environment where religions and science are unified in order to make the world ready for the second coming of the Messiah;" and that "it also appears that petitioner is opposed to the constitutionally mandated separation of church and State." Following a recital of illustrative examples of "political" activities, the report continues, "The petitioner's involvement in these political activities is not an escalated mobilization in behalf of a political cause. Each activity is consistent with the expression of political motives set forth in the Divine Principle and is part of an over-all plan and it is petitioner's deployment of its cadre and administrators for these activities that mark its involvement in political causes". "One of the principal tenets advanced in the Divine Principle is that there be complete integration of all economic, social and religious activities."

The Appellate Division described the referee as reporting, "that petitioner's primary purpose is religious, but that petitioner's theology, as expressed in Reverend Moon's writings binds it to a course of political activity." * * * That court itself concluded that "religious and nonreligious themes are inextricably intertwined in the doctrine", and that, "[t]herefore, despite the religious content of the doctrine, and the leitmotif of religion with which the eclectic teachings are tinged, the doctrine, to the extent that it analyzes and instructs on politics and economics has substantial secular elements." * * *

We conclude that it has been sufficiently demonstrated that what have been characterized below as political and economic beliefs and activities are in the view of the Church integral aspects of its religious doctrine and program.

We turn then to the second avenue of our restricted inquiry. No serious question can be raised on the record before us that the Church has demonstrated the sincerity and the bona fides of its assertions that in its view the political beliefs and activities of the Church and its members and the efforts which they devote to fund raising and recruitment are at the core of its religious beliefs. The Tax Commission found that the Church "does in certain aspects bespeak of a religious association"; the Special Referee reported that the Church's "primary purpose is religious" and that "it is religious in nature and nothing contained in this report should be considered as constituting a comment on the sincerity or lack of sincerity with which any members of [the Church] practices his faith." The Appellate Division concluded "that one of [the Church's] purposes is religious." We do not confront in this case an organization every aspect of whose claim to being religious is challenged, and whose bona fides might accordingly be said to be suspect.

The error of the majority of the Tax Commission, of the Special Referee and of the majority at the Appellate Division is that each asserted the right of civil authorities to examine the creed and theology of the Church and to factor out what in its or his considered judgment are the peripheral political and economic aspects, in contradistinction to what was acknowledged to be the essentially religious component. Each then took the view that beliefs and activities which could be objectively and accurately described by knowledgeable outsiders as "political" and "economic" were by that fact precluded from being classified as "religious."[6]

As stated, it is not the province of civil authorities to indulge in such distillation as to what is to be denominated religious and what political or economic. It is for religious bodies themselves, rather than the courts or administrative agencies, to define, by their teachings and activities, what their religion is. The courts are obliged to accept such characterization of the activities of such bodies, including that of the Church in the case before us, unless it is found to be insincere or sham.

Applying this principle, we conclude that on the record before us, as a matter of law, the primary purpose of the Church (much of whose doctrine, dogmas and teachings and a significant part of whose activities are recognized as religious) is religious and that the determination of the Tax Commission to the contrary is both arbitrary and capricious and affected by error of law.

Determinations with respect to the use to which each of the three individual properties is put, however, cannot be made as a matter of law. Accordingly, inasmuch as such determinations should be made in the first instance by the Tax Commission rather than by the courts, the case must be remitted to Supreme Court with directions to it to remand to the Tax Commission to make determination as to the use of each of the three properties in conformity with the views expressed in this opinion.

For the reasons stated, the judgment of the Appellate Division should be reversed, without costs, and the case remitted to Supreme Court for further remand in accordance with this opinion. * * *

General Counsel Memorandum 36993

February 3, 1977.

[A General Counsel Memorandum ("GCM") is a legal memorandum prepared by the Chief Counsel's office of the Internal Revenue Service. Although a GCM does not have the force of law and is not as authoritative as a treasury regulation or published revenue ruling, it reflects the IRS National Office's legal position on the issue under scrutiny and offers guidance in areas where there are no applicable regulations or rulings. This

---

6. If such categorization were to be undertaken we note that substantial arguments are advanced that traditional theology has always mandated religious action in social, political and economic matters. Numerous illustrations are cited of essentially religious concern and activity in areas of political and economic action in Judeo–Christian history. The point is made that virtually all of the recognized religions and denominations in America today address political and economic issues within their basic theology. (See, e.g., the briefs of the amici curiae filed in support of the position of the Church on this appeal: American Civil Liberties Union and New York Civil Liberties Union; American Jewish Congress; The Catholic League for Religion and Civil Rights; The National Association of Evangelicals, and The Center for Law and Religious Freedom of the Christian Legal Society; and National Council of Churches of Christ in the U.S.A., and New York State Council of Churches.) As reiterated, however, it is not for the courts to make judgments with reference to these substantive matters.

GCM addressed the provocative question of whether a witch's coven qualifies as a "religious organization" for purposes of § 501(c)(3) and a "church" for purposes of § 170(b)(1)(A)(i). Eds.]

* * *

FACTS

The * * * [in a GCM, the Service deletes the name of the taxpayer and certain other confidential material to maintain privacy, Eds.] was incorporated under the laws of * * * on * * * as a nonprofit religious organization. The purpose of the organization is to promote the * * * religion and the worship of deities recognized by the * * * to train priests, priestesses and other leaders of the * * * religion and to instruct members of the religious association in the history, philosophy and all other components of the stated religion. Members of the organization consider themselves to be pagans engaged in the practice of witchcraft. The organization has published a pagan manifesto, which sets forth standards of behavior for its followers. In the manifesto the members are urged to live according to the laws of nature. Judging by the available information these beliefs are sincerely held and there is no evidence in the file that the organization engages in activities that violate any laws or contravene any clearly defined public policy or policies.

The organization holds weekly services following a set ritual. There are also seasonal festivals and marriage ceremonies. The file does not show whether these ceremonies are recognized as valid marriages under applicable state laws. The organization's members worship "the horned god", but it is specifically alleged that this horned god is not the devil. Magic, healing and clairvoyance are practiced and certain animals and plants are sacred to the organization's members.

ANALYSIS

1. Code § 501(c)(3) provides that organizations organized and operated exclusively for religious, charitable and educational purposes, no part of the net earnings of which inure to the benefit of any private shareholder or individuals, are exempt under Code 501(a).

The First Amendment to the United States Constitution provides that Congress is forbidden from enacting any "law respecting an establishment of religion, or prohibiting the free exercise thereof * * *."

There are various definitions of "pagan" and "paganism" to be found in dictionaries. One definition of a "pagan" is "an irreligious person." A more frequently found definition, perhaps, is that a "pagan" is a "follower of a polytheistic religion." In the instant case the primary issue is whether the organization, whose members consider themselves to be "pagans engaged in the practice of witchcraft," may be said to be "religious" as that term is used in Code § 501(c)(3). By the preponderance of dictionary definitions, the beliefs professed by the * * * would qualify as "religious beliefs."

An analysis of the First Amendment to the Constitution of the United States indicates that it is logically impossible to define "religion". It appears that the two religious clauses of the First Amendment define "religious freedom" but do not establish a definition of "religion" within recognized parameters. An attempt to define religion, even for purposes of statutory construction, violates the "establishment" clause since it necessarily delineates and, therefore, limits what can and cannot be a religion. The judicial system has struggled with this philosophic problem throughout the years in a variety of contexts.

In Reynolds v. United States, 98 U.S. 145 (1878), the issue of the constitutionality of a law passed by Congress making the practice of polygamy by persons residing in United States Territories a criminal act was before the Supreme Court. The Court interpreted the constitutional prohibition in this way: "Congress was deprived of all legislative power over mere opinion, but was left free to reach actions which were in violation of social duties or subversive of good order." 98 U.S. at 164. Thus, finding that for some 100 years polygamy had been considered an offense against society in all the states of the union, the Court held that the statute under consideration was constitutional and valid as prescribing a rule of action for all those residing in the territories. In holding that religious belief did not except persons from operation of the statute, the Court said: " * * * while they [laws] cannot interfere with mere religious belief and opinions, they may with practices." Id. at 166. In Cantwell v. Connecticut, 310 U.S. 296 (1940), the Court endorsed Reynolds, stating " * * * the [First] Amendment embraces two concepts, freedom to believe and freedom to act. The first is absolute but, in the nature of things, the second cannot be." 310 U.S. at 303–4. See also Davis v. Beason, 133 U.S. 333, 10 S.Ct. 299, 33 L.Ed. 637 (1890) and Mormon Church v. United States, 136 U.S. 1 (1890) where the Court grappled with the same issue. While continuing to affirm the right of freedom of religious belief, the Court nevertheless held that legislation for the punishment of acts "inimical to the peace, good order and morals of society" did not violate the First Amendment.

In the last three decades the Court continued to struggle for a definition of "religion." [The GCM then discusses a line of cases, none in the tax area, in which the Supreme Court declined to define religion or determine the truth of religious beliefs. Eds.]

* * *

We have concluded that the proper rule as reflected by the above cases is that in the absence of a clear showing that the beliefs or doctrines under consideration are not sincerely held by those professing or claiming them as a religion, the Service cannot question the "religious" nature of those beliefs. This rule has been uniformly followed by the Tax Court in examining organizations claiming tax exemption as religious organizations.

In the early case of Unity School of Christianity, 4 B.T.A. 61 (1926), the Board set the tenor for later Tax Court cases when it stated: Religion is not confined to a sect or ritual. The symbols of religion to one are anathema to another. What one may regard as charity another may scorn as foolish waste. * * * Congress left open the door of tax exemption to all corporations meeting the test, the restrictions not being as to the specie of religion, charity, science or education under which they might operate, but as to the use of its profits and the exclusive purpose of its existence.

Some twelve years after the Supreme Court looked at the "I AM" movement in United States v. Ballard, supra, the movement was before the Tax Court. In Saint Germain Foundation, 26 T.C. 648 (1956), the Commissioner had revoked the exemption of taxpayer on the basis of inurement. With respect to the characterization of the organization as religious, the court noted that the Commissioner's revocation of exemption was not on the ground that taxpayer lacked the necessary religious character. The court then quoted the above excerpt from Unity School and concluded that the evidence established that the organization was organized exclusively for religious purposes.

The rule was again followed in A. A. Allen Revivals, Inc., 22 CCH Tax Ct. Mem. 1435 (1963) where the Tax Court held that under the First Amendment to the Constitution, the decisions of the Supreme Court of the United States and prior decisions of the Tax Court, it was "not free to distinguish between or to approve or disapprove of one form or expression of religious faith."

Thus, when examining an organization claiming a religious character such as the organization in the instant case, the primary rule as to religiosity is whether the organization's adherents are sincere in their beliefs. If that question is resolved affirmatively, the rule of Unity School becomes applicable to test the use of the profits of the organization and the exclusive purposes of its existence.

In addition to the foregoing tests, an organization must conform to basic principles of charity law to qualify for recognition of exemption under Code § 501(c)(3). Thus, for example, its organizational documents cannot authorize it to engage, nor can it engage, in activities that are illegal or contrary to clearly defined public policy. See Restatement (Second), Trusts § 377 (1959); IV A. Scott, The Law of Trusts § 377 (3d ed. 1967).

Applying the above rules to this case, we have concluded on the basis of the evidence available in the administrative file that the organization's members are sincere in their beliefs, the organization is organized and operated exclusively for the claimed purposes, and there is no evidence that its organizational documents authorize it to engage in, or that it in fact engages in, activities that are illegal or contrary to any clearly defined public policy. Accordingly, and on the assumption that it otherwise qualifies, we see no reason to disagree with your proposed conclusion that the organization qualifies for recognition of exemption under Code § 501(c)(3) as a religious organization.

2. The Service has previously considered whether a particular organization constituted a "church." In Rev. Rul. 59–129, 1959–1 C.B. 58 , the * * * was held to be a church within the meaning of Code § 170(b)(1)(A).

In connection with this ruling, it was observed that the * * * had (1) a distinct legal existence; (2) a recognized creed and form of worship; (3) a definite and distinct ecclesiastical government; (4) a formal code of doctrine and discipline; (5) a distinct religious history; (6) a membership not associated with any church or denomination; (7) a complete organization of ordained ministers ministering to their congregations; (8) ordained ministers selected after completing prescribed courses of study; (9) a literature of its own; (10) established places of worship; (11) regular congregations; (12) regular religious services; (13) Sunday Schools for the religious instruction of the young; and (14) schools for the preparation of its ministers. Rev. Rul. 59–129 was published in digest form and did not set forth these characteristics. These characteristics normally would be attributed to a "church" in the commonly accepted meaning of that term. In view of the fact that "church" is not defined in the Code or regulations, the above criteria are useful in determining whether, on balance, a particular religious organization, if tax–exempt, constitutes a "church." The determination is necessarily one of fact and must be made on a case by case basis.

Since it is doubtful that an organization need have all of the above characteristics in order to constitute a "church", it is helpful to examine the few court decisions relevant to this issue in order to ascertain which characteristics have been emphasized.

In Vaughn v. Chapman, 48 T.C. 358 (1967), the court was called upon to determine, inter alia, whether a religious and charitable organization was a "church" within the meaning of Code § 170(b)(1)(A)(i). The organization was interdenominational and was not affiliated with any church group or denomination. The purpose of the organization was twofold: (1) to perform dental work for missionaries, religious workers, and natives, and (2) to promote " * * * the Gospel of the Lord Jesus Christ, around the world, and the evangelization of the world on the basis of the principles of the Protestant Faith."

The organization conducted regular services in the United literature. The members of the organization were all trained in the Bible and church work. While many of its members were ordained ministers, the organization did not conduct a seminary or Bible School. All members were required to be licensed dentists.

The court, after examining the legislative history of Code § 170(b), determined that a more limited concept was intended for the term "church" than that denoted by the term "religious organization." The court stated that Congress did not intend "church" to be used in a generic or universal sense but rather in the sense of a "denomination" or "sect". The court added that a group need not necessarily have an organizational hierarchy or maintain church buildings to constitute a "church."

In holding that the organization was not a church, the court emphasized that (1) the organization's individual members maintained their affiliation with various churches; (2) the organization was interdenominational and did not seek converts to the principles of christianity generally; (3) the organization did not ordain its own ministers; and (4) the conducting of religious services by its members was not conclusive per se that the organization was a church.

In Christian Echoes National Ministry, Inc. v. United States, * * * the United States sought to revoke the Code § 501(c)(3) exempt status of a religious organization. The organization was founded and administered by an ordained minister of the Gospel of Jesus Christ. Other ordained ministers staffed the organization and were empowered to perform all sacerdotal functions on its behalf. The organization conducted numerous religious revivals in various churches throughout the United States sponsored by local congregations, and it also held regular Sunday services in Tulsa, Oklahoma. It conducted annual conventions, leadership schools, and summer sessions for the young. In upholding the organization's tax–exempt status, the [district] court concluded that [p]laintiff's organization and structure, its practices and precepts, and activities provide all the necessary elements of a "church" in the ordinary acceptance of the term and as used in the Internal Revenue Code of 1954, its amendments and applicable regulations. Plaintiff's followers together with its ordained pastors clearly constitute a congregation the same as any local church. [The court of appeals, however, upheld the revocation of Christian Echoes § 501(c)(3) exemption. Its decision was based on the organization's substantial lobbying and political campaign activities. See Section F2 of this chapter, infra, at pp. 289–297. Eds.]

In De La Salle Institute v. United States, 195 F.Supp. 891 (N.D.Cal. 1961), the court employed a "common sense" approach in determining whether a particular organization constituted a church for purposes of Code § 511: To exempt churches, one must know what a church is. Congress must either define "church" or leave the definition to the common meaning and usage of the word; otherwise, Congress would be unable to exempt churches. The court held in that case that an incorporated religious teaching order that performs no sacerdotal functions is not a church, and the income derived by the order from the ownership and operation of a separately incorporated winery is not the income of a church, notwithstanding that both corporations were formed under church auspices.

In comparing the rationale of *Chapman*, *Christian Echoes*, and *De La Salle* to the Salvation Army characteristics underlying Rev. Rul. 59–129, it is evident that some of these characteristics have been considered more significant than others. Thus, *Chapman*, in equating "church" with denomination, stresses both the fact that the organization did not seek to attract individuals into the ranks of its membership and the fact that its members were also members of other church denominations. The court did not, on the other hand, believe that it was necessary to have a church hierarchy or church building. *Christian Echoes*, in a similar approach, emphasized that the religious organization in question had an established congregation ministered to by ordained ministers. The *De La Salle* court, rather than commenting on what a church is, analyzed the issue from the opposite point of view: what a church is not, i.e., it is not a separately incorporated teaching order that performs no sacerdotal functions, or the order's separately incorporated winery.

In the instant case the organization seeks to attract individuals into its ranks and to be accepted such individuals need not abandon their affiliation with other churches. Notwithstanding the nonabandonment factor, we have concluded that it represents a "denomination" within the *Chapman* rationale. Under the facts presented, it has trained priests and priestesses to minister to an established congregation and thus satisfies the *Christian Echoes* requirements.

Application of the other criteria underlying Rev. Rul. 59–129 to the * * * shows the following: (1) It has incorporated and has a distinct legal existence. (2) It has a recognized creed entitled "pagan manifesto" and a distinct form of worship, both unique. (3) It has a definite ecclesiastical government headed by an individual entitled "elder." (4) It has a code of doctrine and discipline. (5) It has adopted the history relating to Welsh mythology. (6) It alleges it has a complete organization with trained priests who have completed prescribed courses of study. (7) It has a vast bulk of literature relating to paganism. (8) It at the present time neither owns or leases property, however it alleges it carries on regular services. (9) It has no separate organization for the religious instruction of the young.

In addition to the above criteria it may be helpful to evaluate this organization in the light of a draft of proposed regulations defining a church for purposes of Code § 170(b)(1)(A) that was prepared, (but never issued as a notice of proposed rule–making), in 1974 * * * .

The draft provides in part: (a) Church or a convention or association of churches. A church or convention or association of churches as described in section 170(b)(1)(A)(i) if it is an organization of individuals having commonly held religious beliefs, engaged solely in religious activities in furtherance of such beliefs. The activities of the organization must include the conduct of religious worship and the celebration of life cycle events such as births, deaths and marriage. The individuals engaged in the religious activities of a church are generally not regular participants in activities of another church, except when such other church is a parent or subsidiary organization of their church. * * * Available information indicates that the * * * meets the above tests other than the "abandonment of other church" criterion, evidently adopted from *Chapman*.

Based on an overall weighing of the "normal characteristics" of churches we believe that the * * * may qualify as a church for purposes of Code § 170.

* * *

[The Los Angeles Times later publicized the Service's permissive policy toward witches with the following headline: "Out of Closet, Into Kitchen: Witches Win Nonprofit Tax Status as a Religion, Hope to Shed Evil Image." L.A. Times, Aug. 20, 1989, Part I, at 4, reprinted in Developments in the Law–Nonprofit Corporations, 105 Harv. L. Rev. 1578 (1992). Eds.]

NOTES AND QUESTIONS

1. *Religious Distinctions.* The Internal Revenue Code includes a large number of religious distinctions, some of which are significant for federal tax purposes. For example, although virtually all bona fide religious organizations qualify for exemption under § 501(c)(3), only "churches, their integrated auxiliaries and conventions or associations of churches" are relieved from filing annual informational returns with the Internal Revenue Service. I.R.C. § 6033(a)(2)(A)(i). An "integrated auxiliary" is a separate § 501(c)(3) organization, such as a school, mission society or youth group, that is affiliated with a church, internally supported, and meets one of the tests for avoiding private foundation status in § 509(a). Treas. Reg. § 1.6033–2(h)(1). More specifically, an organization qualifies as an integrated auxiliary if it either: (1) offers admissions, goods, services, or facilities for sale, other than on an incidental basis, to the general public and not more than 50 percent of its support comes from a combination of government sources, contributions from the general public, and receipts other than those from an unrelated business; or (2) does not offer admissions, goods, services, or facilities for sale, other than on an incidental basis, to the general public. Treas. Reg. § 1.6033–2(h)(4). See also Rev. Proc. 86–23, 1986–1 C.B. 564.

Churches and their integrated auxiliaries are conclusively presumed not to be private foundations, and they are not required to file a formal application in order to be recognized as tax–exempt. I.R.C. § 508(c)(1)(A). They also enjoy special immunities from IRS audits. I.R.C. § 7611. Even though churches are not required to apply for exempt status, many choose to do so to assure contributors that their contributions are tax–deductible.

2. *Personal Churches.* Beginning in the 1970's, the "personal church" emerged as an often comic but generally lamentable vehicle of tax protest. Taxpayers ranging from airline pilots and chiropractors to welders and electricians piously attempted to shelter normally taxable income by assigning their wages and property to a newly–chartered church that in turn provided lodging and a living allowance to the freshly ordained ministers. The charter often was obtained from a mail–order "parent" ministry.

Mail–order ministries received a notable blessing in 1974 when a federal district judge upheld the tax–exempt status of the Universal Life Church of Modesto, California. See Universal Life Church, Inc. v. United States, 372 F.Supp. 770 (E.D.Cal.1974). The Church had no dogma other than "to do whatever's right, to stay within the confines of the law." 372 F.Supp. at 772–773. Its founder, Kirby Hensley, proudly explained that his church was deliberately designed to exploit the tax laws in the hope that Congress and state legislatures would terminate all religious tax exemptions. In upholding the parent ULC's exemption, the district court was reluctant to impose any limits on a purported religion:

> Neither this Court, nor any branch of this Government, will consider the merits or fallacies of a religion. Nor will this Court compare the beliefs, dogmas, and practices of a newly organized religion with those

of an older, more established religion. Nor will the Court praise or condemn a religion, however excellent or fanatical or preposterous it may seem. Were the court to do so, it would impinge upon the guarantees of the First Amendment.

372 F.Supp. at 776. The court's conclusion was questionable because it was not being asked to praise or condemn the "church" or pass judgment on the verity of its beliefs. The more important point was that the church had no doctrines or tenets and did not purport to offer any explanation of the ultimate meaning of life.

It took a while, but the Service ultimately was successful in revoking the exemptions of Universal Life Church "affiliates" and other personal churches whose minister and parishioners consisted of only one or two families. See, e.g., Universal Life Church, Inc. (Full Circle) v. Commissioner, 83 T.C. 292 (1984); Church of Ethereal Joy v. Commissioner, 83 T.C. 20 (1984). Rather than attempting to define religion or question religious beliefs, the courts denied exempt status on the ground that personal churches either were operated for a substantial non–exempt purpose (e.g., to run a business) or violated the inurement of private gain limitation. The cases have become far too numerous even to cite, but an instructive example is Ecclesiastical Order of the Ism of Am v. Commissioner, 80 T.C. 833 (1983), where the Tax Court denied an exemption to a promoter of religious tax benefits on the ground that the organization served a substantial non–exempt purpose. The "church" had no worship services. Rather, its theology was devoted to counseling its local chapters on the tax benefits of religious tax exemptions. The court purported not to question the sincerity of the church but nonetheless denied exempt status on the ground that it was "nothing more than a commercial tax service * * * operating under the cover of a professed religious purpose." 80 T.C. at 843.

3. *Other Grounds for Denying Exemption.* When religious organizations are denied tax exemptions, it usually is because they have violated one or more requirements that apply to all organizations seeking § 501(c)(3) status. As developed later in this chapter, exemptions have been revoked on the ground of inurement of private gain (see, e.g., Church of Scientology of California v. Commissioner, infra p. 217), commerciality (see, e.g., Presbyterian and Reformed Publishing Co. v. Commissioner, infra p. 255), and excessive lobbying and political campaign activities (see, e.g., Christian Echoes National Ministry, Inc. v. United States, and Branch Ministries v. Rossotti, infra pp. 289 & 325).

On rare occasions, religious exemptions are denied on the ground that a claimed church is "secular" rather than "religious." A case in point is Church of the Chosen People (Demigod Socko Pantheon) v. United States, 548 F.Supp. 1247 (D.Minn.1982), where a federal district court rejected the religious claims of an organization which preached the "gay imperative" as a means of controlling overpopulation. The court held that the organization's program was "secular" because it did not address fundamental questions regarding the human condition, and because its beliefs were neither comprehensive in nature nor manifested in external forms.

Another notable case, albeit in a nontax setting, is United States v. Kuch, 288 F.Supp. 439 (D.D.C.1968), which involved the drug prosecution of a leader of the Neo–American Church, an organization of some 20,000 members who considered psychedelic drugs to be sacramental foods. The court held that the church was not a religion because the record presented "[n]o solid evidence of a belief in a supreme being, a religious discipline, a ritual, or tenets to guide one's daily existence." Id. at 444. The court was assisted in reaching these conclusions by its findings that the church had a "Catechism" ("we have a right to practice our religion, even if we are a bunch of filthy drunken bums"), official songs ("Puff, the Magic Dragon" and "Row, Row, Row Your Boat"), a church key (a bottle opener), a bulletin (known as "Divine Toad Sweat"), and a motto ("Victory Over Horseshit"). Id. at 443–44.

4. *A Test of Time?* Are tax administrators and the courts too lax in failing to define what constitutes "religion" or a "church?" Or would a governmental definition result in overly favorable treatment of mainstream religions? How should taxing authorities handle cults that may engage in brainwashing or illegal activities? Dean M. Kelley, a minister and longtime official of the National Council of Churches, has suggested a "simple, objective, external test which can be applied without entanglement to determine the bona fides of groups claiming to be churches"—the test of time. He proposes that provisional religious tax exemptions might be granted to new organizations but that the highly preferred "church" status not be attainable until the organization shows continuing support from its adherents for a minimum period of time—such as 20, 30 or up to 50 years. During the "probationary" period, the "would–be religion" would be subject to all the information reporting, disclosure, audit and other requirements generally applicable to nonprofits. Only after the test of time is satisfied would the group be granted the preferred status of a "church." See Dean M. Kelley, Why Churches Should Not Pay Taxes 58–69 (1977).

5. *For Further Reading.* Charles M. Whelan, "Church" in the Internal Revenue Code: The Definitional Problem, 45 Ford.L. Rev. 885 (1977); Stephen Schwarz, Limiting Religious Tax Exemptions: When Should the Church Render Unto Caesar, 29 U.Fla.L.Rev. 50 (1976); Boris I. Bittker, Churches, Taxes and the Constitution, 78 Yale L.J. 1285 (1969); Tax Guide for Churches and Other Religious Organizations, IRS Publication 1828 (2002).

PROBLEMS

Consider whether each of the following organizations is a religious organization under § 501(c)(3) and, if so, whether the organization also is a "church":

(a) The Free Spirit Church, which was organized three years ago by David Caress, a former low budget movie producer. The church congregation, numbering 150, consists primarily of estranged children and former homeless people who reside with Caress in a compound in a rural area of the Pacific Northwest. The church's stated doctrine is to "free the spirit and enjoy life to the fullest." Local law enforcement authorities believe that illegal drug activities are being conducted inside the compound, and they are concerned that Caress may be sexually exploiting some young congregants.

(b) The Moral Message, a fundamentalist organization that conducts religious services, operates a network of radio stations with religious programming and publishes a weekly newsletter, and solicits funds for its operations. In the course of spreading the gospel, it often takes positions on political and social questions but does not seek to influence legislation or intervene in political campaigns.

(c) The Church of Atheism, an organization with 5,000 members that is dedicated to propagating the belief that there is no Supreme Being. It operates bookstores and conducts meetings for its members at which the writings of prominent atheists are discussed.

7.   OTHER EXEMPT PURPOSES

Internal Revenue Code: §§ 501(e), (f), (j).

Treasury Regulations: § 1.501(c)(3)–1(d)(4) & (5).

The § 501(c)(3) family of exempt organizations has expanded over the years. In addition to the traditional exempt purposes of "religious," "charitable" and "educational," the list of permissible purposes includes "scientific," "literary," and the more specialized categories of testing for public safety, prevention of cruelty to children or animals and fostering of national or international amateur sports competition. In addition, § 501(e) deems certain "cooperative hospital service organizations"—such as an entity created by a consortium of nonprofit hospitals to perform specified services (e.g., data processing, bill collection, food preparation)—to be "charitable," while § 501(f) extends charitable status to common investment funds formed by exempt educational institutions. "Charitable risk pools," a specialized type of nonprofit entity that self-insures the insurable risks of § 501(c)(3) charities, recently has been added to the list of deemed charitable organizations. I.R.C. § 501(n).

Several of these additional exempt purposes were included in an abundance of caution. For example, "prevention of cruelty to children and animals" was added in 1918 without explanation. The Service has ruled that this category includes organizations providing funds for spaying or neutering pets (Rev. Rul. 74–194, 1974–1 C.B. 129) or ensuring humane treatment for laboratory animals (Rev. Rul. 66–359, 1966–2 C.B. 219), but does not include a club formed to promote the ownership and training of purebred dogs (Rev. Rul. 71–421, 1971–1 C.B. 229). "Literary" was added in 1921 for no discernible reason, and since that time the Service has never paused to define the term, allowing controversies over literary publications to be decided under the criteria applicable to "educational" organizations.

"Testing for public safety" was added in 1954 to overturn a case that denied exemption to the Underwriters' Laboratory, a nonprofit organization formed by fire insurance companies to test electrical appliances. See Underwriters' Laboratories v. Commissioner, 135 F.2d 371 (7th Cir.1943), cert. denied, 320 U.S. 756, 64 S.Ct. 63 (1943). The provision has been extended to organizations that test other consumer products, even if there is a benefit provided to the manufacturer (Treas. Reg. § 1.501(c)(3)–1(d)(4)), but not to drug testing organizations because of the Service's view that testing to meet Food and Drug Administration requirements serves primarily the interest of the manufacturer rather than the public (Rev. Rul. 68–373, 1968–2 C.B. 206).

Organizations operated for "scientific" purposes have raised relatively few qualification issues. The regulations provide that scientific organizations may engage in applied or fundamental research provided that they serve public rather than private interests, but exemption is denied for activities, such as testing or inspection, that are ordinarily incident to commercial operations. Treas. Reg. § 1.501(c)(3)–1(d)(5)(i), (ii).

The materials below illustrate some interpretational issues raised by the amateur sports category.

Hutchinson Baseball Enterprises, Inc. v. Commissioner

United States Court of Appeals, Tenth Circuit, 1982.
696 F.2d 757.

■ HOLLOWAY, CIRCUIT JUDGE.

This is an appeal by the Commissioner of Internal Revenue from a decision by the United States Tax Court that the taxpayer Hutchinson Baseball Enterprises, Inc., is organized for the promotion, advancement, and sponsorship of recreational and amateur athletics and therefore qualifies as a charitable organization under § 501(c)(3) of the Internal Revenue Code. 26 U.S.C.A. § 501(c)(3). * * *

I

The taxpayer Hutchinson Baseball Enterprises, Inc., was incorporated on August 31, 1970, as a not–for–profit corporation under the laws of Kansas. The amended articles of incorporation provide that one of the purposes of the corporation is to "[p]romote, advance and sponsor baseball, which shall include Little League and Amateur Baseball, in the Hutchinson, Kansas area." (Certificate of Amendment to Articles of Incorporation of Hutchinson Baseball Enterprises, Inc., attached to the by–laws of Hutchinson Baseball Enterprises, Inc.). The taxpayer is involved in a variety of activities, including owning and operating the Hutchinson Broncos baseball team (the Broncos), leasing and maintaining a playing field for the use of the Broncos, American Legion teams, and a baseball camp, and furnishing instructors and coaches for the Little League and baseball camp. The taxpayer also leases the baseball field to a local junior college for a nominal fee.

The Broncos baseball team, owned by the taxpayer, plays in a semi-professional league. The Tax Court found that the Broncos is an amateur team, and that determination is not challenged on appeal. The team plays in a league consisting of seven teams based in a three–state area. The Bronco team is composed of collegiate baseball players. These players are recruited from various states around the country to play for the team during the summer. They receive no compensation for playing baseball, but they are guaranteed jobs at the minimum wage either with Hutchinson Enterprises in a non–playing capacity or with other organizations in Hutchinson, Kansas. Additionally, all team members receive free housing in a Hutchinson Junior College dormitory.

The Broncos practice and play their home games on Bud Detter Field, which is owned by the City of Hutchinson. The taxpayer Hutchinson Enterprises leases the field from the City for a monthly rental fee, with the proviso that it maintain the field and keep it in good repair. The taxpayer assumed the American Legion's lease of the field from the City of Hutchinson under an agreement with the American Legion which permits the Legion baseball team to use the field rent free and which grants Hutchinson Enterprises exclusive concession rights and profits therefrom for all events held at Detter Field. Since the taxpayer has assumed care of the field, it has improved the facility by installing new fences and screens, and by constructing new dugouts and offices, and additional bleachers to accommodate the larger crowds.

In addition to allowing the American Legion the free use of the baseball field, the taxpayer permits the Little League and the youth baseball camp run by the City of Hutchinson to have free use of the baseball field and also provides Bronco team members to serve as coaches and instructors for these activities. Moreover, the taxpayer has made Bud Detter Field available during the school year to the Hutchinson Junior College for the fee of $500. The taxpayer raises money through sales of tickets, advertising, and concessions, through contribution solicitation, and through operation of the Broncos.

On October 5, 1973, the taxpayer filed an application for exempt status under § 501(c)(3). Effective as of October 5, 1973, the Commissioner recognized the taxpayer as an exempt organization under § 501(c)(3), by a determination letter dated October 24, 1973. * * * As a result of an examination of the taxpayer's activities for the fiscal years ended July 31, 1974, and July 31, 1975, the Commissioner concluded that the taxpayer no longer qualified for exemption under § 501(c)(3) and notified the taxpayer to that effect. The Commissioner issued a final adverse determination on August 28, 1978.

The taxpayer challenged the ruling in this declaratory judgment in the Tax Court. The court's opinion stated that the term "charitable" is to be construed in its generic sense, and is not limited to classifications enumerated in the statute. The court found that the taxpayer was organized for one or more exempt purposes, that the Broncos was an amateur baseball team, and that the purpose of the taxpayer's activities with respect to the

Broncos—as with those engaged in with respect to the Little League, the baseball camp, the American Legion program and the Hutchinson Community Junior College—was to advance amateur athletics, i.e., baseball, in the Hutchinson community. The court therefore held that the taxpayer satisfied the operational test and should be classified as a § 501(c)(3) organization.

II

The only issue on this appeal is whether the Tax Court erred in holding that the taxpayer qualified as a tax–exempt organization under § 501(c)(3) of the Internal Revenue Code. The facts are not in dispute and the subsidiary findings of the Tax Court are not questioned. The Commissioner challenges only the court's conclusion in favor of the taxpayer on its exempt status.

Section 501(a) provides tax exempt status for organizations described in § 501(c). [The language of § 501(c)(3) has been omitted, Eds.]

Section 501(c)(3) thus sets forth three requirements a taxpayer must meet to achieve exempt status: (1) the corporation must be organized and operated exclusively for exempt purposes; (2) no part of the corporation's net earnings may inure to the benefit of any shareholder or individual; and (3) the corporation must not engage in political campaigns or, to a substantial extent, in lobbying activities. Only the first requirement is at issue in this case. In deciding whether the taxpayer here satisfied requirement (1), we will treat in turn the Commissioner's argument that (a) the Tax Court erred in holding that the promotion of an amateur sport, without more, is a qualifying charitable activity; and (b) by reason of the fact that its predominant activity is support of the Broncos, the taxpayer is disqualified for the § 501(c)(3) exemption for organizations furthering educational or other charitable purposes.

A

The Commissioner challenges the Tax Court's conclusion that the taxpayer was entitled to the § 501(c)(3) exemption by being organized for the promotion, advancement, and sponsoring of recreational and amateur baseball.

The Commissioner argues that the sole support cited by the Tax Court for its decision is the legislative history of the amendment of § 501(c)(3) as effected by the Tax Reform Act of 1976. He says the 1976 amendment added to the organizations already enumerated in § 501(c)(3), those whose purpose is to "foster national or international amateur sports competition (but only if no part of its activities involve the provision of athletic facilities or equipment)," and stresses the more favorable treatment for fostering national and international amateur sports; that the history does not indicate that Congress was of the view that under existing law the mere promotion of amateur sports was a qualifying charitable purpose; that Congress actually recognized that promotion of amateur sports had not been viewed as a charitable purpose except where the organization engaged in sufficient instructional activities so as to qualify as an educational organization, or where the sports program was part of an overall recognized charitable activity such as the reduction of juvenile delinquency.

The Commissioner maintains that under existing law, consisting basically of revenue rulings, the fostering of amateur sports competition, without more, had not been regarded by the Commissioner as a qualifying charitable purpose; otherwise the amendment to § 501(c)(3) would have been unnecessary. He says that the Tax Court decision under the 1976 Act has the effect of imposing an added burden on such organizations generally. The anomalous result is that organizations like the taxpayer which promote local amateur sports qualify without regard to whether they provide facilities or equipment, while organizations promoting national and international sports are ineligible if they provide such facilities or equipment. Hence the Tax Court's interpretation is illogical and should be reversed.

At the outset we note that the Tax Court did not rely wholly on the legislative history of the 1976 amendment. The court persuasively reasoned that the organization's purposes in promoting numerous phases of recreational and amateur baseball for the community were of a "charitable" nature and within the broad meaning of the term "charitable" and the penumbra of § 501(c)(3). [S]ee § 1.501(c)(3)–1(d)(2), Income Tax Regulations, 26 CFR 1.501(c)(3)–1(d)(2). The regulation is pertinent in that it recognizes that the term "charitable" is to be construed in its "generally accepted legal sense and is, therefore, not to be construed as limited by the separate enumeration in section 501(c)(3) of other tax exempt purposes which may fall within the broad outlines of 'charity' as developed by judicial decisions."

The Tax Court cited Peters v. Commissioner, 21 T.C. 55. There a charitable contribution was held to have been made. The foundation benefitted was a corporation organized to furnish free public swimming facilities at a beach for residents of Cold Spring Harbor, New York, not having private facilities and not having means to acquire such facilities. A contribution was not a condition for use of the facility, which was open to contributors and noncontributors alike. The corporation was held to have been organized and operated exclusively for charitable purposes. The court found that the organization's dominant purpose was to provide convenient swimming and recreation facilities and was within the broad meaning of the term "charitable," stating (21 T.C. at 59): In its broader meaning, charity is not so limited but also embraces any benevolent or philanthropic objective not prohibited by law or public policy which tends to advance the well–doing and well–being of man.

The Commissioner cites statements from IV Scott on Trusts 2d § 374.6A (1967 ed.) and the Restatement of the Law, Trusts 2d § 374, comment n., that a trust for the mere promotion of sports is not charitable. However both authorities recognize that it has been held that a trust to promote sports among children may be upheld on the ground that it is a part of the education of children to improve their bodies as well as their minds. See also College Preparatory School for Girls of Cincinnati v. Evatt,

144 Ohio St. 408, 59 N.E.2d 142, 145. We are persuaded that in view of the various activities of the taxpayer furthering the development and sportsmanship of children and young men, Hutchinson Baseball Enterprises was properly held to qualify for the exemption as being organized and operated exclusively for charitable purposes.

Thus, on the wording of § 501(c)(3) and proper interpretation of the term "charitable," we agree with the Tax Court's ruling here. Moreover, we agree with the Tax Court's analysis of the legislative history. The Joint Committee explained the purpose of the 1976 amendment to § 501(c)(3) in statements set out in the margin.[2] In interpreting the legislative history, the Tax Court pointed to the concluding portion of the committee's "Explanation of Provision" statement, emphasized in note 2, supra, as showing that amateur athletic organizations could be exempt under 501(c)(3) prior to the 1976 amendment. We agree that the Joint Committee appeared to recognize that under prior law some amateur sports organizations did receive the favored tax–exempt status while other organizations did not. As the taxpayer points out, this recognition illustrates that Congress considered that under the existing law, the advancement of amateur athletics was a permissible charitable activity. The 1976 amendment added a further clarifying provision that organizations which foster national or international amateur sports competition are also within the exemption, subject to the restriction that they not provide athletic equipment or facilities.[3]

2. The Joint Committee stated:

Prior Law. Under prior law, organizations which teach youth or which are affiliated with charitable organizations have been able to qualify for exemption under Section 501(c)(3) and have been eligible to receive tax–deductible contributions. Other organizations which foster national or international amateur sports competition may be exempt from taxation under other provisions (such as Section 501(c)(4)(relating to social welfare organizations) or 501(c)(6)(relating to business leagues)) but often do not qualify to receive tax–deductible contributions.

Reasons for Change. Prior policy on the qualification for Section 501(c)(3) status has been a source of confusion and inequity for amateur sports organizations whereby some gained favored tax–exempt status while others, apparently equally deserving, did not. The failure of some of these organizations to obtain Section 501(c)(3) status and to qualify to receive tax–deductible contributions has discouraged contributions to these organizations, and has deterred other organizations from going through the legal expense of applying to the Internal Revenue Service for recognition of Section 501(c)(3) status. Congress believes that it is, in general, appropriate to treat the fostering of national or international amateur sports competition as a charitable purpose.

Explanation of Provision. The Act permits an organization the primary purpose of which is to foster national or international amateur sports competition to qualify as an organization described in Section 501(c)(3) and to receive tax–deductible contributions, but only if no part of the organization's activities involves the provision of athletic facilities or equipment. This restriction on the provision of athletic facilities and equipment is intended to prevent the allowance of these benefits for organizations which, like social clubs, provide facilities and equipment for their members. This provision is not intended to adversely affect the qualification for charitable tax–exempt status or tax deductible contributions of any organization which would qualify under the standards of prior law. * * *

3. As the Tax Court noted, 73 T.C. at 153, the legislative history demonstrates that this restriction was intended to prevent the providing of facilities and equipment to members of organizations such as social clubs.

We thus are in agreement with the interpretation of the legislative history by the Tax Court instead of that of the Government. However, we prefer not to base our conclusion as to the state of earlier law on that subsequent legislative history. We are persuaded nevertheless that on the wording of the statute and its proper construction, the Tax Court reached the right conclusion in holding that "the furtherance of recreational and amateur sports, falls within the broad outline of 'charity' and should be so classified."

B

There remains for consideration the Commissioner's contention that the taxpayer is disqualified for the § 501(c)(3) exemption because its predominant activity is the operation of the Hutchinson Broncos. He maintains this activity does not serve an educational or other recognized charitable purpose and was pursued to field the best team possible and win the championship of the league.

The Tax Court rejected the argument made along this line. It found that the Broncos was an amateur baseball team. The court found also that the purpose of the taxpayer's activities with respect to the Broncos—as with those it engaged in for the Little League, the baseball camp, the American Legion program and the Hutchinson Community Junior College—was to advance amateur baseball in the Hutchinson community.

The presence of a single nonexempt purpose, if substantial in nature, will destroy the exemption, regardless of the number or importance of truly exempt purposes. Nevertheless we agree with the views of the Tax Court concerning the taxpayer's support of Broncos. While the Commissioner contended in the Tax Court that the Broncos is a semi-professional team, he now expressly states in his brief that the Government is not contesting on appeal the finding that the Broncos are an amateur team. Thus we have the established fact that it is an amateur team which the taxpayer promotes.

The circumstances underlying that fact demonstrate the taxpayer's purpose of aiding development of these young athletes. The Bronco players are acquired by recruiting efforts or tryouts. They are often discovered by their high school or college coaches. The players receive free lodging in the Hutchinson Junior College dormitories during the season at the expense of Hutchinson Baseball Enterprises. The players have jobs in local industry at the minimum wage during the season. In college a large percentage of the players continue to play for college teams during their school years. Finally, an important function of the Broncos team members was that they served as instructors and coaches for Little League teams and the baseball camps.

Considering all these circumstances, we agree with the conclusion of Tax Court. The support of the Broncos and the taxpayer's other activities were for the purpose of advancing amateur baseball and served proper charitable purposes within the § 501(c)(3) exception.

AFFIRMED.

NOTES

1. *Amateur Athletics as a Charitable Purpose.* The Hutchinson Broncos qualified under § 501(c)(3) because they were "charitable" without regard to the 1976 amendment that added fostering of national and international amateur sports competition as an exempt purpose. For a contrary result, see Wayne Baseball, Inc. v. Commissioner, 78 T.C.M. 437 (1999), where the Tax Court found that more than an insubstantial part of an amateur baseball team's activities furthered the nonexempt social and recreational interests of its members. Unlike the Hutchinson Broncos, the team in *Wayne Baseball* did not promote amateur athletics by providing instruction or facilities to the community or engaging in other charitable activities.

The Service also has granted charitable or educational exemptions to organizations that develop youth sports programs to combat juvenile delinquency and provide a "recreational outlet." See Rev. Rul. 80–215, 1980–2 C.B. 174; Rev. Rul. 65–2, 1965–1 C.B. 227. The 1976 amendment was added to extend § 501(c)(3) exempt status to other types of amateur sports organizations, such as support groups for athletes competing in the Olympics and other national and international competitions, which previously could qualify only as § 501(c)(4) social welfare organizations or § 501(c)(6) business leagues.

2. *Qualified Amateur Sports Organizations.* To qualify as an amateur sports organization under the 1976 amendment to § 501(c)(3), no part of the organization's activities may involve the provision of athletic facilities or equipment. According to the legislative history, this strange limitation was intended to preclude social clubs providing facilities and equipment for their members from sneaking into § 501(c)(3). Read literally, however, the language was broad enough to disqualify legitimate athletic support organizations that provided training facilities and equipment. This caused Congress to call a "time out" while it added yet another category—the § 501(j) "qualified amateur sports organization" ("QASO"). A QASO must be organized and operated exclusively to foster national or international amateur sports competitions by conducting the competitions or developing and supporting the competing athletes. A QASO's exemption is not adversely affected because it has a local or regional membership, and it is relieved of the restriction on providing facilities and equipment.

3. *Professional Baseball as a Charitable Purpose.* Can a professional sports team serve a charitable purpose? The estate of Ewing Kaufman, the late former owner of the Kansas City Royals baseball team, received the Service's approval of a complex transaction under which the team was donated to The Greater Kansas City Community Foundation. The Foundation owned and operated the Royals in a limited partnership with local civic leaders until a local buyer was found. Additional funds were contributed to the Foundation to help cover the team's projected operating losses. The "charitable" goal was to hold the team until it could be sold to a buyer who would keep the Royals in Kansas City. The Foundation's share of any sales proceeds were to be used for its charitable purposes. In approving the

transaction, the Service did not rule that the team, despite its win/loss record, qualified for § 501(c)(3) exemption. The Royals continued to be operated by a separate taxable corporation owned by the Foundation in partnership with private investors. It did find, however, that the transfer of an ownership interest in the team to the Foundation and the resulting joint venture with private investors was motivated by a charitable purpose because it "lessened the burdens of government" within the meaning of Treas. Reg. § 1.501(c)(3)–1(d)(2). See, e.g., P.L.R 9530024 (July 28, 1995). While conceding that the same could be said about retaining any large business enterprise, the ruling concluded that historically there was an "intense and unique" interest shown by several different governmental bodies in keeping the Royals in Kansas City.

One premise of the ruling—that preserving a professional sports franchise is a quasi-governmental function—is debatable, but it appears to be the reality in Kansas City and many other communities. Lost in the controversy over this questionable extension of the "reducing the burdens of government" rationale for exemption is the extraordinary generosity of the Royals' late owner, Ewing Kaufman. Largely as a result of Kaufman's gift, the Greater Kansas City Community Foundation ranked second in gifts received by U.S. community foundations in 1995. Columbus Foundation, 1995 Community Foundation Survey (1996). Gifts of this magnitude by owners of other professional sports franchises are unlikely to become a recurring phenomenon.

For a lively critique of the Royals rulings, see Myreon Sony Hodur, Ball Four: The IRS Walks the Kansas City Royals, 19 Hastings Comm/ent L.J. 483 (1997).

PROBLEMS

Consider whether the following organizations qualify for tax exemption under either § 501(c)(3) or § 501(j):

(a) The Mixing Bowl Association, which operates an annual post-season nationally televised college football game ("The Pillsbury Mixing Bowl") in collaboration with a for-profit corporate sponsor. Net revenues from the game are distributed to the participating universities for their athletic and scholarship programs.

(b) The Butterfly Booster Club, an organization that provides moral and financial support to local swimming teams to aid in the personal development of their members, and to foster national and international swimming competition. The Club hosts meets, pays travel expenses for swimmers and coaches who attend competitions, provides training equipment, and rents time at a for-profit swim club where swimmers supported by the club train on a daily basis. The Club's board consists of ten individuals, eight of whom have children on the sponsored teams and the other two of whom own the for-profit swim club. The Club's revenues are generated from fundraising activities and contributions from parents and friends of the competitive swimmers.

(c) The Newport Harbor Foundation, which was founded by Ira Lewis, a wealthy patron of yachting, to finance the entry of his yacht, Viking Two, in the America's Cup sailing competition. Lewis personally contributed $10 million to the Foundation, and an additional $10 million will be raised from corporations, individuals, and private foundations. The Foundation will use the funds to maintain Viking Two, to compensate and house its crew, and for other expenses related to the competition. Lewis is the skipper of Viking Two but does not receive any compensation from the Foundation. Crew members are paid $35,000 per year, on average, plus living expenses.

8. STATE AND LOCAL TAX EXEMPTIONS

Nonprofit organizations that derive their federal income tax exemption under § 501(c)(3) also are likely to enjoy exemption from state and local taxes. All states with a corporate income or franchise tax provide exemptions for charitable organizations and grant exemptions from state and local property taxes, at least if the organization uses the property for its exempt purposes. Public benefit organizations also may be exempt from sales and use taxes. See W. Harrison Wellford and Janne G. Gallagher, Unfair Competition? The Challenge to Charitable Tax Exemption 122–138 & App. B (1988) for a state-by-state summary of property and income tax exemptions. See also E.C. Lashbrooke, Tax–Exempt Organizations 86–119 (1985). Because of the wide variety of state and local taxing schemes, this discussion is necessarily selective, but it should be kept in mind that for many organizations, state tax benefits, especially property or sales tax exemptions, may be more important than exemption from federal income tax or even eligibility to receive tax-deductible contributions.

Income and Franchise Taxes. States vary in their approaches to granting exemption from income and corporate franchise taxes. Some, like California, import most of the requirements imposed by § 501(c)(3) but require a separate application for state income tax exemption. Others, like Delaware, provide that organizations recognized as exempt under § 501(a) and described in § 501(c) are automatically exempt from state taxes without having to file for exemption. Del. Code Ann. tit. 30, 1133. New York exempts certain nonprofit organizations from the state corporate franchise tax by regulation. 20 N.Y. Comp. Codes R. & Regs. tit. 20, § 1–3.4(b)(6). A separate application is required, but New York generally follows the Internal Revenue Service's determination. Most states have provisions comparable to the federal unrelated business income tax.

Real Property Taxes. The most dynamic area of state and local taxation affecting nonprofits is the real property tax exemption. A study by the New York University School of Law's Philanthropy and the Law program, drawing upon an earlier survey by W. Harrison Wellford and Janne

Gallagher, provides a good general description of state property tax exemption schemes:

> [T]hirty-six state constitutions exempt nonprofit charities from property taxes or permit the legislature to grant such exemptions. The remaining state constitutions either generally permit granting exemptions, without restrictions on the class of eligible entities, or, if they contain no provision addressing the issue, have been interpreted as permitting exemptions for organizations carrying on activities similar to those enumerated in Code Section 501(c)(3). Generally, all states condition exemption upon prohibition of private inurement and the irrevocable dedication of assets to exempt purposes. To be exempt, most states require that the property be used either exclusively or primarily for exempt purposes. As the proportion of non-exempt use increases, so does the likelihood that all or a portion of the property will lose its exempt status. In virtually every state, property owned by an exempt entity, but dedicated to entirely non-exempt uses, will be taxed.

Bazil Facchina, Evan Showell & Jan E. Stone, Privileges & Exemptions Enjoyed by Nonprofit Organizations 45–46 (NYU Program on Philanthropy and the Law, 1993).

In reaction to their own fiscal problems and the entrepreneurial activities of many nonprofit organizations, states and municipalities have been reexamining these traditional property tax exemptions. The dollar impact of local tax exemptions on municipalities is substantial. For example, in 1993 non-governmental nonprofits in Philadelphia were exempted from nearly $45.6 million in city property taxes, $55.1 million in school district property taxes, as well as from the City's net profits tax, business privilege tax, business use and occupancy tax and parking tax. Tax exempt property constituted 25.2 percent of the city's property assessment. The assessed value of nonprofit property in Philadelphia grew from $1.2 billion in 1963 to $3.1 billion in 1993. Report of the Philadelphia Mayor's Special Committee on Nonprofits, 94 State Tax Notes 132–28, July 11, 1994. State and local officials have proceeded on several fronts: (1) tightening statutory definitions of the type of activity that qualifies as "charitable;" (2) broadening the sales tax base to include services provided by nonprofits; and (3) enacting municipal service fees or entering into agreements with nonprofits to receive payments in lieu of taxes or services in lieu of taxes to reimburse the municipality for the cost of providing essential services. See Boyd J. Black, Searching for the Revenue: Eroding State and Local Tax Exemptions, in ALI–ABA, Not-for Profit Organizations: The Challenge of Governance in an Era of Retrenchment 229 (1992). In early 1995, the District of Columbia, faced with a $600 billion budget deficit, called for a study of all tax exemptions granted to nonprofits. Prominent targets were George Washington University (holding property with an assessed value of $601 million), the World Bank ($517 million), and Georgetown University ($398.5 million). Also threatened were government instrumentalities such as the Federal National Mortgage Association and leading trade associations such as the Motion Picture Association of America. See David A. Vise, District to Go After Tax–Exempt Groups, Wash. Post, Jan. 25, 1995, A1.

While opposition to tax exemptions of nonprofit hospitals has been the primary focus of attack by state and local tax authorities, challenges have also focussed on YMCAs, nonprofit nursing facilities, residential retirement facilities, educational institutions and even churches. A common pattern is that an assessor, tax board, or lower court reflecting local pressures will revoke an exemption only to be reversed on appeal after years of litigation and substantial expense to the charity. See, e.g., Medical Center Hospital of Vt., Inc. v. City of Burlington, 152 Vt. 611, 566 A.2d 1352 (1989); City of Pittsburgh v. Board Property Assessment Appeals, 129 Pa.Cmwlth. 69, 564 A.2d 1026 (1989); and cases discussed in Black, supra at 242–245. Several states have tightened their exemption standards. For example, New Hampshire now defines ''charitable'' in relation to the services performed by the organization for public good or welfare of the general public or an indefinite segment of it. It requires that an organization not provide any pecuniary profit or limit its benefits to officers or members. N.H. Rev. Stat. Ann. 72:23–1.

Other states have created statutory presumptions. In California, for example, a nonprofit hospital is presumed to be entitled to the welfare property tax exemption if it earns less than ten percent surplus revenues in a year or makes an appropriate showing of how the profit is used. Cal. Rev. & Tax'n Code § 214(a)(1); but see Rideout Hospital Foundation v. County of Yuba, 8 Cal.App.4th 214, 10 Cal.Rptr.2d 141 (1992)(hospital that earned surplus revenue in excess of ten percent can still qualify for welfare exemption from property tax if surplus is used for actual operation of exempt entity). Other states have required nonprofit hospitals to demonstrate their charitable deeds to retain exempt status. See Tex. Health & Safety Code Ann. § 311.045. The Utah State Tax Commission, in response to the Utah Supreme Court's decision in Utah County v. Intermountain Health Care, Inc., 709 P.2d 265 (Utah 1985) has issued guidelines to be applied in determining whether hospitals and nursing homes qualify for exemption from Utah real property taxes. The standards generally require a hospital to be: (1) organized as a nonprofit, (2) prohibit the inurement of net earnings and donations to the benefit of any private individuals, (3) ensure open access to medical services, regardless of race, religion, gender or ability to pay, (4) demonstrate that its policies reflect the public interest by having a broad-based governing board that meets at least annually to address community needs, and (5) enumerate and total the various ways in which it provides unreimbursed service to the community in accordance with certain measurement criteria. These standards were upheld in Howell v. County Board of Cache County, 881 P.2d 880 (Utah 1994).

Local municipalities have attempted to impose Payments-in-Lieu-of-Taxes (Pilots), Services-in-Lieu-of-Taxes (Silots) or user fees on nonprofits. Boston negotiates Pilots agreements at a uniform rate equal to the percentage of the City's operating budget devoted to essential services. In 1991, 27 nonprofits paid over $11.4 million and donated an additional $6.8 million in Silots. In 1998, Harvard University paid $1.3 million to the City of Boston as compensation for lost revenue on student housing. In 1991, it agreed to pay compensation for ten years to Cambridge for any university-owned property removed from the city's tax rolls, and in 1999 Harvard agreed to pay $40 million to Boston over 20 years as payment in lieu of property taxes on otherwise exempt property. In 1994 Philadelphia created a Pilots/Silots program which asked nonprofits to make voluntary payments to make voluntary payments of forty percent of the annual property tax they would owe if they were not tax exempt. Nonprofits would have the option of substituting up to 33% of their Pilots obligations with Silots.

No state has been more forceful in challenging nonprofit tax exemptions than Pennsylvania. The Pennsylvania Constitution allows the state legislature to exempt from taxation only "institutions of purely public charity." Pa. Constit. Art. VIII, Section 2(a)(v). In Hospital Utilization Project v. Commonwealth, 507 Pa. 1, 487 A.2d 1306 (1985), the Pennsylvania Supreme Court held that the Hospital Utilization Project (HUP), a § 501(c)(3) organization which provided statistical information to hospitals, was not a purely public charity under the Pennsylvania Constitution and therefore not entitled to a sales and use tax exemption. (A similar standard is applied for property tax exemption purposes.) The court held that for an entity to qualify as a purely public charity it must: (1) advance a charitable purpose; (2) donate or render gratuitously a substantial portion of its services; (3) benefit a substantial and indefinite class of persons who are legitimate subjects of charity; (4) relieve the government of some of its burden; and (5) operate entirely free from private profit motive. Id. at 1317. In applying these criteria to HUP, the court found that the organization did not donate its services; its beneficiaries were not an indefinite class or legitimate subjects of charity; its executives were paid too well; and its accumulation of excess revenue for capital investment suggested it did not operate entirely free from private profit motive.

Subsequent Pennsylvania cases, construing the property tax exemption statutes strictly in favor of the taxing authority, have held that all these criteria must be met. Board of Revision of Taxes of the City of Philadelphia v. American Board of Internal Medicine, 154 Pa.Cmwlth. 204, 623 A.2d 418 (1993). In School District of Erie v. Hamot Medical Center, 144 Pa.Cmwlth. 668, 602 A.2d 407 (1992), the court upheld the revocation of the tax-exempt status of a nonprofit hospital, finding that it failed to meet four of the five HUP criteria. Tax assessors have challenged other nonprofit hospitals, many of whom offered to make payments of cash or services in lieu of property taxes in order to save their exemption. In perhaps the most extraordinary case, a lower court revoked the real property exemption of Washington & Jefferson College, the nation's sixth oldest, finding the College met only one of the HUP criteria—it was operated entirely free from private profit motive. City of Washington v. Board Assessment Appeals, No. 93–7033 (Washington Co. Com. Pleas, Aug. 5, 1994).

On appeal, however, the Commonwealth Court reversed the trial court, and a divided Pennsylvania Supreme Court affirmed the Commonwealth Court, holding that the College qualified for a property tax exemption as "an institution of purely public charity." Applying the five-part *Hospital Utilization Project* test, the court found that the College: (1) advanced a charitable purpose by providing education for youths in Pennsylvania; (2) donated or rendered gratuitously a substantial portion of its services by absorbing massive tuition charges (through scholarships and the use of endowment funds for operating expenses) that otherwise would be charged to students; (3) benefitted a substantial and indefinite class of persons who are legitimate objects of charity by providing substantial aid to students who, while not poor, would not otherwise be able to afford a college education; (4) relieved the burdens of government because, like other independent colleges and universities, the College relieved the load placed on state-funded schools of higher learning; and (5) operated entirely free from private profit motive. City of Washington v. Board of Assessment, 550 Pa. 175, 704 A.2d 120 (1997).

At about the same time that the Pennsylvania Supreme Court rendered its opinion in *City of Washington*, the Commonwealth enacted a new law (Act 55) redefining the criteria for nonprofits seeking to qualify for property and sales tax exemptions in Pennsylvania. The new law incorporates the five-part *HUP* test and provides elaboration for each prong. As an example of the level of detail, nonprofits may show that they offer a substantial portion of their services for free by meeting any one of seven tests, one of which requires that an institution have a written and reasonably publicized policy that it will not turn anyone away because of inability to pay. Another provision of the new law is aimed at charities carrying on commercial business activities that are unrelated to the charity's purposes as stated in its charter or governing legal documents. The Pennsylvania legislation may be a harbinger of developments nationwide as state and local governments continue to grapple with the increased commercialism of the nonprofit sector. See Grant Williams, New Pa. Law and Court Ruling Specify Standards for Tax Exemption, Chron. Philanthropy, Dec. 11, 1997, at 41.

Constitutional Issues. In a case that has been hailed as a major victory for charities, the Supreme Court held in a 5–to–4 opinion that a state may not deny a property tax exemption to a nonprofit organization because most of the people it serves are nonresidents. Camps Newfound/Owatonna, Inc. v. Town of Harrison, Maine, 520 U.S. 564, 117 S.Ct. 1590 (1997). The case involved a constitutional challenge by a nonprofit church-operated summer camp to a Maine law that limited or denied property tax exemptions to organizations operated principally for the benefit of nonresidents of Maine. The Court held that an otherwise generally applicable state property tax law violates the Commerce Clause if its charitable exemption excludes organizations operated primarily for the benefit of nonresidents. The Court majority reasoned that if the taxing scheme had discriminated against for-profit entities, it clearly would violate the Commerce Clause, and the same protections should extend to the nonprofit sector. In so ruling, the Court observed that it has frequently applied laws regulating commerce (e.g., labor and antitrust laws) to nonprofit organizations.

The Court was not persuaded by the Town's argument that it should be able to give special benefits to charities that cater to local needs, especially those offering services the state itself otherwise would to provide. Relying on Walz v. Tax Commission, 397 U.S. 664, 90 S.Ct. 1409 (1970), where it upheld the constitutionality of religious tax exemptions, the Court stated that there is a constitutionally significant difference between subsidies and tax exemptions.

Justice Scalia, joined by Chief Justice Rehnquist and Justices Thomas and Ginsburg, dissented, complaining that the Commerce Clause should not be invoked to prevent a state from giving tax benefits to charities that serve the state's inhabitants. Justice Thomas also wrote a separate dissent.

Camp Newfound/Owatonna attracted the attention of many large nonprofit organizations, who were concerned that a ruling in favor of Maine's property tax scheme would encourage other state and local governments to discriminate against nonprofits with a national or international presence.

For Further Reading: Property Tax Exemption for Charities: Mapping the Battlefield (Evelyn Brody ed. 2002); Boyd J. Black, Searching for the Revenue: Eroding State & Local Tax Exemptions in Not-for-Profit Organizations: The Challenge of Governance in an Era of Retrenchment (A.L.I. ed. 1992); Margaret A. Potter & Beaufort B. Longest, Jr. The Divergence of Federal and State Policies on the Charitable Tax Exemption of Nonprofit Hospitals, 19 J. Health Pol. Pol'y & L. 393 (1994); Rebecca S. Rudnick, State and Local Taxes on Nonprofit Organizations, 22 Cap. U. L.Rev. 321 (1993); Peter Swords, Charitable Real Property Tax Exemptions in New York State–Menace or Measure of Social Progress (1981); Janne Gallagher, Sales Tax Exemptions for Charitable, Educational, and Religious Organizations, 7 Exempt Org. Tax Rev. 429 (1993).

D.   INUREMENT, PRIVATE BENEFIT AND INTERMEDIATE SANCTIONS

1.   INUREMENT AND PRIVATE BENEFIT

Treasury Regulations: § 1.501(c)(3)–1(c)(2).

Section 501(c)(3) organizations are prohibited from engaging in activities that result in "inurement" of the organization's net earnings to insiders, such as founders, directors, and officers. The related "private benefit" doctrine prohibits a § 501(c)(3) organization from providing a substantial economic benefit to individuals who do not exercise any control over the organization. As interpreted by the IRS, however, "private benefit" must be more than incidental to disqualify an organization as contrasted with the absolute ban on private inurement.

Historically, the Service has invoked the inurement limitation only in the most egregious cases of insider misconduct. Since the only sanction was the ultimate death sentence-revocation of exemption-enforcement was lax. Congress gave the Service a new and more effective weapon in 1996 when it enacted the § 4958 intermediate sanctions regime. Insiders who receive excess economic benefits now are subject to monetary penalties, as are organization managers who approve of such transactions. The materials below survey the historical and contemporary aspects of inurement and private benefit and then turn to intermediate sanctions.

Church of Scientology of California v. Commissioner

United States Court of Appeals, Ninth Circuit, 1987.
823 F.2d 1310.

■ TANG, CIRCUIT JUDGE:

The Church of Scientology (Church) appeals a judgment of the Tax Court which affirmed the Commissioner's assessment of tax deficiencies and late filing penalties against the Church for the years 1970, 1971 and 1972. At issue is whether the Commissioner properly revoked the Church's tax exempt status.

I.

The Church was incorporated as a nonprofit corporation in the State of California in 1954. In 1957, the Commissioner recognized it as a tax exempt organization under § 501(c)(3) of the Internal Revenue Code of 1954. The Commissioner revoked the Church's tax exempt status in 1967. The letter of revocation stated that the Church was "engaged in a business for profit," and was "operated in a manner whereby a portion of [its] earnings inure[d] to the benefit of a private individual," and was "serving a private, rather than a public interest." * * *

On March 28, 1978, the Church filed suit in United States Tax Court challenging the Commissioner's determination of tax deficiency. In an extensive opinion, the Tax Court substantially upheld the determination of the Commissioner. 83 T.C. 381 (1984). It held that the Church did not qualify for exemption from taxation under §§ 501(a) & 501(c)(3) because: (1) the Church was operated for a substantial commercial purpose; (2) its earnings inured to the benefit of L. Ron Hubbard, his family, and OTC, a private non-charitable corporation controlled by key Scientology officials; and (3) it violated well defined standards of public policy by conspiring to prevent the IRS from assessing and collecting taxes owed by the Church. The Court also upheld the validity of the Notice of Deficiency. Finally, the Court upheld the penalties for failure to file tax returns.

II.

During the years in question, the Church of Scientology of California was the "Mother Church" of the many Scientology churches around the country. The Church propagated the Scientology faith, a religion founded by L. Ron Hubbard, through such means as the indoctrination of laity, training and ordination of ministers, creation of congregations, and provision of support to affiliated organizations.

Scientology teaches that the individual is a spiritual being having a mind and body. Part of the mind, called the "reactive mind" is unconscious and filled with mental images that are frequently the source of irrational behavior. Through the administration of a process known as "auditing" a parishioner, called a "pre-clear," is helped to erase his or her reactive mind and gain spiritual awareness. Auditing is administered individually by a trained "auditor." The auditor poses questions to the pre-clear and measures the latter's response with an electronic device called an "E–Meter" that is attached to the skin. The E–Meter assists in the identification of spiritual difficulty. Scientology teaches that spiritual awareness is achieved in stages. A disciple achieves different levels of awareness through additional auditing. The religion also offers courses to train auditors.

Scientology teaches that people should pay for whatever of value they receive. This is called the "Doctrine of Exchange." Toward the realization of this doctrine, branch churches exacted a "fixed donation" for training and auditing. Fixed donations were not based on ability to pay and with few exceptions, services were not given for free.

Scientology is an international religion with numerous churches around the world. In the 1970's, these churches were organized along hierarchical lines according to the level of services they were authorized to provide. Churches that delivered services at the lowest levels were called "franchises" and later "missions." "Class IV orgs" delivered auditing through "grade IV" and training through "level IV." "St. Hill organizations" and "advanced organizations" offered intermediate and higher level services. The branch known as "Flag" offered the highest level of training and auditing.

The California Church consisted of several divisions. The San Francisco Organization and the Los Angeles Organization were both class IV organizations. The American St. Hill Organization was located in Los Angeles and offered intermediate auditing and training. The Advanced Organization of Los Angeles provided high levels of auditing and training to persons who had completed services at a class IV organization. The Flag Operations Liaison Office, located in Los Angeles, was an administrative unit of the California Church.

In addition to auditing and training, the Church provided assistance to prisoners, ex-offenders, the elderly, the mentally ill and drug addicts. On occasion the Church assisted the poor and the sick. The Church performed christenings, funerals and wedding ceremonies free of charge, and conducted regular Sunday services. The Church's chaplain provided marriage and family counseling free of charge. The Church also provided free a specialized form of auditing geared to help people in crisis.

Flag was the highest division of the California Church. It provided spiritual leadership. It also acted as the Church's administrative center.

The Flag division was headquartered aboard the ship Apollo, which cruised the Mediterranean Sea and docked in various countries along its shores. L. Ron Hubbard, his wife, Mary Sue, and their family lived aboard the Apollo with other members of the ship's crew and staff. Besides performing the highest levels of auditing and training, Flag staff members performed a variety of management functions. * * *

The Church derived income from four sources: (1) auditing and training; (2) sales of Scientology literature, recordings and E-meters; (3) franchise operations; and (4) management services. Franchise operators were required to remit ten percent of gross income to the Church. The Church offered its managerial services to branch organizations around the world for a fixed fee.

One of the policy directives of the Church was to "MAKE MONEY". The Church frequently engaged in aggressive promotion of its products and services. This promotion included market surveys and advertisements. In addition, the Church trained staff members in salesmanship techniques.

L. Ron Hubbard officially resigned his position as executive head of the California and other Scientology churches in 1966. Despite his official resignation, the Tax Court found that he continued to exert significant control over the Church by making policy statements, directives, and orders. In addition, his approval was required for all financial planning. He was the sole trustee of a major Scientology trust fund into which the Church made substantial payments. He or Mary Sue Hubbard were signatories on many Church bank accounts.

During the tax years at issue, L. Ron Hubbard and Mary Sue Hubbard received salaries from the California Church and its affiliate, the United Kingdom Church, in the following amounts * * * [the total amounts received were $20,249 in 1970, $49,648 in 1971 and $115,680 in 1972, Eds.]

During these years, L. Ron Hubbard, Mary Sue Hubbard and their four children resided for the most part aboard the Apollo. While aboard ship, the Church provided the Hubbards with free lodging, food, laundry, medical services and vitamins.

The Church made royalty payments to L. Ron Hubbard for sales of his books, tapes and E-meters. The royalties amounted to ten percent of the retail price. The Church, for example, made $104,618.27 in royalty payments to Hubbard in 1972. Additionally, Church policy required that all work pertaining to Scientology and Dianetics be copyrighted to L. Ron Hubbard. As the result of this policy, a number of publications copyrighted by L. Ron Hubbard were actually written by others. For example, Ruth Mitchell wrote the book Know Your People and Peter Gillum wrote the book How to be Successful. Additionally, a series of books called the OEC series contained policy letters, some written by L. Ron Hubbard and others written by paid employees of the Church. L. Ron Hubbard received royalty payments on the sale of all of these publications.

During the 1960's, Scientology organizations around the world were required to pay directly to L. Ron Hubbard, ten percent of their income.

These payments were termed "debt repayments" because they were designed to compensate Hubbard for his work in originating the Scientology religion. The Tax Court concluded that during 1971–1972 the Church continued to make debt repayments to Hubbard.

In 1968, L. Ron Hubbard, Mary Sue Hubbard, and Leon Steinberg incorporated a Panamanian corporation called Operation Transport Corp., Ltd. (OTC). OTC was a for-profit corporation. Shortly after the corporation's formation, Hubbard, Mary Sue Hubbard and Steinberg resigned and were replaced by three Flag employees. During the years in question, the new directors performed only one function. In the summer of 1972, they approved L. Ron Hubbard's decision to transfer approximately two million dollars from an OTC bank account in Switzerland to the Apollo. The money was stored in a locked file cabinet to which Mary Sue Hubbard had the only set of keys.

Between 1971 and 1972, the Church made payments in excess of three and a half million dollars to OTC. During these years, the Church also made payments totaling nearly $175,000 to the Central Defense and Dissemination Fund. According to the Church, these payments were placed in the United States Church of Scientology Trust of which L. Ron Hubbard was the sole trustee. The trust funds were deposited in several Swiss bank accounts. L. Ron Hubbard and Mary Sue Hubbard were signatories of the accounts and L. Ron Hubbard kept the trust checkbooks.

III.

* * *

B.   Inurement

Congress conferred tax exemption on churches and other organizations in recognition of the benefit society derives from the activities of these organizations. The government leaves funds in the hands of charitable organizations rather than taxing them and spending the funds on public projects. Implicit in this purpose is that charities must promote the public good to qualify for tax exemption.

Section 501(c)(3) embodies this policy. Churches are eligible for tax exempt status only if no part of their net earnings inure to the benefit of private individuals. Each phrase of the statute has significance. The term "no part" is absolute. The organization loses tax exempt status if even a small percentage of income inures to a private individual. The sole beneficiary of the church's activities must be the public at large.

Courts have construed broadly the term "net earnings". "Net earnings" includes more than gross receipts minus disbursements as shown on the books of the organization. Only those ordinary expenses necessary to the operation of the church are not included in net earnings.

The heart of § 501(c)(3) tax exempt status is the phrase "inures to the benefit." Payment of reasonable salaries to church officials does not constitute inurement. However, payment of excessive salaries will result in a finding of inurement. Inurement can also result from distributions other than the payment of excessive salaries. Unaccounted for diversions of a charitable organization's resources by one who has complete and unfettered control can constitute inurement.

Finally, the regulations define "private shareholder or individual" broadly as any person "having a personal and private interest in the activities of the organization." 26 C.F.R. § 1.501(a)–1(c).

While we remain solicitous of Congress' intent to confer tax exempt status on religious organizations, this court has previously affirmed the denial of tax exemption where church income inures to private individuals. * * *

The finding of the Tax Court that a portion of the Church's net earnings inured to the benefit of L. Ron Hubbard, his family, and OTC, a private for-profit corporation, is a factual finding. We review this finding for clear error.

The taxpayer has the burden to demonstrate that it is entitled to tax exempt status. This is especially true in situations where there is a great potential for abuse created by one individual's control of the church. The Church must come forward with candid disclosure of the facts bearing on the exemption application. Doubts will be resolved in favor of the government.

In finding that a portion of the Church's net earnings inured to the benefit of L. Ron Hubbard, his family and OTC, the court isolated two indicia of inurement, overt and covert. The overt indicia included salaries, living expenses, and royalties. The covert indicia included "debt repayments" and L. Ron Hubbard's unfettered control over millions of dollars of Church assets. The court concluded that these indicia, when viewed in light of the self-dealing associated with them, coupled with the Church's failure to carry its burden of proof and to disclose the facts candidly, proved conclusively that the Church was operated for the benefit of L. Ron Hubbard and his family.

The Church challenges the overt indicia of inurement on the ground that the salaries, expenses and royalties, were reasonable. It notes that the court did not find them unreasonable, considered separately. The Church questions the logic of the finding that several reasonable payments add up to inurement.

The Church paid L. Ron Hubbard and Mary Sue Hubbard combined salaries of $20,249 in 1970, $49,648 in 1971 and $115,680 in 1972. We cannot say that these salaries were excessive.

In addition to Hubbard's salary, the Church paid for all of the Hubbards' living and medical expenses aboard the cruise ship Apollo. These expenses amounted to about $30,000 per year. Because it is unnecessary to our decision, we express no opinion on whether supporting a Church's founder and his family aboard a yacht cruising the Mediterranean constitutes a reasonable Church expense.

The Church also paid substantial royalties to L. Ron Hubbard for his books, recordings and E-meters. Churches, especially less established ones, rely on the distribution of church literature to propagate their beliefs. Financing church operations through the sale of religious literature does not necessarily violate the requirements for tax exemption. Furthermore, a church may pay the author reasonable compensation in the form of royalties for his literary works. However, the payments in this case, cross the line between reasonable and excessive. Here, the evidence indicates that Hubbard used the Church to generate copyrighted literature and market his products. Scientology policy mandated that any book on Dianetics and Scientology be copyrighted in the name of L. Ron Hubbard. Pursuant to this policy, a number of publications copyrighted by L. Ron Hubbard were actually written by Church employees. Furthermore, the Church encouraged its staff members to market aggressively his products. We agree with the Tax Court that the royalty payments support a finding of inurement.

The Church argues that the evidence does not support the Tax Court's finding of covert inurement. However, the record reveals that L. Ron Hubbard had unfettered control over millions of dollars in Church assets. The Church transferred several million dollars to OTC during 1970–72. These payments were designated as "charter mission expenses." L. Ron Hubbard and Mary Sue Hubbard controlled OTC funds. Sometime during 1972, OTC transferred approximately two million dollars from OTC bank accounts in Switzerland to the Apollo. The finding that OTC was a sham corporation is sustained. During the tax years in question OTC funneled millions of dollars of Church assets to L. Ron Hubbard.

The record also supports the Tax Court's conclusion that L. Ron Hubbard had unfettered control over Church of Scientology Trust Fund assets. The Church deducted payments of $28,930.34 in 1970, $67,892.40 in 1971, and $77,986.62 in 1972 to the Central Defense and Dissemination Fund. According to the Church, these payments were made to the United States Church of Scientology Trust. L. Ron Hubbard was the sole trustee of the Trust during the years in question. Trust funds were deposited in several Swiss bank accounts. L. Ron Hubbard and Mary Sue Hubbard were two of the three signatories on the Trust accounts. L. Ron Hubbard kept the Trust checkbooks. In 1972, over a million dollars was withdrawn from the Trust accounts in Switzerland and brought aboard the Apollo where it was kept in a locked file cabinet. Mary Sue Hubbard had the only keys to the cabinet.

The Church disputes that control over assets compels a finding of inurement. It argues that every Sunday morning pastors all over America collect money from parishioners and hold that money for Church uses. It asserts that OTC funds were used for expenses associated with operation of the Apollo and in providing banking services for Flag. Witnesses testified that the Church used Trust monies to defend Scientology against attack and to propagate the religion. Finally, the Church argues that the three million dollars brought aboard the Apollo from the OTC and Trust accounts remained on the Apollo during the years in question. It cites the testimony of a Trust accountant who counted the cash aboard the Apollo and testified that none of it was missing.

We find these arguments unpersuasive. Unlike the typical Saturday or Sunday when parishioners donate their money to the church, here the Church transferred millions of dollars to bank accounts controlled by a private individual who had no official responsibility for managing church assets. Although witnesses testified that the money was used for Church purposes, the Church presented little documentation to show that the majority of Trust or OTC money was actually spent on bona-fide Church activities. Finally, the self-serving testimony of a Church employee that the three million dollars remained in the Apollo safe proves nothing. The fact that there were three million dollars in the safe on the day the Church accountant checked, is not inconsistent with the Tax Court's finding that L. Ron Hubbard had unfettered control over millions of dollars in money that originated with the Church. The Church failed to come forward with testimony from key individuals such as L. Ron Hubbard and Mary Sue Hubbard and failed to present the documentation necessary to trace the source and use of OTC and Trust monies. In sum, the Church failed to carry its burden of proof in a situation where "the potential for abuse created by the [founder's] control of the Church required open and candid disclosure of facts bearing on the exemption application."

The Tax Court found that Church income inured to the benefit of L. Ron Hubbard in a "grand scale" in the form of "debt repayments." During the 1950's, Hubbard was paid a portion of the gross income of Scientology congregations, franchises and organizations. This compensation scheme was called the "proportional pay plan." During the 1960's these tithes became known as "Founding Debt Payments" (sometimes also called "LRH RR" or "LRH 10").

Although the form changed, the payments continued through the years at issue in this case. Church records indicate that between October 9, 1972 and December 28, 1972, it made debt repayments totaling $19,324.41. A policy letter dated September 7, 1972 entitled "Repayment or Due Money Collected for LRH Personally" set out a program to reimburse Hubbard for past use of Hubbard's personal income and capital; research and development of the technology of Dianetics and Scientology; and the use of Hubbard's goodwill and high credit rating. The letter establishes the post of "LRH accounts officer" to monitor collection of debt repayments.

* * *

In sum, we hold that significant sums of Church money inured to the benefit of L. Ron Hubbard and his family during the tax years 1970, 1971 and 1972. Although neither the salaries nor the living expenses necessarily constituted evidence of inurement, the cumulative effect of Hubbard's use of the Church to promote royalty income, Hubbard's unfettered control over millions of dollars of church assets, and his receipt of untold thousands of dollars worth of "debt repayments" strongly demonstrate inurement. We find no clear error.

* * *

NOTES AND QUESTIONS

1. *Scientology Update.* For almost 30 years, the Church of Scientology and the Internal Revenue Service engaged in a bitter holy war. Even while conceding that Scientology was a bona fide religion, the Service generally was successful in the courts except for a few procedural setbacks. Its earliest substantive victory was in Founding Church of Scientology v. United States, 188 Ct.Cl. 490, 412 F.2d 1197 (1969), where the court denied exemption to what was then the parent church of the Scientology movement. On another front, the Service consistently denied income tax deductions (as either a business or medical expense, or a charitable contribution) to taxpayers who paid for "auditing" and other services provided by the Church of Scientology. See, e.g., Rev. Rul. 78–189, 1978–1 C.B. 68 (no business deduction because auditing did not maintain or improve skills in an existing trade or business); Rev. Rul. 78–188, 1978–1 C.B. 40 (no charitable deduction because taxpayer received a return benefit); Rev. Rul. 78–190, 1978–1 C.B. 74 (no medical expense deduction). In a decision with potential ramifications for other religions, the Supreme Court upheld the disallowance of charitable deductions on the ground that the taxpayers were receiving a quid pro quo. Hernandez v. Commissioner, 490 U.S. 680, 109 S.Ct. 2136 (1989).

In a surprising reversal of policy, however, the Service announced in 1993 that it had "obsoleted" its previous rulings and agreed to permit charitable deductions for auditing fees paid to the Church of Scientology. See Rev. Rul. 93–73, 1993–2 C.B. 75. At the same time, the Service granted retroactive exemptions to 25 Scientology-related organizations. These developments are discussed in Chapter 6B3, infra, at pp. 733–734.

2. *Churches and Inurement.* Applying the inurement limitation to churches is difficult because they are exempt from the usual information reporting requirements generally applicable to exempt organizations and they enjoy special protection from audits. See I.R.C. 6033; 7611. The situation is ripe for abuse. Consider, for example, the Divine Light Mission, a cult once headed by the Guru Maharaj Ji, who was reported to reside in a lavish estate and drive among the parishioners in a fleet of expensive sports cars. In the heyday of the personal church as a vehicle of tax protest, the Service had some success in revoking exemptions on inurement grounds. See, e.g., Unitary Mission Church of Long Island v. Commissioner, 74 T.C. 507 (1980)(excessive wages, loans, reimbursement of founder's travel expenses); Bubbling Well Church of Universal Love, Inc. v. Commissioner, 74 T.C. 531, aff'd 670 F.2d 104 (9th Cir.1981)(living, medical and European travel expenses).

3. *State Law Safeguards*. In addition to the general body of law regulating the fiduciary duties of officers and directors, some state nonprofit corporation laws have specific safeguards against activities that might constitute inurement of private gain for tax purposes. For example, § 5227 of the California Corporations Code provides that no more than 49 percent of the directors of a public benefit corporation may consist of certain "interested persons" such as employees, compensated directors and members of their families. A public benefit corporation in California thus must have a majority (51 percent) of directors who only serve on the board or, if they serve in any other capacity (e.g., as an employee), are not compensated for these services. Additional rules patrol against self-dealing transactions between the corporation and one or more directors who have a material financial interest in the transaction.

4. *Executive Compensation Excess?*. In the early 1990's, it was revealed that William Aramony, then President of United Way of America, earned a base salary of $463,000 and generous fringe benefits. He quickly became the poster boy in a national debate over the appropriate level of compensation for nonprofit executives. The press, the public and Congress during hearings held in 1993 discovered that other nonprofit executives received handsome compensation by any standard. These perceptions of excess served as a lightening rod of public dissatisfaction with the nonprofit sector, and the dialogue continues. Defenders of the trend toward higher compensation argue that nonprofit executives should not be forced to take a vow of poverty and point to the challenges of recruiting and retaining talented people to lead complex organizations.

For many years, The Chronicle of Philanthropy has published an annual survey of compensation and benefits paid to top executives at the nation's largest § 501(c)(3) organizations. The data, which is highly selective, is culled from annual information returns (Form 990's and, for private foundations, Form 990–PFs) filed with the IRS and available for public inspection. Form 990 requires organizations to report the compensation and benefits paid to their officers, directors, trustees, and key employees, and to report separately compensation of the five highest paid employees other than officers, directors or trustees. "Compensation" includes salaries, bonuses and severance payments. Benefits include medical and insurance benefits, deferred compensation, future retirement benefits, and provisions for housing or care. In some unusual situations, the reported amounts may be misleading, such as where a large severance payment is made or extraordinary housing assistance is provided in connection with the recruitment of a new chief executive.

Of the 282 nonprofit groups included in the latest Chronicle of Philanthropy survey available as this text went to press (for 2001), 34 paid their chief executive officer $500,000 or more. At 30 organizations, the highest paid employee other than the chief executive also was paid more than $500,000. The very highest salaries were paid to chief executives and senior physicians at large urban hospital centers, with several receiving salary and benefits in excess of $1 million. Compensation for University presidents also is on the rise; the highest-paid in the 2001 survey earned a base salary of $690,405, along with $117,616 in benefits. Chief executives at the 20 largest private grantmaking and operating foundations also are well compensated, with 8 receiving base pay of over $500,000. At some universities, employees other than the president, such as chief investment officers, medical school professors, or even football and basketball coaches, are the highest paid. See Harvy Lipman & Martha Voelz, Big Rise in Pay for CEO's, Chron. Philanthropy, Oct. 3, 2002, at 33–47.

While the public focus has been upon excesses in the nonprofit sector, the reality is that the compensation of nonprofit employees (at all levels) is still considerably less than salaries paid to private sector employees. Should it be? What is the appropriate benchmark? Pay for performance in the form of stock options or bonuses is the norm in the corporate world. Are such incentives appropriate for employees of nonprofits? A portion of the compensation received by many fundraisers is based on the amount of money they raise. Holly Hall, More than 10% of Fundraisers Get Bonuses, but the Idea Worries Charities, Chron. Philanthropy, July 13, 1993, at 34. Similarly, in-house money managers for charities with large endowments often received performance-based bonuses. In 1996, for example, a portfolio manager for Harvard University's investment management company earned $6.1 million based on his portfolio's performance. Jonathan N. Axelrod & Stephen E. Fran, One Money Manager's Pay is in the Ivy League of Its Own, Wall St. J., July 15, 1996, at C1. Do performance-based bonuses create ethical issues?

One approach suggested to control excessive compensation is to place an absolute limit on nonprofit pay. Pablo Eisenberg, a knowledgeable observer of the nonprofit sector, has suggested limits on nonprofit compensation with a tax imposed on salaries above the limit. IRS Must Slam Door on High Salaries, Chron. Philanthropy, Aug. 13, 1998, at 43. In a thorough examination of compensation of business executives and professionals, Derek Bok, former president of Harvard, urges that the nation must rethink its deepest values, motivations and priorities to harness the movement for ever higher and excessive compensation. The Cost of Talent 294–297 (1993). Are salary caps desirable, or even workable? Would they limit compensation or merely lead to the creation of subsidiaries and affiliated nonprofit corporations with overlapping executives to avoid the maximum? In the business world, the $1 million limit on deductibility of executive compensation imposed by § 162 has proven to be ineffective because of an enormous loophole exempting performance-based pay such as stock options. Or should nonprofit governing boards, as a matter of "best practices," couple any performance-based compensation package with a cap to curb excesses that may send a bad signal about the organization's values?

United Cancer Council, Inc. v. Commissioner

United States Court of Appeals, Seventh Circuit, 1999.
165 F.3d 1173.

■ Posner, Chief Judge.

The United Cancer Council is a charity that seeks, through affiliated local cancer societies, to encourage preventive and ameliorative approaches to cancer, as distinct from searching for a cure, which has been the emphasis of the older and better-known American Cancer Society, of which UCC is a splinter. The Internal Revenue Service revoked UCC's charitable exemption and the Tax Court upheld the revocation, precipitating this appeal.

So far as relates to this case, a charity, in order to be entitled to the charitable exemption from federal income tax, and to be eligible to receive tax-exempt donations, must be "organized and operated exclusively for * * * [charitable] purposes" and "no part of the net earnings of [the charity may] inure[ ] to the benefit of any private shareholder or individual." The IRS claims that UCC (which is defunct) was not operated exclusively for charitable purposes, but rather was operated for, or also for, the private benefit of the fundraising company that UCC had hired, Watson & Hughey Company (W & H). The Service also claims that part of the charity's net earnings had inured to the benefit of a private shareholder or individual—W & H again. The Tax Court upheld the Service's second ground for revoking UCC's exemption—inurement—and did not reach the first ground, private benefit. The only issue before us is whether the court clearly erred in finding that a part of UCC's net earnings inured to the benefit of a private shareholder or individual.

It is important to understand what the IRS does not contend. It does not contend that any part of UCC's earnings found its way into the pockets of any members of the charity's board; the board members, who were medical professionals, lawyers, judges, and bankers, served without compensation. It does not contend that any members of the board were owners, managers, or employees of W & H, or relatives or even friends of any of W & H's owners, managers, or employees. It does not contend that the fundraiser was involved either directly or indirectly in the creation of UCC, or selected UCC's charitable goals. It concedes that the contract between charity and fundraiser was negotiated at an arm's length basis. But it contends that the contract was so advantageous to W & H and so disadvantageous to UCC that the charity must be deemed to have surrendered the control of its operations and earnings to the noncharitable enterprise that it had hired to raise money for it.

The facts are undisputed. In 1984, UCC was a tiny organization. It had an annual operating budget of only $35,000, and it was on the brink of bankruptcy because several of its larger member societies had defected to its rival, the American Cancer Society. A committee of the board picked W & H, a specialist in raising funds for charities, as the best prospect for raising the funds essential for UCC's survival. Another committee of the board was created to negotiate the contract. Because of UCC's perilous financial condition, the committee wanted W & H to "front" all the expenses of the fundraising campaign, though it would be reimbursed by UCC as soon as the campaign generated sufficient donations to cover those expenses. W & H agreed. But it demanded in return that it be made UCC's exclusive fundraiser during the five-year term of the contract, that it be given co-ownership of the list of prospective donors generated by its fundraising efforts, and that UCC be forbidden, both during the term of the contract and after it expired, to sell or lease the list, although it would be free to use it to solicit repeat donations. There was no restriction on W & H's use of the list. UCC agreed to these terms and the contract went into effect.

Over the five-year term of the contract, W & H mailed 80 million letters soliciting contributions to UCC. Each letter contained advice about preventing cancer, as well as a pitch for donations; 70 percent of the letters also offered the recipient a chance to win a sweepstake. The text of all the letters was reviewed and approved by UCC. As a result of these mailings, UCC raised an enormous amount of money (by its standards)—$28.8 million. But its expenses—that is, the costs borne by W & H for postage, printing, and mailing the letters soliciting donations, costs reimbursed by UCC according to the terms of the contract—were also enormous—$26.5 million. The balance, $2.3 million, the net proceeds of the direct-mail campaign, was spent by UCC for services to cancer patients and on research for the prevention and treatment of cancer. The charity was permitted by the relevant accounting conventions to classify $12.2 million of its fundraising expenses as educational expenditures because of the cancer information contained in the fundraising letters.

Although UCC considered its experience with W & H successful, it did not renew the contract when it expired by its terms in 1989. Instead, it hired another fundraising organization—with disastrous results. The following year, UCC declared bankruptcy, and within months the IRS revoked its tax exemption retroactively to the date on which UCC had signed the contract with W & H. The effect was to make the IRS a major creditor of UCC in the bankruptcy proceeding. The retroactive revocation did not, however, affect the charitable deduction that donors to UCC since 1984 had taken on their income tax returns.

The term "any private shareholder or individual" in the inurement clause of section 501(c)(3) of the Internal Revenue Code has been interpreted to mean an insider of the charity. A charity is not to siphon its earnings to its founder, or the members of its board, or their families, or anyone else fairly to be described as an insider, that is, as the equivalent of an owner or manager. The test is functional. It looks to the reality of control rather than to the insider's place in a formal table of organization. The insider could be a "mere" employee—or even a nominal outsider, such as a physician with hospital privileges in a charitable hospital, or for that matter a fundraiser, National Foundation, Inc. v. United States, 13 Cl.Ct. 486, 494–95 (1987)—though the court in that case rejected the argument that the fundraiser controlled the charity.

The Tax Court's classification of W & H as an insider of UCC was based on the fundraising contract. Such contracts are common. Fundraising has become a specialized professional activity and many charities hire specialists in it. If the charity's contract with the fundraiser makes the latter an insider, triggering the inurement clause of section 501(c)(3) and so destroying the charity's tax exemption, the charity sector of the economy is in trouble. The IRS does not take the position that every such contract has this effect. What troubles it are the particular terms and circumstances of UCC's contract. It argues that since at the inception of the contract the charity had no money to speak of, and since, therefore, at least at the beginning, all the expenses of the fundraising campaign were borne by W & H, the latter was like a founder, or rather refounder (UCC was created in 1963), of the charity. The IRS points out that 90 percent of the contributions received by UCC during the term of the contract were paid to W & H to defray the cost of the fundraising campaign that brought in those contributions, and so argues that W & H was the real recipient of the contributions. It argues that because W & H was UCC's only fundraiser, the charity was totally at W & H's mercy during the five-year term of the contract—giving W & H effective control over the charity. UCC even surrendered the right to rent out the list of names of donors that the fundraising campaign generated. The terms of the contract were more favorable to the fundraiser than the terms of the average fundraising contract are.

Singly and together, these points bear no relation that we can see to the inurement provision. The provision is designed to prevent the siphoning of charitable receipts to insiders of the charity, not to empower the IRS to monitor the terms of arm's length contracts made by charitable organizations with the firms that supply them with essential inputs, whether premises, paper, computers, legal advice, or fundraising services.

Take the Service's first point, that W & H defrayed such a large fraction of the charity's total expenses in the early stages of the contract that it was the equivalent of a founder. Pushed to its logical extreme, this argument would deny the charitable tax exemption to any new or small charity that wanted to grow by soliciting donations, since it would have to get the cash to pay for the solicitations from an outside source, logically a fundraising organization. We can't see what this has to do with inurement. The argument is connected to another of the Service's points, that W & H was UCC's only fundraiser during the period of the contract. If UCC had hired ten fundraisers, the Service couldn't argue that any of them was so large a recipient of the charity's expenditures that it must be deemed to have controlled the charity. Yet in terms of the purposes of the inurement clause, it makes no difference how many fundraisers a charity employs. W & H obtained an exclusive contract, and thus was the sole fundraiser, not because it sought to control UCC and suck it dry, but because it was taking a risk; the exclusive contract lent assurance that if the venture succeeded, UCC wouldn't hire other fundraisers to reap where W & H had sown.

And it was only at the beginning of the contract period that W & H was funding UCC. As donations poured into the charity's coffers as a result of the success of the fundraising campaign, the charity began paying for the subsequent stages of the campaign out of its own revenues. True, to guarantee recoupment, the contract with W & H required UCC to place these funds in an escrow account, from which they could be withdrawn for UCC's charitable purposes only after W & H recovered the expenses of the fundraising campaign. But this is a detail; the important point is that UCC did not receive repeated infusions of capital from W & H. All the advances that W & H had made to UCC to fund the fundraising campaign were repaid. Indeed, it is an essential part of the government's case that W & H profited from the contract.

The other point that the Service makes about the exclusivity provision in the contract—that it put the charity at the mercy of the fundraiser, since if W & H stopped its fundraising efforts UCC would be barred from hiring another fundraiser until the contract with W & H expired—merely demonstrates the Service's ignorance of contract law. When a firm is granted an exclusive contract, the law reads into it an obligation that the firm use its best efforts to promote the contract's objectives. If W & H folded its tent and walked away, it would be in breach of this implied term of the contract and UCC would be free to terminate the contract without liability.

The Service also misses the significance of the contract's asymmetrical treatment of the parties' rights in the donor list. The charitable-fundraising community distinguishes between "prospect files" and "housefiles." A prospect file is a list of people who have not given to the charity in question but are thought sufficiently likely to do so to be placed on the list of addressees of a direct-mail fundraising campaign. If the prospect responds with a donation, his or her name is transferred to the housefile, that is, the list of people who have made a donation to the charity. A housefile is very valuable, because people who have already donated to a particular charity are more likely to donate to it again than mere prospects are likely to donate to it for the first time. The housefile's value to the charity is thus as a list of people who are good prospects to respond favorably to future solicitations. Its value to the fundraiser is quite different. The fundraiser is not a charity. The value to it of a housefile that it has created is the possibility of marketing it (as a prospect file—but as a prospect file in which all the prospects are charitable donors rather than a mere cross-section of potential donors) to another charity that hires it. So it made perfect sense for the contract to give the fundraiser the exclusive right to use the UCC housefile that it created in raising money for other charities, while reserving to UCC the right to use the housefile to solicit repeat donations to itself.

The Service's point that has the most intuitive appeal is the high ratio of fundraising expenses, all of which went to W & H because it was UCC's only fundraiser during the term of the contract, to net charitable proceeds. Of the $28–odd million that came in, $26–plus million went right back out, to W & H. These figures are deceptive, because UCC got a charitable "bang" from the mailings themselves, which contained educational materials (somewhat meager, to be sure) in direct support of the charity's central charitable goal. A charity whose entire goal was to publish educational materials would spend all or most of its revenues on publishing, but this would be in support rather than in derogation of its charitable purposes.

Even if this point is ignored, the ratio of expenses to net charitable receipts is unrelated to the issue of inurement. For one thing, it is a ratio of apples to oranges: the gross expenses of the fundraiser to the net receipts of the charity. For all that appears, while UCC derived a net benefit from the contract equal to the difference between donations and expenses plus the educational value of the mailings, W & H derived only a modest profit; for we know what UCC paid it, but not what its expenses were. The record does contain a table showing that W & H incurred postage and printing expenses of $12.5 million, but there is nothing on its total expenses.

To the extent that the ratio of net charitable proceeds to the cost to the charity of generating those proceeds has any relevance, it is to a different issue, one not presented by this appeal, which is whether charities should be denied a tax exemption if their operating expenses are a very high percentage of the total charitable donations that they receive. To see that it's a different issue, just imagine that UCC had spent $26 million to raise $28 million but that the $26 million had been scattered among a host of suppliers rather than concentrated on one. There would be no issue of inurement, because the Service would have no basis for singling out one of these suppliers as being in "control" of UCC (or the suppliers as a group, unless they were acting in concert). But there might still be a concern either that the charity was mismanaged or that charitable enterprises that generate so little net contribution to their charitable goals do not deserve the encouragement that a tax exemption provides. Recall that most of UCC's fundraising appeals offered the recipient of the appeal a chance to win a sweepstake, a form of charitable appeal that, we are told, is frowned upon. There may even be a question of how reputable W & H is (or was). But these points go to UCC's sound judgment, not to whether W & H succeeded in wresting control over UCC from the charity's board.

UCC's low net yield is no doubt related to the terms of the fundraising contract, which were more favorable to the fundraiser than the average such contract. But so far as appears, they were favorable to W & H not because UCC's board was disloyal and mysteriously wanted to shower charity on a fundraiser with which it had no affiliation or overlapping membership or common ownership or control, but because UCC was desperate. The charity drove (so far as the record shows) the best bargain that it could, but it was not a good bargain. Maybe desperate charities should be encouraged to fold rather than to embark on expensive campaigns to raise funds. But that too is a separate issue from inurement. W & H did not, by reason of being able to drive a hard bargain, become an insider of UCC. If W & H was calling the shots, why did UCC refuse to renew the contract when it expired, and instead switch to another fundraiser?

We can find nothing in the facts to support the IRS's theory and the Tax Court's finding that W & H seized control of UCC and by doing so became an insider, triggering the inurement provision and destroying the exemption. There is nothing that corporate or agency law would recognize as control. A creditor of UCC could not seek the satisfaction of his claim from W & H on the ground that the charity was merely a cat's paw or alter ego of W & H, as in Pepper v. Litton, 308 U.S. 295, 311–12, 60 S.Ct. 238, 84 L.Ed. 281 (1939), or Freeman v. Complex Computing Co., 119 F.3d 1044, 1051–53 (2d Cir.1997). The Service and the Tax Court are using "control" in a special sense not used elsewhere, so far as we can determine, in the law, including federal tax law. It is a sense which, as the amicus curiae briefs filed in support of UCC point out, threatens to unsettle the charitable sector by empowering the IRS to yank a charity's tax exemption simply because the Service thinks the charity's contract with its major fundraiser too one-sided in favor of the fundraiser, even though the charity has not been found to have violated any duty of faithful and careful management that the law of nonprofit corporations may have laid upon it. The resulting uncertainty about the charity's ability to retain its tax exemption—and receive tax-exempt donations—would be a particular deterrent to anyone contemplating a donation, loan, or other financial contribution to a new or small charity. That is the type most likely to be found by the IRS to have surrendered control over its destiny to a fundraiser or other supplier, because it is the type of charity that is most likely to have to pay a high price for fundraising services. It is hard enough for new, small, weak, or marginal charities to survive, because they are likely to have a high expense ratio, and many potential donors will be put off by that. The Tax Court's decision if sustained would make the survival of such charities even more dubious, by enveloping them in doubt about their tax exemption.

We were not reassured when the government's lawyer, in response to a question from the bench as to what standard he was advocating to guide decision in this area, said that it was the "facts and circumstances" of each case. That is no standard at all, and makes the tax status of charitable organizations and their donors a matter of the whim of the IRS.

There was no diversion of charitable revenues to an insider here, nothing that smacks of self-dealing, disloyalty, breach of fiduciary obligation or other misconduct of the type aimed at by a provision of law that forbids a charity to divert its earnings to members of the board or other insiders. What there may have been was imprudence on the part of UCC's board of directors in hiring W & H and negotiating the contract that it did. Maybe the only prudent course in the circumstances that confronted UCC in 1984 was to dissolve. Charitable organizations are plagued by incentive problems. Nobody owns the right to the profits and therefore no one has the spur to efficient performance that the lure of profits creates. Donors are like corporate shareholders in the sense of being the principal source of the charity's funds, but they do not have a profit incentive to monitor the care with which the charity's funds are used. Maybe the lack of a profit motive made UCC's board too lax. Maybe the board did not negotiate as favorable a contract with W & H as the board of a profitmaking firm would have done. And maybe tax law has a role to play in assuring the prudent management of charities. Remember the IRS's alternative basis for yanking UCC's exemption? It is that as a result of the contract's terms, UCC was not really operated exclusively for charitable purposes, but rather for the private benefit of W & H as well. Suppose that UCC was so irresponsibly managed that it paid W & H twice as much for fundraising services as W & H would have been happy to accept for those services, so that of UCC's $26 million in fundraising expense $13 million was the equivalent of a gift to the fundraiser. Then it could be argued that UCC was in fact being operated to a significant degree for the private benefit of W & H, though not because it was the latter's creature. That then would be a route for using tax law to deal with the problem of improvident or extravagant expenditures by a charitable organization that do not, however, inure to the benefit of insiders.

That in fact is the IRS's alternative ground for revoking the exemption, the one the Tax Court gave a bye to. It would have been better had the court resolved that ground as well as the inurement ground, so that the case could be definitively resolved in one appeal. But it did not, and so the case must be remanded to enable the court to consider it. We shall not prejudge the proceedings on remand. The usual "private benefit" case is one in which the charity has dual public and private goals, and that is not involved here. However, the board of a charity has a duty of care, just like the board of an ordinary business corporation, and a violation of that duty which involved the dissipation of the charity's assets might (we need not decide whether it would—we leave that issue to the Tax Court in the first instance) support a finding that the charity was conferring a private benefit, even if the contracting party did not control, or exercise undue influence over, the charity. This, for all we know, may be such a case.

REVERSED AND REMANDED.

NOTES AND QUESTIONS

1. *Episode 2: Back to the Tax Court.* The *United Cancer Council* case was pending in the Tax Court for over seven years, but the Seventh Circuit issued its reversal only five weeks after hearing oral argument. Judge Posner strongly disagreed with the IRS's attempt to extend the reach of the inurement limitation to outsiders whose only relationship to an exempt organization is the product of an arm's length agreement negotiated in good faith. The unseemly ratio of fundraising expenses to charitable dollars was not enough to convince the court to turn outsiders into insiders.

2. *The Final Episode: Settlement on Remand.* The Tax Court was deprived of the opportunity to reconsider the case when the IRS and UCC settled their longstanding exemption dispute in February, 2000. UCC, which had filed for bankruptcy, conceded that it was not entitled to exemption under § 501(c)(3) for the years 1986–1989, and the IRS restored UCC's exemption from 1990 forward. As a condition to the settlement, UCC agreed to stop raising funds from the general public and to limit its activities to accepting charitable bequests and transmitting them to local cancer councils for direct care of patients.

Although no Tax Court guidance will be forthcoming on the private benefit issue in *UCC*, its precedential value would have been minimal in any event because the IRS's focus has shifted away from the inurement and private benefit doctrines with the enactment of the § 4958 intermediate sanctions regime. For a discussion of the UCC settlement, see Carolyn D. Wright, UCC, IRS Settle Decade–Long Exemption Dispute: 501(c)(3) Status Revoked for Three Years, 28 Exempt Org. Tax Rev. 189 (2000). For the text of the settlement agreement, see 28 Exempt Org. Tax Rev. 250 (2000).

How should the Tax Court have resolved the private benefit issue on remand? Did UCC violate its duty of care, resulting in a dissipation of the charity's assets, or did it simply make a bad deal that, bad as it was, still allowed UCC to make some charitable grants rather than just dissolve? And who should regulate the excesses of professional fundraisers—the IRS or the states?

3. *Implications.* Judge Posner's decision may influence the development of standards under § 4958. Unlike the "insiders" who can cause an organization to lose its § 501(c)(3) exemption, § 4958 penalizes a potentially broader group of individuals and firms who wield substantial influence over the organization. Judge Posner recognized that being an insider for inurement purposes does not require having a formal title or position—a view consistent with the § 4958 regulations. The more important issue may be whether the definition of "disqualified person" extends further to firms such as Watson & Hughey, who have the economic power to overwhelm a weak charity and exploit its appealing name.

2.   INTERMEDIATE SANCTIONS ON EXCESS BENEFIT TRANSACTIONS

Internal Revenue Code: §§ 4958; 6033(b)(11), (12).

Treasury Regulations: § 1.4958–1 through –8.

Background. The extreme nature of the sanctions for inurement and private benefit—revocation of exemption—and the uncertain scope of those limitations caused enforcement difficulties for the IRS. During hearings held in 1993 by the Oversight Subcommittee of the House Ways and Means Committee, then IRS Commissioner Margaret Richardson addressed the problem, observing that revocation of an exemption for minor or isolated instances of inurement can be a sanction that is greatly disproportionate to the crime. In theory, for example, a university would violate the inurement limitation by paying its president or football coach excessive compensation, but revocation of the university's exemption would be a severe penalty that would adversely affect a large and innocent community of students, faculty, staff, and alumni. And even if the organization lost its exemption, the overcompensated president or coach would not be penalized.

At the 1993 Hearings, IRS officials provided titillating examples of abusive transactions, including the following summaries of actual cases:

* * * (1) a health care organization, in a clinic-type setting, controlled by a CEO and small board, all of the members of which have substantial dealings with the CEO and the organization, paid the CEO more

than $1 million, including a substantial distribution from an executive compensation plan and premium payments on several hundreds of thousands of dollars in life insurance. The organization made substantial credit card payments and cash disbursements for personal expenses. The organization sold its charitable assets and began purchasing physicians' private practices at prices in excess of fair market value, and the physicians and their staffs became employees of the organization. * * * (3) An organization which provided educational services gave its CEO a residence, including maid service and a significant compensation package, including salary, deferred compensation, expense accounts, and loans (one of which is noninterest bearing). * * * (6) A television ministry paid personal expenses for the minister, including a home mortgage, household expenses, country club membership dues, additional homes, and a house for a member of the minister's family. * * * (8) A number of organizations, nearly all of which were viable organizations with ongoing charitable programs, had virtually all of their donations absorbed by a for-profit fundraiser with very little money being made available for the organizations' charitable programs. The true fundraising costs were not discernible from looking at the annual information return, Form 990, because a substantial portion of the costs were allocated to and reported as program services rather than fundraising costs.

Report on Reforms to Improve the Tax Rules Governing Public Charities, Subcomm. on Oversight of House Comm. on Ways and Means, 103d Cong., 2d Sess. 14–15 (1994).

In response to these concerns and revelations, a consensus emerged in favor of a new regulatory scheme that would impose excise tax sanctions short of exemption revocation where a § 501(c)(3) or § 501(c)(4) organization provided excessive economic benefits to "insiders." After several false starts, Congress enacted intermediate sanctions legislation in 1996 by adding § 4958 to the Internal Revenue Code. Section 4958 is modelled on the excise taxes for self-dealing and other transgressions by private foundations (see I.R.C. §§ 4941–4945, and Chapter 3C, infra, at pp. 456–489), and the penalties for excessive lobbying by public charities (see I.R.C. §§ 501(h), 4911, and Section F4 of this chapter, infra, at pp. 308–317). After a four-year gestation and comment period, the IRS in 2002 issued lengthy final regulations that have become required reading for legal advisors to exempt organizations. The highlights of these regulations and some of the more important details are summarized in the text that follows.

Overview of § 4958. Section 4958 applies to an "applicable exempt organization," a category limited to organizations described in § 501(c)(3) and § 501(c)(4) other than private foundations. I.R.C. § 4958(e)(1). To prevent organizations from converting to taxable status to avoid penalties, § 4958 also applies to organizations that are not tax-exempt at the time of the excess benefit transaction under scrutiny but were described in § 501(c)(3) or § 501(c)(4) during a five-year lookback period ending on the date of the transaction. I.R.C. § 4958(e)(2); Treas. Reg. § 53.4958–2(a)(1).

Governmental units or affiliates that are not subject to income tax without regard to § 501(c), including state colleges and universities, are not subject to the § 4958 regime even if they may have voluntarily applied for and received a § 501(c)(3) exemption. Treas. Reg. § 53.4958–2(a)(2)(ii).

The § 4958 sanction—"intermediate" in that it almost always is in lieu of any revocation of exemption—is an excise tax penalty on any "excess benefit transaction" between the exempt organization and a "disqualified person." I.R.C. § 4958(a), (c). The initial penalty is 25 percent of the excess benefit. It is imposed on the disqualified person, not the organization. Lesser penalties also may be imposed on one or more of the organization's "managers" who knowingly permit the organization to engage in an excess benefit transaction. I.R.C. § 4958(a)(2). The disqualified person may be liable for an additional second-tier tax of 200 percent of the excess benefit if the violation is not "corrected" within a specified period of time. I.R.C. § 4958(b). "Correction" essentially means undoing the excess benefit to the extent possible—e.g., restoring the organization to a financial position no worse than it would have been in if the disqualified person had been dealing under the highest fiduciary standards. I.R.C. § 4958(f)(6); Treas. Reg. § 53.4958–1(c)(2).

Effect on Exempt Status. The legislative history indicates that the § 4958 excise taxes are intended to be the sole sanction where the excess benefit does not rise to the level where it calls into question the organization's status. H.R. Rep. No. 506, 104th Cong., 2d Sess. 59, n. 15 (1996) (hereinafter "House Report"). Revocation of an organization's exemption on the ground of inurement thus will occur only in the most egregious situations where the organization is no longer "charitable." The preamble to proposed regulations issued in 1998 elaborated by listing four factors to be considered in determining whether revocation of exemption was appropriate: (1) whether the organization has been involved in repeated excess benefit transactions; (2) the size and scope of the excess benefit; (3) whether, after discovering its initial noncompliance, the organization has implemented safeguards to prevent recurrence; and (4) whether the organization complied with other applicable laws. 63 Fed. Reg. 41486, 41488 (Aug. 4, 1998). The final regulations removed these factors and are silent on this important question. The preamble states that the IRS is still considering what other guidance to provide and, until it does so, it will consider "all relevant facts and circumstances." T.D. 8978, 67 Fed. Reg. 3076 (Jan. 23, 2002).

Disqualified Persons. As is the norm with much recent tax legislation, deciphering § 4958 requires a mastery of a new statutory vocabulary. The "insiders" who are potentially subject to the 25 percent tax are called "disqualified persons" ("DQPs"). A DQP is "any person who was, at any time during the five-year period [preceding the excess benefit transaction] in a position to exercise substantial influence over the affairs of the organization." I.R.C. § 4958(f)(1)(A); Treas. Reg. § 53.4958–3(a)(1). The DQP category also includes certain members of the family of the person with substantial influence and controlled entities (e.g., a corporation or partnership where more than 35 percent of the voting power is held by DQPs). I.R.C. § 4958(f); Treas. Reg. § 53.4958–3(b).

DQPs include officers, directors, trustees and their close relatives, but the lack of a formal title does not immunize an individual from DQP status if that person is in a position to exercise substantial influence. Conversely, individuals holding honorary titles are not DQPs if in reality they have no powers or ultimate responsibility. I.R.C. § 4958(f); Treas. Reg. § 53.4958–3(c). The statutory "substantial influence" standard is potentially quite broad, and soon after § 4958 was enacted, questions arose as to exactly who was or was not a DQP. For example, can a newly hired person with no prior relationship to an organization be a DQP, or are first-timers protected by a "one-free-bite" principle? What about outsiders, such as a for-profit fundraiser or partner in a joint venture, who can influence an exempt organization's activities by virtue of a contractual relationship negotiated at arm's length? Cf. United Cancer Council v. Commissioner, supra p. 226.

The regulations provide many answers. For example, they make it clear, overturning a prior IRS legal opinion, that staff physicians at a hospital are DQPs only if they are in a position to exercise substantial influence over the affairs of the organization. Treas. Reg. § 53.4958–3(g) Examples (10) & (11). Independent contractors, such as attorneys, accountants and investment advisors, will not be DQPs if their sole relationship to an organization is rendering professional advice and they do not have decisionmaking authority with respect to transactions from which they derive no personal economic benefit other than customary fees. Treas. Reg. § 53.4958–3(e)(3)(ii); see also Treas. Reg. § 53.4958–3(g) Example 12.

The regulations also deem three categories of "persons" as not having enough substantial influence to be DQPs: (1) other applicable § 501(c)(3) exempt organizations with respect to organizations with which, for example, they may be affiliated, (2) as to § 501(c)(4) social welfare organizations, any other § 501(c)(4) organization (leaving open the possibility that a "(c)(4)" may be a DQP with respect to transactions with a related "(c)(3)"), and (3) employees who are not statutorily-defined DQPs (such as directors, officers, or substantial contributors to the organization or related family members) and who, for the taxable year in which the benefits are provided, are not "highly compensated"—i.e., they do not receive economic benefits of more than an indexed cap ($90,000 in 2002). Treas. Reg. § 53.4958–3(d).[1] Apart from these specifically included and excluded categories, the determination of a person's DQP status is based on all the facts and circumstances bearing on the question of substantial influence. Treas. Reg. § 53.4958–3(a), (e). The regulations provide a list of factors tending to show that a person does or does not have such influence, along with numerous examples. See Treas. Reg. § 53.4958–3(e)(2)–(3), (g).

---

1. See I.R.C. § 414(q)(1)(B)(i) for the definition of "highly compensated," which § 4958 borrows from the rules governing qualified retirement plans. Note that being paid more than the "highly compensated" cap does not automatically make one a DQP. See Treas. Reg. § 53.4958–3(g) Example (9).

Initial Contract Exception. The regulations address the "first timer" question with an initial contract exception crafted in response to the Seventh Circuit's *United Cancer Council* decision. Although *United Cancer Council* was not a § 4958 case, it influenced the Service to conclude that a one-free bite rule was appropriate in certain situations.

The regulations generally provide that § 4958 does not apply to any fixed payment made to a person with respect to an initial contract, regardless of whether the payment would otherwise constitute an EBT. Treas. Reg. § 53.4958–4(a)(3)(i). For this purpose, an "initial contract" is a binding written contract between an exempt organization and a person who was not a DQP immediately prior to entering into the contract. Treas. Reg. § 53.4958–4(a)(3)(iii). A "fixed payment" is an amount of cash or other property specified in the contract or determined by a specified objective "fixed formula" (e.g., a nondiscretionary bonus based on future revenue generated by the organization's activities), which is to be paid or transferred in exchange for the provision of specified services or property. Treas. Reg. § 53.4958–4(a)(3)(ii)(A). If an initial contract provides for both fixed and non-fixed (e.g., discretionary) payments, the fixed payments will not be subject to § 4958 while the non-fixed payments may be scrutinized, taking into account the DQP's entire compensation package. Treas. Reg. § 53.4958–4(a)(3)(vi).

The theory of the initial contract exception is that a person who negotiates in good faith before he is in a position to exercise substantial influence should not be subject to sanctions even if the consideration received turns out to be excessive. But immunity is not considered to be appropriate with respect to payments where future discretion must be exercised (and thus may be subject to the DQP's substantial influence) in calculating the amount or deciding whether to make a payment. For 11 examples illustrating the application of the initial contract rule, see Treas. Reg. § 53.4958–4(a)(3)(vii).

Excess Benefit Transactions: In General. An "excess benefit transaction" is any transaction in which an economic benefit is provided by an exempt organization directly or indirectly (e.g., by a taxable subsidiary) to or for the use of any DQP if the value of the benefit exceeds the value of the consideration received by the organization for providing the benefit. I.R.C. § 4958(c)(1); Treas. Reg. § 53.4958–4(a)(1), (2). Obvious examples are payment of unreasonable compensation, bargain sales, or below-market loans that benefit a DQP. In adopting a market-driven standard for compensation, Congress rejected an earlier proposal to impose a fixed dollar cap (e.g., the salary paid to the President of the United States) on compensation paid by charitable and social welfare organizations. Indeed, the legislative history states unequivocally that an individual need not accept reduced compensation because he or she renders services to a tax-exempt as opposed to a taxable organization. House Report, supra, at 56.

The regulations incorporate existing tax-law standards under § 162 in determining reasonableness of compensation.[2] Compensation is reasonable if it is comparable to what "would ordinarily be paid for like services by like enterprises under like circumstances." Treas. Reg. § 53.4958–4(b)(1)(ii)(A). The regulations elaborate at length, providing a list of items to be considered (e.g., all forms of cash and noncash compensation, whether or not taxable, including bonuses, deferred compensation and many fringe benefits. Treas. Reg. § 53.4958–4(b)(1)(B).

Disguised Benefits. Several types of benefits are disregarded in evaluating compensation for § 4958 purposes, including: (1) most employee fringe benefits that are excluded from gross income under § 132 (such as an employer's payments of professional dues and other employee business expenses); (2) certain expense reimbursement arrangements; (3) benefits provided to a DQP solely as a member of or volunteer for the exempt organization if the same benefit is available to the public in exchange for a membership fee of no more than $75 per year (e.g., discounts at a museum gift shop); and (4) economic benefits provided to a DQP solely as a member of a charitable class that the organization intends to benefit in connection with the accomplishment of its exempt purposes. Treas. Reg. § 53.4958–4(a)(4)(i)–(iv). An organization's payment of premiums for liability insurance covering § 4958 excise taxes or indemnification for such taxes will not constitute an EBT if the premium or indemnification is treated as compensation to the DQP when paid and the DQP's total compensation is reasonable. Treas. Reg. § 53.4958–4(a)(4).

Establishing Intent to Treat Economic Benefit as Compensation. To monitor disguised compensation, an economic benefit is not treated as consideration for services for § 4958 purposes unless the exempt organization clearly indicates its intent to treat the benefit as compensation when it is paid. To establish its intent, an organization must provide "written substantiation that is contemporaneous with the transfer of the economic benefits at issue." Treas. Reg. § 53.4958–4(c)(1). Contemporaneous substantiation can be accomplished by including the value of the benefit as wages or nonemployee compensation on an original or amended information return, such as a W–2 or 1099, unless the benefit is nontaxable, such as employer-provided medical insurance or qualified pension plan contributions. I.R.C. § 4958(c)(1)(A); Treas. Reg. § 53.4958–4(c)(1). Under a safe harbor, an organization is not required to substantiate its intent to provide an economic benefit as compensation if the benefit is excluded from the DQP's income for income tax purposes. Treas. Reg. § 53.4958–4(c)(2). As a result, although contributions to qualified retirement plans and other nontaxable benefits must be taken into account in determining if compensation is reasonable (unless specifically disregarded—e.g., de minimis and certain other fringe benefits excluded from gross income under § 132), they

---

2. See Treas. Reg. § 1.162–7(b)(3). These "existing standards" are used to determine whether a taxpayer, usually a corporation, may deduct compensation paid to employees as a business expense. "Unrea- sonable" compensation, which typically represents a disguised (nondeductible) dividend to employees who also are shareholders, is not tax-deductible.

are not subject to the contemporaneous written substantiation requirement. All of this is supposed to make it easier for exempt organizations, but the regulations are sufficiently detailed and technical that moderately sophisticated tax advice will be required to follow the regulatory roadmap.

All these rules on establishing intent are intended to prevent an organization from claiming, after an IRS challenge, that an excess benefit was actually compensation and that the DQP's overall compensation was reasonable. Such an argument is essentially foreclosed unless the benefit was part of an authorized compensation package and was treated as such for tax compliance purposes. For example, assume an organization pays its executive director a $200,000 base salary plus $40,000 in various fringe benefits, and the overall compensation package is reasonable. Assume that the organization also pays $20,000 of the executive director's personal living expenses and does not include this benefit as compensation, but if it had done so the director's overall compensation still would have been reasonable. The organization's failure to establish its intent to treat the $20,000 as compensation at the time it was paid causes the payment of the living expenses to be treated as an excess benefit transaction unless the organization can show reasonable cause for the oversight.[3] See Treas. Reg. § 53.4958–4(c)(3)(i)(B), –4(c)(4) Example 2.

If the requisite intent to treat an economic benefit as compensation is not established, the regulations permit a DQP who discovers the failure to amend his or her federal income tax return to report a benefit as income at any time prior to when the Service commences an audit of the DQP or the exempt organization. Treas. Reg. § 53.4958–4(c)(3)(i)(B).

Revenue-Sharing Transactions. A more specialized type of excess benefit transaction may result from revenue-sharing arrangements that constitute inurement to the DQP. I.R.C. § 4958(c)(2). The scope of this rule is uncertain. It potentially affects performance-based compensation arrangements and more complex deals to share revenue from intellectual property or other income-producing activities.

The proposed § 4958 regulations looked to all the facts and circumstances, including the relationship between the size of the benefit provided and the quality and quantity of services provided, as well as the service provider's ability to control the revenue-generating activities on which the compensation was based. Prop. Treas. Reg. § 53.4958–5(a). For example, incentive compensation paid to an exempt organization's in-house money manager was not an EBT when it was based on performance of the portfolio because the employee's compensation increased only when the organization received a proportional benefit. Prop. Treas. Reg. § 53.4958–5(d) Example 1. But a percentage of net revenue arrangement where the DQP controlled the revenue-generating activity and has no incentive to maximize benefits and minimize costs to the exempt organization would trigger a penalty. Prop. Treas. Reg. § 53.4958–5(d) Example 2. All this

---

3. The executive director also may have other income tax problems resulting from the failure to include the $20,000 of benefits in gross income.

helpful guidance was removed from the final regulations while the IRS gives the issue more thought. In the meantime, revenue-sharing arrangements will be evaluated by applying the general rules governing excess benefits, leaving a lingering fog of uncertainty.

Rebuttable Presumption of Reasonableness. The regulations provide that the parties to a transaction may rely on a rebuttable presumption of reasonableness with respect to a compensation arrangement with a DQP if certain procedures are followed. See Treas. Reg. § 53.4958–6. The emphasis is on process. A transaction is presumed not to be an excess benefit transaction if:

(1) its terms are approved in advance by a governing board (or board committee) composed entirely of individuals who have no conflict of interest with respect to the transaction;

(2) prior to making a determination, these disinterested individuals obtained and relied upon appropriate comparability data (e.g., compensation levels paid by similarly situated organizations, both taxable and tax-exempt, for functionally comparable positions; independent compensation surveys by nationally recognized firms; or actual written offers from similar institutions competing for the services of the DQP); and

(3) the board adequately documented the basis for its determination (e.g., the record includes an evaluation of the individual whose compensation was being established and the basis for determining that the individual's compensation was reasonable in light of that evaluation and data).

Treas. Reg. § 53.4958–6(a)(1)–(3). A similar presumption is provided for purposes of valuing property transfers between an exempt organization and a DQP when the transaction is approved by an independent board using appropriate comparability data and adequately documenting its determination. See Id.

From a planning standpoint, the rebuttable presumption of reasonableness is the most important feature of the new regulatory scheme. Organizations are well advised to follow the prescribed procedures to shift the burden of proof to the Service, which must develop sufficient contrary evidence to rebut the probative value of the evidence put forth by the parties to the transaction. Treas. Reg. § 53.4958–6(b). For example, in an unreasonable compensation controversy where the presumption applied, the Service would need to establish that the compensation data relied upon by the parties was not for a functionally comparable position or that the DQP did not substantially perform the responsibilities of the position.

The rebuttable presumption is the product of lobbying by large mainstream exempt organizations with the resources and legal expertise to follow the prescribed procedures. It has the potential of providing full employment for compensation consultants who offer their services, often at great expense, to provide adequate comparability data and help nonprofit boards document the salary packages offered to their key insiders. In response to concerns about the expense of compliance, the regulations offer flexibility on the type of comparability data on which the governing body may rely. A governing body will have appropriate comparability data if, given the knowledge and expertise of its members, it has information sufficient to determine whether the compensation arrangement is reasonable or a property transfer is at fair market value. Treas. Reg. § 53.4958–6(c)(2)(i). This would permit the use of less customized or internally developed data, such as an industry compensation survey or even documented phone calls, as long as the comparables were relevant to the position under scrutiny. See, e.g., Treas. Reg. § 53.4958–6(c)(iv) Examples.

For organizations with average annual gross receipts (including contributions) of less than $1 million (on average over the three years preceding the taxable year), the regulations provide additional relief by permitting these smaller nonprofits to rely on data obtained from three comparable organizations. Treas. Reg. § 53.4958–6(c)(2)(ii), (iii).

Either through ignorance or lack of resources, many affected exempt organizations will fail to satisfy the conditions for the rebuttable presumption. In those cases, the failure will not create any inference that the penalties should be imposed, but the taxpayer will bear the burden of proof, at least at the administrative level. Treas. Reg. § 53.4958–6(e).

Penalties on Organization Managers. Although exempt organizations are not penalized (except for loss of exemption in the most egregious cases) for participating in excess benefit transactions, organization managers are subject to a tax equal to 10 percent of the excess benefit (with the tax capped at $10,000) if their participation was knowing, willful, and not due to reasonable cause. I.R.C. § 4958(a)(2), (d)(2). Organization managers include officers, directors, trustees, and individuals with similar powers or responsibilities regardless of title, but not independent contractors such as attorneys, accountants, and investment advisors, and not middle managers with the power to make recommendations but not to implement decisions without approval of a superior. I.R.C. § 4958(f)(2); Treas. Reg. § 53.4958–1(d)(2)(i). If two or more managers share responsibility for the violation, they are jointly and severally liable. I.R.C. § 4958(d)(1). The best protection for an organization manager seeking to avoid an intermediate sanction is to fully disclose all the facts to a professional advisor and rely on that professional's advice, expressed in a reasoned written legal opinion, that a transaction with a DQP is not an excess benefit transaction. For that purpose, advisors include not merely lawyers but also accountants, accounting firms with expertise in valuation matters, and independent valuation experts. Treas. Reg. § 53.4958–1(d)(4)(iii). See also Treas. Reg. § 53.4958–1(d)(3)–(6) for more details and other defenses to organization manager sanctions.

Correction and Abatement. Once it is established that an excess benefit transaction has occurred, the DQP will be subject to an additional tax equal to 200 percent of the excess benefit unless the transaction is corrected promptly. I.R.C. § 4958(b). In general, the DQP must repay an amount of money equal to the excess benefit plus any additional amount needed to compensate the organization for loss of the use of the money or other property during a period beginning on the date of the excess benefit transaction and ending on the date of correction. Treas. Reg. § 53.4958–1(c)(2)(ii). The Service also is authorized under § 4962 to abate § 4958 penalties if it is established that the violation was due to reasonable cause and not willful neglect, and the transaction at issue was corrected within the specified correction period. Treas. Reg. § 53.4958–1(c)(2)(iii).

Disclosure Requirements. Section 501(c)(3) and § 501(c)(4) organizations must disclose on their annual informational tax returns (Form 990) the names of each DQP who received an excess benefit during the taxable year and such other information as the Service may require. I.R.C. § 6033(b)(11)–(12).

Judicial Interpretation of § 4958. The first reported intermediate sanctions case involved a Mississippi family and a group of health care organizations acquired by the family in a conversion transaction. At issue was the value of the nonprofit entities when they converted to for-profit status. The IRS argued that the nonprofits were significantly undervalued, resulting in excess benefits to the insiders who orchestrated the deal.

In Caracci v. Commissioner, 118 T.C. 379 (2002), the Tax Court held that the value of the transferred assets exceeded the value of the consideration received by the § 501(c)(3) organizations and upheld $11.6 million in intermediate sanctions penalties against various disqualified persons. The decision is a lengthy and fact-bloated valuation opinion—a typical battle of the experts—with extreme positions on both sides as "opening bids." The taxpayers' appraiser determined that the nonprofit organizations had a negative fair market value, while the Service contended that, despite operating losses, the organizations had substantial values to potential purchasers. The court sided with the Service on the intermediate sanctions issues. But it declined to revoke the exempt status of the organizations, finding that intermediate sanctions were sufficient in the circumstances. The court noted that it would be preferable to preserve the exemption and permit the organizations to benefit from the "correction" provisions made available through I.R.C. §§ 4961–4963. This aspect of the decision may influence the development of the relationship between § 4958 and revocation of tax exemption.

PROBLEMS

1. In each of the alternative situations described below, determine whether the organization risks loss of exemption under § 501(c)(3) because of inurement of private gain or substantial private benefit, and consider whether any of the parties would be subject to intermediate sanctions penalties under § 4958:

   (a) Urban Medical Center pays its chief executive officer a base annual salary of $700,000, and provides rent-free housing worth $40,000, free use of a car, a club membership, a standard fringe benefit package (medical and disability insurance, pension plan), and up to

$100,000 in low-interest loans for personal expenses. The Medical Center also pays the physician who heads its radiology department a fixed percentage of the department's gross income. In each case, the compensation package was approved by the Medical Center's board of directors, which consists of a broad group of prominent citizens in the community.

(b) Northern Exposure Hospital ("Hospital") is the only hospital within a 100–mile radius in a rural area of Montana. Hospital has a shortage of primary care physicians. Hospital wishes to entice Dr. Joel Fishbein, who recently completed an ob/gyn residency in Seattle, to establish his practice near Hospital and become a non-employee member of its staff. Hospital's board has agreed to offer the following recruitment incentives to Dr. Fishbein: a one-time bonus of $5,000, payment of his malpractice insurance premium for one year, free office space in a building owned by Hospital for three years, a low-interest home mortgage loan, and reimbursement of moving expenses.

(c) Private University ("University") hires Coach for an initial term as head coach of its highly successful men's collegiate basketball team. They agree to a three-year employment contract, with the following elements: $400,000 base salary paid by the University; an additional $100,000 paid by University's separately incorporated alumni association; a $50,000 bonus if the basketball team advances beyond the first round of the NCAA Tournament; and free use of a car, a country club membership, and a standard fringe benefit package (including medical and disability insurance and a qualified pension plan). University expects that Coach's presence will greatly increase fundraising and so it also agrees to pay him an amount equal to five percent of the gross amount raised for the basketball program. Finally, Coach receives an additional $500,000 pursuant to a contract with a for-profit company that provides shoes and other athletic apparel for use by student-athletes at University. What if the employment contract and other benefits were in connection with a five-year contract renewal? Would the analysis be any different if Coach was employed by a state university?

(d) Church TV is a nonprofit organization that produces a weekly religious television program on various cable television networks. It was formed by Minister to carry his messages to a mass audience. The board of directors of Church TV consists of Minister, his wife and his elderly mother. Minister's brother-in-law, a recent college graduate, serves as Church TV's chief financial officer. Church TV receives $40 million in annual contributions from the public. Its annual expenses average $43 million, including a $500,000 salary and $250,000 bonus to Minister, $250,000 to Minister's wife for secretarial services, a $100,000 director's fee paid to Minister's mother, and $400,000 paid to a fashion designer to design Minister's personal and professional clothing. Church TV's assets include a broadcast studio with a cost of $2 million and a $2 million parsonage for Minister and his family. Minister's son, a contractor, built the broadcast studio under an agreement providing for cost plus 200%.

(e) World Missionaries ("World") is a nonprofit religious corporation organized to provide financial assistance, through direct grants and interest-free loans, to missionaries of Church. The organization was founded by Frank Young, a former missionary, who plans to raise funds based on mail solicitations to church and community leaders, business people and others. Missionary work is an essential component of the church's doctrine. To attract fund raisers, World proposes to offer commissions of "up to 20 percent" of any money raised on the theory that "paying a commission gets the job done better than just hiring solicitors at a set salary." Mr. Young, one of three World trustees, has already raised $200,000 and is entitled to a $20,000 (10%) commission by agreement of the board of trustees.

(f) Same as (e), above, except in addition Telemarketers, Inc., an outside for-profit fundraising firm, raised $5 million but incurred $3.5 million in fundraising expenses. Pursuant to a negotiated agreement with World's board, Telemarketers was paid a $300,000 commission, representing 20 percent of the $1.5 million raised after expenses. As a result, World netted $1.2 million from the arrangement.

(g) The Political Campaign Academy is a nonprofit school and job placement service formed and funded to train professional staff to work in political campaigns. Its purpose is "to benefit the public by fostering the training of competent professional staff in the American political process." The Academy's board is controlled by members of the Democratic National Committee. Applicants are not required to state any political affiliation, and the Academy does not engage in any actual political campaign activity, but virtually all graduates end up working for Democratic candidates.

(h) The Foothills Land Trust, a conservation organization in the Sierra foothills of California, is organized and operated to preserve land as a living resource. Fleming James, one of its trustees, has proposed to donate a 300–acre parcel to the organization. James owns adjoining land that may increase in value as a result of the preservation of the donated parcel as open space. To induce James to make the donation, the organization will obtain an appraisal of the parcel and pay the appraiser's fee.

2. Jill Woods, a resident of New York, is a member of the board of trustees of Redwoods Forever, a large public charity based in California. Jill receives no salary, but Redwoods pays all travel costs (business class air fare, lodging and meals) to attend its quarterly board meetings. In keeping with its policy to foster better camaraderie, Redwoods encourages board members to bring their spouses to meetings and pays all the spouses' travel expenses. Spouses do not attend the formal meetings but they do partici-

pate in all meals and other social events. Redwoods also pays premiums for a directors and officers liability policy that covers Jill and her fellow board members. No Form 1099's or other tax information statements are provided to board members with respect to these travel reimbursements and insurance premiums. On the advice of her tax preparer, Jill does not include these items on her income tax return.

Is Jill liable for any intermediate sanctions penalties under § 4958?

3. Private University ("PU") is negotiating the renewal of an employment contract with Franz Arbitrage, its chief investment officer. Arbitrage is the highest paid employee of PU, earning a base salary and also an incentive fee based on the performance of the university's endowment relative to a benchmark. PU wishes to invoke the rebuttable presumption of correctness if Arbitrage's compensation package is ever challenged by the IRS. The university has requested your law firm to render a written opinion that the employment agreement with Arbitrage is not and will never be an excess benefit transaction.

(a) Who is your client? Does it matter?

(b) Is it appropriate for your firm to render a legal opinion on the reasonableness of Arbitrage's compensation? If so, what should that opinion include (and not include)?

E. COMMERCIAL ACTIVITIES AND JOINT VENTURES

1. THE COMMERCIALITY AND COMMENSURATE-IN-SCOPE DOCTRINES

Internal Revenue Code: § 502

Treasury Regulations: § 1.501(c)(3)–1(b)(1)(i), –1(c)(1), –1(e).

As previewed in Chapter 1, a nonprofit organization is not prohibited from making an economic profit. Many nonprofits engage in activities that are "commercial" in the sense that they resemble income-producing businesses conducted by for-profit firms. A business-like activity may be the exempt organization's very reason for existence (e.g., a health care provider or religious publisher), a support function that may or may not raise revenue (e.g., a museum cafeteria or gift shop), a wholly unrelated business activity conducted to raise funds for exempt purposes, or (worst case) an unrelated business that dedicates its profits to expand or buy other companies.

The "commercialization" of the nonprofit sector has been widely publicized and hotly debated for years. For-profit firms complain that they are victims of unfair competition, while nonprofit organizations counter that entrepreneurial activities are necessary to support their missions and reduce dependence on government and private philanthropy. Some major charities, principally in health care, higher education and the arts, have raised the stakes by conducting commercial activities through complex structures, such as corporate subsidiaries and joint ventures with for-profit entities and private investors. The IRS has responded by devoting more of its resources to patrolling the charity/business border. Congress has barked but rarely bitten, confining itself in recent years to occasional inquiries and threats, usually followed by inaction or special interest relief legislation.

The conduct of a business by an otherwise qualified § 501(c)(3) organization raises two distinct issues under current federal income tax law: first, does the activity adversely affect the organization's exempt status and, if not, should the net income from the business nonetheless be taxed. The materials in this section consider the impact of commercial activities on a § 501(c)(3) organization's exempt status and then turn to the special problem of joint ventures between nonprofits and for-profit partners. The Service's principal border patrol sentry, the unrelated business income tax, is only previewed here and considered in depth in Chapter 5, as are the issues and planning opportunities presented by complex structures. The special problem of concentrated business ownership by private foundations is discussed in Chapter 6.

The impact of commercial activity on tax exemption is an untidy area of the law. No intelligent discussion can begin without at least a glimpse at the unrelated business income tax, familiarly known as the UBIT. Since the UBIT's enactment in 1950, charitable and most other tax-exempt organizations have been taxable on any net income from an "unrelated" trade or business. Very generally and ignoring many specialized exceptions, an unrelated trade or business is an income-producing activity (other than passive investing) that is regularly carried on and not "substantially related" to an organization's exempt purposes apart from the need for income to support its charitable or other exempt mission. See I.R.C. §§ 511–514. The UBIT was enacted in response to real and perceived abuses by tax-exempt organizations, charges of unfair competition from the business community, and—like many tax bills—to raise revenue. At the same time, Congress added § 502, which provides that an organization operated for the primary purpose of carrying on a trade or business for profit shall not be exempt from tax under § 501 on the ground that all of its profits are payable to one or more tax-exempt organizations. This provision denies exemption to "feeder corporations," which usually are entities that operate a business as their sole activity and are obligated to pay over their profits to an affiliated § 501(c)(3) organization.

Under pre-UBIT case law, a charity conducting an unrelated business, even as its sole activity, could qualify for exemption if its net profits were used to support an exempt purpose or were paid over to a bona fide charity. Thus, even feeder corporations could qualify for § 501(c)(3) exemption— e.g., a shoe store obligated by its charter to distribute its profits to support a school. The theory, as articulated by the Supreme Court in dictum and then with greater clarity in later circuit court decisions, was that the destination of income, not its source, was the ultimate test of exemption. See Trinidad v. Sagrada Orden, 263 U.S. 578, 44 S.Ct. 204 (1924); Roche's

Beach v. Commissioner, 96 F.2d 776 (2d Cir.1938); C.F. Mueller Co. v. Commissioner, 190 F.2d 120 (3d Cir.1951). When it enacted the UBIT and decided to tax "unrelated" business income, Congress discarded the destination of income test for UBIT purposes. But the standards for § 501(c)(3) exemption were not altered except in the narrow case of feeder corporations described in § 502.

Against this background, we return to the question of whether and to what extent the conduct of commercial activity jeopardizes qualification for exemption under § 501(c)(3). The question is not resolved by the Internal Revenue Code, which merely requires an organization to be organized and operated "exclusively" for one or more of the enumerated exempt purposes. Looking first at the "organizational test" regulations, an organization's articles of incorporation (or trust agreement) may not "expressly empower" it to "engage, other than as an insubstantial part of its activities, in activities which in themselves are not in furtherance of one or more exempt purposes." Treas. Reg. § 1.501(c)(3)–1(b)(1)(i). Notably, the focus here is on substantial nonexempt *activities*, not on whether or not an organization's primary purpose is charitable. The regulations later warn that an organization will fail the organizational test if its articles empower it to "engage in a manufacturing business." Treas. Reg. § 1.501(c)(3)–1(b)(1)(iii). Read literally, these regulations seem to say that there is little leeway for "substantial" unrelated business activities.

Similarly, the operational test regulations, after interpreting "exclusively" as used in § 501(c)(3) to mean "primarily," go on to provide that an organization will not qualify for exemption "if more than an insubstantial part of its activities is not in furtherance of an exempt purpose." Treas. Reg. § 1.501(c)(3)–1(c)(1). Although the regulations offer no guidance on what types of activities do or do not further an exempt purpose, they seem to leave some leeway for insubstantial commercial activity, whatever its motivation. They later elaborate by providing that an organization will qualify for § 501(c)(3) exemption "although it operates a trade or business as a substantial part of its activities, if the operation of such trade or business is in furtherance of the organization's exempt purpose or purposes and if the organization is not organized or operated for the primary purpose of carrying on an unrelated trade or business, as defined in Section 513." Treas. Reg. § 1.501(c)(3)–1(e). An organization's primary purpose is to be determined by all the facts and circumstances, "including the size and extent of the trade or business and the size or extent of the activities which are in furtherance of one or more exempt purposes." Id.

The regulations raise more questions than they answer and are susceptible to varying interpretations. Some courts and commentators see them as importing a "commerciality" doctrine into § 501(c)(3). Under this theory, an otherwise qualified § 501(c)(3) organization does not lose its exemption by engaging in insubstantial business activities, even if they are unrelated to its exempt purposes. Substantial business activities also are permissible if they are "in furtherance of" (does that mean "related to"?) exempt purposes. But exemption is denied when the organization's "primary purpose" is the conduct of an unrelated trade or business. It follows that if an organization's "unrelated" business activities are "insubstantial," such as less than a specified percentage (of what?), its exemption is secure and the only sanction is the UBIT. But if unrelated business income (net or gross?) exceeds some unarticulated benchmark (some cautious advisors assume it is 50% of total revenue for planning purposes), the organization no longer qualifies for exemption, whether or not the revenue is used to subsidize a charitable activity. This theory loosely links the exemption qualification question with the UBIT relatedness standard, and it has caused risk-averse charities to conduct any substantial unrelated businesses in a separate taxable subsidiary. In many of the cases and IRS rulings, however, the inquiry begins and ends with an amorphous "all the facts and circumstances," smell test that never even mentions the UBIT, leaving charities confused and overly cautious.

A contrary and more permissive view is that current law does not impose any per se limit on the amount of unrelated business income or activity for § 501(c)(3) qualification purposes. Proponents of this theory point to an IRS ruling holding that an organization relying on commercial revenue for its sole source of support qualifies for § 501(c)(3) exemption if it conducts a charitable grantmaking program "commensurate in scope with its financial resources." Rev. Rul. 64–182, infra p. 263. This theory assumes that Congress, in enacting the UBIT, did not intend to overturn the destination of income test for exemption qualification purposes except in the narrow case of § 502 feeder corporations. It follows that any amount of unrelated business income is permissible provided that the organization's "primary purpose" is charitable, as measured (somehow) by the commensurate-in-scope standard.

As we said, this area is untidy. The materials below elaborate on this introductory snapshot, illustrating the tension between charity and commerce as it relates to § 501(c)(3) exemption in a variety of typical settings.

Goldsboro Art League v. Commissioner

Tax Court of the United States, 1980.
75 T.C. 337.

OPINION

■ TIETJENS, JUDGE: Respondent determined that petitioner is not exempt from Federal income tax under section 501(c)(3). The prerequisites for declaratory judgment having been satisfied, petitioner has, pursuant to section 7428, invoked the jurisdiction of this Court. The issue for our determination is whether petitioner is operated exclusively for one or more exempt purposes delineated in section 501(c)(3).

Petitioner, a nonprofit North Carolina corporation incorporated on May 24, 1971, has its principal office in Goldsboro, N.C. On November 20, 1978, the District Director of Internal Revenue, Atlanta, EP/EO Service Unit, received petitioner's application for recognition of exemption. On

October 26, 1979, respondent issued to petitioner a final adverse ruling letter which denied petitioner tax-exempt status for the following reasons: "You are not operated exclusively for any exempt purpose within the meaning of section 501(c)(3) of the Code. You are operated in furtherance of a substantial commercial purpose. Further, you serve private rather than public interests."

Petitioner's charter states that it is organized for the following purposes: to promote the appreciation of and participation in the visual arts; to promote and encourage the expression of creativity through the creative arts; to promote education in the fine arts; to sponsor a creative arts center to provide a facility for instruction, creation and display of paintings, statuary and objects of creative arts; but the corporation shall not pursue any purpose or carry on any activity inconsistent with Sections 501(c)(3) and 170(c)(2) of the Internal Revenue Code.

Petitioner has 12 board members whose professional backgrounds include careers in business, law, education, art, and religion. The president of petitioner, for 1978–79, has a master of divinity degree from Duke University and is Director of Continuing Education at Wayne Community College. Petitioner's vice president is an attorney; its secretary, an interior designer; and its treasurer, an accountant.

Petitioner is the hub of many art activities in Wayne County and is known throughout the State for the quality of its programs. There are no other art museums, galleries, or similar facilities of significant note available within Wayne, or any contiguous, county.

Petitioner operates the Goldsboro Art Center (hereinafter center) which furnishes various educational and charitable services to the community. Specifically, the Center sponsors art classes in conjunction with Wayne Community College (hereinafter college), in such areas as watercolor, oil, and acrylic painting; pottery; interior design; macrame and weaving. The center offers an average of 20 to 25 classes quarterly for approximately 250 students. In addition, on its own, petitioner offers courses for children in pottery, drawing, discovering art, puppetry, creative stitchery, and painting.

The center sponsors art demonstrations, including one at the Wayne County Agricultural Fair each year, and workshops in, for example, Japanese watercolor techniques and Ink Resist (wash techniques). In conjunction with the college and the North Carolina Art Society, the center sponsors film series, including the 13–part "Civilization" series narrated by Sir Kenneth Clark.

Petitioner owns 52 pieces of art as a permanent collection[5] which it displays in various public buildings throughout Wayne County, including the college, Wayne Memorial Hospital, the Wayne County administration building, the Goldsboro City Hall Annex, the Goldsboro fire and police

---

5. On petitioner's books, these works are valued at $614.70, but most were donated by the artists themselves and are, therefore, valued at cost and at significantly less than their fair market value. Petitioner estimates their market value to be more than $30,000.

complex, the Wayne County revenue building, city parks and recreation, and the Wayne County Public Library. The artwork is hung and maintained by members of petitioner. Local Scout troops, school groups, clubs, and other interested persons are given tours of the center, and an estimate of over 400 people are involved in the center's activities each week.

The director of the center gives a series of lectures on art at the Goldsboro High School humanities classes and speaks to both elementary and secondary Goldsboro and Wayne County public school classes. The director of the center also participates in Wayne County and Goldsboro school system's "career day" each year. Likewise, petitioner conducts art oriented workshops for teachers in Goldsboro and Wayne County and public exhibits of the artwork of Goldsboro and Wayne County public school children. Petitioner offers the Goldsboro Camera Club space for a darkroom. Petitioner organizes bus tours to the North Carolina Museum of Art in Raleigh. Petitioner also sponsors tours to the two local State-supported mental institutions.

Petitioner has some paid employees, but it relies heavily on volunteer help. It also hires some of its staff through the Youth Improvement Program, CETA, the Retired Senior Volunteer Program, and the Community College Work Study Program.

Besides these activities, petitioner operates two public galleries, the Art Market and the Art Gallery. All artworks in these galleries are selected by jury procedures to insure artistic quality and integrity. The Art Market and the Art Gallery are similar in that they both exhibit and sell artwork except that the former invites displays from numerous artists, while the latter only features one artist each month. The Art Market has paintings, drawings, sculpture, etchings, serigraphs, lithographs, weavings, pottery, and mobiles. These galleries often exhibit an artist's more daring work.

Petitioner's sales are made pursuant to a mutual understanding between petitioner and the artist without a written contract specifying the terms of sales. Petitioner collects any sales proceeds and turns over that money, less approximately 20–percent commission for estimated expenses, to the artist. In the fiscal year ended June 30, 1976, gross receipts from the sales in the Art Gallery and Art Market were, respectively, $5,624.50 and $3,662.33. After subtracting the amounts paid to artists, however, petitioner's receipts were, respectively, $1,005.14 and $398.34. In the fiscal year ended June 30, 1977, gross receipts from the Art Gallery and Art Market were, respectively, $5,984 and $3,309; deducting the amounts paid to artists, petitioner received, respectively, $1,147 and $860. In the fiscal year ended June 30, 1978, gross receipts from the Art Gallery and Art Market were, respectively, $6,281.86 and $5,106.19; reducing these amounts by the amounts paid to the artists, petitioner received, respectively, $1,204.55 and $849.53.

Petitioner lists as its expenses associated with the Art Gallery and Art Market for the fiscal year ended June 30, 1976, respectively, $497.30 and $38.35 and, therefore, shows profits of $507.84 and $359.99, respectively, for that year. Similarly, in the 1977 fiscal year, petitioner's books show expenses relating to the Art Gallery to be $611 and to the Art Market, $184; subtracting these expenses, petitioner's books show, respectively, profits of $536 and $676. In the fiscal year ended June 30, 1978, petitioner's Art Gallery expenses are indicated to be $553.48 and its Art Market expenses shown as $112.42; petitioner's profits for that year, therefore, are $651.07 and $737.11. However, petitioner's books appear only to include as expenses those costs covering supplies, invitations, and receptions relating to these galleries. Petitioner's books do not show what proportion of rent, utilities, insurance, etc., paid by petitioner to maintain the center, is attributable to the maintenance of the two galleries. In order to maintain the center, petitioner paid a total of $9,700.95 for the fiscal year 1976, $9,826 for the fiscal year 1977, and $10,369.83 for the fiscal year 1978. The center houses three classrooms in addition to the two galleries, but these total expenses must in some part be connected with the Art Gallery and Art Market.

Petitioner's total revenues from all sources in these years were, respectively, approximately $47,109, $47,440, and $57,289.

Various classes of membership in petitioner are entitled to a 2-to 10-percent discount in sales prices of artworks in the two galleries. Two of petitioner's members are among the more than 100 artists who have exhibited their art in the galleries.

Petitioner contends that it is operated exclusively for exempt purposes, that the sale of artwork in its galleries is an incidental activity but one which helps it pursue its exempt purposes, that petitioner is not operated in furtherance of a substantial commercial purpose, and that the primary purpose of the sales, as well as petitioner's other activities, is to further the public's appreciation of art and not to serve private interests.

Respondent, by contrast, argues that since petitioner's activities are indistinguishable from activities required in operating a commercial art gallery for profit, petitioner is operated for a substantial commercial purpose; therefore, respondent asserts, under Better Business Bureau v. United States, 326 U.S. 279 (1945), petitioner may not qualify for exemption under section 501(c)(3) despite the presence of any number of truly exempt purposes.

Moreover, respondent maintains that providing individual artists with direct monetary benefits derived from the sale of created artworks serves more than incidentally the private interests of designated individuals.

Respondent's final ruling letter denied petitioner exempt status on the grounds that it is not operated exclusively for any exempt purpose, that it is operated in furtherance of a substantial commercial purpose, and that it serves private rather than public interests. Petitioner has the burden of proof to show that respondent's determination is wrong.

We find that petitioner has sustained its burden and is exempt from Federal taxation under section 501(c)(3).

In order to be exempt under section 501(c)(3), an organization must qualify under both the organizational and the operational tests. Sec.

1.501(c)(3)–1(a)(1), Income Tax Regs. Respondent does not question that petitioner qualifies for exemption under the organizational test; rather, respondent's denial of exemption is based on his conclusion that petitioner does not satisfy the operational test.

The operational test requires an organization's activities to be primarily those which accomplish one or more exempt purposes as specified in section 501(c)(3) and not, except to an insubstantial part, those which do not further an exempt purpose. Sec. 1.501(c)(3)–1(c)(1), Income Tax Regs. A substantial nonexempt purpose will disqualify an organization from tax exemption despite the number or the importance of its exempt purposes. Better Business Bureau v. United States, supra. The operational test focuses on the purpose and not on the nature of the activity. An organization may engage in a trade or business as long as its operation furthers an exempt purpose and its primary objective is not the production of profits. An organization is not operated exclusively for one or more exempt purposes, however, unless it serves a public rather than a private interest. Sec. 1.501(c)(3)–1(d)(1)(ii), Income Tax Regs. * * * Whether an organization satisfies the operational test is a question of fact.

Included among the exempt purposes are "educational" and "charitable" purposes. Sec. 1.501(c)(3)–1(d)(1)(i)(b) and (f), Income Tax Regs. "Educational" is defined as:

(a) The instruction or training of the individual for the purpose of improving or developing his capabilities; or

(b) The instruction of the public on subjects useful to the individual and beneficial to the community.

Sec. 1.501(c)(3)–1(d)(3), Income Tax Regs. The promotion of the arts has consistently been recognized as both charitable and educational. Indeed, respondent does not question that the overwhelming purpose of petitioner's art classes, films, museum tours, and display of its permanent collection is charitable or educational. Respondent, however, contends that two of petitioner's activities, the operations of its Art Market and Art Gallery, further a substantial commercial purpose and serve the private interests of individual professional artists. He argues that the evidence indicates that the sales activity is an end in itself rather than a means of accomplishing an exempt purpose.

We disagree with respondent's conclusions and find that the evidence presented here confirms, as petitioner suggests, that the purpose of the Art Gallery and Art Market is primarily to foster community awareness and appreciation of contemporary artists and to provide a constant flow of art for students to study art and painting techniques.

Among the factors we consider in determining whether an organization is operated to further a substantial commercial purpose are the particular manner in which an organization's activities are conducted, the commercial hue of these activities, and the existence and amount of profit from these activities.

In the instant case, since there are no other art museums or galleries in the area, petitioner has found difficulty attracting artists to exhibit their work without the incentive of the Art Gallery and Art Market.[6] Petitioner has a jury to select which works will be displayed, and we find it significant that the works are chosen not for their salability but for their representation of modern trends. Exhibiting an artist's more daring works in a part of the country where there are no nearby art museums or galleries illustrates that petitioner's purpose is primarily to educate rather than to sell.

Moreover, petitioner's activities with respect to the Art Market and Art Gallery must be viewed in connection with petitioner's other activities. The clear impression that we get from the record is one of petitioner's dedication to teach the public, through a variety of means, to appreciate art. We find that petitioner's sales activities are incidental to its other activities and serve the same overall objective of art education. This is not a case where the other activities are adjunct to petitioner's sales, but, rather, where petitioner's sales activities are secondary and incidental to furthering its exempt purpose. * * *

We are convinced, moreover, that petitioner is not operating these galleries for a profit. Petitioner retains only approximately 20 percent of the gross receipts from the sales and uses this amount to defray its expenses. A review of petitioner's books for 3 years shows that petitioner has either made no profit or, at most, a negligible one, for these years.

Finally, we reject respondent's contention that petitioner is operated for the private benefit of individuals.[9] Firstly, we find that petitioner's purpose in operating these two galleries is art education for the benefit of the public. Secondly, the private benefit prohibited under section 501(c)(3) relates to a benefit to "designated individuals, the creator or his family, shareholders of the organization, or persons controlled, directly or indirectly, by such private interests." Sec. 1.501(c)(3)–1(d)(1)(ii), Income Tax Regs. The artists exhibited in these two galleries had their works selected by a jury which these artists did not control. Similarly, the proscription against private inurement to the benefit of any shareholder or individual does not apply to unrelated third parties.[10] Of the more than 100 artists exhibited in the two galleries, only 2 members of petitioner have exhibited their works in these galleries and neither of these members is on petitioner's board of directors.

6. That there may be other possible means of attracting artists to exhibit their work is not, as respondent suggests, determinative. It is sufficient that we find that petitioner's purpose in these activities is an exempt one.

9. In support of its position, among other references, respondent cites two revenue rulings, Rev. Rul. 71–395, 1971–2 C.B. 228, and Rev. Rul. 76–152, 1976–1 C.B. 152. We find the earlier revenue ruling inapposite and the 1976 ruling distinguishable from the instant case. In any event, a revenue ruling states respondent's position and need not be followed by this Court. Browne v. Commissioner, 73 T.C. 723 (1980)(concurring opinion).

10. The prohibitions against private inurement and private purposes encompass many of the same elements. * * *

Because petitioner is organized and operated exclusively for an exempt purpose, is not operated in furtherance of a substantial commercial purpose, and serves public rather than private interests, petitioner is entitled to exemption from Federal taxation under sections 501(a) and 501(c)(3).

Decision will be entered for the petitioner.

Presbyterian and Reformed Publishing Co. v. Commissioner

United States Court of Appeals, Third Circuit, 1984.
743 F.2d 148.

■ ADAMS, CIRCUIT JUDGE.

This is an appeal from a decision of the United States Tax Court affirming the Internal Revenue Service's (IRS) revocation of tax-exempt status for a religiously-oriented publishing house. The Tax Court's decision affirming the termination of the publisher's 52–year-old tax-exemption under 26 U.S.C.A. § 501(c)(3)(1982), was based on its conclusion that the publisher had become a profitable venture with only an attenuated relationship to the church with which it claims an affiliation. For the reasons set forth below, the decision of the Tax Court will be reversed.

I.

In 1931, the Presbyterian and Reformed Publishing Company (P & R) was incorporated to

> * * * state, defend and disseminate (through every proper means connected with or incidental to the printing and publishing business) the system of belief and practice taught in the Bible, as that system is now set forth in the Confession of Faith and Catechisms of the Presbyterian Church in the United States of America.

P & R's charter requires that any income otherwise available as a dividend be used to improve its publications, extend their influence, or assist institutions "engaged in the teaching or inculcating" of the "system of belief and practice" of the Orthodox Presbyterian Church (OPC).

> The IRS granted P & R tax-exempt status in 1939, stating,

> Your actual activities consist of publishing a religious paper known as "Christianity Today," a Presbyterian journal devoted to stating, defending, and furthering the gospel. Your income is derived from subscriptions, contributions and gifts and is used to defray maintenance and general operating expenses.

From the beginning, P & R has been closely linked—although not formally affiliated—with the OPC, a Presbyterian group dedicated to its view of reformed Presbyterian theology and, in particular, to the doctrine of Biblical Christianity set forth in the Westminster Confession of Faith. P & R's central editorial criterion is whether a book chosen for publication would make a "worthy contribution * * * to the reformed [Presbyterian] community." One independent publisher characterized P & R's books as lacking in "common ground" with the "nonreformed mind" and "offensive" to all but the "truly reformed."

One of P & R's three incorporators and original directors founded the OPC in 1932, one year after P & R's incorporation. Seven of P & R's nine directors are either officials at Westminster Theological Seminary of Philadelphia or pastors of OPC or OPC-affiliated denominations. On January 1, 1976, P & R changed its charter to specify OPC's seminary, the Westminster Theological Seminary of Philadelphia, as the recipient of all P & R assets in case of dissolution, citing Westminster's common dedication to Biblical Christianity and the Westminster Confession.

The organizational structure of P & R further underscores its close ties to the OPC. Since 1931, the publishing house has been run by three successive generations of the Craig family. Samuel, Charles, and Bryce Craig each worked without compensation at what amounted to a family concern whose business was conducted at the Craigs' kitchen table; all three Craigs were ministers. The record is devoid of evidence indicating any lessening of ties between P & R and the OPC.

From its inception until 1969, the company could claim no income over and above expenses. Indeed, the Craigs themselves often contributed personal funds in order to keep the corporation afloat (Samuel donated $500 in 1939 and $3,000 in 1954; Charles donated a total of $19,600 from 1955 to 1963). Until 1973, P & R relied exclusively on volunteers to help the Craigs with editing, packing, shipping, and clerical work.

Beginning in 1969, however, P & R experienced a considerable increase in economic activity as a result of the sudden and unexpected popularity of books written by Jay Adams, a Westminster Theological faculty member. P & R reported gross profits of over $20,000 for 1969, almost twice as much in 1970, and subsequent escalations culminating in over $300,000 in gross profits in 1979. By 1979, P & R had seven paid employees assisting Bryce Craig, one with a salary of $12,500, and five with salaries under $6,250 (all five full-time employees were OPC officials or members). Bryce Craig himself began receiving a salary of $12,000 in 1976, which increased, to $15,350 by 1979.

As early as March 2, 1974, P & R notified the Internal Revenue Service that it was accumulating surplus cash as a "building fund." In 1976, P & R used this fund to purchase 5-1/2 acres of land in Harmony, New Jersey, close to both an OPC community and Harmony Press, the printer for both P & R and OPC. In 1978, construction of a combined warehouse and office building in Harmony was completed at a cost of $263,000; an additional $27,000 was spent in 1979 for equipment.

After an audit, the IRS issued a revocation of P & R's tax-exempt status in 1980 on the grounds that P & R was not "operating exclusively for purposes set forth in 501(c)(3)" and was "engaged in a business activity which is carried on similar to a commercial enterprise." The IRS made this revocation retroactive, to apply from January 1, 1969 onward.

The Tax Court affirmed the revocation in a December 23, 1982 opinion, but held that the IRS abused its discretion in making the revocation retroactive to 1969. Instead, it set the effective revocation date at 1975, based upon its declaration that as of that year P & R "had acquired a truly commercial hue" and the company "was aware * * * that IRS agents had been raising serious questions [about its exemption]." To support its determination that P & R came to be "animated" by a "substantial commercial [and thus nonexempt] purpose" in 1975, the Tax Court relied primarily on three lines of evidence: first, P & R's "soar[ing] net and gross profits" between 1969 and 1979; second, the fact that P & R set prices which generated "consistent and comfortable net profit margins," rather than lowering prices to encourage a broader readership; and, third, P & R's purchase and sale of books to and from Baker Book Stores (a commercial publishing house), which "must have * * * overlapp[ed] in subject matter" with commercial publishers. * * * The Tax Court deemed this sufficient to support the proposition that P & R was in "competition with commercial publishers." * * *[2]

On P & R's motion for reconsideration, the Tax Court issued a second opinion on April 8, 1983, leaving its prior judgment intact and rejecting P & R's argument that its "profit" figures should have been adjusted to reflect accumulations for the building fund. The Tax Court suggested that the new building furthered commercial purposes as much as religious purposes, and noted that "gross profit margins" did not fall after the building was completed. Finally, the Tax Court emphasized that P & R's accumulations exceeded its expenditures for the new building. P & R's motion to reconsider also sought to distinguish its OPC-affiliated activity from that of generic Christian publishers. The Tax Court rejected this point, stating that "the denominational or nondenominational character of an organization has never been a controlling criterion." * * *.

II.

The principal issue we must address is at what point the successful operation of a tax-exempt organization should be deemed to have trans-

---

2. The Tax Court appended a list of additional "profit motivated" decisions: Other activities as well indicate that petitioner was animated by a substantial commercial purpose. It consciously attempted to transform itself into a more mainline commercial enterprise: It searched out more readers; it employed paid workers; it dropped money-losing plans; it paid substantial royalties; it made formal contracts with some authors; and, of course, it expanded into a new facility from which it could continue to reap profits. Further, petitioner was not affiliated or controlled by any particular church organization and this nondenominational character "contributes to the resemblance between its publishing activities and those of commercial, non-exempt publishers of Christian literature with whom * * * [it] competes." Inc. Trustees of Gospel Wkr. Soc. v. United States, [510 F.Supp. 374,] 379, n. 16 [D.D.C. (1981)]. Petitioner argues that it accumulated profits to expand so that it could publish more books and thus reach more readers. We recognize that petitioner used a large amount of its accumulated profits for the new Harmony facility; this new facility probably aided petitioner in increasing its productivity and distribution. Such increase, however, may also be indicative of a commercial enterprise. We are not convinced that one of the significant reasons for expansion was not the commercial one of wishing to expand production for profit.

formed that organization into a commercial enterprise and thereby to have forfeited its tax exemption. The Tax Court answered this question by looking at the composite effects of the broad-scale increase in commercial activity, the accumulation of capital, the company's "profitability," and the development of a professional staff. Although these indicia of non-exempt business activity are all relevant, we are troubled by the inflexibility of the Tax Court's approach. It is doubtful that any small-scale exempt operation could ever increase its economic activity without forfeiting tax-exempt status under such a definition of non-exempt commercial character. Thus, we believe that the statutory inclusion or exclusion of P & R should be considered under a two-prong test: first, what is the purpose of an organization claiming tax-exempt status; and, second, to whose benefit does its activity inure?

This two-prong inquiry is drawn directly from the wording of 501(c)(3) and the legislative history of its enactment. The statute explicitly cites as qualifying for tax exemption those entities "organized exclusively for religious, charitable * * * or educational purposes." Indeed, the statute's original sponsor cited the religious publishing house as the archetypal example of the contemplated tax-exempt organization. In the words of the sponsor, Senator Bacon:

> [T]he corporation which I had particularly in mind as an illustration at the time I drew this amendment is the Methodist Book Concern, which has its headquarters in Nashville, which is a very large printing establishment, and in which there must necessarily be profit made, and there is a profit made exclusively for religious, benevolent, charitable, and educational purposes, in which no man receives a scintilla of individual profit. Of course if that were the only one, it might not be a matter that you would say we would be justified in changing these provisions of law to meet a particular case, but there are in greater or less degree such institutions scattered all over this country. If Senators will mark the words, the amendment is very carefully guarded, so as not to include any institution where there is any individual profit, and further than that, where any of the funds are devoted to any purpose other than those which are religious, benevolent, charitable, and educational.

44 Cong.Rec., pt. 4, at 4151 (1909).

This passage directly supports the two-part test set forth today. The legislative history refers to a "very large printing establishment * * * in which there must necessarily be profit made" as within the scope of the exemption. Significantly, Senator Bacon's remarks point to the purpose of the publishing house and the absence of personal profit, rather than the volume of business, as the hallmarks of non-taxable activity. Assuming that large religious or educational publishers may qualify for an exemption, and assuming that not all such publishers are created as large entities, the question becomes one of defining the standards by which the growth in volume of a publisher will not in itself jeopardize the tax exemption.

In the case at hand, the "purpose" prong of the two-part test is the more difficult to administer. Therefore, we will turn first to the question of inurement, and then return to the question of purpose.

A.

[The court held that there was no basis for concluding that P & R's increased commercial activity inured to the personal benefit of any individual. Eds.]

Therefore, if P & R is to be denied tax-exempt status, it must be as a result of the first prong of the test set forward today: the purpose of P & R would have to be incompatible with 501(c)(3).

B.

In order to come within the terms of § 501(c)(3), an organization seeking tax-exempt status must establish that it is organized "exclusively" for an exempt purpose. In the leading case elucidating the purposes considered exempt under § 501(c)(3), the Supreme Court in Better Business Bureau v. U.S., 326 U.S. 279, 283, 66 S.Ct. 112, 114, 90 L.Ed. 67 (1945), stated, "[t]he presence of a single [non-exempt] purpose, * * * substantial in nature, will destroy the exemption." The Court found that the Better Business Bureau of the District of Columbia was not exempt because a substantial purpose was "the mutual welfare, protection and improvement of business methods among merchants." Id. at 281, 66 S.Ct. at 113. Nevertheless, Better Business Bureau is a relatively straightforward case because of the presence of an explicit non-exempt commercial purpose by the organization claiming the exemption. P & R, to the contrary, claims that it is animated by no commercial motive and therefore falls squarely within the statutory exemption. Thus, the Tax Court's decision in the present case rests on the evaluation of what it deemed to be the true but unspoken motive of P & R.

Any exploration of unarticulated or illicit purpose necessarily involves courts in difficult and murky problems. When the legality of an action depends not upon its surface manifestation but upon the undisclosed motivation of the actor, similar acts can lead to diametrically opposite legal consequences. In the field of equal protection law, for instance, similar state actions having disproportionate impacts upon minorities may be upheld or struck down depending upon the weighing of various indicia of "discriminatory intent." * * *

The difficulties inherent in any legal standard predicated upon the subjective intent of an actor are further compounded when that actor is a corporate entity. In such circumstances, courts forced to pass upon a potentially illicit purpose have looked for objective indicia from which the intent of the actor may be discerned. In reviewing the decision of the Tax Court in the present case, therefore, the question is whether the proper indicia were relied upon in concluding that P & R was animated by a purpose alien to the statutory exemption of § 501(c)(3).

The Tax Court properly framed the inquiry as to whether P & R's purpose was within § 501(c)(3) as follows: Where a nonexempt purpose is not an expressed goal, courts have focused on the manner in which activities themselves are carried on, implicitly reasoning that an end can be inferred from the chosen means. If, for example, an organization's management decisions replicate those of commercial enterprises, it is a fair inference that at least one purpose is commercial, and hence nonexempt. And if this nonexempt goal is substantial, tax exempt status must be denied. Clearly, petitioner's conduct of a growing and very profitable publishing business must imbue it with some commercial hue. How deep a tint these activities impart can best be evaluated by looking at certain factors deemed significant in cases involving religious publishing companies, as well as in other pertinent cases.

There are two aspects of the Tax Court's opinion regarding P & R's purpose that require careful examination. First is the Tax Court's conclusion that "petitioner was not affiliated or controlled by any particular church and [that] this nondenominational character 'contributes to the resemblance between its publishing activities and those of commercial, nonexempt publishers of Christian literature with whom * * * [it] competes.' " * * * Given the close connection between P & R and the OPC, the absence of formal control of P & R by any particular church is not dispositive of the question of the fundamental ties between its goals as a publishing house and the dogma espoused by the OPC. In Inc. Trustees [v. United States, 510 F.Supp. 374 (D.D.C.1981), Eds.], the court's decision that a gospel-oriented press failed to qualify for § 501(c)(3) status did not turn on the extent of the press' formal affiliation with a church. Rather, the court focused on the virtually complete cessation of religious activity by the church, the church's unexplained accumulation of millions of dollars, and the fact that some officers of the affiliated publishing concern were drawing salaries ranging from $42,000 to over $100,000. The Tax Court itself seems to have recognized the non-dispositive nature of formal affiliation in its decision on the motion for reconsideration, where it stated, "the denominational or nondenominational character of an organization has never been a controlling criterion."

The second point, P & R's accumulation of "profits," causes greater difficulty. Although the profits of P & R constituted only one of the factors enumerated and discussed by the Tax Court in its opinion, the memorandum filed upon P & R's motion for reconsideration makes clear that the Tax Court's principal concern was the "presence of substantial profits." The Tax Court computed P & R's profits by subtracting the cost of goods sold from the gross sales of books to arrive at the gross profits. The sum of other expenses was in turn subtracted from the gross profits to derive the net profit schedule used by the Tax Court in determining P & R's profitability. These net profits peaked at $106,180 in 1975, the year the Tax Court decided that P & R had acquired a truly commercial character. On reconsideration, the Tax Court added that the gross profits margin of P & R did not fall even after the new building was constructed.

We do not read § 501(c)(3) or its legislative history to define the purpose of an organization claiming tax-exempt status as a direct derivative of the volume of business of that organization. Rather, the inquiry must remain that of determining the purpose to which the increased business activity is directed. As the Tax Court itself observed, "the presence of profitmaking activities is not per se a bar to qualification of an organization as exempt if the activities further or accomplish an exempt purpose." Aid to Artisans, Inc. v. Commissioner, 71 T.C. 202, 211 (1978). Despite the long history of § 501(c)(3) and the numerous organizations that have claimed its coverage, no regulation or body of case law has defined the concept of "purpose" under this provision of the Tax Code with sufficient clarity to protect against arbitrary, ad hoc decision-making.

The Tax Court's analysis of P & R's accumulation of profits in the present context could, absent a clearer articulation of the legal standard for tax-exempt status, lead to such arbitrary or ad hoc treatment. We are particularly concerned that although the Tax Court acknowledged that P & R informed the IRS as early as March 2, 1974 of its accumulation of funds to purchase or build an office and warehouse, the opinion tabulates the company's cash-on-hand, and cites this as an important factor in concluding that P & R was motivated by a non-exempt purpose.

There is no doubt that unexplained accumulations of cash may properly be considered as evidence of commercial purpose. Although no regulations govern cash accumulations in the 501(c)(3) context, we are guided by the accumulated earnings tax, 26 U.S.C.A. § 531 et seq. (1982). [The court's discussion of the accumulated earnings tax is omitted. Eds.]

Although we recognize that the Tax Court is entitled to deference in determining the existence of a substantial, non-exempt purpose, that court must focus on facts which indicate a purpose falling outside the ambit of section 501(c)(3). In this case, the Tax Court focused primarily on two factors—the lack of affiliation with a particular church and the accumulation of profits. As we have shown, neither factor indicates the presence of a non-exempt purpose here. Therefore, we must consider the balance of the record to determine whether all the evidence taken together supports a finding of non-exemption. Such an examination reveals no additional evidence of improper motives.

III.

Two competing policy considerations are present in situations where tax-exempt organizations begin to expand the scope of their profit-generating activities. On the one hand, the simple act of accumulating revenues may properly call into question the ultimate purpose of an organization ostensibly dedicated to one of the enumerated pursuits under § 501(c)(3). On the other hand, success in terms of audience reached and influence exerted, in and of itself, should not jeopardize the tax-exempt status of organizations which remain true to their stated goals.

Our concern is that organizations seeking § 501(c)(3) status may be forced to choose between expanding their audience and influence on the one hand, and maintaining their tax-exempt status on the other. If this were a stagnant society in which various ideas and creeds preserve a hold on a fixed proportion of the population, this concern would evaporate. A large religious institution with a broad base of support, such as one of the more established churches, could be the springboard for large-scale publishing houses dedicated to advancing its doctrines and be assured of qualifying for § 501(c)(3) coverage. A small denomination, such as the OPC, could then have within its penumbra only a small-scale operation run off a kitchen table. In such circumstances, any attempt by a publisher adhering to the views of the small denomination to expand its scope of activities would properly raise questions relating to its continued eligibility for tax-exempt status.

This view does not reflect either the dynamic quality of our society or the goals that generated the grant of tax-exempt status to religious publishers. The sudden popularity of an erstwhile obscure writer, such as Jay Adams, cannot, by itself, be the basis for stating that P & R has departed from its professed purpose any more than an increase in congregations would call into question the OPC's continued designation as a church. Such a standard would lead to an inequitable disparity in treatment for publishers affiliated with mainstream churches as opposed to small offshoots.

Accordingly, the decision of the Tax Court will be reversed.

Revenue Ruling 67–4

1967–1 Cum. Bull. 121.

Advice has been requested whether a nonprofit organization formed and operated as described below qualifies for exemption from Federal income tax under section 501(c)(3) of the Internal Revenue Code of 1954.

The organization was formed to encourage scientific research in, and to disseminate educational information about, specific types of physical and mental disorders. This is accomplished by publishing a journal which contains abstracts of current information from the world's medical and scientific publications. The journal is sold, below cost, to the public.

The organization's staff consists of leading pathologists, other medical specialists, and teachers, most of whom donate their services. The organization receives income from the sale of subscriptions, contributions, and government grants. Its operating deficits are defrayed by contributions.

Section 501(c)(3) of the Code provides for the exemption from Federal income tax of organizations organized and operated exclusively for charitable, educational, and scientific purposes.

Section 1.501(c)(3)–1(d)(2) of the Income Tax Regulations defines the term "charitable" as used in section 501(c)(3) of the Code as including the advancement of education or science.

Revenue Ruling 66–147, C.B. 1966–1, 137, holds that the publication of abstracts of scientific and medical articles by an organization contributes to the advancement of education and science by providing an effective means for the increased dissemination and application of such knowledge.

An organization engaged in publishing scientific and medical literature may qualify for exemption from Federal income tax under section 501(c)(3) of the Code if (1) the content of the publication is educational, (2) the preparation of material follows methods generally accepted as "educational" in character, (3) the distribution of the materials is necessary or valuable in achieving the organization's educational and scientific purposes, and (4) the manner in which the distribution is accomplished is distinguishable from ordinary commercial publishing practices.

The methods used in preparing and presenting the abstracts conform to methods traditionally accepted as "educational" in character. The organization provides a reference to literature on the research undertaken in the area, and enables the afflicted to receive improved instruction and treatment. The distribution of the abstracts is carried out essentially in a "charitable" manner, in the sense that there is a public benefit derived from the distribution. The charges for the publication recover only a portion of the costs.

Accordingly, the organization qualifies for exemption from Federal income tax under section 501(c)(3) of the Code.

* * *

This case is distinguishable from that in Revenue Ruling 60–351, C.B. 1960–2, 169, involving an organization which is publishing a magazine and selling it to the general public in accordance with ordinary commercial publishing practices.

Revenue Ruling 64–182

1964–1 Cum. Bull. 186.

A corporation organized exclusively for charitable purposes derives its income principally from the rental of space in a large commercial office building which it owns, maintains and operates. The charitable purposes of the corporation are carried out by aiding other charitable organizations, selected in the discretion of its governing body, through contributions and grants to such organizations for charitable purposes. Held, the corporation is deemed to meet the primary purpose test of section 1.501(c)(3)–1(e)(1) of the Income Tax Regulations, and to be entitled to exemption from Federal income tax as a corporation organized and operated exclusively for charitable purposes within the meaning of section 501(c)(3) of the Internal Revenue Code of 1954, where it is shown to be carrying on through such contributions and grants a charitable program commensurate in scope with its financial resources.

* * *

NOTES AND QUESTIONS

1. *Commercial Hue and Primary Purpose.* As the commerciality cases and rulings demonstrate, the IRS and the courts are often preoccupied with whether an activity under scrutiny has a "commercial hue." Efficiently managed businesses that make money, retain earnings for expansion, and compete with for-profit firms are especially vulnerable, whether or not the activity also might be characterized as "charitable," "educational," "religious," or by one of the other enumerated § 501(c)(3) purposes. Is this analysis consistent with the operational test regulations? They seek to determine, first, whether a "trade or business" is a substantial part of the organization's activities (if not, then no problem, whether or not the business is related or unrelated) and, if so, whether it is "in furtherance of" the organization's exempt purpose. Does "in furtherance of" mean "substantially related to" an exempt purpose (importing standards used for the UBIT), or is it enough that business profits are used to subsidize a charitable activity? Can an unrelated business ever be in furtherance of an organization's exempt purposes? In what circumstances does a business become an organization's "primary purpose?" And what if the business is, in and of itself, the organization's exempt purpose? The problems following this Note grapple with many of these questions in a practical context.

2. *Commensurate-in-Scope.* Revenue Ruling 64–182 has been interpreted as clearly demonstrating that the destination of income test is alive and well. But was the rental activity in that ruling even a "trade or business?" As developed in Chapter 5, most rental income is excluded from the UBIT tax base, as are dividends, interest and royalties, presumably on the theory that passive investing does not present any border patrol problem.

Revenue Ruling 64–182 is brief and relatively uninformative. It evolved from an internal IRS debate culminating in a detailed legal memorandum which concluded that the operational test regulations permit an organization to qualify for exemption despite substantial unrelated business activities if its primary purpose is charitable. See G.C.M. 32869 (Oct. 9, 1963). Under this analysis, "in furtherance of" does not mean "related," and an organization's "primary purpose" is to be determined based on whether it has a "real, bona fide, or genuine charitable purpose, as manifested by the charitable accomplishments of the organization, and not a mathematical measuring of business purpose as opposed to charitable purpose." Id.

In a 1971 General Counsel Memorandum, the IRS effectively "gave away the store" in considering this hypothetical fact pattern that goes well beyond the 1964 published ruling:

> A large department store creates a nonprofit corporation to take over and operate its business assets. The articles of incorporation and bylaws of the nonprofit corporation contain a statement that the purpose of the organization is to engage in charitable works by contributing to those exempt organizations exempt under section 501(c)(3) which are selected by the officers of the nonprofit corporation

in their role as trustees. The articles and bylaws further provide that all proceeds derived from the business operation commensurate with its financial resources will be expended annually in its program of charitable giving. Is the corporation deemed a feeder organization? Is it, on the other hand, considered to be primarily engaged in charitable activities within the meaning of the regulations?

* * *

Assuming that all the assets of the organization referred to in your first series of questions have been effectively dedicated to some charitable objective, we believe that, aside from section 502, such organization could engage in an indeterminate amount of business and still be exempt under section 501(c)(3) so long as it can be said that there is a reasonable operation of the property for the beneficial use of charity. In such case, we would regard it as being operated exclusively for charitable purposes, and not for the primary purpose of carrying on unrelated trade or business within the meaning of regulations section 1.501(c)(3)–1(e). Thus, we would hold that, in accord with Rev. Rul. 64–182, the organization would be entitled to exemption under Code section 501(c)(3).

G.C.M. 34682 (Nov. 17, 1971). For some other authorities applying the commensurate-in-scope doctrine, see Help the Children, Inc. v. Commissioner, 28 T.C. 1128 (1957)(organization contributing less than one percent of bingo revenues to charity did not qualify for exemption because its principal activity was the profitable operation of a commercial bingo business); T.A.M. 200021056 (organization formed to give financial assistance to needy women qualifies for § 501(c)(3) exemption even though 66 percent of its revenue was from operation of an unrelated business; IRS reasons that an unrelated business used to raise funds for a charitable purpose is "in furtherance of" a charitable purpose and does not constitute a substantial non-exempt purpose). For a contrary view, see Orange County Agricultural Society v. Commissioner, 893 F.2d 529 (2d Cir.1990)(organization that received one-third of its income from an automobile racetrack was operated for a substantial non-exempt purpose, but revocation of exemption also was based on inurement of private gain).

Are GCM 34682 and the other cited authorities correct statements of the law? Do they properly interpret the § 501(c)(3) operational test regulations? If the answer is no, how much unrelated business is (or should be) permissible?

Assuming that the commensurate-in-scope doctrine is good law, its scope is unclear because the IRS does not consistently or coherently apply the doctrine. An updated published ruling is badly needed. Would it be possible to quantify the doctrine, or at least establish a safe harbor? Or is best to muddle through with the "facts and circumstances" smell test used in many of the decided cases and rulings?

3. *What's a Feeder?* The quoted portion of the 1971 GCM discussed in Note 2, above, seems to finesse (avoid?) the question of whether the

organization under scrutiny was a § 502 feeder corporation. If it were a feeder, it could not qualify for exemption. A thorough reading of the GCM reveals that it narrowly construed § 502, concluding that it only applies to organizations that are legally obligated (e.g., by their charter or contract) to pay over their profits to a specific charity. On the other hand, an organization would not be a feeder if the distribution of its income was discretionary in the sense that the trustees or directors were under no legal or equitable duty to distribute income to a specific (affiliated?) charity. GCM 34682 (Nov. 17, 1971). As a practical matter, these "non-feeder" grantmaking organizations would have to qualify as a public charity because of the limits in § 4943 on excess business holdings of private foundations. See Chapter 3C4, infra. One approach would be to qualify as a supporting organization under § 509(a)(3) by establishing a support relationship with one or more public charities. See Chapter 3B4, infra.

4. *Other Approaches to Reform.* Are the IRS and the courts too lenient in their treatment of commercial activity? Charities have become very imaginative in broadening their tax-exempt purposes to encompass activities that are virtually indistinguishable from for-profit businesses. Is this a problem? If so, how might the tax exemption border be more effectively patrolled? By narrowing the definition of charity, or refining what is meant by "commercial?" Would it be sufficient to rely on the UBIT to tax "insubstantial" unrelated business income and revoke exemption only when such income becomes substantial, as measured by an agreed upon mathematical benchmark? These are difficult questions and further discussion is best deferred until the UBIT is studied and mastered in Chapter 5.

5. *For Further Reading.* John D. Colombo, Regulating Commercial Activity by Exempt Charities: Resurrecting the Commensurate-in-Scope Doctrine, 39 Exempt Org. Tax Rev. 341 (2003); John D. Colombo, Commercial Activity and Charitable Tax Exemption, 44 Wm. & Mary L. Rev. 487 (2002); Jessica Pena & Alexander L.T. Reid, Note: A Call for Reform of the Operational Test for Unrelated Commercial Activity in Charities, 76 N.Y.U. L. Rev. 1855 (2001); Thomas C. Troyer, Quantity of Unrelated Business Consistent with Charitable Exemption—Some Clarification, 56 Tax Notes 1075 (1992); Kenneth C. Eliasberg, Charity and Commerce: Section 501(c)(3)—How Much Unrelated Business Activity?, 21 Tax L. Rev. 53 (1965).

PROBLEMS

Consider whether the following nonprofit organizations, all of which receive little or no financial support from charitable donations, qualify for tax exemption under § 501(c)(3).

(a) Alcoholic Artifacts is engaged in the purchase and sale of products made by alcoholics, drug addicts, and other ex-convicts. The purpose of the organization is to provide employment opportunities for individuals handicapped by alcoholism, drug dependence and other problems of urban poverty.

(b) The Downtown YMCA is located near the financial district of a major city and offers memberships to the general public for an initiation fee of $250 plus dues of $100 per month. Its facilities include a gymnasium, fitness center, racquetball courts, swimming pool and sun deck, and carpeted locker room facilities with showers, spas and saunas. Located nearby are several for-profit health clubs offering comparable facilities.

(c) Charitable Consultants of Topeka provides managerial and consulting services on a cost basis to an unrelated group of § 501(c)(3) charities in Eastern Kansas. The services of the organization include writing job descriptions and training materials, recruiting personnel, advising on fund raising and endowment management and other administrative and accounting matters.

(d) The Joan's Mother Foundation publishes a monthly magazine ("Joan's Mother") with nationwide circulation. The magazine emphasizes women's issues, politics, the environment, and human rights. The Foundation purchased the magazine from a for-profit corporation that was about to terminate publication of Joan's Mother because of declining profits. The Foundation's revenues come from subscription income, advertising, and a few small grants from private foundations.

(e) The Christian Charter School, an religious educational institution not affiliated with any particular denomination, which has 2,500 students from pre-school through 12th grade, and a profitable publishing division that produces and markets religious textbooks throughout the world. Gross receipts from the publishing division represent 60% of the organization's total gross receipts, while publishing division expenditures are less than half of overall expenditures. Assume that the publishing activity is an unrelated trade or business.

(f) The Rubber Soul Conservancy, founded five years ago to provide financial support to arts and cultural organizations in New York City, derives 75% of its gross revenue from investment income and 25% from the operation of a fashionable shoe store in Manhattan. Annual grants average 4% of the value of the Conservancy's net assets, including the shoe store business.

(g) Same as (f), above, except all the Conservancy's revenue is from operation of the shoe store.

(h) Same as (g), above, except average annual grants ($10,000 per year) are less than 1% of the value of the Conservancy's net assets.

(i) Same as (g), above, except the Conservancy is controlled by the Manny Planetarium, a § 501(c)(3) public charity, and it is obligated by its charter to distribute all its net profits annually to the Planetarium.

2. JOINT VENTURES

Plumstead Theatre Society, Inc. v. Commissioner

United States Tax Court, 1980.
74 T.C. 1324.

OPINION

■ WILBUR, JUDGE:

Respondent determined that petitioner does not qualify for exemption from Federal income tax as a charitable or educational organization under section 501(c)(3). Petitioner challenges respondent's determination and has invoked the jurisdiction of this Court under section 7428 for a declaratory judgment. All of the prerequisites for declaratory judgment have been satisfied. The issue for our decision is whether petitioner is operated exclusively for charitable or educational purposes within the meaning of section 501(c)(3).

[Plumstead Theatre Society was a nonprofit corporation organized to present classical professional theater productions, conduct workshops for new American playwrights, and establish a fund to assist new and established playwrights in writing plays for the organization to produce. Plumstead's nonprofit status enabled it to pay less than union scale compensation to its accomplished performers, directors and technicians. Shortly after it was founded, Plumstead entered into an agreement with another tax-exempt organization to sponsor three family-oriented plays in Pasadena, California. It also agreed with the John F. Kennedy Center for the Performing Arts in Washington, D.C., to coproduce the play, *First Monday in October*, a fictional account of the first woman justice of the U.S. Supreme Court. Plumstead and the JFK Center each were to provide half the capital required for production and split equally any profits or losses. Plumstead's president, the actor Henry Fonda, starred in the play and agreed to accept a lesser salary than he could have received from a commercial theater. When Plumstead found that had insufficient capital to meet its obligations under the agreement with the JFK Center, it sold some of its rights to the play to a limited partnership for which it was the general partner and for-profit investors were the limited partners. The limited partners invested cash in exchange for a 63.5 percent share of the partnership's profits and losses, while Plumstead contributed its rights to coproduce the play in exchange for a 36.5 percent share. The play premiered at the JFK Center in December, 1977, but it was not a commercial success.

The Service denied § 501(c)(3) exempt status to Plumstead on the ground that it was operated for a substantial commercial purpose. An additional ground for denial was that Plumstead was operated for private rather than public interests because of the joint venture with for-profit investors. The Tax Court, citing several revenue rulings granting exemptions to nonprofit theaters, held that Plumstead was operated for exempt purposes and rejected the Service's contention that the organization was indistinguishable from a commercial enterprise. It then considered whether Plumstead's production of "First Monday in October" was indicative of a substantial commercial purpose and analyzed the impact of Plumstead's joint venture with the JFK Center and the for-profit investors. Eds.]

* * *

Nor do we agree with respondent that the activity of coproducing the play, "First Monday in October," with the Kennedy Center is indicative of a substantial commercial purpose. In fulfilling its goals of promoting and fostering the American dramatic arts, petitioner plans not only to resurrect past literary works, but to encourage and develop new and original theatre productions. Indeed, developing new works of artistic quality is considered one of the obligations of a nonprofit performing arts organization.

Respondent has not alleged that petitioner should not be allowed to produce and present original plays. Rather, it points to the manner in which First Monday was presented—that it was advertised in newspapers, that tickets were sold, that professionals were used in the productions—to argue that petitioner has a substantial commercial purpose.

We feel that respondent is completely misdirected in his objections. The Kennedy Center is a tax-exempt organization chartered by Congress and built partially with Federal funds. For major theatrical performances, it generally advertises in the newspaper, charges the public for tickets, and uses paid professionals. Symphony orchestras are considered per se educational under section 501(c)(3). See sec. 1.501(c)(3)–1(d)(3)(ii), example (4), Income Tax Regs. Yet, they too advertise performances, sell tickets, and pay their musicians, and such activity does not render them "substantially commercial." Indeed, all nonprofit performing arts organizations, from opera to ballet to theatre to symphony orchestras, depend upon ticket sales to cover a portion of their operating budgets. The purpose of presenting dramatic productions is for the public to see, to appreciate, to reflect, and to be educated. Nothing in section 501(c)(3) dictates that the public find out about petitioner's performances through word of mouth, that they be forced to watch amateurs act, or that they be seated totally free of charge. The kind of activity respondent deems objectionable in the instant case is no different from that which he has sanctioned on public record. See Rev. Rul. 73–45, 1973–1 C.B. 220; Rev. Rul. 64–175, 1964–1 C.B. (Part 1) 185.

Admittedly, the line between commercial enterprises which produce and present theatrical performances and nonprofit, tax-exempt organizations that do the same is not always easy to draw. Indeed, the theatre is the most prominent area of the performing arts in which commercial enterprises coexist, often in the same city, with nonprofit, tax-exempt charitable organizations that also sponsor professional presentations. See B. Hopkins, Law of Tax Exempt Organizations, sec. 6.9, p. 38 (3d ed. 1979).[6]

6. Hopkins uses by way of illustration, the John F. Kennedy Center for the Performing Arts, a nonprofit, tax-exempt organization, and the National Theatre, a commercial enterprise, both located in Washington, D.C.; and New York City's nonprofit Lincoln Cen-

However, there are differences. Commercial theatres are operated to make a profit. Thus, they choose plays having the greatest mass audience appeal. Generally, they run the plays so long as they can attract a crowd. They set ticket prices to pay the total costs of production and to return a profit. Since their focus is perennially on the box office, they do not generally organize other activities to educate the public and they do not encourage and instruct relatively unknown playwrights and actors.

Tax-exempt organizations are not operated to make a profit. They fulfill their artistic and community obligations by focusing on the highest possible standards of performance; by serving the community broadly; by developing new and original works; and by providing educational programs and opportunities for new talent. Thus, they keep the great classics of the theatre alive and are willing to experiment with new forms of dramatic writing, acting, and staging. Usually, nonprofit theatrical organizations present a number of plays during a season for a relatively short specified time period. Because of a desired quality in acoustics and intimacy with the audience, many present their performances in halls of limited capacity. The combination of the shortness of the season, the limited seating capacity, the enormous costs of producing quality performances of new or experimental works, coupled with the desire to keep ticket prices at a level which is affordable to most of the community, means that, except in rare cases, box office receipts will never cover the cost of producing plays for nonprofit performing arts organizations.[7] See Rockefeller Panel Report, supra at 53–62. We feel that petitioner has shown that it is organized and operated similar to other nonprofit theatre organizations, rather than as a commercial theatre.

Respondent's last argument is that because of the partnership petitioner entered into with two private individuals and a corporation, whereby the limited partners provided capital in exchange for an interest in the profits and losses of First Monday, petitioner is operated for private, rather than public interests. We do not agree. After entering into an agreement with the Kennedy Center, petitioner discovered it was in need of funds for its share of the capitalization costs of First Monday. The record shows that in an arm's-length transaction, it obtained those funds by selling a portion of its interest in the play itself, for a reasonable price. Petitioner is not obligated for the return of any capital contribution made by the limited partners from its own funds, and the partnership has no interest in petitioner or in any other plays it is planning to produce. The limited partners have no control over the way petitioner operates or manages its affairs, and none of the limited partners nor any officer or director of

ter which coexists adjacent to the quintessence of commercial theatre, Broadway. See B. Hopkins, Law of Tax Exempt Organizations, sec. 6.9, pp. 85–86 (3d ed. 1979).

7. On the average, earned income (mainly box office receipts) for the larger, better known nonprofit theatres accounts for approximately two-thirds of their annual budgets; the rest must come from other sources. See R. Anderson and S. Maltezou, "The Economic Condition of the Live Professional Theatre in America," Research in the Arts, Proceedings of the Conference on Policy Related Studies of the National Endowment for the Arts, pp. 63–65 (1977).

Pantheon Pictures, Inc., is an officer or director of petitioner. We find this arrangement, limited to one play produced by petitioner, is no more intrusive or indicative of private interests than the contractual, percentage arrangement approved of in Broadway Theatre League of Lynchburg, Va. v. United States, 293 F.Supp. 346 (W.D.Va.1968).[8]

Therefore, we find that petitioner is organized and operated exclusively for charitable and educational purposes under section 501(c)(3).

An appropriate order will be entered.

Revenue Ruling 98–15

1998–1 Cum. Bull. 718.

ISSUE

Whether, under the facts described below, an organization that operates an acute care hospital continues to qualify for exemption from federal income tax as an organization described in § 501(c)(3) of the Internal Revenue Code when it forms a limited liability company (LLC) with a for-profit corporation and then contributes its hospital and all of its other operating assets to the LLC, which then operates the hospital.

FACTS

Situation 1

A is a nonprofit corporation that owns and operates an acute care hospital. A has been recognized as exempt from federal income tax under § 501(a) as an organization described in § 501(c)(3) and as other than a private foundation as defined in § 509(a) because it is described in § 170(b)(1)(A)(iii). B is a for-profit corporation that owns and operates a number of hospitals.

A concludes that it could better serve its community if it obtained additional funding. B is interested in providing financing for A's hospital, provided it earns a reasonable rate of return. A and B form a limited liability company, C. A contributes all of its operating assets, including its hospital to C. B also contributes assets to C. In return, A and B receive ownership interests in C proportional and equal in value to their respective contributions.

C's Articles of Organization and Operating Agreement ("governing documents") provide that C is to be managed by a governing board

---

8. We note that respondent has quite properly abandoned his initial argument that this arrangement resulted in private inurement. He now simply contends the agreement reflects a private rather than a public purpose—apparently arguing petitioner has commercial rather than artistic objectives. However, even assuming that these objections may be so neatly bifurcated and that First Monday was a commercial venture, the play was only one of many to be produced, and plays were only one of the contemplated means through which petitioner intends to advance the arts. At most, any profits from the play might under this theory be subject to the tax on unrelated business income, but it would not be inimical to exempt status. * * *

consisting of three individuals chosen by A and two individuals chosen by B. A intends to appoint community leaders who have experience with hospital matters, but who are not on the hospital staff and do not otherwise engage in business transactions with the hospital.

The governing documents further provide that they may only be amended with the approval of both owners and that a majority of three board members must approve certain major decisions relating to C's operation, including decisions relating to any of the following topics: A. C's annual capital and operating budgets; B. Distributions of C's earnings; C. Selection of key executives; D. Acquisition or disposition of health care facilities; E. Contracts in excess of $x per year; F. Changes to the types of services offered by the hospital; and G. Renewal or termination of management agreements.

The governing documents require that C operate any hospital it owns in a manner that furthers charitable purposes by promoting health for a broad cross section of its community. The governing documents explicitly provide that the duty of the members of the governing board to operate C in a manner that furthers charitable purposes by promoting health for a broad cross section of the community overrides any duty they may have to operate C for the financial benefit of its owners. Accordingly, in the event of a conflict between operation in accordance with the community benefit standard and any duty to maximize profits, the members of the governing board are to satisfy the community benefit standard without regard to the consequences for maximizing profitability.

The governing documents further provide that all returns of capital and distributions of earnings made to owners of C shall be proportional to their ownership interests in C. The terms of the governing documents are legal, binding, and enforceable under applicable state law.

C enters into a management agreement with a management company that is unrelated to A or B to provide day-to-day management services to C. The management agreement is for a five-year period, and the agreement is renewable for additional five-year periods by mutual consent. The management company will be paid a management fee for its services based on C's gross revenues. The terms and conditions of the management agreement, including the fee structure and the contract term, are reasonable and comparable to what other management firms receive for similar services at similarly situated hospitals. C may terminate the agreement for cause.

None of the officers, directors, or key employees of A who were involved in making the decision to form C were promised employment or any other inducement by C or B and their related entities if the transaction were approved. None of A's officers, directors, or key employees have any interest, including any interest through attribution determined in accordance with the principles of § 318, in B or any of its related entities.

Pursuant to § 301.7701–3(b) of the Procedure and Administrative Regulations, C will be treated as a partnership for federal income tax purposes.

A intends to use any distributions it receives from C to fund grants to support activities that promote the health of A's community and to help the indigent obtain health care. Substantially all of A's grantmaking will be funded by distributions from C. A's projected grantmaking program and its participation as an owner of C will constitute A's only activities.

Situation 2

D is a nonprofit corporation that owns and operates an acute care hospital. D has been recognized as exempt from federal income tax under § 501(a) as an organization described in § 501(c)(3) and as other than a private foundation as defined in § 509(a) because it is described in § 170(b)(1)(iii). E is a for-profit hospital corporation that owns and operates a number of hospitals and provides management services to several hospitals that it does not own.

D concludes that it could better serve its community if it obtained additional funding. E is interested in providing financing for D's hospital, provided it earns a reasonable rate of return. D and E form a limited liability company, F. D contributes all of its operating assets, including its hospital to F. E also contributes assets to F. In return, D and E receive ownership interests proportional and equal in value to their respective contributions.

F's Articles of Organization and Operating Agreement ("governing documents") provide that F is to be managed by a governing board consisting of three individuals chosen by D and three individuals chosen by E. D intends to appoint community leaders who have experience with hospital matters, but who are not on the hospital staff and do not otherwise engage in business transactions with the hospital.

The governing documents further provide that they may only be amended with the approval of both owners and that a majority of board members must approve certain major decisions relating to F's operation, including decisions relating to any of the following topics: A. F's annual capital and operating budgets; B. Distributions of F's earnings over a required minimum level of distributions set forth in the Operating Agreement; C. Unusually large contracts; and D. Selection of key executives.

F's governing documents provide that F's purpose is to construct, develop, own, manage, operate, and take other action in connection with operating the health care facilities it owns and engage in other health care-related activities. The governing documents further provide that all returns of capital and distributions of earnings made to owners of F shall be proportional to their ownership interests in F.

F enters into a management agreement with a wholly-owned subsidiary of E to provide day-to-day management services to F. The management agreement is for a five-year period, and the agreement is renewable for additional five-year periods at the discretion of E's subsidiary. F may terminate the agreement only for cause. E's subsidiary will be paid a management fee for its services based on gross revenues. The terms and conditions of the management agreement, including the fee structure and the contract term other than the renewal terms, are reasonable and comparable to what other management firms receive for similar services at similarly situated hospitals.

As part of the agreement to form F, D agrees to approve the selection of two individuals to serve as F's chief executive officer and chief financial officer. These individuals have previously worked for E in hospital management and have business expertise. They will work with the management company to oversee F's day-to-day management. Their compensation is comparable to what comparable executives are paid at similarly situated hospitals.

Pursuant to § 301.7701–3(b). F will be treated as a partnership for federal tax income purposes.

D intends to use any distributions it receives from F to fund grants to support activities that promote the health of D's community and to help the indigent obtain health care. Substantially all of D's grantmaking will be funded by distributions from F. D's projected grantmaking program and its participation as an owner of F will constitute D's only activities.

LAW

Section 501(c)(3) provides, in part, for the exemption from federal income tax of corporations organized and operated exclusively for charitable, scientific, or educational purposes, provided no part of the organization's net earnings inures to the benefit of any private shareholder or individual.

Section 1.501(c)(3)–1(c)(1) of the Income Tax Regulations provides that an organization will be regarded as operated exclusively for one or more exempt purposes only if it engages primarily in activities which accomplish one or more of such exempt purposes specified in § 501(c)(3). An organization will not be so regarded if more than an insubstantial part of its activities is not in furtherance of an exempt purpose. In Better Business Bureau of Washington, D.C. v. United States, 326 U.S. 279, 283 (1945), the Court stated that "the presence of a single ... [non-exempt] purpose, if substantial in nature, will destroy the exemption regardless of the number or importance of truly ... [exempt] purposes."

Section 1.501(c)(3)–1(d)(1)(ii) provides that an organization is not organized or operated exclusively for exempt purposes unless it serves a public rather than a private interest. It further states that "to meet the requirement of this subdivision, it is necessary for an organization to establish that it is not organized and operated for the benefit of private interests...."

Section 1.501(c)(3)–1(d)(2) provides that the term "charitable" is used in § 501(c)(3) in its generally accepted legal sense. The promotion of health has long been recognized as a charitable purpose. See Restatement (Second) of Trusts, §§ 368, 372 (1959); 4A Austin W. Scott and William F. Fratcher, The Law of Trusts 368, 372 (4th ed. 1989). However, not every activity that promotes health supports tax exemption under § 501(c)(3). For example, selling prescription pharmaceuticals certainly promotes health, but pharmacies cannot qualify for recognition of exemption under § 501(c)(3) on that basis alone. Federation Pharmacy Services, Inc. v. Commissioner, 72 T.C. 687 (1979), aff'd, 625 F.2d 804 (8th Cir.1980) ("Federation Pharmacy"). Furthermore, "an institution for the promotion of health is not a charitable institution if it is privately owned and is run for the profit of the owners." 4A Austin W. Scott and William F. Fratcher, The Law of Trusts § 372.1 (4th ed. 1989). See also Restatement (Second) of Trusts, § 376 (1959). This principle applies to hospitals and other health care organizations. As the Tax Court stated, "[w]hile the diagnosis and cure of disease are indeed purposes that may furnish the foundation for characterizing the activity as 'charitable,' something more is required." * * *

In evaluating whether a nonprofit hospital qualifies as an organization described in § 501(c)(3), Rev. Rul. 69–545, 1969–2 C.B. 117, compares two hospitals. The first hospital discussed is controlled by a board of trustees composed of independent civic leaders. In addition, the hospital maintains an open medical staff, with privileges available to all qualified physicians; it operates a full-time emergency room open to all regardless of ability to pay; and it otherwise admits all patients able to pay (either themselves, or through third party payers such as private health insurance or government programs such as Medicare). In contrast, the second hospital is controlled by physicians who have a substantial economic interest in the hospital. This hospital restricts the number of physicians admitted to the medical staff, enters into favorable rental agreements with the individuals who control the hospital, and limits emergency room and hospital admission substantially to the patients of the physicians who control the hospital. Rev. Rul. 69–545 notes that in considering whether a nonprofit hospital is operated to serve a private benefit, the Service will weigh all the relevant facts and circumstances in each case, including the use and control of the hospital. The revenue ruling concludes that the first hospital continues to qualify as an organization described in § 501(c)(3) and the second hospital does not because it is operated for the private benefit of the physicians who control the hospital.

Section 509(a) provides that the term "private foundation" means a domestic or foreign organization described in § 501(c)(3) other than an organization described in § 509(a)(1), (2), (3), or (4). The organizations described in § 509(a)(1) include those described in § 170(b)(1)(A)(iii). An organization is described in § 170(b)(1)(A)(iii) if its principal purpose is to provide medical or hospital care.

Section 512(c) provides that an exempt organization that is a member of a partnership conducting an unrelated trade or business with respect to the exempt organization must include its share of the partnership income and deductions attributable to that business (subject to the exceptions, additions, and limitations in § 512(b)) in computing its unrelated business income. * * *

In Butler v. Commissioner, 36 T.C. 1097 (1961), acq. 1962–2 C.B. 4 ("Butler"), the court examined the relationship between a partner and a partnership for purposes of determining whether the partner was entitled to a business bad debt deduction for a loan he had made to the partnership that it could not repay. In holding that the partner was entitled to the bad debt deduction, the court noted that "[b]y reason of being a partner in a business, petitioner was individually engaged in business." Butler, 36 T.C. at 1106 citing Dwight A. Ward v. Commissioner, 20 T.C. 332 (1953), aff'd 224 F.2d 547 (9th Cir.1955).

In Plumstead Theatre Society, Inc. v. Commissioner, 74 T.C. 1324 (1980), aff'd, 675 F.2d 244 (9th Cir.1982) ("Plumstead"), the Tax Court held that a charitable organization's participation as a general partner in a limited partnership did not jeopardize its exempt status. The organization co-produced a play as one of its charitable activities. Prior to the opening of the play, the organization encountered financial difficulties in raising its share of costs. In order to meet its funding obligations, the organization formed a limited partnership in which it served as general partner, and two individuals and a for-profit corporation were the limited partners. One of the significant factors supporting the Tax Court's holding was its finding that the limited partners had no control over the organization's operations.

In Broadway Theatre League of Lynchburg, Virginia, Inc. v. U.S., 293 F.Supp. 346 (W.D.Va.1968) ("Broadway Theatre League"), the court held that an organization that promoted an interest in theatrical arts did not jeopardize its exempt status when it hired a booking organization to arrange for a series of theatrical performances, promote the series and sell season tickets to the series because the contract was for a reasonable term and provided for reasonable compensation and the organization retained ultimate authority over the activities being managed.

In Housing Pioneers v. Commissioner, 65 T.C.M. (CCH) 2191 (1993), aff'd, 49 F.3d 1395 (9th Cir.1995), amended 58 F.3d 401 (9th Cir.1995) ("Housing Pioneers"), the Tax Court concluded that an organization did not qualify as a § 501(c)(3) organization because its activities performed as co-general partner in for-profit limited partnerships substantially furthered a non-exempt purpose, and serving that purpose caused the organization to serve private interests. The organization entered into partnerships as a one percent co-general partner of existing limited partnerships for the purpose of splitting the tax benefits with the for-profit partners. Under the management agreement, the organization's authority as co-general partner was narrowly circumscribed. It had no management responsibilities and could describe only a vague charitable function of surveying tenant needs.

In est of Hawaii v. Commissioner, 71 T.C. 1067 (1979), aff'd in unpublished opinion 647 F.2d 170 (9th Cir.1981) ("est of Hawaii"), several for-profit est organizations exerted significant indirect control over est of Hawaii, a non-profit entity, through contractual arrangements. The Tax Court concluded that the for-profits were able to use the non-profit as an "instrument" to further their for-profit purposes. Neither the fact that the for-profits lacked structural control over the organization nor the fact that amounts paid to the for-profit organizations under the contracts were reasonable affected the court's conclusion. Consequently, est of Hawaii did not qualify as an organization described in § 501(c)(3).

In Harding Hospital, Inc. v. United States, 505 F.2d 1068 (6th Cir. 1974) ("Harding"), a non-profit hospital with an independent board of directors executed a contract with a medical partnership composed of seven physicians. The contract gave the physicians control over care of the hospital's patients and the stream of income generated by the patients while also guaranteeing the physicians thousands of dollars in payment for various supervisory activities. The court held that the benefits derived from the contract constituted sufficient private benefit to preclude exemption.

ANALYSIS

For federal income tax purposes, the activities of a partnership are often considered to be the activities of the partners. See, e.g., Butler. Aggregate treatment is also consistent with the treatment of partnerships for purpose of the unrelated business income tax under § 512(c). * * * In light of the aggregate principle discussed in *Butler* and reflected in § 512(c), the aggregate approach also applies for purposes of the operational test set forth in § 1.501(c)(3)–1(c). Thus, the activities of an LLC treated as a partnership for federal income tax purposes are considered to be the activities of a nonprofit organization that is an owner of the LLC when evaluating whether the nonprofit organization is operated exclusively for exempt purposes within the meaning of § 501(c)(3).

A § 501(c)(3) organization may form and participate in a partnership, including an LLC treated as a partnership for federal income tax purposes, and meet the operational test if participation in the partnership furthers a charitable purpose, and the partnership arrangement permits the exempt organization to act exclusively in furtherance of its exempt purpose and only incidentally for the benefit of the for-profit partners. See Plumstead and Housing Pioneers. Similarly, a § 501(c)(3) organization may enter into a management contract with a private party giving that party authority to conduct activities on behalf of the organization and direct the use of the organization's assets provided that the organization retains ultimate authority over the assets and activities being managed and the terms and conditions of the contract are reasonable, including reasonable compensation and a reasonable term. See Broadway Theatre League. However, if a private party is allowed to control or use the non-profit organization's activities or assets for the benefit of the private party, and the benefit is not incidental to the accomplishment of exempt purposes, the organization will fail to be organized and operated exclusively for exempt purposes. See est of Hawaii; Harding; § 1.501(c)(3)–1(c)(1); and § 1.501(c)(3)–1(d)(1)(ii).

Situation 1

After A and B form C, and A contributes all of its operating assets to C, A's activities will consist of the health care services it provides through C and any grantmaking activities it can conduct using income distributed to

C. A will receive an interest in C equal in value to the assets it contributes to C, and A's and B's returns from C will be proportional to their respective investments in C. The governing documents of C commit C to providing health care services for the benefit of the community as a whole and to give charitable purposes priority over maximizing profits for C's owners. Furthermore, through A's appointment of members of the community familiar with the hospital to C's board, the board's structure, which gives A's appointees voting control, and the specifically enumerated powers of the board over changes in activities, disposition of assets, and renewal of the management agreement. A can ensure that the assets it owns through C and the activities it conducts through C are used primarily to further exempt purposes. Thus, A can ensure that the benefit to B and other private parties, like the management company, will be incidental to the accomplishment of charitable purposes. Additionally, the terms and conditions of the management contract, including the terms for renewal and termination are reasonable. Finally, A's grants are intended to support education and research and give resources to help provide health care to the indigent. All of these facts and circumstances establish that, which A participates in forming C and contributes all of its operating assets to C, and C operates in accordance with its governing documents. A will be furthering charitable purposes and continue to be operated exclusively for exempt purposes.

Because A's grantmaking activity will be contingent upon receiving distributions from C, A's principal activity will continue to be the provision of hospital care. As long as A's principal activity remains the provision of hospital care. A will not be classified as a private foundation in accordance with § 509(a)(1) as an organization described in § 170(b)(1)(A)(iii).

Situation 2

When D and E form F, and D contributes its assets to F, D will be engaged in activities that consist of the health care services it provides through F and any grantmaking activities it can conduct using income distributed by F. However, unlike A, D will not be engaging primarily in activities that further an exempt purpose. "While the diagnosis and cure of disease are indeed purposes that may furnish the foundation for characterizing the activity as 'charitable,' something more is required." Sonora, 46 T.C. at 525–526. See also Federation Pharmacy; Sound Health; and Geisinger. In the absence of a binding obligation in F's governing documents for F to serve charitable purposes or otherwise provide its services to the community as a whole. F will be able to deny care to segments of the community, such as the indigent. Because D will share control of F with E, D will not be able to initiate programs within F to serve new health needs within the community without the agreement of at least one governing board member appointed by E. As a business enterprise, E will not necessarily give priority to the health needs of the community over the consequences for F's profits. The primary source of information for board members appointed by D will be the chief executives, who have a prior relationship with E and the management company, which is a subsidiary of

E. The management company itself will have broad discretion over F's activities and assets that may not always be under the board's supervision. For example, the management company is permitted to enter into all but "unusually large" contracts without board approval. The management company may also unilaterally renew the management agreement. Based on all these facts and circumstances, D cannot establish that the activities it conducts through F further exempt purposes. "[I]n order for an organization to qualify for exemption under § 501(c)(3) the organization must 'establish' that it is neither organized nor operated for the 'benefit of private interests.'" Federation Pharmacy, 625 F.2d at 809. Consequently, the benefit to E resulting from the activities D conducts through F will not be incidental to the furtherance of an exempt purpose. Thus, D will fail the operational test when it forms F, contributes its operating assets to F, and then serves as an owner to F.

HOLDING

A will continue to qualify as an organization described in § 501(c)(3) when it forms C and contributes all of its operating assets to C because A has established that A will be operating exclusively for a charitable purpose and only incidentally for the purpose of benefiting the private interests of B. Furthermore, A's principal activity will continue to be the provision of hospital care when C begins operations. Thus, A will be an organization described in § 170(b)(1)(A)(iii) and thus, will not be classified as a private foundation in accordance with § 509(a)(1), as long as hospital care remains its principal activity.

D will violate the requirements to be an organization described in § 501(c)(3) when it forms F and contributes all of its operating assets to F because D has failed to establish that it will be operated exclusively for exempt purposes.

NOTE: WHOLE HOSPITAL JOINT VENTURES

Revenue Ruling 98–15 was the Service's first published ruling on the tax consequences of whole hospital joint ventures. Its principles apply beyond the health care sector, especially to low income housing and shared technology joint ventures. Whole hospital joint ventures became popular as resistance grew to nonprofit hospital conversions. The joint venture is "whole" in the sense that a § 501(c)(3) nonprofit hospital transfers all of its assets and activities to a joint venture entity (usually a limited liability company) in exchange for an ownership interest in the entity. At the same time, a for-profit company contributes cash and possibly other assets, also receiving an interest in the joint venture entity. The § 501(c)(3) organization remains in existence but no longer operates the hospital. A similar structure is the hospital subsidiary joint venture, where an exempt hospital creates a wholly-owned nonprofit subsidiary whose only activity is to participate in a joint venture arrangement with a for-profit partner.

The principal tax issue raised by a whole hospital joint venture is whether the nonprofit partner continues to qualify for exempt status under § 501(c)(3). Revenue Ruling 98–15 focuses primarily on the level of control retained by the tax-exempt partner and provides examples at the good and bad ends of the spectrum. It has been criticized for offering little guidance on the far more prevalent middle ground situations.

In Redlands Surgical Services v. Commissioner, 113 T.C. 47 (1999), aff'd, 242 F.3d 904 (9th Cir.2001), the Tax Court endorsed the IRS's position that a nonprofit organization may lose its tax-exempt status by engaging in a joint venture with a for-profit partner in which the nonprofit lacks effective control. The court held that the Service properly denied exemption to a § 501(c)(3) hospital's nonprofit subsidiary whose sole activity was participating in a joint venture with a for-profit corporation to operate an ambulatory surgery center. In a lengthy opinion that relied heavily on detailed findings of fact, the court reasoned that the nonprofit partner, by ceding effective control over the operation of the activity to private parties, conferred an impermissible private benefit and thus was not operated exclusively for exempt purposes within the meaning of § 501(c)(3).

The facts of *Redlands* typify the complex structures that have become the norm in the health care sector. Redlands Health Systems ("RHS") was a California nonprofit public benefit organization with several wholly-owned subsidiaries, including a nonprofit community hospital, a hospital foundation, and a for-profit subsidiary. To raise capital to acquire and expand a nearby outpatient ambulatory surgery facility ("the Surgery Center"), RHS entered into a joint venture with SCA Centers ("SCA"), a for-profit subsidiary of a publicly traded company that operated surgery facilities throughout the country. As a first step, RHS and SCA formed a general partnership in which RHS received a 46 percent interest and SCA received a 54 percent interest in exchange for their contributions of cash and, in SCA's case, cash and stock of SCA's parent. The RHS–SCA general partnership then acquired a 61 percent general partnership interest in a California limited partnership ("the Operating Partnership") that owned and operated the Surgery Center, which previously had been a successful for-profit enterprise. The other 39 percent of the Operating Partnership was owned by 32 limited partners, all physicians on the staff of Redlands Hospital.

To limit its liability exposure, RHS subsequently transferred its interest in the first-tier general partnership to Redlands Surgical Services ("RSS"), a nonprofit subsidiary formed for the sole purpose of acting as co-general partner in the joint venture. The Service denied RSS's application for § 501(c)(3) status, contending that it had ceded effective control over the Surgery Center to SCA, a for-profit company with no history of charity care. In arguing that the joint venture provided a community benefit by promoting health, RSS contended that its deal with SCA, negotiated at arm's length, ensured that RSS had sufficient influence to further its charitable purposes. In evaluating qualification for exemption, RSS viewed the critical factor as the type of conduct in which the joint venture was engaged, not whether private parties had the ability to control the activity. Alternatively, RSS argued that it qualified for exemption under the "integral part" test of Treas. Reg. § 1.502–1(b), because it was organized and operated to perform services that were integral to the exempt purposes of its parent hospital.

In finding that RSS failed the operational test, the court agreed with the IRS that effective control was critical:

> We disagree with [RSS's] thesis. It is patently clear that the Operating Partnership, whatever charitable benefits it may produce, is not operated "in an exclusively charitable manner". As stated by Justice Cardozo (then Justice of the New York Court of Appeals), in describing one of the "ancient principles" of charitable trusts, "It is only when income may be applied to the profit of the founders that business has a beginning and charity an end." Butterworth v. Keeler, 219 N.Y. 446, 449–450, 114 N.E. 803, 804 (1916). The Operating Partnership's income is, of course, applied to the profit of [RSS's] co-general partner and the numerous limited partners. It is no answer to say that none of [RSS's] income from this activity was applied to private interests, for the activity is indivisible, and no discrete part of the Operating Partnership's income-producing activities is severable from those activities that produce income to be applied to the other partners' profit.

> Taken to its logical conclusion, [RSS's] thesis would suggest that an organization whose main activity is passive participation in a for-profit health-service enterprise could thereby be deemed to be operating exclusively for charitable purposes. Such a conclusion, however, would be contrary to well-established principles of charitable trust law. Frequently, a business enterprise may have charitable effects. * * * A private hospital relieves sickness and suffering. * * * However, the primary object of these institutions is the pecuniary gain of the operators. Hence trusts to aid in the founding or maintenance of private hospitals or clinics * * *, which are business enterprises operated for the purpose of making profits for stockholders or owners, are not charitable even though they involve incidentally some public benefits. "It is not charity to aid a business enterprise." * * *

> Clearly, there is something in common between the structure of petitioner's sole activity and the nature of petitioner's purposes in engaging in it. An organization's purposes may be inferred from its manner of operations; its "activities provide a useful indicia of the organization's purpose or purposes." * * * The binding commitments that petitioner has entered into and that govern its participation in the partnerships are indicative of petitioner's purposes. To the extent that petitioner cedes control over its sole activity to for-profit parties having an independent economic interest in the same activity and having no obligation to put charitable purposes ahead of profit-making objectives, petitioner cannot be assured that the partnerships will in fact be operated in furtherance of charitable purposes. In such a circumstance,

we are led to the conclusion that petitioner is not operated exclusively for charitable purposes.

Based on the totality of factors described below, we conclude that petitioner has in fact ceded effective control of the partnerships' and the Surgery Center's activities to for-profit parties, conferring on them significant private benefits, and therefore is not operated exclusively for charitable purposes within the meaning of section 501(c)(3).

113 T.C. at 77–78.

The Tax Court's conclusions on the extent of for-profit control over the joint venture were influenced by these factors: (1) the partnership agreement failed to establish any obligation of the partnership to put charitable purposes ahead of economic objectives; (2) RSS lacked voting control and was unable unilaterally to cause the Surgery Center to respond to community needs (RSS's power to veto expansion was an insufficient mitigating factor, as was an arbitration process to break deadlocks); (3) a revenue-based management contract with an affiliate of SCA provided an incentive to maximize profits; (4) RSS lacked other informal indicia of control sufficient to ensure furtherance of charitable purposes; and (5) the arrangement restricted the hospital's future ability to provide outpatient services without the approval of its for-profit partner (the resulting market advantages and lesser competitive pressures constituted a private benefit). The Tax Court also rejected RSS's integral part argument, finding that its activity was not so substantially and closely related to the purposes of its exempt affiliates as to warrant disregarding the substantial private benefit conferred on SCA.

Those who were expecting meaningful appellate court guidance on joint ventures from the Ninth Circuit's widely anticipated opinion in *Redlands Surgical Services* were sorely disappointed. In a per curiam opinion issued a mere ten days after oral argument, the court affirmed the Tax Court's decision, noting briefly that it was specifically adopting the trial court holding that RSS had ceded effective control over the operations of the partnerships and the surgery center to private parties, conferring impermissible private benefit. Redlands Surgical Services v. Commissioner, 242 F.3d 904 (9th Cir.2001).

The Service did not fare as well in St. David's Health Care System, Inc. v. United States, 2002–1 USTC ¶ 50,452 (W.D.Tex.2002), another whole hospital joint venture case, where a Texas federal district court overturned the Service's revocation of exemption of St. David's Health Care System. St. David's, which had enjoyed exempt status under § 501(c)(3) since 1938, owned and operated an acute care hospital in Austin, Texas. In 1996, it entered into a limited partnership with an affiliate of HCA, Inc., a nationwide for-profit health care provider, to operate the hospital. St. David's contributed all its assets in exchange for a 45.9 percent interest in the venture (based on an independent valuation of the contributed assets). It was one of two general partners (though an HCA affiliate was the managing general partner) and had equal representation on the governing board. The partnership agreement included certain safeguards to preserve the "charitable" nature of the facility, and St. David's had the unilateral legal right to dissolve the venture if the partnership did not act in accordance with standards for tax exemption.

The Service revoked St. David's exemption on the ground that, by entering into the joint venture, it no longer was operated exclusively for charitable purposes and was providing an impermissible private benefit to its for-profit partner. At trial, the Service argued that, to qualify as "charitable," a health care organization must have a "community board," a requirement not met here because a for-profit entity had the power to appoint 50 percent of the hospital's governing body. It also contended that a health care provider could not be "charitable" unless it provided sufficient care to those without ability to pay. Finally, the Service advanced a private benefit argument as an alternative ground for revocation of exemption.

After pausing to characterize the operational test (Treas. Reg. § 1.501(c)(3)–1(c)(1)) as "a horrible amalgamation of negatives arranged like an inside joke prompting laughter only from seasoned and sadistic bureaucrats," the court rejected the Service's arguments. It found that "the presence of a community board is a point in favor of exemption" but not an "absolute requirement" and, even if it were, the joint venture was in compliance through the rights and safeguards preserved to St. David's through the partnership agreement. Significantly, the court found that St. David's had "substantially more control than the for-profit partner" despite its lack of formal voting control in the 50:50 board structure. As for the Service's argument that St. David's failed to provide sufficient charity care, the court found that the hospital met the community benefit standard articulated in Revenue Ruling 69–545 (see supra p. 122) by providing emergency care regardless of ability to pay.

St. David's is a notable taxpayer victory insofar as it holds that an exempt partner's control of a joint governing board is not essential if sufficient safeguards are included in the agreement. But the Service has not yet retreated from the position articulated in Revenue Ruling 98–15. As this edition went to press, *St. David's* was pending on appeal to the Fifth Circuit.

NOTES AND QUESTIONS

1. *Better Planning? Redlands Surgical Services* involved the tax-exempt status of a nonprofit subsidiary formed solely to act as general partner of the joint venture. Would the result have been different if RHS, the nonprofit parent, or its hospital subsidiary, had acted as general partner in addition to continuing its other activities?

2. *Ancillary Joint Ventures.* A far more common arrangement not addressed by Revenue Ruling 98–15 is the ancillary joint venture. The typical structure of an ancillary joint venture was described by the I.R.S. in its 1998 training manual for exempt organization specialists:

A hospital ancillary joint venture refers to those joint venture arrangements where an exempt organization that operates a hospital or other health care facility owns an interest in a joint venture with a for-profit entity to operate a particular service. The exempt organization, usually part of a health care system, owns and operates a hospital as well as other health care facilities or services, such as ambulatory surgery center, MRI, or home health care services. It transfers the assets of the health care facility or service to the joint venture; or contributes funds to establish the ancillary service. The for-profit partner contributes cash equal to the fair market value of the exempt organization facility transferred to the joint venture. The joint venture owns and operates the health care facility or service. The exempt organization still owns and operates the hospital facility.

Thus, unlike the whole hospital joint venture structure, or the hospital subsidiary joint venture arrangement, the exempt organization does not contribute all of its operating assets nor is the participation by the exempt organization in the joint venture its sole activity. In the hospital ancillary joint venture, the activity conducted by the exempt organization through the joint venture arrangement is generally not the sole activity of the exempt organization, and it may not be a substantial part of the organization's activities. Instead, the exempt partner will continue to operate its hospital and other health care facilities and services.

Mary Jo Salins, Judy Kindell & Marvin Friedlander, Whole Hospital Joint Ventures, FY 1999 IRS Exempt Organizations Professional Education Technical Instruction Program 1 (1998).

Do Rev. Rul. 98–15 and the whole hospital joint ventures cases shed any light on the tax treatment of ancillary joint ventures? What additional issues are raised by this type of structure? If the activities of an ancillary joint venture are substantially related to the exempt partner's charitable purposes and the arrangement is structured to avoid any inurement or private benefit, of what relevance is the exempt partner's control over the venture?

3. *For Further Reading.* John D. Colombo, Private Benefit, Joint Ventures, and the Death of Healthcare as an Exempt Purpose, 34 J.Health Law 505 (2001); Douglas M. Mancino, Exempt Entities: Joint Ventures, Virtual Mergers and Conversions of Status, 50 U.S.C. Tax Inst. (Major Tax Planning), ch. 8 (1998).

PROBLEM

Sturdley University, long recognized as tax-exempt under § 501(c)(3), is a private, nonprofit university with an undergraduate college and professional schools in law, business and medicine. To further its educational mission and raise revenue, Sturdley's business school is exploring whether to enter into a joint venture with ExecutiveEd.com ("Dot Com"), a for-profit provider of on line education to business executives. Under the proposal, the Sturdley School of Business will develop the courses and contribute its name, logo and the services of selected faculty. Dot Com will contribute cash, and a Dot Com subsidiary will manage the venture for a fee under a five-year renewable contract. All operational decisions, including marketing and fee structure, will be made by Dot Com. The venture will be structured as a limited liability company ("LLC") under state law. In exchange for their respective contributions, Sturdley and Dot Com each will take back a 50% LLC interest and have equal representation on the LLC's governing board. Disputes will be resolved through binding arbitration. Income, expenses and distributions will be allocated equally.

Will this joint venture have an adverse effect on Sturdley's tax-exempt status? What factors are relevant in making this determination? Accepting the IRS's current position on joint ventures, what safeguards or other steps would you suggest to protect Sturdley's tax exemption?

F. LIMITATIONS ON LOBBYING AND POLITICAL CAMPAIGN ACTIVITIES

1. BACKGROUND

A nonprofit organization qualifies for tax-exempt status under § 501(c)(3) only if: (1) "no substantial part" of its activities consists of carrying on propaganda or otherwise attempting to influence legislation, and (2) it does not participate or intervene in "any political campaign on behalf of (or in opposition to) any candidate for public office." In lieu of the vague "no substantial part" lobbying limitation, most publicly supported charities may elect to be regulated by more objective expenditure tests that permit the organization to spend certain amounts on lobbying without penalty and then imposes gradual sanctions—first an excise tax on excessive lobbying expenditures and then loss of exemption for more serious transgressions. See generally I.R.C. §§ 501(h), 4911. The Service also may impose excise tax penalties on organizations that make certain impermissible political expenditures, and on officers and trustees of the organization who are aware of these violations. See I.R.C. § 4955. These longstanding restrictions are another aspect of the border patrol function of federal tax law. They limit but do not eliminate the ability of nonprofits to influence the political process.

As a practical matter, the lobbying restrictions are relevant only to § 501(c)(3) organizations classified as public charities. A far more restrictive regime applies to private foundations, which are subject to punitive excise tax penalties if they engage in *any* lobbying, regardless of its relationship to the foundation's charitable program. See I.R.C. § 4945, discussed in Chapter 3C6, infra, at pp. 480–489. By contrast, most noncharitable exempt organizations are free to lobby with respect to legislation germane to their purposes without threatening their exemption, but lobbying activities may result in partial disallowance of business deductions for dues paid to some of these organizations (e.g., trade associations and labor unions) by their for-profit members. See I.R.C. § 162(e) and Chapter 4C3, infra, at pp. 533–536.

Lobbying by charitable organizations was first limited by a 1919 Treasury regulation providing that "associations formed to disseminate controversial or partisan propaganda are not educational within the meaning of the statute." Treas. Reg. 45, art. 517 (1919 ed.). The government advanced this position with varying success in a number of cases, the most notable of which was Slee v. Commissioner, 42 F.2d 184 (2d Cir.1930). In *Slee*, the Second Circuit held that the American Birth Control League failed to qualify for exemption because it had disseminated propaganda to legislators and the public supporting the repeal of laws against birth control. In holding that the League was not operated exclusively for charitable or educational purposes, Judge Learned Hand stated that "political agitation as such" was prohibited unless the lobbying was ancillary to an organization's "end-in-chief." The court apparently would have permitted a birth control society to lobby to remove legal obstacles from its hospital work or allowed a church to lobby against a proposal to repeal Sunday blue laws because these activities were ancillary to the accomplishment of each organization's exempt purposes. But lobbying to shape public policy was viewed as a substantial noncharitable purpose. In a much quoted portion of the opinion, Judge Hand articulated a neutrality justification for this restriction:

> Political agitation as such is outside the statute, however innocent the aim, though it adds nothing to dub it "propaganda," a polemical word used to decry the publicity of the other side. Controversies of that sort must be conducted without public subvention; the Treasury stands aside from them.

42 F.2d at 185.

In 1934, Congress added the "no substantial part" lobbying limitation as a condition on § 501(c)(3) exemption, but its rationale is clouded in obscurity. Some contend that it codifies *Slee*'s distinction between permissible ancillary lobbying and impermissible independent lobbying. Others construe it as relaxing the *Slee* test by permitting insubstantial lobbying for any purpose but prohibiting "substantial" lobbying, whatever the motive. Still others believe that Congress only intended to limit lobbying that served the selfish private interests of an organization's insiders. In 1987 Congressional hearings, a Treasury official conceded that the legislative history was "inconclusive" and that the rationale for the no substantial part limitation had "never been clearly articulated." Lobbying and Political Activities of Tax–Exempt Organizations: Hearings Before the Subcomm. on Oversight of the House Comm. on Ways and Means, 100th Cong., 1st Sess. 87 (1987)(statement of J. Roger Mentz).

In 1987, Congress concluded that these limitations were ineffective in curbing the lobbying activities of some exempt organizations and, in other circumstances, they were unduly harsh by requiring the Service to revoke exemptions for isolated political campaign activity. The Congressional response was a set of additional excise taxes that are summarized later in this chapter.

The history of the political campaign limitation is even more obscure. The absolute ban originated as a Senate floor amendment to the Internal Revenue Code of 1954 and passed without explanatory comment apart from a statement from its sponsor, then Senator Lyndon B. Johnson, that the rule was intended to "extend" the limitation of § 501(c)(3). 100 Cong. Rec. 9604 (1954). The conventional wisdom is that Senator Johnson was out to curb the activities of a Texas foundation which had provided indirect financial support to his opponent in a senatorial election campaign. See Bruce R. Hopkins, The Law of Tax–Exempt Organizations 504 (7th ed. 1998).

This section of the chapter focuses principally on the federal tax law restrictions on lobbying and political campaign activities of § 501(c)(3) organizations. It then discusses the opportunities for greater political involvement through the use of § 501(c)(4) social welfare organizations and § 527 political organizations, and provides an overview of the impact of nontax rules on the politically active nonprofit.

2.   THE LOBBYING LIMITATION: NO SUBSTANTIAL PART TEST

Internal Revenue Code: §§ 501(c)(3); 504; 4912.

Treasury Regulations: § 1.501(c)(3)–1(c)(3).

An organization does not qualify for exemption under § 501(c)(3) unless "no substantial part of [its] activities * * * is carrying on propaganda, or otherwise attempting, to influence legislation." Two principal issues are thus presented: (1) what constitutes "influencing legislation" (lobbying) and (2) when does lobbying become a "substantial" part of the organization's activities?

Influencing Legislation. The Service has attempted, with limited success, to give meaning to the terms "influencing legislation" and "substantial." The regulations provide that an organization will not qualify under § 501(c)(3) if it is an "action organization"—a status attained either by:

(1) engaging in substantial attempts to influence legislation by contacting legislators or urging the public to contact them to propose, support, or oppose legislation, or advocating the adoption or rejection of legislation; or

(2) having primary objectives which may be attained only by legislation or the defeat of proposed legislation (e.g., an organization formed specifically to promote a constitutional amendment permitting prayer in the schools) and campaigning for the attainment of that objective rather than engaging in nonpartisan analysis and research and making the results available to the public.

Treas. Reg. § 1.501(c)(3)–1(c)(3).

The regulations define "legislation" to include action by Congress, state legislatures, local governing bodies or by the public in a referendum, initiative, constitutional amendment or similar procedure. Treas. Reg. § 1.501(c)(3)–1(c)(3)(ii). "Legislation" does not include action by the executive branch or independent administrative agencies. In general, attempts to influence legislation include direct contacts with legislators and their staffs to propose, support or oppose legislation ("direct lobbying") and efforts to urge the general public to contact legislators or their staffs to propose, support or oppose legislation ("grassroots lobbying").

Although generalizations are perilous in this area, cases and revenue rulings over the years provide some additional line-drawing guidance. The early cases interpreting the lobbying limitation took the position that Congress only intended to proscribe the "evil" type of lobbying that served selfish interests and was characterized by factual distortions. Lobbying for the general good would be permissible under this analysis. The Code, however, simply speaks in terms of attempts to influence legislation, whether they be good, bad or indifferent. Most courts came to the view that an organization's motives for lobbying are irrelevant. The League of Women Voters, for example, was stripped of its 501(c)(3) exemption because of excessive lobbying even though it was an integral part of its educational mission. See League of Women Voters v. United States, 148 Ct.Cl. 561, 180 F.Supp. 379 (1960), cert. denied 364 U.S. 822, 81 S.Ct. 57 (1960). In addition, if an organization's primary objective is only attainable through legislation (e.g., repeal of the federal income tax), it will be disqualified as an action organization even if it never mentions a specific bill. See Fund for the Study of Economic Growth and Tax Reform v. IRS, 161 F.3d 755 (D.C.Cir.1998).

An organization is not lobbying when it merely communicates with its members on issues of common interest, at least if the membership group is confined to bona fide followers. But the line is crossed if the organization exhorts its members to contact legislators or their staffs or urges the general public to do so in support of or opposition to specific pending legislation. Section 501(c)(3) organizations also are not treated as lobbying if they engage in nonpartisan analysis, study or research on legislative matters and communicate their analysis to legislators, at least if the analysis is not intended to support a particular position. Rev. Rul. 70–79, 1970–1 C.B. 127. Finally, an organization may give expert testimony or technical assistance in response to a formal request from a legislative body without jeopardizing its exemption. See, e.g., Rev. Rul. 70–449, 1970–2 C.B. 111. But an unsolicited appearance before a congressional committee to endorse or oppose a particular bill is regarded as lobbying.

When is Lobbying "Substantial?" It is not enough to define "influencing legislation." Lobbying activities lead to revocation of an organization's exemption under the general limitation only if they are a "substantial" part of the organization's activities, relative to whatever else the organization does. Nobody (including the Service) knows for sure when lobbying becomes "substantial." A few early cases attempted to devise a quantitative test, and one court held that devoting less than five percent of an organization's time and effort to lobbying was insubstantial. Seasongood v. Commissioner, 227 F.2d 907 (6th Cir.1955). In later cases, the courts opted for a subjective balancing test, under which all the facts and circumstances are sifted "in the context of the objectives and circumstances of the organization." See, e.g., Haswell v. United States, 500 F.2d 1133 (Ct.Cl.1974), cert. denied, 419 U.S. 1107, 95 S.Ct. 779 (1975). Relevant factors include the percentage of an organization's budget (or employee time) spent on lobbying; the continuous or intermittent nature of the organization's legislative involvement; the nature of the organization and its aims; and, realistically, the controversial nature of the organization's position and its visibility.

This balancing approach is a version of what tax lawyers refer to as the "smell test." It provides virtually no guidance to an organization wishing to influence legislation as part of its program without endangering its exempt status.

The Christian Echoes Case. Prior to the 1960's, the lobbying limitations were only sporadically enforced. The Service became more aggressive in the early days of the Kennedy administration when an "ideological organizations" project was initiated for the purpose of scrutinizing the political activities of primarily right-wing exempt organizations. The *Christian Echoes* case, below, was an outgrowth of that project.

Christian Echoes National Ministry, Inc. v. United States

United States Court of Appeals, Tenth Circuit, 1972.
470 F.2d 849.

■ BARRETT, CIRCUIT JUDGE.

Christian Echoes sued for refund of Federal Insurance Contribution Act (FICA) taxes for 1961 and 1963 through 1968 amounting to $103,493.08 plus statutory interest. On June 24, 1971 the District Court held that the taxpayer qualified for tax exemption under 26 U.S.C.A. Section 501(c)(3). The Government appealed to the United States Supreme Court which vacated the judgment and remanded for entry of a new decree. United States v. Christian Echoes National Ministry, Inc., 404 U.S. 561, 92 S.Ct. 663, 30 L.Ed.2d 716 (1972). The District Court entered the same decision on February 24, 1972. The Government takes this appeal therefrom.

Christian Echoes is a nonprofit religious corporation organized in 1951 under the laws of Oklahoma by Dr. Billy James Hargis, its president, chief spokesman and an ordained minister. The Articles of Incorporation state in part that the corporation is founded "to establish and maintain weekly religious, radio and television broadcasts, to establish and maintain a national religious magazine and other religious publications, to establish and maintain religious educational institutions, * * * "Article III of the Articles of Faith in the corporate by-laws reads as follows:

"We believe in God, Supreme and Eternal, and in Jesus Christ as His Son, perfect Deity, and in the Holy Comforter and Challenger of this age, The Holy Ghost, and in the Bible as the inspired Word of God.

We believe that the solution of the World's problems, economic, political and spiritual, is found by the application of Christian Teachings in the lives of men and nations rather than in political ideologies of any kind.

We believe in the Twentieth Century Reformation to combat apostate conditions with the Church. We realize atheistic world forces seek the destruction and overthrow of all the religions of the World, including particularly that founded upon the teachings of Jesus Christ. The same forces seek also the destruction of all free governments, in which the lives and property of the people are protected by civil, moral and spiritual law.

We associate ourselves together to educate and proclaim the essential truths of Christianity, and the doctrine: Jesus Christ is the Hope of the World and America is God's Greatest Nation under the Living Son. We believe in the real spiritual unity in Christ of all redeemed by His precious blood.

We believe in constitutional government, whereby religious as well as other freedoms of mankind are preserved and protected. We believe in the fundamentals of New Testament Christianity, and we propose to promulgate the eternal truths thereof at all costs."

The activities of the organization have been addressed to that theology ever since the date of incorporation.

Christian Echoes maintains religious radio and television broadcasts, authors publications, and engages in evangelistic campaigns and meetings for the promotion of the social and spiritual welfare of the community, state and nation. Dr. Hargis has stated that its mission is a battle against Communism, socialism and political liberalism, all of which are considered arch enemies of the Christian faith. Dr. Hargis testified that Christian Echoes supports "Christian conservative statesmen * * * "without regard to party political labels. The organization publishes a monthly anti-Communist magazine, Christian Crusade, a weekly "intelligence report", Weekly Crusader, and a newspaper column, "For and Against". It also distributes pamphlets, leaflets and broadcast reprints on aspects of anti-Communist activity; it distributes tapes and records of selected broad casts; and it conducts an annual anti-Communist leadership school whose goal is to answer the question, "What can my community do to stem the forces of liberalism and thus stop the growth of socialism and communism?" In 1962 it established a Summer Anti–Communist University and formed youth groups, Torchbearer Chapters, to educate the public on the threat of Communism. In 1964 Christian Echoes encouraged adults to organize local Christian Crusade chapters. Christian Echoes appealed for contributions from the public to carry on its campaign. It earned money from the sale of its publications, tapes, films and admission fees at rallies. From 1961 through 1966 its gross receipts ranged from about $677,000 to $1,000,000 per year. It spent 52% of this income on radio, television, publications and postage.

On March 12, 1953 the Internal Revenue Service ruled that Christian Echoes qualified as a tax-exempt religious and educational organization under Section 501(c)(3) of the 1954 Code, formerly Section 101(6) of the 1939 Code. Section 501(c)(3) states as follows:

> "Corporations, and any community chest, fund, or foundation, organized and operated exclusively for religious, charitable, scientific, testing for public safety, literary, or educational purposes, or for the prevention of cruelty to children or animals, no part of the net earnings of which inures to the benefit of any private shareholder or individual, no substantial part of the activities of which is carrying on propaganda, or otherwise attempting, to influence legislation, and which does not participate in, or intervene in (including the publishing or distributing of statements), any political campaign on behalf of any candidate for public office."

In 1962 and 1963 the National Office of the Internal Revenue Service requested that the activities and financial affairs of Christian Echoes be re-examined. The IRS agents recommended no change in its exempt status. The National Office, after reviewing and analyzing the activities of Christian Echoes, recommended that the exemption be revoked. On November 13, 1964 the District Director in Oklahoma City advised Christian Echoes in a letter of the revocation of its exemption and of its protest rights. Christian Echoes filed a formal protest on June 25, 1965 after conferences with the District Director and the National Office. The District Director notified Christian Echoes on September 22, 1966 that its exempt status was being revoked for three reasons: (1) it was not operated exclusively for charitable, educational or religious purposes; (2) it had engaged in substantial activity aimed at influencing legislation; and (3) it had directly and indirectly intervened in political campaigns on behalf of candidates for public office. Christian Echoes filed further protests without avail. It paid the taxes as assessed. Christian Echoes then filed this refund suit, claiming its right to exemption.

The District Court held that the taxpayer was entitled to tax-exempt status under Section 501(c)(3). The Court ruled that Christian Echoes qualified in that no substantial part of its activities had been devoted to attempts to influence legislation or intervene in political campaigns. The Court found that the only activity of Christian Echoes relating to an attempt to influence legislation was in support of the Becker Amendment urging support of restoration of prayers in the public schools. The Trial Court accepted Dr. Hargis's interpretation of the "attempts to influence legislation" prohibition in 501(c)(3), wherein Dr. Hargis testified on cross-examination that:

> " * * * it's my interpretation that as long as I don't lobby in Washington, which I never have, as long as I don't get behind a bill or post a bill which I never have, as long as I don't endorse a political candidate,

which I never have * * * that by no stretch of the imagination could you say what I am doing is political * * * "

It also held that all of its activities were motivated by sincere religious convictions; that the First Amendment prohibits the Government and courts from determining whether the activities are religious or political; and that the IRS had revoked Christian Echoes' exempt status without evidence to support its action and without constitutionally justifiable cause in violation of the First Amendment. It found that the taxpayer had been denied its right to due process under the Fifth Amendment because the Government had arbitrarily selected it from organizations engaged in similar activities and had violated its published administrative procedures in the steps leading to the revocation.

The Government appealed directly to the United States Supreme Court which dismissed the appeal for lack of jurisdiction, vacated the District Court's judgment and remanded for entry of a new decree. The IRS appeals from the District Court's holding in favor of Christian Echoes following remand. The Government contends that: (1) the taxpayer failed to qualify as tax-exempt under Section 501(c)(3); (2) its interpretation and application of Section 501(c)(3) did not violate the taxpayer's rights under the First Amendment; (3) its revocation of tax-exempt status to the taxpayer under Section 501(c)(3) did not violate the taxpayer's rights of due process under the Fifth Amendment; and (4) the Commissioner did not abuse his discretion in revoking the exemption with retroactive effect.

I.

The Government contends that Christian Echoes failed to qualify as tax-exempt under Section 501(c)(3) because: (1) a substantial part of its activities consisted of carrying on propaganda, or otherwise attempting to influence legislation; and (2) it participated or intervened in political campaigns on behalf of candidates for public office. The issue raises the interpretation and application of Section 501(c)(3).

Almost since the earliest days of the federal income tax, Congress has exempted certain corporations from taxation. The exemption to corporations organized and operated exclusively for charitable, religious, educational or other purposes carried on for charity is granted because of the benefit the public obtains from their activities and is based on the theory that:

"* * * the Government is compensated for the loss of revenue by its relief from financial burden which would otherwise have to be met by appropriations from public funds, and by the benefits resulting from the promotion of the general welfare." H.R.Rep.No.1860, 75th Cong., 3d Sess. 19 (1939).

Tax exemptions are matters of legislative grace and taxpayers have the burden of establishing their entitlement to exemptions. The limitations in Section 501(c)(3) stem from the Congressional policy that the United States Treasury should be neutral in political affairs and that substantial activities directed to attempts to influence legislation or affect a political campaign should not be subsidized.

The limitation in Section 501(c)(3) originated in the Revenue Act of 1934, allowing tax exempt status to organizations, if "no substantial part of the activities of which is carrying on propaganda, or otherwise attempting, to influence legislation." The case which led to the 1934 legislation was Slee v. Commissioner of Internal Revenue, 42 F.2d 184 (2d Cir.1930). There the Court held that the American Birth Control League was not entitled to a charitable exemption because it disseminated propaganda to legislators and the public aimed at the repeal of laws preventing birth control. The IRS denied tax exempt status because the Birth Control League's purposes were not exclusively charitable, educational or scientific. In 1954 Congress attached a further condition to exempt status by adding the bar against participation or intervention in political campaigns on behalf of candidates for public office.

A religious organization that engages in substantial activity aimed at influencing legislation is disqualified from tax exemption, whatever the motivation. The Government has at all times recognized Christian Echoes as a religious organization. Indeed, the Government acknowledges that in all of its activities, Christian Echoes has been religiously motivated.

The critical issue is whether the limitation on attempts to influence legislation should be given the narrow interpretation applied by the District Court or a broader construction. The District Court held that the only attempt to influence legislation by Christian Echoes was in its support of the Becker Amendment relating to restoration of prayers in the public schools. By this construction, there must be specific legislation before Congress in order for the "attempt to influence legislation" prohibition to come into play. We disagree. We hold that the Trial Court was clearly erroneous in this interpretation of law.

Treasury Regulation 1.501(c)(3)–1(c)(3)(ii) states that an organization will be regarded as attempting to influence legislation if the organization:

(a) Contacts, or urges the public to contact, members of a legislative body for the purpose of proposing, supporting, or opposing legislation; or

(b) Advocates the adoption or rejection of legislation. Legislation is defined in the regulations as: " * * * action by the Congress, by any State legislature, by any local council or similar governing body, or by the public in a referendum, initiative, constitutional amendment, or similar procedure." Treas.Reg. 1.501(c)(3)–1(c)(3)(ii)(b).

The Regulation goes well beyond the District Court's interpretation of Section 501(c)(3). It includes direct and indirect appeals to legislators and the public in general. We hold that the Regulation properly interprets the intent of Congress. A capsule review of the "substantial" activities of Christian Echoes will adequately demonstrate, we believe, that Congress intended that the limitations be given a broad or liberal interpretation.

Christian Echoes' publications, such as the Christian Crusade, contained numerous articles attempting to influence legislation by appeals to the public to react to certain issues. These articles were either authored by Dr. Hargis, members of his organization, solicited contributors, or unsolicited authors—but all such articles had the stamp of approval of Dr. Hargis before acceptance for publication. The fact that specific legislation was not mentioned does not mean that these attempts to influence public opinion were not attempts to influence legislation. For example, Christian Echoes appealed to its readers to: (1) write their Congressmen in order to influence the political decisions in Washington; (2) work in politics at the precinct level; (3) support the Becker Amendment by writing their Congressmen; (4) maintain the McCarran–Walter Immigration law; (5) contact their Congressmen in opposition to the increasing interference with freedom of speech in the United States; (6) purge the American press of its responsibility for grossly misleading its readers on vital issues; (7) inform their Congressmen that the House Committee on UnAmerican Activities must be retained; (8) oppose an Air Force Contract to disarm the United States; (9) dispel the mutual mistrust between North and South America; (10) demand a congressional investigation of the biased reporting of major television networks; (11) support the Dirksen Amendment; (12) demand that Congress limit foreign aid spending; (13) discourage support for the World Court; (14) support the Connally Reservation; (15) cut off diplomatic relations with communist countries; (16) reduce the federal payroll by discharging needless jobholders, stop waste of public funds and balance the budget; (17) stop federal aid to education, socialized medicine and public housing; (18) abolish the federal income tax; (19) end American diplomatic recognition of Russia; (20) withdraw from the United Nations; (21) outlaw the Communist Party in the United States; and (22) to restore our immigration laws.

The taxpayer also attempted to mold public opinion in civil rights legislation, medicare, the Postage Revision Act of 1967, the Honest Election Law of 1967, the Nuclear Test Ban Treaty, the Panama Canal Treaty, firearms control legislation, and the Outer Space Treaty. These appeals urging the readers to action all appeared in Christian Echoes' publications between 1961 and 1968. They were all attempts to influence legislation through an indirect campaign to mold public opinion. This was directly evidenced by Dr. Hargis' keynote address delivered at the Anti–Communist Leadership School on February 11, 1963, entitled "Counter Strategy for Counter Attack." After setting forth a 10–point program, he stated that "Your opinion isn't worth a nickel without your action to back it up."

The political activities of an organization must be balanced in the context of the objectives and circumstances of the organization to determine whether a substantial part of its activities was to influence or attempt to influence legislation. A percentage test to determine whether the activities were substantial obscures the complexity of balancing the organization's activities in relation to its objectives and circumstances. An essential part of the program of Christian Echoes was to promote desirable governmental policies consistent with its objectives through legislation. The activities of Christian Echoes in influencing or attempting to influence legislation were not incidental, but were substantial and continuous. The hundreds of exhibits demonstrate this. These are the activities which Congress intended should not be carried on by exempt organizations.

In addition to influencing legislation, Christian Echoes intervened in political campaigns. Generally it did not formally endorse specific candidates for office but used its publications and broadcasts to attack candidates and incumbents who were considered too liberal. It attacked President Kennedy in 1961 and urged its followers to elect conservatives like Senator Strom Thurmond and Congressmen Bruce Alger and Page Belcher. It urged followers to defeat Senator Fulbright and attacked President Johnson and Senator Hubert Humphrey. The annual convention endorsed Senator Barry Goldwater. These attempts to elect or defeat certain political leaders reflected Christian Echoes' objective to change the composition of the federal government.

II.

The Government contends that its application of Section 501(c)(3) does not violate the free exercise clause in the First Amendment. Christian Echoes argues strenuously that denial of its tax-exempt status is a direct infringement upon its First Amendment right of free exercise of religion, and discrimination against the religion of its followers. The District Court agreed. The District Court held that the First Amendment forbids the Government and courts from deciding whether such activities are religious or political, and if political, whether substantial. The District Court held that the Government revoked the taxpayer's exempt status without a constitutionally justifiable cause, denying the taxpayer the free exercise of religion. We disagree. We hold that the Court erred.

If we were to adopt the District Court's findings and the arguments advanced by Christian Echoes, we would be compelled to hold that Congress is constitutionally restrained from withholding the privilege of tax exemption whenever it enacts legislation relating to a nonprofit religious organization. This is fully evidenced by the trial court's Conclusion of Law No. 4 which is both clearly erroneous and irrelevant to the substantive issue relating to substantial activity for the purpose of attempting to influence legislation. There the Court concluded in part: "The Court having found as fact that plaintiff through its followers believes in the religious nature of its activities, neither defendant nor this Court may inquire into such activities and work product of plaintiff for the purpose of determining whether those activities claimed by plaintiff to be religious are religious or political and, if political, whether substantial, for the purpose of denying tax exempt status to plaintiff. To make such an inquiry would first require this Court to define the terms 'religious' and 'political,' then separate plaintiff's activities into these two categories applying those labels thereto under definitions established by this Court. This action would require both a quantitative and qualitative analysis of plaintiff's activities. To do so would require an interpretation of the meaning of the church doctrine espoused by plaintiff and a determination of the relative significance of the religion of plaintiff to its activities." We know of no legal authority supporting the conclusion set forth above. Such conclusion is tantamount to the proposition that the First Amendment right of free exercise of religion, ipso facto, assures no restraints, no limitations and, in effect, protects those exercising the right to do so unfettered. We hold that the limitations imposed by Congress in Section 501(c)(3) are constitutionally valid. The free exercise clause of the First Amendment is restrained only to the extent of denying tax exempt status and then only in keeping with an overwhelming and compelling Governmental interest: That of guarantying [sic] that the wall separating church and state remain high and firm. We reject both the District Court's findings and conclusions on the First Amendment constitutional issue just as the United States Supreme Court put down attacks against the enforcement of the provisions of the "Hatch Act" predicated on First Amendment free speech and assembly rights, restraining political activities by certain federal officers and employees in United Public Workers of America (C.I.O.) v. Mitchell, 330 U.S. 75, 67 S.Ct. 556, 91 L.Ed. 754 (1947) and Oklahoma v. United States Civil Service Commission, 330 U.S. 127, 67 S.Ct. 544, 91 L.Ed. 794 (1947). In these decisions the courts held that the First Amendment rights are not absolutes and that courts must balance First Amendment freedoms against the congressional enactment in order to protect society against political partisanship by Government employees.

In light of the fact that tax exemption is a privilege, a matter of grace rather than right, we hold that the limitations contained in Section 501(c)(3) withholding exemption from nonprofit corporations do not deprive Christian Echoes of its constitutionally guaranteed right of free speech. The taxpayer may engage in all such activities without restraint, subject, however, to withholding of the exemption or, in the alternative, the taxpayer may refrain from such activities and obtain the privilege of exemption. The parallel to the "Hatch Act" prohibitions relating to political activities on the part of certain federal and state employees is clear: The taxpayer may opt to enter an area of federal employment subject to the restraints and limitations upon his First Amendment rights. Conversely, he may opt not to receive employment funds at the public trough in the areas covered by the restraints and thus exercise his First Amendment rights unfettered. The Congressional purposes evidenced by the 1934 and 1954 amendments are clearly constitutionally justified in keeping with the separation and neutrality principles particularly applicable in this case and, more succinctly, the principle that government shall not subsidize, directly or indirectly, those organizations whose substantial activities are directed toward the accomplishment of legislative goals or the election or defeat of particular candidates. From a review of the entire record we hold that the trial court's findings of fact and conclusions of law in this area are clearly erroneous.

III.

The Government also contends that its application of Section 501(c)(3) did not arbitrarily discriminate against Christian Echoes in violation of the

Fifth Amendment due process clause as found by the District Court. The Court found that the Government had arbitrarily selected Christian Echoes in violation of the due process clause. The Fifth Amendment provides that no person shall be deprived of life, liberty or property without due process of law. An organization is being discriminated against in violation of the due process clause only when there is no reasonable relationship to a proper governmental objective. In order to establish discrimination violating the due process clause, the taxpayer must show discrimination based on differences of religion, race, politics or an unacceptable classification. No discrimination is apparent in the record. The fact that the Commissioner has not proceeded against other organizations similar to Christian Echoes does not amount to a denial of due process.

The District Court also erred in its holding that the IRS's departure from its administrative procedures constituted a denial of due process. The taxpayer has not shown any prejudice by deviations from normal procedures.

* * *

Reversed.

NOTES AND QUESTIONS

1. *Policy Issues.* What is the rationale for the lobbying limitation? Consider the following justifications:

   a. Excessive lobbying and other political activity is inconsistent with the concept of "charity."

   b. The Treasury should be neutral in political matters and avoid subsidizing, through tax exemption and the charitable deduction, the lobbying activities of charities.

   c. Charities exist to serve the public at large rather than the self-interests of their founders, members, managers or donors. They should limit their political involvement to purely nonpartisan analysis rather than taking sides in particular controversies.

   d. It is "undemocratic" and "countermajoritarian" to permit charities to use public funds to influence the outcome of governmental decisions because it intensifies the disproportionate influence of their wealthy donors in the political process.

   e. Excessive involvement in political controversies is divisive and polarizing, leading to a decline in the independence and strength of the charitable sector.

Are your responses to these questions influenced by the rationale for charitable tax exemptions? Does it make any difference, for example, if one justifies tax exemptions by Bittker and Rahdert's income measurement theory as opposed to one of the subsidy theories? See Section B of this chapter, supra, at pp. 72–77.

Or should there be no restraints on lobbying? Why shouldn't § 501(c)(3) organizations be permitted, as part of their charitable and educational mission, to advocate policy changes through legislation as a principal means of representing their charitable beneficiaries? Doesn't the political activity of nonprofits provide a coherent voice for otherwise underrepresented groups, enhancing the quality of public debate and leveling the playing field? Or should the restrictions be revised to permit lobbying only by those § 501(c)(3) organizations that are "charitable" in the narrower sense of representing the "public interests" of underprivileged or underrepresented groups? If so, what standards would be used to identify the "public interest" charities that would be permitted to lobby without limitation?

2. *What's Lobbying?* Did the court in *Christian Echoes* go too far in equating the phrase "attempting to influence legislation" with any expression of opinion on a public issue, including those where no specific legislation was pending? Many § 501(c)(3) organizations express views on current issues, on which legislation may or may not be pending. When is this prohibited? In fact, the regulations expressly permit an organization to advocate social change or take positions on broad public issues. Treas. Reg. § 1.501(c)(3)–1(d)(2). The lobbying limitation does not extend to attempts to influence administrative agencies? Should it?

3. *When is Lobbying Substantial?* How did the Tenth Circuit define "substantial?" How does an organization plan its activities to avoid violating the general lobbying limitation?

4. *Influencing Judicial Nominations.* In Notice 88–76, 1988–1 C.B. 392, the Service ruled that attempts to influence the Senate confirmation of an individual nominated by the President to serve as a federal judge constituted "carrying on propaganda or otherwise attempting to influence legislation" within the meaning of § 501(c)(3). It reasoned that "legislation" included action with respect to acts, bills, resolutions and similar items, and the Senate's action of advice and consent on judicial nominations was with respect to a "resolution or similar item." At the same time, however, the Service concluded that attempts to influence judicial confirmation proceedings did not constitute participation or intervention in a political campaign because Federal judicial nominees are not candidates for elective office. For the possibility that expenditures to influence judicial confirmations may trigger a tax under § 527, see Section F6 of this chapter, infra, at p. 335.

5. *Excise Tax on Excess Lobbying Expenditures.* In 1987, Congress concluded that revocation of exemption for excessive lobbying was an ineffective deterrent in some cases. Consider, for example, a charitable organization that uses funds raised from tax-deductible contributions for a substantial lobbying effort and then ceases operations. If the organization has little or no taxable income, it may be indifferent to revocation once its political objectives are met, and its donors' earlier charitable deductions likely would be unaffected.

To combat this problem, § 4912(a) imposes an excise tax on the organization in an amount equal to five percent of all "lobbying expenditures" for the year in which an organization loses its exemption because of substantial lobbying. The definition of "lobbying expenditures" tracks the limitation in § 501(c)(3); it includes all amounts "paid or incurred * * * in carrying on propaganda, or otherwise attempting to influence legislation." I.R.C. § 4912(d)(1). The penalty applies to all § 501(c)(3) organizations other than private foundations, churches and organizations that elect to be governed by the § 501(h) expenditure test.

An additional five percent excise tax is imposed on managers of an organization who agree to make the lobbying expenditures knowing that they were likely to cause revocation of the organization's exemption. "Managers" generally include an organization's officers, directors, trustees or employees with authority or responsibility over lobbying expenditures. A manager is not liable for the penalty, however, if his or her action was not "willful" and was due to "reasonable cause"—for example, where the manager relied on a "reasoned" opinion of counsel that the expenditures were proper. I.R.C. § 4912(b).

6. *No Conversion to § 501(c)(4) Status.* A § 501(c)(3) organization that loses its exemption because of excessive lobbying is not permitted to shift to exempt status as a social welfare organization under § 501(c)(4) even though social welfare organizations generally are permitted to lobby without limitation. I.R.C. § 504. The purpose of this lifetime ban is to prevent an organization from raising tax-deductible funds, then engaging in substantial lobbying which leads to loss of its § 501(c)(3) exemption, and then shifting to § 501(c)(4) status where it may continue to lobby, using the accumulated funds raised during its earlier charitable days. A charity that loses its exemption for excessive political activity is permitted to reapply for § 501(c)(3) status if it ceases to engage in the impermissible activities.

7. *For Further Reading.* Miriam Galston, Lobbying and the Public Interest: Rethinking the Internal Revenue Code's Treatment of Legislative Activities, 71 Tex.L.Rev. 1269 (1993); Laura Brown Chisolm, Exempt Organizations Advocacy: Matching the Rules to the Rationales, 63 Ind. L.Rev. 201 (1987); Elias Clark, The Limitation on Political Activities: A Discordant Note in the Law of Charities, 46 Va.L.Rev. 439 (1960). The history of the ideological organizations project that resulted in the revocation of Christian Echoes' exempt status is chronicled in John A. Andrew III, The Other Side of the Sixties 157–164 (1997).

3.   CONSTITUTIONAL ISSUES

Church groups and other First Amendment advocates were distressed by the Tenth Circuit's opinion in *Christian Echoes*, particularly its constitutional holding. Joining in an odd alliance with Reverend Billy James Hargis, many mainstream Protestant and Jewish organizations urged the Supreme Court to grant certiorari. Their constitutional objections can be summarized as follows:

1. As applied generally, the lobbying limitations violate the First Amendment rights of free speech and freedom to petition. More particularly, they are unconstitutional insofar as the government conditions a benefit upon the agreement of a charity and its contributors to surrender a First Amendment right without justifying such action by a compelling national policy.

2. As applied to religious organizations, the limitations violate the Establishment and Free Exercise clauses of the First Amendment in that they: (a) reflect a lack of governmental neutrality toward religion by discriminating in favor of religions that refrain from becoming involved in issues of public concern; (b) necessitate excessive surveillance by the government in the affairs of religious groups; and (c) impinge upon the free exercise rights of politically active religions by making the sacrifice of these rights a condition for tax benefits.

3. The limitations are void for vagueness and overbreadth. The principal defect is the uncertain meaning of "substantial" but similar ambiguities stem from the phrase "carrying on propaganda," "attempting to influence legislation," and "participate in ... any political campaign." The net effect is that charitable and religious organizations are left without any guidance as to permissible conduct, chilling the exercise of their First Amendment rights.

4. The limitations violate the equal protection notions inherent in the due process clause of the Fifth Amendment insofar as they discriminate between those charities (including churches) that engage in substantial legislative activities and those that are politically inactive. The no substantial part test also discriminates on the basis of size and wealth by allowing larger organizations to devote considerable time and money to legislative involvement while jeopardizing the exemption of a smaller group that may engage in far fewer political activities in an absolute sense.

An unmoved Supreme Court denied certiorari in *Christian Echoes,* but constitutional challenges continued on more general grounds. In 1981, a panel for the D.C. Circuit held, over a strong dissent by Judge Abner Mikva, that the lobbying restrictions did not violate the First Amendment. Taxation with Representation v. Blumenthal, 81–1 USTC ¶ 9329 (D.C.Cir. 1981). On rehearing en banc, however, the Mikva position prevailed in a sweeping though short-lived 7–3 decision. Taxation With Representation v. Regan, 676 F.2d 715 (D.C.Cir.1982). The D.C. Circuit majority found that the lobbying limitations did not abridge the First Amendment rights of charitable organizations because the government was not obligated to subsidize speech. But the court held that the disparate treatment of § 501(c)(3) charities and § 501(c)(19) veterans organizations resulted in an unconstitutional classification that was not supported by any governmental interest. Veterans organizations may lobby without limitation and are eligible to receive tax-deductible contributions under § 170. Unsure of the proper remedy, the court remanded the case with instructions "to cure the constitutionally invalid operation of Section 501(c) after inviting veterans organizations to participate in framing the relief."

The Supreme Court noted probable jurisdiction in *Taxation With Representation*. Its unanimous decision upholding the constitutionality of the lobbying limitations silenced the debate.

Regan v. Taxation with Representation of Washington

Supreme Court of the United States, 1983.
461 U.S. 540, 103 S.Ct. 1997.

■ JUSTICE REHNQUIST delivered the opinion of the Court.

Appellee Taxation With Representation of Washington (TWR) is a nonprofit corporation organized to promote what it conceives to be the "public interest" in the area of federal taxation. It proposes to advocate its point of view before Congress, the Executive Branch, and the Judiciary. This case began when TWR applied for tax exempt status under § 501(c)(3) of the Internal Revenue Code, 26 U.S.C.A. § 501(c)(3). The Internal Revenue Service denied the application because it appeared that a substantial part of TWR's activities would consist of attempting to influence legislation, which is not permitted by § 501(c)(3).

TWR then brought this suit in District Court against the appellants, the Commissioner of Internal Revenue, the Secretary of the Treasury, and the United States, seeking a declaratory judgment that it qualifies for the exemption granted by § 501(c)(3). It claimed the prohibition against substantial lobbying is unconstitutional under the First Amendment and the equal protection component of the Fifth Amendment's Due Process Clause. The District Court granted summary judgment for appellants. On appeal, the en banc Court of Appeals for the District of Columbia Circuit reversed, holding that § 501(c)(3) does not violate the First Amendment but does violate the Fifth Amendment.

TWR was formed to take over the operations of two other non-profit corporations. One, Taxation With Representation Fund, was organized to promote TWR's goals by publishing a journal and engaging in litigation; it had tax exempt status under § 501(c)(3). The other, Taxation With Representation, attempted to promote the same goals by influencing legislation; it had tax exempt status under § 501(c)(4). Neither predecessor organization was required to pay federal income taxes. For purposes of our analysis, there are two principal differences between § 501(c)(3) organizations and § 501(c)(4) organizations. Taxpayers who contribute to § 501(c)(3) organizations are permitted by § 170(c)(2) to deduct the amount of their contributions on their federal income tax returns, while contributions to § 501(c)(4) organizations are not deductible. Section 501(c)(4) organizations, but not § 501(c)(3) organizations, are permitted to engage in substantial lobbying to advance their exempt purposes.

In this case, TWR is attacking the prohibition against substantial lobbying in § 501(c)(3) because it wants to use tax-deductible contributions to support substantial lobbying activities. To evaluate TWR's claims, it is necessary to understand the effect of the tax exemption system enacted by Congress.

Both tax exemptions and tax-deductibility are a form of subsidy that is administered through the tax system. A tax exemption has much the same effect as a cash grant to the organization of the amount of tax it would have to pay on its income. Deductible contributions are similar to cash grants of the amount of a portion of the individual's contributions.[5] The system Congress has enacted provides this kind of subsidy to non profit civic welfare organizations generally, and an additional subsidy to those charitable organizations that do not engage in substantial lobbying. In short, Congress chose not to subsidize lobbying as extensively as it chose to subsidize other activities that non profit organizations undertake to promote the public welfare.

It appears that TWR could still qualify for a tax exemption under § 501(c)(4). It also appears that TWR can obtain tax deductible contributions for its non-lobbying activity by returning to the dual structure it used in the past, with a § 501(c)(3) organization for non-lobbying activities and a § 501(c)(4) organization for lobbying. TWR would, of course, have to ensure that the § 501(c)(3) organization did not subsidize the § 501(c)(4) organization; otherwise, public funds might be spent on an activity Congress chose not to subsidize.[6]

TWR contends that Congress' decision not to subsidize its lobbying violates the First Amendment. It claims, relying on Speiser v. Randall, 357 U.S. 513, 78 S.Ct. 1332, 2 L.Ed.2d 1460 (1958), that the prohibition against substantial lobbying by 501(c)(3) organizations imposes an "unconstitutional condition" on the receipt of tax-deductible contributions. In Speiser, California established a rule requiring anyone who sought to take advantage of a property tax exemption to sign a declaration stating that he did not advocate the forcible overthrow of the Government of the United States. This Court stated that "[t]o deny an exemption to claimants who engage in speech is in effect to penalize them for the same speech." Id., at 518, 78 S.Ct., at 1338.

---

5. In stating that exemptions and deductions, on one hand, are like cash subsidies, on the other, we of course do not mean to assert that they are in all respects identical. See, e.g., Walz v. Tax Commission, 397 U.S. 664, 674–676, 90 S.Ct. 1409, 1414–1415, 25 L.Ed.2d 697 (1970); id., at 690–691, 90 S.Ct., at 1422 (Brennan, J., concurring); id., at 699, 90 S.Ct., at 1427 (opinion of Harlan, J.).

6. TWR and some amici are concerned that the IRS may impose stringent requirements that are unrelated to the congressional purpose of ensuring that no tax-deductible contributions are used to pay for substantial lobbying, and effectively make it impossible for a § 501(c)(3) organization to establish a § 501(c)(4) lobbying affiliate. No such requirement in the code or regulations has been called to our attention, nor have we been able to discover one. The IRS apparently requires only that the two groups be separately incorporated and keep records adequate to show that tax deductible contributions are not used to pay for lobbying. This is not unduly burdensome. We also note that TWR did not bring this suit because it was unable to operate with the dual structure and seeks a less stringent set of bookkeeping requirements. Rather, TWR seeks to force Congress to subsidize its lobbying activity.

TWR is certainly correct when it states that we have held that the government may not deny a benefit to a person because he exercises a constitutional right. But TWR is just as certainly incorrect when it claims that this case fits the Speiser–Perry model. The Code does not deny TWR the right to receive deductible contributions to support its non-lobbying activity, nor does it deny TWR any independent benefit on account of its intention to lobby. Congress has merely refused to pay for the lobbying out of public monies. This Court has never held that the Court must grant a benefit such as TWR claims here to a person who wishes to exercise a constitutional right.

This aspect of the case is controlled by Cammarano v. United States, 358 U.S. 498, 79 S.Ct. 524, 3 L.Ed.2d 462 (1959), in which we upheld a Treasury Regulation that denied business expense deductions for lobbying activities. We held that Congress is not required by the First Amendment to subsidize lobbying. In this case, like in Cammarano, Congress has not infringed any First Amendment rights or regulated any First Amendment activity. Congress has simply chosen not to pay for TWR's lobbying. We again reject the "notion that First Amendment rights are somehow not fully realized unless they are subsidized by the State." Id., at 515, 79 S.Ct., at 534 (Douglas, J., concurring).

TWR also contends that the equal protection component of the Fifth Amendment renders the prohibition against substantial lobbying invalid. TWR points out that § 170(c)(3) permits taxpayers to deduct contributions to veterans' organizations that qualify for tax exemption under § 501(c)(19). Qualifying veterans' organizations are permitted to lobby as much as they want in furtherance of their exempt purposes.[8] TWR argues that because Congress has chosen to subsidize the substantial lobbying activities of veterans' organizations, it must also subsidize the lobbying of § 501(c)(3) organizations.

Generally, statutory classifications are valid if they bear a rational relation to a legitimate governmental purpose. Statutes are subjected to a higher level of scrutiny if they interfere with the exercise of a fundamental right, such as freedom of speech, or employ a suspect classification, such as race. Legislatures have especially broad latitude in creating classifications and distinctions in tax statutes. More than forty years ago we addressed these comments to an equal protection challenge to tax legislation:

"The broad discretion as to classification possessed by a legislature in the field of taxation has long been recognized * * *. The passage of

---

8. The rules governing deductibility of contributions to veterans' organizations are not the same as the analogous rules for § 501(c)(3) organizations. For example, an individual may generally deduct up to 50% of his adjusted gross income in contributions to § 501(c)(3) organizations, but only 20% in contributions to veterans' organizations. Compare § 170(b)(1)(A) with § 170(b)(1)(B). Taxpayers are permitted to carry over excess contributions to § 501(c)(3) organizations, but not veterans' organizations, to the next year. § 170(d). There are other differences. If it were entitled to equal treatment with veterans' organizations, TWR would, of course, be entitled only to the benefits they receive, not to more.

time has only served to underscore the wisdom of that recognition of the large area of discretion which is needed by a legislature in formulating sound tax policies. Traditionally classification has been a device for fitting tax programs to local needs and usages in order to achieve an equitable distribution of the tax burden. It has, because of this, been pointed out that in taxation, even more than in other fields, legislatures possess the greatest freedom in classification. Since the members of a legislature necessarily enjoy a familiarity with local conditions which this Court cannot have, the presumption of constitutionality can be overcome only by the most explicit demonstration that a classification is a hostile and oppressive discrimination against particular persons and classes. The burden is on the one attacking the legislative arrangement to negative every conceivable basis which might support it."

We have already explained why we conclude that Congress has not violated TWR's First Amendment rights by declining to subsidize its First Amendment activities. The case would be different if Congress were to discriminate invidiously in its subsidies in such a way as to "aim at the suppression of dangerous ideas." But the veterans' organizations that qualify under § 501(c)(19) are entitled to receive tax-deductible contributions regardless of the content of any speech they may use, including lobbying. We find no indication that the statute was intended to suppress any ideas or any demonstration that it has had that effect. The sections of the Internal Revenue Code here at issue do not employ any suspect classification. The distinction between veterans' organizations and other charitable organizations is not at all like distinctions based on race or national origin.

The Court of Appeals nonetheless held that "strict scrutiny" is required because the statute "affect[s] First Amendment rights on a discriminatory basis." Its opinion suggests that strict scrutiny applies whenever Congress subsidizes some speech, but not all speech. This is not the law. Congress could, for example, grant funds to an organization dedicated to combatting teenage drug abuse, but condition the grant by providing that none of the money received from Congress should be used to lobby state legislatures. Under Cammarano, such a statute would be valid. Congress might also enact a statute providing public money for an organization dedicated to combatting teenage alcohol abuse, and impose no condition against using funds obtained from Congress for lobbying. The existence of the second statute would not make the first statute subject to strict scrutiny.

Congressional selection of particular entities or persons for entitlement to this sort of largesse "is obviously a matter of policy and discretion not open to judicial review unless in circumstances which here we are not able to find." * * * For the purposes of this case appropriations are comparable to tax exemptions and deductions, which are also "a matter of grace [that] Congress can, of course, disallow * * * as it chooses."

These are scarcely novel principles. We have held in several contexts that a legislature's decision not to subsidize the exercise of a fundamental right does not infringe the right, and thus is not subject to strict scrutiny. Buckley v. Valeo upheld a statute that provides federal funds for candidates for public office who enter primary campaigns, but does not provide funds for candidates who do not run in party primaries. We rejected First Amendment and equal protection challenges to this provision without applying strict scrutiny. Harris v. McRae and Maher v. Roe considered legislative decisions not to subsidize abortions, even though other medical procedures were subsidized. We declined to apply strict scrutiny and rejected equal protection challenges to the statutes.

The reasoning of these decisions is simple: "although government may not place obstacles in the path of a [person's] exercise of * * * freedom of [speech], it need not remove those not of its own creation." Although TWR does not have as much money as it wants, and thus cannot exercise its freedom of speech as much as it would like, the Constitution "does not confer an entitlement to such funds as may be necessary to realize all the advantages of that freedom." As we said in Maher, "[c]onstitutional concerns are greatest when the State attempts to impose its will by force of law * * *." Where governmental provision of subsidies is not "aimed at the suppression of dangerous ideas," its "power to encourage actions deemed to be in the public interest is necessarily far broader."

We have no doubt but that this statute is within Congress' broad power in this area. TWR contends that § 501(c)(3) organizations could better advance their charitable purposes if they were permitted to engage in substantial lobbying. This may well be true. But Congress—not TWR or this Court—has the authority to determine whether the advantage the public would receive from additional lobbying by charities is worth the money the public would pay to subsidize that lobbying, and other disadvantages that might accompany that lobbying. It appears that Congress was concerned that exempt organizations might use tax-deductible contributions to lobby to promote the private interests of their members. See 78 Cong.Rec. 5861 (1934)(remarks of Senator Reed); Id., at 5959 (remarks of Senator La Follette). It is not irrational for Congress to decide that tax exempt charities such as TWR should not further benefit at the expense of taxpayers at large by obtaining a further subsidy for lobbying.

It is also not irrational for Congress to decide that, even though it will not subsidize substantial lobbying by charities generally, it will subsidize lobbying by veterans' organizations. Veterans have "been obliged to drop their own affairs and take up the burdens of the nation," "subjecting themselves to the mental and physical hazards as well as the economic and family detriments which are peculiar to military service and which do not exist in normal civil life." Our country has a long standing policy of compensating veterans for their past contributions by providing them with numerous advantages. This policy has "always been deemed to be legitimate."

The issue in this case is not whether TWR must be permitted to lobby, but whether Congress is required to provide it with public money with which to lobby. For the reasons stated above, we hold that it is not. Accordingly, the judgment of the Court of Appeals is Reversed.

■ Justice Blackmun, with whom Justice Brennan and Justice Marshall join, concurring.

I join the Court's opinion. Because 26 U.S.C. § 501's discrimination between veterans' organizations and charitable organizations is not based on the content of their speech, I agree with the Court that § 501 does not deny charitable organizations equal protection of the law. The benefit provided to veterans' organizations is rationally based on the Nation's time-honored policy of "compensating veterans for their past contributions." As the Court says, a statute designed to discourage the expression of particular views would present a very different question.

I also agree that the First Amendment does not require the Government to subsidize protected activity, and that this principle controls disposition of TWR's First Amendment claim. I write separately to make clear that in my view the result under the First Amendment depends entirely upon the Court's necessary assumption—which I share—about the manner in which the Internal Revenue Service administers § 501.

If viewed in isolation, the lobbying restriction contained in § 501(c)(3) violates the principle, reaffirmed today, "that the Government may not deny a benefit to a person because he exercises a constitutional right." Section 501(c)(3) does not merely deny a subsidy for lobbying activities; it deprives an otherwise eligible organization of its tax-exempt status and its eligibility to receive tax-deductible contributions for all its activities, whenever one of those activities is "substantial lobbying." Because lobbying is protected by the First Amendment, § 501(c)(3) therefore denies a significant benefit to organizations choosing to exercise their constitutional rights.

The constitutional defect that would inhere in § 501(c)(3) alone is avoided by § 501(c)(4). As the Court notes, TWR may use its present § 501(c)(3) organization for its nonlobbying activities and may create a § 501(c)(4) affiliate to pursue its charitable goals through lobbying. The § 501(c)(4) affiliate would not be eligible to receive tax-deductible contributions.

Given this relationship between § 501(c)(3) and § 501(c)(4), the Court finds that Congress' purpose in imposing the lobbying restriction was merely to ensure that "no tax-deductible contributions are used to pay for substantial lobbying." Consistent with that purpose, "[t]he IRS apparently requires only that the two groups be separately incorporated and keep records adequate to show that tax deductible contributions are not used to pay for lobbying." As long as the IRS goes no further than this, we perhaps can safely say that "[t]he Code does not deny TWR the right to receive deductible contributions to support its nonlobbying activity, nor does it deny TWR any independent benefit on account of its intention to lobby." A

§ 501(c)(3) organization's right to speak is not infringed, because it is free to make known its views on legislation through its § 501(c)(4) affiliate without losing tax benefits for its nonlobbying activities.

Any significant restriction on this channel of communication, however, would negate the saving effect of § 501(c)(4). It must be remembered that § 501(c)(3) organizations retain their constitutional right to speak and to petition the Government. Should the IRS attempt to limit the control these organizations exercise over the lobbying of their 501(c)(4) affiliates, the First Amendment problems would be insurmountable. It hardly answers one person's objection to a restriction on his speech that another person, outside his control, may speak for him. Similarly, an attempt to prevent § 501(c)(4) organizations from lobbying explicitly on behalf of their § 501(c)(3) affiliates would perpetuate § 501(c)(3) organizations' inability to make known their views on legislation without incurring the unconstitutional penalty. Such restrictions would extend far beyond Congress' mere refusal to subsidize lobbying. In my view, any such restriction would render the statutory scheme unconstitutional.

I must assume that the IRS will continue to administer §§ 501(c)(3) and 501(c)(4) in keeping with Congress' limited purpose and with the IRS' duty to respect and uphold the Constitution. I therefore agree with the Court that the First Amendment questions in this case are controlled by *Cammarano v. United States*, 358 U.S. 498, 513, 79 S.Ct. 524, 533, 3 L.Ed.2d 462 (1959), rather than by *Speiser v. Randall*, 357 U.S. 513, 518–519, 78 S.Ct. 1332, 1338, 2 L.Ed.2d 1460 (1958), and *Perry v. Sindermann*, 408 U.S. 593, 597, 92 S.Ct. 2694, 2697, 33 L.Ed.2d 570 (1972).

NOTES AND QUESTIONS

1. *Tax Exemption as Subsidy—Revisited.* In *Taxation With Representation*, the Court unequivocally stated that the tax exemption and charitable deduction are a "form of subsidy that is administered through the tax system" having "much the same effect as a cash grant to the organization of the amount of tax it would have to pay on its income." If tax exemptions are equivalent to cash grants from the Treasury, how could Justice Rehnquist have justified, as a constitutional matter, tax exemptions to racially discriminatory schools in the *Bob Jones University* case, supra p. 94? If the Court believes that tax exemptions are subsidies, how did religious tax exemptions pass constitutional muster in Walz v. Tax Commission?

2. *Unconstitutional Conditions.* If the right to participate in the legislative process is protected by the First Amendment, can Congress constitutionally condition that right, or any governmental benefit, on a waiver of a constitutional right? How can even a discretionary government subsidy be conditioned on a waiver of First Amendment rights? Is this the effect of the lobbying limitations in § 501(c)(3)? Or may the government constitutionally control the use of subsidized funds? In *Taxation With Representation* and the later case of *Rust v. Sullivan*, 500 U.S. 173, 111 S.Ct. 1759 (1991), where the Court rejected a First Amendment challenge

to regulations banning the use of federal funds in counseling and referral programs where abortion was a method of family planning, the Supreme Court has strongly suggested that these classic "unconstitutional conditions" arguments do not apply to conditions placed on the use of public funds to subsidize an activity, at least if the conditions do not result in discrimination based on the speaker's viewpoint. This position is premised on the notion that tax exemptions and charitable contributions result in a 100 percent subsidy to the benefited organizations. Is this necessarily so? Charitable contributions only result in a subsidy, if at all, to the extent of the donor's tax savings—no more than roughly 40 percent of the gift under our current rate structure. Why shouldn't the Code at least permit § 501(c)(3) organizations to lobby with the portion of funds raised (e.g., 60 percent) from contributions that do not result in tax savings to their donors?

3. *Planning.* Although the constitutional debate over the lobbying limitations ended with a resounding thud in *Taxation With Representation*, the case has not adversely affected politically active nonprofits. The Supreme
Court pointed the way to a common planning strategy—the use of a § 501(c)(4) affiliate to carry out the lobbying mission of a § 501(c)(3) charity. Some organizations also have created political action committees within their § 501(c)(4) lobbying affiliates. See Section F6 of this chapter, infra, at pp. 335–338. Moreover, as we are about to discover, most § 501(c)(3) organizations may elect to be governed by objective statutory tests which permit specified expenditures for direct and grassroots lobbying.

4. *For Further Reading.* Thomas Troyer, Charities, Law–Making, and the Constitution: The Validity of the Restrictions on Influencing Legislation, 31 N.Y.U. Inst. on Fed. Tax'n 1415 (1973); Note, The Tax Code's Differential Treatment of Lobbying Under Section 501(c)(3): A Proposed First Amendment Analysis, 66 Va.L.Rev. 1513 (1980).

4. THE § 501(h) EXPENDITURE TEST ELECTION

Internal Revenue Code: §§ 501(h); 504; 4911; 6033(b)(8).

Treasury Regulations: §§ 1.501(h)–1, –2, –3; 56.4911–1, –2, –3, –4, –5, –6, –7(a) & (b).

a. INTRODUCTION

The vagueness of the "no substantial part" test prompted Congress to provide more definitive guidance for charities willing to test their lobbying under what purports to be a more precise mathematical test. Section 501(h) permits most § 501(c)(3) organizations to opt out of the "no substantial part" test and instead be governed by mechanical rules that set ceilings for different types of lobbying expenditures. Lesser violations trigger a 25 percent excise tax on excess lobbying expenditures; more flagrant excesses may trigger revocation of exemption. The election is available to most "public charities"—i.e., all organizations (except churches) not classified as "private foundations." I.R.C. §§ 501(h)(3) & (4). The exclusion of churches was the result of constitutional objections by major religious organizations to any type of limitation on their activities. Private foundations are excluded because any lobbying activity subjects them to severe excise tax penalties under § 4945. See Chapter 3C6, infra, at pp. 480–482.

The § 501(h) election is made by filing a simple one-page form (Form 5768) with the Service. Treas. Reg. § 1.501(h)–2(a). The election is effective for all taxable years which end after the date the form is filed and begin prior to the date that the election is revoked. I.R.C. § 501(h)(6). Thus, an organization may make an effective election in the middle of the year, but a mid-year revocation will not be effective until the following year. Id.

The Treasury has issued an extensive and generally helpful set of regulations interpreting the expenditure test election rules. These regulations only apply to electing charities and not to organizations subject to the no substantial part test (I.R.C. § 501(h)(7)), but they likely will serve as guidelines for the vast majority of nonelecting charities that remain subject to the "no substantial part" test.

b.   SPENDING LIMITS AND PENALTIES

Understanding the § 501(h) expenditure test election requires a working knowledge of numerous definitions, all of which are intended to establish a permissible amount of overall lobbying expenditures (direct and grassroots combined) and a separate, more restrictive, level of grassroots expenditures. To avoid the excise tax imposed by § 4911, an organization must keep its overall and grassroots lobbying expenditures below specified dollar levels. Significantly, volunteer time and other subjective factors that clouded interpretation of the no substantial part limitation are not included in this test, which looks solely to monetary expenditures. Although the rules are detailed and daunting, they are extremely permissive, and deciphering them is well worth the effort for a politically active nonprofit organization.

"Exempt purpose expenditures" are the overall measuring rod against which an organization's lobbying expenses are tested. Included are all amounts spent by the organization during the taxable year to accomplish its exempt purposes, excluding capital expenditures or the expenses of a separate fundraising unit, or investment management expenses. I.R.C. 4911(e)(1), (4); Treas. Reg. § 56.4911–4. Simply put, exempt purpose expenditures represent the organization's actual operating budget, including any lobbying expenses.

The *"lobbying nontaxable amount"* ("LNTA") is the overall amount that an organization may spend on direct and grassroots lobbying without being penalized. The LNTA is a specific percentage of the organization's exempt purpose expenditures measured by the following sliding scale:

20%   of the first $500,000 of exempt purpose expenditures

15%   of the next $500,000

10%   of the next $500,000

5%   of the excess over $1,500,000

In no event, however, may the LNTA exceed $1,000,000, a cap reached when an organization's annual budget is $17 million. I.R.C. § 4911(c)(2).

To illustrate, assume an organization has annual expenses (excluding any separate fund-raising unit) of $250,000. Its LNTA is $50,000, which is 20 percent of its budget. If the budget were $750,000, the LNTA would be $137,500—20 percent of $500,000 ($100,000) plus 15 percent of the next $250,000 ($37,500).

The *"grassroots nontaxable amount"* ("GNTA") is 25 percent of the LNTA and thus represents a separate and stricter cap on expenditures for grassroots lobbying. I.R.C. § 4911(c)(4). For example, if an organization has an LNTA of $50,000, its GNTA would be $12,500, and grassroots lobbying expenditures in excess of that cap would be subject to the 25 percent excise tax. The LNTA and GNTA are applied separately to determine an organization's exposure to the excise tax. In the example above, the organization could spend less than $50,000 on general lobbying and not exceed the LNTA, but it nonetheless would be subject to the excise tax if its grassroots expenditures exceeded $12,500.

Armed with the above definitions, the excise tax now can be explained. If overall or grassroots lobbying expenditures exceed either the LNTA or the GNTA, the organization is subject to a 25 percent excise tax on "excess lobbying expenditures"—i.e., whichever excess is greater relative to the applicable limitation. I.R.C. § 4911(a), (b).

Consider one final example. Assume an organization has an LNTA of $50,000 and a GNTA of $12,500. During the current year, its overall lobbying expenditures are $60,000, of which $35,000 are grassroots expenditures. Excess lobbying expenditures are the greater of:

(1) Lobbying Expenditures minus LNTA

($60,000 − $50,000 = $10,000); or

(2) Grassroots Expenditures minus GNTA

($35,000 − $12,500 = $22,500).

The greater of these two numbers, $22,500, is subject to the excise tax, which would be $5,625 (25 percent of $22,500). If none of the lobbying expenditures in the example had been in the grassroots category, the greater excess would have been $10,000, resulting in an excise tax of $2,500.

Expenditures exceeding the respective nontaxable amounts only trigger the excise tax, not loss of exemption. But organizations which "normally" (i.e., over a four year measuring period) make lobbying or grassroots expenditures in excess of 150 percent of the respective nontaxable amounts (higher limits, referred to as "lobbying ceiling amounts") will lose their § 501(c)(3) exemptions. I.R.C. § 501(h)(2); Treas. Reg. § 1.501(h)–3(b). If an organization loses its exemption because of lobbying, it may not thereafter qualify for exempt status as a § 501(c)(4) social welfare organization. I.R.C. § 504(a).

Without inflicting any more detail, it should be obvious that an organization making the § 501(h) election must lobby excessively and repeatedly before it risks losing its exemption.

To prevent circumvention of the dollar limitations, § 4911(f) applies consolidation principles—aggregating expenditures of an "affiliated group" of § 501(c)(3) organizations—to determine the applicable caps on lobbying expenditures. In general, organizations are "affiliated" if they are subject to common control. For example, affiliation will exist if one organization is bound by decisions of the other on legislative issues, or the governing board of one organization includes enough representatives of the other to cause or prevent action on legislative issues. I.R.C. § 4911(f)(2). Rules also apply to aggregate lobbying expenditures of different organizations even where there is limited affiliation—e.g., where one organization controls another solely with respect to national legislation. The regulations fill in the details. See Treas. Reg. § 56.4911–7.

c. LOBBYING EXPENDITURES

Having described the spending limits and penalties for exceeding them, we turn next to the what activities are defined as lobbying and some valuable exceptions.

Lobbying Expenditures—In General. "Lobbying expenditures" are expenditures for the purpose of "influencing legislation," which is defined to include both direct lobbying (i.e., communications with legislators, their employees and other government officials who may participate in the formulation of legislation) and grassroots lobbying (attempting to influence public opinion). I.R.C. § 4911(c)(1), (e)(1). "Legislation" includes action by Congress, any state legislature, local council, or similar legislative body, and action by the public in referenda, ballot initiatives, constitutional amendments, and the like. I.R.C. § 4911(e)(2). "Action" is limited to the introduction, amendment, enactment, defeat, or repeal of legislation. I.R.C. § 4911(e)(3). Significantly, attempts to influence executive, judicial, or administrative bodies do not constitute lobbying unless the principal purpose of the communication is to influence legislation. I.R.C. § 4911(d)(2)(E); Treas. Reg. § 56.4911–2(d)(2)–(4).

Direct Lobbying. A direct lobbying communication is any attempt to influence any legislation through communication with any member or employee of a legislative body, or any other government official or employee who may participate in the formulation of the legislation but only if the principal purpose of the communication is to influence legislation. I.R.C. § 4911(d)(1)(B); Treas. Reg. § 56.4911–2(b)(1)(i). These communications are treated as direct lobbying only if they refer to specific legislation and reflect a view on the legislation. Treas. Reg. § 56.4911–2(b)(1)(ii).

Grassroots Lobbying. Grassroots lobbying is any attempt to influence legislation through communications that attempt to affect the opinion of the general public or any segment thereof. Treas. Reg. § 56.4911–2(b)(2)(i). The regulations provide that a communication will be treated as grassroots lobbying only if it: (1) refers to specific legislation (i.e., legislation that already has been introduced and specific proposed legislation that the organization either supports or opposes); (2) reflects a view on the legislation; and (3) encourages the recipient to take action with respect to the legislation. Treas. Reg. § 56.4911–2(b)(2)(ii). This definition is much more generous than a prior version of the regulations, which would have classified any communication that merely "pertained" to legislation as grassroots lobbying.

Under the three-pronged test, a communication is not grassroots lobbying unless it includes "a call to action" with respect to specific legislation. A communication encourages its recipients to take action only if it: (1) states that the recipient should contact a legislator or employee of a legislative body or other governmental representative involved in the legislative process; (2) states the address, telephone number or similar information about a legislator or legislative staff person; (3) provides a petition, tear-off postcard or similar material for the recipient to communicate his or her views to legislators or their staffs; or (4) specifically identifies one or more legislators who will vote on the legislation as opposing the legislation, being undecided with respect to it, being the recipient's representative in the legislature or being a member of the legislative committee that will consider the legislation. Treas. Reg. § 56.4911–2(b)(2)(iii). The first three types of communications not only "encourage" but "directly encourage" the recipient to take action; communications in the fourth category only "encourage" action. The significance of this distinction is that communications in the fourth category may be within the exceptions for nonpartisan analysis, study or research or member communications (both discussed below) and thus may not be grassroots lobbying communications. Treas. Reg. § 56.4911–2(b)(2)(iv).

To illustrate the generosity of the regulations, assume an organization opposing handgun control pays for an advertisement stating:

> The State Assembly is considering a bill to make gun ownership illegal. This outrageous legislation would violate your constitutional rights and the rights of other law-abiding citizens. If this legislation is passed, you and your family will be criminals if you want to exercise your right to protect yourselves.

Under the regulations, this normally is not grassroots lobbying because it does not include any call to action. Treas. Reg. § 56.4911–2(b)(5)(iv) Example (4).

The regulations include one exception to the "call to action" requirement. Under the "mass media communication" rule, an organization is presumed to engage in grassroots lobbying if, within two weeks before a vote by a legislative body or committee on a "highly publicized piece of legislation", the organization makes a communication in the "mass media" (i.e., television, radio, general circulation newspapers and magazines) that "reflects a view" on the general subject of the legislation and either refers to the legislation or encourages members of the public to communicate with their legislators on the general subject of the legislation. This presumption is rebuttable if the organization can demonstrate that the communication is a type regularly made by the organization in the mass media without regard to the timing of the legislation. Treas. Reg. § 56.4911–2(b)(5)(ii).

Another helpful rule makes it clear that communications to the public with respect to referenda, initiatives, and other ballot measures are treated as direct rather than grassroots lobbying on the theory that the public itself is the legislative body on such matters. Treas. Reg. § 56.4911–2(b)(1)(iii).

The regulations elaborate on these rules with numerous examples. See Treas. Reg. § 56.4911–2(b)(4), –2(b)(5)(iv).

d.   EXCEPTED COMMUNICATIONS

Another way to pose the critical definitional question is: "what isn't lobbying?" In an attempt to provide charities with more guidance and protection, § 4911(d) and the regulations provide that the following activities are not treated as "influencing legislation" for purposes of the elective regime:

(1) making available the results of nonpartisan analysis, study or research;

(2) discussion of broad social, economic, or similar problems;

(3) providing technical advice to a governmental body or committee in response to a written request;

(4) "self-defense" lobbying, such as direct communications to the legislature with respect to issues that may affect the organization's existence, tax exemption or eligibility to receive deductible contributions;

(5) communications between the organization and its bona fide "members" with respect to legislation of direct mutual interest, unless the purpose of the communication is to directly encourage the members themselves to lobby or to urge nonmembers to do so; and

(6) communications with members of the executive branch of government, unless the principal purpose is to influence specific legislation.

Nonpartisan Analysis. Nonpartisan analysis, study or research is generally defined as "an independent and objective exposition of a particular subject matter." Treas. Reg. § 56.4911–2(c)(1)(ii). Significantly, neutrality is not required. An organization may advocate a position on legislation as long as it presents sufficient facts to allow the audience to reach its own conclusion, and the results of the research may be distributed by "any suitable means" provided the communication is not targeted to those interested in only one side of the issue. Treas. Reg. § 56.4911–2(c)(1)(ii), (iv). But communications that otherwise might qualify for the exception are disqualified if they include a "call to action" by expressly encouraging the general public to contact their legislators on the specific legislative matters.

Treas. Reg. § 56.4911–2(c)(1)(vi). Moreover, even though certain analysis may be within the nonpartisan exception when it is initially prepared, subsequent use in a grassroots lobbying effort may cause the entire cost of preparing the "advocacy communication" to be treated as a grassroots expenditure. Treas. Reg. § 56.4911–2(b)(2)(v). Under a valuable safe harbor, the subsequent use rule does not apply if the organization either: (1) demonstrates a primary nonlobbying purpose (e.g., by making a substantial distribution of a study to the academic community at the same time or before it is used for lobbying), or (2) paid all the expenses for the paper at least six months before it was used for lobbying. Treas. Reg. § 53.4911–2(b)(2)(v)(D), (E). For more examples illustrating the scope of the nonpartisan analysis exception and the "subsequent use" trap, see Treas. Reg. § 56.4911–2(c)(1)(vii), –2(b)(2)(v)(H).

Discussions of Broad Social Problems. Examinations and discussions of broad social, economic and similar problems are neither direct nor grassroots lobbying communications even if the problems are of the type with which government might ultimately deal. As long as the "discussions" do not relate to the merits of specific legislation or directly encourage recipients to take action, they are not lobbying. Treas. Reg. § 56.4911–2(c)(2).

Technical Advice. A communication is not direct lobbying if it is in response to a written request by a governmental body or committee to provide technical advice or assistance. Treas. Reg. § 56.4911–2(c)(3).

Self-Defense. The self-defense exception protects an organization's appearances before or communications with any legislative body with respect to a possible action that might affect the existence of the organization, its powers and duties, its tax-exempt status, or its eligibility to receive tax-deductible contributions. Treas. Reg. § 56.4911–2(c)(4). For example, an appearance by representatives of a § 501(c)(3) organization before the Senate Finance Committee to oppose a proposed bill to scale back the charitable deduction would not constitute direct lobbying. Id.

Member Communications. A particularly valuable exception permits an organization to communicate with its bona fide "members" on legislative issues of mutual interest. I.R.C. § 4911(d)(2)(D). A "member" must have more than a nominal connection with the organization; an individual whose name simply appears on a mailing list normally does not qualify. Payment of dues or donations of volunteer time (in more than a nominal amount) will help to establish an individual's "member" status. See Treas. Reg. § 56.4911–5(f).

The practical impact of this exception is that certain member communications are treated more leniently than if they had been with nonmembers. For example, a communication directed only to members that refers to and reflects a view on specific legislation of direct interest to the organization and its members is not lobbying if it does not "directly encourage" the members to engage in direct or grassroots lobbying. Treas. Reg. § 56.4911–5(b). The implication is that communications may "encourage" such lobbying (see Treas. Reg. § 56.4911–2(b)(2)(iv)) by identifying key legislators. If the same communication had been directed to nonmembers, it would have been grassroots lobbying. Similarly, assume that an organization encourages its members to contact their legislators to support a bill of direct interest to the organization. Under the more lenient member communication rules, the expenses of this communication would be treated as direct lobbying. I.R.C. § 4911(d)(3)(A); Treas. Reg. § 56.4911–5(c). If the communication had been directed to nonmembers, it would have been grassroots lobbying. But when an organization urges members to engage in grassroots lobbying on specific legislation, the costs of the communication are treated as grassroots expenditures. I.R.C. § 4911(d)(3)(B); Treas. Reg. § 56.4911–5(d).

The intellectually curious then would ask—what if a communication refers to and reflects a view on specific legislation and directly encourages the recipient to take action, and it is directed to both members and nonmembers? The regulations do not disappoint, providing that if more than half the recipients are members, the costs of the communication may be allocated between direct and grassroots lobbying under rules that vary depending on what type of lobbying is being directly encouraged! Treas. Reg. § 56.4911–5(e)(1). Significantly, if the communication urges recipients to engage in direct lobbying and 15 percent or less of the distribution is to nonmember subscribers, then none of the cost of preparation or distribution is treated as a grassroots expenditure. Treas. Reg. § 56.4911–5(e)(2)(ii). For the gruesome details, see Treas. Reg. § 56.4911–5(e)(2), (3).

Allocation of Mixed–Purpose Expenditures. It should be apparent by now that charities making the § 501(h) election must allocate certain mixed-purpose expenses among nonlobbying pursuits and the two types of lobbying activities. Types of expenses requiring allocation include salaries of employees who devote part of their time to lobbying activities; costs of preparing and mailing pamphlets; costs of newspaper advertising; newsletter costs; and general overhead. Treas. Reg. § 56.4911–3(a)(1). The regulations are typically detailed on this point. If a communication is sent primarily (more than half) to bona fide members, an organization may make any reasonable allocation between lobbying and nonlobbying expenses, such as an allocation based on column inches in the publication. If the audience is primarily nonmembers, however, more stringent allocation rules apply—e.g., costs attributable to the communication that are on the same specific subject as the lobbying message must be allocated to lobbying. Treas. Reg. § 56.4911–3(a)(2).

To illustrate, consider an example in the regulations involving a nonmembership organization ("T") that prepares a three-page document mailed to 3,000 persons on T's mailing list. The first two pages of the mailing (titled "The Need for Child Care") advocates additional child care programs and includes statistics on the number of children living in single-parent or two-worker parent homes. The third page (titled "H.R. 1") indicates T's support for a bill pending in the U.S. House, notes that the bill will provide for $10 million in additional subsidies for child care providers and ends with T's request that recipients contact their representatives to support the legislation. The entire communication is treated as grassroots lobbying (note the "call to action") on one specific subject and the expenditures of preparing and distributing all three pages are treated as "grassroots lobbying expenditures." Treas. Reg. 56.4911–3(b) Example (8). If the document has a fourth page that does not refer to the same specific subject as the lobbying message, the costs of that page would not be treated as a lobbying expenditure. Id. Example (9).

If T in the above example were a "membership" organization, and 75 percent of the recipients of the three-page document were bona fide members, T could treat half the cost of preparing and distributing the document as a nonlobbying expenditure because its purpose is to educate T's members about the need for child care. The other half would be a lobbying expenditure, of which 75 percent (attributable to the request to members to contact legislators) is "direct" lobbying and 25 percent (attributable to the request to nonmembers to contact legislators) is grassroots lobbying. Id. Example (10); Treas. Reg. § 56.4911–3(b) Example (10); see also Treas. Reg. § 56.4911–5(e)(2)(i)–(iii). If in this same example, T allocated only one percent of the costs as a lobbying expenditure because only two out of 200 printed lines in the document mentioned legislation, that allocation of expenses would be considered unreasonable. Treas. Reg. § 56.4911–3(b) Example (11); see also Treas. Reg. § 56.4911–3(a)(2)(ii).

e. REPORTING REQUIREMENTS

Organizations making the § 501(h) election must report their lobbying and grassroots expenditures on a special schedule included on the Form 990 information return filed by § 501(c)(3) organizations. Excise tax liability, if any, must be reported on IRS Form 4720.

These reporting requirements require an electing organization to adopt a relatively sophisticated accounting system, allocating expenditures and general overhead to the direct and grassroots lobbying categories. This is no small chore, particularly because many expenditures may be difficult to categorize. Organizations that lobby should require employees to keep detailed time records so their salaries and benefits can be properly allocated. Expenses for facilities, publications, and other activities should be apportioned on some reasonable basis. Failure to keep careful records will cause difficulties in the event of an audit.

f. TO ELECT OR NOT TO ELECT

After absorbing all this detail about the § 501(h) election, it may appear that the no substantial part test is not so bad after all. Indeed, some charities prefer the vagueness of the general rules to the specificity and recordkeeping requirements of the § 501(h) election. Organizations with large budgets also may be inhibited by the regressive sliding scale and the overall $1 million ceiling on lobbying expenditures. In fact, it has been reported that only a handful of eligible § 501(c)(3) organizations have made the expenditure test election.

Is the election worth the trouble? It may be for an organization planning a highly visible lobbying program. The officers and directors will sleep more soundly knowing that the lobbying activities have not exceeded the statutory ceilings. An organization that relies primarily on volunteers also would be well advised to consider the election because time and energy are not factored into the expenditure limits. The regulations, with their permissive definitions and examples, are an additional reason why a politically active charity might prefer the "safe harbor" of the expenditure test election.

An organization contemplating a one-shot lobbying effort on an issue of great importance might choose to exceed the expenditure limits for a year or two at the price of a modest excise tax. As long as the excesses are temporary, loss of exemption should not result. A similar lobbying program evaluated under the general limitation might cause the organization to lose its exemption and be subject to the 5 percent excise tax under 4912 on all of its lobbying expenditures in the year its exemption is revoked.

Some charities have feared that they will draw too much attention and risk an IRS audit by making the § 501(h) election. IRS officials have repeatedly denied that electing charities are an audit target. And if an organization were audited for excessive lobbying, it almost always would prefer the protection offered by the § 4911 regulations as opposed to the vagaries of the no substantial part test.

5. POLITICAL CAMPAIGN LIMITATIONS

Internal Revenue Code: §§ 501(c)(3); 4955.

Treasury Regulations: §§ 1.501(c)(3)–1(c)(1)(iii); 53.4955–1.

Unlike the lobbying limitations, the ban on participation or intervention in political campaign activities purports to be absolute, although the Service has been known to ignore de minimis violations. In addition, § 4955 authorizes the Service to impose excise tax penalties on § 501(c)(3) charities and their managers if the organization incurs certain proscribed political expenditures discussed in more detail below.

As illustrated by the materials below, the principal interpretive questions are: (1) what constitutes participation or intervention in a political campaign, and how are these prohibited activities distinguished from permissible voter education?; (2) who is a candidate for public office; (3) under what circumstances are political campaign activities of leaders or members attributed to an organization; and (4) does the IRS discriminate in its enforcement of the political campaign limitations?

Revenue Ruling 78–248

1978–1 Cum. Bull. 154.

Advice has been requested whether certain organizations, which otherwise qualify for exemption from Federal income tax under section 501(c)(3) of the Internal Revenue Code of 1954, will be considered "action" organizations and not exempt under section 501(c)(3) if they undertake "voter education" activities in the situations described below.

Section 501(c)(3) of the Code provides for the exemption from Federal income tax of organizations that are organized and operated exclusively for charitable purposes and "that do not participate in, or intervene in (including the publishing or distributing of statements), any political campaign on behalf of any candidate for public office."

Section 1.501(c)(3)–1(c)(3)(i) of the Income Tax Regulations states that an organization is not operated exclusively for one or more exempt purposes if it is an "action" organization. Section 1.501(c)(3)–1(c)(3)(iii) defines an "action" organization as an organization which

> participates or intervenes, directly or indirectly, in any political campaign on behalf of or in opposition to any candidate for public office. * * * Activities which constitute participation or intervention in a political campaign on behalf of or in opposition to a candidate include, but are not limited to, the publication or distribution of written statements or the making of oral statements on behalf of or in opposition to such a candidate.

Whether an organization is participating or intervening, directly or indirectly, in any political campaign on behalf of or in opposition to any candidate for public office depends upon all of the facts and circumstances of each case. Certain "voter education" activities conducted in a non-partisan manner may not constitute prohibited political activity under section 501(c)(3) of the Code. Other so-called "voter education" activities, however, may be proscribed by the statute. The following situations are illustrative:

SITUATION 1

Organization A has been recognized as exempt under section 501(c)(3) of the Code by the Internal Revenue Service. As one of its activities, the organization annually prepares and makes generally available to the public a compilation of voting records of all Members of Congress on major legislative issues involving a wide range of subjects. The publication contains no editorial opinion, and its contents and structure do not imply approval or disapproval of any Members or their voting records.

The "voter education" activity of Organization A is not prohibited political activity within the meaning of section 501(c)(3) of the Code.

SITUATION 2

Organization B has been recognized as exempt under section 501(c)(3) of the Code by the Internal Revenue Service. As one of its activities in election years, it sends a questionnaire to all candidates for governor in State M. The questionnaire solicits a brief statement of each candidate's position on a wide variety of issues. All responses are published in a voters guide that it makes generally available to the public. The issues covered are selected by the organization solely on the basis of their importance and interest to the electorate as a whole. Neither the questionnaire nor the voters guide, in content or structure, evidences a bias or preference with respect to the views of any candidate or group of candidates.

The "voter education" activity of Organization B is not prohibited political activity within the meaning of section 501(c)(3) of the Code.

SITUATION 3

Organization C has been recognized as exempt under section 501(c)(3) of the Code by the Internal Revenue Service. Organization C undertakes a "voter education" activity patterned after that of Organization B in Situation 2. It sends a questionnaire to candidates for major public offices and uses the responses to prepare a voters guide which is distributed during an election campaign. Some questions evidence a bias on certain issues. By using a questionnaire structured in this way, Organization C is participating in a political campaign in contravention of the provisions of section 501(c)(3) and is disqualified as exempt under that section.

SITUATION 4

Organization D has been recognized as exempt under section 501(c)(3) of the Code. It is primarily concerned with land conservation matters.

The organization publishes a voters guide for its members and others concerned with land conservation issues. The guide is intended as a compilation of incumbents' voting records in selected land conservation issues of importance to the organization and is factual in nature. It contains no express statements in support of or in opposition to any candidate. The guide is widely distributed among the electorate during an election campaign.

While the guide may provide the voting public with useful information, its emphasis on one area of concern indicates that its purpose is not non-partisan voter education.

By concentrating on a narrow range of issues in the voters guide and widely distributing it among the electorate during an election campaign, Organization D is participating in a political campaign in contravention of the provisions of section 501(c)(3) and is disqualified as exempt under that section.

* * *

Revenue Ruling 80-282

1980-2 Cum. Bull. 178

ISSUE

Would the publication of a newsletter, by an organization otherwise described in section 501(c)(3) of the Internal Revenue Code, containing the voting records of congressional incumbents on selected issues, in the manner described below, constitute participation or intervention in any political campaign within the meaning of section 501(c)(3)?

FACTS

The organization is exempt from federal income tax under section 501(c)(3) of the Code. The organization engages in a number of different educational and charitable activities. As one of its activities, the organization maintains an office that monitors and reports on legislative, judicial, administrative, and other governmental activities and developments considered to be of important social interest. As part of the office's activities, it distributes a monthly newsletter to interested members and others, who together number only a few thousand nationwide.

The monthly newsletter contains expressions of the organization's views on a broad range of legislative, judicial, and administrative issues it considers significant. In discussing a particular issue, the reader is sometimes encouraged to contact various governmental officials to express his or her views on the issue.

As soon as practical after the close of each congressional session, the organization intends to publish in an issue of its newsletter a summary of the voting records of all incumbent Members of Congress on selected legislative issues important to it, together with an expression of the organization's position on those issues. Each member's votes will be reported in a way which illustrates whether he or she voted in accordance with the organization's position on the issue. The newsletter is politically nonpartisan, and will not contain any reference to or mention of any political campaigns, elections, candidates, or any statements expressly or impliedly endorsing or rejecting any incumbent as a candidate for public office. No mention will be made of an individual's overall qualification for public office, nor will there be any comparison of candidates that might be competing with the incumbents in any political campaign. The voting records of all incumbents will be presented and candidates for re-election will not be identified. The newsletter will point out the limitations of judging the qualifications of an incumbent on the basis of a few selected votes and will note the need to consider such unrecorded matters as performance on subcommittees and constituent service.

Publication usually will occur after congressional adjournment and will not be geared to the timing of any federal election. The newsletter will be distributed to the usual subscribers, and will not be targeted toward particular areas in which elections are occurring.

LAW

Section 501(c)(3) of the Code provides for the exemption from federal income tax of organizations organized and operated exclusively for charitable purposes, no substantial part of the activities of which is carrying on propaganda, or otherwise attempting to influence legislation, and which do not participate in, or intervene in (including the publishing or distributing of statements), any political campaign on behalf of any candidate for public office.

Section 1.501(c)(3)–1(c)(3)(i) of the Income Tax Regulations states that an organization is not operated exclusively for one or more exempt purposes if it is an "action" organization. Section 1.501(c)(3)–1(c)(3)(iii) defines an "action" organization as an organization that participates or intervenes, directly or indirectly, in any political campaign on behalf of or in opposition to any candidate for public office. The regulations further provide that activities that constitute participation or intervention in a political campaign on behalf of or in opposition to a candidate include, but are not limited to, the publication or distribution of written statements or the making of oral statements on behalf of or in opposition to such a candidate.

ANALYSIS

Whether an organization is participating or intervening, directly or indirectly, in any political campaign on behalf of or in opposition to any candidate for public office depends upon all of the facts and circumstances of each case. Certain "voter education" activities conducted in a non-partisan manner may not constitute prohibited political activities under section 501(c)(3) of the Code. Other so-called "voter education" activities, however, may be proscribed by the statute. Rev. Rul. 78–248, 1978–1 C.B. 154, sets forth several situations illustrating when an organization has or has not engaged in prohibited political activities within the meaning of section 501(c)(3).

In Situation 3 of Rev. Rul. 78–248, the organization prepared a questionnaire to all candidates for major public offices that contained questions evidencing a bias on certain issues and made the responses generally available to the public during an election campaign. It was considered to be participating in prohibited political campaign activity. In Situation 4 of Rev. Rul. 78–248, an organization primarily concerned with land conservation matters published a compilation of incumbents' voting records on selected land conservation issues and widely distributed it to the electorate during an election campaign. It was held that by concentrating on a narrow range of issues and widely distributing the publication among the electorate during an election campaign, the organization was participating in a prohibited political activity.

In this case the format and content of the publication are not neutral, since the organization reports each incumbent's votes and its own views on selected legislative issues and indicates whether the incumbent supported or opposed the organization's view. On the other hand, the voting records of all incumbents will be presented, candidates for reelection will not be identified, no comment will be made on an individual's overall qualifications for public office, no statements expressly or impliedly endorsing or rejecting any incumbent as a candidate for public office will be offered, no comparison of incumbents with other candidates will be made, and the organization will point out the inherent limitations of judging the qualifications of an incumbent on the basis of certain selected votes by stating the need to consider such unrecorded matters as performance on subcommittees and constituent service.

In view of the foregoing, other factors must be examined to determine whether in the final analysis the organization is participating or intervening in a political campaign.

In the instant case, the organization will not widely distribute its compilation of incumbents' voting records. The publication will be distributed to the organization's normal readership who number only a few thousand nationwide. This will result in a very small distribution in any particular state or congressional district. No attempt will be made to target the publication toward particular areas in which elections are occurring nor to time the date of publication to coincide with an election campaign.

In view of these facts, Situations 3 and 4 of Rev. Rul. 78–248 are distinguishable from the present case, and the organization will not be considered to be engaged in prohibited political campaign activity.

HOLDING

The publication of a newsletter, by an organization otherwise described in section 501(c)(3) of the Code, containing the voting records of Congressional incumbents on selected issues, in the manner described above, will not constitute participation or intervention in any political campaign within the meaning of section 501(c)(3).

EFFECT ON OTHER REVENUE RULINGS

Rev. Rul. 78–248 is amplified.

Revenue Ruling 86–95

1986–2 Cum. Bull 73.

ISSUE

Would the conduct of public forums involving qualified congressional candidates by an organization otherwise described in section 501(c)(3) of the Internal Revenue Code, in the manner described below, constitute participation or intervention in any political campaign within the meaning of section 501(c)(3)?

FACTS

The organization is an educational membership organization exempt from federal income tax under section 501(c)(3) of the Code. As one of its programs, the organization monitors and reports on legislative, judicial, administrative, and other governmental activities and developments considered to be of important interest to its members.

The organization proposes to conduct a series of public forums. These forums will be conducted in congressional districts during congressional election campaigns. All legally qualified candidates for the House of Representatives from the congressional districts in question will be invited to participate in a forum.

The agenda at each of the forums will cover a broad range of issues, including, but not limited to, those issues considered to be of important educational interest to the organization's members. Questions to forum participants will be prepared and presented by a nonpartisan, independent panel of knowledgeable persons composed of representatives of the media, educational organizations, community leaders, and other interested persons. Each candidate will be allowed an equal opportunity to present his or her views on each of the issues discussed. The organization will select a moderator for each forum whose sole function will be limited to assuring that the general ground rules are followed. At both the beginning and end of each forum, the moderator will state that the views expressed are those of the candidates and not those of the organization and that the sponsorship of the forum is not intended as an endorsement of any candidate.

LAW AND ANALYSIS

Section 501(c)(3) of the Code provides for the exemption from federal income tax of organizations organized and operated exclusively for charitable or educational purposes, no substantial part of the activities of which is carrying on propaganda, or otherwise attempting to influence legislation, (except as otherwise provided in section 501(h)), and which do not participate in, or intervene in (including the publishing or distributing of statements), any political campaign on behalf of any candidate for public office.

Section 1.501(c)(3)–1(c)(3)(i) of the Income Tax Regulations states that an organization is not operated exclusively for one or more exempt purposes if it is an "action" organization. Section 1.501(c)(3)–1(c)(3)(iii) defines an "action" organization as an organization that participates or intervenes, directly or indirectly, in any political campaign on behalf of or in opposition to any candidate for public office. The regulations further provide that activities that constitute participation or intervention in a political campaign on behalf of or in opposition to a candidate include, but are not limited to, the publication or distribution of written statements or the making of oral statements on behalf of or in opposition to such a candidate.

Rev. Rul. 66–256, 1966–2 C.B. 210, holds that a nonprofit organization formed to conduct public forums at which lectures and debates on social, political, and international matters are presented qualifies for exemption from federal income tax under section 501(c)(3) of the Code.

Rev. Rul. 74–574, 1974–2 C.B. 160, holds that a section 501(c)(3) organization operating a broadcast station is not participating in political campaigns on behalf of public candidates by providing reasonable amounts of air time equally available to all legally qualified candidates for election to public office in compliance with the reasonable access provisions of the Communications Act of 1934, 47 U.S.C.A. § 312(a)(7), (1982).

Whether an organization is participating or intervening, directly or indirectly, in any political campaign on behalf of or in opposition to any candidate for public office depends upon all of the facts and circumstances of each case. For example, certain "voter education" activities conducted in a non-partisan manner may not constitute prohibited political activities under section 501(c)(3) of the Code. Other so-called "voter education" activities may be proscribed by the statute. Rev. Rul. 78–248, 1978–1 C.B. 154, contrasts several situations illustrating when an organization that publishes a compilation of a candidate's position or voting record has or has not engaged in prohibited political activities based on whether the questionnaire or voting guide in content or structure shows a bias or preference with respect to the views of a particular candidate. See also Rev. Rul. 80–282, 1980–2 C.B. 178, that amplified Rev. Rul. 78–248 regarding the timing and distribution of voter education materials.

The presentation of public forums or debates is a recognized method of educating the public. See Rev. Rul. 66–256. Providing a forum for candidates is not, in and of itself, prohibited political activity. See Rev. Rul. 74–574. However, a forum for candidates could be operated in a manner that would show a bias or preference for or against a particular candidate. This could be done, for example, through biased questioning procedures. On the other hand, a forum held for the purpose of educating and informing the voters, which provides fair and impartial treatment of candidates, and which does not promote or advance one candidate over another, would not constitute participation or intervention in any political campaign on behalf of or in opposition to any candidate for public office.

The facts and circumstances of this case establish that both the format and content of the proposed forums will be presented in a neutral manner. All legally qualified congressional candidates will be invited to participate in the forum. The questions will be prepared and presented by a nonpartisan, independent panel. The topics discussed will cover a broad range of issues of interest to the public, notwithstanding that the issues discussed may include issues of particular importance to the organization's members. Each candidate will receive an equal opportunity to present his or her views on each of the issues discussed. Finally, the moderator selected by the organization will not comment on the questions or otherwise make comments that imply approval or disapproval of any of the candidates. In view of these facts, the organization will not be considered to be engaged in prohibited political activity.

This conclusion is based on the totality of the circumstances described. The presence or absence of a particular fact here in other similar situations is not determinative of other cases but would have to be considered in light of all the surrounding factors in that case.

HOLDING

The conduct of public forums involving qualified congressional candidates in the manner described above, by an organization otherwise described in section 501(c)(3) of the Code, will not constitute participation or intervention in any political campaign within the meaning of section 501(c)(3).

Branch Ministries, Inc. v. Rossotti

United States Court of Appeals, District of Columbia Circuit, 2000.
211 F.3d 137.

■ BUCKLEY, SENIOR JUDGE:

Four days before the 1992 presidential election, Branch Ministries, a tax-exempt church, placed full-page advertisements in two newspapers in which it urged Christians not to vote for then-presidential candidate Bill Clinton because of his positions on certain moral issues. The Internal Revenue Service concluded that the placement of the advertisements violated the statutory restrictions on organizations exempt from taxation and, for the first time in its history, it revoked a bona fide church's tax-exempt status because of its involvement in politics. Branch Ministries and its pastor, Dan Little, challenge the revocation on the grounds that (1) the Service acted beyond its statutory authority, (2) the revocation violated its right to the free exercise of religion guaranteed by the First Amendment and the Religious Freedom Restoration Act, and (3) it was the victim of selective prosecution in violation of the Fifth Amendment. Because these objections are without merit, we affirm the district court's grant of summary judgment to the Service.

I. BACKGROUND

A. Taxation of Churches

The Internal Revenue Code ("Code") exempts certain organizations from taxation, including those organized and operated for religious purposes, provided that they do not engage in certain activities, including involvement in "any political campaign on behalf of (or in opposition to) any candidate for public office." 26 U.S.C. § 501(a), (c)(3) (1994). Contributions to such organizations are also deductible from the donating taxpayer's taxable income. Id. § 170(a). Although most organizations seeking tax-exempt status are required to apply to the Internal Revenue Service ("IRS" or "Service") for an advance determination that they meet the requirements of section 501(c)(3), id. § 508(a), a church may simply hold itself out as tax exempt and receive the benefits of that status without applying for advance recognition from the IRS. Id. § 508(c)(1)(A).

The IRS maintains a periodically updated "Publication No. 78," in which it lists all organizations that have received a ruling or determination letter confirming the deductibility of contributions made to them. See Rev. Proc. 82–39, 1982–1 C.B. 759, §§ 2.01, 2.03. Thus, a listing in that publication will provide donors with advance assurance that their contributions will be deductible under section 170(a). If a listed organization has subsequently had its tax-exempt status revoked, contributions that are made to it by a donor who is unaware of the change in status will generally be treated as deductible if made on or before the date that the revocation is publicly announced. Id. § 3.01. Donors to a church that has not received an advance determination of its tax-exempt status may also deduct their contributions; but in the event of an audit, the taxpayer will bear the burden of establishing that the church meets the requirements of section 501(c)(3). See generally id. § 3.04; Rev. Proc. 80–24, 1980–1 C.B. 658, § 6 (discussing taxpayers' obligations in seeking a ruling or determination letter).

The unique treatment churches receive in the Internal Revenue Code is further reflected in special restrictions on the IRS's ability to investigate the tax status of a church. The Church Audit Procedures Act ("CAPA") sets out the circumstances under which the IRS may initiate an investigation of a church and the procedures it is required to follow in such an investigation. 26 U.S.C. § 7611. Upon a "reasonable belief" by a high-level Treasury official that a church may not be exempt from taxation under section 501, the IRS may begin a "church tax inquiry." Id. § 7611(a). A church tax inquiry is defined, rather circularly, as any inquiry to a church (other than an examination) to serve as a basis for determining whether a church-(A) is exempt from tax under section 501(a) by reason of its status as a church, or (B) is ... engaged in activities which may be subject to taxation.... Id. § 7611(h)(2). If the IRS is not able to resolve its concerns through a church tax inquiry, it may proceed to the second level of investigation: a "church tax examination." In such an examination, the IRS may obtain and review the church's records or examine its activities "to determine whether [the] organization claiming to be a church is a church for any period." Id. § 7611(b)(1)(A), (B).

B. Factual and Procedural History

Branch Ministries, Inc. operates the Church at Pierce Creek ("Church"), a Christian church located in Binghamton, New York. In 1983, the Church requested and received a letter from the IRS recognizing its tax-exempt status. On October 30, 1992, four days before the presidential election, the Church placed full-page advertisements in USA Today and the Washington Times. Each bore the headline "Christians Beware" and asserted that then-Governor Clinton's positions concerning abortion, homosexuality, and the distribution of condoms to teenagers in schools violated Biblical precepts. The following appeared at the bottom of each advertisement: This advertisement was co-sponsored by the Church at Pierce Creek, Daniel J. Little, Senior Pastor, and by churches and concerned Christians nationwide. Tax deductible donations for this advertisement gladly accepted. Make donations to: The Church at Pierce Creek. [mailing address].
* * *

The advertisements did not go unnoticed. They produced hundreds of contributions to the Church from across the country and were mentioned in a New York Times article and an Anthony Lewis column which stated that the sponsors of the advertisement had almost certainly violated the Internal Revenue Code. Peter Applebome, Religious Right Intensifies Campaign for Bush, N.Y. Times, Oct. 31, 1992, at A1; Anthony Lewis, Tax Exempt Politics?, N.Y. Times, Dec. 1, 1992, at A15.

The advertisements also came to the attention of the Regional Commissioner of the IRS, who notified the Church on November 20, 1992 that he had authorized a church tax inquiry based on "a reasonable belief ... that you may not be tax-exempt or that you may be liable for tax" due to political activities and expenditures. Letter from Cornelius J. Coleman, IRS Regional Commissioner, to The Church at Pierce Creek (Nov. 20, 1992), reprinted in App. at Tab 5, Ex. F. The Church denied that it had engaged in any prohibited political activity and declined to provide the IRS with certain information the Service had requested. On February 11, 1993, the IRS informed the Church that it was beginning a church tax examination. Following two unproductive meetings between the parties, the IRS revoked the Church's section 501(c)(3) tax-exempt status on January 19, 1995, citing the newspaper advertisements as prohibited intervention in a political campaign.

The Church and Pastor Little (collectively, "Church") commenced this lawsuit soon thereafter. This had the effect of suspending the revocation of the Church's tax exemption until the district court entered its judgment in this case. See 26 U.S.C. § 7428(c). The Church challenged the revocation of its tax-exempt status, alleging that the IRS had no authority to revoke its tax exemption, that the revocation violated its right to free speech and to freely exercise its religion under the First Amendment and the Religious Freedom Restoration Act of 1993, 42 U.S.C. § 2000bb (1994) ("RFRA"), and that the IRS engaged in selective prosecution in violation of the Equal Protection Clause of the Fifth Amendment. After allowing discovery on the Church's selective prosecution claim, Branch Ministries, Inc. v. Richardson, 970 F.Supp. 11 (D.D.C.1997), the district court granted summary judgment in favor of the IRS. Branch Ministries, Inc. v. Rossotti, 40 F.Supp.2d 15 (D.D.C.1999).

The Church filed a timely appeal, and we have jurisdiction pursuant to 28 U.S.C. § 1291. We review summary judgment decisions de novo, see Everett v. United States, 158 F.3d 1364, 1367 (D.C.Cir.1998), cert. denied, 526 U.S. 1132, 119 S.Ct. 1807, 143 L.Ed.2d 1010 (1999), and will affirm only if there is no genuine issue as to any material fact and the moving party is entitled to judgment as a matter of law. Fed.R.Civ.P. 56(c).

II.   ANALYSIS

The Church advances a number of arguments in support of its challenges to the revocation. We examine only those that warrant analysis.

A.   The Statutory Authority of the IRS

The Church argues that, under the Internal Revenue Code, the IRS does not have the statutory authority to revoke the tax-exempt status of a bona fide church. It reasons as follows: section 501(c)(3) refers to tax-exempt status for religious organizations, not churches; section 508, on the other hand, specifically exempts "churches" from the requirement of applying for advance recognition of tax-exempt status, id. § 508(c)(1)(A); therefore, according to the Church, its tax-exempt status is derived not from section 501(c)(3), but from the lack of any provision in the Code for the taxation of churches. The Church concludes from this that it is not subject to taxation and that the IRS is therefore powerless to place conditions upon or to remove its tax-exempt status as a church.

We find this argument more creative than persuasive. The simple answer, of course, is that whereas not every religious organization is a church, every church is a religious organization. More to the point, irrespective of whether it was required to do so, the Church applied to the IRS for an advance determination of its tax-exempt status. The IRS granted that recognition and now seeks to withdraw it. CAPA gives the IRS this power.

That statute, which pertains exclusively to churches, provides authority for revocation of the tax-exempt status of a church through its references to other sections of the Internal Revenue Code. The section of CAPA entitled "Limitations on revocation of tax-exempt status, etc." provides that the Secretary [of the Treasury] may "determine that an organization is not a church which [ ] (i) is exempt from taxation by reason of section 501(a), or (ii) is described in section 170(c)." 26 U.S.C. § 7611(d)(1)(A)(i), (ii). Both of these sections condition tax-exempt status on non-intervention in political campaigns. Section 501(a) states that "[a]n organization described in subsection (c) ... shall be exempt from taxation...." Id. § 501(a). Those described in subsection (c) include corporations ... organized and operated exclusively for religious ... purposes ... which do[ ] not participate in, or intervene in (including the publishing or distributing of statements), any political campaign on behalf of (or in opposition to) any candidate for public office. Id. § 501(c)(3). Similarly, section 170(c) allows taxpayers to deduct from their taxable income donations made to a corporation organized and operated exclusively for religious ... purposes ... which is not disqualified for tax exemption under section 501(c)(3) by reason of attempting to ... intervene in (including the publishing or distributing of statements), any political campaign on behalf of (or in opposition to) any candidate for public office. Id. § 170(c)(2)(B), (D).

The Code, in short, specifically states that organizations that fail to comply with the restrictions set forth in section 501(c) are not qualified to receive the tax exemption that it provides. Having satisfied ourselves that the IRS had the statutory authority to revoke the Church's tax-exempt status, we now turn to the free exercise challenges.

B.   First Amendment Claims and the RFRA

The Church claims that the revocation of its exemption violated its right to freely exercise its religion under both the First Amendment and the RFRA. To sustain its claim under either the Constitution or the statute, the Church must first establish that its free exercise right has been substantially burdened. See Jimmy Swaggart Ministries v. Board of Equalization, 493 U.S. 378, 384–85, 110 S.Ct. 688, 107 L.Ed.2d 796 (1990) ("Our cases have established that the free exercise inquiry asks whether government has placed a substantial burden on the observation of a central religious belief or practice and, if so, whether a compelling governmental interest justifies the burden.") (internal quotation marks and brackets omitted); 42 U.S.C. § 2000bb–1(a), (b) ("Government shall not substantially burden a person's exercise of religion" in the absence of a compelling government interest that is furthered by the least restrictive means.). We conclude that the Church has failed to meet this test.

The Church asserts, first, that a revocation would threaten its existence. See Affidavit of Dan Little dated July 31, 1995 at P 22, reprinted in App. at Tab 8 ("The Church at Pierce Creek will have to close due to the revocation of its tax exempt status, and the inability of congregants to deduct their contributions from their taxes."). The Church maintains that a loss of its tax-exempt status will not only make its members reluctant to contribute the funds essential to its survival, but may obligate the Church itself to pay taxes.

The Church appears to assume that the withdrawal of a conditional privilege for failure to meet the condition is in itself an unconstitutional burden on its free exercise right. This is true, however, only if the receipt of the privilege (in this case the tax exemption) is conditioned upon conduct proscribed by a religious faith, or ... denie[d] ... because of conduct mandated by religious belief, thereby putting substantial pressure on an adherent to modify his behavior and to violate his beliefs. Jimmy Swaggart Ministries, 493 U.S. at 391–92 (internal quotation marks and citation omitted). Although its advertisements reflected its religious convictions on certain questions of morality, the Church does not maintain that a withdrawal from electoral politics would violate its beliefs. The sole effect of the loss of the tax exemption will be to decrease the amount of money available to the Church for its religious practices. The Supreme Court has declared, however, that such a burden "is not constitutionally significant." Id. at 391; see also Hernandez v. Commissioner, 490 U.S. 680, 700, 109 S.Ct. 2136, 104 L.Ed.2d 766 (1989) (the "contention that an incrementally larger tax burden interferes with [ ] religious activities ... knows no limitation").

In actual fact, even this burden is overstated. Because of the unique treatment churches receive under the Internal Revenue Code, the impact of the revocation is likely to be more symbolic than substantial. As the IRS confirmed at oral argument, if the Church does not intervene in future political campaigns, it may hold itself out as a 501(c)(3) organization and receive all the benefits of that status. All that will have been lost, in that event, is the advance assurance of deductibility in the event a donor should be audited. See 26 U.S.C. § 508(c)(1)(A); Rev. Proc. 82–39 § 2.03. Contributions will remain tax deductible as long as donors are able to establish that the Church meets the requirements of section 501(c)(3).

Nor does the revocation necessarily make the Church liable for the payment of taxes. As the IRS explicitly represented in its brief and reiterated at oral argument, the revocation of the exemption does not convert bona fide donations into income taxable to the Church. See 26

U.S.C. § 102 ("Gross income does not include the value of property acquired by gift....''). Furthermore, we know of no authority, and counsel provided none, to prevent the Church from reapplying for a prospective determination of its tax-exempt status and regaining the advance assurance of deductibility—provided, of course, that it renounces future involvement in political campaigns.

We also reject the Church's argument that it is substantially burdened because it has no alternate means by which to communicate its sentiments about candidates for public office. In Regan v. Taxation With Representation, 461 U.S. 540, 552–53, 103 S.Ct. 1997, 76 L.Ed.2d 129 (1983) (Blackmun, J., concurring), three members of the Supreme Court stated that the availability of such an alternate means of communication is essential to the constitutionality of section 501(c)(3)'s restrictions on lobbying. The Court subsequently confirmed that this was an accurate description of its holding. See FCC v. League of Women Voters, 468 U.S. 364, 400, 104 S.Ct. 3106, 82 L.Ed.2d 278 (1984). In Regan, the concurring justices noted that "TWR may use its present § 501(c)(3) organization for its nonlobbying activities and may create a § 501(c)(4) affiliate to pursue its charitable goals through lobbying.'' 461 U.S. at 552.

The Church has such an avenue available to it. As was the case with TWR, the Church may form a related organization under section 501(c)(4) of the Code. See 26 U.S.C. § 501(c)(4) (tax exemption for "[c]ivic leagues or organizations not organized for profit but operated exclusively for the promotion of social welfare''). Such organizations are exempt from taxation; but unlike their section 501(c)(3) counterparts, contributions to them are not deductible. See 26 U.S.C. § 170(c); see also Regan, 461 U.S. at 543, 552–53. Although a section 501(c)(4) organization is also subject to the ban on intervening in political campaigns, see 26 C.F.R. § 1.501(c)(4)–1(a)(2)(ii) (1999), it may form a political action committee ("PAC'') that would be free to participate in political campaigns. Id. § 1.527–6(f), (g) ("[A]n organization described in section 501(c) that is exempt from taxation under section 501(a) may, [if it is not a section 501(c)(3) organization], establish and maintain such a separate segregated fund to receive contributions and make expenditures in a political campaign.'').

At oral argument, counsel for the Church doggedly maintained that there can be no "Church at Pierce Creek PAC.'' True, it may not itself create a PAC; but as we have pointed out, the Church can initiate a series of steps that will provide an alternate means of political communication that will satisfy the standards set by the concurring justices in Regan. Should the Church proceed to do so, however, it must understand that the related 501(c)(4) organization must be separately incorporated; and it must maintain records that will demonstrate that tax-deductible contributions to the Church have not been used to support the political activities conducted by the 501(c)(4) organization's political action arm. See 26 U.S.C. § 527(f)(3); 26 C.F.R. § 1.527–6(e), (f).

That the Church cannot use its tax-free dollars to fund such a PAC unquestionably passes constitutional muster. The Supreme Court has consistently held that, absent invidious discrimination, "Congress has not violated [an organization's] First Amendment rights by declining to subsidize its First Amendment activities." Regan, 461 U.S. at 548; see also Cammarano v. United States, 358 U.S. 498, 513, 79 S.Ct. 524, 3 L.Ed.2d 462 (1959) ("Petitioners are not being denied a tax deduction because they engage in constitutionally protected activities, but are simply being required to pay for those activities entirely out of their own pockets, as everyone else engaging in similar activities is required to do under the provisions of the Internal Revenue Code.").

Because the Church has failed to demonstrate that its free exercise rights have been substantially burdened, we do not reach its arguments that section 501(c)(3) does not serve a compelling government interest or, if it is indeed compelling, that revocation of its tax exemption was not the least restrictive means of furthering that interest.

Nor does the Church succeed in its claim that the IRS has violated its First Amendment free speech rights by engaging in viewpoint discrimination. The restrictions imposed by section 501(c)(3) are viewpoint neutral; they prohibit intervention in favor of all candidates for public office by all taxexempt organizations, regardless of candidate, party, or viewpoint. Cf. Regan, 461 U.S. at 550–51 (upholding denial of tax deduction for lobbying activities, in spite of allowance of such deduction for veteran's groups).

C. Selective Prosecution (Fifth Amendment)

The Church alleges that the IRS violated the Equal Protection Clause of the Fifth Amendment by engaging in selective prosecution. In support of its claim, the Church has submitted several hundred pages of newspaper excerpts reporting political campaign activities in, or by the pastors of, other churches that have retained their tax-exempt status. These include reports of explicit endorsements of Democratic candidates by clergymen as well as many instances in which favored candidates have been invited to address congregations from the pulpit. The Church complains that despite this widespread and widely reported involvement by other churches in political campaigns, it is the only one to have ever had its tax-exempt status revoked for engaging in political activity. It attributes this alleged discrimination to the Service's political bias.

To establish selective prosecution, the Church must "prove that (1) [it] was singled out for prosecution from among others similarly situated and (2) that [the] prosecution was improperly motivated, i.e., based on race, religion or another arbitrary classification." United States v. Washington, 705 F.2d 489, 494 (D.C.Cir.1983). This burden is a demanding one because "in the absence of clear evidence to the contrary, courts presume that [government prosecutors] have properly discharged their official duties." United States v. Armstrong, 517 U.S. 456, 464, 116 S.Ct. 1480, 134 L.Ed.2d 687 (1996) (internal quotation marks and citation omitted).

At oral argument, counsel for the IRS conceded that if some of the church-sponsored political activities cited by the Church were accurately reported, they were in violation of section 501(c)(3) and could have resulted in the revocation of those churches' tax-exempt status. But even if the Service could have revoked their tax exemptions, the Church has failed to establish selective prosecution because it has failed to demonstrate that it was similarly situated to any of those other churches. None of the reported activities involved the placement of advertisements in newspapers with nationwide circulations opposing a candidate and soliciting tax deductible contributions to defray their cost. As we have stated, [i]f . . . there was no one to whom defendant could be compared in order to resolve the question of [prosecutorial] selection, then it follows that defendant has failed to make out one of the elements of its case. Discrimination cannot exist in a vacuum; it can be found only in the unequal treatment of people in similar circumstances. Attorney Gen. v. Irish People, Inc., 684 F.2d 928, 946 (D.C.Cir.1982); see also United States v. Hastings, 126 F.3d 310, 315 (4th Cir.1997) ("[D]efendants are similarly situated when their circumstances present no distinguishable legitimate prosecutorial factors that might justify making different prosecutorial decisions with respect to them.") (internal quotation marks and citation omitted).

Because the Church has failed to establish that it was singled out for prosecution from among others who were similarly situated, we need not examine whether the IRS was improperly motivated in undertaking this prosecution.

III.   CONCLUSION

For the foregoing reasons, we find that the revocation of the Church's tax-exempt status neither violated the Constitution nor exceeded the IRS's statutory authority. The judgment of the district court is therefore

Affirmed.

NOTES

1. *Who's a Candidate?* "Candidates" for public office generally include individuals offering themselves or proposed by others for national, state, or local elective public office. Treas. Reg. § 1.501(c)(3)–1(c)(3)(iii). The election need not be contested nor must it involve the participation of political parties. Rev. Rul. 67–71, 1967–1 C.B. 125. An individual who declares his or her intention to run for public office is clearly a candidate, and the term "candidate" also was construed in the *Christian Echoes* case to include incumbents who had not formally announced their candidacy but were likely to do so. But a person's status as a prominent public figure does not automatically equate to "candidate" status despite public speculation about a future run for office. See Tech. Adv. Mem. 9130008. Individuals nominated for appointment to a judgeship are not candidates. Notice 89–76, 1988–2 C.B. 392.

2. *What's Nonpartisan?* The IRS permits § 501(c)(3) organizations to engage in nonpartisan activities such as voter education and get-out-the-vote drives. "Nonpartisan" has never been clearly defined, and attempts at a bright line test are probably futile. At the very least, an organization may

not expressly advocate for or against particular candidates or parties. Voter registration efforts, however, are considered nonpartisan even if they are targeted at groups (e.g., minorities, low-income, the homeless) who are likely to favor a particular political party but apparently registration drives are partisan if they target people with a viewpoint on a particular issue (e.g., pro-life or fiscal conservative). Much of the law here is anecdotal. For a good source on the IRS's thinking, see Judith E. Kindell & John F. Reilly, Election Year Issues, FY 1993 IRS Exempt Organizations Continuing Professional Education Technical Instruction Program 400 (1992); Judith E. Kindell & Amy Hinchey, Election Year Issues, FY 1996 IRS Exempt Organizations Continuing Professional Education Technical Instruction Program 365 (1995); Judith E. Kindell & John Francis Reilly, Election Year Issues, FY 2002 IRS Exempt Organizations Continuing Professional Education Technical Instruction Program 321 (CCH ed. 2001).

3. *Rating Candidates.* The political campaign limits extend to the rating of candidates for elective judgeships, even if the election is nonpartisan and the rating activity is conducted by a politically neutral local bar association to educate the public. See Association of the Bar of the City of New York v. Commissioner, 858 F.2d 876 (2d Cir.1988), where the court held that the term "candidate for public office" includes anyone who is running in an election even if no political parties are involved.

4. *Issue Advocacy.* Some § 501(c)(3) organizations may attempt to influence a political campaign by engaging in well-timed "issue advocacy" that expresses a position on an issue of concern to the organization that coincides with a particular candidate or party's viewpoint. One goal of a carefully crafted "issue advocacy" message is to avoid federal election law regulations discussed later in this chapter. For tax exemption purposes, the question is: when does issue advocacy cross the line and become electioneering? A visible single-issue § 501(c)(3) charity, such as a pro-choice advocacy group, may jeopardize its exempt status if it impliedly endorses or opposes a candidate through aggressive advocacy in the midst of a hotly contested political campaign. The IRS has warned charities using "code language" as part of issue advocacy that they may be engaging in impermissible electioneering even if particular candidates are never mentioned. FY 1993 EO CPE, at 411–412. Issue advocacy is more defensible if it is a year-round activity, or if an organization's message relates to a broad range of topics.

5. *Excise Taxes on Political Expenditures.* Section 4955 authorizes the Service to impose excise tax penalties on certain political expenditures of § 501(c)(3) organizations. These taxes may be imposed in addition to or, perhaps in the case of isolated violations, in lieu of revocation. The § 4955 tax and two additional penalties (§ 6852 and § 7409) discussed below were enacted in response to publicized examples of § 501(c)(3) organizations operated under the guise of "think tanks" and used by candidates to support their political ambitions. See Subcomm. on Oversight, House Comm. on Ways and Means, Hearings on Lobbying and Political Activities of Tax–Exempt Organizations (1987). In addition, concerns had been raised

about a § 501(c)(3) organization that used tax-deductible contributions to oppose the reelection of members of Congress who had not supported aid to the Nicaraguan Contras.

Section 4955 provides for a two-tiered excise tax on specified political expenditures of a § 501(c)(3) organization and on the agreement of its managers to make the expenditure. Two types of expenditures are targeted: (1) amounts paid or incurred to participate or intervene in a political campaign on behalf of any candidate for public office (sound familiar?), and (2) certain expenditures of organizations formed primarily for the purpose of promoting a person's candidacy, or used primarily for that purpose and effectively controlled by the candidate. I.R.C. § 4955(d). The first category tracks the § 501(c)(3) limitation. The second is more specific and includes amounts paid for a candidate's speeches and travel, expenses of conducting polls and surveys, advertising expenses, and any other expense that has the primary effect of promoting public recognition of the candidate. I.R.C. § 4955(d)(2). One wonders how an organization incurring any of the second type of taxable expenditure could have qualified for exemption under § 501(c)(3) in the first place!

The § 4955 initial excise tax on the organization is 10 percent of each forbidden political expenditure is imposed on the organization. A separate tax of 2½ percent of the expenditure (up to a ceiling of $5,000 per expenditure) is imposed on any organization "manager" who agrees to the expenditure knowing that it is impermissible—unless the manager's agreement is "not willful and is due to reasonable cause." Second-tier taxes (100 percent of the expenditure for the organization, 50 percent, with a $10,000 cap, on the knowing manager) are imposed if the political expenditure is not "corrected" within a specified period of time. "Correction" is accomplished by recovering part or all of the expenditure to the extent possible and by establishing safeguards to prevent future political expenditures. If all these steps are taken, even the first-tier taxes may be waived if the expenditure was not "willful and flagrant." I.R.C. § 4962(c). See Treas. Reg. § 53.4955–1(d), (e).

If the Service determines that an organization's violation of the limitation on political campaign expenditures is flagrant, it may immediately assess the excise taxes described above as well as any income taxes due and also may file an action in federal district court to enjoin or halt any future political expenditures by the organization if certain procedural requirements are met. I.R.C. § 6852; § 7409.

Although these new rules are designed to broaden the enforcement powers of the Service against wrongdoers, the excise taxes also might be applied as an alternative to revocation of exemption in the case of an organization that, perhaps inadvertently, makes political expenditures but is willing to undo the damage by recovering the funds (e.g., from the benefited candidate) and promising never to do it again. The Service, however, believes that § 4955 should not be used as an intermediate sanction except in very limited circumstances. See FY 1993 EO CPE, supra, at 417.

6. *For Further Reading*. Bob Boisture & Beth Seller, Power, Politics & Nonprofits (Independent Sector, 1998); Laura Brown Chisolm, Sinking the Think Tanks Upstream: The Use and Misuse of Tax Exemption Law to Address the Use and Misuse of Tax–Exempt Organizations by Politicians, 51 U.Pitt.L.Rev. 577 (1990); Laura Brown Chisolm, Politics and Charity: A Proposal for Peaceful Coexistence, 58 Geo.Wash.L.Rev. 308 (1990); Milton Cerny, Campaigns, Candidates and Charities: Guideposts for All Charitable Institutions, 19 NYU Conf. on Tax Planning for 501(c)(3) Organizations, ch. 5 (1991).

6. The § 501(c)(4) Alternative

Internal Revenue Code: §§ 501(c)(4); 527.

A § 501(c)(3) organization may conclude that it is unable to meet its political objectives within the strictures of either the no substantial part test or § 501(h) expenditure test election. It also may wish to influence political campaigns or engage in more targeted issue advocacy. In those cases, the § 501(c)(3) charity should consider forming an affiliated § 501(c)(4) organization to conduct lobbying and other political activities. This type of dual structure was specifically noted by the Supreme Court in the *Taxation With Representation* case, supra p. 301, when it upheld the constitutionality of the lobbying limitations on § 501(c)(3) organizations.

Section 501(c)(4) confers tax-exempt status on "[c]ivic leagues and organizations not organized for profit but operated exclusively for the promotion of social welfare." As illustrated by Revenue Ruling 71–530, below, "social welfare" has been defined liberally to include virtually any charitable or educational cause that does not violate the law. More importantly, social welfare organizations qualify for exemption even if a substantial part of their activities consists of lobbying or political activities provided those activities are germane to the organization's social welfare purposes. The principal disadvantage of § 501(c)(4) status is that contributions to the organization are not tax-deductible.

Revenue Ruling 71–530

1971–2 Cum. Bull. 237.

Advice has been requested whether the nonprofit organization described below qualifies for exemption from Federal income tax under section 501(c)(4) of the Internal Revenue Code of 1954.

The organization was formed to promote the common good and welfare of the general public through the presentation, at legislative and administrative hearings on tax matters, of views directed at the improvement of the tax system. It selects individuals who the organization believes qualified to represent the interests of the general public in matters of tax policy. Such individuals include members of the tax bar, public finance economists, teachers of accounting and tax law, and other tax specialists. The organization alerts them as soon as tax issues arise in their fields of expertise, and aids them in preparing and publicizing their testimony. It receives contributions from the general public which are used to cover the cost of transporting witnesses, reproducing witness statements, publicizing recommendations on proposed tax changes, and the payment of salaries and other office expense.

Section 501(c)(4) of the Code provides for the exemption from Federal income tax of civic leagues or organizations not organized for profit but operated exclusively for the promotion of social welfare.

Section 1.501(c)(4)–1(a)(2) of the Income Tax Regulations provides that an organization is operated exclusively for the promotion of social welfare if it is primarily engaged in promoting in some way the common good and general welfare of the people of the community.

Section 1.501(c)(4)–1(a)(2)(ii) of the regulations states that a social welfare organization may qualify under section 501(c)(4) even though it is an "action" organization described in 1.501(c)(3)–1(c)(3)(iv) if it otherwise qualifies under the section.

Section 1.501(c)(3)–1(c)(3)(iv) of the regulations provides that an organization is an "action" organization if it has the following two characteristics: (a) its main or primary objective or objectives (as distinguished from its incidental or secondary objective) may be attained only by legislation or a defeat of proposed legislation; and (b) it advocates, or campaigns for, the attainment of such main or primary objective or objectives as distinguished from engaging in nonpartisan analysis, study, or research and making the results thereof available to the public.

Through presentations by qualified witnesses on pending or proposed tax legislation, the organization is promoting the common good and general welfare of the community by assisting legislators and administrators concerned with tax policy. Such activity helps the legislators and administrators form better judgments about the legislation.

The fact that the organization's only activities may involve advocating changes in law does not preclude the organization from qualifying under section 501(c)(4) of the Code. See regulations cited above.

Accordingly, it is held that the organization qualifies for exemption from Federal income tax as a social welfare organization under section 501(c)(4) of the Code. Contributions to it are not deductible by donors under the provisions of section 170(c)(2) of the Code.

* * *

NOTES

1. *Relationship Between a § 501(c)(3) Organization and its § 501(c)(4) Affiliate.* A § 501(c)(3) organization can control its § 501(c)(4) affiliate provided that the "(c)(4)" is a separate legal entity whose activities are not supported by tax-deductible contributions. "Control" is often ensured by a governance structure that gives the § 501(c)(3) parent the authority to

appoint all or a majority of the § 501(c)(4) subsidiary's board of directors. The two organizations may operate side-by-side if they keep separate books, avoid commingling funds, and provide that, upon any dissolution, the assets of the § 501(c)(3) organization may not be distributed to the lobbying affiliate. The board of directors of the two organizations may overlap, and the "(c)(3)" can effectively control the "(c)(4)'s" policies as long as the finances of each organization are kept separate. Sharing of space and personnel is permitted, provided that the "(c)(4)" reimburses the "(c)(3)" for its share of direct costs and general overhead.

2. *Political Campaign Activities.* A § 501(c)(4) social welfare organization may engage in political campaign activities as long as political campaigning is not the organization's primary activity. Rev. Rul. 81–95, 1981–1 C.B. 332. A good rule of thumb is to limit electioneering to less than 50 percent of an organization's total activities.

Social welfare organizations also may create separate political action committees ("PACs") to engage in campaign activities and make contributions to candidates. To protect its tax-exempt status, a § 501(c)(3) parent must not involve itself in these electoral activities. For example, a charity's tax-deductible contributions should not be diverted to a PAC, and a PAC should not be controlled directly by a charity.

3. *Other Tax Consequences of Political Activities.* Although a properly structured § 501(c)(3)/§ 501(c)(4)/PAC combination will not threaten the tax-exempt status of the affiliated organizations, certain types of expenditures may trigger a tax liability under rules designed to ensure that politically active § 501(c) organizations are taxed comparably to political organizations.

Section 527 political organizations generally are organizations having as their principal purpose the support or opposition of one or more candidates for public office. I.R.C. § 527(e)(1), (2). In general, political organizations are not taxed on the dues and contributions they receive for their electioneering and other political activities, but they are taxed at the highest corporate income tax rate on any business or investment income. I.R.C. § 527(b), (c). Contributions by individual donors to political organizations are not tax-deductible nor are they subject to federal gift tax. I.R.C. § 2501(a)(5). Gifts to § 501(c)(4) advocacy organizations also are not tax-deductible, but they may be taxable gifts for federal gift tax purposes if they exceed the annual exclusion (currently $10,000 per donor).

Tax-exempt organizations become subject to the § 527 political organization tax regime if they make expenditures for an "exempt function"— defined as "influencing or attempting to influence the selection, nomination, election, or appointment of any individual to any Federal, State, or local public office, or office in a political organization, or the election of Presidential or Vice–Presidential electors, whether [the] individual or electors are selected, nominated, elected, or appointed." I.R.C. 527(e)(2). As used for this purpose, the term "exempt" has nothing to do with "exempt purposes" under § 501(c)(3) but rather is a reference to the exempt functions of a typical political organization. For more details on the scope of "exempt function" activities, see Treas. Reg. § 1.527–2(c). The amount taxed is the lesser of the organization's net investment income or the aggregate amount spent for exempt functions. I.R.C. § 527(f)(1). "Net investment income" consists of dividends, interest, rent, royalties, and capital gains, less directly related expenses. I.R.C. § 527(f)(2).

To illustrate, assume a § 501(c)(4) advocacy organization has $400,000 of net income, of which $100,000 is net investment income, and it spends $150,000 during the year on political campaign activities that constitute "exempt functions" as defined in § 527(e)(2). The organization will be subject to tax at the highest applicable corporate rate (currently 35%) on the lesser of: (1) its exempt function expenditures, or (2) the organization's net investment income. In the example, the § 501(c)(4) organization would be subject to an income tax of $35,000 (35% x $100,000 net investment income). If its political expenditures had been only $80,000, the tax would be 35 percent of that lesser amount, or $28,000.

An organization with no investment income does not need to be concerned with this tax. An organization with a large endowment can avoid the tax by establishing a separate segregated fund (which need not be a separate legal entity) and allocating to it a share of the organization's dues. I.R.C. § 527(f)(3). For tax purposes, the fund will be treated as a separate organization and, if it has no investment income, it will not be taxable with respect to its political expenditures. Care must be taken not to commingle funds or "loan" money to the segregated fund to preserve its separate tax status.

7.   USE OF THE INTERNET FOR LOBBYING AND CAMPAIGN ACTIVITIES

In Announcement 2000–84, 2000–42 I.R.B. 385, the Service requested comments on areas for which guidance was necessary to clarify the application of federal tax law to use of the Internet by exempt organizations. With the explosive growth of the Internet as a communications medium, the scope of this request was wide ranging. Three areas where the need for guidance is particularly compelling are: (1) lobbying and political activities; (2) the unrelated business income tax; and (3) charitable contributions (see Chapter 6, infra, at pp. 739–740). This discussion, which assumes familiarity with Internet basics, highlights some of the major issues relating to lobbying and political activity.

Because it is a convenient and relatively inexpensive communications medium, the Internet has proven to be an effective vehicle for exempt organizations to lobby and otherwise attempt to influence the political process. The following examples, posed as hypothetical questions, illustrate the range of issues:

- A § 501(c)(3) educational organization with an advocacy mission that has not made the § 501(h) election devotes over half of its web site but a relatively insignificant portion of its budget to grassroots lobbying. How is this lobbying activity evaluated in applying the "no substantial part" test? Is the location of the lobbying communication (e.g., home page or several clicks away) or number of hits relevant in making the "substantial part" determination?

- A § 501(c)(3) charity that has made the § 501(h) lobbying election maintains an extensive (but inexpensive) web site that includes (in a prominent place) all the elements of grassroots lobbying communications on a wide range of issues. Alternatively, the various elements are spread around separate locations on the web site, but navigation is easy (or not) for those with an interest in the issue. The site also contains links to the web sites of other non-§ 501(c)(3) exempt organizations, and those sites include calls to action that meet all the elements of grassroots lobbying. Variations abound, as do issues which include: (a) how to apply the definitions of lobbying to web site communications; (b) when do statements on a web site constitute a "call to action" or a mass media communication for purposes of the mass media rule in Treas. Reg. § 56.4911–2(b)(5)(ii); (c) under what circumstances should information transmitted on or from the Internet be treated as a favored member communication for purposes of the § 501(h) election regime; (d) when should statements on a linked web site be attributed back to the originating exempt organization; and (e) how should expenses of the web site be allocated to lobbying communications?

- A § 501(c)(3) charity's web site includes, as part of the organization's educational mission, links to an affiliated § 501(c)(4) advocacy organization or, alternatively, to a § 527 political action committee for a candidate for public office. The web site contains no overt statements supporting or opposing candidates, but many of the links (reached with just one click) include statements (or voter guides, etc.) whose content clearly violates the political campaign limitations in § 501(c)(3). Can these links be treated as nonpartisan voter education? What is required to make them nonpartisan? What if a § 501(c)(3) educational organization and its § 501(c)(4) lobbying affiliate share a web site that includes, in the (c)(4)'s cyberspace, statements that are proper for the (c)(4) but would warrant revocation of the (c)(3)'s exemption?

Any guidance that is forthcoming from the Service should be grounded in the developed law, such as it is, regulating lobbying and political activities by § 501(c)(3) organizations. Thus, a voter's guide that passes muster under the Service's ruling policy should be similarly evaluated if it is communicated through a web site. Similarly, a well advised § 501(c)(3) organization should avoid including overt statements on its web site that support or oppose candidates for public office, but its exemption should not be threatened if the links to candidate sites are incident to a nonpartisan educational mission. Beyond these obvious principles, however, the trouble spots (e.g., impact of hyperlinks, allocation of expenses) raise challenging questions that in the end will best be resolved by regulations or published rulings containing bright line safe harbors with a facts and circumstances fallback focusing on the organization's objective intent.

8. NONTAX REGULATION OF POLITICAL ACTIVITIES

Federal laws impose various other restrictions on lobbying and other political activity by nonprofit organizations. Some of these restrictions were enacted in response to real and perceived abuses and reflect the persistent theme that lobbying, despite its prevalence throughout American history, is undesirable or at least must be closely regulated. This discussion is limited to an overview of the major nontax statutes and regulations applicable to the nonprofit sector.

Lobbying Disclosure Act. The Lobbying Disclosure Act of 1995 ("the Act") establishes a comprehensive regime for registration and reporting of lobbying activities at the federal level. Among other things, the Act requires exempt and non-exempt organizations to register and file semi-annual reports on their lobbying activities if: (1) the organization has at least one employee who is a "lobbyist" (as defined), and (2) the organization incurs or expects to incur expenditures on "lobbying activities" of $20,000 or more in a six-month period. A "lobbyist" is an employee who makes at least two "lobbying contacts" and devotes at least 20 percent of his or her time to "lobbying activities."

The question remains—what is lobbying for purposes of the Act? Charities that have made the § 501(h) election for federal tax purposes may elect to use the federal tax definition of "influencing legislation" and the tax rules for computing lobbying expenditures for purposes of determining their obligations under the Lobbying Disclosure Act. The definition of lobbying under the Act, however, differs significantly from the tax definitions in §§ 4911 and 162(e). For example, the Act does not cover efforts to influence state and local legislative bodies or grassroots lobbying at any level, but it does include most "self-defense" lobbying and efforts to influence executive branch decisions through contacts with members of Congress or with executive branch officials. Politically active charities thus are faced with a strategical choice as to which definition to use in determining their obligations under the Act.

Churches and their integrated auxiliaries are exempt from the registration and reporting requirements of the Act, but outside lobbyists retained by a church are subject to it. Although private foundations are not permitted to lobby, as that term is defined for federal tax purposes, they are still subject to the Act if they engage in activities that are treated as lobbying under the Act but not under federal tax law.

In addition to the registration and reporting requirements, the Act includes monetary sanctions for violations and a prohibition on receipt of federal funds by § 501(c)(4) organizations that lobby, but they may establish a separate § 501(c)(4) affiliate to engage in privately-funded lobbying.

For a summary of the impact of the Lobbying Disclosure Act on nonprofit organizations, see Robert A. Boisture, What Charities Need to

Know to Comply with the Lobbying Disclosure Act of 1995 (Independent Sector, 1995); Bob Smucker, The Nonprofit Lobbying Guide (Independent Sector, 2d ed. 1999).

Restrictions on Use of Federal Funds for Lobbying. Rules promulgated by the Office of Management and Budget prohibit some nonprofits from using federal funds for lobbying at the federal and state levels. See OMB Circular A–122, Cost Principles for Nonprofit Organizations, 49 Fed.Reg. 18,260 (April 27, 1984). The definitions of lobbying are similar but not identical to those employed under the federal tax laws. The OMB regulations do not restrict a nonprofit's overall lobbying expenses if none of those expenses are paid with funds obtained through federal grants or contracts. Legislation enacted in 1989 under the sponsorship of Senator Robert Byrd of West Virginia also forbids the use of federally appropriated funds for lobbying purposes and requires disclosure of lobbying activities and expenses by organizations that are seeking federal grants, contracts, loans, and the like. This legislation covers attempts to influence executive agencies as well as the legislature. Nonprofit organizations are specifically subject to the Byrd Amendment. See generally 31 U.S.C.A. § 1352 (1988).

Federal Election and Campaign Finance Law Restrictions. Federal election and campaign finance laws, and the election laws of some states, restrict the ability of corporations (including nonprofit organizations) to make certain types of campaign contributions and other political expenditures and limit the amount that individuals may contribute to political candidates. They also regulate political action committees at the federal level and require disclosure of most political contributions in federal elections. See generally Federal Election Campaign Act, 2 U.S.C.A. §§ 431–455 (1988). The federal election laws are a confusing maze. In general, they distinguish between "express advocacy"—i.e., advocating the election or defeat of a specific candidate by using certain magic words—and more generalized activities. In Buckley v. Valeo, 424 U.S. 1, 96 S.Ct. 612 (1976), the Supreme Court upheld the constitutionality of federal election law limits on "hard money" contributions to candidates, political parties, and other organizations that engage in express advocacy, but ruled that it was constitutionally impermissible to restrict "soft money" contributions used for more general party-building activities, voter registration efforts, and issue advocacy, and other grassroots effort that do not involve "express advocacy" on behalf of candidates. This "soft money" loophole has been widely exploited by both political parties and is the principal target of those advocating campaign finance reform.

Section 501(c)(3) organizations are generally unaffected by federal election laws because the tax law already bars them from engaging in express advocacy on behalf of candidates. Except in one situation discussed below, other nonprofit organizations may not spend money to engage in express advocacy on behalf of candidates. But they can engage in issue advocacy and support political parties with soft money through their separate political action committees.

A narrow sub-category of § 501(c)(4) organization may spend money directly for express advocacy—i.e., they may expressly advocate the election or defeat of federal candidates. This exception to the normal ban on hard money spending by corporations is the result of several Supreme Court decisions addressing the application of Federal Election Law restrictions to nonprofit advocacy groups. In Federal Election Commission v. Massachusetts Citizens for Life, 479 U.S. 238, 107 S.Ct. 616 (1986), the Court held that it was unconstitutional to restrict the electioneering activities of a nonprofit "pro-life" § 501(c)(4) advocacy organization. The Court distinguished the advocacy group from a business corporation, finding that it was "formed to disseminate political ideas, not to amass capital." Id. at 259.

In Austin v. Michigan Chamber of Commerce, 494 U.S. 652, 110 S.Ct. 1391 (1990), however, the Court held that state-imposed restrictions on political expenditures were constitutionally applied to a § 501(c)(6) business league. Rejecting the First Amendment free speech arguments of the Michigan Chamber of Commerce, the Court found that a nonprofit corporation must be organized "to promot[e] political ideas" rather than engage in business activities in order to be constitutionally exempt from political expenditure limitations. Id. at 662. The Court reasoned that the free speech rights of corporations, including their tax-exempt trade associations, were outweighed by the state's compelling interest to ensure that the political process was not corrupted by undue influence of wealthy corporate interests.

In response to these decisions, the Federal Election Commission allows a § 501(c)(4) organization to make independent (i.e., independent of a candidate's campaign) expenditures to expressly advocate on behalf or in opposition to federal candidates if the organization was formed for the express purpose of promoting identified political ideas, and provided that it does not take corporate or labor donations and refrains from any related or unrelated business activities. See 11 C.F.R. § 114.10.

Is the distinction drawn by the Supreme Court in *Massachusetts Citizens for Life* and *Austin* persuasive? Would an organization like the Sierra Club, which engages in political activities, publishes a magazine, sells books, and promotes outdoor vacation experiences, come within the Federal Election Commission's exception?

For Further Reading: Bruce R. Hopkins, Charity, Advocacy and the Law (1992); Developments in the Law–Nonprofit Corporations, 105 Harv. L.Rev. 1578, 1666–1677 (1992).

NOTE: USE AND ABUSE OF NONPROFIT ORGANIZATIONS FOR PARTISAN POLITICAL ACTIVITIES

The use of tax-exempt organizations as fronts for political causes and candidates has been widely reported for decades. The ongoing debate over campaign finance reform has focused attention on the use of "religious" or "educational" organizations to raise tax-deductible contributions for partisan political activity, and shows how both § 501(c)(3) and § 501(c)(4) organizations have been formed to circumvent federal and state election law contribution limits and disclosure requirements. The following selection of well publicized cases highlights the problem:

- In the early 1990's, a Republican Party political action committee (GOPAC) developed a voter outreach project to disseminate the Republican Party's agenda. The project included a course (Renewing American Civilization) taught at two small colleges by then House Speaker Newt Gingrich. The thrust of Gingrich's message was that the United States should replace its current welfare state with an "opportunity society." With funding provided first by the Abraham Lincoln Opportunity Fund and later by the Progress and Freedom Foundation, both § 501(c)(3) organizations with close ties to GOPAC, the course was broadcast nationwide by satellite television. The House Ethics Committee charged Rep. Gingrich with violating House rules by failing to seek the advice of tax counsel regarding the use of tax-deductible funds for political purposes and for providing inaccurate information to the committee when he said the course was completely nonpartisan. See In the Matter of Representative Newt Gingrich, H.Rep. No. 105–1, 105th Cong., 1st Sess. (1997). After a lengthy investigation, Rep. Gingrich accepted a reprimand and fine without conceding any violation of tax law. Three years later, the IRS ruled that the Progress and Freedom Foundation had not engaged in any impermissible political activity by sponsoring Gingrich's course. Calling it a "close case," the Service concluded that the course was nonpartisan and that the private interests of Mr. Gingrich and the Republican Party were served only incidentally by the use of tax-exempt funds. It noted that the content of the course "was educational and never favored or opposed a candidate for public office." Tech. Adv. Mem. (unreleased) (Dec. 1, 1998), reprinted in 23 Exempt Org. Tax Rev. 512 (1999). At the same time, however, the IRS revoked the tax-exempt status of the Abraham Lincoln Opportunity Fund, but in 2003 changed its mind and retroactively restored ALOF's exemption.

- In 1995, Senate majority leader Bob Dole and House speaker Newt Gingrich created the National Commission for the Study of Economic Growth and Tax Reform, directing it to make recommendations on federal tax reform and appointing Jack Kemp as chairman. After applying for § 501(c)(3) status and soliciting tax-deductible contributions, the Commission held public hearings and issued a report recommending repeal of the federal income tax and its replacement with a "flat" tax. The IRS denied tax-exempt status to the Commission, and the denial was upheld by the courts. See Fund for the Study of Economic Growth and Tax Reform v. Internal Revenue Service, 161 F.3d 755 (D.C.Cir.1998).

- According to news reports and Congressional testimony, during the 1996 Presidential campaign White House officials advised a prospective donor that he could receive favorable tax benefits and anonymity by making large gifts to several § 501(c)(3) organizations that were friendly to the reelection of President Clinton. Included in the list of potential donees was Vote Now '96, an allegedly nonpartisan organization formed to increase voter turnout in areas that typically vote Democratic. Jill Abramson, Tax–Exempt Group's Links to Democrats are Examined, N.Y. Times, Sept. 20, 1997, at A1.

- A principal activity of the Christian Coalition, which was founded by Rev. Pat Robertson and sought tax-exempt status under § 501(c)(4), was the distribution of millions of voter guides in churches on the Sunday before major elections. The guides evidenced a bias for or against particular political candidates and legislative proposals. After a lengthy examination, the IRS ruled in 1999 that the Coalition did not qualify under § 501(c)(4). The Coalition promptly reorganized, forming both a § 527 political organization for election-related activities and an affiliated § 501(c)(4) organization to engage in education and advocacy. See Carolyn D. Wright, Christian Coalition Fails to Obtain Tax–Exempt Status, 25 Exempt Org. Tax Rev. 9 (1999).

- Some legal expenses for the sexual harassment suit brought in the late 1990's by Paula Jones against President Clinton reportedly were paid from funds contributed by wealthy donors to § 501(c)(3) organizations. James Bennet, Group Aiding Paula Jones Alleges Tax Intimidation, N.Y. Times, Jan. 3, 1998, at A7.

- In May 1999, a gala was held at the John F. Kennedy Center in Washington to raise millions of dollars for the Trent Lott Leadership Institute at the University of Mississippi, founded to honor and support the philosophy of Senator Majority Leader Trent Lott. Among major contributors were Lockheed Martin Corporation and MCI Worldcom, both of which were lobbying Congress on matters affecting their business. John Mintz & Helen Dewar, Firms Invest in Philanthropy of Self–Interest, Wash. Post, May 8, 1999, at A03.

The use of § 501(c)(3) organizations to disguise political activity is generally motivated by several overlapping goals: (1) to give donors a charitable deduction for what otherwise would be a nondeductible political contribution; (2) to avoid federal election law limitations on "hard money" contributions and other regulation by the Federal Election Commission; and (3) to avoid the public disclosure of political contributions mandated by federal and state election laws. In more aggressive scenarios, a § 501(c)(4) organization is used; although no tax deduction is allowed, contributions and expenditures are not subject to the federal election law disclosure requirements.

It should be apparent by now that the law in this area is hopelessly murky and thus ripe for exploitation. Newt Gingrich's satellite seminar is a good example of how experts disagree on the scope of the political campaign limitations in § 501(c)(3). The special counsel to the House Ethics Committee, after consultation with experienced tax counsel, concluded that Gingrich's course conferred more than insubstantial benefits to GOPAC and Republican candidates. Although conceding that the content of the course was more ideological than politically partisan, the report pointed to Gingrich's political motivation and the role of Republican Party officials and financial support of GOPAC. Other tax specialists argued, however, that the course was no different than the strategically timed issue advocacy conducted by a broad range of § 501(c)(3) organizations. See, e.g., Leslie Lenkowsky, Newt Tax Violation Hard to Find, and Terrence Scanlon & William J. Lehrfeld, And Don't Believe the Partisan Spin, Wall St. J., Jan. 3, 1997, at A8. Should resolution of the Gingrich matter have turned on subjective factors, such as partisan intent? It appears that the IRS's decision to clear the organizations that funded the Gingrich seminar of any tax law violations was based on its evaluation of the content of the course rather than the underlying political motives.

The use of nonprofit organizations to circumvent federal election and tax laws raises policy issues that have yet to be addressed in any comprehensive manner. Both § 501(c)(3) and § 501(c)(4) organizations are increasingly serving as conduits for huge sums of money that support issue advocacy, voter registration activities, and other grassroots political activity, much of which is hard to distinguish from the express advocacy regulated by the Federal Election Commission or the electioneering prohibited by § 501(c)(3).

For Further Reading. Robert Paul Meier, The Darker Side of Nonprofits: When Charities and Social Welfare Groups Become Political Slush Funds, 147 U.Pa.L.Rev. 971 (1999); Brent Coverdale, A New Look at Campaign Finance Reform: Regulation of Nonprofit Organizations Through the Tax Code, 46 U.Kans.L.Rev. 155 (1997).

NOTE: § 527 POLITICAL ORGANIZATIONS—REPORTING AND DISCLOSURE REQUIREMENTS

As discussed earlier in this chapter, § 527 provides a form of limited tax-exempt status for "political organizations," a broad category embracing political parties, political action committees, and funds created to support candidates and causes at the federal, state and local levels. Section 527 organizations are exempt from federal income tax on contributions they receive, and donors are exempt from federal gift tax on their contributions. Net investment income of political organizations is taxable at the highest corporate income tax rate (currently 35 percent).

Unlike § 501(c) tax-exempt organizations, § 527 organizations have not been required to apply for their special exempt status or file annual Form 990 information returns. Section 527 organizations with taxable investment income must file an annual return (Form 1120–POL), which reports taxable income and deductible expenses but does not include information on the specific activities of the organization or the sources of its revenue. Tax returns filed by political organizations have not been subject to the public disclosure and inspection requirements applicable to § 501(c) organizations, and § 527 organizations that seek to influence federal campaigns by engaging in "express advocacy" must disclose their activities and contributors to the Federal Election Commission. "Express advocacy," however, generally is limited to advocating the election or defeat of specific candidates for federal elective office by using the magic words "vote for" and "vote against," and thus many § 527 groups need not file reports with the FEC.

Beginning in the mid–1990's, political activists, exploiting inconsistencies in the tax and election laws, began to form § 527 organizations to funnel vast sums of unregulated "soft money" to benefit political causes and candidates through activities such as voter education and issue advocacy. The principal goals of these new stealth vehicles were to: (1) avoid public disclosure of their activities and sources of income under both tax and election laws, (2) avoid federal election law limits on contributions, and (3) allow donors to contribute unlimited amounts without the gift tax exposure that they would face if the contributions were made to a § 501(c)(4) advocacy organization.

The emergence of § 527 organizations was the subject of some scholarly discourse during the 1998 election campaign. See, e.g., Frances R. Hill, Probing the Limits of Section 527 to Design a New Campaign Finance Vehicle, 22 Exempt Org. Tax Rev. 205 (1998). But it was not until the 2000 primary season that campaign finance reformers and the media began to expose these secretive groups as the loophole of choice for raising and spending unlimited amounts on political activity without any tax liability or disclosure obligation. See John M. Broder & Raymond Bonner, A Political Voice, Without Strings, N.Y. Times, March 29, 2000, at A1. Among the specific groups exposed by journalists and reform advocates were Republicans for Clean Air, which broadcast advertisements critical of Senator John McCain before the March 2000 Super Tuesday primaries and reportedly was financed by a major supporter of George W. Bush; Citizens for a Republican Congress, which was said to raise and spend $35 million on ads in competitive Congressional races; Business Leaders for Sensible Priorities, created by the founders of Ben and Jerry's ice cream to argue for less spending on weapons and more on education; and Peace Action, an antiwar group which raised $250,000 in seed money from a few anonymous donors to influence the policy debate in a handful of contested Congressional races. Id.; see also Common Cause, Under the Radar: The Attack of the "Stealth PACs" on Our Nation's Elections, available at <www.commoncause.org/publications/utr/>.

In June, 2000, Congress responded by passing narrowly tailored legislation (H.R. 4762, 106th Cong., 2d Sess.) to require § 527 organizations to disclose their activities and donors. Among other things, the legislation requires § 527 groups to: (1) notify the IRS within 24 hours of their creation; (2) file periodic reports (more frequently in election years) of their activities and expenses; and (3) disclose their contributors unless they are already required to do so with the Federal Election Commission. Sanctions, including monetary penalties and possible loss of exempt status, will be imposed for noncompliance. Expanded disclosure rules require the IRS to make all this information available to the public on the Internet. As a result of subsequent legislation enacted in 2002, some entities operating solely at the state or local level are exempted from the disclosure rules.

Although this legislation will bring the most secretive § 527 groups into the sunshine, it does not extend to other tax-exempt organizations often used for political advocacy, such as § 501(c)(4) social welfare organizations, § 501(c)(5) labor unions, and § 501(c)(6) trade associations. Conservative opponents of campaign finance reform failed in their attempt to extend the expanded disclosure requirements (e.g., publicly identifying donors) to § 501(c) organizations. They were targeting liberal advocacy groups and labor unions that also receive soft money for political purposes but, unlike § 527 groups, may not exist solely to engage in political campaign activities. With the passage of legislation limited to § 527 groups, secret soft money was expected to migrate back to § 501(c)(4) organizations and, possibly, even to § 501(c)(3) charities (under the guise of "education") and for-profit entities.

For Further Reading. Frances R. Hill, Softer Money: Exempt Organizations and Campaign Finance, 32 Exempt Org. Tax Rev. 27 (2001); Martin A. Sullivan, More Disclosure From 501(c)'s: Poison Pill or Good Policy, 29 Exempt Org. Tax Rev. 10 (2000).

PROBLEMS

1. Seniors Association for Gerontological Endeavor ("SAGE") is a nonprofit § 501(c)(3) membership organization organized and operated to study the problems of the aging population and assist senior citizens. SAGE's board of trustees recently decided that the organization should become more politically active. During the current year, the board passed a resolution expressing SAGE's support for proposed legislation that would prohibit certain types of age discrimination in employment, and it developed an intense interest in legislation affecting social security benefits and medicare. From time to time, SAGE also has taken positions on local issues affecting senior citizens.

SAGE's expenditures for the current year, apart from certain additional items to be described separately below, were as follows:

Construction of New Building	$ 500,000
Administrative Expenses	200,000
Straight Line Depreciation	100,000
Services to Elderly	600,000
Fundraising Expenses	100,000
TOTAL	$1,500,000

In addition, SAGE spent the following amounts in the current year for the purposes indicated:

(1) $150,000 for a special "Public Impact Program" designed to promote SAGE's advocacy priorities by outlining the organization's position on age discrimination and social security legislation and urging members to contact their legislators to encourage them to vote in accordance with SAGE's position on specific pending bills.

(2) $50,000 to finance a study of the problems of aged workers and to publish a report of the findings for distribution to all members of Congress and other interested persons, including foundations, think tanks, and academic institutions.

(3) $50,000 to distribute literature to the general public in California urging support for local measures to ban age discrimination. The literature advocated SAGE's position on several pending bills and did not specifically request recipients to contact their legislators, but it identified the members of the key legislative committees that are considering the bills.

(4) $50,000 to publish a newsletter; 25% of the space in the newsletter was devoted to reporting on the prospects for passage of legislation supported by SAGE and identifying the main sponsors of the bills in the legislature; the other 75% of the newsletter reported on SAGE's many social service activities. The newsletter was mailed to SAGE's 20,000 members and to 5,000 paid subscribers (mostly libraries). Minimum SAGE membership dues are $50 per year and 80% of SAGE's members paid the minimum.

(5) $15,000 for billboards near major urban freeways with a picture of an active and healthy older American and the inscription "Don't Put Mom and Dad Out to Pasture: Eliminate Age Discrimination," and, in smaller print, "No on 39." No other mention was made on the billboard of any pending legislation, nor was SAGE identified as the proponent of the message, but the billboards were displayed for the three weeks preceding the vote on a statewide ballot measure (known as Proposition 39) relating to age discrimination.

(6) $10,000 for full-page newspaper advertisements opposing a bill pending in Congress to reduce Medicare benefits for older Americans. The ads were strategically published during the two weeks preceding the vote but did not include any specific "call to action" or mention any legislators by name.

(7) $25,000 for mailings, radio advertisements, web site postings, e-mails, faxes, and other activities opposing a nominee for the United States Supreme Court whom SAGE regarded as an opponent of the employment rights of older Americans.

Consider the following questions:

(a) Assuming SAGE does not make the § 501(h) election, has it jeopardized its tax-exempt status as a result of its activities in the current year?

(b) If SAGE made an effective election under § 501(h), would it be liable for any excise taxes under § 4911 in the current year? If so, how might SAGE have restructured its activities to avoid excise tax exposure?

(c) If SAGE made an effective § 501(h) election and all of its expenses described above remained constant for the four years following the current year, would it jeopardize its exempt status? Will making the election serve as a "red flag" to the Internal Revenue Service, prompting a likely audit of SAGE's lobbying activity?

(d) If SAGE makes the § 501(h) election, will that complicate its ability to receive grants from private foundations?

(e) If SAGE loses its exempt status because of excessive lobbying, could it then become a § 501(c)(4) organization? Would it be subject to any other sanctions? Could SAGE promise never to lobby again and reapply for § 501(c)(3) status?

2. Consider whether the proposed activities described below would jeopardize SAGE's tax-exempt status under § 501(c)(3) or subject SAGE to excise tax liability under § 4955. If you are concerned about any of the activities, please advise SAGE how it might make changes to minimize any tax risks.

(a) SAGE formally endorses a candidate for Governor who is sympathetic to the organization's positions.

(b) The chair of SAGE's board of directors signs a statement formally opposing the reelection of an incumbent Senator who is not sympathetic to SAGE's positions.

(c) SAGE publishes a voter's guide, listing state legislators and informing SAGE's members how each legislator voted on subjects of interest to SAGE. Is the timing of this publication relevant?

(d) SAGE allows some of its members and employees to use the organization's telephones and copying machine to encourage people to attend a rally on behalf of a candidate who is widely known to share SAGE's position on issues affecting older Americans.

(e) SAGE conducts a voter registration project urging senior citizens to register to vote and assisting them to obtain absentee ballots.

(f) SAGE sponsors candidates' forums in legislative districts with large senior citizen populations. All major party candidates are invited to participate (minor party candidates are excluded). SAGE selects the moderator and controls the format.

(g) SAGE rents its mailing lists to political candidates who favor SAGE's position on public issues.

(h) SAGE establishes and supports a political action committee for the purpose of influencing specific campaigns.

(i) SAGE forms a § 501(c)(4) affiliate, known as SAGE Advocates, which engages in lobbying, and it also establishes the SAGE Political Action Committee to support candidates for public office. SAGE makes grants to its § 501(c)(4) affiliate for lobbying purposes, but the affiliate otherwise raises its own funds. SAGE makes its mailing list available to the PAC without charge.

3. The Institute for Public Policy is a "think tank" founded by Lute Stormy, a prominent member of the U.S. House of Representatives, to

conduct research on economics and public policy. The Institute relies on gifts and grants from individuals, corporations, and foundations, most of whom also have directly and indirectly supported Rep. Stormy's political agenda. Funds are used to publish reports, conduct symposia, and sponsor a weekly closed-circuit television seminar taught by Rep. Stormy. The Institute is not directly involved in any partisan political activity, but its activities and emphasis are consistent with the legislative initiatives of interest to Rep. Stormy and supported by his political party. Does the Institute qualify for tax-exempt status under § 501(c)(3)? Should it?

G. SOCIAL WELFARE ORGANIZATIONS

Section 501(c)(4) broadly confers exempt status on "civic leagues or organizations not organized for profit but operated exclusively for the promotion of social welfare." Social welfare organizations are another breed of public service organization, but they differ markedly from § 501(c)(3) charities in their inability to receive tax-deductible contributions as well as their ability to engage in substantial lobbying activities.

To qualify under § 501(c)(4), an organization must be primarily engaged in promoting in some way the common good and general welfare of the community, such as "by bringing about civic betterments and social improvements." Treas. Reg. § 1.501(c)(4)–1(a)(2). "Social welfare" is thus quite similar to "charitable," the major difference being that attempts to influence legislation are not considered "charitable" purposes but are nonetheless regarded as compatible with the promotion of social welfare. This distinction is rather odd in view of the fact that promotion of social welfare is an example of a charitable purpose. See Treas. Reg. § 1.501(c)(3)–1(d)(2).

As previously discussed, "social welfare" does not include direct or indirect participation in political campaigns on behalf of candidates for public office; social activities for the benefit, pleasure or recreation of members; or the conduct of a business with the general public in a manner similar to commercial operations. Treas. Reg. § 1.501(c)(4)–1(a)(2)(ii). Lobbying is permissible, of course, but illegal activities such as civil disobedience are regarded as an impermissible means of promoting social welfare.

As a practical matter, apart from its role as the Code section of choice for advocacy groups, § 501(c)(4) has become the "dumping ground" for organizations that fail to make the grade as a § 501(c)(3) charity but nonetheless provide a substantial public benefit. For example, the Service routinely has granted § 501(c)(4) status to nonprofit health maintenance organizations that fail to provide the requisite "community benefit" required by § 501(c)(3). Certain neighborhood groups and homeowners associations that enforce restrictive covenants and preserve open space for a limited geographical area have been held to qualify under § 501(c)(4) even though they would not benefit a sufficiently broad charitable class to fit within § 501(c)(3). See, e.g., Rev. Rul. 75–286, 1975–2 C.B. 210 (organization engaged in preserving and beautifying a city block); Rancho Santa Fe Association v. United States, 589 F.Supp. 54 (S.D.Cal.1984) (homeowner's association).

H. PROCEDURAL ISSUES

1. JUDICIAL DETERMINATIONS OF EXEMPT STATUS

Internal Revenue Code: § 7428.

Prior to 1976, organizations that failed to obtain a favorable exemption ruling from the Internal Revenue Service or were threatened with revocation of their exemption had great difficulty obtaining judicial review of the IRS's adverse determination. As a practical matter, the organization's only legal recourse was to await a monetary controversy involving an income or employment tax deficiency or a disallowed charitable contributions deduction for one of its donors. This could take years and, in the meantime, the organization would be unable to assure its contributors that their gifts were tax-deductible. Attempts by organizations to obtain more immediate relief were rebuffed by the courts on procedural grounds. See, e.g., Bob Jones University v. Simon, 416 U.S. 725, 94 S.Ct. 2038 (1974) and Alexander v. "Americans United" Inc., 416 U.S. 752, 94 S.Ct. 2053 (1974), where the Supreme Court held that declaratory judgment actions were precluded by the Anti–Injunction Act (I.R.C. § 7421(a)) and other procedural barriers.

In *Bob Jones University v. Simon*, the Supreme Court invited Congress to remove these obstacles to dispute resolution:

> Congress has imposed an especially harsh regime on 501(c)(3) organizations threatened with loss of tax-exempt status and with withdrawal of advance assurance of deductibility of contributions. * * * The degree of bureaucratic control that, practically speaking, has been placed in the Service over those in [the position of Bob Jones University] is susceptible to abuse, regardless of how conscientiously the Service may attempt to carry out its responsibilities. Specific treatment of not-for-profit organizations to allow them to seek preenforcement review may well merit consideration.

416 U.S. at 749–750. In a dissenting opinion in the companion *Americans United* case, Justice Blackmun lamented the "unfettered power of the Commissioner [of Internal Revenue]" to issue exemption rulings in a system that did not provide a meaningful avenue for judicial review. 416 U.S. at 774.

Prompted by these Supreme Court decisions and the lobbying efforts of the exempt organizations community, Congress enacted § 7428 as part of the Tax Reform Act of 1976. Under that section, organizations may bring declaratory judgment actions in the Tax Court, the U.S. Court of Federal Claims and the Federal District Court for the District of Columbia in actual controversies relating to qualification for exemption under § 501(c)(3), classification as a private foundation or private operating foundation, and eligibility to receive tax-deductible charitable contributions under § 170(c)(2). This remedy enables aggrieved organizations to proceed directly to court from an administrative controversy without having to await a specific monetary dispute with the IRS.

Section 7428 confers jurisdiction only in cases where there is an "actual controversy," such as when the organization has obtained an adverse notice of final determination, or the IRS has failed to make a timely determination on the organization's initial or continuing exemption qualification or private foundation classification. There is no jurisdiction to review rulings regarding the effect of a proposed transaction, at least where no formal steps have been taken by the IRS to revoke the organization's exemption. The Tax Court has liberally interpreted the "actual controversy" requirement. It has accepted jurisdiction, for example, in cases where the IRS granted a favorable advance nonprivate foundation ruling to an organization based on its public support while simultaneously declining to issue a definitive ruling that the organization qualified as a church. See, e.g., Foundation of Human Understanding v. Commissioner, 88 T.C. 1341 (1987). An actual controversy existed in these cases because church classification is more favorable.

Congress did not intend that § 7428 would supplant the normal administrative process. Section 7428(b)(2) thus requires that a declaratory judgment is not available unless an organization demonstrates to the court that it has exhausted all administrative remedies available to it within the IRS. Specifically, it must show that it filed a substantially completed Form 1023, timely submitted all additional information requested to complete the application, and exhausted all administrative appeals within the Service, including appeals to the National Office. If the Service fails to take action on an application, the organization is not deemed to have satisfied the exhaustion requirement until the expiration of 270 days from the date on which a substantially completed application or request for determination has been filed. I.R.C. § 7428(b)(2). If the organization hears nothing from the IRS after the 270–day period expires, it ordinarily may bring an action under § 7428, unless it has been uncooperative at the administrative level—for example, by failing to supply requested information.

Most § 7428 declaratory judgment actions are brought in the Tax Court, which has promulgated a detailed set of rules to govern this procedure. See Tax Court Rule 210 et seq. The Tax Court has expressed a strong preference for disposing of declaratory judgment actions on the basis of the administrative record. Tax Court Rule 217. Additional evidence will be admitted only for good cause shown, and the court rarely finds good cause. See, e.g., Houston Lawyer Referral Service v. Commissioner, 69 T.C. 570 (1978). The administrative record includes the organization's request for a determination (the Form 1023 on an original application), all documents submitted in connection with the request, all protests and related papers submitted during the appeals process, any relevant tax and informational returns, the adverse IRS notice, and the organization's charter and other enabling documents.

Contributions Made During Judicial Proceedings. If a previously exempt organization loses its status as an eligible charitable donee under § 170(c)(2) and challenges the IRS's action in a § 7428 proceeding, contributions made to the organization while the litigation is pending will continue to be deductible up to the date of the final judicial determination even though the court ultimately upholds the IRS's position. I.R.C. § 7428(c)(1). This relief is only available where the IRS has revoked an organization's exempt status and not where an initial application is denied. The notice of revocation must have been formally published by the IRS, and the organization must have initiated a timely declaratory judgment proceeding.

To obtain relief under § 7428(c), a contributor must have clean hands. Thus, a deduction will not be allowed if the contribution was made by an individual who was responsible for the activities that were the basis for the revocation of exemption. I.R.C. § 7428(c)(3). In addition, the maximum amount of contributions to an organization made by any one individual (husbands and wives are treated as one contributor for this purpose) that are allowed during the entire pendency of the litigation may not exceed $1,000. I.R.C. § 7428(c)(2).

2. INFORMATION RETURN AND DISCLOSURE REQUIREMENTS

Internal Revenue Code: §§ 6033(a), (b); 6104(a)(1)(A) & (C), (b), (d); 6652(c).

Treasury Regulations: § 301.6104(d)–3, –4, –5.

Information Returns. Section 6033(a) generally requires exempt organizations to file an annual informational return that reports all receipts and disbursements and any other information that the Service may require by forms or regulations. Most exempt organizations must file Form 990; organizations with gross receipts of less than $100,000 and total assets of less than $250,000 may file its short-form equivalent, Form 990–EZ. Private foundations must file Form 990–PF. Any exempt organization that is liable for the unrelated business income tax (see Chapter 5, infra) also must file Form 990–T and, if it expects its tax for the year to exceed $500, the organization must make quarterly payments of estimated tax on unrelated business income. Complete copies of recent versions of Form 990, Form 990–PF and their instructions are reproduced in the Statutes, Regulations and Forms Supplement.

Mandatory exemptions from the filing requirement are granted to churches, their integrated auxiliaries, and conventions or associations of churches; certain organizations that are not private foundations and have annual gross receipts that normally do not exceed $5,000; and religious orders, with respect to their exclusively religious activities. I.R.C. § 6033(a)(2)(A). The Service also has discretionary authority under § 6033(a)(2)(B) to grant filing exemptions, and it has done so by increasing the annual gross receipts threshold from $5,000 to $25,000 for all exempt organizations that are not private foundations and for most state and U.S. governmental organizations, and for certain organizations affiliated with governmental units, such as state colleges and universities, and public libraries and museums. I.R.S. Ann. 82–88, 1982–25 I.R.B 23; I.R.S. Ann. 94–117, 1994–39 I.R.B. 19. In 1997, the Service proposed raising the Form 990 filing threshold to reduce the paperwork burden on small nonprofits. The proposal was dropped after objections of state regulators and others who argued that small nonprofits often need the annual reporting requirement to ensure proper recordkeeping and to provide a medium for public scrutiny of their activities.

Disclosure and Inspection. In a continuing effort to make exempt organizations more accountable, Congress has enacted and expanded a variety of public disclosure and inspection requirements that apply to both the Internal Revenue Service and the organization.

The IRS must make available for public inspection at the National Office and the appropriate field offices all Forms 990 and approved applications for exemption. I.R.C. § 6104(a)(1)(A), (b). Trade secrets and information that would adversely affect national defense are exempt from disclosure, as is the schedule of major contributors that is required as an attachment to the Form 990. I.R.C. § 6104(a)(1)(D), (b).

All organizations exempt from tax under § 501(c) or § 501(d) must make available for inspection their application for exemption, along with all supporting documents, and their annual informational returns for the most recent three years. The documents must be made available at the organization's principal office during regular business hours and at regional or district offices with three or more employees. I.R.C. 6104(d)(1)(A). Exempt organizations also must provide copies of their exemption applications and Form 990's for the three most recent tax years to anyone who requests them. The copies ordinarily must be provided immediately if the request is made in person or within 30 days if in writing. I.R.C. § 6104(d)(1)(B). Under prior law, requestors only could inspect these documents at the organization's office and had no right to demand copies. If a copy is requested, the organization may charge only for reasonable copying and mailing costs. For the many details on the obligation to make copies, see Treas. Reg. § 301.6104(d)–3(d).

Organizations that make their documents widely available, such as by posting an exact and downloadable reproduction on a World Wide Web site, are not required to provide photocopies, but they still must make returns available for inspection at their offices. I.R.C. § 6104(d)(4); Treas. Reg. § 301.6104(d)–4. In response to this opportunity, more organizations are exploring use of the Internet to meet the "widely available" standard.

In expanding the disclosure requirements, Congress was mindful that some highly visible charities would be the target of harassment campaigns, and it authorized the IRS to issue regulations providing relief in appropriate cases. I.R.C. § 6104(d)(4). The regulations define a harassment campaign as "a single coordinated effort to disrupt the operations of a tax-exempt organization, rather than to collect information about the organization." Treas. Reg. § 301.6104(d)–5(b). Examples of harassment include a sudden increase in the number of request for copies, an extraordinary number of requests made through form letters, or numerous requests containing language "hostile" to the organization. Id. If a sudden increase in requests for copies is the result of national media attention and there is no evidence that the requests are part of an organized campaign to disrupt the organization's operations, no relief will be available even if the requests place a burden on the organization. Treas. Reg. § 301.6104(d)–5(f) Example 1. The regulations elaborate on the procedures an organization must follow to establish that it is the victim of a harassment campaign. Treas. Reg. § 301.6104(d)–5(d).

Form 990's of public charities and private foundations are now widely accessible on the Internet. One of the best sources is the Guidestar Directory of Philanthropic Research, Inc., which posts information on most § 501(c)(3) organizations on its Web page (http://www.guidestar.org). The greater availability of financial data provides a wealth of information to journalists and scholars and is bound to result in a heightened level of scrutiny of the nonprofit sector.

Joint Committee on Taxation Disclosure Study. Despite periodic reforms, calls for still greater public disclosure by exempt organizations continue to reverberate from Washington. A study published in January, 2000, by the Joint Committee on Taxation staff proposes that nearly every piece of paper exchanged between tax-exempt organizations and the IRS be made public with very few redactions. See Joint Committee on Taxation, Study of Present–Law Taxpayer Confidentiality and Disclosure Provisions as Required by Section 3802 of the Internal Revenue Service Restructuring and Reform Act of 1998, Volume II: Study of Disclosure Provisions Relating to Tax–Exempt Organizations (JCS–1–00), Jan. 28, 2000, reprinted in 27 Exempt Org. Tax Rev. 567 (2000).

The JCT proposals are based on the premise that the public interest is best served by greater disclosure of information relating to tax-exempt organizations. Full disclosure, in the JCT's view, generally outweighs privacy concerns by enabling the general public to provide greater oversight of exempt organization activities, and it assists donors in determining whether organizations should be supported and whether changes in the law are needed.

Among the more significant recommendations in the JCT study are:

- Form 990 should be revised to provide more information and should be designed to be more understandable by the public.
- All written determinations and background file documents involving tax-exempt organizations should be disclosed without redaction.
- The results of IRS audits and all settlement agreements with tax-exempt organizations should be disclosed.
- Applications for exempt status and supporting documents should be disclosed when the application is submitted.

- Exempt organizations should be required to disclose not just their basic Form 990 information return but also any Form 990–T reporting unrelated business taxable income, and any UBIT returns filed by affiliates.
- Whether or not they make the § 501(h) election, all public charities should be required to provide a general description of their lobbying activities, expenses for self-defense lobbying and expenses for non-partisan study, analysis or research if a "call to action" is included.
- The IRS should have more authority to share audit information with nontax state officials and agencies that have jurisdiction over exempt organizations.

Although the Joint Committee's proposals have received scattered applause from a handful of long-time disclosure proponents, they have been met with an icy reception from the mainstream nonprofit sector. Among the concerns expressed are that the mandatory disclosure of audit files and closing agreements would have a chilling effect on the settlement process; releasing unredacted private rulings and background documents would invade the privacy of exempt organizations, curtail the letter ruling process, and contribute to the dissemination of misleading and inaccurate information by the press; and the disclosure of UBIT returns will give an unfair advantage to an exempt organization's privately owned for-profit competitors. Critics also have questioned whether it is good policy to enlist the general public as vigilantes, as opposed to the IRS and other governmental agencies, to oversee the activities of the nonprofit sector. For a thoughtful critique of the JCT study, see Peter L. Faber, The Joint Committee Staff Disclosure Recommendations: What They Mean for Exempt Organizations, 28 Exempt Org. Tax Rev. 31 (2000).

Penalties. An exempt organization that fails to file a required information return is subject to a penalty of $20 per day, with a maximum penalty of the lesser of $10,000 or 5 percent of gross receipts. I.R.C. § 6652(c)(1)(A). The penalties are increased for organizations with gross receipts exceeding $1 million. Id. Penalties also may be imposed on the managers of the organization who knowingly fail to file a return or provide information after a request from the Service. I.R.C. § 6652(c)(1)(B). Responsible officials of an exempt organization who refuse to provide copies of documents or allow public inspection are subject to penalties of $10 for each day the failure continues up to a maximum of $5,000 per return. I.R.C. § 6652(c)(1)(C), (D). Additional penalties may be imposed for willful noncompliance or fraud. I.R.C. §§ 6685; 7207.

3. STANDING BY THIRD PARTIES TO CHALLENGE EXEMPT STATUS

Some of the most provocative substantive tax exemption controversies have never been decided on the merits because of insurmountable procedural obstacles. The courts generally are only willing to entertain controversies involving adverse determinations by the Internal Revenue Service with respect to particular organizations. Interested third parties whose taxes are not directly affected by the Service's actions or administrative policy have met with little success in their attempts to challenge tax benefits granted to others.

But it is not for lack of trying. As discussed earlier in this chapter, low-income individuals and their representatives were held to lack standing to challenge the Service's shift from a "relief of the poor" to a "community benefit" exemption standard for hospitals. Simon v. Eastern Kentucky Welfare Rights Organization, 426 U.S. 26, 96 S.Ct. 1917 (1976). The Supreme Court held in Allen v. Wright, 468 U.S. 737, 104 S.Ct. 3315 (1984) that parents of black children attending public schools lacked standing to challenge the Service's procedures for denying exemption to racially discriminatory private schools. A group of for-profit travel agents failed in their attempt to enjoin the Service from granting exempt status on non-profit organizations that offered travel tour packages to their members at below-market prices. American Society of Travel Agents v. Blumenthal, 566 F.2d 145 (D.C.Cir.1977), cert. denied, 435 U.S. 947, 98 S.Ct. 1533 (1978). Dr. Lenora Fulani, a minor party candidate for President in 1988, met with mixed success in challenging the tax-exempt status of organizations that failed to include her in nationally televised candidates' debates. The Second Circuit held that Dr. Fulani did have standing to challenge the exempt status of the League of Women Voters Education Fund for failing to include her in Presidential primary debate, but dismissed her case on the merits. Fulani v. League of Women Voters Educ. Fund, 882 F.2d 621 (2d Cir.1989). But Dr. Fulani was denied standing in a related case brought to challenge the exempt status of the Commission on Presidential Debates, which sponsored later debates after the League of Women Voters temporarily receded from the process. Fulani v. Brady, 935 F.2d 1324 (D.C.Cir.1991). And she failed again in a challenge to her exclusion from a 1992 Democratic party debate co-sponsored by the League of Women Voters Education Fund and Cable News Network. Fulani v. Bentsen, 35 F.3d 49 (2d Cir.1994)(Dr. Fulani suffered no injury traceable to League's conduct because CNN still would have prevented her from participating; prior Second Circuit decision distinguished on ground that League was sole sponsor of 1988 debates and its action caused actual harm to Dr. Fulani's campaign).

The obstacles faced by third parties are well summarized in the *Abortion Rights Mobilization* case, which follows. The suit was brought by a consortium of abortion rights groups, civil liberties organizations, clergy, and individual taxpayers acting in various capacities, all seeking to challenge the tax exemption of the Roman Catholic Church, which the plaintiffs alleged was engaging in political activities on abortion issues that were inconsistent with the Church's tax-exempt status. The litigation took a circuitous route, but it ended predictably when the Second Circuit denied standing, and the Supreme Court later denied certiorari.

In re United States Catholic Conference

United States Court of Appeals, Second Circuit, 1989.
885 F.2d 1020, cert. denied 495 U.S. 918, 110 S.Ct. 1946.

■ CARDAMONE, CIRCUIT JUDGE:

This appeal is before us for a second time. The Supreme Court has remanded the matter for a determination of whether the United States

District Court for the Southern District of New York (Carter, J.) had subject matter jurisdiction over the instant lawsuit that challenged the tax-exempt status of the Roman Catholic Church in the United States. The specific issue is whether the plaintiffs, who initiated this litigation to force the government to revoke the Catholic Church's tax-exempt status, satisfy the standing requirements of Article III. For the reasons discussed below, we hold that they do not.

I.   Background

A.   The Plaintiffs

Plaintiffs in this appeal are united in their commitment to a woman's right to obtain a legal abortion. This suit was instituted originally by 20 individuals and nine organizations. We assume familiarity with their specific identities as set forth in the district court's opinion. See Abortion Rights Mobilization, Inc. v. Regan, 544 F.Supp. 471, 474 (S.D.N.Y.1982). Some are no longer parties. Of the nine original organizational plaintiffs, for example, the district court held that five abortion clinics lacked standing and dismissed their complaints. The district court did grant standing to an organization called the Women's Center for Reproductive Health, because it is run by a Presbyterian minister who is also a plaintiff. We discuss the Women's Center with the clergy plaintiffs. The three remaining organizations are Abortions Rights Mobilization Inc. (ARM), the National Women's Health Network Inc. (NWHN) and the Long Island National Organization For Women–Nassau, Inc. (Nassau–NOW). The former two are pro-choice organizations that are non-profit, tax-exempt organizations as defined in § 501(c)(3) of the Internal Revenue Code (Code). 26 U.S.C.A. § 501(c)(3). Nassau–NOW shares ARM's and NWHN's objectives, but is exempt from taxes under § 501(c)(4), rather than (c)(3).

Twenty individual plaintiffs also bring this suit. They include Protestant ministers and Jewish rabbis. In contrast to the views of the Catholic Church, they believe that abortion is morally permissible under some circumstances. Many of the individual plaintiffs donate money to or serve as directors of the organizational plaintiffs. The individual plaintiffs vote and pay taxes.

B.   Pertinent Statutory Framework

Before reciting the history of the prior legal proceedings, an understanding of two pertinent sections of the Code is necessary, as a preliminary matter, to appreciate what is at stake in this litigation. As noted, the Catholic Church and organizational plaintiffs ARM and NWHN are tax-exempt under § 501(c)(3). That section states that qualifying religious or civic public interest organizations need not pay federal taxes. The trade-off for the benefit of this exemption is that no substantial part of the organization's activities may include "carrying on * * * propaganda, or otherwise attempting, to influence legislation * * * [nor may it] participate in, or intervene in (including the publishing or distributing of statements), any political campaign on behalf of any candidate for public office." Thus, the quid pro quo for § 501(c)(3) tax-exemption is a restraint on an organization's right to try to influence the political process. This limitation has been held constitutional. Section 501(c)(3) status is advantageous to the supporters of an organization as well as the organization itself because § 170 of the Code permits donors to § 501(c)(3) entities to claim a deduction for their contributions. This deduction gives the donor an economic incentive to contribute. For example, a donor in a 28 percent tax bracket actually pays only 72 cents for every dollar contributed to the Catholic Church because of the deduction. Consequently, organizations like the Church and plaintiffs ARM and NWHN have enhanced fundraising abilities because they are able to offer donors the lure of the § 170 deduction.

C.   The Dispute

The plaintiffs object to the Internal Revenue Service's (IRS) enforcement—or, as they describe it, nonenforcement—of § 501(c)(3)'s prohibition on lobbying and campaigning. Because this appeal arises from a motion to dismiss for want of standing, we must accept all of the plaintiffs' allegations as true and draw all inferences in their favor.

Plaintiffs first allege that the Catholic Church is repeatedly violating § 501(c)(3)'s prohibition on campaigning in order to promote the tenet that abortion is immoral and should therefore be made unlawful. For instance, plaintiffs point to the Church's "Pastoral Plan for Pro–Life Activities," which they claim is an organized effort to mobilize the entire Church in a "three-fold educational, pastoral and political effort to outlaw abortions in the United States." The complaint also alleges that through its priests and officials, the Catholic Church has endorsed or supported pro-life political candidates and opposed pro-choice candidates by publishing articles in its bulletins, attacking or endorsing candidates from the pulpit, distributing partisan letters to parishioners, and urging its members to donate to and sign petitions of "right to life" committees and candidates. Similarly, plaintiffs contend that the Church has contributed substantial sums of money to "right to life" and other political groups which have, directly or indirectly, supported the political candidacies for public office of persons favoring anti-abortion legislation.

Plaintiffs' other major contention is that the IRS knows about the Catholic Church's alleged political activities and has ignored these activities rather than either revoking the Church's tax-exempt status under § 501(c)(3), or not renewing the Church's annual exemption. They therefore assert that the government has "exempted the Roman Catholic Church from the strictures of the law and from the government's enforcement efforts," and that the IRS treats the Catholic Church more favorably than those organizations that are pro-choice. Yet plaintiffs do not allege that the IRS has penalized them for violating the Code; in fact, they assert that they have not violated § 501(c)(3) by electioneering, and do not intend to. Rather, they want the government to enforce the strictures of

§ 501(c)(3) against the Catholic Church. Thus, plaintiffs do not complain about their own tax status—their challenge is directed solely against the Catholic Church's exemption.

The complaint and affidavits also spell out the asserted harms plaintiffs suffer as a result of the Church's and the IRS' acts. Because the nature of the claimed harm is an integral component in standing analysis, it will be fully analyzed in the later discussion of standing.

D. Prior Proceedings

In the amended complaint of January 30, 1981 the plaintiffs sued then-Secretary of the Treasury Donald T. Regan, then-Commissioner of Internal Revenue Roscoe L. Egger, Jr., the United States Catholic Conference, Inc., and the National Conference of Catholic Bishops (the latter two collectively the Catholic Church or the Church). The Catholic Church is composed of approximately 30,000 parishes, schools and other entities in the United States whose tax-exemption is granted collectively in a group ruling. The plaintiffs sought declarations that the defendants had violated both § 501(c)(3) of the Code and the Establishment Clause of the First Amendment to the United States Constitution. They also sought injunctive relief to compel the government to enforce the Code and Constitution by revoking the Church's group tax-exemption, to collect the resulting back taxes, and to notify contributors to the Catholic Church that they may no longer claim their donations as deductions on their income tax returns.

The defendants moved to dismiss the complaint on several grounds, including standing. In 1982 the district court held that the clergy and voter plaintiffs had standing, see Abortion Rights Mobilization, Inc. v. Regan, 544 F.Supp. at 491 (S.D.N.Y.1982)(ARM I), and three years later—following a rehearing to consider the impact of the Supreme Court's subsequent decision in Allen v. Wright, 468 U.S. 737, 104 S.Ct. 3315, 82 L.Ed.2d 556 (1984)—reiterated this holding. See Abortion Rights Mobilization, Inc. v. Regan, 603 F.Supp. 970 (S.D.N.Y.1985)(ARM II). The defendant Catholic Church's motion to dismiss it as a defendant in the suit was granted. See ARM I, 544 F.Supp. at 487. As the litigation progressed, plaintiffs requested substantial discovery from the Church as a non-party witness. Upon its refusal to comply, the Catholic Church was held in contempt in May, 1986. See 110 F.R.D. 337 (S.D.N.Y.1986).

On appeal, the Church argued that it was improperly held in contempt in the action because the district court lacked subject matter jurisdiction over the case before it due to plaintiffs' lack of standing. We held that, as a non-party contemnor, the Church itself lacked standing to challenge plaintiffs' standing in the main suit, and that as a non-party witness it could only challenge a contempt finding when the district court was without even colorable jurisdiction. Hence, we had no occasion to reach the underlying question now before us of plaintiffs' standing. See In re United States Catholic Conference, 824 F.2d 156 (2d Cir.1987). The Supreme Court reversed, holding that a non-party witness held in contempt had standing to challenge the district court's subject matter jurisdiction. United States

Catholic Conference v. Abortion Rights Mobilization, Inc., 487 U.S. 72, 108 S.Ct. 2268, 101 L.Ed.2d 69 (1988). Upon remand from the Supreme Court, we now must analyze whether plaintiffs have standing to sue the government for conferring tax-exempt status to the Catholic Church.

II. DISCUSSION

A. Standing Analysis

In Allen v. Wright, 468 U.S. 737, 104 S.Ct. 3315, 82 L.Ed.2d 556 (1984), the Supreme Court made clear that standing is not merely a prudential inquiry into whether a court should exercise jurisdiction, but is rooted in Article III's "case" or "controversy" requirement and reflects separation of powers principles. Thus, when a plaintiff lacks standing to bring suit, a court has no subject matter jurisdiction over the case. Deceptively simple to state, standing entails a complex three-pronged inquiry. First, plaintiffs must show that they have suffered an injury in fact that is both concrete in nature and particularized to them. Second, the injury must be fairly traceable to defendants' conduct. Third, the injury must be redressable by removal of defendants' conduct. The second and third prongs-traceability and redressability—often dovetail; essentially, both seek a causal nexus between the plaintiff's injury and the defendant's assertedly unlawful act. To establish standing, a plaintiff must plead all three elements.

B. Application to This Case

Standing in the case at hand is alleged under a number of theories that require a general overview in order to match the category of plaintiff to the asserted basis for standing. The prior proceedings have distilled standing theories that view plaintiffs as clergy, voters, and taxpayers. We first address those theories relied upon by the district court in finding that plaintiffs had standing, and then consider a fourth theory—competitive advocate standing—not explicitly addressed below.

1. Clergy Standing

Clergy plaintiffs claim standing under the Establishment Clause of the First Amendment. That clause provides: "Congress shall make no law respecting an establishment of religion * * *." The amended complaint alleges that "The failure of the government defendants to apply the Code equally to the * * * Church is in effect a subsidy of the Church's efforts to further its religious aims in the political sphere, a subsidy not granted to law-abiding * * * plaintiffs, who hold contrary religious beliefs." This constitutes an unconstitutional establishment of religion. Without reaching the merits, the district court held that the clergy plaintiffs and the religiously affiliated Women's Center for Reproductive Health (collectively clergy plaintiffs) had standing under the Establishment Clause because they were "denigrated by government favoritism to a different theology." Thus, it concluded that the IRS "hampers and frustrates these plaintiffs' ministries." The appropriateness of this holding turns on whether the stigma plaintiffs allege is a cognizable injury in fact. We think the district court erred by translating plaintiffs' genuine motivation to sue into a personalized injury in fact.

It is true that an injury claimed to derive from a violation of the Establishment Clause can be spiritual in nature. Nonetheless, the injury must be particularized to the individuals who sue. * * * The Establishment Clause does not exempt clergy or lay persons from Article III's standing requirements. Here, the clergy plaintiffs have not been injured in a sufficiently personal way to distinguish themselves from other citizens who are generally aggrieved by a claimed constitutional violation. For that reason, they lack standing.

Both Valley Forge and Allen v. Wright support this conclusion. In Valley Forge, an organization dedicated to ensuring separation of church and state sued the Secretary of Health, Education and Welfare for conveying, without consideration, surplus government property to a religiously affiliated college. The Valley Forge plaintiffs made the same argument as the instant clergy plaintiffs—that by conferring a benefit to a third party that was a religious entity, the government had violated the Establishment Clause. The Supreme Court considered whether plaintiffs had been injured as taxpayers—a subject we address below—and as "separationists" bent on policing the Establishment Clause. Accepting the sincerity of plaintiffs' ire at the alleged violation of the Establishment Clause, it held that such distress was not cognizable unless plaintiffs could "identify any personal injury suffered by them as a consequence of the alleged constitutional error * * *." It was not enough to point to an assertedly illegal benefit flowing to a third party that happened to be a religious entity. Absent a particularized injury, plaintiffs could not maintain suit.

In Allen v. Wright, the plaintiffs were parents of black children who attended public schools. They sued the IRS, asserting that it was duty-bound to deny tax-exempt status to racially discriminatory private schools, and its failure to do so impaired desegregation of the public school system. In Allen v. Wright, as here, plaintiffs' complaint centered on the tax-exempt status of a third party. The parents asserted two injuries, only one of which is pertinent to this case—harm from the fact that the government was giving financial assistance to private discriminatory schools. The Supreme Court held that the parents did not have standing and made several points on the injury in fact requirement.[9] Relying on Schlesinger v. Reservists Committee to Stop the War, 418 U.S. 208, 94 S.Ct. 2925, 41 L.Ed.2d 706 (1974)(Reservists), the Court stated that "an asserted right to have the Government act in accordance with law is not sufficient, standing alone, to confer jurisdiction on a federal court." Parents did not derive standing by claiming "stigmatizing injury" caused by racial discrimination because "such injury accords a basis for standing only to 'those persons who are personally denied equal treatment' by the challenged discriminato-

---

9. The Supreme Court held that although diminished opportunity for plaintiffs' children to obtain desegregated public education stated a cognizable injury in fact, the complaint failed to satisfy the standing requirement of traceability and redressability.

ry conduct." The Supreme Court then emphasized that when the injury asserted is an "abstract stigmatic injury," the requirement that a plaintiff be personally injured takes on heightened importance.

The clergy plaintiffs' complaint in the instant case suffers from the same defects as the parents' complaint in Allen v. Wright and the separationists' complaint in *Valley Forge*: The primary injury of which they complain is their discomfiture at watching the government allegedly fail to enforce the law with respect to a third party. As in *Valley Forge*, the instant plaintiffs state that defendants have violated their "sincere and deeply held belief in the separation of church and state." This injury can hardly be called personalized to the clergy plaintiffs. They can point to no illegal government conduct directly affecting their own ministries. Thus, the injury the clergy complain of could be asserted by any member of the public who disagrees with the views of the Catholic Church and the IRS in granting it a tax exemption.

Similarly, because the clergy have neither been personally denied equal treatment under the law nor in any way prosecuted by the IRS, their self-perceived "stigma" does not amount to a particularized injury in fact. To hold the clergy plaintiffs' injury cognizable would turn the federal court into "a forum in which to air * * * generalized grievances about the conduct of government." Hence, the clergy's complaint collapses into that of an offended bystander, insufficient to meet Article III's standing requirements. A mere "claim that the Government has violated the Establishment Clause does not provide [plaintiffs] a special license to roam the country in search of governmental wrongdoing and to reveal their discoveries in federal court."

This analysis is unchanged by the fact that the plaintiffs in this case are clergy. To rebut the argument that they have not suffered a particularized injury, these plaintiffs contend that what distinguishes them from the ordinary member of the public who takes issue with the Church and IRS is that they are members of the clergy. In our view, the holding in *Valley Forge* and its progeny would have been the same even had those plaintiffs been members of the clergy rather than Americans United For Separation of Church and State because "standing is not measured by the intensity of the litigant's interest or the fervor of his advocacy."

Moreover, granting standing to clergy qua clergy raises several troubling issues. Granting standing to the instant ministers and rabbis on the basis that they were directly and personally injured by the IRS' actions solely on account of their stature within their churches and synagogues would require us to give greater credence to the clergy's beliefs than the beliefs of their parishioners. Thus, to hold that a religious leader is more qualified to bring an Article III "case" or "controversy" than a member of his congregation seemingly entails an impermissible invasion into a church's or a synagogue's internal hierarchy and its autonomy. And, as the district court correctly noted, the Establishment Clause protects religions from secular interference.

Second, granting standing to enforce the Establishment Clause to clergy qua clergy might itself violate the same clause by constituting governmental favoritism of religion over non-religion. The Supreme Court has made clear that the Establishment Clause prohibits not only government endorsement of a given sect, but also forbids the government from generally favoring religion over secularism. Thus, the strength, intensity, or knowledge of one's religious beliefs obviously is not a criterion upon which to confer standing because such a rule would deny to non-believers the same benefits of maintaining suit. As Thomas Jefferson stated in his much quoted metaphor, the Establishment Clause was designed to build "a wall of separation between church and State." Plaintiffs point to no authority for a standing doctrine exception to this principle of separation between church and state. To read plaintiffs' complaint as stating a particularized injury simply because it is dressed in clerical garb would only weaken the foundation of Jefferson's metaphorical wall. As a consequence, stripped of the assertedly unique status of clergy, plaintiffs' injury is as generalized as that asserted in *Valley Forge* and Allen v. Wright, and their complaint must be similarly dismissed.

2. Taxpayer Standing

The taxpayer plaintiffs allege that they are "harmed because the government's subsidy of the * * * Church's illegal political activities is the equivalent of a government expenditure to establish a religion in violation of the First Amendment to the Constitution." In essence, they complain that not only is the government making illegal use of tax revenue, but also that they, as taxpayers, are forced to contribute to the government's asserted subsidy of the Catholic Church.

We set forth briefly the requirements for taxpayer standing, which are somewhat more specific than those for standing generally. The basic rule is that taxpayers do not have standing to challenge how the federal government spends tax revenue. See Frothingham v. Mellon, 262 U.S. 447, 488, 43 S.Ct. 597, 601, 67 L.Ed. 1078 (1923). In Flast v. Cohen, the Supreme Court created an exception to the *Frothingham* rule, holding that taxpayer standing is available to challenge Establishment Clause violations when the allegedly unconstitutional action was authorized by Congress under the taxing and spending clause of Art. I, § 8. Subsequent cases made clear the narrowness of *Flast's* exception to *Frothingham's* rule against taxpayer standing.

Then *Valley Forge*—handed down in the interim between the filing of the instant complaint and the motion to dismiss—caused some commentators to conclude that the taxpayer standing theory was virtually a dead letter. Hence, plaintiffs abandoned this theory in the district court. Following the Supreme Court's more recent decision in Bowen v. Kendrick, 108 S.Ct. 2562, 101 L.Ed.2d 520 (1988)(holding that taxpayers had standing to challenge the application of the Adolescent Family Life Act (AFLA)), plaintiffs renew before us their taxpayer standing arguments. In light of the protracted history of this litigation, it is appropriate to consider this issue now, if for no other reason than to prevent a third appeal.

The Supreme Court in *Kendrick* distinguished *Valley Forge* by emphasizing that in the latter case the decision by the executive agency to dispose of the surplus federal property—though made pursuant to a federal statute—was not a challenge to Congress' taxing and spending power because the statute's mandate derived from the property clause of Art. IV, § 3. In so doing, the Supreme Court clarified that taxpayer standing exists to challenge the executive branch's administration of a taxing and spending statute; the challenge need not be directed exclusively at Congress. But *Kendrick's* discussion of *Valley Forge* does not breathe new life into plaintiff's moribund taxpayer standing theory, as shall become evident.

In *Kendrick*, it was Congress that decided how the AFLA funds were to be spent, and the executive branch, in administering the statute, was merely carrying out Congress' scheme. See id. at 2580 ("[A]ppellees' claims call into question how the funds authorized by Congress are being disbursed pursuant to the AFLA's statutory mandate."). Thus, the Supreme Court held that taxpayers had standing to challenge whether Congress' decision under the taxing and spending clause had violated the limits imposed by the Establishment Clause.

Plaintiffs in the instant case do not challenge Congress' exercise of its taxing and spending power as embodied in § 501(c)(3) of the Code; they do not contend that the Code favors the Church. The Supreme Court, as noted, has already upheld the constitutionality of that section. Instead, they argue that the IRS, in allegedly closing its eyes to violations by the Church, is disregarding the Code's mandate and the Constitution. The complaint centers on an alleged decision made solely by the executive branch that in plaintiffs' view directly contravenes Congress' aim. The instant case is therefore distinguishable from *Kendrick*. In that case, there was "a sufficient nexus between the taxpayer's standing as a taxpayer and the congressional exercise of taxing and spending power, notwithstanding the role the Secretary plays in administering the statute." Here, there is no nexus between plaintiffs' allegations and Congress' exercise of its taxing and spending power. Hence, *Kendrick* does not alter the requirements of taxpayer standing to allow the instant plaintiffs to challenge how the IRS administers the Code. Consequently, plaintiffs fall within *Frothingham's* general rule denying taxpayer standing.

3.   Voter Standing

The voter plaintiffs allege that they are injured because the IRS' refusal to revoke the Catholic Church's tax-exempt status "impairs and diminishes plaintiffs' right to vote." When it granted plaintiffs' "voter standing," the district court relied on Baker v. Carr, 369 U.S. 186, 82 S.Ct. 691, 7 L.Ed.2d 663 (1962). The district court's appellation of this theory as "voter standing" as applied to this case is a misnomer; plaintiffs' asserted basis for standing has nothing to do with voting. In Baker v. Carr, the Supreme Court held that disadvantaged voters had standing to challenge

Tennessee's apportionment plan. The wrong that plaintiffs sought to vindicate in Baker v. Carr and in those cases that construed it was the dilution of their vote relative to the vote of other citizens of the same state—a direct, cognizable injury.

The Supreme Court has also held that disadvantaged voters may challenge an apportionment plan that is gerrymandered, that is, a plan whose voting district lines are drawn to reduce or eliminate the voting leverage of a given group of voters. It is undisputed that the instant plaintiffs do not allege that their vote has been diluted or that voting district lines have been gerrymandered to favor the Church or that anyone has "stuffed the ballot box" with votes for Church-backed candidates or that anyone has been prevented from voting. In short, plaintiffs here do not allege the particularized and objectively ascertainable injury in fact that sustained standing in the malapportionment cases. We therefore hold that Baker v. Carr and its progeny are inapposite and provide no basis for granting voter standing to these plaintiffs.

4.   Competitive Advocate Standing

We consider finally whether the plaintiffs may have standing under a theory that the district court did not explicitly consider, yet which derives from its discussion of "voter standing." This theory may be labeled as "Competitive Advocate Standing." It is addressed separately from voter standing for analytical clarity and because it presents a closer question.

Plaintiffs allege that they are injured "by the unequal enforcement of the Code by [the government] * * * which constitutes an illegal, unfair and unconstitutional distortion of the political process by the government * * *." They argue that their chance of electoral success is diminished because they do not receive the advantage that the Church receives from the government's asserted non-enforcement of the Code: The ability to campaign without losing tax-exemption under § 501(c)(3), and the ability nonetheless to offer their contributors a tax deduction for donating. "In the inherently competitive political arena an advantage granted to one competitor automatically constitutes a hardship to the others." The essence of this charge is that the IRS' non-enforcement of the Code creates an uneven playing field, tilted to favor the Catholic Church. The fatal flaw in the argument is that plaintiffs are not players in that arena or on that field.

The Supreme Court has found cognizable injuries to economic competitors. Implicit in the reasoning of those opinions is a requirement that in order to establish an injury as a competitor a plaintiff must show that he personally competes in the same arena with the party to whom the government has bestowed the assertedly illegal benefit. Only then does the plaintiff satisfy the rule that he was personally disadvantaged.

The economic competitor cases arose as banks diversified their functions, moved into new business areas, and became competitors of firms that had traditionally provided those services into which the banks sought to expand. The Supreme Court held that the organizations from which the banks sought to take away business—that is, with whom they sought to compete—had standing to challenge the banks' expansion into non-banking functions.

In each of these cases the banks obtained governmental rulings allowing them to compete on the same "playing field" as the plaintiffs. The results would have been different had the travel agents, for example, sought to complain about the bank's incursion into the data processing business. It is equally inappropriate to allow the present plaintiffs to challenge the IRS' treatment of the Church, since by their own admission they choose not to match the Church's alleged electioneering with their own. Therefore, they are not competitors.

* * * Plaintiffs' allegations of a political system biased against them by illegal government conduct are troubling. But, just as the Supreme Court has refused to recognize an Establishment Clause exception to standing doctrine, so must the requirements of Article III be applied with equal rigor to cases concerning participation in the political process. There is "no principled basis on which to create a hierarchy of constitutional values or a complementary 'sliding scale' of standing which might permit respondents to invoke the judicial power of the United States."

Like the claims of the clergy plaintiffs, the instant competitor claims lack particularized injury in fact. By asserting that an advantage to one competitor adversely handicaps the others, plaintiffs have not pleaded that they were personally denied equal treatment. They concede their tax status was correctly assessed by the IRS. Moreover, the complaint indicates that no plaintiff is currently a political candidate for public office. Plainly, the whole point of this lawsuit is plaintiffs' contention that it is illegal for the Catholic Church as a § 501(c)(3) recipient to participate actively in the political process. And, recognizing that potential illegality and the value of their own exemptions under §§ 501(c)(3) and (c)(4), plaintiffs state that they have refused to engage in electioneering to counter the Church's pro-life stance. Partly as a result of this self-imposed restraint, plaintiffs chose not to compete.

It may be argued that to qualify as competitor advocates plaintiffs need not go so far as to run for office or lobby; rather, they may simply advocate the pro-choice cause and stop short of supporting candidates. But that argument fails to answer the nagging question of why these individuals and organizations are then the appropriate parties to call a halt to the alleged wrongdoing. It is obvious that plaintiffs express their pro-choice views strongly and articulately. Yet such strongly held beliefs are not a substitute for injury in fact.

A further problem with recognizing a competitor advocate theory of standing in the present case is that it would be difficult to deny standing to any person who simply expressed an opinion contrary to that of the Catholic Church. Affording standing on that basis would lack a limiting principle, and would effectively give standing to any spectator who supported a given side in public political debate. Cf. J.H. Ely, Democracy and Distrust 103 (1980)(courts should intervene when the playing field is tilted, not when they think the wrong side has scored). This is precisely the problem the Supreme Court addressed in *Valley Forge* when it denied standing to plaintiffs who sued as taxpayers and citizens. We think that result would have been the same even had they called themselves "competitor advocates"—as proponents of a theory of the Establishment Clause different than that held by the government or the college that received the government benefit.

* * *

We do not foreclose the possibility that political competitors may state a cognizable injury; instead, we simply hold that the theory cannot be sustained here. Putting out into the stormy sea of this litigation, it is prudent to closely hug the shores of the pleaded facts and established law, and not venture out any further than we must. As a consequence, because we hold that plaintiffs have not pleaded a direct injury in fact, we need not decide whether the two other standing requirements of traceability and redressability have been met.

III. CONCLUSION

It could be argued that if no one among this diverse group of plaintiffs has standing to challenge the IRS' application of 501(c)(3) to the Church, then perhaps no one could ever have standing to raise this issue. But such is irrelevant for determining whether the "case" or "controversy" requirement has been satisfied. As the Supreme Court noted, that "view would convert standing into a requirement that must be observed only when satisfied." Moreover, the lack of a plaintiff to litigate an issue may suggest that the matter is more appropriately dealt with by Congress and the political process.

Without reaching or deciding whether there are prudential reasons not to exercise jurisdiction, we conclude that plaintiffs have not met the Article III minimum requirements for standing. In sum, we hold that none of the plaintiffs has standing, that the district court therefore did not have subject matter jurisdiction, that the contempt adjudication must be vacated, and that the order denying the motion to dismiss the case must be reversed and the plaintiffs' complaint dismissed.

Reversed and complaint dismissed.

■ Jon O. Newman, Circuit Judge, dissenting:

The Court today rules that tax-exempt organizations advocating the right to an abortion have no standing to challenge the actions of the Internal Revenue Service in failing to enforce against the Catholic Church the statutory requirement that prohibits tax-exempt organizations from "participat[ing] in, or interven[ing] in * * * any political campaign * * *." 26 U.S.C.A. § 501(c)(3)(1982). The Court reaches this result by concluding that the "pro-choice" organizations are not competitors of the Catholic Church in the political arena on the subject of abortion. Because I believe that conclusion is incorrect—indeed, that it is contrary to the undisputed facts of the abortion controversy in Twentieth Century America, I respectfully dissent.

The majority begins its analysis by labeling the issue that divides us as "Competitive Advocate Standing." I think that is an admirable designation. The majority then recognizes that standing is frequently recognized for those who seek to challenge the lawfulness of governmental actions that inure to the benefit of their competitors. The majority then concludes that the competitor standing rule of these cases does not apply to the tax-exempt "pro-choice" organizations that are plaintiffs in this suit because they do not intervene in political campaigns.

That conclusion rests on a needlessly narrow view of both the realities of American political life and the contours of the doctrine of competitive advocate standing. To be an advocate in the political arena in this country, organizations and their members need not intervene in the campaign of any particular candidate for public office. Political advocacy takes many forms. To promote their views, a few people run for office. Others support candidates. But most Americans advocate their side of public issues by standing up for what they believe through a wide range of activities beyond the formal processes of electoral politics. They speak to their friends and neighbors; they participate in community activities; they devote their time, their energy, and sometimes their money to their causes. All who engage in these activities are competing in the arena of public advocacy with those who choose to support differing points of view by various forms of advocacy, including backing like-minded political candidates.

The competition necessary to confer competitor standing need not be in the identical activity of one's economic or philosophical opponent. When the Texas Monthly challenged the tax exemption of religious magazines, it did not wish to compete in the precise activity of publishing religious magazines. It wished to compete in the broader field of magazine publishing, and it was accorded standing to challenge the economic benefit of a tax exemption conferred upon the competitive publisher of a religious magazine. So here, plaintiffs Abortion Rights Mobilization, Inc. and the National Women's Health Network, Inc. do not wish to compete in the political arena with the Catholic Church on the issue of abortion by the precise technique of supporting candidates for public office. Instead, they have chosen to compete in advocating their side of the abortion issue by distributing information on the availability of abortions, by speaking, writing, and marching, and by championing in countless other ways the cause of abortion rights.

If the words are to have any meaning at all, these plaintiffs are indisputably "competitive advocates" of the Catholic Church on the issue of abortion.

The majority reckons with the argument that the plaintiff 501(c)(3) organizations might qualify as competitive advocates if they "simply advocate the pro-choice cause and stop short of supporting candidates." The argument is dismissed by the assertion that the strongly held beliefs of the plaintiffs "are not a substitute for injury in fact." Of course, they are not. But no one claims they are. The injury in fact is the competitive disadvantage the plaintiff organizations are obliged to endure when, accepting at this stage the allegations of the complaint, the Catholic Church is permitted to violate the tax laws by using tax-exempt donations to support the "anti-abortion" side of the national debate through contributions to like-minded political candidates, while the plaintiff organizations must confine their advocacy of the "pro-choice" side to those insubstantial lobbying activities that the tax laws permit. If the allegations of the complaint are true, and plaintiffs seek only the opportunity to prove them, the plaintiff organizations are seriously injured both in the eyes of the law and in the real world of political advocacy by the significant advantage currently enjoyed by the Catholic Church as a result of governmental action that violates the tax laws. According to the complaint, the Catholic Church is using its tax-free funds to support political candidates who oppose the right to an abortion; the plaintiff 501(c)(3) organizations, abiding by the terms of the tax law, are limited to other forms of advocacy. Both sides are competing in the arena of public advocacy, but governmental action is tolerating a law violation that enables one side to promote its cause with a significant technique denied to the other side. That should be sufficient to permit the claim of law violation to be litigated.

In the majority's view, the plaintiff 501(c)(3) organizations and the Catholic Church are not competitors in the arena of public advocacy on the issue of abortion because the plaintiffs "choose not to match the Church's alleged electioneering with their own." That makes it sound as if the plaintiff 501(c)(3) organizations have simply decided as a matter of personal preference that they do not wish to match the Church's alleged electioneering. But the decision to forgo electioneering is not a matter of personal preference, it is obedience to a requirement of an act of Congress. I fail to understand why any person or organization, seeking to challenge a violation of federal law, should be denied access to a federal court for the reason that it is obeying the law.

The majority further supports its rejection of competitive advocate standing by expressing concern that such standing would be too extensive, that "it would be difficult to deny standing to any person who simply expressed an opinion contrary to that of the Catholic Church." I think this fear is groundless. The competition that most clearly creates standing in this case is not between the Catholic Church and every citizen who holds a contrary view on the issue of abortion. Such citizens are not limited by a statute that they are prepared to prove the Catholic Church is violating to their disadvantage. The competition is between those tax-exempt organizations that are abiding by the limitations of section 501(c)(3) in their advocacy on the abortion issue and the Catholic Church, which is violating these limitations in the advocacy of its point of view on the issue. Whether an individual citizen could challenge the Church's tax exemption on the theory that its unlawful support of political candidates is aided by tax-free donations unavailable to the ordinary citizen is a question far beyond the narrow issue we are required to decide in this case. A standing doctrine is entirely within manageable bounds when it recognizes the competition among organizations all of which are subject to the same statutory restraint and permits the law-abiding competitors to challenge the governmental action that enables one organization to violate that restraint to the detriment of the others.

A variant of the competitive advocate doctrine should also confer standing on the one plaintiff that is a 501(c)(4) organization, Long Island National Organization for Women–Nassau ("Nassau NOW"). This plaintiff, by qualifying as a tax-exempt organization under section 501(c)(4), is not subject to the restraints on political activity imposed by section 501(c)(3), but is obliged to solicit donations that are not tax deductible to the donors. Like the 501(c)(3) plaintiffs, Nassau–NOW competes with the Catholic Church in the arena of public advocacy on the issue of abortion, but does so under a competitive disadvantage that is different from the one existing between the Church and the 501(c)(3) plaintiffs. The latter may not support political candidates at all, while the Church, though barred from doing so, provides such support (according to the complaint). Nassau–NOW may engage in political activity but only with donations that cost its donors 100 cents on the dollar, while the Church supports political candidates with tax deductible donations that cost its donors only 67, 72, or 85 cents for every dollar contributed, depending on whether they are in the 33%, 28% or 15% bracket. That competitive disadvantage, arising from what plaintiffs are prepared to prove is a violation of law, is also sufficient to confer standing on the entity that is disadvantaged.

Whether any of the other plaintiffs have standing presents issues that I need not decide. We are asked to adjudicate the lawfulness of a contempt citation for refusing lawful discovery requests that has been challenged solely on the ground that the District Court lacks jurisdiction over the subject matter of the complaint. If any one plaintiff has standing to bring this lawsuit, the jurisdiction of the District Court to require compliance with the discovery requests is established, and the contempt judgment against the recalcitrant witnesses should be affirmed. For these reasons, I respectfully dissent.

ON REHEARING

PER CURIAM:

Appellants have sought rehearing, alleging inconsistency between the opinion in this case and an opinion issued by another panel in Fulani v. League of Women Voters Education Fund, 882 F.2d 621 (2d Cir.1989). In *Fulani*, competitor standing was accorded to a political candidate to challenge her exclusion from a televised debate in which her political rivals were invited to participate. A majority of the panel concluded that she suffered sufficient injury to establish standing. In the present case, though this panel is divided as to whether the plaintiffs are sufficiently in competition with the Catholic Church to have suffered injury that confers standing, we are in agreement that the competition in *Fulani* is more direct and immediate than that shown here.

The petition for rehearing is denied.

NOTES AND QUESTIONS

1. *Postscript.* The day after the Supreme Court denied certiorari in *Abortion Rights Mobilization*, the organization's president, Lawrence Lader, was quoted as saying, "I just don't know how you'd come up with a plaintiff to fit the Court's definition of standing." Linda Greenhouse, Supreme Court Roundup; Suit on Church Tax Status and Abortion Fails, N.Y. Times, May 1, 1990, at A18. Was Mr. Lader correct? Could the plaintiffs have positioned themselves more effectively to obtain standing? What if they had sought tax exemption under § 501(c)(3) for an organization that stated unequivocally that it intended to engage in political activities on abortion issues? Once the application was denied, could the organization survive a standing challenge in its suit to enjoin the Catholic Church's exemption?

2. *For Further Reading.* Note, Standing to Challenge Tax–Exempt Status: The Second Circuit's Competitive Political Advocate Theory, 58 Fordham L. Rev. 723 (1990); Note, Voter Standing: A New Means for Third Parties to Challenge the Tax–Exempt Status of Nonprofit Organizations?, 16 Hastings Const. L.Q. 453 (1989).

CHAPTER 3

PRIVATE FOUNDATIONS

A. THE UNIVERSE OF PRIVATE FOUNDATIONS

1. INTRODUCTION

Within the extended family of § 501(c)(3) organizations, the Internal Revenue Code makes a critical distinction between private foundations and public charities. Defined generically, a philanthropic foundation is a fund of private wealth established for charitable purposes, usually in perpetuity. Most private foundations receive their support from a single individual or corporate source or from a close-knit family group. The principal function of most private foundations is to make grants to other nonprofit organizations, qualified individuals and government entities, but some "operating foundations" directly engage in one or more active programs, such as research or the operation of a museum. Public charities, by contrast, derive most of their support from government or the general public, or the nature of their activities makes them accountable to a broader constituency.

Although the warning signs came earlier, it was not until 1969 that Congress singled out private foundations for special regulation through the federal tax system. The intricate regime examined in this chapter was the result of a growing impression, supported more by anecdotal evidence than thoughtful empirical analysis, that private foundations were more susceptible to abuse than public charities. Congress has since relaxed some of the punishment inflicted on foundations and is shifting its scrutiny to public charities. But the Code continues to police private foundations more strictly. The details will follow, but it is useful at the outset to summarize the principal badges of tax inferiority.

First, the income tax treatment of gifts to private foundations is less favorable than for contributions to public charities. For purposes of determining an individual donor's income tax charitable deduction, stricter percentage limitations are imposed on charitable gifts to private grantmaking foundations. Gifts of cash and ordinary income property to public charities are subject to an annual limitation of 50 percent of adjusted gross income with a five-year carryover of any excess. I.R.C. § 170(b)(1)(A). This limitation is reduced to 30 percent for gifts to private foundations. I.R.C. § 170(b)(1)(B). Gifts of long-term capital gain property (such as stock and most real estate) to private foundations are subject to a 20 percent limitation, as compared to the 30 percent cap applicable to public charities. I.R.C. § 170(b)(1)(B), (D). Income tax deductions for gifts of appreciated capital gain property (other than certain publicly traded stock) to private foundations are limited to the donor's basis in the contributed property, while taxpayers generally may deduct the full fair market value if capital gain property is donated to a public charity. I.R.C. § 170(e)(1)(B)(ii). These distinctions, however, are limited to the income tax charitable deduction. Gifts and bequests to both public charities and private foundations are fully deductible for federal gift and estate tax purposes. I.R.C. §§ 2055; 2522.

Second, private foundations are subject to a two percent excise tax on their net investment income, including capital gains. I.R.C. § 4940. The rate can be reduced to one percent for foundations that increase their charitable distributions by a specified amount. I.R.C. § 4940(e).

Third, private foundations are subject to federal excise tax sanctions if they engage in various proscribed activities such as self-dealing, excessive ownership of business interests, and investments that jeopardize the organization's charitable purposes, or if they make certain forbidden "taxable expenditures." Penalties also may be imposed if a private foundation fails to meet income distribution requirements designed to ensure that the foundation's charitable payout is reasonably related to its endowment. I.R.C. §§ 4941–4945.

Finally, private foundations must comply with reporting and disclosure requirements that can be somewhat more onerous than those imposed on public charities. I.R.C. §§ 6033(c); 6104.

This chapter has been designed to accommodate coverage of the tax rules regulating private foundations in varying degrees of depth. For those seeking a user-friendly overview, this introductory section should suffice. It describes the universe of private foundations in the United States, summarizes the history and policy of the current regulatory scheme, provides an overview of the technical definition of a private foundation and the scope of the private foundation excise taxes, and explores the positive role that family foundations play in the world of philanthropy. Subsequent sections flesh out the details and consider planning strategies that enable an organization to avoid private foundation status or, if that is not feasible, to navigate successfully around the tax landmines.

The excerpt below, from a handbook published by The Council on Foundations,[1] sets the stage.

David F. Freeman, The Handbook on Private Foundations

The Council on Foundations 1–9 (Rev. Ed. 1991).

The roots of philanthropy go back many centuries, and philanthropic organizations exist in many cultures. In the United States, many individuals, families, and corporations have chosen a unique institution—the pri-

---

1. The Council on Foundations, based in Washington, D.C., is a membership organization of foundations established in 1949 to promote and strengthen organized philanthropy. It includes most major U.S. foundations among its members.

vate foundation—to carry out their charitable purposes. Private foundations have played an important role in U.S. history during the last century, supporting cultural, social, and scientific efforts. Today private foundations continue to offer donors special opportunities to contribute to society.

Foundations in the United States date from the end of the nineteenth century, when Andrew Carnegie, John D. Rockefeller, and other industrial pioneers first chose to apply parts of their accumulating wealth to public purposes. Unlike European philanthropists, they faced no governmental restrictions or royal monopoly on good works. The corporate form or organization had served them well in the pursuit of profits, and with no public agency to direct them otherwise, they found it only natural to adapt this same device for the achievement of charitable objectives.

These early foundations were created years before income or estate taxes became a serious factor. Moreover, when federal progressive taxes on income, gifts, and estates were enacted in the second decade of the twentieth century, our government not only exempted charities, including foundations, from income tax but also encouraged gifts to them by permitting donors' deductions from income, gift, and estate taxes. Such deductions, intended as incentives, had their desired effect. By the late 1980s, nearly 30,000 foundations were in existence, many of them created by persons of relatively modest wealth.

A prime reason for this remarkable growth has been the foundation's flexibility. It can respond to a need as it becomes manifest, it can strike out quickly in new directions, and it can give in a single community or throughout the world.

WHAT'S IN A NAME?

In 1957, two foundation watchers offered very different answers to the question, "What is a foundation?" To author Dwight MacDonald, the Ford Foundation was "a large body of money completely surrounded by people who want some."

F. Emerson Andrews developed the second definition in his pioneering work, *Philanthropic Foundations*. It was adopted by the Foundation Center in the first edition of *The Foundation Directory* and remains substantially unchanged today:

A foundation [is] a nongovernmental, nonprofit organization with its own funds (usually from a single source, either an individual, family, or corporation) and program managed by its own trustees and directors, which was established to maintain or aid educational, social, charitable, religious, or other activities serving the common welfare primarily by making grants to other nonprofit organizations.

This definition readily fits most of the organizations described in this handbook. But the grantmaking field has no copyright on the name *foundation*—it is a term freely used by noncharitable organizations, by other kinds of charities, and increasingly by governmental agencies. Ordinarily this confusion is a minor irritant, making problems for statisticians of the field, but not a matter of general concern. On occasion, however, the public image of grantmaking foundations is damaged by the publicized misdeeds or excesses of other types of "foundations" not subject to the same close regulation.

Just as the presence of the word foundation in an organization's name is no guarantee that it is a grantmaking foundation, the reverse is also true. The titles of many foundations contain synonyms such as *fund, endowment*, and *trust*, but others use no such identifier at all—for example, Carnegie Corporation of New York; DeRance, Inc.; and Research Corporation.

* * *

TYPES OF FOUNDATIONS

The *independent foundation* is a term coined by the Council on Foundations to distinguish private foundations established and funded by individuals or families from those funded by corporations. Also adopted for statistical use by the Foundation Center, the independent foundation category is by far the largest and most varied. It includes the large, long-established foundations as well as the smallest foundations.

Most independent foundations are established by contributions from an individual donor or family. In many instances, the donor and other family members participate actively in the foundation's direction. Large foundations usually have professional staff, but the smaller ones typically do not and are run entirely by their directors or trustees on a volunteer basis. Over time, a foundation launched with close ties to a donor and family often tends to develop a character and style of its own, becoming less personalized and more of an institution in its own right.

Most independent foundations are endowed, that is, they have a principal fund and make their grants essentially from investment income. Some, particularly smaller foundations, make grants from funds that are contributed periodically by living donors. Foundations that operate initially on this pass-through basis often receive an endowment at a later stage.

Corporate foundations are those established by business corporations as a means of carrying out systematic programs of charitable giving. They are classified as private foundations and are legally separate from the corporation. Corporations, whether giving through a foundation or direct giving program, frequently focus on the educational, cultural, and social welfare needs of communities where the company facilities and employees are located. They often sponsor programs to match employee gifts to charity. The corporate foundation board of directors is usually composed of senior executives and directors of the company, and staff is often recruited from within the company—although in recent years some corporations have hired staff from outside the corporation who are experienced in community work. Few corporate foundations have large endowments. Most receive and distribute funds each year from current profits of the parent company and have endowments equivalent to only one or two years of annual giving. * * *

Community foundations differ significantly in structure and in other respects from independent and corporate foundations. Community foundations have multiple sources of funding and a local or regional focus in their giving. Commonly they administer investments and charitable distributions separately; investments are managed professionally, often by trustee banks. The grantmaking and other charitable activities are directed by a governing body or distribution committee representative of community interests. The assets of a community foundation consist of a number of component funds with varying charitable purposes.

Community foundations are classified as public charities under the 1969 Tax Reform Act and accordingly are subject to fewer and different regulations than private foundations. Gifts to them qualify for maximum income tax deductibility. The number and size of community foundations have grown tremendously in the last 20 years. This is in part because of the requirement that they raise funds to meet a public support test. It may also have partly resulted from the help provided to newly forming or revitalizing community foundations by special programs sponsored by the Council on Foundations, the Ford Foundation, and the C.S. Mott Foundation. However, a major reason for their popularity among donors is the ease with which funds can be established and the variety of giving options available to donors. * * *

An *operating foundation* is a private foundation that primarily conducts programs of its own, expending its funds directly for the conduct of its own charitable activities rather than making grants to others. Examples include the J. Paul Getty Trust, which operates museum activities, and the Russell Sage Foundation, which conducts and publishes research. The distinction between operating foundations and those that are primarily grantmaking has long been recognized in the foundation field. The 1969 Tax Reform Act recognized this distinction by establishing a separate category, with more favorable tax status, for operating foundations. Approximately 3,000 organizations are classified by the Internal Revenue Service (IRS) as private operating foundations. The vast majority of private foundations are classified as private "nonoperating" * * *.

GENERAL AND SPECIAL PURPOSE FOUNDATIONS

Most donors charter their foundations with general purposes to support a wide range of charitable activities that change from time to time, as the directors or trustees determine. Others, either by choice of the managers or by virtue of the charter, may have one or more special purposes. A special purpose may be extremely broad, such as the advancement of science or health, or quite limited and specific, such as research into the causes and cure of alcoholism. Frequently, foundation managers select trustees and staff for a special-purpose foundation because of their interest or expertise in the field of emphasis.

Whether or not they incorporate geographic limitations into their charters, most small general-purpose foundations and a few large ones restrict their giving to a region, state, or city. Many special-purpose foundations and the largest of the general-purpose foundations, however, give regionally, nationally, and internationally.

FOUNDATIONS IN SOCIETY

The Andrews/Foundation Center definition of a private foundation * * * is helpful in describing the range of organizations in which we are primarily interested. However, it fails to position foundations in the voluntary sector of our society. The voluntary, independent nonprofit, or third sector, as it is variously called, is an important partner with government and business in the myriad activities that collectively make up our way of life. Within the voluntary sector, foundations play both a supportive and an innovative role, serving as important channels through which profits earned by individuals and businesses are distributed to the public in goods and services. Their influence within the voluntary sector is not dependent on the dollar volume of their grants, which is small in comparison to government spending. Rather, it lies in their flexibility in responding to needs, their willingness to take risks, and in the pluralistic nature of foundation decision making.

No other country has so many alternatives to government funding for a good idea or a new approach to an old problem. The value of foundations as alternative funding sources lies in the likelihood that at least one grantmaker will be willing to take a chance on a particular organization or individual, making possible an experiment that may gain public acceptance and broad support.

This is not to suggest that it is easy to get a grant from a foundation. Some of the staffed foundations that keep track of the number of qualified requests they decline each year report the percentage of turndowns is about 85 percent and rising. This trend is partly due to increased demand for private contributions in the wake of government cutbacks during the 1980s. But the adage, "if at first you don't succeed, try, try again," is still sound advice to the grantseeker.

The range of activities recognized by the IRS as within a charitable organization's exempt purposes constantly widens. Even contributions to businesses that operate for profit can qualify as charitable if made, for example, to help racial minorities establish themselves in the free enterprise system. Foundation grants have triggered other extensions of the definition of what is charitable, such as special guidelines including public interest work in law and voter education activities.

There is much discussion among scholars and practitioners about foundation grantmaking philosophy. Some say foundations are more concerned with research on the underlying causes of social or health problems, while others contend that they are more involved in funding the delivery of needed services. It is probably more accurate to say that they are concerned with both. Thus, while some foundations working on the problems of the inner city may fund studies of economic or demographic trends, others seek to help new community organizations wrestling with immediate problems such as homelessness, drug abuse, or unemployed young people.

We can learn valuable lessons from the relatively short experience of organized grantmaking. For example, a few foundations have traditionally shown considerable willingness to stay with a particular problem or project over a period of years—a capability that distinguishes them from most government funding sources. The Rockefeller Foundation's long and successful battle against yellow fever is a favorite example. That same foundation and others have shown equal persistence in the funding of agricultural research leading to the miracle rice and grain strains that have increased crop yields so markedly as part of the "green revolution" in Asia, Africa, and Latin America. And, in future years we may find that long-term commitments from private foundations such as the Robert Wood Johnson Foundation and others will be instrumental in finding a cure and developing prevention strategies for AIDS.

Although grantmaking may be their primary function, many foundations offer more than money. Staffed foundations and actively involved trustees of unstaffed ones frequently develop expertise in a special area of interest and become informal clearinghouses of information about new approaches to problems and funding sources other than their own. Often foundations bring together people working in the same or related fields for mutually helpful discussion and planning.

Although most foundations are blessed with broad charters, in practice many narrow their areas of current interest. This sharpening of focus serves several useful purposes. If these interests are clearly defined and publicized, it helps grantseeking agencies to target their appeals for support. And the grantmaker, having become familiar with both the problems and the imaginative people who are working toward solutions in a special field, is able to make better-informed grant decisions.

Examples of both the "staying power" of foundations and the advantages of selecting areas of special interest (taken from a long list of past accomplishments) include reform of medical education, early work on population problems, and development of policy-oriented research institutes such as the Brookings Institution and the Institute of Medicine of the National Academy of Sciences.

Nonprofit organizations look to grantmaking foundations to provide funding for experimental and high-risk projects. But with many research, educational, and service agencies heavily dependent on government project funding, general support grants from smaller foundations are also vitally important. In these and many other ways, foundations are demonstrating their continuing usefulness.

FOUNDATIONS AND GOVERNMENT

Much has been written about the degree to which government has "taken over" the funding of the voluntary sector. It is true that government support of nonprofit institutions equals that of private contributions, and government spending on charitable activities such as health care and job training dwarfs private spending. But since foundations are able to change the direction and emphasis of their programs with little or no lead time, many new opportunities have opened up *because* of heavy government funding in fields traditionally thought of as the concern of the private sector. For example, government funding of health services through Medicare and Medicaid has created demand for new types of health practitioners; Robert Wood Johnson, Commonwealth, Kaiser, and other foundations have conducted studies, made grants to educational institutions, funded demonstration projects, and otherwise moved to help identify ways to meet the demand.

In the environmental field, foundations have long played an important role by preserving wilderness areas, barrier islands, and historic buildings. This function continues to be an important one, especially because of the speed with which foundations and grantees such as the Nature Conservancy and Trust for Public Land can move. In addition, foundations monitor government conservation programs and allow environmental disputes between government agencies to be ventilated. And on occasion, powerful coalitions of public interest law firms and voluntary membership organizations (many of whom were launched by or are funded by foundations) generate lawsuits to force corporations or government agencies to comply with environmental protection laws and regulations. Foundations have been willing to take risks in this area and in others through support of pilot projects, studies, and investigative reporting. These and similar activities have often influenced or changed public policies.

Trends in the 1980s indicated that government funding in certain areas may have reached its limit, resulting in a larger demand for foundation dollars for basic services, especially for the disadvantaged. Foundation boards and staffs find themselves in new roles, sometimes working in tandem with government agencies to fund programs. Foundations are also contributing more dollars to issues such as public education—areas that have traditionally been considered to be the concern of the public sector.

LEGAL STATUS OF FOUNDATIONS

Foundations in the United States typically are created and organized under state law either as corporations or trusts and enjoy federal tax exemption under the Internal Revenue Code. Neither these laws nor others give the term *foundation* a precise or fixed legal meaning. Indeed, many of the state statutes under which foundations are created and operate do not use the word at all.

The Internal Revenue Code refers to foundations in various contexts related to not-for-profit organizations, but it leaves the term undefined. However, the relatively new phrase *private foundation*, introduced by the 1969 Tax Reform Act, does have a technical meaning. Unfortunately, the code defines private foundations not by what they are, but by what they are not. Moreover, the phrase private foundation creates confusion because the word *private* tends to blur an essential fact: Foundations are committed to public purposes, even though their assets are derived from private sources.

The code's definition by exclusion of private foundation operates in this fashion. Starting with the universe of voluntary organizations described in Section 501(c)(3), the code excludes broad groups such as churches, schools, hospitals, government, and publicly supported charities and their affiliates. (Publicly supported charities derive much of their support from the general public and reach out in other ways to a public constituency.) The code refers to all of the above kinds of excluded organizations as *public charities*. Section 501(c)(3) organizations remaining after these exclusions are considered private foundations.

Thus, organizations are included in the remainder as private foundations that are not really grantmaking foundations at all. These may include museums, homes for the aged, and libraries, among others. The IRS considers these organizations private foundations if they have been endowed by an individual or a single family or if they were established as public charities and lose that status by failing to prove that they have received ongoing financial support from the general public.

———

NOTE: DIMENSIONS OF THE FOUNDATION COMMUNITY

According to the latest authoritative count as this text went to press in early 2003, there were an estimated 56,582 private grantmaking foundations in the United States. These foundations had approximately $486 billion in total assets and made aggregate annual grants of $27.6 billion in 2000. Most foundations have less than $1 million in assets and make annual grants of less than $100,000. The largest foundations (e.g., with assets of $50 million or more), although representing less than 2 percent of all foundations, control roughly two-thirds of the assets and award almost 50 percent of all grants.

Based on public filings available as of the end of 2001, the ten wealthiest U.S. private foundations, measured by the value of their assets, were:

Rank	Foundation	Total Assets
1	Bill and Melinda Gates Foundation	$ 23,299,544,119
2	Lilly Endowment	12,626,153,000
3	The Ford Foundation	11,310,262,000
4	Robert Wood Johnson Foundation	8,850,561,262
5	David and Lucille Packard Foundation	6,200,000,000
6	William and Flora Hewlett Foundation	5,943,495,000
7	W. K. Kellogg Foundation	5,484,469,005
8	Pew Charitable Trusts	4,338,580,605
9	John D. and Catherine D. MacArthur Foundation	4,200,000,000
10	Andrew W. Mellon Foundation	4,033,000,000

Sources: Foundation Yearbook (Foundation Center 2002 ed.); Chronicle of Philanthropy, April 4, 2002.

2.   The Distinction Between Private Foundations and Public Charities: Historical Origins*

The first harbingers of Congress's desire to treat private foundations as second class citizens came in the Revenue Act of 1950, which added to the Internal Revenue Code a set of rules withdrawing tax-exempt status from organizations that engaged in certain "prohibited transactions," such as loans without adequate security, payment of unreasonable compensation, bargain sales, and preferential rendering of services to related parties. Rules also were enacted to patrol against unreasonable accumulations of income, substantial expenditures for nonexempt purposes, or investments that jeopardized the ability of a charity to carry out its exempt purposes. The legislative history reveals Congress's concern that some charities—specifically, certain charitable trusts and private foundations—were abusing the privileges of their exempt status by benefiting donors, their families and other insiders. Congress exempted churches, schools, hospitals and certain publicly supported organizations from the potential sanctions, apparently because they were viewed as less susceptible to the perceived abuses.

By the mid–1950's, these distinctions between charitable organizations were incorporated in the rules governing the income tax charitable deduction. Historically, an individual donor's annual charitable deduction has been limited to a certain percentage of the donor's adjusted gross income. In 1954, the overall percentage limitation was raised from 20 to 30 percent, but only for gifts to religious orders, schools and colleges, hospitals, and churches. The change was justified as a way to help the favored institutions obtain "the additional funds they need, in view of their rising costs and the relatively low rate of return they are receiving on endowment funds." S.Rep.No. 1622, 83d Cong., 2d Sess. 29 (1954); H.Rep.No. 1337, 83d Cong., 2d Sess. 25 (1954). In 1956, the higher limitation was extended to a narrow type of medical research organization and, in 1962, to organizations that supported state universities. The extra 10–percent deduction (along with several other benefits, such as eligibility for a five-year carryover of contributions that exceeded the annual ceiling) was extended again in 1964 to other organizations that derived a substantial part of their total support from governmental sources or from direct or indirect contributions from the general public. These incremental changes had the effect of narrowing the *disfavored* category to private foundations and a miscellany of other

* Much of this history is derived from Laurens Williams and Donald V. Moorehead, An Analysis of the Federal Tax Distinctions Between Public and Private Charitable Organizations, in IV U.S. Dept. of the Treasury, Research Papers Sponsored by the [Filer] Commission on Private Philanthropy and Public Needs 2099 (1977), and Peter Dobkin Hall, A Historical Overview of the Private Nonprofit Sector, in The Nonprofit Sector: A Research Handbook 3, 19–20 (Walter W. Powell ed., 1987).

§ 501(c)(3) organizations that could not demonstrate the requisite public support.

Professor Boris Bittker has explained this caste system as embodying two distinctions, resting on different rationales suggested but not clearly articulated in the legislative history. First, Congress may have intended to benefit operating over nonoperating charities on the theory that the operating charities needed special assistance to maintain or expand their activities at accustomed levels in the face of increased costs and declining endowment yields. Grantmaking charities, it seemed, could more easily retrench or postpone their activities. Second, the distinction between public and private charities may have been based on the view that public charities satisfied more pressing social needs, or had been endorsed by a form of public referendum. Churches, schools and hospitals fell into the "charmed circle" irrespective of their public support—presumably because they were the most venerable (and influential) members of the charitable sector. See Boris I. Bittker, Should Foundations Be Third–Class Charities?, in The Future of Foundations 132, 142–143 (Fritz F. Heimann ed., 1973).

The increasing regulation of private foundations was not entirely unexpected. Throughout the first half of the 20th century, large pools of philanthropic wealth were periodically subjected to critical scrutiny by a diverse ideological coalition. In 1916, a commission investigating industrial relations concluded that the small group of wealthy families controlling American industry were extending their reach to education and "social service" by creating "enormous privately managed funds for indefinite purposes." Among other things, the Walsh Commission recommended that these institutions be required to obtain a federal charter that limited their size, prohibited accumulations of unexpended income, and opened their books to government inspection. Two Congressional investigations in the 1950's were somewhat more balanced, but concerns remained about public accountability, the unhealthy influence of foundations over social science research and education, and the leftist and collectivist leanings of some foundations. In 1952, the Cox Commission concluded its report by asking whether foundations had supported persons and projects that "tended to weaken or discredit the capitalistic system as it exists in the United States and to favor Marxist socialism." The 1954 Reece Commission recommended a limit on the life of a foundation, and it would have required mandatory distribution of income, restrictions on corporate control, and a complete prohibition on all political activity.

The movement against private foundations picked up considerable steam in the 1960's, primarily because of the efforts of populist Congressman Wright Patman of Texas. The barrage began in 1962 with extensive hearings culminating in a lengthy report that identified abuses ranging from misuse of funds to operation of businesses at a competitive advantage. A 1965 Treasury Department report concluded that private foundations played an important and valuable role in American philanthropy but identified three broad areas for legislative attention. First, the Treasury concluded that the use of foundations produced an undue lag between the charitable gift generating the tax benefit (the transfer of wealth to the foundation) and the use of the funds for charitable purposes. Second, the Treasury was concerned that foundations were becoming a disproportionate segment of the national economy. Third, foundations were said to represent dangerous concentrations of social and economic power. Among the recommended legislative solutions were a ban on self-dealing, an annual charitable payout requirement, a limit on foundation holdings in business enterprises, less beneficial tax treatment for gifts of appreciated property to private foundations, prohibitions on borrowing by foundations, and a rule requiring the family of the founding donor to reduce its representation on the governing board to no more than 25 percent after the first 25 years of a foundation's existence.

It was against this background that Congress mounted the attack on private foundations that culminated in the Tax Reform Act of 1969. The excerpt below, from Waldemar Nielsen's 1972 Twentieth Century Fund study of private foundations, is a lively and informative chronicle of the political climate during the gestation period of the 1969 legislation. An appreciation of the setting in which the regulatory regime emerged can only enhance understanding of the technical material to follow.

Waldemar A. Nielsen, The Big Foundations

7–17 (The Twentieth Century Fund, 1972).

By 1969, foundations were once again under assault not only from the ideological barricades but also in the arena of practical politics. The setting was the U.S. Congress, and the context a debate over tax reform legislation. The leader of the anti-foundation forces was the sturdy old Populist from Texas, Wright Patman, who for more than thirty years—with considerable success—has carried on a personal crusade against Wall Street, chain stores, monopolies, banks, and "greedy millionaires" in general. Patman is a blue-eyed, cherubic-looking man (he has been called a mixture of Father Christmas and Foxy Grandpa) of gentle manner and deceptively quiet voice. But in exposing and condemning what he regards as the evils of Big Money, he is tenacious and tough.

Patman had begun his campaign against the foundation eight years before with a mild speech in the House on May 2, 1961, praising their "wonderful work," but deploring their rapid growth and questioning the motives of some of their donors. In the following months his attacks became less restrained; he made use of all available charges of financial misconduct as well as the contradictory allegations of both capitalistic and communistic bias among foundations. In early 1962, the House Small Business Committee authorized him to hire a staff, conduct studies, and hold hearings. Over the next several years, with unflagging energy, he prepared massive (and not always accurate) compilations of data, on the basis of which he charged foundations with short sales of securities, speculation in commodity futures and oil wells, manipulation of stock prices, and the use of their assets to carry on proxy fights for the control of corporations.

Through his skill in making headlines Patman began to attract public and congressional attention to the general subject of foundation conduct. He also succeeded in badgering the Treasury Department and the Internal Revenue Service into more vigorous surveillance. In July 1964 he held his first series of public hearings, calling only government witnesses. He charged that the Treasury's statistics on foundations were totally inadequate and that as a result of its "indefensible apathy and its archaic procedures" it had actually encouraged abuses by some donors and foundations. At Patman's demand, the Treasury undertook a new study of foundations and issued a report in 1965 that identified a number of spreading financial abuses among foundations and analyzed their basic structural faults, such as the unduly close ties among foundations, donor families, and certain associated companies. For this major accomplishment the Treasury—and Patman—must be given full credit.

The recommendations in the report were moderate, but foundation response was divided. A number of the big philanthropies approved them, but rather passively; others, however, immediately dispatched their lawyers to Washington to try to block any legislative action on the basis of them, which they succeeded in doing. Nonetheless, the Treasury's report had a deep effect on public opinion and generally seemed to validate Patman's charges. In a succession of further reports in 1966, 1967, and 1968, the Texas congressman presented a stream of new allegations and cases of flagrant foundation misconduct.

Nevertheless, it began to appear that Patman's crusade was running out of steam; it had produced no significant legislation, and Congress and the public were becoming fatigued by his antics. But in 1968 it suddenly revived, riding the wave of a spontaneous public revolt against the burdens and injustices of the tax laws, especially their loopholes for the rich. Half the letters then being deposited on congressional desks were taxpayers' protests. The public mood was reflected in the response to a statement late that year by Joseph W. Barr, then Secretary of the Treasury, to a congressional committee that in 1967 there had been 155 individual tax returns filed with adjusted gross income above $200,000 on which no income tax had to be paid: and 21 returns were filed with incomes above $1 million on which no tax had to be paid. These startling figures, when reported by the press and television, provoked a new torrent of outraged letters, telegrams, and telephone calls to Washington.

This, then, was the atmosphere in which the House Ways and Means Committee under Chairman Wilbur Mills of Arkansas opened its tax reform hearings on February 18, 1969. It began by taking up the question of tax-exempt foundations and thereby got off to a lively start. The first witness called was Wright Patman, who fired a shotgun blast full into their flank:

> Today, I shall introduce a bill to end a gross inequity which this country and its citizens can no longer afford: the tax-exempt status of

the so-called privately controlled charitable foundations, and their propensity for domination of business and accumulation of wealth.

Put most bluntly, philanthropy—one of mankind's most noble instincts—has been perverted into a vehicle for institutionalized, deliberate evasion of fiscal and moral responsibility to the nation.

This has been accomplished by tax immunities granted by the U.S. Congress. The use of the tax-free status * * * reveals the continuing devotion of some of our millionaires to greed, rather than conversion to graciousness.

Mr. Chairman, when a privilege is abused, it should be withdrawn. And the onerous burdens of 65 million taxpayers demand that Congress curb the tax-exempt foundations which, in unwitting good faith, it helped to create.

On the second day of the hearings, the committee heard Representative John J. Rooney, a Democrat from Brooklyn, New York. He told a story to agitate the heart of any politician. Apparently a wealthy opponent of his in the previous primary campaign had used his own private foundation as a weapon of partisan attack. According to Rooney, the Frederick W. Richmond Foundation had swooped into his district just before the election and handed out tax-free gifts to such politically potent groups as the Puerto Rican Trade Committee, the Hispanic Society of the Fire Department, and the Zion Negro Baptist Church. In addition the foundation created Neighborhood Study Clubs, Inc., which Rooney charged was simply a political machine "oiled" by charity dollars. In concluding his testimony he said:

> In other words, to sum up my experience in the primary campaign of 1968, for the first time in anyone's knowledge, a congressional political campaign was subsidized by all United States taxpayers and in defiance, if not in violation, of laws governing campaign moneys * * *.

> This time, Mr. Chairman, it happened in my district. It can—and probably will—happen in your districts. In fact, the appeal of this political gimmick is a threat to every officeholder, in Congress or elsewhere, who does not have access to a fat bankroll or to a business or to a tax-exempt foundation.

On the third day McGeorge Bundy, president of the Ford Foundation, was the witness before a chamber packed with hundreds of intent spectators. Bundy had left his post as dean of Harvard College to go to Washington in 1961 with President John F. Kennedy and the New Frontier. Over the following five years, under President Kennedy and then under President Lyndon Johnson, he served as the White House assistant for national security affairs. Many in Congress and elsewhere had come to believe that Bundy had played a key role in the Bay of Pigs and the Dominican Republic interventions and in the escalation of the Vietnam War.

In 1966, Bundy moved from the White House to the Ford Foundation, and the hawkish strategic planner seemed almost instantly to be transformed into an activist domestic reformer, a change that some of his liberal critics charged to bad conscience. In any event, the foundation under this leadership began a series of grants that plunged it into sensitive areas. In the South, Ford supplemented the funds of the Southern Regional Council to enlarge its voter registration drives for blacks. And as the number of newly registered black voters swelled, many traditional Southern political leaders felt their power was being undermined by the foundation. In the Southwest, Ford gave help to a militant Mexican–American organization which, brandishing radical slogans, then entered local politics, causing even the leading liberal Democrats of the area to protest Ford's actions.

In Cleveland in 1967, Ford gave substantial funds to the local chapter of the Congress on Racial Equality to be spent, among other things, for a voter registration drive. The preponderance of new voters registered were black—and when a black was elected mayor in the next election, there were charges from both Democratic and Republican party regulars that Ford money had put him in office. In New York City, the foundation financed a school decentralization experiment which, by the time it was over, had detonated black-Jewish tensions in the city, brought about a bitter confrontation between the black community and the powerful United Federation of Teachers, and resulted in a destructive citywide school strike that nearly cost John Lindsay his second term as mayor.

To make the atmosphere at the Washington hearings still more volatile, the New York *Times* just the week before had reported Ford grants to eight prominent members of the staff of the late Senator Robert F. Kennedy. They had received awards aggregating $131,000, personally approved by Bundy. According to a foundation press release issued after the first news stories appeared, "the grants were provided under a foundation program of long standing that aims to ease the transition from public to private life. They provide up to a year of leisure and freedom from immediate financial concern."

The members of the House committee immediately pounced on Bundy about them. He got off to a bad start because his discursive defense of the grants as purely "educational" and not tinged with political or personal favoritism was singularly unpersuasive. His replies to subsequent questions were equally unconvincing to the committee. According to private statements made later by five members who were present, Bundy conveyed a strong impression of arrogance and condescension. One congressman said, "I went into that hearing this morning basically friendly to the foundations; I came out feeling that if Bundy represents the prevailing attitude among them, they are going to have to be brought down a peg. For all their Ph.D.'s they are not above the law."

John D. Rockefeller 3d appeared a week later—and in so far as the committee at any point seriously discussed nonpolitical issues of philanthropy, it was largely in the exchange between him and Representative John W. Byrnes of Wisconsin, the ranking Republican member.

For example, in reply to Rockefeller's earnest and self-effacing plea for continued tax inducements for private philanthropy, Representative Byrnes posed some serious questions:

The real problem here * * * is that certain people have a choice as to how the tax aspect of their income is going to be spent * * *. The great vast array of the American people do not have this choice. They are not only paying for things about which some of them are not very enthusiastic, but they must also pay a higher price to carry on these services simply because some people with wealth have said that they do not want to support any of these services.

Should we permit a segment of our society to set up a government of its own to render philanthropic services? Our tax laws have given one group a chance to * * * make their own determination as to what is in the public good, and to decide how to spend that money.

How do we cope with the choice that we have given to some people when we haven't given that choice to the great mass of citizens?

But even that interval of sobriety in the proceedings was interrupted by a nerve-jangling distraction. In making his case, the witness had happened to mention, almost in passing, that because of the unlimited deduction privilege for charitable contributions permitted under existing legislation, he had not had to pay any income tax since 1961. That statement by a Rockefeller in 1969, a year of tax rebellion, brought the committee bolt upright and sent newspapermen racing for the telephones.

Once the hearings were over, the committee and its staff, with the help of a number of Treasury experts, set to work to draft proposals for new legislation. Three months later, in a press release dated May 27, 1969, the committee issued a harsh judgment upon foundations. The foundations were shocked by some of the specific recommendations, but even more so by the evidence of the extent to which they were mistrusted.

Their predicament was made still worse a month later by the disclosure of a relationship between Supreme Court Justice Abe Fortas and the Wolfson Family Foundation, whose donor—the notorious corporation raider and stock manipulator, Louis E. Wolfson—was then under federal indictment. Fortas, it was learned, had agreed to accept a $20,000 annual fee from the foundation after he joined the Supreme Court. Shortly thereafter it was revealed that another member of the Court, Justice William O. Douglas, was on the payroll of the Parvin Foundation, whose donor, Albert Parvin, had extensive holdings in hotels and gambling casinos in Las Vegas. On May 9 the Los Angeles Times reported an interconnection between the two cases; Wolfson and Parvin had once been named co-conspirators in a stock manipulation case. In addition, Fortas' wife, Carolyn Agger Fortas, had been retained as an attorney by the Parvin Foundation. A few days later Fortas resigned from the Court—and a new charge had been added against philanthropic foundations, namely that they had become instruments for the corruption of public officials.

As the congressional battle shifted from the House to the Senate the odds against the foundations were heavy. Years of bombardment by Patman, the foundations' stumbling performance before the House Committee, and such incidents as the Fortas case had thrown them on the defensive.

More ominous, once it was realized in Washington that the tax reform drive might threaten even such hallowed loopholes as the oil depletion allowance and the excess depreciation rules for real estate, big politics took over. Tax lobbyists representing major industries and interest groups from all over the country began a mass assault on the members of Congress. In this atmosphere, foundations became a convenient scapegoat and even the few political friends on whom they could ordinarily rely suddenly became unwilling to speak up. Southern conservatives, led by George Wallace, were furious about grants for black voter registration and school desegregation, and northern conservatives were equally upset by foundation activism in the ghettos; at the same time the vigorous opposition of the AFL–CIO to foundations as tax shelters for the wealthy undermined the support of a number of liberal congressmen. The large and politically influential state universities, long resentful of foundation favoritism for Ivy League schools, decided not to exert themselves in behalf of the foundations. And in a few cases, strong opponents of the Vietnam War were put off by the prominence of McGeorge Bundy among the spokesmen for private philanthropy. Most members of Congress, confronted with the necessity of choice, made a simple political calculation: foundations, compared to oil, banking, and real estate, represented a small and weak constituency that presumably could be ignored.

Another major handicap to the foundations was the contradictory position of the Nixon administration. During his presidential campaign, Nixon had been skeptical of the significance of the tax revolt, and when he took office he put tax reform near the bottom of his priorities. His top appointees in the Treasury, scarcely noted as reformers, did little to persuade him otherwise. Thus both the White House and the Treasury were surprised by the storm that broke over Capitol Hill. Forced to submit legislative proposals, the Treasury did so hurriedly and with little preparation. Later, as the tax fight heated up and the various pressure groups went to work, the White House embarrassed the Treasury by reversing its position even on the mild reforms that had been proposed. Assistant Secretary Edwin Cohen, the principal Treasury participant in the technical work of the Ways and Means Committee, consistently displayed an anti-foundation bias that by early fall had become so marked that it produced a split within the Administration. The Secretary of Health, Education and Welfare, Robert Finch, on September 17, 1969, wrote a strong letter, which he also made public, to Treasury Secretary David M. Kennedy, asserting that the bill approved by the House committee threatened to undermine American foundations and even to destroy them. The gravest dangers, he said, were posed by the provisions—apparently supported by the Treasury—prohibiting any activity by foundations that might influence legislation. In his view the language could be "interpreted in such a way as to preclude any foundation impact on public opinion formation" and render illegal a broad and important range of foundation activities directed to social and educational problems.

Secretary Kennedy, in a superbly bland reply drafted in Cohen's office, said: "While the line between education and the influencing of legislation may not always be easy to draw, I am confident that the Internal Revenue Service will continue to exercise sound discretion in this respect as it has in the past."

Handicapped by a dubious public, an irritated and harassed Congress, and an unsympathetic administration, the foundations in September prepared to face the Senate Finance Committee. A blue-ribbon lineup of leaders from universities, research centers, the business community, and civil rights groups was organized to pay individual calls to key members of the House and the Senate. In addition, a coordinated series of statements was prepared defending the foundation position, and a panel of witnesses was organized consisting of some of the most eminent names in American life. A useful buttress to these efforts was the report issued on October 22 by a private study group headed by Peter G. Peterson, a prominent Chicago businessman. The commission had been organized several months before at the prompting of John D. Rockefeller 3d to make an independent appraisal of foundations, and its findings and recommendations were critical but constructive.

The well-planned testimony of the foundation witnesses certainly did no harm. But how much good it accomplished for their case was difficult to measure because by the time the Senate committee met, the political winds generated by a multitude of aroused interest groups were howling so loudly around the tax bill that the small voice of the pro-foundation spokesmen could scarcely be heard. In the end the Finance Committee, although it dropped some of the features of the House bill that were most objectionable to the foundations, added a provision putting a mandatory forty-year limitation on their life.

Although the provision was eventually rejected, it produced a lively but bewildering debate on the floor of the Senate which revealed the full depth of congressional division if not confusion regarding philanthropy. Among the liberals, for example, Senator Walter F. Mondale, a Democrat from Minnesota, defended the foundations in these terms: "In health, in education, in the cultural field, in social welfare, in noncommercial television, in legal rights for the poor and the consumer, in civil rights, in social sciences, in the National Merit Scholarships, in population problems—wherever we look, the cutting edge of the liberal dynamic thought in this country today is being supported by the private foundations."

Senator Charles H. Percy, a liberal Republican from Illinois, defended them on opposite grounds, citing their sound traditionality: "The heart of foundation giving is not generally the glamorous, pioneering variety * * *. Instead, grants are made year in and year out to the YMCA, Boys' Clubs, the Cancer Society, educational institutions and hospitals, symphonies, museums, welfare agencies, and the myriad of other institutions which contribute to the development of a better society."

A dean of the liberal group, Senator Albert Gore, Democrat of Tennessee [father of 2000 Presidential Candidate Albert Gore, Jr., Eds.], then attacked the liberal defenders of foundations: "One of the strangest anomalies in our history is that my liberal friends think this is a liberal cause for which they are fighting. They are fighting for the vested interest of this country, for the vested wealth of this country, to be tied up in perpetuity for the descendants of a few people who have waxed rich, sometimes by chance or inheritance, from this society of ours.''

After the Senate passed the tax bill without the forty-year "death sentence," the conference committee of the two houses under Chairman Mills worked long hours on the final compromises. At 3:30 Tuesday afternoon, December 23, the cluster of lobbyists and newspapermen outside the committee room knew from a burst of applause inside that the Tax Reform Act of 1969 needed only President Nixon's signature to become reality.

NOTES AND QUESTIONS

1. *The Role of Private Foundations.* Do private foundations represent a "shadow government" that acts as a political force partially financed by public funds, without accountability to the electorate? Should they steer clear of public controversy and limit their activities to support of traditional charitable activities such as scientific and medical research? Is it fundamentally undemocratic for foundations to exert their influence in a democratic society? Or do foundations inform democracy by offering different and innovative solutions to social problems?

Most private foundations exist in perpetuity. Would it be preferable if the law required them to have a limited life span, such as 50 to 100 years? Would term limits protect against departure from the original donor's grantmaking intent?

2. *For Further Reading.* Thomas A. Troyer, The 1969 Private Foundations Law: Historical Perspectives on Its Origin and Underpinnings, 27 Exempt Org. Tax Rev. 52 (2000); John A. Edie, Congress and Foundations, in Teresa Odendahl (ed.), America's Wealthy and the Future of Foundations (1987); John G. Simon, Charity and Dynasty Under the Federal Tax System, 5 The Probate Lawyer 1 (Summer 1978); Fritz F. Heimann (ed.), The Future of Foundations (1973); Marion R. Fremont–Smith, Foundations and Government (1965).

3.   THE FEDERAL TAX TREATMENT OF PRIVATE FOUNDATIONS: AN OVERVIEW

a.   THE TAX DEFINITION OF A PRIVATE FOUNDATION

Considering the vast regulatory scheme aimed at private foundations, one might have assumed that Congress would have told us what a private foundation "is." Curiously, it did just the opposite. The Code defines private foundations by exclusion, providing in § 509(a) that all § 501(c)(3) domestic or foreign organizations are private foundations unless they come within any of the following four categories of "nonprivate" foundations:

(1) § 509(a)(1) "traditional public charities"—more specifically, those organizations described in 170(b)(1)(A)(i)–(vi). Very generally, this group includes churches, schools, hospitals, medical research institutions, support arms of state universities, governmental units, and broad publicly supported organizations that enjoy favored treatment for purposes of the charitable income tax deduction.

(2) § 509(a)(2) "broad publicly supported organizations"—another breed of public charity, sometimes referred to as "gross receipts" or "membership" organizations, that receive more than one-third of their support from gifts, grants, fees and "gross receipts" from admissions, sales of goods or services, where the fee-generating activity is related to the performance of the organization's exempt purposes.

(3) § 509(a)(3) "supporting organizations," which are not publicly supported but have a closely defined control or programmatic relationship with one or more public charities.

(4) § 509(a)(4) "testing for public safety" organizations, a specialized category of no great consequence that will not be discussed further.

All of these organizations share the characteristic of "publicness" in that they rely on public support or are accountable to a broad constituency. As such, they are seen as less susceptible to the abuses that motivated Congress to regulate private foundations more stringently. The excerpt below, from a guidebook published by The Council on Foundations, elaborates on the three major types of "nonprivate" foundations.

John A. Edie, First Steps in Starting a Foundation

Council on Foundations 8–13 (4th ed. 1997).

Exception 1: Traditional Charities and Publicly Supported Organization #1

The traditional charity exception contains the largest number of organizations. The term traditional is not used in the tax code, but is offered here to distinguish the various categories in shorthand form.

The first exception is really a list of many different legal exceptions that include many traditional institutions: churches, colleges, universities, schools, nonprofit hospitals, medical research institutes, support organizations to schools and governmental units. If the organization qualifies under the legal definition of any one of these traditional institutions, it is sufficiently public and will not be classified as a private foundation.

Congress felt that churches were sufficiently public because by definition they were composed of a broad segment of the community that actively participated in the day-to-day operations of the organization and contributed funds to it regularly. Similarly, educational institutions by definition include faculty and student bodies and parents paying tuition. Medical institutions (such as nonprofit hospitals) also could fall under the definition of public based on the involvement of the medical profession, and the fact that patients constantly use the institution for medical care. In short, each institution could not survive without continually convincing a reasonably large segment of the public that its operation and services are worthwhile. By similar reasoning, governmental units were sufficiently public, because their continued existence depended upon the oversight and approval of publicly elected officials. Note that all governmental units escape private foundation status through Exception 1. Governmental units are treated as public charities even though they are not classified under Section 501(c)(3).

A newly formed organization also can fall under this first exception as a traditional charity in another way. Even though it may not satisfy the legal definition of the various institutions just noted, it may qualify by being publicly supported. The test of publicness here is different. It is not the inherent nature (or definition) of the church, school or hospital that is important here. The question is whether the organization can meet certain public support tests. Can the organization demonstrate that a certain portion of its total support comes directly or indirectly from public contributions?

If one is contemplating the formation of an organization whose primary source of funding will be public donations and/or government support, the traditional charity format is the preferred type of organization to form. The organization will not be classified as a private foundation (through Exception 1—Traditional) because it will meet one of two public support tests. Traditional charities such as the Red Cross, the YMCA, the United Way and the Audubon Society meet this definition. However, certain organizations whose purpose primarily is grantmaking (such as community foundations) also can satisfy the rules for this classification.

For publicly supported charities under this first exception, there are two tests. If the charity fails to meet the first test, it may fall back to the second test. The first test is called the **mechanical test** because it relies on a mathematical formula. If over the most recent four-year period, public support equals or exceeds one-third of total eligible support, the charity has met the test and will qualify as a public charity.

Public support divided by total support equals the support fraction. The rules for what counts as public support and what does not are complex; this is one of many areas where legal counsel is especially important. Generally, the types of support that count as *public* support and are included in both the top and the bottom half of the support fraction are:

1. Contributions from individuals, foundations, trusts or corporations.
2. Support from governmental units.
3. Membership dues, if the basic purpose of such payment is to support the organization rather than to purchase admissions, merchandise, services or the use of facilities.

All public support counts as part of total support. The types of support that *cannot* count as public support but are included in *total* support making up the bottom half of the fraction are:

1. Gross investment income.

2. Contributions and dues from individuals, foundations, trusts or corporations that exceed two percent of total support for the applicable period.

3. Net income from unrelated business activities.

In constructing the support fraction to see if the one-third test has been met, the organization must exclude from both the top and bottom half any income received from the exercise of the exempt function of the foundation (admission fees, fees for services, etc.). * * *

If the organization fails to meet the mechanical test, it has a second chance and may resort to the **facts and circumstances test.** Under this test, the organization may fall below the one-third test, but—as the name suggests—it may still qualify depending on all the facts and circumstances. To qualify under this test, the organization must demonstrate adequate evidence of three different elements:

1. The total amount of government and public support must equal or exceed an absolute minimum ten percent of total support for the applicable period.

2. It must be organized and operated to attract new and additional public and governmental support on a continuous basis; and

3. It must demonstrate by other facts and circumstances that it is entitled to be recognized as public rather than private. Two of several factors considered here are: to what degree the board of directors represents the general public (rather than merely the donors), and to what extent services or facilities of the organization are available to the general public.

In summary, the first exception (Traditional Charities and Publicly Supported Organization #1) is quite flexible, and meeting the public support requirements is not onerous. Consequently, it is the most frequently used form of public charity.

* * *

Exception 2: Gross Receipts Charities or Publicly Supported Organization #2

The second type of public charity also must meet a public support test. Part of the legacy of the 1969 tax legislation was recognizing that certain organizations that relied in large part on gross receipts from tax-exempt activities also should qualify for the more favored tax advantages of the traditional charities. As noted above, the traditional charity may not include as public support any receipts obtained from carrying out its exempt function. A Gross Receipts charity—as the name suggests—can count such support as public. Again, the term gross receipts is not actually used in this section of the tax code, but it is offered here to avoid the use of more technical language.

To qualify as a Gross Receipts charity, two tests must be met. The first is a different **public support test.** To satisfy this test, the organization normally must receive more than one-third of its total support from any combination of (1) qualifying gifts, grants, contributions or membership fees, *and* (2) gross receipts from admissions, sales of merchandise, performance of services or furnishing of facilities in activities related to its exempt functions. Examples of public charities that commonly fall under this classification are symphonies, opera companies and a wide variety of organizations that provide charitable services for a fee.

As with traditional charities, the support fraction is calculated over the previous four-year period. However, you have *no* facts and circumstances test to fall back on. The one-third public support percentage is an absolute minimum.

The second test that must be met is the **investment income test.** Under this test, the organization must show that the total of its investment income and net unrelated business income does not exceed one-third of its total support.

It bears repeating that what constitutes total support versus public support for both Traditional charities and Gross Receipts charities is highly technical and complex and, therefore, skilled counsel is essential. Two examples of this complexity for Publicly Supported Charity #2 are worth noting:

Limits on Substantial Contributors: In adding up public support to qualify as a Publicly Supported Charity #2, the contribution of *any* amount from a disqualified person (including substantial contributors) cannot count as public support (in the top half) but nonetheless counts as total support (in the bottom half). A substantial contributor to a Publicly Supported Charity #2 is one who contributes more than $5,000; and that amount must exceed two percent of the total support ever received by the organization by the close of that tax year. Contributions from substantial contributors can count as public support for a traditional charity (subject to the two percent limit described above).

$5,000 or One Percent Limit on Gross Receipts: A Gross Receipts charity cannot count as *public* support gross receipts from any person or governmental unit that exceeds the greater of $5,000 or one percent of total support for that year. However, any gross receipts that exceed this limit must be counted as part of *total* support in meeting the one-third test. As noted above, gross receipts received by a traditional charity may not count as public support.

If this discussion of public support leaves you hopelessly confused, do not feel alone. The U.S. Tax Court stated that these rules are "almost frighteningly complex and technical." * * * However, you should be left with the understanding that: (1) two different types of publicly supported organization classifications are available, each with different advantages and disadvantages, and (2) sound legal advice on which option best fits the reader's needs is indispensable.

Exception 3: Supporting Organization

The supporting organization is a third type of public charity category. Because of the complexity of the rules, an attempt to provide details on how to qualify as a supporting organization would be foolish in the context of this book. Instead, the intent here is to provide a rough understanding of what a supporting organization is and how it can be used.

Four important points should be stressed. First, this option is becoming a popular choice among those starting foundations. Second, its requirements are flexible, enabling it to be used in a variety of different circumstances. Third, its great advantage is that it does not require meeting any public support test and, *at the same time*, it enables the organization to obtain the advantages of being a public charity. Finally, establishing a supporting organization without expert legal counsel is virtually impossible.

How does a supporting organization acquire sufficient publicness to qualify as a public charity? A supporting organization is like a barnacle; it attaches itself to (or supports) another public charity (or charities), and—in effect—acquires the public charity status of the organization or organizations it supports. The biggest problem is to make sure the barnacle sticks. In other words, the supporting organization must be carefully constructed to meet the complex tests required by the law and regulations. The two essential tests are a **purpose test** and a **control test.** The purpose test requires the supporting organization to benefit or carry out a purpose of the supported organization, ordinarily a public charity. The control test requires that the supported organization control the supporting organization. However, the definition of control is fairly broad and can be satisfied easily in most cases. Perhaps two examples of typical supporting organizations will aid the reader's understanding.

> **Trust example:** Mr. and Mrs. X endow a trust with $1 million to provide scholarships to public high school students in a particular city. The sole trustee is the local community foundation. No public support or fundraising is provided. The scholarships are paid from the investment income. The trust can qualify as a public charity because it is a supporting organization of a community foundation (one example of a traditional charity).

> **Corporate example:** Mr. and Mrs. Y establish a nonprofit corporation with an endowment of $1 million to help a local church in eliminating poverty in a particular city. In the articles of incorporation, they name a local church as the supported organization, and the church appoints three of five members to the foundation's board. Mr. and Mrs. Y are the other two board members. This foundation can qualify as a public charity since it is a supporting organization of another public charity.

Two other general limitations are worth mentioning:

Specified public charities: Normally it is expected that the charity or charities that will be supported will be specifically identified in the governing instruments by name. However, under some circumstances, specific identification can be avoided by identifying beneficiary organizations by class or purpose so long as other more technical tests are also met.

Limitation on control: A supporting organization may not be controlled directly or indirectly by one or more disqualified persons (meaning substantial contributors to the foundation and their families). Control in this context means having 50 percent or more of the voting power of the organization or the right to exercise veto power over the activities of the foundation.

* * *

———

b.   PRIVATE OPERATING FOUNDATIONS

The Internal Revenue Code distinguishes between traditional grantmaking foundations and private operating foundations. Operating foundations do more than just make grants for charitable purposes; they also conduct their own charitable programs. The typical operating foundation receives its funding from a large gift or bequest from the founding donor. The income from the resulting endowment is used to support an active charitable enterprise, such as the operation of a museum, library, research institute, or public park. An example of a large private operating foundation is the J. Paul Getty Museum in Los Angeles.

Private operating foundations are subject to the entire regulatory regime applicable to private foundations, but they enjoy several notable advantages. The principal benefit is that donors to operating foundations may take advantage of the more favorable income tax charitable deduction rules applicable to public charities. Contributions to operating foundations qualify for the higher 50 percent limitation on contributions of cash and ordinary income property and the 30 percent limitation on contributions of capital gain property, and they are not subject to the reduction for unrealized built-in gain on certain gifts of appreciated capital gain property. I.R.C. § 170(b)(1)(A)(vii). Operating foundations also are exempt from the income distribution requirement applicable to nonoperating foundations under 4942.

Qualification as a private operating foundation requires satisfying an "income test," which generally requires the foundation to use "substantially all" (85 percent or more) of its income directly for the active conduct of charitable activities rather than for grantmaking. In addition, a private operating foundation must meet one of the following three tests, each of which is described only generally:

1.   The **assets test**, under which a foundation must show that at least 65 percent of all its assets are devoted directly to the active conduct of the foundation's exempt function activities (e.g., opera-

tion of a museum) or to functionally-related businesses (e.g., low-income housing), or both, or consist of stock of a foundation-controlled corporation, 65 percent or more of the assets of which are so devoted. I.R.C. § 4942(j)(3)(B)(i). Investment assets are included in the denominator of the testing fraction but may not be counted in satisfying the 65 percent test.

2. The **endowment test**, under which the foundation normally must expend funds directly for the active conduct of its exempt purposes in an amount equal to 3–1/3 percent of the fair market value of its net investment assets. I.R.C. § 4942(j)(3)(B)(ii).

3. The **support test**, under which the foundation must receive at least 85 percent of its support from the general public and five or more unrelated exempt organizations, provided that not more than 25 percent of the foundation's support is received from any one exempt organization and not more than half of the support is normally received from gross investment income. I.R.C. § 4942(j)(3)(B)(iii).

The regulations elaborate considerably on these requirements, covering such matters as the relevant testing periods and the treatment of various receipts and expenses for purposes of the numerous tests. See Treas. Reg. § 53.4942(b).

c. PRIVATE FOUNDATION EXCISE TAXES

The centerpiece of the 1969 legislation was a set of excise taxes imposed on private foundations and their managers (e.g., trustees, officers and other insiders) for the types of infractions that Congress concluded were susceptible to the greatest abuse. These taxes impose gradual punishment, beginning with a slap on the wrist (an "initial tax") and the opportunity to seek absolution by a process known as "correction." Those who do not correct are subject to a far more confiscatory second-level tax. Only the most flagrant violators risk loss of tax-exempt status and, in the very worst cases, confiscation of all their assets. An abatement procedure provides relief from the first-tier taxes in some cases, but ignorance of the law ordinarily does not justify exoneration. Congress also enacted a modest excise tax on a private foundation's net investment income, ostensibly to pay for all the bureaucracy needed to audit and monitor the new regime.

The excise taxes are extremely intricate and go beyond whatever abuses had been prevalent in the foundation community. The following description briefly summarizes the regulatory system, stripped of details. To ease comprehension, the text avoids the use of limiting language such as "in general" and "ordinarily," but it should be understood that exceptions and refinements abound in this area, and a legal advisor to a private foundation should never rely on a mere overview.

Excise Tax on Investment Income (§ 4940). Section 4940 imposes a tax of two percent on a private foundation's net investment income, a tax base that includes items such as dividends, interest, royalties, and net capital gains, less directly related expenses. At one time the rate was four percent, but Congress reduced it in 1978 after discovering that the tax raised far more than what was needed to administer the system. Beginning in 1985, foundations may reduce their excise tax rate to one percent by making additional distributions for charitable purposes.

Self-Dealing (§ 4941). The self-dealing provisions are perhaps the best example of legislative overkill. They penalize virtually any transaction between a private foundation and its "disqualified persons," even if the dealings are at arm's length. Section 4946 defines "disqualified person" broadly to include major donors (known technically as "substantial contributors"), trustees and officers of the foundation, members of their families, some of their business associates and related business entities such as corporations and partnerships. In theory, the penalty can apply even if the act of self-dealing benefits the foundation. Among the prohibited transactions are sales, exchanges and leases of property; lending of money; and furnishing of goods, services or facilities. A foundation may pay reasonable compensation to a disqualified person, however, for services necessary to carry out the foundation's exempt purposes.

The initial penalty is 5 percent of the amount involved in the transaction on the self-dealer and 2–1/2 percent (with a $10,000 cap) on foundation managers who participate and know what they are doing. Second—tier taxes of 200 percent and 50 percent (with a $10,000 cap), respectively, of the amount involved are imposed if the self-dealing act is not corrected within a specified period.

Minimum Distribution Requirements (§ 4942). Private foundations must make annual "qualifying distributions" in an amount equal to 5 percent of the fair market value of their net investment assets. The penalty for failure to meet this charitable payout requirement is an excise tax of 15 percent of the undistributed income, with a second-tier penalty of 100 percent if the shortfall is not distributed within a specified correction period. Qualifying distributions include grants for charitable purposes, reasonable administrative costs related to the grantmaking process (e.g., staff salaries), payments to acquire assets used in the conduct of the foundation's exempt activities, and expenses of conducting direct charitable activities (e.g., a research project). Certain amounts set-aside for future projects and "program-related investments" (e.g., scholarship loans or an equity investment in a community development project) also satisfy the payout requirement. A foundation generally has two years (the current taxable year and the following year) to make the required distributions.

Excess Business Holdings (§ 4943). Congress concluded that it was inappropriate for a private foundation to hold a substantial stake in the principal donor's family business. To implement this policy, § 4943 imposes a tax on a foundation's "excess business holdings," which are defined for most purposes as any holdings that exceed a 20 percent ownership interest in the enterprise, reduced by the percentage owned by disqualified persons. For example, if disqualified persons own 11 percent, the foundation's interest must be limited to 9 percent. If disqualified persons own more than

20 percent, the foundation must completely divest, except under a de minimis rule a foundation can always own less than 2 percent of any business irrespective of the percentage held by disqualified persons. Grace periods of from 5 to 10 years are provided to divest holdings received by gift or bequest. If effective control of the business is held by owners who are not disqualified persons, the limit may be raised to 35 percent. The initial tax is 5 percent of the value of the excess holdings. An additional tax of 200 percent is imposed if the foundation fails to make the required divestiture within a correction period. Section 4943 also includes mind-numbing transitional rules that provide relief to foundations with large business holdings as of the date of enactment of the Tax Reform Act of 1969.

Jeopardy Investments (§ 4944). Private foundations are subject to a 5 percent penalty on amounts invested in a manner that jeopardizes the carrying out of their exempt purposes. Foundation managers who knowingly participate in the jeopardy investment also are subject to a 5 percent penalty (with a $5,000 cap). Failure to correct will result in a second-tier tax of 25 percent against the foundation and 5 percent (with a $10,000 cap) against any sinning foundation managers. Determining whether an investment crosses the jeopardy line is a factual question, with the emphasis placed on the care and prudence of the board of directors. Often cited examples of investments likely to be scrutinized are commodities futures and short sales. An exception is granted for program-related investments made to achieve a charitable objective rather than to produce income (e.g., a low-interest loan to a minority business).

Taxable Expenditures (§ 4945). Section 4945 contains a list of expenditures that Congress believed were inconsistent with a private foundation's proper mission. Taxable expenditures include any expenditures for lobbying; electioneering and voter registration; grants to individuals; grants to any organization that is not classified as a public charity; and (lest anything be forgotten) any other expenditure for noncharitable purposes. An initial tax of 10 percent of the prohibited expenditure is imposed on the foundation and 2-½ percent on foundation managers (with a $5,000 cap) who agree to the expenditure and know it is subject to a penalty. Additional taxes of 100 percent on the foundation and 50 percent on the foundation manager (with a $10,000 cap) are imposed if the action is not corrected. This only begins to tell the story. Section 4945 contains numerous exceptions—for example, grants to individuals are permitted if certain grantmaking procedures are pre-approved by the IRS. Grants to organizations that are not public charities are allowed if the foundation exercises "expenditure responsibility"—a bureaucratic but ultimately surmountable legal requirement designed to ensure that the funds are used solely for charitable purposes.

4. The Present (and Future) of Private Foundations

The birth rate of private foundations declined sharply after the Tax Reform Act of 1969. A study by the Council on Foundations and the Yale Program on Nonprofit Organizations revealed that wealthy donors were deterred by the increased regulation, the tax disincentives for lifetime gifts, the administrative burdens, and the availability of alternative philanthropic vehicles such as community foundations, donor-advised funds, and supporting foundations. According to the study, attorneys played a major role in discouraging the formation of foundations during the 1970's and early 1980's. Overreacting to the 1969 legislation, they conveyed the message that foundations were expensive, time consuming, inefficient and complicated—"a mine field for somebody who doesn't know what they are doing." Francie Ostrower, The Role of Advisors to the Wealthy in The Future of Foundations 247 et seq. (Teresa Odendahl ed., 1987). This negative environment caused many existing private foundations to dissolve or transfer their assets to community foundations.

By the 1990's, however, private foundations began to enjoy a resurgence as Congress relaxed some of the disincentives and philanthropists and their advisors adapted to the regulatory regime. The enormous wealth accumulated by entrepreneurs and investors in the bull market that peaked in early 2000 was a major stimulus to the foundation birth and growth rates. The total number of foundations increased nearly 70 percent (from 32,401 to 56,582) between the beginning and end of the decade. Foundation Yearbook (Foundation Center 2002). And in an ironic twist, various expirations and temporary reinstatements of the now permanent full fair market value income tax charitable deduction (see I.R.C. § 170(e)(5)) for gifts of appreciated publicly traded stock to private foundations encouraged procrastinators to take action. See Monica Langley, A Tax Break Prompts Millionaires' Mad Dash to Create Foundations, Wall St. J., Jan. 27, 1997, at A1 and A5. Financial service companies, consultants, and sophisticated estate planners also have played a role by including foundations in their list of attractive "products." Publicity surrounding several enormous gifts to new and existing foundations has contributed to a bandwagon effect among the actual and aspiring affluent. All these developments have confirmed the emergence of the family foundation as a growth industry and a powerful force within the world of philanthropy.

Why did philanthropists rediscovered private foundations despite the legal "mine field" that almost caused their extinction? The nontax motivations for creating a foundation are many, including: (1) providing a formal structure to administer family charitable giving and a strategic buffer between an affluent family and the many charities who seek contributions; (2) building a charitable endowment that will last well beyond the founder's life and serve as a permanent memorial to the family's values; (3) giving a donor greater influence and control over donated funds; (4) providing a vehicle for family unity; (5) offering younger family members a meaningful role in their communities (and sometimes a job); (6) personal fulfillment; and (7) status.

Wealth transfer tax savings also are influential. With the prospect of a 49 percent (in 2003 and decreasing down to 45 percent by 2007) federal estate tax rate on wealth transfers over $2.5 million, a substantial bequest to a private foundation often becomes the culminating event in a wealthy individual's estate plan. This type of "philanthropic inheritance" avoids turning family assets over to the government through taxes and permits enormous pools of wealth to remain under family control for generations. (Needless to say, the proposed repeal of the federal estate tax would alter the planning agenda and reduce the tax incentive to form a family foundation.) Many private foundations are initially funded during the wealth creator's life at a relatively modest level ($2 to $5 million) and receive the bulk of their endowment at the founder's death, when they qualify for a 100 percent estate tax charitable deduction.

Despite these advantages, foundations still have their detractors, even from within the world of philanthropy. Some critics argue that private foundations are self-indulgent status symbols that support "pet projects" of the donor and are motivated largely by tax avoidance. They view public charities as more deserving of favorable tax treatment because they are more broadly representative of and thus accountable to the community at large. Congress, however, has gradually relaxed some of the rules governing private foundations and seems to be shifting its scrutiny to the real and perceived abuses of public charities.

For Further Reading. Jerry J. McCoy & Kathryn W. Miree, Family Foundation Handbook (2001); Bruce R. Hopkins & Jody Blazek, Private Foundations: Tax Law and Compliance (1997).

5. PRIVATE FOUNDATION ALTERNATIVES

The major advantages of a private foundation are flexibility and control. For donors who are willing to relinquish a measure of control, several alternative vehicles offer many of the advantages of private foundations without the added expense, reduced tax benefits, or additional regulation.

a. COMMUNITY FOUNDATIONS

A community foundation is a § 501(c)(3) organization that is created to receive and administer funds contributed by members of a particular community and to disburse those funds for charitable purposes within that community. The typical community foundation has a broadly representative governing board and its funds are administered professionally, often by a group of banks that act as trustees. Because they receive their support from a broad constituency, community foundations are public charities and, as explained in the excerpt below, donors often find them to be a desirable alternative to a private foundation.

John A. Edie, First Steps in Starting a Foundation

Council on Foundations 35–38 (4th ed.1997).

THE COMMUNITY FOUNDATION OPTION

As one type of traditional charity, the community foundation has the tax advantages of being publicly supported and does not have the disadvantages of being a private foundation. This section explains how the community foundation differs from other public charities and why it is an attractive option in a variety of circumstances.

Community foundations do not have a separate, legal classification in the tax code. In almost every circumstance community foundations are classified as traditional charities under Section 509(a)(1). However, their history goes back to 1914 and thus predates the tax code itself. The Council on Foundations defines a community foundation as a tax exempt, nor-for-profit, autonomous, publicly supported philanthropic institution comprised primarily of permanent funds endowed by many separate donors for the long-term benefit of the residents of a defined geographic area. Even though community foundations do not have a separate legal classification, the Treasury regulations defining publicly supported organizations of the Traditional charity variety provide great detail about the rules governing community trusts or community foundations. In contemplating the formation of a new foundation focusing on local needs, one would be well advised to learn the advantages of utilizing an existing community foundation or creating a new one to service the local community.

Community foundations develop, receive and administer endowment funds from private sources and manage them under community control for charitable purposes primarily focused on local needs. Their grants are normally limited to charitable organizations within a specific identified region or local community, and their charitable giving and other charitable activities are overseen by a board of directors representing the diversity of community interests. Originally conceived as a vehicle primarily for those desiring to leave property by will in perpetuity, community foundations have broadened their range over the years to accept more lifetime and short-term gifts.

Community foundations have two major purposes: to seek funds from private sources to build a pool of capital for local philanthropic purposes, and to allocate and distribute such funds for public needs.

Developers of a Capital Pool for Philanthropy

A community foundation attracts capital in ways not intended to impede the efforts of local service organizations to raise annual operating support. It is a supplement to federated funds and other agencies, not a competitor. It seeks its resources from testators, living donors, business corporations, other nonprofit organizations, trade associations, clubs and occasionally from units of government.

In bringing resources into a pool, the community foundation enhances the utility of each fund by developing an endowment of size sufficient to tackle community problems. By pooling resources, a community foundation can support one joint staff (as opposed to different staffs for each fund), and can take advantage of the obvious economies of scale.

Distributors of Funds for Philanthropy

Having drawn capital resources together, a community foundation distributes funds as its governing body determines or to charitable agencies and fields of interest designated by donors at the time of making their gifts. Its staff, supported by pooled resources, is able to become well acquainted with the emerging and changing needs of the local community, and thus provides professional expertise rarely available otherwise to private donors, corporations, unstaffed private foundations and other grantmakers. The permanence of a community foundation ensures the ongoing presence of such expertise; and the public structure of both its governing body and its procedures ensures that its grantmaking choices are responsive to community needs.

Since the formation of the first community foundation in Cleveland in 1914, this institution has grown in popularity around the nation. In 1997, there were more than 400 community foundations with assets ranging from a few thousand dollars to over $1 billion. Together, community foundations hold assets in excess of $13 billion and distribute annually more than $900 million. In addition to the main purpose just outlined, each community foundation has certain basic characteristics in common, as summarized here.

Form

Community foundations are created as trusts or nonprofit corporations whose charitable distributions are made by a distribution committee in the trust form, or by a board of directors in the corporate form. In the trust form, banks or other investment firms serve as trustees under a common governing instrument that may be executed using similar language by each local institution that agrees to accept funds constituting a part of that community's foundation. In some communities, one bank serves as sole trustee; but in most areas, a number of institutions with trust powers accept funds under the declaration of trust of their community's foundation. In the trust form, banks or other institutions, as trustees, manage the investment function; a distribution committee or board of directors manages the distribution function. In the nonprofit corporation form, the board of directors often performs both functions.

Geography and Size

A community foundation operates primarily to serve a chosen area, but on occasion it may accept funds for distribution outside that area. Generally, each community foundation serves an area of natural cohesion whether it be a city, greater metropolitan area, county or state. While there is no specific minimum geographic size required, the smaller the population, the fewer the number of potential donors and corporations likely to be available to provide the basic support.

Governing Body

The Treasury regulations governing most community foundations require that all the combined or pooled funds (component parts) be subject to a common governing body or distribution committee which directs or, in the case of a fund designated for specific beneficiaries, monitors the distribution of all of the funds exclusively for charitable purposes. The governing body must represent the broad interests of the public rather than the personal or private interests of a limited number of donors. Community foundations frequently satisfy this public representation requirement by filling positions on the governing body with: 1) public officials, 2) members appointed by public officials, 3) persons with special knowledge in a particular field or discipline in which the community foundation operates, and/or 4) community leaders such as members of the clergy, educators or civic leaders.

Range of Service to Donors

Community foundations provide a wide variety of ways to respond to the needs of donors whether the gifts are permanent or short-term. Unrestricted funds are most sought after by community foundations because they provide the governing body with the maximum amount of flexibility to respond to the most pressing needs of the community. Designated funds are created by the donor *at the time of transferring the assets* and specifically name the agency or agencies to receive the benefit of the fund. Donor-advised funds are created by the donor, reserving at the time of making the gift the privilege (from time to time thereafter) to recommend agencies to receive grants. However, the ultimate power to make all grant decisions must lie with the governing body and such recommendations can be redirected. Field-of-interest funds are established by a donor by specifying at the time of asset transfer some broadly identified field of charitable concern. Examples would be health, education or cultural arts. In any of the various funds noted above, a donor can name the fund thereby providing an opportunity to give his or her family name a place in the philanthropic history of the community. Community foundations normally charge a fee for these donor services, often based on a percentage of the value of the corpus of the fund.

Variance Power

Treasury regulations for most community foundations require that the governing body have a variance power. Specifically, the rules state that the governing body must have the power (alone or with court approval) "to modify any restriction or condition on the distribution of funds for any specified charitable purposes or to specified organization if in the sole judgment of the governing body * * * such restriction or condition becomes, in effect, unnecessary, incapable of fulfillment, or inconsistent with the charitable needs of the community or area served." The concept of including a variance power in the design of a community foundation has been present since the first one was formed in Cleveland. In fact, providing a variance power was a major reason for starting a community foundation since it provided a reasonable mechanism to avoid having the donor's restriction become obsolete or impossible to fulfill (sometimes called the rule of the dead hand).

* * *

NOTES

1. *Growth of Community Foundations.* There are now over 650 community foundations in the United States, and virtually every major metropolitan area is served by one or more. Community foundations have enjoyed tremendous growth. According to a survey by the Columbus Foundation, the assets of community foundations reached $31.4 billion in 2001, a 47.4 percent increase from five years earlier, while grants paid in 2001 reached an all-time high of $2.6 billion. 2001 Community Foundation Survey, The Columbus Foundation. As this text went to press in early 2003, the top 10 community foundations, ranked by market value of assets, were:

Rank	Foundation	Total Assets
1.	New York Community Trust	$1,785,215,504
2.	Cleveland Foundation	1,499,767,419
3.	Chicago Community Trust	1,157,517,684
4.	Marin Community Foundation (California)	1,035,125,000
5.	San Francisco Foundation	741,241,110
6.	Columbus Foundation	656,714,613
7.	Boston Foundation	645,602,875
8.	Saint Paul Foundation (Ohio)	638,286,519
9.	Greater Kansas City Community Foundation	636,106,000
10.	Communities Foundation of Texas	627,493,000

Source: The Columbus Foundation.

2. *For Further Reading.* Christopher R. Hoyt, Legal Compendium for Community Foundations (1996).

b. DONOR–ADVISED FUNDS

Traditional Donor–Advised Funds. Donor-advised funds within a community foundation (or other public charity) have become another attractive alternative to private foundations. Assets held by the largest donor-advised funds in the United States rose to $12.3 billion in 2001. Chron. of Philanthropy, May 30, 2002. The structure of advised funds varies, but all funds must be operated in compliance with IRS regulations that seek to ensure that the public charity retains the final authority to determine the grants to be made from the fund. See generally Treas. Reg. § 1.170A–9(e)(10) & (11). A fund typically bears the name of the donor or another individual that the donor selects. The donor is permitted to make grant recommendations for distributions of the fund's income or corpus under flexible guidelines established by the community foundation. Recommendations are usually accepted if they are made to public charities within the area served by the community foundation or, in some cases, even if they are beyond the geographic area but provide the type of activity that the community foundation seeks to support. All investment management and recordkeeping is handled by the public charity. Most donor-advised funds terminate at the death of the donor (or the donor's spouse), and any remaining assets are then available for the community foundation's general programs. Some funds permit a member of one younger generation to act as a donor adviser if assets remain after the original donor's death.

Gifts to donor-advised funds qualify for current income tax deductions, but the donor may defer selecting the ultimate recipients until later years. A donor thus may make a large gift (e.g., of highly appreciated stock) in high-income years and use the fund to make grants over time without being subject to the private foundation rules. In addition, earnings within each donor-advised fund are not subject to income tax.

A related vehicle is the donor-designated fund, where a donor makes an irrevocable gift to a community foundation and designates specific charitable organizations to which grants will be made, and field-of-interest funds established to support a particular charitable purpose, such as the arts or education.

Commercially Sponsored Funds. A controversial newcomer to the list of private foundation alternatives is the self-standing donor-advised fund created by a financial services firm. The prototype for this new breed of charity is the Fidelity Charitable Gift Fund, a § 501(c)(3) organization that in less than 15 years has amassed over $2.6 billion, making it one of the wealthiest public charities in the United States. The Fidelity Charitable Gift Fund consists almost exclusively of donor-advised funds. For a minimum initial tax-deductible gift of $10,000, donors may "bank" their charitable dollars in a named or anonymous fund and recommend grants to virtually any charity on the IRS approved list. All the Fund's investments are managed by the Fidelity mutual fund group, the nation's largest, for a fee that varies based on the balance in the fund and the number of annual transactions. Several other mutual fund families and a handful of other financial services companies are offering similar philanthropic "products" that are said to provide all the advantages of a private foundation without the expense (or the regulation).

Although commercially sponsored funds contributed to the growth in the charitable giving in the 1990's, they were not warmly received within the world of philanthropy. Community foundations expressed particular concern about the close relationship between these funds and their commercial sponsors. The funds also are criticized for their marketing emphasis and failure to carry out any charitable program or to monitor the grantmaking of their donor-advisers. Initially, the Fidelity Charitable Gift Fund allegedly gave almost unbridled discretion to donors, allowing them to make grants to their own private foundations or to foreign charities. Unlike community foundations, which purport to regulate their donor-advised grants, some commercial funds were permitting donors to pay off legally binding pledges or receive personal benefits in return for their grants without reducing their charitable deduction. When these practices were publicized, Fidelity adopted several new rules prohibiting donors from funnelling money to private foundations and mandating the annual distribution of at least 5 percent of the Fund's assets for charitable purposes. Despite these changes, critics remained dissatisfied, asserting that the sole purpose of creating the commercial funds was to generate fees for the sponsor.

Other Legal Developments. Although the process for granting tax-exempt status to the Fidelity Charitable Gift Fund was somewhat casual, the IRS now takes a closer look at organizations that do nothing other than administer donor-advised funds. The principal focus is on who has ultimate control. The IRS fears that funds acting merely as conduits permit easy avoidance of the private foundation rules. See, e.g., Ronald J. Shoemaker & Amy Henchey, Donor Directed Funds, FY 1996 IRS Exempt Organizations Continuing Professional Education Technical Instruction Program 328 (1995). Although the law is far from developed in this area, the courts have declined to revoke the exempt status of organizations that administer donor-advised funds, at least if they can demonstrate that the donors have no legal control over grants or investments and the fund is not merely serving as a grant laundering device. See, e.g., National Foundation v. United States, 13 Cl.Ct. 486 (1987); Fund for Anonymous Gifts v. Internal Revenue Service, 194 F.3d 173 (D.C.Cir.1999).

In 1999, the Joint Committee on Taxation and the IRS announced that they were beginning a comprehensive review of this area. One proposal would have established a new category of quasi-private foundation, to be known as a Foundation Management Organization (FMO). An FMO would be any § 501(c)(3) organization with 25 percent or more of its assets in donor-advised funds. FMOs would be subject to many of the same regulations as private foundations, including the § 4941 self-dealing rules, the § 4942 minimum payout requirement, and the § 4943 prohibition on excess business holdings, but not the 2 percent excise tax on net investment income. The proposal stimulated some discussion but has not yet been seriously considered by Congress.

For Further Reading. Victoria B. Bjorklund, Charitable Giving to a Private Foundation: The Alternatives—The Supporting Organization, and the Donor–Advised Fund, 27 Exempt Org. Tax Rev. 107 (2000); Albert R. Rodriguez, William C. Choi & Ingrid P. Mittermaier, The Tax–Exempt Status of Commercially Sponsored Donor–Advised Funds, 17 Exempt Org. Tax Rev. 95 (1997); Monica Langley, You Don't Have to be a Rockefeller to Set Up Your Own Foundation, Wall St. J., Feb. 12, 1998, at A1; Monica Langley, Fidelity Plans to Limit Donors' Ability to Benefit From Gifts to Public Charity, Wall St. J., July 14, 1998, p. A4.

c. PASS–THROUGH FOUNDATIONS AND POOLED COMMON FUNDS

Internal Revenue Code: § 170(b)(1)(A)(vii), (b)(1)(E)(ii), (iii).

Two types of private grantmaking foundations—the pass-through (or conduit) foundation and the pooled common fund—are subject to the entire private foundation regulatory regime except for the limitations, on the charitable deduction in § 170. More specifically, they are entitled to the more liberal percentage limitations and their donors are not required to reduce their deductions for gifts of appreciated capital gain property by the amount of the built-in gain.

Pass–Through Foundations. A pass-through foundation must pass through all contributions made to it during the taxable year within two and one-half months after the end of the tax year in which the gifts are made. The definition is actually a bit more technical in that the requirement is to make "qualifying distributions," as defined in § 4942(g), equal to 100 percent of the value of its contributions received. For this purpose, qualifying distributions include grants to other charities and certain costs of administering the grantmaking program. See I.R.C. § 170(b)(1)(E)(ii).

Pass-through foundations are used by philanthropists who wish to launch a charitable entity during their lives, enjoying the favorable income tax benefits, and then more fully endow the foundation at death. The trade-off for the more liberal income tax treatment is the pass-through requirement, but this vehicle presents a few advantages over direct gifts from the donor. First, reasonable administrative costs, such as salaries to foundation staff, count as qualifying distributions but might not be tax-deductible if paid directly by an individual donor. Second, donors achieve a current income tax deduction but have a grace period of several months to decide the ultimate recipients of their charitable largesse. Third, a foundation may elect in and out of pass-through status from year to year. Thus, in years where the liberal deduction rules in § 170 are desirable, it can make the election; in other years, the foundation may elect out and only be required to meet the minimum distribution requirements (generally, five percent of its endowment) of § 4942. See Section C3 of this chapter, infra, at pp. 469–472.

Pooled Common Funds. The pooled common fund is a little-known charitable vehicle with the following characteristics:

1. One or more donors may make contributions that are pooled into a common fund.

2. The donor (or his or her spouse) may retain the right to designate annually the organizations to which the income attributable to his or her contribution shall be given. This is similar (though not identical) to the donor-advised fund concept discussed earlier.

3. The donee organizations must be public charities described in § 509(a)(1).

4. The fund's governing instrument must require it to distribute, and it in fact must pay out (including administrative costs):

   a. All of its adjusted net income (as defined) to one or more eligible charities not later than two and one-half months after the end of the taxable year in which the income was earned or realized.

   b. All the corpus attributable to any donor's contribution to the fund to one or more eligible charities not later than one year after the death of the donor (or the donor's surviving spouse if that spouse has the right to designate the recipients of corpus). I.R.C. § 170(b)(1)(E)(iii).

The pooled common fund offers donors the advantage of the more liberal charitable income tax deduction rules without the requirement to pass through all gifts on a relatively current basis. It allows donors to retain full control over the ultimate recipients of their gifts and, if desired, to pool funds with close family members and other donors. Like the donor-advised fund within a community foundation, the pooled common fund also permits donors with fluctuating income to coordinate their annual giving levels, giving more in high income years while retaining a steady level of giving overall. They also can "bank" charitable funds for a major gift in the future while achieving current charitable deductions. But a pooled common fund is not a suitable vehicle for establishing an endowed grantmaking foundation in perpetuity because the corpus must be paid out to qualifying public charities within a year of the donor's death.

d. SUPPORTING ORGANIZATIONS

Yet another attractive private foundation alternative is a § 509(a)(3) supporting organization. Supporting organizations are separate legal entities established to support one or more existing public charities. They can be quite useful when a donor needs the tax benefits of a lifetime gift to a public charity but desires the structure of independent charitable entity. Supporting organizations were previewed earlier in this chapter (see supra pp. 396–397); their use (and possible abuse) is discussed in more detail in Section B4, infra, at pp. 422–447.

B. AVOIDING PRIVATE FOUNDATION STATUS

The preceding section provided an overview of the federal tax treatment of private foundations. For those with the fortitude, intellectual curiosity, or professional obligation to explore further, we turn here to a more technical examination of the tax definition of a private foundation—and some strategies for avoiding private foundation status. Because this chapter has been designed to provide both a self-standing overview along with this more detailed coverage, some repetition is unavoidable for those who read on. Any overlap is likely to be pedagogically beneficial, however, because the private foundation rules are seldom mastered on a first reading.

1. THE DISQUALIFIED PERSON RULES

Internal Revenue Code: §§ 4946; 507(d)(2).
Treasury Regulations: §§ 53.4946–1(a); 1.507–6(b)(1).

Like any complex tax statute, the private foundation rules are littered with terms of art. A term of particular importance is "disqualified person."

For example, in testing the level of an organization's public support, contributions from disqualified persons count less than gifts from outsiders, and in some cases they do not count at all. The self-dealing penalty in 4941 applies to transactions between a private foundation and disqualified persons, and the holdings of disqualified persons in a business enterprise may affect a foundation's permissible business holdings.

A "disqualified person" with respect to a private foundation includes the following: a "substantial contributor" (defined below), a "foundation manager" (also defined below), a more than 20 percent owner of a business entity that is a substantial contributor, a member of the family (yet another definition) of any of the foregoing, and corporations, partnerships, trusts or estates in which any of the foregoing (as a group) have greater than 35 percent ownership interests. I.R.C. § 4946(a).

A few specialized categories of "disqualified person" apply for purposes of the self-dealing and excess business holdings rules. They will be discussed in the context of the penalties to which they relate. See I.R.C. § 4946(a)(1)(H), (I).

Substantial Contributor. The major category of disqualified person consists of substantial contributors to the foundation and members of the family of substantial contributors. A substantial contributor is any person (including natural persons as well as entities, such as corporations or other private foundations) who has contributed or bequeathed an aggregate amount of more than $5,000 to the foundation, if that amount is more than 2 percent of the total contributions and bequests received by the foundation from its inception through the end of its taxable year in which the contribution or bequest is received. The creator of a charitable trust is always a substantial contributor. I.R.C. § 507(d)(2). The determination of a donor's substantial contributor status is made annually on the last day of a foundation's taxable year, but a donor "joins the club" as of the first date that the foundation received from the donor an amount sufficient to make him a substantial contributor. Id.; Treas. Reg. § 1.507–6(b)(1). With one exception described below, the donor remains a substantial contributor for time immemorial (including after one's death!), even if the person's aggregate gifts fall short of the 2 percent threshold in the future. Id.

In identifying substantial contributors, contributions and bequests are taken into account at their fair market value on the date the foundation receives the gift, except that any gifts received before October 9, 1969 are treated for valuation purposes as having been received on that date. I.R.C. § 507(d)(2)(B)(i) & (ii). Individuals are treated as making all contributions and bequests made by their spouse, but not by other members of their family. I.R.C. § 507(d)(2)(B)(iii).

The principal donors to a private foundation almost always are substantial contributors. For example, assume Mr. and Mrs. Donor each give $1 million in appreciated stock to fund the Donor Foundation. Each is treated as giving $2 million—an amount well in excess of $5,000 and constituting 100 percent of the foundation's total gifts. The inquiry is more challenging for smaller donors. To illustrate, assume that Giver makes a mid-year gift of $6,000 cash to Foundation, which has received a total of $100,000 of gifts and bequests as of the end of that year. Since Giver's gift exceeds $5,000 and is more than 2 percent of the year-end total (2% of $100,000 = $2,000), he is a substantial contributor. But if Giver made the same $6,000 mid-year gift at a time when the foundation's total gifts were $100,000, but subsequent gifts raised the foundation's total to $1,000,000 by year-end, Giver would not be a substantial contributor because his gift does not exceed $20,000 (2% of $1,000,000) as of the end of the year.

At one time, the rule was—"once a substantial contributor, always a substantial contributor." As will become clearer below, this status could taint related family members and their spouses even though they had nothing to do with the foundation. In the meantime the foundation may have received large gifts from other donors, diluting any historic influence a substantial contributor may have once derived from his or her contribution. Section 507(d)(2)(C) addresses this problem by providing that a person ceases to be treated as a substantial contributor as of the close of a foundation's taxable year if, for a ten-year period ending at the close of that year, the contributor or any related person neither makes any contribution to the foundation nor serves as its foundation manager. In addition, the Service must determine that the aggregate contributions made by the contributor and related persons (including appreciation of contributed property while held by the foundation) are "insignificant" when compared with the aggregate amount of contributions made by "one other person." I.R.C. § 507(d)(2)(C)(i)(III). To illustrate, assume Donor makes a $10,000 cash gift to Foundation, which has received total contributions of $100,000 as of the end of Year 1. Donor makes no further gifts and, as of the end of Year 11, Foundation's aggregate gifts are $1,000,000, of which $500,000 was received from a person unrelated to Donor. Donor would lose substantial contributor status at the end of Year 11 because no gifts had been made for 10 years and Donor's $10,000 gift is "insignificant" when compared with the $500,000 received from the unrelated person.

Foundation Manager. A "foundation manager" is another type of disqualified person. Foundation managers include officers, directors, trustees, or individuals having similar powers or responsibilities. I.R.C. § 4946(a)(1)(B), (b)(1). Other foundation employees with authority or responsibility regarding particular matters also are treated as managers with respect to any act, or failure to act, within their scope of authority or responsibility, but the regulations make it clear that a person who is a foundation manager solely under this "responsible employee" rule is not a disqualified person for any other purpose. Treas. Reg. § 53.4946-1(f)(4).

Owners of Substantial Contributors. As noted above, corporations, partnerships, trusts and other entities may become substantial contributors. In addition, persons owning more than 20 percent of these entities are also treated as disqualified persons. Specifically, the ownership threshold is crossed by owning more than 20 percent of the voting stock of a corporation, of the profits interests of a partnership, or of the beneficial interests of other entities. I.R.C. § 4946(a)(1)(C). Nothing is simple. Stock ownership is determined by applying the § 267(c) attribution rules, with the definition of "family" modified slightly to include only an individual's spouse, ancestors, children, grandchildren, great grandchildren, and the spouses of these lineal descendants (siblings and more distant lineal descendants are dropped). I.R.C. § 4946(a)(3). Additional technical rules are provided to determine constructive ownership of interests in partnerships, trusts and other entities. See I.R.C. § 4946(a)(4).

Family Members. "Members of the family" of a substantial contributor, a foundation manager, or a more than 20 percent owner of a substantial contributor also are disqualified persons. I.R.C. § 4946(a)(1)(D). An individual's "family" includes his or her spouse, ancestors, children, grandchildren, great grandchildren, and the spouses of children, grandchildren and great grandchildren. I.R.C. § 4946(d). At one time, the disqualified person taint meandered forever through the family tree, but Congress— perhaps fearful that all of civilization ultimately would become disqualified people—revised the rule to halt the virus at the great grandchildren's generation.

Related Entities. To ensure that Congressional intent could not be circumvented through the use of related entities, the term "disqualified person" includes any corporation, partnership, trust, or estate if more than 35 percent of the corporation's voting stock, the partnership's profits interests, or the trust or estate's beneficial interests is owned by the four types of disqualified persons discussed above—i.e., substantial contributors, more than 20 percent owners of substantial contributors, foundation managers, and members of the family of any of the foregoing. I.R.C. § 4946(a)(1)(E), (F), (G). The § 267 attribution rules once again apply in determining ownership interests.

2. TRADITIONAL PUBLIC CHARITIES: § 509(a)(1)

Internal Revenue Code: §§ 509(a)(1), (d); 170(b)(1)(A)(i)–(vi).

Treasury Regulations: §§ 1.170A–9(a), (b), (c)(1), (d), (e)(1)–(4)(v), (6), (7), (8), (9).

Most organizations that avoid private foundation status come within the exception provided by § 509(a)(1) for traditional and publicly supported charities described in § 170(b)(1)(A)(i) through (vi). These organizations historically have been favored for charitable income tax deduction purposes. They sometimes are referred to as "50 percent charities" because cash contributions to them may be deducted by individual donors up to an annual limit of 50 percent of adjusted gross income. Traditional public charities fall into six sub-categories, five of which are exempted because of the nature of their activities and the sixth because of the level of public financial support that they receive.

a.   ORGANIZATIONS ENGAGING IN INHERENTLY PUBLIC ACTIVITIES

Churches or Conventions or Associations of Churches. The first exclusion from private foundation status is for churches and conventions and associations of churches. I.R.C. 170(b)(1)(A)(i). As discussed in Chapter 2, not every religious organization is a "church." The regulations do not define "church," but the courts occasionally have been forced to do so, usually applying 14 church characteristics suggested by the Internal Revenue Service. According to the Tax Court, a minimum requirement for "church" status is a body of believers or communicants that assemble regularly in order to worship. See, e.g., Foundation of Human Understanding v. Commissioner, 88 T.C. 1341 (1987) (acq.); Chapter 2C6, supra, at pp. 199–201. A "convention or association of churches" is a regional or national umbrella organization that consists of member churches, usually of the same denomination, such as the National Council of Churches, the Union of American Hebrew Congregations, and the National Catholic Conference. See Rev. Rul. 74–224, 1974–1 C.B. 61.

Educational Organizations. Traditional public charities also include educational organizations that maintain a "regular faculty and curriculum" and normally have a "regularly enrolled body of pupils or students in attendance * * *." I.R.C. § 170(b)(1)(A)(ii). This category includes primary and secondary schools, colleges, universities and nonprofit vocational schools. Treas. Reg. § 1.170A–9(b). Advocacy organizations that qualify as "educational" under 501(c)(3) would not fall into this narrower classification. The primary function of an educational organization must be "the presentation of formal instruction." Id. The Service has construed this requirement liberally in several published rulings. See, e.g., Rev. Rul. 73–434, 1973–2 C.B. 71 (26–day survival course for young people); Rev. Rul. 78–309, 1978–2 C.B. 123 (martial arts school).

Hospitals and Medical Research Organizations. The hospitals that avoid private foundation status include any organization for which the "principal purpose or function is the providing of medical or hospital care." I.R.C. § 170(b)(1)(A)(iii). Inpatient care need not be provided, but the term "hospital" is not broad enough to include convalescent homes, homes for children or the aged, or facilities for training the handicapped. Treas. Reg. § 1.170A–9(c)(1).

"Medical research organizations" qualify if they are directly engaged in the continuous active conduct of medical research in conjunction with a hospital and if they commit contributions received to such research for use within five years of the time of the gift. I.R.C. § 170(b)(1)(A)(iii). Formal affiliation with a hospital is not required—only an "understanding" that the research organization and the hospital will cooperate and engage in a "joint effort." Treas. Reg. § 1.170A–9(c)(2)(vii). For more guidance on the nature of "medical research" and the extent of pursuits necessary to qualify under this provision, see Treas. Reg. § 1.170A–9(c)(2). This specialized exemption reportedly was created to cover organizations founded by Howard Hughes and the DuPont family, but it has a wider net.

Support Organizations for State Colleges and Universities. Organizations formed to support state colleges and universities are not private foundations if they normally receive a substantial part of their support from governmental sources or from direct or indirect contributions from the general public, or from a combination of those sources. I.R.C. 170(b)(1)(A)(iv). This category includes separately incorporated entities formed to conduct building fund drives, maintain scholarship funds, support athletic programs and the like. The determination of public support generally follows the guidelines applicable to § 170(b)(1)(A)(vi) organizations (see discussion below), although permitted sources of support from governmental entities are somewhat narrower. See Treas. Reg. § 1.170A–9(b)(2).

Governmental Units. This category of nonprivate foundation includes the United States, its political subdivisions, the District of Columbia, and all other governmental bodies listed in § 170(c)(1). I.R.C. § 170(b)(1)(A)(v). Singling out governmental units in § 170 is significant for purposes of the charitable income tax deduction, but excluding them from private foundation status is unnecessary because most governmental units derive their federal tax exemption from § 115 rather than § 501(c)(3), and only § 501(c)(3) organizations can be private foundations.

b. PUBLICLY SUPPORTED ORGANIZATIONS

Section 170(b)(1)(A)(vi) describes the first of two types of publicly supported organizations excluded from private foundation status because of the breadth of their financial support. The exclusion is based on the notion that an organization dependent upon the general public or government for its support will be publicly accountable. This category of public charity must:

> [n]ormally receive a substantial part of its support (exclusive of income received in the exercise or performance by such organization of its charitable, educational, or other purpose or function constituting the basis for its exemption under § 501(a)) from a governmental unit * * * or from direct or indirect contributions from the general public.

I.R.C. § 170(b)(1)(A)(vi).

The regulations elaborate considerably, providing two alternative sub-tests to measure the requisite public support and defining the critical statutory terms. See generally Treas. Reg. § 1.170A–9(e). We shall first outline the two sub-tests and then flesh out the remaining details.

Mathematical Test. An organization will be treated as a public charity for a taxable year if public and governmental contributions equal at least one-third of the total support received by the charity over a testing period that generally consists of the four taxable years preceding the year under scrutiny. Treas. Reg. 1.170A–9(e)(2), (4).

Facts and Circumstances Test. An organization that fails to meet the mathematical test still can qualify as a public charity if it generates at least 10 percent public support during the testing period and is "so organized and operated as to attract new and additional public or governmental support on a continuous basis." Treas. Reg. § 1.170A–9(e)(3)(i), (ii). An active fund raising program, including a membership structure, is helpful in meeting the "attraction of public support" requirement.

In addition to the 10 percent and attraction of public support requirements, the organization must establish, based on "all pertinent facts and circumstances," that it is publicly supported. Treas. Reg. § 1.170A–9(e)(3)(ii). The regulations list five factors, stating that the weight accorded to any one of them may differ depending upon the nature and purpose of the organization and the length of time it has been in existence:

(1) *Percentage of Financial Support*. The higher the percentage of public support above 10 percent, the lesser is the organization's burden of establishing its publicly supported nature through other factors. The burden increases, conversely, as public support approaches 10 percent. Treas. Reg. § 1.170A–9(e)(3)(iii).

(2) *Sources of Support*. Public support is best demonstrated by a representative number of supporters rather than members of a single family group. In considering breadth of support, the regulations consider "the type of organization involved, the length of time it has been in existence, and whether it limits its activities to a particular community or region or to a special field which can be expected to appeal to a limited number of persons." Treas. Reg. § 1.170A–9(e)(3)(iv).

(3) *Representative Governing Body*. A governing board that is representative of broad public or community interests is preferable to a narrow group. The regulations suggest a board comprised of public officials acting in that capacity; of individuals selected by public officials; of persons having special knowledge or expertise in the foundation's field of interests; of community leaders and others representing a broad cross-section of community views; and, in the case of membership organizations, of individuals elected by a broadly based membership. Treas. Reg. § 1.170A–9(e)(3)(v).

(4) *Availability of Public Facilities or Services and Public Participation*. Organizations that generally provide facilities or services directly for the benefit of the general public on a continuing basis— e.g., museums, libraries, symphonies—are more easily able to demonstrate that they are publicly supported. In addition, the fact that educational or research organizations regularly publish and disseminate scholarly studies is considered evidence that they are publicly supported. The regulations list a number of other factors that are considered evidence of public support. Treas. Reg. § 1.170A–9(e)(3)(vi).

(5) *Additional Factors Pertinent to Membership Organizations*. Membership organizations can demonstrate their public support by soliciting a broad cross-section of the public and having activities that are likely to appeal to persons having some broad common

interest, such as educational activities in the case of alumni associations, or musical activities in the case of symphonies. Treas. Reg. § 1.170A–9(e)(3)(vii).

Both the mechanical and the facts and circumstances tests require the organization to calculate its public support over a testing period by using a fraction that compares public support (the numerator) with total support (the denominator). The regulations provide the definitions needed to make this calculation.

Total Support. Total support includes gifts and grants from individuals, corporate donors, public charities, private foundations, and other nonprofit organizations; bequests; government grants made to enable the organization to provide a service to or maintain a facility for the direct benefit of the public; membership fees paid for general support of the organization; net income from unrelated business activities; gross investment income (excluding capital gains); tax revenues levied by a governmental unit for the benefit of the organization; and the value of services or facilities furnished without charge to the organization by a government unit (exclusive of what is generally provided free to the public). All income derived by the organization from the performance of its exempt functions—such as tuition, admission fees to a museum or theater, proceeds from the sale of merchandise—is excluded from total support for purposes of § 170(b)(1)(A)(vi). I.R.C. § 509(d); Treas. Reg. § 1.170A–9(e)(7)(i). Also excluded are the value of donated services (e.g., a volunteer's time) and certain "unusual grants," which are discussed below.

Public Support. Public support includes gifts, bequests and grants from the general public, government grants, membership fees, tax revenues levied specifically to benefit the organization, and the value of government provided services or facilities. Donations from any private source (e.g., a corporation, individual, trust or private foundation) are included in public support only to the extent they do not exceed two percent of the total support received by the organization over the measuring period. In applying the two percent limitation, an individual's contributions are aggregated with gifts made during the measuring period by certain members of the donor's family. Significantly, contributions from government entities and other public charities are not subject to the two percent limitation. Treas. Reg. § 1.170A–9(e)(6), (7) & (8).

Unusual Grants. An "unusual grant" may be excluded from both the top and bottom of the public support fraction if including the grant would cause the organization to fail the public support test. An unusual grant is a substantial gift or bequest to an organization that: (1) is attracted by reason of the organization's publicly supported nature, (2) is unusual or unexpected with respect to its amount, and (3) by reason of its size, adversely affects the organization's public charity status. Treas. Reg. § 1.170A–9(e)(6)(ii). Because gifts and grants are fully included in total support but are not included in public support to the extent they exceed the two percent cap, the ability to exclude unusual grants can be very helpful in preserving the public charity status of an organization receiving an unexpected windfall from a generous donor.

In evaluating whether a contribution qualifies as an unusual grant, the Service considers a long list of factors, no one of which is determinative. For example, a grant is more likely to be unusual if: (1) it is made by a person with no prior connection to the organization rather than by a member of the founding family or a member of the board of directors, (2) it is a bequest rather than a lifetime gift, (3) the gift is of cash or marketable securities rather than an illiquid asset that is unrelated to the organization's exempt purposes, (4) the organization regularly solicits funds, (5) if the organization has a broad based governing board, and (6) no material restrictions are imposed on the grant. Treas. Reg. § 1.170A–9(e)(6)(iii); Rev. Proc. 81–7, 1981–1 C.B. 621.

Testing Period. The statute cryptically requires that a public charity "normally" must receive substantial public support. The term "normally" is construed by the regulations to require a testing period of four consecutive taxable years in order to level the peaks and valleys that an organization may encounter in attracting public support. An organization qualifies as a public charity for the current year and the succeeding year if it meets either of the support sub-tests for the four years immediately preceding the current year. Treas. Reg. § 1.170A–9(e)(4)(i), (ii). To illustrate, if an organization meets the one-third support test for the years 1996–1999 (calculated in the aggregate, not year-by-year), it qualifies as a public charity for 2000 and 2001. Or looking backwards, an organization would qualify as a public charity for 2001 if it met the public support tests for the years 1996–1999 or 1997–2000. As a result of the flexibility of the testing period rules, a year of poor public support will not necessarily jeopardize an organization's status as a public charity if it is able to make up the slack before and after the bad year.

Special testing period rules apply to new organizations. If an organization has been in existence for at least eight months but fewer than five taxable years, the testing period consists of the entire period of the organization's existence immediately preceding the year being tested. Treas. Reg. § 1.170A–9(e)(4)(vi).

Substantial and Material Changes in Support. Because the testing period rules look backwards, not including the year under scrutiny, the regulations provide an exception in cases where substantial and material changes in support occur in the current year other than from unusual grants. In that event, the four-year testing period is expanded to five years, consisting of the current year and the four preceding years. An example of a substantial and material change in support is the receipt of an unusually large contribution or bequest that does not qualify as an unusual grant. See Rev. Proc. 81–7, 1981–1 C.B. 621. To illustrate, if substantial and material changes occur in an organization's support for the 2000 tax year, then, even though the organization may meet the requirements of the public support test based on a computation period of tax years 1995–1998 or 1996–1999, the organization will not meet either test unless it also meets the test for a computation period consisting of the tax years 1996–2000. Treas. Reg. § 1.170A–9(e)(4)(v)(a).

Under a safe harbor rule, a grantor or contributor will not be considered as responsible for a substantial and material change in support if the aggregate of her contributions for a taxable year is 25 percent or less of the aggregate support received by the donee organization from all sources (except prior gifts from the donor and certain related persons) for the four taxable years preceding the year of the contribution (or the years of the organization's existence, if less). Rev. Proc. 81–6, 1981–1 C.B. 620. The safe harbor is not available, however, if the contributor is an insider (e.g., foundation manager) or obtains a position of authority (e.g., a seat on the board of directors) as a result of the contribution. Id.

A donor generally may rely upon the Service's recognition of an organization's public charity status until notice of a change is formally published in the Internal Revenue Bulletin. But a donor who is responsible for, or aware of, a substantial and material change in support that adversely affects public charity status is not entitled to such protection. Reg. § 1.170A–9(e)(4)(v)(b).

3. "GROSS RECEIPTS" AND MEMBERSHIP ORGANIZATIONS: § 509(a)(2)

Internal Revenue Code: § 509(a)(2). Review §§ 507(d)(2); 509(d); 4946.

Treasury Regulations: § 1.509(a)–3(a).

A different type of publicly supported organization is described in § 509(a)(2). To come within this escape hatch, an organization must enjoy broad public support measured by a positive support test and a negative investment income test. Specifically, a § 509(a)(2) organization first must demonstrate that it "normally" receives more than one-third of its total support from any combination of gifts, grants, contributions, membership fees, admission charges, and fees from the performance of exempt functions. I.R.C. § 509(a)(2)(A). Second, it must establish that it normally does not receive more than one-third of its support from the sum of net investment income and unrelated business income less federal taxes imposed on that income. I.R.C. § 509(a)(2)(B). Congress included the additional category of public charity at the behest of certain organizations that derive substantial public support through their exempt function activities but are not heavily dependent on investment income. Because § 170(b)(1)(A)(vi) excludes exempt function income in testing for public support, another test was necessary to protect organizations that traditionally derived much of their revenue from tax-exempt activities. The legislative history indicates that § 509(a)(2) was intended to cover "symphony societies, garden clubs, alumni associations, Boy Scouts, Parent–Teacher Associations and many other membership organizations." S.Rep. No. 552, 91st Cong., 2d Sess. 461 (1969).

Total Support. The "total support" denominator of both the positive and negative fractions in § 509(a)(2) includes gifts, grants, contributions, and membership fees; "gross receipts" from admissions, sales of merchandise, performance of services or furnishing of facilities in an activity which is not an unrelated trade or business; net income from unrelated business activities; gross investment income, excluding capital gains; tax revenues levied for the organization's benefit and either paid to or expended on behalf of the organization; and the value of services or facilities furnished by the government specifically to the organization without charge. I.R.C. § 509(d).

Good Support. The numerator of the positive support fraction includes gifts, grants, contributions and fees received from governmental sources, public charities, or any other person who is not a disqualified person with respect to the organization as well as gross receipts from the conduct of exempt functions. I.R.C. § 509(a)(2)(A). Thus, gifts from substantial contributors or other insiders do not count as good support. Gross receipts from the conduct of exempt functions also are excluded from the numerator in any taxable year to the extent that they exceed the greater of $5,000 or one percent of the organization's support for that year. This limitation is intended to ensure that organizations relying on § 509(a)(2) maintain a broad-based program of income-generating sales or services.

The regulations go on at some length to distinguish grants (which are not subject to this limitation) and gross receipts. "Gross receipts" are amounts received from an activity where the organization provides a specific service, facility or product to serve the direct and immediate needs of the payor rather than to confer a direct benefit upon the general public. See Treas. Reg. § 1.509(a)–3(g).

Gross Investment Income. The negative support test set forth in § 509(a)(2)(B) provides that no more than one-third of the organization's total support may consist of: (1) gross investment income (consisting of interest, dividends, payments with respect to securities loans, rents, and royalties) and (2) the net of unrelated business taxable income over the unrelated business tax imposed by Section 511. The regulations also provide that an organization's gross investment income includes amounts distributed from the gross investment income of another organization. See Treas. Reg. § 1.509(a)–5(a)(1) for the details.

Unusual Grants. In measuring support for both the positive public support and negative investment income tests, an organization may exclude any unusual grants if they would have an adverse effect. The criteria for determining whether a particular contribution is an unusual grant are the same as those already discussed under § 170(b)(1)(A)(vi). See p. 417, supra, and Treas. Reg. § 1.509(a)–3(c)(3) & (4).

Testing Period. The positive and negative support fractions are calculated by aggregating the organization's sources of support over the same rolling four-year testing period discussed earlier in connection with the § 170(b)(1)(A)(vi) public support test. Reg. § 1.509(a)–3(c)(1)(i). If the tests are met for the testing period, the organization avoids private foundation status under § 509(a)(2) for the two taxable years following the close of that period. Id. Rules similar to those applicable under § 170(b)(1)(A)(vi) also apply to newly created organizations. Reg. § 1.509(a)–3(c)(1)(iv). For any taxable year in which there are substantial and material changes in the organization's support, the testing period becomes the current year and the four preceding years. Treas. Reg. § 1.509(a)–3(c)(1)(ii).

PROBLEM

This problem offers an opportunity to apply the tests for public charity status under §§ 170(b)(1)(A)(vi) and 509(a)(2).

The Burbank Foundation, a § 501(c)(3) organization, was organized in New York by Amanda Burbank and her husband, Earl, each of whom became "substantial contributors" as a result of their founding gifts. The purposes of the Foundation are to support a broad range of charitable activities, concentrating specifically on the problems of the environment. The Foundation has six directors, including three members of the Burbank family and three local community leaders. The Foundation's President is Walter Russell, the husband of Aretha Burbank Russell, who is the daughter of Amanda and Earl Burbank.

For the years 1997–2000, the Foundation's gross revenues were as follows (figures are in thousands of dollars):

	1997	**1998**	**1999**	**2000**
Dividends	125	125	125	125
Government grants	25	25	25	25
Sierra Club grant	—	25	—	25
Individual donations	50	25	150	25
Fundraising dance	25	25	20	30
Sale of environmental posters	25	25	30	20
Total	$250	$250	$350	$250

No one person purchased more than $100 in tickets to the fundraising dance, an annual event. Half the price of each ticket to the dance was treated as a charitable contribution, and the other half was for the food and entertainment provided at the event. The posters were sold to a diverse group of people except for the Sierra Club, a § 501(c)(4) organization, which made an annual bulk purchase of $10,000 worth of posters (included in the above totals). The Foundation has received a letter ruling that the poster sales were an activity substantially related to its exempt purposes and thus did not constitute an unrelated trade or business.

Individual donations to the Foundation came from a diverse group of supporters and were in amounts of $500 or less. No person gave more than $500 except that in both 1997 and 1999, Walter Russell made $10,000 in cash gifts, and in 1999 the Foundation received a $100,000 bequest from Willard Ginsburg, a Vermont philanthropist, who had never made any previous gifts to the Foundation. The Sierra Club's grants to date have not exceeded two percent of the total contributions and bequests received by the Foundation.

(a) Who are the disqualified persons with respect to the Burbank Foundation?

(b) Is the Burbank Foundation a "private foundation" as of January 1, 2001? Consider §§ 170(b)(1)(A)(vi) and 509(a)(2).

4.   Supporting Organizations: § 509(a)(3)

Internal Revenue Code: § 509(a)(3).

Treasury Regulations: § 1.509(a)–4.

a.   INTRODUCTION

Section 509(a)(3) provides a final refuge from private foundation status to organizations that maintain a support relationship with one or more publicly supported charities or governmental entities. An organization avoids private foundation status under § 509(a)(3) if it is:

1. Organized and continuously operated exclusively for the benefit of, to perform the functions of, or to carry out the purposes of one or more public charities that have avoided private foundation status under § 509(a)(1) or § 509(a)(2).

2. Operated, supervised, or controlled by, or in connection with, one or more of these nonprivate foundations.

3. Not controlled, directly or indirectly, by one or more "disqualified persons" other than foundation managers and the public charities that it supports.

A supporting organization can be an attractive vehicle for involving a family with a public charity through an independent entity that bears the family's name and yet it avoids the disadvantages of private foundation status. For example, a philanthropist may wish to fund a charitable foundation with lifetime gifts of stock in a closely held corporation. Unlike a private foundation, a supporting organization is not required to dispose of "excess business holdings," such as stock in a family company, and it is not subject to the two percent tax on its net investment income. In addition, contributions of appreciated long-term capital gain property, including closely-held stock, are generally deductible to the extent of 30 percent of the donor's adjusted gross income, without reduction by the amount of the built-in gain. The trade-off is that donors who establish supporting organizations give up the level of control they would have with a private foundation.

The specific requirements for qualifying as a supporting organization are found in § 509(a)(3) and a challenging set of regulations, all summarized below.

b.   PERMISSIBLE RELATIONSHIPS

A critical step in deciphering the regulations is to understand that three alternative types of relationships between the supporting and supported organization are sanctioned by § 509(a)(3). The type of relationship on which an organization relies may have an impact on the other statutory tests that must be met. A supporting organization may be: (1) operated, supervised or controlled by, (2) supervised or controlled in connection with, or (3) operated in connection with, one or more publicly supported organizations. Treas. Reg. § 1.509(a)–4(f)(2). Thus, it is possible to satisfy the statute by establishing a relationship of tight control (analogous to a parent owning a subsidiary), or to provide virtual autonomy to the supporting organization ("operated in connection with"). Any relationship must insure, however, that the supporting organization is "responsive to the needs or demands of one or more publicly supported organizations" and that the supporting organization "will constitute an integral part of, or maintain a significant involvement in, the operations of one or more publicly supported organizations." Treas. Reg. § 1.509(a)–4(f)(3).

Operated, supervised, or controlled by. The first and most restrictive type of relationship is established when a majority of the officers, directors or trustees of the supporting organization must be appointed or elected by the governing body or officers of the supported organization. The regulations give the example of a separately incorporated university press whose board of governors is selected by the university's trustees on recommendation of the university president. Treas. Reg. § 1.509(a)–4(g)(2) Example (1). The organization or organizations that control the supporting organization need not be those directly benefited by it, provided that the purposes of the controlling organizations are carried out by means of the benefits afforded the latter organizations. See Treas. Reg. § 1.509(a)–(4)(g)(1)(ii). An example from the regulations is a trust that pays its net income to three hospitals in a particular community for research, and its trustees are appointed by the president of a local university, some of whose faculty members do research in the hospitals. Treas. Reg. § 1.509(a)–4(g)(2) Example (3).

Supervised or controlled in connection with. This relationship is analogous to that of brother-sister corporations—i.e., there must be common supervision or control over both the supporting and supported organizations. Mere payments (mandatory or discretionary) to one or more named public charities will not suffice to establish this type of relationship. Rather, the control or management of the supporting organization must be vested in the same persons that control or manage the supported public charity. Treas. Reg. § 1.509(a)–4(h).

Operated in connection with. This is the most amorphous of the permissible statutory relationships and also the most flexible. The supporting organization must demonstrate its "responsiveness" to the needs of its beneficiary, and show that its programs are significant enough to be an "integral part" of the functions of the supported organization. Treas. Reg. § 1.509(a)–4(i). Not surprisingly, the regulations provide a "responsiveness" test and an "integral part" test, each of which must be met to establish this type of relationship.

"Responsiveness" is established through interlocking boards or officer structures, or by a "close and continuous working relationship" between the officers, directors or trustees of both organizations. Treas. Reg. § 1.509(a)–4(i)(2). By reason of this symbiosis, the supported organization must have a "significant voice" in the investment policies, the timing of grants, the manner of making grants, and the selection of recipients, "and in otherwise directing the use of the income or assets" of the supporting organization. If the supporting organization is a charitable trust under state law, then the "responsiveness" test is met by naming each beneficiary under the trust's governing instrument, and by each beneficiary organization's power to enforce the trust. Id.

The "integral part" test requires a "significant involvement" by the supporting organization in the operations of one or more public charities, which in turn must be dependent upon the supporting organization for the type of support that it provides. Treas. Reg. § 1.509(a)–4(i)(3)(i). One way to satisfy the test is by showing that the supporting organization's activities carry out the purposes of the supported public charities and otherwise would have been carried on by those charities but for the involvement of the supporting organization. Treas. Reg. 1.509(a)–4(i)(3)(ii). Alternatively, the integral part test is met by showing that the supporting organization pays "substantially all" of its income for support purposes, and that amount of support is "sufficient to insure the attentiveness [of the supported organization] to the operations of the supporting organization." Treas. Reg. § 1.509(a)–4(i)(3)(iii)(*a*). Obviously, the greater the resources of the supporting organization, the more likely it is to engage the attention of its beneficiary. The regulations flesh out the integral part test with considerably more detail and several examples. Treas. Reg. § 1.509(a)–4(i)(3)(iii).

The regulations describing what it takes to establish a "Type 3" ("in connection with") relationship require highly subjective determinations. Aggressive practitioners have exploited this aspect of the "Type 3" structure by creating supporting organizations that have very attenuated relationships with their supported public charities. The *Lapham Foundation* case, which follows, suggests that the Tax Court is prepared to require a strong factual showing that the required relationship exists.

Lapham Foundation v. Commissioner

United States Tax Court, 2002.
84 T.C.M. 586.

MEMORANDUM OPINION

■ NIMS, J.

[The Lapham Foundation, Inc. was formed by Charles and Maxine Lapham ("the Laphams") as a Michigan nonprofit corporation in 1998. As provided in its Articles of Incorporation, the purpose of the Foundation was to operate exclusively for the benefit of The American Endowment Foundation ("AEF"), an Ohio public charity that operated a donor-advised fund program under which donors could make nonbinding recommendations regarding the charitable use or beneficiaries of contributions made to AEF. The Foundation's five-person board of directors consisted of the Laphams and three other individuals, none of whom had a family or employment relationship with the Laphams. One of the three unrelated board members was appointed by AEF and one was nominated by a local church.

The Laphams' first gift to the Foundation was an interest-bearing promissory note in the amount of $1,554,244. The Laphams were the payees, and the maker was the Laphams' wholly-owned corporation, Estate Storage, Inc. The note was due in full no later than December 30, 2013. In connection with their contribution of the note, the Laphams entered into a charitable gift annuity agreement under which the Foundation agreed to pay the Laphams an annual annuity over their joint lives.

In its application for § 501(c)(3) exemption, the Foundation requested classification as a § 509(a)(3) supporting organization. It indicated that it would support AEF and other qualified charities by receiving and administering funds for the benefit of AEF. Specifically, the Foundation stated that it would be "operated in connection with" AEF and that it intended to pay at least 85 percent of its income to AEF. In later correspondence with the IRS, the Foundation stated that it intended to recommend that one-third of its contributions to a donor-advised fund administered by AEF would be used to support charitable activities in southeastern Michigan and two-thirds would be used to support charities in the Laphams' hometown, Northville, Michigan.

The IRS granted the Foundation's application for § 501(c)(3) exemption but adversely ruled on its request for classification as a "Type 3" ("operated in connection with") supporting organization. The IRS contended that because the Foundation's primary asset was a promissory note from the Laphams' corporation, it was controlled by disqualified persons and that the AEF-appointed director lacked a "significant voice" in the Federation's activities. In a response submitted during the administrative process, the Foundation proposed to amend its Articles and include a church and a local chapter of the Boy Scouts of America as additional supported organizations. It stated that it would give at least $10,000 to the church; $1,000 to a music endowment fund (40 percent of that fund's $2,500 budget for the year 2000) and $9,000 to a real estate acquisition fund (80 percent of that fund's year 2000 budget). Eds.]

Discussion

I. General Rules

Section 509(a) defines a private foundation as any organization described in section 501(c)(3) except those excluded under section 509(a)(1) through (4). Paragraphs (1) and (2) of section 509(a) detail what are referred to as publicly supported entities, sec. 1.509(a)–4(a)(5), Income Tax Regs., and encompass religious, educational, medical, and governmental entities and institutions which receive substantial public support. Paragraph (3) of section 509(a) describes what are termed supporting organizations, sec. 1.509(a)–4(a)(5), Income Tax Regs., as follows:

an organization which—

(A) is organized, and at all times thereafter is operated, exclusively for the benefit of, to perform the functions of, or to carry out the purposes of one or more specified organizations described in paragraph (1) or (2),

(B) is operated, supervised, or controlled by or in connection with one or more organizations, described in paragraph (1) or (2), and

(C) is not controlled directly or indirectly by one or more disqualified persons (as defined in section 4946) other than foundation managers and other than one or more organizations described in paragraph (1) or (2); * * *

As a practical matter, organizations classified as private foundations are subject to an excise tax regime and to deductibility limits on contributions not applicable to publicly supported charities and other excepted entities. Secs. 170, 4940–4948. The rationale underlying this distinction, and its relationship to supporting organizations in particular, has been encapsulated by the Court of Appeals for the Seventh Circuit:

Public charities were excepted from private foundation status on the theory that their exposure to public scrutiny and their dependence on public support would keep them from the abuses to which private foundations were subject. Supporting organizations are similarly excepted in so far as they are subject to the scrutiny of a public charity. The Treasury Regulations therefore provide that the supporting organization must be responsive to the needs of the public charity and intimately involved in its operations. * * *

A. Section 509(a)(3)(A)

Regulations promulgated under section 509(a)(3) set forth tests expounding on the requirements recited in subparagraphs (A) through (C) above. Section 1.509(a)–4(b) through (e), Income Tax Regs., specifies organizational and operational tests that relate to the criteria of section 509(a)(3)(A). The organizational test is not at issue in this proceeding, and because respondent raises no arguments under the operational test distinct from those addressed more fully by respondent in connection with subparagraphs (B) and (C), we do not separately discuss the elements and tests of section 509(a)(3)(A).

B. Section 509(a)(3)(B)

Section 509(a)(3)(B) prescribes the nature of the relationship that must exist between the supporting organization and the publicly supported organization. [The court then discussed the three types of permissible relationships and proceeded to elaborated on the "operated in connection with" relationship under which the Foundation was seeking to qualify. Eds.]

The regulations further impose two specific tests that must be satisfied in order for an organization to qualify as operated in connection with a publicly supported entity; namely, the responsiveness test and the integral part test. Sec. 1.509(a)–4(i), Income Tax Regs. The responsiveness test is designed to ensure that the supporting organization is responsive to the needs of the publicly supported organization by requiring that the supported organization have the ability to influence the activities of the supporting organization. Sec. 1.509(a)–4(i)(2), Income Tax Regs. As relevant herein, the test mandates that:

(a) One or more officers, directors, or trustees of the supporting organization are elected or appointed by the officers, directors, trustees, or membership of the publicly supported organizations;

(b) One or more members of the governing bodies of the publicly supported organizations are also officers, directors or trustees of, or hold other important offices in, the supporting organizations; or

(c) The officers, directors or trustees of the supporting organization maintain a close and continuous working relationship with the officers, directors or trustees of the publicly supported organizations; and

(d) By reason of (a), (b), or (c) of this subdivision, the officers, directors or trustees of the publicly supported organizations have a significant voice in the investment policies of the supporting organization, the timing of grants, the manner of making them, and the selection of recipients of such supporting organization, and in otherwise directing the use of the income or assets of such supporting organization. [Sec. 1.509(a)-4(i)(2)(ii), Income Tax Regs.]

The integral part test seeks to ensure that the supporting organization "maintains a significant involvement in the operations of one or more publicly supported organizations and such publicly supported organizations are in turn dependent upon the supporting organization for the type of support which it provides." Sec. 1.509(a)–4(i)(3)(i), Income Tax Regs. Two alternative sets of criteria exist under the regulations for satisfying this test. Id. The first alternative (sometimes referred to for convenience by the parties (with different punctuation) and herein as the "but-for subtest") is set forth in section 1.509(a)–4(i)(3)(ii), Income Tax Regs.:

The activities engaged in for or on behalf of the publicly supported organizations are activities to perform the functions of, or to carry out the purposes of, such organizations, and, but for the involvement of the supporting organization, would normally be engaged in by the publicly supported organizations themselves.

The second alternative (referred to as the "attentiveness subtest") is laid out in section 1.509(a)–4(i)(3)(iii), Income Tax Regs.:

(a) The supporting organization makes payments of substantially all of its income to or for the use of one or more publicly supported organizations, and the amount of support received by one or more of such publicly supported organizations is sufficient to insure the attentiveness of such organizations to the operations of the supporting organization. In addition, a substantial amount of the total support of the supporting organization must go to those publicly supported organizations which meet the attentiveness requirement of this subdivision with respect to such supporting organization. Except as provided in (b) of this subdivision, the amount of support received by a publicly supported organization must represent a sufficient part of the organization's total support so as to insure such attentiveness. In applying the preceding sentence, if such supporting organization makes payments to, or for the use of, a particular department or school of a university, hospital or church, the total support of the department or school shall be substituted for the total support of the beneficiary organization.

(b) Even where the amount of support received by a publicly supported beneficiary organization does not represent a sufficient part of the beneficiary organization's total support, the amount of support received from a supporting organization may be sufficient to meet the requirements of this subdivision if it can be demonstrated that in order to avoid the interruption of the carrying on of a particular function or activity, the beneficiary organization will be sufficiently attentive to the operations of the supporting organization. This may be the case where either the supporting organization or the beneficiary organization earmarks the support received from the supporting organization for a particular program or activity, even if such program or activity is not the beneficiary organization's primary program or activity so long as such program or activity is a substantial one.

All pertinent factors are to be considered under the foregoing subtest in order to determine whether the amount of support received by the beneficiary organization is sufficient to ensure attentiveness. Sec. 1.509(a)–4(i)(3)(iii)(d), Income Tax Regs. Factors highlighted by the regulations include the number of beneficiaries, the length and nature of the relationship between the organizations, the purpose to which the funds are put, and the imposition of a requirement that the supporting organization furnish reports to the supported organization. Id. As a general premise, the regulations provide that the greater the amount involved as a percentage of the beneficiary organization's total support, the greater the likelihood that the required degree of attentiveness will be present. Id. There is, however, the caveat that "evidence of actual attentiveness by the beneficiary organization is of almost equal importance." Id.

C.   Section 509(a)(3)(C)

Section 509(a)(3)(C) specifies the third basic requirement for all charitable entities wishing to be classified as supporting organizations. A supporting organization may not be controlled directly or indirectly by disqualified persons, including substantial contributors; their family members; and corporations, partnerships, or trusts in which interests of more than 35

percent are owned by disqualified persons. Secs. 509(a)(3)(C), 4946(a);
* * *

II. Preliminary Considerations

As a threshold matter, we first address a dispute between the parties regarding whether the tests set out above are to be applied with or without taking into consideration certain alleged changes to petitioner's intended operations and governing documents. [The court concluded that it was required to base its ruling solely on the materials exchanged by the parties during the administrative process. Since those materials did not establish implementation of certain proposed changes, the court reached its decision by applying the § 509(a)(3) tests to the Foundation's original organizational documents. Eds.]

III. Responsiveness Test

As previously mentioned, petitioner claims to be an organization "operated in connection with" a supported organization, AEF, for purposes of the relationship requirement prescribed in section 509(a)(3)(B). See sec. 1.509(a)–4(f)(2), Income Tax Regs. To qualify as such, petitioner must satisfy both the responsiveness test of section 1.509(a)–4(i)(2), Income Tax Regs., and the integral part test of section 1.509(a)–4(i)(3), Income Tax Regs. We consider each of these tests seriatim.

The responsiveness test is structured to ensure that the supported organization will have the ability to influence the supporting organization, thereby ensuring that the supporting organization will be responsive to the needs of the supported organization. Cockerline Meml. Fund v. Commissioner, 86 T.C. 53, 59, 1986 WL 22074 (1986); Nellie Callahan Scholarship Fund v. Commissioner, 73 T.C. 626, 633, 1980 WL 4573 (1980); Roe Found. Charitable Trust v. Commissioner, T.C. Memo.1989–566; sec. 1.509(a)–4(i)(2), Income Tax Regs.

Under the circumstances of this case, the pertinent requirements are found in subdivisions (a) and (d) of section 1.509(a)–4(i)(2)(ii), Income Tax Regs. Subdivision (a) specifies that at least one officer, director, or trustee of the supporting organization must be appointed or elected by the supported organization. Here the administrative correspondence indicates that Mr. Gallina was appointed to petitioner's board of directors by AEF. Petitioner also offers a proposed finding of fact to that effect, to which respondent has "No objection." In addition, petitioner's bylaws mandate that "one or more members of the Board of Directors shall be appointed by the Board of Directors of the publicly supported organization(s) for whose benefit the Corporation exists." We are satisfied that petitioner is in conformity with section 1.509(a)–4(i)(2)(ii)(a), Income Tax Regs.

Subdivision (d) of 1.509(a)–4(i)(2)(ii), Income Tax Regs., then requires that, by reason of the above relationship, the supported organization have a "significant voice" in the investment policies of the supporting organization; in the timing, manner, and recipients of grants made by the supporting organization; and in otherwise directing the use of the income or assets of the supporting organization. The term "significant" in this context has been interpreted to mean " 'likely to have influence,' not control." Cockerline Meml. Fund v. Commissioner, supra at 60 (quoting Webster's Third New International Dictionary 2116 (1981)); see also Roe Found. Charitable Trust v. Commissioner, supra.

Respondent by answer raised the issue of failure to satisfy the responsiveness test, alleging therein that the director appointed by AEF lacked a significant voice in the activities specified in section 1.509(a)–4(i)(2)(ii)(d), Income Tax Regs. On brief respondent argues that no facts have been given to show Mr. Gallina will have a significant voice in determining petitioner's investment policies or when and where petitioner's funds will be paid. Respondent similarly states that there is no evidence that nondisqualified directors will have any control over the income or assets of petitioner. In particular, respondent focuses on the fact that the only asset held by petitioner is the Estate Storage note and observes that the charitable gift annuity obligation will require payments equal to the majority of the note's annual income. Hence, it is respondent's view that there are, as a practical matter, no meaningful assets or investments for the board to manage.

At the outset, we reiterate that respondent bears the burden of proof on this issue, which creates a situation quite different from that in Roe Found. Charitable Trust v. Commissioner, supra, cited favorably by respondent. In Roe Found. Charitable Trust v. Commissioner, supra, we relied in significant part on the taxpayer's failure to indicate how the relevant trustee would have a significant voice. Here respondent must demonstrate that AEF will not have the requisite significant voice, and we conclude respondent has not done so.

Mr. Gallina is one of five directors, and petitioner has represented that the AEF director will have a voice equal to any of the remaining four. Respondent has not established otherwise. Petitioner's articles of incorporation empower the corporation through its board of directors to carry out the purposes of the entity by, among other things, owning, acquiring, transferring, and disposing of property; receiving and administering property by gift, devise, or bequest; and entering into contracts. Furthermore, although petitioner currently has few assets requiring active management, respondent has not shown that principal payments on the note or additional annual contributions, etc., estimated by petitioner will not occur to render the management role increasingly material. Certain of respondent's statements also seem to conflate influence with control to a degree unsupported by the regulations and caselaw.

Moreover, as pertains to the timing, manner, and recipients of grants, petitioner indicated during the administrative process that the AEF director would serve on the advisory committee of the donor-advised fund and would thereby have a significant voice in recommending grants. Again, respondent has introduced nothing proving to the contrary. We further are mindful that AEF exercises final authority over distributions from the donor-advised fund. Hence, we cannot find that AEF lacks the necessary ability to influence petitioner's activities in these matters. Accordingly, we conclude that petitioner's governance and affairs are structured to satisfy the responsiveness test of section 1.509(a)–4(i)(2)(ii), Income Tax Regs.

IV.   Integral Part Test

The complementary and interrelated roles of the responsiveness and integral part tests have been expressed by this Court as follows:

> While the responsiveness test guarantees that the supported organization will have the ability to influence the supporting organization's activities, the integral part test insures that the supported organization will have the motivation to do so. The general thrust of this regulation is that the supporting organization must maintain a significant involvement in the operations of the supported organization so that the latter will be attentive to the supporting organization's operations. [Nellie Callahan Scholarship Fund v. Commissioner, 73 T.C. at 637–638.]

As previously discussed, the regulations in section 1.509(a)–4(i)(3), Income Tax Regs., offer two alternative sets of criteria for satisfying the integral part test, which we for convenience refer to as the "but-for subtest" of subdivision (ii) and the "attentiveness subtest" of subdivision (iii).

A.   But–For Subtest

The but-for subtest will be met where: (1) The activities engaged in for or on behalf of the supported organization are activities to perform the functions of or to carry out the purposes of the supported organization, and (2) but for the involvement of the supporting entity, such activities would normally be engaged in by the supported organization itself. Sec. 1.509(a)–4(i)(3)(ii), Income Tax Regs.

With respect to the first prong set forth above, we have stated that "This rule generally applies only to situations where the supporting organization *actually* engages in activities that benefit the supported organization, such as performing a specific function for one or more publicly supported organizations." Roe Found. Charitable Trust v. Commissioner, T.C. Memo.1989–566. In a similar vein, respondent maintains that the but-for subtest applies only in cases where the involvement of the supporting organization extends beyond merely making grants or monetary donations. Petitioner, on the other hand, contends that "activities" in section 1.509(a)–4(i)(3)(ii), Income Tax Regs., should be construed in a manner consistent to its use elsewhere in the regulations under section 509(a), with the result that the term should encompass grant making. Petitioner cites section 1.509(a)–4(e)(1), Income Tax Regs., which uses the word and then explains: "Such activities may include making payments to or for the use of, or providing services or facilities for, individual members of the charitable class benefited by the specified publicly supported organization."

We, however, need not resolve this dispute. Even if we were to assume arguendo that grant making is properly characterized as an activity for purposes of section 1.509(a)–4(i)(3)(ii), Income Tax Regs., a matter which is by no means clear, the administrative record establishes that petitioner cannot satisfy the second prong set out above. Before setting forth the reasons for our conclusion, it is necessary to describe petitioner's argument in more detail.

Petitioner summarizes its position on the but-for subtest as follows:

Petitioner is providing the only support the American Endowment Foundation receives for the support of activities in Northville, Michigan. "But for" Petitioner's support, those activities would not exist, and would not be funded unless the American Endowment Foundation found funding elsewhere. * * *

Petitioner also states that AEF "is dependent upon Petitioner for its grants to perform the functions of the public charities in the Northville, Michigan area." Thus, petitioner views the pertinent activities narrowly, i.e., in terms of support of the Northville, Michigan, region, and not broadly, i.e., in terms of AEF's mission to assist the community of U.S. inhabitants.

We reject petitioner's argument on the ground that it is based upon a faulty factual premise; namely, that petitioner's support to AEF is dedicated to activities in Northville, Michigan, or southeastern Michigan. This premise is based upon the fact that petitioner intends to recommend to AEF that petitioner's contributions to the donor-advised fund be used to support charities in Northville, Michigan, or southeastern Michigan. However, as found above, AEF is not bound by such recommendations and can use the support received from petitioner to fund charitable activities anywhere in the United States.

AEF endeavors through its grant making to benefit communities throughout the United States. Yet such grant-making activities cannot properly be characterized as something in which AEF *would be* engaged *but for* petitioner's support. Rather, distributing grant moneys is something in which AEF *is* and will continue to be engaged *regardless* of support from petitioner. Hence, the record reveals no but-for relationship between petitioner's operations and those of AEF and, accordingly, cannot establish the type of dependency sought by the integral part test.

B. Attentiveness Subtest

Under the attentiveness subtest, (1) the supporting organization must make payments of substantially all of its income to or for the use of the supported organization, and (2) either (a) the amount of support must be sufficient to ensure the attentiveness of the supported entity or (b) the funds must be earmarked for a substantial program or activity of the supported entity, such that the supported organization will be attentive to avoid interruption thereof. Sec. 1.509(a)–4(i)(3)(iii)(a) and (b), Income Tax Regs.

In addition, a substantial amount of the total support of the supporting organization must go to those publicly supported organizations which meet the attentiveness requirement. Sec. 1.509(a)–4(i)(3)(iii)(a), Income Tax Regs.

The phrase "substantially all of its income", as used in the integral part test, has been interpreted to mean 85 percent or more of net income. Rev. Rul. 76–208, 1976–1 C.B. 161 (stating that the terminology should be given the same meaning as in sec. 53.4942(b)–1(c), Foundation Excise Tax Regs.). Since petitioner has indicated that it will distribute at least 85 percent of its net annual income, we focus on the further criteria intended to cultivate attentiveness.

With respect to the first method for ensuring attentiveness, support significant in amount relative to the beneficiary's total support is generally the defining characteristic. Sec. 1.509(a)–4(i)(3)(iii)(d), Income Tax Regs. By this standard, we conclude that petitioner's proposed contributions to AEF do not rise to the requisite level. Anticipated annual contributions of approximately $7,600 from petitioner, when measured against the total annual contributions received by AEF of more than $7 million, are not sufficient to guarantee attentiveness.

Additionally, while evidence of actual attentiveness can be equally important, id., the record on this score is less than persuasive. Petitioner has mentioned that it will furnish financial reports to AEF and cites AEF's appointment of a Northville resident to petitioner's board as evidence of actual attentiveness. On these facts, however, we remain unconvinced that the two features highlighted portend the type of ongoing monitoring and attentiveness envisaged in the regulation. Given the vast difference in the size and scope of the two entities' programs, establishing actual attentiveness would require more than pointing to a few administrative formalities.

We now turn to the earmarking facet of the attentiveness subtest, noting that petitioner appears on brief to emphasize this argument over the support-based considerations just addressed, as follows:

> Petitioner's support to the American Endowment Foundation has been earmarked for use in Northville, Michigan. This is the only support that the American Endowment Foundation received to support activities in Northville, Michigan. Without Petitioner's support, the Northville activities will be interrupted. Therefore, even though the percentage of support provided by Petitioner to American Endowment Foundation's overall budget is small, it is 100% of the support that American Endowment Foundation provides to Northville residents. * * *

On the present facts, there exist at least two barriers to petitioner's ability to satisfy the integral part test through the alleged earmarking. The first is the requirement that either petitioner or AEF earmark the funds for a particular program or activity. Because the contributions are made to a donor-advised fund, petitioner cannot definitively earmark the moneys for any specific project. Rather, petitioner is limited to making recommendations which AEF is not bound to, and will not necessarily, implement.

Moreover, petitioner has not established that AEF has in fact earmarked petitioner's contributions for a particular venture.

Second, the regulations mandate that the payments be earmarked for a *substantial* program or activity of the supported organization. Again, the administrative record belies that supporting Northville, Michigan, is a substantial activity of AEF. Even benefiting Michigan as a whole has not been shown to be a substantial focus of AEF, and there is no evidence that the rather minimal expenditures made in that State by AEF ($5,500 in 1998) would be interrupted absent petitioner's support. Petitioner therefore has failed to prove that its operations will ensure AEF's attentiveness.

V.   Control Test

In view of our holding above that the integral part test is not met on the record presented, we need not reach the control test. * * *

To reflect the foregoing,

Decision will be entered for respondent.

NOTES

1.   *The Integral Part Test.* The Tax Court also strictly interpreted the integral part test in Cuddeback v. Commissioner, 84 T.C.M. 623 (2002). *Cuddeback* involved a charitable trust created to distribute 10 percent of its income to each of two churches and 80 percent to a multi-care facility that qualified as a public charity. The court held that the trust failed to qualify as a § 509(a)(3) supporting organization because it was unable to demonstrate that the support it provided was sufficient to assure the attentiveness of the supported charities or that a reduction of support would interrupt a particular program.

2.   *For Further Reading.* David A. Shevlin, Recent Court Decisions Analyze the Rules Governing "Type 3" Supporting Organizations, 39 Exempt Org. Tax Rev. 181 (2003).

c.   ORGANIZATIONAL AND OPERATIONAL TESTS

A supporting organization must be organized and operated exclusively for the benefit of one or more public charities. Treas. Reg. § 1.509(a)–4(b). The regulations enforce this statutory requirement with an "organizational" and an "operational" test.

Organizational Test. The organizational test is concerned solely with the language used in the supporting organization's articles of incorporation or other governing instrument. The articles must limit the organization's purposes to exclusively benefitting, performing the functions of, or carrying out the purposes of the supported organization or organizations, all of which must be public charities described in §§ 509(a)(1) and (a)(2). The articles may not empower the organization to engage in any activities that do not further those purposes. Treas. Reg. § 1.509(a)–4(c)(1)–(3).

A critical element of the organizational test is the general requirement that the supported organizations be designated specifically by name. Treas. Reg. § 1.509(a)–4(d)(2). A specific designation is not required, however, if there has been a historic and continuing relationship between the supporting and supported organizations so that a substantial identity of interest has developed between them. Treas. Reg. § 1.509(a)–4(d)(2)(iv). In addition, the beneficiary charities can be identified by "class or purpose" (e.g., "all the institutions of higher learning" in a particular state) rather than by name if the organizations' relationship satisfies either the "operated, supervised or controlled by" or "supervised or controlled in connection with" test. Treas. Reg. § 1.509(a)–4(d)(2)(i). The regulations also elaborate on the circumstances when a substitution of specified beneficiaries will be permitted. Treas. Reg. § 1.509(a)–4(d)(3) & (4).

As illustrated by Revenue Ruling 75–437, below, the Service has been known to interpret the organizational test rather strictly, with unfortunate ramifications for otherwise worthy organizations that commit a technical foot fault in drafting their articles of incorporation.

Operational Test. The operational test requires that the supporting organization must engage "solely in activities which support or benefit the specified publicly supported organizations." Treas. Reg. § 1.509(a)–4(e)(1). The supporting organization need not pay its income to the supported organization to meet this requirement. Instead, it may carry on an independent activity or program benefiting the supported organization. Treas. Reg. § 1.509(a)–4(e)(2). The example in the regulations is of a separately incorporated alumni association of a university that uses its dues and other income "to support its own program of educational activities for alumni, faculty, and students * * * and to encourage alumni to maintain a close relationship with the university and to make contributions to it." Treas. Reg. § 1.509(a)–4(e)(3) Example (1).

Revenue Ruling 75–437

1975–2 Cum. Bull. 218.

Advice has been requested whether the charitable trust described below is a supporting organization within the meaning of section 509(a)(3) of the Internal Revenue Code of 1954 and thus not a private foundation.

An individual recently established the charitable trust which has been recognized as exempt from Federal income tax under section 501(c)(3) of the Code. The sole purpose of the trust is to provide college scholarships to graduates of the high schools in a particular county. Recipients of scholarships are selected by a committee composed of the superintendent of schools of the county, the superintendent of schools of one city within the county, and a third member selected by the two superintendents. The selection committee has no authority with respect to the administration and operation of the trust. This responsibility is vested in a bank that has been designated as trustee of the trust.

The income of the trust is derived from interest and dividends; expenditures are for scholarships and administrative expenses.

Those high schools in the county which are separately incorporated and which have only educational purposes are organizations described in section 170(b)(1)(A)(ii) of the Code. Those which are not separately incorporated but are operated by either the county or one of the cities within the county are not section 170(b)(1)(A)(ii) organizations; however, the governmental units of which they are a part are section 170(b)(1)(A)(v) organizations. Thus, all of the high schools in the county or the governmental units of which they are a part are organizations described in sections 170(b)(1)(A) and 509(a)(1).

Section 509(a)(3) of the Code excludes from the definition of a "private foundation" an organization which—(A) is organized, and at all times thereafter is operated, exclusively for the benefit of, to perform the functions of, or to carry out the purposes of one or more specified organizations described in paragraph (1) or (2), (B) is operated, supervised, or controlled by or in connection with one or more organizations, described in paragraph (1) or (2) and (C) is not controlled directly or indirectly by one or more disqualified persons (as defined in section 4946) other than foundation managers and other than one or more organizations described in paragraph (1) or (2).

Section 1.509(a)–4(c)(1) of the Income Tax Regulations provides that an organization is organized exclusively for one or more of the purposes specified in section 509(a)(3)(A) of the Code only if its articles of organization: (i) Limit the purposes of such organization to one or more of the purposes set forth in section 509(a)(3)(A); (ii) Do not expressly empower the organization to engage in activities which are not in furtherance of the purposes set forth in subdivision (1) of this subparagraph; (iii) State the specified publicly supported organizations on whose behalf such organization is to be operated within the meaning of paragraph (d) of this section; and (iv) Do not expressly empower the organization to operate to support or benefit any organization other than the specified publicly supported organizations referred to in subdivision (iii) of this subparagraph.

Under section 1.509(a)–4(c)(2) of the regulations, the supporting organization's governing instrument must state that the organization is formed for the benefit of, to perform a function of, or to carry out a purpose of an organization described in section 509(a)(1) or (2) of the Code.

The trust in the instant case does not satisfy this requirement of the "organizational test," because the trust instrument does not contain the requisite statement of purpose. Since the trust is not "operated, supervised, or controlled by" or "supervised or controlled in connection with" the publicly supported schools and governmental units, the fact that the educational purposes of the trust are consistent with those of the schools and governmental units is not sufficient to satisfy the organizational test.

Under section 1.509(a)–4(d)(2) of the regulations, if the supporting organization is neither "operated, supervised, or controlled by" nor "supervised or controlled in connection with" a publicly supported organization, then the "specified" publicly supported organization must be designated by name in the supporting organization's articles unless there has been an historic and continuing relationship between the supporting organization and the supported organization and by reason of such relationship there has developed a substantial identity of interests between such organizations.

Because the trust in the instant case does not bear one of the above prescribed relationships to the publicly supported schools and governmental units, the failure of the trust instrument to name the supported organizations prevents it from satisfying this requirement of the organizational test.

Since the trust does not meet either of the two basic requirements of the organizational test, it is not an organization described in section 509(a)(3) of the Code.

Section 1.509(a)–4(e)(1) of the regulations provides that a supporting organization will be regarded as "operated exclusively" to support one or more specified publicly supported organizations only if it engages solely in activities which support or benefit the specified publicly supported organizations. This may include making payments to or for the use of, or providing services or facilities for, individual members of the charitable class benefited by the specified publicly supported organizations.

In granting scholarships to the graduates of the high schools in the county, the trust is benefiting members of the charitable class benefited by the schools and governmental units which operate the schools. See Example (1) of section 1.509(a)–4(e)(3) of the regulations. Thus, aside from the fact that the schools and governmental units are not properly specified, the trust meets the requirements of the "operational test."

Section 1.509(a)–4(f)(1) of the regulations provides that in order to meet the requirements of section 509(a)(3) of the Code, an organization must be operated, supervised, or controlled by or in connection with one or more publicly supported organizations. This test is met if the organization is: (1) "operated, supervised, or controlled by" one or more publicly supported organizations (section 1.509(a)–4(g)); (2) "supervised or controlled in connection with" one or more publicly supported organizations (section 1.509(a)–4(h)); or (3) "operated in connection with" one or more publicly supported organizations (section 1.509(a)–4(i)).

Because of the complete independence of the trustee in the instant case, the trust is neither "operated, supervised, or controlled by" nor "supervised or controlled in connection with" the publicly supported schools and governmental units.

To be considered as "operated in connection with" one or more section 509(a)(1) or (2) organizations, an organization must meet both the "responsiveness test" of section 1.509(a)–4(i)(2) of the regulations and the "integral part test" of section 1.509(a)–4(i)(3).

With exceptions not here relevant, the responsiveness test is satisfied only if the organization meets the requirements of either section 1.509(a)–4(i)(2)(ii) or (iii) of the regulations. The first of these tests requires that: (a) One or more officers, directors, or trustees of the supporting organization are elected or appointed by the officers, directors, trustees, or membership of the publicly supported organizations; (b) One or more members of the governing bodies of the publicly supported organizations are also officers, directors, or trustees of, or hold other important offices in, the supporting organization; or (c) The officers, directors, or trustees of the supporting organization maintain a close and continuous working relationship with the officers, directors, or trustees of the publicly supported organizations; and (d) By reason of (a), (b) or (c) of this subdivision, the officers, directors, or trustees of the publicly supported organizations have a significant voice in the investment policies of the supporting organization, the timing of grants, the manner of making them, and the selection of recipients by such supporting organization, and in otherwise directing the use of the income or assets of such supporting organization.

Because the trustee of the trust is completely independent of the publicly supported schools and governmental units, requirements (a) and (b) are not satisfied. Requirement (c) may be satisfied because of the working relationship between the representatives of the publicly supported organizations on the selection committee and the trustee. However, requirement (d) is not satisfied because the publicly supported organizations do not have a significant voice in the investment policies of the trust or the timing and making of grants. The selection committee's authority extends only to the selection of grant recipients.

The alternative method of satisfying the responsiveness test provided by section 1.509(a)–4(i)(2)(iii) of the regulations, requires that: (a) The supporting organization is a charitable trust under State law; (b) Each specified publicly supported organization is a named beneficiary under such charitable trust's governing instrument; and (c) The beneficiary organization has the power to enforce the trust and compel an accounting under State law.

Although the trust in the instant case satisfies requirement (a), it does not satisfy either (b) or (c). The publicly supported organizations are not named beneficiaries and, under the applicable state law, there is no authority supporting the right of organizations such as these to enforce the trust or compel an accounting.

Under section 1.509(a)–4(i)(3) of the regulations, an organization will satisfy the integral part test (with exceptions not here relevant) only if it maintains a significant involvement in the operations of one or more publicly supported organizations and these organizations are dependent upon the supporting organization for the type of support which it provides. The integral part test will not be satisfied unless: (1) the activities engaged in for or on behalf of the publicly supported organizations are ones which, but for the involvement of the supporting organization, would normally be engaged in by the publicly supported organizations themselves: or (2) the supporting organization makes payments of substantially all of its income to or for the use of one or more publicly supported organizations and the amount received by one or more of the publicly supported organizations is sufficient to insure their attentiveness to the operations of the supporting organization.

The first of these tests is not met in the instant case because the granting of scholarships is not an activity which would normally be engaged in by the publicly supported schools and governmental units. Cessation of the operation of this trust would not cause the schools and governmental units to assume the trust's scholarship program.

The second test is not applicable because the trust is not making grants to or for the use of a school or governmental unit, but is carrying on its own independent scholarship program. Thus, the integral part test of section 1.509(a)–4(i)(3) of the regulations is not satisfied.

Because neither the responsiveness test nor the integral part test is satisfied, the trust is not 'operated in connection with' the publicly supported schools and governmental units.

In summary, the trust is not an organization described in section 509(a)(3) of the Code because it does not meet the organizational test of section 1.509(a)–4(c) and (d) of the regulations and because it is not "operated, supervised, or controlled by," "supervised or controlled in connection with" or "operated in connection with" one or more publicly supported organizations as required by section 1.509(a)–4(f) of the regulations.

Accordingly, the trust is not a supporting organization within the meaning of section 509(a)(3) of the Code and is a private foundation.

NOTE

The courts have been more lenient than the Service in interpreting the organizational test for scholarship-granting organizations. For example, the Tax Court has held that no particular magic language is required in a foundation's organizational documents to state that a § 509(a)(3) organization is organized to benefit a specified public charity. See Warren M. Goodspeed Scholarship Fund v. Commissioner, 70 T.C. 515 (1978), nonacq. 1981–2 C.B. 3, where a charitable trust (established by a Will) whose net income was to be used to pay for the education at Yale College of graduates of a Massachusetts public high school qualified under § 509(a)(3) even though the Will did not specifically state that the trust was organized exclusively for Yale's benefit. In Cockerline Memorial Fund v. Commissioner, 86 T.C. 53 (1986), the court held that the historic relationship between a scholarship granting trust and colleges and universities in Oregon was sufficient to qualify the trust under 509(a)(3) even though the Will creating the trust did not specify the benefited organizations.

d. CONTROL TEST

Although a supporting organization may achieve substantial autonomy by operating "in connection with" more than one public charity, it may not be controlled "directly or indirectly" by one or more disqualified persons (other than foundation managers and/or the charities it is required to support). I.R.C. § 509(a)(3)(C). Control is determined with reference to the aggregate power of disqualified persons to require the organization to perform any significant act or prevent such an act. See Treas. Reg. § 1.509(a)–4(j). The revenue ruling that follows is a good example of the concept of "indirect" control.

Revenue Ruling 80–207

1980–2 Cum. Bull 193.

ISSUE

Is an organization which makes distributions to a university, under the circumstances described below, a supporting organization within the meaning of section 509(a)(3) of the Internal Revenue Code if it is controlled by a disqualified person and the employees of a disqualified person?

FACTS

The organization is exempt from federal income tax under section 501(c)(3) of the Code. Its purpose is to make distributions to a university described in section 509(a)(1) and section 170(b)(1)(A)(ii).

The organization is controlled by a four member board of directors. One of these directors is a substantial contributor to the organization. Two other directors are employees of a business corporation of which more than 35 percent of the voting power is owned by the substantial contributor. The remaining director is chosen by the university. None of the directors has a veto power over the organization's actions.

LAW AND ANALYSIS

Section 509(a)(3)(C) of the Code provides that in order to qualify as other than a private foundation under section 509(a)(3), an organization may not be controlled directly or indirectly by one or more disqualified persons (as defined in section 4946) other than foundation managers and other than one or more organizations described in section 509(a)(1) or (2).

Section 4946 provides that the term "disqualified person" includes a substantial contributor to an organization, and a corporation of which a substantial contributor owns more than 35 percent of the total combined voting power.

Section 1.509(a)–4(j) of the Income Tax Regulations provides that a supporting organization will be considered to be controlled directly or indirectly by one or more disqualified persons if the voting power of such persons is 50 percent or more of the total voting power of the organization's governing body or if one or more of such persons has the right to exercise veto power over the actions of the organization. However, all pertinent facts and circumstances will be taken into consideration in determining whether a disqualified person does in fact indirectly control an organization.

Because only one of the organization's directors is a disqualified person and neither the disqualified person nor any other director has a veto power over the organization's actions, the organization is not directly controlled by a disqualified person under section 1.509(a)–4(j) of the regulations. However, in determining whether an organization is indirectly controlled by one or more disqualified persons, one circumstance to be considered is whether a disqualified person is in a position to influence the decisions of members of the organization's governing body who are not themselves disqualified persons. Thus, employees of a disqualified person will be considered in determining whether one or more disqualified persons controls 50 percent or more of the voting power of an organization's governing body.

Two of the organization's four directors are also employees of a corporation that is itself a disqualified person because more than 35 percent of its voting power is owned by a disqualified person. Because a majority of its board of directors consists of a disqualified person and employees of a disqualified person, the organization is indirectly controlled by disqualified persons within the meaning of section 509(a)(3)(C) of the Code.

HOLDING

Since the organization is controlled by a disqualified person and the employees of a disqualified person, under the circumstances described above, it is not a supporting organization within the meaning of section 509(a)(3) of the Code.

e. USE (AND ABUSE) OF SUPPORTING ORGANIZATIONS

Supporting foundations largely have existed in the shadows of the nonprofit sector. Until recently, the arcane and barely intelligible regulations that you have just studied (mastered?) were enough to discourage generalist lawyers from recommending supporting foundations (assuming they even knew about § 509(a)(3)), or Congress or the IRS from scrutinizing them (same assumption). The handful of attorneys who did understand the rules quietly counselled their clients on the advantages of the supporting organization. More aggressive advisors devised creative structures that allowed donors to maintain the same level of practical control that they would have with a private foundation, but without the regulatory regime.

In 1998, however, supporting foundations were "outed" in a front page story in the Wall Street Journal, excerpts of which follow.

Monica Langley, The SO Trend: How to Succeed in Charity Without Really Giving: a "Supporting Organization" Lets the Wealthy Donate Assets, Still Keep Control

Wall St. Journal, May 29, 1998, A1.

How can ex-raider Carl Icahn bear to part with $100 million? Why did famed defense lawyer Gerry Spence give up his cherished Wyoming ranch? And whatever caused real-estate investor David Cammack to relinquish his beloved fleet of antique Tucker automobiles?

The answer: They can give these assets to charity—and retain control of them at the same time.

Messrs. Icahn, Spence and Cammack are just three of those taking advantage of a suddenly hot charitable vehicle with a not-so-sexy name: supporting organizations, or SO, for short.

Though its mechanics are complex, the allure of the SO is straightforward. It provides all the big tax breaks designed to encourage public philanthropy, yet it operates much like a private foundation. By parking their land, art or money in this form of charitable entity, donors can maintain an unusual degree of influence for years: The SO's board, typically appointed by the donor, oversees the assets' use or income into perpetuity.

Through an SO, Mr. Icahn can thus turn over cash and stock generated in a corporate-takeover deal, get a substantial tax deduction, and continue to manage the stock as if it were still his own. Mr. Spence can donate his 220–acre ranch and still enjoy the views overlooking the Little Wind River when he hosts meetings with other lawyers. And Mr. Cammack, an antique-car enthusiast, is able to give his valuable Tuckers to charity, yet dictate how and when they are displayed, keeping them in his garage in the meantime.

* * *

The rich enjoyed a good, long run with the private foundation: After all, it could be named for their families; it let them dole out the money when and to whom they wanted; and it afforded them far more prestige and influence than they would get by simply writing a check to charity.

But in recent years, private foundations have been hit with some onerous and changing restrictions, while public charities (or tax-exempt, publicly supported organizations) have maintained the glow—and the special tax benefits—of representing true philanthropy. And so wealthy benefactors and their advisors have been scrambling for alternatives in the public charity realm.

Their discovery: a largely unnoticed law enacted in 1969, whereby an SO is deemed "public," without the prohibitions against "self dealing" (giving loans to family members, for instance) that one runs up against with a private foundation. With an SO, donors get a lot of leeway, as well as the considerable tax advantages they would get if they gave to a recognized public charity such as the Salvation Army or United Way: namely, hefty income-tax deductions, and none of the excise taxes or minimum-payout rules required of private foundations. After transferring assets into the SO, donors can later pass control to their heirs, making provisions for subsequent generations to continue picking the SO's governing board.

The law set up three categories of SO, but the so-called Type III—which allows for the most sweeping donor control—is what really caught the attention of financial advisors.

Probably most important in spurring the recent spate of SO activity, donors to public charities can contribute any form of property—real estate, art, a family business—and get immediate tax breaks for the full appreciated value. (A similar contribution to a private foundation [except for publicly traded securities] yields deductions just for the cost basis.)

The newfound popularity of the SO is a mixed blessing, according to financial advisers and charities themselves. At best, SO's encourage more people to part with their money and property for the ultimate benefit of charity. "Often the donors are initially motivated for tax and estate-planning benefits, but they soon realize the SO can be a real tool for carrying out charitable goals," says Gerald Treacy, an attorney in Seattle and one of the first to dust off the law.

But at worst, the SO surge is about exploiting a charitable vehicle for immediate tax breaks while the money languishes without any clear philanthropic direction, or any legal imperative to spend down the original gift amount—or corpus—for charity. Distribution rules vary depending on the type of SO: Some are required to give away 85% of the asset's net income annually; for the others, the regulations on timing and payout are vague. Because the developments are so current, the jury is still out, yet the tensions are beginning to show.

The latest SO activity "is a lot of smoke and mirrors," says Jim Luck, president of the Columbus Foundation, a community foundation in Ohio. "Many of these SO's name numerous and disparate charities to support, with the effect of fragmenting the responsibility of the supported charities and ensuring greater donor control. The question becomes: Is there any real accountability to charity?"

Marcus Owens, the Internal Revenue Service's director of tax-exempt organizations, warns that people may "set up a supporting organization that meets the required technical structure, but the real test will be if it's carried out correctly. The IRS will look for evidence whether the organization is really supporting charities or is a vehicle of enrichment for private individuals," he says. "Our bottom line: is there a real charitable purpose?"

The extent to which the wealthy have managed to keep control over their donations through the SO shows how easily public-charity rules can be manipulated for private purposes. It is exactly this kind of influence that Congress and the IRS have tried to stem by implementing strict restrictions covering private foundations.

Because the scope of SOs—and the kind of assets they can hold—are so varied, motivations for establishing them are equally diverse. The ultimate goal must be charitable, because the assets will some day pass to the charity—but the tax benefits are immediate.

Take the ex-raider Carl Icahn. The 62–year-old billionaire wanted to contribute stock of a privately held company he won't name. He was looking for a bigger deduction than just the cost basis of the stock. "I don't like giving to the government," he says, explaining why he chose not to donate to his own private foundation. Instead, he threw the stock into an SO, giving him the tax advantages of the public charity with many of the operational features of a private foundation.

Moreover, the transfer of appreciated stock to the SO meant he avoided capital gains taxes. And Mr. Icahn can be fairly certain that donating a minority stake in his closely held company won't pose a challenge to his management, because the new shareholder is the SO of his own creation.

The only disadvantage to the SO, Mr. Icahn says, is that the majority of the board has to be made up of four outsiders representing charities. His control isn't legally insured, though he chose the board members. "You don't like to give up *total* control," he says, "but you get the benefit of putting in top people who can give you advice on your charity." And Mr. Icahn exercises practical control of his SO, which is located at his corporate offices in Manhattan. Besides himself, the other inside directors are his uncle and his employee-turned-fiancee Gail Golden. (Mr. Icahn and his wife are in divorce proceedings.)

"Though I'm on the board, they (Mr. Icahn's office) are basically running their foundation," says Marcia Lowry, executive director of Children's Rights Inc. Two outside directors acknowledge that in the year that Mr. Icahn's SO has existed, the board hasn't yet held a meeting. "I have to focus on it," Mr. Icahn says, "We're due for a board meeting."

[The article then described the supporting organization created by real estate investor David Cammack to hold his antique automobile collection. The cars ultimately are to be displayed in the Cammack family wing of a museum to be constructed by the American Automobile Club of America Inc. in Hershey, Pennsylvania. Eds.]

* * *

Mr. Spence, the lawyer, isn't even sure how he's given away his 220–acre ranch near Dubois, Wyoming. "I don't understand what I've done," he says in his booming voice. "We conveyed the ranch to a charitable whatever-it-is." He says he followed the advice of his legal and financial advisers. He doesn't recall "who's on the board, but they're good people."

The 69–year-old trial guru's concern was simple: "I can't live forever, so I want to have this beautiful ranch around in perpetuity * * * or some jerk will buy it and make it into a bunch of little ranchettes," he says. "When I'm gone, this property will continue my cause."

That cause is his Trial Lawyers College, where young lawyers spend a month on the ranch with Mr. Spence to learn trial tactics and he says, to "beat up corporate America and big government." To that end, the stalls in the cow barn have been converted to meeting rooms; the open area in the barn serves as a courtroom, the loft as an auditorium, and the cookhouse as the group's dining room.

"The training * * * is free of charge for the month-long institute," which is held twice a year, Mr. Spence says, although the students pay for costs such as food. Mr. Spence started the Trial Lawyers College with his own money, and it is now one of the main charities supported by the SO.

NOTE

The Wall Street Journal article highlights the more aggressive and colorful uses of supporting organizations. It neglects to mention the many conventional "SOs" created to support community foundations, religious federations, schools, and the like, and are legally controlled by one public charity. Nonetheless, the article caused the staff of the Joint Committee on Taxation to begin considering legislation to limit the abuses of supporting organizations. As this edition went to press, no specific written proposal has yet surfaced. Based on comments of its staff, the Joint Committee is considering legislation that would allow SOs to support only one named charity (as opposed to a class of charities), with a possible exception for multiple organizations of a single religious faith, and would eliminate the looser (Type 3) "operated or controlled in connection with" relationship.

For Further Reading. Antonia M. Grumbach & Susan D. Brown, Creative Planning Opportunities with Section 509(a)(3) Supporting Organizations—A Flexible Organizational Tool, 22 N.Y.U. Conf. on Tax Planning for 501(c)(3) Organizations ch. 1 (1994); Thomas J. Brorby & Brian W. Crozier, Section 509(a)(3) Supporting Organizations: Advantages and Planning Opportunities, 18 N.Y.U. Conf. on Tax Planning for 501(c)(3) Organizations ch. 3 (1990).

PROBLEM

Paul and Frances Ross are a wealthy couple in their early 60's. They have three children, all in their 30's. Mr. and Mrs. Ross have been discussing estate planning options with their attorney and are interested in establishing a family charitable foundation. Their major asset is $30 million of common stock in Ross Cosmetics, Inc., a closely-held family corporation. Members of the Ross family own 85 percent of the stock; the remaining 15 percent is owned by employees of the company.

Mr. and Mrs. Ross have been advised that serious problems would be presented if they were to donate their Ross Cosmetics stock to a family foundation. Because the stock is their major asset, they are exploring techniques to avoid private foundation status but still establish a philanthropic vehicle over which their family would have substantial influence and control. The Rosses are anxious to involve their descendants in the activities of the foundation, which they hope will serve as a continuing memorial to the Ross Cosmetics dynasty.

Mr. and Mrs. Ross are major donors to their local Jewish Community Federation, which is classified as a public charity under § 170(b)(1)(A)(vi). The Federation, in turn, makes grants to a wide variety of Jewish and some secular charities in the community. The Ross children are interested in supporting environmental organizations and in establishing scholarship funds for disadvantaged students.

The Rosses recently attended an estate planning seminar where they learned about the advantages in establishing a "supporting foundation" for the benefit of a public charity. It is their understanding that such a foundation would not be a "private foundation" if it were carefully structured. Based on this information, Mr. and Mrs. Ross have decided to create The Ross Family Supporting Foundation, to be operated exclusively for charitable, educational or religious purposes by supporting activities for the benefit of or to carry out the purposes of the Jewish Community Federation. The new entity gradually will be funded with a $10 million gift of Ross Cosmetics stock. All the income from the stock will be distributed in the discretion of the board of directors. The board will consist of Paul, Frances, their daughter Rhoda, and two unrelated family friends, one of whom is vice-president of Ross Cosmetics, Inc. None of the proposed directors is currently an employee, officer or director of the Jewish Community Federation.

(a) Why are Mr. and Mrs. Ross so anxious to avoid private foundation status?

(b) Will the Ross Foundation, as currently proposed, qualify for exemption under § 501(c)(3)?

(c) Will the Ross Foundation qualify as a supporting organization under § 509(a)(3)? If not, is it possible to restructure the proposal to achieve § 509(a)(3) status?

(d) If the Rosses are willing to limit their financial support to the Jewish Community Federation, why don't they simply donate the funds directly? Why should they go to the trouble of creating a separate entity?

(e) Suppose the Ross children express concern about the emphasis of the Foundation and propose to broaden the purposes as follows: "to further the dual causes of Jewish philanthropy and arresting the problems of urban poverty." Is this feasible? If not, how might the same objectives be achieved and how should the Foundation's organizational documents reflect those objectives?

(f) What if the Ross children wished to create a separate foundation whose sole purpose was to support the purely educational activities of a § 501(c)(5) labor organization? Would this type of supporting organization qualify under §§ 501(c)(3) and 509(a)(3)?

(g) Suppose the Rosses wished their foundation to have as its sole purpose the creation and maintenance of a public interest law program at the Vanguard College of the Law, a well-established independent nonprofit law school. Officials of the law school have been reluctant to expand public interest programs in the past but, tempted by the Rosses' generosity, they have informally agreed to undertake such a program. What considerations should be taken into account in structuring this type of supporting organization? Could the foundation, once formed, later amend its articles and shift its support to another law school if it becomes dissatisfied with Vanguard's program?

(h) What if the Rosses wished to create a charitable trust, the sole purpose of which is to provide college scholarships to graduates of public high schools in Los Angeles County, California. Recipients will be selected by a committee composed of the Superintendent of the Unified School District, the principal of the largest public high school in the county and a third member selected by the other two. The trust will be administered by a reputable bank. Would the trust qualify as a § 509(a)(3) supporting organization?

5.   PRIVATE OPERATING FOUNDATIONS

Internal Revenue Code: § 4942(j)(3).

Treasury Regulations: §§ 53.4942(b)–1(a)(1), (b), (c); –2, –3(a), (b)(1).

Within the private foundations family, the Code distinguishes between private operating foundations, such as foundations which directly engage in charitable or educational activities, and nonoperating or grantmaking foundations. Very generally, a private operating foundation ("POF") is a § 501(c)(3) organization that has not escaped private foundation status, often because of an abundance of investment income, but which meets certain statutory tests that entitle it to avoid some of the strictures that burden grantmaking foundations. The distinctive characteristics of private operating foundations include:

(1) Contributions to POFs are deductible by individual donors to the same extent as contributions to public charities—i.e., they are not subject to the special 30 percent limitation on contributions of cash and ordinary income property, the 20 percent limitation on contributions of capital gain property, and the reduction of unrealized built-in gain on gifts of appreciated capital gain property.

(2) Certain POFs, known as "exempt operating foundations," are exempt from the 2 percent excise tax on investment income.

(3) POFs are not subject to the § 4942 payout requirement.

(4) Grants to POFs ordinarily may be counted by the donor foundation as "qualifying distributions" in satisfaction of the § 4942 payout requirement.

(5) Other private foundations that make grants to "exempt operating foundations" are relieved from exercising "expenditure responsibility" with respect to the grants.

A POF is defined in § 4942(j)(3) as a foundation that makes "qualifying distributions directly for the active conduct" of its exempt-function activities that are equal in value to substantially all of the lesser of its "adjusted net income" or its "minimum investment return" (five percent of the value of its investment assets). For this purpose, "substantially all" means 85 percent. Treas. Reg. § 53.4942(b)–1(c). Where "qualifying distributions" exceed the foundation's minimum investment return, substantially all of those distributions must be made directly for the conduct of exempt function activities. Treas. Reg. § 53.4942(b)–1(a)(1)(ii).

This initial test for POF status, known as the "income test," requires an understanding of several statutory terms of art that are amplified in the regulations. For example, are capital expenditures to acquire assets to be used directly in the conduct of the foundation's exempt activities considered as qualifying distributions? The answer is yes; the conduct of such activities also qualify. But payments to individuals (e.g., scholarships or grants) ordinarily fail to qualify unless the foundation maintains a "significant involvement" in a charitable, educational or other activity within the context of which those grants are made. Thus, where an exempt purpose of the foundation is the relief of poverty or human distress, and its exempt activities are designed to "ameliorate conditions among a poor or distressed class of persons or in an area subject to poverty or natural disaster," and the foundation maintains a salaried or volunteer staff to supervise its activities on a continuing basis, the grants will qualify for purposes of the substantially all test. For elaboration and other examples, see Treas. Reg. § 53.4942(b)–1(b)(2).

In addition to meeting the "income" test, a POF must satisfy one of three alternative tests relating to its use of assets, operating expenditures or support.

Assets Test. Under the assets test, substantially more than half (i.e., 65 percent or more) of the assets of the foundation must be devoted directly to the foundation's exempt function activities or to functionally-related businesses, or both, or consist of stock of a corporation controlled by the foundation, substantially all of the assets of which are so devoted. I.R.C. § 4942(j)(3)(B)(i).

Expenditures Test. The organization normally must spend an amount that is not less than two-thirds of its minimum investment return directly for the active conduct of its exempt activities. I.R.C. § 4942(j)(3)(B)(iii).

Support Test. The organization must receive substantially all of its support (other than gross investment income) from the general public and from five or more exempt organizations that are not related to one another, and not more than 25 percent of the foundation's support may be received from any one such exempt organization, and not more than half the foundation's support may normally be received from gross investment income. I.R.C. § 4942(j)(3)(B)(iii).

The above tests may be applied on a year-by-year basis. A foundation qualifies as a POF by satisfying the activity test, and either the assets, expenditures or support test, for any three taxable years during a four-year period consisting of the taxable year in question and the three immediately preceding taxable years. Alternatively, the foundation may aggregate all pertinent items for the four-year period and qualify on the basis of those aggregate amounts. It may not, however, use one method (for example, the three-out-of-four-year test) to satisfy the income test and the other to satisfy the assets, expenditures or support test. Reg. § 53.4942(b)-3(a).

6. PROCEDURAL ASPECTS

a. PRIVATE FOUNDATION CLASSIFICATION RULINGS

Treasury Regulations: §§ 1.170A–9(e)(5); 1.509(a)–3(d), (e).

With limited exceptions for churches and public charities with gross receipts of $5,000 or less, a newly formed organization seeking to avoid private foundation status must obtain a determination letter to that effect from the Service or the organization will be presumed to be a private foundation. I.R.C. § 508(a)–(c). A classification ruling is requested on the application for 501(c)(3) exemption (Form 1023), which gives the organization the choice of obtaining a definitive or an advance ruling. Organizations that base their nonprivate foundation status on the nature of their activities or their support relationship with a public charity may request a definitive ruling if they have completed a tax year of at least 8 months. A definitive ruling is essentially a final determination. If it is adverse, the organization has various appeal rights, including the opportunity to seek a judicial determination under § 7428.[1]

New organizations relying on the public support tests of either § 170(b)(1)(A)(vi) or § 509(a)(2) do not have enough of a track record to obtain a definitive ruling, but they may request an advance ruling based on their reasonable expectations. The excerpt below, from IRS Publication 557, summarizes the advance ruling process.

IRS Publication 557, Tax–Exempt Status for Your Organization
Rev. July '01, pp. 32–33

Advance rulings to newly created organizations—initial determination of status. Many newly created organizations cannot meet either the four-year normally publicly supported provisions or the provisions for newly created organizations to qualify as normally publicly supported because they have not been existence long enough. However, a newly

---

1. See Chapter 2H1, supra, at pp. 351–353.

created organization may qualify for an advance ruling that it will be treated as an organization described in section 170(b)(1)(A)(vi) during an advance ruling period sufficient to enable it to develop an adequate support history on which to base an initial determination as to foundation status.

Generally, the type of newly created organization that would qualify for an advance ruling is one that can show that its organizational structure, proposed programs and activities, and intended method of operation are likely to attract the type of broadly based support from the general public, public charities, and governmental units that is necessary to meet the public support requirements discussed earlier.

An advance ruling or determination will provide that an organization will be treated as an organization described in section 170(b)(1)(A) for an advance ruling period of 5 years.

5–year advance ruling period. A newly created organization may request a ruling or determination letter that it will be treated as a section 170(b)(1)(A)(vi) organization for its first 5 tax years. The request must be accompanied by a consent to extend the statute [of limitations] (on Form 872–C) that, in effect, states the organization will be subject to the taxes imposed under section 4940 if it fails to qualify as not a private foundation during the 5–year advance ruling period. The organization's first tax year, regardless of length, will count as the first year in the 5–year period. The advance ruling period will end on the last day of the organization's 5th tax year.

Between 30 and 45 days before the end of the advance ruling period, the EP area manager will contact the organization and request the financial support information necessary to make a final determination of foundation status. In general, that is the information requested in Part IV–A of Form 1023.

Failure to obtain advance ruling. If a newly created organization has not obtained an advance ruling or determination letter, it cannot rely upon the possibility that it will meet the public support requirements discussed earlier. Thus, in order to avoid the risk of being classified as a private foundation, the organization may comply with the rules governing private foundations by paying any applicable private foundation taxes. If the organization later meets the public support requirements for the applicable period, it will be treated as a section 170(b)(1)(A)(vi) organization from its inception and any private foundation tax that was imposed may be refunded.

Reliance period. The newly created organization will be treated as a publicly supported organization for all purposes other than sections 507(d)(relating to total tax benefit resulting from exempt status) and 4940 (relating to tax on net investment income) for the period beginning with its inception and ending 90 days after its advance ruling period expires. The period will be extended until a final determination is made of an organization's status only if the organization submits, within the 90–day period, information needed to determine whether it meets either of the support tests for its advance ruling period (even if the organization fails to meet either test). However, this reliance period does not apply to the excise tax imposed on net investment income. If it is later determined that the organization was a private foundation from its inception, that excise tax will be due without regard to the advance ruling or determination letter. Consequently, if any amount of the tax is not paid on or before the last date prescribed for payment, the organization is liable for interest on the tax due for years in the advance ruling period. However, since any failure to pay the tax during the period is due to reasonable cause, the penalty imposed for failure to pay the tax will not apply.

If an advance ruling or determination letter is terminated by the IRS before the expiration of the reliance period, the status of grants or contributions with respect to grantors or contributors to the organization will not be affected until notice of change of status of the organization is made to the public (such as by publication in the Internal Revenue Bulletin). However, this will not apply if the grantor or contributor was responsible for, or aware of, the act or failure to act that resulted in the organization's loss of classification as a publicly supported organization.

Also, it will not apply if the grantor or contributor knew that the IRS had given notice to the organization that it would be deleted from this classification. Before any grant or contribution is made, a potential grantee organization may request a ruling on whether the grant or contribution may be made without loss of classification as a publicly supported organization.

The ruling request may be filed by the grantee organization with the key EO area manager. The issuance of the ruling will be at the sole discretion of the IRS. The organization must submit all information necessary to make a determination on the support factors previously discussed. If a favorable ruling is issued, the ruling may be relied upon by the grantor or contributor of the particular contribution in question. The grantee organization also may rely on the ruling for excluding unusual grants.

b.   INFORMATION REPORTING AND DISCLOSURE REQUIREMENTS

Internal Revenue Code: § 6033(c); 6104(d).

As discussed in Chapter 2, most exempt organizations must file an annual information return with the Internal Revenue Service. I.R.C. § 6033. These returns (Form 990 for public charities, Form 990–PF for private foundations) are public documents that are available for inspection at various designated IRS offices and on the Internet. Unlike public charities, private foundations must include an itemized statement of all grants made or approved for future payment, with the name and address of grantees and the purpose and amount of each grant, and they must complete a detailed schedule showing that they have complied with the five percent payout requirement. Like most public charities, private foundations must make their annual Form 990–PF (as well as their application for exemption) available for public inspection at their principal office during regular business hours. I.R.C. § 6104(a).

To enhance oversight and public accountability, Congress expanded the public inspection requirements by requiring all tax-exempt organizations, except churches and certain smaller organizations, to provide to any individual who makes a request a "take home" copy of Form 990 and Form 990–PF (in the case of a private foundation) for the three most recent taxable years, and a copy of the organization's exemption application (Form 1023). Monetary penalties are imposed on the foundation and its managers for failure to comply with these requirements. I.R.C. § 6685. These rules, which were extended to private foundations in 1998, were discussed earlier in the text. See Chapter 2H2, supra, at pp. 353–356.

Because of the unusual amount of detail required, the annual information return filed by any large foundation is likely to be quite bulky, making duplication and mailing of the returns expensive and administratively burdensome. When it expanded the disclosure requirements, Congress directed the Treasury to consider the unique issues that private foundations might face. In January, 2000, the Service issued final regulations governing the public disclosure of private foundation annual information returns and exemption applications. T.D. 8861, 65 Fed. Reg. 2030 (Jan. 12, 2000). These regulations, which took effect on March 13, 2000, are very similar to the generally applicable disclosure rules governing other exempt organizations except that private foundations, unlike public charities, must disclose the names and addresses of their contributors. Under the final regulations, a private foundation must provide copies of its three most recent annual information returns and its exemption application in response to an in-person request or within 30 days of receipt of a written request. For returns filed after March 13, 2000, private foundations no longer are required to publish a notice in a local newspaper announcing that their information return is available for inspection.

A more significant development on the disclosure front has been the posting on the Internet of the most recent tax information returns for virtually every U.S. private foundation. The full collection of Form 990–PFs is available to scholars, grantseekers, journalists and voyeurs thanks to a joint project of Philanthropic Research, Inc. and the Urban Institute's National Center for Charitable Statistics. Their respective web sites are: <www.guidestar.org> and <www.nccs.urban.org>. The Form 990's of most public charities are also being posted on these two sites. Form 990's and other financial information for California charities are available on the California Attorney General's web site: <caag.state.ca.us/charities/>.

C.   Private Foundation Excise Taxes

Sections 4940 through 4945 impose excise taxes on private foundations, foundation managers, and in some cases principal donors and government officials. With one exception (the § 4940 tax on net investment income), these excise taxes impose monetary sanctions for specific abuses enumerated in the statute. The initial sanctions serve as a warning and an invitation to "correction" of the abuse. If correction does not occur within a designated time period, much larger second-tier penalties are imposed. Repeated transgressions that go uncorrected may lead to termination of the foundation and confiscation of all its assets by the government. Exceptions, monetary caps, opportunities for abatement, and other relief provisions abound throughout the complex scheme.

Mastery of the excise tax rules—a highly technical but obligatory exercise for legal advisors to private foundations—requires familiarity with the statutory provisions and a daunting set of regulations.

1. TAX ON NET INVESTMENT INCOME: § 4940

Internal Revenue Code: § 4940.

Treasury Regulations: § 53.4940(a)–1(a), (c), (d), (e), (f).

In General. Section 4940 imposes a two percent excise tax on a private foundation's net investment income. The tax was justified as a special fee to finance the expenses of auditing private foundations and enforcing the regulatory scheme. It thus has become known as the "audit tax" even though the revenue raised is not earmarked for the IRS's budget. The § 4940 tax rate initially was four percent, but Congress reduced it to two percent in 1978 after discovering that the higher rate produced more than twice the revenue needed to administer all of the exempt organizations provisions. When subsequent studies revealed that audit tax receipts continued to far exceed the costs of administration, Congress reduced the rate to one percent for foundations making additional distributions for charitable purposes. The audit tax is a persistent source of controversy. The foundation community sees it as a punitive measure that reduces funds available for charitable purposes and unfairly singles out foundations. Supporters of the tax argue that foundations, especially those with large endowments, should pay for some of the costs of government.

Net Investment Income. The audit tax is imposed on "net investment income," which is the sum of "gross investment income" and "capital gain net income," less related expenses of producing and collecting the income. I.R.C. § 4940(c)(1). Gross investment income includes dividends, interest, rents, royalties, and payments with respect to loans of securities, but not tax-exempt bond interest and any income subject to the unrelated business tax. I.R.C. § 4940(c)(2), (5).

"Capital gain net income" is the excess of capital gains over capital losses from dispositions of property used for the production of interest, dividends, rents and royalties and of income-producing property used in an unrelated business unless that gain is already subject to the unrelated business income tax. I.R.C. § 4940(c)(4)(A). Capital losses may be netted against capital gains for the taxable year, but excess capital losses are not deductible against gross investment income, and no capital loss carryovers are allowed. I.R.C § 4940(c)(4)(C). Capital gain net income includes gains from the sale of property "used" for the production of the various types of investment income if the property "is of a type that generally produces" such income, even if the foundation sells the income-producing property immediately after receiving it in a gift or bequest. Treas. Reg. § 53.4940–1(f)(1). See Greenacre Foundation v. United States, 762 F.2d 965 (Fed.Cir. 1985). It also includes gain from the sale of property that may be currently unproductive but is "of a type which generally produces * * * capital gain through appreciation," at least where the property was capable of producing interest, dividends, rents, or royalties. Treas. Reg. § 53.4940–1(f)(1). See Zemurray Foundation v. United States, 687 F.2d 97 (5th Cir.1982); Zemurray Foundation v. United States, 755 F.2d 404 (5th Cir.1985).

In computing net investment income, the foundation may deduct ordinary and necessary expenses (including straight line depreciation and cost depletion) paid or incurred for the production or collection of gross investment income or for the management, conservation or maintenance of property held for the production of such income. I.R.C. § 4940(c)(3). The deduction provision is derived from § 212, which permits individual taxpayers to deduct various investment expenses. Typical deductible expenses would be investment advisory fees, salaries paid to foundation employees who manage the endowment, depreciation on property used to manage investments, and investment interest. See Treas. Reg. § 53.4940–1(e).

Rate Reduction. Section 4940(e) reduces the audit tax rate from two to one percent for foundations that make equivalent increases in their qualifying distributions for charitable purposes. The term "qualifying distributions" has the same meaning as in § 4942(g)—very generally, it refers to amounts distributed or set aside for charitable purposes and expenses of administering the foundation's charitable program. Specifically, to qualify for the rate reduction a foundation's qualifying distributions for the year must equal or exceed the sum of: (1) the value of the foundation's assets for that year multiplied by the foundation's average percentage charitable payout for a "base period" consisting of the five taxable years preceding the current year (or the foundation's existence, if it has less than a five-year history), and (2) one percent of net investment income. I.R.C. § 4940(e)(2)(A). Foundations in their first year of existence do not qualify for any rate reduction. To illustrate, assume that a foundation has investment assets with a value of $10 million at all times during the current year and the preceding five years. Assume further that, on average, the foundation has made $500,000 of qualifying distributions for the five-year base period, and that its net investment income for the current year is $600,000. The foundation will qualify for the one percent rate reduction (a savings of $6,000) if its qualifying distributions for the current year equal or exceed the sum of: $500,000 (net investment assets multiplied by average payout) plus $6,000 (one percent of net investment income), or $506,000. In effect, a foundation that is able to maintain its historical distribution level may substitute additional qualifying distributions for the extra one percent of audit tax.

Two other operating rules complete the picture. First, to prevent the general formula described above from requiring continually higher payout rates to qualify for the rate reduction (a "distributions escalator"), § 4940(e)(3)(C) provides that, for any year in the base period that the audit tax rate was reduced, the amount of qualifying distributions made by the foundation during that year also is reduced by the amount of the rate reduction. In practice, this rule provides at best only partial relief, and foundations that have made grants in excess of their payout requirement may find it increasingly difficult to achieve a rate reduction. Second, the reduction is not available for a given year if, at any time during the base period, the foundation has incurred a penalty under § 4942 for failing to meet the minimum payout requirement. I.R.C. § 4940(e)(2)(B).

Exempt Operating Foundations. Exempt operating foundations are wholly exempt from the audit tax. I.R.C. § 4940(d)(1). An organization qualifies as an exempt operating foundation if:

(a) It had private operating foundation status on January 1, 1983, or qualified as an operating foundation for its last taxable year ending before January 1, 1983,[1] or it is a private operating foundation in the taxable year and met the public support tests of either § 170(b)(1)(A)(vi) or § 509(a)(2) for at least ten years prior to the taxable year;

(b) The organization's governing body, at all times during the taxable year, consisted of individuals at least 75 percent of whom were not "disqualified individuals;"

(c) The organization's governing body, throughout the taxable year, was broadly representative of the general public; and

(d) No officer of the organization was, at any time during the taxable year, a "disqualified individual."

I.R.C. § 4940(d)(2).

For this purpose, a "disqualified individual" is an individual who is either a substantial contributor to the foundation, a more than 20 percent owner of a business enterprise (corporation, partnership or trust) that is a substantial contributor, or a member of the family of one of the foregoing individuals. I.R.C. § 4940(d)(3)(B).

Only operating foundations in existence at the beginning of 1983 or with a previous history as a public charity are within the narrow group eligible for this benefit, provided they have a sufficiently public governing board. Newly created foundations do not qualify.

PROBLEM

The Lifton Foundation, a § 501(c)(3) organization classified as a private nonoperating foundation, had the following assets (all acquired after 1969) on January 1 of the current year:

---

1. This transitional rule, which is not in the Internal Revenue Code, can be found in § 302(c)(3) of the Tax Reform Act of 1984, P.L. 98—369.

	Basis	**Value**
Lifton Pea Co. stock	$10,000	$4,500,000
Real Estate	80,000	200,000
Cash	50,000	50,000
Undeveloped parcel	200,000	300,000
Works of art (on loan to museum)	25,000	75,000
Office furniture	10,000	8,000
State of Connecticut bonds	300,000	250,000

During the current year, the Foundation had the following income, expenses and losses:

Income

Dividends on Lifton Pea stock	$225,000
Capital gain from sale of parcel	100,000
Rentals from real estate	20,000
Interest on Connecticut bonds	12,000

Expenses and Loss

General administrative expenses	$ 40,000
Scholarship grants	120,000
Maintenance of real estate (including straight line depreciation)	10,000
Purchase of various works of art	25,000
Loss on sale of Connecticut bonds	50,000

Assume that no expenses are directly related to producing either the dividend or the interest income.

(a) What is the Lifton Foundation's § 4940 excise tax liability for the current year?

(b) In general, what steps can be taken by the Foundation to reduce its tax rate from 2 to 1 percent?

2. SELF-DEALING: § 4941

Internal Revenue Code: § 4941(a), (b), (c), (d)(1), (2)(A)–(G), (e).

Treasury Regulations: §§ 53.4941(a)–1(a), (b), (c); 53.4941(d)–1(a), (b)(1), (2), (4)–(8); 53.4941(d)–2(a), (b)(1) & (2), (c), (d), (e), (f), (g); 53.4941(d)–3.

Much of the criticism of private foundations that influenced the 1969 legislation was directed at the ability of foundation insiders and related persons to use the foundation's resources for private gain. Prior law had penalized self-dealing transactions by certain § 501(c)(3) organizations if they favored substantial contributors and other insiders. The only federal sanction, however, was revocation of the organization's exempt status, and regulation of self-dealing under state nonprofit law was uneven and largely ineffective. The arm's length standard of prior law was subjective, and enforcement efforts proved ineffective, inhibited by the draconian sanction. Congress also believed that even arm's-length transactions permitted insid-

---

ers to benefit improperly, such as when an insider sells property to a foundation at a fair price but the sale is made to provide liquidity to the insider at a time when other buyers can't be found. In response to these concerns, Congress decided to penalize a broad range of self-dealing transactions, whether or not they disadvantaged the foundation.

a. ACTS OF SELF–DEALING

Section 4941(d)(1) identifies five categories of self-dealing transactions between a private foundation and its disqualified persons, and one additional category limited to certain dealings with government officials. The "special rules" in § 4941(d)(2) offer several helpful exceptions for innocent transactions that otherwise would fall within the broad sweep of the self-dealing concept. As is the norm in the private foundations area, the regulations elaborate considerably.

Sales and Exchanges. A sale or exchange of property between a private foundation and a disqualified person is an act of self-dealing even if the transaction is at fair market value or, remarkably, even if the foundation receives a bargain. I.R.C. § 4941(d)(1)(A). Transfers of encumbered real or personal property by a disqualified person to the foundation are treated as sales or exchanges if the foundation expressly assumes the debt or takes subject to a mortgage or lien placed on the property within the 10–year period preceding the transfer. I.R.C. § 4941(d)(2)(A).

An important exception is provided for certain transactions between a private foundation in its capacity as a shareholder of a corporation that is a disqualified person. Liquidations, mergers, redemptions, recapitalizations and similar corporate transactions are not treated as acts of self-dealing if all the securities of the same class as that held by the foundation are subject to the same terms and those terms provide for receipt by the foundation of not less than fair market value. I.R.C. § 4941(d)(2)(F).

Leases. A lease of property between a private foundation and a disqualified person is an act of self-dealing. The regulations carve out an exception for rent-free leases by a disqualified person to a foundation if payments by the foundation for janitorial services, utilities and other maintenance costs are not made to the disqualified person. Treas. Reg. § 53.4941(d)–2(b)(2).

Loans. The "lending of money or other extension of credit" between a private foundation and a disqualified person is an act of self-dealing. Interest-free loans by a disqualified person to a foundation are excepted where the loan proceeds are used exclusively by the foundation in pursuit of its exempt purposes. I.R.C. § 4941(d)(1)(B) & (d)(2)(B).

Furnishing of Goods, Services or Facilities. The furnishing of goods, services or facilities between a private foundation and a disqualified person is an act of self-dealing, except where the goods, services or facilities are furnished by the disqualified person without charge and used by the foundation in pursuit of its exempt purposes. I.R.C. § 4941(d)(1)(C) & (d)(2)(C). A second exception applies where the goods, services or facilities are furnished by the private foundation to the disqualified person on terms not more favorable than those made available to the general public. I.R.C. § 4941(d)(2)(D).

Payment of Compensation. The payment of compensation or reimbursement of expenses by a foundation to a disqualified person is an act of self-dealing unless the payment is not excessive and is for personal services which are "reasonable and necessary to carrying out the exempt purpose" of the foundation. In no event may the foundation pay any compensation to a "government official." I.R.C. § 4941(d)(1)(D) & (d)(2)(E).

Use or Transfer of Assets or Income. Congress did not want to leave any stone unturned. Its final catch-all category provides that any transfer by a private foundation of its income or assets to or for the use or benefit of a disqualified person is an act of self-dealing. I.R.C. § 4941(d)(1)(E). For example, the Service has ruled that the placing of paintings owned by a private foundation in the residence of a substantial contributor comes within this category. Rev. Rul. 74–600, 1974–2 C.B. 385.

Payments to Government Officials. Any agreement by a private foundation to make a payment of money to a government official, even if the payment is reasonable in amount, is an act of self-dealing. I.R.C. § 4941(d)(1)(F). An individual is a "government official" if, at the time of any particular act of self-dealing, he or she holds various elective or appointive offices specified in § 4946(c). This long list includes the President and Vice President of the United States, all members of Congress, federal judges and cabinet members, high-level employees of all three branches of the federal government, staff members in the U.S. Senate or House who earn at least $15,000 a year in compensation, elected or appointed state and local governmental officials who earn at least $20,000 a year, and any "personal or executive assistant or secretary" to any of the foregoing. For more details, see Treas. Reg. § 53.4946–1.

The government official self-dealing rule is subject to several exceptions. For example, a foundation may agree to employ or make a grant to a government official for any period after termination of government service if the agreement is made no more than 90 days before that service terminates. See Treas. Reg. § 53.4941(d)–3(e)(8). Other exceptions cover certain narrowly defined types of scholarships, prizes, awards, pension benefits, de minimis gifts, and travel expense reimbursements. See I.R.C. § 4941(d)(2)(G) and Treas. Reg. § 53.4941(d)–3(e).

Disaster-Relief Payments. Prior to September 11, 2001, it was unclear whether disaster-relief payments by company-sponsored private foundations to employees were acts of self-dealing. The concern was that such assistance was tantamount to an employee benefit program that provided an impermissible private benefit. For example, the IRS had ruled that a private foundation established, funded and controlled by a particular employer for the purpose of providing disaster relief for employees of a particular employer did not qualify as a charitable organization under § 501(c)(3) because the foundation was not operated solely for charitable purposes and was providing a benefit on behalf of the employer in violation of the prohibition on private inurement. See, e.g., P.L.R. 199914040.

The Victims of Terrorism Tax Relief Act of 2001 (§ 111) eases the path for employer-sponsored foundations that make relief payments in connection with disasters resulting from certain terrorist or military actions, Presidentially declared disasters, disasters resulting from an accident involving a common carrier, or any other event determined by the Secretary of the Treasury to be catastrophic (collectively defined as a "qualified disaster.") The Service now must presume that such qualified disaster payments made by company foundations to employees or their families are consistent with the foundation's charitable purposes if: (1) eligible beneficiaries are a sufficiently large or indefinite group to constitute a "charitable class;" (2) the recipients are selected based on an objective determination of need; and (3) the selection is made by an independent selection committee or adequate substitute procedure to ensure that any benefit to the employer is incidental or tenuous. If the requirements of this presumption are met, the foundation's payments will be treated as made for charitable purposes and will not constitute acts of self-dealing.

b. THE TAX COST OF SELF-DEALING

Initial Tax. In keeping with the general scheme of the foundation excise taxes, penalties for self-dealing are imposed at two levels. An initial tax is imposed on the self-dealer and, in some circumstances, on a foundation manager who knowingly participates in the act on behalf of the foundation. Notably, a penalty is not imposed on the foundation itself. Failure to correct the evil act within an appropriate period of time triggers the second-level tax.

The initial tax on the self-dealer is five percent of the "amount involved" with respect to the act of self-dealing for each year or part of a year in the taxable period. I.R.C. § 4941(a)(1). The "amount involved" is the greater of the amount of money and the fair market value of the other property given, or the amount of money and the fair market value of the other property received, valued as of the date of the act of self-dealing. I.R.C. § 4941(e)(2). A tax of 2-½ percent of the amount involved is imposed on a foundation manager who knowingly engaged in the act for each year (or part thereof) in the taxable period. I.R.C. § 4941(a)(2). The "taxable period" begins with the act of self-dealing and ends on the earliest of: (1) the date of mailing of an IRS deficiency notice, (2) the date on which the first-level tax is assessed, or (3) the date on which the act of self-dealing is fully corrected. I.R.C. § 4941(e)(1).

Correction. "Correction" requires undoing the transaction to the extent possible, provided there is no detriment to the foundation after assuming that the disqualified person is acting under the "highest fiduciary standards." I.R.C. § 4941(e)(3). The regulations provide amplification, essentially imposing a restitution plus profits (if any) requirement. Treas. Reg. § 53.4941(e)–1(c). Failure to correct triggers the second-level tax of 200 percent of the amount involved on the self-dealer and 50 percent on the obstinate or ignorant foundation manager who refuses to agree to all or part of the correction. I.R.C. § 4941(b)(1), (b)(2). For this purpose, the "amount involved" means the greater of the amount of money paid or the highest fair market value during the taxable period. I.R.C. § 4941(e)(2)(B).

Abatement of First–Tier Excise Taxes. In connection with its 1984 reexamination of the private foundation sanctions, Congress concluded that the first-level excise tax should be abated in certain cases if the "taxable event was due to reasonable cause and not to willful neglect" and correction is accomplished within the appropriate correction period. I.R.C. § 4962(a). Congress found no justification for extending abatement relief to acts of self-dealing, however, because the penalty tax is payable by the self-dealer and not the foundation, and since "commercial transactions between disqualified persons and foundations are generally prohibited." H.R. Rep. No. 98–432 (Part 2), 98th Cong., 2d Sess. 1472 (1984). See I.R.C. § 4962(b). The conferral of abatement authority reflects an awareness that innocent transgressions of the private foundation rules commonly occur, and that a rigid penalty is often inappropriate. Query whether the most appealing case for equitable consideration can be made on behalf of the "innocent" self-dealer, to whom abatement relief is not available?

* * *

The *Madden* case, which follows, is a real-world example of the reach of the § 4941 self-dealing penalty regime. It demonstrates the importance of carefully interpreting the statute and regulations before advising a private foundation and its managers about their potential exposure to self-dealing penalties.

Madden v. Commissioner

United States Tax Court, 1997.
74 T.C.M. (CCH) 440.

■ Fay, Judge:

MEMORANDUM FINDINGS OF FACT AND OPINION

[The taxpayers in this case were John Madden, his wife, Marjorie, their daughter, Cynthia, and several business entities controlled by the Madden family. Mr. Madden was the founder of John Madden Co., which developed and managed commercial properties including Greenwood Plaza, a major office complex in Denver, Colorado. The taxpayers formed a private foundation to operate an outdoor museum (hereinafter "Museum") located in Greenwood Plaza. Mr. and Mrs. Madden and their daughter all served as directors or officers of Museum and thus were "foundation managers" within the meaning of § 4946(b). John Madden also owned a 75 percent stake in GMC, a maintenance and janitorial company that performed services for many of the buildings in the complex, including Museum. Because it was controlled by Mr. Madden, GMC was a "disqualified person" with respect to Museum.

Museum's collection consisted primarily of sculptures and other exhibits designed to withstand the outdoor elements. Most of the pieces were located along public thoroughfares running through the complex or in atriums on the ground floor of some of the buildings. In addition to displaying its works, Museum conducted tours and offered art courses to the community.

John Madden Co. furnished office space to Museum, rent-free, and allowed Museum to use the company's accounting system free of charge. Museum also relied on building owners, including John Madden Co., to provide space free of charge for displays of its collection. Museum often held special events, such as wedding receptions and bar mitzvahs, in the complex and charged a fee for the use of space furnished by building owners. In connection with these events, it paid GMC fees for maintenance and janitorial services. The fee arrangement was entered into after John Madden Co.'s chief executive officer, Sherry Manning, told Cynthia Madden that GMC could charge Museum for its services as long as the fee was no higher than the fair market rate for comparable services rendered.

Museum also mistakenly made small payments for repairs to artwork owned by John Madden personally, but Mr. Madden promptly reimbursed Museum, and Museum made a $3,000 payment to an unrelated company (Form, Inc.) in connection with an art exhibit, fulfilling a contractual obligation of John Madden Co.

The IRS asserted that GMC was liable for § 4941(a)(1) self-dealing penalties and that John, Marjorie and Cynthia Madden were liable for § 4941(a)(2) foundation manager self-dealing penalties in connection with payments made by Museum to GMC. The IRS also claimed that Museum owed unrelated business income tax on its revenue from the special events and the leasing of space; the excerpts from the opinion below are limited to the self-dealing issues. Eds.]

OPINION

* * *

Issue 3. Payments to GMC

Section 4941 imposes an excise tax for acts of "self-dealing" that occur between a private foundation and a "disqualified person". Sec. 4941(a)(1). The parties agree that GMC is a "disqualified person" with respect to the Museum, a private foundation. For the purposes of this section, "self-dealing" includes the "furnishing of goods, services, or facilities between a private foundation and a disqualified person". Sec. 4941(d)(1)(C). However, section 4941(d)(2) provides several exceptions for certain arrangements that would otherwise constitute self-dealing transactions. Specifically, section 4941(d)(2)(E) provides:

the payment of compensation (and the payment or reimbursement of expenses) by a private foundation to a disqualified person for personal services which are reasonable and necessary to carrying out the exempt purpose of the private foundation shall not be an act of self-dealing if

the compensation (or payment or reimbursement) is not excessive
* * *

Throughout the years at issue, the Museum contracted with GMC to perform general maintenance, janitorial, and custodial functions. Respondent maintains that payments to GMC for services performed are self-dealing transactions within the ambit of section 4941(d)(1)(C). Petitioner replies that these transactions fit within the exception in section 4941(d)(2)(E) as "personal services" which are reasonable and necessary to carry out the Museum's exempt functions. As might be expected, respondent disagrees.

The resolution of this issue depends solely on whether or not the functions that GMC performed fall within the definition of "personal services" of section 4941(d)(2)(E). Before making this determination, a review of the legislative history of section 4941 is helpful.

Prior to 1969, sections 501(a) and 503(a), (b), and (d) had imposed severe sanctions for transactions that resulted in the diversion of funds to a creator or substantial contributor of a tax-exempt organization. Further, in order to prevent tax-exempt foundations from being used to benefit their creators or substantial contributors, Congress had established a set of arm's-length standards for dealings between the foundations and these disqualified individuals. H. Rept. 91–413 (Part 1), at 21 (1969), 1969–3 C.B. 200, 214.

Nevertheless, Congress noted that abuses involving tax-exempt organizations continued. Congress believed the abuses resulted from the significant enforcement problems posed by the arm's-length standards. Id. Therefore, section 4941 was enacted as part of subchapter A of a new chapter 42 added to the Internal Revenue Code by the Tax Reform Act of 1969 (the 1969 Act), Pub.L. 91–172, sec. 101(b), 83 Star. 487, 499.

One of the stated goals of the 1969 Act was to minimize the need for an arm's-length standard by generally prohibiting self-dealing transactions. Specifically, the 1969 Act prohibited the following transactions between a foundation and a disqualified person: (1) The sale, exchange or lease of property; (2) the lending of money; (3) the furnishing of goods, services or facilities; (4) the payment of compensation to a disqualified person; (5) the transfer or use of foundation property by a disqualified person; and (6) payments to Government officials. S. Rept. 91–552, at 29 (1969), 1969–3 C.B. 423, 443. If the foundation and a disqualified person entered into a prohibited transaction, then the 1969 Act imposed various levels of sanctions.

The question before us is whether the functions performed by GMC qualify as "personal services" under section 4941(d)(2)(E). Thus, we must construe what activities Congress intended would qualify as personal services. At the outset, we can look to the regulations interpreting the statute. While those regulations do not define the term "personal services", they offer several examples of activities that constitute "personal services". See sec. 53.4941(d)–3(c)(2), Foundation Excise Tax Regs. The activities set out in the examples include legal services, investment management services, and general banking services. Id.

Respondent argues that the character of the services performed by GMC, namely maintenance, janitorial, and security, are different than those outlined in the regulations. We agree. The services in the regulations are essentially professional and managerial in nature. These types of services contrast with the nature of the services rendered by GMC.

GMC contends any activity is a service where capital is not a major factor in the production of income. Under this interpretation, as set out in the brief, "the sale of goods is not the rendering of personal services, but certainly all other services which assist the private foundation in carrying on its legitimate business are personal services." We cannot agree with GMC's interpretation of the statute. First, this position would nullify the prohibition against furnishing services contained in section 4941(d)(1)(C), because almost any service would be a "personal service" and fall within the exception. The statute draws an explicit distinction between a "charge" for "furnishing of goods, services, or facilities", see sec. 4941(d)(1)(C) and (2)(C), and the payment of "compensation" "for personal services", see sec. 4941(d)(1)(D) and (2)(E). GMC's argument equating a charge for services with compensation for personal services significantly erodes this distinction.

Second, GMC's interpretation of the term "personal services" contravenes congressional intent, as expressed in the above legislative history. We think it is clear that Congress intended to prohibit self-dealing. Consequently, any exceptions to the self-dealing transactions rules should be construed narrowly. We therefore reject GMC's broad interpretation of the term "personal services" and conclude that the janitorial services provided by GMC do not meet the definition of "personal services". Accordingly, we find that the payments made by the Museum to GMC constitute "self-dealing" within the meaning of section 4941(d)(1)(C), and, as a consequence, GMC is liable for the self-dealing excise tax under section 4941(a)(1).

Issue 4. Excise Tax on Payments Made by the Museum to GMC

We shall next turn our attention to whether petitioner, petitioner's wife, and petitioner's daughter (the foundation managers)[8] are liable under section 4941(a)(2) for payments made to GMC by the Museum. In general, section 4941(a)(1) imposes an excise tax on the self-dealer for each self-dealing transaction. When an excise tax is imposed under section 4941(a)(1), then section 4941(a)(2) may impose excise taxes on the management of the foundation as well. Section 4941(a)(2) provides:

8. A separate excise tax was imposed on petitioner, on petitioner's wife, and on petitioner's daughter (the foundation managers). However, the legal issues and relevant facts are identical with respect to each of the foundation managers. For brevity, we will combine our examination of each tax into a single discussion and refer to the above-named parties collectively as the foundation managers where possible.

In any case in which a tax is imposed by [section 4941(a)] paragraph (1), there is hereby imposed on the participation of any foundation manager in an act of self-dealing between a disqualified person and a private foundation, knowing that it is such an act, a tax equal to 20 percent of the amount involved with respect to the act of self-dealing for each year (or part thereof) in the taxable period, unless such participation is not willful and is due to reasonable cause. * * *

Thus, this tax is imposed only when (1) a tax is imposed under section 4941(a)(1), (2) the participating foundation manager knows that the act is an act of self-dealing, and (3) the participation by the foundation manager is willful and is not due to reasonable cause. Sec. 53.4941(a)-l(b)(1), Foundation Excise Tax Regs. Respondent must prove, by clear and convincing evidence, that the foundation managers participated knowingly in the self-dealing transaction. Sec. 7454(b); Rule 142(c).

We first turn to the regulations to provide the initial guidance in applying section 4941(a)(2). The regulations interpret what the statute requires for knowing participation. Section 53.4941(a)-l(b)(3), Foundation Excise Tax Regs., states:

a person shall be considered to have participated in a transaction "knowing" that it is an act of self-dealing only if—

 (i)   He has actual knowledge of sufficient facts so that, based solely upon such facts, such transaction would be an act of self-dealing,

 (ii) He is aware that such an act under these circumstances may violate the provisions of federal tax law governing self-dealing, and

 (iii) He negligently fails to make reasonable attempts to ascertain whether the transaction is an act of self-dealing, or he is in fact aware that it is such an act.

The regulations specify that the term "knowing" does not mean "having reason to know", but evidence that shows a person has a reason to know a fact is relevant in determining whether that person has actual knowledge of that fact. Id. These regulations were adopted in 1972, 3 years after the passage of the statute, and have not been substantially modified since that time. Therefore, we must give appropriate weight to the regulations in interpreting the statute. Commissioner v. South Texas Lumber Co., 333 U.S. 496, 68 S.Ct. 695, 92 L.Ed. 831 (1948).

We have found no other cases that have analyzed the foundation manager excise tax under section 4941(a)(2). However, the Tax Court analyzed the foundation manager excise tax under section 4945(a)(2) in Thorne v. Commissioner, 99 T.C. 67, 1992 WL 166157 (1992). These statutes were both enacted as part of the chapter 42 reforms of the 1969 Act, and the statutes, as well as the respective regulations promulgated thereunder, contain nearly identical language. Thus, the analysis contained in Thorne v. Commissioner, supra, is highly probative in interpreting the excise tax of section 4941(a)(2). We concluded in Thorne v. Commissioner that the threshold determination under the knowledge requirement is ascertaining the extent of the taxpayer's factual knowledge concerning the expenditures and not whether the taxpayer actually knew the expenditures were prohibited under the statute.

The parties have stipulated that the foundation managers were aware both that GMC was a disqualified person vis-a-vis the Museum, and that some transactions between a private foundation and a disqualified person are considered "self-dealing" under section 4941(d). Further, the parties have agreed that the foundation managers were aware self-dealing is defined as, inter alia, a direct furnishing of goods, services, or facilities between a private foundation and a disqualified person. In addition, the parties have agreed that the foundation managers were aware the Museum was making payments to GMC, and the managers did not oppose the making of these payments. On the basis of these facts, we conclude respondent has proven, by clear and convincing evidence, that the foundation managers possessed actual knowledge of sufficient facts concerning the transactions to establish the arrangements with GMC were self-dealing transactions.

Respondent has satisfied both the first and second requirements of section 4941(a)(2). First, we have concluded that, under section 4941(a)(1), an excise tax should be imposed on the payments from the Museum to GMC. Second, respondent has established that the foundation managers possessed sufficient "knowledge" concerning the self-dealing payments to GMC. Next, we shall evaluate whether the foundation managers made the payments willfully and without reasonable cause, the third requirement under section 4941(a)(2).

The regulations define "willful" participation by the foundation manager as conduct that is "voluntary, conscious, and intentional." Sec. 53.4941(a)–1(b)(4), Foundation Excise Tax Regs. On the basis of the facts, we conclude the foundation managers voluntarily and intentionally caused the Museum to enter into the transactions with GMC. Accordingly, we sustain respondent's determination that the participation of the foundation managers was willful.

Additionally, the foundation managers' participation in these transactions must not be due to reasonable cause. The regulations explain that "A foundation manager's participation is due to reasonable cause if he has exercised his responsibility on behalf of the foundation with ordinary business care and prudence." Sec. 53.4941(a)–1(b)(5), Foundation Excise Tax Regs. The foundation managers were aware that GMC was a disqualified person with respect to the Museum, and they were aware that tax laws prohibited self-dealing transactions. Nevertheless, they proceeded to contract with GMC to provide services to the Museum without first attempting to get advice from their counsel concerning the implications of these arrangements. This demonstrates a failure to exercise their responsibilities with ordinary business care and prudence.

The foundation managers argue that they acted on the advice of Dr. Sherry Manning. Dr. Manning, a former president of a women's college,

has experience with nonprofit organizations. Thus, the foundation managers claim that they exercised ordinary prudence in relying on Dr. Manning's advice. We cannot agree. Dr. Manning is not a lawyer, and she does
not otherwise have any special expertise in foundation tax law. Further,
although she had been the president of a college, there is no indication in
the record that Dr. Manning gained any experience in running foundations.
Clearly, the foundation managers were aware of the potential problems
with paying fees to GMC, as prior to the hiring of Dr. Manning, GMC had
simply rendered the services for free. We conclude the foundation managers
did not exercise ordinary prudence by relying on the advice of Dr. Manning
and not seeking the advice of counsel regarding these payments. Accordingly, we hold that the foundation managers are liable for the foundation
manager excise tax under section 4941(a)(2) for payments made by the
Museum to GMC.

Issue 5. Excise Tax on Other Payments Made by the Museum

Respondent determined that the foundation managers are liable for the
foundation manager excise tax under section 4941(a)(2) for two payments
made by the Museum that benefited petitioner and a third payment by the
Museum that benefited the Company. Specifically, the two payments which
benefited petitioner, in the amounts of $2,304 and $1,343, were made by
the Museum for work done to petitioner's artwork. A third payment, in the
amount of $3,000, related to a financial obligation of the Company which
was actually paid by the Museum. As discussed supra, a foundation
manager excise tax under section 4941(a)(2) may be imposed where (1) a
tax should be imposed under section 4941(a)(1), (2) the participating
foundation manager knows that the act is an act of self-dealing, and (3) the
participation by the foundation manager is willful and is not due to
reasonable cause. Sec. 53.4941(a)–1(b)(1), Foundation Excise Tax Regs.
Respondent must carry the burden of proving by clear and convincing
evidence that the foundation managers participated knowingly in the
transaction. Sec. 7454(b); Rule 142(c).

The foundation managers have conceded that each of these payments
constitutes self-dealing under section 4941(a)(1). However, respondent
must still prove that the foundation managers knew the act was an act of
self-dealing. Also, the participation by the foundation managers must be
willful and not due to reasonable cause.

As noted supra, the Company provided accounting services to the
Museum. Two invoices relating to artwork repairs were received by the
accounting department of the Company. The accounting personnel, assuming that the work had been performed on artwork owned by the Museum,
made payments of $2,304 and $1,343 by checks drawn upon the Museum's
bank account. In fact, the artwork belonged to petitioner, and the payments should have been made from petitioner's personal account.

Far from having actual knowledge of sufficient facts about the two
transactions, the evidence indicates that the foundation managers lacked
any knowledge concerning these transactions. Immediately upon learning

of the payments a few days after they were made, petitioner's daughter corrected both of the transactions, and petitioner reimbursed the Museum for the expense. Under these circumstances, we conclude respondent erred in imposing the foundation manager excise tax on these two transactions.

The record is less than complete regarding the $3,000 payment made for the benefit of the Company. The payment was made by the Museum on behalf of the Company, a disqualified person. The Company has not reimbursed the Museum. Respondent, again, must prove by clear and convincing evidence that the foundation managers participated knowingly in this transaction. Sec. 7454(b); Rule 142(c). Respondent has failed to carry this burden. First, respondent has not shown that petitioner or petitioner's wife had any knowledge of this transaction. We refuse to presume that, because the transaction occurred, petitioner or petitioner's wife must have known about it. Consequently, we do not sustain respondent's determination with respect to petitioner or petitioner's wife as it relates to this transaction.

As for petitioner's daughter, the facts must be examined more closely. The $3,000 payment related to a contract with Form, Inc., for the creation of an outdoor art exhibit. The subject matter of the contract comports directly with the Museum's exempt purpose, and the contract was signed by petitioner's daughter as a director of the Museum. However, the John Madden Co. is the named party in the contract, not the Museum. The payment by the Museum for setting up the outdoor exhibit satisfied a financial obligation of the Company under the contract with Form, Inc., and the parties agree that it is a self-dealing payment to the Company.

Petitioner's daughter testified that she was aware of the payment made by the Museum. As evidenced by this testimony, she was knowledgeable about the subject matter of the contract. However, based on the testimony and surrounding facts, we conclude that her actions do not constitute knowing participation in a self-dealing transaction. Petitioner's daughter testified that the foundation managers intended to have the Museum shoulder the responsibility for the exhibit, not the Company. She believed, at the time of the payment, that responsibility for the financial obligation rested with the Museum. As a consequence, petitioner's daughter did not view this payment as benefiting the Company. Given these circumstances, we conclude respondent has failed to prove by clear and convincing evidence that petitioner's daughter knowingly entered into a self-dealing transaction. Accordingly, we do not sustain respondent's determination with respect to petitioner's daughter as it relates to this $3,000 transaction.

PROBLEMS

1. The Lifton Foundation ("the Foundation") is a § 501(c)(3) organization classified as a private nonoperating foundation. The Foundation's President is Olga Lifton Rothschild, granddaughter of Archibold Lifton, who created the Foundation in 1970 with a substantial gift of Lifton Pea Corporation stock. Other substantial gifts have been made by Archibold's

wife, Claribel, and by Roger Ogleby, a distant cousin of Olga Rothschild. Assume that Archibold and Claribel Lifton and Roger Ogleby are "substantial contributors." The Foundation's net assets are $25 million.

Which of the following transactions during the current year are likely to create excise tax liability for self-dealing under § 4941? In each case in which you conclude that there is such liability, determine: (a) against whom the tax will be imposed; (b) the probable amount of the tax; and (c) the procedure and time period in which to correct the act and the ramifications of failing to do so within the prescribed period.

(a) Payment of $75,000 per year compensation to Olga for her services as President, and $5,000 in reimbursement of travel expenses for other family members and their spouses to attend the annual meeting of the board of directors at the family's summer retreat.

(b) Leasing of office space by the Foundation on a rent-free basis in a townhouse owned by Olga Rothschild.

(c) Sharing of office space with Lifton family members in a commercial building owned by an unrelated party; the Foundation reimburses the family members for its share of rent and related expenses.

(d) Payment by the Foundation of a legally binding charitable pledge made by Olga to her alma mater to commemorate her 25th college reunion.

(e) Hanging of paintings from the Foundation's collection at the home of Peggy Rothschild, Olga and Dick's daughter.

(f) Sale by the Foundation of an undeveloped parcel on March 15 to Olga's husband, Dick, for $300,000, its fair market value. As foundation manager, Olga was aware of the sale but did not know that a sale at fair market value would constitute an act of self-dealing. For this purpose, assume that the IRS issues a statutory notice of deficiency three years after March 15 of the current year, asserting that the sale is an act of self-dealing and assume, alternatively, that:

(1) Dick continues to own the land, which is now worth $500,000.

(2) Dick develops the land, now a shopping center worth $1,500,000.

(3) Dick's plan to develop the land fails and he sells the land for $250,000 seven months after its acquisition.

(g) Payment by the Foundation of $5,000 in directors and officers liability insurance premiums to cover the potential liability of its trustees for wrongful acts committed in their official capacity.

(h) Indemnification of the Foundation's officers and directors against penalties imposed by the Internal Revenue Service under § 4941 and reimbursement of their legal expenses in connection with the imposition of those penalties.

(i) Receipt by Olga and other Lifton family members of preferred seating at opera and symphony performances, and member benefits at museums, resulting from the Foundation's substantial grants to these cultural institutions.

(j) Scholarship grant of $1,000 to Olga's granddaughter, Henrietta.

(k) Payment of an honorarium of $1,000 plus travel expenses to Hiram Goldsmith, legislative assistant to a United States Senator, for a speech sponsored by the Foundation and delivered for the Senator by Mr. Goldsmith.

2.   If the transactions described in Problem 1, above, all occur in the current year, is it likely that the Foundation or any other person will be liable for taxes or penalties in addition to those imposed by § 4941? See, e.g., I.R.C. §§ 507(c); 6684.

3.   CHARITABLE DISTRIBUTION REQUIREMENTS: § 4942

Internal Revenue Code: § 4942(a), (b), (c), (d), (e), (g)(1)–(3), (h), (j)(1), (2) & (4).

a.   INTRODUCTION

It always has been assumed that a § 501(c)(3) organization will regularly disburse its funds for charitable purposes. Prior to 1969, however, some charities held unproductive assets or accumulated income, neglecting their charitable commitment. Although the Code provided that some foundations would lose their exemption if its accumulations of income were "unreasonable" in amount and duration, the standards were vague and sanctions were difficult to enforce.

To encourage more consistent generosity, § 4942 requires all private nonoperating foundations to make certain minimum annual distributions for charitable purposes. The required payout is measured with reference to a percentage of the foundation's investment assets. A foundation that fails to meet the minimum payout requirement is subject to an excise tax on its "undistributed income." If any of the required payout remains undistributed as of the beginning of the second (or any succeeding) taxable year following the current taxable year, a first-level tax equal to 15 percent of that undistributed amount is imposed; continuing failure to satisfy the statute gives rise to a more severe second-level penalty equal to 100 percent of the undistributed income. I.R.C. § 4942(a), (b).

To illustrate, assume that a private foundation formed on January 1, 1998, is required by § 4942 to distribute $100,000 for that year. The foundation would be subject to the initial excise tax under § 4942 if all or part of the 1998 distributable amount were not distributed as of January 1, 2000. If, however, the foundation had a $50,000 shortfall as of the beginning of 2000, it would be subject to a tax of $7,500 (15% x $50,000 of undistributed income) and the liability would continue for each succeeding taxable year in which the remaining payout requirement were not met. Continuing transgressions would also trigger the more severe second-level penalty equal to 100 percent of the undistributed income.

b. OPERATION OF § 4942

Distributable Amount. To avoid the § 4942 tax, a foundation must not have "undistributed income," which is defined by § 4942(c) as the foundation's "distributable amount" for the taxable year less "qualifying distributions" attributable to that year. The "distributable amount" is equal to the foundation's "minimum investment return" reduced by the § 4940 audit tax and any unrelated business income tax imposed on the foundation. I.R.C. § 4942(d).

Minimum investment return ("MIR") is equal to five percent of the excess of the fair market value of all assets of the foundation (other than those used directly in carrying out its exempt purposes) over any acquisition indebtedness to which those assets are subject. I.R.C. § 4942(e)(1). The "MIR" concept guarantees that a foundation's charitable activity, as measured by its grant-making or more direct expenditures for charitable purposes, bears some reasonable relationship to its size. The specific determination of MIR presents inevitable questions of valuation. For example, readily marketable securities are valued on a monthly basis, and the annual valuation must be an average of the monthly values determined. I.R.C. § 4942(e)(2)(A). Other assets may be valued less frequently—e.g., real property may be valued by independent appraisals at five-year intervals. Treas. Reg. § 53.4942(a)–2(c)(4)(iv). For securities, reductions in value for blockage or similar factors are appropriate where the foundation establishes that a reduction in value would accompany any liquidation, but blockage discounts are limited to 10 percent of market prices. I.R.C. § 4942(e)(2)(B).

Assets used directly to carry out a foundation's exempt purposes are excluded in determining MIR on the theory that they do not produce any income that is available for distribution. Examples of excluded assets are the buildings, equipment and supplies used in managing a foundation's exempt activities—but not the facilities used in administering a foundation's investments. Treas. Reg. § 53.4942(a)–2(c)(3). Also excluded are assets "held for use" in an exempt activity (e.g., an office building purchased for use as a national headquarters but temporarily rented to commercial tenants) and "program-related investments" (e.g., low-interest student loans). Id. Other examples of excluded related-function assets include: paintings loaned to museums and schools (Rev. Rul. 1974–2 C.B. 387); an island preserved for ecological and historical purposes (Rev. Rul. 75–207, 1975–1 C.B. 361); and assets of a business for which substantially all of the work is performed by volunteers (Rev. Rul. 76–85, 1976–1 C.B. 357).

Qualifying Distributions. A foundation satisfies its payout requirement by making "qualifying distributions." In general, a "qualifying distribution" is any amount paid to accomplish a proper charitable purpose, or any amount paid to acquire an asset to be used in carrying out such a purpose. I.R.C. § 4942(g)(1). Most qualifying distributions are grants, but direct expenditures to advance the foundation's proper purposes also qualify. Excluded, however, are (1) distributions to an organization controlled by the foundation or one or more disqualified persons, and (2) distributions to other nonoperating foundations, unless the distributee commits to passing such amount through by the end of the succeeding year. I.R.C. § 4942(g)(1), (3).

Qualifying distributions include reasonable and necessary administrative expenses paid to accomplish the foundation's exempt purposes, but not investment expenses and other costs of managing the foundation's endowment. Treas. Reg. § 53.4942(a)–3(a)(2). "Grant administrative expenses" include expenses allocable to the making of grants, such as costs of evaluating grant applications, expenses incurred to administer and evaluate grants, and expenses for post-grant review. From 1985 to 1990, § 4942(g)(4) imposed a ceiling generally equal to .65 percent of the foundation's net assets on the amount of grant administrative expenses that could be treated as qualifying distributions, but the ceiling—adopted out of fear that administrative costs were getting out of hand—was allowed to expire in 1991.

Set-Asides. From time to time a foundation may find it advisable to establish an internal fund for future expenditures in a charitable activity. For example, it may choose to fund a scientific research program of such magnitude that it requires an accumulation of funds before the project commences. Or it may wish to accumulate funds in connection with a matching-grants program in which the distributee is expected to raise an amount to match the foundation's future contribution. Section 4942(g)(2) permits such "set-aside" amounts to qualify as current distributions provided that the amount will be paid for a specific project within five years (and the foundation satisfies the Service as to that prospect), and that either:

a. the foundation establishes that the project is one which can better be accomplished by such set-aside than by immediate payment; or

b. each of the following requirements is met:

   (i) the project will not be completed within the year in which the set-aside is made;

   (ii) the foundation has, in post–1976 years, met certain statutory distribution requirements; and

   (iii) the foundation has also met certain pre–1976 distribution requirements.

The advantage of the alternative (albeit complicated) determination of the foundation's right to use a current set-aside is that the Service need not be satisfied that the set-aside is more appropriate than an immediate grant. § 4942(g)(2)(B).

The amount set aside need not be an accumulation of income. It is sufficient if the foundation sets aside, by means of a bookkeeping entry, the amount of its minimum investment return for the preceding year and earmarks it for a specific project. Rev. Rul. 78–148, 1978–1 C.B. 380. But the set-aside must advance the project. In Rev. Rul. 79–319, 1979–2 C.B.

388, a set-aside made so that the foundation could control the funds during a three-year museum construction period and receive income thereon, was held not to be a qualifying distribution. Compare Rev. Rul. 74–450, 1974–2 C.B. 388 (conversion of land into park under four-year construction contract justified set-asides against future payments).

Incorrect valuation. Where a foundation fails to make adequate qualifying distributions solely because it incorrectly valued assets for purposes of determining minimum investment return, the statute affords relief from tax provided that:

a. the failure to value the asset properly was not willful and was due to reasonable cause, and

b. "make-up" distributions are made within the "allowable distribution period" (as defined by 4942(j)(2)); the foundation notifies the Service that the necessary amount has been distributed; and the make-up distribution is treated, under the tracing rules of the statute, as made out of income for the year as to which the incorrect valuation occurred.

I.R.C. § 4942(a)(2).

Source of qualifying distributions. The initial § 4942 tax is imposed only if the "distributable amount" for the taxable year is not expended by qualifying distributions made by the end of the following year. I.R.C. § 4942(a). The statute provides that qualifying distributions are treated as first made out of the undistributed income for the immediately preceding year, then out of the undistributed income for the present year, and finally out of corpus. To enable a foundation to correct a distributions deficiency for a year prior to the immediately preceding year, however, the foundation may elect to treat any distribution that otherwise would be treated as out of the current year's distributable amount, or out of corpus, as a distribution for the year in which correction is necessary. I.R.C. § 4942(h).

If by chance the foundation's distributions during the preceding five years (the "adjustment period") exceed its distributable amount for those years, then the excess distributions may be used to reduce the foundation's distributable amount for the taxable year. I.R.C. § 4942(i).

PROBLEM

The Wang Foundation ("Wang"), a private operating foundation, commenced operations on January 1, 1999, when it was funded with the following gifts:

Asset	Donor	Adj. Basis	F.M.V.
10,000 shs. Wang Inc. stock (10% of total shs. outstanding)	Tom Wang	$370,000	$3,970,000
Cash	Mary Wang	30,000	30,000
Office Building	Lemon, Inc.	80,000	150,000
Furniture/Fixtures	Lemon, Inc.	20,000	20,000

Unless otherwise indicated, assume for convenience that the assets and values remain unchanged throughout the years covered by the problem, and that no blockage discount is allowed for the Foundation's stock in Wang, Inc.

Wang was organized to encourage the education of underprivileged youth in Northern California by seeking to identify urban high schools with a high percentage of disadvantaged students, to make grants to these schools to establish special educational programs, to award college scholarships, and to make student loans. Wang administers its programs in a building donated by a for-profit corporation, and employs a full-time director, a secretary, and one staff member who spends virtually all of her time visiting schools and counseling students. The building also is frequently used for meetings between high school students and representatives of various colleges.

In 1999, Wang's income consisted of $250,000 of dividends and a $360,000 long-term capital gain from the sale of 1,000 shares of Wang, Inc. stock on December 31, 1999. The foundation's expenses were as follows:

Administrative expenses	$7,000
Salaries	50,000
Maintenance of building	10,000
Depreciation	6,000
Grants to schools	18,000
Scholarship awards	40,000
Student loans	20,000
Investment advisory fee	5,000

On January 1, 2000, Wang used the $380,000 gross proceeds from the sale of Wang, Inc. stock to purchase all the outstanding common stock of a small company engaged in preparing students for standardized college entrance examinations. Wang hoped that it could use the resources of this company to increase the test scores of disadvantaged students, but it had no immediate plans to change the nature of the business. At the same time, the remaining Wang, Inc. stock was sold and the proceeds were reinvested in a diversified portfolio of securities. Assume that the average value of the portfolio during 2000 was $3,420,000.

Dividends	$160,000
Interest	80,000
Long-term Capital Gain	3,240,000
Short-term Capital Gain	20,000
Repayment of Student Loans	6,000

Expenditures in 2000 were exactly the same as in 1999 in each category except that scholarships were $50,000 and student loans were $30,000.

Consider the following questions:

(a) Should Wang have made additional distributions in 1999 or 2000 to avoid the § 4942(a) tax?

(b) To avoid any tax under § 4942, what amount must Wang distribute in 2001?

(c) May Wang satisfy its distribution requirements by creating an account on its books of $500,000 and earmarking the amount for an accelerated summer school tutoring program on the condition that the City of San Jose, before January 1, 2007, appropriates an equal amount for the same purpose?

4. EXCESS BUSINESS HOLDINGS: § 4943

Internal Revenue Code: § 4943(a), (b), (c)(1)–(3), (5)–(7), (d); skim § 4943(c)(4).

Treasury Regulations: § 53.4943–1, –3(a), (b), –6(a).

a. INTRODUCTION

One of the principal abuses that Congress sought to curb in 1969 was the perpetuation of control of a closely-held family business through substantial private foundation ownership of equity or proprietary interests. Foundation managers, often wearing shareholder and officer hats as well, were said to place the interests of the business ahead of the charitable responsibilities of the foundation. The legislative history of the 1969 Act cited several egregious examples, including one where a foundation controlled 45 separate businesses: fifteen were clothing manufacturers, seven engaged in the real estate business, six operated retail stores, one owned and managed a hotel, and others carried on printing, hardware and jewelry businesses. See S.Rep. No. 552, 91st Cong., 1st Sess. (1969).

The income-distribution mandate of § 4942 represents one solution to this problem. Congress went further, however, by limiting the extent to which a business may be controlled by a private foundation and its major donors. Section 4943 generally provides that a foundation and its disqualified persons together may not own more than 20 percent of the voting stock of a corporation or equivalent interests in a partnership. The value of holdings in excess of those permitted are subject to an initial tax of 5 percent, and a second-level tax of 200 percent for failure to dispose of the excess holdings during a statutorily prescribed correction period. I.R.C. § 4943(a), (b).

b. OPERATION OF § 4943

Permitted and excess holdings. Section 4943(c)(1) defines "excess business holdings" as the amount of stock that a private foundation must dispose of to a person other than a disqualified person in order for its remaining holdings to be "permitted holdings." "Permitted holdings" in a corporation are 20 percent of the corporation's voting stock less the percentage of such stock held by all disqualified persons. I.R.C. § 4943(c)(2)(A). A private foundation is thus permitted to own 20 percent of the voting stock of a corporation, reduced by the percentage of voting stock owned by all disqualified persons. Where all disqualified persons together do not own more than 20 percent of voting stock, the private foundation may own nonvoting stock in any amount. Id.

To illustrate, assume that the Stewart Foundation owns 11 percent of the voting stock of Rainbow Fabrics, Inc.; the chair of the Stewart board owns 3 percent; and other disqualified persons (descendants of a substantial contributor) own 9 percent. Since the aggregate holdings of the foundation and its disqualified persons are 23 percent, the foundation has excess business holdings. But since all disqualified persons together do not own more than 20 percent, any nonvoting shares held by the foundation are treated as permitted holdings.

Congress apparently selected 20 percent as the critical benchmark on the theory that more than 20 percent ownership may represent control of a corporation when shares are otherwise widely dispersed. The same policy prompted Congress to relax the rules when effective control can be shown to reside elsewhere. If the private foundation and all disqualified persons together do not own more than 35 percent of the voting stock, and it can be established that effective control of the corporation is in other nondisqualified persons, then the overall limitation is 35 percent rather than 20 percent. I.R.C. § 4943(c)(2)(B). See Rev. Rul. 81–111, 1981–1 C.B. 509 (may qualify for 35% limit by proving unrelated party or "cohesive group" exercises control, but not by showing that foundation and disqualified persons cannot exercise control).

Both the 20 percent and 35 percent rules are modified by a de minimis rule, which provides that if the foundation, together with any other private foundations to which it is considered related under § 4946(a)(1)(H), does not own more than two percent of the voting stock and not more than two percent in value of all outstanding shares of the corporation, it will not be treated as having any excess business holdings without regard to the holdings of disqualified persons. I.R.C. § 4943(c)(2)(C).

Similar albeit less precise rules are provided for unincorporated business enterprises. To determine permitted holdings in a partnership, the foundation's "profits interest" is aggregated with the profits interests of all disqualified persons and substituted for the voting stock measure applicable to corporations, and "capital interest" is used in lieu of nonvoting stock. I.R.C. § 4943(c)(3)(A); Treas. Reg. § 53.4943–3(c). No business whatsoever may be conducted as a proprietorship. I.R.C. § 4943(c)(3)(B). In the highly unusual event that a business in which the foundation has an interest is conducted in the form of a trust, the foundation's beneficial interest in such trust, together with those of its disqualified persons, is substituted for the voting stock measure applicable to corporate stock ownership. I.R.C. § 4943(c)(3)(C).

Excluded from the definition of "business enterprise" and thus not subject to the excess business holdings penalties are businesses that are functionally related (e.g., a business that is related to the foundation's exempt purposes) or a business where at least 95 percent of the gross income is derived from passive sources (e.g., dividends, interest, rent and the like). I.R.C. § 4943(d)(3).

Attribution rules. In computing the holdings of any business enterprise, stock or other interests owned directly or indirectly by a corporation, partnership, estate, or trust are considered as owned proportionately by the beneficial owners. I.R.C. § 4943(d)(1). In order to establish the extent of a foundation's permitted holdings, therefore, it often is necessary to undertake a rather extensive fact-finding mission, and to inquire, particularly of trustees and estate administrators, as to the extent of their holdings in the business in question. The responsibility of the foundation managers is considerable—and so, too, are the enforcement problems. The regulations suggest that the foundation send an annual questionnaire to each foundation manager, substantial contributor, etc., requesting a listing of all actual and beneficial holdings of interests in enterprises in which the foundation has interests in excess of the 2 percent de minimis rule. Treas. Reg. § 53.4943–2(a)(1)(v)(B).

Disposal of excess business holdings. The Code and regulations offer several avenues of avoidance from the excess business holdings tax. The simplest method allows a foundation a 90–day correction period from the time it discovers an excess business holdings problem. The 90–day period begins to run on the date "on which [the foundation] knows, or has reason to know, of the event which caused it to have such excess business holdings." Treas. Reg. § 53.4943–2(a)(1)(ii). Even a purchase by the foundation will not subject it to liability, where the excess can be shown to be attributable to prior acquisitions by disqualified persons of which the foundation managers were unaware. The foundation's innocence, which is crucial to the 90–day escape, is established on the basis of all relevant "facts and circumstances." Treas. Reg. § 53.4943–2(a)(1)(v).

Transitional Rules. A far more complex route is available to foundations that had business holdings as of May 26, 1969. The transitional rules for these "present holdings" were designed to provide ample time for foundations to dispose of their interests without the economic loss that might result from an immediate forced divestiture. Fortunately, the importance of the transitional rules has waned considerably, and only a brief overview will be provided here.

Business interests held by a foundation on May 26, 1969, or acquired subsequently under a will executed before that date or pursuant to a trust that was irrevocable on that date, are subjected to more liberal divestiture schedules. In general, the more extensive the holdings of the foundation and its disqualified persons, the longer the period allowed.

During the first phase of divestiture, all interests held by a private foundation on May 26, 1969 were treated as held by disqualified persons rather than the foundation. I.R.C. § 4943(c)(4)(B). As a result, these interests were not considered excess business holdings. If the foundation and all disqualified persons held more than 95 percent of the voting stock on May 26, 1969, the foundation was permitted a 20–year period before it was required to dispose of any of those holdings I.R.C. § 4943(c)(4)(B)(i); if the foundation and all disqualified persons had more than a 75 percent voting interest on May 26, 1969, it had 15 years before any dispositions were required under I.R.C. § 4943(c)(4)(B)(ii); in all other cases, the foundation was entitled to a 10–year disposition period. I.R.C. § 4943(c)(4)(B)(iii). By now, Phase I has expired for all private foundations.

The Phase I period is followed, in all cases, by a 15–year Phase II during which the foundation is subject to limits on permitted holdings that may be considerably higher than those prescribed by the general rules in § 4943(c). In general, the limit for the aggregate holdings of the foundation and its disqualified persons during Phase II is 50 percent or the actual holdings on May 26, 1969, whichever is less. This substituted percentage is reduced (but not below the normal 20 percent) if disqualified persons should purchase shares after May 26, 1969, or if the foundation or a disqualified person disposes of shares. See I.R.C. § 4943(c)(4)(A)(i), (ii). If disqualified persons own more than 2 percent of the voting stock at any time during Phase II, the substituted percentages described above are modified so that the aggregate ceiling for the foundation and its disqualified persons is 50 percent, of which not more than 25 percent may be voting stock held directly by the foundation. I.R.C. § 4943(c)(4)(D)(i).

By the end of Phase II, the foundation and its disqualified persons must bring their combined holdings down to 35 percent of the voting stock unless disqualified persons owned more than 2% during Phase I, in which case the foundation's direct holdings may be no more than 25 percent. I.R.C. § 4943(c)(4)(D)(iv).

Gifts and bequests. Business interests received by gift or bequest after May 26, 1969 that cause a foundation to have excess business holdings are treated, along with prior holdings of the foundation if it was not then in an excess business holdings position, as held by a disqualified person (rather than by the foundation) during the five-year period beginning on the date such holdings are received. The foundation thus has a five-year period to correct the problem created by the gift or bequest. I.R.C. § 4943(c)(6). Where a foundation receives "an unusually large gift or bequest of diverse business holdings or holdings with complex corporate structures," the Service may extend the five-year disposition period to ten years. I.R.C. § 4943(c)(7). An extension will be granted, however, only if the foundation establishes that it has made diligent attempts to dispose of the excess holdings within the initial five-year period and that disposition was not possible other than at a distress sale price. Id.

PROBLEM

The James Irving Foundation, a private foundation, was organized in 1994 by James Irving and his wife, Esther, each of whom contributed 9,000 shares of Irving Co. common stock. On that date and at the present time, the outstanding Irving Co. common stock (totalling 100,000 shares) was held as follows:

Irving Foundation	18,000 shares
James Irving	3,000 shares
Esther Irving	3,000 shares
Leola Irving Smythe	3,000 shares
Craft Industries	22,000 shares
Unrelated shareholders	51,000 shares

Leola Irving Smythe is the daughter of James and Esther Irving. Craft Industries is not related to the Irving family; it acquired all of its shares last year in a tender offer. None of the "unrelated shareholders" owns as much as one percent of the stock.

(a) Do the Foundation's present holdings create any excess business holdings problem? If so, how could the problem be avoided? Consider, among other things, the possibility of the Foundation selling all or part of its stock to other shareholders, or the corporation redeeming stock held by the Foundation in order to achieve any necessary divestiture.

(b) Same as (a), above, except that the Foundation owns only 2,000 shares, and James and Esther and Leola Irving Smythe own 25,000 shares in the aggregate.

(c) Same as (a), above, except that the Foundation received its 18,000 shares two years ago as a bequest from the late Rosalie Irving, the mother of James Irving.

5. JEOPARDY INVESTMENTS: § 4944

Internal Revenue Code: § 4944.

Treasury Regulations: § 53.4944–1, –3(a).

In theory, the income distribution requirements and the sanctions against excess business holdings should guarantee a diversified and reasonably productive investment portfolio. But Congress also was concerned that a foundation manager might make investments that would jeopardize the foundation's endowment. To ensure that the foundation's portfolio strategy creates no more than a tolerable level of risk, § 4944 imposes an excise tax of five percent on any amount invested by a private foundation "in such a manner as to jeopardize the carrying out of any of its exempt purposes * * *." I.R.C. § 4944(a). As defined by the regulations, a jeopardy investment occurs:

> if it is determined that the foundation managers, in making such investment, have failed to exercise ordinary business care and prudence, under the facts and circumstances prevailing at the time of making the investment, in providing for the long-and short-term financial needs of the foundation to carry out its exempt purposes.

Treas. Reg. § 53.4944–1(a)(2)(i).

Jeopardy can be a quantitative matter. Thus, a foundation with $10 million in assets which carries in its portfolio $1 million in speculative growth stocks in various industries and shows a significantly higher total return on those investments than on its more conservative portfolio, is not likely to be subject to any sanctions. On the other hand, a foundation that risks nearly all of its endowment in speculative ventures is not likely to survive close audit scrutiny. The standards to be applied on audit are not precise. Despite extensive regulations, the determination of jeopardy turns on all the facts and circumstances, including "the need for diversification." Treas. Reg. § 53.4944–1(a)(2)(i).The following investments are considered worthy of "close scrutiny:" margin trading; commodity futures; working interests in oil and gas wells; options and straddles; warrants; and short sales.

Notably excepted from the prohibitions of § 4944 are program-related investments, which are defined as investments "the primary purpose of which is to accomplish one or more of the [charitable, religious, etc.] purposes described in section 170(c)(2)(B) and no significant purpose of which is the production of income or the appreciation of property." I.R.C. § 4944(c). The regulations suggest a "but for" test-i.e., would the investment have been made but for the relationship between the investment and the accomplishment of the foundation's exempt activities. Treas. Reg. § 53.4944–3(a)(2)(i). For example, assume a foundation invests in an urban renewal project in a deteriorating inner-city neighborhood. Assistance in the financing of such a project involves significant risks, to be sure, and probably an unfavorable interest rate, but the project is intended to advance a charitable purpose of the foundation. See Treas. Reg. § 53.4944–3(b).

A private foundation that makes a jeopardy investment is subject to an initial tax of five percent of the amount invested for each taxable year or part thereof. Additional taxes may be imposed if the investment is "not removed from jeopardy." I.R.C. § 4944(a)(1), (b)(1). In addition, participating foundation managers are subject to a five percent first-level tax (up to a maximum of $5,000) and a five percent second-level tax (up to $10,000), unless such participation is not willful and is due to reasonable cause. I.R.C. § 4944(a)(2), (d)(2). Under the regulations, however, managers are protected if they act on the advice of legal counsel "expressed in a reasoned written legal opinion" that the particular investment will not jeopardize the foundation's exempt purposes. Similarly, reliance upon the advice of investment counsel, expressed in writing, that a particular investment will provide for the "long-and short-term financial needs of the foundation" will provide a defense to the penalty even though the investment turns out badly. Reg. § 53.4944–1(b)(2)(v).

PROBLEM

The Prudence Foundation has net assets worth $10 million, of which $2 million is cash recently received as a gift from Maude Prudence, the President of its board. The remaining $8 million is invested in a diversified portfolio of stocks and bonds.

Evaluate whether the following investments being considered by the Foundation's board for the $2 million cash would be treated as jeopardy investments:

(a) High-yield (and high-risk) subordinated corporate debentures.

(b) Commodity futures, stock index futures, options, and other derivative instruments.

(c) Undeveloped real estate.

(d) Below-market loans to low-income farmers in a depressed rural area.

6.   TAXABLE EXPENDITURES: § 4945

Internal Revenue Code: §§ 4945; 4946(c).

Treasury Regulations: §§ 53.4945–1(a), (d), –4, –5, –6; skim § 53.4945–3.

a.   INTRODUCTION

Section 4945 penalizes a private foundation for making certain expenditures that Congress considered to be inappropriate even when the expenditures may be consistent with the foundation's charitable purposes. The obligations created by § 4945 are constant, necessitating evaluation of each foundation grant or expenditure against the requirements of the statute. Some expenditures are forbidden entirely, while others are permitted if the foundation satisfies additional guidelines. Section 4945 thus may influence private foundations to limit their grants to public charities to escape the burdens of oversight responsibility and the possibility of penalty.

If a private foundation makes a taxable expenditure, it is subject to an initial tax of 10 percent of the amount expended. I.R.C. § 4945(a)(1). Foundation managers who "knowingly" agree to the making of a taxable expenditure are subject to a 2–1/2 percent tax, up to a $5,000 ceiling. I.R.C. § 4945(a)(2), (c). Additional sanctions (100 percent on the foundation, 50 percent of the amount on the manager up to $10,000) are imposed for failures to correct the initial transgression. I.R.C. § 4945(b), (c).

b.   TYPES OF TAXABLE EXPENDITURES

Section 4945(d) lists the following five categories of proscribed expenditures, each of which is discussed in more detail below: (1) propaganda and lobbying, (2) influencing legislation and financing voter registration drives, (3) grants to individuals, (4) grants to organizations other than public charities, and (5) expenditures for noncharitable purposes.

Propaganda and Lobbying. Any amount paid (i) for grassroots lobbying, or (ii) to "influence legislation through communication with any member or employee of a legislative body, or with any other government official or employee who may participate in the formulation of the legislation" (except technical advice provided pursuant to written request) will be a taxable expenditure. I.R.C. § 4945(e). The statute and regulations, however, carve out several qualifications and exceptions.

"Legislation" includes action by legislatures but not by executive, judicial or administrative bodies. Treas. Reg. § 53.4945–2(a), referring to Treas. Reg. § 56.4911–2(d). Quasi-legislative entities, such as school boards, housing authorities, etc., whether elective or appointive, are considered administrative bodies. Id.

Expenditures by a private foundation for nonpartisan analysis, study, or research, are not considered to be "lobbying communications" and thus are not taxable expenditures. Treas. Reg. § 53.4945–2(d)(1). As long as the foundation presents a "sufficiently full and fair exposition of the pertinent facts" that enables the public to form an independent opinion, no penalty will attach, whether the communication is to the public at large or is directed to legislators. Treas. Reg. § 53.4945–2(d)(1)(ii). Expenditures in connection with examinations and discussions of broad social, economic, and similar problems also are not considered to be lobbying. Treas. Reg. § 53.4945–2(d)(4).

Another valuable exception is provided for amounts expended in connection with providing technical assistance to a governmental body or committee in response to a written request. Treas. Reg. § 53.4945–2(d)(2). Thus, whenever possible, a foundation seeking to communicate with a legislature should do so by invitation. Another exception is provided for amounts expended to influence proposed legislation that may affect the powers or duties of a foundation. Note, however, that the possible decision sought to be influenced by the foundation must affect the foundation's existence, its powers and duties, its tax-exempt status, or the deductibility of contributions to it—not merely a matter or policy as to which the foundation has an ideological or programmatic interest. Treas. Reg. § 53.4945–2(d)(3).

Where a foundation makes a program-related investment (see I.R.C. § 4944(c)), and the recipient engages in lobbying, the investing foundation will not be liable for any penalty, provided that funds were not earmarked for lobbying, and the recipient obtains a § 162 (ordinary and necessary business) deduction for the lobbying expenditure. Treas. Reg. § 53.4945–2(a)(4). Grants to public charities also create no liability, provided that there is no earmarking for a use which would violate any § 4945(d) provision and no agreement whereby the granting foundation may cause the grantee to engage in any such prohibited activity. Treas. Reg. § 53.4945–2(a)(5).

Elections and Voter Registration Drives. Section 4945(d)(2) somewhat redundantly proscribes expenditures to "influence the outcome of any specific public election or to carry on * * * any voter registration drive." As discussed earlier in connection with qualification for tax-exempt status, electioneering expenses should cause an organization to lose its exempt status under § 501(c)(3). Congress nonetheless included them in § 4945's forbidden list in response to reports that foundations were using their funds to finance voter registration drives in limited geographical areas or publicizing the views of certain political candidates. See S. Rep. No. 552, 91st Cong., 1st Sess. 454 (1969).

Under a narrow exception, amounts paid in connection with certain nonpartisan and broadly supported voter registration activities, if carried on in five or more states, are not taxable expenditures. I.R.C. § 4945(f); Treas. Reg. § 53.4945–3(b). Although it has been suggested that this exception furnishes the only means by which a private foundation may support voter registration, a non-earmarked general purpose grant to a public charity (e.g, a community development organization) which conducts voter registration as an educational (and nonpartisan) aspect of its general programs seems likely to create a problem for the foundation only if its grantee is deemed to have engaged in prohibited political campaign activities. See Treas. Reg. § 53.4945–2(a)(5).

Grants to Individuals. Historically, private foundations have made grants to individuals, typically in the form of scholarships. This traditional activity is impeded somewhat by § 4945(d)(3), which treats grants to an individual "for travel, study, or other similar purposes" as a taxable expenditure unless the grant is made pursuant to a procedure approved "in advance" by the Service, which must be satisfied that the grant either: (1) constitutes a scholarship or fellowship excludable from gross income by the grantee under § 117(a) and is used for study at a § 170(b)(1)(A)(ii) institution (i.e., a regular college, university, etc.); (2) constitutes a prize or award (as defined in § 74(b)); or (3) is made to "achieve a specific objective, produce a report or other similar product, or improve or enhance a * * * capacity, skill or talent of the grantee." I.R.C. § 4945(g).

As explained by the drafters of the 1969 legislation, the rule was designed to preclude foundations from making ostensibly educational grants which are made "to enable people to take vacations abroad, to have paid interludes between jobs, and to subsidize the preparation of materials furthering specific political viewpoints." S.Rep. No. 91–552, 91st Cong., 1st Sess. 47 (1969).

A principal exception to the prohibition on grants to individuals relates to scholarships. To secure approval of a scholarship-granting procedure, the foundation must demonstrate not only a sensible and objective selection procedure but also must show that its scholarship program is genuinely charitable—e.g., does not constitute a disguised fringe benefit to the children of the employees of a corporate contributor. Service guidelines indicate that the number of scholarships awarded should not exceed 25 percent of eligible applicants, or in the case of a company foundation scholarship plan, 10 percent of the number of employees' children who can be shown to be eligible for grants. Rev. Proc. 76–47, 1976–2 C.B. 670. See also Rev. Proc. 80–39, 1980–2 C.B. 772, as to employer-related foundation loan programs. Note that approval of "scholarship" grant procedures carries no guarantee that grants will be excluded from grantees' gross income as "scholarships" under 117. See, e.g., Rev. Rul. 77–44, 1977–1 C.B. 355. The foundation also must monitor the academic performance of its scholarship grantees by making arrangements to receive reports of grades at least once a year or, as to advanced studies, to receive a brief progress report. Treas. Reg. § 53.4945–4(c)(2).

The regulations require the Service to respond to a request for approval of grant-making procedures within 45 days. Treas. Reg. § 53.4945–4(d)(3). If no response is received, the procedures are deemed approved until notice is received. See Rev. Rul. 81–46, 1981–1 C.B. 514. Conversely, even though a grant-making procedure is ultimately approved, grants made prior to submission to the Service will constitute taxable expenditures. German Society of Maryland, Inc. v. Commissioner, 80 T.C. 741 (1983).

Given the relative ease with which grants may be made to public charities, it might be tempting for a private foundation simply to select such an organization as the recipient of a grant ultimately destined to support the study or research of a particular individual. The regulations provide a surprising latitude to do so, provided that the grantee organization exercises ultimate discretion over the selection of the individual recipients and the terms of the award. See Examples at Treas. Reg. § 53.4945–4(a)(4)(iv).

Payments for services of consultants are not considered grants. Treas. Reg. § 53.4945–4(a)(2); Rev. Rul. 74–125, 1974–1 C.B. 327. Nor are payments to research assistants of the foundation's individual grantee, if not selected by the foundation. Rev. Rul. 81–293, 1981–2 C.B. 218.

Grants to Other Organizations. If a private foundation makes a grant to an organization that is not a public charity, it must exercise "expenditure responsibility" in order to avoid taxable expenditure treatment. I.R.C. § 4945(d)(4). Under § 4945(h) and the accompanying regulations, that responsibility involves pre-grant investigations and adequate follow-up procedures to determine that the grant is appropriately spent, and that the grantee has adequately reported upon its progress. The granting foundation is obligated to report to the Service in some detail as to the use of all grants subject to expenditure responsibility.

Public charities have benefited from the burden of the expenditure responsibility requirement. Indeed, many private foundations, as a matter of policy, decline to make grants to organizations other than public charities to avoid the expenditure responsibility requirement. But as explained below, the burden may not be so great for the well-advised foundation.

Expenditures for Noncharitable Purposes. To make certain that nothing was forgotten, Congress added a final category of taxable expenditures-amounts paid "for any purpose other than one specified in section 170(c)(2)(B)." I.R.C. § 4945(d)(5). In effect, this covers all foundation outlays that are not made for a charitable purpose. The regulations provide considerable elaboration. Thus, expenditures to acquire and manage investments, payment of taxes, and any payment which constitutes a qualifying distribution are excepted. Treas. Reg. § 53.4945–6(b). But unreasonable administrative expenses or fees (unless incurred in the good faith belief of reasonableness and necessity), and certain payments to noncharitable organizations are listed as examples of forbidden outlays. Id.

c. EXPENDITURE RESPONSIBILITY

John A. Edie, Expenditure Responsibility: "It's Easier Than You Think"

in The Handbook on Private Foundations 248–253 (1991).

Expenditure responsibility "can't get no respect." It's the Rodney Dangerfield of grantmaking. Maids don't do windows, and private foundations don't do expenditure responsibility. Yet, a growing number of private foundations are finding the exercise of expenditure responsibility to be a regular and surprisingly routine part of their grantmaking.

Last spring in the middle of a speech in New York City, I was asked to explain what steps were required to do expenditure responsibility. When I finished a brief explanation, several members of the audience expressed amazement at how simple it sounded. One questioner said, "We do most of that already with every grant." Despite this common reaction, once the procedure is explained, I am continually confronted with grantmakers who avoid expenditure responsibility like the plague.

* * *

This potential penalty [under § 4945] for giving to a nonpublic charity has created the misconception among many in the foundation field that a private foundation can give only to a Section 501(c)(3) organization. This simply is not true. There are many organizations to which a private foundation may make a grant even though the grantee is not a public charity. Examples include chambers of commerce, labor unions, trade associations, fraternal orders (such as Rotary), other private foundations, or even for-profit companies. However, to avoid the penalty when giving to nonpublic charity grantees, the private foundation must, in Congress's words, "exercise expenditure responsibility."

In other words, the private foundation must exercise the oversight job normally done by IRS for public charities. Since such a grant is going to a private foundation or to an organization that is *not* organized and operated exclusively for charitable purposes, the grantor foundation must take the steps necessary to see that the funds are appropriately spent. Before spelling out the basic steps required to exercise expenditure responsibility correctly, it is important to make clear that this process is not as easy nor as safe as simple grants to universities or to the United Way. The required procedures and documents must be designed with care and should definitely be approved by your legal counsel. But once established, procedures are very similar to what many foundations already undertake for many, if not all, of their grants. While it is certainly true that staffed foundations are more likely to make expenditure responsibility grants, more and more smaller foundations are finding this procedure to be much easier than they had first thought.

There are four basic requirements for expenditure responsibility: (1) a pregrant inquiry, (2) a written agreement, (3) regular reports from the grantee, and (4) a report to IRS by the grantor. A brief summary of each of these requirements is set out below, and the reader can obtain sample procedures and documents from the Council on Foundations. However, it bears repeating that any system for exercising expenditure responsibility should be approved by legal counsel.

As a first step, a private foundation must conduct an inquiry of the potential grantee that is complete enough to give a reasonable person assurance that the grantee will use the grant for proper, charitable purposes. As Treasury regulations state, such a pregrant inquiry "should concern itself with matters such as (a) the identity, prior history and experience (if any) of the grantee organization and its managers; and (b) any knowledge which the private foundation has (based on prior experience or otherwise) of, or other information which is readily available concerning the management, activities, and practices of the grantee organization." Some foundations design a simple pregrant inquiry check sheet that is completed by a foundation official and kept on file. The regulations also make clear that the "scope" of the inquiry will vary from case to case depending on "the size and purpose of the grant, the period over which it is to be paid, and the prior experience which the grantor has had with the capacity of the grantee to use the grant for the proper purposes."

WRITTEN AGREEMENT

In making an expenditure responsibility grant, the foundation may not simply write a check. Rather, a written agreement (or contract) must be signed by "an appropriate officer, director or trustee of the grantee organization." This requirement for a written agreement is where legal counsel is most vital because the regulations are quite specific about what must be included.

However, once a "form" contract (or "boilerplate" as lawyers call it) has been developed and approved, completing the rest of the blank spaces in the "form" contract is fairly easy. The blanks to fill in can be as simple as name of grantee, name and title of grantee official signing the agreement, the date of the agreement, the length of the grant period, the date (or dates) by which a written report (or reports) on the status of the grant must be submitted, and the grant's specific charitable purpose (or purposes). The regulations are clear in indicating that the purpose of the grant must be spelled out in writing.

The rest of the private foundation's standard expenditure responsibility agreement will never change (unless amended by counsel). However, the regulations require that the grantee sign an agreement that includes each of the following four commitments:

1. To repay any portion of the amount granted that is not used for the purposes of the grant.

2. To submit full and complete annual reports on the manner in which the funds are spent and the progress made in accomplishing the purposes of the grant.

3. To maintain records of receipts and expenditures and to make its books and records available to the grantor at reasonable times.

4. Not to use any of the funds:

To undertake any activity that is not charitable;

To carry on propaganda, or otherwise attempt to influence legislation;

To influence the outcome of any specific public election, or to carry on, directly or indirectly, any voter registration drive;

To make any grants to individuals for travel, study or similar purposes unless such grants comply with the requirements to which private foundations are subject; or

To make any grants that would require expenditure responsibility unless such grants comply with the requirements to which private foundations are subject.

There may be other provisions of agreement that your legal counsel may wish to include. For example, a foundation may wish to state that the grantee understands that the grantor intends to monitor and evaluate the activities funded by the grant, and that the grantor may discontinue, modify, or withhold part or all of the grant funds when, in its judgment, such action is necessary to comply with the law or regulations.

REPORTS FROM THE GRANTEE

Since Treasury regulations do not spell out the details of what must be included in the grantee's report, it is probably wise for your legal counsel to include them in the "form" contract.

The regulations state, "The grantee shall make such reports as of the end of its annual accounting period within which the grant or any portion thereof is received and all such subsequent periods until the grant funds are expended in full or the grant is otherwise terminated." For example, if grantee X receives a two-year expenditure responsibility grant on May 1, 1990 and grantee X has an accounting period ending on June 30, reports would be due "within a reasonable period of time" after June 30, 1990; after June 30, 1991; and after June 30, 1992. The grantee must make a final report (the June 30, 1992, report in the example above) with respect to "all expenditures made from such funds (including salaries, travel, and supplies) and indicating the progress made toward the goals of the grant." The grantor is not required to conduct "any independent verification" of such reports "unless it has reason to doubt their accuracy or reliability," and may rely on adequate records or other sufficient evidence (such as a statement by an appropriate officer, director, or trustee of the grantee organization).

Finally, if the grantee receiving the expenditure responsibility grant is other than a private foundation, the grantee must agree to maintain continuously the grant funds "in a separate fund dedicated to one or more charitable purposes." In other words, the noncharitable grantee may not simply commingle funds that are dedicated exclusively for charitable purposes with those that are not.

Failure by the grantee to provide the required reports could subject the grantor to a penalty unless the grantor makes a reasonable effort to obtain the reports and withholds any future payments until they are received.

REPORTING TO THE IRS

Every private foundation is required to file a tax return within four and one-half months after the end of its tax year. For each year in which it has made an expenditure responsibility grant, it must answer "yes" to the appropriate question * * *. In addition, it must add a schedule to the tax return, providing a brief summary paragraph on each expenditure responsibility grant's status. An example, as suggested by the IRS, is Form 990–PF for the hypothetical Oak Foundation:

Grantee: Allen Reid Museum of Fine Arts, 31 Meyers St., Atlanta, Ga. 30301.

Date paid: April 7, 1985. Amount $15,000.

Purpose: For the partial support of a major renovation and expansion of the museum facilities.

Amount of grant spent by grantee: $15,000.

Diversion: To the knowledge of the foundation, and based on the report furnished by the grantee, no part of the grant has been used for other than its intended purpose.

Date of report for grantee: Final report January 8, 1986.

* * *

For some, the requirements of expenditure responsibility will seem more complicated than their normal grantmaking procedures. But many will note, for any grant, that a pregrant inquiry is regularly performed, their foundation requires use of a standard grant agreement form, and some kind of written report is required from the grantee. For these foundations, the added steps of satisfying the requirements of expenditure responsibility will be relatively easy to accomplish.

PROBLEMS

In each part of this problem, determine whether the described private foundation may properly make the proposed grant or other expenditure and, if so, whether any conditions should attach to the grant for the protection of the foundation:

(a) The Eli Stern Foundation, formed in 1937 "to advance the welfare and education of the employees of Eli Stern & Co.," a shoe manufacturer which employs 7,000 persons, intends to announce its annual grant of 200 scholarships in the amount of $1,000 each to children of employees.

(b) Exploring for Peace, Inc., intends to make a $100,000 grant to support an expedition to map several of the uncharted Amazon River tributaries. It wants the project to be led by Dr. Ferris Murple, a prominent geographer and cartographer of the University of New Hampshire. Would your advice be the same if Dr. Murple were on the faculty of a Canadian university?

(c) The Blue Dolphin Foundation, which has long supported marine research, has been approached by a private operating foundation, Friends Under the Sea, Inc., which seeks a grant of $50,000 to study the sounds of whales.

(d) The Wilderness Fund proposes to place a full-page advertisement in the Sunday Los Angeles Times criticizing the Governor of California for proposing cutbacks in the public recreation budget and urging the legislature to pass a scenic rivers bill which would create 40,000 acres of state parks.

(e) The Public Conscience Trust, which has in the past supported research in American history, is considering a grant of $500,000 to a recently organized § 501(c)(3) organization, The Citizens' Crusade, which will conduct as its sole activity voter registration drives. Such drives will soon begin in New York, Florida, California and Pennsylvania, and will concentrate on registration of voters who will be eligible to cast their ballots for the first time in the next Presidential election.

(f) The Public Conscience Trust also is considering a grant of $250,000 to finance an empirical study by Simon Catchpole, an authority on the mass media, as to the effect of digital satellite dishes on (a) the gross national product, (b) the national divorce rate, (c) the national birth rate, and (d) the incidence of violent crimes. If the study tends to prove that the new dishes are inimical to the well-being of the nation, may the Trust:

    (1) publish it?

    (2) send copies to each member of Congress?

    (3) send Mr. Catchpole, study in hand, to the Federal Communications Commission?

(g) The Bakst Foundation, created in 1966 by M. Charles Bakst for the purpose of encouraging investigative journalism, wishes to make grants to the person whose work represents the best example of investigative reporting on matters concerning the Federal government. All U.S. journalists will be eligible for the award, and the winner would be chosen by majority vote of an independent selection committee appointed by the Foundation's trustees.

(h) What if the grants in (g), above, were to outstanding journalists to be used for financing a three-month trip throughout Europe for the purpose of broadening the recipient's understanding of the common market?

(i) The Human Rights Foundation wishes to make a $50,000 grant to the Southeast Asia Refugee Coalition, an organization formed in Indonesia,to investigate and remedy human rights violations. See Treas. Reg. § 53.4945–5(a)(4).

D. TERMINATION OF PRIVATE FOUNDATION STATUS

Internal Revenue Code: § 507.

Section 507 governs the tax consequences of a termination of a § 501(c)(3) organization's status as a private foundation. Foundations may give up the status voluntarily, or they may be terminated involuntarily for "willful repeated acts" or a "willful and flagrant act (or failure to act)" giving rise to liability for a Chapter 42 tax. See I.R.C. § 507(a)(2).

1. INVOLUNTARY TERMINATION

Involuntary termination is not a joyous event. The Code imposes a confiscatory "termination tax" equal to the lower of: (1) the aggregate historical tax benefits of exemption to the foundation and its substantial contributors (dating back to its organization or February 28, 1913, whichever is later), plus interest, or (2) the value of the net assets of the foundation. So much for the foundation! I.R.C. § 507(c), (d).

The Service has the authority to abate any portion of the termination tax if the private foundation distributes all of its net assets to one or more public charities, each of which has been in existence as such for at least 60 months, or upon assurance that appropriate corrective action has been initiated under state law. I.R.C. § 507(g). The regulations provide no indication as to how liberally the Service may exercise its authority. See Treas. Reg. § 1.507–1(b)(9).

2. VOLUNTARY TERMINATION

A private foundation may avoid the dreaded termination tax by transferring its assets to one or more public charities or by operating itself as an organization described in §§ 509(a)(1), (2) or (3). Many smaller private foundations chose voluntary termination after becoming frightened by the 1969 legislation. By far the simplest route to relief from the burdens of private foundation status is simply to distribute all the foundation's assets to one or more public charities each of which has been in existence and so described for at least 60 months. I.R.C. § 507(b)(1)(A). In order to do so, however, notice must be given to the Service.

If the foundation wishes to convert to public charity or supporting organization status, it must give notice to the Service and embark upon a five-year qualification measuring period. I.R.C. § 507(b)(1)(B). An advance ruling based on the expectancy of operating as a public charity may be obtained under Treas. Reg. § 1.507–2(e). If the organization fails to qualify for the entire 60–month period, it nonetheless will escape the private foundation regime for any year within that period for which it does meet the public charity requirements.

A final alternative is abdication. A foundation may accomplish a voluntary termination simply by notifying the Service of its intent to do so, without proposing to transfer its assets to other public charities, or to operate itself as such an organization. In that case, the foundation becomes liable for the § 507(c) termination tax. The regulatory burdens persist until rigor mortis fully sets in. The regulations provide that the foundation's notice must "set forth in detail the computation and amount" of tax owing, and, unless a request for abatement is made, full payment of the tax must be made when the statement is filed. Treas. Reg. § 1.507–1(b)(1).

Common situations where a private foundation may wish to terminate include: (1) disagreements within the founding family, or a desire for branches of the family to go their separate ways, (2) a desire to change the legal form (e.g., from trust to corporation), (3) simplicity, such as eliminating the expense and responsibility of administering a separate entity, or (4) a preference, possibly to achieve greater tax benefits, to make grants through a donor-advised fund or supporting organization.

For many years, foundations wishing to terminate incurred the expense of obtaining a private ruling as an insurance policy against the § 507 termination tax. The IRS finally responded by issuing the two published rulings below. Although they are highly technical (and also offer a good review of many of the private foundation rules previously studied), they provide several different toll-free exit ramps from private foundation status.

Revenue Ruling 2002–28

2002–1 Cum. Bull. 941.

ISSUES

(1) If a private foundation transfers all of its assets to one or more private foundations, is the transferor foundation required to notify the Manager, Exempt Organizations Determinations, Tax Exempt and Government Entities Division (TE/GE), that it plans to terminate its private foundation status pursuant to § 507(a) of the Internal Revenue Code and pay the tax under § 507(c)?

(2) What are a private foundation's tax return filing obligations after it transfers all of its assets to one or more transferee private foundations and:

(a) terminates, or

(b) does not terminate?

(3) If a private foundation transfers all of its assets to one or more private foundations that are effectively controlled (within the meaning of

the Income Tax Regulations under § 507), directly or indirectly, by the same person or persons who effectively control the transferor foundation, what are the implications under:

(a) § 4940,

(b) § 4941,

(c) § 4942,

(d) § 4943,

(e) § 4944, and

(f) § 4945?

(4) If a private foundation transfers all of its assets to one or more private foundations that are effectively controlled (within the meaning of the regulations under § 507), directly or indirectly, by the same person or persons who effectively control the transferor foundation, what are the implications for the transferor foundation's aggregate tax benefits under § 507(d)?

FACTS

In each of the following situations: (i) the transferee private foundations are effectively controlled (within the meaning of the regulations under § 507), directly or indirectly, by the same persons who effectively controlled the transferor private foundations; (ii) the private foundations have not committed either willful repeated acts (or failures to act), or a willful and flagrant act (or failure to act), giving rise to liability for tax under chapter 42; (iii) the private foundations have not terminated under § 507(a)(2) or (b)(1); (iv) prior to the transactions described below, the transferor private foundations made outstanding grants to organizations not described in § 4945(d)(4)(A), which required the transferor foundations to exercise expenditure responsibility in accordance with § 4945(h); and (v) the private foundations are not operating foundations within the meaning of § 4942(j)(3).

SITUATION 1

P is recognized as exempt from federal tax under § 501(c)(3) and is classified as a private foundation under § 509(a). P's current directors have divergent charitable objectives.

X, Y, and Z are recognized as exempt from federal tax under § 501(c)(3) and are classified as private foundations under § 509(a). Pursuant to a plan of dissolution, after satisfying all of its outstanding liabilities, P distributes all of its remaining assets in equal shares to X, Y, and Z. As part of the plan of dissolution, X agrees to exercise expenditure responsibility for all outstanding grants made by P. The day after P distributes all of its assets, P files articles of dissolution with the appropriate state authority.

SITUATION 2

T, a charitable trust, is recognized as exempt from federal tax under § 501(c)(3) and is classified as a private foundation under § 509(a). The trustees of T determine that T's charitable purposes can be more effectively accomplished by operating in corporate form.

The trustees of T create W, a not-for-profit corporation, for the purpose of carrying on T's activities. W is recognized as exempt from federal tax under § 501(c)(3) and is classified as a private foundation under § 509(a). T transfers all of its assets and liabilities to W.

SITUATION 3

J and K are not-for-profit corporations that are recognized as exempt from federal tax under § 501(c)(3) and are classified as private foundations under § 509(a). J and K generally confine their grantmaking activities to supporting charitable programs in the city in which both J and K are located.

V, a newly-formed entity, is recognized as exempt from federal tax under § 501(c)(3) and is classified as a private foundation under § 509(a). To eliminate the costs of maintaining two private foundations with identical charitable purposes, J and K transfer all of their assets and liabilities to V.

LAW

Section 507(a) provides that, except as provided in § 507(b), the status of any organization as a private foundation shall be terminated only if: (1) such organization notifies the Secretary of its intent to accomplish such termination, or (2) with respect to such organization, there have been either willful repeated acts (or failures to act), or a willful and flagrant act (or failure to act), giving rise to a liability for tax under chapter 42, and the Secretary notifies such organization that it is liable for the tax imposed by § 507(c). Under § 507(a)(1) and (2), the organization's private foundation status is terminated when the organization pays the tax imposed by § 507(c) or the entire amount of such tax is abated under § 507(g). The person currently designated to receive the notice of termination described in § 507(a)(1) is Manager, Exempt Organizations Determinations (TE/GE).

Section 507(b)(2) provides that in the case of a transfer of assets of any private foundation to another private foundation pursuant to a liquidation, merger, redemption, recapitalization, or other adjustment, organization or reorganization, the transferee foundation shall not be treated as a newly created organization.

Section 507(c) imposes a tax on each organization whose private foundation status is voluntarily or involuntarily terminated under § 507(a). The tax imposed is equal to the lower of: (1) the amount which the private foundation substantiates by adequate records or other corroborating evidence as the aggregate tax benefit resulting from the § 501(c)(3) status of such foundation, or (2) the value of the net assets of the foundation.

Section 1.507–1(b)(6) of the Income Tax Regulations provides that if a private foundation transfers all or part of its assets to one or more other private foundations pursuant to a transfer described in § 507(b)(2) and

§ 1.507–3(c), such transferor foundation will not have terminated its private foundation status under § 507(a)(1).

Section 1.507–1(b)(7) provides that a transfer of all the assets of a private foundation does not result in a termination of the transferor private foundation under § 507(a), unless the transferor private foundation elects to terminate pursuant to § 507(a)(1), or § 507(a)(2) is applicable.

Section 1.507–3(a)(1) provides that, in a § 507(b)(2) transfer, a transferee organization will not be treated as a newly created organization. The transferee organization is treated as possessing those attributes and characteristics of the transferor organization which are described in § 1.507–3(a)(2), (3) and (4).

Section 1.507–3(a)(2)(i) provides that a transferee organization shall succeed to the aggregate tax benefit of the transferor organization in an amount equal to the amount of such aggregate tax benefit multiplied by a fraction the numerator of which is the fair market value of the assets (less encumbrances) transferred to such transferee and the denominator of which is the fair market value of the assets of the transferor (less encumbrances) immediately before the transfer.

Section 1.507–3(a)(3) provides that, in the event of a transfer of assets under § 507(b)(2), any person who is a substantial contributor with respect to the transferor foundation shall be treated as a substantial contributor with respect to the transferee foundation, regardless of whether such person meets the $5,000 two-percent test with respect to the transferee at any time. If a private foundation makes a transfer described in § 507(b)(2) to two or more transferee private foundations, any person who is a substantial contributor with respect to the transferor foundation prior to such transfer shall be considered a substantial contributor with respect to each transferee.

Section 1.507–3(a)(4) provides that if a private foundation incurs liability for one or more of the taxes imposed under chapter 42 (or any penalty resulting therefrom) prior to, or as a result of, making a transfer of assets described in § 507(b)(2) to one or more private foundations, in any case where transferee liability applies each transferee foundation shall be treated as receiving the transferred assets subject to such liability to the extent that the transferor foundation does not satisfy such liability.

Section 1.507–3(a)(5) provides that, except as provided in § 1.507–3(a)(9), a private foundation is required to meet the distribution requirements of § 4942 for any taxable year in which it makes a § 507(b)(2) transfer of all or part of its net assets to another private foundation.

Section 1.507–3(a)(6) provides that whenever a private foundation makes a § 507(b)(2) transfer of all or part of its net assets to another private foundation, the applicable period of time described in § 4943(c)(4), (5), or (6) shall include both the period during which the transferor foundation held such assets and the period during which the transferee foundation holds such assets.

Section 1.507–3(a)(7) provides that, except as provided in § 1.507–3(a)(9), where the transferor has disposed of all of its assets, during any period in which the transferor has no assets, § 4945(d)(4) and (h) shall not apply to the transferee or the transferor with respect to any expenditure responsibility grants made by the transferor. However, the information reporting requirements under § 4945 will apply for any year in which any such transfer is made.

Section 1.507–3(a)(9)(i) provides that if a private foundation transfers all of its net assets to one or more private foundations that are effectively controlled, directly or indirectly, by the same person or persons that effectively controlled the transferor private foundation, the transferee private foundation will be treated as if it were the transferor private foundation for purposes of §§ 4940 through 4948 and §§ 507 through 509. However, where proportionality is appropriate, such a transferee foundation shall be treated as if it were the transferor in the proportion which the fair market value of the assets (less encumbrances) transferred to such transferee bears to the fair market value of the assets (less encumbrances) of the transferor immediately before the transfer.

Section 1.507–3(a)(9)(ii) provides that § 1.507–3(a)(9)(i) shall not apply to the requirements under § 6033, which must be complied with by the transferor foundation, nor to the requirement under § 6043 that the transferor foundation file a return with respect to its liquidation, dissolution or termination.

Section 1.507–3(a)(9)(iii) (example 2) provides that if the transferees of a § 507(b)(2) transfer are effectively controlled by the same persons who control the transferor, each transferee is required to exercise expenditure responsibility with respect to the transferor's outstanding grants, unless, as part of the transfer, the transferor assigns and one or more transferees assume the transferor's expenditure responsibility, in which case, only the transferees assuming the transferor's expenditure responsibility are required to exercise such expenditure responsibility. Section 1.507–3(a)(9)(iii) (example 2) also provides that because such transferee foundations are treated as the transferor, rather than as recipients of expenditure responsibility grants, there are no expenditure responsibility requirements which must be exercised under § 4945(d)(4) and (h) with respect to the § 507(b)(2) transfer.

Section 1.507–3(a)(10), by reference to § 1.507–1(b)(9), provides that a private foundation that transfers all of its net assets is required to file the annual information return required by § 6033 for the taxable year in which such transfer occurs. However, the foundation will not be required to file such return for any taxable year following the taxable year in which the last of such transfers occurred, provided the foundation does not hold equitable title to any assets or engage in any activity during such subsequent taxable year.

Section 1.507–3(c)(1) provides that for purposes of § 507(b)(2), the terms "other adjustment, organization, or reorganization" shall include any partial liquidation or any other significant disposition of assets to one or more private foundations, other than transfers for full and adequate consideration or distributions out of current income.

Section 1.507–3(c)(2) provides that the term "significant disposition of assets to one or more private foundations" includes any disposition (or series of related dispositions) by a private foundation to one or more private foundations of 25 percent or more of the fair market value of the net assets of the transferor foundation at the beginning of the taxable year in which the transfers occur.

Section 1.507–3(d) provides that unless a private foundation voluntarily gives notice pursuant to § 507(a)(1), a transfer of assets described in § 507(b)(2) will not constitute a termination of the transferor's private foundation status under § 507(a)(1).

Section 1.507–4(b) provides that private foundations which make transfers described in § 507(b)(2) are not subject to the tax imposed under § 507(c) with respect to such transfers unless the provisions of § 507(a) become applicable.

Section 1.507–7(a) provides that the net value of assets for purposes of § 507(c) shall be determined at whichever time such value is higher: (1) the first day on which action is taken by the organization which culminates in its ceasing to be a private foundation, or (2) the date on which it ceases to be a private foundation.

Sections 1.507–7(b)(1) and 1.507–8 provide that in the case of a termination under § 507(a)(1), the date referred to in § 1.507–7(a)(1) shall be the date on which the terminating foundation gives the notification described in § 507(a)(1).

Section 4940(a) generally imposes an excise tax on a private foundation's net investment income for the taxable year.

Section 4940(c)(1) defines net investment income as the amount by which the sum of the gross investment income and the capital gain net income exceeds the deductions allowed under § 4940(c)(3).

Section 4941(a)(1) imposes a tax on each act of self-dealing between a disqualified person and a private foundation. Section 53.4946–1(a)(8) provides that, for purposes of § 4941, the term "disqualified person" shall not include any organization described in § 501(c)(3) (other than an organization described in § 509(a)(4)).

Section 4942(a) generally imposes a tax on the undistributed income of a private foundation (other than an operating foundation under § 4942(j)(3)) for any taxable year, which has not been distributed before the first day of the second (or any succeeding) taxable year following such taxable year.

Section 4942(c) defines "undistributed income" for any taxable year as the amount by which the distributable amount for such taxable year exceeds the qualifying distributions made out of such distributable amount for such taxable year.

Section 4942(d) defines "distributable amount" as the amount equal to the sum of the minimum investment return, plus certain other amounts, reduced by the sum of the taxes imposed on such private foundation for the taxable year under subtitle A and § 4940.

Section 4942(g)(1)(A) defines "qualifying distribution" as any amount (including that portion of reasonable and necessary administrative expenses) paid to accomplish one or more purposes described in § 170(c)(2)(B) other than a contribution to: (i) an organization controlled directly or indirectly by the foundation or by one or more disqualified persons with respect to the foundation, unless certain requirements are satisfied, or (ii) any private foundation which is not an operating foundation under § 4942(j)(3), unless certain requirements are satisfied.

Section 4942(i) provides for a carry-over of the amount by which qualifying distributions during the five preceding taxable years (other than amounts required to be distributed out of corpus under § 4942(g)(3)) have exceeded the distributable amounts for such years.

Rev. Rul. 78–387 (1978–2 C.B. 270) holds that when a private foundation transfers all its assets to another private foundation that is controlled by the same persons who controlled the transferor foundation, the transferee foundation may reduce its distributable amount under § 4942(d) by the amount of the transferor's excess qualifying distributions as described in § 4942(i).

Section 4943(a)(1) imposes a tax on the "excess business holdings" (as defined in § 4943(c)) of any private foundation in a business enterprise.

Section 4944(a)(1) imposes a tax on any amount invested by a private foundation in a manner that jeopardizes the carrying out of any of the foundation's exempt purposes.

Section 4945 imposes a tax on any "taxable expenditure" (as defined in § 4945(d)) made by a private foundation.

Section 4945(d)(4) provides that the term "taxable expenditure" includes any amount paid or incurred as a grant to a private non-operating foundation unless the grantor foundation exercises expenditure responsibility with respect to such grant in accordance with § 4945(h).

Section 4945(h) provides that the expenditure responsibility referred to in § 4945(d)(4) means a private foundation is responsible to exert all reasonable efforts and to establish adequate procedures to: (1) see that the grant is spent solely for the purpose for which made, (2) obtain full and complete reports from the grantee on how the funds are spent, and (3) make full and detailed reports with respect to such expenditures to the Secretary.

Section 4946(a)(1) defines a "disqualified person" for purposes of subchapter A of chapter 42.

Section 6033(a)(1) provides that, with certain exceptions, every organization exempt from taxation under § 501(a) shall file an annual return.

Section 6043(b) and § 1.6043–3(a)(1) provide that, with certain exceptions, a private foundation must provide information with respect to a liquidation, dissolution, termination or substantial contraction as required by the instructions accompanying the foundation's annual return.

ANALYSIS

SECTION 507

Section 507(b)(2) applies to a significant disposition of assets by one private foundation to one or more private foundations, other than transfers for full and adequate consideration or distributions out of current income. See § 1.507–3(c)(1). A transfer of all of a private foundation's assets to one or more private foundations constitutes a significant disposition. See § 1.507–3(c)(2). In Situations 1, 2 and 3, each transferor foundation transfers all of its assets to one or more private foundations. The transfers are not for full and adequate consideration and are not distributions out of current income. Thus, the transfers in Situations 1, 2 and 3 are § 507(b)(2) transfers.

A transfer of assets described in § 507(b)(2) does not constitute a termination of the transferor's private foundation status under § 507(a)(1) unless the transferor voluntarily gives notice pursuant to § 507(a)(1). See §§ 1.507–1(b)(6) and 1.507–3(d). The transferor foundation is not required to provide such notice. In Situation 1, P's dissolution under state law has no effect on whether P has terminated its private foundation status for federal tax purposes.

In Situations 1, 2, and 3, if the transferor foundation does not give notice to the Manager, Exempt Organizations Determinations (TE/GE), of its intent to terminate, the transferor retains its private foundation status and the § 507(c) tax does not apply. See § 507(a)(1) and § 1.507–4(b). The transferor foundation is required to file a Form 990–PF for the taxable year of the transfer(s), but is not required to file a Form 990–PF for subsequent taxable years during which it does not have equitable title to any assets and does not engage in any activity. See §§ 6033(a)(1) and 6043(b), and §§ 1.507–1(b)(9) and 1.507–3(a)(10). If, at any time following the transfer(s), the transferor foundation receives additional assets or engages in any activity, the transferor foundation must file a Form 990–PF. Additionally, because the transferor foundation has not terminated its private foundation status, the transferor foundation continues to be treated as a private foundation.

In Situations 1, 2, and 3, if the transferor foundation does give notice to the Manager, Exempt Organizations Determinations (TE/GE), of its intent to terminate, then the § 507(c) tax applies on the date such notice is given. See § 1.507–7(a) and (b)(1). Thus, in Situations 1, 2, and 3, if the transferor foundation provides notice at least one day after it transfers all of its assets, the tax imposed by § 507(c) will be zero. The transferor foundation is required to file a Form 990–PF for the taxable year of the transfer(s). See §§ 6033(a)(1) and 6043(b).

Regardless of whether the transferor foundation provides notice of its intent to terminate, the transferee foundations are treated as possessing the aggregate tax benefit of the transferor foundations. See § 1.507–3(a)(1) and (2)(i). In Situation 1, X, Y, and Z succeed to P's aggregate tax benefit in proportion to the assets transferred to each. See § 1.507–3(a)(2)(i).

Moreover, regardless of whether the transferor foundation provides notice of its intent to terminate, where transferee liability applies, each transferee foundation is treated as receiving the transferred assets subject to the transferor foundation's prior excise tax liabilities under chapter 42 (and any penalties resulting therefrom), if any, to the extent the transferor did not previously satisfy those liabilities. See § 1.507–3(a)(1) and (4).

SECTION 4940

In Situations 1, 2 and 3, the transfers do not constitute investments of the transferor for purposes of § 4940; therefore, the transfers do not give rise to net investment income subject to tax under § 4940(a).

In Situations 1, 2, and 3, because each transferor foundation transfers all of its assets to one or more private foundations effectively controlled by the same persons that effectively control the transferor, any excess § 4940 tax paid by the transferor may be used by the transferees to offset the transferees' § 4940 tax liability. See § 1.507–3(a)(9)(i). In Situation 1, where there are several transferees, proportionality is appropriate, and X, Y, and Z will each succeed to one third of any excess § 4940 tax paid by P. See § 1.507–3(a)(9)(i).

SECTION 4941

In Situations 1, 2 and 3, the transfers are to § 501(c)(3) organizations, which are not treated as disqualified persons for purposes of § 4941. See § 53.4946–1(a)(8). Thus, the transfers do not constitute self-dealing transactions and are not subject to tax under § 4941(a)(1).

SECTION 4942

In Situations 1, 2 and 3, because each transferor foundation transfers all of its assets to one or more private foundations effectively controlled by the same persons that effectively control the transferor, the transferee foundations are treated as though they were the transferor for purposes of § 4942. See § 1.507–3(a)(9)(i). Accordingly, the transfers to the transferee foundations are not treated as qualifying distributions of the transferor foundation. In addition, in Situations 2 and 3, each transferee foundation assumes all obligations with respect to the transferor's "undistributed income" within the meaning of § 4942(c), if any, and reduces its own distributable amount under § 4942 by the transferor foundation's excess qualifying distributions under § 4942(i). In Situation 1, where there are several transferee foundations, proportionality is appropriate, and X, Y and Z each becomes responsible for one third of P's undistributed income and succeeds to one third of P's excess qualifying distributions, if any. See § 1.507–3(a)(9)(i) and Rev. Rul. 78–387.

SECTION 4943

Whether the transfers cause a transferee foundation to have excess business holdings and be subject to tax under § 4943(a) depends on the facts and circumstances. In Situations 1, 2, and 3, because each transferor foundation transfers all of its assets to one or more private foundations effectively controlled by the same persons that effectively control the transferor, the transferee foundations are treated as though they were the transferor for purposes of §§ 4943 and 4946. See § 1.507–3(a)(9)(i). Accordingly, in determining whether a transferee foundation has excess business holdings, the disqualified persons of the transferee foundation are determined in part by treating the transferee as though it were the transferor. For example, both the substantial contributors of the transferee and the substantial contributors of the transferor are treated as a disqualified persons of the transferee in determining whether the transferee has excess business holdings as a result of the transfer. See § 4946(a)(1)(A) and § 1.507–3(a)(9)(i); see also § 1.507–3(a)(3). In addition, in determining whether a transferee foundation is subject to tax under § 4943, the transferee's holding period in the transferred assets for purposes of § 4943(c)(4), (5), and (6) includes both the period during which the transferor foundation held such assets and the period during which the transferee foundation holds such assets. See § 1.507–3(a)(6).

SECTION 4944

In Situations 1, 2, and 3, the transfers do not constitute investments for purposes of § 4944; therefore the transfers do not constitute investments jeopardizing the transferor foundation's exempt purposes and are not subject to tax under § 4944(a)(1).

SECTION 4945

In Situations 1, 2, and 3, because each transferor foundation transfers all of its assets to one or more private foundations effectively controlled by the same persons that effectively control the transferor, the transferee foundations are treated as though they were the transferor for purposes of § 4945. See § 1.507–3(a)(9)(i). Because the transferee foundations are treated as the transferor foundation rather than as recipients of expenditure responsibility grants, there are no expenditure responsibility requirements that must be exercised under § 4945(d)(4) or (h) with respect to the transfers to the transferee foundations. See § 1.507–3(a)(9)(i) and (iii)(example 2).

The transferor foundation is required to exercise expenditure responsibility over the transferor's outstanding grants until the transferor disposes of all of its assets. Thereafter, during any period in which the transferor foundation has no assets, the transferor foundation is not required to exercise expenditure responsibility over any outstanding grants. See § 1.507–3(a)(7). However, the transferor foundation still must meet the § 4945(h) reporting requirements for the outstanding grants for the year in which the transfers are made. See § 1.507–3(a)(7).

The transferee foundations assume expenditure responsibility for all the transferor's outstanding grants. See § 1.507–3(a)(9)(i). In Situation 1, because X agreed to exercise expenditure responsibility for all of P's outstanding grants, Y and Z have no expenditure responsibility over P's grants. However, in the absence of such an agreement, X, Y and Z each would be required to exercise expenditure responsibility with respect to all of P's outstanding grants. See § 1.507–3(a)(9)(i) and (iii) (example 2).

HOLDINGS

(1) A private foundation that transfers all of its assets to one or more private foundations in a transfer described in § 507(b)(2) is not required to notify the Manager, Exempt Organizations Determinations (TE/GE), that it plans to terminate its private foundation status under § 507(a)(1). If the private foundation does not provide notice and does not terminate, the private foundation is not subject to the § 507(c) termination tax. If the private foundation chooses to provide notice, and therefore terminates, it is subject to the § 507(c) tax; however, if the private foundation has no assets on the day it provides notice (e.g., it provides notice at least one day after it transfers all of its assets), the § 507(c) tax will be zero.

(2) (a) A private foundation that has disposed of all of its assets and terminates its private foundation status must file a Form 990–PF for the taxable year of the disposition and must comply with any expenditure responsibility reporting obligations on such return.

(b) A private foundation that has disposed of all of its assets and does not terminate its private foundation status must file a Form 990–PF for the taxable year of the disposition and must comply with any expenditure responsibility reporting obligations on such return, but does not need to file returns in the following taxable years if it has no assets and does not engage in any activities. If, in later taxable years, it receives additional assets or resumes activities, it must resume filing a Form 990–PF for those taxable years in which it has assets or activities.

(3) Where transferee liability applies, each transferee foundation is treated as receiving the transferred assets subject to the transferor foundation's prior excise tax liabilities under chapter 42 (and any penalty resulting therefrom), if any, to the extent the transferor foundation did not previously satisfy those liabilities.

(a) The transfers do not give rise to net investment income and are not subject to tax under § 4940(a). The transferee foundations may use their proportionate share of any excess § 4940 tax paid by the transferor to offset their own § 4940 tax liability.

(b) The transfers do not constitute self-dealing and are not subject to tax under § 4941(a)(1).

(c) The transfers do not constitute qualifying distributions for the transferor foundation under § 4942. The transferee foundations assume their proportionate share of the transferor foundation's undistributed income under § 4942 and reduce their own distributable amount for

such organization notifies the Secretary of its intent to accomplish such termination, or (2) with respect to such organization, there have been either willful repeated acts (or failures to act), or a willful and flagrant act (or failure to act), giving rise to a liability for tax under chapter 42, and the Secretary notifies such organization that it is liable for the tax imposed by § 507(c). Under § 507(a)(1) and (2), the organization's private foundation status is terminated when the organization pays the tax imposed by § 507(c) or the entire amount of such tax is abated under § 507(g).

Section 507(b)(1)(A) provides that the private foundation status of any organization, with respect to which there have not been either willful repeated acts (or failures to act) or a willful and flagrant act (or failure to act) giving rise to a liability for tax under chapter 42, shall be terminated, if the private foundation distributes all its net assets to one or more organizations described in § 170(b)(1)(A) (other than clauses (vii) and (viii)) each of which has been in existence and so described for a continuous period of at least 60 calendar months immediately preceding such distribution.

Section 507(c) imposes a tax on each organization whose private foundation status is voluntarily or involuntarily terminated under § 507(a). The tax imposed is the lower of (1) the amount that the private foundation substantiates by adequate records or other corroborating evidence as the aggregate tax benefit resulting from the § 501(c)(3) status of such foundation, or (2) the value of the net assets of the foundation.

Section 1.507–1(b)(1) provides that in order to terminate its private foundation status under § 507(a)(1), an organization must submit a statement to the Manager, Exempt Organizations Determinations, Tax Exempt and Government Entities Division (TE/GE), of its intent to terminate its private foundation status under § 507(a)(1). Such statement must set forth in detail the computation and amount of tax imposed under § 507(c). Unless the organization requests abatement of such tax pursuant to § 507(g), full payment of such tax must be made at the time the statement is filed under § 507(a)(1). An organization may request the abatement of all of the tax imposed under § 507(c), or may pay any part thereof and request abatement of the unpaid portion of the amount of tax assessed. If the organization requests abatement of the tax imposed under § 507(c) and such request is denied, the organization must pay such tax in full upon notification by the Service that such tax will not be abated.

Section 1.507–1(b)(7) provides that a transfer of all the assets of a private foundation does not result in a termination of the transferor private foundation under § 507(a), unless the transferor private foundation elects to terminate pursuant to § 507(a)(1), or § 507(a)(2) is applicable.

Section 1.507–2(a)(1) provides that under § 507(b)(1)(A), a private foundation, may terminate its private foundation status by distributing all its net assets to one or more organizations described in § 170(b)(1)(A) (other than clauses (vii) and (viii)) each of which has been in existence and so described for a continuous period of at least 60 calendar months immediately preceding such distribution. As § 507(a) does not apply to such a termination, a private foundation that makes such a termination is not required to give the notification described in § 507(a)(1). A private foundation that terminates its private foundation status under § 507(b)(1)(A) does not incur tax under § 507(c) and, therefore, no abatement of such tax under § 507(g) is required.

Section 1.507–2(a)(4) provides that an organization that terminates its private foundation status pursuant to § 507(b)(1)(A) will remain subject to the provisions of chapter 42 until it distributes all its net assets to distributee organizations described in § 507(b)(1)(A).

Section 1.507–2(a)(7) provides that a private foundation will meet the requirement that it "distribute all of its net assets" within the meaning of § 507(b)(1)(A) only if it transfers all its right, title, and interest in and to all its net assets to one or more organizations referred to in § 507(b)(1)(A).

Section 1.507–2(a)(8)(i) provides, in part, that to effectuate a transfer of "all of its right, title, and interest in and to all of net assets," a transferor private foundation may not impose any material restriction or condition that prevents the transferee organization from freely and effectively employing the transferred assets, or the income derived therefrom, in furtherance of its exempt purposes.

Section 1.507–3(e) provides that if a private foundation transfers all or part of its assets to one or more organizations described in § 509(a)(1), (2), or (3) and, within a period of 3 years from the date of such transfers, one or more of the transferee organizations lose their § 509(a)(1), (2), or (3) status and become private foundations, then the transfer will be treated as a transfer described in § 507(b)(2) and the provisions of § 1.507–3(a) shall be treated as applying to such transferee from the date any such transfer was made to it.

Section 1.507–4(b) provides that private foundations that make transfers described in § 507(b)(1)(A) or (2) are not subject to the tax imposed under § 507(c) with respect to such transfers unless the provisions of § 507(a) become applicable.

Section 1.507–7(a) provides that the value of net assets for purposes of § 507(c) shall be determined at whichever time such value is higher: (1) the first day action is taken by the organization that culminates in its ceasing to be a private foundation, or (2) the date it ceases to be a private foundation.

Section 1.507–7(b)(1) provides that in the case of a termination under § 507(a)(1), the date of action referred to in § 1.507–7(a)(1) shall be the date the terminating foundation gives the notification described in § 507(a)(1).

[The ruling then summarizes pertinent provisions of §§ 4940–4945 and the accompanying regulations. Essentially the same provisions are set forth in Rev. Rul. 2002–28, supra, at pp. 495–497. Eds.]

* * *

In Rev. Rul. 75–289, 1975–2 C.B. 215, a private foundation defined in § 509 distributed all its net assets to an organization, described in

§ 170(b)(1)(A)(vi), that had been in existence for only 20 months. The organization was formed as a result of a consolidation of two organizations each of which would have been an organization described in § 170(b)(1)(A)(vi) and in existence for a continuous period of 60 calendar months before the distribution had they continued in existence. The ruling held that the private foundation had terminated its private foundation status under § 507(b)(1)(A).

ANALYSIS

SECTION 507

Under § 507(b)(1)(A), an organization's status as a private foundation is terminated if the organization distributes all its net assets to one or more organizations described in § 509(a)(1) (i.e., organizations described in § 170(b)(1)(A) (other than in clauses (vii) and (viii))) each of which has been in existence and so described for a continuous period of at least 60 calendar months immediately preceding the distribution. An organization that terminates its private foundation status under § 507(b)(1)(A) is not required to give notice under § 507(a)(1) and is not subject to the tax described in § 507(c). See § 1.507–2(a)(1).

If a private foundation distributes all its net assets to one or more public charities, at least one of which is described in § 509(a)(1) and has been so described for fewer than 60 calendar months immediately preceding the distribution or is described in §§ 509(a)(2) or (3), then the rules of § 507(b)(1)(A) do not apply. In this case, the distributions do not cause the private foundation to terminate its private foundation status. See § 1.507–1(b)(7). The private foundation may choose to terminate its private foundation status by submitting a statement of its intent to terminate its private foundation status under § 507(a)(1) to the Manager, Exempt Organizations Determinations, Tax Exempt and Government Entities Division (TE/GE). See § 1.507–1(b)(1). Such statement must set forth in detail the computation and amount of tax imposed under § 507(c). See § 1.507–1(b)(1). If the private foundation has no net assets on the day it provides notice (e.g., it provides notice at least one day after it distributes all its net assets), the tax imposed by § 507(c) will be zero. See § 507(a)(1) and § 507(c); and §§ 1.507–7(a) and (b). A submission of a Form 990–PF marked "Final" does not constitute notice of termination of private foundation status under § 507(a)(1). See § 1.507–1(b)(1).

In Situation 1, P transfers all its net assets to X, which is described in § 509(a)(1) and has been so described for a continuous period of at least 60 calendar months immediately preceding the distribution. Accordingly, the distribution is subject to the rules of § 507(b)(1)(A), rather than the rules of § 507(a)(1). See § 507(b)(1)(A) and § 1.507–2(a)(1).

Because the distribution is described in § 507(b)(1)(A), P's status as a private foundation is terminated upon the distribution and P is not subject to the tax described in § 507(c). See § 1.507–2(a)(1) and § 1.507–4(b). P is not required to give notice under § 507(a)(1) to terminate its private foundation status.

In Situation 2, X is an organization described in § 509(a)(1) that has been in existence and so described for fewer than 60 calendar months immediately preceding the distribution. In Situation 3, X is an organization described in § 509(a)(2). In Situation 4, X is an organization described in § 509(a)(3). Accordingly, the distributions in Situations 2, 3, and 4 are not subject to the rules of § 507(b)(1)(A). See § 507(b)(1)(A) and § 1.507–2(a)(1).

Because the distributions in Situations 2, 3, and 4 are not described in § 507(b)(1)(A), P's status as a private foundation is not terminated unless it gives notice under § 507(a)(1). See § 1.507–1(b)(1) and § 1.507–1(b)(7). If P does not provide notice and does not terminate, P is not subject to the tax under § 507(c).

If P chooses to provide notice, and therefore terminates, it is subject to the tax under § 507(c) on the date it provides notice; however, if P has no net assets on the day it provides notice (e.g., it provides notice at least one day after it distributes all its net assets), the tax imposed by § 507(c) will be zero. See § 507(a)(1) and § 507(c); and §§ 1.507–7(a) and (b).

SECTION 4940

In Situations 1, 2, 3, and 4, the distributions do not constitute an investment of P for purposes of § 4940; therefore the distributions do not give rise to net investment income under § 4940(a). See § 53.4940–1(f)(1).

SECTION 4941

In Situations 1, 2, 3, and 4, the distributions are to § 501(c)(3) organizations, which are not treated as disqualified persons for purposes of § 4941. See § 53.4946–1(a)(8). Thus, the distributions do not constitute self-dealing transactions and are not subject to tax under § 4941(a)(1).

SECTION 4942

In Situations 1, 2, 3, and 4, the distributions are paid to accomplish one or more purposes described in § 170(c)(2)(B) and are not made to organizations controlled directly or indirectly by P or by one or more disqualified persons with respect to P. Thus, the distributions are qualifying distributions for purposes of § 4942(g)(1)(A).

SECTION 4943

In Situations 1, 2, 3, and 4, the distributions do not cause P to have excess business holdings subject to tax under § 4943(a).

SECTION 4944

In Situations 1, 2, 3, and 4, the distributions do not constitute investments for purposes of § 4944 and therefore are not jeopardizing investments subject to tax under § 4944(a)(1).

SECTION 4945

In Situations 1, 2, 3, and 4, the distributions are to organizations described in §§ 509(a)(1), (2), or (3). Therefore, the distributions are not taxable expenditures under § 4945. See § 4945(d)(4)(A). P will not be required to exercise expenditure responsibility with respect to the distributions under § 4945(d)(4) or (h).

HOLDINGS

Under the facts of the ruling:

1. A private foundation that distributes all its net assets to one or more organizations described in § 509(a)(1) (i.e., organizations described in § 170(b)(1)(A) (other than in clauses (vii) and (viii))) each of which has been in existence and so described for a continuous period of at least 60 calendar months immediately preceding the distribution terminates its private foundation status under § 507(b)(1)(A). The private foundation is not required to file a notice of termination under § 507(a)(1) and is not liable for tax under § 507(c).

A private foundation that distributes all its net assets to one or more public charities, at least one of which is described in § 509(a)(1) and has been so described for fewer than 60 calendar months immediately preceding the distribution or is described in §§ 509(a)(2) or (3), does not terminate its private foundation status unless it gives notice under § 507(a)(1). If the private foundation does not provide notice and does not terminate, the private foundation is not subject to tax under § 507(c). If the private foundation chooses to provide notice, and therefore terminates, it is subject to the tax under § 507(c) on the date notice is given; however, if the private foundation has no net assets on the day it provides notice (e.g., it provides notice at least one day after it distributes all its net assets), the tax imposed by § 507(c) will be zero.

If the private foundation elects to terminate its private foundation status under § 507(a)(1), it must submit a statement to the Manager, Exempt Organizations Determinations, Tax Exempt and Government Entities Division (TE/GE), of its intent to terminate its private foundation status under § 507(a)(1). Such statement must set forth in detail the computation and amount of tax imposed under § 507(c). The submission of a Form 990–PF marked "Final" does not constitute notice of termination of private foundation status under § 507(a)(1).

2. (a) The distribution does not give rise to net investment income and is not subject to tax under § 4940(a).

(b) The distribution does not constitute a self-dealing transaction and is not subject to tax under § 4941(a)(1).

(c) The distribution constitutes a qualifying distribution for the transferor private foundation under § 4942.

(d) The distribution does not result in excess business holdings and is not subject to tax under § 4943(a).

(e) The distribution does not constitute an investment jeopardizing the transferor private foundation's exempt purposes and is not subject to tax under § 4944(a)(1).

(f) The distribution is not a taxable expenditure described in § 4945.

CHAPTER 4

Tax Exemption: Mutual Benefit Organizations

A. The Rationale for Tax Exemption

In this chapter, we turn to the taxation of mutual benefit organizations, the diverse family of "noncharitable" nonprofits that exists primarily to further the common goals of its members rather than the public at large. Mutual benefit organizations include labor unions, trade and professional associations, social clubs, fraternal lodges, cooperatives, and a myriad of other more specialized entities ranging from cemetery companies to black lung trusts. Unlike charitable nonprofits, mutual benefit organizations generally are not eligible to receive tax-deductible contributions,[1] and they do not share most of the other tax benefits enjoyed by § 501(c)(3) charities, such as exemption from unemployment taxes and the ability to issue tax-exempt bonds.

Since mutual benefit organizations are viewed as providing only an incidental public benefit and may not be subject to the nondistributional constraint, one might ask why this chapter is even necessary. Is there a normative principle that explains why organizations serving the narrow economic or social interests of their members have long been exempt from federal income tax? Can tax exemptions for mutual benefit nonprofits be explained by the traditional subsidy theories that justify the charitable exemption? Perhaps because their tax benefits are not as generous or extensive as those enjoyed by their charitable counterparts, mutual benefit organizations have not been as closely scrutinized by the taxing authorities or legal scholars. The excerpt below is one of the few attempts in the tax literature to articulate a coherent rationale for exemption.

Boris I. Bittker and George K. Rahdert, The Exemption of Nonprofit Organizations From Federal Income Taxation

85 Yale L.J. 299, 348–357 (1977).

In general terms, mutual benefit organizations are operated to provide goods and services to their members at cost. Any excess of gross revenues over costs may appear to violate this purpose, but since they do not

---

1. The few exceptions are veterans organizations, fraternal societies (if the gift is used for charitable purposes), and cemetery companies. I.R.C. § 170(c)(3)(5).

endeavor to generate profits from membership patronage, a year-end surplus could be viewed as an overcharge which, if promptly refunded to the members, should not be classified as "income." This is in fact how patronage refunds by consumers' cooperative societies are treated, reflecting the fact that the society would have had nothing resembling "income" if it had reduced its prices in order to avoid a year-end surplus. And since actual price reductions would have prevented the society from having any income, one might favor the same tax-free result if the "overcharges" are retained by the mutual society to benefit the members in future years by permitting charges to be reduced or facilities to be expanded without additional cost. Alternatively, but with the same nontaxable result—a mutual society's "profit" from membership patronage might be regarded as a deposit or capital contribution by the members to finance future activities or facilities. If the members of a commune estimate their expenses for food at $500 per person and pay this amount in advance to their purchasing agent, one would not expect the group, as an entity, to realize income if the cost turned out to be only $450 per person, even if the excess was retained for the commune's future needs rather than refunded to the members. To classify the excess as income would be tantamount to taxing the members because they were astute shoppers or because they performed unpaid services for the society.

Much could be said for a comprehensive statutory rule embodying the foregoing rationale, but—as is often true of the Internal Revenue Code—Congress has preferred piecemeal legislation to broad generalizations. Similarly, Congress did not prescribe a set of across-the-board rules governing the investment income, profit-oriented activities and transactions with nonmembers, of mutual benefit organizations, but instead established many divergent taxing systems, which turn on such variables as the organization's size, function, history, and occupational or geographic characteristics. The most important categories of mutual benefit organizations are discussed hereafter.

A.   Social Clubs

Clubs organized and operated exclusively "for pleasure, recreation, and other nonprofitable purposes" have been exempt since 1916. As originally enacted, the exemption was denied if any part of the club's net earnings inured to the benefit of any "private shareholder or member." In 1924, the word "member" was excised from this restriction, and the door was opened to two substantial tax advantages: the building up of a tax-free endowment, and the exemption from tax of profits derived from dealings with nonmembers.

First, the members of a social club could build up its capital with their initiation fees and dues, immunizing the income generated by these contributions from tax, even though it served to reduce the club's charges to its members in later years. Of course, if the dues and fees were invested in such assets as a golf course or a clubhouse, the use of the exempt organization to acquire these properties would not result in a tax savings for the members, because if the members invested in recreational or social property individually or as joint tenants rather than through a "conduit" organization, their ownership and use of these facilities would not itself create taxable income. But if the club converted the contributions into income-producing endowment, it got an exemption that was not available to the members as individuals. In effect, therefore, they could earmark part of their own income-producing capital to be used, free of income taxes, to pay for their pleasure or recreation.[136] Second, social clubs enjoyed an even more dramatic advantage in that profits generated by their transactions with nonmembers were also exempt from tax, despite use of these profits to reduce the fees paid by members or to provide better facilities without cost to them.

Before 1969, when this state of affairs was drastically altered by legislation, the courts intervened from time to time to limit the scope of these tax advantages. Although the adjective "social" is a label rather than an operative statutory phrase, the statutory term "club," in conjunction with the Code's references to "pleasure" and "recreation," was held to require "some sort of commingling of members," with the result that groups like automobile clubs serving a mutual interest without social contact among the members were held not to qualify. The courts found another restraint in the statutory requirement that a club be operated exclusively for "nonprofitable purposes," which was interpreted to disqualify clubs with excessive amounts of income from nonmembership patronage or separate business activities. Even if a social club avoided these pitfalls, however, the Tax Reform Act of 1969 substantially reduced its tax advantages by expanding the reach of the tax on "unrelated business taxable income." With minor exceptions, a social club's income from investments and from non-member patronage is now taxable.

As a consequence of the 1969 changes, the major significance of a social club's exemption at present is that it is not taxed on "profits" arising from goods, facilities, and services furnished to members and their dependents and guests. This residual tax advantage is minimal if the club is regarded as a true association of its members, since any profit from one year's operations will at most be used to reduce membership charges in another year. A relentless search for income in this context, of course, would disclose that some members derive an economic advantage from expenditures by their fellow members. Thus, if the club's sole charge is an annual membership fee, those who use the club's facilities frequently are subsidized by the other members, just as a trencherman benefits from splitting a restaurant bill equally after dining with a group of abstemious friends. But if the friends' overpayment is subjected to analysis, it qualifies as a tax-free gift to the person paying less than his true share of the bill. Perhaps the

---

136. A nonexempt club might attempt to achieve the same result, by using endowment or business income to reduce its charges to members for their use of its social facilities, and deducting the maintenance expenses under § 162 in a manner reminiscent of the incorporated country estates and yachts that gave rise to § 543(a)(6) of the personal holding company provisions. * * *

benefits accruing to a member of a social club who pays less than his share of its costs, at the expense of members paying more than their share, can also be characterized as a gift, even though the bonds of affection among the members are more attenuated than is customary in the case of most gifts.

B.   Consumers' Cooperatives and Similar Organizations

The Internal Revenue Code contains a single set of rules to govern the tax treatment of two quite different types of cooperative societies-consumers' cooperatives, organized primarily to supply food and other household goods to their members; and marketing cooperatives, organized by farmers, dairymen, and other producers to market their agricultural products. The far greater economic importance of marketing cooperatives, coupled with a risk that agricultural profits may slip untaxed through a statutory crevice between the cooperative and its members, has given rise to elaborate provisions to ensure that all income will be reported by one or the other of these potential taxpayers. The tax status of consumers' cooperatives emerges almost as an afterthought from the same network of rules.

Under the basic statutory scheme, as applied to consumers' cooperatives, the organization enjoys no explicit tax exemption, but it is allowed to exclude patronage dividends from its taxable income. These distributions are not taxed to the members, on the theory that they represent belated reductions in the cost of household goods. The net effect is that the organization is taxed in full on income from business with nonmembers; it is taxed on transactions with its members only to the extent that overcharges are not refunded, and it can reduce its taxable income from membership transactions by either charging less or refunding more. Earnings from membership patronage retained by the organization to provide working capital or expand its facilities, however, are subject to tax, even though, as suggested earlier, they might be appropriately exempted on the ground that they represent savings by the members to reduce their future living expenses.

Although they perform substantially the same functions as consumers' cooperatives, various other organizations are granted blanket tax exemption (save for their unrelated business income) by the Internal Revenue Code. This miscellaneous group of exempt organizations includes:

1.   Fraternal lodges and employee associations providing life, sickness, accident, or other benefits to members and dependents.

2.   Local life insurance associations, and mutual irrigation, telephone, and similar companies, if at least 85 percent of their income is paid by members to defray expenses and losses.

3.   Cemetery companies operated for the benefit of their members, or not for profit.

4.   Credit unions.

5.   Insurance companies (primarily fire and casualty companies) whose premiums and investment income do not exceed $150,000.

Profits accruing to these organizations from membership patronage, which is probably the sole or dominant source of their income in most cases, qualify for exemption under the rationale outlined above for exclusion of the patronage dividends of cooperatives. Income from investment or nonmembership patronage, however, would not be immune from tax under this conduit rationale, and the statutory exemption of income from these sources probably reflects benign neglect more than thoughtful attention.[148]

C. Labor Unions

Section 501(c)(5) exempts "labor organizations" in unqualified language, carrying forward a provision of the Revenue Act of 1913. The Regulations state that the organization's net earnings must not inure to the benefit of any member, a restriction of doubtful validity unless loosely construed, since the statutory provision must have been intended, and has been consistently interpreted, to exempt labor unions engaged in collective bargaining on behalf of their members. The prohibition is also virtually retracted by another part of the Regulations themselves, conditioning the exemption on the organization's dedication to "the betterment of the conditions" of its membership. Moreover, the Internal Revenue Service has ruled that unions do not lose their exemption by paying sickness, death, accident, or other benefits to members. In revoking an earlier ruling to the contrary, the Service said that "labor organizations were exempted for the very reason that they operated, in part, as mutual benefit organizations providing [such] benefits to their members."

Approached ab initio, the exemption of labor unions is best examined in the context of the principles governing business expenses. Dues paid by a union member are deductible as ordinary and necessary business expenses under § 162 because the organization serves as his collective bargaining agent in a profit-seeking endeavor and in otherwise seeking to improve his conditions of employment. If the dues are not immediately spent by the union, but are invested and retained for future contingencies (in a strike fund, for example), the member's share of the union's investment income might be imputed back to him. But then the member should be allowed an offsetting deduction when the income so imputed is later spent by the

---

148. In addition to consumer cooperatives, agricultural and horticultural organizations have been consistently included in the statutory list of exempt organizations since 1913. Although the statute does not describe these organizations further, the Regulations state that their objectives must be "the betterment of the conditions of those engaged in such pursuits, the improvement of the grade of their products, and the development of a higher degree of efficiency in their respective occupations" and that they must not allow their net earnings to inure to the benefit of their members. Treas. Reg. § 1.501(c)(5)–1(a)(1958).

Given these limitations, organizations qualifying under § 501(c)(5) have much in common with business leagues, exempt under § 501(c)(6), and with social welfare organizations exempt under § 501(c)(4). * * *

Farmers' cooperatives, whether engaged in purchasing supplies and equipment for their members or in marketing their produce, are subject to special rules. * * * Hence the organizations qualifying under § 501(c)(5) are probably of minor importance. The few published rulings refer to the sponsorship of county fairs, improvement of livestock, and soil testing as appropriate objectives of these organizations. * * *

organization on his behalf, because he could deduct similar expenditures from his own private (and taxable) investment income.

As in the case of business leagues, exempting the organization's accumulated income is the equivalent of currently imputing its income to its members but allowing them to deduct these amounts when they are ultimately used by the union, except that the time value of the money slips past the tax collector. Alternatively, if the union's accumulated income permits dues to be reduced in future years (or activities to be expanded without additional cost to the membership), the fact that the members will deduct a smaller amount for dues in these years than if they paid in full for the union's activities will compensate the Treasury, albeit belatedly, for the revenue lost by exempting the union's income when realized-again, except for the time value of the money.[155]

D. Business Leagues

Since 1913, business leagues, chambers of commerce, and boards of trade have been exempt from income taxation if not organized for profit and if their net earnings do not inure to the benefit of any private shareholder or individual. Real estate boards were added to the statutory list in 1928 and professional football leagues in 1966.[156] Trade associations are the most common instances of exempt "business leagues," along with professional groups like the American Bar Association and the American Medical Association.

For most qualifying organizations, the statutory prohibitions of § 501(c)(6) against a profit orientation and the inurement of net earnings to private benefit must be loosely interpreted, as was no doubt intended by Congress from the outset. Strictly construed, these limits would close the door to organizations serving the business interests of an industry, since these activities inure to the benefit of their profit-motivated members. Such a construction would confine § 501(c)(6) to organizations not in need of its protection-those devoted to the general welfare of society, which qualify for exemption as charitable or social welfare organizations under § 501(c)(3) or (4). The statutory prohibitions of § 501(c)(6), therefore, have not been interpreted to preclude the commonly understood objectives of chambers of commerce and similar organizations.

As summarized by the Regulations, the activities of a business league

should be directed to the improvement of business conditions of one or more lines of business as distinguished from the performance of particular services for individual persons. An organization whose pur-

---

155. * * * Since the membership's composition changes over time, the group to whom the union's investment income would be imputed is not identical with the group that will benefit from future lower dues. As pointed out earlier * * *, there is a similar disparity in the case of social clubs.

156. §501(c)(6). The 1966 committee reports do not disclose why baseball was not given the same treatment as football. If the House Committee on Un-American Activities were still on the warpath, surely it would want to investigate this disparagement of our national sport.

pose is to engage in a regular business of a kind ordinarily carried on for profit, even though the business is conducted on a cooperative basis or produces only sufficient income to be self-sustaining, is not a business league.

In administration, the interpretative problems under § 501(c)(6) have primarily concerned the boundary between business leagues and taxable joint business ventures. Although § 501(c)(6) does not by any means impose a high standard of altruism, it has been held to exclude organizations created by business competitors to coordinate or centralize their advertising or purchasing activities, engage in research for their exclusive benefit, furnish credit reports and collect delinquent accounts, or otherwise advance their special business interests; § 501(c)(6) does require some showing of benefit to the public. Less frequently, it is necessary to decide whether a business league's devotion to the public interest so outweighs its service to its membership as to justify classification as a charitable or educational organization. Charitable status is ordinarily of minor importance, however, since tax exemption as a business league is usually as satisfactory as exemption under § 501(c)(3). To be sure, the latter status permits gifts to be deducted by the donors as charitable contributions, but this is no more (and, occasionally, less) advantageous than deducting them as business expenses under § 162. While charitable status would be preferred to a § 501(c)(6) exemption if gifts are sought from exempt foundations or other nonmember donors, a business league could obtain deductible contributions by organizing an affiliated entity devoted solely to its charitable objectives. An example is the American Bar Association's American Bar Endowment.

Once it is recognized that § 501(c)(6) organizations ordinarily serve the business objectives of their members, the justification for their statutory exemption is exposed as rickety. There would be no great difficulty in applying familiar principles of income computation to their activities, nor in fixing an appropriate level of taxation for an organization whose membership is composed of corporations whose income is taxed predominantly at a fixed rate. On the other hand, the exercise would, to a large degree, be self-defeating. First, their charges to members would no doubt be increased to offset the tax, and the additional amounts would be deductible by the members as business expenses; their own taxes would thus be reduced by about one-half of the taxes paid by the organization. Second, as a more drastic response, the organization could operate at or near its breakeven point, generating little or no income to be taxed, and increasing its charges to its members when necessary.

Viewed as an alternative to the hypothetical charges that could be deducted by its members, a business league's tax exemption, which covers its investment income, is not without a plausible rationale. The principal residual objection to the § 501(c)(6) exemption is that if large reserves are currently being accumulated by the organization against nebulous and distant future needs, its members are able to delay income tax liability—and thus save the time value of the deferred taxes—by taking immediate deductions for the league's future business expenditures and by excluding from income the organization's endowment income.

NOTES AND QUESTIONS

1. *Subsidy and Capital Formation Theories.* To what extent does the traditional subsidy theory explain the exemption for mutual benefit organizations? Is Congress trying to encourage mutual benefit nonprofits to perform their various roles? Or is the income tax exemption the product of historical factors, inattention, or the political power of the benefited groups? Some academic theorists justify the exemption by arguing that mutual benefit organizations arise in response to the failure of the private markets. Because mutual benefits are the most efficient suppliers of their goods and services, these theorists assert, they should be granted exemption from tax in order to increase their retained earnings available for growth. See, e.g., Henry Hansmann, The Rationale for Exempting Nonprofit Organizations from Corporate Income Taxation, 67 Yale L.J. 54, 95–96 (1981).

2. *Investment Income.* Why should the passive investment income of mutual benefit organizations be exempt from tax? Do Bittker and Rahdert adequately explain why the exemption reaches this far? In 1987, the staff of the Joint Committee on Taxation floated a proposal to tax the investment income of trade associations and labor unions, but it was never seriously considered. The idea remained largely dormant outside of academic circles until the Clinton Administration, in its fiscal year 2000 budget submission, proposed to raise revenue by taxing investment income of trade associations in excess of $10,000. The arguments for and against this proposal are summarized by the staff of the Joint Committee on Taxation in the excerpt that follows.

Excerpt From Joint Committee on Taxation, Description of Revenue Provisions Contained in the President's Fiscal Year 2000 Budget Proposal

106th Cong., 1st Sess. 279–281 (JCS 1–99, Feb. 22, 1999).

1. Subject investment income of trade associations to tax

In general

Under present law, dues payments by members of an organization described in section 501(c)(6) generally are deductible. In addition, the organization generally is not subject to tax on its investment income. Thus, members of such an organization are able to fund future operations of the organization through deductible dues payments, even though the members would have been subject to tax on the earnings attributable to such dues payments if they had been retained and invested by the members and paid at the time the organization had expenses. Supporters of the Administration proposal argue that the tax-exempt treatment accorded to organizations described in section 501(c)(6) should not extend to the accumulation of assets on a tax-free basis. Thus, it can be argued that such organizations should be subject to tax on earnings attributable to amounts collected in excess of the amounts needed to fund current operations of the organization.

Opponents of the proposal will argue that the proposal does not permit organizations described in section 501(c)(6) to plan for anticipated expenditures, such as the purchase of a headquarters building. Thus, it could be argued that the proposal has the effect of forcing such an organization to collect substantial dues from members in the year in which an extraordinary expense arises and that this will have the effect of penalizing those individuals who are members at the time of an extraordinary expense. On the other hand, the Administration proposal does not subject the first $10,000 of investment earnings to tax, and thus allows an organization described in section 501(c)(6) to accumulate some assets to meet future expenses.

Opponents of the proposal also may contend that it is not appropriate to extend the tax treatment of social clubs (and other mutual benefit organizations) to other organizations described in section 501(c)(6), because the purposes and activities of these types of entities are not analogous. The purpose of a social club is to provide to its members benefits of a recreational or social nature, which generally would not be deductible if directly paid for by the members. Accordingly, it is considered appropriate to prevent such benefits from being provided through tax-free investment income. In contrast, expenditures for many of the activities of a trade association (e.g., although not expenditures for lobbying or political activities * * *) would be deductible by the association's members if carried on by the members directly, because the expenditures would constitute ordinary and necessary business expenses under section 162(a).

Alternatively, opponents might argue the proposal is too narrow because it would not impose tax on the investment income of organizations exempt under other provisions of section 501 (for example, labor, agricultural or horticultural organizations under sec. 501(c)(5)). On the other hand, it could be argued that such organizations are not analogous to the ones taxed under the proposal, or to organizations subject to [the unrelated business income tax] under present law on all gross income other than exempt function income.

* * *

Economic analysis of proposal

In general, the dues collected by a trade association are established at levels that are intended to provide sufficient funds to carry out the exempt purposes of the trade association. That is, the trade association ultimately spends all dues collected on the exempt purposes of the trade association. The effect of the present-law exclusion from UBIT for certain investment income of trade associations is that if the trade association collects $1.00 of dues today, but does not incur expenses until some point in the future, the association will have an amount with a present value of $1.00 available to meet those expenses. For example, if interest rates are 10 percent and the trade association collects $1.00 in January 1999, but incurs no expenses until January 2000, at that time it will have $1.10 available to meet expenses.

The deductibility of dues paid by the trade association member to the trade association effectively reduces the cost of paying such dues. Depending upon whether investment earnings of trade associations predominantly are earned and used to fund current year operations or whether substantial balances of assets are carried forward for a number of years, the present-law exclusion from UBIT for investment income of trade associations may permit the trade association and its members to effectively lower the cost of the trade associations's dues below the cost reduction created solely by deductibility of dues.

* * *

NOTES AND QUESTIONS

1. *Lobbying Against Taxing the Lobbyists.* The Clinton Administration's proposal would have taxed the wealthiest special-interest trade associations—namely, lobbyists. Not surprisingly, the intended targets responded by lobbying against the proposal. A spokesman for the Chamber of Commerce described the plan as "a stake driven at the very heart of nonprofit organizations." Jacob M. Schlesinger, Clinton Plan to Tax Lobbyists' Investment Gains Hits Home in a Fury of Faxes, Letters, Web Sites, Wall St. J., Feb. 17, 1999, at A24. Trade groups argued that their investment income is derived from funds accumulated as a result of "prudent fiscal planning" and used for public services. Id. Despite its theoretical appeal, the proposal was not well received and is unlikely to be revived any time soon. For a thoughtful discussion of the issue, see Analysis of Administration's Year 2000 Budget Proposal to Tax the Investment Income of Trade Associations, ABA Tax Section, in 25 Exempt Org. Tax Rev. 138 (1999).

2. *Why Not Labor Unions?* Why was the Clinton Administration's proposal limited to § 501(c)(6) trade associations? Shouldn't the investment income of labor unions also be taxed? Do individual members of labor unions receive the same tax benefits from their dues payments as corporate members of trade associations?

B. LABOR, AGRICULTURAL AND HORTICULTURAL ORGANIZATIONS

Internal Revenue Code: § 501(c)(5).

Treasury Regulations: § 1.501(c)(5)–1.

Section 501(c)(5) provides a tax exemption for labor, agricultural and horticultural organizations. In general, these groups must "have as their objects the betterment of the conditions of those engaged in such pursuits, the improvement of the grade of their products, and the development of a higher degree of efficiency in their respective occupations." Treas. Reg. § 1.501(c)(5)–1(a)(2). Section 501(c)(5) embraces not only the typical collective bargaining unit but also includes associations formed to educate union members, process grievances, and engage in litigation and lobbying activities. See, e.g., Rev. Rul. 76–31, 1976–1 C.B. 157. Inurement of net earnings to any member is prohibited, but the payment of death, sickness, accident or similar benefits to members is permitted if provided under a plan aimed at bettering the conditions of the members. See, e.g., Rev. Rul. 62–17, 1962–1 C.B. 87.

The case that follows, involving a foreign pension fund's efforts to achieve tax-exempt status under § 501(c)(5), is one of the few contemporary controversies over the definition of a labor organization.

Stichting Pensioenfonds Voor de Gezondheid v. United States

United States Court of Appeals, District of Columbia Circuit, 1997.
129 F.3d 195, cert. denied, 525 U.S. 811, 119 S.Ct. 43 (1998).

■ TATEL, CIRCUIT JUDGE:

A Dutch pension fund jointly controlled by employers and unions and claiming to be a "labor organization" as described in section 501(c)(5) of the Internal Revenue Code challenges the Internal Revenue Service's denial of its application for exemption from federal income taxation. Because tax exemptions require unambiguous proof and because we can find no authority directly entitling the pension fund to an exemption, we affirm the district court's grant of summary judgment to the United States.

I

Appellant Stichting Pensioenfonds Voor de Gezondheid, Geestelijke en Maatschappelijke Belangen (the "Fund") is a Dutch pension plan formed in 1969 following negotiations between labor unions representing hospital workers and the Dutch national hospital employers' association. Soon after the Fund's formation, the Dutch government granted it "compulsory treatment," thus requiring all private hospitals and their employees to participate. The Fund has since expanded to include fourteen health and social welfare sectors in the Netherlands. The Fund has no principal place of business in the United States, nor does it engage in any trade or business here.

A board of directors controls the Fund's management and assets. Pursuant to Dutch law, employers and unions each appoint half of the board's twelve directors. The six employer directors and the six union directors enjoy equal voting power. If all directors are not present at a meeting, each side may only cast as many votes as the side with the fewer directors. On all policy issues, employer and union directors must agree, or the board may not act. Unions and employers also designate equal numbers of directors to all committees formed by the board.

As the second largest private pension fund in the Netherlands, the Fund covered approximately one million people as of December 31, 1993, some of whom were union members and some of whom were not. About 600,000 were active contributing members. Some 330,000 of the remaining members were "sleepers," a Dutch idiom referring to employees no longer working in industry sectors covered by the Fund but entitled to receive pension benefits upon retirement by virtue of previous employment. The remaining members were retirees already receiving pension benefits.

Both employers and employees contribute to the Fund. The board of directors establishes required contribution rates, as well as the respective portions of the total contribution paid by employers and employees.

The Fund invests in U.S. stocks and mutual funds. In 1993, its U.S. security custodians withheld and paid to the U.S. Treasury over eight million dollars in income tax. Claiming tax-exempt status as a labor organization under section 501(c)(5) of the Internal Revenue Code, the Fund filed a claim for this amount. Receiving no response from the Service, the Fund filed suit in the U.S. District Court for the District of Columbia.

Noting that taxpayers must prove exemptions "unambiguously," and finding that the Fund lacked "a sufficient nexus with a more traditional labor organization to qualify as a tax-exempt labor organization itself," the district court granted summary judgment for the United States. In doing so, the district court rejected the Fund's alternative argument that, even if not entitled to tax-exempt status, it should have received a refund pursuant to section 7805(b) of the Code. We review the district court's grant of summary judgment de novo.

II

Because the Constitution confers upon Congress exclusive authority to collect taxes to provide for the general welfare of the United States, U.S. Const. art. I, § 8, cl. 1, only Congress itself may create exemptions from federal tax laws. Given the importance of taxation and the general presumption in favor of taxing all sources of income, courts may not infer exemptions when Congress has not clearly provided for them. See 1 Jacob Mertens, Jr., The Law of Federal Income Taxation § 3.49 (Nov. 1991). For this reason, the Supreme Court has consistently held for over a century that a taxpayer must "unambiguously" prove entitlement to an exemption: "[E]xemptions from taxation are not to be implied; they must be unambiguously proved," United States v. Wells Fargo Bank, 485 U.S. 351, 354, 108 S.Ct. 1179, 1182, 99 L.Ed.2d 368 (1988); "[T]hose who seek an exemption from a tax must rest it on more than a doubt or ambiguity. Exemptions from taxation cannot rest upon mere implications," United States v. Stewart, 311 U.S. 60, 71, 61 S.Ct. 102, 109, 85 L.Ed. 40 (1940); "As taxation is the rule, and exemption the exception, the intention to create an exemption must be expressed in clear and unambiguous terms* * *. Legislation which relieves any species of property from its due proportion of the burdens of the government must be so clear that there can be neither reasonable doubt nor controversy in regard to its meaning," Yazoo & Miss. Valley R.R. Co. v. Thomas, 132 U.S. 174, 183, 10 S.Ct. 68, 72, 33 L.Ed. 302 (1889). As Justice Cardozo said for a unanimous court over sixty years ago, "Exemptions from taxation are not to be enlarged by implication if doubts are nicely balanced." Trotter v. Tennessee, 290 U.S. 354, 356, 54 S.Ct. 138, 139, 78 L.Ed. 358 (1933). With this extremely high standard in mind, we search for some direct authority that unquestionably and conclusively entitles the Fund to the exemption it seeks.

We begin, of course, with the Internal Revenue Code. Section 501(c)(5) exempts labor, agricultural, and horticultural organizations from taxation. The Code neither defines the term "labor organization" nor elaborates on its meaning. The legislative history, moreover, provides no unambiguous guidance. The early twentieth-century congressional debates on whether to include the term "labor organization" in section 501(c)'s precursor had nothing to do with whether jointly controlled entities providing pension benefits should be exempt from federal taxation. Instead, the debates focused on whether the Code's exemption for "fraternal beneficiary societies * * * providing for the payment of life, sick, accident, or other benefits to members" would be understood as covering all labor organizations, a question that Congress answered negatively when it explicitly exempted labor organizations. See 44 Cong. Rec. 4154–55 (1909). We agree with the district court that this legislative history provides "little help" in understanding the scope of the term "labor organization."

We next turn to the Treasury Regulation that defines the term "labor organization," but which is ultimately unhelpful. It says: The organizations contemplated by section 501(c)(5) as entitled to exemption from income taxation are those which: (1) Have no net earnings inuring to the benefit of any member, and (2) Have as their objects the betterment of the conditions of those engaged in such pursuits, the improvement of the grade of their products, and the development of a higher degree of efficiency in their respective occupations. 26 C.F.R. § 1.501(c)(5)–1(a) (1997). A nonprofit entity, the Fund clearly satisfies sub-paragraph (1). While the Fund may also satisfy the first of sub-paragraph (2)'s requirements—it has as its object the betterment of employee financial conditions—it cannot meet the other two requirements: it works neither to improve products nor to develop higher degrees of efficiency. The Fund urges us to read subparagraph (2) disjunctively, but given the plain meaning of the word "and" we cannot do so. See C.K. Ogden, Basic English International Second Language 132 (1968) ("And is used for joining words together: The man and the woman are married. Or is used for the idea of one of two: The man or the woman is married."). Although this conclusion would otherwise end this case—the regulation does not unambiguously entitle the Fund to an exemption—the Service did not rely on the regulation in its brief or at oral argument. Because the Service itself does not argue that the regulation excludes the Fund from labor organization status, we decline to decide the case on that basis.

Finding help in neither the Code nor the regulation, we look next to the IRS's Revenue Rulings, the second most important agency pronouncements that interpret the Code. Applying the Code to specific situations, Revenue Rulings bind both the Service and the taxpayer. Although Revenue Rulings "do not have the force and effect of Treasury Department Regulations," they are "published to provide precedents to be used in the disposition of other cases, and may be cited and relied upon for that purpose." 26 C.F.R. § 601.601(d)(2)(v)(d) (1997). But because "each Revenue Ruling represents the conclusion of the Service as to the application of the law to the entire state of facts involved, taxpayers, Service personnel, and others concerned are cautioned against reaching the same conclusion in other cases unless the facts and circumstances are substantially the same." 26 C.F.R. § 601.601(d)(2)(v)(e). The Fund can thus prevail only by identifying a Revenue Ruling awarding an exemption in a case having facts and circumstances "substantially the same" as this case. Examining the relevant Revenue Rulings carefully, we find no such controlling authority.

The Service has issued fifteen Revenue Rulings under section 501(c)(5). Eleven deal with organizations completely controlled by unions and thus do not involve facts and circumstances substantially similar to those in this case. Of the four that concern jointly controlled organizations, three award tax exemptions, but none of the organizations covered by those rulings is substantially similar to the Fund. See Rev. Rul. 78–42, 1978–1 C.B. 158; Rev. Rul 75–473, 1975–2 C.B. 213; Rev. Rul. 59–6, 1959–1 C.B. 121. To begin with, the organizations do not provide pension benefits. Rulings 78–42 and 59–6 deal with apprenticeship committees that provide training and education to employees, while Ruling 75–473 involves a jointly controlled dispatch hall that allocates work assignments to union members and adjudicates grievances over working conditions. Moreover, the labor organizations that the Service found exempt in these three rulings focus primarily on improving employee conditions on the job, while the Fund has as its purpose improving employee benefits after the job, i.e. pension benefits. The three Rulings also differ from this case because none involves organizations governed by foreign law. Simply because the Service has awarded tax exemptions to labor organizations dually controlled under American law does not mean that it would necessarily have to reach the same conclusion for organizations dually controlled under foreign law, particularly since exempting foreign pension plans means that their earnings will escape all U.S. taxation. Earnings of exempt domestic funds, by comparison, are taxed when benefits are paid to recipients.

The Fund argues that it should receive an exemption because it conducts appropriate labor organization activities. That an organization performs activities "appropriate" to labor organizations, however, does not make it a labor organization under these Revenue Rulings. The Service has said only that a labor organization not itself a labor union that engages in appropriate labor union activities "may" qualify for an exemption. Rev.

Rul. 75–473. The Service does not end its inquiry upon finding that the organization carries out an "appropriate" union activity. Instead, the Service examines the specific facts of each case, looking to other factors such as the organization's purpose, see Rev. Rul. 78–42; Rev. Rul. 59–6, and the nexus between the organization's activities and the parent labor union's objectives, see Rev. Rul. 75–473. Although providing and administering pension plans for workers is certainly an appropriate and traditional union function, we find no basis for an exemption in this case because the Revenue Rulings do not unambiguously stand for the proposition that any organization bearing some connection to a traditional labor union and performing appropriate or traditional union functions is necessarily an exempt labor organization.

The fourth Revenue Ruling dealing with a jointly controlled labor organization casts even more doubt on the Fund's claim. Rev. Rul. 77–46, 1977–1 C.B. 147. In that Ruling, the Service denied an exemption to an organization that withheld money from union members' pay and invested it, later paying it back annually with interest. Although the Fund argues, perhaps correctly, that this kind of savings plan differs from a pension plan, the Fund's claim for an exemption still ultimately rests on inference and implication rather than unambiguous authority.

The Fund also relies heavily on several General Counsel Memoranda. These "GCMs," however, have no precedential value. * * * They therefore cannot provide a basis for the Fund's claim.

The Fund has failed to meet its heavy burden of demonstrating unambiguous entitlement to tax-exempt status. We find nothing in the Code, the regulation, or the Revenue Rulings that even comes close to stating that a jointly controlled pension plan governed by foreign law is a labor organization exempt from federal taxation. Our doubts about the Fund's entitlement to tax-exempt status are not even "nicely balanced."

We recognize that in Morganbesser v. United States, 984 F.2d 560 (2d Cir.1993), the Second Circuit, with one judge dissenting, held that a jointly controlled pension fund is entitled to tax-exempt status under section 501(c)(5). Unlike this case, however, *Morganbesser* involved a pension fund organized under U.S. law. The Second Circuit, moreover, relied on the precedentially dubious GCMs, never mentioning or applying the "unambiguous" standard that we find controlling. In any event, the Treasury Department has now promulgated a regulation providing that "[a]n organization is not an organization described in section 501(c)(5) if the principal activity of the organization is to receive, hold, invest, disburse, or otherwise manage funds associated with * * * pension or other retirement savings plans or programs." 62 Fed.Reg. 40,447, 40,449 (1997) (adding proposed 26 C.F.R. § 1.501(c)(5)–1(b)(1)). Although both parties agree that this purely prospective regulation has no relevance to the case before us, we mention it to point out that Morganbesser had a brief life.

III

[The court then rejected the Fund's alternative argument that the Service had engaged in unfair discrimination by denying the Fund an exemption while granting favorable private rulings to two comparable British multiemployer pension funds.]

NOTES

1. *Pension Funds.* Qualified pension trusts are exempt from tax under § 501, but they must satisfy a long list of technical requirements in I.R.C. § 401 et seq. The *Stichting* case was an attempted end run around these rules by a foreign multiemployer pension fund seeking to avoid tax on its U.S. investment income. As noted in the opinion, the Second Circuit's opinion in Morganbesser v. United States reached a contrary result, suggesting the possibility of a conflict in the circuits. The Supreme Court resisted the temptation to address this fascinating issue, however, by denying certiorari in *Stichting*. The issue may well be resolved prospectively by the regulation discussed at the end of the *Stichting* opinion.

2. *Agricultural Organizations.* Agricultural organizations are exempt if they engage in the art or science of cultivating land, harvesting crops or aquatic resources, or raising livestock. See I.R.C. § 501(g). To be exempt under § 501(c)(5), an agricultural organization must be devoted to encouraging the development of better agricultural and horticultural products and to the betterment of the conditions of persons engaged in agriculture. If the organization's activities are directed toward the improvement of marketing or other business conditions, it must pass muster under the qualification standards for a business league under § 501(c)(6).

3. *Political Activities.* Section 501(c)(5) organizations do not jeopardize their exempt status by lobbying and seeking to influence political campaigns as long as these pursuits do not become the organization's primary activities. This longstanding policy withstood a constitutional challenge by aerospace workers who sought to strip their union's tax exemption because part of their dues were being used for partisan political purposes. In denying standing, the D.C. Circuit concluded that tax exemptions to labor unions did not amount to a government subsidy and that consequently there was an insufficient nexus between the exemption and any government involvement in the union's political activities. See Marker v. Shultz, 485 F.2d 1003 (D.C.Cir.1973). Certain political expenditures of § 501(c)(5) organizations are subject to federal and state election regulation law restrictions, however, and direct political expenditures may trigger a tax on a union's investment income under § 527(f). See chapter 2F6, supra, at pp. 337–338.

C. TRADE ASSOCIATIONS AND OTHER BUSINESS LEAGUES

Internal Revenue Code: §§ 501(c)(6); 162(e); 6033(e).
Treasury Regulations: § 1.501(c)(6)–1; 1.162–29.

Section 501(c)(6) exempts nonprofit business leagues, chambers of commerce, real estate boards, boards of trade and professional football leagues. This important category includes many influential trade associations, such as the American Medical Association, the American Bar Association, the National Association of Manufacturers, and The National Football League. The primary advantages of § 501(c)(6) status are that dues and investment income received by the organization are exempt from tax, and similar income tax exemptions frequently are available from state and local taxes. Exempt status also may provide an intangible advantage for a trade association in the eyes of the general public and governmental officials.

A business league is defined as an association of persons organized to promote a common business interest provided the organization does not engage in a regular business of a kind ordinarily carried on for profit. Its activities must be directed to the improvement of business conditions of "one or more lines of business" as distinguished from the performance of particular services for individuals. Treas. Reg. § 1.506(c)(6)–1. No part of the net earnings of the organization may inure to the benefit of any private individual. Section 501(c)(6) organizations must provide benefits to an entire industry (e.g., plastics manufacturers) or a component geographical branch (e.g., California hot tub contractors). But they may limit their membership provided there is a common business interest (e.g., business and professional women or candidates for a professional degree in a particular field). See Rev. Rul. 76–400, 1976–2 C.B. 153; Rev. Rul. 77–112, 1977–1 C.B. 149.

1.   THE LINE OF BUSINESS REQUIREMENT

Guide International Corporation v. United States

United States Court of Appeals, Seventh Circuit, 1991.
948 F.2d 360.

■ KANNE, CIRCUIT JUDGE.

Guide International Corporation is a nonprofit organization whose purpose is to develop data processing products and services, and to provide a forum for the exchange and dissemination of information concerning data processing equipment and systems. In 1971, the Internal Revenue Service determined that Guide was exempt from tax as a nonprofit business league under § 501(c)(6) of the Internal Revenue Code. However, Revenue Ruling 83–164, 1983–2 C.B. 95 put Guide's tax-exempt status into question.[2] To obtain a binding determination of its tax-exempt status, Guide filed income tax returns for the years 1984, 1985, and 1986, and, thereafter, filed for refund of taxes paid with those returns. No action was taken on Guide's

---

2. The ruling held that an organization whose members represent diversified businesses that own, rent, or lease computers produced by a single computer manufacturer does not qualify for exemption from federal income tax as a business league under § 501(c)(6).

claim and Guide brought suit. On cross-motions for summary judgment, the district court found that Guide failed to qualify as a business league and granted summary judgment in favor of the government. Guide appeals and we affirm.

* * *

The facts are undisputed. Guide was formed in 1956 and incorporated in Missouri in 1969 as a nonprofit association. Guide's purposes, as set forth in its Articles of Incorporation, are the following: (a) The promotion of sound professional practices with respect to the uses of data processing equipment and systems. (b) The exchange and dissemination of information concerning data processing equipment and systems. (c) The participation with manufacturers of data processing equipment (including hardware, software and peripheral equipment) in the improvement and development of products, standards, and education. Guide's By-laws state that its primary purposes include "communicat[ing] to the IBM Corporation user needs in all technical areas of interest" and "review[ing], comment[ing] and exchang[ing] information on products and services related to the equipment needed to qualify for GUIDE membership." The By-laws restrict membership to organizations who own large-scale computer equipment manufactured by International Business Machines (IBM mainframes).

Guide's membership includes major corporations from diverse fields, as well as educational and governmental organizations. Many of the members compete against each other, and some compete against IBM. Guide is managed by a board of directors, who are members of the organization. Guide's principal activity is the sponsorship of week-long conferences that are held three times a year and focus on data processing matters. Representatives of IBM and other persons are invited to speak at the conferences on topics chosen by Guide's management. Although IBM and manufacturers of compatible peripheral equipment present data processing products at the conferences, all sales and recruitment activities are prohibited. IBM provides administrative personnel, a personal computer, copiers and refreshments at the meetings. The information presented and discussed at the conferences is communicated to IBM.

Guide also conducts research involving data processing equipment manufactured by IBM and other companies. Project papers and other resource materials prepared by Guide are maintained in a library and are generally available to all interested parties, including non-members.

Guide argues that the district court erred in determining it was not a business league under § 501(c)(6). The principal issue before the district court was whether Guide satisfies the requirement of Treasury Regulation § 1.501(c)(6)–1 (26 C.F.R. § 1.501(c)(6)–1) that its activities "be directed to the improvement of business conditions of one or more lines of business as distinguished from the performance of particular services for individual persons."

Relying on National Muffler Dealers Ass'n, Inc. v. United States, 440 U.S. 472, 99 S.Ct. 1304, 59 L.Ed.2d 519 (1979), the district court found that Guide fails to meet the line of business test because it primarily serves the interests of IBM and the users of IBM computers rather than the data processing industry as a whole.

In *National Muffler*, the United States Supreme Court adopted the Internal Revenue Commissioner's interpretation of the line of business test that an association which is not industrywide should not be exempt. 440 U.S. at 484, 99 S.Ct. at 1310. But see Pepsi-Cola Bottlers' Ass'n v. United States, 369 F.2d 250 (7th Cir.1966)(not followed by Rev.Rul. 68–182, 1968–1 C.B. 263 (1968), and disapproved by *National Muffler*, 440 U.S. at 476, 99 S.Ct. at 1306). Accordingly, the Court denied a tax exemption to an association of franchisees of one brand of muffler because the association did not improve conditions of an industrial line, but, instead, promoted a particular product at the expense of others in the industry.

Here, the district court acknowledged that although Guide's stated purpose is to facilitate the use and exchange of information regarding data processing equipment in general, the primary benefit inures to IBM which is only a segment (70 to 75%) of the mainframe computer business, not a line of business.

Guide argues that this case is distinguishable from *National Muffler* because its activities improve several lines of business by enabling its members to perform data processing more efficiently. This argument is in direct conflict with Revenue Ruling 83–164 and was rejected in National Prime Users Group, Inc. v. United States, 667 F.Supp. 250 (D.Md.1987). Revenue Ruling 83–164 held that an organization that directs its activities to the users of one brand of computers improves the business conditions in only segments of the various lines of business to which its members belong. Similarly, in *National Prime Users Group*, the court denied a tax exemption to an association whose members consisted of users of computers of a single manufacturer because the association only improved conditions for members in those lines of businesses that used the particular computers. The court found an inherent competitive advantage for the computer manufacturer. We believe that the Revenue Ruling and the decision of the district court in Maryland were correct.

Therefore, while Guide's members reflect a wide variety of businesses, no single business is enhanced and Guide only benefits IBM and those individuals within various lines of business who use IBM mainframes. Moreover, the district court found that Guide primarily advances IBM's interests and that any benefit to its members and other data processing companies who use information prepared by Guide is incidental.

We agree with the district court's characterization of Guide as a powerful marketing tool for IBM. Guide's conferences provide IBM customers with the opportunity to learn about IBM products and services and IBM receives feedback about those products and services which influences product development. The district court properly found that Guide fails to qualify as an exempt business league under § 501(c)(6).

The judgment of the district court is Affirmed.

2.   NO CONDUCT OF BUSINESS FOR PROFIT REQUIREMENT

Associated Master Barbers & Beauticians of America v. Commissioner

United States Tax Court, 1977.
69 T.C. 53.

■ DAWSON, JUDGE:

[Associated Master Barbers & Beauticians of America was organized in 1924 for the purpose of "promoting such unity of sentiment and action among the Master Barbers throughout America, joining them closer together for united protection." Among its activities were the administration of certain insurance programs for its members and the publication of a magazine, first known as Master Barber and Beautician Magazine and later as The Professional Men's Hairstylist and Barber's Journal. The magazine included news and information of the trade, such as shampooing methods and shaving techniques, and articles dealing with the various benefits, goods, services and insurance programs offered to members. The association also sent representatives to "The World Hairstyling Olympics," an international conclave held for the purpose of exchanging hairstyling techniques with professionals in foreign countries. The Service revoked the organization's exempt status under § 501(c)(6) on the ground that it had engaged in a regular business for profit. Eds.]

OPINION

Issue 1. Tax–Exempt Status Under Section 501(c)(6)

Section 501(c)(6) defines as tax-exempt organizations:

Business leagues, chambers of commerce, real-estate boards, boards of trade, or professional football leagues (whether or not administering a pension fund for football players), not organized for profit and no part of the net earnings of which inures to the benefit of any private shareholder or individual.

Section 1.501(c)(6)–1, Income Tax Regs., provides:

A business league is an association of persons having some common business interest, the purpose of which is to promote such common interest and not to engage in a regular business of a kind ordinarily carried on for profit. It is an organization of the same general class as a chamber of commerce or board of trade. Thus, its activities should be directed to the improvement of business conditions of one or more lines of business as distinguished from the performance of particular services for individual persons. An organization whose purpose is to engage in a regular business of a kind ordinarily carried on for profit, even though the business is conducted on a cooperative basis or produces only sufficient income to be self-sustaining, is not a business league. * * *

These regulations have remained basically unchanged for many years and have been held valid by various courts. They may be deemed to have been approved in effect by reenactment of the statutory exemption provision in the same terms since their adoption and permitting the administrative interpretation to become settled. American Automobile Association v. Commissioner, 19 T.C. 1146, 1158 (1953).

Petitioner has the burden of proving that it meets the requirements of the statute. A statute creating an exemption must be strictly construed, and any doubt must be resolved in favor of the taxing power. The essential requirements of an organization exempt under section 501(c)(6) were spelled out in American Automobile Association v. Commissioner, as follows:

> (1) It must be an association of persons having a common business interest.

> (2) Its purpose must be to promote that common business interest.

> (3) It must not be organized for profit.

> (4) It should not be engaged in a regular business of a kind ordinarily conducted for a profit.

> (5) Its activities should be directed toward the improvement of business conditions of one or more lines of business as opposed to the performance of particular services for individual persons.

> (6) Its net earnings, if any, must not inure to the benefit of any private shareholder or individual.

Petitioner must meet each of these requirements in order to qualify as a tax-exempt business league.

* * *

Petitioner is clearly an association of persons having a common business interest. Members of the Associated Master Barbers & Beauticians of America, Inc., associate themselves in order to professionalize their services and ensure the establishment of an adequate income for services provided. The purpose for which petitioner was formed was to promote the common business interests of its members. That purpose was set forth in its constitution and rule book. In addition, petitioner was not organized for profit. It was incorporated in 1924 as a nonprofit organization. Its intention to operate as a nonprofit organization was stated in its articles of incorporation. Thus, the petitioner meets the first three requirements set out above.

The crux of respondent's position, however, is that the petitioner fails to meet the last three requirements. He contends that the services provided by the petitioner to both members and nonmembers were activities which are of a kind ordinarily carried on for profit. In particular, respondent points to petitioner's self-insurance programs and its involvement with the various insurance programs underwritten by independent insurance companies as evidence that it is engaged in a regular business of a kind ordinarily conducted for profit.

To the contrary, the petitioner maintains that the income from its insurance programs is related to the exempt function of its organization. Central to its position is that an association promotes the good of a profession as a whole when it provides proper protection and fringe benefits for the members of a profession who would otherwise not have any security, protection, or benefits. Thus the operation of an insurance program, argues petitioner, is related to the exempt purpose of the organization.

We agree with the respondent. Petitioner established a basic death benefit plan in 1928 and a basic sick benefit plan in 1932. In addition, a voluntary supplemental benefit plan was initiated in 1955. From October 1, 1966, to September 30, 1971, petitioner administered and self-insured the basic sick and death benefit plans and the supplemental benefit plan. Its national officers and employees kept records on what insurance program each member participated in, processed claims for benefits, and paid benefits with respect to the numerous insurance programs provided by the petitioner.

A new basic benefit program, approved on August 15, 1972, was underwritten by Globe Life Insurance Co. Those members age 66 and above were not eligible for the new program. They continued to receive benefits under the old basic benefit program. Petitioner continued to operate and administer its self-insurance programs including the basic sick and death benefit plans for those members age 66 and above. In addition, Globe Life Insurance Co. required petitioner to collect premiums from its members, keep records of payments made, determine whether the insured was still a member, and process claims for benefits.

A large majority of petitioner's members participated in the self-insurance plans offered by petitioner. During the taxable year ended September 30, 1967, 6,971 of petitioner's 9,041 members participated in the sick and death benefit plans, while 2,220 participated in the voluntary supplemental benefit plan. During the taxable year ended September 30, 1970, 5,010 of petitioner's 6,832 members participated in the sick and death benefit plans, while 941 participated in the voluntary supplemental benefit plan. During the taxable year ended September 30, 1971, 4,366 of petitioner's 5,964 members participated in the sick and death benefit plans, while 960 participated in the voluntary supplemental benefit plan.

In addition, the number of claims processed by petitioner was substantial. During the taxable year ended September 30, 1967, it processed and paid 596 claims under the basic plan (sick and death) and 124 claims under the voluntary supplemental plan. During the taxable year ended September 30, 1970, it processed 497 claims under the basic plan and 104 claims under the voluntary supplemental plan. During the taxable year ended September

30, 1971, it processed 453 claims under the basic plan and 91 claims under the voluntary supplemental plan.

We think the evidence clearly demonstrates that petitioner was engaged in a regular business of a kind ordinarily carried on for profit during all the taxable years in question. Its officers and employees were involved on a daily basis with recordkeeping, processing claims for benefits, paying claims, and performing other administrative duties in connection with such insurance activities. As we see it, the petitioner was engaging in an insurance business—a business of the type which is ordinarily carried on for profit.

* * *

In our judgment the petitioner herein is engaged in a regular business of a kind ordinarily carried on for profit, namely, the insurance business. However, it is true that an organization whose principal purpose and activity is such as to qualify for "business league" exemption does not lose its exempt status by engaging in incidental activities which standing alone would be subject to taxation. It is therefore necessary for us to examine the extent of petitioner's insurance activities to see if they constitute only incidental, as opposed to substantial, activities.

Petitioner argues that the time which the employees of an association devote to its various functions is a proper measure of "activity." It further argues that the evidence here shows that the time petitioner's employees devoted to its insurance activities was only 15 percent for the taxable years ended September 30, 1967, September 30, 1970, and September 30, 1971, and only 10 percent for the taxable year ended September 30, 1973. Thus, it is asserted that the insurance activities were only "incidental."

Respondent, on the other hand, contends that we should look to petitioner's financial data, such as its statement of receipts and disbursements for the taxable years at issue, to determine the extent of petitioner's insurance activities. See Evanston-North Shore Board of Realtors v. United States, supra.

During the taxable year ended September 30, 1967, receipts from the basic sick and death benefit funds and the voluntary supplemental benefit fund amounted to $115,876.32; and disbursements totaled $96,720.95. These amounts constituted 43 percent and 35 percent, respectively, of total receipts and total disbursements during that year. During the taxable year ended September 30, 1970, receipts and disbursements from the basic sick and death benefit funds and the voluntary supplemental benefit fund amounted to $94,547 and $95,584, respectively. These amounts constituted 31 percent and 30 percent, respectively, of total receipts and disbursements for that year. During the taxable year ended September 30, 1971, receipts and disbursements from the basic sick and death benefit funds and the voluntary supplemental benefit fund amounted to $87,400 and $85,931, respectively. These amounts constituted 31 percent and 32 percent, respectively, of total receipts and disbursements for that year. During the taxable year ended September 30, 1973, receipts and disbursements from the basic sick and death benefits funds and the voluntary supplemental benefit fund amounted to $22,549 and $47,363, respectively. These amounts constituted 11 percent and 21 percent, respectively, of total receipts and disbursements for that year.

While we think that both time and financial data should be considered in determining the extent of an organization's nonexempt activities, we view the petitioner's evidence, consisting of the testimony of Chris Hood, an employee, J. Nelson Snyder, a former employee, and Gerald St. Onge, petitioner's national president at the time he testified, as having little probative value with regard to the percentage of time spent on the insurance programs. What is clear from the record is that numerous clerical duties had to be performed and voluminous records were kept on the petitioner's various insurance programs. Evidence as to the numerous records that had to be kept, the entries that had to be made on each record, and the processing of claims for benefits establishes to our satisfaction that a substantial amount of time was devoted to the insurance programs. The time spent, combined with the persuasive financial data available, convinces us that the petitioner's insurance activities were not merely incidental. They were substantial.

For these reasons we conclude that the petitioner failed to meet the fourth requirement necessary to qualify for exemption under section 501(c)(6). In our opinion it was engaging in a regular business of a kind ordinarily carried on for profit.

With respect to the fifth requirement for exemption, the record contains substantial evidence of the performance of "particular services" for individual persons and comparatively little evidence of activities designed to promote the hairstyling profession. In all of the years at issue the petitioner provided and offered numerous benefits to individual members in the form of various types of insurance, goods, and services. In addition to the self-insurance programs it administered and financed, the petitioner initiated a new basic benefit program in 1972 which was underwritten by Globe Life Insurance Co. In July 1967, the major benefit insurance program was initiated and underwritten by Zurich Insurance Co. This program provided, on a voluntary basis to the members, monthly disability income protection and death benefits. During the years at issue, the petitioner also offered a cancer insurance policy underwritten by an insurance company to its members; a malpractice and personal liability insurance policy underwritten by an insurance company; and a hospitalization insurance plan underwritten by Craftsman Life Insurance Co., and later, by Hanover Insurance Co. The petitioner also offered to its members a voluntary retirement insurance program which was in effect only during its taxable years ended September 30, 1970, and September 30, 1971.

Besides the numerous insurance programs, the petitioner offered its members an eyeglass and prescription lens replacement service. It sold its local chapters certain supplies. It sold its members hair and beard styling charts, a "carlow book," style of the month binders, appointment books, and white nylon hair cloths. It sold its members shop emblems and association jewelry. It also sold a standard textbook and an examination for the textbook, as well as a special hairstyling book.

These insurance and other activities, which formed the bulk of the activities performed by petitioner during the years of issue, did not contribute to the improvement of business conditions in one or more lines of business as opposed to the performance of particular services for individuals. Consequently, we conclude that the petitioner has failed to satisfy the fifth requirement for exempt status under section 501(c)(6). The record contains substantial evidence of activities of a type termed "particular services" by the regulations, but little evidence of activities designed to improve business conditions in the barbering and beautician professions. Because these activities serve as a convenience or economy to petitioner's members in the operation of their businesses, we think they constitute "particular services" as proscribed by the regulation. By providing insurance or textbooks for its members, the petitioner relieves its members of obtaining insurance or textbooks on an individual basis from a nonexempt commercial business. If the petitioner did not provide these goods and services, its individual members would have to obtain them from nonexempt businesses at a substantially increased cost. Thus, the organization is rendering "particular services" for the individual members as distinguished from an improvement of business conditions in the barbering and beautician professions generally.

Accordingly, we sustain respondent's determination revoking the exempt status of petitioner under section 501(c)(6) for the years at issue herein. The petitioner is taxable as a corporation under section 11 of the Code.

NOTES

1. *Monopoly Businesses.* What if a nonprofit organization seeking § 501(c)(6) status engages in a business but does not compete with other commercial enterprises because it constitutes a monopoly? The Service contends that *potential* competition with for-profit businesses is fatal. See, e.g., Jockey Club v. United States, 133 Ct.Cl. 787, 137 F.Supp. 419 (1956), denying § 501(c)(6) status to a thoroughbred racing organization which published "The American Stud Book," a popular volume listing bloodlines of purebreds, and "Racing Calendar," an almanac for the horsey set. Although Jockey Club had a monopoly, the court found that commercial competition was foreseeable.

In M.I.B., Inc. v. Commissioner, 80 T.C. 438 (1983), the Tax Court upheld the § 501(c)(6) exemption of an organization that collected and exchanged confidential underwriting information about applicants for life insurance among its members in order to deter fraud and misrepresentation. The membership consisted of virtually the entire U.S. life insurance industry, and there were no competing organizations providing the same service. Revenues, including "assessments" to members and service charges, were substantial ($11,400,000 in 1978) but there was no foreseeable competition. On appeal, however, the First Circuit reversed, holding that the modus operandi of M.I.B. was to perform direct services for its individual members rather than improving business conditions as a whole. M.I.B., Inc. v. Commissioner, 734 F.2d 71 (1st Cir.1984). The court reasoned that the ultimate inquiry is "whether the association's activities advance the members' interests generally, by virtue of their membership in the industry, or whether they assist members in the pursuit of the individual businesses." 734 F.2d at 78. A negative factor was that members' assessments were not uniform but varied in approximate proportion to the specific services received.

2. *Unrelated Business Income Tax.* Even if an organization qualifies for exemption under § 501(c)(6), it remains taxable on the net income from any business activities unrelated to its exempt purposes. Treas. Reg. § 1.506(c)(6)–1. Since enactment of the unrelated business income tax, there have been fewer reported controversies involving qualification for § 501(c)(6) status and far more disputes over whether particular income-generating activities are taxable. See Chapter 5, infra.

3. LOBBYING AND OTHER POLITICAL ACTIVITIES

The Internal Revenue Code does not impose any express limitation on the lobbying or other political activities of § 501(c)(6) organizations. Indeed, the Service has ruled that a trade association may qualify for exemption under § 501(c)(6) even though its sole or principal activity is the advocacy of legislation beneficial to the common business interests of its members. Rev. Rul. 61–177, 1961–2 C.B. 117. But the nature and extent of a trade association's lobbying and other political activities may adversely affect the ability of its for-profit members to deduct their dues as business expenses.

Impact of Lobbying on Deduction of Membership Dues. In general, trade association membership dues are tax-deductible under § 162. For many years, § 162(e) disallowed a business deduction for expenses incurred in connection with either attempts to influence the general public on legislation ("grassroots" lobbying) or participation or intervention in political campaigns on behalf of or in opposition to candidates for public office. Consistent with that policy, the portion of trade association membership dues attributable to grassroots lobbying or political campaign activities also was not deductible. In 1993, Congress extended the deduction disallowance to all amounts paid in connection with "influencing legislation" and direct communications with high-level executive branch officials to influence their official actions or positions. I.R.C. § 162(e)(1). In so doing, it further limited the membership dues deduction.

As amended, § 162(e) has become a minefield of rules that only will be summarized here to provide a sense of their impact on tax-exempt trade associations. "Influencing legislation" is defined as "any attempt to influence any legislation through communicating with any member or employee of a legislative body or with any government official or employee who may participate in the formulation of legislation." I.R.C. § 162(e)(4)(A). This definition is expanded to include research, preparation, planning or coordination of an attempt to influence legislation. I.R.C. § 162(e)(5)(C). A "lobbying communication" must refer to and reflect a view on specific legislation, or it must clarify, modify, or provide support for views reflected in a prior lobbying communication. Treas. Reg. § 1.162–29(b)(3). "Legislation" includes the usual actions with respect to Acts, bills, and resolutions, as well as proposed treaties submitted by the President to the Senate for its advice and consent. I.R.C. §§ 162(e)(4)(B); 4911(e)(2); Treas. Reg. § 1.162–29(b)(4).

An exception excludes from the definition of "influencing legislation" any attempts to influence local bodies, such as county or city councils. I.R.C. § 162(e)(2). A de minimis rule excludes from disallowance "in-house expenditures" provided that they do not exceed $2,000 (without regard to overhead). I.R.C. § 162(e)(5)(B)(i). In-house expenditures are lobbying expenditures other than payments to a professional lobbyist or association dues that are allocable to lobbying. I.R.C. § 162(e)(5)(B)(ii).

These rules affect trade associations in several different ways. First, § 162(e)(3) disallows a business deduction for the portion of membership dues paid to any noncharitable exempt organization that is allocable to the kinds of lobbying and political campaign expenses ("§ 162(e) expenses") that are not deductible under § 162(e). To illustrate, assume that Corporation pays $1,000 in annual dues to exempt Trade Association, which spends 30 percent of its annual budget on direct lobbying. Corporation would not be able to deduct $300 (30 percent) of its dues. See Treas. Reg. § 1.162–28 for permissible methods of allocating costs to lobbying activities. Second, noncharitable exempt organizations must include on their annual Form 990 informational return their total § 162(e) expenses and the total amount of membership dues allocable to those expenses. I.R.C. § 6033(e)(1)(A)(i). Third, unless they are protected by the de minimis rule described above, these organizations must make a reasonable estimate of the portion of dues attributable to § 162(e) expenses and notify dues paying members at least annually of the amount that is not deductible. I.R.C. § 6033(e)(1)(A)(ii). Alternatively, an exempt organization may avoid the notification requirement by electing to pay a "proxy tax," at the highest corporate tax rate applicable for the taxable year, on the total amount of its § 162(e) expenditures (up to the amount of dues received during the year). The proxy tax is imposed automatically if an organization fails to notify its members of the nondeductible portion of their dues. § 6033(e)(2)(A).

In a final burst of complexity, § 6033(e)(3) waives the reporting requirement for organizations that establish to the Service's satisfaction that substantially all (90 percent or more, according to the legislative history) of the dues paid to the organization are "not deductible without regard to section 162(e)." This apparently means that an organization receiving the bulk of its dues from individuals who cannot deduct them is exempt from any reporting requirement.

Constitutional Issues. Prior to the enactment of § 162(e), the Treasury had promulgated regulations disallowing any business deduction for lobbying expenditures, be they direct or grassroots. In Cammarano v. United States, 358 U.S. 498, 79 S.Ct. 524 (1959), the Supreme Court upheld the constitutionality of these regulations, which the Service had applied to disallow a deduction claimed by beer and liquor dealers for expenses incurred in attempts to urge voters to defeat state initiative measures that would have put them out of business. In rejecting the taxpayer's First Amendment challenge, the Court said:

> Petitioners are not being denied a tax deduction because they engage in constitutionally protected activities, but are simply being required to pay for those activities entirely out of their own pockets, as everyone else engaging in similar activities is required to do under the provisions of the Internal Revenue Code. Nondiscriminatory denial of deduction from gross income to sums expended to promote or defeat legislation is plainly not "aimed at the suppression of dangerous ideas." * * * Rather, it appears to us to express a determination by Congress that since purchased publicity can influence the fate of legislation which will affect, directly or indirectly, all in the community, everyone in the community should stand on the same footing as regards its purchase so far as the Treasury of the United States is concerned.

After *Cammarano* was decided, Congress enacted the pre–1994 version of § 162(e), which expressly permitted the deduction of direct lobbying expenses but continued to disallow a deduction for grassroots expenses. In the 1993 legislation, Congress reverted to the Treasury's earlier policy by disallowing business deductions for both direct and grassroots lobbying. Is this constitutional? Is it sound tax policy? Does it unfairly limit the expression of views on legislative matters by the corporate community? Are the tax rules that apply to business taxpayers consistent with the treatment of nonprofit organizations and their donors or members?

Some of these constitutional questions were revisited when a coalition of trade associations challenged the provisions in §§ 162(e) and 6033(e) that forbid members of tax-exempt organizations from deducting the portion of their dues allocable to lobbying expenses and require organizations either to notify members of the nondeductible portion of their dues or pay a 35 percent proxy tax on lobbying expenses. Applying "rational basis" scrutiny, the D.C. Circuit, affirming the federal district court, held that the challenged provisions did not violate First Amendment free speech rights or discriminate against organizations that lobby because the statutory scheme bore a rational relationship to the legislative goal of eliminating any tax subsidy for lobbying and preventing taxpayers from circumventing that goal. In finding no free speech burden, the court emphasized that a § 501(c)(6) organization could avoid any obligation to allocate dues or pay a proxy tax by dividing itself into two separate tax-exempt entities, one of which engages exclusively in lobbying and one that completely refrains from lobbying. American Society of Association Executives v. United States, 195 F.3d 47 (D.C.Cir.1999). Is § 501(c)(6) tantamount to a subsidy? Would it be a subsidy if the Clinton Administration's proposal to tax investment income of § 501(c)(6) organizations had been enacted?

Other Political Activities. Nothing in the Code or regulations specifically prohibits § 501(c)(6) organizations from engaging in political campaign activities. The conventional wisdom is that a business league will not jeopardize its exempt status by engaging in political activities that promote the common business interests of its members provided that campaign activity is not the organization's primary purpose. Section 501(c)(6) organizations are subject to federal and state election laws, however, and their investment income may be taxable under § 527 to the extent the organization incurs certain types of political expenditures. See Chapter 2F6, supra, at pp. 337–338, for the tax treatment of political activities of § 501(c) organizations and for an overview of federal election law regulations.

For Further Reading. Jasper L. Cummings, Jr., Tax Policy, Social Policy, and Politics: Amending Section 162(e), 9 Exempt Org. Tax Rev. 137 (1994); Miriam Galston, Lobbying and the Public Interest: Rethinking the Internal Revenue Code's Treatment of Legislative Activities, 71 Tex.L.Rev. 1269 (1993); George Cooper, The Tax Treatment of Business Grassroots Lobbying: Defining and Attaining Public Policy Objectives, 68 Colum.L.Rev. 801 (1968).

PROBLEMS

1.   Determine whether the following organizations are exempt from tax under § 501(c)(6):

   (a) Dialogue, a nonprofit membership organization of business and professional women formed to promote the acceptance of women in business and the professions. The group sponsors luncheons and dinner meetings devoted to discussion of career opportunities for women; awards scholarships to promising women in local professional schools; and presents a "young-woman-of-the-month" award.

   (b) Merchants of the Mall, Inc., an association composed of all the business tenants and the corporate owner of a suburban shopping center. Membership in the organization is mandatory under the terms of the tenants' leases, and no businesses other than tenants of the center are permitted to join. The purpose of the organization is to serve as a means of communication and exchange of views between the developer and the tenants and to serve as the governing body for enforcing rules respecting the common areas of the center. Income is from membership dues assessed according to the amount of business space rented.

2.   The National Association of Industrialists ("NAI") is a nationwide trade association exempt from tax under § 501(c)(6). It has taken a strong position that recent proposals in the state legislature to impose a timetable for implementation of new occupational safety standards will have a drastic economic impact, forcing layoffs and causing some businesses to cease

operations. The Association has contacted its members to urge them to ask their employees and customers to oppose enactment of the legislation because of its detrimental effect on their businesses. It also has paid a professional lobbyist to monitor the legislation and to help draft position papers that will be sent to all members of the legislature. Do these activities constitute "lobbying communications" and, if so, what in general are the tax consequences to NAI and its members?

D.   SOCIAL CLUBS AND FRATERNAL ORGANIZATIONS

Internal Revenue Code: §§ 501(c)(7), (8) & (10); 501(i).
Treasury Regulations: § 1.501(c)(7)–1.

1.   INTRODUCTION

Section 501(c)(7) grants exempt status to "clubs organized for pleasure, recreation, and other nonprofitable purposes" provided that substantially all of the club's activities serve these exempt purposes and no part of its net earnings inures to the benefit of any private shareholder. As previewed earlier and developed at greater length later in this text, the exemption under § 501(c)(7) does not extend to a club's investment income (e.g., dividends, interest and most capital gains) or to its net revenue from dealings with non-members. See I.R.C. § 512(a)(3), which in effect limits a club's exemption to "exempt function income," such as dues and charges for goods and services to members and their guests, and Chapter 5F2, infra, at pp. 663–664.

To qualify as a "club," the Service requires personal contacts and fellowship. "Commingling" of the members must play a material part in the life of the organization. See Rev. Rul. 69–635, 1969–2 C.B. 126. The membership must evidence an "identity of purpose"—for example, a flying club consisting of members who enjoy flying for recreation. Rev. Rul. 74–30, 1974–1 C.B. 137. An organization will not qualify if it is operated primarily as a service to its members-for example, a flying club operated to save money for pilots by sharing facilities. Rev. Rul. 70–32, 1970–1 C.B. 132.

Two types of fraternal organizations qualify for exemption. The first category—organizations providing life, sickness, accident or other benefits to their members or dependents and which operate under the lodge system or for the exclusive benefit of members of a fraternal society under the lodge system—are exempt as "fraternal beneficiary societies" under § 501(c)(8). Organizations that operate under the lodge system and devote all their net earnings exclusively to religious, charitable, scientific, literary, educational and fraternal purposes and which do not provide for the payment of life, sickness, accident or other benefits are exempt as "domestic fraternal societies" under § 501(c)(10). This second category reportedly was added to cover the Masons, who engage in many charitable pursuits but do not offer insurance programs for their members.

The exemption for fraternal organizations is not limited to their exempt function income; investment income also is exempt from tax. Moreover, contributions by an individual to a fraternal society operating under the lodge system are tax-deductible if the donation is "used exclusively for religious, charitable, scientific, literary or educational purposes, or for the prevention of cruelty to children or animals." I.R.C. § 170(c)(4).

As demonstrated by the *Zeta Beta Tau* case, which follows, the more generous tax treatment of fraternal organizations can motivate a college fraternity or sorority to contend that it is more fraternal than social.

Zeta Beta Tau Fraternity, Inc. v. Commissioner

United States Tax Court, 1986.
87 T.C. 421.

■ SWIFT, JUDGE:

In a timely statutory notice of deficiency respondent determined a deficiency in the unrelated business income tax of petitioner for its taxable year ending June 30, 1971, in the amount of $1,936. The only issue for decision is whether petitioner, a tax-exempt social club described in section 501(c)(7), also qualifies as a tax-exempt domestic fraternal society described in section 501(c)(10). If so, petitioner's income from investments is not taxable as unrelated business income and petitioner is not liable for an underpayment of tax.

FINDINGS OF FACT

* * *

Petitioner was organized as a New York corporation in 1907. Petitioner is the central organization of the Zeta Beta Tau national college fraternity (hereinafter referred to as "Zeta Beta"). Associated with Zeta Beta are approximately 80 local chapters. Also associated with Zeta Beta are approximately 80 corporations (hereinafter referred to as the "house corporations") that individually own each building in which the local fraternity houses are located. Zeta Beta also operates the Zeta Beta Tau Foundation, Inc., and the NFEF Foundation, Inc. Zeta Beta, its associated local chapters, and the house corporations were granted tax-exempt status by respondent in 1940 under the provisions of section 101(a), Internal Revenue Code of 1939, the predecessor to section 501(c)(7).

Under the provisions of its national constitution and code of rules, the officers and directors of Zeta Beta's governing body, the supreme council, are selected by representatives of the local chapters who meet annually at a national convention. The supreme council meets periodically and acts as the legislative, executive, and judicial authority of Zeta Beta. Zeta Beta also employs an administrative staff. The principal purpose of Zeta Beta's central staff is to serve as the coordinating and governing organization of the local chapters, house corporations, and private foundations that comprise the Zeta Beta national college fraternity.

Zeta Beta also provides various programs, services, and publications to the local chapters, their members, and the house corporations. The services and publications provided by Zeta Beta include a philanthropic and social service programming guide, a dance marathon guide, a fraternity magazine, awards to local chapters and members for scholastic and public service achievements, information concerning scholarship and emergency student loan programs, a leadership school for undergraduate members, and a monthly newsletter containing articles on professional schools, study tips, financial aid information, and social news from local chapters throughout the United States. Zeta Beta itself does not engage in any significant social activities.

Each local chapter of Zeta Beta adopts its own constitution and bylaws and generally exercises substantial autonomy in the governance of its affairs. The local chapter may not, however, adopt any rule that contravenes Zeta Beta's constitution or code of rules. Generally, each local chapter does not incorporate as a separate entity. Each chapter, however, files its own annual Federal tax returns (Forms 990, Return of Organization Exempt from Tax). The assets, liabilities, receipts, and expenses of local chapters are not included on Zeta Beta's Federal tax returns. Zeta Beta also does not file a separate group information return with respondent on behalf of local chapters.

Each house corporation associated with Zeta Beta is separately incorporated and serves as the owner and manager of the local fraternity house. The house corporations individually file annual Federal tax returns (Forms 990), and Zeta Beta does not include the assets, liabilities, receipts, or expenses of the individual house corporations in its Federal tax returns. Each house corporation is, however, subordinate to Zeta Beta and subject to its general supervision.

The Zeta Beta Tau Foundation, Inc. (hereinafter referred to as the "ZBT Foundation") provides scholarship and loan assistance to undergraduate students who belong to the fraternity. The ZBT Foundation also issues fellowship grants to graduate students in return for their management advice to local chapters of Zeta Beta. The NPEF Foundation, Inc., supports Zeta Beta research and publication programs, chapter house libraries, and leadership development workshops. Both the ZBT Foundation and the NPEF Foundation are recognized by respondent as exempt from Federal income taxes under section 501(c)(3).

As of 1985, Zeta Beta had approximately 104,500 members, of which 4,500 were undergraduate college students and 100,000 were alumni members. Zeta Beta's local chapters provide the undergraduate student members of Zeta Beta housing and meals, social activities, and opportunities for charitable service within their communities. Usually, only a portion of the members of a local chapter reside at the fraternity house. Local chapters generally provide daily meals to its members.

Social activities of each chapter typically include homecoming weekend for alumni and parents, a fall "football weekend," a winter carnival, and a formal dance in the spring. Depending on budgetary considerations and the calendar of social events sponsored by the college, local chapters sponsor additional social events at the fraternity house. The costs of the social events typically are borne by individual members of the chapter.

Local chapters of Zeta Beta also participate in public service activities, such as blood drives, Easter Seal drives, and the transportation of elderly citizens to the polls on election day. Some local chapters regularly sponsor an annual dance marathon to raise funds for charity.

Local chapters of Zeta Beta compete with other college fraternities in scholastic achievement. Chapter members help each other adjust to college life and generally aid in each other's personal development. At times, upperclassmen and graduate student members of Zeta Beta assist and supervise other members of Zeta Beta in their studies. Most Zeta Beta fraternity houses contain a library for use by members. Of the approximately 100,000 alumni, approximately 5,100 contributed money in 1984 to Zeta Beta. An additional 600 alumni participated in Zeta Beta activities in 1984.

The parties agree that Zeta Beta and its subordinate local chapters operate under the lodge system and do not pay insurance benefits to members within the meaning of section 501(c)(10). Zeta Beta concedes that (together with its subordinate local chapters and house corporations) it is a national college fraternity within the meaning of section 1.501(c)(10)–1, Income Tax Regs.

On August 18, 1972, Zeta Beta filed a Return of Organization Exempt from Tax (Form 990) for its taxable year ended June 30, 1971. On June 15, 1973, Zeta Beta filed its Exempt Organization Business Income Tax Return (Form 990–T) for its taxable year ended June 30, 1971. In November of 1975, Zeta Beta filed with respondent an application for a determination that it was tax exempt as a domestic fraternal society under section 501(c)(10). Zeta Beta's application was denied on June 26, 1976. In his letter denying the application, respondent noted that Zeta Beta had 'always operated * * * exclusively for educational, charitable, or fraternal purposes,' but that as a national college fraternity, it was precluded from tax exemption under section 501(c)(10) by section 1.501(c)(10)–1, Income Tax Regs.

On July 8, 1976, Zeta Beta protested respondent's denial of its application for tax-exempt classification as a domestic fraternal society under section 501(c)(10), and requested reconsideration thereof. On September 30, 1977, respondent reaffirmed its denial of Zeta Beta's application. Respondent's notice of deficiency at issue herein followed.

Respondent's computation of the deficiency herein is based on his inclusion in Zeta Beta's unrelated business income the investment income Zeta Beta received in its taxable year ending June 30, 1971.

OPINION

Generally, tax-exempt organizations described in section 501(c) are taxed at regular corporate rates on unrelated business income. Sec. 511(a).

The term "unrelated business taxable income" is defined as the gross income derived from any unrelated trade or business regularly carried on by an organization, less allowable deductions that are directly connected with the conduct of the trade or business. Sec. 512(a). In general, investment income such as dividends, interest, annuities, royalties, rents derived from real property, and capital gains, are excluded from the exempt organization's unrelated business income. Sec. 512(b)(1).

Unrelated business income is described differently, however, for, among other organizations, tax-exempt social clubs described in section 501(c)(7). In the case of a section 501(c)(7) social club, unrelated business taxable income includes all income generated by the organization other than "exempt function income" less expenses related to exempt function income. Sec. 512(a)(3)(A). Exempt function income is defined as the gross income derived from dues, fees, charges, or similar amounts received from organization members or their guests for goods, facilities, or services in furtherance of the tax-exempt purposes of the organization. Sec. 512(a)(3)(B). The result of this difference in the computation of unrelated business taxable income is that investment income of section 501(c)(7) social clubs is taxed as unrelated business income, whereas investment income of section 501(c)(10) fraternal organizations generally is not taxed as unrelated business income.

Zeta Beta, as the central organization of a national college fraternity, received its long-standing tax exemption under the predecessor of section 501(c)(7). Zeta Beta argues, however, that it also properly may be classified as a domestic fraternal society under section 501(c)(10), and that its investment income, therefore, should not be subject to the unrelated business income tax.

Section 501(c)(10), a new category of tax-exempt organizations that was added to the Internal Revenue Code by the Tax Reform Act of 1969, provides a tax exemption for—

> (10) Domestic fraternal societies, orders, or associations, operating under the lodge system—
>
> > (A) the net earnings of which are devoted exclusively to religious, charitable, scientific, literary, educational, and fraternal purposes, and
> >
> > (B) which do not provide for the payment of life, sick, accident, or other benefits.

Treasury regulations relating to section 501(c)(10) expressly state that national college fraternities do not qualify under section 501(c)(10). Section 1.501(c)(10)–1, Income Tax Regs., provides as follows:

* * *

Any organization described in section 501(c)(7), such as, for example, a national college fraternity, is not described in section 501(c)(10) and this section. [Emphasis added.]

Zeta Beta argues that it is an organization that is precisely described by the language of section 501(c)(10) because it is a fraternal society that operates under the lodge system, it does not provide insurance benefits to members, and because its net earnings are devoted exclusively to religious, charitable, scientific, literary, educational, and fraternal purposes. Zeta Beta further argues that it cannot be distinguished factually from organizations such as the Masons, Moose, or Elks clubs which usually are classified by respondent as tax exempt under section 501(c)(10). Zeta Beta, therefore, contends that section 1.501(c)(10)–1, Income Tax Regs., in its exclusion of national college fraternities from tax exemption under section 501(c)(10), establishes an arbitrary distinction that discriminates between two similarly situated taxpayers (namely, national college fraternities and organizations such as the Masons) and is, therefore, to that extent invalid.

Zeta Beta also contends that its classification as a tax-exempt organization described in section 501(c)(7) does not preclude its additional classification under section 501(c)(10). Zeta Beta concludes that if it meets the precise description of a section 501(c)(10) organization, there is no express or implied legislative policy that would deny it an exemption thereunder just because it also may be classified as a section 501(c)(7) social club.

Respondent argues that Zeta Beta is not an organization described in section 501(c)(10) because of the clear congressional intent that national college fraternities be exempt from tax as social clubs under section 501(c)(7). Respondent contends that national college fraternities such as Zeta Beta are fundamentally different from those fraternal organizations, such as the Masons, that Congress intended to qualify for tax exemption under section 501(c)(10). Finally, respondent argues that even if a national college fraternity could qualify for tax exemption under section 501(c)(10), the net earnings of Zeta Beta herein are not exclusively devoted to the exempt purposes listed in section 501(c)(10)(A). For the above reasons, respondent argues that Zeta Beta properly may be classified only as a section 501(c)(7) tax-exempt social club.

After careful review of the relevant statutory provisions, the legislative history thereof, and the facts of this case, we agree with respondent that a national college fraternity such as Zeta Beta may not properly be classified as a domestic fraternal society described in section 501(c)(10).

Contrary to Zeta Beta's contention, the relevant statutory language is not clear and unambiguous. As we recently stated—

> Trying to understand the various exempt organization provisions of the Internal Revenue Code is as difficult as capturing a drop of mercury under your thumb. There are currently 23 categories of exempt organizations under section 501(c) and five categories of organizations recognized as qualified donees of tax deductible contributions under section 170(c). Rarely is it clear that an organization would qualify only under one of the categories of section 501(c), and often it is clear that an organization would qualify under a number of the categories, even though a particular organization may have applied for

and actually received its exemption letter under a single provision of section 501(c).

There is an extensive body of legislative history explaining the changes in 1969 to the unrelated business income tax provisions of the Code and of the addition of paragraph 10 to section 501(c). A decision herein based solely on the statutory language would be based on a mere 'toss of the coin.' Reference to the relevant legislative history, on the other hand, provides significant insight into the relevant statutory language. Under such circumstances, we would be remiss if we were to ignore such assistance.

As explained, the tax exemption for domestic fraternal organizations in section 501(c)(10) had its genesis in the Tax Reform Act of 1969 and arose specifically out of the imposition of the unrelated business income tax on investment income of membership organizations described in sections 501(c)(7) and (c)(9). Congress recognized that a tax-exempt social club or similar group organized for recreational or social purposes merely was an extension of the individual members and that it would be inappropriate to impose a tax on the social club as a separate entity. S. Rept. No. 91–552 (1969), 1969–3 C.B. 423, 429. One court summarized the rationale as follows:

> Congress has determined that in a situation where individuals have banded together to provide recreational facilities on a mutual basis, it would be conceptually erroneous to impose a tax on the organization as a separate entity. The funds exempted are received only from the members and any "profit" which results from overcharging for the use of the facilities still belongs to the same members. No income of the sort usually taxed has been generated; the money has simply been sifted from one pocket to another, both within the same pair of pants. * * * McGlotten v. Connally, 338 F.Supp. 448, 458 (D.D.C.1972).

Where, however, the tax-exempt membership organization receives investment income and uses the tax free income to pay for recreational services offered to its members, the members receive an unintended benefit. As explained in the Senate committee report—

> where the organization receives income from sources outside the membership, such as income from investments (or in the case of employee benefit associations, from the employer), upon which no tax is paid, the membership receives a benefit not contemplated by the exemption in that untaxed dollars can be used by the organization to provide pleasure or recreation (or other benefits) to its membership. For example, if a social club were to receive $10,000 of untaxed income from investment in securities, it could use that $10,000 to reduce the cost or increase the services it provides to its members. In such a case, the exemption is no longer simply allowing individuals to join together for recreation or pleasure without tax consequences. Rather, it is bestowing a substantial additional advantage to the members of the club by allowing tax-free dollars to be used for their personal recreational or pleasure purposes. The extension of the exemption to such

investment income is, therefore, a distortion of its purpose. (S. Rept. No. 91–552, supra at 470.)

The House report accompanying the Tax Reform Act of 1969 notes similar concern with respect to fraternal societies, as follows:

> The receipt of untaxed income by fraternal beneficiary societies for use in providing recreational or social facilities in furtherance of the organization's fraternal purpose creates a similar problem to that of social clubs. * * * (H. Rept. No. 91–413 (1969), 1969–3 C.B. 199, 231.)

Congress recognized, however, that investment income also could be used by tax exempt membership organizations to further the exempt purposes of the organizations and that in such cases the tax on investment income would be inappropriate. Accordingly, the statutory exception found in section 512(a)(3)(B)(i) and (ii) for such income was enacted. As originally proposed by the House, only investment income of fraternal beneficiary associations and employees' beneficiary associations would have been eligible to qualify for this exception. In the Senate Finance Committee, however, the House version was changed to include investment income of social clubs where the investment income of social clubs was set aside for educational or charitable purposes. The Senate committee report explains the change as follows:

> In extending the exemption, the committee intends in the case of *national organizations of college fraternities and sororities* that amounts set aside for scholarships, student loans, loans on local chapter housing, leadership and citizenship schools and services, and similar activities, be classified as amounts used for educational or charitable purposes under this provision. [Emphasis added].

The express reference in the above legislative history to investment income of "national organizations of college fraternities and sororities," makes it very clear that Congress considered the investment income of such organizations to be generally subject to the new unrelated business income tax provisions.

In the general explanation of the 1969 Act issued in 1970 by the Joint Committee on Taxation it was expressly noted that the tax on investment income would apply to national organizations of college fraternities and sororities, unless the investment income thereof is set aside for certain educational or charitable purposes. Staff of Joint Comm. on Taxation, 91st Cong., 1st Sess., General Explanation of the Tax Reform Act of 1969 at 70 (J. Comm. print 1970).

* * *

Zeta Beta's emphasis on its similarity to section 501(c)(10) organizations such as the Masons also is not persuasive. Clearly, like the Masons, Zeta Beta operates under the lodge system and its local chapters engage in some activities that concededly further the charitable and educational goals of the fraternity. We agree with respondent, however, that the predominant purpose of Zeta Beta and its local chapters is to provide housing, board, and social activities for its undergraduate student members. In that respect, Zeta Beta is fundamentally different from fraternal organizations such as the Masons.

Even if we could find no relevant distinction between the purposes and activities of Zeta Beta and the Masons, it is not for this Court to counteract by judicial decision what we conclude is the congressional intent to treat national college fraternities in a manner different from fraternal organizations such as the Masons. Congress has "broad latitude in creating classifications and distinctions in tax statutes." Regan v. Taxation with Representation of Washington, 461 U.S. 540, 547–548 (1983).

Zeta Beta argues that its existing tax exemption under section 501(c)(7) does not preclude it from receiving an additional tax-exempt classification under section 501(c)(10), if it meets the qualifications thereof. As we stated earlier, in some situations an organization may qualify for tax exemption under a number of paragraphs of section 501(c). We have concluded, however, that national college fraternities are intended by Congress to be treated as exempt under section 501(c)(7) and not under section 501(c)(10).

Zeta Beta concedes that college fraternities historically have been granted tax-exempt classification under section 501(c)(7). If Congress had intended in 1969 to change that policy and to allow national college fraternities to be exempt under section 501(c)(10), it is reasonable to conclude that some mention of such a policy change would have been made in the extensive legislative history that accompanied the passage of the Tax Reform Act of 1969. To the contrary, that history (as well as the legislative history accompanying the 1976 amendments to section 501(c)(7)) reiterates the long-standing treatment of national college fraternities as tax-exempt organizations under section 501(c)(7) and the predecessors thereof.

We also note the agreement among commentators that national college fraternities and sororities are tax-exempt social clubs described in section 501(c)(7) and are subject to the unrelated business income tax on investment income. See, e.g., P. Treusch & N. Sugarman, Tax-Exempt Charitable Organizations, ch. 3, sec. E2.03 at 128 (1983); B. Hopkins, The Law of Tax-Exempt Organizations, sec. 18.1 at 303 (1983).

The prohibition in section 1.501(c)(10)–1, Income Tax Regs., on national college fraternities obtaining their tax exemption under section 501(c)(10) is a valid and reasonable interpretation of the statutory provisions as explained above. Treasury regulations must be sustained unless unreasonable and plainly inconsistent with the language, history, and purpose of a statute.

In light of the congressional intent that national college fraternities qualify for their tax-exempt status under section 501(c)(7), and not section 501(c)(10), we agree with respondent that Zeta Beta is not an organization described in section 501(c)(10), and that Zeta Beta is taxable on its investment income under section 512(a)(3)(A).

Accordingly,

Decision will be entered for the respondent.

2. DISCRIMINATION

McGlotten v. Connally

United States District Court, District of Columbia, 1972.
338 F.Supp. 448.

■ BAZELON, CHIEF JUDGE.

[Plaintiff, an African-American allegedly denied membership in a local lodge of the Benevolent and Protective Order of Elks solely because of his race, brought this class action to enjoin the granting of federal tax benefits to fraternal and non-profit organizations that excluded non-whites from membership. After rejecting various jurisdictional arguments raised by the Service, the court turned to the merits. Eds.]

* * *

II. *Failure to State a Claim Upon Which Relief Can Be Granted*

As noted above, plaintiff advances three separate theories in support of his right to relief. He challenges the constitutionality of the statute if, and to the extent that, it authorizes the grant of tax exempt status to nonprofit clubs and fraternal orders, and makes deductible contributions to such fraternal orders. He alternatively claims that the Internal Revenue Code does not authorize the deductibility of contributions to fraternal orders. Finally, plaintiff claims that both exemption from taxation and deductibility of contributions are federal financial assistance in violation of Title VI of the Civil Rights Act of 1964. Since a motion to dismiss for failure to state a claim tests the legal sufficiency of each count of the complaint, we must consider the counts separately.

A. *Constitutionality of Federal Tax Benefits to Segregated Organizations*

Better than one hundred years ago, this country sought to eliminate race as an operative fact in determining the quality of one's life. The decision has yet to be fully implemented. As Mr. Justice Douglas has pointedly stated: "Some badges of slavery remain today. While the institution has been outlawed, it has remained in the minds and hearts of many white men." The minds and hearts of men may be beyond the purview of this or any other court; perhaps those who cling to infantile and ultimately self-destructive notions of their racial superiority cannot be forced to maturity. But the Fifth and Fourteenth Amendments do require that such individuals not be given solace in their delusions by the Government. Nor is this emphasis on the conduct of the Government misplaced. "Government is the social organ to which all in our society look for the promotion of liberty, justice, fair and equal treatment, and the setting of worthy norms and goals for social conduct. Therefore something is uniquely amiss in a society where the government, the authoritative oracle of community values, involves itself in racial discrimination." Where that involvement is alleged, the courts have exercised the most careful scrutiny to ensure that the State lives up to its own promise.

Here plaintiff challenges the constitutionality of various provisions of the Internal Revenue Code to the extent that they authorize the grant of Federal tax benefits to organizations which exclude nonwhites from membership. These provisions exempt from income taxation nonprofit clubs (§ 501(c)(7)) and fraternal orders (§ 501(c)(8)) and make individual contributions to such fraternal orders deductible for income, estate, and gift taxes if the contributions are used "exclusively for religious, charitable, scientific, literary or educational purposes, or for the prevention of cruelty to children or animals." §§ 170(c)(4), 642(c), 2055, 2106(a), 2522. Plaintiff's claim thus leads us into the murky waters of the "state action" doctrine, for we must determine whether by granting tax benefits to private organizations which discriminate on the basis of race in membership, the Federal Government has supported or encouraged private discrimination so as to have itself violated plaintiff's right to the equal protection of the laws.

While a century ago, the phrase "state action"[31] may have sufficiently demarcated the extent of lawful state participation in private discrimination, that clarity has long since vanished in the wake of the greatly expanded role of government in a modern, industrial society. Whether by licensing, contract, or tax, few activities are left wholly untouched by the arm of Government. The responsibilities of the Government under the Fifth and Fourteenth Amendments, however, are not diluted by the expanded scope of Government, and our inquiry has become necessarily more detailed. "[O]nly by sifting facts and weighing circumstances can the nonobvious involvement of the State in private conduct be attributed its true significance." Burton v. Wilmington Parking Authority, 365 U.S. 715, 722, 81 S.Ct. 856, 860, 6 L.Ed.2d 45 (1961).

1. *The Deductibility of Contributions to Fraternal Orders.*

To demonstrate the unconstitutionality of the challenged deductions plaintiff must, of course, show that they in fact aid, perpetuate, or encourage racial discrimination. He alleges, subject to proof at trial, both the substantiality of the benefits provided[37] and a causal relation to the

---

31. Since the grant of tax benefits is certainly an act of the state, it might be more accurate to state the question as whether the act of exemption violates the Fifth Amendment. Cf. Reitman v. Mulkey, 387 U.S. 369, 392, 87 S.Ct. 1627, 18 L.Ed.2d 830 (Harlan, J. dissenting). Nonetheless, the determination of when state involvement is sufficient either to bring otherwise private discrimination within the aegis of the Fifth or Fourteenth Amendment, or to evoke a duty on the part of the government to prevent that discrimination, has traditionally been styled one of "state action." Little clarity is gained at this stage by attaching a different label to the same inquiry depending on who is the defendant.

37. There is no question that allowing the deduction of charitable contributions in fact confers a benefit on the organization receiving the contribution. The court in Green v. Kennedy, supra note 11, described "the impact of Federal tax * * * deduction" as a "matching grant," and we agree.

discrimination practiced by the segregated organizations.[38] But more is required to find a violation of the Constitution. Every deduction in the tax laws provides a benefit to the class who may take advantage of it. And the withdrawal of that benefit would often act as a substantial incentive to eliminate the behavior which caused the change in status. Yet the provision of an income tax deduction for mortgage interest paid has not been held sufficient to make the Federal Government a "joint participant" in the bigotry practiced by a homeowner. An additional line of inquiry is essential, one considering the nature of the Government activity in providing the challenged benefit and necessarily involving the sifting and weighing prescribed in Burton.

The rationale for allowing the deduction of charitable contributions has historically been that by doing so, the Government relieves itself of the burden of meeting public needs which in the absence of charitable activity would fall on the shoulders of the Government. "The Government is compensated for its loss of revenue by its relief from financial burdens which would otherwise have to be met by appropriations from public funds." H.Rep. No. 1860, 75th Cong., 3rd Sess. 19 (1938). And here the Government does more than simply authorize deduction of contributions to any cause which the individual taxpayer deems charitable. The statute, regulations, and administrative rulings thereunder, define in extensive detail not only the purposes which will satisfy the statute, but the vehicles through which those purposes may be achieved as well. A contribution, even for an approved purpose, is deductible only if made to an organization of the type specified in § 170 and which has obtained a ruling or letter of determination from the Internal Revenue Service. Thus the government has marked certain organizations as "Government Approved" with the result that such organizations may solicit funds from the general public on the basis of that approval.

In our view, the Government has become sufficiently entwined with private parties to call forth a duty to ensure compliance with the Fifth Amendment by the parties through whom it chooses to act. We see no difference in the degree to which the Government has "place[d] its power, property and prestige behind the admitted discrimination," Burton v. Wilmington Parking Authority, supra, at 725, 81 S.Ct. at 862, where a private restaurant in a government owned parking facility refuses service to black patrons, and where a tax supported organization by its constitution admits only "white male citizens."[43]

---

38. We do not find it significant that plaintiff does not allege, as was the case in Green v. Kennedy, that the charitable purposes to which the federal funds are put are in themselves discriminatory. Plaintiff alleges that he and others in his position are denied the opportunity to help determine the purposes to which the funds are devoted. Paternalism should not be confused with equality.

43. See Pitts v. Department of Revenue, * * *. The court there held that the grant of exemption from property taxation to organizations which discriminate on the basis of race in their membership violates the Fourteenth Amendment. The statute in question, Wis.Stat. § 70.11(4), made exemption available only to particular organizations, and the parties agreed "that the exemptions are granted on the reasoning that the organizations benefitted serve a public purpose."

The public nature of the activity delegated to the organization in question, the degree of control the Government has retained as to the purposes and organizations which may benefit, and the aura of Government approval inherent in an exempt ruling by the Internal Revenue Service, all serve to distinguish the benefits at issue from the general run of deductions available under the Internal Revenue Code. Certain deductions provided by the Code do not act as matching grants, but are merely attempts to provide for an equitable measure of net income. Others are simply part of the structure of an income tax based on ability to pay. We recognize that an additional class of deductions—such as accelerated depreciation for rehabilitated low income rental property, or deductions for mortgage interest-do act as "incentives" favoring certain types of activities. But unlike the charitable deductions before us, these provisions go no further than simply indicating the activities hoped to be encouraged; they do not expressly choose fraternal organizations as a vehicle for that activity and do not allow such organizations to represent themselves as having the imprimatur of the Government. This seems to us a significant difference of degree in an area where no bright-line rule is possible.

2.   *The Exemption From Income Tax for Nonprofit Clubs and Fraternal Orders.*

The exemptions from income taxation for nonprofit clubs (§ 501(c)(7)) and fraternal orders (§ 501(c)(8)) present more difficult problems. Because their tax treatment is not identical, we consider the exemptions for the two types of groups separately.

Nonprofit Clubs

Plaintiff's claim of unconstitutional aid to private discrimination rests on the following syllogism: Since the Government imposes a tax on all income, § 61(a), and then exempts from taxation the income of nonprofit clubs, an affirmative benefit or subsidy has been provided the exempted groups. After the Tax Reform Act of 1969, the treatment of exempt nonprofit clubs is that all their income, including passive investment income, is taxed at regular corporate rates. They are, however, allowed the equivalent of a deduction for "exempt function income," defined essentially as income derived from members. It is therefore this deduction which provides the allegedly unconstitutional aid.

Unlike the deduction for charitable contributions, the deduction for "exempt function income" does not operate to provide a grant of federal funds through the tax system. Rather, it is part and parcel of defining appropriate subjects of taxation. Congress has determined that in a situation where individuals have banded together to provide recreational facilities on a mutual basis, it would be conceptually erroneous to impose a tax on the organization as a separate entity. The funds exempted are received only from the members and any "profit" which results from overcharging for the use of the facilities still belongs to the same members. No income of the sort usually taxed has been generated; the money has simply been shifted from one pocket to another, both within the same pair of pants. Thus the exclusion of member generated revenue reflects a determination that as to these funds the organization does not operate as a separate entity.

That the Government provides no monetary benefit does not, however, insulate its involvement from constitutional scrutiny. The lease in Burton was, as far as the record shows, entirely arm's length with no provision of federal property at less than market value. Encouragement of discrimination through the appearance of governmental approval may also be sufficient involvement to violate the Constitution. But here the necessary involvement is not readily apparent. Section 501(c)(7) does not limit its coverage to particular activities; exemption is given to "[c]lubs organized and operated exclusively for pleasure, recreation and other nonprofitable purposes * * * "(emphasis added.) Thus there is no mark of Government approval inherent in the designation of a group as exempt. Congress has simply chosen not to tax a particular type of revenue because it is not within the scope sought to be taxed by the statute. And however dysfunctional the "state action" limitation is at a time when the nation has sufficiently matured that the elimination of racial discrimination is a cornerstone of national policy, it still means that Congress does not violate the Constitution by failing to tax private discrimination where there is no other act of Government involvement. To find a violation solely from the State's failure to act would, however laudably, eliminate the "state action" doctrine and that must come from the Supreme Court. The motion to dismiss is granted as to the claim that the exemption for § 501(c)(7) nonprofit clubs violates the Constitution.

Fraternal Orders

The exemption given to fraternal organizations under § 501(c)(8) stands on different footing. Unlike nonprofit clubs, fraternal organizations are taxed only on "unrelated business taxable income" defined as "any trade or business the conduct of which is not substantially related (aside from the need of such organization for income or funds or the use it makes of the profits derived) to the exercise or performance by such organization of its charitable, educational, or other purpose or function constituting the basis for the exemption under section 501 ... " The crucial impact of this differential treatment is that the passive investment income of fraternal orders is not taxed. This exemption cannot be explained simply by the inappropriateness of taxing the organization as a separate entity in this situation. Here individuals are providing funds which are then invested for the purposes of benefiting the contributing members, and the exemption of this income is a "benefit" provided by the Government.

We think this exclusion, provided only to particular organizations with particular purposes, rather than across the board, is sufficient government involvement to invoke the Fifth Amendment. By providing differential treatment to only selected organizations, the Government has indicated approval of the organizations and hence their discriminatory practice, and aided that discrimination by the provision of federal tax benefits.

B. *Claim that the Internal Revenue Code Does Not Authorize the Deductibility of Contributions to Segregated Fraternal Organizations*

Plaintiff also alleges that the deductibility of contributions to fraternal organizations which exclude nonwhites from membership is not authorized by the Internal Revenue Code.[59] Contributions to fraternal organizations exempt under § 501(c)(8) are deductible under §§ 170(c)(4), 642(c), 2055, 2106(a), and 2522, if used exclusively for the purposes there listed. Plaintiff argues that because such contributions also perpetuate the existence of an organization which discriminates on the basis of race, the exclusivity requirement is not satisfied.

Only recently a three-judge court of this District considered the application of the statutes in question to the benefits granted to segregated private schools. Green v. Connally, 330 F.Supp. 1150 (D.D.C.1971), aff'd sub nom. Coit v. Green, 404 U.S. 997, 92 S.Ct. 564, 30 L.Ed.2d 550 (1971)(mem.). The Court there held that since "the Congressional intent in providing tax deductions and exemptions is not construed to be applicable to activities that are either illegal or against public policy," the overwhelming federal policy against segregated education required that the Internal Revenue Code "no longer be construed so as to provide private schools operating on a racially discriminatory premise the support of the exemptions and deductions which Federal tax law affords to charitable organizations and their sponsors."

In *Green*, the Court felt its construction of the Code was "underscored by the fact that it obviates the need to determine * * * serious constitutional claims." Since the constitutional claim here, unlike in *Green*, was challenged by a motion to dismiss, and since we therefore cannot avoid plaintiff's serious constitutional claim, we have already determined that the tax deductions in question, if authorized, would violate the Fifth Amendment. As such, we would be bound to interpret the Code as not allowing the deduction of contributions to segregated fraternal orders. We do not think, however, that the correctness of that construction depends on the finding of state action which underlies our constitutional determination. The Thirteenth Amendment clothed "Congress with power to pass all laws necessary and proper for abolishing all badges and incidents of slavery in the United States," Civil Rights Cases, 109 U.S. 3, 20, 3 S.Ct. 18, 28, 27 L.Ed. 835 (1883), and that expression of constitutional concern has been held to include acts of private discrimination. Jones v. Alfred H. Mayer Co., 392 U.S. 409, 88 S.Ct. 2186, 20 L.Ed.2d 1189 (1968). Further, in what we find an analogous area, Congress, by Section 601 of the Civil Rights Act of 1964, 42 U.S.C.A. § 2000d, has provided that racial discrimination cannot be practiced by those receiving "federal financial assistance." Whether or

59. Under Count 3 of the complaint, unlike the other counts, Plaintiff attacks only the deductibility of contributions and not the tax exempt status of the organizations themselves.

not tax benefits of the sort at issue here are "federal financial assistance" within the terms of the Civil Rights Act, see Part IIC infra, there is a clearly indicated Congressional policy that the beneficiaries of federal largesse should not discriminate. We think this overriding public policy, even in the absence of our constitutional holding in Part IIA, requires that the Code not be construed to allow the deduction of contributions to organizations which exclude nonwhites from membership.

[The Court then considered the plaintiff's allegations that the granting of federal tax benefits to organizations excluding non-whites from membership was a form of federal financial assistance in violation of Title VI of the 1964 Civil Rights Act (46 U.S.C.A. § 2000d et seq.) It concluded that while the tax deduction for charitable contributions and the tax exemption for fraternal orders constituted "federal financial assistance," the exemption of social clubs did not. Eds.]

III.   *Conclusion*

We have no illusion that our holding today will put an end to racial discrimination or significantly dismantle the social and economic barriers that may be more subtle, but are surely no less destructive. Individuals may retain their own beliefs, however odious or offensive. But the Supreme Court has declared that the Constitution forbids the Government from supporting and encouraging such beliefs. By eliminating one more of the "nonobvious involvement[s] of the State in private conduct," we obey the Court's command to quarantine racism.

NOTES

1. *Section 501(i).* After *McGlotten* was decided, Congress enacted § 501(i), which disqualifies a social club from exemption if at any time during its taxable year the charter, bylaws, or other governing instruments of the organization, or any written policy statement, contain a provision which provides for discrimination against any person on the basis of race, color or religion. The prohibition is intended to extend to discrimination against guests and other persons, such as employees. In 1980, at the behest of the Knights of Columbus, Congress added an exception to § 501(i) permitting clubs and certain auxiliaries of fraternal societies to discriminate on the basis of religion, if they in good faith limit their membership to members of a particular religion in order to further their principles, rather than to exclude individuals of a particular race or color.

2. *Other Legal Issues: Private Associations and the Constitution.* State and local governments have been more aggressive than the IRS in seeking to eliminate discrimination by private membership associations through public accommodation laws and property tax exemption measures. Many of these efforts have been challenged as violative of First Amendment freedom of association rights. The resulting Supreme Court jurisprudence has drawn a distinction between the constitutional protection granted for "expressive" and "non-expressive" association. Affected groups range from

§ 501(c)(3) membership organizations, such as the Junior Chamber of Commerce and Boy Scouts of America, to private social clubs.

In its first major constitutional decision on private associations and the Constitution, the Supreme Court rejected a challenge by the United States Jaycees, which at one time limited its regular membership to young men between the ages of 18 and 35, to a Minnesota law that prohibited discrimination in places of public accommodation on the basis of race, color, creed, religion, disability, national origin, or sex. Finding that the Jaycees were neither small nor selective, the Court held that they did not foster the type of intimate relationship that was worthy of constitutional protection. The Court went on to conclude that the Minnesota law, enacted to remove barriers to economic advancement from historically disadvantaged groups, was not aimed at the suppression of speech. As a result, it held that requiring the Jaycees to admit women did not impinge on any right to freedom of expression. Roberts v. United States Jaycees, 468 U.S. 609, 104 S.Ct. 3244 (1984). See also Board of Directors of Rotary International v. Rotary Club of Duarte, 481 U.S. 537, 107 S.Ct. 1940 (1987)(application of California's Unruh Act, requiring equal accommodations regardless of sex in any state "business establishment," did not violate Rotary Club members' First Amendment associational rights; the Rotary Club did not deserve constitutional protection because of its large size, high turnover rate, inclusive nature of its membership, the public purpose behind its service activities, and the compelling state interest in eliminating discrimination against women and assuring them equal access to public accommodation).

State and local public accommodation laws also have profoundly affected the membership practices of many private social and luncheon clubs. In New York State Club Association v. City of New York, 487 U.S. 1, 108 S.Ct. 2225 (1988), the Supreme Court rejected a challenge to a New York City ordinance that extended its prohibition on discrimination to private clubs that were determined to be sufficiently "public." An exemption was provided for "any institution, club or place of accommodation which is in is nature distinctly private." Specifically covered by the antidiscrimination law were clubs with more than 400 members that provided regular meal services, or regularly received payments for dues, fees, use of space, facilities, services, meals or beverages from nonmembers "for the furtherance of trade or business." N.Y.C. Admin. Code § 8–102(9) (1986). The Court upheld the law, finding that it employed the least restrictive means to achieve its goal of eliminating discrimination against women and minorities. It was significant that the law only affected relatively large clubs that had a commercial hue and it exempted religious and benevolent organizations. The larger clubs, particularly those that provided a regular setting for business meals or generated revenue from dealing with non-members, did not have a strong case that they were formed for an expressive purpose deserving of constitutional protection. See also Frank v. Ivy Club, 120 N.J. 73, 576 A.2d 241 (1990), cert. denied, 498 U.S. 1073, 111 S.Ct. 799 (1991), where the New Jersey Supreme Court, upholding a state law banning gender discrimination in public accommodations, required Princeton University's Ivy and Tiger Inn eating clubs to admit women.

What then, does it take, to mount a successful constitutional challenge to a state public accommodations law? One controversial answer can be found in the Supreme Court's decision in Boy Scouts of America v. Dale, 530 U.S. 640, 120 S.Ct. 2446 (2000), where the Court held that application of New Jersey's public accommodation law violated the First Amendment insofar as it required local Boy Scout chapters to admit homosexuals as members. The New Jersey Supreme Court, determining that the state had a compelling interest in eliminating the destructive consequences of discrimination from society, had found that the Boy Scouts' ability to disseminate its message and adhere to its moral values would not be adversely affected by admitting homosexual boys as members and scoutmasters. It emphasized the Boy Scouts' large size, nonselectivity, inclusive purpose, and practice of allowing nonmembers to attend meetings. The New Jersey Supreme Court was not persuaded that a shared goal of Boy Scout members was to associate in order to preserve the view that homosexuality is immoral

A divided U.S. Supreme Court disagreed, stressing that a critical element of the Boy Scouts' mission was to instill values in young people—a form of expressive activity that would be significantly affected by the New Jersey law because of the Boy Scouts' assertion that homosexual conduct was inconsistent with the values embodied by the Scout Oath and Law (to be "morally straight" and "clean"). After finding that the Boy Scouts was an expressive association and that the forced inclusion of a gay assistant scoutmaster would significantly affect its expression, the Court majority had little difficulty taking the final step and held that application of the New Jersey public accommodation law ran afoul of the Scouts' freedom of expressive association, outweighing New Jersey's compelling interest in eliminating discrimination.

Subsequent events suggest that the Boy Scouts may have won a Phyrric victory in the Supreme Court. Shortly after the decision was rendered, various state and local governments, corporations and individuals withdrew their support. Some local jurisdictions went so far as to prohibit the Boy Scouts from using public facilities or conducting programs in conjunction with public schools. Further litigation is likely.

3. *For Further Reading.* Boris I. Bittker & Kenneth M. Kaufman, Constitutionalizing the Internal Revenue Code, 82 Yale L.J. 51 (1972).

3. NONMEMBER ACTIVITIES

At one time, a social club qualified for exemption under § 501(c)(7) only if it was "organized and operated exclusively for pleasure, recreation * * * and similar exempt purposes." In 1976, Congress relaxed the "exclusively" requirement. A club now qualifies if "substantially all" of its activities are for the recreational and other exempt purposes listed in the

Code. This amendment was intended to make it clear that a social club may receive outside income, including investment income, without losing its exempt status and to permit clubs to derive a somewhat higher level of income from the use of their facilities or services by non-members. The trade-off is that this type of income may be taxable as unrelated business income.

The legislative history provides the following guidelines to measure the permissible extent of nonmember income:

(1) A club may receive up to 35 percent of its gross receipts, including investment income, from nonmember sources.

(2) In applying the 35 percent test above, not more than 15 percent of total gross receipts may be derived from the use of the club's facilities or services by the general public.

(3) If a club has outside income that exceeds either the 35 or 15 percent limits, a facts and circumstances test will be applied to determine qualification for exemption under § 501(c)(7).

(4) For purposes of these tests, "gross receipts" means receipts from normal and usual activities of the club, including charges, admissions, membership fees, dues, assessments, investment income and normal recurring capital gains on investments but excluding initiation fees and capital contributions. Where a club receives unusual amounts of bunched income—e.g., gain from the sale of its clubhouse-that income will not be included in the gross receipts formula.

See S. Rep. No. 94–1318, 94th Cong., 2d Sess. (1976).

It is important to remember that satisfying the safe harbor tests for nonmember income does not automatically protect a club from loss of exemption. A club still may be disqualified if its members do not "commingle" sufficiently or if the club engages in excessive activities, even of a non-income producing nature, that do not serve its exempt purposes. Private inurement is also prohibited. For example, the Service takes the position that where a club has different membership classes which enjoy the same rights and privileges but are treated differently for purposes of dues and initiation fees, inurement of private gain may result because the classes paying the lower dues are being subsidized by the members of the classes paying more. See Rev. Rul. 70–48, 1970–1 C.B. 133.

PROBLEMS

1.   Consider whether the following organizations are exempt as social clubs under § 501(c)(7):

(a) The Suburban Golf and Country Club has 450 members, none of whom are African-American or Jewish. Neither the club's charter nor any written policy statements authorize discrimination on the basis of race or religion, but new members must obtain five "sponsors" who already belong to the club. This policy has been in effect during the club's 92 years of operation.

(b) The Oyster Cracker Club, a luncheon club in a major U.S. city, has male members of all races, creeds and colors but no women members. Women are not permitted in the main dining room or bar, but they may be guests at functions held in the club's private rooms.

(c) Same as (b), above, except the club has only women members.

2. The Argonaut Club, which has both men and women members, provides traditional services that include a dining room, lounges and private rooms for meetings and parties. The club is known for its wonderful food. In an effort to provide more services for members (and raise revenue), the club is considering the activities described below. Which, if any, of these activities will jeopardize the club's tax-exempt status?

(a) Sale of food products, such as turkey and ham platters and baked goods, to members to be consumed off the club's premises. The products could be packaged as gift items or for the convenience of members seeking "take out" service.

(b) Sale of flower arrangements to be taken off club property.

(c) Renting club parking spaces to members to be used while they are at work.

(d) Renting rooms to members who live in the suburbs but wish to stay overnight in the city while attending the theater, symphony or club functions.

(e) Engaging in any of the foregoing transactions with nonmembers.

E. OTHER MUTUAL BENEFIT ORGANIZATIONS

1. VETERANS ORGANIZATIONS

Until 1972, veterans organizations were exempt as social welfare organizations under § 501(c)(4) or as social clubs under § 501(c)(7). To protect veterans organizations from exposure to the unrelated business tax on income derived from insuring their members, Congress created a new exemption category in § 501(c)(19) and added a specific unrelated business tax exemption for veterans groups in § 512(a)(4). In addition, contributions to veterans organizations are tax-deductible under § 170(c)(3).

A veterans organization qualifies for exemption under § 501(c)(19) if:

(1) It is organized in the United States or its possessions;

(2) At least 75 percent of its members are past or present "members of the Armed Forces" (whether or not "war veterans") and substantially all the other members are cadets or spouses, widows or widowers of members of the Armed Forces or cadets;

(3) At least 97.5 percent of its members are veterans, students in college or university ROTC programs, students at armed services academies, and spouses and surviving spouses of these veterans or students; and

(4) No part of the net earnings of the organization inures to the benefit of any private shareholder or individual.

See also Treas. Reg. § 1.501(c)(19)–1(b).

The regulations elaborate on the permissible exempt purposes of a veterans organization. They include assisting disabled veterans and current members of the armed forces and their dependents, entertaining and caring for hospitalized veterans, perpetuating the memory of deceased veterans and comforting their survivors, carrying on traditional charitable and educational programs, sponsoring patriotic activities, providing insurance benefits, and providing social and recreational activities for members. Treas. Reg. § 1.501(c)(19)–1(c). Significantly, veterans organizations historically have been permitted to lobby in furtherance of these exempt purposes without limitation. The Supreme Court has upheld the constitutionality of this favorable treatment of veterans organizations as compared to § 501(c)(3) public charities. See Regan v. Taxation With Representation of Washington, 461 U.S. 540, 103 S.Ct. 1997 (1983), supra, at p. 301.

Section 501(c)(23) confers exempt status on a separate (and narrow) category of organization that was founded before 1880 and whose principal purpose is to provide insurance and other benefits to veterans or their dependents provided that more than 75 percent of the organization's members are present or past members of the armed forces.

2. POLITICAL ORGANIZATIONS

Political organizations are a hybrid form of tax-exempt organization. For tax purposes, a political organization is a group or fund organized and operated primarily to accept contributions or make expenditures for an "exempt function." I.R.C. § 527(e)(1). Exempt functions include influencing or attempting to influence the selection, nomination, election, or appointment of individuals to any Federal, state, or local public office or office in a political organization, or the election of Presidential or Vice Presidential electors, whether or not these individuals are selected, nominated, elected, or appointed. I.R.C. § 527(e)(2).

Political organizations are taxable on their "political organization taxable income," which is defined as the organization's gross income other than "exempt function income" less directly related expenses of the nonexempt income. I.R.C. § 527(b), (c)(1). Exempt function income includes: (1) contributions, (2) membership dues, fees, and assessments, (3) proceeds from political fundraising events and sales of campaign materials, and (4) proceeds of bingo games, to the extent all these amounts are segregated for use for the organization's exempt functions. I.R.C. § 527(c)(3).

As a practical matter, all of this means that political organizations are not taxed on contributions and other income generated by their political activities, but they are taxable, at the highest corporate rate (currently 35 percent), on their net investment income. I.R.C. § 527(b)(1). Even if a political organization has investment income, it may be able to avoid tax under § 527 by establishing a "separate segregated fund" (a simple checking or savings account would suffice) to receive contributions and make political expenditures. I.R.C. § 527(f)(3); Treas. Reg. § 1.527–2(b)(1). Segregated funds are treated as separate entities for tax purposes.

Section 527(f) links the taxing scheme outlined above to those § 501(c) organizations-primarily § 501(c)(4) social welfare organizations, § 501(c)(5) labor unions, and § 501(c)(6) business leagues—that make expenditures for an exempt function, such as participating in a political campaign or seeking to influence a nomination of a Supreme Court appointee. These organizations generally are taxed on the lesser of their net investment income, or the aggregate amount spent for exempt functions. I.R.C. § 527(f)(1). The application of § 527 to an exempt organization that controls an affiliated political action committee is discussed in Chapter 2F6, supra, at pp. 337–338.

3.   Title Holding Companies

Exempt organizations occasionally form separate nonprofit entities to hold title to their property, collect the income, pay expenses, and distribute the net earnings to the exempt parent-beneficiary. Nonprofits first formed title holding companies to overcome state law obstacles to direct holding of title to real property. More recently, title holding companies have served to insulate exempt organizations from liability, enhance the owner's ability to borrow against the property, simplify accounting and management, and facilitate compliance with state property law requirements.

Section 501(c)(2) grants exempt status to a title holding company that may hold any type of property (not just real estate), usually for the benefit of one exempt organization. Section 501(c)(25) confers exemption to corporations or trusts organized for the exclusive purpose of holding title to real property, and collecting and remitting the income to one or more qualified exempt organizations (including pension trusts and § 501(c)(3) organizations) provided that the entity has no more than 35 shareholders or beneficiaries. The purpose of § 501(c)(25), which was added to the Code in 1986, was described as follows by the Joint Committee on Taxation staff:

> The Congress concluded that smaller, unrelated tax-exempt organizations should be able to pool investment funds for purposes of investing in real property through a title-holding company * * * with generally the same tax treatment as is available to a larger tax-exempt organization having a title-holding subsidiary that is tax-exempt as an organization described in section 501(c)(2).

Staff of Joint Comm. on Taxation, 99th Cong., 2d Sess., General Explanation of the Tax Reform Act of 1986 at 1328 (Comm. Print 1987).

Prior to 1993, title holding companies lost their exempt status if they generated any unrelated business income from activities other than collecting income from their property and remitting it to their exempt parent-beneficiary. Treas. Reg. § 1.501(c)(2)–1. In 1993, however, Congress enacted an obscure but important amendment that permits all § 501(c)(2) and § 501(c)(25) title holding companies to receive up to 10 percent of gross income from incidental unrelated business activities without affecting their exempt status. I.R.C. § 501(c)(25)(G). The change was intended to provide relief to title holding companies holding large properties, such as apartment houses or shopping centers, that derived income from parking garages and vending machines. H.R.Rep. No. 103–111, 103d Cong., 1st Sess. 618–619 (1993).

4. OTHER EXEMPT ORGANIZATIONS

The remaining categories of mutual benefit organizations may be vitally important to their founders and members, but they are highly specialized and thus beyond the scope of our coverage. They include: nonprofit cemetery companies (I.R.C. § 501(c)(13)); employee benefit organizations, such as voluntary employee beneficiary associations (I.R.C. § 501(c)(9)); trusts to provide group legal services (I.R.C. § 501(c)(20)); trusts to provide supplemental unemployment compensation benefits (I.R.C. § 501(c)(17)); local teachers' retirement funds (I.R.C. § 501(c)(11)); trusts to compensate coal miners for disability or death due to certain diseases covered by the Black Lung laws (I.R.C. § 501(c)(21)); and various types of mutual insurance, ditch and irrigation, cooperative electric, and telephone companies (I.R.C. § 501(c)(12), (14)–(16)). In addition, homeowners associations may elect to be treated as exempt organizations, limiting their tax liability to 30 percent of their investment income and amounts received from nonmembers for the use of association property. I.R.C. § 528.

*

PART THREE

TAXATION OF BUSINESS AND INVESTMENT INCOME

CHAPTER 5 The Unrelated Business Income Tax

CHAPTER 5

THE UNRELATED BUSINESS INCOME TAX

A. INTRODUCTION

A nonprofit organization does not necessarily lose its exempt status by engaging in commercial activities. Even the conduct of a highly profitable business is not fatal if it furthers the organization's exempt purposes. But what if an exempt organization earns a profit from the active conduct of a business that has no discernible relationship to its exempt purposes and directly competes with for-profit businesses? Consider, for example, a university-owned pizza parlor that solicits business from the general public, underpricing an off-campus establishment that must pay taxes on its income. Should the university's exemption extend to its pizza profits on the theory that, like tuition and endowment income, the profits are used for educational purposes? Or should those earnings be taxed to eliminate the potential for unfair competition? And if unfair competition is the problem, why not tax profits from any competitive business, such as a prosperous university bookstore, even if it is closely related to the school's educational mission? These questions set the stage for a study of one of the most contentious topics in the law of tax-exempt organizations—the unrelated business income tax. Subject to a host of exceptions, the "UBIT," as it is familiarly known, is generally imposed on the net income of any trade or business that is regularly carried on by an exempt organization and which is not substantially related to the organization's exempt purposes. I.R.C. § 511 et seq.

The UBIT has been the subject of lively discussion for decades. Over 50 years ago, much like today, the popular press warned of the perceived abuses of tax exemption. A December, 1948 front-page story in The New York Times described how universities were being used as tax shelters for business profits.[1] Two years later, an article in Fortune magazine was titled with the exhortation: "The Abuse of Tax Exemption: It Has Got to the Point Where Something Has to Be Done About It."[2] As this chapter will reveal, something *was* done in 1950. But the entrepreneurial pursuits of nonprofits continued, attracting the attention of the small business community, Congressional taxwriting committees, the Internal Revenue Service,

---

1. Benjamin Fine, University Dollars Yielding Tax-Free Business Profits, N.Y. Times, Dec. 13, 1948, at A1, A29.

2. Fortune, May 1950, at 74.

muckraking journalists, *New Yorker* cartoons[3] and last, but not least, economists and legal scholars.

The contemporary conventional wisdom is that the nonprofit sector has undergone a commercial transformation. To replace traditional sources of revenue, more nonprofits are said to be straying from their stated mission as they increasingly mimic for-profit firms. The excerpt that follows, from a study by economists and social scientists, describes this phenomenon.

Burton A. Weisbrod, The Nonprofit Mission and Its Financing: Growing Links Between Nonprofits and the Rest of the Economy

To Profit or Not to Profit: The Commercial Transformation of the Nonprofit Sector 1–4 (Burton A. Weisbrod, ed. 1998).

Massive change is occurring in the nonprofit sector. Seemingly isolated events touching the lives of virtually everyone are, in fact, parts of a pattern that is little recognized but has enormous impact; it is a pattern of growing commercialization of nonprofit organizations:

Nonprofit *hospitals* are launching health clubs open to the public, with the latest exercise equipment and Olympic-size swimming pools, generating substantial profits and threatening the for-profit fitness center industry.

Nonprofit *museums* are opening glitzy retail shops, generating revenue that is now a larger percentage of operating income than that from federal funding or admissions and memberships.

Nonprofit *universities* are engaging in research alliances with private firms and suppressing research findings that are unfavorable to those firms' profit prospects.

Nonprofits in various industries are forming for-profit subsidiaries, engaging in joint ventures with private firms, and paying executives compensation at "Fortune 500" levels.

Commercialism in the nonprofit sector sounds like a paradox: Nonprofits are supposed to be different from private firms, for whom commercialism is their very lifeblood. To some people, though, the uniqueness of nonprofit organizations is by no means self-evident; perhaps they are really not different from private firms, but are just as influenced by business motives and opportunities for self-aggrandizement.

Late in 1997 two apparently unrelated events brought front-page headlines. One involved a contract between the American Medical Association and the Sunbeam Corporation, a manufacturer of consumer electronic products, with the AMA promising to endorse Sunbeam products, such as

---

3. December 15, 1976 cartoon depicted Santa Claus saying to his elves, "I've been thinking. This year, instead of *giving* every- thing away, why don't we charge a little something." The authors thank Professor John Simon for this discovery.

heating pads and vaporizers, in return for payments expected to yield millions of dollars. The other involved the purchase by Chicago's Field Museum of Natural History of "Sue," the largest complete *Tyrannosaurus rex* fossil in existence—the $8.3 million cost being financed largely by McDonald's and the Walt Disney Company. McDonald's will get several "life-size replicas of the ferocious dinosaur, one of the most widely recognized dinosaurs and a powerful promotional tool," and one of the replicas will be displayed at McDonald's DinoLand USA attraction at Disney's new Animal Kingdom theme park. In addition, the museum will display the original in its new McDonald's Fossil Preparatory Laboratory, and there is talk of miniatures, with the Field Museum name, being included in hamburger Happy Meals.

Both the AMA and Field Museum cases involved nonprofit, tax-exempt organizations contracting to receive multimillion-dollar payments from private firms. Both arrangements generated money but also criticism. The criticism of the AMA was so intense that its top leadership resigned and the AMA broke the agreement with Sunbeam, resulting in a $20 million breach-of-contract lawsuit.

The nonprofit sector has been both criticized and acclaimed. The rationale for its special tax treatment and subsidies rests on the belief that it provides services that are materially different from, and preferred to, the services that private enterprise provides. * * * [Prof. Weisbrod then describes the growth of the nonprofit sector and suggests that it reflects an increase in the gap between perceived social needs and the capacity of government to provide these public-type services. Eds.]

As the nonprofit sector grows, the debate over its proper role in a modern economy continues, periodically grabbing public attention: private firms claim they are victims of "unfair competition" from subsidized, tax-exempt, nonprofits, pressuring lawmakers to restrict nonprofits' commercial activities; the federal government considers revising the personal income tax in ways that will affect incentives to donate to charitable nonprofits; local governments introduce the latest device for extracting money from supposedly tax-exempt nonprofits.

In short, what brings the activities into the limelight is their links with the rest of the economy. Contrary to the common view, nonprofits are far from independent of private enterprise and government. They compete with and collaborate with these other organizations in countless ways in their efforts to finance themselves, to find workers, managers, and other resources to produce their outputs, and to develop markets for those outputs.

————

Professor Weisbrod's study proceeds to examine the extent to which the increasing commercialization affects the behavior of nonprofit organizations, both generally and in specific sectors such as health, education and the arts. This chapter has a narrower focus, limiting its coverage to the tax system's response to the pursuit of profits by nonprofits. We begin with a brief history of the UBIT and a survey of the current tax policy debate. The chapter then considers the application and scope of the tax, with an emphasis on contemporary controversies, and concludes by evaluating proposals for reform.

1.   HISTORICAL BACKGROUND

When the unrelated business income tax was added to the Internal Revenue Code in 1950, it represented a legislative retreat from unbridled tax exemption for nonprofit organizations. Previously, the prevailing view was that an organization conducting a business nonetheless qualified for exemption if its profits were dedicated to charitable or other exempt purposes. The origins of this destination of income test can be traced back to a dispute between the Insular Collector of the Philippine Islands, then under U.S. jurisdiction, and Sagrada Orden de Predicadores, an ancient Philippine religious order with missions throughout the Far East. The order derived the bulk of its income from large real estate and securities holdings and more modest revenue from the sale of wine, chocolates and other articles for use within its religious missions. The Insular Collector, even while conceding that the religious charity was organized and operated for exempt purposes, argued that it was not operated "exclusively" for such purposes because it derived significant revenue from commercial sources. In Trinidad v. Sagrada Orden,[1] the Supreme Court ruled that the charity qualified for tax exemption, holding that the earliest predecessor of § 501(c)(3) permitted exempt organizations to have net income and "said nothing about the source of the income, but makes the destination the ultimate test of exemption."[2] In discussing the organization's income from the sale of wines and chocolates, the court observed that all goods sold by Sagrada Orden were either for religious use or "incidental" to the charity's missionary activities.[3]

An important principle from *Sagrada Orden*—that an organization may be "exclusively" operated for exempt purposes even if it engages in some insubstantial income-producing activities—already has been discussed in Chapter 2.[4] A close reading of *Sagrada Orden* does not reveal that the religious charity was engaged in any business that was unrelated to its exempt purposes. The bulk of its revenue was from passive investments, and its sales of wine and chocolates apparently were related to its religious mission. Yet this landmark case gave birth to another principle: a tax-exempt organization does not lose its exemption by virtue of the conduct of an unrelated business as long as its profits are dedicated to charitable or other exempt purposes.

Sagrada Orden's "destination of income" test had its heyday in the 1930's and 1940's as a handful of exempt organizations began engaging in

---

1. 263 U.S. 578, 44 S.Ct. 204 (1924).

2. Id. at 581, 44 S.Ct. at 205.

3. Id. at 582, 44 S.Ct. at 206.

4. See Chapter 2E1, supra, at pp. 246–249.

commercial activities, either directly or through separate entities (known as "feeders") that operated a business and distributed the profits to their tax-exempt owners. In one of the earliest cases, the Second Circuit upheld the exempt status of a corporation operating a large bathing beach business near Far Rockaway in New York City. The organization's revenues, which came from the rental of bath houses, bathing suits, towels and beach-related concessions, all were paid over to a charitable foundation created by the late owner of the beach. The court held that a corporation engaged exclusively in commercial activities qualified for tax-exempt status so long as all of its net profits were turned over to a legitimate charitable organization.[5] In a later and more notorious case, the Third Circuit held that C.F. Mueller Co., then the nation's largest manufacturer of noodles and macaroni, qualified for exemption under § 501(c)(3) because its pasta profits were distributed to its sole shareholder, New York University, for the exclusive benefit of its School of Law.[6] This case was working its way through the courts as Congress debated the first UBIT bill. It prompted Representative John Dingell to warn that unless action was taken "the macaroni monopoly will be in the hands of the university * * * and eventually all the noodles produced in this country will be produced by corporations held or created by universities," depriving the Treasury of any tax revenue from an entire industry.[7]

Relying on the destination of income test, more nonprofits began engaging in commercial activities having no relationship to their exempt purposes. Although New York University was best known for its School of Law's macaroni business, the university also owned Howes Leather Company, American Limoges China, and Ramsey Corporation, a manufacturer of piston rings.[8] Other nonprofits acquired real estate from for-profit taxpayers, usually borrowing to finance the purchase, and then leased the property back to the seller for a lengthy term. In 1942, the Treasury Department prodded Congress to hold hearings on the subject, and two perceived abuses were identified: loss of revenue and unfair competition. But it was not until the Revenue Act of 1950 that Congress finally responded. First, it imposed a tax on the "unrelated business income" of most (but not all)[9] tax-exempt organizations. Second, it withdrew exempt status from feeder corporations by providing, in the predecessor to current § 502, that an organization primarily engaged in a trade or business for profit does not qualify for exemption merely because its profits are destined for charitable ends. The

---

5. Roche's Beach v. Commissioner, 96 F.2d 776 (2d Cir.1938). Judge Learned Hand dissented, noting correctly that Trinidad v. Sagrada Orden was distinguishable because the business income in that case was "very trifling." 96 F.2d at 779. Judge Hand believed that a "business subsidiary" should not be exempt, without regard to where its income was destined.

6. C.F. Mueller Co. v. Commissioner, 190 F.2d 120 (3d Cir.1951).

7. Hearings Before the House Comm. on Ways and Means, 81st Cong., 2d Sess. 579–80 (1950).

8. For more on this early history, see Donald L. Sharpe, Unfair Business Competition and the Tax on Income Destined for Charity: Forty–Six Years Later, 3 Fla. Tax Rev. 367, 380–383 (1996).

9. Churches, social clubs, and fraternal beneficiary societies were exempt from the earliest version of the UBIT.

legislative history indicates that Congress's primary concern was the perceived problem of unfair competition. Both the House and Senate Reports stated that:[10]

> The problem at which the tax on unrelated business income is directed is primarily that of unfair competition. The tax-free status of [section 501(c)(3)] organizations enables them to use their profits tax-free to expand operations, while their competitors can expand only with the profits remaining after taxes. Also, a number of examples have arisen where these organizations have, in effect, used their tax exemptions to buy an ordinary business. That is, they have acquired the business with little or no investment on their own part and paid for it in installments out of subsequent earnings—a procedure which usually could not be followed if the business were taxable.

The statutory regime that we are about to study, however, says little or nothing about competition, and it is apparent that the need for revenue to finance the Korean War and more generalized fairness concerns also influenced enactment of the UBIT.[11]

The 1950 legislation forever altered the economic stakes of unrelated business activity by most nonprofits, but it did not completely address the problem. Churches had successfully lobbied for a complete exemption from the UBIT, as did social clubs and fraternal beneficiary societies. When churches began exploiting their favored status, even the sensibilities of religious leaders were offended, a condition that was exacerbated by unfavorable publicity and constitutional challenges.[12] After much deliberation, the mainstream religious community shifted its position and, in 1969, the National Council of Churches and the United States Catholic Conference urged Congress to eliminate the UBIT church exemption. Congress willingly obliged in the Tax Reform Act of 1969 by extending the tax to churches as well as social clubs and fraternal beneficiary societies. At the same time, it expanded the scope of the tax to patrol against a new form of abusive debt-financed acquisition by tax exempt organizations that had been endorsed by the Supreme Court.[13] The 1969 legislation significantly tightened the UBIT in several other respects but any business activities that were substantially related to the exempt purposes of an organization were left untouched, even if they were in direct competition with a for-profit taxpayer.

The subsequent history of the UBIT is a series of piecemeal changes, most of which are specialized exemptions added at the behest of lobbyists

---

10. H.R.Rep. No. 2319, 81st Cong., 2d Sess. 38 (1950); S.Rep. No. 2375, 81st Cong., 2d Sess. 28–29 (1950).

11. See particularly President Truman's admonitions "to improve the fairness of the tax system, to bring in some additional revenue, and to strengthen [the] economy." 96 Cong. Rec. 769, 771 (1950) (President's Message to Congress).

12. For much of this history, see Stephen Schwarz, Limiting Religious Tax Exemptions: When Should the Church Render Unto Caesar?, 29 U.Fla.L.Rev. 50, 94–96 (1976).

13. Commissioner v. Brown, 380 U.S. 563, 85 S.Ct. 1162 (1965). For further discussion of these "bootstrap acquisition" transactions, see Section E2 of this chapter.

representing a particular nonprofit sub-sector. At least once a decade, complaints about unfair competition from segments of the small business community are sufficiently loud to prompt Congress to engage in a comprehensive review. The last such episode was in 1987, when Representative J.J. Pickle of Texas presided over extensive hearings by the House Ways and Means Committee's Oversight Subcommittee. The Hearings resulted in three volumes of fascinating testimony and a discussion draft (excerpted at the end of this chapter) proposing significant reforms but resulting in no immediate legislation.

As the rest of this chapter will demonstrate, the commercial activities of exempt organizations raise profoundly complex and perhaps insoluble policy issues about the role of the nonprofit sector and the rationale for tax exemption. The policy debate inevitably will continue as long as nonprofits successfully compete with private firms while straying from their stated mission.

NOTES AND QUESTIONS

1. *Destination of Income Test.* What was so bad about the destination of income test? If the rationale for exempt status under § 501(c)(3) is to subsidize organizations that provide a public benefit, relieve the burdens of government and foster pluralism, why shouldn't the tax exemption extend to all the organization's sources of revenue? Is the destination of income still alive and well for purposes of determining whether an organization qualifies for exemption? See Chapter 2E1, supra, at pp. 246–249. Some of the academic theories discussed in Chapter 2 explain tax exemption as a subsidy to correct the undersupply of goods and services that suffer from the twin failures of the private market and government? Do those theories justify subsidizing an unrelated business? For example, under Hall and Colombo's donative theory, is taxing unrelated business income irrelevant as long as the organization has the requisite level of donative support? See John D. Colombo & Mark A. Hall, The Charitable Tax Exemption 175–179 (1995).

2. *Unfair Competition or Profit Motive?* Is income from an unrelated business taxable only if the exempt organization is competing with a for-profit firm? Most courts considering this question have concluded that the presence or absence of competition with for-profits, while an important objective of the tax, is not determinative. In their view, the more critical question is whether the organization has a profit motive and operates the business in a commercial manner. Noting that the statutory language has never required a showing of unfair competition, these decisions emphasize that the UBIT was enacted not only to eliminate a form of unfair competition but also to raise revenue by closing a loophole. See, e.g, Clarence LaBelle Post No. 217, Veterans of Foreign Wars of the United States v. United States, 580 F.2d 270 (8th Cir.1978)(income from bingo games subject to UBIT even though organization did not compete because only nonprofit entities may operate bingo games under local law); Louisiana

Credit Union League v. United States, 693 F.2d 525 (5th Cir.1982). For a contrary view that requires a showing of unfair competition, see Hope School v. United States, 612 F.2d 298 (7th Cir.1980).

3. *For Further Reading.* Harvey P. Dale, About the UBIT, N.Y.U. 18th Conf. on Tax Planning for 501(c)(3) Organizations § 9 (1990); Donald L. Sharpe, Unfair Business Competition and the Tax on Income Destined for Charity: Forty–Six Years Later, 3 Fla. Tax Rev. 367 (1996); Kenneth C. Eliasberg, Charity and Commerce: Section 501(c)(3)-How Much Unrelated Business Activity?, 21 Tax L.Rev. 53 (1965); Note, The Macaroni Monopoly: The Developing Concept of Unrelated Business Income of Exempt Organizations, 81 Harv.L.Rev. 1280 (1968).

2. POLICY CONSIDERATIONS: FAIRNESS AND EFFICIENCY

Echoing the theme that pervades the legislative history of the UBIT, the regulations state that "the primary objective of [the tax] was to eliminate a source of unfair competition by placing the unrelated business activities of certain exempt organizations upon the same tax basis as the non-exempt business endeavors with which they compete." Treas. Reg. § 1.513–1(b). The small business community, led by the Office of Advocacy of the U.S. Small Business Administration and a consortium of other trade groups, has emphasized competitive imbalance in urging Congress to expand the reach of the UBIT and improve its enforcement. These concerns gained prominence during hearings held in 1987 by the Oversight Subcommittee of the House Ways and Means Committee.

Some tax law scholars and economists, however, have questioned the underlying economic assumptions that appear to have influenced the enactment and expansion of the UBIT. The following materials survey the policy debate.

Statement of Joseph O'Neil, Chairman, Business Coalition for Fair Competition, at Hearings Before the Subcommittee on Oversight, House Ways and Means Committee

100th Cong. 1st Sess. 217–220 (Ser. 100–26, 1987).

[The Business Coalition for Fair Competition is an alliance of trade and professional associations and businesses formed in 1983 to articulate the concerns of the business community on the subject of unfair competition. This excerpt is from testimony of BCFC's chairman at the 1987 House UBIT hearings. Eds.]

The Importance of Nonprofits in Our Society

At the outset, let me make clear what this testimony is *not* about, and why BCFC believes legislative solutions are needed.

Our purpose is not to denigrate the vital role of nonprofits. The spirit of voluntarism, our ability to balance a system which emphasizes self-reliance with the common welfare of all, is what makes this nation unique. We acknowledge the importance of the independent nonprofit sector and its essential contributions in education, basic research, and charitable endeavors. We are particularly proud of the participation of our small businesses in charitable endeavors. Small business owners serve on the boards of many local nonprofit institutions such as the YMCA, the university, the hospital, or the United Way. At the annual pancake festival you will most likely find that the local restaurant owner has contributed the maple syrup. Many nonprofits play a critical role in society. For example, universities educate the highly trained engineers, scientists and other professionals needed for the jobs of the future. Nonprofit trade and professional associations promote professional and ethical conduct as well as improvements in the quality of goods and services.

* * *

What Are the Unfair Advantages?

Unfair competition itself is easy to define, yet difficult to quantify. The unfair advantage is derived from the granting of special status by an external source, almost always the government, which either permits the entity to avoid governmental "burdens" (e.g., taxes) or to obtain direct support (e.g., grants). The exemption from federal taxation is the most significant of these advantages. Others include exemption from state and local taxes, lower subsidized postal rates, and antitrust exemptions, to name a few. Congress only recently granted another privilege to nonprofits, the ability to obtain contracts from the government on a sole source basis.

Tax-exemption is the most recognized unfair advantage, but it is difficult to measure the extent of that advantage. The Internal Revenue Code includes a provision that requires the nonprofit to pay an unrelated business income tax on activities deemed to be unrelated. Only 22,000 reported any unrelated activity in 1984. Although the income of nonprofits surpassed $300 billion they reported only $27.5 million as unrelated income. Although a lower postal rate or an antitrust exemption is important, there is no doubt that tax-exemption drives the nonprofit issue. It is the linchpin of the nonprofit system.

A significant "benefit" of nonprofit status is the aura of the government imprimatur. While the "aura" has been described as a rationale for the existence of nonprofits, it, in fact, has emerged as a major business advantage. The "contract failure" theory suggests nonprofits assure the public of quality and performance in services for which the consumer is not able to make such judgments. The evidence now suggests that, increasingly, the aura serves as a marketing tool as much as a method of quality control and protection.

The Impact of Unfair Competition

How do these exemptions or privileges provide advantage within the marketplace? The obvious answer is that the exemptions allow the nonprofit to lower the price of the goods or services. A less obvious advantage is the ability to sustain the costs of market entry. The chance to devote more resources to advertising, to produce a better product and to underwrite new products is a tremendous advantage. The National Geographic Society, for example, through nonprofit donations is able to commit vast sums to the production of the magazine, which in turn creates new donors.

The damage of unfair competition is difficult to assess because the problem is national in scope, but local in impact. This explains, in part, why the phenomenon hits the small business sector particularly hard. The competition takes place on an institution-by-institution basis. A small business competes against one university or one hospital. The central activity is the provision of service. Service, except for a limited number of franchise operations, does not lend itself to a national marketing strategy. A key index, if one were able to compile the data, is "opportunity lost." How many sales were not made by the for-profit, how many jobs were not created as the result of the sales not made, or the taxes not paid on those sales? In a growing market, if a firm's sales increase 50% but a nonprofit has siphoned off another 50% of the potential growth, how is one to know?

What is clear is that nonprofits have become increasingly reliant on income-producing activities. Contributions as a percentage of income have decreased from 17 to 13 percent, and dues have decreased from 26 to 12 percent between 1946 and 1978. Other income has increased from 57 to 75 percent. The nonprofit sector has gained marketshare, and it is easier to document their gain rather than small business' loss. The correlation is clear, and not surprisingly, the concept of the for-profit business community regarding unfair competition has risen in direct proportion to the increase in the sale of goods and services by nonprofits.

How Nonprofits Compete

Areas in which businesses go head to head with nonprofits include food service, testing laboratories, retail sales of books and computers, travel, recreation, nurseries, day care, hearing aids, veterinarians, blood banks, consulting engineers, medical equipment suppliers, pencil makers, specialty advertisers, hotels, bus operators, printing, construction, laundries, janitorial services, waste hauling, electrical, plumbing and heating contracting to name a few. * * *

Why Nonprofits Compete

There are two types of competitors. In a number of fields, such as health care, the nonprofit has been dominant provider of the service and it is the for-profit that has sought a foothold in the market. In the second case, the nonprofit has expanded, entering a thriving for-profit market. The reasons for this latter expansion are clear. "Escalating expenses, declining revenue and a rising demand for highly technical services have forced many exempt organizations into the commercial arena." More accurately it is escalating expenses, declining revenue, and *excess* capacity that have forced the exempts to look to the commercial arena. Nonprofits are professionally operated, and sophisticated management will adapt to maximize resources. At the same time, self interest dictates that managers and employees will seek to protect their efforts. The laundry industry provides a classic example. Nonprofit hospital laundries have learned to capitalize on their resources. Consider the statements of these nonprofit managers: "We intend to turn St. Elizabeth's into a profit making operation." "This guarantees employment for our staff of 32 and allows us to think about hiring more." Meanwhile for-profit laundries have been able to document a corresponding loss of marketshare. One such business owner reports a drop of marketshare from approximately 28–30 percent to 20 percent shortly after the nonprofit laundry expanded its marketing efforts.

The trend towards for-profit performance of activities which have been the province of nonprofits presents an entirely different set of questions. Changes in our society, particularly the growth of health insurance, have created a situation where ability to pay is no longer the dominant factor in determining who receives health care. Either way, there is no organized body of law or economics to explain adequately why nonprofits exist or why governments grant such status to particular enterprises. As early as 1601, the British had conferred preferred status on charitable institutions through the Statute of Uses. In the U.S., the first tax-exemptions surfaced in the Tariff of 1894. Since that time Congress has added over twenty-five specific statutory categories but "not [as] the result of any planned legislative scheme, and [exemptions] have never been set forth as part of any unified concept of exemption."

Academicians have advanced a number of theories to explain the existence of nonprofits. The predominant explanation is the contract failure theory, which states that a consumer "needs an organization that he can trust", and the nonprofit, because of the legal constraints under which it must operate, is likely to serve that function better than its for-profit counterpart. The second theory is the "public goods" theory, which suggests that nonprofits provide services the government would otherwise have to provide to the citizenry. Both the Congress and the courts have provided added credibility to this theory. Small business counters with the assertion that the public good rationale actually begs the question. The existence of for-profits should be prima facie evidence that the government would not have to provide the service. Further, one can ask why the Government does not subsidize all providers, whether for-profit or nonprofit.

One rationale for tax-exemption is that it fosters volunteerism and the principle of volunteerism is part and parcel of our society and culture. What makes the U.S. economy truly unique is the balance between self reliance and the common good. However, tax-exemption does not have an inherent bearing on the relationship. Nonprofit status without the tax-exemption should foster volunteerism under this theory. The motivation of the volunteer, in addition to the desire to contribute to the common good, is the knowledge that no individual will benefit or profit from the work of volunteers. Two commentators have succinctly summed up the common justifications for a tax-exemption and the counter arguments thereto:

"**Nonprofits are better suited than for-profits to produce public good because everyone should have access to public goods at the lowest possible price**. The classic example of a public good is a lighthouse; society is served when all boats use its light. It is very difficult to charge a price for the service because you cannot deny the light to those who do not pay. Some observers think of health care services as this kind of public good. A nonprofit organization, theoretically freed from worrying too much about costs and from raising money, can better deliver such services at the lowest possible price.

"This argument confuses funding with production. Government funding underwrites public goods and services that the private marketplace would otherwise not produce in sufficient quantity. The organizational form whose output is most cost effective-whether for-profit, nonprofit, or public-should receive such government funding to produce the needed services.

"**Nonprofit organizations have the same motives and rationales—and are subject to the same controls—as public organizations**. But nonprofits are not the same as public organizations because they have few outside controls on their activities. The free market sector is watchdogged by everything from the stock market to government regulatory agencies and consumer advocate organizations. Government institutions have somewhat fewer controls on their performance, like the voting process and bureaucratic budgetary control. Nonprofits have even fewer; boards of trustees appoint their members who are then subjected to little outside scrutiny. Although some observers believe donors act as a control, in reality they are hardly involved with the impact or results of their donations.

"**Nonprofit managers operate from a moral base that makes them more trustworthy than for-profit managers because the mission of their organization is not to make money but to serve society**. Nonprofits are supposedly more worthy to receive private donations than for-profits because their managers will not divert them into the organization's bottom line. Given the weaker controls on nonprofits, however, it is unclear why nonprofit managers should not be equally likely to direct such funds into larger salaries, organizational perquisites, and excessively large staffs.

"**Nonprofits are better suited than for-profits to provide services their customers cannot evaluate, such as education or health care, in part because they sacrifice growth to quality**. This argument assumes a naive consumer whose existence we doubt. Given a choice between two organizations that offer the same service, the American customer is more likely than ever to pick the one with the better performance no matter what its form. More consumers are well-educated today than ever before. Recent sharp declines in deaths from heart disease in the United States, for example, are caused primarily by self-induced changes in life-styles, not from counsel by the medical profession. Further, no one has proven that nonprofits are reluctant to grow; they have tripled since World War II, and their income now represents more than 9% of GNP."

[Mr. O'Neil went on to propose "solutions" to the unfair competition problem, some of which are discussed in Section G of this chapter, infra, at pp. 664–670. Eds.]

NOTES AND QUESTIONS

1. *Why and How is the Competition Unfair?* How, specifically, are for-profit businesses harmed by their tax-exempt competitors? Is it because nonprofits charge lower prices for comparable services? For-profit firms also could lower their prices. Is it because nonprofits can accumulate earnings and expand faster if they are exempt from income tax while for-profits only can expand with after-tax profits? Economically, who is adversely affected by unfair competition? Would repeal of the UBIT result in widespread displacement of for-profit firms?

2. *Economic Perspectives: Fairness.* In tax policy parlance, "horizontal equity" is the principle that taxpayers with equal income should pay the same amounts of tax. In questioning the underlying economic assumptions in the UBIT policy debate, Professor Susan Rose-Ackerman has identified two different claims based on the notion of horizontal equity. The first compares firms within the same industry and asserts that it is unfair for the tax system to favor one competitor over another. The second approach compares for-profit firms across different industries—those with and those without tax-exempt competitors—and asserts that for-profits that compete with both taxable and tax-exempt firms are disadvantaged. Susan Rose-Ackerman, Unfair Competition and Corporate Income Taxation, 34 Stan. L.Rev. 1017, 1019–1021 (1982).

Professor Rose-Ackerman argues that unfairness does not result from competition between firms in the same industry. In her view, the impact of tax exemption is less upon the for-profit firms than upon their investors, and the unfair competition is with investors in industries that do not face competition from tax favored firms. As a result, similarly situated investors earn different returns. Investors in an industry with competition from nonprofits are asked to bear a greater share of the social costs of tax favoritism to nonprofits than investors in firms without nonprofit competition. Rose-Ackerman suggests that the only way nonprofits can affect profits is through excessive entry into a particular industry so that the industry has more firms earning lower gross returns than the for-profit investors anticipated. In other words, nonprofits will enter a field, causing marginally profitable for-profit firms to leave because they will be earning subcompetitive returns. She concludes that if the nonprofit sector's productive business investments were spread across the economy, they would be unlikely to have any competitive impact. But since the UBIT prevents such dispersion, nonprofits must concentrate their profitable endeavors on those few lines of business that are substantially related to their exempt purposes. It thus is more likely that the permissible business activities of nonprofits will impose losses on competitive for-profit firms.

And so what does one conclude from all of this? Professor Rose-Ackerman's thesis is that the UBIT creates more unfairness than it can possibly prevent and should be repealed. Id. at 1038. Other commentators also have questioned the effectiveness of the UBIT in preventing unfair competition by nonprofits. But this debate has proceeded on a wholly theoretical level. As the commentators concede, empirical work is virtually non-existent. See also Boris I. Bittker & George K. Rahdert, The Exemption of Nonprofit Organizations from Federal Income Taxation, 85 Yale L.J. 299, 316–326 (1976); William A. Klein, Income Taxation and Legal Entities, 20 UCLA L.Rev. 13, 61–68 (1972).

3. *Economic Perspectives: Efficiency.* Professor Henry Hansmann believes that the UBIT policy debate has been muddled by casting the issue in terms of fairness. In his view, the more fundamental concern is economic efficiency. From that perspective, he concludes that the argument for retaining the UBIT in roughly its present form is overwhelming. Henry B. Hansmann, Unfair Competition and the Unrelated Business Income Tax, 75 Va.L.Rev. 605, 607 (1989).

Professor Hansmann agrees with Rose-Ackerman that repeal of the UBIT would not result in widespread displacement of for-profit firms. Id. at 610. But he argues that failure to apply the corporate income tax to unrelated businesses operated by nonprofits could result in a number of inefficiencies. For example, if the UBIT were repealed, universities, foundations and pension funds that now invest a substantial portion of their endowments in a diversified portfolio of common stocks would have a strong incentive to invest in wholly owned businesses. The result would be an incentive for nonprofits to increase their investment risk through decreased diversification. Id. at 615.

Hansmann also argues that repeal of the UBIT would lead to managerial inefficiency because nonprofits have no stockholders and thus less incentive to minimize costs or maximize revenues. Moreover, repeal would give nonprofits too great an incentive to accumulate assets rather than spend for their exempt purposes. Finally, Hansmann maintains that repeal of the UBIT would shrink the corporate tax base because nonprofits would purchase wholly owned exempt businesses through debt-financed acquisitions. Id. at 622. Although Hansmann concludes that the case for repealing or considerably broadening the UBIT is weak, he urges that serious reform is needed in defining (and contracting) the scope of the basic underlying exemption. Id. at 634–635.

4. *For Further Reading.* Office of Advocacy, U.S. Small Business Administration, Unfair Competition by Nonprofit Organizations with Small Business: An Issue for the 1980s (1984); General Accounting Office, Tax Policy: Competition Between Taxable Business and Tax-Exempt Organizations (1987); W. Harrison Wellford and Janne G. Gallagher, Unfair Competition? The Challenge to Tax Exemption (1988).

B.   The Nature of an Unrelated Trade or Business

1.   Imposition and Rates of Tax

Internal Revenue Code: § 511(a), (b).

The unrelated business income tax applies to virtually all organizations otherwise exempt from tax under § 501(a), including qualified pension and profit-sharing plans, and state colleges, universities, and their subsidiaries. I.R.C. § 511(a)(2). The UBIT does not apply to certain United States instrumentalities, such as the Federal Deposit Insurance Corporation and the Federal National Mortgage Association. I.R.C. §§ 511(a)(2); 501(c)(1). See Gen. Couns. Mem. 38737 (June 1, 1981). Except in the case of trusts, unrelated business taxable income is taxable at corporate income tax rates, which range from 15 percent on the first $25,000 of taxable income to 34 percent for taxable income over $75,000 and peak at 35 percent for taxable income over $10 million. I.R.C. §§ 511(a)(1); 11(b). Trusts are taxable at the compressed trust rates in § 1(e), which in 2003 reached the top 35 percent bracket at a mere $9,350 of taxable income. I.R.C. § 511(b)(1). In view of the differences in rates, an exempt organization with substantial unrelated business taxable income will save taxes by conducting the business in a corporation.

2.   Taxable and Excepted Activities

Internal Revenue Code: § 513(a), (c), (f), (h), (i).

Treasury Regulations: § 1.513–1, –4.

The principal target of the UBIT is income derived from profit-seeking activities not related to an organization's exempt purposes. Congress did not intend to tax income from the activities related to an organization's charitable or other exempt mission—e.g., admission fees to theaters and museums, college tuition, fees paid by hospital patients, or dues paid by members of labor unions, trade associations, and social clubs. And since the tax was aimed at the problem of unfair competition, most forms of passive investment income, such as dividends, interest, rents and royalties, are exempt from the UBIT, except in the case of social clubs and a few more specialized types of exempt organizations.

Three conditions must be met for an activity to be classified as an unrelated trade or business: (1) the activity must be a "trade or business"; (2) it must be "regularly carried on"; and (3) it must not be substantially related to an organization's exempt purposes, aside from the need for funds derived from the activity. I.R.C. § 513(a); Treas. Reg. § 1.513–1(a).

The threshold question is whether the organization is engaged in a trade or business. In general, a "trade or business" includes "any activity carried on for the production of income from the sale of goods or performance of services." Treas. Reg. § 1.513–1(b). An activity will not lose its identity as a trade or business merely because it is carried on within a larger aggregate of similar activities which may or may not be related to the exempt purposes of the organization. I.R.C. § 513(c); Treas. Reg. § 1.513–1(b). Under this fragmentation approach, an "unrelated" business need not be wholly separate from the exempt activities of the organization. Thus, the sale of pharmaceutical supplies to the general public by a hospital pharmacy does not escape characterization as an unrelated business merely because the pharmacy also furnishes supplies to the hospital and its patients. Similarly, even though the publication of a magazine is related to the exempt purposes of an organization, its advertising revenue may be taxable.

The "regularly carried on" test relates to the frequency and continuity of the activity as compared with similar activities of nonexempt organizations. Congress believed that intermittent activities would not pose any threat of unfair competition. Treas. Reg. § 1.513–1(c). An organization thus will not be subject to the UBIT if it briefly conducts an income-producing activity of a kind that a taxable business would conduct on a year-round basis (e.g., a fundraising auction). But if income-producing activities are of a kind normally undertaken by for-profit firms only on a "seasonal" basis, the conduct of comparable activities by an exempt organization during a significant portion of the season ordinarily will constitute the regular conduct of a trade or business. Id. Some of the special problems raised by the "regularly carried on" test are illustrated later in this chapter.

The "substantially related" test is far more difficult to apply. The regulations offer little more than abstract generalizations, requiring an examination of the relationship between the business and the organization's exempt purposes. To be "related" to an exempt purpose, there must be a substantial causal relationship—i.e., the activity must "contribute importantly" to the accomplishment of the exempt purpose. Treas. Reg. § 1.513–1(d). All the facts and circumstances control, but particular emphasis is placed on the size and extent of the activity. Thus, if a business is conducted on a scale larger than necessary to carry out an exempt purpose, it is more likely to be treated as unrelated. The potential for competition with a commercial counterpart is another important factor. Id.

These general rules are subject to numerous qualifications, conditions, and exceptions. Three activities are specifically excluded from the definition of an unrelated trade or business: (1) any trade or business where substantially all of the labor is performed by unpaid volunteers, (2) any trade or business carried on by a § 501(c)(3) organization or a state college or university primarily for the convenience of members, students, patients, officers or employees (e.g., a university cafeteria), and (3) any trade or business which consists of selling donated merchandise (e.g., a thrift shop). See I.R.C. § 513(a)(1)–(3). More specialized exceptions are provided for activities such as bingo (I.R.C. § 513(f)), certain corporate sponsorship payments that do not constitute advertising (I.R.C. § 513(i)), convention and trade shows (I.R.C. § 513(d)(3)(A)), distribution of low-cost items as part of fundraising solicitations (I.R.C. § 513(h)(1)), public entertainment at events such as state fairs (I.R.C. § 513(d)(2)(A)), services for small hospitals (I.R.C. § 513(e)), and rental of telephone poles (I.R.C. § 513(g)). The Code also contains numerous "modifications" which have the effect of exempting virtually all forms of passive income from the UBIT provided the income is not derived from debt-financed property. I.R.C. §§ 512(b); 514.

The concept of an unrelated trade or business has been evolving in recent years as the Internal Revenue Service concentrates more of its attention on the business activities of exempt organizations. The materials that follow illustrate the range of current issues.

United States v. American College of Physicians

Supreme Court of the United States, 1986.
475 U.S. 834, 106 S.Ct. 1591.

■ JUSTICE MARSHALL delivered the opinion of the Court.

A tax-exempt organization must pay tax on income that it earns by carrying on a business not "substantially related" to the purposes for which the organization has received its exemption from federal taxation. The question before this Court is whether respondent, a tax-exempt organization, must pay tax on the profits it earns by selling commercial advertising space in its professional journal, The Annals of Internal Medicine.

I

Respondent, the American College of Physicians, is an organization exempt from taxation under § 501(c)(3) of the Internal Revenue Code. The purposes of the College, as stated in its articles of incorporation, are to maintain high standards in medical education and medical practice; to encourage research, especially in clinical medicine; and to foster measures for the prevention of disease and for the improvement of public health. The principal facts were stipulated at trial. In furtherance of its exempt purposes, respondent publishes The Annals of Internal Medicine (Annals), a highly regarded monthly medical journal containing scholarly articles relevant to the practice of internal medicine. Each issue of Annals contains advertisements for pharmaceuticals, medical supplies, and equipment useful in the practice of internal medicine, as well as notices of positions available in that field. Respondent has a longstanding policy of accepting only advertisements containing information about the use of medical products, and screens proffered advertisements for accuracy and relevance to internal medicine. The advertisements are clustered in two groups, one at the front and one at the back of each issue.

In 1975, Annals produced gross advertising income of $1,376,322. After expenses and deductible losses were subtracted, there remained a net income of $153,388. Respondent reported this figure as taxable income and paid taxes on it in the amount of $55,965. Respondent then filed a timely claim with the Internal Revenue Service for refund of these taxes, and when the Government demurred, filed suit in the United States Claims Court.

The Claims Court held a trial and concluded that the advertisements in Annals were not substantially related to respondent's tax-exempt purposes. Rather, after finding various facts regarding the nature of the College's advertising business, it concluded that any correlation between the advertisements and respondent's educational purpose was incidental because "the comprehensiveness and content of the advertising package is entirely dependent on each manufacturer's willingness to pay for space and the imagination of its advertising agency." Accordingly, the court determined that the advertising proceeds were taxable.

The Court of Appeals for the Federal Circuit reversed. It held clearly erroneous the trial court's finding that the advertising was not substantially related to respondent's tax-exempt purpose. The Court of Appeals believed that the trial court had focused too much on the commercial character of the advertising business and not enough on the actual contribution of the advertisements to the education of the journal's readers. It held that respondent had established the requisite substantial relation and its entitlement to exemption from taxation. We granted the Government's petition for certiorari, and now reverse.

II

The taxation of business income not "substantially related" to the objectives of exempt organizations dates from the Revenue Act of 1950. The statute was enacted in response to perceived abuses of the tax laws by tax-exempt organizations that engaged in profit-making activities. Prior law had required only that the profits garnered by exempt organizations be used in furtherance of tax-exempt purposes, without regard to the source of those profits. * * * As a result, tax-exempt organizations were able to carry on full-fledged commercial enterprises in competition with corporations whose profits were fully taxable. * * * See Revenue Revision of 1950 * * * (describing universities' production of "automobile parts, chinaware, and food products, and the operation of theatres, oil wells, and cotton gins"). Congress perceived a need to restrain the unfair competition fostered by the tax laws.

Nevertheless, Congress did not force exempt organizations to abandon all commercial ventures, nor did it levy a tax only upon businesses that bore no relation at all to the tax-exempt purposes of an organization, as some of the 1950 Act's proponents had suggested. Rather, in the 1950 Act it struck a balance between its two objectives of encouraging benevolent enterprise and restraining unfair competition by imposing a tax on the "unrelated business taxable income" of tax-exempt organizations. 26 U.S.C. § 511(a)(1).

"Unrelated business taxable income" was defined as "the gross income derived by any organization from any unrelated trade or business * * * regularly carried on by it * * *." § 512(a)(1). Congress defined an "unrelated trade or business" as "any trade or business the conduct of which is not substantially related * * * to the exercise or performance by such organization of its charitable, educational, or other purpose or function constituting the basis for its exemption * * *." § 513(a). Whether respondent's advertising income is taxable, therefore, depends upon (1) whether the publication of paid advertising is a "trade or business," (2) whether it is regularly carried on, and (3) whether it is substantially related to respondent's tax-exempt purposes.

III

A

Satisfaction of the first condition is conceded in this case, as it must be, because Congress has declared unambiguously that the publication of paid advertising is a trade or business activity distinct from the publication of accompanying educational articles and editorial comment.

In 1967, the Treasury promulgated a regulation interpreting the unrelated business income provision of the 1950 Act. The regulation defined "trade or business" to include not only a complete business enterprise, but also any component activity of a business. Treas.Reg. § 1.513–1(b), 26 CFR § 1.513–1(b)(1985). This revolutionary approach to the identification of a "trade or business" had a significant effect on advertising, which theretofore had been considered simply a part of a unified publishing business. The new regulation segregated the "trade or business" of selling advertising space from the "trade or business" of publishing a journal, an approach commonly referred to as "fragmenting" the enterprise of publishing into its component parts:

> "[A]ctivities of soliciting, selling, and publishing commercial advertising do not lose identity as a trade or business even though the advertising is published in an exempt organization periodical which contains editorial matter related to the exempt purposes of the organization." 26 CFR § 1.513–1(b)(1985).

In 1969, Congress responded to widespread criticism of those Treasury regulations by passing the Tax Reform Act of 1969, Pub.L. 91–172, 83 Stat. 487 (1969 Act). That legislation specifically endorsed the Treasury's concept of "fragmenting" the publishing enterprise into its component activities, and adopted, in a new § 513(c), much of the language of the regulation that defined advertising as a separate trade or business:

> "Advertising, etc., activities * * * an activity does not lose identity as a trade or business merely because it is carried on * * * within a larger complex of other endeavors which may, or may not, be related to the exempt purposes of the organization." 26 U.S.C. § 513(c).

The statute clearly established advertising as a trade or business, the first prong of the inquiry into the taxation of unrelated business income.

The presence of the second condition, that the business be regularly carried on, is also undisputed here. The satisfaction of the third condition, however, that of "substantial relation," is vigorously contested, and that issue forms the crux of the controversy before us.

B

According to the Government, Congress and the Treasury established a blanket rule that advertising published by tax-exempt professional journals can never be substantially related to the purposes of those journals and is, therefore, always a taxable business. Respondent, however, contends that each case must be determined on the basis of the characteristics of the advertisements and journal in question. Each party finds support for its position in the governing statute and regulations issued by the Department of the Treasury.

In its 1967 regulations, the Treasury not only addressed the "fragmentation" issue discussed above, but also attempted to clarify the statutory "substantially related" standard found in § 513(a). It provided that the conduct of a tax-exempt business must have a causal relation to the organization's exempt purpose (other than through the generation of income), and that "the production or distribution of the goods or the performance of the services from which the gross income is derived must *contribute importantly* to the accomplishment of [the exempt] purposes." Treas.Reg. § 1.513–1(d)(2)(emphasis added). In illustration of its new test for substantial relation, the Treasury provided an example whose interpretation is central to the resolution of the issue before us. Example 7 of Treas.Reg. § 1.513–1(d)(4)(iv) involves "Z," an exempt association formed to advance the interests of a particular profession and drawing its membership from that profession. Z publishes a monthly journal containing articles and other editorial material that contribute importantly to the tax-exempt purpose. Z derives income from advertising products within the field of professional interest of the members:

> "Following a practice common among taxable magazines which publish advertising, Z requires its advertising to comply with certain general standards of taste, fairness, and accuracy; but within those limits the form, content, and manner of presentation of the advertising messages are governed by the basic objective of the advertisers to promote the sale of the advertised products. While the advertisements contain certain information, the informational function of the advertising is incidental to the controlling aim of stimulating demand for the advertised products and differs in no essential respect from the informational function of any commercial advertising. Like taxable publishers of advertising, Z accepts advertising only from those who are willing to pay its published rates. Although continuing education of its members in matters pertaining to their profession is one of the purposes for which Z is granted exemption, the publication of advertising designed and selected in the manner of ordinary commercial advertising is not an educational activity of the kind contemplated by the exemption statute; it differs fundamentally from such an activity both in its governing objective and in its method. Accordingly, Z's publication of advertising does not contribute importantly to the accomplishment of its exempt purposes; and the income which it derives from advertising

constitutes gross income from unrelated trade or business." § 1.513–1(d)(4)(iv), Example 7.

The Government contends both that Example 7 creates a per se rule of taxation for journal advertising income and that Congress intended to adopt that rule, together with the remainder of the 1967 regulations, into law in the 1969 Act. We find both of these contentions unpersuasive.

Read as a whole, the regulations do not appear to create the type of blanket rule of taxability that the Government urges upon us. On the contrary, the regulations specifically condition tax exemption of business income upon the importance of the business activity's contribution to the particular exempt purpose at issue, and direct that "[w]hether activities productive of gross income contribute importantly to the accomplishment of any purpose for which an organization is granted an exemption depends *in each case* upon the facts and circumstances involved," § 1.513–1(d)(2) (emphasis added). Example 7 need not be interpreted as being inconsistent with that general rule. Attributing to the term "example" its ordinary meaning, we believe that Example 7 is best construed as an illustration of one possible application, under given circumstances, of the regulatory standard for determining substantial relation.

The interpretative difficulty of Example 7 arises primarily from its failure to distinguish clearly between the statements intended to provide hypothetical facts and those designed to posit the necessary legal consequences of those facts. Just at the point in the lengthy Example at which the facts would appear to end and the analysis to begin, a pivotal statement appears: "the informational function of the advertising is incidental to the controlling aim of stimulating demand for the advertised products." The Government's position depends upon reading this statement as a general proposition of law, while respondent would read it as a statement of fact that may be true by hypothesis of "Z" and its journal, but is not true of Annals.

We recognize that the language of the Example is amenable to either interpretation. Nevertheless, several considerations lead us to believe that the Treasury did not intend to set out a per se statement of law. First, when the regulations were proposed in early 1967, the Treasury expressed a clear intention to treat all commercial advertising as an unrelated business. When the regulations were issued in final form, however, following much criticism and the addition of Example 7, they included no such statement of intention. Second, a blanket rule of taxation for advertising in professional journals would contradict the explicit case-by-case requirement articulated in Treas.Reg. § 1.513–1(d)(2), and we are reluctant to attribute to the Treasury an intention to depart from its own general principle in the absence of clear support for doing so. Finally, at the time the regulations were issued, the 1950 Act had been interpreted to mean that business activities customarily engaged in by tax-exempt organizations would continue to be considered "substantially related" and untaxed. A per se rule of taxation for the activity, traditional among tax-exempt journals, of carrying commercial advertising would have been a significant departure from that prevailing view. Thus, in 1967 the idea of a per se rule of taxation for all journal advertising revenue was sufficiently controversial, its effect so substantial, and its statutory authorization so tenuous, that we simply cannot attribute to the Treasury the intent to take that step in the form of an ambiguous example, appended to a subpart of a subsection of a subparagraph of a regulation.

It is still possible, of course, that, regardless of what the Treasury actually meant by its 1967 regulations, Congress read those regulations as creating a blanket rule of taxation, and intended to adopt that rule into law in the 1969 Act. The Government appears to embrace this view, which it supports with certain statements in the legislative history of the 1969 Act. For example, the Government cites to a statement in the House Report, discussing the taxation of advertising income of journals published by tax-exempt organizations:

> "Your committee believes that a business competing with taxpaying organizations should not be granted an unfair competitive advantage by operating tax free unless the business contributes importantly to the exempt function. It has concluded that by that standard, advertising in a journal published by an exempt organization is not related to the organization's exempt functions, and therefore it believes that this income should be taxed." H.R.Rep. No. 91–413, pt. 1, p. 50 (1969), U.S.Code Cong. & Admin.News 1969, pp. 1645, 1695.

Similar views appear in the Senate Report:

> "Present law.—In December 1967, the Treasury Department promulgated regulations under which the income from advertising and similar activities is treated as 'unrelated business income' even though such advertising for example may appear in a periodical related to the educational or other exempt purpose of the organization."

> "General reasons for change.—The committee agrees with the House that the regulations reached an appropriate result in specifying that when an exempt organization carries on an advertising business in competition with other taxpaying advertising businesses, it should pay a tax on the advertising income. The statutory language on which the regulations are based, however, is sufficiently unclear so that substantial litigation could result from these regulations. For this reason, the committee agrees with the House that the regulations, insofar as they apply to advertising and related activities, should be placed in the tax laws." S.Rep. No. 91–552, p. 75 (1969), U.S.Code Cong. & Admin. News 1969, p. 2104.

Based on this language, the Government argues that the 1969 Act created a per se rule of taxation for advertising income. The weakness of this otherwise persuasive argument, however, is that the quoted discussion appears in the Reports solely in support of the legislators' decision to enact § 513(c), the provision approving the fragmentation of "trade or business." Although § 513(c) was a significant change in the tax law that removed one barrier to the taxation of advertising proceeds, it cannot be construed as a comment upon the two other distinct conditions-"regularly carried on" and "not substantially related"—whose satisfaction is prerequisite to taxation of business income under the 1950 Act. Congress did not incorporate into the 1969 Act the language of the regulation defining "substantial relation," nor did the statute refer in any other way to the issue of the relation between advertising and exempt functions, even though that issue had been hotly debated at the hearings. Thus, we have no reason to conclude from the Committee Reports that Congress resolved the dispute whether, in a specific case, a journal's carriage of advertising could so advance its educational objectives as to be "substantially related" to those objectives within the meaning of the 1950 Act.

It is possible that the Committees' discussion of advertising reflects merely an erroneous assumption that the "fragmentation" provision of § 513(c), without more, would establish the automatic taxation of journal advertising revenue. Alternatively, the quoted passages could be read to indicate the Committees' intention affirmatively to endorse what they believed to be existing practice, or even to change the law substantially. The truth is that, other than a general reluctance to consider commercial advertisements generally as substantially related to the purposes of tax-exempt journals, no congressional view of the issue emerges from the quoted excerpts of the Reports. Thus, despite the Reports' seeming endorsement of a per se rule, we are hesitant to rely on that inconclusive legislative history either to supply a provision not enacted by Congress, or to define a statutory term enacted by a prior Congress. * * * We agree, therefore, with both the Claims Court and the Court of Appeals in their tacit rejection of the Government's argument that the Treasury and Congress intended to establish a per se rule requiring the taxation of income from all commercial advertisements of all tax-exempt journals without a specific analysis of the circumstances.

IV

It remains to be determined whether, in this case, the business of selling advertising space is "substantially related"—or, in the words of the regulation, "contributes importantly"—to the purposes for which respondent enjoys an exemption from federal taxation. Respondent has maintained throughout this litigation that the advertising in Annals performs an educational function supplemental to that of the journal's editorial content. Testimony of respondent's witnesses at trial tended to show that drug advertising performs a valuable function for doctors by disseminating information on recent developments in drug manufacture and use. In addition, respondent has contended that the role played by the Food and Drug Administration, in regulating much of the form and content of prescription-drug advertisements, enhances the contribution that such advertisements make to the readers' education. All of these factors, respondent argues, distinguish the advertising in Annals from standard commercial advertising. Respondent approaches the question of substantial relation from the perspective of the journal's subscribers; it points to the benefit that they may glean from reading the advertisements and concludes that benefit is substantial enough to satisfy the statutory test for tax exemption. The Court of Appeals took the same approach. It concluded that the advertisements performed various "essential" functions for physicians, and found a substantial relation based entirely upon the medically related content of the advertisements as a group.

The Government, on the other hand, looks to the conduct of the tax-exempt organization itself, inquiring whether the publishers of Annals have performed the advertising services in a manner that evinces an intention to use the advertisements for the purpose of contributing to the educational value of the journal. Also approaching the question from the vantage point of the College, the Claims Court emphasized the lack of a comprehensive presentation of the material contained in the advertisements. It commented upon the "hit-or-miss nature of the advertising," and observed that the "differences between ads plainly reflected the advertiser's marketing strategy rather than their probable importance to the reader." "[A]ny educational function [the advertising] may have served was incidental to its purpose of raising revenue." Id., at 535.

We believe that the Claims Court was correct to concentrate its scrutiny upon the conduct of the College rather than upon the educational quality of the advertisements. For all advertisements contain some information, and if a modicum of informative content were enough to supply the important contribution necessary to achieve tax exemption for commercial advertising, it would be the rare advertisement indeed that would fail to meet the test. Yet the statutory and regulatory scheme, even if not creating a per se rule against tax exemption, is clearly antagonistic to the concept of a per se rule for exemption for advertising revenue. Moreover, the statute provides that a tax will be imposed on "any trade or business the conduct of which is not substantially related," 26 U.S.C. § 513(a)(emphasis added), directing our focus to the manner in which the tax-exempt organization operates its business. The implication of the statute is confirmed by the regulations, which emphasize the "manner" of designing and selecting the advertisements. See Treas.Reg. § 1.513–1(d)(4)(iv), Example 7, 26 CFR § 1.513–1(d)(4)(iv), Example 7 (1985). Thus, the Claims Court properly directed its attention to the College's conduct of its advertising business, and it found the following pertinent facts:

> "The evidence is clear that plaintiff did not use the advertising to provide its readers a comprehensive or systematic presentation of any aspect of the goods or services publicized. Those companies willing to pay for advertising space got it; others did not. Moreover, some of the advertising was for established drugs or devices and was repeated from one month to another, undermining the suggestion that the advertising was principally designed to alert readers of recent developments [citing, as examples, ads for Valium, Insulin and Maalox]. Some ads even concerned matters that had no conceivable relationship to the College's tax-exempt purposes." 3 Cl.Ct., at 534 (footnotes omitted).

These facts find adequate support in the record. * * * Considering them in light of the applicable legal standard, we are bound to conclude that the advertising in Annals does not contribute importantly to the journal's educational purposes. This is not to say that the College could not control its publication of advertisements in such a way as to reflect an intention to contribute importantly to its educational functions. By coordinating the content of the advertisements with the editorial content of the issue, or by publishing only advertisements reflecting new developments in the pharmaceutical market, for example, perhaps the College could satisfy the stringent standards erected by Congress and the Treasury. In this case, however, we have concluded that the Court of Appeals erroneously focused exclusively upon the information that is invariably conveyed by commercial advertising, and consequently failed to give effect to the governing statute and regulations. Its judgment, accordingly, is

Reversed.

■ CHIEF JUSTICE BURGER, with whom JUSTICE POWELL joins, concurring.

Most medical journals are not comparable to magazines and newspapers published for profit. Their purpose is to assemble and disseminate to the profession relevant information bearing on patient care. The enormous expansion of medical knowledge makes it difficult for a general practitioner—or even a specialist—to keep fully current with the latest developments without such aids. In a sense these journals provide continuing education for physicians—a "correspondence course" not sponsored for profit but public health.

There is a public value in the widest possible circulation of such data, and advertising surely tends to reduce the cost of publication and hence the cost to each subscriber, thereby enhancing the prospect of wider circulation. Plainly a regulation recognizing these realities would be appropriate. Such regulations, of course, are for the Executive Branch and the Congress, not the courts. I join the opinion because it reflects a permissible reading of the present Treasury regulations.

Hi-Plains Hospital v. United States

United States Court of Appeals, Fifth Circuit, 1982.
670 F.2d 528.

■ CLARK, CHIEF JUDGE:

Hi-Plains Hospital (Hi-Plains) appeals from the district court's decision holding that pharmaceutical sales to nonhospital patients generated taxable business income unrelated to the tax-exempt operations of Hi-Plains. We reverse in part and remand in part.

I

Hi–Plains was established in 1945 to provide hospital and other related services to its members. Hi–Plains is located in Hale Center, Texas, a small town of about 2,250 people. Prior to 1937, Hale Center had been served by a resident doctor. From 1937, when the doctor died, until 1945, when Hi-Plains was established, Hale Center lacked medical services. The establishment of Hi-Plains both provided a physical facility in which patients could be treated and served as an inducement to doctors to practice in Hale Center. Toward this end, Hi-Plains offered to provide a doctor who would work on its staff with furnished offices in the hospital, complete nursing assistance, and a bookkeeping and billing service for the benefit of his private practice. Although it is undisputed that the cost of such facilities and services would normally consume 40% of a doctor's fees, Hi-Plains offered these services in return for five percent of a doctor's collected fees. Moreover, the hospital made certain of its own services, such as x-ray, laboratory facilities and a pharmacy, available to its doctor's private patients. Thus, if the doctor wanted a patient who had come in for an office visit to be x-rayed, the doctor would refer that patient to the hospital which would make the x-ray and bill the patient.

The pharmacy, the income of which is questioned in this case, makes sales to hospital patients, to private patients of the doctors located in the hospital and to the general public. The bulk of these sales consists of prescription drugs. Only a small percentage of the pharmacy's income is derived from the sale of nonprescription items. The pharmacy neither advertises nor uses display areas to attract customers. It maintains only a counter where orders can be placed. A small cardboard sign, which the state requires be displayed, is the pharmacy's only identifying mark.

The Commissioner of Internal Revenue assessed a tax, for the years 1973, 1974, 1975 and 1976, on sales by the pharmacy both to the private patients of the staff doctors and to the general public. He claimed that these sales constituted a trade or business which is unrelated to the exempt function of Hi-Plains. Hi-Plains paid the tax and then sued for a refund in federal district court.

The district court rejected Hi–Plains' claim for a refund because it found that sales by the pharmacy to nonhospital patients were not substantially related to Hi–Plains' exempt purpose, "namely that of providing a hospital." The district court also rejected Hi–Plains' claim that provision of a pharmacy was itself an exempt activity. The court found that it was providing a hospital which gave rise to the exemption and that any added benefits must relate to the hospital.

II

Although Section 501(a) of the Internal Revenue Code exempts the income of certain charitable organizations from tax, section 511 imposes a tax on any income generated by an unrelated trade or business conducted by a charitable organization. See I.R.C. § 511. Section 513(a) of the Code defines an unrelated trade or business as: any trade or business the conduct of which is not substantially related (aside from the need of such organization for income or funds or the use it makes of the profits derived) to the exercise or performance by such organization of its charitable, educational, or other purpose or function constituting the basis for its exemption under section 501 * * * I.R.C. § 513(a). This definition is in turn explained by Treasury Regulation § 1.513–1(a) which sets forth three elements which are required to prove an unrelated trade or business. It must be: i) a trade or business within the meaning of section 162 of the Code; ii) which is regularly carried on; and iii) which is not substantially related to the exempt function of the organization. See Treas.Reg. § 1.513–1(a). There is little question that the sale of drugs by Hi-Plains to nonhospital patients is a trade or business which is regularly carried on. The question turns on whether such sales are substantially related to the exempt function of Hi-Plains.

Section 1.513–1(d) provides guidelines for determining whether an activity is substantially related to the exempt function of a charitable organization. See Treas.Reg. § 1.513–1(d). The activity must be causally related to the exempt function of the organization. See Treas.Reg. § 1.513–1(d)(2). Moreover, the causal connection must be one which "contributes importantly" to the accomplishment of that function. The regulations provide that this determination "depends in each case upon the facts and circumstances involved." Id. Finally, the regulations note that even if an activity is "related in part" it is not substantially related if it is conducted on a scale larger than is "reasonably necessary" to accomplish the organization's purpose. See Treas.Reg. § 1.513–1(d)(3). The regulations thus require a case-by-case identification of the exempt purpose, an analysis of how the activity contributes to that purpose and an examination of the scale on which the activity is conducted.

In making this inquiry, the district court identified the exempt purpose of Hi-Plains as "that of providing a hospital." It rejected Hi-Plains' claim that pharmacy sales to private patients were substantially related because it reasoned that pharmacy sales could only be related to the hospital's exempt purpose if the sales were made as an incident of a person's use of the hospital. Because the sales in this case did not arise in connection with a customer's direct use of the hospital, the district court held that such sales were substantially unrelated to Hi-Plains' exempt function. The district court erred, however, in not considering this question, as the Treasury Regulations require, in light of the particular facts and circumstances of this case. It is only by looking at the particular problems Hi-Plains faced in providing medical services in Hale Center that we can determine whether the pharmacy sales to the staff doctors' patients contributed significantly to achieving that goal. Whether an activity contributes importantly to achieving an exempt purpose turns in each case on the particular problems encountered in attempting to achieve that purpose.

Not only did Hale Center lack any medical facilities when Hi-Plains was established, it was also subject to a problem shared by many rural communities, the inability to attract doctors to staff those facilities and administer medical care. It is undisputed that Hale Center had lacked a doctor for eight years before Hi-Plains was established and that no doctors, other than those associated with Hi-Plains, have come to Hale Center since then. It is also undisputed that Hi-Plains has engaged in a variety of measures designed to induce doctors to settle in Hale Center. It provided doctors with facilities and service personnel at a fraction of their normal cost. It has also made its own services available for the use of the doctors' private patients. The government concedes that: (t)he record is abundantly clear that these services are provided to the doctors as a convenience to lower their overhead in private practice * * *. (T)he hospital provides support services for the doctors in their private practices, as an inducement for the doctors to staff the hospital.

In capsule, the purpose of Hi-Plains is to provide medical services and attracting and holding doctors is essential to the accomplishment of that purpose.

The availability of the hospital's pharmacy for use by the doctor's private patients is causally related to inducing doctors to practice at Hi-Plains. Such sales facilitate the practice of medicine and thus contribute importantly to the goal of making medical services available at Hi-Plains. The ready availability of prescription drugs for the doctor's patients, no less than the availability of the hospital's x-ray and laboratory facilities for their service creates an inducement to practice medicine at Hi-Plains. Indeed, doctors practicing at Hi-Plains testified that the availability of the pharmacy had been a material factor in their decision to settle in Hale Center. Although pharmacy sales to nonhospital patients will generally not be considered to contribute importantly towards providing hospital services, see Rev.Rul. 68–375, 1968–2 C.B. 245, the problems faced by Hi-Plains indicate that in this case such sales do play an important role.

Finally, there is no indication that these sales are conducted on a larger scale than is reasonably necessary to accomplish Hi-Plains' exempt purpose. See Treas.Reg. § 1.513–1(d)(3). The pharmacy primarily sells prescription drugs to the patients of the hospital and to the private patients of the staff doctors. It has not sought to expand its market or the type of products it sells. It does not advertise nor does it use display areas to attract customers. In short, it lacks the indicia of a modern commercial drug store and appears to have directed its efforts solely at meeting the needs of the hospital and its staff doctors.

The government argues that the legislative history of section 513, the Treasury Regulations and the case law require a different result. We disagree. The government states that the purpose of the unrelated business tax was to alleviate the unfair competitive advantage given to tax-exempt organizations that compete with tax paying businesses. In this context, the government notes that sales by a hospital pharmacy to nonhospital patients were specifically mentioned as an unrelated trade or business in the Senate Report on the Tax Reform Act of 1969, P.L. 91–172, 83 Stat. 487. The difficulty with this argument, as explained below, is that the Senate Report refers to an amendment that was eventually rejected by the Conference Committee. See Conf.Rep.No. 782, 91st Cong., 1st Sess., reprinted in (1969) U.S. Code Cong. & Ad. News 2392, 2406.

Both the House and the Senate were concerned that business income from a collateral function might be insulated from taxation because an unrelated trade or business was carried on as a part of an exempt activity. The version of the bill proposed by the Senate identified three specific business activities which were being shielded from taxation by their relation to other exempt activities. See S.Rep.No. 552, 91st Cong., 1st Sess., reprinted in (1969) U.S. Code Cong. & Ad. News 2027, 2104. One activity was sales by a hospital pharmacy to the general public. See id. The Conference Committee, however, rejected the per se Senate bill in favor of a more general version proposed by the House. See Conf.Rep.No. 782, 91st Cong., 1st Sess., reprinted in (1969) U.S. Code Cong. & Ad. News 2392, 2406. The House Bill, and the bill ultimately enacted, provided that "an activity does not lose identity as a trade or business merely because it is carried on within a larger aggregate of similar activities * * * which may, or may not, be related to the exempt purpose of the organization." Tax Reform Act of 1969, § 121(c)(codified at I.R.C. § 513(c)). While the rejection of the Senate version does not imply that sales by a hospital pharmacy to the general public were not within the ambit of section 513, it does indicate that the Congress rejected a mechanical application of section 513 to such sales in favor of a more general approach. Moreover, the purpose of this amendment was to identify particular activities as a trade or business within the meaning of section 513. Such identification does not answer the remaining question of whether that activity is substantially related to the exempt purpose of the charitable organization.

The government also notes that section 1.513–1(b) of the Treasury Regulations expressly refers to sales by a hospital pharmacy to the general public. However, the context of this reference indicates that it is inapposite to the issue before us. In a subsection explaining what constitutes the first of the three required elements, "a trade or business," the regulations state that an activity does not lose its identity as a trade or business merely because it is incorporated in a larger aggregate of similar activities and give, as an example, sales by a hospital pharmacy to nonhospital patients. See Treas.Reg. § 1.513–1(b). The regulations essentially incorporate the amendment to section 513 enacted in the Tax Reform Act of 1969. This reference to sales by a hospital pharmacy, like the reference in the Senate Report, does no more than establish that sales by Hi-Plains' pharmacy constitute an identifiable trade or business. The fact that such sales satisfy the first element of a three part test does not answer the question of whether they satisfy the last part—are they substantially related to Hi-Plains' exempt purpose?

The government finally relies on Carle Foundation v. United States, 611 F.2d 1192 (7th Cir.1979), cert. denied, 449 U.S. 824, 101 S.Ct. 85, 66 L.Ed.2d 27 (1980). In Carle, a pharmacy in a tax exempt hospital sold drugs to both hospital patients and to the private patients of doctors who operated an independent clinic association on a for-profit basis in offices located in the hospital complex. The Seventh Circuit rejected a claim that sales to these private patients were exempt. It found that the "stated purpose of (Carle) Foundation is to conduct 'a hospital for the treatment of sick and disabled persons.' * * * There is no evidence that the sale of pharmaceuticals to the (independent) Clinic and its private patients substantially furthers that purpose." 611 F.2d at 1199.

Carle, however, is not inconsistent with our holding. The facts present in *Carle* give no indication that the hospital had any difficulty in attracting doctors to its staff. The *Carle* court considered that pharmacy services might be used to induce doctors to staff the hospital but found that there was no evidence in that case to support that proposition. Here, the evidence shows that a small rural community which was without medical services chose to make its hospital pharmacy available to service the private patients of any doctor who would serve in the community. This was only one, though an important component, of a bundle of benefits designed to attract and hold the medical doctor whose presence was essential to accomplish the broad goal of providing a hospital.

III

Our holding, that the pharmacy sales to private patients of the doctors are substantially related to the provision of hospital service and therefore not taxable under section 511 of the Code, does not dispose of this case. It appears from Hi-Plains' brief that a small portion of the pharmacy's income is derived from sales to the general public. Because sales to the general public, as opposed to sales to the private patients of the staff doctors, are not substantially related to Hi-Plains' exempt purpose, we must address Hi-Plains' other arguments.

Hi-Plains contends that the sale of drugs was itself an exempt activity. Hi-Plains relies on statements in its articles of incorporation and in the exemption letter from the IRS that Hi-Plains was organized to provide hospitalization and related services. It also relies on the fact that for a majority of the years which Hi-Plains has been in operation, Hale Center has lacked a pharmacy. The district court considered Hi-Plains' arguments but found that "it is the providing of a hospital that gives rise to the exemption and the added benefits must relate to the hospital." We cannot say that the district court's finding is clearly erroneous and therefore reject Hi-Plains' argument.

The parties below did not apparently distinguish between pharmacy sales to the private patients of the staff doctors and sales to the general public. Instead, they treated all nonhospital sales as one category. It is unclear whether sales to the general public, which involve only a small amount of money, were only made occasionally and thus not taxable. See Rev.Rul. 68–374, 1968–2 C.B. 242. We remand this issue to the district court. If the parties are unable to resolve this minor issue, the district court must give further consideration to the matter in light of what we have held here.

Reversed in part and remanded in part.

■ TATE, CIRCUIT JUDGE, dissenting:

The majority's scholarly and pragmatic opinion makes a persuasive presentation for its holding that, under the highly individualized facts presented to us, the profits from the sales by the tax-exempt hospital's pharmacy to private patients of the staff doctors should likewise be regarded as tax-exempt, because "substantially related" to the tax-exempt purpose of the charitable institution. I.R.C. §§ 501(a), 511, 513(a). The majority concludes that the activity meets this test essentially because it "contributes importantly" to the accomplishment of the tax-exempt function, see Treas.Reg. § 1.513–1(d)(2), under the narrow facts before us-that, to accomplish the tax-exempt purposes of affording hospital facilities in this small (pop. 2,250) community, it was necessary to provide substantial inducements to physicians to practice at the hospital center.

The majority therefore concludes that the sale of prescriptions at a profit to the private non-hospitalized patients of these medical practitioners (engaged in a private medical practice, not part of the tax-exempt function) can be considered substantially related to the tax-exempt purposes of the hospital itself—just as is, concededly, the sale of prescriptions to hospital patients, or (to entice the doctors to come) the furnishing by the hospital of office space to the doctors and of substantial below-cost assistance (nursing, bookkeeping, and billing) to them for their private and for-profit medical practices.

I respectfully disagree. The hospital pharmacy is open for sales at a profit to the general public and to private patients of the doctors (already furnished offices and other services by the hospital in aid of its tax-exempt purpose). I think the sales of prescriptions at a profit to non-hospital patients of doctors engaged in that regard in the practice of medicine for their personal profit is too attenuated in connection with the tax-exempt purpose so as to itself be tax-free.

The determinative issue is whether this activity "contributes importantly" to the accomplishment of the tax-exempt purpose, Treas.Reg. § 1.513(d)(2), so as to be considered as "substantially related * * * to the exercise or performance * * * of its charitable * * * function constituting the basis for its exemption under section 501." I.R.C. § 513(a). I would not disturb the administrative determination to the negative, nor the district court's findings to the negative (which, insofar as factual, are not clearly erroneous). The majority concedes that the sale of drugs to the general public, at least if on a non-occasional basis, would not be substantially related (i.e., contribute importantly) to the tax-exempt purpose. No more, in my opinion, should be the sale at profit of drugs by prescription to the private patients of doctors (themselves in this regard engaged in a medical practice for their own profit)—prescriptions that could as well be filled by pharmacies elsewhere (although, admittedly, more conveniently at the hospital's own pharmacy).

I therefore agree with the findings and conclusions of the district court, as follows: The court finds the evidence clearly establishes that the sales by the pharmacy to the private patients of the physicians were incidental to the purchaser's visit to his private physician and not incidental to the use of services provided by the hospital. Consequently, these sales constitute a trade or business which is not substantially related to the exercise or performance of plaintiff's exempt purpose, namely that of providing a hospital. The mere fact that the doctors operated out of the hospital under the arrangement described above and that these pharmacy sales were made by employees of the hospital does not qualify such sales as being a portion of the exempt purpose of the hospital. Since the sales are related to the private practices of the physicians and are substantially unrelated to the hospital, the income produced is taxable under 26 U.S.C. § 511. It is noted that the legislative history of these pertinent statutes indicates that one of the bases of their enactment was to prevent unfair competition. This court finds that this purpose would be served by denying plaintiff recovery in this case. During the period of years in question, the evidence indicated that two or more pharmacies had commenced their operation in Hale Center but were unable to continue in business for any lengthy period of time. To the contrary, the hospital's pharmacy was able to sustain its business, show a profit, and continue in business to this date. It would have a favored status in the event a tax exempt privilege were to be allowed for the hospital pharmacy income. This court has guidance from Carle Foundation v. United States of America, 611 F.2d 1192 (7th Cir.1979), in which the Seventh Circuit expressly held that pharmaceutical sales such as those presently in question give rise to unrelated business taxable income. The pharmaceuticals which were purchased by the doctors' private patients were as an incident of that person's visit to the private physician rather than as an incident to the hospital. The material facts of this case are the same as those in *Carle* and this court elects to follow that holding. Therefore, pharmacy sales to all persons who are not patients of the hospital, whether they are private patients of the physicians who office in the hospital or members of the community who come into the hospital for the sole purpose of purchasing pharmaceuticals, are taxable as unrelated business income.

In concluding, I must nevertheless admit the attractiveness of the individualized case-by-case consideration espoused by the majority. Bright-line ease of administration of the tax laws should yield to individualized equitable application, if indeed that was the intention of the Congress.

In my opinion, however, the danger of the majority's approach is that the judicial subjectivity in weighing the graduated factors—how small the town, how "important" the contribution, how "substantial" the relationship—will lead to uncertain and unequal applications, and also, to much greater judicial involvement in the ultimate determination of whether income from an unrelated trade or business conducted by a charitable organization is taxable. Compare majority opinion (income not taxable) with the Seventh Circuit's *Carle Foundation*, supra, (income taxable under generally similar circumstances). The majority's approach is further open to a more substantive objection. By hair-splitting judge-determined distinctions with regard to generically similar facts, profit-making activities conducted by charitable institutions separate from their tax-exempt purpose will be permitted to enjoy a competitive advantage over tax-paying businesses attempting to afford the same service, contrary to the Congressional intent made manifest by the legislative history and statutory provisions requiring taxation of such profit-making subsidiary operations.

I therefore respectfully dissent.

Revenue Ruling 80–296

1980–2 Cum. Bull. 195.

ISSUE

Is the sale of broadcasting rights to an annual intercollegiate athletic event by an organization exempt from federal income tax under section 501(c)(3) of the Internal Revenue Code unrelated trade or business within the meaning of section 513?

FACTS

The organization was created by a regional collegiate athletic conference, made up of universities exempt under section 501(c)(3) of the Code, for the purpose of conducting an annual competitive athletic game between the champion of the conference and another collegiate team. The annual game generates income from various sources including admission charges and the sale of exclusive broadcasting rights to a national radio and television network.

LAW AND ANALYSIS

Section 513(a) of the Code defines the term "unrelated trade or business" as any trade or business the conduct of which is not substantially related (aside from the need of an organization for income or funds or the use it makes of the profits derived) to the exercise or performance by an organization of its exempt function.

Section 1.513–1(d)(2) of the Income Tax Regulations provides that a trade or business is "substantially related" only if the production or distribution of the goods or the performance of the service from which the gross income is derived contributes importantly to the accomplishment of the purposes for which exemption is granted. Whether activities productive of gross income contribute importantly to the accomplishment of any purpose for which an organization is granted exemption depends in each case upon the facts and circumstances involved.

College and university athletic organizations that promote certain aspects of athletic competition have generally been held to be educational and thus exempt from federal income tax. An athletic program is considered to be an integral part of the educational process of a university, and activities providing necessary services to student athletes and coaches further the educational purposes of the university. See Rev. Rul. 67–291, 1967–2 C.B. 184. See also Rev. Rul. 64–275, 1964–2 C.B. 142.

The Service has traditionally taken the position that income from paid admissions to college and university athletic events, regardless of the number of persons in attendance or the amount of paid admissions, is not taxable as income from unrelated trade or business because the events themselves are related to the educational purposes of the colleges and universities. This position is consistent with the following language contained in the Committee Reports on the Revenue Act of 1950, in which the predecessor to section 513 of the Code was enacted.

> Athletic activities of schools are substantially related to their educational functions. For example, a university would not be taxable on income derived from a basketball tournament sponsored by it, even where the teams were composed of students from other schools. (H.R. Rep. No. 2319, 81st Cong., 2d Sess. 37, 109 (1950), 1950–2 C.B. 380, 458.)

> Of course, income of an educational organization from charges for admissions to football games would not be deemed to be income from an unrelated business, since its athletic activities are substantially related to its athletic program. (S. Rep. No. 2375, 81st Cong., 2d Sess. 29, 107 (1950), 1950–2 C.B. 483, 505.)

On the basis of the facts and circumstances presented in this case the educational purposes served by intercollegiate athletic activities are identical whether conducted directly by individual universities or by their regional athletic conference. Also, the educational purposes served by exhibiting a game before an audience that is physically present and exhibiting the game on television or radio before a much larger audience are substantially similar. Therefore, the sale of the broadcasting rights and the resultant broadcasting of the game contributes importantly to the accomplishment of the organization's exempt purposes.

HOLDING

The sale of broadcasting rights, under the circumstances described, is substantially related to the purpose constituting the basis for the organization's exemption and is not unrelated trade or business within the meaning of section 513 of the Code.

National Collegiate Athletic Ass'n v. Commissioner

United States Court of Appeals, Tenth Circuit, 1990.
914 F.2d 1417.

■ SEYMOUR, CIRCUIT JUDGE.

The National Collegiate Athletic Association (NCAA), the petitioner in this case, appeals from the decision of the tax court, which determined a deficiency of $10,395.14 in unrelated business income tax due for the 1981–1982 fiscal year. On appeal, the NCAA challenges the court's conclusion that revenue received from program advertising constituted unrelated business taxable income under I.R.C. § 512, not excludable from tax as a royalty under section 512(b)(2), I.R.C. § 512(b)(2). We reverse.[2]

---

2. Our determination that the advertising revenue is not unrelated business taxable income obviates the need to consider whether the income should nonetheless be excluded from taxation as a royalty under I.R.C. § 512(b)(2).

I.

The NCAA is an unincorporated association of more than 880 colleges, universities, athletic conferences and associations, and other educational organizations and groups related to intercollegiate athletics, for which it has been the major governing organization since 1906. The NCAA is also an "exempt organization" under section 501(c)(3) of the Code, I.R.C. § 501(c)(3), and hence is exempt from federal income taxes. One of the purposes of the NCAA, as described in the organization's constitution, is "to supervise the conduct of * * * regional and national athletic events under the auspices of this Association." Pursuant to this purpose, the NCAA sponsors some seventy-six collegiate championship events in twenty-one different sports for women and men on an annual basis. The most prominent of these tournaments, and the NCAA's biggest revenue generator, is the Men's Division I Basketball Championship. The tournament is held at different sites each year. In 1982, regional rounds took place at a variety of sites, and the Louisiana Superdome in New Orleans was the host for the "Final Four," the tournament's semifinal and final rounds. In that year, the Championship consisted of forty-eight teams playing forty-seven games on eight days over a period of almost three weeks. The teams played in a single-game elimination format, with each of the four regional winners moving into the Final Four.

The NCAA contracted with Lexington Productions, a division of Jim Host and Associates, Inc. ("Host" or "Publisher"), in 1981 to print and publish the program for the 1982 Final Four games.[3] The purpose of such programs, according to the NCAA's then-director of public relations, is

> "to enhance the experience primarily for the fans attending the game * * *. [It also] gives the NCAA an opportunity to develop information about some of its other purposes that revolve around promoting sports [as a] part of higher education and demonstrating that athletes can be good students as well as good participants."

Prior to the middle of the 1970s, the host institution produced the Final Four program. The NCAA took over production until the late 1970s, when it began contracting with Host for the Final Four program. In 1982, Host began producing the programs for all rounds of the Championship. The motive for contracting the program production to Host was, according to the NCAA, to achieve consistency and quality at each round's game sites; making a profit was not the primary incentive.

The "Official Souvenir Program" for the 1982 Final Four round of the tournament was some 129 pages long, and it featured pictures of NCAA athletes such as Michael Jordan and articles on the NCAA itself, on New

---

3. The agreement read in part: [Under the agreement, the NCAA granted Host the exclusive right to publish the Final Four program and to act as the NCAA's exclusive agent for the sale of advertising. Advertising in the program was not to exceed 35% of the total pages, and the NCAA reserved the right of final approval for all advertising. Host agreed to pay to the NCAA the sum of $50,000 or 51% of net revenues, whichever was greater]. The parties also entered into an oral agreement under which Host produced a uniform program for the regional tournament games.

Orleans, on individual athletes, on championships from prior years, and on the Final Four teams: Georgetown, Houston, Louisville, and North Carolina. Advertisements made up a substantial portion of the program, some of which were placed by national companies. Among the products and services so displayed were Buick automobiles, Miller beer, Texaco motor oil, Fuji film, Maxwell House coffee, Nike sneakers, McDonald's fast food, Coca-Cola soda, Xerox photocopiers, ESPN cable network, and Popeye's Famous Fried Chicken. Other advertisers were local New Orleans merchants. A number of the New Orleans advertisements, including those for restaurants, hotels, and rental cars, apparently were directed at out-of-town tournament attendees. But these advertisements were exceeded in number by those placed by New Orleans/Louisiana companies not specifically related to the tourist industry. Among the local advertisers were the Canal Barge Company, the National Bank of Commerce in Jefferson Parish, Breit Marine Surveying, Inc., Pontchartrain Materials Corp., McDermott Marine Construction, and Tri-Parish Construction & Materials, Inc.[4]

The NCAA's total revenue from the 1982 Men's Division I Basketball Championship was $18,671,874. The NCAA reported none of this amount as unrelated business taxable income on its federal income tax return for the fiscal year ending August 31, 1982. The Commissioner mailed the NCAA a notice of deficiency in which he determined that the NCAA was liable for $10,395.14 in taxes on $55,926.71 of unrelated business taxable income from the program advertising revenue. The NCAA petitioned the tax court for a redetermination of the deficiency set forth by the Commissioner. The tax court determined that this revenue was unrelated business taxable income, and that it was not excludable from the tax as a royalty.

* * *

III.

Section 511 of the Code imposes a tax on the unrelated business taxable income of exempt organizations. Section 512(a)(1) of the Code defines the term "unrelated business taxable income" as "the gross income derived by any organization from any unrelated trade or business * * * regularly carried on by it * * *." The term "unrelated trade or business" means "any trade or business the conduct of which is not substantially related * * * to the exercise or performance by such organization" of its exempt function. I.R.C. § 513(a). Under the heading "Advertising, etc., activities," section 513(c) provides that "the term 'trade or business' includes any activity which is carried on for the production of income from the sale of goods or the performance of services * * *. An activity does not lose identity as a trade or business merely because it is carried on * * * within a larger complex of other endeavors which may, or may not, be related to the exempt purposes of the organization." I.R.C. § 513(c).

4. Only the Final Four program was included in the record, and so we use it as an example. The NCAA's director of public relations testified that the program for the earlier rounds differed very little from the Final Four program. See rec., vol. II, at 33.

The NCAA's advertising revenue therefore must be considered unrelated business taxable income if: "(1) It is income from trade or business; (2) such trade or business is regularly carried on by the organization; and (3) the conduct of such trade or business is not substantially related (other than through the production of funds) to the organization's performance of its exempt functions." Treas. Reg. § 1.513–1(a). If a taxpayer shows that it does not meet any one of these three requirements, the taxpayer is not liable for the unrelated business income tax.

The NCAA concedes that its program advertising was a "trade or business" not "substantially related" to its exempt purpose. The only question remaining, therefore, is whether the trade or business was "regularly carried on" by the organization. The meaning of the term "regularly carried on" is not defined by the language of the statute. Accordingly, we turn to the Treasury Regulations for assistance.[5]

Section 1.513–1(c) of the Treasury Regulations provides a discussion of the phrase "regularly carried on." The general principles set out there direct us to consider "the frequency and continuity with which the activities productive of the income are conducted and the manner in which they are pursued." Treas. Reg. § 1.513–1(c)(1)(emphasis added). As a cautionary note, the regulations emphasize that whether a trade or business is regularly carried on must be assessed "in light of the purpose of the unrelated business income tax to place exempt organization business activities upon the same tax basis as the nonexempt business endeavors with which they compete." Id.

The regulations then move beyond the general principles and set out a process for applying the principles to specific cases. The first step is to consider the normal time span of the particular activity, and then determine whether the length of time alone suggests that the activity is regularly carried on, or only intermittently carried on. See id. § 1.513–1(c)(2)(i). If the activity is "of a kind normally conducted by nonexempt commercial organizations on a *year-round* basis, the conduct of such [activity] by an exempt organization over a period of only a few weeks does not constitute the regular carrying on of trade or business." Id. (emphasis added). As an example of a business not regularly carried on, the regulations describe a hospital auxiliary's operation of a sandwich stand for only two weeks at a state fair. In contrast, the regulations deem the operation of a commercial parking lot every Saturday as a regularly-carried-on activity. Id.

If the activity is "of a kind normally undertaken by nonexempt commercial organizations only on a seasonal basis, the conduct of such activities by an exempt organization during a significant portion of the season ordinarily constitutes the regular conduct of trade or business." Id.

5. We of course accord the Treasury Regulations deference unless they are unreasonable or plainly inconsistent with the Code. See Commissioner v. Portland Cement Co., 450 U.S. 156, 169, 101 S.Ct. 1037, 67 L.Ed.2d 140 (1981). Neither party challenges the validity of the regulations, and both argue that they provide the analytical framework for our inquiry here.

(emphasis added). The operation of a horse racing track several weeks a year is an example of a regularly-conducted seasonal business, because such tracks generally are open only during a particular season. Id.

A primary point of contention in this case is whether the NCAA's advertising business is normally a seasonal or year-round one, and whether it is intermittent or not. The tax court noted that the Commissioner looked at the short time span of the tournament, concluded that it was as much a "seasonal" event as the operation of a horse racing track, and then argued that the time involved in the tournament program advertising made it a regularly carried on business. The court observed that the NCAA, which did not agree with the Commissioner's "season" conclusion, also focused on the tournament itself in contending that the event's short time span made the activity in question intermittent. The tax court rejected these arguments as "plac[ing] undue emphasis on the tournament itself as the measure for determining whether petitioner regularly carried on the business at issue * * *. Although sponsorship of a college basketball tournament and attendant circulation of tournament programs are seasonal events, the 'trade or business' of selling advertisements is not."

We agree that to determine the normal time span of the activity in this case, we should consider the business of *selling advertising space*, since that is the business the Commissioner contends is generating unrelated business taxable income. There is no dispute that the tournament itself is substantially related to the NCAA's exempt purpose and so, unlike the horse racing track, it should not be the business activity in question. See American College of Physicians, 475 U.S. at 839 ("Congress has declared unambiguously that the *publication of paid advertising* is a trade or business activity *distinct* from the publication of accompanying * * * articles")(emphasis added). Since the publication of advertising is generally conducted on a year-round basis, we conclude that if the NCAA's sale of program advertising was conducted for only a few weeks, that time period could not, standing alone, convert the NCAA's business into one regularly.

In regard to the question of how long the NCAA conducted its advertising business, the tax court stated that "it is inappropriate to decide whether the trade or business at issue is regularly carried on solely by reference to the time span of the tournament itself." The tax court, observing that the agency relationship between the NCAA and Host allowed the court to attribute Host's activities to the NCAA, noted that the NCAA had "not produced any evidence * * * regarding the extent or manner of Host's conduct in connection with the solicitation, sale, and publication of advertising for the tournament programs." The court went on to conclude that "without such evidence [the NCAA] has not proven that neither it nor Host carried on the activity of selling program advertising regularly. [The tax court] will not assume Host's conduct in this regard was infrequent or conducted without the competitive and promotional efforts typical of other commercial endeavors." We believe the tax court focused its analysis in the wrong direction.

The tax court held, and the Commissioner argues, that the amount of preliminary time spent to solicit advertisements and prepare them for publication is relevant to the regularly-carried-on determination, and that the length of the tournament is not relevant. This position is contrary to the regulations and to existing case law. The language of the regulations alone suggests that preparatory time should not be considered. The sandwich stand example in the regulations, for instance, included a reference only to the two weeks it was operated at the state fair. See Treas. Reg. § 1.513–1(c)(a)(i). The regulations do not mention time spent in planning the activity, building the stand, or purchasing the alfalfa sprouts for the sandwiches.

The case closest to the one here also does not evaluate preparatory time. In that case, Suffolk County Patrolmen's Benevolent Ass'n v. Commissioner, 77 T.C. 1314 (1981), an exempt organization staged a professional vaudeville show every year as a fundraising event, using a company with which it had contracted. The organization derived the vast majority of its receipts from the sale of advertising in a program guide distributed to show patrons and to anyone who requested it. The shows generally consisted of three or four performances stretching over two weekends. The tax court found that preparation for the shows and the program, including the solicitation of advertisements, lasted eight to sixteen weeks, but it then emphasized that "nowhere in the regulations or the legislative history of the tax on unrelated business income is there any mention of time apart from the duration of the event itself * * *. The fact that an organization seeks to insure the success of its fundraising venture by beginning to plan and prepare for it earlier should not adversely affect the tax treatment of the income derived from the venture."

As in *Suffolk County*, the advertising here was solicited for publication in a program for an event lasting a few weeks. The NCAA did put on evidence as to the duration of that event. While the length of the tournament is irrelevant for purposes of assessing the normal time span of the business of selling advertising space, we hold that, contrary to the tax court's conclusion, the tournament must be considered the actual time span of the business activity sought to be taxed here. The length of the tournament is the relevant time period because what the NCAA was selling, and the activity from which it derived the relevant income, was the publication of advertisements in programs distributed over a period of less than three weeks, and largely to spectators.[7] Obviously, the tournament is the relevant time frame for those who chose to pay for advertisements in the program. This case is unlike American College of Physicians, 475 U.S. at 836, where advertisements were sold for each issue of a monthly medical journal. Accordingly, we conclude that the NCAA's involvement in the sale

7. There was testimony that some programs also were sold to members of the public not attending the tournament, but who wanted the program as a souvenir of the tournament. See Suffolk County Patrolmen's Benevolent Ass'n v. Commissioner, 77 T.C. 1314, 1317 (1981)(vaudeville show program made available to any nonpatron who requested it).

of advertising space was not sufficiently long-lasting to make it a regularly-carried-on business solely by reason of its duration.

The next step of the regulation's analysis is to determine whether activities which are intermittently conducted are nevertheless regularly carried on by virtue of the manner in which they are pursued. In general, according to the regulations, "exempt organization business activities which are engaged in only discontinuously or periodically will not be considered regularly carried on if they are conducted without the competitive and promotional efforts typical of commercial endeavors." Treas. Reg. § 1.513–1(c)(2)(ii). As an example of an activity not characteristic of commercial endeavors, the regulations refer to "the publication of advertising in programs for sports events or music or drama performances." Id. (emphasis added). The NCAA places considerable emphasis on this latter sentence and criticizes the tax court, which stated only that there was insufficient evidence from which the court could draw conclusions on the manner of Host's conduct of its advertising activities. As the NCAA stresses, the tax court did not distinguish the 1982 Basketball Championship from the "sports events" referred to in the regulation above.

On appeal, the Commissioner initially agreed with the tax court that the record was devoid of evidence with which the NCAA could show that Host's efforts were not of a sufficiently competitive and promotional nature. But the Commissioner then went on to focus on the Final Four program, a part of the record. He characterized the program's advertisements as "typical print media advertisements," and distinguished them from the advertisements in the vaudeville show programs, which " 'more closely resembled complimentary contributions than commercial selling agents.' "The sentence referring to sports events in the regulations was, according to the Commissioner, directed more at advertising in high school sports programs than at the type of advertising in the program here.

Addressing first the tax court's conclusion, we fail to see what evidence in addition to the advertisements themselves the tax court could require. The regulations discuss the business of advertising but refer only to advertisements published in programs, and not to any efforts to secure the advertisements. In *Suffolk County*, the tax court disregarded all but the advertisements themselves and stated that it is "entirely reasonable for an exempt organization to hire professionals in an effort to insure the success of a fundraiser, and there are no indications [in the applicable statutes and regulations] * * * that the use of such professionals would cause an otherwise infrequent intermittent activity to be considered regularly carried on." 77 T.C. at 1323.

The Commissioner's assertion that the advertisements themselves are of a commercial nature deserves more discussion. It is true that a number of the advertisements are virtually indistinguishable from those that might appear in magazines like Sports Illustrated. A substantial number of other advertisements, however, particularly those placed by Louisiana companies not engaged in the tourist industry, seem to us to resemble more closely the "complimentary contributions" of Suffolk County.

The difficult question of whether the NCAA's advertising is of the type envisioned as commercial in nature, or instead as consistent with that connected to the "sports events" referred to in the regulations, is not one which we must answer now, however. For the final step in the process spelled out by the regulations requires us to consider whether, promotional efforts notwithstanding, an intermittent activity occurs "so infrequently that neither [its] recurrence nor the manner of [its] conduct will cause [it] to be regarded as trade or business regularly carried on." Treas. Reg. § 1.513–1(c)(2)(iii). We conclude that the advertising here is such an infrequent activity. The programs containing the advertisements were distributed over less than a three-week span at an event that occurs only once a year. We consider this to be sufficiently infrequent to preclude a determination that the NCAA's advertising business was regularly carried on.

Our conclusion is buttressed by the regulation's admonition that we apply the regularly-carried-on test in light of the purpose of the tax to place exempt organizations doing business on the same tax basis as the comparable nonexempt business endeavors with which they compete. See Treas. Reg. § 1.513–1(c)(1). The legislative history of the unrelated business income tax also convinces us that we must consider the impact an exempt organization's trade or business might have on its competition. The tax was a response to the situation prevailing before 1950, when an exempt organization could engage in any commercial business venture, secure in the knowledge that the profits generated would not be taxed as long as the destination of the funds was the exempt organization. The source of those funds did not affect their tax status. * * * As more and more exempt organizations began acquiring and operating commercial enterprises, there were rumblings in Congress to do away with the perceived advantage enjoyed by these organizations. The case which most forcefully brought this point home was that involving the C.F. Mueller Co. That company, a leading manufacturer of macaroni products, was in 1947 acquired and organized for the purpose of benefitting the New York University's School of Law, a tax-exempt educational institution.[8] See C.F. Mueller, 190 F.2d at 121. This acquisition prompted an outcry from a number of sources.

In President Truman's 1950 message to Congress, for example, he stated that " 'an exemption intended to protect educational activities has been misused in a few instances to gain competitive advantage over private enterprise through the conduct of business * * * entirely unrelated to educational activities.' "Primarily to "restrain the unfair competition fos-

8. New York University also owned a leather company and chinaware manufacturing operations. Other educational institutions operated a number of enterprises: automobile parts, cotton gins, oil wells, theaters, an airport, a radio station, a hydroelectric plant, haberdasheries, citrus groves, and cattle ranches. See Kaplan, Intercollegiate Athletics and the Unrelated Business Income Tax, 80 Colum. L. Rev. 1430, 1432 & n.8 (1980).

tered by the tax laws," Congress imposed a tax on the business income of exempt organizations, but only on that income substantially unrelated to the organization's exempt purposes.[9] See Revenue Act of 1950, Pub. L. No. 814, § 301, 64 Stat. 906, 947.

Although we have observed that the purpose of the unrelated business income tax was to prevent unfair competition[10] between companies whose earnings are taxed and those whose are not, it is not necessary to prove or disprove the existence of actual competition. But analyzing the business in question in terms of its possible effect on prospective competitors helps to explain why an activity can occur "so infrequently" as to preclude a designation as a business regularly carried on. While the operation of a parking lot on a weekly basis occurs sufficiently frequently to threaten rival parking lot owners, the hospital auxiliary's annual sandwich stand is too infrequent a business to constitute a threat to sandwich shop owners. The competition in this case is between the NCAA's program and all publications that solicit the same advertisers. The competition thus includes weekly magazines such as Sports Illustrated and other publications which solicit automobile, beverage, photocopier, and fried chicken advertisements, to name a few. Viewed in this context, we conclude that the NCAA program, which is published only once a year, should not be considered an unfair competitor for the publishers of advertising. Application of the unrelated business tax here therefore would not further the statutory purpose. We hold that the NCAA's advertising business was not regularly carried on within the meaning of the Code.

The decision of the tax court is REVERSED.

NOTE

The Service did not acquiesce to the Tenth Circuit's decision in *NCAA*. See A.O.D. 1991–015. Although it strongly disagreed with the decision, the Service announced that it would not seek Supreme Court review because there was no conflict between the circuits but it would continue litigating the issue "in appropriate cases." Id.

9. Although prevention of unfair competition was the main purpose behind the unrelated business income tax, revenue raising concerns also played a role in Congress' actions, for Congress feared that exempt organizations, with a tax-induced competitive advantage, would drive other enterprises out of business. Congress believed this would mean that " 'eventually all the noodles produced in this country will be produced by corporations held or created by universities * * * and there will be no revenue to the Federal Treasury from this industry. That is our concern.' "

10. The term "unfair competition" is the hallmark of the unrelated business income tax, but the content of that term has been called into question. As one commentator has noted, "different tax treatment * * * implies only that N.Y.U. would keep a larger share of Mueller's profits than would Ronzoni's owners * * *. Why must a fair tax code treat students and scholars who are the beneficiaries of Mueller's profits as if they were 'equal to' Ronzoni's investors?" Rose-Ackerman, Unfair Competition and Corporate Income Taxation, 34 Stan. L. Rev. 1017, 1020 (1982).

Revenue Ruling 73–104

1973–1 Cum.Bull. 263.

Advice has been requested whether, under the circumstances described below, the sales activities of an educational organization that is exempt from Federal income tax under section 501(c)(3) of the Internal Revenue Code of 1954 constitutes unrelated trade or business within the meaning of section 513 of the Code.

The organization maintains and operates an art museum devoted to the exhibition of modern art. The museum offers for sale to the general public greeting cards that display printed reproductions of selected works from the museum's collection and from other art collections. The proportions of the reproductions are determined by the form of the original work and care is taken with respect to other technical aspects of the reproduction process. Each card is imprinted with the name of the artist, the title or subject matter of the work, the date or period of its creation, if known, and the museum's name. The cards contain appropriate greetings and are personalized on request.

The organization sells the cards in the shop it operates in the museum. It also publishes a catalogue in which it solicits mail orders for the greeting cards. The catalogue is available at a small charge and is advertised in magazines and other publications throughout the year. In addition, the shop sells the cards at quantity discounts to retail stores. As a result, a large volume of cards are sold at a significant profit.

Section 511(a) of the Code imposes a tax upon the unrelated business taxable income (as defined in section 512) of organizations exempt from Federal income tax under section 501(c)(3). Section 512(a) of the Code defines "unrelated business taxable income" as income from any "unrelated trade or business" regularly carried on by the organization as computed in the manner provided in section 512.

The term "unrelated trade or business" is defined in section 513 of the Code as any trade or business the conduct of which is not substantially related (aside from the need of such organization for income or funds or the use it makes of the profits derived) to the exercise or performance by such organization of its exempt functions.

Section 513(c) of the Code and section 1.513–1(b) of the Income Tax Regulations provide that trade or business includes any activity which is carried on for the production of income from the sale of goods.

Section 1.513–1(d)(2) of the regulations provides that a trade or business is "substantially related" to purposes for which exemption is granted only if the production or distribution of the goods from which the gross income is derived "contributes importantly" to the accomplishment of those purposes.

The museum is exempt as an educational organization on the basis of its ownership, maintenance, and exhibition for public viewing of works of art. The sale of greeting cards displaying printed reproductions of art works contributes importantly to the achievement of the museum's exempt educational purposes by stimulating and enhancing public awareness, interest, and appreciation of art. Moreover, a broader segment of the public may be encouraged to visit the museum itself to share in its educational functions and programs as a result of seeing the cards. The fact that the cards are promoted and sold in a clearly commercial manner at a profit and in competition with commercial greeting card publishers does not alter the fact of the activity's relatedness to the museum's exempt purpose.

Accordingly, it is held that these sales activities do not constitute unrelated trade or business under section 513 of the Code.

Revenue Ruling 73–105

1973–1 Cum.Bull. 264.

Advice has been requested whether, under the circumstances described below, the sales activities of an art museum exempt from Federal income tax as an educational organization under section 501(c)(3) of the Internal Revenue Code of 1954 constitute unrelated trade or business within the meaning of section 513 of the Code.

The organization maintains and operates an art museum devoted to the exhibition of American folk art. It operates a shop in the museum that offers for sale of the general public: (1) reproductions of works in the museum's own collection and reproductions of artistic works from the collections of other art museums (these reproductions take the form of prints suitable for framing, postcards, greeting cards, and slides); (2) metal, wood, and ceramic copies of American folk art objects from its own collection and similar copies of art objects from other collections of art works; and (3) instructional literature concerning the history and development of art and, in particular, of American folk art. The shop also rents originals or reproductions of paintings contained in its collection. All of its reproductions are imprinted with the name of the artist, the title or subject matter of the work from which it is reproduced, and the museum's name.

Also sold in the shop are scientific books and various souvenir items relating to the city in which the museum is located.

Section 511(a) of the Code imposes a tax upon the unrelated business taxable income (as defined in section 512) of organizations exempt from Federal income tax under section 501(c)(3). Section 512(a) of the Code defines "unrelated business taxable income" as the gross income from any "unrelated trade or business" regularly carried on by the organization as computed in the manner provided in section 512.

The term "unrelated trade or business" is defined in section 513 of the Code as any trade or business the conduct of which is not substantially related (aside from the need of such organization for income or funds or the use it makes of the profits derived) to the exercise or performance by such organization of its exempt functions.

Section 1.513–1(d)(2) of the Income Tax Regulations provides that trade or business is "substantially related" to purposes for which exemption is granted only if the production or distribution of the goods from which the gross income is derived "contributes importantly" to the accomplishment of those purposes.

Section 513(c) of the Code and section 1.513–(b) of the regulations provide that trade or business includes any activity which is carried on for the production of income from the sale of goods. An activity does not lose its identity as trade or business merely because it is carried on within a larger aggregate of similar activities or within a larger complex of other endeavors which may not be related to the exempt purposes of the organization.

Thus, sales of a particular line of merchandise any be considered separately to determine their relatedness to the exempt purpose. Section 1.513–1(d)(2) of the regulations emphasizes that it is the particular facts and circumstances involved in each case which determines whether the activities in question contribute importantly to the accomplishment of any purpose for which the organization is exempt.

An art museum is exempt as an educational organization on the basis of its ownership, maintenance, and exhibition for public viewing of an art collection. The sale and rental of reproductions of works from the museum's own collection and reproductions of artistic works not owned by the museum contribute importantly to the achievement of the museum's exempt educational purpose by making works of art familiar to a broader segment of the public, thereby enhancing the public's understanding and appreciation of art. The same is true with respect to literature relating to art.

Accordingly, it is held that these sales activities do not constitute unrelated trade or business under section 513 of the Code.

On the other hand, scientific books and souvenir items relating to the city where the museum is located have no causal relationship to art or to artistic endeavor and, therefore, the sale of these items does not contribute importantly to the accomplishments of the subject organization's exempt educational purpose which, as an art museum, is to enhance the public's understanding and appreciation of art. The fact that some of these items could, in a different context, be held related to the exempt educational purpose of some other exempt educational organization does not change the conclusion that in this context they do not contribute to the accomplishment of this organization's exempt educational purpose.

Additionally, under the provisions of section 513(c) of the Code, the activity with respect to sales of such items does not lose identity as trade or business merely because the museum also sells articles which do contribute importantly to the accomplishment of its exempt function.

Accordingly, it is held that the sale of those articles having no relationship to American folk art or to art generally, constitutes unrelated trade or business under section 513 of the Code.

NOTE: CORPORATE SPONSORSHIP ACTIVITIES

Background. In the early 1990's, the Internal Revenue Service provoked a major controversy by threatening to tax the income received by exempt organizations from corporate sponsorship arrangements. In a celebrated technical advice memorandum, the Service ruled that two § 501(c)(3) organizations that conducted college football bowl games were taxable on amounts received from corporations paying substantial sums to "sponsor" the annual events. Tech. Adv. Memo 9147007. Although the ruling deleted the names of the affected organizations, it was well known that they were the Mobil Cotton Bowl and the John Hancock Bowl. See, e.g., Bowl Ruling May Affect Others, Chron. of Philanthropy (Dec. 17, 1991). It was reported that the Mobil Oil Corporation paid over $1 million to sponsor the "Mobil Cotton Bowl," in return for which Mobil's name and logo were prominently displayed on the playing field, scoreboards, uniforms, paper cups, and all related print material connected with the New Year's Day event. Id.

In its "Cotton Bowl ruling" the Service concluded that the corporate sponsor's payment was made with an expectation of receiving a substantial return benefit for the "well-positioned visual images" displayed at the bowl game. Tech. Adv. Memo 9147007. The ruling's premise was that the activity went beyond mere "donor acknowledgment" and was more akin to advertising—thus, it was a trade or business, regularly carried on and not substantially related to the organization's exempt purposes.

College football fans and other nonprofit sector advocates reacted with alarm, fearing that the UBIT might be extended to a wide range of donor acknowledgement activities such as corporate sponsored art exhibits, Little League teams, walkathons, public broadcasting programs, and even named professorships at universities. After reading piles of mail, the Service first issued somewhat threatening audit guidelines and then retreated considerably in proposed regulations issued in 1993. Finally, Congress entered the fray in 1997 by enacting § 513(i), a specific statutory exclusion that is largely based on the generous proposed regulations. Final regulations interpreting § 513(i) were issued in 2002. Treas. Reg. § 1.513–4.

Qualified Sponsorship Payments. Section 513(i) excludes from the term "unrelated trade or business" the activity of soliciting and receiving "qualified sponsorship payments" (QSPs). A QSP is any payment (including cash payments, transfers of property and performance of services) made by a person engaged in a trade or business ("the sponsor") with respect to which there is no arrangement or expectation that the sponsor will receive any substantial return benefit other than the use or acknowledgement of the sponsor's name, logo, or product lines in connection with the activities of the exempt organization that receives the payment. I.R.C. § 513(i)(2)(A); Treas. Reg. § 1.513–4(c)(1) & 2(iv). A "substantial return benefit" does not include any goods or service that have an insubstantial value, such as complimentary tickets, pro-am playing slots in a golf tournament, or donor receptions. Return benefits also are deemed to be "insubstantial" and thus are disregarded if their aggregate fair market value is not more than 2 percent of the payment. Treas. Reg. § 1.513–4(c)(2)(ii).

Activities covered by the QSP exclusion may include a single event (such as a bowl game, walkathon or television program); a series of related events (such as a concert series or sports tournament); an activity of extended or indefinite duration (such as an art exhibit); or continuing support of an exempt organization's operation. See Preamble to Regulations on Corporate Sponsorship, T.D. 8991, F.R. 20433, reprinted in 36 Exempt Org. Tax Rev. 419 (2002). A payment may be a QSP even if the sponsored activity is not substantially related to the recipient organization's exempt purposes. Treas. Reg. § 1.513–4(c)(1).

Section 501(i) acts as a safe harbor, insulating payments that come within its reach from the UBIT. If the QSP safe harbor does not apply, a sponsorship payment is not necessarily taxable but must be evaluated under general UBIT principles apart from § 513(i). For example, a payment may not be taxable because the activity generating it is not regularly carried on. Treas. Reg. § 1.513–4(d)(1)(i).

Advertising. The QSP exclusion does not extend to payments received for advertising the sponsor's products or services. For this purpose, "advertising" means messages that include qualitative or comparative language, price information, etc., or other indications of savings or value, endorsements, and the like. I.R.C. § 513(i)(2)(A). Treas. Reg. § 1.513–4(c)(2)(v). Payments contingent upon the level of attendance at one or more events, broadcast ratings, or other factors indicating the degree of public exposure, also do not qualify for the QSP exclusion. I.R.C. § 513(i)(2)(B)(i); Treas. Reg. § 1.513–4(e)(2). But the fact that a sponsorship payment is contingent on an event taking place or being broadcast is not, in and of itself, fatal, nor is the distribution or display of a sponsor's products to the general public at a sponsored event. See id. and Joint Committee on Taxation, General Explanation of Tax Legislation Enacted in 1997 ("1997 General Explanation"), 105th Cong., 1st Sess. (1997).

A payment does not qualify as a QSP if it entitles the sponsor to the use or acknowledgement of its name, logo, or product lines in a regularly published periodical of the exempt organization that is not related to and primarily distributed in connection with a specific sponsored event. I.R.C. § 513(i)(2)(B)(ii)(I); Treas. Reg. § 1.513–4(b). Whether or not such a payment is taxable depends upon an application of general UBIT principles relating to periodical advertising, as developed in the regulations (see Treas. Reg. § 1.513–1(d)(4)(iv) Example 7) and the case law (see, e.g., United States v. American College of Physicians, supra p. 578). In addition, the QSP safe harbor does not apply to payments made in connection with any qualified convention or trade activity, as defined in § 512(d)(3). I.R.C. § 513(i)(2)(B)(ii)(II); Treas. Reg. § 1.513–4(b).

Dual Purpose Payments. To the extent that a portion of a payment (if made as a separate payment) would be a qualified sponsorship payment, that portion and the other portion will be treated separately for purposes of the QSP exclusion. I.R.C. § 513(i)(3); Treas. Reg. § 1.513–4(d)(1), –4(f)

Examples 2 and 3. Thus, if a payment entitles the sponsor to both product advertising and the use or acknowledgement of the sponsor's name or logo by an exempt organization, the amount of the payment that exceeds the fair market value of the product advertising would not be taxable. The regulations place the burden of establishing the fair market value of any substantial return benefit on the exempt organization. Id. To illustrate, assume a corporate sponsor pays $100,000 to a museum to sponsor an art exhibit and receives in return $5,000 of "pure" advertising. Under a tainting rule in an earlier version of the regulations, the entire $100,000 would have been taxable, but § 501(i) only taxes the $5,000 in advertising revenue and not the $95,000 sponsorship income.

Exclusive Sponsorship and Provider Arrangements. The right to be an exclusive sponsor of an activity (without any advertising or other substantial return benefit to the payor)—such as for a museum exhibit or bowl game with a single corporate sponsor—is generally not considered to be a substantial return benefit. Treas. Reg. § 1.513–4(c)(2)(vi)(A), –4(f) Example 4. But an exclusive *provider* agreement—such as where, in return for a payment, an exempt organization agrees that products or services that compete with the payor's products or services will not be sold in connection with one or more of the exempt organization's activities—generally results in a substantial return benefit, causing the arrangement to fall outside the QSP safe harbor. Treas. Reg. § 1.513–4(c)(2)(vi)(B). If a payor receives both exclusive sponsorship and exclusive provider rights in exchange for making a payment, the fair market value of the exclusive provider arrangement and any other substantial return benefit is determined first in making the required allocation between taxable and excluded payments. Treas. Reg. § 1.513–4(f) Example 6. To illustrate, assume the increasingly common situation where a university receives a substantial payment from a soft drink company or athletic gear manufacturer and agrees in return that only that company's products may be sold on campus. Under the regulations, the payment would not come within the QSP safe harbor, but that does not necessarily resolve the ultimate question of whether the payment is taxable under general UBIT principles.

Web Sites and Hyperlinks. Another important question is whether links between Internet sites of an exempt organization and a sponsor constitute potentially taxable advertising. The regulations respond with two helpful examples. In the first, the mere posting of a list of sponsors along with hyperlinks to their web sites on an exempt organization's web site is treated as an acknowledgement if there is no promotion of products or advertising. But if the exempt organization provides a hyperlink to a sponsor's web site where the organization then endorses the sponsor's product, the endorsement is advertising and falls outside the QSP safe harbor. See Treas. Reg. § 1.513–4(f) Examples 11 and 12.

Impact on Public Charity Status. QSPs in the form of money or property (but not services) qualify as public support in determining whether an organization qualifies as a public charity and thus avoids private foundation status under §§ 170(b)(1)(A)(vi) or 509(a)(2). Treas. Reg. § 1.509(a)–3(f)(1), (3) Examples 2 and 3. See Chapter 3, supra.

For Further Reading. Frances R. Hill, Corporate Sponsorship in Transactional Perspective: General Principles and Special Cases in the Law of Tax-Exempt Organizations, 13 U. Miami Ent. & Sports L. Rev. 5 (1995); David A. Brennen, The Proposed Corporate Sponsorship Regulations: Is the Treasury Department "Sleeping with the Enemy?" 6 Kan. J.L. & Pub. Pol'y (1996); Nathan Wirtschafter, Note, Fourth Quarter Choke: How the IRS Blew the Corporate Sponsorship Game, 27 Loy.L.A.L.Rev. 1465 (1994).

NOTES AND QUESTIONS

1. *The Substantially Related Test.* Is substantial "relatedness" the appropriate standard for determining whether an exempt organization's business activity should be taxed? Does the test offer adequate guidance to exempt organizations and the Service? Have the courts and the Service applied the test too leniently, causing exempt organizations to exploit it? For example, is it reasonable to conclude that a symphony gift shop's sale of T-shirts with the likeness of a composer, an art museum's sale of Rodin pasta, Monet olive oil, or Cezanne baseballs, or an environmental organization's mail order sale of panda bears "contribute importantly" to the exempt purposes of these organizations?

At the 1987 Hearings of the House Ways and Means Oversight Subcommittee, Treasury Department officials testified that the relatedness test had "conceptual merit," but they expressed concern that its "inherent generality is a source of administrative difficulty." Although the Treasury made no substantive legislative recommendations, it proposed more detailed reporting rules to serve as a source of data for a more informed study of the adequacy of the relatedness test. See Statement of O. Donaldson Chapoton, 1 Hearings Before the Subcomm. on Oversight of the House Committee on Ways and Means, Unrelated Business Income Tax, 100th Cong., 1st Sess. 37–39 (Ser. 100–26, 1987) (hereinafter "1987 House Hearings"). For additional proposed reforms, which remain on the legislative back burner, see Section G of this chapter, infra, at pp. 664–670.

2. *The Convenience Exception.* The legislative history indicates that the exception for businesses carried on primarily for the convenience of members, students, patients, officers or employees was enacted to exempt university dining halls and dormitories, hospital cafeterias, and laundries serving students and patients. Why is this exception necessary? Why don't these activities escape the UBIT because they are substantially related to the organization's exempt purposes?

3. *Low-Cost Articles Exception.* Under another special exception, the distribution by charitable and veterans organizations of certain low-cost items incident to the solicitation of charitable contributions is not a taxable activity. I.R.C. § 513(h)(1); Treas. Reg. § 1.513–1(b). Congress enacted this safe harbor rule to protect organizations that distribute small items (such as greeting cards) as part of a fundraising campaign. In general, a low-cost

article is one costing the organization not more than $5 (this amount is indexed); in 2002 it was $7.90. I.R.C. § 513(h)(2). The charitable solicitation requirement is met if the distribution is made without the recipient's request or consent, the distributed items are accompanied by a request for a donation, and the solicitation includes a statement that the recipient may keep the article, whether or not a contribution is made. I.R.C. § 513(h)(3).

4. *Bingo Exception.* Income from bingo games, but not from other games of chance, is exempt from the UBIT if the bingo game is "not an activity ordinarily carried out on a commercial basis," and conduct of the game does not violate any state or local law. I.R.C. § 513(f). If these tests are not met, a regularly conducted bingo or other gambling activity is an unrelated business. Not all bingo qualifies for the § 513(f) exception. The courts have held that "instant" or pull tab bingo, a game of chance in which individuals place wagers by purchasing a card and pulling off sealed tabs to determine if the revealed numbers match a preprinted winning combination, does not qualify for the UBIT exception. See, e.g., Julius M. Israel Lodge of B'nai B'rith No. 2113 v. Commissioner, 98 F.3d 190 (5th Cir.1996).

5. *Tip Jars and Pickle Cards.* In addition to bingo, many small nonprofit organizations raise funds from more esoteric (at least to the uninitiated, which includes the authors) gambling activities. For example, tip jars are gambling devices in which players purchase sealed pieces of paper containing numbers or symbols entitling the player to a prize. In Vigilant Hose Co. of Emmitsburg v. United States, 87 A.F.T.R.2d 2001–2398 (D.Md.2001), the court found that proceeds from tip jars placed in taverns for the benefit of a volunteer fire department did not constitute UBTI. The for-profit taverns administered the activity, with the nonprofit's role being limited to obtaining a county permit and taking a share of the profits. On these facts, the court concluded that the organization's activities did not rise to the level of a trade or business and, in so doing, it declined to impute the taverns' activities to the nonprofit organization under an agency theory.

Pickle cards are another legal gambling activity for nonprofit organizations in Nebraska. In Education Athletic Ass'n v. Commissioner, 77 T.C.M. (CCH) 1525 (1999), the Tax Court held that a § 501(c)(3) educational organization that received all of its financial support from the sale of pickle cards to Nebraska liquor establishments was engaged in an unrelated trade or business even though state law prohibited for-profit firms from the activity. Despite the lack of any unfair competition, the court concluded that the organization's sale of the pickle cards was not substantially related to its exempt purposes and thus the profits were taxable. As a result, the organization failed to qualify as a public charity under § 509(a)(2) but, notably, its § 501(c)(3) exemption was not challenged.

6. *Associate Member Dues.* Trade associations, labor unions, and some agricultural organizations have attempted to avoid the UBIT by disguising revenue for certain services or benefits as dues paid by "associate members." Several federal postal unions pushed the envelope by charging dues

to associate members who were not even required to be postal workers but joined the unions primarily to obtain access to low-cost group insurance. In most cases, associate members have no voting rights, but occasionally they may have limited legal rights that on closer scrutiny are devoid of substance. The courts have been unreceptive to these arrangements. See, e.g., National League of Postmasters of the United States v. Commissioner, 86 F.3d 59 (4th Cir.1996); National Ass'n of Postal Supervisors v. United States, 944 F.2d 859 (Fed.Cir.1991); American Postal Workers Union v. United States, 925 F.2d 480 (D.C.Cir.1991). After a period of further controversy (and lobbying), Congress enacted § 512(d), which provides that § 501(c)(5) agricultural and horticultural organizations will not be taxable on any portion of membership dues not exceeding $100 by reason of any benefits or privileges to which the members are entitled. In Rev. Proc. 97–12, 1997–1 Cum. Bull. 631, the Service extended this statutory safe harbor by indicating that it would not treat income from associate member dues paid to § 501(c)(5) or § 501(c)(6) organizations as UBTI unless the associate member category was formed or availed of for the principal purpose of avoiding the UBIT.

7. *Feeder Corporations.* A "feeder corporation" generally is a controlled subsidiary of an exempt organization that carries on a trade or business for profit. Section 502(a) makes it clear that a feeder corporation will not be entitled to tax-exempt status on the ground that all of its profits are payable to one or more exempt organizations. Feeders are thus fully taxable entities even if *part* of their income might have been exempt if it had been earned directly by the exempt parent. Section 502 has been extended to deny exemption to certain shared-service organizations formed by several unrelated entities to serve special needs—e.g., a laundry serving a group of hospitals. See HCSC-Laundry v. United States, 450 U.S. 1, 101 S.Ct. 836 (1981). As discussed later in this chapter (see infra pp. 641–642), feeders are not necessarily bad. Indeed, if an exempt organization is clearly engaged in an unrelated business, a taxable subsidiary may be quite desirable from a planning standpoint.

Not all subsidiaries of exempt organizations are taxable "feeders." If the subsidiary is operated exclusively (i.e., primarily) for exempt purposes, it may obtain exempt status—e.g., where it carries on a trade or business that is substantially related to an exempt mission. In addition, a separate corporation can avoid taxable feeder status if its activities are an "integral part" of its exempt parent's activities, such as an organization operated for the sole purpose of furnishing electric power to a tax-exempt university. Treas. Reg. § 1.502–1(b). The integral part test is discussed in Chapter 2C4a, supra, at p. 142.

8. *UBIT Compliance.* Exempt organizations with $1,000 or more of gross income from an unrelated trade or business are required to file a Form 990—T (Exempt Organization Business Income Tax Return) on which they compute and pay their tax. I.R.C. § 6012(a)(2); Treas. Reg. § 1.6012–2(e). Quarterly payments of estimated tax also are required for organizations that anticipate $500 or more of UBIT liability for a taxable

year. I.R.C. § 6154(h). Information collected for the 1987 House Hearings revealed that very few organizations actually paid the UBIT. In 1986, for example, IRS data reveals that only 32,000 organizations (less than 5% of those organizations then listed in the IRS Master File) reported UBIT liability, and tax collected was a mere $53 million. Federal tax laws applicable to the activities of tax-exempt charitable organizations, hearings before Subcomm. on Oversight of House Comm. on Ways and Means, 103d Cong., 1st Sess. 27–28 (Ser. 103–39, 1993). By 1997, the last year for which reliable data is available, collected UBIT revenues increased to $418.4 million and returns were filed by 39,302 organizations (of which 10,614 were § 501(c)(3) organizations), but 47 percent of those filing UBIT returns in 1997 reported a net loss. Overall, form 990–T filers in 1997 reported $7.8 billion of gross unrelated business income, which was offset by $8.5 billion of total deductions, resulting in an overall net loss of $700 million. Margaret Riley, Unrelated Business Income of Nonprofit Organizations, 1997, in IRS Statistics of Income Division, Compendium of Studies of Tax–Exempt Organizations, 1989–1998, at 634 et seq. Significantly, these figures do not reflect any unrelated businesses conducted through for-profit, taxable subsidiaries.

PROBLEMS

1. Sturdley University is a prominent private university, with an undergraduate college and graduate colleges of law, medicine and agriculture. Sturdley controls several separately incorporated entities, some of which are described below. Evaluate the unrelated business tax consequences of the following activities:

(a) The Sturdley University Alumni Association, a separately incorporated § 501(c)(3) organization, operates a travel tour program open to all members of the Association and their immediate families. Last year, the Association made four mailings to its approximately 30,000 members announcing nine tours to various destinations around the world. The brochures described a special discount fare arrangement and stated that the tours included sightseeing and visits to historic sites. No formal educational program was conducted in connection with any trip. The Association works with various commercial travel agencies in planning the tours under arrangements whereby each participating travel agent pays the Association a per person fee.

(b) The University athletic department operates a campus golf course, used by the college golf team (3%), other students (27%), faculty and staff (20%) and the general public (50%). Public users are required to pay fees comparable to those charged by nearby commercial golf courses.

(c) The Sturdley College of Agriculture operates a commercial dairy adjacent to the campus. The primary purpose of the dairy is to teach the art of farming. The dairy has a store on campus where it sells products such as milk, butter, cheese and ice cream.

(d) The University has a large auditorium on campus that is used for class registrations, intercollegiate athletic events and commencement exercises. On average, the auditorium is used 75 days a year for events for which tickets are sold, including rock concerts, closed-circuit television presentations of boxing matches, and professional basketball games. All these events are open to the public and generate substantial revenues for the University.

(e) The University's athletic department operates a tennis club during the summer for the general public, charging membership and court fees.

(f) The University operates a summer sports camp for high school students, charging fees comparable to those charged by for-profit summer camps.

(g) The University's intercollegiate football and basketball programs generate substantial revenues, including admission fees, radio and television receipts, and the sale of advertising in programs and advertising space at the football stadium and basketball arena. The advertisements are for fast food restaurants, insurance companies, soft drinks, automobiles, and banks.

(h) The Sturdley Medical Center, a large teaching hospital, operates a 500-car parking garage adjacent to the hospital for the use of patients, staff, visitors and the general public. On many weekends, the garage also is used by spectators attending various concerts and sporting events at the auditorium and Sturdley Stadium.

(i) The Medical Center operates a pharmacy, primarily to sell drugs to patients and persons visiting private physicians in an adjacent medical office building owned by the hospital.

(j) The Sturdley Daily News, the student daily newspaper, derives revenue from advertising for local businesses serving the university community.

2.   The Museum of Provocative Art is a large urban museum with a wide variety of modern and traditional exhibits. Will it be subject to the unrelated business income tax if it realizes income from the operation of:

(a) A cafeteria and snack bar on museum premises for use by its staff, employees, visiting members of the public and employees of nearby businesses.

(b) A gift shop and bookstore, where it sells greeting cards, expensive books for coffee table display, art reproductions, jewelry, ceramics, stuffed animals and t-shirts with the museum logo.

(c) Same as (b), above, except that the museum also sells all the items available in the gift shop through a mail order catalog that is distributed nationwide.

(d) Same as (b), above, except the shop is a "satellite" facility located 25 miles from the museum in a suburban shopping mall.

(e) A theater on museum premises used for the showing of educational films during museum hours and as an ordinary motion picture theater for public entertainment during the evening.

(f) Sponsorship of a major new exhibit by a leading soft drink manufacturer. In exchange for a $500,000 payment, the corporate sponsor's name is included in the title of the event and is prominently displayed in all promotional literature and publicity. Special VIP showings and receptions are provided for the corporation's executives and their friends, and the corporate sponsor has the exclusive right to sell its soft drinks at the museum's cafeteria and vending machines.

C.   EXCLUSIONS FROM UNRELATED BUSINESS TAXABLE INCOME

Internal Revenue Code: §§ 512(a)(1), (b)(1)–(5), (7)–(9), (13), (15).

Treasury Regulations: §§ 1.512(b)–1(a)(1), (b), (c)(2)–(5), (d)(1).

The computation of unrelated business taxable income ("UBTI") is governed by § 512(a)(1), which defines UBTI as the gross income derived from the unrelated business less expenses directly connected with the carrying on of the trade or business, both computed with certain modifications in § 512(b). Most of these "modifications" are actually exclusions from the unrelated business tax base. As such, they are appropriately examined first, before turning to the more mechanical computation and expense allocation issues.

1.   PASSIVE INVESTMENT INCOME

When it first enacted the UBIT in 1950, Congress stated that passive investment income was long recognized as a proper source of revenue for charitable and educational organizations and was not likely to cause competitive problems for taxable businesses. S.Rep. No. 2375, 81st Cong., 2d Sess. (1950). In keeping with this policy, the most significant exclusions from UBTI are for traditional forms of passive investment income, such as dividends, interest, annuities, rents and royalties. I.R.C. § 512(b)(1)–(4). The exclusion extends to all gains from the sale, exchange or other disposition of property other than inventory and property primarily held for sale to customers in the ordinary course of a trade or business. I.R.C. § 512(b)(5). In effect, all capital gains are excluded unless the property is debt-financed. Gain on the sale of depreciable property used in an unrelated trade or business is taxable to the extent it is treated as ordinary income under the depreciation recapture provisions. Treas. Reg. § 1.1245–6(b).

In recognition of the growing investment sophistication of the nonprofit sector, this traditional list has been expanded to exclude income from modern investment and risk management strategies such as options, securities lending transactions, notional principal contracts and short sales. Treas. Reg. § 1.512(b)–1(a)(1); see also I.R.C. §§ 512(a)(5); 512(b)(5). As to short sales, see Rev. Rul. 95–8, 1995–1 C.B. 107.

As developed later in this chapter (see infra pp. 643–658), the passive investment income exclusions generally are unavailable if the income is derived from debt-financed property (e.g., dividends from securities purchased with borrowed funds). I.R.C. § 512(b)(4). In addition, some forms of investment income received by an exempt organization from a 50 percent or more controlled subsidiary may be taxable. See I.R.C. § 512(b)(13).

2. RENTS

The rules for the rent exclusion vary, depending on whether the rent is derived from real or personal property, or from a mixed lease. Real property rents are excludable in full, even if they are derived from an actively managed real estate rental business. I.R.C. § 512(b)(3)(A)(i). Personal property rents (e.g., from a lease of computer or medical equipment) are excludable only if derived from a mixed lease and the rents attributable to the personal property are an "incidental" (not more than 10 percent) part of the total rents received under the lease. I.R.C. § 512(b)(3)(A)(ii); Reg. § 1.512(b)–1(c)(2)(ii). If the amount attributable to personal property is more than incidental but not more than 50 percent of the total, the real property rent is excludable but the personal property rent is not. But if the personal property rent exceeds 50 percent of the total, then none of the rent is excludable. I.R.C. § 512(b)(3)(B)(i); Treas. Reg. § 1.512(b)–1(c)(2)(iii)(a). In making these determinations, the terms of the lease are not necessarily conclusive if the amounts allocated are unrealistic. See Treas. Reg. § 1.512(b)–1(c)(2)(iv), Example.

Rents dependent on profits or income derived by any person from the real property do not qualify for the exclusion unless they are based on a fixed percentage of gross receipts or sales. I.R.C. § 512(b)(3)(B)(ii). To prevent an obvious end-run around these requirements, multiple leases (i.e., separate leases with respect to real and personal property) are considered as one lease if the real and personal property covered by the lease have an "integrated use." Treas. Reg. § 1.512(b)–1(c)(3)(iii).

Amounts paid for the occupancy of space do not qualify for the rent exclusion if the property owner renders services for the convenience of the occupant, as in a hotel, boarding house, parking lot, or warehouse. Services are considered rendered to the occupant if they are "primarily for his convenience and are other than those usually or customarily rendered in connection with the rental of rooms or other space for occupancy only." Treas. Reg. § 1.512(b)–1(c)(5).

3.   ROYALTIES

The royalty exclusion is exceedingly broad, extending to virtually all payments for the right to use intangible property, including income received for the use of valuable intellectual property rights, such as patents, trademarks, and copyrights, but not to mineral royalties connected with working interest arrangements. See Treas. Reg. § 1.512(b)–1(b). Because the royalty concept is so elastic, exempt organizations have been encouraged to enter into licensing arrangements to exploit their valuable forms of intangible property rather than developing them directly. As illustrated by the materials that follow, the Service has attempted with very limited success to recharacterize some of these licensing arrangements as joint ventures, product endorsements, or the rendering of services for compensation.

Sierra Club, Inc. v. Commissioner

United States Court of Appeals, Ninth Circuit, 1996.
86 F.3d 1526.

■ WIGGINS, CIRCUIT JUDGE:

Sierra Club, Inc., a tax-exempt organization under I.R.C. § 501(c)(4), must pay taxes on "unrelated business taxable income" ("UBTI") under I.R.C. §§ 511–13. I.R.C. § 512(b)(2), however, excludes "all royalties" from UBTI, thus rendering the royalty income of a tax-exempt organization nontaxable. The Commissioner of Internal Revenue ("Commissioner") contends that the Tax Court erred in determining on summary judgment that Sierra Club's income from the rental of its mailing lists and from participation in an affinity credit card program constituted "royalties" and therefore was not taxable for the years 1985, 1986, and 1987. We have jurisdiction under 26 U.S.C. § 7482 and we AFFIRM in part, REVERSE in part, and REMAND.

I.

The income Sierra Club received from the following two business arrangements is at the center of this dispute.

A.   Mailing List Rentals

In order to communicate with its members in furtherance of its exempt purpose, Sierra Club developed and maintained a list of its members, donors, and other supporters; it also maintained a list of its catalog purchasers. Sierra Club had exclusive ownership rights in these mailing lists, including the right to all net income derived from them. Sierra Club retained Triplex Marketing Corporation ("Triplex"), a computer service bureau, to maintain the lists and update the lists by adding new names and removing stale names from the lists. Sierra Club also inserted "seed names" in its mailing lists to protect against abuse and unauthorized use of the lists.

Moreover, like many organizations, Sierra Club raised funds by permitting other organizations to "rent" the names from its mailing lists for a fee. Sierra Club retained Names in the News ("Names") and Chilcutt Direct Marketing Corporation ("Chilcutt")—both list managers—to administer and oversee the external uses of its lists. Sierra Club set the rates for the rental of the lists (the names on the lists could only be used once per rental); it also retained the right to review requests to rent the lists and to approve the proposed mailing material and schedule for the mailing.

Names and Chilcutt promoted the rental of Sierra Club's lists through solicitations, personal sales calls, advertising and seminars. Those who wished to rent Sierra Club's lists placed a list order with Chilcutt or Names, which Chilcutt or Names forwarded to Sierra Club. Sierra Club in turn filled the list rental order through Triplex, who would perform services requested by the list renter such as selecting names based on zip code, gender, or frequency of contribution. Triplex provided the membership list or catalog list on magnetic tape, cheshire labels, or pressure sensitive labels as instructed by the list renter. Triplex billed Names or Chilcutt for the performance of these services; Names or Chilcutt in turn billed the list renter for these costs.

Names and Chilcutt received a commission of ten percent of the base price of the list (the cost of renting the list excluding the Triplex service charges). Typically, the list broker arranging for the rental on behalf of the list user would also receive a commission of ten or twenty percent of the base list price. Sierra Club thus received payment for the rental of the list less the commissions for Names or Chilcutt, the list broker's commission and Triplex's service charges.

In the tax years 1985, 1986, and 1987, Sierra Club received $142,636, $317,579, and $452,042 respectively for the rental of its mailing lists.

B. Affinity Credit Card Program[2]

On February 20, 1986, after intermittent discussions, Sierra Club entered into an agreement (the "Sierra Club Bankcard Agreement") with American Bankcard Services, Inc. ("ABS"). The parties agreed that ABS would offer Sierra Club members a "Sierra Club Visa and/or Mastercard" with the name of Sierra Club on the front of the card and its logo on the reverse side. Sierra Club "agree[d] to cooperate with ABS on a continuing basis in the solicitation and encouragement of SC members to utilize the Services provided by ABS."

In exchange, ABS agreed to pay Sierra Club a monthly fee, designated in the agreement as a "royalty fee," of one-half percent of the total cardholder sales volume provided that the fees received by ABS from the financial institution issuing the card were between one-half and one per-

2. An affinity credit card program is an arrangement by which an organization such as Sierra Club agrees that a credit card issuer may use the organization's name and logo to market an affinity credit card—i.e., the Sierra Club Visa Card—in exchange for a small percentage of total amounts charged on the affinity card.

cent of total cardholder sales volume.[3] ABS was responsible for the development of promotional and solicitation materials for the card program, subject to Sierra Club's approval. ABS agreed to bear the cost of such materials; however, Sierra Club had the right to elect to pay for the production and mailing costs associated with the solicitations to its members, in which case Sierra Club would receive an increased payment. ABS also was required to maintain complete accounts for the program.

Moreover, ABS agreed to indemnify Sierra Club and its members from all liability arising out of participation in the affinity card program. Sierra Club agreed to indemnify ABS and its agents for all liability arising from Sierra Club's participation in the program to the extent that the liability was a result of gross or willful negligence. The agreement specifically states that it does not establish a partnership or agent/principal relationship between ABS and Sierra Club.

In addition, the Sierra Club Bankcard Agreement notes that ABS had entered into an agreement with Chase Lincoln First Bank ("Chase Lincoln") in which Chase Lincoln agreed "to issue bankcards for [Sierra Club]." In the event Chase Lincoln ceased to be the issuer of Sierra Club bankcards, ABS would recommend additional financial institutions from which Sierra Club could select a successor to Chase Lincoln.

After entering into the Sierra Club Bankcard Agreement, on March 9, 1986, ABS assigned its right to solicit Sierra Club's members to Concept I, Inc. On March 26, 1986, Sierra Club and Chase Lincoln entered into an agreement in which they agreed that if ABS failed to perform its duties under the Sierra Club Bankcard Agreement, Chase Lincoln would have the right to assume ABS's responsibilities. Sierra Club also agreed not to authorize the issuance of other affinity cards by any other bank during the terms of its agreement with ABS.

Further, in a March 28, 1986 agreement between Chase Lincoln and Concept I, Chase Lincoln agreed to issue the Sierra Club Visa; Concept I agreed to solicit Sierra Club members at least twice a year using names and addresses supplied by Sierra Club. The parties acknowledged that all promotional materials were to be approved by Sierra Club. "In consideration for the solicitation of Members to participate in the Card Program," Chase Lincoln agreed to pay Concept I one percent of the total retail purchase volume generated by the card program. In a separate agreement dated March 28, 1986 between ABS, Concept I, and Chase Lincoln, Chase Lincoln secured the right (but not the responsibility) to assume the rights and responsibilities of either ABS or Concept I in the event that either or both failed to perform its obligations under the Sierra Club Bankcard Agreement as well as under the March 7, 1986 agreement between Concept I and ABS. Finally, on July 7, 1986, Concept I reassigned its right to solicit Sierra Club members for the affinity card program to ABS.

---

3. The payment Sierra Club received increased if ABS received a greater percentage of total cardholder sales as a fee from the financial institution issuing the card. Sierra Club also received additional payments for Sierra Club members' use of an 800 number travel service.

ABS initially solicited Sierra Club members for the credit card program in letters dated June 15, 1986. The letters were written on Sierra Club's letterhead, contained Sierra Club's return address and were signed by Sierra Club's president.[5] The letters were mailed using Sierra Club's non-profit postage permit, although ABS stated that this was a "mistake" because "[i]t might have been better to have had the mailing delivered all at once rather than spread out over the entire month." ABS also placed advertisements in Sierra magazine, which ABS paid for at the standard commercial advertising rate. Members sent their credit card applications to Chase Lincoln; inquiries about the program were directed to a toll free number answered by Chase Lincoln or ABS. Members who applied for the Sierra Club Premier VISA received a letter on joint Sierra Club and Chase Lincoln letterhead, signed by the Vice President of Chase Lincoln and the Executive Director of Sierra Club, thanking them and welcoming them to the program.[6]

After the tax years at issue, ABS was unable to persuade Chase Lincoln to continue to waive its annual fee of $30. ABS mailed rebate checks to cardholders, many of which were not honored. Sierra Club declared ABS in default under their agreement on October 26, 1987 and terminated the agreement in late 1987. Sierra Club subsequently reimbursed its members for the annual fee. Sierra Club and Chase Lincoln entered into a new agreement, under which Sierra Club agreed, inter alia, to endorse the card program and encourage participation by its members, to include program information in its new member mailings and to advertise in Sierra magazine at its own expense.

For the tax years 1986 and 1987, Sierra Club received $6,021 and $303,225 respectively from the credit card program.

C.   Proceedings Before the Tax Court

On February 11, 1991, the Commissioner issued a notice of deficiency to Sierra Club for the 1985, 1986, and 1987 tax years based upon a determination that the income from the above described activities was UBTI and thus was taxable. After paying the additional tax, Sierra Club filed a petition before the Tax Court on May 7, 1991, challenging the Commissioner's deficiency determination and alleging that the income at issue constituted royalties which were excludable from UBTI.

Sierra Club and the Commissioner filed cross-motions for partial summary judgment on the issue of whether the income from the rental of mailing lists constituted royalties under I.R.C. § 512(b)(2) and therefore was excludable from UBTI. In a memorandum opinion dated May 10, 1993, the Tax Court held that the rental income from the mailing lists constitut-

---

5. The letters stated in part: As a member of the Sierra Club, you are eligible to apply for a new member service—The Sierra Club Premier VISA card. There are important advantages to both you and the Sierra Club when you use this card.

6. This letter reads in part: Thank you for joining with the Sierra Club and Chase Lincoln First in this important new program. We hope you'll enjoy the benefits and savings provided with your new Sierra Club Premier VISA.

ed royalties. In reaching this decision, the court defined royalties as " 'payments for the use of intangible property rights' "and thus are not limited solely to passive income, relying upon Disabled American Veterans v. Commissioner, 94 T.C. 60, 70 (1990) ("DAV II"), rev'd on other grounds, 942 F.2d 309 (6th Cir.1991).

The parties then filed cross-motions for summary judgment on the issue of whether the income from the affinity credit card program constituted royalties as well. In a second memorandum opinion dated August 24, 1994, the Tax Court held that the "consideration received by [Sierra Club] on account of its participation in the affinity credit card program was for the use of intangible property ([Sierra Club's] name, logo, and mailing list)."

* * *

The Commissioner appeals both decisions of the Tax Court.

II.

* * *

B.

The crux of the parties' dispute is how to define "royalties" for the purpose of I.R.C. § 512(b)(2). A tax-exempt organization under I.R.C. § 501(c) must pay taxes at normal corporate rates on "unrelated business taxable income." I.R.C. § 511(a). UBTI is defined as "the gross income derived by any organization from any unrelated trade or business * * * regularly carried on by it, less the deductions allowed * * * both computed with the modifications provided in subsection (b)." I.R.C. § 512(a)(1). Section 512(b)(2) provides that "[t]here shall be excluded all royalties (including overriding royalties) whether measured by production or by gross or taxable income from the property, and all deductions directly connected with such income."

"Royalties" as used in § 512(b)(2) is not further defined by statute or by regulation. Texas Farm Bureau v. United States, 53 F.3d 120, 123 (5th Cir.1995). Thus, we look to the "ordinary, everyday senses" of the word. Commissioner v. Soliman, 506 U.S. 168, 174, 113 S.Ct. 701, 705, 121 L.Ed.2d 634 (1993). Webster's Ninth New Collegiate Dictionary defines "royalty" in pertinent part as "a share of the product or profit reserved by the grantor esp. [sic] of an oil or mining lease * * * a payment made to an author or composer for each copy of his work sold or to an inventor for each article sold under a patent." Webster's Ninth New Collegiate Dictionary 1028 (1984).

Black's Law Dictionary provides a more comprehensive definition of a royalty as [c]ompensation for the use of property, usually copyrighted material or natural resources, expressed as a percentage of receipts from using the property or as an account per unit produced. A payment which is made to an author or composer by an assignee, licensee or copyright holder in respect of each copy of his work which is sold, or to an inventor in respect of each article sold under the patent. Royalty is share of product or profit reserved by owner for permitting another to use the property. Black's Law Dictionary 1330–31 (6th Ed.1979).

From the above, we can glean that "royalty" commonly refers to a payment made to the owner of property for permitting another to use the property. The payment is typically a percentage of profits or a specified sum per item sold; the property is typically either an intangible property right—such as a patent, trademark, or copyright—or a right relating to the development of natural resources.[12]

Revenue Ruling 81–178, relied upon by the parties, supports defining royalty as a payment which relates to the use of a property right. It states that "[p]ayments for the use of trademarks, trade names, service marks, or copyrights, whether or not payment is based on the use made of such property, are ordinarily classified as royalties for federal tax purposes." * * * Thus, according to Revenue Ruling 81–178, by definition, "royalties do not include payments for personal services." Rev. Rul. 81–178, 1981–2 C.B. 135.

The parties agree that the above definition of royalty is correct—up to this point. The Commissioner argues that "royalty" must be further defined, claiming that a payment for the use of intangible property is not necessarily a royalty unless the subject of the payment is "passive in nature." Sierra Club, on the other hand, contends that any payment for the use of an intangible property right constitutes a royalty. For the following reasons, we hold that under § 512(b)(2) "royalties" are payments for the right to use intangible property. We further hold that a royalty is by definition "passive" and thus cannot include compensation for services rendered by the owner of the property.

First, the circuits that have considered whether or not income received by a tax-exempt organization constitutes royalties under § 512(b)(2) have consistently excluded income received as compensation for services-income that is not "passive"—from royalty income. In Disabled American Veterans v. United States, 227 Ct.Cl. 474, 650 F.2d 1178 (1981) ("DAV I"), the Court of Claims upheld the Tax Court's determination that DAV's income from the rental of its donor lists to other organizations was not royalty income under § 512(b)(2). The court reasoned that § 512(b) as a whole "excludes from taxation the conventional type of passive investment income tradition-ally earned by exempt organizations (dividends, interest, annuities, real property rents)." Id. Because DAV's rental of its donor lists was "the product of extensive business activity by DAV" (such as preparing rate cards, sending the rate cards to list brokers, sorting the lists, and providing the information on magnetic tape or labels), the court held that the list rental income did "not fit within the types of 'passive' income set forth in section 512(b)."[14]

---

12. Thus, "royalty" is differentiated from "rent" by the nature of the property the owner is permitting another to use.

14. This analysis was confirmed by the Sixth Circuit in Disabled American Veterans v. Commissioner, 942 F.2d 309 (6th Cir.1991) (DAV III). In DAV III, the Sixth Circuit re-

Similarly, in Fraternal Order of Police, the Seventh Circuit held that income from the sale of space for business listings in The Trooper magazine was not royalty income excludable from UBTI under § 512(b)(2). The court noted that the Fraternal Order of Police ("FOP") had the final authority over the editorial content of each issue of The Trooper, could appoint the magazine's executive editor, could prepare the editorials and feature articles, could oversee and control the solicitor's activities in the business listings program, could control the program's bank account and the reprint of any material published in The Trooper, and shared the proceeds of the business listings program with the organization that published the magazine. Thus, the court upheld the Tax Court's finding that FOP "was an active participant in the publication of The Trooper" and therefore the income received from the business listings program was not passive in nature and, consequently, not royalty income under § 512(b)(2).

Most recently, in Texas Farm Bureau, the Fifth Circuit held that income received by the Farm Bureau from its agreement with two life insurance companies to help promote the insurance companies' life insurance plans was not royalty income. The agreements at issue demonstrated that the Farm Bureau was paid in exchange for (1) granting the insurance companies the exclusive right to use the Farm Bureau name and logo in Texas, (2) agreeing to "use its good offices, influence, and prestige in promoting the general welfare" of the insurance companies, and (3) providing clerical, telephone and administrative services. Id. Accordingly, the court concluded that, as a matter of law, "the plain language of the agreements demonstrates that the agreements were strictly for services and did not contemplate a royalty payment."

This distinction between payments for services and payments for the right to use an intangible property right is supported by Rev. Rul. 81–178. The ruling discusses and applies the exclusion of royalty income from UBTI in two factual scenarios. In the first, a tax-exempt organization of professional athletes solicits and negotiates licensing agreements which authorize the use of the organization's trademarks, trade names, service marks, as well as its members' names, photographs, likenesses and facsimile signatures; under the terms of the agreements, the organization has the right to approve the quality and style of the use of the licensed product. In the second, the same organization solicits and negotiates agreements to endorse the products and services offered by the other party to the agreement; the agreements require personal appearances by the members of the organization. The ruling states that the income generated by the agreements in the first situation is royalty income within the meaning of § 512(b).[15] However, the income received in the second situation is not

versed the Tax Court's holding that DAV's rental income from its donor lists constituted "royalties" under the recently issued Revenue Ruling 81–178. Although different tax years were involved, the court held that collateral estoppel barred DAV from relitigating the issue of whether the rental income consti-

tuted royalty income because Rev. Rul. 81–178 did not offer additional guidance on the issue of whether royalty income must be passive.

15. It notes that "the fact that the organization has the right to approve the quality or style of the licensed products and ser-

royalty income because the agreements "require the personal services of the organization's members in connection with the endorsed products and services." Rev. Rul. 81–178, 1981–2 C.B. 135.

Lastly, differentiating between passive royalty income and income which is compensation for services comports with the purpose of I.R.C. §§ 511–513. As discussed by the Commissioner, the imposition of the tax on unrelated business income was in response to a concern that tax-exempt organizations were competing unfairly with taxable businesses. * * * Certain categories of income, however, were excluded from UBTI because "[the] committee believe[d] that they are 'passive' in character and are not likely to result in serious competition for taxable businesses having similar income." S.Rep. No. 2375, 81st Cong., 2d Sess., 28, 30–31 (1950), reprinted in 1950 U.S.S.C.A.N. 3053, 3083. The purpose of the tax on UBTI to prevent unfair competition coupled with the exclusion of income believed to be "passive" in character from that tax provides additional support for excluding payment for services from royalty income.

Sierra Club's argument against "narrowly" interpreting the definition of royalties in § 512(b)(2) is threefold. First, Sierra Club argues that the IRS has previously rejected a "passivity test" in its own rulings. IRS internal memoranda, however, are not binding on the IRS or on this court. See DAV III, 942 F.2d at 315 n. 5 ("Such informal, unpublished opinions of attorneys within the IRS are of no precedential value."). Second, Sierra Club, in arguing that Congress intended to exclude all royalty income from UBTI, not simply royalty income passively derived, points to legislative history that states: All dividends, interest, annuities, and royalties, and the deductions directly connected therewith, are excluded from the concept of unrelated business net income. This exception applies not only to investment income, but also to such items as business interest on overdue open accounts receivable. S.Rep. No. 2375, 81st Cong., 2d Sess. at 108, reprinted in 1950 U.S.S.C.A.N. at 3166. We agree with Sierra Club that the legislative history, as well as the language of the statute, indicates that Congress intended to exclude "all royalties." Acknowledging this, however, does not aid in determining whether by definition "all royalties" means payments (for the use of a property right) that are passive in nature.

Third, Sierra Club claims that in order for the exception to UBTI to apply, the royalty income must be derived from an unrelated business activity, or it would not be taxable as UBTI in the first place. Thus, if the exclusion of royalties from UBTI were only meant to encompass passively derived royalties, § 512(b)(2) would never apply. In other words, because a trade or business is defined to exclude passive activities, see American Bar Endowment, 477 U.S. at 110, 106 S.Ct. at 2429 ("Congress defined 'trade or business' as 'any activity which is carried on for the production of income from the sale of goods or the performance of services.' ") (quoting

vices does not change this result. The mere retention of quality control rights by a licensor in a licensing agreement situation does not cause payments to the licensor under the agreements to lose their characterization as royalties." Rev. Rul. 81–178, 1981–2 C.B. 135.

I.R.C. § 513(c)), a tax-exempt organization must be engaged in an active trade or business before a royalty could possibly be taxed under § 511.

This last argument highlights why royalties should be defined as "passive" only to the extent that a royalty cannot be compensation for services. Sierra Club could be engaged in a trade or business such as manufacturing t-shirts. The income from selling the t-shirts would be taxable as UBTI. However, if Sierra Club copyrighted the designs on its t-shirts and then licensed the designs to a t-shirt manufacturer in exchange for a one percent royalty fee on gross sales, the royalty fees would be excluded from UBTI under § 512(b)(2).

Thus, to the extent the Commissioner claims that a tax-exempt organization can do nothing to acquire such fees (e.g., providing a rate sheet listing the fee charged for use of each copyrighted design or retaining the right to approve how the design is used and marketed), the Commissioner is incorrect. However, to the extent that Sierra Club appears to argue that a "royalty" is any payment for the use of a property right—such as a copyright—regardless of any additional services that are performed in addition to the owner simply permitting another to use the right at issue, we disagree.

In sum, we hold that "royalties" in § 512(b) are defined as payments received for the right to use intangible property rights and that such definition does not include payments for services.

III.

Given the above definition of royalties, we must now decide whether the district court erred in granting summary judgment on the issue of whether the payments received by Sierra Club for one-time rentals of its lists constitute "royalties" or payments for services performed by Sierra Club. [The court found that the Sierra Club did not itself perform the services relating to the rental of mailing lists or market the mailing lists. Rather, it hired others to maintain the lists on a computerized data base, to administer the list rentals, and to perform various other ministerial tasks. Ed.]

* * * Sierra Club did not itself perform the services relating to the rental of mailing lists. Nor did it market the mailing lists. It did nothing more than collect a fee for the rental of its mailing lists. Thus, Sierra Club's activities with regard to the mailing list rentals were far less substantial than the activities other courts have found to prevent a claim that income was royalty income. Cf. Texas Farm Bureau, 53 F.3d at 124 (Farm Bureau provided offices, clerical help, supplies, and agreed to promote insurance companies' policies); Fraternal Order of Police, 833 F.2d at 723–24 (FOP was an active participant in the publication of the magazine because it could appoint the executive editor, prepare editorials and feature articles, oversee and control solicitations of business listings and control the bank account and reprint of articles). To hold otherwise would require us to hold that any activity on the part of the owner of intangible property

to obtain a royalty, renders the payment for the use of that right UBTI and not a royalty.

IV.

We now address whether, given the definition of "royalties" discussed above, the district erred in granting summary judgment on the issue of whether the income from the affinity credit card program constituted "royalties." Because the Tax Court improperly resolved disputed factual issues in favor of Sierra Club, rather than viewing the evidence in the light most favorable to the Commissioner, we reverse the Tax Court's grant of partial summary judgment and remand to the Tax Court for findings of fact regarding whether Sierra Club's income from the affinity card program constituted royalties under § 512(b).

[The court observed that Sierra Club's agreement to cooperate with ABS on a continuing basis in soliciting and encouraging Sierra Club members to use the credit cards would permit a factfinder to infer that Sierra Club was performing endorsement services and not simply licensing its name, logo, and mailing lists. In addition, the court concluded that ABS's use of Sierra Club's postal permit to send initial solicitation materials, and Sierra Club's reimbursement of its members for ABS's dishonored checks, could cause a factfinder to infer that Sierra Club was performing services. Ed.]

In sum, the Tax Court failed to view the facts regarding the affinity credit card program in the light most favorable to the Commissioner. Therefore, we reverse the grant of partial summary judgment on the issue of whether the income generated by the affinity credit card program was royalty income and remand this issue for trial before the Tax Court. As a consequence, the Tax Court failed to recognize that there remain genuine issues of material fact as to whether the payments Sierra Club received in connection with the program were payments for services.

V.

Therefore, we REVERSE the partial grant of summary judgment on the question of whether the income generated by the affinity credit card program constitutes "royalties" and is therefore non-taxable.

NOTES AND QUESTIONS

1. *Subsequent Developments: Mailing Lists and Affinity Cards.* After the adverse Ninth Circuit decision in *Sierra Club,* the Justice Department filed a rare petition for rehearing, claiming that a distinction drawn by the court—that mailing list rental income is not an excludable royalty if the business activities are conducted by the organization's own employees but is a royalty if the activities are performed by entities hired by the organization—does not withstand analysis. Is this a valid point? Should it matter if the outside entities were acting as agents of the Sierra Club? The government argued that the computer service bureau and list managers were

agents and that the Ninth Circuit's opinion provides an easy end run around the unrelated business tax. The Ninth Circuit denied the petition. In a later mailing list case, the Tax Court held generally that independent list brokers and list managers were not acting as agents of an exempt organization that derived revenue from mailing list rentals. See Common Cause v. Commissioner, 112 T.C. 332 (1999).

As for the affinity card issue, the Tax Court held on remand that all payments received by the Sierra Club were royalties and not consideration for services rendered. The Service once again argued that the Sierra Club controlled the marketing of the affinity cards, offered the cards as a member service, advertised the cards in magazines and local publications, and performed other administrative and endorsement services. In a lengthy and fact specific opinion, the Tax Court rejected all these arguments, finding that the Sierra Club's activities were confined to safeguarding its intangible property interests by approving marketing proposals and that all revenues from the affinity card program were for the use of its name and logo rather than for services rendered. Sierra Club v. Commissioner, 77 T.C.M. (CCH) 1569 (1999).

Although the government did not seek Supreme Court review of the Ninth Circuit's decision in *Sierra Club*, IRS officials indicated that they would continue litigating the mailing list and affinity card issues in other cases with more favorable facts. See, e.g., Carolyn D. Wright, IRS Looking to Pursue Sierra Club Issues in Another Case, Owens Says, 16 Exempt Org. Tax Rev. 564 (1997). The Service's continuing efforts were unsuccessful. See, e.g., Oregon State University Alumni Ass'n v. Commissioner, 71 T.C.M. (CCH) 1935 (1996), aff'd, 193 F.3d 1098 (9th Cir.1999); Alumni Ass'n of the University of Oregon v. Commissioner, 71 T.C.M. (CCH) 2093 (1996), aff'd, 193 F.3d 1098 (9th Cir.1999); and Mississippi State University Alumni, Inc. v. Commissioner, 74 T.C.M. (CCH) 458 (1997). In all these cases, the Tax Court held that income derived by university alumni associations from affinity card programs qualified for the royalty exclusion because the fees received from the bank marketing the cards were for the use of valuable intangible property rights, not for services rendered. The two Oregon cases were affirmed on appeal, and the Service decided not to appeal the *Mississippi State* case. In December, 1999, the IRS surrendered when the National Office instructed area managers to stop litigating affinity card and mailing list cases except where the exempt organization performs significant marketing or administrative services and there is a good case for allocating the payment between the services and the intangible. See Fred Stokeld, IRS Memo Tells Area Managers to Stop Litigating Affinity Card, Mailing List Cases, 28 Exempt Org. Tax Rev. 18 (2000).

2. *Statutory Mailing List Exception.* Section 513(h)(1)(B), enacted in 1986, exempts amounts derived by most § 501(c)(3) and veterans organizations from the rental or exchange of donor lists to or with other such exempt organizations. The exception does not extend to § 501(c)(4) organizations, such as the Sierra Club, and it does not exempt income from mailing list rentals to for-profit organizations. In enacting this amendment,

Congress included a typical reminder in the legislative history that no inference was intended as to whether or not revenue from mailing list activities other than those expressly described in § 513(h)(1)(B) were taxable. Staff of the Joint Committee on Taxation, General Explanation of the Tax Reform Act of 1986, 100th Cong., 1st Sess. 1325 (Jt. Comm. Print 1987). The issue thus lives on.

3. *Policy Issues.* Should exempt organizations be allowed to use licensing or endorsement arrangements to convert the earnings of an unrelated trade or business into an excludable royalty that likely is tax-deductible by the for-profit payor? Is the exempt organization receiving passive investment income in these royalty arrangements or is it acting more like a joint venturer? Should it make any difference if the royalty is based on net or gross income, or whether the exempt organization has the right to control the manufacture and marketing of the licensed product? Why isn't licensing a trademark or logo a commercial exploitation of the organization's goodwill?

4. RESEARCH INCOME

Most educational and scientific organizations that derive income from their research activities are not subject to the UBIT because their research income is substantially related to the organizations' exempt purposes. Congress also has provided the following three statutory exclusions from UBTI for research income, whether or not the underlying activity is "related:"

(1) The research is performed for the United States, any agency or instrumentality of the federal government, or a state or local government. I.R.C. § 512(b)(7).

(2) The research is performed by a college, university or hospital "for any person." I.R.C. § 512(b)(8).

(3) The research is "fundamental" (as distinguished from "applied") and the results are freely made available to the general public. I.R.C. § 512(b)(9).

The regulations limit the reach of these exclusions by distinguishing "research" activities from other activities "of a type ordinarily carried on as an incident to commercial or industrial operations, for example, the ordinary testing or inspection of materials or products or the designing or construction of equipment, buildings, etc." Treas. Reg. § 1.512(b)–1(f)(4). In addition, the term "fundamental research" does not include research carried on for the primary purpose of commercial or industrial applications. Id.

In a 1976 ruling, the Service set forth factors to be considered in determining whether income from commercially sponsored research conducted by a scientific organization would be subject to the UBIT. See Rev. Rul. 76–296, 1976–2 C.B. 141. If the results of commercially sponsored research projects are published in a form available to the public within a reasonably short time after completion, the organization is treated as engaging in scientific research in the public interest even if the sponsor retains ownership rights in the research results. But if the scientific organization agrees to withhold publication beyond the time reasonably necessary to obtain patents or agrees to forego publication entirely, its income from conducting the commercially sponsored research is subject to the UBIT.

5.   PAYMENTS FROM CONTROLLED ORGANIZATIONS

An exempt organization operating an unrelated trade or business might be tempted to segregate its business activities in a wholly owned subsidiary and then convert otherwise taxable business income into excluded income through the payment of interest, rent, royalties or other items that are deductible by the taxable subsidiary and excludable by the exempt parent.

Section 512(b)(13) largely blocks this opportunity by tracing the passive income back to the subsidiary's business operations and treating it as UBTI to the parent to the extent it was not taxed to the subsidiary. This result is accomplished by including all or part of certain investment income items received from controlled entities in the parent's UBTI.

These special rules apply to interest, annuities, royalties and rent (but not dividends) received by a "controlling organization" from a "controlled entity." I.R.C. § 512(b)(13)(C). In the case of a stock corporation, "control" is defined as ownership (by vote or value) of more than 50 percent of the stock of the corporation. I.R.C. § 512(b)(13)(D)(i)(I). In the case of a partnership, "control" requires ownership of more than 50 percent of the profits or capital interests. I.R.C. § 512(b)(13)(D)(i)(II). In all cases, "control" means ownership of more than 50 percent of the beneficial interests in the entity. I.R.C. § 513(b)(13)(D)(i)(III). These control tests were tightened in 1997 to prevent several avoidance opportunities that were available under prior law.

Significantly, constructive ownership rules, borrowed from the corporate tax world (see I.R.C. § 318), apply in determining control. I.R.C. § 512(b)(13)(D)(ii). To illustrate with one simple example, assume Charity owns 100 percent of the stock of Holding Company, which in turns owns 100 percent of the stock of one or more second-tier subsidiaries that conduct unrelated businesses. Charity is treated under § 318 as owning 100 percent of the second-tier subsidiary. Under prior law, which did not provide any indirect ownership rules, Charity would not have been in control of a second-tier subsidiary and thus could have received tax-free payments of rent, interest, royalties, or annuities. This "double drop down" strategy was utilized successfully by several well-known exempt organizations. In a widely publicized case, the National Geographic Society, a § 501(c)(3) organization best known for its National Geographic magazine, created a for-profit holding company that in turn controlled second-tier subsidiaries engaged in various television, film, on-line and map-making businesses. See Marlis L. Carson, Exploring the UBIT's Frontier: A National Geographic Production, 69 Tax Notes 1432 (1995); Constance L. Hays,

Seeing Green in a Yellow Border: Quest for Profits Is Shaking a Quiet Realm, N.Y. Times, Aug. 3, 1997, § 3, at 1, 12, 13.

If § 512(b)(13) applies, the taxable portion of the otherwise excluded payments received by the controlling exempt organization is determined under "look-through" rules that seek to preserve one level of tax within the affiliated structure. The rules apply to a "specified payment" (interest, annuity, royalty, or rent) from a controlled entity to the controlling organization. I.R.C. § 512(b)(13)(A), (C). If the controlled entity is itself an exempt organization, the parent must include a specified payment in its gross income to the extent that the payment reduced the net UBTI or increased any net unrelated loss of the exempt subsidiary. I.R.C. § 512(b)(13)(A), (B)(i)(II). If the controlled entity is not tax-exempt, a similar "matching" principle requires the subsidiary first to determine the portion of its taxable income that would have been UBTI if it were an exempt organization with the same exempt purposes as the parent. The parent then includes in its gross income that portion of the payment that reduced the hypothetical UBTI (or increased net unrelated loss) of the controlled entity. I.R.C. § 512(b)(13)(A), (B)(i)(I). In either case, the parent is allowed all deductions directly connected with amounts treated as derived from an unrelated trade or business. I.R.C. § 512(b)(13)(A).

NOTES AND QUESTIONS

1. *Policy Concerns.* Is § 512(b)(13) based on a flawed premise– Assume that an exempt organization leases space or licenses its logo to an unrelated third party in exchange for rent or a royalty. These payments may be deducted by the payor and will not be taxable to the exempt organization. Why should the same type of payment, assuming it is not excessive, be included in UBTI if it is received from a controlled entity? To date, these arguments have been considered and rejected by Congress, most recently when it tightened the control test in § 512(b)(13). As explained by the Joint Committee on Taxation staff, one purpose of § 512(b)(13) is to prevent taxable subsidiaries from reducing their otherwise taxable income by borrowing, leasing, or licensing assets from a tax-exempt parent at inflated levels. But even if the payments are not inflated, the provision "is intended to prevent a tax-exempt parent from obtaining what is, in effect, a tax-free return on capital invested in the subsidiary" if the subsidiary is conducting an active business. Staff of Joint Committee on Taxation, General Explanation of Tax Legislation Enacted in 1997, 105th Cong., 1st Sess. 239–240 (1997). Does this explanation make sense?

2. *Fair Market Value Exception.* Ever since § 512(b)(13) was tightened, a group of adversely affected nonprofit organizations have been lobbying for a "fair market value" exception that would allow payments of interest, rent, royalties and annuities from controlled subsidiaries to their tax-exempt parents to be excluded from UBTI as long as they were made at "fair market value." Supporters of this proposal argue that § 512(b)(13) makes no sense in cases where transactions between affiliated organiza-

tions are determined on an arm's length basis. Consider, however, an exempt organization that is engaged in a profitable unrelated business. If that business is operated directly by the organization, the profits undoubtedly are taxable. Why should the organization be able to eliminate all or part of the taxable income from this same business simply by conducting it through a taxable subsidiary that arranges to make payments of interest, rent and royalties to its tax-exempt parent?

3. *For Further Reading.* Fred Stokeld, Nonprofits Push Fair Market Value Exception, 24 Exempt Org. Tax Rev. 475 (1999); Fred Stokeld, EO Specialists Have Doubts About Section 512(b)(13) Modification, 17 Exempt Org. Tax Rev. 246 (1997).

6. A MONOGRAMMED EXCLUSION

Section 512(b)(15) contains a curious "modification" excluding from UBTI the income and deductions of any trade or business of providing certain "federally licensed services" by a religious order that carried on the business prior to May 27, 1959, provided that less than 10 percent of the net income is used for other than the order's exempt purposes and the Service is satisfied that competitive rates are being charged. It is widely believed that this exclusion was enacted (embroidered?) for a radio station in New Orleans that is owned and operated by Jesuit-affiliated Loyola University. The call letters of the station are monogrammed into three separate sub-sections of Section 512(b)(15) ("which ... ; which ... ; less ... "). See Philip M. Stern, The Rape of the Taxpayer 40–41 (1973), which attributes this provision to the cultivated sense of humor of Senator Russell Long of Louisiana.

PROBLEMS

1. Sturdley University has a vast complex of athletic facilities, including a superb football stadium, 20 lighted tennis courts with dressing room facilities, an art museum, a variety of eating facilities, and a large on-campus bookstore. What are the tax consequences to the University of the following activities:

(a) Leasing the football stadium as a practice facility to a professional football team during July and August. Under the lease agreement, the University will maintain the playing surface and provide dressing room, linen and security services.

(b) "Renting" the art museum for special events such as corporate receptions, cocktail parties, weddings and dinners. In a normal year, the museum is used for 25 to 30 outside events. The University makes available its personnel for furniture set-up and, as required by its liquor license, University personnel are required to purchase and serve any alcoholic beverages. Volunteer docents are available at most events to lead tours and discuss exhibits at the museum.

(c) An exclusive marketing agreement with a soft drink company under which the University, in exchange for a fee, agrees to grant the company exclusive rights to sell its products and display its logo and familiar slogan, at all University eating facilities, vending machines and concession stands.

(d) Leasing the tennis complex to a local country club, which will operate a satellite facility and pay the University rent based on a fixed percentage of the gross receipts derived by the club from the use of the complex.

(e) Licensing the University's name and logo for use on Sturdley University athletic apparel (T-shirts, shorts, sweatshirts) and a University-label wine ("Sturdley Cabernet") that is sold in the on-campus bookstore and through mail-orders to alumni, parents and others on the alumni association's mailing list. The University retains the right to approve all the merchandise and is paid a royalty based on a percentage of the net income from sales.

(f) Providing the University's mailing list, logo, and a photograph of the campus to Bancorp, which offers a no-fee Sturdley VISA credit card to all alumni of the University. The alumni association, through an unrelated list manager, provides mailing labels for all "Sturdley card" marketing materials. Bancorp provides all other services related to the credit cards and pays the University a fee based on a small percentage of total cardholder sales volume.

2. Golden Gate Hospital leases space in its adjacent medical building to a group of doctors who provide medical services to private patients. It also leases medical equipment to various doctors and for-profit medical partnerships. Is the income derived by the Hospital taxable as unrelated business income?

D. Computation and Planning Issues

Internal Revenue Code: § 512(a).

Treasury Regulations: § 1.512(a)–1(a), (b), (c), (d), (e), (f)(1).

1. Allocation of Expenses

As previewed above, UBTI, the base on which the UBIT is computed, is defined in § 512(a)(1) as the gross income derived from any unrelated trade or business less allocable deductions for business expenses, losses, depreciation and other items "directly connected" with the unrelated business. I.R.C. § 512(a)(1). The computation is not as simple as the statute suggests. Reaching the bottom line is complicated by the necessity of allocating deductions between the unrelated trade or business and the exempt activities of the organization. If an exempt organization is unable to avoid the

UBIT under the myriad exclusions already discussed, it often can utilize the expense allocation rules to reduce or eliminate the bottom line figure.

Directly Connected. To be "directly connected" with the carrying on of an unrelated trade or business, an expense generally must have a "proximate and primary relationship" to that business. Treas. Reg. § 1.512(a)–1(a). This relationship exists in two situations: (1) the expenses are attributable solely to an unrelated business, in which case they are fully deductible (Treas. Reg. § 1.512(a)–1(b)), or (2) the expenses are attributable to the dual use of facilities or personnel, requiring an allocation between exempt and business functions on a "reasonable basis" (Treas. Reg. § 1.512(a)–1(c)). Thus, if employees are used for both exempt and business activities, their compensation must be allocated on a reasonable basis, and the amount allocated to the business is considered to be "directly connected." Treas. Reg. § 1.512(a)–1(c). The regulations suggest an allocation based on time devoted to the various activities. Depreciation and other expenses on a building can be allocated by reference to the space used for the various activities unless there is a more reasonable basis for the allocation. Id.

Exploitation of Exempt Functions. Organizations engaging in an unrelated business that "exploits" an exempt function may be able to minimize their UBIT exposure by allocating expenses of the exempt activity to the taxable business. The regulations permit this type of allocation in certain limited situations.

In general, expenses attributable to the exploitation of an exempt function are not deductible in computing UBTI on the theory that the items are incident to the conduct of an exempt purpose and thus do not possess a sufficient relationship to the unrelated trade or business. Treas. Reg. § 1.512(a)–1(d). Under a special and very generous rule, if an unrelated trade or business is of a kind carried on for profit by a taxable organization and if the exempt activity exploited by the business also is comparable to activities normally conducted by taxable organizations in pursuance of such a business, the expenses attributable to the exempt activity are deductible to the extent that: (1) they exceed the income (if any) attributable to the exempt activity, and (2) the allocation of the excess expenses to the unrelated activities does not result in a loss from the unrelated trade or business. Treas. Reg. § 1.512(a)–1(d)(2).

To illustrate, assume that Friends of the Sea, an exempt environmental organization with 20,000 members, mails advertising literature for consumer products to its members under a contract with an advertising agency. The mailing activity is an unrelated business that exploits the membership list developed in the conduct of the organization's exempt functions. The expenses solely attributable to the advertising business are deductible. But since development of the membership lists is not an activity usually conducted by for-profit organizations, no part of the cost of developing the membership list is deductible in computing UBTI. Treas.Reg. § 1.512(a)–1(e), Example.

Advertising in an exempt organization's journal is a typical example of exploitation of an exempt function. May the expenses attributable to the production and distribution of the journal be deducted against the taxable advertising income? Within limits, the answer is yes since the exempt activity (publication of the journal) is of "a type normally conducted by taxable organizations in pursuance of such [a] business." Treas. Reg. § 1.512(a)–1(d)(2). The regulations provide elaborate rules for allocating expenses in the advertising area. Treas. Reg. § 1.512(a)–1(f)(2)–(7). See also Treas. Reg. § 1.512(a)–1(e) Example 2 (net loss related to a museum's publication of an exhibition catalog may be deducted against UBTI from museum's sale of advertising in catalog because sale of advertising exploits an activity—the publication of editorial material—normally conducted by taxable entities that sell advertising; but net expenses of the exhibition itself may not be deducted against advertising income because cost of presenting exhibition is not directly connected with the conduct of the advertising activity and does not have a proximate and primary relationship to that activity).

If expenses of an exempt activity are deductible in computing UBTI, the regulations provide an allocation procedure that may limit the deductible amount. Exempt function expenses first must be allocated to the income derived from or attributable to that function—e.g., expenses of publishing a journal first must be allocated to subscription income, if any. Any excess then may be allocated to the unrelated business income. But no allocation of the excess is permitted to the extent that such an allocation would result in a net operating loss from the unrelated business. Finally, the excess may not be allocated to any other unrelated trade or business that does not exploit the same exempt function—e.g., excess expenses attributable to a periodical may not be applied against income from a manufacturing activity. Treas. Reg. § 1.512(a)–1(d)(2). But several businesses exploiting the same exempt function may be consolidated. Treas. Reg. § 1.512(a)–1(f)(7).

As illustrated by the *Rensselaer Polytechnic Institute* case, which follows, the allocation of expenses between related and unrelated activities of dual use facilities has proven to be one of the more difficult aspects of computing unrelated business taxable income.

Rensselaer Polytechnic Institute v. Commissioner

United States Court of Appeals, Second Circuit, 1984.
732 F.2d 1058.

■ Pratt, Circuit Judge:

The issue before us is not only one of first impression; it is also of considerable financial significance to many of our colleges and universities. When a tax-exempt organization uses one of its facilities, as in this case a fieldhouse, for both tax-exempt purposes and for the production of unrelated business income, what portion of its indirect expenses such as depreciation may it deduct from its unrelated business income pursuant to I.R.C. § 512 (1982)? May it allocate those expenses, as prescribed by Treas. Reg. § 1.512(a)–1(c), on any "reasonable" basis? Or must it first establish, as the commissioner here argues, that the expense would not have been incurred in the absence of the business activity? Finding no conflict between the regulation and the statute and finding no error in the determination of the tax court that RPI's method of allocation was reasonable, we reject the commissioner's position and affirm the tax court's judgment, which approved apportioning the fieldhouse's idle time in proportion to the hours devoted to exempt and not exempt uses.

The facts are undisputed. Rensselaer Polytechnic Institute (RPI) is a non-profit educational organization entitled to tax-exempt status under I.R.C. § 501(c)(3). It owns and operates a fieldhouse which it devotes to two broad categories of uses: (1) student uses, which include physical education, college ice hockey, student ice skating, and other activities related to RPI's tax-exempt educational responsibilities; and (2) commercial uses, which include activities and events such as commercial ice shows and public ice skating, that do not fall within its tax-exempt function. For the fiscal year 1974, the net income from commercial use of the fieldhouse constituted "unrelated business taxable income" which was subject to taxation under I.R.C. § 511(a)(1).

The dispute is over the amount of unrelated business tax due from RPI for 1974 and, since there is no disagreement over the gross income, $476,613, we must focus on the deductible expenses. The parties have classified RPI's applicable deductible expenses in three groups. The first group, "direct expenses," are those that can be specifically identified with particular commercial uses. For the year in question direct expenses amounted to $371,407, and the parties have always agreed to their deductibility.

The second group, "variable expenses", are those which vary in proportion to actual use of the fieldhouse, but which cannot be identified with particular events. They were originally in dispute before the tax court, but neither side has appealed that part of the decision below which (a) found the total variable expenses to be $197,210; and (b) allocated them on the basis of actual use, as claimed by RPI, rather than total availability, as claimed by the commissioner.

This appeal involves the third group, "fixed expenses", which do not vary in proportion to actual use of the facility. The amounts of fixed expenses incurred with respect to the fieldhouse were stipulated to be:

Salaries and fringe benefits	$ 59,415
Depreciation	29,397
Repairs and Replacements	14,031
Operating Expenditures	1,356
	$104,199

Narrowly stated, the issue is how these fixed expenses should be allocated between RPI's dual uses: the exempt student use and the taxable commercial use. RPI contends it is entitled to allocate the fixed expenses on the basis of relative times of actual use. Thus, in computing that portion of its deductible expenses, RPI multiplies the total amount of fixed expenses by a fraction, whose numerator is the total number of hours the fieldhouse was used for commercial events, and whose denominator is the total number of hours the fieldhouse was used for all activities and events-student and commercial combined.

The commissioner argues that the allocation of fixed expenses must be made not on the basis of times of actual use, but on the basis of total time available for use. Thus, he contends the denominator of the fraction should be the total number of hours in the taxable year. In practical terms, the difference between the two methods of allocation amounts to $9,259 in taxes.

Below, the tax court agreed with RPI's method of allocating on the basis of actual use, finding it to be "reasonable" within the meaning of Treas. Reg. § 1.512(a)–1(c). The commissioner appeals, contending (a) that the tax court's otherwise reasonable allocation based on actual use does not satisfy the statutory requirement that in order to be deductible an expense must be "directly connected with" the unrelated business activity; (b) that the cases the tax court relied on below, dealing with allocation of home office expenses between business and personal use, are inapposite; and (c) that strict application of the "directly connected with" language of the statute is "necessary to prevent serious abuse of the tax exemption privilege."

It has been the consistent policy of this nation to exempt from income taxes a corporation, like RPI, that is "organized and operated exclusively for * * * educational purposes * * * ". I.R.C. § 501(c)(3). This preferred treatment to educational, as well as religious, charitable, and scientific institutions, was established simultaneously with the first income tax enacted by congress in 1913, and has been continued in identical language through a series of revenue acts down to and including the current provision contained in I.R.C. § 501. * * * So firm was the policy shielding educational institutions from taxation that, despite repeated challenges by the commissioner, the statute was consistently interpreted to exempt from taxation all income earned by an exempt corporation, even that obtained from activities unrelated to its tax-exempt educational purposes.

Recognizing, however, the unfair competitive advantage that freedom from income taxation could accord tax-exempt institutions that entered the world of commerce, congress, in 1950, extended the income tax to the "unrelated business income" of certain tax-exempt institutions, including educational corporations. Pub. L. No. 81–814, § 301, 64 Stat. 906, 947 (1950)(codified at I.R.C. § 511–513). Its objective in changing the law was to eliminate the competitive advantage educational and charitable corporations enjoyed over private enterprise, without jeopardizing the basic purpose of the tax-exemption. * * *

With this historical background in mind, we turn to the applicable statute and regulations. Section 512 of the code defines as "unrelated business taxable income" gross income derived from unrelated business activities less deductions "directly connected with" such activities. Treas. Reg. § 1.512(a)–1(a) further defines the term "directly connected with", and provides that "to be 'directly connected with' the conduct of unrelated business for purposes of section 512, an item of deduction must have proximate and primary relationship" to that business. Two subsequent subsections of that regulation define "proximate and primary relationship" in the context of (a) items that are attributable solely to the unrelated business, Treas. Reg. § 1.512(a)–1(b); and (b) as in this case, items that are attributable to facilities or personnel used for both exempt and unrelated purposes, Treas. Reg. § 1.512(a)–1(c). The latter regulation provides:

> (c) Dual use of facilities or personnel. Where facilities are used both to carry on exempt activities and to conduct unrelated trade or business activities, expenses, depreciation and similar items attributable to such facilities (as, for example, items of overhead), shall be allocated between the two uses on a reasonable basis. Similarly, where personnel are used both to carry on exempt activities and to conduct unrelated trade or business activities, expenses and similar items attributable to such personnel (as, for example, items of salary) shall be allocated between the two uses on a reasonable basis. The portion of any such items so allocated to the unrelated trade or business activity is proximately and primarily related to that business activity, and shall be allowable as a deduction in computing unrelated business taxable income in the manner and to the extent permitted by section 162, section 167 or other relevant provisions of the Code.

Treas. Reg. § 1.512(a)–1(c)(emphasis added).

Thus, when allocated "on a reasonable basis," expenses attributable to such facilities or personnel-which expressly include such "indirect expenses" as depreciation and overhead—are by definition "proximately and primarily related" to the business. They are therefore "directly connected with" the unrelated business activity and expressly made deductible by the regulation.

Under this regulation, therefore, the critical question is whether the method of allocation adopted by RPI was "reasonable". The tax court found that it was, and, giving due regard to its expertise in this area, ABKCO Industries, Inc. v. Commissioner, 482 F.2d 150, 155 (3d Cir.1973), we see no error in that conclusion. Apportioning indirect expenses such as depreciation on the basis of the actual hours the facility was used for both exempt and taxable purposes sensibly distributes the cost of the facility among the activities that benefit from its use. In addition, the method is consistent with that followed by the tax court in the most common dual-use situation, home office deduction cases. * * *

Indeed, the commissioner does not claim that RPI's allocation method is factually unreasonable, but instead contends solely that the method is not "reasonable", because by permitting depreciation during "idle time", when the fieldhouse is not being used at all, it contravenes the statutory requirement that deductible expenses be "directly connected with" RPI's unrelated business activities. By advancing this argument, however, the commissioner ignores his own definition of the concept "directly connected with" included in Treas. Reg. § 1.512(a)–1(a) discussed above. In addition, the commissioner would have us adopt a more stringent interpretation of "directly connected with" in § 512 than has been applied for over sixty years to the same concept in the commissioner's regulations governing the deductibility of ordinary and necessary business expenses. See Treas. Reg. § 1.162–1(a). Moreover, the logical extension of his position would require the commissioner to deny depreciation deductions to all businesses for those periods when their assets are idle. Such a view, however, would contravene the basic concepts underlying the commissioner's elaborate regulations governing depreciation generally. See Treas. Reg. § 1.167(a)–1 et seq.

For an expense to be "directly connected with" an activity, the commissioner argues that it must be one that would not have been incurred in the absence of the activity. But whether or not the fieldhouse is actually put to any business use, depreciation of the facility continues. We cannot accept the commissioner's argument, therefore, because it would in effect eliminate entirely all deductions for indirect expenses such as depreciation, a result that is not required by statute and that is directly contrary to the regulation.

* * *

Some concern has been expressed that RPI's allocation method would provide an incentive for educational institutions to abuse their tax-exempt status. The argument is a red herring. Use of educational facilities for producing unrelated business income is not tax abuse; on the contrary, as we have pointed out above, such non-exempt activities have been consistently permitted and, since 1950, expressly approved by congress. Moreover, should the trustees of a particular tax-exempt educational institution so pervert its operations that the institution no longer "engages primarily in activities which accomplish * * * [its exempt purposes]", Treas. Reg. § 1.501(c)(3)–1(c)(1), the commissioner has adequate remedies available to correct any abuse or even terminate the exemption.

The judgment appealed from is affirmed.

■ MANSFIELD, CIRCUIT JUDGE (Dissenting):

I respectfully dissent.

Rensselaer Polytechnic Institute ("RPI") is a tax-exempt institution only because it has dedicated itself and its property in perpetuity to "charitable" and "educational purposes." 26 U.S.C. § 501(c). Its unrelated business income less "deductions * * * which are directly connected with the carrying on of such trade or business" is taxable. 26 U.S.C. § 501(b), 512(a). We are here asked to permit the college to deduct from its commercial business income fixed expenses that would normally be allocated on a time basis to periods when the college's property is not being used for trade or business but for its educational purposes.

In my view such expenses are not "directly connected" with the institution's commercial business activities within the meaning of § 512(a) and are therefore not deductible form its business income. On the contrary, they are attributable to time when the facilities exist for educational purposes. Indeed, it could reasonably be argued that since RPI would, absent part-time use of its fixed assets for commercial purposes, be required to absorb all depreciation of such assets, no such depreciation is "directly connected" with its commercial business operations. RPI represented in its petition to the Tax Court that "[t]he main function of the fieldhouse is to provide a suitable facility necessary to allow petitioner to carry out *its total educational responsibilities*." (Emphasis added). Although some allocation may be permissible, I do not believe RPI should be allowed to give its commercial use any credit for time when its facilities exist for educational use. To do so would give a tax exempt institution an unfair tax advantage over commercial institutions. The majority reaches this result only by what appears to be a misinterpretation of the governing statute and regulations.

In my view the fundamental error underlying the majority's decision is its assumption that tax-exempt institutions are governed for tax deduction purposes by the same standards as those governing taxable businesses. That assumption conflicts with legislative intent, economic reality, and the express wording of the pertinent statute and regulations. When Congress in 1950 passed legislation subjecting tax-exempt organizations to income tax on unrelated business income, it was concerned both with removing the unfair competitive advantage enjoyed by tax-exempt institutions and with assuring that the unrelated business income would produce a fair amount of revenue for the public fisc. However, it was confronted with inherent differences between regular taxable business and a non-profit university engaged mainly in educational activity and only partially in income-producing commercial activities. These differences precluded a wholesale transfer and application to a university of the same deduction principles as those governing regular commercial businesses.

In the case of a commercial business devoted solely to making a profit, its entire operation is subject to a tax on its income. Regardless how it chooses to allocate its business expenses between divisions, the net income from all divisions is taxable. The IRS therefore has no quarrel with an "reasonable" allocation of deductible expenses between branches of the operation. The tax-exempt university, on the other hand, is fundamentally different in that one of its "divisions"—the educational function—is not subject to taxation. The university will therefore always have an incentive to minimize the allocation of expenses attributed to the educational function, and correspondingly to maximize the deduction for unrelated business activity. This incentive, which is not present in the ordinary business setting, requires a stricter standard of deductibility for tax-exempt organizations than for purely profit-seeking firms. The government cannot, in the case of an educational institution engaged in unrelated commercial business activity, afford to take the same relaxed approach as with wholly-taxable businesses and to accept any allocation the taxpayer may deem "reasonable."

Thus, the majority achieves parity only in the most superficial sense. The identical rule of deductibility is imposed, but it is imposed on organizations that have different characteristics and are therefore affected differently by the same rule. To whatever extent Congress sought to place wholly taxable and exempt organizations on the same footing, it was concerned not with such technical legal tests but with the real after-tax situations of the two different types of organization. Yet the majority's approach, which claims to provide equal treatment, actually leaves the tax-exempt organizations with the very advantage that the majority claims Congress was trying to eliminate.

That Congress adopted a narrower test of deductibility for the tax-exempt organization is clearly reflected in the statute. 26 U.S.C. § 512 allows such an organization to take those "deductions allowed by this chapter which are directly connected with" its unrelated business income (emphasis added). The underlined language is imposed as an additional requirement for tax-exempt institutions not faced by purely profit-oriented businesses.

* * *

For these reasons, I would reverse the Tax Court's decision.

2.   Other Computation Issues

Several of the modifications in § 512(b) affect the computation of unrelated business taxable income. Net operating losses ("NOLs") are allowable as a deduction in computing UBTI and may be carried back and forward as in a normal business activity. I.R.C. § 512(b)(6). Only income and deduction items not excluded from the UBIT are taken into account for NOL purposes, and any preceding years in which the organization was not an exempt organization are ignored in computing NOLs, including carrybacks and carryforwards. For the details, see Treas. Reg. § 1.512(b)–1(e).

Nonprofit corporations subject to the UBIT generally may deduct charitable contributions in an amount up to 10 percent of UBTI computed without regard to the contributions. I.R.C. § 512(b)(10). Contributions in excess of the 10 percent limit may be carried over for five years, but no carryover is allowed to the extent it increases a net operating loss carryover. The contributions need not be connected to the unrelated business but they must be paid to another qualified organization. I.R.C. § 512(b)(10); Treas. Reg. § 1.512(b)–1(g). Trusts may deduct contributions in the same amounts as allowed for individuals, but the percentage limitations in § 170(b) are determined in relation to UBTI rather than adjusted gross income. I.R.C. § 512(b)(11); Treas. Reg. § 1.512(b)–1(g)(2).

A "specific deduction" of $1,000 is allowed in computing UBTI, but this deduction may not create or increase a net operating loss. I.R.C. § 512(b)(12). The deduction is limited to $1,000 irrespective of the number of unrelated businesses in which the organization engages. Church units may be eligible for separate $1,000 deductions (per parish, diocese, province, etc.) provided that the local units are not separate entities and the parent organization files a consolidated return. I.R.C. § 512(b)(12); Treas. Reg. § 1.512(b)–1(h)(2).

3. UBIT PLANNING: THE USE OF CONTROLLED SUBSIDIARIES

It has become increasingly common for well-advised exempt organizations to conduct unrelated business activities through a for-profit taxable subsidiary. These complex structures are not motivated solely by tax considerations. The exempt parent may wish to insulate itself from the liabilities of the business activity, adopt different compensation arrangements, fringe benefit plans or accounting methods, employ different management structures for its various activities, expand access to investment capital, or avoid public disclosure of certain sensitive financial information. Tax considerations also may play a large role in the decision to use a controlled subsidiary. Dropping the taxable activity into a subsidiary may protect an exempt organization against a challenge to its exempt status. Under current exemption qualification standards, the activities and income of separate controlled entities generally are not taken into account in determining whether an organization's "primary purpose" is a tax-exempt purpose-at least if the parent does not exercise day-to-day operational control over the subsidiary's activities. Exempt organizations thus may conduct substantial unrelated business activities through subsidiaries without risking their exemption even though their favored tax status might be threatened if they conducted the same activities directly. Moreover, taxable subsidiaries are frequently formed to serve as the general partner when an exempt organization engages in a joint business venture with for-profit entrepreneurs and investors. The organization might jeopardize its exemption if it served directly as a general partner in ventures where the partnership activity does not otherwise further the organization's exempt purposes.

A second planning strategy is to use a controlled subsidiary to reduce the overall tax burden resulting from an unrelated business activity. For example, an exempt organization could use a for-profit subsidiary to conduct both an unprofitable exempt activity and a taxable business, enabling losses from the related business to offset profits of the unrelated activity. This helpful allocation of expenses could not be accomplished if all the activities were conducted directly by the exempt organization.

Under current law, the separate identity of a controlled subsidiary is almost always respected by the Service. In this area, the venerable tax doctrine of substance over form gives way to an equally hoary line of cases that respect a corporation's separate existence.[1] The business activities of the subsidiary ordinarily are not attributed to the parent if (1) the purposes for which the subsidiary is formed are the equivalent of business activities,

---

1. See, e.g., Moline Properties, Inc. v. Commissioner, 319 U.S. 436, 63 S.Ct. 1132, 87 L.Ed. 1499 (1943); National Carbide Corp. v. Commissioner, 336 U.S. 422, 69 S.Ct. 726, 93 L.Ed. 779 (1949). For a rare case where the Service successfully denied a § 501(c)(3) exemption because of the activities of a for profit subsidiary, see Orange County Agric. Soc'y v. Commissioner, 893 F.2d 529 (2d Cir. 1990).

or (2) the subsidiary subsequently carries on business activities. G.C.M. 39326 (Jan. 17, 1985).[2] But if the parent so controls the affairs of the subsidiary that it is merely an instrumentality of the parent, the separate corporate status of the subsidiary can be disregarded. Id. Against this permissive background, the use of complex structures has proliferated, particularly in the health care sector, where a medical center often consists of a tax-exempt parent acting essentially as a holding company for a multitude of taxable and tax-exempt subsidiaries.

During its scrutiny of the UBIT in the late 1980's, the Oversight Subcommittee of the House Ways and Means Committee made several specific proposals to limit the use of these controlled subsidiary tax avoidance strategies. A particularly controversial recommendation would have required the activities of an exempt parent and its controlled subsidiaries to be treated as an integrated enterprise in determining whether an organization's primary purpose was a tax-exempt purpose. This and other proposals never were enacted, but the controversy over complex structures lingers as a major policy issue in the law of tax-exempt organizations. The policy issues are discussed further in Section G of this chapter, infra, at pp. 664–670, infra.

For Further Reading. Michael I. Sanders, Partnerships & Joint Ventures Involving Tax-Exempt Organizations (1994); James J. McGovern, The Use of Taxable Subsidiary Corporations by Public Charities—A Tax Policy Issue for 1988, 41 Tax Notes 1125 (1988); Ellen P. Aprill, Lessons from the UBIT Debate, 45 Tax Notes 1105 (1989), reprinted in 2 Exempt Org. Tax Rev. 687 (1990).

PROBLEMS

1. State College uses its multi-purpose indoor athletic center for intercollegiate basketball and hockey games, student intramural activities, professional athletic events and commercial entertainment. During the current year the College earned $500,000 in gross revenue from commercial use of the facility. Assume that this revenue is subject to the unrelated business tax.

Expenses for the facility for the current year were as follows: $300,000 of direct expenses for commercial events (setting up the facility, paying extra security guards, etc.), $100,000 of variable expenses (e.g., expenses that vary with the use of the facility), and $100,000 of fixed expenses (e.g., expenses, such as depreciation, repairs, and salaries) that do not vary with the use of the facility.

2. In GCM 39326, an exempt organization was formed to provide hospital management and support activities to nonprofit hospitals. The business became successful and the organization wished to expand its operation to include governmental and educational agencies and for-profit entities. Since the expanded activities likely would be viewed as inconsistent with the organization's charitable purposes, it dropped down the management business to a for-profit subsidiary.

Assume for convenience that there are 9,000 hours during the year, and the use of the athletic facility is as follows: 600 hours for commercial events, 4,200 hours for activities substantially related to the College's exempt purposes, and 4,200 hours of idle time.

Compute the College's unrelated business taxable income from this facility for the current year.

2.   Save the Porpoise ("STP") is a § 501(c)(3) environmental organization. One of its activities is the publication of a quarterly journal, The Porpoise, that is distributed to its 10,000 members who pay annual dues of $40 per year. STP also distributes 5,000 additional copies of The Porpoise to nonmembers (such as libraries), who pay $20 per year. During the current year, STP derived $600,000 in gross revenue from the sale of commercial advertising in the Porpoise. Its direct costs of selling and publishing the advertising were $400,000. STP's other costs in producing and distributing The Porpoise were $350,000.

(a) What is STP's unrelated business taxable income from its advertising activity?

(b) Same as (a), above, except assume STP sold only 500 copies of The Porpoise to nonmembers at $20 per year and STP's members could elect not to receive the journal, in which case their dues would be reduced from $40 per year to $24 per year. During the current year, 3,000 members elected to receive the journal and pay the full $40 annual dues.

(c) Same as (a), above, except that STP had a net loss from the advertising activity of $30,000 and also earned $50,000 of unrelated business taxable income from another business activity (not advertising). What is STP's aggregate UBTI from the two activities?

E.   UNRELATED DEBT-FINANCED INCOME

Internal Revenue Code: §§ 514(a); (b); (c)(1)–(4), (7), (9)(A)–(D), (E).

Treasury Regulations: § 1.514(b)–1(a), (b), (d).

If an exempt organization borrows in order to acquire income-producing property, all or part of that income, less allocable deductions, may be included in UBTI under § 514 even if it otherwise would have been excluded under § 512(b). This expansion of the unrelated business tax to embrace income from debt-financed investments was in response to a variety of transactions aimed at circumventing the UBIT and exploiting an organization's tax-exempt status. A few words of background may be helpful to introduce this technical topic.

When the UBIT was first enacted, charities were viewed as being in a unique position to trade on their tax exemptions by acquiring property such as real estate on credit and then renting the property through a long-term leaseback to the seller, without payment of taxes by either party. A typical transaction might have been structured as follows:

> Charity buys rental property from Taxpayer, paying little or nothing down and financing the balance of the purchase price with a 20–year purchase money mortgage. Charity then enters into a net lease arrangement with Taxpayer, who agrees to pay all expenses on the property and remit a net rental to Charity. The tax-free rent received by Charity enables it to amortize the mortgage and still realize a profit. Taxpayer, in turn, enjoys capital gains treatment on the sale (often spreading his gain via the installment method of reporting) and is able to reduce its income from operating the property to a nominal amount through the deductions for rent and other expenses.

In 1950, Congress responded by imposing the UBIT on rentals from leases of real property and certain personal property if the lease term exceeded five years and the property was acquired with borrowed funds. The amount taxed generally was the gross rent multiplied by a percentage computed by dividing the total outstanding debt by the adjusted basis of the property, less a similar percentage of expenses attributable to the property. See Revenue Act of 1950, ch. 994, § 301(a). Creative tax advisors devised other transactions to circumvent this early legislation. For example, some exempt organizations made debt-financed acquisitions of going businesses that were liquidated tax-free by the charity, which then leased the assets back to a new entity created by the former owners of the for-profit business. Attempts by the Service to curb these transactions by requiring sellers to report their gains as ordinary income or revoking the charity's tax exemption were generally unsuccessful. See, e.g., Commissioner v. Brown, 380 U.S. 563, 85 S.Ct. 1162, 14 L.Ed.2d 75 (1965).

Fearing an erosion of the tax base and an unchecked growth of charitable organizations without any commensurate increase in their level of donative support, Congress expanded § 514 in 1969 to include in UBTI any passive investment income of an exempt organization to the extent that the property generating the income was acquired, directly or indirectly, with borrowed funds. But § 514 goes far beyond the transactions at which it was originally aimed. For example, stocks and bonds purchased on margin may constitute debt-financed property and, as a result, their dividend and interest income will be partially taxable.

Section 514 provides that an exempt organization must include in its UBTI a certain percentage§known as the "debt/basis fraction"—of gross income from debt-financed property, less a similar percentage of allocable deductions. I.R.C. § 514(a)(1)–(3). The types of income items potentially covered are rent, royalties, interest, dividends, and capital gains. "Debt-financed property" is defined as any tangible or intangible property held for the production of income with respect to which there exists an "acquisition indebtedness" at any time during the taxable year. I.R.C. § 514(b)(1); Treas. Reg. § 1.514(b)–1(a). Property is considered held for the production of income if it is held for operating profit or gain on a disposition of the property. Treas. Reg. § 1.514(b)–1(a). Familiar examples of debt-financed property are rental real estate subject to a mortgage and corporate stock purchased in part with borrowed funds. The statutory definition is qualified by numerous exceptions, most of which are intended to exempt property related to the organization's exempt purposes. I.R.C. § 514(b)(1); Treas. Reg. § 1.514(b)–1(b).

"Acquisition indebtedness" is generally defined as any unpaid debt incurred to acquire or improve property, including in some cases debt incurred before or after the acquisition or improvement. The most obvious example of acquisition indebtedness occurs when an organization acquires or improves income-producing property with borrowed funds, but the definition is broader in order to cover other borrowing that is closely connected with the acquisition or improvement of the property. The regulations provide that the "facts and circumstances" of each situation will determine whether the incurrence of a debt is reasonably foreseeable. The fact that the need to incur a debt may not have been foreseen before the acquisition does not necessarily mean that a later incurrence of the debt was not reasonably foreseeable. Treas. Reg. § 1.514(c)–1(a)(1).

The debt-basis fraction is used to determine the percentage of debt-financed income that must be included in UBTI. The fraction is generally determined by comparing the "average acquisition indebtedness" with respect to the debt-financed property to its adjusted basis. The fraction varies with the passage of time, as the debt is amortized and the basis is adjusted through depreciation, improvements, etc. I.R.C. § 514(a)(1).

Although § 514 was aimed at real estate, it has a much broader reach, as illustrated by the *Bartels Trust* case, which follows.

Bartels Trust v. United States

United States Court of Appeals, Second Circuit, 2000.
209 F.3d 147, cert. denied, 531 U.S. 978, 121 S.Ct. 426 (2000).

■ WEXLER, DISTRICT JUDGE:

Plaintiff-appellant, The Henry E. & Nancy Horton Bartels Trust for the Benefit of the University of New Haven ("Taxpayer"), appeals from a judgment of the United States District Court for the District of Connecticut (Eginton, J.), upon an order granting Taxpayer's motion for reconsideration and, on reconsideration, affirming an order granting the government's motion for summary judgment and denying Taxpayer's cross-motion for summary judgment in Taxpayer's refund action. Because we agree with the district court that Taxpayer's securities purchased on margin constitute debt-financed property and that income derived therefrom is subject to the unrelated business income tax ("UBIT") under §§ 511–14 of the Internal Revenue Code ("Code"), 26 U.S.C. §§ 511–14, we affirm.

I. BACKGROUND

The relevant facts, which are undisputed, may be summarized as follows: Taxpayer was created by a Declaration of Trust, dated November

30, 1988. The Internal Revenue Service ("IRS") granted Taxpayer tax-exempt status under § 501(c)(3) of the Code on April 24, 1989. Taxpayer was formed to provide support for the University of New Haven ("UNH") and qualified as a "supporting organization" under § 509(a)(3) of the Code. The Declaration of Trust gave Taxpayer's trustees broad discretion in investing its funds.

During the 1991, 1992, and 1993 tax years, Taxpayer invested in securities purchased "on margin," i.e., using funds borrowed from Taxpayer's stockbroker, Gilder, Gagnon, Howe & Co. ("Gilder, Gagnon"). In January 1995, Taxpayer filed Form 990–T, Exempt Organization Business Income Tax Return, for tax years 1991, 1992, and 1993, showing unrelated business income tax due on income derived from its margin-financed securities of $417, $2,948, and $6,123, respectively. Taxpayer paid the tax in full, with interest and penalties, but on May 22, 1995, Taxpayer filed a claim for refund of those payments. On April 25, 1996, the IRS denied taxpayer's refund claim. Taxpayer then brought this refund action.

In the district court, the government filed a motion for summary judgment, and Taxpayer filed a cross-motion for summary judgment. On March 17, 1998, the district court entered an order granting the government's motion and denying Taxpayer's cross-motion. The district court ruled that Taxpayer's income derived from securities purchased on margin is unrelated business taxable income under § 511 of the Code.

Taxpayer moved for reconsideration. The district court granted the motion for reconsideration and, on reconsideration, affirmed its earlier order. Judgment was entered, and Taxpayer filed this appeal.

We now affirm the district court's judgment.

II.   DISCUSSION

A.   Standard of Review

We review the district court's grant of the government's motion for summary judgment and denial of Taxpayer's cross-motion for summary judgment de novo. Eisenberg v. Commissioner, 155 F.3d 50, 53 (2d Cir. 1998).

B.   Unrelated Business Income Tax

An organization exempt from tax under § 501 of the Code may be subject to the UBIT on income it derives from a trade or business unrelated to its exempt purpose. See 26 U.S.C. § 501(b). Section 511(b) imposes the UBIT on tax-exempt trusts for "unrelated business taxable income," as defined in § 512. Id. § 511(b). Under § 512(a), "unrelated business taxable income" is defined, in general, as the "gross income derived by any organization from any unrelated trade or business (as defined in section 513) regularly carried on by it, less the deductions ... directly connected with the carrying on of such trade or business." Id. § 512(a)(1). Section 513, in turn, defines "unrelated trade or business" to include any trade or business "the conduct of which is not substantially related (aside from the need of such organization for income or funds or the use it makes of the profits derived) to the exercise or performance by such organization of its charitable, educational, or other purpose or function constituting the basis for its exemption under section 501"—subject to certain exceptions not applicable here. Id. § 513(a).

As a general rule, § 512 excludes from tax passive investment income, such as interest, dividends, and royalties, received by exempt organizations. Nevertheless, such investment income is taxable if derived from "debt-financed property," as defined in § 514. Thus, while § 512(b) generally excludes certain items of income from "unrelated business taxable income," it nullifies these exclusions for income derived from "debt-financed property," providing: "Notwithstanding paragraph (1), (2), (3), or (5), in the case of debt-financed property (as defined in section 514) there shall be included, as an item of gross income derived from an unrelated trade or business, the amount ascertained under section 514(a)(1)...." Id. § 512(b)(4). Section 514(a)(1) requires that income earned from "debt-financed property" be treated as income derived from an unrelated trade or business (in the proportion that the basis of the property bears to the amount financed) for purposes of determining unrelated business taxable income. Id. § 514(a)(1). The taxability of income from debt-financed property has no effect on the tax-exempt organization's tax-exempt status, but the income the organization derives from debt-financed property is subject to the UBIT as income from an unrelated trade or business. See id. § 501(b).

"Debt-financed property" is defined as "any property which is held to produce income and with respect to which there is an acquisition indebtedness (as defined in subsection (c)) at any time during the taxable year." Id. § 514(b)(1). Expressly excluded from debt-financed property is "any property substantially all the use of which is substantially related (aside from the need of the organization for income or funds) to the exercise or performance by such organization of its charitable, educational, or other purpose or function constituting the basis for its exemption under section 501." Id. § 514(b)(1)(A)(i).

Section 514(c)(1), in turn, defines "acquisition indebtedness" generally as "the indebtedness incurred by the organization in acquiring or improving [debt-financed property]." Id. § 514(c)(1)(A). Expressly excluded from acquisition indebtedness is "indebtedness the incurrence of which is inherent in the performance or exercise of the purpose or function constituting the basis of the organization's exemption, such as the indebtedness incurred by a credit union described in section 501(c)(14) in accepting deposits from its members." Id. § 514(c)(4).

C. Imposition of UBIT on Taxpayer's Income Derived from Securities Purchased on Margin

Taxpayer argues that the income it derived from securities purchased on margin is not subject to the UBIT because: (1) Taxpayer's securities investment activities, including margin trading, do not constitute conduct of a "trade or business" under the Code; (2) neither Taxpayer nor any third-party (i.e., UNH or Gilder, Gagnon) derived a direct or indirect "unfair competitive advantage" over taxable entities from Taxpayer's margin trading and the income derived therefrom; (3) Taxpayer's securities purchased on margin are not "debt-financed property" under § 514(b)(1); and (4) the exceptions to "debt-financed property" and "acquisition indebtedness" under § 514(b)(1)(A)(i) and § 514(c)(4), respectively, apply to exclude Taxpayer's income derived from securities purchased on margin from the UBIT. We disagree with Taxpayer's arguments, each of which we address below, and hold, as did the district court, that Taxpayer's income derived from margin-financed securities is subject to the UBIT under §§ 511–14 of the Code.

1.   Unrelated Trade or Business

Taxpayer initially argues that its securities investment activities, particularly its margin trading, do not constitute a "trade or business" under the Code, and, therefore, the income it derived from margin-financed securities is not subject to the UBIT. In this respect, Taxpayer argues that in determining whether an exempt organization's income is subject to the UBIT as "unrelated business taxable income" the following three requirements must be met: "(1) [i]t is income from trade or business; (2) such trade or business is regularly carried on by the organization; and (3) the conduct of such trade or business is not substantially related (other than through the production of funds) to the organization's performance of its exempt functions." Treas.Reg. § 1.513–1(a); see United States v. American College of Physicians, 475 U.S. 834, 838–39, 106 S.Ct. 1591, 89 L.Ed.2d 841 (1986). Taxpayer maintains that the first prong of this test is not met because Supreme Court decisions, such as Higgins v. Commissioner, 312 U.S. 212, 61 S.Ct. 475, 85 L.Ed. 783 (1941), and Whipple v. Commissioner, 373 U.S. 193, 83 S.Ct. 1168, 10 L.Ed.2d 288 (1963), hold that securities investing is not the conduct of a "trade or business." As further set out below, we find no merit to Taxpayer's argument.

Under the plain language of the UBIT, the purchase of securities on margin is a purchase using borrowed funds; therefore, under § 514(c), the securities are subject to an "acquisition indebtedness." See Elliot Knitwear Profit Sharing Plan v. Commissioner, 614 F.2d 347, 348–51 (3d Cir.1980). Thus, the margin-financed securities constitute "debt-financed property" under § 514(b)(1). As "debt-financed property," § 512(b)(4) and § 514(a)(1) require that the income derived from these securities be treated "as an item of gross income derived from an unrelated trade or business" (in the proportion that the basis of the property bears to the amount financed), and, therefore, this income is included in the § 512 computation of unrelated business taxable income. See, e.g., id. (holding securities purchased on margin are subject to UBIT, as margin-financed securities are debt-financed property, and § 514(a) requires treating income derived therefrom as income from unrelated trade or business). Thus, Taxpayer's reliance on Supreme Court decisions construing "trade or business" in other contexts and under the general test for determining unrelated business taxable income is misplaced because § 512(b)(4) and § 514(a)(1) require that Taxpayer's income derived from margin-financed securities be treated as income derived from an unrelated trade or business.

2. Unfair Competition

Despite the plain language of the UBIT, and its straightforward applicability to the income Taxpayer derived from margin-financed securities, Taxpayer argues that the UBIT does not apply here because neither Taxpayer nor any third-party derived, directly or indirectly, an "unfair competitive advantage" over taxable entities. Taxpayer asserts that because there has been no showing of "unfair competition," the income it derived from margin-financed securities is not subject to the UBIT. We find no merit to this argument.

First, and foremost, there is nothing in the plain language of the UBIT requiring a showing of unfair competition. Nevertheless, Taxpayer maintains that the legislative history of the UBIT compels such a requirement because Congress's "sole" purpose in enacting the UBIT was to prevent the business activities of tax-exempt organizations from gaining an unfair competitive advantage over taxable entities. Taxpayer relies on Greene v. United States, 79 F.3d 1348 (2d Cir.1996), in which this Court stated: "Although a statute's plain language is generally dispositive, it sometimes will yield when evidence of legislative history is so strong to the contrary that giving a literal reading to the statutory language will result in defeating Congress' purpose in enacting it." Id. at 1356. Although we believe that the plain language of the UBIT is dispositive here and should end our inquiry, resort to the legislative history does not, in any event, assist Taxpayer.

Since the first income tax, various organizations, including those established for charitable and educational purposes, have received exemption from income taxes. Rensselaer Polytechnic Institute v. Commissioner, 732 F.2d 1058, 1060 (2d Cir.1984) (citing relevant revenue acts). Prior to 1950, the tax-exemption provisions were interpreted to allow tax-exempt organizations to acquire commercial business enterprises and avoid paying taxes on the income generated. See C.F. Mueller Co. v. Commissioner, 190 F.2d 120 (3d Cir.1951). As this Court later observed in *Rensselaer Polytechnic*, Congress "[r]ecogniz[ed] ... the unfair competitive advantage that freedom from income taxation could accord tax-exempt institutions that entered the world of commerce," and so, in 1950, "extended the income tax to the 'unrelated business income' of certain tax-exempt institutions." Rensselaer Polytechnic, 732 F.2d at 1061 (citing Pub.L. No. 81–814, § 301, 64 Stat. 906, 947 (1950)). As this Court further observed: "[Congress's] objective in changing the law was to eliminate the competitive advantage educational and charitable corporations enjoyed over private enterprise, without jeopardizing the basic purpose of the tax-exemption." Id. (citing H.R.Rep. No. 81–2319 at 36–38 (1950); S.Rep. No. 81–2375 at 28–30 (1950)).

One of the earliest cases addressing the legislative history of the UBIT was Clarence LaBelle Post No. 217 v. United States, 580 F.2d 270 (8th

Cir.1978). In Clarence LaBelle, a tax-exempt organization sued for a refund of tax paid on its income from bingo games, after the IRS treated the bingo games as an unrelated trade or business under § 513 and taxed the income under § 511. The organization argued, inter alia, that income from an unrelated trade or business may be taxed only if the trade or business competes with a taxpaying entity, and that it was not subject to the tax because only tax-exempt nonprofit organizations may operate bingo games under the applicable state law. Id. at 271. The Eighth Circuit disagreed and held that "the tax on unrelated business income is not limited to income earned by a trade or business that operates in competition with taxpaying entities." Id. at 272. In reviewing the legislative history of the UBIT, the Eighth Circuit concluded that Congress enacted §§ 511–513 in order to "close a tax loophole" and raise additional revenue, as well as to eliminate a form of unfair competition. Id.

As for § 514, this section initially was "designed to prevent, inter alia, an exempt organization from trading in real estate on its exemption." Elliot Knitwear, 614 F.2d at 350–51. In 1969, Congress amended § 514 as part of the Tax Reform Act of 1969, Pub.L. No. 91–172, 83 Stat. 487, to broaden its reach beyond "debt-financed leases" in order to encompass income from property subject to acquisition indebtedness, i.e., "debt-financed property." Elliot Knitwear, 614 F.2d at 351. As the legislative history shows, Congress intended to remedy "weaknesses" in the then-existing UBIT to discourage the exploitation of an exempt organization's tax-exempt status for the benefit of a non-exempt organization in situations such as those addressed in Commissioner v. Brown, 380 U.S. 563, 85 S.Ct. 1162, 14 L.Ed.2d 75 (1965), and University Hill Foundation v. Commissioner, 51 T.C. 548, 1969 WL 1730 (1969), rev'd, 446 F.2d 701 (9th Cir.1971). See H.R.Rep. No. 91–413 at 44–46 (1969), reprinted in 1969 U.S.C.C.A.N. 1645, 1690–91. The House Ways and Means Committee explained the provision as follows:

> [U]nfair business competition [through use of tax-exempt organizations] should be discouraged.... [The] way to do so is by eliminating the incentive for owners desiring to sell a business to exploit the tax exemption of nonprofit organizations. This objective can be achieved by imposing the unrelated business income tax on the income received by the exempt organization in proportion to the debt existing on the income-producing property.

> Under the bill, the unrelated debt-financed income is included in "unrelated business income." It would be subject to tax, however, only if the income arises from property acquired or improved with borrowed funds and the production of the income is unrelated to the educational, charitable, religious, or other purpose constituting the basis of the organization's tax exemption.

Id. at 46, reprinted in 1969 U.S.S.C.A.N. at 1691.

While some courts of appeals, including the Eighth Circuit in *Clarence LaBelle*, have concluded that eliminating unfair competition was one purpose among many that motivated Congress to enact the UBIT, other courts of appeals have concluded that eliminating unfair competition was Congress's "primary" purpose. See Louisiana Credit Union League v. United States, 693 F.2d 525, 540–41 (5th Cir.1982) (recognizing two lines of authority: one where courts find prevention of unfair competition to be "primary purpose" and other where courts "prescribed a broader interpretation of the statute, focusing on the multiple objectives of Congress in enacting the unrelated business income tax," and concluding that a "study of the statute, the regulations, the legislative history, and the cases inclines us toward the latter view"); * * * .

The Supreme Court also has observed that the "undisputed purpose" of the UBIT was to prevent unfair competition. Portland Golf Club v. Commissioner, 497 U.S. 154, 161–62, 110 S.Ct. 2780, 111 L.Ed.2d 126 (1990) (citing S.Rep. No. 81–2375 at 28 (1950); H.R.Rep. No. 81–2319 at 36 (1950)); United States v. American Bar Endowment, 477 U.S. 105, 114, 106 S.Ct. 2426, 91 L.Ed.2d 89 (1986); American College of Physicians, 475 U.S. at 837–38, 106 S.Ct. 1591.

Although Taxpayer argues that *Portland Golf, American Bar Endowment*, and *American College of Physicians* "overruled" Clarence LaBelle's determination that the elimination of unfair competition was not the "sole" purpose of the UBIT, we find these cases unavailing to Taxpayer, as the Supreme Court did not hold in these cases that unfair competition must be shown for imposition of the UBIT, particularly as applied to "debt-financed property." Similarly, although Taxpayer argues that this Court "held" in Rensselaer Polytechnic, 732 F.2d at 1061, and People's Educational Camp Society, Inc. v. Commissioner, 331 F.2d 923, 935 (2d Cir.1964), that "the" purpose of the UBIT was the elimination of unfair competition, these cases also do not assist Taxpayer, as both involved undisputed evidence of unfair competition and did not address whether unfair competition must be shown for imposition of the UBIT. Moreover, Taxpayer cites no court of appeals case holding that unfair competition must be shown for imposition of the UBIT, and our review of the applicable case law reveals that no court of appeals has required such a showing. * * *

Taxpayer also argues that the "mischief rule" of statutory construction, as exemplified in Elliot Coal Mining Co. v. Director, Office of Workers' Compensation Programs, 17 F.3d 616, 631 (3d Cir.1994), requires that we bear in mind the mischief that Congress had in view when it enacted the UBIT and interpret the UBIT to tax only that category of conduct within the mischief Congress was attacking, namely, elimination of unfair competition. We reject Taxpayer's argument. Even though Congress enacted the UBIT primarily to eliminate unfair competition, it chose language going beyond the evil which it sought to correct in closing a loophole when it imposed the UBIT on "debt-financed property." As the tax court observed in Kern County Electrical Pension Fund v. Commissioner, 96 T.C. 845, 1991 WL 106265 (1991), aff'd by unpublished opinion, 988 F.2d 120 (9th Cir.1993):

> We quite agree that Congress was concerned with putting an end to the abuses reflected in Clay Brown and University Hill. But, although it focused on those particular abuses, the provisions which it enacted were couched in broader terms, and were not limited precisely to those situations. This is but another instance of Congress' going beyond the evil which it seeks to correct in closing a loophole. In the words of Judge Friendly in Commissioner v. Pepsi–Cola Niagara Bottling Corp., 399 F.2d 390, 392 (2d Cir.1968), "a legislature seeking to catch a particular abuse may find it necessary to cast a wider net."

Kern County Elec., 96 T.C. at 853; see also Elliot Knitwear, 614 F.2d at 350 (holding that although purchase of securities on margin does not seem to present source of unfair competition, both plain meaning of statute and congressional intent support imposition of UBIT on this type of income). In short, we find no basis for ignoring the plain language of the statute and its applicability to Taxpayer's income derived from debt-financed property even absent a showing of unfair competition. Despite Taxpayer's argument, we cannot say that the legislative history of the UBIT is so "strong to the contrary" that such an application of the statute would defeat Congress's purpose in enacting it.

Accordingly, we reject Taxpayer's argument that unfair competition must be shown for the imposition of the UBIT on income it derived from margin-financed securities.

3. "Held to Produce Income"

Next, Taxpayer argues that its margin-financed securities are not "debt-financed property" because § 514(b)(1) defines "debt-financed property" as property that is "held to produce income," and this phrase should be interpreted to include only "periodic" income. We find no merit to this argument for at least two reasons. First, Taxpayer cites no authority for this construction of § 514(b)(1), and there is nothing in the statutory language or legislative history of the UBIT supporting this restrictive interpretation. Second, the applicable regulation specifically construes "income" under § 514(b)(1) as including both capital gains and recurring or "periodic" income (e.g., dividends). In this respect, Treasury Regulation § 1.514(b)–1(a) defines "debt-financed property" as

> any property which is held to produce income (e.g., rental real estate, tangible personal property, and corporate stock), and with respect to which there is an acquisition indebtedness (determined without regard to whether the property is debt-financed property) at any time during the taxable year. The term "income" is not limited to recurring income but applies as well to gains from the disposition of the property.

Treas. Reg. § 1.514(b)–1(a) (emphasis added). Although Taxpayer urges us to reject the Commissioner's interpretation of the UBIT, we must sustain the regulation unless it is "unreasonable and plainly inconsistent" with the statute.

Section 61(a) of the Code broadly defines income to include "all income from whatever source derived," and lists, as examples, both periodic income (e.g., dividends and interest) and nonperiodic income (e.g., compensation for services; gross income derived from business; and gains derived from dealings in property). 26 U.S.C. § 61(a)(1), (2), (3), (4), (7). There is nothing in the statutory language to suggest that this general definition of "income" is inapplicable to § 514(b)(1) or to justify limiting § 514(b)(1) to "periodic" income. Moreover, the legislative history of the UBIT does not indicate that Congress intended to tax only "periodic" income under those provisions. Accordingly, we reject Taxpayer's argument that § 514(b)(1)'s reference to "debt-financed property" includes only "periodic" income.

4.   Exceptions to Acquisition Indebtedness and Debt–Financed Property

Finally, Taxpayer argues that even if the income it derived from margin-financed securities would otherwise constitute unrelated business income under §§ 511 and 512, the exceptions to "debt-financed property" and "acquisition indebtedness" under § 514(b)(1)(A)(i) and § 514(c)(4), respectively, apply to exclude this income. In this respect, Taxpayer argues that its income is not taxable because (1) the securities it purchased on margin are "substantially related" to its exempt purpose under the § 514(b)(1)(A)(i) exception to "debt-financed property"; and (2) its purchase of securities on margin is "inherent" to its exempt purpose under the § 514(c)(4) exception to "acquisition indebtedness." We find no merit to Taxpayer's argument, as both exceptions are inapplicable here.

The leading case addressing these exceptions is *Elliot Knitwear*, which involved a tax-exempt employee profit-sharing plan which derived income from margin-financed securities. See Elliot Knitwear, 614 F.2d at 348. In holding the income subject to the UBIT, the Third Circuit rejected the plan's argument that its margin account fell within the § 514(c)(4) exception to acquisition indebtedness because the margin account was "inherent" in the plan's exempt purpose, and the plan's further argument that the margin account fell within the § 514(b)(1)(A)(i) exception to debt-financed property because the margin account was "substantially related" to the plan's exempt purpose, namely, accumulation of income for employees for their retirement. *See id.* at 349–51. The court held that "inherent," as used in § 514(c)(4), is synonymous with "essential," and concluded that, while investing on margin may have been desirable for the plan, it was not essential to its tax-exempt purpose of providing employee participation in the employer's profits. Id. at 349–50. The court reasoned that "while investment of the fund probably is inherent to its tax-exempt purpose, debt-financed investment is not." Id. at 350. Thus, the court held that the "purchase of securities on margin is not inherent to the purpose of a tax-exempt profit-sharing plan within the meaning of section 514(c)(4)" and, therefore, not within the exception to "acquisition indebtedness." Id.

As for the plan's argument that the § 514(b)(1)(A)(i) exception to debt-financed property applied, the court first observed that "[i]t is the property itself, and not the income generated by the property, that must be substantially related to the exempt purpose of the organization." Id. In rejecting the plan's argument, the court reasoned:

> It is expected that the buying and selling of income-producing property will be a method utilized to increase and accumulate income and gains, but such investment activity is a means to accomplish the purpose of deferred compensation it is not the purpose itself of the Plan. Even assuming, arguendo, that investment of contributions for accumulation of income is a function of the Plan, indebtedness or acquisition of securities on margin is not necessary for such accumulation or that purpose.

Id. Moreover, the court recognized that the "statute does not exclude property that is substantially related by virtue of 'the need of the organization for income or funds.' "Id. (quoting 26 U.S.C. § 514(b)(1)(A)(i)).

We find the *Elliot Knitwear* court's reasoning persuasive, and accordingly conclude that Taxpayer's purchase of securities on margin does not fall within the "inherent" purpose exception or the "substantially related" exception to § 514.

Taxpayer's exempt purpose is to provide funds to support UNH's educational programs. Taxpayer's purchase of securities on margin is not "inherent" or essential to that purpose. Indeed, many alternative investments, whether involving borrowed funds or not, are available to Taxpayer for generating income. Taxpayer's indebtedness incurred from its margin borrowing is readily distinguishable from the statute's example of indebtedness that is "inherent" to an organization's exempt purpose, namely, "the indebtedness incurred by a credit union * * * in accepting deposits from its members." 26 U.S.C. § 514(c)(4). Taxpayer need not purchase securities on margin to generate income from trading in securities.

For similar reasons, Taxpayer's securities purchased on margin are not "substantially related" to Taxpayer's exempt purpose of supporting UNH's educational programs. As the Third Circuit noted in Elliot Knitwear, the use of the property itself, not the income generated by the property, must be substantially related to the exempt purpose. Elliot Knitwear, 614 F.2d at 350. Taxpayer's argument ignores that the exception does not apply to property "substantially related" merely by virtue of "the need of the organization for income or funds." While margin-financed securities may be useful to accomplish that exempt purpose by their ability to generate income, their purchase and use is not substantially related to Taxpayer's tax-exempt purpose within the meaning of § 514(b)(1)(A)(i). See id.

Thus, Taxpayer's borrowing to purchase securities is not "inherent" to its exempt purpose; and its margin-financed securities are not "substantially related" to its exempt purpose. Accordingly, the district court correctly held that the exceptions in § 514(b)(1)(A)(1) and § 514(c)(4) do not apply.

III. CONCLUSION

We have reviewed Taxpayer's remaining arguments raised on appeal and find them to be without merit. For the above reasons, we affirm the judgment of the district court.

NOTES AND QUESTIONS

1. *Avoiding § 514.* In many typical situations, § 514 is avoidable because of the numerous exceptions summarized in this Note.

Substantially Related Use. If "substantially all" of the use of the property is "substantially related" to the exercise or performance of the organization's exempt purposes, no part of the property is treated as debt-financed. I.R.C. § 514(b)(1)(A)(i). "Substantially all" is defined by the regulations to be 85 percent or more. The extent to which property is used for a particular purpose is determined on the basis of all the facts, particularly time and space. Treas. Reg. § 1.514(b)–1(b)(1)(ii). "Related use" does not include the need of the organization for income or the use it makes of the profits derived from the property. Treas. Reg. § 1.514(b)–1(b)(1)(i). For example, assume that University owns an office building that is debt-financed. If at least 85 percent of the building is used for university activities, the fact that 15 percent may be rented to outsiders will not cause the property to be debt-financed.

Dual Use. If property is used for both exempt activities and to produce income (but less than 85 percent of the property is substantially related to exempt activities), the property will be considered debt-financed only in proportion to the non-exempt use. I.R.C. § 514(b)(1)(A)(ii). For example, assume that University owns an office building subject to a large mortgage. Two floors are used for university administration; the other two floors are rented to the public. Only the rented portion of the building is debt-financed. Treas. Reg. § 1.514(b)–1(b)(1)(iii) Example (2).

Unrelated Business Income. If the income from the property is subject to the UBIT under the general rules in §§ 511 to 513, it is not debt-financed unless the income results from the sale or exchange of non-inventory property. I.R.C. § 514(b)(1)(B). For example, an exempt organization that provided substantial services in connection with a rental real estate activity, as in the case of an apartment hotel, would be taxable on its rental income even if the property were not debt-financed.

Research Income. In keeping with prior themes, property used in certain research activities is not debt-financed if the income is excludable from UBTI under §§ 512(b)(7), (8) or (9). I.R.C. § 514(b)(1)(C).

Volunteers, Convenience Activities and Thrift Shops. Mirroring the general UBIT exceptions for these activities, property used in a trade or business described in § 513(a)(1)(relating to services performed by volunteers), § 513(a)(2)(activities conducted for the convenience of students, patients, customers, etc.) and § 513(a)(3)(sale of donated merchandise) is not debt-financed. I.R.C. § 514(b)(1)(D).

Neighborhood Land Property. A rather elaborate exception to the definition of debt-financed property applies in cases where an organization acquires income-producing real estate for future use for exempt purposes. Known as the "neighborhood land rule," this exception is available if the following requirements are met:

(1) The real property must be acquired for the principal purpose of using the land but not the improvements in the exempt activities of the organization within ten years after it is acquired. The intent to use the property in an exempt manner may not be abandoned within the 10–year period. I.R.C. § 514(b)(3)(A).

(2) The property must be in the "neighborhood" of other property owned and used by the organization for its exempt purposes. Id. Property is considered in the "neighborhood" if it is contiguous to the other property or would be but for the intervention of a road, street, railroad, stream, etc. Treas. Reg. § 1.514(b)–1(d)(1)(ii).

(3) If the acquired property is not contiguous with the exempt purpose property, it is still treated as "in the neighborhood" if it is within one mile of the property and the facts and circumstances indicate that the acquisition of contiguous property was not feasible. Id.

(4) If structures exist on the property when it is purchased, the organization's intended use requires the structures to be demolished. I.R.C. § 514(b)(3)(C)(i).

The neighborhood land exception applies for no more than ten years after the property is acquired. It applies for years 6–10 only if the organization can establish to the satisfaction of the Service that conversion for use in an exempt activity within ten years after the purchase is "reasonably certain." (Churches have 15 years.) I.R.C. § 514(b)(3)(A), (E). This special burden of proof must be met by a ruling request filed at least 90 days before the end of the fifth year after acquisition. Treas. Reg. § 1.514(b)–1(d)(1)(iii).

If the organization fails the above tests, either because the property is not in the neighborhood or the organization is unable to prove in years 6–10 that it is "reasonably certain" that the land will be converted, the exception nonetheless applies (and is given retroactive effect) if the organization in fact converts the land to exempt use within ten years of its purchase. I.R.C. § 514(b)(3)(B).

Exception for Certain Leveraged Real Property. Section 514(c)(9) contains an important exception for indebtedness incurred with respect to real estate held by qualified pension and profit sharing trusts, certain educational organizations described in § 170(b)(1)(A)(ii) and their affiliated support organizations described in § 509(a)(3), and certain § 501(c)(25) holding companies.[1] Stripped of detail, debt incurred by these "qualified organizations" to acquire or improve any real property is not "acquisition indebtedness" provided that:

(1) The acquisition price is a fixed amount determined as of the date of acquisition or completion of the improvement;

---

1. Section 501(c)(25) title holding companies pass through their income to their shareholders or beneficiaries. These beneficial owners may utilize the § 514(c)(9) exception with respect to amounts passed through to them only if they are qualified pension trusts, or the types of educational organizations described in § 170(b)(1)(A)(ii). I.R.C. § 514(c)(9)(F).

(2) The amount of the debt, or the time for making payment, is not dependent on profits derived from the property;

(3) The property is not leased back to the seller or to any person related to the seller within the § 267(b) attribution rules, except that a qualified exempt organization may lease back to the seller up to 25 percent of a debt-financed property if the lease is on a commercially reasonable basis and is independent of the sale and other transactions between the parties;

(4) In the case of a qualified pension or profit sharing trust, the property is not acquired from or leased back to certain "disqualified persons," as defined in § 4975(e)(2);

(5) Neither the seller, a party related to the seller, nor a disqualified person provides financing in connection with the acquisition or improvement;

(6) If the real property is held by a partnership, the partnership must meet all the foregoing requirements and, in addition, all the partners must be qualified organizations as defined in § 514(c)(9)(C), and certain other mind boggling requirements must be met. Since those requirements require a mastery of partnership tax, this explanation will go no further.

I.R.C. § 514(c)(9)(B) & (c)(9)(G)(i).

2. *Policy for the Leveraged Real Estate Exception.* It has been suggested that the only reason why the generous exemption in § 514(c)(9) was enacted is that "some people wanted it" in order to achieve greater investment diversification for the nonprofit organizations that they represented! 4 Bittker & Lokken, Federal Taxation of Income, Estates and Gifts § 103.4.3 (2d ed. 1992). When first enacted in 1980, the exception only applied to qualified pension trusts. Their lobbyists argued that they were at a competitive disadvantage relative to banks and insurance companies. Over the Treasury's objection, the exception was extended to schools (as narrowly defined in § 170(b)(1)(A)(ii)) in 1984, and in 1986 to certain real estate title holding companies. Employee retirement plans at least can make the argument that their income eventually will be taxed to the employees and the beneficiaries. That same rationale does not extend to educational organizations and title holding companies.

The § 514(c)(9) exception includes anti-abuse rules. For example, the purchase price may not be contingent on earnings, leasebacks to the seller are not permitted, and the seller may not finance the acquisition. Why should the exception be limited to pension plans, schools, and their title holding companies? Why shouldn't it extend to all § 501(c)(3) organizations and to debt-financed property other than real estate?

3. *For Further Reading.* Suzanne Ross McDowell, Taxation of Unrelated Debt–Financed Income, 34 Exempt Org. Tax Rev. 197 (2001); Suzanne Ross McDowell, Taxing Leveraged Investments of Charitable Organizations: What is the Rationale? 39 Case West.L.Rev. 705, 712–723 (1988);

Douglas Mancino, How to Acquire and Operate Debt-Financed Property, 5 J. Tax'n Exempt Org. 78 (1993).

PROBLEM

Law School owns a 20–story building one block from its urban campus. Law School's cost basis in the building is $800,000, and the property is encumbered by a $600,000 seller-financed mortgage. Consider whether the rentals from the building are subject to the unrelated business income tax in the following alternative situations:

(a) Law School rents 90 percent of the building to students for residential use and 10 percent to commercial tenants.

(b) Same as (a), above, except 60 percent of the use is by students and 40 percent by commercial tenants.

(c) Same as (b), above, except Law School received the building as a contribution from Benefactor, who had owned it for ten years before making the lifetime gift.

(d) Law School operates the building as a hotel and restaurant.

(e) Law School operates the building as an apartment house for the general public.

(f) Assume Law School acquired the building, which previously had been operated as a residential hotel, with the intent of demolishing the structure and using the property for a new student residence facility. It continues to rent space to the general public for seven years while seeking city approval for the project.

(g) Same as (e), above, except that the building is never demolished and Law School eventually renovates it for student use.

(h) Would the result be different in any of the above alternatives if the debt had not been seller-financed?

F. SPECIAL PROBLEMS

1. PARTNERSHIPS AND S CORPORATIONS

Internal Revenue Code: § 512(c)(1), (e).
Treasury Regulations: § 1.512(b)–1(h)(2).

Service Bolt & Nut Co. v. Commissioner

United States Tax Court, 1982.
78 T.C. 812.

OPINION

■ NIMS, JUDGE: * * *.

[The primary issue in this case was whether a tax-exempt profit-sharing trust realized "unrelated business taxable income" in its capacity as a limited partner in various partnerships that were engaged in a wholesale fastener distribution business. The same issue is raised with respect to other § 501(c) organizations which realize income from limited partnership investments. Eds.]

Notwithstanding their general income tax exemption under section 501(a), section 511 imposes a tax on profit-sharing trusts qualified under section 401(a) to the extent such trusts receive "unrelated business taxable income." The primary dispute in this case is whether petitioners received any unrelated business taxable income within the meaning of section 511 as a result of holding limited partnership interests in various wholesale fastener distributing partnerships.

Petitioners argue that a limited partnership interest is a passive investment that cannot, unlike a general partnership interest, produce unrelated business taxable income.

Respondent, on the other hand, contends that a limited partnership interest is no different from a general partnership interest for purposes of the section 511 tax: Both can produce unrelated business taxable income.

The concept of and tax imposed upon unrelated business income of exempt organizations derives essentially from Supplement U of the 1939 Code. In its latter codification, this concept appears at sections 511 through 515. Section 511 imposes a tax on the unrelated business taxable income (as defined in section 512) of certain tax-exempt organizations. As regards the treatment of income from partnership interests held by exempt organizations, the relevant provisions of the 1954 Code are sections 512(c) and 513(b). Section 512(c) provides:

(c) SPECIAL RULES APPLICABLE TO PARTNERSHIPS.—If a trade or business regularly carried on by a partnership of which an organization is a member is an unrelated trade or business with respect to such organization, such organization in computing its unrelated business taxable income shall, subject to the exceptions, additions, and limitations contained in subsection (b), include its share (whether or not distributed) of the gross income of the partnership from such unrelated trade or business and its share of the partnership deductions directly connected with such gross income. If the taxable year of the organization is different from that of the partnership, the amounts to be so included or deducted in computing the unrelated business taxable income shall be based upon the income and deductions of the partnership for any taxable year of the partnership ending within or with the taxable year of the organization.

Section 513(b) provides in relevant part:

(b) SPECIAL RULE FOR TRUSTS.—The term "unrelated trade or business" means, in the case of?

* * *

(2) a trust described in section 401(a), or section 501(c)(17), which is exempt from tax under section 501(a); any trade or business regularly carried on by such trust or by a partnership of which it is a member.

Petitioners contend that these references to partnerships in sections 512(c) and 513(b) apply only in the case of general partnership interests held by exempt organizations and not to limited partnership interests. They argue that limited partnership income is analogous to such passive-income items as dividends, interest, royalties, and some rents. Congress, petitioners argue, could not have meant to make taxable the income from a passive investment such as a limited partnership interest, where the exempt organization could not actively manage the business in a fashion to result in unfair competition. We disagree.

In examining the application of a particular statute, our first reference must be to the words of that statute. Here, the provisions in question (secs. 512(c) and 513 (b)) impose a tax on an exempt organization's distributive share of partnership gross income (less allocable deductions) attributable to a partnership's regularly carrying on a trade or business unrelated to the exempt organization's purpose. The only statutory requirement for the imposition of this tax is that the organization be a "member" of such a partnership. Petitioners would limit the meaning of the word "member" to "general partner." There is nothing in the language or structure of these sections to demand or even justify reading into them petitioners' narrower requirement. * * *

Additionally, the legislative history of these sections does not support petitioners' narrow reading. In discussing the application of the Supplement U tax in the case of partnership interests, both the House and Senate reports from 1950 contain the following example: For example, if an exempt educational institution is a silent partner in a partnership which runs a barrel factory and such partnership also holds stock in a pottery manufacturing corporation, the exempt organization would include in its unrelated business income its share of the barrel factory income, but not its proportionate share of any dividends received by the partnership from the pottery corporation. * * * While, as petitioners point out, a "silent partner" is not necessarily the same thing as a "limited partner," we think the above example clearly demonstrates Congress' intent to include exempt organizations' distributive shares of partnership income within the Supplement U tax, regardless of whether, as partners, they behaved in an active or passive manner with regard to the management of the partnership's unrelated trades or businesses.

Indeed, it would have been unlikely for Congress to have thought otherwise. One problem which Congress was addressing in the Supplement U tax was the availability of pools of tax-exempt income which gave previously nontaxable trades or businesses unfair competitive advantages over their taxable counterparts. In the case of a partnership, these pools of income can be created when a partner who otherwise would have to withdraw some of his partnership income each year to pay the tax on his distributive share of partnership income does not have to withdraw any cash from the partnership because he has no income tax to pay. Whether the tax-exempt partner actively manages the underlying unrelated partnership business or not is thus irrelevant to the issue of whether the partnership as a whole has an unfair competitive advantage from the accumulation of an unwithdrawn pool of tax-exempt income.

* * *

In short, we decline to strain the construction of the word "member" in sections 512(c) and 513(b) and defeat the intent of Congress. Therefore, we hold that an exempt trust which is a limited partner may receive unrelated business taxable income (within the meaning of section 512) through a limited partnership upon which the trust is taxable under section 511. Since it is undisputed that the wholesale fastener partnerships in which petitioners were members engaged in the type of activity which falls within the section 513(a) definition of unrelated trade or business, respondent's determinations of petitioners' liabilities for the tax imposed by section 511 must be sustained.

* * *

NOTES AND QUESTIONS

1. *Policy Considerations.* What is the policy of § 512(c)? Exempt organizations generally are not taxed on income derived from passive investments. If an exempt organization chooses to invest in an active business as a limited partner, why is it subject to the UBIT when it would not be taxed on dividends and interest from other types of investments? The answer lies in the need to ensure that income from an unrelated business is subject to at least one level of tax. If the business is conducted by a typical "C corporation," its net income will be subject to the corporate income tax, and thus earnings distributed as dividends to tax-exempt investors need not be taxed again as they would be if they were received by taxable shareholders. Partnerships and limited liability companies (which are taxed as partnerships), by contrast, are not subject to tax but rather pass through their income and deductions to their partners or members. Section 512(c) treats any unrelated business income of a partnership as if it were realized directly by its tax-exempt partners, even if they do not actively participate in management of the enterprise. This rule is faithful to the pass-through principles of partnership taxation and precludes an easy end run around the policy of the UBIT.

2. *Investment Partnerships.* Many wealthy exempt organizations, such as private foundations or universities with large endowments, engage in a variety of sophisticated investment strategies, often through investment pools known generically as "hedge funds." See Thomas J. Billitteri, Hedging Their Bets: Big Foundations and Universities Turn to Non-Traditional Investments, Chron. of Philanthropy, Oct. 22, 1998, at 1, 33–35. These investment pools are unregulated in the sense that, unlike mutual funds, they are exempt from most regulation under federal and state securities

and investment company laws. To qualify for this special status, access to private investment partnerships must be limited to wealthy individuals and large institutional investors who meet certain tests qualifying them as "sophisticated" under federal securities laws.

Virtually all domestic investment pools are structured as limited partnerships or limited liability companies in order to avoid the corporate income tax. The specific investment strategies of these funds vary widely, ranging from the classic hedge fund that seeks to minimize risk by holding both long and short market positions, to real estate and venture capital funds, and to more exotic investments in risk and event arbitrage transactions, debt of financially distressed companies, foreign currency, and harvestable timber.

If an exempt organization is a limited partner in an investment partnership, its share of dividends, interest, rent, capital gains and other forms of passive investment income is not included in UBTI because the reach of § 512(c) is limited to active business income. If a hedge fund uses leverage, however, a tax-exempt partner likely will be taxable on at least part of its otherwise excluded investment income because of the unrelated debt-financed property rules in § 514. To avoid these tax problems, large investment pools catering to tax-exempt investors typically incorporate offshore funds, often in the Cayman Islands. For example, a Cayman Islands Exempted Company can be structured to avoid corporate income tax either in the United States or its offshore domicile. Since the fund is a corporation, its net income does not pass-through to the tax-exempt investors, and problems with unrelated debt-financed income are avoided. Distributions by offshore funds to their investors are ordinarily treated as dividends excluded from UBTI by § 512(b).

If debt-financed real estate is held by a partnership, any tax-exempt partners that are "qualified organizations" (e.g., pension trusts and schools) may qualify for the § 514(c)(9)(A) exception from acquisition indebtedness (see Section E of this chapter, supra at pp. 656–657), but only if certain additional requirements are met. I.R.C. § 514(c)(9)(B)(vi), (E); 168(h)(6). Very generally, the Congressional agenda is to prevent partnerships consisting of both taxable and tax-exempt partners from making strategic allocations to realize tax benefits that could not be achieved using a more direct route. Understanding the details requires a mastery of the arcane world of partnership allocations, a topic mercifully beyond the scope of this Note.

3. *S Corporations.* Like partnerships and limited liability companies, S corporations are generally not subject to federal income tax at the entity level. The income, deductions, and other tax items of an S corporation pass through to its shareholders in proportion to their ownership interests. Unlike partnerships and LLCs, S corporations are subject to strict eligibility limitations. For example, an S corporation may have no more than 75 shareholders; its shareholders are limited to individuals, estates, certain types of trusts, and a few specialized categories; and it may only have one class of stock. See I.R.C. §§ 1361 et seq. Over the years, however, Congress

has been relaxing these limitations and, effective on January 1, 1998, S corporations may have exempt organizations as shareholders. I.R.C. § 1361(c)(6).

In liberalizing the S corporation eligibility requirements, Congress took steps to preclude tax-exempt shareholders from circumventing the UBIT. To preserve at least one level of tax, § 512(e)(1) provides that an exempt organization's interest in an S corporation "shall be treated as an interest in an unrelated trade or business." As a result, the organization's share of the corporation's income, loss, deduction, and other tax items, as well as any gain or loss on a disposition of S corporation stock, is taken into account in computing the exempt organization's UBTI. The items passing through to a tax-exempt shareholder's UBTI include its pro rata share of the corporation's dividends, interest, rents, and capital gains. These passive investment income items would be excluded from UBTI if they were realized through a partnership or LLC. S corporations raise a host of other unique UBIT issues that must be considered by an organization in evaluating whether it should purchase or accept a gift of S corporation stock. For a good discussion of this largely uncharted area, see Christopher R. Hoyt, Subchapter S Stock Owned by Tax-Exempt Organizations: Solutions to Legal Issues, 22 Exempt Org. Tax Rev. 25 (1998).

2.   SOCIAL CLUBS

Internal Revenue Code: § 512(a)(3).

The UBIT has a much broader reach in the case of § 501(c)(7) social clubs and a handful of other exempt organizations. A social club's UBTI includes all of its gross income other than "exempt function income," less directly related deductions. I.R.C. § 512(a)(3)(A). This rule has the effect of taxing social clubs on their investment income. The theory is that the club's members would be individually taxable on their dividends and interest and must pay for social and recreational activities with after-tax income. They should not be able to obtain a more favorable result by pooling their investments in an exempt entity that uses the resulting income to support the members' recreational pursuits.

"Exempt function income" includes dues, fees and charges paid by the club's members for goods, facilities and services that are related to the club's exempt functions. It also includes amounts set aside for charitable purposes, such as where a college fraternity or sorority sets aside funds for scholarships. I.R.C. § 512(a)(3)(B). Finally, gain from the sale of assets used in the performance of a social club's exempt functions (e.g., the sale of a club house) are not taxable to the extent that the proceeds are reinvested in assets used for a comparable function within a specified period of time. I.R.C. § 512(a)(3)(D).

Computation of the unrelated business taxable income of a social club requires an allocation of business expenses and depreciation between exempt function income and taxable receipts. One common strategy used by social clubs to reduce their bottom line UBTI is to deduct net losses from nonmember activities, such as the sale of food and beverages, against taxable investment income. Some clubs claimed these deductions even when the nonmember business was not carried out with a profit motive. This issue worked its way up to the Supreme Court, which held in a 6–3 opinion that social clubs may offset losses incurred from nonmember activities against investment income only if the nonmember sales were motivated by an intent to make a profit. Portland Golf Club v. Commissioner, 497 U.S. 154, 110 S.Ct. 2780 (1990). Profit motive, for this purpose, was interpreted by the Court to mean an intent to generate receipts in excess of costs.

G.   PROPOSALS FOR REFORM

As previewed at the beginning of this chapter, the scope and application of the unrelated business income tax attracted increasing scrutiny in the 1980's, culminating in extensive hearings by the Subcommittee on Oversight of the House Ways and Means Committee in 1987 and 1988. In mid-1988, the Subcommittee circulated a draft report and recommendations, which were quickly leaked to the press. See Subcommittee on Oversight of the House Committee on Ways and Means, 100th Cong., 2d Sess., Draft Report Describing Recommendations on the Unrelated Business Income Tax (Comm. Print 1988)(hereinafter "Draft Report"). By 1989, the momentum had shifted, and UBIT reform began moving to the back burner, where it remained during the budget-driven tax legislative gridlock that typified much of the 1990's. The Draft Report nonetheless remains "on the shelf" and is poised to serve as the focal point for discussion if and when the UBIT debate is resurrected.

After flirting with some alternative formulations (e.g., a "directly related" test), the Oversight Subcommittee recommended the retention of the conceptual framework of the UBIT, including the "substantially related" test. It observed, however, that the test had proven to be vague, difficult to administer and unevenly enforced. Draft Report at 29–34. The Subcommittee concluded that further clarification was needed to identify particular income-producing activities that were fundamentally not "related" in nature. The excerpt below sets forth some of the Subcommittee's specific recommendations to supplant the substantially related test with respect to the certain categories of revenue-producing activities.

Subcommittee on Oversight of House Ways and Means Committee, Draft Report Describing Recommendations on the Unrelated Business Income Tax

100th Cong., 2d Sess. (Comm. Print 1988).

* * *

b.   Gift shop, bookstore, catalog and mail order activities.

Recommendation: Income derived from the sale of goods through gift shop, bookstore, catalog, and mail order activities (whether the sale takes place on or off the premises of the exempt organization) should be treated as income derived from an unrelated trade or business, subject to the exceptions described below. For this purpose, the term sale of goods includes rental of goods (e.g., the rental of video cassettes by a bookstore or gift shop). However, the sale or rental of medical equipment and devices, or pharmaceutical drugs and goods, is governed by the rule described at c., below.

[The Report then carved out several limited exceptions. For all exempt organizations other than schools and hospitals, the UBIT would not apply to: (1) sales of "mementos" (e.g., T-shirts, tote bags, etc., with the organization's logo) costing not more than $15, (2) sales of reproductions by museums, libraries, historical societies, or other organizations maintaining collections if the reproductions cost no more than $50 and the object reproduced was part of the organization's own collection or exhibits, and (3) items, whatever their cost, that are "primarily educational" and whose content relates to the exempt purposes of the organization (e.g., income derived by a museum of modern sculpture from a bookstore sale of a general art history textbook, but items of a "primarily decorative or functional" nature would be taxable). In the case of hospital gift shops, the UBIT would not apply to income from the sale of goods used primarily by or for patients, such as flowers, candy, toiletries, reading materials and pajamas, whether or not the items were purchased for a patient. In the case of educational institutions, the UBIT would not apply to income from the sale to students of goods with a retail price of $15 or less or to income from the sale of higher priced goods to students that furthered the institution's educational programs and "are not common consumer goods." Books and computer software would be exempted, but not appliances, cameras, televisions, VCRs and recreational sports equipment. Special rules were provided for the sale of computers by an educational institution. Sales to students would be exempted if the student submitted a statement signed by a faculty member that the computer was required for the student's course work, but income from the sale of computers to students would be taxable "to the extent that the number of otherwise exempt sales made by the institution during a year exceeds half the total number of full-time students attending the institution during that year." Eds.]

c. Activities related to medical equipment and devices, pharmaceutical drugs and goods, and laboratory testing

Recommendation: Income derived from the sale or rental of medical equipment and devices (including hearing aids, portable X-ray units, and oxygen tanks), the sale of pharmaceutical drugs and goods, and the performance of laboratory testing should be treated as income derived from an unrelated trade or business, subject to the following two exceptions.

First, the UBIT should not apply to income from the sale or rental of such items to patients of the organization deriving the income (e.g., to patients of the hospital), or from the performance of laboratory testing for such patients. For this purpose, the term patient has the same meaning as used for UBIT purposes under present law. * * *

Second, the UBIT should not apply to income from the sale or rental of such an item to, or the providing of laboratory testing for, persons who are not patients of the organization if such item or service is not otherwise available in the immediate geographic area.

d.   Fitness, exercise, and similar health-promotion activities

Recommendation: Income derived by a charitable organization from fitness, exercise, and similar health-promotion activities (such as classes or programs in aerobics, weightlifting, racquetball, or swimming) should be treated as income derived from an unrelated trade or business unless the facility at which the activity is conducted independently serves a primarily charitable purpose. The required charitable purpose could be demonstrated by various factors, such as service to low-income, elderly, or handicapped individuals, youth, or by providing service to the community as a whole.

The present-law treatment of "special-fee" activities should be retained. For example, if members of a section 501(c)(3) community recreational organization could use the organization's weightlifting or exercise room only by paying an additional charge that precludes participation by the general community, income from the special-fee activity would be unrelated business income.

e.   Travel and tour service activities

Recommendation: Income derived from travel and tour activities should be treated as income derived from an unrelated trade or business, subject to the exception described below. For purposes of this rule, the term travel and tour activities would not include local transportation activities of a charitable nature, such as the transportation of needy individuals to medical facilities for treatment of the transportation of elderly individuals to senior citizen centers for meals or to pharmacies to purchase medicine, but would include such activities as the transportation of individuals to tourist attractions or vacation spots.

Under the exception, the UBIT should not apply (1) to income derived by an educational institution from travel or tour activities conducted for the benefit of its students or faculty members ("students") if the travel or tour is part of the degree program curriculum of the institution, or (2) to a de minimis amount of income attributable to participation in such travel or tours by individuals who are neither its students nor faculty members ("nonstudents"). For this purpose, de minimis should be defined as income attributable to five percent or less of the available participation in the qualified travel or tour. For example, if a university arranges a bus trip with seating for 40 persons to an art museum in connection with its art history degree program, sells 38 tickets to students, and makes the two seats not purchased by students available to other individuals, then income from the two nonstudents would not be subject to UBIT. If students purchased only 35 tickets and the remaining five seats were sold to nonstudents, the income attributable to three of the five nonstudent tickets would be treated as unrelated business income.

f. Ancillary food sale or service activities

Recommendation: Income derived from food sale or service activities that are ancillary to an organization's exempt purpose should be treated as income derived from an unrelated trade or business, subject to the exception described below. For example, if a museum operates a sidewalk cafe or other food facility that can be patronized by the general public without entering the museum building, or provides catering services for a private reception held in a museum when it is not open to the general public (or in a part of the museum closed to the general public), income from such activities would be subject to the UBIT. Similarly, income derived by a hospital from a catering-type service whereby the hospital prepares and delivers meals to members of the general public would be treated as unrelated business income. Under this rule, the UBIT would not apply where food services are provided as part of the organization's primary exempt function, such as where a charitable organization delivers meals to elderly individuals at their residences (or serves meals to the elderly at a senior citizen's center) as a charitable activity, or provides food at shelters for the homeless.

Under the exception, the UBIT should not apply to income derived from food sale or service activities of a section 501(c)(3) organization (or State college or university) that both (1) are provided on the organization's premises, and (2) are provided primarily for students, faculty, patients, employees, or members of the organization, or visitors to the organization. For example, food sales at a cafeteria within a museum while the museum is open to the public, or at on-premises hospital or school cafeterias, would qualify for the exception, as would on-premise food vending machine sales and concession sales at sports or cultural events.

g. Veterinary activities

Recommendation: Income derived from veterinary activities should be treated as income derived from an unrelated trade or business, subject to three exceptions. The UBIT should not apply to income from (1) spaying and neutering, (2) measures to protect the public health (such as rabies shots), and (3) emergency surgery (or other emergency services) if determined by a veterinarian to be necessary for the health of the animal.

h. Hotel facility activities

Recommendation: Income derived from operation of a hotel facility that is patronized by the general public should be treated as income derived from an unrelated trade or business. The term hotel facility does not include hospitals, nursing homes, hospices, youth homes and hostels, away-from-home lodging (based on need) for parents of hospitalized children, or dormitories, fraternities, or sororities of educational institutions (to the extent such educational institution facilities are used by students, faculty, or staff).

i.   Retail sales of condominiums and time-sharing units

Recommendation: Income derived from retail sales of condominiums or time-sharing units should be treated as income derived from an unrelated trade or business. The term retail sale does not include a sale of a condominium or time-sharing unit that has been donated as a charitable contribution to the organization if such income otherwise would be excludable from the UBIT pursuant to sections 512(b)(5) and 514.

j.   Affinity credit card and other affinity merchandising activities

Recommendation: Income derived from affinity credit card or other affinity merchandising activities (whether or not such income is labeled as "royalties") should be treated as income derived from an unrelated trade or business.

For this purpose, the term affinity credit card refers to a credit card that carries the name or identifying logo of an exempt organization; the term other affinity merchandising refers to a catalog or similar sales literature that carries the name or identifying logo of an exempt organization and that offers ordinary commercial merchandise (such as household or gardening items) or services (such as long-distance telephone service). Under these so-called affinity arrangements, the exempt organization typically furnishes its membership or contributor mailing list to the credit card or merchandising business, enters into a contractual arrangement for exclusive use of the exempt organization's name or logo, and in effect endorses or promotes obtaining and using the particular company's credit card, ordering catalog items from the merchandising company, or using services of the commercial business.

These affinity arrangements are distinguishable from, and this recommendation does not apply with respect to, a practice sometimes referred to as "cause-related fund raising." Under this practice, charitable contributions (qualifying for deduction under section 170) are made by a business which merely has informed the public that an amount will be donated to the charity based on the sales of its products or use of its services, and has not entered into a contractual arrangement with the charity under which the business receives any consideration from the charity (such as the exclusive right to use the charity's name or logo on a particular type of product). For example, if a retail fast-food chain advertises that for each soft drink purchased at its restaurants it will donate one cent to a named charity, and subsequently makes a charitable contribution to the charity measured by the number of such sales, and the charity does not endorse the product except by allowing use of its name or logo, the donation received by the charity would not constitute unrelated business income.

k.   Theme or amusement park activities

Recommendation: Income from theme or amusement park activities should be treated as income derived from an unrelated trade or business.

* * *

NOTES

1. *Other Recommendations.* The Draft Report also recommended repeal of the "convenience" exception in § 513(a)(2), concluding that its unduly broad interpretation had the effect of freeing exempt organizations from the responsibility for deciding whether particular activities were substantially related to the organization's exempt functions. Draft Report at 49–50. The Subcommittee concluded that activities traditionally covered by this exception, such as college dining halls and dormitories and hospital parking lots, would remain exempt under the substantially related test, but that more tangential revenue-producing activities, such as the operation of gas stations and the sale of common consumer goods, would no longer be protected. Id.

One of the more controversial recommendations was to tax any royalty income measured by net or taxable income derived from the licensed property, except for research income. Even royalty income not measured by net or taxable income (e.g., a flat fee royalty arrangement) would have been taxed if the organization either created the property right being licensed or was active in marketing the property right, with exceptions for licensing arrangements furthering the organization's exempt purpose and for research. Draft Report at 51–52. The Report specifically stated that licensing a trademark or logo in an attempt to foster name recognition would not, in itself, be treated as furthering an organization's exempt function. Id. But a children's educational organization that licensed its name or self-created intangible property for use on books or video cassettes would continue to be exempt on the theory that the arrangement furthered the organization's educational purposes. Id. at 52.

The Report also recommended several reforms that would more closely regulate the use of taxable subsidiaries. Under one proposal, the taxable income of a nonexempt controlled subsidiary could be no less than the amount of unrelated business taxable income if the income-producing activity had been carried on directly by the tax-exempt parent. Draft Report at 54–55. This rule was designed to preclude a taxable subsidiary from carrying on a profitable unrelated business along with a money-losing business activity that would be "related" if carried on directly by the exempt parent. Another proposal—to modify the "control" test in § 512(b)(13)—was adopted by Congress in the Taxpayer Relief Act of 1997. See Section D5 of this chapter, supra, at p. 629.

The Report recommended far more specific rules for allocation of expenses. In the case of dual use facilities, only the marginal costs attributable to the taxable activity would be deductible if the facility were used 25 percent or less of the time (measured by actual, not total available, use) for a taxable activity. If the facility were used 26 to 75 percent of the time for a taxable activity, then a portion of all costs attributable to the facility (including depreciation and general administrative costs) would be allocable to the taxable activity based on that activity's percentage of actual use. If the facility were used more than 75 percent of the time for a taxable activity, then all costs attributable to the facility would be deductible except for marginal costs related to tax-exempt use. In that case, however, any losses generated by the unrelated taxable activity could not be used to offset taxable income from other sources. Id. at 56–57. In the case of advertising, the Report recommended that publication and circulation expenses of an exempt organization periodical should not be deductible against advertising revenue.

The Oversight Subcommittee's final recommendation was an "aggregation rule" under which the Service, in determining whether an organization's "primary purpose" was a tax-exempt purpose under § 501(c), could take into account the activities of any of the organization's 80 percent or more subsidiaries. This determination, which could lead to revocation of exemption, was to be made based on a variety of factors, including the time and attention given by the parent's governing board and staff to taxable and unrelated business activities, the organization's mix of income and expenditures, and its expectation of earning a profit. Id. at 63–65.

2. *For Further Reading.* Thomas A. Troyer, Changing UBIT: Congress in the Workshop, 41 Tax Notes 1221 (1988).

PART FOUR

CHARITABLE GIVING

CHAPTER 6

CHARITABLE CONTRIBUTIONS

A. INTRODUCTION

1. HISTORICAL ORIGINS[1]

The first charitable income tax deduction was enacted in 1917 as part of a tax bill that raised federal tax rates to help finance the costs of entering World War I. Ever since, the charitable deduction has been a prominent feature of our income tax system. The legislative history is typically sparse, but excerpts from the floor debate reveal Congress's belief that the steeper tax rates would reduce funds donated to needy schools, hospitals, churches, and other charitable organizations. Proponents of the charitable deduction argued that private donations came from the "surplus" of an individual's income. As Senator Hollis of New Hampshire put it:

> * * * After they have done everything else they want to do, after they have educated their children and traveled and spent their money on everything they really want or think they want, then, if they have something left over, they will contribute it to a college or to the Red Cross or for some scientific purposes. Now, when war comes and we impose these very heavy taxes on incomes, that will be the first place where the wealthy men will be tempted to economize, namely, in donations to charity. They will say, "Charity begins at home."[2]

The estate and gift tax charitable deduction has an equally venerable history. The unlimited deduction for charitable bequests now found in § 2055 was added in 1918, two years after enactment of the first federal estate tax. The deduction was justified on the familiar ground that wealth transferred for charitable, educational and religious uses should not be burdened by a tax because the funds would be used for a public purpose.[3] The gift tax charitable deduction in § 2522 is similarly entrenched in our wealth transfer tax system.

In succeeding tax bills, Congress has justified the charitable deduction, like tax exemptions generally, as an efficient alternative to government

---

1. Much of this early history of the charitable deduction is derived from John A. Wallace & Robert W. Fisher, The Charitable Deduction Under Section 170 of the Internal Revenue Code, in IV Research Papers Sponsored by the [Filer] Commission on Private Philanthropy and Public Needs 2131 (1977).

2. Remarks of Senator Hollis, 55 Cong. Rec. 6728 (1917).

3. See John Holt Myers, Estate Tax Deduction for Charitable Benefits: Proposed Limitations, in IV Research Papers Sponsored by the [Filer] Commission on Private Philanthropy and Public Needs 2299 (1977).

support for those nonprofit organizations providing a public benefit. Early Congressional advocates also believed that individuals should not be taxed on the portion of their income devoted to charity. The underlying premise of this argument was that the income tax should be imposed only upon consumable income—i.e., the taxpayer's gross income, less the costs of earning it *and* the taxpayer's charitable contributions. As developed later in this chapter, these theories continue to be advanced whenever critics seek to curtail or eliminate the charitable deduction.

The 1917 predecessor of current § 170 allowed an income tax deduction for:

> Contributions or gifts made within the year to corporations or associations organized and operated exclusively for religious, charitable, scientific, or educational purposes, or to societies for the prevention of cruelty to children or animals, no part of the net income of which inures to the benefit of any private stockholder or individual, to an amount not in excess of 15 per centum of the taxpayer's taxable net income as computed without the benefit of this paragraph.

The current version of § 170 expands this once elegant concept to more than 22 pages in the most recent Commerce Clearing House edition of the Internal Revenue Code, and the regulations exceed 100 pages, small print, double column! This once inspired a prominent law professor to suggest that an entire four-unit basic income tax course could be taught solely by studying § 170. Our goals here are somewhat more modest. After a survey of the policy issues, this chapter provides an overview of the tax aspects of charitable giving, emphasizing those issues of greatest interest to donors, charitable fundraisers, trustees of nonprofit organizations, and their legal and financial advisors.

2.   POLICY ISSUES

The policy debate over the charitable deduction is reminiscent of the controversy surrounding the rationale for tax exemptions. A central question is whether the charitable deduction is a subsidy—a "tax expenditure" in modern tax policy parlance—and, if so, whether it is a proper mechanism for providing government support to the charitable sector. Some critics of the deduction ask why the government should provide undifferentiated support to all public charities without evaluating their relative needs, or why it should provide any support to religious organizations. And even if a subsidy is appropriate, the question remains whether it should come from the tax system and, if so, whether the structure of the current tax regime is defensible as a policy matter. Other critics claim that the system violates principles of equity and fairness in a democratic society because organizations benefiting the most from the charitable deduction cater to the tastes of the upper class "cultural elite." The charitable deduction also has been challenged as an inefficient incentive because it principally benefits higher income taxpayers and does not significantly influence the giving patterns of low and middle-income donors.

Defenders of the charitable deduction reject the notion of an inefficient subsidy and argue that contributions do not constitute personal consumption and thus are not appropriately included in a normative income tax base. They answer the claims of upper class privilege by emphasizing the contributions of private philanthropy to a dynamic pluralistic society and the range of innovative options offered beyond those provided by the government and business sectors.

The first excerpt below, from the 1975 report of the Commission on Private Philanthropy and Public Needs (the Filer Commission), summarizes the debate. It is followed by excerpts from the writing of Professor William Andrews, who argues that charitable contributions are not properly included in a normative income tax base, and Teresa Odendahl, who offers an anthropologist's perspective on the role of philanthropy in American culture.

Giving in America: Toward a Stronger Voluntary Sector
Report of the [Filer] Commission on Private Philanthropy and Public Needs 107–111 (1975).

Philosophical Challenge

A major challenge to the philosophical basis of the charitable deduction lies in the contention that charitable giving is not that different from other kinds of personal outlays and therefore should not be treated differently under the income tax. This viewpoint is summarized in a study for the Commission by Paul R. McDaniel of Boston College Law School. " * * * Most economists and social psychologists," he writes, "take the 'scientific' view that charitable contributions are not simply individual sacrifices for the public good, but are actually consumption spending * * * In making a charitable gift, the individual is seen as purchasing status, the perpetuation of his social values, or on a less mercenary level, the satisfaction resulting from doing a 'good deed.' * * * And one can inquire as to whether the deduction operates equitably as an incentive system to induce this form of consumption."

Overlapping this argument in recent years has been the more vigorous and somewhat less abstract contention of tax reformers that the charitable deduction is not distinct from a number of other deductions that have been built into the income tax, and that all of them are wanting by the yardstick of equity.

According to this viewpoint, all tax immunities are forms of government subsidy to whatever activity benefits from nontaxation. This is not a new idea. A president of Harvard University, Charles William Eliot, acknowledged and attacked this way of looking at tax immunity a century ago. "It has been often asserted," he said, "that to exempt an institution from taxation is the same thing as to grant it money directly from the public treasury. This statement is sophistical and fallacious." But the tax-immunity-as-subsidy viewpoint has gained considerable influence among tax analysts in recent years. It was adopted by the federal government in

1968 when the Treasury Secretary's annual report included a "tax expenditure" section. This section lists the amounts by which the government is seen to be subsidizing various areas through forms of nontaxation or reduced taxes. * * *

Nor is the tax expenditure viewpoint limited to tax analysts or government ledgers. A ghetto activist in Hartford who challenges the pattern of corporation and foundation philanthropy in that city was quick to evoke the viewpoint during an interview for a Commission report. His position: "These corporations and foundations are tax exempt. Therefore, part of the money they spend is my money. Therefore, they should have regulatory restrictions placed upon them that will force them to meet specific social criteria * * *." The result of one foundation's practices, he charged later, was "to use charitable giving—a form of federal subsidy-to perpetuate the effects of past discrimination."

When seen as a form of government subsidy or expenditure, the charitable deduction, like other personal income tax deductions, is open to charges of inequity because of a pattern that is, in effect, the inverse of the progressive structure of the income tax. The higher a person's income the higher the rate of taxation under the income tax and therefore the more the government forgoes—or "spends" in the tax-expenditure view—for any portion of such income not taxed. In other words, the government adds proportionately more of the subsidy to a high-income taxpayer's giving and proportionately less to the low-income taxpayer's contribution.

Stanley S. Surrey of Harvard Law School, formerly Assistant Secretary of the Treasury for Tax Policy, is the foremost proponent of this way of looking at tax deductions, starting with his advocacy of a tax-expenditure budget while he was in the Treasury Department. Talking of the charitable deduction in a Commission discussion, Surrey illustrated the tax-expenditure viewpoint in this way:

"Let us look at this subsidy to charities which is given by the charitable deduction. Well, it was a very peculiar subsidy. It's sort of an upside-down affair. As you know, if a person in the 70 per cent bracket [the highest marginal bracket at the time] gives a sum of money, he is able to deduct that sum of money from his tax base, and in effect he is only giving 30 per cent, whereas when a person in the 14 per cent bracket gives a sum of money, he is giving 86 per cent. Or to put it differently, if a $200,000 person gives 10 per cent of his income to charity, it really costs the government $14,000 to get $6,000 out of that person * * * If a $12,000 person gives 10 per cent of his income to charity, it costs the government $324 to get $876 from this person. The charitable deduction works just upside down." * * *

The tax-expenditure viewpoint and its implications are by no means universally accepted. A major argument that has been raised against the whole notion of tax "expenditures" is that it implies that all income covered by tax laws is government money. It is only in this light, it is contended, that non-taxation can be seen as a subsidy or expenditure.

The equity implications of the tax-expenditure viewpoint are also challenged by those who argue that the alleged disparity of tax expenditures in favor of high-income taxpayers is merely the mirrored reflection of the progressive income tax, which is structured against them. In other words, nontaxation of portions of higher incomes because of tax exemptions or deductions is only higher, can only be viewed as a greater government expenditure, because the tax rates are set higher for upper-income levels to begin with.

Perhaps the principal counter-argument to the tax-expenditure viewpoint as far as its application to the charitable deduction goes rests with the "income definition" rationale for the deduction. According to this reasoning, tax allowances for philanthropic giving cannot be looked at or measured in the same way as tax privileges for other purposes because money given to charity is not an element of income that should be subject to government's taxing power to begin with. Boris I. Bittker of Yale Law School posed the "income definition" argument against the "tax-expenditure" viewpoint this way in the same Commission discussion in which Stanley Surrey took part:

" * * * The concept of income is not settled, cannot be settled the way one can define water as H_2O or lay down the laws of gravity * * * Income is a political, economic, social concept which takes its meaning from the society in which the term is used, in my view. And there are many definitions of income * * * But at the very core of the only definition that has the benefit of a consensus, there is a concept of consumption * * * I would assert that consumption certainly consists of what one spends on food, shelter and clothing for himself, his family, friends, what one saves to pass on to heirs and so on * * * But 2,000 years of religious, philosophical and ethical views suggest that what one gives to charity can properly be viewed differently * * * If, as I think, we have a powerful sense of difference between giving to charity and spending in other respects, I see no reason at all why in defining income one shouldn't exclude those items like charitable contributions that our whole history tells us represent a special kind of use of one's funds."

Yet another view that the Commission heard expressed by tax experts was that those who support the charitable deduction should have no argument with the tax-expenditure viewpoint, but should be willing to view tax savings from the charitable deduction as a form of tax expenditure and simply assert that, for special reasons associated with philanthropic giving, it was a desirable form of tax expenditure, whereas other forms were not necessarily desirable. This view in turn has been challenged on the grounds that to regard charitable tax savings as a form of government expenditure is to undermine the "income definition" case for the deduction, because it means conceding that the charitable deduction is not fundamentally different from other deductions and allowances.

The pros and cons of the tax-expenditure viewpoint continue to be argued, often heatedly, as do its implications for the charitable and other deductions. Meanwhile, however, the viewpoint seems to be taking an even firmer hold within government. The tax-expenditure part of the Treasury Secretary's report was instituted in 1968 by administrative decision. In 1974, Congress wrote the tax-expenditure viewpoint into law: it passed legislation requiring that as of 1975 a tax-expenditure section be included in the federal budget. In all likelihood, tax exemptions, deductions, credits—including those benefiting nonprofit organizations—will be increasingly scrutinized by Congress as if they were forms of government spending, whatever the implications.

William D. Andrews, Personal Deductions In an Ideal Income Tax

86 Harv.L. Rev. 309, 344–348, 356–358, 371–372, 374–375 (1972).

The charitable contribution deduction is generally described as a subsidy to charitable giving and thus to the activities of qualified charitable organizations. The effect of the deduction has been likened to a matching gift program under which an employer makes matching gifts to charities supported by its employees. There is something peculiar, of course, about the Government spending funds with so little control over their allocation or use. Furthermore, this is an unusual matching gift program because the rate at which gifts are matched varies directly with the taxpayer's marginal tax rate bracket: wealthy taxpayers find their gifts much more generously matched than do lower bracket taxpayers. * * *

But I do not believe, nor do I think most serious practical students of the subject believe, that the charitable contribution deduction is as irrational as this explanation makes it sound. To be sure, there are anomalies arising out of the allowance of a deduction for the fair market value of appreciated property without any offsetting recognition of gain. But as to simple cash contributions, the charitable deduction makes more sense than tax expenditure analysis would indicate. If we want our theories to express our judgments, therefore, we should seek to give the deduction a better explanation.

* * * [T]here are substantial grounds for excluding from our definition of taxable personal consumption whatever satisfactions a taxpayer may get from making a charitable contribution. * * * [T]here are * * * good reasons why a charitable contribution may rationally be excluded from the concept of taxable personal consumption. In the case of alms for the poor, for instance, the charitable contribution results in the distribution of real goods and services to persons presumably poorer and in lower marginal tax brackets than the donor. These goods and services, therefore, should not be taxed at the higher rates intended to apply to personal consumption by the donor. In the case of philanthropy more broadly defined—the support of religion, education, and the arts–benefits often do not flow exclusively or even principally to very low bracket taxpayers. But the goods and services produced do have something of the character of common goods whose enjoyment is not confined to contributors nor apportioned among contributors according to the amounts of their contributions. There are a number of

reasons for defining taxable personal consumption not to include the benefit of such common goods and services. The personal consumption at which progressive personal taxation with high graduated rates should aim may well be thought to encompass only the private consumption of divisible goods and services whose consumption by one household precludes their direct enjoyment by others.

Various objections can be made to this analysis. It can be argued that the exercise of power over the distribution of goods and services is what constitutes taxable personal consumption even if that power is exercised in favor of somebody else. Or it can be argued that the pleasure or satisfaction one presumably gets from supporting philanthropic enterprises is a component of consumption. But at least this analysis and the objections to it focus on the problem of how to treat philanthropy as an intrinsic issue of personal tax policy, instead of just assuming that the purpose underlying the deduction must be something outside the realm of tax policy.

It is convenient to take up first the case of alms for the poor, then philanthropy more broadly defined, and finally the special problems that arise when charitable contributions are made out of accumulated wealth rather than current earnings.

A.   Alms for the Poor

Consider a taxpayer who simply contributes some of his earnings to an organization which redistributes them to or for the needy. In such a case the consumption or accumulation of real goods and services represented by the funds in question has been shifted to the recipients rather than the donor and should not be subjected to taxation at rates designed to apply to the donor's standard of living and saving. If the redistributed funds are used for ordinary consumption by the recipients, then in principle the funds should be taxed to the recipients at their rates—although in practice the recipients' total income may often fall below a taxable level. The matter is essentially one of rates. Under a graduated rate schedule the personal consumption and accumulation of well-to-do taxpayers is intended to be curtailed much more than that of the poor. Yet if a wealthy taxpayer were to be taxed at his high rate even on the income that he donated to the poor, the probable effect would be a reduction in the amount received by the donees. For all practical purposes, such a scheme would tax the consumption of the poor at the rate intended for the wealthy taxpayer. The effect of the charitable contribution is to avoid this result.

Moreover, the charitable contribution deduction operates to treat a taxpayer who redistributes his income by giving alms like other taxpayers who effect a redistribution of income directly. A businessman, for example, may pay generous wages, higher than he would have to pay in order to secure the services he needs. If he does so, within reason, we would not tax him on the additional income he could have earned by paying less. He has arranged his business in a way that diverts more income to employees and less to himself; the tax law generally will deal with the income as so redistributed.

More to the point, perhaps, a doctor might choose to spend one day a week in a clinic without charging for his services. More generally he might simply treat impecunious patients for less than the going rate. In either case he has foregone in favor of the patients whom he treats some of the personal consumption and accumulation he could have had. We do not tax the doctor on the value of his services or the excess of the value of his services over the fee he charges. We tax the doctor only on the personal consumption and accumulation he achieves by the exercise of his profession, not on what he could have achieved if he chose to maximize his personal financial gain.

Another professional man, a tax lawyer for example, may have skills that are not so directly useful to the poor as those of the doctor. If he wishes to devote part of his professional energies to the welfare of the poor, the efficient way to do it may well be to continue practicing his profession for paying clients but to turn over part of his fees for distribution among the poor or for the purchase of other services to meet their needs. The charitable contribution deduction operates to treat the tax lawyer like the doctor, by taxing him only on the amount of personal consumption and accumulation he realizes from the practice of his profession, not on what he could have realized if he had not given part of his fees away.

* * *

B. Philanthropy More Broadly Defined

For many kinds of charitable contributions the foregoing analysis will not quite do because the benefits of the contributions do not go entirely to the poor. More than half of all charitable deductions are for contributions to churches, whose activities are conducted for rich and poor alike and often on a more comfortable and expensive scale in wealthy neighborhoods than in poor ones. Many contributions are to private schools, whose student bodies are probably still disproportionately representative of the affluent part of the population. Some contributions go to support artistic enterprises, ordinary and esoteric, in which most of the poor are likely to have little interest. Moreover, the activities of such organizations are frequently ones in which contributors participate more or less directly for their own edification or pleasure.

Such contributions also differ from alms for the poor because they represent an affirmative allocation of resources by the contributor to a particular activity whose benefits are not taxed to the recipients. In theory, though not in practice (and it is typically not important in practice), alms should be counted as income to the recipient, so that deduction by the donor is only a matter of reassigning taxability to the person whose consumption is supported, as in the case of alimony. But when a group of wealthy people support a church, a school, a research institute, or a symphony orchestra, the effect of the charitable contribution deduction is to eliminate the enjoyment of the output of that activity from the tax base altogether. A community of people that supports a church will pay less in taxes than a community of people with the same total income, similarly distributed, that spends less on its church and more on its private homes.

Nevertheless, the benefits produced by charitable contributions have certain shared characteristics which provide the basis for principled arguments in favor of deduction. Almost all charitable organizations other than those that distribute alms to the poor produce something in the nature of common or social goods or services. The benefit produced by a contribution to a private school, for example, may not inure primarily to the poor, but neither does it inure solely to the contributor. Even when contributors are almost all members who share in the product of the organization, as in the case of a church, the product is essentially a common good to be enjoyed by the members without regard to relative contributions and usually is at least open to enjoyment by others.

Common goods have several characteristics relevant for our purposes. Principally, their enjoyment is not limited exclusively or even primarily to those who pay for them. That might be stated merely as a matter of external benefits: a wealthy man cannot purchase and enjoy the sound of a new church organ without conferring a benefit on his fellow parishioners. Unlike the typical external effect of private consumption, however, the benefit conferred on others is of the same kind as that enjoyed by the contributor himself.

Moreover, it is typically the case that the benefits produced by a charitable organization are free goods in the sense that one person's enjoyment of them will not directly impair another's enjoyment. Attendance at church on a particular Sunday, use of the town library, or listening to a symphony orchestra broadcast will not immediately prevent someone else from doing the same thing. Of course, pure public goods are relatively rare. Use of the library does not immediately prevent others from using it; but if too many use it too much, then its utility will be impaired. The conditions under which a town common can serve effectively for common use are very limited. And students' places in schools are sometimes quite scarce. But as among the students, once admitted to a school or to a particular class, many of the educational opportunities offered have this quality of common goods.

The underlying problem with respect to contributions to churches, schools, museums, and similar charities is whether the common goods they produce should be reflected in the consumption component of personal income of any of the individuals associated with them.

* * *

C. Charity by the Idle Rich

The discussion thus far has dealt with a taxpayer who contributes part of his earnings to a charitable organization, and it has been pointed out that the effect of the deduction is to treat such a taxpayer as if he had devoted part of his energies directly toward the promotion of charitable enterprises, instead of earning money. Many charitable contributions, however, are made by wealthy people from accumulated wealth or unearned income. Thus, the question arises whether a deduction for them can be justified on grounds such as those we have been exploring.

1. *Contributions Out of Investment Income.* Consider first a taxpayer with an income solely from dividends who contributes one third to charity and lives on the rest. It cannot be argued very directly that a charitable deduction will operate to treat him as if he were performing services for the charity instead of earning money and turning it over, since he is not earning any money in any event. Nor can it be argued in this situation that the incentive effect of the charitable contribution deduction serves to offset the disincentive effect of the tax on remunerative employment. There may seem to be more reason, therefore, to take the taxpayer's income as fixed and to tax it without regard to use in order to make the tax neutral with respect to expenditure choices.

But I think the deduction is still justified along the lines indicated in this paper for two reasons. First, most taxpayers in the long run do face earnings or investment decisions with respect to which the tax is not neutral and which may have some relation to their level of charitable giving. The deduction will therefore operate to offset the bias of the tax itself insofar as income is devoted to charitable uses. Second, even if that is not so for a particular taxpayer, considerations of equity require that he be allowed a charitable contribution deduction if other taxpayers are. For reasons that include a consideration of incentive effects on most taxpayers, we have decided that taxable consumption should embrace only private, preclusive, household consumption. To make income a measure of consumption thus defined, plus accumulation, a deduction must be allowed for expenditures for other things, whatever the source of the income. The deduction should be allowed, therefore, whenever charitable contributions are made out of taxable ordinary income, whether earned or unearned.

2. *Unrealized Capital Appreciation.* In the case of a donation of appreciated capital assets to a charitable organization, present law generally allows a deduction for fair market value without taking into account that there is unrealized gain represented by the excess of fair market value over the taxpayer's basis. The argument in this paper will not support that rule. The argument here is concerned only with adjusting gross income to make it a more accurate measure of private consumption plus accumulation by allowing a deduction to offset the inclusion in gross income of receipts that have been turned over to philanthropic use. Since the effect of the fair market value rule is to allow a tax deduction for an amount, the unrealized gain, that will never be included in gross income, it clearly goes beyond that rationale.

Whatever its origin, the fair market value rule must now be viewed as a subsidy or artificial inducement, above and beyond mere tax exemption, for philanthropic giving. The magnitude of the subsidy is a function of the amount of unrealized appreciation in relation to the basis of the property and the taxpayer's rates of tax, being greatest for taxpayers in highest brackets and with most appreciation. For a taxpayer in the top rate brackets whose property has a nominal basis, the rule operates in a sense to make the Government take over the whole cost of a charitable donation. * * *

* * *

5. *Conclusion.* In general, then, the argument of this paper, that the purpose of the deduction is to help create an income tax that imposes a uniform graduated burden on aggregate personal private consumption and accumulation, supports a deduction for contributions only to the extent that funds out of which each contribution is made have otherwise been included in computing taxable income. That limitation is clearly exceeded in the case of the deduction of fair market value of appreciated capital assets without recognition of the unrealized gain. It raises difficulties in other cases where some current receipts or prior accumulations may have been taxed at less than current ordinary rates. But the difficulties are not solely, or even primarily, a product of the charitable contributions deduction, since they already exist with respect to capital gains or prior accumulations that may be devoted to current private consumption without ever bearing tax at current ordinary income rates. The capital gain rules in particular are inconsistent with the underlying thesis that the tax should be evenly laid on total consumption plus accumulation without distinctions according to differences in source, and the charitable contribution deduction only puts that inconsistency into sharper focus.

Teresa Odendahl, Charity Begins at Home: Generosity and Self Interest Among the Philanthropic Elite
3–5, 232–240 (1990).

CULTURE, GENEROSITY, AND POWER

Elite American philanthropy serves the interests of the rich to a greater extent than it does the interests of the poor, disadvantaged, or disabled. * * * Voluntary organizations supported and directed by wealthy philanthropists divert decision making in the arts, culture, education, health, and welfare from public representatives to a private power elite.

Paradoxically, although people of all classes participate in nonprofit groups, most of these organizations are controlled by a few, and many charities benefit the rich more than they do the poor. The vast majority of nonprofit agencies and programs do not primarily serve the needy. Many elite philanthropists are civic-minded and sincere, but the system they help to maintain may actually reduce the extent to which basic human services are provided on a democratic basis.

By studying rich people and their charitable endeavors, I have identified a nationwide "culture of philanthropy." Those who inherited "old money" and the richest Americans, usually with "new money," tend to be the most involved in voluntary activities. But they contribute disproportionately to private universities, the arts, and culture, rather than to community health clinics, legal aid programs, or other projects for the poor. There are thousands of good causes in which millionaires have little interest. Those are not the subject of this book, although they are certainly affected by the neglect of the wealthy.

Not all millionaires in the United States are serious philanthropists. My guess is that fewer than half of the wealthy are charitably minded. Those who regularly contribute large sums of money to nonprofit organizations, serve on several volunteer boards of directors, and spend much of their time raising additional resources for charity from colleagues, friends, and relatives belong to a select social group.

* * *

In addition, and of great importance, is the fact that through their charitable activities, wealthy philanthropists and their advisers sponsor what we think of as "high culture"—ballet, opera, symphony, theater, and the visual arts. Rich children learn to value these "serious" cultural forms that on the whole are produced by nonprofit organizations. But there is more to philanthropic culture than breeding and taste.

Through their donations and work for voluntary organizations, the charitable rich exert enormous influence in society. As philanthropists, they acquire status within and outside of their class. Although private wealth is the basis of the hegemony of this group, philanthropy is essential to the maintenance and perpetuation of the upper class in the United States. In this sense, nonprofit activities are the nexus of a modern power elite.

The culture of philanthropy is manifest in the common behavior and manners, economic status, and sociocultural institutions, as well as in the shared attitudes, ideas, perceptions, tastes, and values of this group whose members frequently interact with one another. The "established" wealthy are socialized in the family and by exclusive preparatory schools and private colleges. Their interaction continues throughout adulthood as business associates, friends, leaders of local and national voluntary organizations, and relatives by birth and marriage. Elite culture is passed from generation to generation, and from those with old money to the newly rich.

Class and culture are related but not identical. Although the elite who participate in the culture of philanthropy are usually members of the upper class, not everyone in this class endorses a particular way of life. And some middle-class individuals—notably certain "professionals," who serve the wealthy as, for example, personal advisors and private foundation staff-often have perspectives and values similar to their employers and exist within the same charitable system.

My use of the term culture in connection with philanthropy is intentional: the word carries so many subtle applicable meanings. The rich are integral members of the wider society. In certain respects the charitable elite are so aware of prevalent middle-class cultural norms that they deny their affluence and privilege and do not present or even think of themselves as being upper-class. This book is primarily about wealthy people who belong to a distinctive culture that is, in the anthropological sense, a subculture.

* * *

THE RESTRUCTURING OF ELITE PHILANTHROPY

The philanthropy of the wealthy serves many purposes, but primarily it assists in the social reproduction of the upper class. Private contributions by the elite support institutions that sustain their culture, their education, their policy formulation, their status—in short, their interests. This is not to say that the charitable giving of the rich is unworthy, or wholly detrimental to the larger society. Funding of the arts may provide the general population with greater access to high culture. Elite schools do not serve the wealthy alone but also enroll a sizable proportion of scholarship students. A new wing at a children's hospital or money for medical research may ultimately save many lives. Corporate and foundation grants for economic development or housing can be worthwhile, especially since the government has moved away from funding in these areas. Small amounts of money to grassroots, poverty, and social-change projects are absolutely basic to their survival.

The vast majority of these nonprofit agencies, groups, organizations, programs, and institutions do good work that is essential in our society. I have not been criticizing them or their performance. The evidence, however, indicates that they have been stretched thin because of federal cutbacks. Social services have suffered more than any others, and philanthropy—elite or otherwise—has not made up the difference. At least half of all private contributions come from the upper class. As I have stressed in the preceding chapters, most of this money does not go to aid the poor, and we must ask whether the funding of the wealthy serves the public good. Is this the type of human service deployment we want in a "pluralistic" society?

Even one of the leading proponents of pluralism, the political scientist Robert A. Dahl, has argued for the necessity of redistributing wealth and income. He acknowledges that in the United States the full achievement of pluralist democracy has been curtailed; all citizens do not have the opportunity to participate effectively in organizations that have an impact on the political process. Because certain groups have greater access than others to resources, "the preferences of their members count for more than the preferences of citizens who belong to weaker organizations." The "final control over the agenda" is not shared equally. "The unequal resources that allow organizations to stabilize injustice also enable them to exercise unequal influence in determining what alternatives are seriously considered." A central ingredient in a solution to the dilemmas posed by Dahl is progressive taxation and redistribution.

The difficulty, of course, is that a majority of elite philanthropists already object to what they consider excessive taxation. They view their charitable giving as an alternative to even higher taxes. In addition they derive immense personal satisfaction from their philanthropic activities.

The rich continue to view any money that was once theirs as still theirs. They think of their contributions as private money going for the public good. It thus follows, the elite earnestly professed during interviews, that they should make decisions about "their" money. In this way the upper class, rather than the majority of the population, through a political process, defines the public good. The wealthy, however, feel entitled to this prerogative. After all, are they not better qualified as leaders, especially given their superior culture and knowledge?

I have argued that the elite control, influence, or want to control the organizations they fund in significant ways. Thus an already powerful group has disproportionate authority in many nonprofit endeavors. Once again, this does not mean that rich people run all the private cultural, educational, health, and welfare organizations in the country. But they do have the strongest voices in many of the biggest, most prestigious enterprises and institutions. When the elite or the foundations they have funded deem projects to be unworthy of their time and money, these causes suffer because they must increase their efforts in order to secure smaller sums from more contributors.

Furthermore, wealthy board members make decisions about the disposition of more than their "own" funds. Many nonprofit groups still take in sizable government revenue as well as smaller contributions from thousands of middle-and working-class donors. The charitable tax break for itemizers has also resulted in lost income to the State. In effect, these are not private efforts but public endeavors.

At its best, the philanthropy system provides a check against corporate or government domination or indifference. It is also inextricably linked with business and political affairs. Individual nonprofit groups can be important players in a kind of balance of power, as "independent centers of thought, action, involvement, and pressure." This is the type of pluralism that we should promote. I would not do away with the system, but I strongly believe that it needs to be restructured.

Given the widespread support for charity, how might the system be reformed to serve the public interest? A variety of policy options and recommendations about elite philanthropy are outlined in the remainder of this chapter. An equitable tax system would lay the foundation for such reforms. Each alternative offered is built upon the need for accountability from donors, the government, intermediaries, and nonprofit service providers as well as the desirability of a representative process. Public awareness, educational, and organizing programs could foster the participation of more citizens in philanthropy and work against elite control. Clear guidelines and standards for foundations, other grant-makers, and nonprofit governance in general would encourage fairness. There is a way for us to continue to be partners with our own government in providing for the common good. And there are several strategies for building individual choice, without elite control, into the process.

EQUITABLE TAXATION

Taxation has been the mechanism that provides revenues for the funding of national defense, public works, and public goods. Almost all Americans these days feel that they suffer from taxation. Curiously, even the wealthy are perturbed, although it is undeniable that the real tax burden is carried disproportionately by the middle class. Within the framework of a modern capitalist system, and leaving aside for the moment the particular responsibilities of a democracy to its citizens, there appears to be no alternative to taxation short of the nationalization of industry. There has to be some source of income. A reformed system could be devised along the following lines.

No Nonprofit Public Policy

Charitable policy is currently enacted through a tax code premised on the notion that individual philanthropy is altruistic and should be rewarded. Yet some contributions are clearly more altruistic than others and some organizations more highly geared than others toward serving the public good. Americans need to rethink the system by which nonprofit groups are categorized as tax-exempt under the rulings of the Internal Revenue Service. The code could, for example, require a more representative decision and governance process within individual charities, and base their exemption status partially on these criteria. Except for due care and fiduciary responsibility, the legal requirements of most voluntary groups are extremely limited; there is little regulation of the field and almost no distinction between the services that the various tax-exempt organizations actually perform.

The main exception is the private foundation, which has been treated differently since the Tax Reform Act of 1969. This act was a specific and fairly successful attempt to limit the power exercised by the wealthy through the grant-making institutions they endow. It did not, however, apply to the individual contributions of the upper class, to the elite organizations they tend to support, or to other charitable trusts and vehicles.

Certain endeavors more clearly fill a public role than others, and they should receive a larger tax break. We do have a precedent in this regard. Those who donate to public charities, for example, receive the largest deduction, 50 percent, whereas those who create or contribute to private foundations are given only a 30 percent deduction. (This disparity represents a recognition of the basic differences in the functions and roles of these types of organizations.) In addition, an individual or family cannot have a controlling business interest in the assets that comprise the endowment of a private foundation, whereas closely held assets may be contributed to other kinds of charitable vehicles, such as support organizations.

We might want to insure that people who donate money to the organizations serving the neediest members of our society will receive the greatest tax benefits. Or, a full tax exemption might be given only if the general population is free to use the services of the agency. A related option would be to require that certain nonprofit groups meet a "public interest" or "public support" test. In order to be accorded public charity status, even grant-making organizations would have to demonstrate that they have widespread support and boards of trustees that are representative of the communities to be served. Gifts to nonprofit institutions that are exclusionary or offer services for high fees would get reduced tax breaks. In the case of private schools, for example, the number of scholarships offered might be required to equal or even exceed the number of tuition-paying students in order for the institution to be accorded a particular tax standing. People of all classes could still have the option to give to whatever nonprofit group they might choose, but the tax benefits would be based on the nature of the work done by that group.

Income Tax

Whether or not philanthropy is to be viewed as an alternative form of taxation, when people are given choice about where "their" money goes, more democratic safeguards need to be instituted. If the income tax system were equitable across classes, there would be a charitable deduction for all citizens or for none. The present system is untenable. A fair income tax system would also be effectively progressive, and corporations would pay their share. * * *

Another consequence of the inequality in the tax system is that it encourages the wealthy to give large contributions which allow them to control nonprofit organizations. An obvious way to limit individual power over specific groups in particular and public policy in general would be to place an annual ceiling on gifts to any one charitable agency, as we do for contributions to national political campaigns. This option would undoubtedly be unpopular with many nonprofit groups that depend heavily on large gifts, especially elite preparatory schools and universities. And the increased work of fundraising could take away from the basic goals or services of the organization. But many groups that are not supported by the wealthy already face this dilemma. Perhaps a compromise would be to allow a fully deductible contribution up to a certain amount, and to limit tax breaks over that sum. It might also be stipulated that there be no limits on contributions to public charities and foundations that meet a public-support test.

In contrast to major donations, smaller gifts do become public because they are immediately absorbed into a common fund, or in the case of single works of art, into a larger collection. It is difficult to be precise about the exact figure that would constitute a major donation, but perhaps $10,000 is a good "dividing line." Or the breakoff point might change depending on the size of the budget of the recipient group. In any event, the specifics of these recommendations would require much discussion among all who would be concerned, and resolution within the political arena.

Estate Taxes

As we have seen, our inheritance system perpetuates inequality and the concentration of wealth. We have a myth in this country that all people are equal at birth. But almost by definition the majority of the poor are unable to accumulate possessions that they can pass on to their children or others when they die. Middle-class individuals, if they do not end up in a nursing home, may have something, perhaps a house, for their offspring to inherit. Only the rich bequeath charitable trust funds, seats on foundation boards, non-charitable trust funds, and vast fortunes to their children. As we have seen, their children grow up in a different world-of culture, good education, and privilege. If we in the United States were to drastically alter or even disallow the inheritance system, then our people might start off more equal at birth.

Another alternative to the present system would be to eliminate loopholes like annuities, special gifts, and split-interest trusts that enable the wealthy to avoid inheritance taxation. For example, charitable lead and remainder trusts enable the wealthy to sidestep taxation by receiving assets tax-free simply because for some period of time their interest income went to charity.

We might, however, want to continue to provide incentives for direct bequests to truly charitable nonprofit organizations or public foundations. The same basic guidelines that are adopted for income tax deductions might be applied to estate plans. Wealthy individuals and others with considerable assets would pay lower or even minimum estate taxes if a bequest were made to a group that clearly met and maintained full tax-exempt status.

NOTE: POLICY ASPECTS OF THE ESTATE TAX CHARITABLE DEDUCTION

Proponents of the tax expenditure concept have extended their analysis to the federal wealth transfer taxes. Viewing the charitable estate and gift tax charitable deduction as a spending measure that departs from a normative transfer tax structure, they contend that the deduction must be justified in terms of need, efficiency, or equity. See, e.g., Paul R. McDaniel, James R. Repetti & Paul L. Caron, Federal Wealth Transfer Taxation: Cases and Materials 558, 598–606 (5th ed. 2003). Professor McDaniel and others have argued that the deduction mechanism concentrates in very wealthy estates the foregone revenue that results from allowing the deduction. This "upside-down effect," they contend, undercuts the fundamental argument in favor of the charitable deduction based on the need for a pluralistic approach to the solution of social problems. See id. Tax expenditures theorists propose to replace the estate and gift tax charitable deductions with a more carefully tailored federal direct matching grant program.

In response, Professor John Simon has attempted to extend the tax-base defining rationales for tax exemptions and the charitable income tax deduction to the wealth transfer taxes. He argues:

> Just as income is based on consumption and accumulation and the [income-defining] rationale asserts that this consumption is the private consumption of non-"public" * * * goods and services, we can perhaps

say that the definition of personal wealth for estate tax purposes should refer to those assets available for the private accumulation or consumption of non-"public" * * * goods and services. A testamentary charitable contribution reduces the amount of assets available for such private consumption and accumulation; hence, under this analysis, it is logical to exclude these contributions from the definition of wealth for purposes of the estate tax. Here, as in the case of the income tax, it would be concluded that the government is subsidizing no one when it affords a charitable deduction.

John G. Simon, Charity and Dynasty Under the Federal Tax System, 5 The Probate Lawyer 22–23 (Summer 1978). Professor Simon also concludes that while the charitable deduction may be a "non-egalitarian law," it still serves to benefit all classes of citizens including those who do not receive direct tax benefits. Id. at 56 et seq.

Unlike the income tax charitable deduction, which is subject to annual percentage limitations, the estate and gift tax deductions are unlimited. As a result, the wealthiest Americans can and often do avoid paying any significant estate tax when they die because they leave virtually all their wealth to charity-usually a private foundation controlled by their family. This has prompted proposals to limit the estate tax charitable deduction to 50 percent of a decedent's gross estate and to restrict or deny a deduction for gifts and bequests to private foundations. Not surprisingly, nonprofit sector advocates and some tax theorists vigorously oppose these suggestions. They argue that limiting the charitable estate tax deduction would reduce charitable bequests, particularly to private colleges and universities, without much offsetting gain in equity or tax revenues. See, e.g., Michael J. Boskin, Estate Taxation and Charitable Bequests, in III Research Papers Sponsored by the Commission on Private Philanthropy and Public Needs 1453 (1977); Boris I. Bittker, Charitable Bequests and the Federal Estate Tax: Proposed Restrictions on Deductibility, 31 Rec. Ass'n B. City N.Y. 159 (1976).

NOTES AND QUESTIONS

1. *The Charitable Deduction as a Tax Expenditure.* Since 1974, Congress has required a listing of tax expenditures in the federal budget. For this purpose, tax expenditures are defined as revenue losses due to preferential provisions of the federal tax laws. As estimated by the Treasury Department for the fiscal 2003 budget, the total revenue loss attributable to the income tax charitable deduction was $40.6 billion. The charitable deduction ranks as one of the largest income tax expenditures. The exclusion of employee contributions for medical insurance premiums and medical care ranked first, costing $108.5 billion. See Tax Expenditures Chapter From President's Fiscal 2004 Budget.

2. *Philanthropy and the Cultural Elite.* Teresa Odendahl's thesis is that elite philanthropy, instead of relieving social and economic inequality, actually exacerbates it. She argues that private schools and other nonprofit

institutions of "high culture" have a disproportionate influence and limited public accountability and that federal tax policy reinforces this syndrome. Odendahl's goal of rethinking the qualification criteria for tax-exempt status presents a challenge similar to that raised by the legal theorists. But her agenda suffers from considerable imprecision. Would private foundations still be eligible charitable donees under her proposed reforms? Should favored tax-exempt status be conditioned on the representative composition of an organization's governing board or a "public interest" test? Would it be appropriate to place a cap on a taxpayer's annual charitable deduction for gifts to a single institution—for example, limit the deduction to $10,000 per year per charitable donee? What would be the impact on charitable giving if the estate tax charitable deduction were subject to a dollar or percentage limitation, or if the federal wealth transfer taxes were repealed?

3. *Charitable Deduction for Non–Itemizers.* Under current law, only taxpayers who itemize deductions obtain any tax benefit from the charitable deduction. Should the deduction also be available to taxpayers who claim the standard deduction? Would this provide a greater inducement for donations from low-income taxpayers? In 1975, the Filer Commission recommended extending the charitable deduction to non-itemizers and went so far as to propose a "double charitable deduction" for families with incomes of less than $15,000 a year. These low-income taxpayers would have been allowed to deduct 200 percent of their gifts to charity! Giving in America: Toward a Stronger Voluntary Sector, Report of the Commission on Private Philanthropy and Public Needs 135 (1975). In 1981, Congress amended the Code to permit non-itemizers to deduct a portion of their charitable contributions, but the provision expired at the end of 1986.

The introduction of bills to resurrect some type of charitable deduction for non-itemizers has become an annual ritual in Congress. Legislation pending as this text went to press in early 2003 would allow non-itemizers to take a charitable deduction of up to $250 ($500 for married filing jointly taxpayers) for contributions made during the year that exceed a $250 floor ($500 for joint filers). Joint Committee on Taxation, Description of the "CARE Act of 2003" (JCX–04–03), Feb. 3, 2003, at 3–4. Proponents, including the Bush Administration, point to the benefits to low and middle-income taxpayers and the incentive to giving. Opponents express concerns about the additional complexity that comes with undermining the policy of the standard deduction and likely compliance problems (e.g., fraudulent deductions).

4. *Itemized Deductions Floor.* Most itemized deductions, including the charitable deduction, are subject to a reduction rule enacted by Congress in 1990 as a phantom tax rate increase for high-income taxpayers. Single individuals and married couples filing joint returns must reduce their total itemized deductions (except for a few exempted items) by three percent of the excess of those deductions over an indexed threshold ($139,500 in 2003), but not by more than 80 percent of itemized deductions subject to the limit. I.R.C. § 68. Beginning in 2006, this limitation is scheduled to phase out and be eliminated by 2009 and then, unless Congress takes

further action, it will reappear in 2010. Whether or not this rule reduces the tax benefits of charitable giving is a matter of some debate. What is not debatable is that this type of phase-out has significant complexity costs and contributes to taxpayer (and student?) confusion. Tax rate increases, by contrast, are easy to understand.

5. *For Further Reading.* Stanley S. Surrey, Pathways to Tax Reform 223–232 (1973); Boris I. Bittker, Charitable Contributions: Tax Deductions or Matching Grants, 28 Tax L.Rev. 37 (1972); Paul R. McDaniel, Federal Matching Grants for Charitable Contributions: A Substitute for the Income Tax Deduction, 27 Tax L. Rev. 377 (1972); John K. McNulty, Public Policy and Private Charity: A Tax Policy Perspective, 3 Va. Tax Rev. 229 (1984); John G. Simon, Charity and Dynasty Under the Federal Tax System, 5 The Probate Lawyer 22 (Summer 1978); Mark P. Gergen, The Case for a Charitable Contributions Deduction, 74 Va.L.Rev. 1393 (1988); Lawrence M. Stone, Federal Tax Support of Charities and Other Exempt Organizations: The Need for a National Policy, 1968 U.S.C. Tax Inst. 27; Mark G. Kelman, Personal Deductions Revisited: Why They Fit Poorly in an "Ideal" Income Tax and Why They Fit Worse in a Far from Ideal World, 31 Stan.L.Rev. 831, 838–851 (1979); Charles T. Clotfelter, Tax–Induced Distortions in the Voluntary Sector, 39 Case West.L.Rev. 663 (1988); Francie Ostrower, Why the Wealthy Give: The Culture of Elite Philanthropy (1996); Symposium: Corporate Philanthropy: Law, Culture, Education and Politics, 41 N.Y.L.Sch.L.Rev. 753 (1997).

B.   CHARITABLE CONTRIBUTIONS: BASIC PRINCIPLES

Internal Revenue Code: § 170(c).

1.   QUALIFIED DONEES

a.   IN GENERAL

The definition of a charitable contribution in § 170(c) consists of a list of the following five categories of organizations that qualify to receive tax-deductible gifts:

1. Governmental entities, including the United States, the District of Columbia, states, possessions and political subdivisions, provided the gift is made for exclusively public purposes. I.R.C. § 170(c)(1).
2. Domestic corporations, community chests, funds, or foundations that are organized and operated exclusively for religious, charitable, scientific, literary or educational purposes, to prevent cruelty to children or animals, or to foster national or international amateur sports competition, provided that no part of the organization's net earnings inure to the benefit of any private shareholder or individual and the organization does not violate the lobbying and political campaign limitations in § 501(c)(3). I.R.C. § 170(c)(2). This is the same group of organizations eligible for tax-exempt status under § 501(c)(3), except that "testing

for public safety" is not a qualifying purpose under § 170. In the case of gifts by corporate donors to a charitable trust or other noncorporate donee, a charitable deduction is allowed only if the gift is to be used within the united states or any of its possessions. I.R.C. § 170(c)(2), flush language. Gifts by corporations to domestic corporate donees, however, are not subject to any place-of-use restriction and thus may be expended outside the United States. Rev. Rul. 69–80, 1969–1 C.B. 65.

3. Veterans organizations (including certain ancillary entities), subject to a no inurement of private gain limitation. I.R.C. § 170(c)(3).

4. Domestic fraternal lodges, if the gift is from an individual and is to be used exclusively for religious, charitable, scientific, literary, or educational purposes, or for the prevention of cruelty to children or animals. I.R.C. § 170(c)(4).

5. Nonprofit cemetery companies owned and operated exclusively for the benefit of their members, which also are subject to a no inurement of private gain limitation. I.R.C. § 170(c)(5).

With a few minor differences, the first four categories of organizations in the above list also are eligible to receive tax-deductible gifts for federal estate and gift tax purposes. I.R.C. §§ 2055(a); 2522(a).

Most qualified donees are included in the IRS's Publication 78, also known as "The Cumulative List," a bulky two-volume book that lists all organizations that have obtained a favorable determination under § 170(c) from the Service. The list is also available on the IRS's web site at <http://www.irs.ustreas.gov>. In general, a contributor may rely upon the Cumulative List and its quarterly supplement until the Service publishes a formal notice of revocation or change of classification (e.g., from public charity to private foundation). If the donor knew the organization's exempt status was revoked, was aware that revocation was imminent, or was responsible for or aware of the circumstances leading to the revocation, the donor may not rely on the Cumulative List. See Rev. Proc. 82–39, 1982–2 C.B. 759.

b. INTERNATIONAL GIVING

The growth of global philanthropy has stimulated greater interest in tax planning for contributions by U.S. donors for use beyond the borders of the United States. The arcane and often formalistic tax regime that regulates international giving places a high premium on knowing the "right way" to structure a gift for use abroad. Section 170 appears to place a geographical limitation on the income tax deduction for individual contributions by requiring qualified donees to be created or organized within the United States, including any state, the District of Columbia, and U.S. possessions. I.R.C. § 170(c)(2)(A). But the Code does not restrict the area in which deductible contributions may be used for charitable purposes. Reg. § 1.170A–8(a)(1). As illustrated by Revenue Ruling 63–152, which follows, U.S. individual taxpayers may deduct contributions made for use abroad provided the gifts are made to a domestic charity that is not legally obligated to pay over the donated funds to a foreign recipient.

Revenue Ruling 63–252

1963–2 Cum.Bull. 101.

Advice has been requested as to the deductibility, under section 170 of the Internal Revenue Code of 1954, of contributions by individuals to a charity organized in the United States which thereafter transmits some or all of its funds to a foreign charitable organization.

* * *

In determining whether contributions to or for the use of a particular corporation, trust, community chest, fund, or foundation are deductible, it must first be determined that the recipient organization was validly created or organized in the United States, a state or territory, the District of Columbia or a possession of the United States, as required by section 170(c)(2)(A) of the Code. If the organization does not qualify under section 170(c)(2)(A) of the Code—that is, it was not created or organized in the United States, etc.—a contribution thereto is not deductible under section 170 of the Code. It must further be found that the recipient was organized and operated exclusively for one of the purposes stated in section 170(c)(2)(B) of the Code, namely, religious, charitable, scientific, literary, or educational purposes or for the prevention of cruelty to children or animals, and that it meets the remaining requirements of section 170(c)(2) of the Code.

Assuming that an organization otherwise meets the requirements set forth in section 170(c)(2) of the Code, a further problem arises where that organization is required to turn all or part of its funds over to a foreign charitable organization. As noted above, contributions directly to the foreign organization would not be deductible. The question presented here is whether the result should differ when funds are contributed to a domestic charity which then transmits those funds to a foreign charitable organization.

Prior to the passage of the Revenue Act of 1938 there were no restrictions as to the place of creation of charitable organizations to which individuals might make deductible contributions. * * * The rule as to individual contributions was changed with the passage of the Revenue Act of 1938. Section 23(o) of that Act provided that contributions by individuals were deductible only if the recipient was a "domestic" organization. Section 224 of the Revenue Act of 1939 substituted for the requirement that a qualifying organization be "domestic," the requirement that it have been "created or organized in the United States or in any possession thereof," etc. In substantially the same form, this requirement was re-enacted as section 170(c)(2)(A) of the 1954 Code.

At the outset, it should be noted that section 170(c)(2)(A) of the Code relates only to the place of creation of the charitable organization to which deductible contributions may be made and does not restrict the area in which deductible contributions may be used. Compare the last sentence in section 170(c)(2) of the Code, which requires that certain corporate contributions be used within the United States. Accordingly, the following discussion should not be construed as limiting in any way the geographical areas in which deductible contributions by individuals may be used.

The deductibility of the contributions here at issue will be discussed in connection with five illustrative examples set out below. The "foreign organization" referred to in each of the examples is an organization which is chartered in a foreign country and is so organized and operated that it meets all the requirements of section 170(c)(2) of the Code excepting the requirement set forth in section 170(c)(2)(A) of the Code. The "domestic organization" in each example is assumed to meet all the requirements in section 170(c)(2) of the Code. In each case, the question to be decided is whether the amounts paid to the domestic organization are deductible under section 170(a) of the Code.

(1) In pursuance of a plan to solicit funds in this country, a foreign organization caused a domestic organization to be formed. At the time of formation, it was proposed that the domestic organization would conduct a fund-raising campaign, pay the administrative expenses from the collected fund and remit any balance to the foreign organization.

(2) Certain persons in this country, desirous of furthering a foreign organization's work, formed a charitable organization within the United States. The charter of the domestic organization provides that it will receive contributions and send them, at convenient intervals, to the foreign organization.

(3) A foreign organization entered into an agreement with a domestic organization which provides that the domestic organization will conduct a fund-raising campaign on behalf of the foreign organization. The domestic organization has previously received a ruling that contributions to it are deductible under section 170 of the Code. In conducting the campaign, the domestic organization represents to prospective contributors that the raised funds will go to the foreign organization.

(4) A domestic organization conducts a variety of charitable activities in a foreign country. Where its purposes can be furthered by granting funds to charitable groups organized in the foreign country, the domestic organization makes such grants for purposes which it has reviewed and approved. The grants are paid from its general funds and although the organization solicits from the public, no special fund is raised by a solicitation on behalf of particular foreign organizations.

(5) A domestic organization, which does charitable work in a foreign country, formed a subsidiary in that country to facilitate its operations there. The foreign organization was formed for purposes of administrative convenience and the domestic organization controls

every facet of its operations. In the past the domestic organization solicited contributions for the specific purpose of carrying out its charitable activities in the foreign country and it will continue to do so in the future. However, following the formation of the foreign subsidiary, the domestic organization will transmit funds it receives for its foreign charitable activities directly to that organization.

It is recognized that special earmarking of the use or destination of funds paid to a qualifying charitable organization may deprive the donor of a deduction. In S.E. Thomason v. Commissioner, 2 T.C. 441 (1943), the court held that amounts paid to a charitable organization were not deductible where the contributions were earmarked for the benefit of a particular ward of the organization. Similarly, see Revenue Ruling 54-580, C.B. 1954-2, 97. These cases indicate that an inquiry as to the deductibility of a contribution need not stop once it is determined that an amount has been paid to a qualifying organization; if the amount is earmarked, then it is appropriate to look beyond the fact that the immediate recipient is a qualifying organization to determine whether the payment constitutes a deductible contribution.

Similarly, if an organization is required for other reasons, such as a specific provision in its charter, to turn contributions, or any particular contribution it receives, over to another organization, then in determining whether such contributions are deductible it is appropriate to determine whether the ultimate recipient of the contribution is a qualifying organization. * * * Moreover, it seems clear that the requirements of section 170(c)(2)(A) of the Code would be nullified if contributions inevitably committed to go to a foreign organization were held to be deductible solely because, in the course of transmittal to the foreign organization, they came to rest momentarily in a qualifying domestic organization. In such cases the domestic organization is only nominally the donee; the real donee is the ultimate foreign recipient.

Accordingly, the Service holds that contributions to the domestic organizations described in the first and second examples set forth above are not deductible. Similarly, those contributions to the domestic organization described in the third example which are given for the specific purpose of being turned over to the foreign organization are held to be nondeductible.

On the other hand, contributions received by the domestic organization described in the fourth example will not be earmarked in any manner, and use of such contributions will be subject to control by the domestic organization. Consequently, the domestic organization is considered to be the recipient of such contributions for purposes of applying section 170(c) of the Code. Similarly, the domestic organization described in the fifth example is considered to be the real beneficiary of contributions it receives for transmission to the foreign organization. Since the foreign organization is merely an administrative arm of the domestic organization, the fact that contributions are ultimately paid over to the foreign organization does not require a conclusion that the domestic organization is not the real recipient of those contributions. Accordingly, contributions by individuals to the domestic organizations described in the fourth and fifth examples are considered to be deductible.

* * *

NOTES

1. *Treaties.* In limited cases, foreign organizations may receive tax-deductible contributions for U.S. tax purposes under a treaty. For example, gifts to certain Canadian and Mexican charities may be deductible under the terms of tax treaties with those countries.

2. *Private Foundation Grants to Foreign Charities.* Private foundations in the United States have become increasingly involved in international philanthropy. In Rev. Proc. 92–94, 1992–2 C.B. 507, the Internal Revenue Service has provided a simplified procedure to assure that foundation grants to foreign grantees will be treated as "qualifying distributions" for purposes of the § 4942 foundation payout requirements and will not be treated as "taxable expenditures" under § 4945. The problem arises because most foreign grantees do not have exemption classification rulings from the Internal Revenue Service. Under the revenue procedure, grants to foreign charities will comply with the private foundation rules if the foundation obtains an affidavit of the grantee or an opinion of counsel of either the grantor or grantee that the grantee's operations and sources of support make it likely that the grantee would have qualified as a public charity or private operating foundation if it had been a domestic organization.

3. *For Further Reading.* Harvey P. Dale, Foreign Charities, 48 Tax Lawyer 657 (1995); Victoria B. Bjorklund, International Philanthropy Exploring New Ways to Accomplish International Goals, Including Activities of U.S. Charities Abroad, 21 NYU Conf. on Tax Planning for 501(c)(3) Organizations § 8 (1993); Kimberly S. Blanchard, U.S. Taxation of Foreign Charities, 8 Exempt Org. Tax Rev. 719 (1993).

c. FISCAL SPONSORS

Assume that an individual or group engaging in a short-term or embryonic project is seeking to raise tax-deductible contributions from individual or corporate donors, or grants from private foundations or government agencies. The project may be an educational film, a theater production, or an international human rights program—all activities that comfortably would qualify as "charitable" if carried out directly by a § 501(c)(3) organization. Because they will be short-lived or are still in the formative stages, these projects might not justify the expense of creating a separate tax-exempt entity. Yet without formal recognition from the Internal Revenue Service, the prospect of raising substantial funds is slim to none.

The nonprofit sector has developed and refined the "fiscal sponsorship" concept to respond to these concerns. As described in a leading guidebook on the subject:

> Fiscal sponsorship arrangements typically arise when a person or group (we will call this a project) wants to get support from a private foundation, a government agency, or tax-deductible donations from individual or corporate donors. By law or preference, the funding source will make payments only to organizations with 501(c)(3) tax status. So the project looks for a 501(c)(3) sponsor to receive the funds and pass them on to the project.

Gregory L. Colvin, Fiscal Sponsorship: 6 Ways to Do it Right (1993).

Fiscal sponsors are sometimes called "fiscal agents," but the latter term is a misnomer. To comply with IRS guidelines, the sponsoring exempt organization should not act as an agent of the nonexempt project. Rather, the charity must retain legal control of the project and ensure that it furthers the charity's exempt purposes and does not result in any inurement of private gain to the project leaders. Id. Contributions to a charity that are simply earmarked by the donor for a particular individual or nonexempt organization would not be deductible where the charity lacks discretion and control over the donated funds.

2.   FORM AND TIMING OF THE CONTRIBUTION

Treasury Regulations: § 1.170A–1(a), (b), (g).

A contribution is tax-deductible if it is made either "to" or "for the use of" a qualified donee. Gifts made directly to individuals, however worthy or needy they may be, are not deductible. The term "for the use of " permits a charitable deduction for gifts that benefit a charity even though not made directly "to" the organization. The term has been interpreted to include gifts made in trust for an organization's benefit. As discussed in Davis v. United States, which follows, it does not extend to gifts to support individuals who perform services for a charity that does not have sufficient control over the donated funds.

Davis v. United States

Supreme Court of the United States, 1990.
495 U.S. 472, 110 S.Ct. 2014.

■ JUSTICE O'CONNOR delivered the opinion of the Court.

We are called upon in this case to determine whether the funds petitioners transferred to their two sons while they served as full-time, unpaid missionaries for the Church of Jesus Christ of Latter-day Saints (Church) are deductible as charitable contributions "to or for the use of" the Church, pursuant to 26 U.S.C. § 170 (1982 ed.).

I

[Harold and Enid Davis were members of the Mormon Church. During the taxable years in controversy, they claimed a charitable deduction for funds transferred to the personal checking accounts of their two sons, who were serving as missionaries. It was customary for a missionary's parents to provide the necessary funds for support during the child's period of service. Missionaries were instructed that the money received for their support was sacred and should be spent only for missionary work and they were encouraged to keep expenses to a minimum.

Mr. and Mrs. Davis claimed that their payments were charitable contributions "for the use of" the Church or, alternatively, that they were deductible as unreimbursed expenditures incident to the rendering of services to a charitable organization. The district court upheld the Service's disallowance of the deductions, and the Ninth Circuit affirmed. Because the Ninth Circuit's decision conflicted with previous decisions of the Tenth and Fifth Circuits, the Supreme Court granted certiorari. Eds.]

II

Under § 170 of the Internal Revenue Code of 1954, a taxpayer may claim a deduction for a charitable contribution only if the contribution is made "to or for the use of" a qualified organization. * * *

Petitioners contend that the funds they transferred to their sons' accounts are deductible as contributions "for the use of" the Church. Alternatively, petitioners claim these funds are unreimbursed expenditures under Treasury Regulation § 1.170A–1(g) and therefore are deductible as contributions "to" the Church. We first consider whether the payments at issue here are "for the use of" the Church within the meaning of § 170.

On its face, the phrase "for the use of" could support any number of different meanings. See, e.g., Webster's New International Dictionary (2d ed. 1950)("use" defined in general usage as "to convert to one's service"; "to employ"; or, in law, "use imports a trust" relationship). Petitioners contend that the phrase "for the use of" must be given its broadest meaning as describing "the entire array of fiduciary relationships in which one person conveys money or property to someone else to hold or employ in some manner for the benefit of a third person." Under this reading, no legally enforceable relationship need exist between the recipient of the donated funds and the qualified donee; in effect, any intermediary may handle the funds in any way that would arguably benefit a charitable organization, regardless of how indirect or tangential the benefit might be. Petitioners also advance a second, somewhat narrower interpretation, specifically that a contribution is "for the use of" a qualified organization within the meaning of § 170 so long as the donee has "a reasonable ability to ensure that the contribution primarily serves the organization's charitable purposes." In this case, petitioners argue that their payments at least meet this second interpretation. They point to the Church's role in requesting the funds, setting the amount to be donated, and requiring weekly expense sheets from the missionaries. The Service, on the other hand, has historically defined "for the use of" as conveying "a similar meaning as 'in trust for.' "

Although the language of § 170 would support the interpretation of either the Service or petitioners, the events leading to the enactment of the 1921 amendment adding the phrase "for the use of" to § 170 indicate that Congress had a specific meaning of "for the use of" in mind. The original version of § 170, promulgated in the War Revenue Act of 1917, ch. 63, § 1201(2), 40 Stat. 330, did not allow deductions for gifts "for the use of" a qualified donee. Rather, it allowed individuals to deduct only "[c]ontributions or gifts * * * to corporations or associations organized and operated exclusively for religious, charitable, scientific, or educational purposes * * *." In interpreting this provision in the Act, the Bureau of Internal Revenue stated that "[c]ontributions to a trust company (a corporation) in trust to invest and disburse them for a charitable purpose are not allowable deductions under [§ 170]." In hearings before the Senate Committee on Finance on the proposed Revenue Act of 1921, representatives of charitable foundations requested an amendment making gifts to trust companies and similar donees deductible even though a trustee, rather than a charitable organization, held legal title to the funds. Testimony before the Committee indicated that numerous communities had established charitable trusts, charitable foundations, or community chests so that individuals could donate money to a trustee who held, invested, and reinvested the principal, and then turned the principal over to a committee that distributed the funds for charitable purposes. Responding to these concerns, Congress overruled the Bureau's interpretation of § 170 (then § 214(a)(11)) by adding the phrase "for the use of * * * any corporation, or community chest, fund, or foundation * * *"to the charitable deduction provision of the Revenue Act of 1921. In light of these events, it can be inferred that Congress' use of the phrase "for the use of" related to its purpose in amending § 170 of allowing taxpayers to deduct contributions made to trusts, foundations, and similar donees. An interpretation of "for the use of" as conveying a similar meaning as "in trust for" would be consistent with this goal.

It would have been quite natural for Congress to use the phrase "for the use of" to indicate its intent of allowing deductions for donations in trust, as this phrase would have suggested a trust relationship to the members of the 67th Congress. From the dawn of English common law through the present, the word "use" has been employed to refer to various forms of trust arrangements. * * * In the early part of this century, the word "use" was technically employed to refer to a passive trust, but less formally used as a synonym for the word "trust." The phrases "to the use of" or "for the use of" were frequently used in describing trust arrangements. Given that this meaning of the word "use" precisely corresponded with Congress' purpose for amending the statute, it appears likely that in choosing the phrase "for the use of" Congress was referring to donations made in trust or in a similar legal arrangement.

* * *

The Commissioner's interpretation of "for the use of" thus appears to be entirely faithful to Congress' understanding and intent in using that phrase. Moreover, the Commissioner's interpretation is consistent with the purposes of § 170 as a whole. In enacting § 170, "Congress sought to provide tax benefits to charitable organizations, to encourage the development of private institutions that serve a useful public purpose or supplement or take the place of public institutions of the same kind." The Commissioner's interpretation of "for the use of" assures that contributions will in fact foster such development because it requires contributions to be made in trust or in some similar legal arrangement. A defining characteristic of a trust arrangement is that the beneficiary has the legal power to enforce the trustee's duty to comply with the terms of the trust. A qualified beneficiary of a bona fide trust for charitable purposes would have both the incentive and legal authority to ensure that donated funds are properly used. If the trust contributes funds to a range of charitable organizations so that no single beneficiary could enforce its terms, the trustee's duty can be enforced by the Attorney General under the laws of most States. Although the Service's interpretation does not require that the qualified organization take actual possession of the contribution, it nevertheless reflects that the beneficiary must have significant legal rights with respect to the disposition of donated funds.

* * *

Although the language of the statute may also bear petitioners' interpretation, they have failed to establish that their interpretation is compelled by the statutory language. To the contrary, there is no evidence that Congress intended the phrase "for the use of" to be interpreted as referring to fiduciary relationships in general or as referring to a type of relationship that gives a qualified organization a reasonable ability to supervise the use of contributed funds. Rather, as noted above, there are strong indications that Congress intended a more specific meaning. Moreover, petitioners' interpretations would tend to undermine the purposes of § 170 by allowing taxpayers to claim deductions for funds transferred to children or other relatives for their own personal use. Because a recipient of donated funds need not have any legal relationship with a qualified organization, the Service would face virtually insurmountable administrative difficulties in verifying that any particular expenditure benefited a qualified donee. Cf. § 170(a)(1). Although there is no suggestion whatsoever in this case that the transferred funds were used for an improper purpose, it is clear that petitioners' interpretation would create an opportunity for tax evasion that others might be eager to exploit. We need not determine whether petitioners' interpretation of "for the use of" would have been a permissible one had the Service decided to adopt it, though we note that the Service may retain some flexibility to adopt other interpretations in the future. It is sufficient to decide this case that the Service's longstanding interpretation is both consistent with the statutory language and fully implements Congress' apparent purpose in adopting it. Accordingly, we conclude that a gift or contribution is "for the use of" a qualified organization when it is held in a legally enforceable trust for the qualified organization or in a similar legal arrangement.

Viewing the record here in the light most favorable to petitioners, as we must after a grant of summary judgment for the United States, we discern no evidence that petitioners transferred funds to their sons "in trust for" the Church. It is undisputed that petitioners transferred the money to their sons' personal bank accounts on which the sons were the sole authorized signatories. Nothing in the record indicates that petitioners took any steps normally associated with creating a trust or similar legal arrangement. Although the sons may have promised to use the money "in accordance with Church guidelines," they did not have any legal obligation to do so; there is no evidence that the guidelines have any legally binding effect. Nor does the record support the assertion, that the Church might have a legal entitlement to the money or a civil cause of action against missionaries who used their parents' money for purposes not approved by the Church. We conclude that, because petitioners did not donate the funds in trust for the Church, or in a similarly enforceable legal arrangement for the benefit of the Church, the funds were not donated "for the use of" the Church for purposes of § 170.

III

Petitioners contend, in the alternative, that their transfer of funds into their sons' account was a contribution "to" the Church under Treas.Reg. § 1.170A–1(g), 26 CFR § 1.170A–1(g)(1989), which provides: "Contributions of services. No deduction is allowable under section 170 for a contribution of services. However, unreimbursed expenditures made incident to the rendition of services to an organization contributions to which are deductible may constitute a deductible contribution. For example, the cost of a uniform without general utility which is required to be worn in performing donated services is deductible. Similarly, out-of-pocket transportation expenses necessarily incurred in performing donated services are deductible. Reasonable expenditures for meals and lodging necessarily incurred while away from home in the course of performing donated services also are deductible. For the purposes of this paragraph, the phrase 'while away from home' has the same meaning as that phrase is used for purposes of section 162 and the regulations thereunder."

Petitioners assert that this regulation allows them to claim deductions for their sons' unreimbursed expenditures incident to their sons' contribution of services. We disagree. The plain language of § 1.170A–1(g) indicates that taxpayers may claim deductions only for expenditures made in connection with their own contributions of service to charities. Unless there is a specific statutory provision to the contrary, a taxpayer ordinarily reports his own income and takes his own deductions. Section 1.170A–1(g) is thus most naturally read as referring to the individual taxpayer, who may deduct only those "unreimbursed expenditures" incurred in connection with the taxpayer's own "rendition of services to [a qualified] organization." This interpretation of the regulation is consistent with the Revenue

Ruling that was the precursor to § 1.170A–1(g). See Rev.Rul. 55–4, 1955–1 Cum.Bull. 291 ("A taxpayer who gives his services gratuitously to an association, contributions to which are deductible under [§ 170] and who incurs unreimbursed traveling expenses * * * may deduct the amount of such unreimbursed expenses in computing his net income * * *"). It would strain the language of the regulation to read it, as petitioners suggest, as allowing a deduction for expenses made incident to a third party's rendition of services rather than to the taxpayer's own contribution of services. Similarly, the taxpayer is clearly intended to be the subject of the other provisions in the regulation. For example, it is most natural to read the regulation as referring to a taxpayer who incurs expenditures for meals and lodging while away from his home, not while a third party is away from his home.

Petitioners' interpretation not only strains the language of the statute, but would also allow manipulation of § 1.170A–1(g) for tax evasion purposes. For example, parents might be tempted to transfer funds to their children in amounts greater than needed to reimburse reasonable expenses incurred in donating services to a charity. Parents and children might attempt to claim a deduction for the same expenditure. Controlling such abuses would place a heavy administrative burden on the Service, which would not only have to monitor the taxpayer's records, but also correlate them with the records of the third party. To the extent petitioners' interpretation lessens the likelihood that claimed charitable contributions actually served a charitable purpose, it is inconsistent with § 170.

Petitioners cite judicial decisions that allowed taxpayers to claim deductions for the expenses of third parties who assisted the taxpayers in rendering services to qualified organizations. These cases are inapposite, as petitioners do not claim that they were independently rendering services to the Church, assisted by their sons.

We conclude that § 1.170A–1(g) does not allow taxpayers to claim a deduction for expenses not incurred in connection with the taxpayers' own rendition of services to a qualified organization. Therefore, petitioners are not entitled to a deduction under § 1.170A–1(g).

Petitioners also assert that because their sons are agents of the Church authorized to receive payments to support their own missionary efforts, payments made to their sons are payments to the Church. Because this argument was neither raised before nor decided by the Court of Appeals, we decline to address it here.

Accordingly, we hold that petitioners' transfer of funds into their sons' accounts was not a contribution "to or for the use of" the Church for purposes of § 170. The judgment of the Court of Appeals is Affirmed.

NOTES

1. *Out-of-Pocket Expenses.* Payments that further an organization's charitable activities, such as unreimbursed expenses of volunteers and

board members, are deductible even if the payment is not made directly to the charity. The out-of-pocket expense deduction extends to travel expenses, subject to a "no smile" rule enacted in 1986 that disallows a deduction for transportation, meals and lodging "unless there is no significant element of personal pleasure, recreation, or vacation in such travel." I.R.C. § 170(j). In determining the deduction for unreimbursed expenses for using a passenger automobile, § 170(i) prescribes a special rate of 14 cents per mile. Unreimbursed expenditures are treated as contributions "to" a charity (rather than "for the use of") and thus are subject to the higher 50 percent limitation on cash contributions in § 170(b)(1)(A). See Rockefeller v. Commissioner, 676 F.2d 35 (2d Cir.1982); Rev. Rul. 84–61, 1984–1 C.B. 39.

2. *Students in the Taxpayer's Household.* Section 170(g) provides a limited charitable deduction (generally $50 per month) for amounts paid to maintain individuals as members of the taxpayer's household. This provision applies to certain arrangements between taxpayers and qualified charitable organizations which provide educational opportunities in the United States for full-time students in the 12th or lower grades.

3. *Payment Requirement.* Whatever their method of accounting, individual taxpayers may deduct charitable contributions only in the year in which they are unconditionally paid. Treas. Reg. § 1.170A–1(a). Payment is accomplished by placing the contributed property beyond the dominion and control of the donor. Thus, a cash contribution made by a check that clears in due course will be effective as of the date of mailing, even if it is not received and deposited by the charity until the following year. Treas. Reg. § 1.170A–1(b). Contributions made by a credit card are deductible when the charge is made to the donor's account, regardless of when the cardholder pays the bank. Rev. Rul. 78–38, 1978–1 C.B. 67. Gifts of stock registered in certificate form in the taxpayer's name are not considered complete until stock is transferred on the corporation's books. Treas. Reg. § 1.170A–1(b). But if a donor mails a properly endorsed stock certificate to a charity or to a broker who is acting as an agent for the charity, the gift will be effective as of the date of mailing if the certificate reaches the charity in the normal course of the mails. Id. If securities held by the donor in "street name" in a brokerage or custody account are transferred to an account in the charity's name, the gift is effective as of the date of the transfer.

4. *Pledges.* Even if a pledge is enforceable under state law, neither the act of making the pledge nor the delivery of the donor's own promissory note will constitute "payment" for purposes of the charitable deduction. Rev. Rul. 68–174, 1968–1 C.B. 81. A deduction is allowable only when the pledge is satisfied or the note is paid. Treas. Reg. § 1.170A–1(a). As to the enforceability of pledges to nonprofit organizations, see Mary Frances Budig, Gordon T. Butler & Lynne M. Murphy, Pledges to Non–Profit Organizations: Are They Enforceable and Must They Be Enforced? (New York University School of Law Program on Philanthropy and the Law, 1993).

5. *Corporate Donors*. A corporation using the accrual method of accounting may elect to deduct contributions authorized by its board of directors before the end of its taxable year and paid on or before the fifteenth day of the third month of the following year. I.R.C. § 170(a)(2); Reg. § 1.170A–11(b).

6. *Options*. An option granted to a charitable donee to purchase property at a bargain price does not produce a charitable deduction at the time of the grant. A deduction is allowed at the time the option is exercised. The amount of the charitable deduction is the excess of the fair market value of the property at that time over the exercise price. Rev. Rul. 82–197, 1982–2 C.B. 72.

3.   What is a Charitable Gift?

Treasury Regulations: § 1.170A–1(h).

To be tax-deductible, a charitable contribution must be made with donative intent. A transfer does not qualify as a gift if the transferor receives a return benefit, such as a good or service with a measurable fair market value. The burden is on the taxpayer to show that she intended to make a gift and in fact donated an amount with a value exceeding the fair market value of any goods or services received from the donee. Treas. Reg. § 1.170A–1(h). In the celebrated *Duberstein* case, the Supreme Court loosely defined a gift as a transfer of money or property without adequate consideration and with no expectation of a return benefit.[1] Under *Duberstein*, the requisite donative intent is present if the transfer is made out of "detached and disinterested generosity," an elusive and highly factual standard. In the more recent *American Bar Endowment* case, the Court stated that "[a] payment of money generally cannot constitute a charitable contribution if the contributor expects a substantial benefit in return. * * * The *sine qua non* of a charitable contribution is a transfer of money or property without adequate consideration."[2]

As illustrated by the materials below, whether a donor has made a gift or is receiving a quid pro quo has become an increasingly important question as the Internal Revenue Service has heightened its scrutiny of the vast array of return benefits provided to donors by charitable organizations.

Revenue Ruling 67–246

1967–2 Cum. Bull. 104.

Advice has been requested concerning certain fund-raising practices which are frequently employed by or on behalf of charitable organizations

---

1. Commissioner v. Duberstein, 363 U.S. 278, 285, 80 S.Ct. 1190, 1196 (1960). In *Duberstein*, the Court was interpreting the appropriate standard for determining whether a transfer qualified as a gift for purposes of § 102, which excludes gifts from gross income.

2. United States v. American Bar Endowment, 477 U.S. 105, 116, 118, 106 S.Ct. 2426, 2433 (1986).

and which involve the deductibility, as charitable contributions under section 170 of the Internal Revenue Code of 1954, of payments in connection with admission to or other participation in fund-raising activities for charity such as charity balls, bazaars, banquets, shows, and athletic events.

Affairs of the type in question are commonly employed to raise funds for charity in two ways. One is from profit derived from sale of admissions or other privileges or benefits connected with the event at such prices as their value warrants. Another is through the use of the affair as an occasion for solicitation of gifts in combination with the sale of the admissions or other privileges or benefits involved. In cases of the latter type the sale of the privilege or benefit is combined with solicitation of a gift or donation of some amount in addition to the sale value of the admission or privilege.

The need for guidelines on the subject is indicated by the frequency of misunderstanding of the requirements for deductibility of such payments and increasing incidence of their erroneous treatment for income tax purposes.

In particular, an increasing number of instances are being reported in which the public has been erroneously advised in advertisements or solicitations by sponsors that the entire amounts paid for tickets or other privileges in connection with fund-raising affairs for charity are deductible. Audits of returns are revealing other instances of erroneous advice and misunderstanding as to what, if any, portion of such payments is deductible in various circumstances. There is evidence also of instances in which taxpayers are being misled by questionable solicitation practices which make it appear from the wording of the solicitation that taxpayer's payment is a "contribution," whereas the payment solicited is simply the purchase price of an item offered for sale by the organization.

Section 170 of the Code provides for allowance of deductions for charitable contributions, subject to certain requirements and limitations. To the extent here relevant a charitable contribution is defined by that section as 'a contribution or gift to or for the use of' certain specified types of organizations.

To be deductible as a charitable contribution for Federal income tax purposes under section 170 of the Code, a payment to or for the use of a qualified charitable organization must be a gift. To be a gift for such purposes in the present context there must be, among other requirements, a payment of money or transfer of property without adequate consideration.

As a general rule, where a transaction involving a payment is in the form of a purchase of an item of value, the presumption arises that no gift has been made for charitable contribution purposes, the presumption being that the payment in such case is the purchase price.

Thus, where consideration in the form of admissions or other privileges or benefits is received in connection with payments by patrons of fund-raising affairs of the type in question, the presumption is that the payments are not gifts. In such case, therefore, if a charitable contribution deduction is claimed with respect to the payment, the burden is on the taxpayer to establish that the amount paid is not the purchase of the privileges or benefits and that part of the payment, in fact, does qualify as a gift.

In showing that a gift has been made, an essential element is proof that the portion of the payment claimed as a gift represents the excess of the total amount paid over the value of the consideration received therefor. This may be established by evidence that the payment exceeds the fair market value of the privileges or other benefits received by the amount claimed to have been paid as a gift.

Another element which is important in establishing that a gift was made in such circumstances, is evidence that the payment in excess of the value received was made with the intention of making a gift. While proof of such intention may not be an essential requirement under all circumstances and may sometimes be inferred from surrounding circumstances, the intention to make a gift is, nevertheless, highly relevant in overcoming doubt in those cases in which there is a question whether an amount was in fact paid as a purchase price or as a gift.

Regardless of the intention of the parties, however, a payment of the type in question can in any event qualify as a deductible gift only to the extent that it is shown to exceed the fair market value of any consideration received in the form of privileges or other benefits.

In those cases in which a fund-raising activity is designed to solicit payments which are intended to be in part a gift and in part the purchase price of admission to or other participation in an event of the type in question, the organization conducting the activity should employ procedures which make clear not only that a gift is being solicited in connection with the sale of the admissions or other privileges related to the fund-raising event, but also, the amount of the gift being solicited. To do this, the amount properly attributable to the purchase of admissions or other privileges and the amount solicited as a gift should be determined in advance of solicitation. The respective amounts should be stated in making the solicitation and clearly indicated on any ticket, receipt, or other evidence issued in connection with the payment.

In making such a determination, the full fair market value of the admission and other benefits or privileges must be taken into account. Where the affair is reasonably comparable to events for which there are established charges for admission, such as theatrical or athletic performances, the established charges should be treated as fixing the fair market value of the admission or privilege. Where the amount paid is the same as the standard admission charge there is, of course, no deductible contribution, regardless of the intention of the parties. Where the event has no such counterpart, only that portion of the payment which exceeds a reasonable estimate of the fair market value of the admission or other privileges may be designated as a charitable contribution.

The fact that the full amount or a portion of the payment made by the taxpayer is used by the organization exclusively for charitable purposes has no bearing upon the determination to be made as to the value of the admission or other privileges and the amount qualifying as a contribution.

Also, the mere fact that tickets or other privileges are not utilized does not entitle the patron to any greater charitable contribution deduction than would otherwise be allowable. The test of deductibility is not whether the right to admission or privileges is exercised but whether the right was accepted or rejected by the taxpayer. If a patron desires to support an affair, but does not intend to use the tickets or exercise the other privileges being offered with the event, he can make an outright gift of the amount he wishes to contribute, in which event he would not accept or keep any ticket or other evidence of any of the privileges related to the event connected with the solicitation.

The foregoing summary is not intended to be all inclusive of the legal requirements relating to deductibility of payments as charitable contributions for Federal income tax purposes. Neither does it attempt to deal with many of the refinements and distinctions which sometimes arise in connection with questions of whether a gift for such purposes has been made in particular circumstances.

The principles stated are intended instead to summarize with as little complexity as possible, those basic rules which govern deductibility of payments in the majority of the circumstances involved. They have their basis in section 170 of the Code, the regulations thereunder, and in court decisions. The observance of these provisions will provide greater assurance to taxpayer contributors that their claimed deductions in such cases are allowable.

Where it is disclosed that the public or the patrons of a fund-raising affair for charity have been erroneously informed concerning the extent of the deductibility of their payments in connection with the affair, it necessarily follows that all charitable contribution deductions claimed with respect to payments made in connection with the particular event or affair will be subject to special scrutiny and may be questioned in audit of returns.

In the following examples application of the principles discussed above is illustrated in connection with various types of fund-raising activities for charity. Again, the examples are drawn to illustrate the general rules involved without attempting to deal with distinctions that sometimes arise in special situations. In each instance, the charitable organization involved is assumed to be an organization previously determined to be qualified to receive deductible charitable contributions under section 170 of the Code, and the references to deductibility are to deductibility as charitable contributions for Federal income tax purposes.

Example 1:

The M Charity sponsors a symphony concert for the purpose of raising funds for M's charitable programs. M agrees to pay a fee which is calculated to reimburse the symphony for hall rental, musicians' salaries, advertising costs, and printing of tickets. Under the agreement, M is entitled to all receipts from ticket sales. M sells tickets to the concert charging $5 for balcony seats and $10 for orchestra circle seats. These prices approximate the established admission charges for concert performances by the symphony orchestra. The tickets to the concert and the advertising material promoting ticket sales emphasize that the concert is sponsored by, and is for the benefit of M Charity.

Notwithstanding the fact that taxpayers who acquire tickets to the concert may think they are making a charitable contribution to or for the benefit of M Charity, no part of the payments made is deductible as a charitable contribution for Federal income tax purposes. Since the payments approximate the established admission charge for similar events, there is no gift. The result would be the same even if the advertising materials promoting ticket sales stated that amounts paid for tickets are "tax deductible" and tickets to the concert were purchased in reliance upon such statements. Acquisition of tickets or other privileges by a taxpayer in reliance upon statements made by a charitable organization that the amounts paid are deductible does not convert an otherwise nondeductible payment into a deductible charitable contribution.

Example 2:

The facts are the same as in Example 1, except that the M Charity desires to use the concert as an occasion for the solicitation of gifts. It indicates that fact in its advertising material promoting the event, and fixes the payments solicited in connection with each class of admission at $30 for orchestra circle seats and $15 for balcony seats. The advertising and the tickets clearly reflect the fact that the established admission charges for comparable performances by the symphony orchestra are $10 for orchestra circle seats and $5 for balcony seats, and that only the excess of the solicited amounts paid in connection with admission to the concert over the established prices is a contribution to M.

Under these circumstances a taxpayer who makes a payment of $60 and receives two orchestra circle seat tickets can show that his payment exceeds the established admission charge for similar tickets to comparable performances of the symphony orchestra by $40. The circumstances also confirm that amount of the payment was solicited as, and intended to be, a gift to M Charity. The $40, therefore, is deductible as a charitable contribution.

Example 3:

A taxpayer pays $5 for a balcony ticket to the concert described in Example 1. This taxpayer had no intention of using the ticket when he acquired it and he did not, in fact, attend the concert.

No part of the taxpayer's $5 payment to the M Charity is deductible as a charitable contribution. The mere fact that the ticket to the concert was not used does not entitle the taxpayer to any greater right to a deduction than if he did use it. The same result would follow if the taxpayer had made a gift of the ticket to another individual. If the taxpayer desired to support M, but did not intend to use the ticket to the concert, he could have made a qualifying charitable contribution by making a $5 payment to M and refusing to accept the ticket to the concert.

Example 4:

A receives a brochure soliciting contributions for the support of the M Charity. The brochure states: "As a grateful token of appreciation for your help, the M Charity will send to you your choice of one of the several articles listed below, depending upon the amount of your donation." The remainder of the brochure is devoted to a catalog-type listing of articles of merchandise with the suggested amount of donation necessary to receive each particular article. There is no evidence of any significant difference between the suggested donation and the fair market value of any such article. The brochure contains the further notation that all donations to M Charity are tax deductible.

Payments of the suggested amounts solicited by M Charity are not deductible as a charitable contribution. Under the circumstances, the amounts solicited as 'donations' are simply the purchases prices of the articles listed in the brochure.

Example 5:

A taxpayer paid $5 for a ticket which entitled him to a chance to win a new automobile. The raffle was conducted to raise funds for the X Charity. Although the payment for the ticket was solicited as a "contribution" to the X Charity and designated as such of the face of the ticket, no part of the payment is deductible as a charitable contribution. Amounts paid for chances to participate in raffles, lotteries, or similar drawings or to participate in puzzle or other contests for valuable prizes are not gifts in such circumstances, and therefore, do not qualify as deductible charitable contributions.

* * *

Example 8:

In order to raise funds, W Charity plans a theater party consisting of admission to a premiere showing of a motion picture and an after-theater buffet. The advertising material and tickets to the theater party designate $5 as an admission charge and $10 as a gift to W Charity. The established admission charge for premiere showings of motion pictures in the locality is $5.

Notwithstanding W's representations respecting the amount designated as a gift, the specified $10 does not qualify as a deductible charitable contribution because W's allocation fails to take into account the value of admission to the buffet dinner.

Example 9:

The X Charity sponsors a fund-raising bazaar, the articles offered for sale at the bazaar having been contributed to X by persons desiring to support X's charitable programs. The prices for the articles sold at the bazaar are set by a committee of X with a view to charging the full fair market value of the articles.

A taxpayer who purchases articles at the bazaar is not entitled to a charitable contribution deduction for any portion of the amount paid to X for such articles. This is true even though the articles sold at the bazaar are acquired and sold without cost to X and the total proceeds of the sale of the articles are used by X exclusively for charitable purposes.

* * *

Example 12:

To assist the Y Charity in the promotion of a Halloween Ball to raise funds for Y's activities, several individuals in the community agree to pay the entire costs of the event, including the costs of the orchestra, publicity, rental of the ballroom, refreshments, and any other necessary expenses. Various civic organizations and clubs agree to undertake the sale of tickets for the dance. The publicity and solicitations for the sale of the tickets emphasize the fact that the entire cost of the ball is being borne by anonymous patrons of Y and by the other community groups, and that the entire gross receipts from the sale of the tickets, therefore, will go to Y Charity. The price of the tickets, however, is set at the fair market value of admission of the event.

No part of the amount paid for admission to the dance is a gift. Therefore, no part is deductible as a charitable contribution. The fact that the event is conducted entirely without cost to Y Charity and that the full amount of the admission charge goes directly to Y for its uses has no bearing on the deductibility of the amounts paid for admission, but does have a bearing on the deductibility of the amounts paid by the anonymous patrons of the event. The test is not the cost of the event to Y, but the fair market value of the consideration received by the purchaser of the ticket or other privileges for his payment.

Hernandez v. Commissioner

Supreme Court of the United States, 1989.
490 U.S. 680, 109 S.Ct. 2136.

■ JUSTICE MARSHALL delivered the opinion of the Court.

Section 170 of the Internal Revenue Code of 1954 (Code), 26 U.S.C. § 170, permits a taxpayer to deduct from gross income the amount of a "charitable contribution." The Code defines that term as a "contribution or gift" to certain eligible donees, including entities organized and operated exclusively for religious purposes. We granted certiorari to determine whether taxpayers may deduct as charitable contributions payments made to branch churches of the Church of Scientology (Church) in order to receive services known as "auditing" and "training." We hold that such payments are not deductible.

I

Scientology was founded in the 1950's by L. Ron Hubbard. It is propagated today by a "mother church" in California and by numerous branch churches around the world. The mother Church instructs laity, trains and ordains ministers, and creates new congregations. Branch churches, known as "franchises" or "missions," provide Scientology services at the local level, under the supervision of the mother Church.

Scientologists believe that an immortal spiritual being exists in every person. A person becomes aware of this spiritual dimension through a process known as "auditing." Auditing involves a one-to-one encounter between a participant (known as a "preclear") and a Church official (known as an "auditor"). An electronic device, the E-meter, helps the auditor identify the preclear's areas of spiritual difficulty by measuring skin responses during a question and answer session. Although auditing sessions are conducted one on one, the content of each session is not individually tailored. The preclear gains spiritual awareness by progressing through sequential levels of auditing, provided in short blocks of time known as "intensives."

The Church also offers members doctrinal courses known as "training." Participants in these sessions study the tenets of Scientology and seek to attain the qualifications necessary to serve as auditors. Training courses, like auditing sessions, are provided in sequential levels. Scientologists are taught that spiritual gains result from participation in such courses.

The Church charges a "fixed donation," also known as a "price" or a "fixed contribution," for participants to gain access to auditing and training sessions. These charges are set forth in schedules, and prices vary with a session's length and level of sophistication. In 1972, for example, the general rates for auditing ranged from $625 for a 12 1/2–hour auditing intensive, the shortest available, to $4,250 for a 100–hour intensive, the longest available. Specialized types of auditing required higher fixed donations: a 12 1/2–hour "Integrity Processing" auditing intensive cost $750; a 12 1/2–hour "Expanded Dianetics" auditing intensive cost $950. This system of mandatory fixed charges is based on a central tenet of Scientology known as the "doctrine of exchange," according to which any time a person receives something he must pay something back. In so doing, a Scientologist maintains "inflow" and "outflow" and avoids spiritual decline.

The proceeds generated from auditing and training sessions are the Church's primary source of income. The Church promotes these sessions not only through newspaper, magazine, and radio advertisements, but also through free lectures, free personality tests, and leaflets. The Church also encourages, and indeed rewards with a 5% discount, advance payment for these sessions. The Church often refunds unused portions of prepaid auditing or training fees, less an administrative charge.

Petitioners in these consolidated cases each made payments to a branch church for auditing or training sessions. They sought to deduct these payments on their federal income tax returns as charitable contributions under § 170. Respondent Commissioner, the head of the Internal Revenue Service (IRS), disallowed these deductions, finding that the payments were not charitable contributions within the meaning of § 170.

Petitioners sought review of these determinations in the Tax Court. * * * Before trial, the Commissioner stipulated that the branch churches of Scientology are religious organizations entitled to receive tax-deductible charitable contributions under the relevant sections of the Code. This stipulation isolated as the sole statutory issue whether payments for auditing or training sessions constitute "contribution[s] or gift[s]" under § 170.

The Tax Court * * * upheld the Commissioner's decision. It observed first that the term "charitable contribution" in § 170 is synonymous with the word "gift," which case law had defined "as a voluntary transfer of property by the owner to another without consideration therefor." It then determined that petitioners had received consideration for their payments, namely, "the benefit of various religious services provided by the Church of Scientology." The Tax Court also rejected the taxpayers' constitutional challenges based on the Establishment and Free Exercise Clauses of the First Amendment.

The Court of Appeals * * * affirmed. The First Circuit rejected Hernandez's argument that under § 170, the IRS' ordinary inquiry into whether the taxpayer received consideration for his payment should not apply to "the return of a commensurate *religious* benefit, as opposed to an *economic or financial* benefit." The court found "no indication that Congress intended to distinguish the religious benefits sought by Hernandez from the medical, educational, scientific, literary, or other benefits that could likewise provide the quid for the quo of a nondeductible payment to a charitable organization." The court also rejected Hernandez's argument that it was impracticable to put a value on the services he had purchased, noting that the Church itself had "established and advertised monetary prices" for auditing and training sessions, and that Hernandez had not claimed that these prices misstated the cost of providing these sessions.

Hernandez's constitutional claims also failed. Because § 170 created no denominational preference on its face, Hernandez had shown no Establishment Clause violation. As for the Free Exercise Clause challenge, the court determined that denying the deduction did not prevent Hernandez from paying for auditing and training sessions and thereby observing Scientology's doctrine of exchange. Moreover, granting a tax exemption would compromise the integrity and fairness of the tax system.

The Ninth Circuit also found that the taxpayers had received a "measurable, specific return * * * as a quid pro quo for the donation" they had made to the branch churches. The court reached this result by focusing on "the external features" of the auditing and training transactions, an analytic technique which "serves as an expedient for any more intrusive inquiry into the motives of the payor." Whether a particular exchange generated secular or religious benefits to the taxpayer was irrelevant, for under § 170 "[i]t is the structure of the transaction, and not the type of benefit received, that controls."

The Ninth Circuit also rejected the taxpayers' constitutional arguments. The tax deduction provision did not violate the Establishment Clause because § 170 is "neutral in its design" and reflects no intent "to visit a disability on a particular religion." Furthermore, that the taxpayers would "have less money to pay to the Church, or that the Church [would] receive less money, [did] not rise to the level of a burden on appellants' ability to exercise their religious beliefs." Indeed, because the taxpayers could still make charitable donations to the branch church, they were "not put to the choice of abandoning the doctrine of exchange or losing the government benefit, for they may have both." Finally, the court noted that the compelling governmental interest in "the maintenance of a sound and uniform tax system" counseled against granting a free exercise exemption.

We granted certiorari to resolve a Circuit conflict concerning the validity of charitable deductions for auditing and training payments. We now affirm.

II

For over 70 years, federal taxpayers have been allowed to deduct the amount of contributions or gifts to charitable, religious, and other eleemosynary institutions. Section 170, the present provision, was enacted in 1954; it requires a taxpayer claiming the deduction to satisfy a number of conditions. The Commissioner's stipulation in this case, however, has narrowed the statutory inquiry to one such condition: whether petitioners' payments for auditing and training sessions are "contribution[s] or gift[s]" within the meaning of § 170.

The legislative history of the "contribution or gift" limitation, though sparse, reveals that Congress intended to differentiate between unrequited payments to qualified recipients and payments made to such recipients in return for goods or services. Only the former were deemed deductible. The House and Senate Reports on the 1954 tax bill, for example, both define "gifts" as payments "made with no expectation of a financial return commensurate with the amount of the gift." Using payments to hospitals as an example, both Reports state that the gift characterization should not apply to "a payment by an individual to a hospital in consideration of a binding obligation to provide medical treatment for the individual's employees. It would apply only if there were no expectation of any quid pro quo from the hospital."

In ascertaining whether a given payment was made with "the expectation of any quid pro quo," the IRS has customarily examined the external features of the transaction in question. This practice has the advantage of obviating the need for the IRS to conduct imprecise inquiries into the motivations of individual taxpayers. The lower courts have generally embraced this structural analysis. We likewise focused on external features in United States v. American Bar Endowment, to resolve the taxpayers' claims that they were entitled to partial deductions for premiums paid to a charitable organization for insurance coverage; the taxpayers contended that they had paid unusually high premiums in an effort to make a contribution along with their purchase of insurance. We upheld the Commissioner's disallowance of the partial deductions because the taxpayers had failed to demonstrate, at a minimum, the existence of comparable insurance policies with prices lower than those of the policy they had each purchased. In so doing, we stressed that "[t]he sine qua non of a charitable contribution is a transfer of money or property *without adequate consideration.*"

In light of this understanding of § 170, it is readily apparent that petitioners' payments to the Church do not qualify as "contribution[s] or gift[s]." As the Tax Court found, these payments were part of a quintessential quid pro quo exchange: in return for their money, petitioners received an identifiable benefit, namely, auditing and training sessions. The Church established fixed price schedules for auditing and training sessions in each branch church; it calibrated particular prices to auditing or training sessions of particular lengths and levels of sophistication; it returned a refund if auditing and training services went unperformed; it distributed "account cards" on which persons who had paid money to the Church could monitor what prepaid services they had not yet claimed; and it categorically barred provision of auditing or training sessions for free. Each of these practices reveals the inherently reciprocal nature of the exchange.

Petitioners do not argue that such a structural analysis is inappropriate under § 170, or that the external features of the auditing and training transactions do not strongly suggest a quid pro quo exchange. Indeed, the petitioners in the consolidated Graham case conceded at trial that they expected to receive specific amounts of auditing and training in return for their payments. Petitioners argue instead that they are entitled to deductions because a quid pro quo analysis is inappropriate under § 170 when the benefit a taxpayer receives is purely religious in nature. Along the same lines, petitioners claim that payments made for the right to participate in a religious service should be automatically deductible under § 170.

We cannot accept this statutory argument for several reasons. First, it finds no support in the language of § 170. Whether or not Congress could, consistent with the Establishment Clause, provide for the automatic deductibility of a payment made to a church that either generates religious benefits or guarantees access to a religious service, that is a choice Congress has thus far declined to make. Instead, Congress has specified that a payment to an organization operated exclusively for religious (or other eleemosynary) purposes is deductible only if such a payment is a "contribution or gift." 26 U.S.C. § 170(c). The Code makes no special preference for payments made in the expectation of gaining religious benefits or access to a religious service. The House and Senate Reports on § 170, and the other legislative history of that provision, offer no indication that Congress' failure to enact such a preference was an oversight.

Second, petitioners' deductibility proposal would expand the charitable contribution deduction far beyond what Congress has provided. Numerous forms of payments to eligible donees plausibly could be categorized as providing a religious benefit or as securing access to a religious service. For example, some taxpayers might regard their tuition payments to parochial schools as generating a religious benefit or as securing access to a religious service; such payments, however, have long been held not to be charitable contributions under § 170. Taxpayers might make similar claims about payments for church-sponsored counseling sessions or for medical care at church-affiliated hospitals that otherwise might not be deductible. Given that, under the First Amendment, the IRS can reject otherwise valid claims of religious benefit only on the ground that a taxpayers' alleged beliefs are not sincerely held, but not on the ground that such beliefs are inherently irreligious, the resulting tax deductions would likely expand the charitable contribution provision far beyond its present size. We are loath to effect this result in the absence of supportive congressional intent.

Finally, the deduction petitioners seek might raise problems of entanglement between church and state. If framed as a deduction for those payments generating benefits of a religious nature for the payor, petitioners' proposal would inexorably force the IRS and reviewing courts to differentiate "religious" benefits from "secular" ones. If framed as a deduction for those payments made in connection with a religious service, petitioners' proposal would force the IRS and the judiciary into differentiating "religious" services from "secular" ones. We need pass no judgment now on the constitutionality of such hypothetical inquiries, but we do note that "pervasive monitoring" for "the subtle or overt presence of religious matter" is a central danger against which we have held the Establishment Clause guards. * * *

Accordingly, we conclude that petitioners' payments to the Church for auditing and training sessions are not "contribution[s] or gift[s]" within the meaning of that statutory expression.[10]

III

We turn now to petitioners' constitutional claims based on the Establishment Clause and the Free Exercise Clause of the First Amendment. [The Court rejected the taxpayers' constitutional arguments. As for the Establishment Clause claim, the Court concluded that § 170 was neutral in design and purpose and neither advanced nor inhibited religion. It found no risk of excessive entanglement from the IRS ascertaining whether a pay-

---

10. Petitioners have not argued here that their payments qualify as "dual payments" under IRS regulations and that they are therefore entitled to a partial deduction to the extent their payments exceeded the value of the benefit received. See American Bar Endowment, 477 U.S., at 117, 106 S.Ct., at 2433 (citing Rev.Rul. 67–246, 1967–2 Cum. Bull. 104). We thus have no occasion to decide this issue.

ment to the church as part of a quid pro quo transaction. The Court also brushed aside the taxpayers' contention that disallowing their charitable deductions violated their right to the free exercise of religion by placing a heavy burden on the central practice of Scientology. Even if the burden were substantial, the Court concluded, it was justified by the broad public interest in maintaining a sound tax system, free of exceptions flowing from a wide range of religious beliefs. The Court then turned to the taxpayers' selective prosecution claim. Eds.]

IV

* * *

In their arguments to this Court, petitioners have shifted emphasis. They now make two closely related claims. First, the IRS has accorded payments for auditing and training disparately harsh treatment compared to payments to other churches and synagogues for their religious services: Recognition of a comparable deduction for auditing and training payments is necessary to cure this administrative inconsistency. Second, Congress, in modifying § 170 over the years, has impliedly acquiesced in the deductibility of payments to these other faiths; because payments for auditing and training are indistinguishable from these other payments, they fall within the principle acquiesced in by Congress that payments for religious services are deductible under § 170.

Although the Commission demurred at oral argument as to whether the IRS, in fact, permits taxpayers to deduct payments made to purchase services from other churches and synagogues, the Commissioner's periodic revenue rulings have stated the IRS' position rather clearly. A 1971 ruling, still in effect, states: "Pew rents, building fund assessments, and periodic dues paid to a church * * * are all methods of making contributions to the church, and such payments are deductible as charitable contributions within the limitations set out in section 170 of the Code." Rev.Rul. 70–47, 1970–1 Cum.Bull. 49. We also assume for purposes of argument that the IRS also allows taxpayers to deduct "specified payments for attendance at High Holy Day services, for tithes, for torah readings and for memorial plaques."

The development of the present litigation, however, makes it impossible for us to resolve petitioners' claim that they have received unjustifiably harsh treatment compared to adherents of other religions. The relevant inquiry in determining whether a payment is a "contribution or gift" under § 170 is, as we have noted, not whether the payment secures religious benefits or access to religious services, but whether the transaction in which the payment is involved is structured as a quid pro quo exchange. To make such a determination in this case, the Tax Court heard testimony and received documentary proof as to the terms and structure of the auditing and training transactions; from this evidence it made factual findings upon which it based its conclusion of nondeductibility, a conclusion we have held consonant with § 170 and with the First Amendment.

Perhaps because the theory of administrative inconsistency emerged only on appeal, petitioners did not endeavor at trial to adduce from the IRS or other sources any specific evidence about other religious faiths' transactions. The IRS' revenue rulings, which merely state the agency's conclusions as to deductibility and which have apparently never been reviewed by the Tax Court or any other judicial body, also provide no specific facts about the nature of these other faiths' transactions. In the absence of such facts, we simply have no way (other than the wholly illegitimate one of relying on our personal experiences and observations) to appraise accurately whether the IRS' revenue rulings have correctly applied a quid pro quo analysis with respect to any or all of the religious practices in question. We do not know, for example, whether payments for other faiths' services are truly obligatory or whether any or all of these services are generally provided whether or not the encouraged "mandatory" payment is made.

The IRS' application of the "contribution or gift" standard may be right or wrong with respect to these other faiths, or it may be right with respect to some religious practices and wrong with respect to others. It may also be that some of these payments are appropriately classified as partially deductible "dual payments." With respect to those religions where the structure of transactions involving religious services is established not centrally but by individual congregations, the proper point of reference for a quid pro quo analysis might be the individual congregation, not the religion as a whole. Only upon a proper factual record could we make these determinations. Absent such a record, we must reject petitioners' administrative consistency argument.

Petitioners' congressional acquiescence claim fails for similar reasons. Even if one assumes that Congress has acquiesced in the IRS' ruling with respect to "[p]ew rents, building fund assessments, and periodic dues," Rev.Rul. 70–47, 1970–1 Cum.Bull. 49, the fact is that the IRS' 1971 ruling articulates no broad principle of deductibility, but instead merely identifies as deductible three discrete types of payments. Having before us no information about the nature or structure of these three payments, we have no way of discerning any possible unifying principle, let alone whether such a principle would embrace payments for auditing and training sessions.

V

For the reasons stated herein, the judgments of the Courts of Appeals are hereby

Affirmed.

■ JUSTICE BRENNAN and JUSTICE KENNEDY took no part in the consideration or decision of these cases.

■ JUSTICE O'CONNOR, with whom JUSTICE SCALIA joins, dissenting.

The Court today acquiesces in the decision of the Internal Revenue Service (IRS) to manufacture a singular exception to its 70–year practice of allowing fixed payments indistinguishable from those made by petitioners to be deducted as charitable contributions. Because the IRS cannot constitutionally be allowed to select which religions will receive the benefit of its past rulings, I respectfully dissent.

The cases before the Court have an air of artificiality about them that is due to the IRS' dual litigation strategy against the Church of Scientology (Church). As the Court notes, the IRS has successfully argued that the mother Church of Scientology was not a tax-exempt organization from 1970 to 1972 because it had diverted profits to the founder of Scientology and others, conspired to impede collection of its taxes, and conducted almost all of its activities for a commercial purpose. In the cases before the Court today, however, the IRS decided to contest the payments made to Scientology under 26 U.S.C. § 170 rather than challenge the tax-exempt status of the various branches of the Church to which the payments were made. According to the Deputy Solicitor General, the IRS challenged the payments themselves in order to expedite matters. As part of its litigation strategy in these cases, the IRS agreed to several stipulations which, in my view, necessarily determine the proper approach to the questions presented by petitioners.

The stipulations, relegated to a single sentence by the Court, established that Scientology was at all relevant times a religion; that each Scientology branch to which payments were made was at all relevant times a "church" within the meaning of § 170(b)(1)(A)(i); and that Scientology was at all times a "corporation" within the meaning of § 170(c)(2) and exempt from general income taxation under 26 U.S.C. § 501(a). As the Solicitor General recognizes, it follows from these stipulations that Scientology operates for "charitable purposes" and puts the "public interest above the private interest." Moreover, the stipulations establish that the payments made by petitioners are fixed donations made by individuals to a tax-exempt religious organization in order to participate in religious services, and are not based on "market prices set to reap the profits of a commercial moneymaking venture." The Tax Court, however, appears to have ignored the stipulations. It concluded, perhaps relying on its previous opinion in Church of Scientology, that "Scientology operates in a commercial manner in providing [auditing and training]. In fact, one of its articulated goals is to make money." The Solicitor General has duplicated the error here, referring on numerous occasions to the commercial nature of Scientology in an attempt to negate the effect of the stipulations.

It must be emphasized that the IRS' position here is not based upon the contention that a portion of the knowledge received from auditing or training is of secular, commercial, nonreligious value. Thus, the denial of a deduction in these cases bears no resemblance to the denial of a deduction for religious-school tuition up to the market value of the secularly useful education received. Here the IRS denies deductibility solely on the basis that the exchange is a quid pro quo, even though the quid is exclusively of spiritual or religious worth. Respondent cites no instances in which this has been done before, and there are good reasons why.

When a taxpayer claims as a charitable deduction part of a fixed amount given to a charitable organization in exchange for benefits that have a commercial value, the allowable portion of that claim is computed by subtracting from the total amount paid the value of the physical benefit received. If at a charity sale one purchases for $1,000 a painting whose market value is demonstrably no more than $50, there has been a contribution of $950. The same would be true if one purchases a $1,000 seat at a charitable dinner where the food is worth $50. An identical calculation can be made where the quid received is not a painting or a meal, but an intangible such as entertainment, so long as that intangible has some market value established in a noncontributory context. Hence, one who purchases a ticket to a concert, at the going rate for concerts by the particular performers, makes a charitable contribution of zero even if it is announced in advance that all proceeds from the ticket sales will go to charity. The performers may have made a charitable contribution, but the audience has paid the going rate for a show.

It becomes impossible, however, to compute the "contribution" portion of a payment to a charity where what is received in return is not merely an intangible, but an intangible (or, for that matter a tangible) that is not bought and sold except in donative contexts so that the only "market" price against which it can be evaluated is a market price that always includes donations. Suppose, for example, that the charitable organization that traditionally solicits donations on Veterans Day, in exchange for which it gives the donor an imitation poppy bearing its name, were to establish a flat rule that no one gets a poppy without a donation of at least $10. One would have to say that the "market" rate for such poppies was $10, but it would assuredly not be true that everyone who "bought" a poppy for $10 made no contribution. Similarly, if one buys a $100 seat at a prayer breakfast receiving as the quid pro quo food for both body and soul-it would make no sense to say that no charitable contribution whatever has occurred simply because the "going rate" for all prayer breakfasts (with equivalent bodily food) is $100. The latter may well be true, but that "going rate" includes a contribution.

Confronted with this difficulty, and with the constitutional necessity of not making irrational distinctions among taxpayers, and with the even higher standard of equality of treatment among religions that the First Amendment imposes, the Government has only two practicable options with regard to distinctively religious quids pro quo: to disregard them all, or to tax them all. Over the years it has chosen the former course.

Congress enacted the first charitable contribution exception to income taxation in 1917. A mere two years later, in A.R.M. 2, 1 Cum.Bull. 150 (1919), the IRS gave its first blessing to the deductions of fixed payments to religious organizations as charitable contributions:

> "[T]he distinction of pew rents, assessments, church dues, and the like from basket collections is hardly warranted by the act. The act reads 'contributions' and 'gifts.' It is felt that all of these come within the two terms.

"In substance it is believed that these are simply methods of contributing although in form they may vary. Is a basket collection given involuntarily to be distinguished from an envelope system, the latter being regarded as 'dues'? From a technical angle, the pew rents may be differentiated, but in practice the so-called 'personal accommodation' they may afford is conjectural. It is believed that the real intent is to contribute and not to hire a seat or pew for personal accommodation. In fact, basket contributors sometimes receive the same accommodation informally."

The IRS reaffirmed its position in 1970, ruling that "[p]ew rents, building fund assessments and periodic dues paid to a church * * * are all methods of making contributions to the church and such payments are deductible as charitable contributions." Rev.Rul. 70–47, 1970–1 Cum.Bull. 49. similarly, notwithstanding the "form" of mass stipends as fixed payments for specific religious services, the irs has allowed charitable deductions of such payments. See Rev.Rul. 78–366, 1978–2 Cum.Bull. 241.

These rulings, which are "official interpretation[s] of [the tax laws] by the [IRS]," flatly contradict the Solicitor General's claim that there "is no administrative practice recognizing that payments made in exchange for religious benefits are tax deductible." Indeed, an Assistant Commissioner of the IRS recently explained in a "question and answer guidance package" to tax-exempt organizations that "[i]n contrast to tuition payments, religious observances generally are not regarded as yielding private benefits to the donor, who is viewed as receiving only incidental benefits when attending the observances. The primary beneficiaries are viewed as being the general public and members of the faith. Thus, payments for saying masses, pew rents, tithes, and other payments involving fixed donations for similar religious services, are fully deductible contributions." Although this guidance package may not be as authoritative as IRS rulings, in the absence of any contrary indications it does reflect the continuing adherence of the IRS to its practice of allowing deductions for fixed payments for religious services.

There can be no doubt that at least some of the fixed payments which the IRS has treated as charitable deductions, or which the Court assumes the IRS would allow taxpayers to deduct, are as "inherently reciprocal," as the payments for auditing at issue here. In exchange for their payment of pew rents, Christians receive particular seats during worship services. Similarly, in some synagogues attendance at the worship services for Jewish High Holy Days is often predicated upon the purchase of a general admission ticket or a reserved seat ticket. See J. Feldman, H. Fruhauf, & M. Schoen, Temple Management Manual, ch. 4, p. 10 (1984). Religious honors such as publicly reading from Scripture are purchased or auctioned periodically in some synagogues of Jews from Morocco and Syria. See H. Dobrinsky, A Treasury of Sephardic Laws and Customs 164, 175–177 (1986). Mormons must tithe their income as a necessary but not sufficient condition to obtaining a "temple recommend," i.e., the right to be admitted into the temple. See The Book of Mormon, 3 Nephi 24:7–12 (1921);

Reorganized Church of Jesus Christ of Latter-day Saints, Book of Doctrine and Covenants § 106:1b (1978); * * *. A Mass stipend—a fixed payment given to a Catholic priest, in consideration of which he is obliged to apply the fruits of the Mass for the intention of the donor—has similar overtones of exchange. According to some Catholic theologians, the nature of the pact between a priest and a donor who pays a Mass stipend is "a bilateral contract known as do ut facias. One person agrees to give while the other party agrees to do something in return." 13 New Catholic Encyclopedia, Mass Stipend, p. 715 (1967). A finer example of a quid pro quo exchange would be hard to formulate.

This is not a situation where the IRS has explicitly and affirmatively reevaluated its longstanding interpretation of § 170 and decided to analyze all fixed religious contributions under a quid pro quo standard. There is no indication whatever that the IRS has abandoned its 70–year practice with respect to payments made by those other than Scientologists. In 1978, when it ruled that payments for auditing and training were not charitable contributions under § 170, the IRS did not cite—much less try to reconcile-its previous rulings concerning the deductibility of other forms of fixed payments for religious services or practices. See Rev.Rul. 78–189, 1978–1 Cum.Bull. 68 (equating payments for auditing with tuition paid to religious schools).

Nevertheless, respondent now attempts to reconcile his previous rulings with his decision in these cases by relying on a distinction between direct and incidental benefits in exchange for payments made to a charitable organization. This distinction, adumbrated as early as the IRS' 1919 ruling, recognizes that even a deductible charitable contribution may generate certain benefits for the donor. As long as the benefits remain "incidental" and do not indicate that the payment was actually made for the "personal accommodation" of the donor, the payment will be deductible. It is respondent's view that the payments made by petitioners should not be deductible under § 170 because the "unusual facts in these cases * * * demonstrate that the payments were made primarily for 'personal accommodation.' "Specifically, the Solicitor General asserts that "the rigid connection between the provision of auditing and training services and payment of the fixed price" indicates a quid pro quo relationship and "reflect[s] the value that petitioners expected to receive for their money."

There is no discernible reason why there is a more rigid connection between payment and services in the religious practices of Scientology than in the religious practices of the faiths described above. Neither has respondent explained why the benefit received by a Christian who obtains the pew of his or her choice by paying a rental fee, a Jew who gains entrance to High Holy Day services by purchasing a ticket, a Mormon who makes the fixed payment necessary for a temple recommend, or a Catholic who pays a Mass stipend, is incidental to the real benefit conferred on the "general public and members of the faith," while the benefit received by a Scientologist from auditing is a personal accommodation. If the perceived difference lies in the fact that Christians and Jews worship in congregations, whereas

Scientologists, in a manner reminiscent of Eastern religions, gain awareness of the "immortal spiritual being" within them in one-to-one sessions
with auditors, such a distinction would raise serious Establishment Clause
problems. The distinction is no more legitimate if it is based on the fact
that congregational worship services "would be said anyway," without the
payment of a pew rental or stipend or tithe by a particular adherent. The
relevant comparison between Scientology and other religions must be
between the Scientologist undergoing auditing or training on one hand and
the congregation on the other. For some religions the central importance of
the congregation achieves legal dimensions. In Orthodox Judaism, for
example, certain worship services cannot be performed and Scripture
cannot be read publicly without the presence of at least 10 men. 12
Encyclopaedia Judaica, Minyan, p. 68 (1972). If payments for participation
occurred in such a setting, would the benefit to the 10th man be only
incidental while for the personal accommodation of the 11th? In the same
vein, will the deductibility of a Mass stipend turn on whether there are
other congregants to hear the Mass? And conversely, does the fact that the
payment of a tithe by a Mormon is an absolute prerequisite to admission to
the temple make that payment for admission a personal accommodation
regardless of the size of the congregation?

Given the IRS' stance in these cases, it is an understatement to say
that with respect to fixed payments for religious services "the line between
the taxable and the immune has been drawn by an unsteady hand." This is
not a situation in which a governmental regulation "happens to coincide or
harmonize with the tenets of some or all religions," but does not violate the
Establishment Clause because it is founded on a neutral, secular basis.
Rather, it involves the differential application of a standard based on
constitutionally impermissible differences drawn by the Government
among religions. As such, it is best characterized as a case of the Government "put[ting] an imprimatur on [all but] one religion." That the Government may not do.

The Court attempts to downplay the constitutional difficulty created by
the IRS' different treatment of other fixed payments for religious services
by accepting the Solicitor General's invitation to let the IRS make case-
specific quid pro quo determinations. * * * As a practical matter, I do not
think that this unprincipled approach will prove helpful. The Solicitor
General was confident enough in his brief to argue that, "even without
making a detailed factual inquiry," Mormon tithing does not involve a quid
pro quo arrangement. At oral argument, however, the Deputy Solicitor
General conceded that if it was mandatory, tithing would be distinguishable
from the "ordinary case of church dues." If the approach suggested by the
Solicitor General is so malleable and indefinite, it is not a panacea and
cannot be trusted to secure First Amendment rights against arbitrary
incursions by the Government.

On a more fundamental level, the Court cannot abjure its responsibility to address serious constitutional problems by converting a violation of
the Establishment Clause into an "administrative consistency argument,"

with an inadequate record. It has chosen to ignore both longstanding, clearly articulated IRS practice, and the failure of the respondent to offer any cogent, neutral explanation for the IRS' refusal to apply this practice to the Church of Scientology. Instead, the Court has pretended that whatever errors in application the IRS has committed are hidden from its gaze and will, in any event, be rectified in due time.

In my view, the IRS has misapplied its longstanding practice of allowing charitable contributions under § 170 in a way that violates the Establishment Clause. It has unconstitutionally refused to allow payments for the religious service of auditing to be deducted as charitable contributions in the same way it has allowed fixed payments to other religions to be deducted. Just as the Minnesota statute at issue in Larson v. Valente, 456 U.S. 228, 102 S.Ct. 1673, 72 L.Ed.2d 33 (1982), discriminated against the Unification Church, the IRS' application of the quid pro quo standard here—and only here—discriminates against the Church of Scientology. I would reverse the decisions below.

Sklar v. Commissioner

United States Court of Appeals, Ninth Circuit, 2002.
282 F.3d 610.

AMENDED OPINION

■ REINHARDT, CIRCUIT JUDGE.

The taxpayer-petitioners in this action, Michael and Marla Sklar, challenge the Internal Revenue Service's ("IRS") disallowance of their deductions, as charitable contributions, of part of the tuition payments made to their children's religious schools. In the notice of deficiency sent to the Sklars, the IRS explained that "[s]ince these costs are personal tuition expenses, they are not deductible." Specifically, the Sklars sought to deduct 55% of the tuition, on the basis that this represented the proportion of the school day allocated to religious education. The Sklars contend that these costs are deductible under section 170 of the Internal Revenue Code, as payments for which they have received "solely intangible religious benefits." They also argue that they should receive this deduction because the IRS permits similar deductions to the Church of Scientology, and it is a violation of administrative consistency and of the Establishment Clause to deny them, as Orthodox Jews, the same deduction.

The Tax Court found that under De Jong v. Commissioner, 309 F.2d 373, 376 (9th Cir.1962), tuition paid for the education of a taxpayer's children is a personal expense which is non-deductible under § 170. The Tax Court also rejected the administrative inconsistency argument and the Establishment Clause claim, and ruled inadmissible several documents supporting the Sklars' contentions with respect to the Church of Scientology on the ground that the Sklars are not similarly situated to the members of the Church of Scientology. The Sklars filed this timely appeal.

We review the Tax Court's conclusions of law and its construction of the tax code de novo, and no deference is owed that court on its application of the law.

I.   The Provisions of the Tax Code Governing Charitable Contribution Deductions Do Not Appear to Permit the Deduction Claimed by the Sklars

The Sklars assert that the deduction they claimed is allowable under section 170 of the Internal Revenue Code which permits taxpayers to deduct, as a charitable contribution, a "contribution or gift" to certain tax-exempt organizations. Not only has the Supreme Court held that, generally, a payment for which one receives consideration does not constitute a "contribution or gift" for purposes of § 170, see United States v. American Bar Endowment, 477 U.S. 105, 118, 106 S.Ct. 2426, 91 L.Ed.2d 89 (1986) (stressing that "[t]he *sine qua non* of a charitable contribution is a transfer of money or property without adequate consideration"), but it has explicitly rejected the contention made here by the Sklars: that there is an exception in the Code for payments for which one receives only religious benefits in return. Hernandez v. Commissioner, 490 U.S. 680, 109 S.Ct. 2136, 104 L.Ed.2d 766 (1989). The taxpayers in *Hernandez,* members of the Church of Scientology, sought to deduct, as charitable contributions under § 170(c), payments made by them to the Church of Scientology in exchange for the religious exercises of "auditing" and "training."[1] The Court affirmed the Tax Court's reading of the statute disallowing the deductions on the following three grounds: (1) Congress had shown no preference in the Internal Revenue Code for payments made in exchange for religious benefits as opposed to other benefits, 490 U.S. at 692–93, 109 S.Ct. 2136; (2) to permit the deductions the taxpayers demanded would begin a slippery slope of expansion of the charitable contribution deduction beyond what Congress intended, 490 U.S. at 693, 109 S.Ct. 2136; and (3) to permit these deductions could entangle the IRS and the government in the affairs and beliefs of various religious faiths and organizations in violation of the constitutional principle of the separation of church and state, 490 U.S. at 694, 109 S.Ct. 2136. Specifically, the Supreme Court stated that to permit these deductions might force the IRS to engage in a searching inquiry of whether a particular benefit received was "religious" or "secular" in order to determine its deductibility, a process which, the Court said, might violate the Establishment Clause. Hernandez, 490 U.S. at 694, 109 S.Ct. 2136.

Despite the clear statutory holding of *Hernandez,* the Sklars contend that recent changes to the Internal Revenue Code have clarified Congressional intent with respect to the deductibility of these payments. We seriously doubt the validity of this argument. The amendments to the Code

---

1. The Supreme Court, in *Hernandez,* described "auditing" as the process by which, through a one-to-one encounter with a Church of Scientology official, one becomes aware of his spiritual dimension. 490 U.S. at 684–85, 109 S.Ct. 2136. The Court describes "training" as one of several "doctrinal courses" in which members study the tenets of the faith and train to become the leaders of auditing sessions. 490 U.S. at 685, 109 S.Ct. 2136.

appear not to have changed the substantive definition of a deductible charitable contribution, but only to have enacted additional documentation requirements for claimed deductions. Omnibus Budget Reconciliation Act of 1993 ("OBRA 93"), P.L. No. 103–66, 107 Stat. 312 (codified as amended in scattered sections of 26 U.S.C.). Section 170(f) of the Code adds a new requirement that taxpayers claiming a charitable contribution deduction obtain from the donee an estimate of the value of any goods and services received in return for the donation, and exempts *from that new estimate requirement* contributions for which solely intangible religious benefits are received.[2] I.R.C. § 170(f)(8)(A) & (B)(ii). Similarly, § 6115 requires that tax-exempt organizations inform taxpayer-donors that they will receive a tax deduction only for the amount of their donation above the value of any goods or services received in return for the donation and requires donee organizations to give donors an estimate of this value, exempting *from this estimate requirement* contributions for which solely intangible religious benefits are received.

Given the clear holding of *Hernandez* and the absence of any direct evidence of Congressional intent to overrule the Supreme Court on this issue, we would be extremely reluctant to read an additional and significant substantive deduction into the statute based on what are clearly procedural provisions regarding the documentation of tax return information, particularly where the deduction would be of doubtful constitutional validity. *Hernandez,* 490 U.S. at 694, 109 S.Ct. 2136; see Lemon v. Kurtzman, 403 U.S. 602, 612–13, 91 S.Ct. 2105, 29 L.Ed.2d 745 (1971) (holding that a statute is unconstitutional under the Establishment Clause if it fosters "an excessive government entanglement with religion"). We need not, however, decide this issue definitively in this case.[3]

II. The IRS Policy Regarding the Church of Scientology May Not Be Withheld from Public Scrutiny and Appears to Violate the Establishment Clause; Further, It Appears That the Sklars Have Not Made Out a Claim of Administrative Inconsistency

Additionally, the Sklars claim that the IRS engages in a "policy" of permitting members of the Church of Scientology to deduct as charitable

---

2. Section 170(f)(8)(C) permits the donee organization to provide this acknowledgment information to the IRS directly on its own tax return instead, thereby relieving the donor of this obligation.

3. Our concurring colleague may well be correct that *Hernandez* is still controlling of this case and that § 170 has not been amended to permit deductions of contributions for which the consideration consists of "intangible religious benefits." As we have stated in the text, we are strongly inclined to that view ourselves. However, we need not issue a definitive holding on the effect of the statutory amendments here, because we can

reject the Sklars' claim on the ground that they have failed to satisfy the requirements for the partial deductibility of dual payments set out in United States v. American Bar Endowment, 477 U.S. 105, 106 S.Ct. 2426, 91 L.Ed.2d 89 (1986). Anderson v. United States, 417 U.S. 211, 218, 94 S.Ct. 2253, 41 L.Ed.2d 20 (finding it "inadvisable ... reach out ... to pass on important questions of statutory construction when simpler, and more settled, grounds are available for deciding the case at hand"). See Section IV, infra (rejecting the Sklars' claim on the "dual payment" ground).

contributions, payments made for "auditing," "training," and other quali- fied religious services, and that the agency's refusal to grant similar religious deductions to members of other faiths violates the Establishment Clause and is administratively inconsistent. They assert that the "policy" is contained in a "closing agreement"[4] that the IRS signed with the Church of Scientology in 1993, shortly after the *Hernandez* decision and the 1993 changes to § 170 of the Internal Revenue Code.[5] Because the IRS errone- ously asserted that it is prohibited from disclosing all or any part of the closing agreement, we assume, for purposes of resolving this case, the truthfulness of the Sklars' allegations regarding the terms of that agree- ment. However, rather than concluding that the IRS's pro-Scientology policy would require it to adopt similar provisions for all other religions, we would likely conclude, were we to reach the issue, that the policy must be invalidated on the ground that it violates either the Internal Revenue Code or the Establishment Clause. See Hernandez, 490 U.S. at 694, 109 S.Ct. 2136; Lemon v. Kurtzman, 403 U.S. at 612–13, 91 S.Ct. 2105.

A. The IRS's Refusal to Disclose the Terms of Its Closing Agreement with the Church of Scientology

We are required, for purposes of our analysis, to assume the contents of the IRS's policy towards the Church of Scientology, because of the IRS's refusal to reveal to the Sklars, to this court, or even to the Department of Justice,[6] the contents of its closing agreement, although that agreement has apparently been reprinted in the Wall Street Journal. See Scientologists and IRS Settle for $12.5 Million, Wall St. J., Dec. 30, 1997, at A12; agreement reprinted in Wall St. J. Interactive Edition (www.wsj.com). The IRS insists that the closing agreement in this case cannot be disclosed as it contains return information which the IRS is required to keep confidential under I.R.C. § 6103. Under § 6103, the IRS is prohibited from disclosing "return information," which is defined to include closing agreements. I.R.C. § 6103(2). The prohibitions of § 6103 are subject to § 6104, where that provision applies, and § 6104 mandates public disclosure by each tax- exempt entity of its application for tax exemption (which itself contains detailed financial information about the entity, including revenues and expenses) as well as all documentation in support of that application. § 6104(a)(1)(A). * * * [The court then discussed whether or not IRS disclosure of closing agreements was categorically prohibited or required. It

---

4. Closing agreements are governed by I.R.C. § 7121, which permits the IRS to enter into "an agreement in writing with any per- son relating to the liability of such person (or of the person or estate for whom he acts) in respect of any internal revenue tax for any taxable period." I.R.C. § 7121(a); 26 C.F.R. § 301–7121–1.

5. The year 1993 also saw the issuance by the IRS of *Church of Scientology,* Revenue Ruling 93–73, 1993 WL 436350 (RRU Nov. 1, 1993), which declared "obsolete" *Church of*

Scientology, Revenue Ruling 78–189, 1978 WL 42290 (RRU 1978), which had explicitly prohibited the deduction of the costs of audit- ing, training and other courses in the Church of Scientology as charitable contribution de- ductions under § 170.

6. At oral argument the Justice Depart- ment lawyer specifically represented to the court that the Department of Justice has not been informed of the contents of the agree- ment, even for purposes of this appeal, be- cause the IRS deems it to be confidential.

concluded that disclosure was not categorically prohibited by § 6103 and, "in appropriate circumstances," such as the Scientology settlement, disclosure may be required under § 6104 "or otherwise." The court then offered the following public policy justification for disclosure of closing agreements. Eds.]

Third, where a closing agreement sets out a new policy and contains rules of general applicability to a class of taxpayers, disclosure of at least the relevant part of that agreement is required in the interest of public policy. That this is the IRS's understanding as well is demonstrated by the fact that public disclosure has been a requirement contained in at least two such policymaking closing agreements. The IRS required publication of its closing agreement with Hermann Hospital of Houston, Texas, a tax-exempt entity, concluded following the hospital's disclosure to the IRS of certain physician recruitment practices which might have constituted prohibited transactions for a tax-exempt entity. John W. Leggett, Physician Recruitment and Retention by Tax Exempt Hospitals: The Hermann Hospital Physician Recruitment Guidelines, 8 Health Law. 1, 6 (Spring 1995). Under the closing agreement, the hospital was required to engage only in permissible physician recruitment activities, as detailed extensively in an attached set of "Guidelines." Public disclosure of the closing agreement put other non-profit hospitals on notice of the IRS's definition of permissible physician recruitment activities.[11] That such was the purpose of requiring publication is clear from the fact that the agreement included provisions that did not apply to Hermann Hospital, but that might in the future be applicable to other tax-exempt hospitals. Similarly, publication on the Internet was required of the IRS's closing agreement with the Kamehameha Schools Bishop Estate, a tax-exempt educational trust in Hawaii. The agreement was concluded after the IRS threatened to revoke the trust's tax-exempt status because the trustees had engaged in serious financial misconduct and self-dealing. Evelyn Brody, A Taxing Time for the Bishop Estate: What is the I.R.S. Role in Charity Governance?, 21 U. Haw. L. Rev. 537, 539–540 (1999). It required that the incumbent trustees be removed, that the estate pay a penalty of nine million dollars, and that future governance of the estate conform to the agreement's provisions, including restrictions on who could become trustees and a requirement that the estate make its financial records publicly available. Brody at 539–40. Because the IRS had not traditionally intervened to this extent in matters of estate governance, the publication of the closing agreement served to put the members of other trusts on notice that the failure to administer trusts along the lines that the IRS required of the Bishop Estate might lead to loss of tax-exempt status.[12] Here, there is a strong public interest in the

---

11. See Robert C. Louthian III, and Elizabeth M. Mills, Physician Recruitment after Hermann Hospital, 4 Annals Health L. 1, *5–* 6 (1995) (discussing the fact that IRS was well within its authority to require disclosure of the agreement and that although closing agreements have no legal precedential value, the Hermann Hospital closing agreement will likely affect both how tax-exempt hospitals conduct their affairs and how IRS agents evaluate the activities of tax-exempt hospitals).

12. Evelyn Brody, The Limits of Charity Fiduciary Law, 57 Md. L. Rev. 1400, 1410–

disclosure of the contents of the IRS's agreement with the Church of Scientology, especially as the agreement establishes a new policy governing charitable contributions to a particular religious organization which, while the pertinent statute may be unclear, clearly contravenes a prior Supreme Court holding.

Therefore, we reject the argument that the closing agreement made with the Church of Scientology, or at least the portion establishing rules or policies that are applicable to Scientology members generally, is not subject to public disclosure. The IRS is simply not free to enter into closing agreements with religious or other tax-exempt organizations governing the deductions that will be available to their members and to keep such provisions secret from the courts, the Congress, and the public.[13]

B. The Constitutionality of the IRS's Agreement with the Church of Scientology

[The court then considered whether the IRS concession to the Church of Scientology constituted an unconstitutional denominational preference and, if so, whether such a discriminatory policy was justified by a compelling governmental interest. After some discussion, the court decided that it need not reach the constitutional issue because, in all events, the Sklars failed to show that their tuition payments constituted a partially deductible "dual payment" under the Tax Code. Ed.]

III. The Sklars' Tuition Payments Do Not Constitute Partially Deductible "Dual Payments" Under the Tax Code

A "dual payment" (or "quid pro quo payment") under the Tax Code is a payment made in part in consideration for goods and services, and in part as a charitable contribution. I.R.C. § 6115. For example, the purchase, for seventy-five dollars, of an item worth five dollars at a charity auction would constitute a dual payment: five dollars in consideration for goods, and seventy dollars as a charitable contribution. The IRS permits a deduction under § 170 for the portion of a dual payment that consists of a charitable contribution, but not for the portion for which the taxpayer receives a benefit in return. Although the Sklars concede that they received a benefit for their tuition payments, in that their children received a secular education, they claim that part of the payment—the part attributable to their

1411 & n. 49 (1998) ("Lately, perhaps responding to criticism that closing agreements create a secret body of law, some [IRS] regulators have conditioned settlement on the charity's assenting to public disclosure of the agreement.").

13. We believe that the Tax Court's ruling that the closing agreement is not relevant is in all likelihood correct. The Tax Court concluded that the Sklars were not similarly situated to the members of the Church of Scientology who benefitted from the closing agreement. While we have no doubt that certain taxpayers who belong to religions other than the Church of Scientology would be similarly situated to such members, we think it unlikely that the Sklars are. Religious education for elementary or secondary school children does not appear to be similar to the "auditing" and "training" conducted by the Church of Scientology. See note 1, supra. Again, however, we need not resolve that issue here.

children's religious education—should be regarded as a charitable contribution because they received only an "intangible religious benefit" in return. Leaving aside both the issue, discussed in section I, of whether the tax code does indeed treat payments for which a taxpayer receives an "intangible religious benefit" as a charitable contribution, as well as any constitutional considerations, we are left with the Sklars' contention that their tuition payment was a dual one: in part in consideration for secular education, and in part as a charitable contribution. The Sklars assert that because 45% of their children's school day was spent on secular education, and 55% on religious education, they should receive a deduction for 55% of their tuition payments.

On the record before this court, the Sklars failed to satisfy the requirements for deducting part of a "dual payment" under the Tax Code. The Supreme Court discussed the deductibility of such payments in United States v. American Bar Endowment, 477 U.S. 105, 106 S.Ct. 2426, 91 L.Ed.2d 89 (1986), and held that the taxpayer must establish that the dual payment exceeds the market value of the goods received in return. * * *

Similarly, the Sklars have not shown that any dual tuition payments they may have made exceeded the market value of the secular education their children received. They urge that the market value of the secular portion of their children's education is the cost of a public school education. That cost, of course, is nothing. The Sklars are in error. The market value is the cost of a comparable secular education offered by private schools. The Sklars do not present any evidence even suggesting that their total payments exceeded that cost. There is no evidence in the record of the tuition private schools charge for a comparable secular education, and thus no evidence showing that the Sklars made an "excess payment" that might qualify for a tax deduction. This appears to be not simply an inadvertent evidentiary omission, but rather a reflection of the practical realities of the high costs of private education. The Sklars also failed to show that they intended to make a *gift* by contributing any such "excess payment." Therefore, under the clear holding of *American Bar Endowment,* the Sklars cannot prevail on this appeal.[14]

IV. Conclusion

We hold that because the Sklars have not shown that their "dual payment" tuition payments are partially deductible under the Tax Code, and, specifically, that the total payments they made for both the secular and religious private school education their children received exceeded the market value of other secular private school education available to those

14. Moreover, as the IRS argues in its brief, the Sklars' deduction was properly denied on the alternative ground that they failed to meet the contemporaneous substantiation requirement of § 170(f)(8)(A), (B) & (C). The Sklars did not present, prior to filing their tax return, a letter from the schools acknowledging their "contribution" and esti- mating the value of the benefit they received, as is required under the statute. As noted earlier, certain reporting requirements are not applicable where intangible religious benefits are received in exchange, but such exemptions apply only where the consideration consists *solely* of such benefits. * * *

children, the IRS did not err in disallowing their deductions, and the Tax Court did not err in affirming the IRS's decision. We affirm the decision of the Tax Court on that ground.

AFFIRMED.

■ SILVERMAN, CIRCUIT JUDGE, CONCURRING:

Why is Scientology training different from all other religious training? We should decline the invitation to answer that question. The sole issue before us is whether the *Sklars'* claimed deduction is valid, not whether members of the Church of Scientology have become the IRS's chosen people.

The majority states that the Church of Scientology's closing agreement is not relevant because "the Sklars [are] not similarly situated to the members of the Church of Scientology. . . ." That may or may not be true, but it has no bearing on whether the tax code permits the Sklars to deduct the costs of their children's religious education as a charitable contribution. Whether the Sklars are entitled to the deduction they claim is governed by 26 U.S.C. § 170, Hernandez v. Commissioner, 490 U.S. 680, 109 S.Ct. 2136, 104 L.Ed.2d 766 (1989), and United States v. American Bar Endowment, 477 U.S. 105, 106 S.Ct. 2426, 91 L.Ed.2d 89 (1986), not by the Church of Scientology closing agreement.

— Section 170 states that quid pro quo donations, for which a taxpayer receives something in return, are not deductible.

— *Hernandez* holds that § 170 applies to religious quid pro quo donations.

— *American Bar Endowment* holds that charitable donations are deductible only to the extent that they exceed the fair market value of what is received in exchange.

The Sklars receive something in return for their tuition payments—the education of their children. Thus, they are not entitled to a charitable deduction under § 170, as Judge Reinhardt carefully shows. *Hernandez* clearly forecloses the argument that § 170 should not apply because the tuition payments are for religious education. Finally, the Sklars have not demonstrated that what they pay for their children's education exceeds the fair market value of what they receive in return; therefore, they have not shown that they are entitled to a deduction under *American Bar Endowment*. It is as simple as that.

Accordingly, under both the tax code and Supreme Court precedent, the Sklars are not entitled to the charitable deduction they claimed. The Church of Scientology's closing agreement is irrelevant, not because the Sklars are not "similarly situated" to Scientologists, but because the closing agreement does not enter into the equation by which the deductibility of the Sklars' payments is determined. An IRS closing agreement cannot overrule Congress and the Supreme Court.

If the IRS does, in fact, give preferential treatment to members of the Church of Scientology—allowing them a special right to claim deductions that are contrary to law and rightly disallowed to everybody else—then the proper course of action is a lawsuit to stop to *that* policy. The remedy is not to require the IRS to let others claim the improper deduction, too.

Revenue Procedure 90–12
1990–1 Cum.Bull. 471.

SECTION 1. PURPOSE
These guidelines are intended to provide charitable organizations with help in advising their patrons of the deductible amount of contributions under section 170 of the Code when the contributors are receiving something in return for their contributions. These guidelines will also be used by agents in determining whether charities have provided accurate information about deductibility to their contributors.

SECTION 2. BACKGROUND
01.   Recently, the Congress expressed concern that charities do not accurately inform their patrons of the extent to which contributions are deductible. In expressing its concern, the Congress stated that it 'anticipates that the Internal Revenue Service will monitor the extent to which taxpayers are being furnished accurate and sufficient information by charitable organizations as to the nondeductibility of payments to such organizations where benefits or privileges are received in return, so that taxpayers can correctly compute their Federal income tax liability.'

* * *

04.   Rev. Rul. 67–246 asks charities to determine the fair market value of the benefits offered for contributions in advance of a solicitation and to state in the solicitation and in tickets, receipts, or other documents issued in connection with a contribution how much is deductible under section 170 of the Code and how much is not. If charities are unable to make an exact determination of the fair market value of the benefits, Rev. Rul. 67–246 indicates that they should use a reasonable estimate of fair market value.

05.   Many charities have suggested that this determination is difficult or burdensome particularly in the case of small items or other benefits that are of token value in relation to the amount contributed. The Service has determined that a benefit may be so inconsequential or insubstantial that the full amount of a contribution is deductible under section 170 of the Code. Under the following guidelines, charities offering certain small items or other benefits of token value may treat the benefits as having insubstantial value so that they may advise contributors that contributions are fully deductible under section 170.

SECTION 3. GUIDELINES
01.   Benefits received in connection with a payment to a charity will be considered to have insubstantial fair market value for purposes of advising patrons if the requirements of paragraphs 1 and 2 are met:

1.   The payment occurs in the context of a fund-raising campaign in which the charity informs patrons how much of their payment is a deductible contribution, and either

2.   (a) The fair market value of all of the benefits received in connection with the payment, is not more than 2 percent of the payment, or $50, whichever is less [the $50 limitation is indexed for inflation; in 2003, it is $80, Eds.], or (b) The payment is $25 [adjusted for inflation; in 2003, the amount is $40, Eds.] or more and the only benefits received in connection with the payment are token items (bookmarks, calendars, key chains, mugs, posters, tee shirts, etc.) bearing the organization's name or logo. The cost (as opposed to fair market value) of all of the benefits received by a donor must, in the aggregate, be within the limits established for 'low cost articles' under section 513(h)(2) of the Code. (Generally, under section 170, the deductible amount of a contribution is determined by taking into account the fair market value, not the cost to the charity, of any benefits received in return. For administrative reasons, however, in the limited circumstances of this subparagraph, the cost to the charity may be used in determining whether the benefits are insubstantial.)

02.   For purposes of paragraph 1 of section 3.01, above, a qualifying fund-raising campaign is one designed to raise tax-deductible contributions, in which the charity determines the fair market value of the benefits offered in return for contributions (using a reasonable estimate if an exact determination is not possible), and states in its solicitations (whether written, broadcast, telephoned, or in person)—as well as in tickets, receipts, or other documents issued in connection with contributions—how much is deductible under section 170 of the Code and how much is not. If a charity is providing only insubstantial benefits in return for a payment, fund-raising materials should include a statement to the effect that: "Under Internal Revenue Service guidelines the estimated value of the benefits received is not substantial; therefore the full amount of your payment is a deductible contribution."

03.   There may be situations in which it is impractical to state in every solicitation how much of a payment is deductible. For example, where a nonprofit broadcasting organization offers a number of premiums in an on-air fund-raising announcement, it may be unduly cumbersome to include information on the fair market value of each premium. If a charity believes that stating how much is deductible in every statement is impractical, it may seek a ruling from the Service concerning an alternative procedure. The Service will rule on whether the alternative procedure meets the Congressionally mandated goal of providing accurate and sufficient information to contributors.

04.   For purposes of paragraph 2 of section 3.01, above, newsletters or program guides (other than commercial quality publications) will be treated as if they do not have a measurable fair market value or cost if their primary purpose is to inform members about the activities of an organization and if they are not available to nonmembers by paid subscription or

through newsstand sales. Whether a publication is considered a commercial quality publication depends upon all of the facts and circumstances. Generally, publications that contain articles written for compensation and that accept advertising will be treated as commercial quality publications having measurable fair market value or cost. Professional journals (whether or not articles are written for compensation and advertising is accepted) will normally be treated as commercial quality publications. For purposes of subparagraph (b) of paragraph 2, the cost of a commercial quality publication includes the costs of production and distribution and must be computed without regard to income from advertising or newsstand or subscription sales.

05.   In applying paragraph 2, the total amount of a pledge payable in installments will be considered to be the amount of the payment. Also, benefits provided by charities in the form of cash or its equivalent will never be considered insubstantial.

06.   For purposes of subparagraph (b) of paragraph 2, an item is a "low cost article" under section 513(h)(2) of the Code if its cost does not exceed $5, increased for years after 1987 by a cost-of-living adjustment under section 1(f)(3). [For 2003, the amount is $8, Eds.] The $25 [$40 in 2003, Eds.] payment required in subparagraph (b) of paragraph 2 must also be increased, in the same manner.

07.   For purposes of subparagraph (b) of paragraph 2, if items offered to contributors are donated to the charity or if services are donated in connection with the production of an item, the cost "to the organization" for purposes of section 513(h)(2) of the Code will be a reasonable estimate of the amount the organization would have to pay for the items or services in question.

08.   These guidelines describe a safe harbor; depending on the facts in each case, benefits received in connection with contributions may be "insubstantial" even if they do not meet these guidelines.

* * *

NOTES AND QUESTIONS

1.   *Scientology Truce.* As the Ninth Circuit noted in *Sklar*, the IRS abruptly ended its long battle against the Church of Scientology in 1993 by entering into a settlement agreement under which numerous Scientology entities were granted tax-exempt status. At the same time, the Service "obsoleted" the 1978 revenue ruling in which it had disallowed charitable deductions for "fixed donations" to the church. Rev. Rul. 93–73, 1993–2 C.B. 75. The settlement agreement was not released to the public, and the Service did not explain why it had abandoned a legal position on the charitable deduction issue that had been sustained by the Supreme Court.

The terms of the 1993 settlement eventually were leaked, first by The Wall Street Journal in an Internet posting and then more broadly in the establishment press. See, e.g, Douglas Frantz, $12.5 Million Deal with IRS

Lifted Cloud Over Scientologists, N.Y. Times, Dec. 31, 1997, A1 and A13. In exchange for a payment of $12.5 million, the Service agreed to discontinue audits of 13 Scientology entities, to abate tax penalties, and to grant exempt status to 114 domestic Scientology branches. In exchange, the church agreed to drop its lawsuits against the Service and to create a special oversight committee to monitor the church's tax compliance and report annually to the Service for three years. This is an unusually high level of government oversight of a religious organization. The entire closing agreement is reprinted in 19 Exempt Org. Tax Rev. 227 (1998).

Response to the details of the settlement was mixed. Some former IRS officials praised the Service for its innovative approach to resolving a long and bitter dispute, while other commentators criticized the Service for "caving" in response to continued harassment by the Church of Scientology. See Fred Stokeld, Purported Closing Agreement Reveals Scientology Paid Government $12.5 Million, 19 Exempt Org. Tax Rev. 152 (1998).

2. *Donee Estimates of Return Benefits.* Charities should provide their donors with a good faith estimate of the value of any return benefits. In so doing, they may use any reasonable method to determine value. If the service or product is available commercially, using a valuation within the range of retail prices normally would be acceptable. If it is not available commercially, the estimate should be made by comparing the return benefit to comparable goods or services. The regulations provide an example of a museum that allows donors to hold private events in exchange for a sufficiently large donation. In this type of case, they authorize a valuation based on the cost of leasing ballrooms in two hotels in the same community with similar amenities and capacity. Treas. Reg. § 1.6115–1(a)(3). The unique qualities of the museum (e.g., its collection) can be disregarded, as may "celebrity presence" at a fundraiser or other special event. Id.

3. *For Further Reading.* Pamela McAllister, The Charity's Guide to Charitable Contributions (1998).

4. Percentage Limitations and Carryovers

Internal Revenue Code: § 170(b), (d)(1).

When it first enacted the charitable income tax deduction in 1917, Congress did not intend the deduction to be unlimited. The earliest predecessor of § 170 limited an individual taxpayer's charitable deduction to 15 percent of the donor's "net income." Since then, Congress has become so enamored of the percentage limitation concept that it has constructed a mind numbing web of often overlapping rules that contributes to the corpulence of § 170. The limitations reflect a judgment that no taxpayer should completely avoid federal income tax by making charitable contributions. As a practical matter, they affect only the most generous philanthropists.

Several different types of percentage limitations apply for purposes of determining an individual taxpayer's income tax charitable deduction. The "basic percentage limitation" varies based on the type of organization receiving the gift. Other limitations apply to gifts of long-term capital gain property. Finally, the percentage limitation applicable to a particular gift also is affected by whether the gift is "to" or merely "for the use of" the charity. The percentage limitations for individual taxpayers are applied with reference to the taxpayer's "contribution base," which is defined as "adjusted gross income * * * computed without regard to any net operating loss carryback to the taxable year * * *." I.R.C. § 170(b)(1)(F).

The Basic 50% and 30% Limitations. Qualified recipients of charitable contributions are divided into two general categories for purposes of the basic percentage limitation. The preferred group-known as "50 percent charities"—includes schools, hospitals, churches, medical research organizations, government entities, publicly supported charities and certain operating and supporting foundations. I.R.C. § 170(b)(1)(A). The second and less favored category—the "30 percent charities"—consists primarily of private foundations. For the background of these distinctions, see Chapter 3A2, supra, at pp. 382–384.

Gifts of cash and ordinary income property to 50 percent charities qualify for the maximum allowable annual charitable deduction–50 percent of a donor's contribution base. Contributions in excess of the 50 percent limit may be carried forward and deducted, subject to the same 50 percent limit, over the five taxable years following the gift. I.R.C. § 170(d)(1). Gifts to private foundations generally may be deducted up to a 30 percent limit, with a five-year carryover of any excess. I.R.C. § 170(b)(1)(C). In addition, gifts "for the use of" even the most favored group of charities (e.g., gifts in trust) are subject to the 30 percent limit.

In applying these limitations, gifts to 50 percent charities are considered first. Gifts to 30 percent charities are currently deductible only to the extent that, when added to gifts to 50 percent charities, they do not result in total gifts exceeding the overall 50 percent limit. Stated more technically, the 30 percent limit is the lesser of: (1) 30 percent of a donor's contribution base for the year, or (2) 50 percent of the contribution base less gifts that qualify for the 50 percent limit. I.R.C. § 170(b)(1)(B).

To illustrate the relationship between the basic limitations, assume Donor ("D") has adjusted gross income (D's "contribution base") of $100,000 and contributes $40,000 cash to Public Charity and $25,000 to Private Foundation. D's gift to Public Charity, which is counted first, is fully deductible because it does not exceed the 50 percent limit, but only $10,000 of D's gift to Private Foundation is currently deductible. Although the private foundation gift did not exceed 30 percent of D's contribution base, it is deductible only to the extent of the difference between 50 percent of D's contribution base ($50,000) and the amount of D's gifts to 50 percent charities ($40,000). The $15,000 excess may be carried over for the five succeeding years.

Gifts of Capital Gain Property. The basic percentage limitations described above apply to gifts of cash and ordinary income property. Additional limitations are imposed on gifts of long-term capital gain property, a category consisting of capital and § 1231 assets (e.g., securities, art and other collectibles, and most investment real estate) which, if sold, would result in long-term capital gain. I.R.C. § 170(b)(1)(C)(iv). A capital asset is "long-term" when it has been held for more than one year. I.R.C. § 1222(3).

A donor may deduct the fair market value of gifts of capital gain property to "50 percent" public charities to the extent that the total amount for the year does not exceed 30 percent of the donor's contribution base. Any excess may be carried forward for five years, subject in each succeeding year to the same percentage limitation. I.R.C. § 170(b)(1)(C). Special rules discussed later in this chapter may reduce the amount of the charitable deduction for gifts of certain tangible personal property that is not used by the donee for its exempt purposes. See I.R.C. § 170(e)(1)(B)(i). See Section C3 of this chapter, infra, at p. 751.

Gifts of capital gain property to private foundations may be subject to double punishment. In general, the amount of the gift first must be reduced by the long-term capital gain that would have been recognized if the donor had sold rather than contributed the property. I.R.C. § 170(e)(1)(B)(ii).[1] This reduced amount (or the fair market value, if property with a basis in excess of its value is contributed) then may be deducted only to the extent of 20 percent of the donor's contribution base. I.R.C. § 170(b)(1)(D).

Special Stepdown Election. A special elective provision permits a donor to avoid the 30 percent limitation on gifts of capital gain property to the favored group of charities and instead be subject to the 50 percent limitation. The trade-off is that the donor must reduce the value of all gifts of appreciated capital gain property to those organizations by the entire gain that would have been recognized if the property had been sold for its fair market value rather than contributed. I.R.C. § 170(b)(1)(C)(iii). If this election is made, it applies to all gifts of capital gain property made during the year and to any carryovers from and to the year in which the election is made.

The effect of the stepdown election is that the charitable deduction is limited to the donor's basis in the donated capital gain property. The election may be useful when the amount of appreciation inherent in the property is small or where the gift is so large that the donor would not have been able to deduct its full value, even over the five-year carryover period, if the gift were subject to the 30 percent limitation.

Relationship Between the Percentage Limitations. The relationship between the various percentage limitations is very technical, especially in years when a donor has both current gifts and contribution carryovers from prior years and has made gifts of both cash and capital gain property to the different categories of donees. Fortunately, excellent computer software is

---

1. The reduction to basis rule does not apply, however, to gifts of "qualified appreciated stock," a category that generally includes publicly traded securities provided that the donor and certain related persons have not contributed more than 10 percent of the corporation's outstanding stock to private foundations. I.R.C. § 170(e)(5).

available to sort out these relationships, either at the planning stage or for purposes of preparing the donor's tax return. For purposes of this overview, it will suffice to summarize the ordering rules that emerge from the many examples in the § 170 regulations. In any given year, a donor's charitable deduction is determined by taking into account contributions in the following order: (1) gifts qualifying under the 50 percent limitation actually made during the year, (2) carryovers of 50 percent contributions made during the preceding five years, (3) contributions of cash and ordinary income property made to 30 percent charities during the current year, (4) carryovers of excess 30 percent cash and ordinary income property contributions made during the preceding five years, (5) contributions of 30 percent capital gain property made during the year, (6) carryovers of excess 30 percent capital gain property from the preceding five years, (7) contributions of 20 percent capital gain property made during the year, and (8) carryovers of excess 20 percent capital gain property from the preceding five years. But as we said, software is available, so never mind—and we'll skip the examples!

Corporate Contributions. The percentage limitation on charitable contributions by corporations is 10 percent of the corporation's taxable income, after certain technical adjustments. I.R.C. § 170(b)(2). Amounts in excess of this limit may be carried forward and deducted in the five years following the gift. I.R.C. § 170(d)(2). Gifts authorized during the year by accrual method corporations may be deducted even if not actually paid up to two months and fifteen days after the close of the year, provided an election to that effect is made. See I.R.C. § 170(a)(2). Contributions by Subchapter S corporations, which generally are not taxable entities, pass through to the shareholders, who may deduct their respective portion subject to the appropriate percentage limitations applicable to individuals. Similar pass-through rules apply to contributions by partnerships and limited liability companies.

5. SUBSTANTIATION AND COMPLIANCE RULES

Internal Revenue Code: §§ 170(f)(8); 6113; 6115; 6710; 6714.

Treasury Regulations: § 1.170A–13(a), (f); 1.6115–1.

Individual taxpayers deduct charitable contributions on Schedule A of Form 1040, listing on separate lines their cash and property contributions. It is sufficient to list the aggregate amount of cash contributions, without providing a list of donees and specific amounts. In the event of an audit, however, taxpayers must substantiate their gifts. Historically, this could be accomplished by providing a cancelled check, a receipt from the donee showing the name of the charity and the amount and date of the gift, or "other reliable written records" showing the information required on a receipt. Treas. Reg. § 1.170A–13(a).

Despite attempts by the Internal Revenue Service to educate charities and their donors, Congress concluded in 1993 that more rigorous substantiation and disclosure requirements were necessary to patrol against inflated charitable deductions and misleading solicitations. The Senate Finance Committee explained why these changes were necessary:[1]

Difficult problems of tax administration arise with respect to fundraising techniques in which an organization that is eligible to receive tax deductible contributions provides goods or services in consideration for payments from donors. Organizations that engage in such fundraising practices often do not inform their donors that all or a portion of the amount paid by the donor may not be deductible as a charitable contribution. Consequently, the committee believes that there will be increased compliance with present-law rules governing charitable contribution deductions if a taxpayer who claims a separate charitable contribution of $250 or more is required to obtain substantiation from the donee indicating the amount of the contribution and whether any goods, service, or privilege was received by the donor in exchange for making the contribution. In addition, the committee believes it is appropriate that when a charity receives a *quid pro quo* contribution in excess of $75 (i.e., a payment exceeding $75 made partly as a gift and partly in consideration for a benefit furnished to the payor), the charity should inform the donor that the deduction under section 170 is limited to the amount by which the payment exceeds the value of the goods or service furnished by the charity, and should provide a good faith estimate of the value of such goods or service.

Substantiation of Gifts of $250 or More. To implement this policy, Congress enacted § 170(f)(8), which provides that no charitable deduction shall be allowed for a separate contribution of $250 or more unless the taxpayer substantiates the contribution with a contemporaneous written acknowledgement from the donee organization. The responsibility for obtaining this substantiation lies with the donor. The acknowledgment must include the following information: (1) the amount of cash and a description (but not the value) of any property other than cash contributed, (2) whether the donee provided any return benefits in the form of goods or services, and (3) a description and good faith estimate of the value of any goods or services provided to the donor in exchange for making the gift, or if such goods or services consist solely of "intangible religious benefits," a statement to that effect. I.R.C. § 170(f)(8)(B); Treas. Reg. § 1.170A–13(f)(2). The term "intangible religious benefit" is defined as any intangible religious benefit provided by an organization organized exclusively for religious purposes and where the benefit is not sold in a commercial transaction outside the donative context. I.R.C. § 170(f)(8)(B). No particular form is prescribed for the charity's acknowledgment, but it is clear that a cancelled check is not sufficient. The contemporaneous requirement is met if the acknowledgement is obtained on or before the earlier of the date that the taxpayer files a return for the year of the contribution, or the due date (including extensions) for filing the return. I.R.C. § 170(f)(8)(C);

---

1. Explanation of Senate Finance Committee Revenue Provisions, Revenue Recon- ciliation Act of 1993, 103d Cong., 1st Sess. 221 (1993).

Treas. Reg. § 1.170A–13(f)(3). These special substantiation rules are waived for the donor if the donee organization files an annual information return reporting all the required information on gifts of $250 or more made during the year. I.R.C. § 170(f)(8)(D).

The substantiation rules raise numerous technical questions that seem trivial when viewed in isolation but can be important to charitable organizations that engage in substantial fundraising. Considerable guidance can be found in the regulations, which make it clear that separate payments are treated as separate contributions and thus are not aggregated for purposes of the $250 threshold, and that contributions made by payroll deductions will be treated as separate payments. Treas. Reg. § 1.170A–13(f)(1), (11).

Information Disclosure for Quid Pro Quo Contributions. A charitable organization that receives a *quid pro quo* contribution in excess of $75 must provide, in connection with the solicitation or receipt of the contribution, a good faith estimate of the value of the goods or services and inform the donor in writing that only the excess of the contribution is deductible. I.R.C. § 6115(a); Treas. Reg. § 1.6115–1(a)(1). A "quid pro quo" contribution is a payment that is "made partly as a contribution and partly in consideration [for return benefits in the form of] goods or services." I.R.C. § 6115(b). For example, if a donor pays $100 to attend a fund raising event and receives in exchange a $40 dinner, the charity must inform the donor that only $60 is tax-deductible. The legislative history states that the disclosure must be made in a manner that is reasonably likely to come to the donor's attention; small print is thus discouraged. The disclosure requirement does not apply if the goods or services provided are de minimis (see Rev. Proc. 90–12, supra, at pp. 731–733), or if the contributor receives solely an intangible religious benefit that is provided by an organization organized exclusively for religious purposes and the benefit generally is not sold in a commercial transaction outside the donative context. I.R.C. § 170(f)(8)(B); Treas. Reg. § 1.6115–1(a)(2), –1(b). Transactions that have no donative element, such as sales of goods by a museum gift shop that are devoid of any donative element, also are not covered.

If a charity fails to make the required disclosure, it is subject to a penalty of $10 per contribution, capped at $5,000 for any particular fundraising event or mailing. I.R.C. § 6714. The penalty is waived if the charity can show that its failure was due to reasonable cause. Id. The penalties are triggered if an organization either fails to make any disclosure in connection with a *quid pro quo* contribution or makes an incomplete or inaccurate disclosure, such as a determination of the value of the return benefits that is not in good faith. Id.

Internet Fundraising: Special Problems. Some charitable solicitations are being made by for-profit firms on behalf of specified charitable organizations. Contributions are collected through secure connections using credit cards and the solicitor remits the gift to the charity after keeping a fee. If the solicitor is acting as the charity's agent, the full amount of the gift should be deductible, with the fee being treated as an expense of the charity. In other cases (and how is the donor to know?), the fee would not be a deductible contribution because the intermediary is the donor's agent. The legal relationship of the solicitor to the charity also may affect the timing of a deduction. If the solicitor is the donor's agent, the gift is not complete until remitted to the charity, but a deduction should be available upon a click of the mouse if the solicitor is the charity's agent.

In a request for comments in Announcement 2000–84, 2000–42 I.R.B. 385, the Service asked whether e-mail acknowledgements and disclosures of "quid pro quo" return benefits satisfied the substantiation and disclosure rules in §§ 170(f)(8) and 6115. The answer in both cases should be yes, at least if the electronic acknowledgements can be printed out and contain the required information. The IRS agrees. See IRS Publication 1771, Charitable Contributions—Substantiation and Disclosure Requirements, which includes examples of proper wording for e-mail acknowledgements. A related question is whether Internet solicitations (either on a web site or by e-mail) are in "written or printed form" within the meaning of I.R.C. § 6113(c)(1)(A), in which case organizations (such as § 501(c)(4) advocacy groups) that are not eligible to receive deductible gifts must include an express statement to that effect in "a conspicuous and easily recognizable format."

What about a web surfer who visits an on line "charity mall" where "commissions" paid by on-line merchants on all purchases made through the site are remitted to charities selected by the purchasers from a list. One charitable mall, in response to a "frequently asked question," once advised donors that they could not take any tax deduction because they were buying goods and services at regular prices and not making a donation directly to the charity. May the merchants (who don't select the donee) take the deduction? In a variation on this theme, another web-based merchant/solicitor (iGive.com) allows members to purchase products from vendors who then send back rebates which the buyer either may keep or designate to selected charities. In this situation, members are told that rebates designated to charities are tax-deductible (because the member may keep the rebate or donate it. But donations over $250 to any single cause are now allowed in any single month (why?).

Information Disclosure of Nondeductibility of Contributions. During its closer scrutiny of fundraising practices of nonprofit organizations in the late 1980's, Congress discovered many nonprofits ineligible to receive tax-deductible contributions were not disclosing their proper status to potential contributors and, in some cases, were actually implying in solicitations that contributions were deductible when in fact they were not. Particular targets of this scrutiny were § 501(c)(4) lobbying organizations. To patrol against these abuses, § 6113 generally requires fundraising solicitations by or on behalf of tax-exempt donees that do not qualify to receive deductible contributions, or by any political organization defined in § 527(e), to include an express statement in a conspicuous and easily recognizable format that contributions to the organization are not tax-deductible. I.R.C. § 6113(a), (b)(1). Exceptions are provided for small organizations (with average annual gross receipts not exceeding $100,000), fraternal organizations with respect to solicitations for exclusively charitable purposes, and any solicitation made by letter or telephone call if the letter or call is not part of a coordinated fundraising campaign soliciting more than 10 persons during the calendar year. I.R.C. § 6113(b)(2), (3) & (c)(2). Monetary penalties are imposed for noncompliance with these rules unless the failure was due to reasonable cause. I.R.C. § 6710.

Gifts of Property. Additional valuation and substantiation rules apply to gifts of property other than cash. These rules are discussed in Section C7 of this chapter, infra at pp. 756–758.

For Further Reading. David M. Donaldson & Carolyn M. Osteen, The Harvard Manual on Tax Aspects of Charitable Giving (8th ed. 1999); Bruce R. Hopkins, The Tax Law of Charitable Giving (1993); Christina L. Nooney, Tax–Exempt Organizations and the Internet, 27 Exempt Org. Tax Rev. 33 (2000); Catherine E. Livingston, Tax–Exempt Organizations and the Internet: Tax and Other Legal Issues, 31 Exempt Org. Tax Rev. 419 (2001).

PROBLEMS

Determine whether the following contributions are tax-deductible under § 170 and, if not, suggest how the transfer might be restructured to achieve an income tax deduction:

(a) Concerned Citizen makes a $1,000 payment to the United States government to help reduce the national debt.

(b) Ira Weisel donates $10,000 to Community Foundation, a § 170(c) charity, on the understanding that the funds will be transferred to a foreign charitable organization that provides food and shelter to needy residents of Third World countries.

(c) Dan Kaye, a prominent geologist, donates $50,000 to the Sturdley University Department of Geology and earmarks the gift to support the research of two graduate students who work in his laboratory under his supervision.

(d) Edith Calderon volunteers five hours a week at St. Anthony's Soup Kitchen, a charitable organization that provides meals for the homeless. She also incurs travel expenses for two cross-country trips per year in connection with her service as an alumni trustee of her undergraduate alma mater.

(e) Barnabas Collins, who has a rare blood type, donates blood with a fair market value of $5,000 to the American Red Cross.

(f) Gordon Haines, a wealthy personal injury lawyer, donates $5 million to State Law School. In recognition of the gift, the Law School renames its library as The Haines Legal Information Center.

(g) Tyrone Johnson, a third-year law student, buys 10 tickets to a raffle sponsored by his school's Public Interest Law Foundation (at $1 per ticket), fully aware that he has only a small chance at winning the first prize: a free bar review course worth $1,200. Each of the raffle tickets states that the "donation" is "tax-deductible as provided by law."

(h) After several glasses of Chablis, Celine Kane makes the winning bid ($2,000) on a baseball autographed by the 1955 New York Yankees at the annual Country Day School Auction. A reliable collector's guide values similar balls at $700.

(i) Donna Davies pays $250 for a "patron" ticket to a benefit concert to benefit The Metropolitan Symphony. A comparable ticket for a regular concert would cost $75. As a "patron," Donna is recognized as such in the printed program and entitled to a Fritos-champagne-and-caviar reception honoring Luciano Pavarotti following the performance.

(j) Same as (i), above, except Donna has no intention of attending the event.

(k) In 1999, Mimi Stone becomes a member of KPBS, her local public broadcasting station for a "contribution" of $40. In return, she receives a KPBS coffee mug (cost to KPBS—$3; fair market value—$5) and a bi-monthly listener's guide (cost of printing and distribution—$4 per year; fair market value—$6 per year). (Hint: see Rev. Rul. 90–12, supra p. 731, for the applicable "low cost article" and "insubstantial benefit" limitations for 2003.)

(l) Dan Stein contributes $5,000 annually to the Sturdley University athletic program booster fund, for which he receives a biweekly newsletter about the college athletic program and the right to purchase preferential seating at football and basketball games. The seats sold to those who donate $5,000 or more are not available to other alumni or the general public.

(m) Rhoda Powell is a member of Temple Sinai, a large urban Jewish synagogue. Her annual dues are $1,250, which are based on her income according to a dues policy approved by the synagogue's board. As a member, she is entitled to attend weekly services and other events (which usually are also open to non-members on a space-available basis) and receives reserved seat tickets to the Jewish High Holy Day services (which non-members may not attend).

(n) Emil Perini makes a $350 cash contribution to Charity by mailing a check on December 31 of Year One. Charity receives and deposits the check on January 5 of Year Two, but it does not mail Emil any acknowledgement. Charity's original solicitation form stated: "Your cancelled check shall serve as your receipt."

(o) Same as (n), above, except that Emil gave $250 on April 1 and another $100 on December 1.

(p) Same as (n), above, except Emil pays $30 monthly through employee payroll reductions.

C.   CHARITABLE CONTRIBUTIONS OF PROPERTY

Internal Revenue Code: §§ 170(a)(3), (b), (e)(1), (3) & (5); 1011(b).

Treasury Regulations: §§ 1.170A–1(c)(1) & (2), –13(b), (c).

1.   CAPITAL GAIN PROPERTY

Subject to the percentage limitations discussed earlier, charitable gifts of property generally are deductible in an amount equal to their fair market value on the date of the gift. Gifts of "capital gain property," such as appreciated stock or real estate held by the taxpayer for more than one year, offer particularly attractive tax benefits. The donor avoids tax on the gain that would have been recognized if the donated property had been sold, and she may deduct the full fair market value of the property subject to the applicable percentage limitations. I.R.C. § 170(b)(1)(C). A full fair market value deduction, however, is not available for gifts of appreciated capital gain property (other than certain publicly traded stock) to a private foundation. In determining the charitable deduction, the donor's gift must be reduced by the amount of long-term capital gain that would have been recognized if the property had been sold for its fair market value rather than contributed. I.R.C. § 170(e)(1)(A) & (B)(ii). As previewed earlier, this "stepdown" rule is one of the most significant disadvantages of making lifetime gifts of property such as closely held stock or real estate to a private foundation. In addition, the deductible amount is subject to a 20 percent limitation with a five-year carryover. I.R.C. § 170(b)(1)(D).

It is not advisable to contribute capital gain property that is worth less than its basis because the donor will be unable to deduct the loss. If a sale of property would result in a deductible loss, the donor should sell the property, deduct the loss, and donate the proceeds to charity.

Philanthropic taxpayers who are about to sell appreciated property occasionally find it attractive to contribute the property and let the charity complete the sale. For example, a donor may own publicly traded stock for which a tender offer is outstanding or may be negotiating the sale of real estate. In these situations, the donor will avoid recognizing the gain inherent in the contributed property only if the contribution is made prior to an unconditional sale. The charity must not be obligated to sell the property as a condition of the gift. Similarly, a contribution of closely held stock followed by a redemption will not be treated as a constructive dividend to the donor-shareholder if the charity is not legally obligated to tender the stock to the company. See, e.g., Rev. Rul. 78–197, 1978–1 C.B. 83. As illustrated by the *Blake* case, which follows, an implied understanding between the donor and the charity may cause the donor's delicate tax plan to self destruct if the Service is able to successfully invoke the step transaction doctrine.

Blake v. Commissioner

United States Court of Appeals, Second Circuit, 1982.
697 F.2d 473.

■ OAKES, CIRCUIT JUDGE:

This appeal presents a familiar problem in the tax law involving step-transaction analysis. The context is one in which a taxpayer "contributes" a substantially appreciated asset to a charitable organization which then liquidates the contribution and purchases another asset from the taxpayer. The question in this case is whether the taxpayer is entitled to treat the transfer of the first asset—corporate stock—as a contribution and treat the transfer of the second asset—a yacht—as a sale, or whether, as the Tax Court held, the transactions here must be recharacterized for tax purposes as a sale of the stock by the taxpayer followed by a contribution to the charity of the vessel. The vessel, it might be noted, was sold by the charity shortly after it had been purchased from the taxpayer for a little less than half of what the charity paid the taxpayer out of the proceeds of the stock. The taxpayer contends that the charity had no legally binding obligation to purchase the yacht and that absent such an obligation the transactions here must be treated according to the form they took: a contribution followed by a sale of an asset. We disagree. We hold that in this case the charity would have been legally obligated to purchase the yacht and that, even if it were not legally obligated, the Tax Court's finding that the transactions were undertaken pursuant to an understanding arrived at in advance is sufficient to sustain the Commissioner's position. We therefore affirm the Tax Court, Arnold Raum, Judge, in its decision that the gain realized on the sale of the stock was attributable to the taxpayer. It follows that only the market value of the yacht, not challenged on this appeal, was deductible as a contribution.

I. Facts

The taxpayer in this case, S. Prestley Blake, was a co-founder and major stockholder in the Friendly Ice Cream Corporation. In 1972, Blake purchased the yacht "America" for $500,000. The America is a replica of the original yacht America, built in 1851, after which the America's Cup race is named. Although not particularly well suited to racing or chartering, the yacht does have a certain mystique owing to its historical associations. Subsequent to the transactions recounted below, the America became familiar nationally because it was featured in the Tall Ships' Sail to New York City during the Bicentennial celebration of 1976. Blake, however, had nothing but trouble with the yacht. The vessel required frequent repair, and Blake found various captains and crews unsatisfactory. With one exception, Blake's ambition to defray expenses associated with owning the boat through chartering was never realized. He ultimately decided to dispose of the yacht; in his own words, he "had to get rid of [the America] at all costs," because it "was taking too much * * * time and concern."

Blake had made a number of charitable gifts throughout his career, particularly in western New England, his home and the place where he started business. He attempted to donate the America to Mystic Seaport in Mystic, Connecticut, but that institution declined the gift. More unhappy cruises followed. Some time later, Blake approached the Kings Point Fund, Inc. (the Fund), a qualified charitable organization associated with the United States Merchant Marine Academy at Kings Point, New York. In January and February of 1975, Blake and the superintendent of the Academy discussed the possibility of the Academy's use of the America as a training vessel, and the Superintendent wrote Blake a letter in late February of 1975 confirming the Academy's interest in the proposition. The letter expressed gratitude for Blake's "extremely generous offer to donate" the America and to "provide an additional annual grant of $10,000 towards its maintenance." The record indicates that the Fund's directors had discussed the possibility of acquiring the America at an earlier meeting where it was suggested that the boat be kept for at least two years and that Blake donate $10,000 annually and that twelve other major donors be solicited to raise an additional $125,000 for upkeep. On March 13, 1975, some two weeks after the Superintendent wrote Blake, the Fund's directors met again. It was reported at the meeting that Blake was "very receptive to donating his YACHT AMERICA to the Kings Point Fund" and the minutes of the meeting indicate that "[f]urther negotiation packages to this acquisition [were] to be discussed." A motion to acquire the America, subject to the consent of the Superintendent and approval of legal counsel, carried the Board unanimously.

In the meanwhile, Blake was apparently consulting with his tax lawyers. Four days after the March 13 meeting, he wrote the Fund that he had transferred 35,000 shares of Friendly stock "to advance your training program for young cadets in a way that you see fit." The stock had an adjusted basis in Blake's hands of $98, but a market value of $686,875 at the time of transfer. The Fund immediately sold the stock in a series of transactions netting $701,688.89. At an April 8, 1975, meeting of the Fund's directors, it was reported that "Mr. Blake had donated * * * $714,000 * * * worth of Friendly Ice Cream stock" to the Fund, that the Fund "then sold same," and that $675,000 "is to be used to purchase the yacht AMERICA and the remainder is to be used toward the maintenance of the vessel." The Board unanimously accepted "the generous donation of Mr. P. Blake to be used for the purchase of the yacht America and her maintenance." Almost immediately, however, the Board set out to sell the yacht; at a June 17, 1975, meeting a possible sale was discussed which would allow the Academy to use the vessel for the Bicentennial "Tall Ships Parade." This sale was approved, the minutes noting that it would "net the Fund over $200,000." Presumably this sale was carried out over the summer; the minutes of a meeting of September 18, 1975, show that, in addition to selling half a dozen other smaller craft, the Fund sold the America for $250,000, netting it some $200,000. The taxpayer does not dispute that, but for his expectation that the Fund would purchase the vessel, he might not have contributed the stock. But he argues that he had, at most, an expectation in this regard because there was no binding, enforceable commitment on the Fund's part to purchase the vessel. He points out that the directors of the Fund were free not to purchase the yacht if they determined that it would not be in the Fund's best interests to do so and that he alone bore the risk that events occurring between the transfer of the stock and either its sale or the purchase of the yacht would reduce the value of the stock or the yacht respectively. Thus, the taxpayer argues, there was a mere "coincidence" of two transactions and the principles underlying the tax treatment of charitable contributions require separate treatment of these transactions in the absence of an obligation binding the charity to purchase an asset of the contribution.

Under Grove v. Commissioner, 490 F.2d 241 (2d Cir.1973), the taxpayer argues reversal is required. *Grove* is presented to us as in a line of cases including, e.g., Palmer v. Commissioner, 62 T.C. 684 (1974), aff'd on other grounds, 523 F.2d 1308 (8th Cir.1975), acq'd in Rev.Rul. 78–197, 1978–1 C.B. 83; * * *. We will first examine whether there was a legally binding agreement in this case, although this point was neither relied upon by the Tax Court nor particularly argued by the Commissioner, because the premise of the taxpayer's argument is that there was no legal obligation whatsoever. We will then address the Tax Court's holding that the understanding between the parties was alone sufficient to justify recharacterization of these transactions, irrespective whether the understanding was legally enforceable.

II.   The Fund's Obligation to Blake

If there was a legally binding agreement on the Fund's part to purchase the vessel with the entirety of the proceeds derived from the sale of the transferred stock, the taxpayer seems to concede that there would be no contribution here in excess of the fair market value of the yacht at the time of its transfer. The existence of such an obligation is determined, of course, with reference to state law. [The court then surveyed the various state laws that might govern the transaction. Eds.]

* * *

We need not decide which of the three states' law would govern, however, because we are certain that each state would consider the Fund legally obligated to purchase the America under a theory of promissory estoppel on the facts of this case. Under this theory, a mere gratuitous promise by the Fund that it would purchase the America became legally binding when Blake acted in reliance on such an assurance. * * *

The taxpayer argues that no legal obligation arose on the charity's part to purchase the vessel because he "gave the shares * * * absolutely, parting with all control over them." But, far from negating the existence of an obligation, the transfer itself gave rise to an obligation, under the decisions cited above, if the taxpayer made the transfer in reliance upon an assurance that the charity would use the proceeds of the asset for a specific purpose. Although the taxpayer maintains that the charity made no commitment upon which the reliance in the form of the transfer could be premised, the Tax Court's findings are to the contrary. The Tax Court concluded, upon the record in its entirety, that the transfer of stock was made "with the understanding that the stock would be sold, that the yacht would be turned over to the fund, and that virtually all of the proceeds of the sale of the stock would end up in [the taxpayer's] hands." The individual who served as the Fund's negotiator in dealing with Blake was unable to testify at trial as to any express oral agreement between the Fund and Blake, but a Fund director testified that it was the Board's understanding that the negotiator had agreed that the stock proceeds would be used to "purchase" the vessel. That the Board's "understanding" accurately reflected an understanding between Blake and the Fund's negotiator is supported by the fact that, as of the March 13, 1975, meeting, the directors agreed to take "such steps as necessary to acquire the YACHT AMERICA" and were aware that "further negotiation packages to acquisition [were] to be discussed." Further support is provided by the minutes of the Fund's April 8, 1975, meeting, which note the approval of a motion "to accept the generous donation of Mr. P. Blake to be used for the purchase of the yacht America and her maintenance." Finally, Blake himself testified on direct examination that he would not have made a donation as substantial as the amount of the market value of the stock he transferred "except for the boat thing."

On the basis of the Tax Court's factual findings as to the understanding between the taxpayer and the charity, we have little difficulty concluding that Blake would have had an enforceable cause of action under a promissory estoppel theory. * * * The same public policy considerations that support the enforcement of promises made by individuals to charitable organizations also support the enforcement of promises made by a charity in connection with a contribution. As the former Assistant Superintendent of the Merchant Marine Academy and twenty-five-year director of the Fund testified at trial, if the Fund had not purchased the America with the proceeds of the stock, if it "had simply taken Mr. Blake's money and run," the "gifting of future yachts would have been severely jeopardized." We therefore reject the taxpayer's contention that the Fund was not legally obligated to "purchase" the yacht, and this is enough to satisfy the case law referred to us. Grove v. Commissioner, supra, and the other cases cited by the taxpayer for the proposition that there must be a legally binding obligation on a charity's part before a transfer that is ostensibly a contribution can be recharacterized are therefore simply inapposite because there was a legal obligation here.

III. The "Understanding" Between Blake and the Fund

The Tax Court found as a factual matter that there existed an "understanding" between Blake and the Fund with respect to the disposition of the proceeds the Fund realized from sale of the stock. Even if this understanding fell short of a legal obligation, it amounted to more than mere wishful thinking on the taxpayer's part and thus refutes the contention that these transactions were merely coincidental. It also serves to distinguish this case from Grove v. Commissioner, supra, if not from all the other cases the taxpayer cites here. In *Grove*, this court relied on the Tax

Court's finding there was not even an informal agreement that the charity would deal with the contributed asset in a manner providing a tax benefit to the taxpayer. The majority opinion in *Grove* declined to infer an understanding from a pattern of activity benefiting the taxpayer in the "absence of any supporting facts in the record," an approach with which the author of this opinion took issue. But this case does not present us with the same difficulty. Here, the Tax Court found an understanding and we are quite firmly convinced that this finding was not clearly erroneous. Our review of the record satisfies us that "[t]here was evidence to support the findings of the Tax Court, and its findings must therefore be accepted."

[The court then proceeded to distinguish several cases relied upon by the taxpayers. Eds.]

* * *

More troublesome is the case of Palmer v. Commissioner, 62 T.C. 684 (1974), aff'd on other grounds, 523 F.2d 1308 (8th Cir.1975), which held that even an expectation of a stock redemption would not warrant denying charitable contribution status. The Service, in Revenue Ruling 78–197, 1978–1 C.B. 83, acquiesced in *Palmer*, stating that it would treat redemption proceeds under facts similar to Palmer as income to the donor "only if the donee is legally bound, or can be compelled by the corporation, to surrender the shares for redemption." The Service cited both *Grove* and *Carrington* as support for its position; what we have said above indicates our belief that this Ruling reads too much into those decisions. Where there is, as here, an expectation on the part of the donor that is reasonable, with an advance understanding that the donee charity will purchase the asset with the proceeds of the donated stock, the transaction will be looked at as a unitary one. A wooden view that would require legal enforceability of an understanding or obligation to purchase the asset contemplated to be donated ab initio is not what the tax law contemplates. At least, this circuit will not take it to do so.

Judgment affirmed.

2. ORDINARY INCOME PROPERTY

Section 170(e)(1) significantly reduces the tax benefits for gifts of ordinary income property. Ordinary income property is property that, if sold by the taxpayer for its fair market value, would result in ordinary income or short-term capital gain. Examples include inventory, other property held primarily for sale to customers in the ordinary course of the taxpayer's trade or business ("dealer property"), depreciable property to the extent that gain on a sale would be "recaptured" and taxed as ordinary income, stock and other capital assets held for one year or less, certain preferred corporate stock (§ 306 stock), and works of art or other intellectual property created by the donor.

Charitable gifts of ordinary income property are not subject to the special 30 percent limitation that applies to most gifts of capital gain property, but the donor is required to reduce the gift by the amount of gain that would not have been long-term capital gain if the property had been sold for its fair market value rather than contributed to charity. I.R.C. § 170(e)(1)(A). Put less technically, taxpayers who donate ordinary income property may only deduct their basis (usually cost) of that property. The purpose of this rule is to place these donors in roughly the same position that they would occupy if the ordinary income property had been sold and the proceeds were contributed to a charity.

To illustrate, assume that Donor contributes to Charity $10,000 of stock that she acquired seven months ago for $4,000. Because the stock has not been held for more than one year and thus would generate short-term capital gain if it were sold, it is ordinary income property. Donor thus must reduce her charitable deduction to $4,000. If she had held the same stock for more than one year at the time of her donation, her deduction (before application of any percentage limitation) would have been $10,000.

The ordinary income property "stepdown" rule is subject to a significant exception for corporate contributions of inventory to a public charity for a use that is related to the donee's exempt purposes and if the inventory is used "solely for the care of the ill, the needy, or infants." I.R.C. § 170(e)(3). Examples include gifts of food or drugs. If this exception applies, the usual reduction for gifts of ordinary income property is limited under a complex formula that has the effect of allowing a deduction for the lesser of (1) twice the basis of the property, or (2) the basis of the property plus 50 percent of the unrealized appreciation.

The ordinary income property rules significantly reduce the tax benefits for contributions of inventory and other "dealer" property. As illustrated by Revenue Ruling 79–256, which follows, the Service has expanded the definition of "dealer" to prevent efforts by taxpayers (and facilitating tax shelter promoters) to circumvent these rules.

Revenue Ruling 79–256

1979–2 Cum.Bull. 256.

ISSUE

In the situations described below, does section 170(e) of the Internal Revenue Code apply and thus require that the amount of the taxpayers' charitable contributions be reduced by any gain that would not have been long-term capital gain if the donated property had been sold by the taxpayer at its fair market value?

FACTS

Situation 1. For a number of years the taxpayer was engaged in the activity of raising ornamental plants, as a hobby. In 1978, as in prior years, the taxpayer donated a large number of plants to various charities, after having held the donated plants for the long-term holding period for a capital asset under section 1222(3) of the Code. The cost of the plants contributed in 1978 was 25x dollars, and they had a total fair market value of 200x dollars when they were contributed. Approximately the same ratio of cost to fair market value existed in the prior years.

Situation 2. The taxpayer is not a dealer in objects of art. In 1977, the taxpayer purchased a substantial part of the total limited edition of a particular lithograph print by an established artist for a total price of 25x dollars. In 1978, after having held the prints for more than a year, the taxpayer donated the prints to various art museums. The total fair market value of the prints was 100x dollars when they were contributed.

LAW AND ANALYSIS

Section 170(a) of the Code allows as a deduction any charitable contribution payment of which is made within the taxable year.

Section 1.170A–1(c)(1) of the Income Tax Regulations provides that, if a charitable contribution is made in property other than money, the amount of the contribution is the fair market value of the property at the time of the contribution.

Section 170(e)(1)(A) of the Code provides that the amount of any charitable contribution of property shall be reduced by the amount of gain that would not have been long-term capital gain if the property had been sold by the taxpayer at its fair market value.

Section 1.170A–4(a)(1) of the regulations provides that section 170(e)(1)(A) requires that the amount of a charitable contribution of "ordinary income property" be reduced by the amount of gain that would not have been recognized as long-term capital gain if the property had been sold by the donor at fair market value at the time such property was contributed.

Section 1.170A–(4)(b)(1) of the regulations provides that the term "ordinary income property" means property on which any of the gain would not have been long-term capital gain if the property had been sold by the donor at its fair market value at the time of its contribution. The term "ordinary income property" includes, for example, property held by a donor primarily for sale to customers in the ordinary course of the donor's trade or business.

Thus, under section 170(e)(1)(A) of the Code and the corresponding regulations, the determination whether property contributed to charity is ordinary income property requires that the donor be placed in the position of a seller of such property. Even though a donor is not engaged in a trade or business, the frequency and continuity of the contributions may be such as to be substantially equivalent to the activities of a dealer selling property in the ordinary course of a trade or business. Under such circumstances, the items contributed would be treated as ordinary income property.

In both Situation 1 and Situation 2, the contributions were not made after a period of accumulation and enjoyment by the taxpayers of the property contributed. On the contrary, the contributed property was produced (Situation 1) or purchased (Situation 2) in bulk and distributed to various donees. In Situation 1, the taxpayer's continuous production and disposition of plants are the equivalent of the activities of a commercial nursery business. In Situation 2, the taxpayer's bulk acquisition and subsequent disposal of a substantial part of the total limited edition of prints are substantially equivalent to the activities of a commercial art dealer. Therefore, under the presumed sale requirement of section 170(e)(1)(A) of the Code, the items contributed in both situations will be treated as ordinary income property.

HOLDING

In both Situation 1 and Situation 2, the amount of each taxpayer's contribution must be reduced, under section 170(e) of the Code, by the excess of the fair market value of the contributed property as of the dates of contribution over each taxpayer's cost. Therefore, the amount of each taxpayer's contribution is limited, for purposes of section 170 of the Code, to its cost to the donor. However, the treatment provided under section 170(e) does not imply that a taxpayer is engaged in a trade or business for the purposes of any other section of the Code. Furthermore, the holding of this revenue ruling is equally applicable to taxpayers who, under comparable circumstances, produce or acquire types of property other than those involved in the two situations.

3.   TANGIBLE PERSONAL PROPERTY

In general, a donor may take a full fair market value deduction for gifts of tangible personal property such as art objects, jewelry, antiques, books or yachts. A reduction rule applies, however, if the donated tangible personal property is not used by the donee in the conduct of its exempt purposes or functions. In that event, the gift must be reduced by the amount of long-term capital gain that the donor would have recognized if the property had been sold for its fair market value rather than contributed. I.R.C. § 170(e)(1)(B). In other words, as with gifts of ordinary income property, the charitable deduction generally is limited to the donor's basis in the contributed property. If this reduction rule applies, the gift is not subject to the 30 percent limitation on gifts of capital gain property (thus, the basic 50 percent limitation applies), but this is of little solace in light of the tax benefits lost from reducing the charitable deduction to the donor's basis.

In evaluating whether contributed property is used in the conduct of a charity's exempt functions, the regulations provide that it must be "reasonable to anticipate" that the organization will use the property for some exempt purpose. Treas. Reg. § 1.170A–4(b)(3)(ii). Examples include a gift of art to a museum for its collection, or rare books to a library. But the reduction rule applies if the donor can reasonably anticipate that the charity will sell the property-e.g., at a fundraising auction.

4.   BARGAIN SALES

A "bargain sale" is a sale of property for less than its fair market value. Bargain sales to charitable organizations offer two major benefits:

(1) a charitable deduction for the bargain element (the fair market value of the property less the sale price), and (2) reduction of the tax that the donor would pay if the property had been sold for its full fair market value. Bargain sales have proven particularly useful where a donor wishes to donate part of a substantial piece of property that is not easily divided (such as real estate) and to receive cash for the remaining portion.

A bargain sale to a charitable organization is bifurcated for tax purposes into a sale and a charitable gift. Under a special rule only applicable to bargain sales to charity, the donor's basis in the property must be allocated between the sale and gift transactions in proportion to the respective fair market values of each portion. I.R.C. § 1011(b). As a result, the donor is taxed on the difference between the sale price and the portion of the basis allocated to the sale part of the transaction.

To illustrate, assume that Donor ("D") owns a parcel of unimproved investment real estate with a fair market value of $100,000 and an adjusted basis of $50,000. D sells the property to Charity for $40,000 cash. D's charitable contribution is the $60,000 "bargain element"—i.e., the $100,000 fair market value of the property less the $40,000 sales proceeds received by D. Because this is a contribution of capital gain property, the $60,000 gift will be subject to the 30 percent limitation in § 170(b)(1)(C). D then must proceed to determine her gain on the sale portion of the transaction. D's amount realized is $40,000. Under § 1011(b), her basis in the sale portion is 40 percent (the ratio of the $40,000 sale price to the $100,000 value of the property) of her $50,000 total basis, or $20,000, and her taxable gain is thus $20,000 ($40,000 amount realized, minus $20,000 adjusted basis). See Treas. Reg. § 1.1011–2(a); 1.170A–4(c)(2).

A charitable gift of encumbered property is treated as a bargain sale to the extent that the outstanding liability exceeds the portion of the donor's adjusted basis allocated to the sale portion of the transaction. See, e.g., Guest v. Commissioner, 77 T.C. 9 (1981). Gifts of limited partnership interests also may constitute bargain sales when the partnership property is subject to indebtedness.

5. PARTIAL INTERESTS (NOT IN TRUST)

Donors historically have favored giving techniques that allow them to take a current income tax deduction for the value of a future interest in property while they retain a right to current income or enjoyment of the donated property. The Code contains intricate rules, summarized later in this chapter, for charitable gifts of income or remainder interests in trust. Section 170(f)(3) imposes comparable restrictions on gifts of partial interests not in trust by providing that the retained present interest either must be a guaranteed annuity or unitrust interest. In addition, § 170(a)(3) provides that a contribution of a remainder interest in tangible personal property is deductible only when all intervening noncharitable interests have expired. This seemingly superfluous rule postpones a charitable deduction for a gift of a remainder interest in tangible personal property, such as a work of art or other collectible, when the donor or a related party retains the right to possess and enjoy the property.

The limitations on deductions for partial interests not in trust are subject to three major exceptions that offer attractive planning opportunities. Two of these exceptions—for contributions of qualified conservation easements and gifts of remainder interests in a personal residence or farm—are discussed later in this chapter. See Section C6, infra, at p. 756, and Section D4, infra, at p. 766. The third exception applies to gifts of an undivided portion of a donor's entire interest in property. I.R.C. § 170(f)(3)(B)(ii); Treas.Reg. § 1.170A–7(b)(1). As demonstrated by the *Winokur* case, which follows, this exception permits donors to obtain a current deduction for a donation of a work of art or real estate by contributing a fractional interest in the property. After the gift, the donor and the charity will be co-owners, often sharing the property on a seasonal basis.

Winokur v. Commissioner

United States Tax Court, 1988.
90 T.C. 733.

■ Swift, Judge.

[The taxpayer was an art collector who served on the board of the Carnegie Institute Museum of Art in Pittsburgh. In December, 1977, he donated to the Institute a 10 percent undivided interest in a collection of 44 works of art. The deed of gift provided that the Institute had the right to possession of the works for a specified number of days each year following the donation. During the 12 months following the 1977 gift, the Institute did not take physical possession of any of the donated works of art.

The taxpayer donated a second 10 percent interest in the same works of art to the Institute in December, 1978 and, once again, the Institute did not take physical possession of any of the art works during the 12–month period following the gift. In December, 1979, the taxpayer donated his remaining 80 percent interest in five of the works of art and the Institute took physical possession. No additional gifts were made with respect to the other 39 pieces.

The Service determined that the 1977 and 1978 donations of 10 percent undivided interests did not qualify as charitable contributions in those years because the Institute did not take physical possession of the works during the 12–month periods following those gifts. The Service also challenged the taxpayers' valuation of some of the donated property. Eds.]

OPINION

Section 170 permits a deduction for contributions to qualifying charitable organizations that are paid within the taxable year. Contributions that constitute an "undivided portion of the donor's entire interest in property" qualify as charitable contribution deductions under section 1.170A–7(b)(1),

Income Tax Regs. The regulations specify, however, that a contribution of an undivided interest will only qualify for a charitable contribution deduction where the donee organization given the right, as a tenant in common with the donor, to possession, dominion, and control of the property contributed for the portion of each year that is equal to the organization's undivided interest in the property. Section 1.170A–7(b)(1), Income Tax Regs., provides, in relevant part, as follows:

> (1) *Undivided portion of donor's entire interest.* (i) A deduction is allowed under section 170 for the value of a charitable contribution not in trust of an undivided portion of a donor's entire interest in property. An undivided portion of a donor's entire interest in property must consist of a fraction or percentage of each and every substantial interest or right owned by the donor in such property and must extend over the entire term of the donor's interest in such property and in other property into which such property is converted. * * * A deduction is allowed under section 170 for a contribution of property to a charitable organization whereby such organization given the right, as a tenant in common with the donor, to possession, dominion, and control of the property for a portion of each year appropriate to its interest in such property. * * *

Consistent with the above requirements, a charitable contribution deduction is not allowed for a donation of a future interest in tangible personal property. Sec. 170(a)(3). A future interest is described in the regulations as a donation "in which a donor purports to give tangible personal property to a charitable organization, but has an understanding, arrangement, agreement, etc., whether written or oral, with the charitable organization which has the effect of reserving to, or retaining in, such donor a right to the use, possession, or enjoyment of the property." Sec. 1.170A–5(a)(4), Income Tax Regs.

Section 1.170A–5(a)(2) provides that transfer of an undivided present interest in property will not be treated as a transfer of a future interest and will not be disallowed under section 170(a)(3) if the "period of initial possession by the donee is not deferred in time for more than one year." Section 1.170A–5(a)(2) also includes an example illustrating a donation of an undivided present interest in a work of art that would qualify for a charitable deduction, as follows:

> (2) Section 170(a)(3) and this section have no application in respect of a transfer of an undivided present interest in property. For example, a contribution of an undivided one-quarter interest in a painting with respect to which the donee is entitled to possession during three months of each year shall be treated as made upon the receipt by the donee of a formally executed and acknowledged deed of gift. However, the period of initial possession by the donee may not be deferred in time for more than one year.

Petitioner argues that the value of the 10–percent undivided interests in the works of art that he donated to the Carnegie Institute in 1977 and 1978 are deductible under section 1.170A–7(b)(1) because the interests donated represent undivided portions of his entire interest in the 44 works of art. Petitioner also argues that under the deeds of gift dated December 28, 1977, and December 7, 1978 (which gave the Carnegie Institute the right to possession of the donated works of art for a portion of each year following the gifts), petitioner and the Carnegie Institute share the donated interests as tenants in common.

Respondent argues that petitioner's donations in 1977 and 1978 of undivided interests in the works of art do not qualify as undivided present interests because the Carnegie Institute did not take physical possession of the works of art for any portion of the years immediately following the donations. Respondent therefore contends that petitioner's donations are future interests of tangible personal property which, under section 170(a)(3), are not deductible.

No cases have addressed the issue before us. The relevant statutory and regulatory language suggest, among other things, that it is the right or entitlement to possession, not actual physical possession, that controls whether a purported present interest will be regarded as a future interest. Section 170(a)(3), speaks of "rights to the actual possession." Section 1.170A–7(b)(1), quoted above, speaks of "right" to possession. The example set forth in section 1.170A–5(a)(2), also quoted above, speaks of "entitle-ment" to possession. Petitioner's donations are very similar to the donation of an undivided interest described in the regulations as a qualifying charitable deduction.

Neither the statute nor the regulations require the donee organization to take physical possession of the donated property during the year immedi-ately following the gift. In order for an undivided interest to be treated as a present interest and not as a future interest, the donee simply must have the right to interrupt the donor's possession and the right to have physical possession of the property during each year following the donation equiva-lent to its undivided interest in the property, in addition to the other rights of a tenant in common.

Petitioner transferred such rights to the Carnegie Institute in 1977 and 1978. Under the deeds of gift, the Carnegie Institute unequivocally was given the right to possess and control the works of art for a portion of each of the years following the donations equivalent to its undivided ownership interest in the works of art. There is no evidence that petitioner deprived the Carnegie Institute of the right of common possession and enjoyment thereof. Apparently, the Carnegie Institute's failure to take physical posses-sion of many of the individual works of art has been voluntary and has not been caused by acts of petitioner. In our view, petitioner and the Carnegie Institute shared the works of art as tenants in common. Accordingly, petitioner's donations of the 10–percent undivided interests in 1977 and 1978 qualify as charitable contribution deductions under section 170.

[The portion of the opinion relating to valuation has been omitted. Eds.]

6. Qualified Conservation Contributions

To encourage the preservation of open space land, including agricultural property, § 170(f)(3)(B)(iii) allows a charitable deduction for gifts of "qualified conservation contributions" that meet certain highly technical rules set forth in § 170(h). The term "qualified conservation contribution" entails these three requirements:

(1) The gift must be of a "qualified property interest," which is defined as the donor's entire interest in the property (except for certain mineral interests), a remainder interest, or a perpetual restriction on the use which may be made of the property. I.R.C. § 170(h)(2).

(2) The contribution must be made to a governmental unit, a public charity, or an organization that is controlled by and supports a public charity or governmental unit. I.R.C. § 170(h)(3).

(3) The contribution must be exclusively for one or more specified "conservation purposes," including: preservation of land areas for outdoor recreation by, or education of, the general public; protection of a relatively natural habitat of fish, wildlife, plants, or similar ecosystems; preservation of open space, including farms and forest land, where the preservation is for the scenic enjoyment of the general public or pursuant to a clearly delineated governmental policy and will yield a significant public benefit; and preservation of an historically important land area or a certified historic structure. I.R.C. § 170(h)(4)(A).

Valuation of a conservation easement ordinarily is based on an appraisal that determines the difference between the fair market value of the property without the restriction and the fair market value after it is encumbered by the easement. Reg. § 1.170A–14(h)(3)(i).

7. Valuation and Appraisal Requirements

A donor's charitable deduction for a noncash contribution generally is the fair market value of the donated property. For this purpose, the regulations adopt the usual definition of fair market value—the price at which property would change hands in an arm's-length transaction between a willing buyer and a willing seller. Reg. § 1.170A–1(c)(2). In the case of publicly traded securities, valuation is easily determined by reference to published quotations. The charitable deduction for a listed security is the mean (i.e., average) of the highest and lowest quoted selling prices on the date of the gift, without regard to the net proceeds realized by the charitable donee on a subsequent sale of the security. Reg. § 20.2031–2(b)(1). Gifts of closely held stock, real estate, art and other hard to value property raise far more difficult valuation questions of valuation and have been susceptible to abuse by donors who are seeking inflated charitable contribution deductions. Congress has responded to these problems by imposing penalties for overvaluations and enacting detailed reporting and appraisal requirements for substantial gifts of property.

Form 8283: Gifts of $5,000 or Less. Noncash charitable contributions in excess of $500 must be reported to the Internal Revenue Service on Form 8283, which is an attachment to the donor's income tax return.[1] The information required on the form varies depending on the type and amount of the gift. Charitable gifts with a claimed value of $5,000 or less per item (or group of similar items) and gifts of publicly traded securities are reported on Schedule A of Form 8283. The information requested includes a description of the donated property, the date of the contribution, the date the property was acquired by the donor, how the donor acquired the property, the donor's cost or other tax basis, the fair market value of the property and the method used to determine fair market value. Additional information is required for gifts of less than entire interest in property or gifts subject to restrictions. See Form 8283, Section A, Part II.

Appraisal Requirements: Gifts in Excess of $5,000. No charitable deduction will be allowed for a contribution of property with a claimed value of more than $5,000 unless the donor obtains a "qualified appraisal" and provides an "appraisal summary" on Part B of Form 8283. A "qualified appraisal" is an appraisal which: (1) is made not earlier than 60 days prior to the date of the contribution (note that this does not restrict the number of days after the contribution but merely limits appraisals made in advance of the gift); (2) is prepared, signed and dated by a "qualified appraiser," who generally must be someone who holds himself out to the public as an appraiser, is familiar with the type of property being appraised, and is unrelated to the donor or donee; (3) includes certain specific information, such as a detailed description of the property and its condition, the valuation method used, the specific basis for the valuation, etc.; and (4) is not based on a percentage of the appraised value of the property or the amount allowed as a deduction. See Treas.Reg. § 1.170A–13(c) for considerably more detail.

Although a qualified appraisal is necessary to substantiate a charitable deduction, the donor is not required to attach the complete appraisal to his or her tax return except in the case of art contributions with a claimed value of $20,000 or more. In all other cases, only the "appraisal summary" required by Part B of Form 8283 must be filed. The summary requests certain general information on the donated property; it requires the appraiser to certify that he or she is qualified under the rules; and it requires the donee to acknowledge that it is a qualified recipient of charitable contributions and received the donated property on the date indicated.

Donee Information Return. The appraisal requirement is buttressed by a donee information return rule. A donee that sells property donated to it with a value in excess of $5,000 within two years of the date of the gift must file an information return (Form 8282) with the Internal Revenue

---

1. A copy of Form 8283, including instructions, is reproduced in the Statutes, Regulations and Forms Supplement which is available to accompany this text.

Service. I.R.C. § 6050L. The reporting requirement is waived for items valued at less than $500 where the donor has signed a declaration to that effect on Form 8283, and for items consumed or distributed without consideration in furtherance of the donee's charitable purpose.

Penalties. If an amount claimed as a charitable deduction is 200 percent or more than the correct value as finally determined, the donor is subject to a substantial valuation misstatement penalty of 20 percent of the amount by which the donor's tax is understated as a result of the inflated valuation. I.R.C. § 6662(e). If the value claimed is 400 percent or more of the correct amount, the penalty is increased to 40 percent of the tax understatement. I.R.C. § 6662(h). The penalty may be waived only if the donor can show that he or she relied on a qualified appraisal and the donor made a good faith investigation of the value of the contributed property. I.R.C. § 6664(c)(2). An appraiser who is found to have provided an appraisal knowing that it will result in an underpayment of tax also may be subject to penalties. See I.R.C. § 6701.

NOTES AND QUESTIONS

1. *Policy Issues.* Why does § 170 permit a charitable deduction for the full fair market value of appreciated capital gain property without requiring the donor to recognize the gain inherent in the property? Without giving the matter much thought, the Internal Revenue Service ruled in 1923 that allowing a full fair market value deduction was an appropriate interpretation of the statute. This rule acts as a powerful inducement for large gifts of stock, real estate and art, particularly by wealthy supporters of private universities and museums. Critics of the appreciated property charitable deduction contend that it sharply departs from normative tax principles and is inequitable. In recommending that the deduction be limited to the lesser of the fair market value of donated property or the donor's basis, indexed for inflation, a 1984 Treasury Department report stated:

> The current treatment of certain charitable gifts of appreciated property is unduly generous and in conflict with basic principles governing the measurement of income for tax purposes. In other circumstances where appreciated property is used to pay a deductible expense, or where such property is the subject of a deductible loss, the deduction allowed may not exceed the taxpayer's adjusted basis plus any gain recognized. Thus, a taxpayer generally may not receive a tax deduction with respect to untaxed appreciation in property. The current tax treatment of certain charitable gifts departs from this principle by permitting the donor a deduction for the full value of the property, including the element of appreciation with respect to which the donor does not realized gain.

U.S. Treasury Department, Report to the President, 2 Tax Reform for Fairness, Simplicity, and Economic Growth 72–74 (1984).

Congress rejected the Treasury's 1984 recommendation but in 1986 it included the unrealized appreciation inherent in contributed capital gain property as a tax preference item for purposes of the alternative minimum tax. For many wealthy donors, this had the effect of significantly reducing the tax benefits of gifts of appreciated property. After a concerted lobbying effort by the nonprofit sector, Congress gradually repealed this provision, initially with respect to gifts of tangible personal property and in 1993 for all gifts of appreciated capital gain property to public charities.

2. *Art Valuations.* The Internal Revenue Service has an Art Advisory Panel that meets several times a year to determine a value for all donated works of art with a claimed value of $20,000 or more. The Panel includes museum curators and directors, art scholars, art dealers, and representatives from major auction houses, all of whom serve without compensation. The recommendations made by the Panel are used by the Service in its audit, administrative appeals, and litigation functions. A taxpayer may obtain an advance "statement of value" for donated works of art after the contribution is made but before the taxpayer files a federal income tax return claiming a charitable deduction. Rev. Proc. 96–15, 1996–1 C.B. 627. The procedure is limited to items for which the taxpayer has obtained an appraisal of $50,000 or more, and requires the taxpayer to pay a $2,500 "user fee" to the Service. Taxpayers must submit their qualified appraisals to the Service, which then issues a statement either approving the appraisal or disagreeing and indicating the basis of its disagreement and its own determination of value. In cases where the Service disagrees, the taxpayer may accept the Service's valuation or submit additional support with the tax return on which the deduction is claimed.

PROBLEMS

1. Donor is a single taxpayer who is considering whether to make a charitable gift of appreciated property with a fair market value of $100,000 and an adjusted basis to Donor of $20,000. Potential donees are Public Charity, which is described in § 170(b)(1)(A)(vi), and Private Foundation. Consider generally the tax consequences of the charitable gift in the following alternative situations:

(a) Donor contributes publicly traded stock acquired more than a year ago to Public Charity.

(b) Same as (a), above, except the contribution is made to Private Foundation.

(c) Public Charity is a library. The donated property is a collection of rare books and Donor is a rare book dealer.

(d) Same as (c), above, except Donor is not a rare book dealer and acquired the books for investment more than one year ago.

(e) Public Charity is a law school. The donated property is an antique automobile that Public Charity intends to sell at a fund-raising auction, using the proceeds for a student scholarship fund.

(f) Public Charity is an art museum, and Donor is an artist. The donated property is a work of art painted by Donor and is being donated for the museum's collection.

(g) Same as (f), above, except that Donor is an art collector who acquired the painting more than a year ago. The Museum intends to keep the painting in storage for a year and then sell it and use the proceeds to acquire works of art that are more compatible with its collection.

(h) For which of the gifts in the alternatives above must Donor complete and attach a Form 8283 to her income tax return?

(i) For which of the gifts in the alternatives above must Donor obtain a qualified appraisal?

(j) Assume that the donated art in (g), above, is fully deductible, but on audit it is determined to have a fair market value of only $50,000 rather than the $100,000 claimed by Donor on her income tax return. To what extent, if any, will Donor be subject to a valuation overstatement penalty?

2. Environmentalist ("E") owns a parcel of undeveloped land in which he has an adjusted basis of $100,000 and which is subject to an outstanding nonrecourse mortgage of $300,000. The fair market value of the land, as determined by a qualified appraisal, is $400,000. E's adjusted gross income for the current year (apart from this transaction) is $150,000. E wishes to contribute the parcel to The Land Trust, a public charity, which will take the property subject to the outstanding mortgage. What are the tax consequences of this contribution to E?

3. Generous Giver ("GG") is a wealthy widow who is contemplating several charitable gifts and is seeking advice on the income tax consequences of the following alternatives:

(a) GG owns a 300–acre ranch in Montana where she spends the months of July and August. She wishes to grant the Girl Scouts the exclusive use of the ranch, on a year-to-year basis, during the remaining 10 months.

(b) GG owns an original Picasso that hangs in her New York apartment, where she resides six months during the year. She proposes to donate the Picasso to the Museum of Modern Art for the other six months.

(c) Same as (b), above, except that GG loans the Picasso to the Museum for an entire year for a special exhibit and then takes it back.

4. Todd Hugo owns a 200 acre property in Western Massachusetts that the Hugo family has used as a summer retreat for many decades. Directly adjacent to the Hugo property is a 500–acre parcel owned by the estate of a recently deceased neighbor. The Berkshire Land Trust ("the Trust") is a § 501(c)(3) organization dedicated to land conservation. Hugo proposes to donate appreciated stock to the Trust in an amount sufficient

to allow the Trust to acquire the 500–acre parcel. The Trust then will convey 250 of those acres to Hugo subject to a conservation easement permitting the construction of only two residences in return for Hugo's grant of a conservation easement restricting development of his 200 acre property. An appraiser is prepared to write a report stating that the exchange is for equal value. Consider generally the tax consequences and risks of these transactions to Mr. Hugo and the Trust, and suggest an alternative plan that would involve less risk to the parties.

D.   Planned Giving Techniques

1.   Introduction

The terms "planned giving" and "deferred giving" do not appear in the Internal Revenue Code or the Treasury Regulations. These terms were created by charitable fundraisers to describe a variety of sophisticated "plans" by which donors make a substantial gift to a charitable organization. The "plan" can be as simple as a pledge during the donor's lifetime to make an outright bequest to endow a chair or scholarship fund at a university. The more typical planned gift involves a more complex arrangement, such as a gift in trust where the donor or his family retains some present or future rights in the property. Planned gifts may be made during the donor's lifetime or at death; in either case, significant tax savings may be achieved if the gift is properly structured.

The topic of planned giving is far too technical for detailed coverage in a survey course on the taxation of nonprofit organizations. The goal here is to become familiar with the planned giving universe by outlining the principal techniques and providing some typical illustrative cases. Bibliographic references are provided at the end of this section for those who might wish to study this area in the considerable depth that is required for charitable fundraisers, philanthropists, and their legal advisors.

The principal vehicles for planned giving are:

(1) *Charitable Remainder Trusts.* A charitable remainder trust is one of several types of planned giving techniques where a donor makes a gift of property in trust and retains an interest for himself and/or other noncharitable beneficiaries for life or a term of years. In general, there are two types of charitable remainder trusts: annuity trusts and unitrusts. An annuity trust pays out a fixed annual dollar amount to the income beneficiary; the amount is a specific percentage (but not less than 5 percent) of the initial fair market value of the property contributed to the trust. Payments may be made annually or at more frequent intervals. A unitrust is similar except that the income beneficiary, who is often the donor, receives annual payments based on a fixed percentage of the trust assets as valued each year, or in some cases the annual net income of the trust if it is less than the fixed percentage. In either format, the

remainder goes to the charity after the death of the income beneficiary or beneficiaries.

(2) *Pooled Income Funds.* A pooled income fund is a common trust to which a donor transfers cash or securities that are commingled for investment purposes with property transferred to the fund by other donors. The donor or any person designated by the donor is paid an annual amount of income based on the rate of return of the fund. After the death of the income beneficiary or beneficiaries, the remainder passes to the charity.

(3) *Remainder Interest in a Personal Residence or Farm.* As discussed earlier, charitable gifts of future interests in property that are not made to one of the trust vehicles described above do not offer any tax benefits. In the case of a personal residence or farm, however, a donor may contribute a remainder interest while retaining lifetime use for himself or others and take a charitable deduction for the actuarial value of the remainder interest.

(4) *Charitable Gift Annuity.* A charitable gift annuity is a contract under which a charitable organization, in exchange for an irrevocable gift of cash or property, promises to pay a fixed amount each year to a designated beneficiary for life. The amount of the annuity is determined by actuarial tables. At the time the gift is made, the donor may take a charitable deduction for the difference between the value of the gift and the value of the annuity.

(5) *Charitable Lead Trusts.* A charitable lead trust is the mirror image of a charitable remainder trust. It is a gift in trust with a specified annuity or unitrust amount payable to a charity or group of charities for a term of years. At the end of the charitable income term, the remainder either reverts to the donor or, more commonly, it passes to younger family members, such as children or grandchildren.

2. CHARITABLE REMAINDER TRUSTS

Apart from simple bequests, charitable remainder trusts are the most widely used planned giving vehicles. In 1969, Congress significantly tightened the requirements to qualify gifts to split-interest trusts for income, gift and estate tax benefits. Prior law permitted donors to claim charitable deductions that did not correlate with the amount that ultimately would be received by the charitable remainder beneficiary. The purpose of the intricate new ground rules was to eliminate these potentially large discrepancies. As a condition to obtaining tax benefits, gifts of partial interests in trust must be made to a "charitable remainder annuity trust" or a "charitable remainder unitrust," as defined in § 664(d). I.R.C. § 170(f)(2)(A). Charitable remainder trusts are most frequently created during a donor's lifetime, but they also may be established at death, in a decedent's will or revocable living trust. In all cases, the charitable deduction—be it for income, gift or estate tax purposes—is determined actuarially and is the present value of the charity's right to receive the corpus of the trust when the noncharitable interests expire. A trust created after July 28, 1997 generally will not qualify as a charitable remainder trust unless the actuarial value of the remainder interest is at least 10 percent of the net fair market value of the property transferred to the trust. I.R.C. §§ 664(d)(1)(D), (d)(2)(D).

Charitable Remainder Annuity Trusts (§ 664(d)(1)). A charitable remainder annuity trust ("CRAT") is a trust from which a specified amount (not less than five percent and not more than 50 percent of the initial fair market value of the assets transferred to the trust) must be paid to the donor and/or other named income beneficiaries, either for the life of the named noncharitable beneficiaries or a specific period of time that may not exceed 20 years. The payments must be made at least annually, but the trust may provide for payments at more frequent intervals, such as quarterly or monthly. The frequency of the payments affects the valuation of the charitable remainder interests.

Since the annuity is fixed, it is unaffected by the trust accounting income actually earned by the trust. If the actual income is insufficient, the Trustee is required to meet the payout requirement from previously accumulated income (including capital gains) or corpus. If the income exceeds the required payout, it accumulates in the trust. If the trust holds real estate, closely held stock or other illiquid assets that may not generate sufficient income to meet the payout requirement, the Trustee is required either to liquidate the assets or transfer fractional portions to the beneficiary. Particularly careful advance planning is thus required for any CRAT that may face a liquidity problem.

No additional gifts may be made to a CRAT after its initial funding, and the trust may not authorize the Trustee to invade corpus for the benefit of the noncharitable income beneficiaries. I.R.C. § 664(d)(1)(B).

Charitable Remainder Unitrusts § 664(d)(2). A unitrust is similar to an annuity trust with the important exception that it pays the donor or other noncharitable beneficiaries a variable annuity computed as a fixed percentage (not less than five percent) of the net fair market value of the trust assets valued at least annually. A unitrust is a better inflation hedge than an annuity trust because the payout fluctuates with the value of the trust assets. On the other hand, the guaranteed payout of an annuity trust provides more security if the value of the trust assets should decline.

Section 664(d)(3) also authorizes an alternative "income only" unitrust format that permits the payment of the lesser of: (1) a fixed percentage of the trust's annual value (not less than five percent and not more than 50 percent), or (2) the net income of the trust. The trust also may (but is not required to) include a "makeup" provision which is triggered if the actual income is lower than the percentage amount for one or more years and is higher in a later year. In that case, the excess income can be paid to the beneficiaries up to the amount necessary to "make up" past shortfalls.

The "net income with make-up" (NIMCRUT) format is a particularly flexible device when the property transferred to the trust does not currently produce income (e.g., raw land or closely held stock) and may not be sold for some time after the gift is made. If a trust is a NIMCRUT, the Trustee is not required to distribute corpus while the low-yielding property is retained and may make larger distributions after the property is sold. An even more attractive variation is the "flip" unitrust, which begins as an income-only CRUT and converts to a standard fixed payout when the illiquid or unproductive asset is sold or on certain other events. The Service will approve a flip if it is triggered by the sale of an unmarketable asset or other events such as marriage, divorce, death, or birth of a child. See Reg. § 1.644–3(a)(1)(i)(c)–(e).

Another feature unique to unitrusts is that additional deductible gifts may be made by the grantor after the trust is initially funded. When the trust is funded with hard-to-value assets such as closely held stock or real estate, a disadvantage of a unitrust is the requirement to value the assets at least annually.

Determining the Donor's Charitable Deduction. The charitable income and gift tax deduction for a donor who makes a lifetime gift to a charitable remainder trust is the present value of the charitable remainder interest, determined from the Service's actuarial and mortality tables. These valuations are based on actuarial tables that incorporate the applicable discount rate for the month in which the valuation date falls or, if the taxpayer elects, either of the two preceding months. I.R.C. § 7520(a). The applicable rate varies monthly and is set at 120 percent of an index known as the "Federal Mid–Term Rate." The amount of the charitable deduction is thus a function of the annuity or unitrust payment; the length of the noncharitable income payout period; and the frequency of payment of the annuity or unitrust amount. A similar approach is used for determining the charitable estate tax deduction for bequests to a charitable remainder trust. See I.R.C. § 2055(e)(2).

To illustrate, assume a 70–year old Donor contributes $300,000 of appreciated stock to a charitable remainder annuity trust, retaining a $15,000 (5 percent) annuity for her life, payable annually, with the remainder passing to a designated public charity. At the time of the gift, assume the applicable discount rate under § 7520 is 6 percent. Using the appropriate actuarial valuation tables, Donor's charitable income tax deduction is determined as follows:

Amount of Annuity	$15,000
Annuity Factor for Age 70	8.4988
Present Value of Annuity	127,482
Present Value of Remainder	172,518

Donor's charitable deduction is thus $172,518, subject to the 30 percent limitation for gifts of capital gain property. If Donor had contributed cash, the 50 percent limitation would have applied. If a private foundation were a potential charitable remainder beneficiary, the percentage limitations would be reduced to 30 percent (for cash gifts) and 20 percent (gifts of capital gain property).

Income Taxation of the Trust and its Beneficiaries. A charitable remainder trust is exempt from all federal income taxes except in the rare and unfortunate case where it has unrelated business income; in that event, all the trust's income is subject to tax. I.R.C. § 664(c) This means that when a charitable remainder trust sells appreciated property contributed by a donor, the gain is not taxable to the trust although, under rules described below, it may be taxable to the life income beneficiaries when it is distributed.

The beneficiaries of a charitable remainder trust are taxable on the amounts distributed to them, but the character of that income is determined based on a unique "tier system" that looks to the historic income of the trust since its creation. Thus, distributions are first taxed as ordinary income to the extent of the trust's ordinary income for the current year and undistributed ordinary income from prior years; next as capital gain to the extent of current and past undistributed capital gains, with short-term gains deemed distributed first; then as "other" (i.e., tax-exempt) income to the extent of current and past exempt income of the trust; and finally as a nontaxable distribution of corpus. I.R.C. § 664(b).

To illustrate, assume Donor contributes $500,000 of nondividend paying publicly traded growth stock with a basis of $100,000 to a charitable remainder annuity trust that pays a 7 percent annuity ($35,000) per year. The CRAT immediately sells the stock, realizing a $400,000 long-term capital gain, and invests the proceeds in a corporate bond yielding 8 percent ($40,000 interest income) annually. The annual $35,000 payout to Donor is deemed to come entirely from the current ordinary income of the trust. If the proceeds had been invested entirely in an 8 percent tax-exempt bond, the trust would have no ordinary income and thus the $35,000 payout would be taxed as "second-tier" long-term capital gain to Donor until the $400,000 long-term capital gain from the sale of the stock is exhausted through distributions.

Application of Private Foundation Restrictions. Section 4947(a)(2) provides that split-interest charitable trusts are subject to some of the restrictions applicable to private foundations. Specifically, a qualifying charitable remainder trust is subject to the prohibitions on self-dealing in § 4941 and the taxable expenditure rules in § 4945. See Chapter 3C2 and 3c6, supra, at pp. 456–469, 480–489.

3.   POOLED INCOME FUNDS

A pooled income fund is a trust, created and administered by a public charity, which consists of commingled property contributed by many donors who retain life income interests in their pro rata shares of the net income earned by the fund. See I.R.C. § 642(c)(5). Pooled income funds are particularly attractive to smaller donors. They provide a means for diversifying investments without incurring the tax that otherwise would result if the donor sold appreciated property and reinvested the proceeds. See I.R.C. § 642(c)(5).

Pooled income funds are like mutual funds. A donor who contributes cash or property to the fund acquires "units" of participation that entitle the donor to periodic distributions of income that usually continue for the life of the donor or one or more other living persons. The annual income received by a beneficiary is dependent on the fund's rate of return. Some larger charities maintain different types of pooled income funds to accommodate their donors' goals—e.g., a relatively stable fixed-income fund along with a lower-yielding balanced fund that seeks moderate growth and thus the potential of higher income in later years.

A donor to a pooled income fund receives a current income tax deduction for the actuarial value of the charitable remainder interest. I.R.C. § 170(f)(2)(A). Valuation is dependent on several variables, including the value of the donated property, the age of the income beneficiary or beneficiaries, the historical rate of return of the fund, or an assumed rate of return for new funds. The fund itself is generally exempt from tax, but income received by the beneficiary is taxable at ordinary income rates.

4. Remainder Interest In Personal Residence or Farm

One of the few partial interests in property that qualifies for charitable income, gift and estate tax deductions is a remainder interest in a personal residence or farm. If the interest is contributed during the donor's lifetime, the donor may take an income tax deduction for the actuarial value of the remainder interest, discounted to reflect straight line depreciation on the improvements. See I.R.C. §§ 170(f)(3)(B)(i), (f)(4); Treas.Reg. § 1.170A–12. In a typical arrangement, the donor continues living in the residence or on the farm during his or her life, and at death the property passes to charity.

To qualify as a personal residence, the property need not be the donor's *principal* residence. Vacation homes also may qualify. A "farm" includes the land and buildings used by the donor for the production of crop, fruits, agricultural products, or sustenance of livestock.

5. Charitable Gift Annuities

A charitable gift annuity involves the transfer of property to a charitable organization in return for the charity's commitment to pay an annual sum certain to the donor for the donor's life, or for the joint lives of the donor and the donor's spouse. A charitable deduction is allowed for the amount transferred to charity that exceeds the actuarially determined present value of the annuity. In general, the annual amounts received by the donor is taxed according to the normal rules for the taxation of annuities. Thus, a portion of each annuity payment is a tax-free return of capital, and a portion is taxable as ordinary income. See I.R.C. § 72.

When a donor transfers appreciated property to acquire the annuity, the transaction is treated as a bargain sale for tax purposes. A portion of the donor's basis in the transferred asset is allocated to the gift portion of the transaction, and the balance is allocated to the purchase of the annuity. The gain from the "sale part" may be spread over the period during which payments are received if the annuitant is the donor or the donor's spouse. If the annuitant is a third party, the entire gain is taxable in the year of the gift. See Treas. Reg. § 1.170A–1(d); 1.1011–2(b).

6.   CHARITABLE LEAD TRUSTS

Charitable lead trusts provide for a gift of income to charity for a period of time with the remainder either returning to the grantor or passing to noncharitable beneficiaries, usually children or grandchildren of the grantor. One type of lead trust—the "grantor lead trust"—is used principally to obtain a current income tax deduction equal to the actuarial value of the charitable income interest. The more widely used format—the "nongrantor lead trust"—is an estate planning technique designed to provide income to charity for a specified term and then to pass the property to family members at little or no wealth transfer tax cost. In either case, the trust must provide for payments to a specified charity or charities not less than annually, and the payments must be in the form of a fixed annuity or a unitrust interest.

Grantor Lead Trusts. A grantor lead trust is useful when the donor is seeking a current income tax charitable deduction in a year when his or her marginal income tax rate is unusually high relative to later years. Grantor lead trusts have little or no appeal when tax rates are relatively flat or are gradually increasing over time because the trade-off for a current income tax deduction for the actuarial value of the charitable income interest is that the donor is taxable on the trust income at a higher rate during the term of the trust even though she does not receive the income. If a donor expects to be in a lower marginal tax bracket in the future, however, the present value of the current deduction may outweigh the present value of the future tax liability on the trust income.

Nongrantor Lead Trusts. The nongrantor lead trust does not provide a current income tax deduction but it may be a useful technique for shifting wealth to younger generations. If properly structured, a nongrantor lead trust allows a donor to benefit a favored charity for a period of time and then pass the property either outright or in a continuing trust to family members at relatively little transfer tax cost. If a nongrantor lead trust is established during the donor's life, a current gift tax deduction is available for the actuarial value of the charitable lead interest. If a lead trust is created upon the donor's death, the donor's estate is entitled to an estate tax charitable deduction for the value of the charitable lead interest. In either case, the remainder passing to family members is a taxable gift or bequest at the time the trust is created. The amount of the taxable gift may be minimized by synchronizing the required charitable payout with the term of the trust—a result more easily accomplished when the applicable discount rate under § 7520 is lower rather than higher.

The problems that follow illustrate some prototype cases where charitable split-interest trusts may be utilized effectively.

PROBLEMS

1. Julius Sims is a 65 year old bachelor with a net worth of approximately $1.6 million and adjusted gross income of $200,000 per year. His assets include 10,000 shares of publicly traded Pacific Wiper Co. stock, which he acquired many years ago for $50,000. The stock is now worth $500,000, but it pays a meager dividend of 50 cents per share. Julius is interested in diversifying his portfolio, but he does not relish the prospect of the large capital gains tax that he would incur if he were to sell or all or part of his Pacific Wiper stock. Julius has no close relatives and plans to leave the bulk of his estate to the Sturdley College of Business Administration to establish the Julius Sims Professorship.

Consider the following proposal that has been suggested by a financial planner. Julius will transfer his entire 10,000 shares of Pacific Wiper stock to a charitable remainder annuity trust. Julius will retain an annual annuity of $35,000, and the remainder will be distributed on Julius's death to Sturdley College, a public charity which will serve as Trustee. During discussions with representatives of Sturdley's development office, an understanding has been reached that Sturdley will sell the Pacific Wiper stock and reinvest the proceeds in a diversified portfolio of stocks and bonds. Assume that at the time the stock is transferred to the trust, the applicable rate under § 7520 for the month of the gift and the two prior months is 6% (and thus the appropriate valuation factor for Julius's annuity is 9.7151).

(a) In general, what are the income tax consequences to Julius when he creates the trust? Would the result be the same if Julius simply retained a life income interest in the trust, with the remainder to go to Sturdley College.

(b) What is the income tax treatment of the trust during Julius's life?

(c) What are the income tax consequences to Julius when he receives his $35,000 annual annuity? Is your answer affected by the Trustee's investment strategy?

(d) Would Julius have jeopardized the tax benefits for himself and the trust if he had reserved the right to change the charitable remainder beneficiary at any time during his life?

(e) Is it appropriate for Sturdley College to serve as Trustee of a charitable remainder trust created for its benefit? Could Julius have served as Trustee?

(f) When Julius dies, will the trust property be included in his gross estate for federal estate tax purposes?

(g) Assume that Julius's lawyer is not competent to draft a charitable remainder trust and would prefer the planning, drafting, and other details to be handled by the development office of Sturdley College.

Is it appropriate for the charity to assist the donor in this manner? May the charity pay the expenses for a competent lawyer to plan and draft the trust?

2.   Garth Coleman is a wealthy 65–year old widower. He has $2 million of his own funds and recently inherited a $10 million estate from his wife, Marian. Garth is a loyal alumnus of Private Law School ("PLS") and was recently named as chair of its Board of Visitors. He regularly makes charitable gifts to PLS averaging about $20,000 per year but will be expected to give more in his role as chair of the Board of Visitors. Garth ultimately would like to leave his wealth to his children and grandchildren. Would it make sense for Garth to consider establishing a nongrantor charitable lead trust that would pay a specific amount to PLS for a period of time and then distribute the assets remaining in trust to his children? Consider generally the design of the trust and the tax consequences of such an arrangement.

*

INDEX

References are to Pages

†

1-58778-595-1

90000

9 781587 785955